WESTERN
CIVILIZATIONS

WORLD · POLITICAL

NATIONAL BOUNDARIES

Winkel Tripel Projection

NORTH
AMERICA

ARCTIC
OCEAN

New Siberian Islands

Victoria
Island

North
Magnetic Pole

ASIA

North Pole ★

North Land

Baffin
Bay

Svalbard

Novaya
Zemlya

Franz
Josef
Land

GREENLAND

Iceland

Laptev
Sea

East
Siberian
Sea

ARCTIC

GREENLAND

Iceland

QUEEN
ELIZABETH
ISLANDS

Baffin
Bay

ARCTIC CIRCLE

Hudson
Bay

Lake
Winnipeg

Lake
Superior

Great Bear
Lake

Island of
Newfoundland

NORTH
AMERICA

NORTH
PACIFIC
OCEAN

NORTH
ATLANTIC
OCEAN

GULF OF
MEXICO

WEST INDIES

Gulf of
St. Lawrence

L. Huron

L. Erie

L. Ontario

TROPIC OF CANCER

Hawaii

ALEUTIAN TRENCH

CENTRAL
AMERICA

MID ATLANTIC RIDGE

EQUATOR

Amazon
Basin

SOUTH
AMERICA

Samoa
Islands

Tahiti

Tuamotu Archipelago

TROPIC OF CAPRICORN

SOUTH
PACIFIC
OCEAN

SOU

ATLA

OCE

ANDES

PERU-CHILE TRENCH

POLYNESIA

MELANESIA

Falkland Islands

Cabo Horn

Drake Passage

ANTARCTIC
PENINSULA

WEDDELL
SEA

Alexander
Island

GLOBAL SATELLITE MOSAIC

The beauty and complexity of Earth's landscapes are both strikingly and sometimes
overshadowed in the Global Satellite Mosaic. The mosaic was produced
for the National Geographic Society by NASA's Jet Propulsion Laboratory, using
more than 500 satellite images from the National Oceanic and Atmospheric
Administration. The cloud-free images show Earth in its natural colors as it would be
seen from space. One can easily identify the world's major glaciers, deserts, mountain
ranges, and rain forests. For example, follow the green ribbon of lush vegetation along
the Nile into the stark, dry Sahara. The mountain ranges seem to rise off this map thanks
to digital elevation databases from the Department of Defense. The deepest areas of the
ocean realm are colored dark blue in contrast to the light blue areas highlighting
continental shelves, submarine ridges, and underwater mountains.

ELLSWORTH LAND

Marie Byrd Land

Vinson Massif
16067 ft

RONNE ICE SHELF

ANTARCTIC CIRCLE

A N T

BIOSPHERE

Thousands of satellite images were
combined to show a picture of biospheric
productivity. In the oranges, red, yellow, and
green indicate waters rich in phytoplankton. On land
green areas show high potential plant productivity; tan
areas suffer from productivity limitations due to aridity and temperature.

TH

SA

SOUTH POLAR REGION

Drake Passage

ANTARCTIC CIRCLE

Weddell Sea

Antarctic Peninsula

Alexander I.

Queen Maud Land

ANTARCTICA

Transantarctic Mountains

Vinson Massif

★ South Pole

WEST ANTARCTICA

EAST ANTARCTICA

Bellingshausen Sea

Marie Byrd Land

Ross Ice Shelf

Ross Sea

Wilkes Land

South Magnetic Pole

ANTARCTIC CIRCLE

ARCTIC CIRCLE

Franz Josef Land

North Land

BARENTS SEA

EUROPE

ASIA

SIBERIA

Kamchatka Peninsula

Ural Mountains

Lake Baikal

Aral Sea

Black Sea

Caspian Sea

NORTH PACIFIC OCEAN

TROPIC OF CANCER

AFRICA

ARABIAN PENINSULA

Plateau of Tibet

INDIA

ARABIAN SEA

BAY OF BENGAL

SOUTH CHINA SEA

PHILIPPINE SEA

MICRONESIA

Congo Basin

Lake Victoria

INDONESIA

EQUATOR

MELANESIA

Lake Tanganyika

Lake Malawi

Madagascar

INDIAN OCEAN

Ninetyeast Ridge

AUSTRALIA

TROPIC OF CAPRICORN

CORAL SEA

New Caledonia

Fiji Islands

SOUTH PACIFIC OCEAN

Kalahari Desert

Cape of Good Hope

SOUTHWEST INDIAN RIDGE

Great Barrier Reef

TASMAN SEA

North Island

NEW ZEALAND

South Island

SOUTHEAST INDIAN RIDGE

KERGUELEN PLATEAU

Tasmania

Wilkes Land

THE NEED FOR SATELLITES

The Global Satellite Mosaic along with the biosphere image (lower left) and surface temperature image (lower right) provides an integrated view of our world. The high elevations of the Himalayas and Tibet show up as a cold area (blue). Temperatures (measured as a plant-poor area (tan, biosphere image). Temperature, moisture, and landscape are interrelated. The need to understand the forces shaping environmental change has led to a space race among various countries. In 1997 alone some 85 rockets launched more than 140 satellites—mostly from China, Europe, Japan, Russia, and the United States. Some satellites provide vital communication links propelling economic development, other satellites supply data on patterns and trends associated with agricultural productivity, pollution monitoring, weather forecasting, and many other environmental concerns.

WINKEL TRIPEL PROJECTION, CENTRAL MERIDIAN 0°

SCALE 1:38,931,000

1 CENTIMETER = 389 KILOMETERS, 1 INCH = 614 MILES AT THE EQUATOR

KILOMETERS

STATUTE MILES

SURFACE TEMPERATURE

Reddish colors vividly show average high temperature on the two largest continents, Africa and Asia, from the Sahara to Central Asia. Latitude, mountains, and oceans influence land temperatures.

RLD

MAP

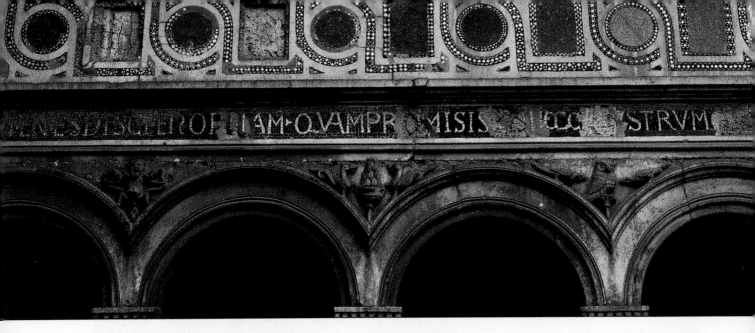

VOLUME II/SIXTEENTH EDITION

JUDITH G. COFFIN

ROBERT C. STACEY

BASED ON *WESTERN CIVILIZATIONS*
BY EDWARD McNALL BURNS

ROBERT E. LERNER

STANDISH MEACHAM

W · W · NORTON & COMPANY · NEW YORK · LONDON

WESTERN
CIVILIZATIONS

THEIR HISTORY
& THEIR CULTURE

W. W. Norton & Company has been independent since its founding in 1923, when William Warder Norton and Mary D. Herter Norton first published lectures delivered at the People's Institute, the adult education division of New York City's Cooper Union. The Nortons soon expanded their program beyond the Institute, publishing books by celebrated academics from America and abroad. By mid-century, the two major pillars of Norton's publishing program—trade books and college texts— were firmly established. In the 1950s, the Norton family transferred control of the company to its employees, and today—with a staff of four hundred and a comparable number of trade, college, and professional titles published each year—W. W. Norton & Company stands as the largest and oldest publishing house owned wholly by its employees.

Composition: TSI Graphics
Manufacturing by R. R. Donnelley & Sons—Willard Division
Book design by Antonina Krass
Layout artist: Paul Lacy
Production manager: Ben Reynolds
Editor: Karl Bakeman
Associate Director, Electronic Media: Steven S. Hoge
Copy Editor: Candace Levy
Project Editor: Lory A. Frenkel
Editorial Assistants: Rebecca Arata, Kate Feighery

The Library of Congress has cataloged the one-volume edition as follows.

Coffin, Judith G., 1952–
    Western civilizations: their history & their culture / by Judith G. Coffin and Robert C. Stacey.—16th ed.
        p. cm.
    Includes bibliographical references and index.
    ISBN 978-0-393-93099-3 (hardcover)
    1. Civilization, Western—Textbooks. 2. Europe—Civilization—Textbooks. I. Stacey,
Robert C. II. Title. III. Title: Western civilizations, their history and their culture.

CB245.C65 2008
909'.09821—dc22   2007042776

ISBN 13: 978-0-393-93098-6 (pbk.)
W. W. Norton & Company, Inc., 500 Fifth Avenue, New York, N.Y. 10110
www.wwnorton.com

W. W. Norton & Company Ltd., Castle House, 75/76 Wells Street, London W1T 3QT
1 2 3 4 5 6 7 8 9 0

To our families—Robin, Will, and Anna Stacey, and Willy, Zoe, and Aaron Forbath—for their patience and support. They reminded us that books such as this are worth the work, and also that there are other things in life.

To Robert Lerner, Standish Meacham, Edward McNall Burns, and Marie Burns, our predecessors who successfully guided *Western Civilizations* for thirteen editions, spanning six decades.

ABOUT THE BOOK

Used by over 1,000,000 students *Western Civilizations* is renowned for its balanced presentation, clear prose, and exceptional treatment of cultural history. Originally published in 1942, the book began as an outgrowth of Edward McNall Burns's Western civilizations course at Rutgers University. Robert Lerner (Northwestern University) and Standish Meacham (University of Texas at Austin) took over authorship in the ninth edition and extended the book's traditional strengths to include the new social history. Beginning with the fourteenth edition, Judith Coffin (University of Texas at Austin) and Robert Stacey (University of Washington) debuted as the third generation of authors to lead this book. While Coffin and Stacey maintain the balanced presentation of *Western Civilizations*, they have enlarged the conception of "Western Civilization" to take in the diversity of the European world.

ABOUT THE AUTHORS

JUDITH G. COFFIN received her Ph.D. in modern French history from Yale University. She has taught at Harvard University and the University of California, Riverside, and is currently associate professor of history at the University of Texas at Austin, where she won a 1999 University of Texas President's Associates' Award for Teaching Excellence. Her research interests focus on the social and cultural history of gender, mass culture, slavery, race relations, and colonialism. She is the author of *The Politics of Women's Work: The Paris Garment Trades, 1750-1915*.

ROBERT C. STACEY is Dean of Humanities and Arts and Professor of History and Jewish Studies at the University of Washington in Seattle. A long-time teacher of western civilization and medieval European history, he has received Distinguished Teaching Awards from both the University of Washington and Yale University, where he taught from 1984 to 1988. The author or coauthor of four books, he is a Fellow of the Royal Historical Society and has held awards from the American Council of Learned Societies and from the Guggenheim Foundation. His current research deals with the history of Jews in medieval England.

CONTENTS

CHAPTER 14 RELIGIOUS WARS AND STATE BUILDING, 1540–1660   502

PART V EARLY MODERN EUROPE

CHAPTER 15 ABSOLUTISM AND EMPIRE, 1660–1789   538

CHAPTER 16 THE NEW SCIENCE OF THE SEVENTEENTH CENTURY   578

CHAPTER 17 THE ENLIGHTENMENT   602

PART VI   THE AGE OF REVOLUTION

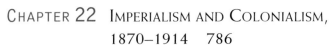

PART VII THE WEST AT THE WORLD'S CENTER

PART VIII   THE WEST AND THE WORLD

Documents

CHRONOLOGIES

MAPS

PREFACE

Since the 1920s, the western civilization survey course has held a central place in the curricula of American universities and high schools. Yet the concept of "western civilization" remains both elusive and controversial. It seems appropriate, therefore, that we begin by defining our terms. How do we, as authors, conceive of our subject?

During much of the twentieth century, "western" civilization meant "the civilization of western Europe," to which the history of the Ancient Near East was somewhat arbitrarily attached. Western civilization was therefore presented as beginning at Sumer, developing in Egypt, and then flowering in Greece. From Greece it spread to Rome, then made its way to France, Germany, England, Italy, and Spain, whose emigrating colonists brought it to the Americas after 1492. Rather like a train passing through stations, western civilization was thus conceived as picking up "cargo" at each of its stops, but always retaining the same engine and the same baggage cars.

This vision of western civilization was not only selective, it was often tied to a series of contentious assumptions. It cast the worldwide dominance of the European imperial powers between roughly 1800 and 1950 as the culmination of several thousand years of historical development, which it was the obligation of historians to explain. It also tended to presume that European global dominance in the nineteenth and twentieth centuries reflected and demonstrated the superiority of western European civilization over the African, Asian, and Native American civilizations the Europeans conquered during the heyday of their imperial expansion.

Historians today are keenly aware of how much such an account leaves out. It slights the use of force and fraud in European expansion. It also ignores the sophistication, dynamism, and humanity of the many cultures it sidelines. By neglecting the crucial importance of Byzantium and Islam, it even gives a misleadingly narrow account of the development of European civilization. It also misleads us about the civilizations created in North and South America after 1492, which were creole, or hybrid, cultures, not simply European cultures transplanted to other shores. This is not to argue that a study of western civilizations must give way to a study of world civilization. It is merely to insist that understanding the historical development of the West requires us to place our subject in a geographical and cultural context that is wider than western Europe alone; and that, shorn of its triumphalism, the history of these various and differing western civilizations becomes vastly more interesting.

Therefore, we mean for the plural in our title, *Western Civilizations*, to be taken seriously. The West cannot be understood as a single, continuous historical culture. Rather, there have been a number of western civilizations whose fundamental characteristics have changed markedly over time. We treat "western" as a geographical designator referring to the major civilizations that developed in and around the Mediterranean Sea between 3500 B.C.E. ("Before the Common Era," equivalent to the Christian dating system B.C., "Before Christ") and 500 C.E. ("Common Era," equivalent to the Christian dating system A.D., "Anno Domini," "the Year of the Lord"). We also treat as "western" the civilizations that emerged out of the Mediterranean world in the centuries after 500 C.E., as the Greco-Roman world of antiquity divided into Islamic, Byzantine, and Latin Christian realms. The interdependence and mutual influences of these three western civilizations upon each other will be a recurring theme of the first half of this book. We take the same approach to describing the complex relationships between Europe and the other world civilizations with which it came into contact after 1500.

Western Civilizations rests on the efforts and learning of three generations of historians. Edward McNall Burns, Robert Lerner, and Standish Meacham constructed a textbook that combined a vigorous narrative style with attention to the diverse ways in which ordinary people responded to changing environments, societies, and cultures. In building upon their work, we have tried to retain these traditional strengths by remaining attentive to narrative, by aiming for clarity and accessibility without compromising on accuracy or ignoring complexity, and by presenting politics and culture as part of a single, shared world of historical experience.

We have also made significant changes to the book that reflect the changing historical interests of teachers, students, and scholars. In keeping with our broadened understanding of western civilizations, we devote much more attention to the world outside western Europe. We continue to integrate new scholarly work in social and cultural history and the history of gender into our narrative, but we have also substantially increased the attention we pay to economic, religious, and military history. We also pay particular attention to the varying ways in which these different western civilizations sought to govern themselves and the territories they conquered. "Empire" has been a consistent

theme in the history of the West for more than four thousand years. In revising this book, we have tried to do justice to its importance.

CHANGES TO THE SIXTEENTH EDITION

Throughout, we have worked to integrate the text, visual material, and pedagogy. That has meant bringing in different images, rewriting focus questions, and adding study questions to the documents as well as updating the text. These changes make the text more user-friendly while still allowing professors and students alike to tailor it to their particular course and interests.

Part I, "The Ancient Near East," was completely reorganized and rewritten for the fifteenth edition. However, we have made a number of changes to the text as well as to the artwork and document selections. In Chapter 1, the discussion of prehistory and the emergence of the earliest towns and villages have been updated, with particular attention to the exciting archaeological work currently underway at Çatal Höyük. We have also revised the presentation of Sumerian religion and added a discussion of Enheduanna, high priestess and daughter of Sargon I of Akkad. In Chapter 2, we have revised the discussion of Hatshepsut's role as a female pharaoh and added many new illustrations, including Hatshepsut's mortuary temple, one of the glories of ancient Egyptian architecture.

In Part II, readers will find a much-improved program of illustrations in all the chapters. Chapter 4 includes a revised account of Hellenistic religions, especially the so-called "mystery cults." Reflecting the consensus of recent scholarly work, Mithraism is now discussed only in Chapter 5, as an example of the new religious devotions that swept through early imperial Roman society. Readers will also find in Chapter 5 a new treatment of the economy of the Roman empire. Chapter 6 offers a completely new account of the fall of the western Roman empire during the fifth century C.E., emphasizing the suddenness of Rome's collapse and the profound consequences this collapse had for the Roman economy and for standards of living within the western Roman empire. Here too, as throughout the book, we are trying to reflect the current balance of scholarly opinion.

In Part III, "The Middle Ages," Chapter 7 now includes a separate section on the Vikings with several new accompanying illustrations. This chapter also features a revised explanation of the split between Shi'ite and Sunni Islam, a revised assessment of the influence of early Islamic civilization on Europe, and a new document box pairing passages from the Qur'an on Jews and Christians with the "Pact of Umar." Chapter 8 features another new document box, on the summoning of the First Crusade in 1096. A number of new illustrations have been added to Chapter 8 to give more students a better sense of daily life during the high middle ages. Readers will also find an improved discussion of climate change during this period. Chapter 9 includes a new document box on kingship as a religious office, which we hope will make it easier for students to grasp the issues at stake in the Investiture Conflict.

Part IV, "From Medieval to Modern," begins with a completely new chapter (10) on the later middle ages, which emphasizes the remarkable resilience and creativity that characterized European responses to the Black Death. The far-reaching consequences of the plague upon social, economic, and religious life are the central themes of this chapter. Interestingly, however, there is now considerable doubt among historians and epidemiologists as to whether the Black Death was in fact an outbreak of bubonic plague, or whether it may have been some other disease entirely. This new chapter includes an up-to-date discussion of this controversy, which remains unresolved as this book goes to press.

In Chapter 13, "Reformations of Religion," readers will find a new section on "Reform and Discipline," and a new selection of paired documents, contrasting Lutheran and Catholic positions on marriage and celibacy.

In Part V, we have rewritten Chapter 16, "The New Science of the Seventeenth Century," to make it clearer and more accessible. It emphasizes the transformation of scientific knowledge, practice, and institutions. Here as in all our discussions of intellectual history, we foreground the context in which new ideas emerged and how those ideas came to matter for a range of people, from philosophers, rulers, and bureaucrats to explorers, artists, and artisans.

In Part VI, we have expanded discussion of Napoleon's empire and its legacy to Europe and the world. We have added to Chapter 21 an extended discussion of slavery and its abolition in the Americas which follows up on the treatment of the Haitian revolution in Chapter 18. Coming as it does before the section on the American Civil War, it places developments in the United States in a larger, comparative perspective. No course can be comprehensive, especially one dealing with a topic as hard to define as the

West, but we have chosen to touch down on a few topics, like the politics of abolition, with an eye to highlighting comparisons and global connections. We have expanded the treatment of U.S. imperialism in Chapter 22 for the same reason.

Part VI continues to be organized thematically. Chapter 19, on industrial society, focuses on the relationship between social, economic, and cultural change—or on industry as a way of life. Chapters 20 and 21 break the tumultuous history of the mid-nineteenth-century revolutions into two parts, to make themes easier to follow. Chapter 20 goes from the reaction against the French Revolution of 1789 to the renewed outbreak of revolution in 1848, and includes a discussion of nineteenth-century political ideologies and cultural movements. Chapter 21 begins with the revolutions of 1848 in central and eastern Europe and then focuses on the issues those revolutions raised, nation and state building, as they played out elsewhere.

In Part VII, we have revised Chapter 24, on World War I. Readers will find more material on the long-term evolution of warfare and the emergence of total war. We have also expanded the treatment of the Paris Peace Conference, another important global moment. The new scope of war summoned global institutions to contend with the war's ramifications. Whether or not those international concerns could be compatible with national interests was an open question, and would become a theme of the history of the twentieth century. So would other issues central to the Peace of Paris, such as the expansion of empire, the mobilization of movements for national self determination, and the protection of minorities within new nation states.

In Part VIII, which was almost entirely rewritten for the previous edition, we added discussion of the history of human rights to conclude the chapter on globalization. Why, suddenly, is the language of human rights so familiar? The change highlights the dramatic political transformation wrought by the end of the cold war; it also reflects the new horizons of a rapidly globalizing world, with all their potential and peril. Finally, a history of human rights provides the occasion to review some of the central debates of the Western political tradition.

INNOVATIVE PEDAGOGICAL PROGRAM

Western Civilizations, Sixteenth Edition, is designed for maximum readability. The crisp, clear, and concise narrative is also accompanied by a pedagogical program to help students study while engaging them in the subject matter. Highlights of this innovative program include:

- **New "Transformations" feature provokes students to consider the implications of major historical events.** Throughout the Sixteenth Edition, we have inserted new material on important "transformations" in the history of western civilizations. Highlighted with an icon, these sections ask students to reflect on the larger political, social, or cultural consequences of major turning points in history. Frequently, they draw on cutting-edge scholarship that has transformed our understanding of these events. New "Tranformations" include:

- Chapter 1: "The Origins of Food Production in the Ancient Near East." This rewritten and expanded section focuses on the disadvantages and the advantages of agriculture.

- Chapter 6: "The German Invasions and the Fall of the Western Roman Empire." The new material on the German-Roman relations elaborates on the economic collapse of western Rome in the fifth century, and explains how aspects of Roman life—the tax and administrative system, agricultural systems, and city life—persisted.

- Chapter 10: "The Black Death." The effects of the plague rippled across Europe. It affected every aspect of life. For example, fewer people were available to work the fields, but there were also fewer people to feed. Prices of grain went up, but because there were fewer people competing for jobs, wages did, too. Consequently, ordinary people could now afford not only to buy more bread, they could also purchase dairy products, meat, fish, fruits and wine on a more regular basis. As a result, the people of Europe in the later middle ages ate a more balanced diet, and were consequently better nourished than they had been for centuries, or than some are today.

- Chapter 16: "Science and Cultural Change." This new "transformation" section deals with the cultural shifts that arose from the Scientific Revolution. Beginning in the 17th century, embracing science and the scientific method was at the heart of what it meant to be "modern." This has implications for the Enlightenment, but it also became the justification for new technologies and for new empires.

- Chapter 24: "The Peace Settlement at Versailles." The Treaty of Versailles marks the emergence of the United States as a world power. But it also repre-

sents the first time so many countries were involved in a peace settlement and marks the scope of the war, the growing national sentiments and aspirations, and the tightening of international communication and economic networks.

- **NEW Document Questions.** Professors requested questions for the documents in the book. We have added questions at the bottom of each box that ask students to engage the primary source or connect it to the larger issues in the chapter.

- **End-of-Chapter Key Terms.** In response to requests from professors, each chapter includes a list of key terms to help students focus on the key ideas, events, or people in the chapter.

- **In-Text Documents.** To add depth to the more focused narrative of *Western Civilizations*, each chapter contains an average of four primary sources, two of which are paired to convey a sense of historical complexity and diversity.

- **Map Program with Enhanced Captions.** Over 130 beautiful maps appear throughout the text, including twenty-five new maps, each accompanied by an enhanced caption designed to engage the reader analytically while conveying the key role that geography plays in the development of history and the societies of the world.

- **In-Chapter Chronologies.** Several brief chronologies built around particular events, topics, or periods appear in each chapter and are designed to provide road maps through the narrative detail.

- **Focus Question System.** To ensure that students remain alert to key concepts and questions on every page of the text, focus questions guide their reading in three ways: (1) a focus question box appears at the beginning of each chapter to preview the chapter's contents; (2) relevant questions reappear at the start of the section in which they are discussed; and (3) running heads on the righthand pages keep these questions in view throughout the chapter.

- **Pull Quotes.** Lifted directly from the narrative, pull quotes appear throughout each chapter to highlight key thoughts and keen insights while keeping students focused on larger concepts and ideas.

RESOURCES FOR STUDENTS

⑤ StudySpace
wwnorton.com/studyspace

This student website provides a rich array of multimedia resources and review materials within a proven, task-oriented study plan.

Each chapter is arranged in an effective *Organize, Learn, and Connect* pedagogy:

Organize
In this section, students can work through Focus Questions, print out Chapter Outlines and summaries, or check in with Progress Reports that help them focus their studies.

Learn
This section encourages active learning with:
- **iMaps and GeoQuizzes that engage and test students' geographic knowledge** with map review worksheets and maps with zoom functions, highlighting, and labels.
- **Multiple-choice quizzes for each chapter.**
- **FlashCards** with audio pronunciations.
- **Interactive Chrono-Sequencers** that challenge students to reassemble sequences of events, reinforcing their understanding of the flow of history.
- **NEW! Document Quizzes** provide a form for students to answer the questions about the in-text documents.

Connect
In this section, students are reminded to connect to additional resources that include:
- **250 additional primary source documents**
- **Research Topics** that combine a writing prompt, documents, headnotes and sample questions.
- **NEW Interactive MapPlayer** with audio introductions, transitions, and conclusions, along with a suite of interactive functions to examine individual maps as they are presented in a progressive sequence.
- **Audio Glossary**

Study Guide
Margaret Minor and Paul Wilson, *Nicholls State University*

The *Study Guide* gives students a comprehensive means for review and self-assessment. Each chapter contains a chapter outline, identifications, multiple-choice questions, matching, and true/false questions, chronologies, and short-answer and essay questions.

RESOURCES FOR INSTRUCTORS

Norton Media Library
This newly expanded resource for multimedia lectures offers:
- PowerPoint presentations for each chapter
- Hi-resolution maps and graphics files from the book
- Art from the book
- Questions for Classroom Response PowerPoints (Clicker Questions)

Instructor's Manual
Steven Kreis, *American Public University*

Each chapter in the *Instructor's Manual* includes lecture outlines, key lecture topics, suggested films, and suggestions for integrating media into the classroom and using media as homework assignments.

Test Bank
April Harper, *State University of New York, Oneonta*

This vastly expanded test bank includes 60% more questions, including true/false and essay questions. It is available in *ExamView® Assessment Suite*, WebCT, and Blackboard formats.

Blackboard and WebCT Coursepacks offer study plans that integrate review materials for each chapter, as well as ready-to-use test banks, maps, PowerPoint lecture presentations, and practice quizzes.

Map Transparencies

ACKNOWLEDGMENTS

The drafts of the manuscript have benefited from careful reading by and suggestions from a group of professors to whom we are greatly indebted. Our sincere thanks to:
- Eric Ash, Wayne State University
- Sacha Auerbach, Virginia Commonwealth University
- Ken Bartlett, University of Toronto
- Benita Blessing, Ohio University
- Chuck Boening, Shelton State Community College
- John Bohstedt, University of Tennessee– Knoxville
- Dan Brown, Moorpark College
- Kevin Caldwell, Blue Ridge Community College
- Jodi Campbell, Texas Christian University
- Annette Chamberlain, Virginia Western Community College
- Jason Coy, College of Charleston
- Benjamin Ehlers, University of Georgia

- Maryann Farkas, Dawson College
- Gloria Fitzgibbon, Wake Forest University
- Tina Gaddis, Onondaga Community College
- Alex Garman, Eastern New Mexico State University
- Norman Goda, Ohio University
- Andrew Goldman, Gonzaga University
- Robert Grasso, Monmouth University
- Sylvia Gray, Portland Community College
- Susan Grayzel, University of Mississippi
- Hazel Hahn, Seattle University
- Derek Hastings, Oakland University
- Dawn Hayes, Montclair State University
- John Houston, Fordham University
- Michael Hughes, Wake Forest University
- Bruce Hunt, University of Texas–Austin
- Ahmed Ibrahim, Southwest Missouri State University
- Kevin James, University of Guelph
- John Kearney, Cy Fair Community College
- Elizabeth Lehfeldt, Cleveland State University
- Thomas Maulucci, State University of New York–Fredonia
- Amy McCandless, College of Charleston
- Nicholas Murray, Adirondack College
- Charles Odahl, Boise State University
- Bill Olejniczak, College of Charleston
- Jeffery Plaks, University of Central Oklahoma
- Peter Pozesky, College of Wooster
- Rebecca Schloss, Texas A&M University
- Patrick Speelman, College of Charleston
- Paul Teverow, Missouri Southern State University
- James Vanstone, John Abbott College
- Kirk Willis, University of Georgia
- Ian Worthington, University of Missouri–Columbia
- Margarita Youngo, Pima Community College

We want to thank Steve Forman and Jon Durbin at W. W. Norton & Company for their faith in this project; Karl Bakeman for his intelligent editing, consistent support, and exceptional good cheer; and Rebecca Arata, Kate Feighery, Ben Reynolds, and Lory Frenkel for their help with all aspects of the production process.

Robert Stacey is principally responsible for Chapters 1–15. He owes special thanks to Jason Hawke of Northern Illinois University for his extraordinary help in drafting Chapters 1–5. He would also like to acknowledge the assistance of a large number of friends and colleagues around the country who have taken the time to answer queries and offer suggestions: Jon Crump, Gerald Eck, Sandra Joshel, Mary O'Neil, Ben Schmidt, Julie Stein, Carol Thomas, Joel Walker, and Dan Waugh of the University of Washington; Michael Halvorson, University of Puget Sound; Michelle Ferry, University of California, Santa Barbara; Byron Nakamura, Southern Connecticut State University; Lawrence Duggan, University of Delaware; and Robert Stiefel, University of New Hampshire.

Judith Coffin is principally responsible for the revisions to Chapter 16–29. Many colleagues have supplied expertise and references, particularly Caroline Castiglione, David Crew, Paul Hagenloh, Tony Hopkins, Bruce Hunt, Standish Meacham, John Merriman, Gail Minault, Joan Neuberger, Paula Sanders, Daniel Sherman, James Sidbury, Robert Stephens, Michael Stoff, and Charters Wynn. Patrick Timmons, Marion Barber, Cori Crider, April Smith, and, especially, Michael Schmidt were terrific research assistants. Special thanks to Dinah Chenven and Norman Chenven who drafted Chapter 16, to James Brophy for his consistently excellent advice, to Geoffrey Clayton and Justin Glasson, who have researched, edited, and written many chapters, and to the students in Western Civ at the University of Texas, Austin.

WESTERN
CIVILIZATIONS

CHAPTER ELEVEN

CHAPTER CONTENTS

COMMERCE, CONQUEST, AND COLONIZATION, 1300–1600

B Y 1300, THE GREAT EUROPEAN expansion of the High Middle Ages was coming to an end. In Iberia, there would be no further conquests of Muslim territory until 1492, when Granada fell to King Ferdinand and Queen Isabella. In the East, the Crusader kingdoms of Constantinople and Acre collapsed, in 1261 and 1291 respectively. Only the German drive into eastern Europe continued; but by the mid-fourteenth century, it too had been slowed by the rise of a new Baltic state in Lithuania. Internal expansion was also ending, as Europe reached the ecological limits of its resources. Thereafter, the pressure on resources was eased only by the dramatic population losses that resulted during the fourteenth century from the combined effects of famine, plague, and war.

But despite these checks, Europeans in the late Middle Ages did not turn inward. Although land-based conquests slowed, new sea-based empires emerged in the Mediterranean world during the fourteenth and fifteenth centuries, with colonies that extended from the Black Sea to the Canary Islands. New maritime trade routes were opened up through the Strait of Gibraltar, resulting in greater economic integration between the Mediterranean and Atlantic economies and increasing the demand in northwestern Europe for Asian spices and African gold. By the late fifteenth century, Mediterranean mariners and colonists had extended their domination out into the Atlantic, from the Azores in the north to the Canary Islands in the south. Portuguese navigators were also pushing down the west coast of Africa. In 1498 one such expedition would sail all the way around the Cape of Good Hope to India.

The fifteenth-century conquest of the "Atlantic Mediterranean" was the essential preliminary to the dramatic events that began in 1492 with Columbus's attempt to reach China by sailing westward across the Atlantic Ocean and that led, by 1600, to the Spanish and Portuguese conquests of the Americas. Because these events are so familiar, we can easily underestimate their importance. For the native peoples and empires of the Americas, the results of European contact were cataclysmic. By 1600, somewhere between 50 and 90 percent of the indigenous peoples of the

FOCUS QUESTIONS

• What impact did the Mongol conquests have on Europe?

• Why were slaves so important to Ottoman society?

 • How were the Portuguese able to control Indian Ocean trade?

• What was the impact of New World silver on the European economy?

Americas had perished from disease, massacre, and enslavement. For Europeans, the results of their conquests were less lethal but no less far reaching. By 1300, Europe had eclipsed both Byzantium and the lands of Islam as a Mediterranean power, but outside the Mediterranean and the north Atlantic European power was negligible. By 1600, however, Europe had emerged as the first truly global power in world history, capable of pursuing its imperial ambitions and commercial interests wherever its ships could sail and its guns could reach. Europeans would not achieve full control over the interiors of the African, Asian, and American land masses until the end of the nineteenth century, and their control would last thereafter for less than a century. By 1600, however, European navies ruled the seas, and the world's resources were increasingly being channeled through European hands—patterns that have continued until the present day.

THE MONGOLS

What impact did the Mongol conquests have on Europe?

Trade between the Mediterranean world and the Far East dated back to antiquity, but it was not until the late thirteenth century that Europeans began to establish direct trading connections with India, China, and the Spice Islands of the Indonesian archipelago. For Europeans, these connections would prove profoundly important, although less for their economic significance than for their impact on the European imagination. For the peoples of Asia, however, the appearance of European traders on the Silk Road between Central Asia and China was merely a curiosity. The really consequential event was the rise of the Mongol Empire that made such connections possible.

THE RISE OF THE MONGOL EMPIRE

The Mongols were one of a number of nomadic peoples inhabiting the steppes of Central Asia. Although closely connected with various Turkish-speaking peoples with whom they frequently intermarried, the Mongols spoke their own distinctive language and had their own homeland to the north of the Gobi Desert in present-day Mongolia. Sheep provided them with shelter (in the form of wool tents), clothing, milk, and meat.

Like many nomadic peoples throughout history, the Mongols were highly accomplished cavalry soldiers who supplemented their own pastoralism and craft production by raiding the sedentary peoples to their south. (It was in part to control such raiding from Mongolia that, many centuries before, the Chinese had built the famous Great Wall.) Primarily, however, China defended itself by attempting to ensure that the Mongols remained internally divided and so turned their martial energies most often against each other.

In the late twelfth century, however, a Mongol chief named Temüjin began to unite the various Mongol tribes under his rule. By incorporating the army of each defeated tribe into his own army, Temüjin quickly built up a large military force. In 1206, his supremacy was formally acknowledged by all the Mongols, and he took the title Chingiz (Genghis) Khan—"the oceanic [possibly meaning "universal"] ruler." Chingiz now turned his enormous army against his non-Mongol neighbors. China at this time was divided into three hostile states. In 1209, Chingiz launched an attack on northwestern China; in 1211 he invaded the Chin Empire in north China. At first these attacks were probably looting expeditions rather than deliberate attempts at conquest, but by the 1230s a full-scale Mongol conquest of northern and western China was under way, culminating in 1234 with the fall of the Chin. In 1279, Chingiz's grandson Qubilai (Kublai) Khan completed the conquest of southern (Sung) China, thus reuniting China for the first time in centuries.

Meanwhile, Chingiz turned his forces westward, conquering much of Central Asia and incorporating the important commercial cities of Tashkent, Samarkand, and Bukhara into his expanding empire. When Chingiz died in 1227, he was succeeded by his third son Ögedei (*EHRG-uh-day*), who completed the conquest of the Chin, conquered the lands between the Oxus River and the Caspian Sea and then laid plans for a massive inva-

CHRONOLOGY

RISE OF THE MONGOL EMPIRE, 1206–1260

Temüjin crowned as Chingiz Khan	1206
Mongols conquer northern China	1234
Mongols conquer southern Russia	1237–1240
Mongol forces withdraw from Europe	1241
Mamluk sultanate halts Mongol advance in Egypt	1260

sion toward the west. Between 1237 and 1240, the Mongol horde (so called from the Turkish word *ordu*, meaning "tent" or "encampment") conquered southern Russia and then launched a two-pronged assault farther west. The smaller of the two Mongol armies swept through Poland toward eastern Germany; the larger army went southwest toward Hungary. In April 1241 the smaller Mongol force met a hastily assembled army of Germans and Poles at the battle of Liegnitz, where

the two sides fought to a bloody standstill. Two days later, the larger Mongol army annihilated the Hungarian army at the River Sajo.

How much farther west the Mongol armies might have pushed will forever remain in doubt, for in December 1241 the Great Khan Ögedei died, and the Mongol forces withdrew from eastern Europe. It took five years before a new great khan could establish himself, and when he died in 1248, the resulting interregnum lasted

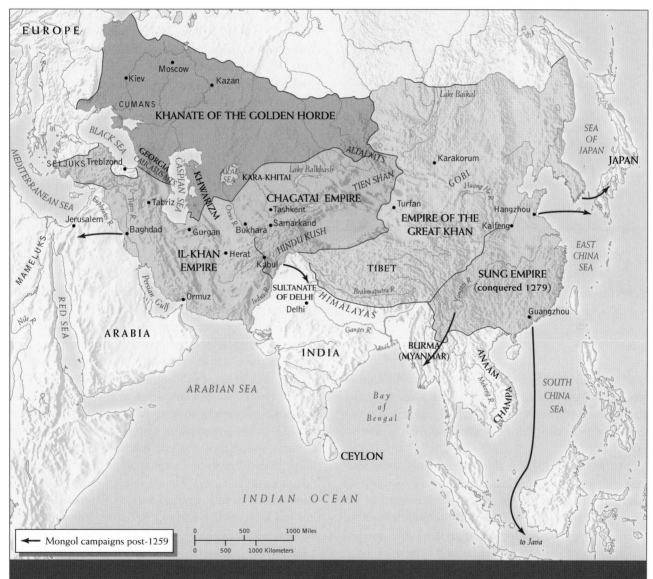

THE MONGOL SUCCESSOR STATES

Consider the breakup of Chingiz Khan's empire after 1259 and the passing similarities its fracture might possess to the disintegration of Alexander's empire, also conquered swiftly and encompassing vast swaths of Europe and Asia. Why did Chingiz Khan's empire splinter? How did the Mongol onslaught against and occupation of major sections of the Arab Muslim world possibly aid the expansion of European civilization and trade into the Mediterranean? At the same time, how did it complicate the situation for the crusader efforts in the Holy Land?

The Head of Timur the Lame. A forensic reconstruction based on his exhumed skull.

for three more years. Mongol conquests continued in Persia, the Middle East, and China; but after 1241 the Mongols never resumed their attacks on Europe. By 1300, the period of Mongol expansion had come to an end.

But the Mongol threat did not suddenly disappear. Descendants of Chingiz Khan continued to rule this enormous land empire (the largest such empire in the history of the world) until the mid-fourteenth century. Later, under the leadership of Timur the Lame (known as Tamerlane to Europeans) it looked briefly as if the Mongol Empire might be reunited. But Timur died in 1405 on his way to invade China; thereafter the various parts of the Mongol Empire fell into the hands of local rulers, including (in Asia Minor) the Ottoman Turks. Mongol cultural influence continued, however, and can be seen in the enormously impressive artwork produced during the fifteenth and sixteenth centuries in Persia and in Mughal India.

The Mongols owed their success to the size, speed, and training of their mounted armies; to the intimi-

dating savagery with which they butchered those who resisted them; and to their ability to adapt the administrative traditions of their subjects to their own purposes. Partly because the Mongols themselves put little store even in their own shamanistic religious traditions, they were also unusually tolerant of the religious beliefs of others—a distinct advantage in controlling an empire that comprised a dizzying array of Buddhist, Christian, and Muslim sects. However, little was distinctively "Mongol" about the way they governed their empire. Except in China, where the Mongol Yuan Dynasty inherited and maintained a complex administrative bureaucracy, the Mongols' rule was relatively unsophisticated, being chiefly directed at securing the steady payment of tribute from their subjects.

EUROPE, THE MONGOLS, AND THE FAR EAST

The Mongols had a keen eye for the commercial advantages their empire could offer them. They took steps to control the caravan routes that led from China through Central Asia to the Black Sea. They also encouraged commercial contacts with European traders, especially through the Iranian city of Tabriz, from which both land and sea routes led on to China. Until the Mongol conquests, the Silk Road to China had been closed to Western merchants and travelers. But almost as soon as the Mongol Empire was established, we find Europeans venturing on these routes. The first such travelers were Franciscan missionaries such as William de Rubruck, sent by King Louis IX of France in 1253 as his ambassador to the Mongol court. But Western merchants quickly followed. The most famous of these early merchants were three Venetians: Niccolo, Maffeo, and Marco Polo. Marco Polo's account of his twenty-year sojourn in China in the service of Qubilai Khan and of his journey home through the Spice Islands, India, and Iran, is one of the most famous travel accounts of all time. Its effect on the imagination of his contemporaries was enormous. For the next two centuries, most of what Europeans knew about the Far East they learned from Marco Polo's *Travels.* Christopher Columbus's copy of this book still survives.

European connections with the western end of the Silk Road would continue until the mid-fourteenth century. The Genoese were especially active in this trade, not least because their rivals, the Venetians, already dominated the Mediterranean trade with Alexandria

MARCO POLO'S DESCRIPTION OF JAVA

The Venetian merchants Niccolo and Maffeo Polo traveled overland from Constantinople to the court of Qubilai Khan between 1260 and 1269. When they returned a few years later, they brought with them Niccolo's son Marco. A gifted linguist, Marco would remain at the Mongol court until the early 1290s, when he returned to Europe after a journey through Southeast Asia, the Spice Islands, and the Indian Ocean. Marco's account of his travels would shape European images of the Far East for centuries.

Departing from Ziamba, and steering between south and south-east, fifteen hundred miles, you reach an island of very great size, named Java. According to the reports of some well-informed navigators, it is the greatest in the world, and has a compass above three thousand miles. It is under the dominion of one king only, nor do the inhabitants pay tribute to any other power. They are worshipers of idols.

The country abounds with rich commodities. Pepper, nutmegs, spikenard, galangal, cubebs, cloves and all the other valuable spices and drugs, are the produce of the island; which occasion it to be visited by many ships laden with merchandise, that yields to the owners considerable profit.

The quantity of gold collected there exceeds all calculation and belief. From thence it is that . . . merchants . . . have imported, and to this day import, that metal to a great amount, and from thence also is obtained the greatest part of the spices that are distributed throughout the world. That the Great Khan [Qubilai] has not brought the island under subjection to him, must be attributed to the length of the voyage and the dangers of the navigation.

The Travels of Marco Polo, rev. and ed. Manuel Komroff (New York, 1926), pp. 267–268.

QUESTIONS FOR ANALYSIS

1. What effect did Marco Polo's *Travels* have on European images of the Far East?
2. Why did Marco Polo refer to various spices as "rich commodities"? Why were spices so highly valued by Europeans?

and Beirut, through which the bulk of Europe's Far Eastern luxury goods continued to pass. But the Mongols of Iran become progressively more hostile to Westerners as the fourteenth century progressed. By 1344, the Genoese had abandoned Tabriz after attacks on Westerners had made their position there untenable. In 1346, the Mongols of the Golden Horde besieged the Genoese colony at Caffa on the Black Sea. Apart from crippling Genoese commerce in the Black Sea, this siege is memorable chiefly because during it the Black Death was passed from the Mongol army (which had inadvertently brought it from the Gobi Desert, where the disease was endemic) to the Genoese defenders, who returned with it to western Europe, where it proceeded to kill at least one third of the entire European population.

The window of opportunity that made Marco Polo's travels possible was thus relatively short. By the middle of the fourteenth century, hostilities between the various parts of the Mongol Empire were already making travel along the Silk Road perilous. After 1368, when the Mongol (Yuan) Dynasty was overthrown, Westerners were excluded from China altogether, and Mongols were restricted to cavalry service in the Ming imperial armies. The overland trade routes from China to the Black Sea continued to operate; Europeans, however, were no longer able to travel along them. But the new, more integrated commercial world the Mongols created had a lasting impact on Europe, despite the relatively short time during which Europeans themselves were able to participate directly in it. European memories of the Far East would be preserved, and the dream of reestablishing direct connections between Europe and China would survive to influence a new round of European commercial and imperial expansion from the late fifteenth century onward.

THE RISE OF THE OTTOMAN EMPIRE

Why were slaves so important to Ottoman society?

Like the Mongols, the Ottoman Turks were initially a nomadic people whose economy continued to depend on raiding even after they had conquered an extensive empire. The peoples who would become the Ottomans were already established in northwestern Anatolia when the Mongols arrived and were already at least nominally Muslims. But unlike the established Muslim powers in the region, whom the Mongols destroyed, the Ottoman Turks were among the principal beneficiaries of the Mongol conquest. By toppling the Seljuk sultanate and the Abbasid caliphate of Baghdad, the Mongols eliminated the two traditional authorities that had previously kept Turkish border chieftains like the Ottomans in check. Now the Ottomans were free to raid along their soft frontiers with Byzantium unhindered. At the same time, however, they remained far enough away from the centers of Mongol authority to avoid being destroyed themselves.

By toppling the Seljuk sultanate and the Abbasid caliphate of Baghdad, the Mongols eliminated the two traditional authorities that had previously kept Turkish border chieftains like the Ottomans in check.

THE CONQUEST OF CONSTANTINOPLE

By the end of the thirteenth century, the Ottoman Dynasty had established itself as the leading family among the Anatolian border lords. By the mid-fourteenth century, it had solidified its preeminence by capturing a number of important cities. These successes brought the Ottomans to the attention of the Byzantine emperor, who in 1345 hired a contingent of Ottomans as mercenaries. Thus introduced into Europe, the Ottomans quickly made themselves at home. By 1370, they had extended their control all the way to the Danube. In 1389 Ottoman forces defeated the powerful Serbian Empire at the battle of Kosovo, enabling them to consolidate their control over Greece, Bulgaria, and the Balkans.

In 1396 the Ottomans attacked Constantinople, but withdrew to repel a Western crusading force that had been sent against them. In 1402, they attacked Constantinople again, but once more were forced to withdraw, this time to confront a Mongolian invasion of Anatolia. Led by Timur the Lame, the Mongol army captured the Ottoman sultan and destroyed his army; for the next decade it appeared that Ottoman hegemony over Anatolia might be gone forever. By 1413, however, Timur was dead, a new sultan had emerged, and the Ottomans were able to resume their conquests. Ottoman pressure on Constantinople continued during the 1420s and 1430s, producing a steady stream of Byzantine refugees who brought with them to Italy the surviving masterworks of classical Greek literature. But it was not until 1451 that a new sultan, Mehmet II, turned his full attention to the conquest of the imperial city. In 1453, after a brilliantly executed siege, Mehmet succeeded in breaching the city's walls. The Byzantine emperor was killed in the assault, the city itself was thoroughly plundered, and its population was sold into slavery. The Ottomans then settled down to rule their new capital in a style reminiscent of their Byzantine predecessors.

The Ottoman conquest of Constantinople was an enormous psychological shock to Christian Europe, but its economic impact on western Europe was minor. Ottoman control over the former Byzantine Empire did reduce European access to the Black Sea, but the bulk of the Far Eastern luxury trade with Europe had never passed through the Black Sea ports in the first place. Europeans got most of their spices and silks through Venice, which imported them from Alexandria and Beirut. These two cities did not fall to the Ottomans until the 1520s. In no sense, therefore, can the Ottomans be seen as the spur that propelled Portuguese efforts during the late fifteenth century to establish a direct sea route between Europe, India, and the Spice Islands. If anything, the opposite is the case. After the Portuguese established a direct sea route between Europe and India, it was their attempts to exclude Muslims from the Indian Ocean spice trade that helped spur the Ottoman conquests of Syria, Egypt, and Hungary during the 1520s and 1530s. To be sure, these Ottoman conquests had other motives also, including the desire to control the Egypt-

ian grain trade. But by eliminating the merchants who had traditionally dominated the overland spice trade through Beirut and Alexandria, the Ottomans also hoped to redirect this trade through Constantinople, and then up the Danube into western Europe.

The effects of the Ottoman conquest of Constantinople on western Europe were modest. On the Ottomans themselves, however, their conquest was transformative. Vast new wealth poured into Ottoman society, which the Ottomans increased by carefully tending to the industrial and commercial interests of their new capital city. Trade routes were redirected to feed the capital, and the Ottomans became a naval power in the eastern Mediterranean and the Black Sea. As a result, Constantinople's population grew from less than 100,000 in 1453 to more than 500,000 in 1600, making it the largest city in the world outside China.

WAR, SLAVERY, AND SOCIAL ADVANCEMENT

Despite the Ottomans' careful attention to commerce, their empire rested on raiding and conquest. Until the end of the sixteenth century, the Ottoman Empire was therefore on an almost constant war footing. To continue its conquests, the size of the Ottoman army and administration grew exponentially. But this growth drew more and more manpower from the empire. Because the Ottoman army and administration were largely composed of slaves, the demand for more soldiers and administrators could best be met through further conquests that would capture yet more slaves. Further conquests, however, required a still larger army and an even more extensive bureaucracy; and so the cycle continued.

Sultan Mehmet II, "The Conqueror" (1451–1481), by Ottoman Artist Siblizade Ahmed. The sultan's pose and handkerchief are Central Asian conventions in portraiture, but the subdued color and three-quarter profile show the influence of Italian Renaissance portraits. The sultan wears the white turban of a scholar but also wears the thumb ring of an archer, neatly reflecting his combination of scholarly and military attainments.

CHRONOLOGY

RISE OF THE OTTOMAN EMPIRE, 1300–1571

Ottomans become leading Anatolian family	1300
Byzantine emperor hires Ottoman mercenaries	1345
Ottomans enter Europe	1350s
Ottomans defeat Serbian empire	1389
Ottomans conquer Constantinople	1453
Ottomans conquer Syria, Egypt, Hungary	1520s
Battle of Lepanto	1571

Slaves were the backbone of the Ottoman army and administration, as they had been in Mamluk Egypt. But slaves were also critical to the lives of the Ottoman upper class. One of the important measures of status in Ottoman society was the number of slaves in one's household. After 1453, new wealth permitted some Ottoman notables to maintain households in which thousands of slaves attended to their masters' whims. In the sixteenth century, the sultan's household alone numbered more than 20,000 slave attendants, not including his bodyguard and his elite infantry units, both of which were also composed of slaves.

The result was an almost insatiable demand for slaves, especially in Constantinople itself. Many of these slaves were captured in war. Many others were taken from Poland and Ukraine in raids by Crimean slave merchants, who then shipped their captives to the slave markets of Constantinople. But slaves were also recruited (some willingly, some by coercion) from rural areas of the Ottoman Empire itself. Because the vast majority of Ottoman slaves were household servants and administrators rather than laborers, some people willingly accepted enslavement, believing that they would be better off as slaves in Constantinople than as impoverished peasants in the countryside. In the Balkans especially, many people were enslaved as children, handed over by their families to pay the infamous child tax the Ottomans imposed on rural areas too poor to pay a monetary tribute. Although unquestionably a wrenching experience for families, this practice did open up opportunities for social advancement. Special academies were created at Constantinople to train the most able of these enslaved children to act as administrators and soldiers, and some rose to become powerful figures in the Ottoman Empire. Slavery therefore carried relatively little social stigma. Even the sultan himself was most often the son of an enslaved woman.

Because Muslims were not permitted to enslave other Muslims, the vast majority of Ottoman slaves were from Christian families (although many converted to Islam later in life). But because so many of the elite positions within Ottoman government were held by slaves, the paradoxical result of this reliance on slave administrators was that Muslims, including Turks, were effectively excluded from the main avenues of social and political advancement in Ottoman society. Nor was Ottoman society characterized by a powerful hereditary nobility of the sort that dominated contemporary European society. As a result, power in the fifteenth- and sixteenth-century Ottoman Empire was remarkably, perhaps even uniquely, open to men of ability and talent, provided

that such men were slaves and therefore not Muslims by birth. Nor was this pattern of Muslim exclusion limited to government and the army. Commerce and business also remained largely in the hands of non-Muslims, most frequently Greeks, Syrians, and Jews. Jews in particular found in the Ottoman Empire a welcome refuge from the persecutions and expulsions that had characterized Jewish life in late medieval Europe. After their 1492 expulsion from Spain, more than 100,000 Spanish (Sephardic) Jews ultimately immigrated into the Ottoman Empire.

Ottoman Orthodoxy. This Ottoman genealogical chart shows the descent of Sultan Mehmet III (1595–1603) from the Prophet Muhammad (shown veiled).

OTTOMAN JANISSARIES

The following account is from a memoir written by a Christian Serb who was captured as a youth by Sultan Mehmet II the Conqueror, converted to Islam, and then served eight years in the Ottoman janissary corps. In 1463, however, the fortress he was defending for the Sultan was captured by the Hungarians, and the author thereupon returned to Christianity.

Whenever the Turks invade foreign lands and capture their people an imperial scribe follows immediately behind them, and whatever boys there are, he takes them all into the Janissaries and gives five gold pieces for each one and sends them across the sea [to Anatolia]. There are about two thousand of these boys. If, however, the number of them from enemy peoples does not suffice, then he takes from the Christians in every village in his land who have boys, having established what is the most every village can give so that the quota will always be full. And the boys whom he takes in his own land are called *cilik*. Each one of them can leave his property to whomever he wants after his death. And those whom he takes among the enemies are called *pendik*. These latter after their deaths can leave nothing; rather, it goes to the emperor, except that if someone comports himself well and is so deserving that he be freed, he may leave it to whomever he wants. And on the boys who are across the sea the emperor spends nothing; rather, those to whom they are entrusted must maintain them and send them where he orders. Then they take those who are suited for it on ships and there they study and train to skirmish in battle. There the emperor already provides for them and gives them a wage. From there he chooses for his own court those who are trained and then raises their wages.

Konstantin Mihailovic, *Memoirs of a Janissary* (Michigan Slavic Translations 3), trans. Benjamin Stolz (Ann Arbor, Mich., 1975), pp. 157–159.

QUESTIONS FOR ANALYSIS

1. What role did the janissary corps play in the Ottoman Empire?
2. Were the Ottoman incursions into the West a serious threat to the European balance of power?

RELIGIOUS CONFLICTS

The Ottoman sultans were relentlessly orthodox Sunni Muslims, who lent staunch support to the religious and legal pronouncements of the Islamic scholarly schools. In 1516, the Ottomans captured the cities of Medina and Mecca, thus becoming the defenders of the holy sites. Soon after, they captured Jerusalem and Cairo, putting an end to the Mamluk sultanate of Egypt. In 1538 the Ottoman ruler formally adopted the title of caliph, thereby declaring himself to be the legitimate successor of the Prophet Muhammad.

In keeping with Sunni traditions, the Ottomans were also religiously tolerant toward non-Muslims, especially during the fifteenth and sixteenth centuries. They organized the major religious groups of their empire into legally recognized units known as *millets*, permitting them considerable rights of religious self-government. After

1453, however, the Ottomans were particularly careful to protect and promote the authority of the Greek Orthodox patriarch of Constantinople over the Orthodox Christians of their empire. As a result, the Ottomans enjoyed staunch support from their Orthodox Christian subjects during their sixteenth-century wars with the Latin Christians of western Europe. Despite the religious diversity of their empire, the Ottomans' principal religious conflicts were therefore not with their own subjects, but with the Shi'ite Muslim Dynasty that ruled neighboring Persia. Time and again during the sixteenth century, Ottoman expeditions against western Europe had to be abandoned when hostilities erupted with the Persians.

THE OTTOMANS AND EUROPE

During the sixteenth century, the Habsburg rulers of Spain, Germany, and Austria were similarly distracted by their own conflicts with the Catholic kings of France (with whom the Ottomans made an alliance) and with the Protestant princes of Germany, the Netherlands, and England. As a result, the contest between the Ottoman Empire and the Western powers never really lived up to the rhetoric of holy war that both sides employed in their propaganda. In 1396, a Western crusader army was annihilated by the Ottomans at the battle of Nicopolis. In the sixteenth and seventeenth centuries, Ottoman armies several times

THE GROWTH OF THE OTTOMAN EMPIRE

Consider the patterns of Ottoman expansion revealed in this map. Did the 1453 capture of Constantinople lead to immediate further conquests? Why do you suppose this was? Compare the extent of the Ottoman Empire in 1566 with that of the Byzantine Empire under Justinian (see the map on page 237). How would you account for these similarities? Why didn't the Ottoman Empire continue its rapid expansion after 1566?

besieged Vienna. But despite these dramatic moments, conflicts between the Ottomans and the rulers of western Europe were fought out mainly through pirate raids and naval battles in the Mediterranean. The main result of this contest was thus a steady escalation in the scale and cost of navies. In 1571, when a combined Habsburg and Venetian force defeated the Ottoman fleet at Lepanto, more than 400 ships took part, with both sides deploying naval forces ten times larger than they had possessed half a century before.

Although undeniably a victory for the Habsburgs and their Venetian allies, the battle of Lepanto was far less decisive than is often suggested. The Ottoman navy was speedily rebuilt; by no means did Lepanto put an end to Ottoman influence over the eastern Mediterranean Sea. Nevertheless, after 1571 both Ottoman and Habsburg interests shifted away from their conflict with each other. The Ottomans embarked on a long and costly war with Persia, while the Spanish Habsburgs turned their attention toward their new empire in the Atlantic. By the mid-seventeenth century, when a new round of Ottoman-European conflicts began, the strength of the Ottoman Empire had been sapped by a series of indolent, pleasure-loving sultans and by the tensions that arose within the Ottoman Empire itself as it ceased to expand. The Ottoman Empire would last until 1918; but from the mid-seventeenth century on, it was no longer a serious rival to the global hegemony the European powers were beginning to achieve.

Mediterranean Colonialism

How were the Portuguese able to control Indian Ocean trade?

During the fifteenth century, Europeans focused their colonial and commercial ambitions more and more on the western Mediterranean and the Atlantic world. Although historians have sometimes argued the contrary, this reorientation was not a result of the rising power of the Ottoman Empire. Instead, this westward orientation was the product of two related developments: the growing importance to late medieval Europe of the African gold trade; and the growth of European colonial empires in the western Mediterranean Sea.

Silver Shortages and the Search for African Gold

Europeans had been trading for African gold for centuries, mainly through Muslim middlemen who transported this precious metal in caravans from the Niger River area where it was produced to the North African ports of Algiers and Tunis. From the thirteenth century on, Catalan and Genoese merchants maintained colonies in Tunis, where they traded woolen cloth for North African grain and sub-Saharan gold.

What accelerated the late medieval demand for gold, however, was a serious silver shortage that affected the entire European economy during the fourteenth and fifteenth centuries. Silver production in Europe fell markedly during the 1340s and remained at a low level thereafter, as Europeans reached the limits of their technological capacity to extract silver ore from deep mines. This shortfall in silver production was compounded during the fifteenth century by a serious balance-of-payments problem: more European silver was flowing east in the spice trade than could be replaced using existing mining techniques on known silver deposits. Gold currencies represented an obvious alternative for large transactions, and from the thirteenth century on European rulers with access to gold were minting gold coins. But Europe itself had few natural gold reserves. To maintain and expand these gold coinages, new and larger supplies of gold were needed. The most obvious source for this gold was Africa.

Mediterranean Empires: Catalunya, Venice, and Genoa

The growing European interest in the African gold trade coincided with the creation of sea-based Mediterranean empires by the Catalans, the Venetians, and the Genoese. During the thirteenth century, the Catalans conquered and colonized a series of western Mediterranean islands, including Majorca, Ibiza, Minorca, Sicily, and Sardinia.

Silver production in Europe fell markedly during the 1340s and remained at a low level thereafter, as Europeans reached the limits of their technological capacity to extract silver ore from deep mines.

Except in Sicily, the pattern of Catalan exploitation was largely the same on all these islands: expropriation or extermination of the native (usually Muslim) population; economic concessions to attract new settlers; and a heavy reliance on slave labor to produce foodstuffs and raw materials for export.

Unlike Catalan colonization efforts, which were mainly carried on by private individuals operating under a crown charter, Venetian colonization was directed by the city's rulers and was focused mainly on the eastern Mediterranean, where the Venetians dominated the trade in spices and silks. The Genoese, by contrast, had more extensive interests in the western Mediterranean world where they traded bulk goods such as cloth, hides, grain, timber, and sugar. Genoese colonies tended to be more informal and family based than Venetian or Catalan colonies, constituting more of a network than an extension of a sovereign empire. They were also more closely integrated into the native societies of North Africa, Spain, and the Black Sea than were the Venetian or the Catalan colonies. Genoese colonies pioneered the production of sugar and sweet Madeira wines in the western Mediterranean, first in Sicily and later in the Atlantic islands off the west coast of Africa. To transport such bulky goods, the Genoese moved away from the oared galleys favored by the Venetians toward larger, fuller-bodied sailing ships that could carry greater volumes of cargo. With further modifications to accommodate the rougher sailing conditions of the Atlantic Ocean, these were the ships that would carry sixteenth-century Europeans around the globe.

> Starting around 1270, however, Italian merchants began to sail through the Strait of Gibraltar and on to the wool-producing regions of England and the Netherlands. This was the essential first step in the extension of Mediterranean patterns of commerce and colonization into the Atlantic Ocean.

FROM THE MEDITERRANEAN TO THE ATLANTIC

Until the late thirteenth century, European maritime commerce had been divided between a Mediterranean and a north Atlantic world. Starting around 1270, however, Italian merchants began to sail through the Strait of Gibraltar and on to the wool-producing regions of England and the Netherlands. This was the essential first step in the extension of Mediterranean patterns of commerce and colonization into the Atlantic Ocean. The second step was the discovery (or possibly rediscovery), during the fourteenth century, of the Atlantic island chains known as the Canaries and the Azores by Genoese sailors. Efforts to colonize the Canary Islands, and to convert and enslave their inhabitants, began almost immediately. But an effective conquest of the Canary Islands did not really begin until the fifteenth century, when it was undertaken by Portugal and completed by Castile. The Canaries, in turn, became the base from which further Portuguese voyages down the west coast of Africa proceeded. They were also the jumping-off point from which Christopher Columbus would sail westward across the Atlantic Ocean in hopes of reaching Asia.

THE TECHNOLOGY OF SHIPS AND NAVIGATION

The European empires of the fifteenth and sixteenth centuries rested on a mastery of the oceans. The Portuguese caravel—the workhorse ship of the fifteenth-century voyages to Africa—was based on ship and sail designs that had been in use among Portuguese fishermen since the thirteenth century. Starting in the 1440s, however, Portuguese shipwrights began building larger caravels of about 50 tons displacement with two masts, each carrying a triangular (lateen) sail. Such ships were capable of sailing against the wind much more effectively than were the older, square-rigged vessels. They also required much smaller crews than did the multi-oared galleys that were still commonly used in the Mediterranean. By the end of the fifteenth century, even larger caravels of around 200 tons were being constructed, with a third mast and a combination of square and lateen sails. Columbus's *Niña* was of this design, having been refitted with two square sails in the Canary Islands to enable it to sail more efficiently before the wind during the Atlantic crossing.

Europeans were also making significant advances in navigation during the fifteenth and sixteenth centuries. Quadrants, which calculated latitude in the Northern Hemisphere by the height of the North Star above the horizon, were in widespread use by the 1450s. As sailors approached the equator, however, the quadrant became less and less useful, and they were forced instead to make use of astrolabes, which reckoned latitude by the height of the sun. Like quadrants, astrolabes

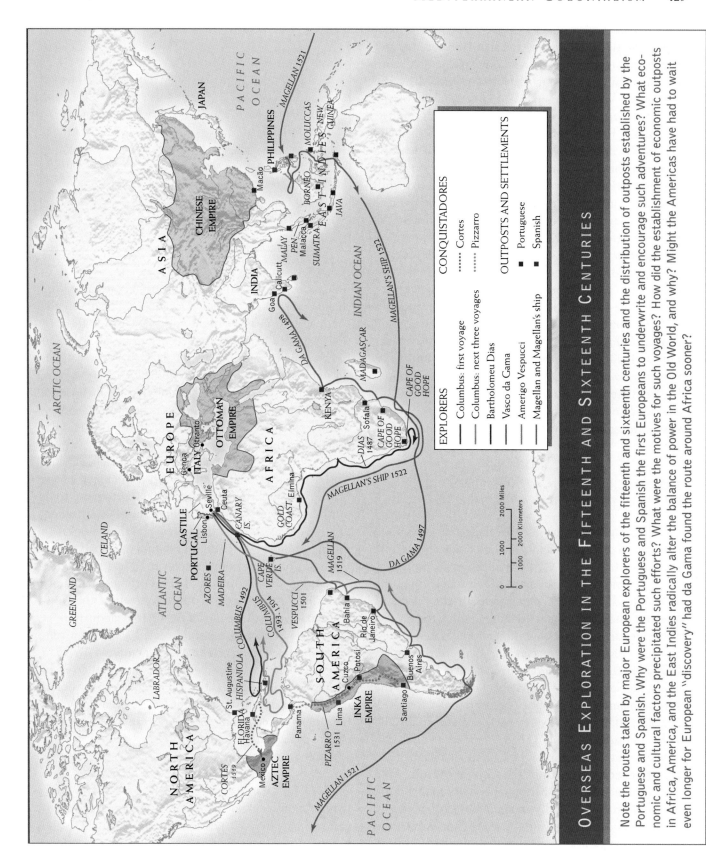

OVERSEAS EXPLORATION IN THE FIFTEENTH AND SIXTEENTH CENTURIES

Note the routes taken by major European explorers of the fifteenth and sixteenth centuries and the distribution of outposts established by the Portuguese and Spanish. Why were the Portuguese and Spanish the first Europeans to underwrite and encourage such adventures? What economic and cultural factors precipitated such efforts? What were the motives for such voyages? How did the establishment of economic outposts in Africa, America, and the East Indies radically alter the balance of power in the Old World, and why? Might the Americas have had to wait even longer for European "discovery" had da Gama found the route around Africa sooner?

had been known in western Europe for centuries. But it was not until the 1480s that the astrolabe became a really useful instrument for seaborne navigation, with the preparation of standard tables sponsored by the Portuguese crown. Compasses too were also coming into more widespread use during the fifteenth century. Longitude, however, remained impossible to calculate accurately until the eighteenth century, when the invention of the marine chronometer finally made it possible to keep accurate time at sea. In the sixteenth century, Europeans sailing east or west across the oceans generally had to rely on their skill at dead reckoning to determine where they were on the globe.

European sailors also benefited from a new interest in maps and navigational charts. Especially important to Atlantic sailors were books known as *rutters* or *routiers*. These contained detailed sailing instructions and descriptions of the coastal landmarks a pilot could expect to encounter on route to a variety of destinations. Mediterranean sailors had had similar books, known as *portolani*, since at least the fourteenth century. In the fifteenth century, however, this tradition was extended to the Atlantic Ocean; by the end of the sixteenth century, rutters spanned the globe.

PORTUGAL, AFRICA, AND THE SEA ROUTE TO INDIA

It was among the Portuguese that these dual interests—the African gold trade and Atlantic colonization—first came together. In 1415, a Portuguese expedition captured the north African port of Ceuta. During the 1420s the Portuguese colonized both the island of Madeira and the Canary Islands. During the 1430s, they extended these colonization efforts to the Azores. By the 1440s they had reached the Cape Verde Islands. In 1444 Portuguese explorers first landed in the area between the Senegal and the Gambia River mouths on the African mainland, where they began to collect cargoes of gold and slaves for export back to Portugal. By the 1470s, Portuguese sailors had rounded the African "bulge" and were exploring the Gulf of Guinea. In 1483 they reached the mouth of the Congo River. In 1488 the Portuguese captain Bartholomeu Dias rounded the southern tip of Africa. Blown around it accidentally by a gale, Dias named the point "Cape of Storms," but the king of Portugal took a more optimistic view of Dias's achievement. He renamed it the Cape of Good Hope and began planning a naval expedition to India. Finally in 1497–1498, Vasco da Gama rounded the cape, and

CHRONOLOGY

PORTUGUESE MARITIME EXPANSION, 1420s–1515

Colonization of Madeira and Canary Islands	1420s
Colonization of the Azores	1430s
Dias rounds the Cape of Good Hope	1488
Da Gama reaches India	1497–1498
Portuguese reach Malacca in Southeast Asia	1511
Portuguese reach Spice Islands	1515

then, with the help of a Muslim navigator named Ibn Majid, crossed the Indian Ocean to Calicut on the southwestern coast of India, opening up for the first time a direct sea route between Europe and the Far Eastern spice trade. Although da Gama lost half his fleet and one third of his men on his two-year voyage, his cargo of spices was so valuable that his losses were deemed insignificant. His heroism became legendary, and his story became the basis for the Portuguese national epic, the *Lusiads*.

Now master of the quickest route to riches in the world, the king of Portugal swiftly capitalized on da Gama's accomplishment. After 1500, Portuguese trading fleets sailed regularly to India. In 1509, the Portuguese defeated an Ottoman fleet and then blockaded the mouth of the Red Sea, attempting to cut off one of the traditional routes by which spices had traveled to Alexandria and Beirut. By 1510 Portuguese military forces had established a series of forts along the western Indian coastline, including their headquarters at Goa. In 1511 Portuguese ships seized Malacca, a center of the spice trade on the Malay peninsula. By 1515 they had reached the Spice Islands and the coast of China. So completely did the Portuguese now dominate the spice trade that by the 1520s even the Venetians were forced to buy their pepper in the Portuguese capital of Lisbon.

ARTILLERY AND EMPIRE

Larger, more maneuverable ships and improved navigational aids made it possible for the Portuguese and other European mariners to reach Africa, Asia, and the Americas by sea. But fundamentally, these sixteenth-century European commercial empires were a military achievement. As such, they reflected what Europeans had learned in their wars against each other during the fourteenth and fifteenth centuries. Perhaps the most critical military advance of the late Middle Ages was the increasing sophistication of artillery, a development made possible not only by gunpowder, but also by improved metallurgical techniques for casting cannon barrels. By the middle of the fifteenth century, the use of artillery pieces had rendered the stone walls of medieval castles and towns obsolete, a fact brought home in 1453 by the successful French siege of Bordeaux (which brought to an end the Hundred Years' War), and by the Ottoman siege of Constantinople (which brought to an end the Byzantine Empire).

One of the reasons the new ship designs (first caravels, and later the even larger galleons) were so important was that their larger size made it possible to mount more effective artillery pieces on them. Increasingly during the sixteenth century, European naval vessels were conceived as floating artillery platforms, with scores of guns mounted in fixed positions along their sides and swivel guns mounted fore and aft. These guns were vastly expensive, as were the ships that carried them; but for those rulers who could afford to possess them, such ships made it possible to project military power around the world. In 1498, Vasco da Gama became the first Portuguese captain to sail into the Indian Ocean; but the Portuguese did not gain control of that ocean until 1509, when they defeated a combined Ottoman and Indian naval force at the battle of Div. Portuguese trading outposts in Africa and Asia were fortifications, built not only to guard against the attacks of native peoples but also to ward off assaults from other Europeans. Without this essential military component, the European maritime empires of the sixteenth century would not have existed.

> Increasingly during the sixteenth century, European naval vessels were conceived as floating artillery platforms, with scores of guns mounted in fixed positions along their sides and swivel guns mounted fore and aft.

PRINCE HENRY THE NAVIGATOR

Because we know that these fifteenth-century Portuguese expeditions down the African coast did ultimately open up a sea route to India and the Far East, it is tempting to presume that this was their goal from the beginning. It was not. The traditional narrative of these events, which presents exploration as their mission, India as their goal, and Prince Henry the Navigator as the guiding genius behind them, no longer commands the confidence of most historians. Only from the 1480s did India clearly become the goal toward which these voyages were directed. Before the 1480s, Portuguese involvement in Africa was driven instead by much more traditional goals: crusading ambitions against the Muslims of North Africa; the desire to establish direct links with the sources of African gold production south of the Sahara Desert; the desire to colonize the Atlantic islands; the burgeoning market for slaves in Europe and in the Ottoman Empire; and the hope that somewhere in Africa they might find the legendary Prester John, a mythical Christian king whom Europeans believed would be their ally against the Muslims if only they could locate him. In the twelfth and thirteenth centuries, they had sought him in Asia. But from the 1340s on, he was believed to reside in Ethiopia, an expansive term that to most Europeans seems to have meant "somewhere in Africa."

Nor does Prince Henry (whose title, "the Navigator," was not assigned to him until the seventeenth century) seem so central a figure in Portuguese exploration as he was once thought to be. In fact, he directed only eight of the thirty-five Portuguese voyages to Africa between 1419 and his death in 1460; and the stories about his gathering a

A Turkish Brass Cannon of the Fifteenth Century. This eighteen-ton gun fired balls twenty-five inches in diameter.

THE LEGEND OF PRESTER JOHN

The Travels of Sir John Mandeville is an almost entirely fictional account of the wonders of the East, written by an English expatriate during the first half of the fourteenth century. Despite the fact that Mandeville (almost certainly a pseudonym) knew almost nothing about the lands he describes, his book became a primary source for European ideas about South and East Asia. Although Mandeville locates the legendary Prester John in Persia, India, or China (his geography is fuzzy, to say the least), by the fifteenth century Europeans were searching for Prester John in Africa.

This emperor Prester John has great lands and has many noble cities and good towns in his realm and many great, large islands. For all the country of India is separated into islands by the great floods that come from Paradise, that divide the land into many parts. And also in the sea he has many islands. . . .

This Prester John has under him many kings and many islands and many varied people of various conditions. And this land is full good and rich, but not so rich as is the land of the Great Khan. For the merchants do not come there so commonly to buy merchandise as they do in the land of the Great Khan, for it is too far to travel to. . . .

[Mandeville then goes on to describe the difficulties of reaching Prester John's lands by sea.]

This emperor Prester John always takes as his wife the daughter of the Great Khan, and the Great Khan in the same way takes to wife the daughter of Prester John. For these two are the greatest lords under the heavens.

In the land of Prester John there are many diverse things, and many precious stones so great and so large that men make them into vessels such as platters, dishes, and cups. And there are many other marvels there that it would be too cumbrous and too long to put into the writing of books. But of the principal islands and of his estate and of his law I shall tell you some part.

This emperor Prester John is Christian and a great part of his country is Christian also, although they do not hold to all the articles of our faith as we do. . . .

And he has under him 72 provinces, and in every province there is a king. And these kings have kings under them, and all are tributaries to Prester John.

And he has in his lordships many great marvels. For in his country is the sea that men call the Gravelly Sea, that is all gravel and sand without any drop of water. And it ebbs and flows in great waves as other seas do, and it is never still. . . . And a three-day journey from that sea there are great mountains out of which flows a great flood that comes out of Paradise. And it is full of precious stones without any drop of water. . . .

He dwells usually in the city of Susa [in Persia]. And there is his principal palace, which is so rich and so noble that no one will believe the report unless he has seen it. And above the chief tower of the palace there are two round pommels of gold and in each of them are two great, large rubies that shine full brightly upon the night. And the principal gates of his palace are of a precious stone that men call sardonyxes [a type of onyx], and the frames and the bars are made of ivory. And the windows of the halls and chambers are of crystal. And the tables upon which men eat, some are made of emeralds, some of amethyst, and some of gold full of precious stones. And the legs that hold up the tables are made of the same precious stones. . . .

Mandeville's Travels, ed. M. C. Seymour (Oxford, 1967), pp. 195–199 (language modernized from Middle English by R. C. Stacey).

QUESTIONS FOR ANALYSIS

1. How persuasive was the myth of Prester John? Would you consider such a myth important enough to serve as a primary motive for European exploration?

Prince Henry the Navigator, by a Fifteenth-Century Portuguese Painter. This portrait is taken from a group portrait of the Portuguese royal family. Although thought to depict Henry, the identification is not certain.

school of navigators and cartographers on the Atlantic coast of Portugal, about his role in designing improved ships and navigational instruments, and about his encouragement of scientific learning generally have all been shown to be false. Henry did play an important role in organizing Portuguese colonization of Madeira, the Canary Islands, and the Azores; and he also pioneered the Portuguese slave trade, first on the Canaries (whose Stone Age population was almost entirely enslaved) and then along the Sene-Gambian coast of Africa. His main goal, however, was to outflank the cross-Saharan African gold trade by intercepting this trade at its source. To this end, he built a series of forts along the African coastline, most famously at Arguim, to which he hoped to divert the cross-Saharan gold caravans. This was also his reason for colonizing the Canary Islands, which he saw as a staging ground for expeditions into the African interior. There is no evidence that he ever dreamed of reaching India by sailing around Africa. Indeed, quite the opposite seems to

be the case. Portuguese progress toward the Cape of Good Hope proceeded much more rapidly in the years after Henry's death than it had during his lifetime. Henry himself was a crusader against Islam, a prince in search of a kingdom, a lord seeking resources to support his followers, and an aspiring merchant who hoped to make a killing in the gold trade but found his main profits in slaving. He was, in all these respects, a man of his time, which is to say, of the fifteenth century. He was not the architect, or even the visionary, of Portugal's sixteenth-century maritime empire.

Atlantic Colonization and the Growth of Slavery

The profits Prince Henry had hoped would come from the African gold trade did not materialize during his lifetime. He therefore had to make his expeditions pay by other means. One of those means was the slave trade. Although slavery in most of western Europe had effectively disappeared by the early twelfth century, slavery continued in Iberia (and to a lesser extent in Italy) throughout the high and late Middle Ages. Until the mid-fifteenth century, however, slavery on the Iberian mainland and in Italy remained very small in scale. The major Mediterranean slave markets of the fourteenth and early fifteenth centuries lay in Muslim lands, and especially in the Ottoman Empire. Relatively few of the slaves who passed through these markets were Africans. Most were European Christians, predominantly Poles, Ukrainians, Greeks, and Bulgarians. Thus the patterns of slavery were not racialized in the late medieval Mediterranean world, except insofar as "primitive" peoples such as the natives of the Canary Islands or of Sardinia were more likely to be regarded as targets for enslavement.

From the mid-fifteenth century on, however, Lisbon began to emerge as a significant market for enslaved Africans. Something on the order of 15,000 to 20,000 Africans were sold in Lisbon during Prince Henry's lifetime, most of them between 1440 and 1460. In the half century after his death, the numbers grew, amounting to perhaps 150,000 African slaves imported into Europe by 1505. For the most part, these slaves were regarded as status symbols—one reason they were so frequently depicted in paintings of the period. Even in the Atlantic colonies—Madeira, the Canaries, and the Azores—the land was worked mainly by European settlers and sharecroppers. Slave labor, if it was employed at all, was generally used only in sugar mills. This meant that on the Azores, which remained a wheat-producing colony, slavery found no real foothold. On Madeira and the Canaries, where sugar became the predominant cash crop during the last quarter of the fifteenth century, some slaves were introduced. But even sugar production did not lead to the widespread introduction of slavery on these islands.

A new style of slave-based sugar plantations began to emerge in Portugal's Atlantic colonies only in the 1460s, starting on the Cape Verde Islands and then extending southward into the Gulf of Guinea. These islands were not populated when the Portuguese began to settle them, and their climate was such as to discourage any large number of Europeans from settling there. They were ideally located, however, to purchase laborers from the slave traders along the nearby West African coast. No comparable system of large-scale, slave-based plantation production had been seen in Europe or Africa since the Roman period. But it was this model of sugar plantations staffed by enslaved Africans that would be exported to the Caribbean islands of the Americas by their Spanish conquerors, with incalculable consequences for Africa, the Americas, and Europe.

EUROPE ENCOUNTERS A NEW WORLD

What was the impact of New World silver on the European economy?

The decision by Spain's rulers to underwrite Columbus's famous voyage was an outgrowth of the progress of these Portuguese ventures. After 1488, when Dias successfully rounded the Cape of Good Hope, it was clear that Portugal would soon dominate the sea lanes leading eastward to Asia. The only alternative for Portugal's Spanish rivals was to finance someone bold enough to try to reach Asia by sailing west. The popular image of Christopher Columbus (1451–1506) as a visionary who struggled to convince hardened ignoramuses that the world was round does not bear up under scrutiny. In fact, the sphericity of the earth had been

widely known throughout European society since at least the twelfth century. What made Columbus's scheme seem plausible to King Ferdinand and Queen Isabella was, first, the discovery and colonization of the Canary Islands and the Azores, which had reinforced a view of the Atlantic as being dotted with islands all the way to Japan; and second, the Genoese mariner's own astonishing miscalculation of the actual size of the earth, which convinced him that he could reach Japan and China in about a month's clear sailing westward from the Canary Islands. America was actually rediscovered by Europeans at the end of the fifteenth century as the result of a colossal error in reckoning. Columbus himself never realized his mistake. When he reached the Bahamas and the island of Hispaniola in 1492 after only a month's sailing, he returned to Spain to report that he had indeed reached the outer islands of Asia.

THE DISCOVERY OF A NEW WORLD

Columbus was not the first European to set foot on the American continents. Viking sailors had reached and briefly settled present-day Newfoundland, Labrador, and perhaps New England around the year 1000. But knowledge of these Viking landings had been forgotten or ignored throughout Europe for hundreds of years. In the fifteenth century, even the Scandinavian settlements in Greenland had been abandoned. It would be perverse, therefore, to deny Columbus credit for his accomplishments. Although Columbus himself never accepted the reality of what he had discovered, those who followed him soon did and busily set out to exploit this new world.

Understandably, Columbus brought back no Asian spices from his voyages. He did, however, return with some small samples of gold and a few indigenous people, whose existence gave promise of entire tribes that might be "saved" (by conversion to Christianity) and enslaved by Europeans. This provided sufficient incentive for the Spanish monarchs to finance three more expeditions by Columbus and many more by others. Soon the mainland was discovered as well as further islands, and the conclusion quickly became inescapable that a new world had indeed been found. Awareness of this new world was most widely publicized by the Italian geographer Amerigo Vespucci. Though he may not have deserved this honor, the continents of the Western Hemisphere became known thereafter as "America" after Vespucci's first name.

WHAT WAS THE IMPACT OF NEW WORLD SILVER ON THE EUROPEAN ECONOMY?

EUROPE ENCOUNTERS A NEW WORLD   435

The realization that this was indeed a new world was at first a disappointment to the Spanish, for with a major land mass lying between Europe and Asia, Spain could not hope to beat Portugal in the race for Asian spices. Any remaining doubt that not one, but two vast oceans separated Europe from Asia was completely removed in 1513, when Vasco Núñez de Balboa first viewed the Pacific Ocean from the Isthmus of Panama. Not entirely admitting defeat, Ferdinand and Isabella's grandson, the Holy Roman emperor Charles V, accepted Ferdinand Magellan's offer in 1519 to see whether a route to Asia could be found by sailing around South America. But Magellan's voyage demonstrated beyond question that the globe was simply too large for any such plan to be feasible. Of the five ships that left Spain under Magellan's command, only one returned three years later, having been forced to circumnavigate the globe. Out of a crew of 265 sailors, only eighteen survived. Most had died from scurvy or starvation; Magellan himself had been killed in a skirmish with native peoples in the Philippines. This fiasco brought to an end all hope of discovering an easy southwest passage to Asia. The dream of a northwest passage survived, however, and continued to motivate European explorers of North America until the nineteenth century.

THE SPANISH CONQUEST OF AMERICA

Although the discovery of this new continent was initially a disappointment to the Spanish, it quickly became clear that the New World had great wealth of its own. From the start, Columbus's gold samples, in themselves rather paltry, had nurtured hopes that somewhere in America gold might lie piled in ingots, ready to enrich whatever European adventurer discovered them. Rumor fed rumor, until a few freelance Spanish soldiers really did strike it rich beyond their most avaricious imaginings. Between 1519 and 1521, the *conquistador* (Spanish for "conqueror") Hernando Cortés, with a force of 600 Europeans but with the assistance of thousands of the Aztecs' unhappy subjects,

Spanish Conquistadors in Mexico. This sixteenth-century drawing of conquistadors massacring Mexican natives emphasizes the advantages that plate armor and steel swords gave to the Spanish soldiers.

overthrew the Aztec Empire of Mexico and carried off its rulers' fabulous wealth. Then in 1533 another conquistador, Francisco Pizarro, this time with only 180 men, toppled the highly centralized South American empire of the Inkas and carried off its great stores of gold and silver. Cortés and Pizarro had the advantage of some cannons and a few horses (both unknown to the native peoples of the Americas), but they achieved their victories primarily by sheer audacity, courage, and treachery. They were aided also by the unwillingness of the indigenous peoples whom the Aztecs and the Inkas had subjected to fight on behalf of their oppressors. Little did the Spaniards' erstwhile allies know how much worse their new conquerors would soon prove to be.

THE PROFITS OF EMPIRE IN THE NEW WORLD

Cortés and Pizarro were plunderers who captured in one fell swoop hoards of gold and silver that had been accumulated for centuries by the native civilizations of Mexico and Peru. Already, however, a search had begun for the sources of these precious metals. The first gold deposits were discovered in Hispaniola, where surface mines were speedily established using native laborers who died in appalling numbers from disease, brutality, and overwork. Of the approximately 1 million native people who lived on Hispaniola in 1492, only 100,000 survived by 1510. By 1538, their numbers were down to 500.

With the loss of so many workers, the Hispaniola mines became uneconomical to operate, and the European colonists turned instead to cattle raising and sugar production. Modeling their sugarcane plantations on those of the Cape Verde Islands and St. Thomas in the Gulf of Guinea, colonists imported African slaves to labor in the new industry. Sugar production was by its nature a highly capital-intensive undertaking. The need to import slave labor added further to its costs, guaranteeing that control over the sugar industry would fall into the hands of a few extremely wealthy planters and financiers.

Despite the importance of sugar production on the Caribbean islands and of cattle ranching on the Mexican mainland, mining shaped the Spanish colonies of Central and South America most fundamentally. Gold was the lure that had initially drawn the Spanish conquerors to the New World, but silver became their most lucrative export. Between 1543 and 1548, vast sil-

ver deposits were discovered north of Mexico City and at Potosí in Bolivia. Even before the discovery of these deposits, the Spanish crown had taken steps to assume direct governmental control over its Central and South American colonies. It was therefore to the Spanish crown that the profits from these astonishingly productive mines accrued. Potosí quickly became the most important mining town in the world. By 1570, it numbered 120,000 inhabitants, despite being located at an altitude of 15,000 feet where the temperature never climbs above 59 degrees Fahrenheit. As in Hispaniola, enslaved native laborers died by the tens of thousands in these mines and in the disease-infested boom towns that surrounded them.

New mining techniques (in particular, the mercury-amalgamation process, introduced into Mexico in 1555 and Potosí in 1571) made it possible to produce even greater quantities of silver, at the cost of even greater mortality among the native laborers. Between 1571 and 1586, silver production at Potosí quadrupled, reaching a peak in the 1590s, when 10 million ounces of silver per year were arriving in Spain from the Americas. In the 1540s, the corresponding figure was only 1.5 million ounces. In the peak years of domestic European silver production, between 1525 and 1535, only about 3 million ounces of silver per year were being produced, and this figure dropped steadily from about 1550 on. Europe's silver shortage came triumphantly to an end during the sixteenth century, but the silver that now circulated there came almost entirely from the New World.

This massive infusion of silver into the European economy accelerated an inflation that had begun already in the later fifteenth century. Initially, this inflation was driven by the renewed growth of the European

CHRONOLOGY	
ENCOUNTERING THE NEW WORLD, c. 1000–1545	
Vikings settle Newfoundland	c. 1000
Columbus reaches Hispaniola	1492
Balboa reaches Pacific Ocean	1513
Magellan's fleet sails around the world	1519–1522
Cortés conquers the Aztecs	1521
Pizarro conquers the Inkas	1533
Potosí silver deposits discovered	1545

ENSLAVED NATIVE LABORERS AT POTOSÍ

Since the Spanish crown received one fifth of all the revenues from mines (as well as maintaining a monopoly over the mercury used to refine the silver ore into silver), it had an important stake in ensuring the productivity of the mines. To this end, the crown granted colonial mine owners the right to conscript native peoples to work in the mines. This account from about 1620 describes the conditions under which these forced native laborers worked. It is not surprising that mortality rates among such laborers were horrendous.

According to His Majesty's warrant, the mine owners on this massive range [at Potosí] have a right to the conscripted labor of 13,300 Indians in the working and exploitation of the mines, both those which have been discovered, those now discovered, and those which shall be discovered. It is the duty of the *Corregidor* (municipal governor) of Potosí to have them rounded up and to see that they come in from all the provinces between Cuzco . . . and as far as the frontiers of Tarija and Tomina. . . .

The conscripted Indians go up every Monday morning to the . . . foot of the range; the *Corregidor* arrives with all the provincial captains or chiefs who have charge of the Indians assigned him for his miner or smelter; that keeps him busy till 1 P.M., by which time the Indians are already turned over to these mine and smelter owners.

After each has eaten his ration, they climb up the hill, each to his mine, and go in, staying there from that hour until Saturday evening without coming out of the mine; their wives bring them food, but they stay constantly underground, excavating and carrying out the ore from which they get the silver. They all have tallow candles, lighted day and night; that is the light they work with, for as they are underground, they have need for it all the time. . . .

These Indians have different functions in the handling of the silver ore; some break it up with bar or pick, and dig down in, following the vein in the mine; others bring it up; others up above keep separating the good and the poor in piles; others are occupied in taking it down from the range to the mills on herds of llamas; every day they bring up more than 8,000 of these native beasts of burden for this task. These teamsters who carry the metal are not conscripted, but are hired.

Antonio Vázquez de Espinosa, *Compendium and Description of the West Indies,* trans. Charles Upson Clark (Washington, D.C.,1968), p. 62.

QUESTIONS FOR ANALYSIS

1. What was the human cost of the Potosí silver mine?

population, an expanding economy, and a relatively fixed supply of food. From the 1540s on, however, inflation was largely the product of the greatly increased supply of silver that was now entering the European economy. The result was what historians have termed "the Price Revolution." Although the effects of this inflation were felt throughout the European continent, Spain was affected with particular severity. Between

1500 and 1560, Spanish prices doubled; between 1560 and 1600, they doubled again. Such exceptionally high prices in turn undermined the competitiveness of Spanish industries. When the flow of New World silver to Spain slowed dramatically during the 1620s and 1630s, the Spanish economy collapsed.

After 1600, lessening quantities of New World silver entered the European economy, but prices continued to rise, albeit more slowly than before. By 1650, the price of grain within Europe had risen to five or six times its level in 1500, producing social dislocation and widespread misery for many of Europe's poorest inhabitants. In England, the period between about 1590 and 1610 was probably the most desperate the country had experienced for 300 years. As the population rose and wages fell, living standards dropped dramatically. If we compute living standards by dividing the price of an average basket of food by the average daily wage of a building laborer, then standards of living were lower in England in 1600 than they had been even in the terrible years of the early fourteenth century. It is no wonder, then, that so many Europeans found emigration to the Americas a tempting prospect. We may wonder, indeed, what might have happened in seventeenth-century Europe had the new world of the Americas not existed as an outlet for Europe's growing population.

CONCLUSION

By 1600, colonization and overseas conquest had profoundly changed both Europe and the wider world. The emergence during the sixteenth century of Portugal and Spain as Europe's leading long-distance traders permanently moved the center of gravity of European economic power away from Italy and the Mediterranean toward the Atlantic. Deprived of its role as the principal conduit for the spice trade, Venice gradually declined. The Genoese moved increasingly into the world of finance, backing the commercial ventures of others, particularly of Spain. By contrast, the Atlantic ports of Spain and Portugal bustled with vessels and shone with wealth. By the mid-seventeenth century, however, economic predominance was passing to the north Atlantic states of England, Holland, and France. Spain and Portugal would retain their American colonies until the nineteenth century. But from the seventeenth century on, it would be the Dutch, the French, and especially the English who would establish new European empires in North America, Asia, Africa, and Australia. By and large, these new empires would last until the World War II.

KEY TERMS

Chingiz Khan	gunpowder	Prince Henry the	New World silver
Marco Polo	Canary Islands	Navigator	Aztecs
Timur the Lame	caravels	Christopher Columbus	Inkas
Ottoman Janissaries	astrolabe	conquistador	

SELECTED READINGS

Abu-Lughod, Janet L. *Before European Hegemony: The World System A.D. 1250–1350.* Oxford and New York, 1989. A study of the trading links among Europe, the Middle East, India, and China, with special attention to the role of the Mongol Empire; extensive bibliography.

Allsen, Thomas T. *Culture and Conquest in Mongol Eurasia.* Cambridge and New York, 2001. A synthesis of the author's earlier studies, emphasizing Mongol involvement in the cultural and commercial exchanges that linked China, Central Asia, and Europe.

Amitai-Preiss, Reuven, and David O. Morgan, eds. *The Mongol Empire and Its Legacy.* Leiden, 1999. A collection of essays that represents some of the new trends in Mongol studies.

The Book of Prophecies, Edited by Christopher Columbus. Trans. Blair Sullivan, ed. Roberto Rusconi. Berkeley and Los Angeles, 1996. After his third voyage, from which Columbus was returned to Spain in chains, he compiled a book of quotations from various sources, selected to emphasize the millenarian implications of his discoveries; a fascinating insight into the mind of the explorer.

Christian, David. *A History of Russia, Central Asia and Mongolia.* Volume 1: *Inner Eurasia from Prehistory to the Mongol Empire.* Oxford, 1998. The authoritative English-language work on the subject.

Coles, Paul. *The Ottoman Impact on Europe.* London, 1968. An excellent introductory text, still valuable despite its age.

Fernández-Armesto, Felipe. *Before Columbus: Exploration and Colonisation from the Mediterranean to the Atlantic, 1229–1492.* London, 1987. An indispensible study of the medieval background to the sixteenth-century European colonial empires.

Fernández-Armesto, Felipe. *Columbus.* Oxford and New York, 1991. An excellent biography that stresses the millenarian ideas that underlay Columbus's thinking. A good book to read after Phillips and Phillips.

Flint, Valerie I. J. *The Imaginative Landscape of Christopher Columbus.* Princeton, N.J., 1992. A short, suggestive analysis of the intellectual influences that shaped Columbus's geographical ideas.

The Four Voyages: Christopher Columbus. Trans. J. M. Cohen. New York, 1992. Columbus's own self-serving account of his four voyages to the Indies.

Goffman, Daniel. *The Ottoman Empire and Early Modern Europe.* Cambridge and New York, 2002. A revisionist account that presents the Ottoman Empire as a European state.

The History and the Life of Chinggis Khan: The Secret History of the Mongols. Trans. Urgunge Onon. Leiden, 1997. A newer version of *The Secret History,* now the standard English version of this important Mongol source.

Inalcik, Halil. *The Ottoman Empire: The Classical Age, 1300–1600.* London, 1973. The standard history by the dean of Turkish historians.

Inalcik, Halil, ed. *An Economic and Social History of the Ottoman Empire, 1300–1914.* Cambridge, 1994. An important collection of essays, spanning the full range of Ottoman history.

Jackson, Peter. *The Mongols and the West, 1221–1410.* Harlow, UK, 2005. A well-written survey that emphasizes the interactions among the Mongol, Latin Christian, and Muslim worlds.

Kafadar, Cemal. *Between Two Worlds: The Construction of the Ottoman State.* Berkeley, Calif., and Los Angeles, 1995. An important study of Ottoman origins in the border regions between Byzantium, the Seljuk Turks, and the Mongols.

Larner, John. *Marco Polo and the Discovery of the World.* New Haven, Conn., 1999. A study of the influence of Marco Polo's *Travels* on Europeans.

Morgan, David. *The Mongols,* 2d ed. Oxford, 2007. An accessible introduction to Mongol history and its sources, written by a noted expert on medieval Persia.

Parker, Geoffrey. *The Military Revolution: Military Innovation and the Rise of the West (1500–1800),* 2d ed. Cambridge and New York, 1996. A work of fundamental importance for understanding the global dominance achieved by early modern Europeans.

Phillips, J. R. S. *The Medieval Expansion of Europe,* 2d ed. Oxford, 1998. An outstanding study of the thirteenth- and fourteenth-century background to the fifteenth-century expansion of Europe. Important synthetic treatment of European relations with the Mongols, China, Africa, and North America. The second edition includes a new introduction and a bibliographical essay; the text is the same as in the first edition (1988).

Phillips, William D., Jr., and Carla R. Phillips. *The Worlds of Christopher Columbus.* Cambridge and New York, 1991. The first book to read on Columbus: accessible, engaging, and scholarly. Then read Fernández-Armesto's biography.

Ratchnevsky, Paul. *Genghis Khan: His Life and Legacy.* Trans. Thomas Nivison Haining. Oxford, 1991. An English translation and abridgment of a book first published in German in 1983. The author was one of the greatest Mongol historians of his generation.

Rossabi, M. *Khubilai Khan: His Life and Times.* Berkeley, Calif., 1988. The standard English biography.

Russell, Peter. *Prince Henry "The Navigator": A Life.* New Haven, Conn., 2000. A masterly biography by a great historian who has spent a lifetime on the subject. The only book one now needs to read on Prince Henry.

Saunders, J. J. *The History of the Mongol Conquests.* London, 1971. Still the standard English-language introduction; somewhat more positive about the Mongols' accomplishments than is Morgan.

Scammell, Geoffrey V. *The First Imperial Age: European Overseas Expansion, 1400–1715.* London, 1989. A useful introductory survey, with a particular focus on English and French colonization.

The Secret History of the Mongols. Trans. F. W. Cleaves. Cambridge, Mass., 1982.

The Secret History of the Mongols and Other Pieces. Trans. Arthur Waley. London, 1963. The later Chinese abridgment of the Mongol original.

The Travels of Marco Polo, trans. R. E. Latham. Baltimore, Md., 1958. The most accessible edition of this remarkably interesting work.

CHAPTER TWELVE

THE CIVILIZATION
OF THE RENAISSANCE,
C. 1350–1550

THE PREVALENT MODERN NOTION that a "Renaissance period" followed western Europe's Middle Ages was first expressed by numerous Italian writers who lived between 1350 and 1550. According to them, 1,000 years of unrelieved darkness had intervened between the Roman era and their own times. During these dark ages the muses of art and literature had fled Europe before the onslaught of barbarism and ignorance. Almost miraculously, however, in the fourteenth century the muses suddenly returned, and Italians happily collaborated with them to bring forth a glorious "renaissance of the arts."

Ever since this periodization was advanced, historians have taken for granted the existence of some sort of renaissance intervening between medieval and modern times. Indeed, from the late eighteenth to the early twentieth centuries many scholars went so far as to argue that the Renaissance was not just an epoch in the history of learning and culture but that a unique Renaissance spirit transformed all aspects of European life—political, economic, and religious as well as intellectual and artistic. Today, however, most experts no longer accept this characterization because they find it impossible to locate any truly distinctive "Renaissance" politics, economics, or religion. Instead, most scholars reserve the term *Renaissance* to describe certain trends in thought, literature, and the arts that emerged in Italy from roughly 1350 to 1550 and then spread to northern Europe during the sixteenth century. That is the approach that we follow here: accordingly, when we refer to a "Renaissance" period in this chapter, we mean to limit ourselves to an epoch in intellectual and cultural history.

FOCUS QUESTIONS

• How did the Italian Renaissance culture differ from the culture of the High Middle Ages?

• Why did the Renaissance occur in Italy?

• What were the principal characteristics of Italian Renaissance art?

• Why did the Renaissance decline around 1550?

• How did the northern and Italian Renaissances differ from one another?

THE RENAISSANCE AND THE MIDDLE AGES

How did Italian Renaissance culture differ from the culture of the High Middle Ages?

Granted this restriction, some further qualifications are still necessary. Since the word *renaissance* literally means "rebirth," it is sometimes thought that after about 1350 certain Italians who were newly cognizant of Greek and Roman cultural accomplishments initiated a rebirth of classical culture after a long period during which that culture had been essentially dead. In fact, however, the High Middle Ages witnessed no "death" of classical learning. Saint Thomas Aquinas considered Aristotle to be "the Philosopher;" Dante revered Virgil. Similar examples could be cited almost without limit. It would be equally false to contrast an imaginary Renaissance paganism with a medieval age of faith because, however much most Renaissance personalities loved the classics, none saw classicism as superseding Christianity. And finally, all discussions of the Renaissance must be qualified by the fact that there was no single Renaissance position on anything. Renaissance thinkers and artists were enormously diverse in their attitudes, achievements, and approaches. As we assess their accomplishments, we need to beware not to force them into too narrow a mold.

In the twelfth and thirteenth centuries Greek scientific and philosophical treatises became available to western Europeans in Latin translations through Islam, but none of the great Greek literary masterpieces and practically none of the major works of Plato were yet known.

RENAISSANCE CLASSICISM

Nonetheless, in the realms of thought, literature, and the arts, we can certainly find distinguishing traits that make the concept of a "Renaissance" meaningful for intellectual and cultural history. First, regarding knowledge of the classics, there was a significant quantitative difference between the learning of the Middle Ages and that of the Renaissance. Medieval scholars knew many Roman authors, such as Virgil, Ovid, and Cicero, but during the Renaissance the works of others such as Livy, Tacitus, and Lucretius were rediscovered and made familiar. Equally if not more important was the Renaissance recovery of the literature of classical Greece from Byzantium. In the twelfth and thirteenth

centuries Greek scientific and philosophical treatises became available to western Europeans in Latin translations through Islam, but none of the great Greek literary masterpieces and practically none of the major works of Plato were yet known. Nor could more than a handful of medieval Westerners read the Greek language. During the Renaissance, on the other hand, large numbers of Western scholars learned Greek and mastered almost the entire Greek literary heritage that is known today.

Second, Renaissance thinkers not only knew many more classical texts than their medieval counterparts but they used them in new ways. Whereas medieval writers presumed that their ancient sources would complement and confirm their own Christian assumptions, Renaissance writers were more aware of the conceptual and chronological gap that separated their own world from that of their classical sources. At the same time, however, the structural similarities between the ancient city-states and those of Renaissance Italy encouraged Italian thinkers in particular to find in these ancient sources models of thought and action directly applicable to their own day. This firm determination to learn from classical antiquity was even more pronounced in the realms of architecture and art, areas in which classical models contributed most strikingly to the creation of fully distinct Renaissance styles.

Third, although Renaissance culture was by no means pagan, it was more worldly and overtly materialistic in its orientation than was the culture of the twelfth and thirteenth centuries. The evolution of the Italian city-states created a supportive environment for attitudes that stressed the importance of the urban political arena and of living well in this world. Such ideals helped create a culture that was increasingly nonecclesiastical. The relative weakness of the church in Italy also contributed to the more secular culture that emerged there. Italian bishoprics were small and for the most part poorly endowed. Italian universities were also largely independent of ecclesiastical supervision and control. Even the papacy was severely limited in its ability to intervene in the cultural life of the Italian city-states, not least because the papacy's role as a political rival in central Italy compromised its moral authority as an arbiter of cultural and religious values. All these factors helped create a space within which the worldly, materialistic culture of the Renaissance could emerge effectively untrammeled by ecclesiastical opposition.

RENAISSANCE HUMANISM

One word above all comes closest to summing up the most common and basic Renaissance intellectual ideals—namely *humanism*. Renaissance humanism was a program of studies that aimed to replace the thirteenth- and fourteenth-century scholastic emphasis on logic and metaphysics with the study of language, literature, rhetoric, history, and ethics. The humanists always preferred ancient literature; although some (notably Francesco Petrarch and Leon Batista Alberti) wrote in both Latin and the vernacular, most humanists regarded vernacular literature as at best a diversion for the uneducated. Serious scholarship and literature could be written only in Latin or Greek. That Latin, moreover, had to be the Latin of Cicero and Virgil. Renaissance humanists were self-conscious elitists who condemned the living Latin of their scholastic contemporaries as a barbarous departure from ancient (and therefore correct) standards of Latin style. Despite their belief that they were thereby reviving the study of the classics, the humanists' position was thus inherently ironic. By insisting on ancient standards of Latin grammar, syntax, and word choice, the humanists of the Renaissance succeeded ultimately in turning Latin into a fossilized language that thereafter ceased to evolve. They thus contributed, quite unwittingly, to the ultimate triumph of the European vernaculars as the primary languages of intellectual and cultural life.

Humanists were convinced that their own educational program—which placed the study of Latin language and literature at the core of the curriculum and then encouraged students to go on to Greek—was the best way to produce virtuous citizens and able public officials. Their elitism was to this extent intensely practical and directly connected to the political life of the city-states in which they lived. Because women were excluded from Italian political life, the education of women was therefore of little concern to most humanists, although some aristocratic women did acquire humanist training. As more and more fifteenth-century city-states fell into the hands of princes, however, the humanist educational curriculum lost its immediate connection to the republican ideals of Italian political life. Nevertheless, humanists never lost their conviction that the study

> By insisting on ancient standards of Latin grammar, syntax, and word choice, the humanists of the Renaissance succeeded ultimately in turning Latin into a fossilized language that thereafter ceased to evolve.

of the "humanities" (as the humanist curriculum came to be known) was the best way to produce leaders for European society.

THE RENAISSANCE IN ITALY

Why did the Renaissance occur in Italy?

Although the Renaissance eventually became a Europe-wide intellectual and artistic movement, it developed first and most distinctively in fourteenth- and fifteenth-century Italy. Understanding why this was so is important not only to explaining the origins of this movement but also to understanding its fundamental characteristics.

THE ORIGINS OF THE ITALIAN RENAISSANCE

The Renaissance originated in Italy for several reasons. The most fundamental reason was that Italy in the later Middle Ages was the most advanced urban society in all of Europe. Unlike aristocrats north of the Alps, Italian aristocrats customarily lived in urban centers rather than in rural castles and consequently became fully involved in urban public affairs. Moreover, since the Italian aristocracy built its palaces in the cities, the aristocratic class was less sharply set off from the class of rich merchants than in the north. Hence, whereas in France or Germany most aristocrats lived on the income from their landed estates while rich town dwellers (*bourgeois*) gained their living from trade, in Italy so many town-dwelling aristocrats engaged in banking or mercantile enterprises and so many rich mercantile families imitated the manners of the aristocracy that by the fourteenth and fifteenth centuries the aristocracy and upper bourgeoisie were becoming virtually indistinguishable. The noted Florentine family of the Medici (*MEH-dih-chee*), for example, emerged as a family of physicians (as the name suggests), made its fortune in banking and commerce, and rose into the aristocracy in the fifteenth century. The results of these developments for the history of education are obvious: not only was there a great demand for education in the skills of reading and counting

THE HUMANISTS' EDUCATIONAL PROGRAM

These three selections illustrate the confidence of civic humanists such as Vergerius, Bruni, and Alberti that their elite educational program would be of supreme value to the state as well as to the individual students who pursued it. Not everyone agreed with the humanists' claims, however, and a good deal of self-promotion lies behind them.

VERGERIUS ON LIBERAL STUDIES

We call those studies *liberal* which are worthy of a free man; those studies by which we attain and practice virtue and wisdom; that education which calls forth, trains, and develops those highest gifts of body and of mind which ennoble men, and which are rightly judged to rank next in dignity to virtue only. . . . It is, then, of the highest importance that even from infancy this aim, this effort, should constantly be kept alive in growing minds. For . . . we shall not have attained wisdom in our later years unless in our earliest we have sincerely entered on its search. [P. P. Vergerius (1370–1444), *"Concerning Excellent Traits."*]

ALBERTI ON THE IMPORTANCE OF LITERATURE

Letters are indeed so important that without them one would be considered nothing but a rustic, no matter how much a gentlemen [he may be by birth]. I'd much rather see a young nobleman with a book than with a falcon in his hand. . . .

Be diligent, then, you young people, in your studies. Do all you can to learn about the events of the past that are worthy of memory. Try to understand all the useful things that have been passed on to you. Feed your minds on good maxims. Learn the delights of embellishing your souls with good morals. Strive to be kind and considerate [of others] when conducting civil business. Get to know those things human and divine that have been put at your disposal in books for good reason. Nowhere [else] will you find . . . the elegance of a verse of Homer, or Virgil, or of some other excellent poet. You will find no field so delightful or flowering as in one of the orations of Demosthenes, Cicero, Livy, Xenophon, and other such pleasant and perfect orators. No effort is more fully compensated . . . as the constant reading and rereading of good things. From such reading you will rise rich in good maxims and good arguments, strong in your ability to persuade others and get them to listen to you; among the citizens you will willingly be heard, admired, praised, and loved. [Leon Battista Alberti (1404–1472), *"On the Family."*]

BRUNI ON THE HUMANIST CURRICULUM

The foundations of all true learning must be laid in the sound and thorough knowledge of Latin: which implies study marked by a broad spirit, accurate scholarship, and careful attention to details. Unless this solid basis be secured it is useless to attempt to rear an enduring edifice. Without it the great monuments of literature are unintelligible, and the art of composition impossible. To attain this essential knowledge we must never relax our careful attention to the grammar of the language, but perpetually confirm and extend our acquaintance with it until it is thoroughly our own. . . .

But the wider question now confronts us, that of the subject matter of our studies, that which I have already called the realities of fact and principle, as distinct from literary form. . . . First among such studies I place History: a subject which must not on any account be neglected by one who aspires to true cultivation. . . . For the careful study of the past enlarges our foresight in contemporary affairs and affords to citizens and to monarchs lessons . . . in the ordering of public policy. From History, also, we draw our store of examples of moral precepts. . . .

The great Orators of antiquity must by all means be included. Nowhere do we find the virtues more warmly extolled, the vices so fiercely decried. From them we may learn, also, how to express consolation, encouragement, dissuasion or advice. . . .

Familiarity with the great poets of antiquity is essential to any claim to true education. For in their writings we find deep speculations upon Nature, and upon the Causes and Origins of things, which must carry weight with us both from their antiquity and from their authorship. . . .

Proficiency in literary form, not accompanied by broad acquaintance with facts and truths, is a barren attainment; whilst information, however vast, which lacks all grace of expression would seem to be put under a bushel or partly thrown away. . . . Where, however, this double capacity exists—breadth of learning and grace of style—we allow the highest title to distinction and to abiding fame. . . . [Leonardo Bruni (1369–1444), "Concerning the Study of Literature."]

Vergerius and Bruni: William Harrison Woodward, ed., *Vittorino da Feltre and Other Humanist Educators* (London:, 1897), pp. 96–110, 124–129, 132–133. Alberti: Eric Cochrane and Julius Kirshner, eds., *University of Chicago Readings in Western Civilization*, Vol. 5: *The Renaissance* (Chicago, 1986), pp. 81–82.

QUESTIONS FOR ANALYSIS

1. Why did the Italian Renaissance produce such a strong spirit of civic humanism?

2. Do you think that Socrates' and Cicero's perceptions of virtue were identical to those of Vergerius and Bruni? Were Renaissance virutes and classical virtues one and the same thing?

3. Why did humanists such as Leonardo Bruni consider the study of history essential to a full education?

necessary to become a successful merchant but the richest and most prominent families sought above all to find teachers who would impart to their sons the knowledge and skills necessary to argue well in the public arena. Consequently, Italy produced a large number of lay educators, many of whom not only taught students but also demonstrated their learning by producing political and ethical treatises and works of literature. Italian schools created the best-educated upper-class public in all of Europe, along with a considerable number of wealthy patrons who were ready to invest in the cultivation of new ideas and new forms of literary and artistic expression.

A second reason why late medieval Italy was the birthplace of an intellectual and artistic renaissance lay in the fact that it had a far greater sense of rapport with the classical past than any other territory in western Europe. Ancient Roman monuments were omnipresent throughout the peninsula, and classical Latin literature referred to cities and sites that Renaissance Italians recognized as their own. Italians were particularly intent on reappropriating their classical heritage in the fourteenth and fifteenth centuries because they were also seeking to establish an independent cultural identity in opposition to a scholasticism most closely associated with France. Not only did the removal of the papacy to Avignon for most of the fourteenth century and then the Great Schism from 1378 to 1417 heighten antagonisms between Italy and France but, during the fourteenth century, an intellectual reaction against scholasticism on all fronts encouraged Italians to prefer the intellectual alternatives offered by classical literary sources. As Roman literature and learning took root in Italy, so too did Roman art and architecture, for Roman models could help Italians create a splendid artistic alternative to French Gothicism just as Roman learning offered an intellectual alternative to French scholasticism.

Finally, the Italian Renaissance could not have occurred without the underpinning of Italian wealth. The Italian economy as a whole was probably more prosperous in the thirteenth century than it was in the fourteenth and fifteenth. But late medieval Italy was wealthier in comparison with the rest of Europe than it had been before, a fact that meant that Italian writers and artists were more likely to stay at home than to seek employment abroad. In late medieval Italy, intensive investment in culture arose both from an intensification of urban pride and the concentration of per capita wealth. During the fourteenth century, cities themselves were the primary patrons of art and learning. During the fifteenth century, however, when most Italian city-states succumbed to the hereditary rule of noble families, patronage was monopolized by the princely aristocracy. Among these great princes were

Pope Julius II, by Raphael. The acorns at the top of the throne posts are visual puns for the pope's family name, della Rovere ("of the oak").

the popes in Rome, who based their strength on temporal control of the Papal States. The most worldly of the Renaissance popes—Alexander VI (1492–1503); Julius II (1503–1513); and Leo X (1513–1521), son of the Florentine ruler Lorenzo de' Medici—employed the greatest artists of the day and for a few decades made Rome the artistic capital of Western Europe.

THE ITALIAN RENAISSANCE: LITERATURE AND THOUGHT

In surveying the accomplishments of Italian Renaissance scholars and writers it is natural to begin with the work of Petrarch (Francesco Petrarca, 1304–1374), the "father of Renaissance humanism." Petrarch was a deeply committed Catholic who believed that scholasticism was entirely misguided because it concentrated on abstract speculation rather than on teaching people how to live virtuously and attain salvation. Petrarch thought that the Christian writer must instead cultivate literary eloquence so that he could inspire people to do good. For him the best models of eloquence were to be found in the classical texts of Latin literature, which were doubly valuable because they were also

filled with ethical wisdom. Petrarch dedicated himself, therefore, to rediscovering such texts and to writing his own poems and moral treatises in a Latin style modeled on classical authors. But Petrarch was also a remarkable vernacular poet. The Italian sonnets—later called Petrarchan sonnets—that he wrote for his beloved Laura in the chivalrous style of the troubadours were widely imitated and admired throughout the Renaissance period, and continue to be read today.

Because he was a very traditional Christian, Petrarch's ultimate ideal for human conduct was the solitary life of contemplation and asceticism. But from about 1400 to 1450, subsequent Italian thinkers and scholars, located mainly in Florence, developed a different vision customarily called civic humanism. Civic humanists such as the Florentines Leonardo Bruni (c. 1370–1444) and Leon Battista Alberti (1404–1472) agreed with Petrarch on the need for eloquence and the value of classical literature, but they also taught that man's nature equipped him for action, for usefulness to his family and society, and for serving the state—ideally a republican city-state after the classical or contemporary Florentine model. In their view ambition and the quest for glory were noble impulses that ought to be encouraged. They refused to condemn the striving for material possessions, for they argued that the history of human progress is inseparable from our success in mastering the earth and its resources.

Perhaps the most famous of the civic humanists' writings is Alberti's *On the Family* (1443), in which he argued that the nuclear family was instituted by nature for the well-being of humanity. Within this framework, however, Alberti consigned women to purely domestic roles, asserting that "man [is] by nature more energetic and industrious," and that woman was created "to increase and continue generations, and to nourish and preserve those already born." Although such dismissals of women's intellectual abilities were fiercely resisted by a few notable women humanists, for the most part Italian Renaissance humanism was characterized by a pervasive denigration of women—a denigration expressed also in the works of classical literature that the humanists so much admired.

THE EMERGENCE OF TEXTUAL SCHOLARSHIP

The civic humanists also went far beyond Petrarch in their knowledge of classical (and especially Greek) literature and philosophy. In this they were aided by a number of Byzantine scholars who had migrated to

SOME RENAISSANCE ATTITUDES TOWARD WOMEN

Italian society in the fourteenth and fifteenth centuries was characterized by marriage patterns in which men in their late twenties or thirties customarily married women in their mid- to late teens. This demographic fact probably contributed to the widely shared belief in this period that wives were essentially children, who could not be trusted with important matters and who were best trained by being beaten. Renaissance humanism did little to change such attitudes. In some cases, it even reinforced them.

After my wife had been settled in my house a few days, and after her first pangs of longing for her mother and family had begun to fade, I took her by the hand and showed her around the whole house. I explained that the loft was the place for grain and that the stores of wine and wood were kept in the cellar. I showed her where things needed for the table were kept, and so on, through the whole house. At the end there were no household goods of which my wife had not learned both the place and the purpose. . . .

Only my books and records and those of my ancestors did I determine to keep well sealed. . . . These my wife not only could not read, she could not even lay hands on them. I kept my records at all times . . . locked up and arranged in order in my study, almost like sacred and religious objects. I never gave my wife permission to enter that place, with me or alone. . . .

[Husbands] who take counsel with their wives . . . are madmen if they think true prudence or good counsel lies in the female brain. . . . For this very reason I have always tried carefully not to let any secret of mine be known to a woman. I did not doubt that my wife was most loving, and more discreet and modest in her ways than any, but I still considered it safer to have her unable, and not merely unwilling, to harm me. . . . Furthermore, I made it a rule never to speak with her of anything but household matters or questions of conduct, or of the children.

Leon Battista Alberti, "On the Family," in *The Family in Renaissance Florence*, trans. and ed. Renée N. Watkins. (Columbia, S.C., 1969), pp. 208–213, as abridged in Julie O'Faolain and Lauro Martines, eds., *Not in God's Image: Women in History from the Greeks to the Victorians* (New York, 1973), pp. 187–188.

QUESTIONS FOR ANALYSIS

1. For what reasons did Leon Battista Alberti argue that his wife should have no access to his books or records?
2. Would you expect Renaissance attitudes toward women to have been more liberal and more modern? Did Alberti's comments refer to Italian society as a whole or merely to a small segment of it?

Italy in the first half of the fifteenth century and gave instruction in the Greek language. Italian scholars also traveled to Constantinople and other Eastern cities in search of Greek masterpieces hitherto unknown in the West. In 1423 one Italian, Giovanni Aurispa, alone brought back 238 manuscript books, including works of Sophocles, Euripides, and Thucydides, which were quickly translated into Latin, not word for word, but sense for sense to preserve the literary force of the original. By 1500, most of the Greek classics, including the writings of Plato, the dramatists, and the historians, were available to western Europe.

Related in his textual interests to the civic humanists, but by no means a full adherent of their movement, was the atypical yet highly influential Renaissance thinker Lorenzo Valla (1407–1457). Born in Rome and active primarily as a secretary in the service of the king of Naples, Valla had no allegiance to the republican ideals of the Florentine civic humanists. Instead, he used his skills in grammar, rhetoric, and the painstaking analysis of Greek and Latin texts to show how the thorough study of language could discredit old verities. Most remarkable in this regard was Valla's brilliant demonstration that the Donation of Constantine was a medieval forgery. Whereas papal propagandists had argued that the papacy's rights to temporal rule in western Europe derived from this charter purportedly granted by the emperor Constantine in the fourth century, Valla proved that the charter was full of nonclassical Latin usages and anachronistic terms. Hence he concluded that the "Donation" was the work of a medieval forger whose "monstrous impudence" was exposed by the "stupidity of his language." This demonstration not only discredited a prize specimen of "medieval ignorance" but, more important, introduced the concept of anachronism into all subsequent textual study and historical thought. In his *Notes on the New Testament* he also applied his expert knowledge of Greek to elucidating the true meaning of Saint Paul's letters, which he believed had been obscured by Saint Jerome's Latin Vulgate translation. This work was to prove an important link between Italian Renaissance scholarship and the subsequent Christian humanism of the north.

RENAISSANCE NEOPLATONISM

From about 1450 until about 1600 Italian thought was dominated by a school of Neoplatonists who sought to blend the ideas of Plato, Plotinus, and various strands of ancient mysticism with Christianity. Foremost among these were Marsilio Ficino (1433–1499) and Giovanni Pico della Mirandola (1463–1494), both of whom were members of the Platonic Academy founded by Cosimo de' Medici in Florence. The academy was a loosely organized society of scholars who met to hear readings and lectures. Their hero was Plato: sometimes they celebrated Plato's birthday by holding a banquet in his honor, after which everybody gave speeches as if they were characters in a Platonic dialogue. From the standpoint of posterity, Ficino's greatest achievement was his translation of Plato's works into Latin, which made them widely available to western Europeans for the first time. Ficino himself, however, regarded his *Hermetic Corpus*, a collection of passages drawn from a number of

Pico della Mirandola. When the young nobleman Pico arrived in Florence at age nineteen he was said to have been "of beauteous feature and shape." This contemporary portrait may have been done by the great Florentine painter Botticelli.

ancient mystical writings including the Hebrew Kabbalah, as his greatest contribution to learning.

It is debatable whether Ficino's own philosophy should be called humanist because he moved away from ethics to metaphysics and taught that the individual should look primarily to the hereafter. In Ficino's opinion, "the immortal soul is always miserable in its mortal body." The same issue arises with respect to Ficino's disciple Giovanni Pico della Mirandola. Pico was certainly not a civic humanist because he saw little worth in mundane public affairs. He also fully shared his teacher's penchant for extracting and combining snippets taken out of context from ancient mystical tracts. But he did also believe—and so argued in his famous *Oration on the Dignity of Man*—that there is "nothing more wonderful than man" because he believed that man is endowed with the capacity to achieve union with God if he so wills.

MACHIAVELLI

Hardly any of the Italian thinkers between Petrarch and Pico were really original: their greatness lay mostly in their manner of expression, their scholarship, and their popularization of different themes of ancient thought. The same, however, cannot be said of Renaissance Italy's greatest political philosopher, the Florentine Niccolò Machiavelli (*mah-kee-uh-VEHL-ee*, 1469–1527). Machiavelli's writings reflect the unstable condition of Italy in his time. At the end of the fifteenth century Italy had become the cockpit of international struggles. Both France and Spain had invaded the peninsula and were competing for the allegiance of the Italian city-states, which in turn were torn by internal dissension. In 1498 Machiavelli became a prominent official in the government of the Florentine republic, set up four years earlier when the French invasion had led to the expulsion of the Medici. His duties largely involved diplomatic missions to other Italian city-states. While in Rome he became fascinated with the attempt of Cesare Borgia, son of Pope Alexander VI, to create his own principality in central Italy. He noted with approval Cesare's ruthlessness and shrewdness and his complete subordination of personal morality to political ends. In 1512 the Medici returned to overthrow the republic of Florence, and Machiavelli was deprived of his position. Disappointed and embittered, he spent the remainder of his life at his country estate, devoting his time to writing.

Machiavelli remains a controversial figure even today. Some modern scholars see him as an amoral theorist of realpolitik, disdainful of morality and Christian piety, caring nothing about the proper purposes of political life, but interested solely in the acquisition and exercise of power as an end in itself. Others see him as an Italian patriot, who viewed princely tyranny as the only way to liberate Italy from its foreign conquerors. Still others see him as a follower of Saint Augustine of Hippo, who understood that in a fallen world populated by sinful people, a ruler's good intentions do not guarantee that his policies will have good results. Instead, Machiavelli insisted that a prince's actions must be judged by their consequences and not by their intrinsic moral quality. Human beings, Machiavelli argued, "are ungrateful, fickle, and deceitful, eager to avoid dangers, and avid for gain." This being so, "the necessity of preserving the state will often compel a prince to take actions which are opposed to loyalty, charity, humanity, and religion. . . . So far as he is able, a prince should stick to the path of good but, if the necessity arises, he should know how to follow evil."

The puzzle is heightened by the fact that, on the surface, Machiavelli's two great works of political analysis appear to contradict each other. In his *Discourses on Livy* he praised the ancient Roman republic as a model for his own contemporaries, lauding constitutional government, equality among the citizens of a republic, political independence for city-states, and the subordination of religion to the service of the state. There is little doubt, therefore, that Machiavelli was a committed republican, who believed in the free city-state as the ideal form of human government. But Machiavelli also wrote *The Prince*, "a handbook for tyrants" in the eyes of his critics, and he dedicated this work to Lorenzo, son of Piero de' Medici, whose family had overthrown the Florentine republic that Machiavelli himself had served.

Because *The Prince* has been so much more widely read than the *Discourses*, interpretations of Machiavelli's political thought have often mistaken the admiration he expressed in *The Prince* for Cesare Borgia as an endorsement of princely tyranny for its own sake. Machiavelli's real position was quite different. In the political chaos of early sixteenth-century Italy, Machiavelli saw a ruthless prince such as Borgia as the only hope for revitalizing the spirit of independence among his contemporaries, and so making them fit, once again, for republican self-rule. However dark his vision of human nature, Machiavelli never ceased to hope that his Italian contemporaries would rise up, expel their French and Spanish conquerors, and restore their ancient traditions of republican liberty and equality. Princes such as Borgia were necessary steps toward that end, but for Machiavelli their rule was not the ideal form of government for humankind. In Italy's sunken political situation, however, a princely state was the best form of government toward which Machiavelli's downtrodden contemporaries could aspire.

> In the political chaos of early sixteenth-century Italy, Machiavelli saw a ruthless prince such as Borgia as the only hope for revitalizing the spirit of independence among his contemporaries, and so making them fit, once again, for republican self-rule.

THE IDEAL OF THE COURTIER

Far more congenial to contemporary tastes than the shocking political theories of Machiavelli were the guidelines for proper aristocratic conduct offered in *The Book of the Courtier* (1528) by the diplomat and count Baldassare Castiglione. This cleverly written forerunner of modern handbooks of etiquette stands in sharp contrast to the earlier civic humanist treatises of Bruni and Alberti. Whereas they taught the sober republican

MACHIAVELLI'S ITALIAN PATRIOTISM

These passages are from the concluding chapter to Machiavelli's treatise The Prince. *Like the book itself, they are addressed to Lorenzo, the son of Piero de' Medici.*

Reflecting on the matters set forth above and considering within myself whether the times were propitious in Italy at present to honor a new prince and whether there is at hand the matter suitable for a prudent and virtuous leader to mold in a new form, giving honor to himself and benefit to the citizens of the country, I have arrived at the opinion that all circumstances now favor such a prince, and I cannot think of a time more propitious for him than the present. If, as I said, it was necessary in order to make apparent the virtue of Moses, that the people of Israel should be enslaved in Egypt, and that the Persians should be oppressed by the Medes to provide an opportunity to illustrate the greatness and the spirit of Cyrus, and that the Athenians should be scattered in order to show the excellence of Theseus, thus at the present time, in order to reveal the valor of an Italian spirit it was essential that Italy should fall to her present low estate, more enslaved than the Hebrews, more servile than the Persians, more disunited than the Athenians, leaderless and lawless, beaten, despoiled, lacerated, overrun and crushed under every kind of misfortune. . . . So Italy now, left almost lifeless, awaits the coming of one who will heal her wounds, putting an end to the sacking and looting in Lombardy and the spoliation and extortions in the Realm of Naples and Tuscany, and cleanse her sores that have been so long festering. Behold how she prays God to send her some one to redeem her from the cruelty and insolence of the barbarians. See how she is ready and willing to follow any banner so long as there be some one to take it up. Nor has she at present any hope of finding her redeemer save only in your illustrious house [the Medici] which has been so highly exalted both by its own merits and by fortune and which has been favored by God and the church, of which it is now ruler. . . .

This opportunity, therefore, should not be allowed to pass, and Italy, after such a long wait, must be allowed to behold her redeemer. I cannot describe the joy with which he will be received in all these provinces which have suffered so much from the foreign deluge, nor with what thirst for vengeance, nor with what firm devotion, what solemn delight, what tears! What gates could be closed to him, what people could deny him obedience, what envy could withstand him, what Italian could withhold allegiance from him? THIS BARBARIAN OCCUPATION STINKS IN THE NOSTRILS OF ALL OF US. Let your illustrious house then take up this cause with the spirit and the hope with which one undertakes a truly just enterprise. . . .

Niccolò Machiavelli, *The Prince,* trans. and ed. Thomas G. Bergin (Arlington Heights, Ill:, 1947), pp. 75–76, 78.

QUESTIONS FOR ANALYSIS

1. Why did Machiavelli argue that Italy needed the type of prince he had outlined in his book *The Prince*?
2. According to Machiavelli, what was wrong with the Italy of his own day?
3. Did Machiavelli espouse the cause of Italian nationalism or the banner of a strong prince like Lorenzo de' Medici? Or were his visions of patriotism and leadership concurrent?

virtues of strenuous service in behalf of city-state and family, Castiglione, writing in an Italy dominated by magnificent princely courts, taught how to attain the elegant and seemingly effortless qualities necessary for acting like a true gentleman. More than anyone else, Castiglione popularized the ideal of the "Renaissance man": one who is accomplished in many different pursuits and is also brave; witty; and "courteous," meaning civilized and learned. Unlike Alberti, Castiglione said nothing about women's role in "hearth and home" but stressed instead the ways in which court ladies could be "gracious entertainers." Widely read throughout Europe for over a century after its publication, Castiglione's *Courtier* spread Italian ideals of civility to princely courts north of the Alps, resulting in the ever-greater patronage of art and literature by the European aristocracy.

Sixteenth-century Italians were also highly accomplished creators of imaginative prose and verse. Machiavelli himself wrote a delightful short story, "Belfagor," and an engagingly bawdy play, *Mandragola;* the great artist Michelangelo wrote many moving sonnets; and Ludovico Ariosto (1474–1533), the most eminent of sixteenth-century Italian epic poets, wrote a lengthy verse narrative called *Orlando Furioso* (The madness of Roland). Although based on the medieval Charlemagne cycle, this work differed radically from any of the medieval epics because it introduced elements of lyrical fantasy and, above all, because it was totally devoid of heroic idealism. Ariosto wrote to make readers laugh and to charm them with descriptions of the quiet splendor of nature and the passions of love. His work embodies the disillusionment of the late Renaissance, the loss of hope and faith, and the tendency to seek consolation in the pursuit of pleasure and aesthetic delight.

THE ITALIAN RENAISSANCE: PAINTING, SCULPTURE, AND ARCHITECTURE

What were the principal characteristics of Italian Renaissance art?

Despite numerous intellectual and literary advances, the longest-lived achievements of the Italian Renaissance were made in the realm of art. Of all the arts, painting was undoubtedly supreme. We have already

seen the artistic genius of Giotto around 1300, but it was not until the fifteenth century that Italian painting began to come fully of age. One reason for this was that in the early fifteenth century the laws of linear perspective were discovered and first employed to give the fullest sense of three dimensions. Fifteenth-century artists also experimented with effects of light and shade (*chiaroscuro*) and for the first time carefully studied the anatomy and proportions of the human body. By the fifteenth century, too, increasing private wealth and the growth of lay patronage had opened the domain of art to a variety of nonreligious themes and subjects. Even subject matter from biblical history was now frequently infused with nonreligious themes. Artists sought to paint portraits that revealed the hidden mysteries of the soul. Paintings intended to appeal primarily to the intellect were paralleled by others whose main purpose was to delight the eye with gorgeous color and beauty of form. The introduction

The Impact of Perspective. Masaccio's painting *The Trinity with the Virgin* illustrates the startling sense of depth made possible by the rules of perspective.

of painting in oil, probably from Flanders, also characterized fifteenth-century painting. The use of the new technique doubtless had much to do with the artistic advance of this period. Because oil does not dry as quickly as fresco pigment, the painter could now work more slowly, taking time with the more difficult parts of the picture and making corrections if necessary as he or she went along.

RENAISSANCE PAINTING IN FLORENCE

The majority of the great painters of the fifteenth century were Florentines. First among them was the precocious Masaccio (1401–1428), known to his contemporaries as "Giotto reborn." Although he died at the age of twenty-seven, Masaccio inspired the work of Italian painters for a hundred years. Masaccio's greatness as a painter is based on his success in "imitating nature," which became a primary value in Renaissance painting. To achieve this effect he employed perspective, perhaps most dramatically in his fresco of the Trinity; he also used chiaroscuro with originality, leading to strikingly dramatic effects.

Masaccio's best-known successor was the Florentine Sandro Botticelli (1445–1510), who depicted both classical and Christian subjects. Botticelli's work excels in linear rhythms and sensuous depiction of natural detail. He is most famous for paintings that portray figures from classical mythology without any overtly Christian frame of reference. His *Allegory of Spring* and *Birth of Venus* employ a style greatly indebted to Roman depictions of gods, goddesses, zephyrs, and muses moving gracefully in natural settings. Consequently, these works were once understood as the expression of Renaissance paganism at its fullest, a celebration of earthly delights breaking sharply with Christian asceticism. More recently, however, scholars have preferred to view them as allegories fully compatible with Christian teachings. According to this interpretation, Botticelli was addressing himself to learned aristocratic viewers, well versed in the Neoplatonic theories of Ficino, which considered ancient gods and goddesses to represent various Christian virtues. Venus, for example, might have stood for a species of chaste love. Although Botticelli's great "classical" works remain cryptic, two points remain certain: any viewer is free to enjoy them on their naturalistic sensuous level,

Birth of Venus, by Botticelli. Botticelli was a mystic as well as a lover of beauty, and this painting is most often interpreted as a Neoplatonic allegory.

and Botticelli had surely not broken with Christianity, since he painted frescoes for the pope in Rome at just the same time.

LEONARDO DA VINCI

Perhaps the greatest of the Florentine artists was Leonardo da Vinci (1452–1519), one of the most versatile geniuses who ever lived. Leonardo personified the Renaissance man: he was a painter, architect, musician, mathematician, engineer, and inventor. The illegitimate son of a notary and a peasant woman, Leonardo set up an artist's shop in Florence by the time he was twenty-five and gained the patronage of the Medici ruler of the city, Lorenzo the Magnificent. But if Leonardo had any weakness, it was his slowness in working and difficulty in finishing anything. This naturally displeased Lorenzo and other Florentine patrons, who thought an artist was little more than an artisan, commissioned to produce a certain piece of work of a certain size for a certain price on a certain date. Leonardo, however, strongly objected to this view because he considered himself to be no menial craftsman

The Virgin of the Rocks, by Leonardo da Vinci. This painting reveals Leonardo's interest in the human face and in the atmosphere of natural settings.

The Last Supper, by Leonardo da Vinci.

but an inspired creator. Therefore in 1482 he left Florence for the Sforza court of Milan where he was given freer rein in structuring his time and work. He remained there until the French invaded Milan in 1499; after that he wandered about Italy, finally accepting the patronage of the French king, Francis I, under whose auspices Leonardo lived and worked in France until his death.

The paintings of Leonardo da Vinci began what is known as the High Renaissance in Italy. His approach to painting was that it should be the most accurate possible imitation of nature. Leonardo was like a naturalist, basing his work on his own detailed observations of a blade of grass, the wing of a bird, a waterfall. He obtained human corpses for dissection and reconstructed in drawing the minutest features of anatomy, which knowledge he carried over to his paintings. Leonardo worshiped nature and was convinced of the essential divinity in all living things. It is not surprising, therefore, that he was a vegetarian and that he went to the marketplace to buy caged birds, which he released to their native habitat.

It is generally agreed that Leonardo's masterpieces are *The Virgin of the Rocks* (which exists in two versions), *The Last Supper,* and his portraits of the Mona Lisa and Ginevra da Benci. *The Virgin of the Rocks* typifies not only his marvelous technical skill but also his passion for science and his belief in the universe as a well-ordered place. The figures are arranged geometrically, with every rock and plant depicted in accurate detail. *The Last Supper,* painted on the walls of the refectory of Santa Maria delle Grazie in Milan, is a study of psychological reactions. A serene Christ, resigned to his terrible fate, has just announced to his disciples that one of them will betray him. The artist succeeds in portraying the mingled emotions of surprise, horror, and guilt in the faces of the disciples as they gradually perceive the meaning

of their master's statement. The third and fourth of Leonardo's major triumphs, the *Mona Lisa* and *Ginevra da Benci,* reflect a similar interest in the varied moods of the human soul.

THE VENETIAN SCHOOL

The beginning of the High Renaissance around 1490 also witnessed the rise of the so-called Venetian school, the major members of which were Giovanni Bellini (c. 1430–1516), Giorgione (1478–1510), and Titian (c. 1490–1576). The work of all these men reflected the luxurious, pleasure-loving life of the thriving commercial city of Venice. Most Venetian painters showed little of the Florentine school's concerns with philosophical and psychological issues. Their aim was to appeal to the senses by painting idyllic landscapes and sumptuous portraits of the rich and powerful. In the subordination of form and meaning to color and elegance they mirrored the sumptuous tastes of the wealthy merchants for whom they were created.

Doge Francesco Venier (1555), by Titian. Titian served as the official painter of the Venetian Republic for sixty years. This superb portrait of Venice's ruler shows Titian's mastery of light and color.

PAINTING IN ROME

High Renaissance painting reached its peak in the first half of the sixteenth century. During this period, Rome became the major artistic center of the Italian peninsula, although the traditions of the Florentine school still exerted a potent influence.

RAPHAEL

Among the eminent painters of this period was Raphael (1483–1520), a native of Urbino, and perhaps the most beloved artist of the entire Renaissance. The lasting appeal of his style is due primarily to his ennobling portrayals of human beings as temperate, wise, and dignified creatures. Although Raphael was influenced by Leonardo, he cultivated a much more symbolical or allegorical approach to his painting. His *Disputà* illustrated the relationship between the church in heaven and the church on earth. In a worldly setting against a brilliant sky, theologians debate the meaning of the Eucharist, while in the clouds above, saints and the Trinity repose in the possession of a holy mystery. Raphael's *School of Athens* depicts the harmony between Platonism and Aristotelianism. Plato (painted as a portrait of Leonardo) is shown pointing upward to emphasize the spiritual basis of his world of Ideas, while Aristotle stretches a hand forward to exemplify his claim that the created world embodies these same principles in physical form. Raphael is noted also for his portraits and Madonnas. To the latter, especially, he gave a softness and warmth that seemed to endow them with a sweetness and piety quite different from Leonardo's enigmatic and somewhat distant Madonnas.

MICHELANGELO

The last towering figure of the High Renaissance was Michelangelo (1475–1564), a native of Florence. If Leonardo was a naturalist, Michelangelo was an idealist; where the former sought to recapture and interpret fleeting natural phenomena, Michelangelo, who

School of Athens, by Raphael.

The Creation of Adam, by Michelangelo (1475–1564). One of a series of frescoes on the ceiling of the Sistine Chapel in Rome. Inquiring into the nature of humanity, it represents Renaissance affirmativeness at its height.

embraced Neoplatonism as a philosophy, was more concerned with expressing enduring, abstract truths. Michelangelo was a painter, sculptor, architect, and poet—and he expressed himself in all these forms with a similar power and in a similar manner. At the center of all of his paintings is the male figure, which is always powerful, colossal, magnificent. If humanity, embodied in the male body, lay at the center of Italian Renaissance culture, then Michelangelo, who depicted the male figure without cease, is the supreme Renaissance artist.

Michelangelo's greatest achievements in painting appear in a single location—the Sistine Chapel in Rome—yet they are products of two different periods in the artist's life and consequently exemplify two different artistic styles and outlooks on the human condition. More famous are the sublime frescoes Michelangelo painted on the ceiling of the Sistine Chapel from 1508 to 1512, depicting scenes from the book of Genesis. All the panels in this series, including *God Dividing the Light from Darkness, The Creation of Adam,* and *The Flood,* exemplify the young artist's commitment to classical Greek aesthetic principles of harmony, solidity, and dignified restraint. Correspondingly, all exude a sense of sublime affirmation regarding the Creation and the heroic qualities of humankind. But a quarter of a century later, when Michelangelo returned to work in the Sistine Chapel, both his style and mood had changed dramatically. In the enormous *Last Judgment,* a fresco done for the Sistine Chapel's altar wall in 1536, Michelangelo repudiated classical restraint and substituted a style that emphasized tension and distortion to communicate the older man's pessimistic conception of a humanity wracked by fear and bowed by guilt.

SCULPTURE

In the realm of sculpture the Italian Renaissance took a great step forward by creating statues that were no longer carved as parts of columns or doorways on church buildings or as effigies on tombs. Instead, Italian sculptors for the first time since antiquity carved free-standing statues "in the round." By freeing sculpture from its bondage to architecture, the High Renaissance reestablished sculpture as a separate and potentially secular art form.

DONATELLO

The first great master of Renaissance sculpture was Donatello (c. 1386–1466). His bronze statue of David triumphant over the head of the slain Goliath, the first free-standing nude since antiquity, imitated classical sculpture not just in the depiction of a nude body but also in the subject's posture of resting his weight on one leg. Yet this David is clearly a lithe adolescent rather than a muscular Greek athlete. Later in his career, Donatello more consciously imitated ancient statuary in his commanding portrayal of the proud warrior Gattamelata—the first monumental equestrian statue in bronze executed in the West since the time of the Romans.

MICHELANGELO

Certainly the greatest sculptor of the Italian Renaissance—indeed, probably the greatest sculptor of all time—was Michelangelo. Believing with Leonardo that the artist was an inspired creator, Michelangelo regarded sculpture as the most exalted of the arts because it allowed the artist to imitate God most fully in re-creating human forms. Furthermore, in Michelangelo's view the most God-like sculptor disdained slavish naturalism, for anyone could make a plaster cast of a human figure, but only an inspired creative genius could endow his sculpted figures with a sense of life. Accordingly, Michelangelo subordinated naturalism to the force of his imagination and sought restlessly to express his ideals in ever more arresting forms.

Like his painting, Michelangelo's sculpture followed a course from classicism to mannerism—that is, from

David, by Donatello (c. 1386–1466). The first free-standing nude statue executed in the West since antiquity.

harmonious modeling to dramatic distortion. The sculptor's most distinguished early work, his *David,* executed in 1501, is surely his most perfect classical statue. Choosing, like Donatello, to depict a male nude, Michelangelo conceived of his own *David* as a public expression of Florentine civic ideals and hence as heroic rather than merely graceful. To this end he worked in marble—the "noblest" sculptural medium—and created a figure twice as large as life. By sculpting a serenely confident young man at the peak of physical fitness, Michelangelo celebrated the Florentine republic's own fortitude in resisting tyrants and upholding

David, by Michelangelo. Over thirteen feet high, this serenely self-confident affirmation of the beauty of the human form was placed prominently by the Florentine government in front of Florence's city hall to proclaim the city's humanistic values.

The Descent from the Cross, by Michelangelo. This portrayal of tragedy was made by the sculptor for his own tomb. Note the distortion for effect exemplified by the elongated body and left arm of the figure of Christ. The figure in the rear is Nicodemus, but was probably intended to represent Michelangelo himself.

ideals of civic justice. The serenity seen in *David* was no longer prominent in the works of Michelangelo's middle period; rather, in a work such as his *Moses* of about 1515, the sculptor had begun to explore the use of anatomical distortion to create effects of emotional intensity—in this case, the biblical prophet's righteous rage. While such statues remained awesomely heroic, as Michelangelo's life drew to a close he experimented more and more with exaggerated stylistic mannerisms for the purpose of communicating moods of brooding pensiveness or outright pathos. The culmination of this trend in Michelangelo's statuary is his unfinished but intensely moving *Descent from the Cross*, a depiction of an old man resembling the sculptor himself grieving over the distorted, slumping body of the dead Christ.

ARCHITECTURE

To a much greater extent than either sculpture or painting, Renaissance architecture had its roots in the past. The new building style was a compound of elements derived from the Middle Ages and from antiquity. It was not the Gothic, however, a style that had never found a congenial soil in Italy, but the Italian Romanesque that

The Villa Rotonda, by Palladio. A highly influential Renaissance private dwelling near Vicenza.

provided the medieval basis for the architecture of the Italian Renaissance. The great architects of the Renaissance generally adopted their building plans from Romanesque churches, some of which they believed, mistakenly, to be Roman rather than medieval. They also copied their decorative devices from the ruins of ancient Rome. The result was an architecture based on the cruciform floor plan of transept and nave, but embodying the decorative features of the column and arch or the column and lintel, the colonnade, and frequently the dome. Renaissance architecture also emphasized geometrical proportion because Italian

builders, under the influence of Neoplatonism, concluded that certain mathematical ratios reflect the harmony of the universe. A fine example of Renaissance architecture is St. Peter's Basilica in Rome, built under the patronage of popes Julius II and Leo X and designed by some of the most celebrated architects of the time, including Donato Bramante (c. 1444–1514) and Michelangelo. Equally impressive are the artfully proportioned aristocratic country houses designed by the northern Italian architect Andrea Palladio (1508–1580), who created secular miniatures of ancient temples such as the Roman Pantheon to glorify the aristocrats who dwelled within them.

CHRONOLOGY

LIVES OF ITALIAN RENAISSANCE SCHOLARS AND ARTISTS

Petrarch	1304–1374
Leon Battista Alberti	1404–1472
Giovanni Pico della Mirandola	1463–1494
Niccolò Machiavelli	1469–1527
Leonardo da Vinci	1452–1519
Titian	c. 1490–1576
Raphael	1483–1520
Michelangelo	1475–1564

THE WANING OF THE ITALIAN RENAISSANCE

Why did the Renaissance decline around 1550?

Around 1550 the Renaissance in Italy began to decline. The causes of this decline were varied. The French invasion of 1494 and the incessant warfare that ensued was one of the major factors. The French king Charles VIII viewed Italy as an attractive target for his expansive dynastic ambitions. In 1494 he led an army of 30,000 well-trained troops across the Alps to press his claims to the Duchy of Milan and the Kingdom of Naples. Florence swiftly capitulated; within less than a year the French had promenaded down the peninsula and conquered Naples. By so doing, however, they aroused the suspicions of the rulers of Spain, who feared an attack on their own territory of Sicily. An alliance among Spain, the Papal States, the Holy Roman Empire, Milan, and Venice finally forced Charles to withdraw from Italy. But the respite was brief. Charles's successor, Louis XII, launched a second invasion, and from 1499 until 1529 warfare in Italy was virtually uninterrupted. Alliances and counteralliances followed each other in bewildering succession, but they managed only to prolong the hostilities. The French won a great victory at Marignano in 1515, but they were decisively defeated by the Spanish at Pavia in 1525. The worst disaster came in 1527 when rampaging troops under the command of the Spanish ruler and Holy Roman emperor Charles V sacked the city of Rome, causing enormous destruction. Only in 1529 did Charles V finally manage to gain control over most of the Italian peninsula, putting an end to the fighting for a time. Once triumphant, Charles retained two of the largest portions of Italy for Spain—the Duchy of Milan and the Kingdom of Naples—and installed favored princes as the rulers of almost all the other Italian political entities except for Venice and the Papal States. These protégés of the Spanish crown continued to preside over their own courts, to patronize the arts, and to adorn their cities with luxurious buildings; but they were puppets of a foreign power and unable to inspire their retinues with a sense of vigorous cultural independence.

To these political disasters was added a waning of Italian prosperity. Italy's virtual monopoly of trade with Asia in the fifteenth century had been one of the chief economic supports for Italian Renaissance culture, but the gradual shifting of trade routes from the Mediterranean to the Atlantic region, following the overseas discoveries of around 1500, slowly but surely cost Italy its supremacy as the center of European trade. Warfare also contributed to Italy's economic hardships, as did Spanish financial exactions in Milan and Naples. As Italian wealth diminished, there was less and less of a surplus to support artistic endeavors.

A final cause of the decline of the Italian Renaissance was the Counter-Reformation. During the sixteenth century the Roman church sought increasingly to exercise firm control over thought and art as part of a campaign to combat worldliness and the spread of Protestantism. In 1542 the Roman Inquisition was established; in 1564 the first Roman Index of Prohibited Books was published. Even Michelangelo's great *Last Judgment* in the Sistine Chapel was criticized for showing too many naked bodies. Therefore, Pope Paul IV ordered a second-rate artist to paint in clothing wherever possible. (The unfortunate artist was afterward known as the "underwear maker.") Although this incident may appear merely grotesquely humorous, the determination of ecclesiastical censors to enforce doctrinal uniformity could lead to death, as in the case of the unfortunate Neoplatonic philosopher Giordano Bruno, whose insistence that there may be more than one world (in contravention of the biblical book of Genesis) resulted in his being burned at the stake by the Roman Inquisition in 1600.

Galileo was not willing to die for his beliefs, but after he publicly retracted his view that the earth revolves around the sun he supposedly whispered, "despite everything, it still moves."

The most notorious example of inquisitorial censorship of intellectual speculation was the disciplining of the great scientist Galileo, whose achievements we will discuss in more detail in Chapter Sixteen. In 1616 the Holy Office in Rome condemned the new astronomical theory that the earth moves around the sun as "foolish, absurd, philosophically false, and formally heretical." When Galileo published a brilliant defense of the heliocentric system in 1632 the Inquisition ordered Galileo to recant his "errors" and sentenced him to house arrest for the duration of his life. Galileo was not willing to die for his beliefs, but after he publicly retracted his view that the earth revolves around the sun he supposedly whispered, "despite everything, it still moves." It is not surprising that the great astronomical discoveries of the next generation were made in northern Europe, not in Italy.

Cultural and artistic achievement was by no means extinguished in Italy after the middle of the sixteenth century. On the contrary, impressive new artistic styles were cultivated between about 1540 and 1600 by painters who drew on traits found in the later work of Raphael and Michelangelo. In the seventeenth cen-

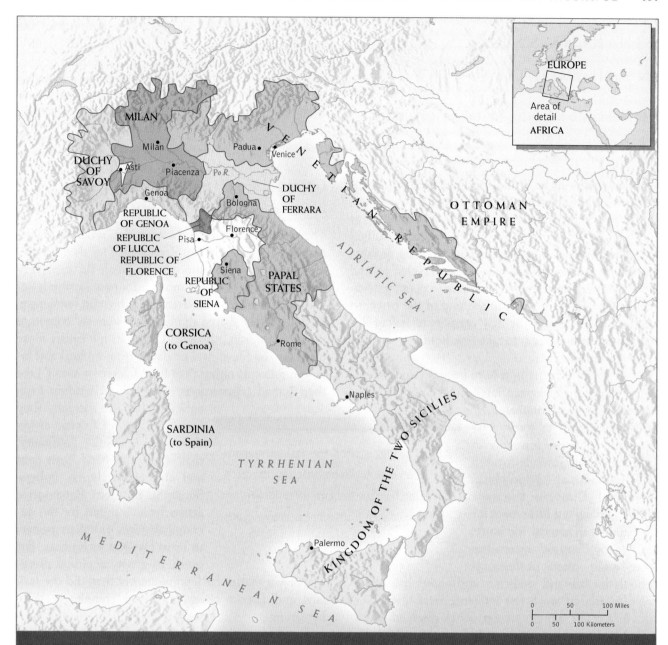

THE STATES OF ITALY DURING THE RENAISSANCE, C. 1494

Note the political divisions of Italy on the eve of the French invasion in 1494. Contemporary observers often described Italy as being divided among five great powers: Milan, Venice, Florence, the Papal States, and the Kingdom of Naples. Which of these powers were most interested in expanding their territory? Which neighboring territories would be most threatened by such attempts at expansion? Why did Florence and the Papal States so often find themselves in conflict with each other?

tury came the dazzling Baroque style, which was born in Rome under ecclesiastical auspices. Similarly, Italian music registered enormous accomplishments virtually without interruption from the sixteenth to the twentieth century. But as Renaissance culture spread from Italy to the rest of Europe, the cultural dominance of the Italians began to wane, and the focus of European high culture shifted toward the princely courts of Spain, France, England, Germany, and Poland.

THE RENAISSANCE IN THE NORTH

How did the northern and Italian Renaissances differ from one another?

Contacts between Italy and northern Europe continued throughout the fourteenth and fifteenth centuries. Italian merchants and financiers were familiar figures at northern courts; students from all over Europe studied at Italian universities such as Bologna or Padua; authors (including Chaucer) and their works traveled to and from Italy; and northern soldiers were frequent participants in Italian wars. Only at the end of the fifteenth century, however, did the new currents of Italian Renaissance learning begin to take firm hold in Spain and northern Europe.

A variety of explanations have been offered for this delay. Northern European intellectual life in the late Middle Ages was dominated by universities such as Paris, Oxford, and Charles University in Prague, whose curricula focused on the study of philosophical logic and Christian theology. This approach left little room for the study of classical literature. In Italy, by contrast, universities were more often professional schools for law and medicine, and universities themselves exercised much less influence over intellectual life. As a result, a more secular, urban-oriented educational tradition took shape in Italy, within which Renaissance humanism was able to develop. Even in the sixteenth century, northern scholars influenced by Italian Renaissance ideals usually worked outside the university system under the patronage of kings and princes.

Before the sixteenth century, northern rulers were also less interested in patronizing artists and intellectuals than were the city-states and princes of Italy. In Italy, such patronage was an important arena for competition between political rivals. In northern Europe, political units were larger and political rivals were fewer. It was therefore more difficult to use art for political purposes in a kingdom than it was in a city-state. In Florence, a statue erected in a central square would be seen by nearly all the city's residents. In Paris, such a statue would be seen only by a tiny minority of the French king's subjects. Only in the sixteenth century, as northern nobles began to spend more time in residence at the royal court, could kings be reasonably certain that their patronage of artists and intellectuals would be noticed by those whom they were trying to impress.

CHRISTIAN HUMANISM AND THE NORTHERN RENAISSANCE

The northern Renaissance was the product of the grafting of certain Italian Renaissance ideals onto pre-existing northern traditions. This can be seen very clearly in the case of the most prominent northern Renaissance intellectual movement, Christian humanism. Although they shared the Italian humanists' contempt for scholasticism, northern Christian humanists more often looked for ethical guidance from biblical and religious precepts rather than from Cicero or Virgil. Like their Italian counterparts, they sought wisdom from antiquity, but the antiquity they had in mind was Christian rather than classical—the antiquity, that is, of the New Testament and the early church fathers. Similarly, northern Renaissance artists were inspired by the accomplishments of Italian masters to learn classical techniques. But northern artists depicted classical subject matter far less frequently than did the Italians and almost never portrayed completely nude human figures.

Although they shared the Italian humanists' contempt for scholasticism, northern Christian humanists more often looked for ethical guidance from biblical and religious precepts rather than from Cicero or Virgil.

DESIDERIUS ERASMUS

Any discussion of northern Renaissance accomplishments in the realm of thought and literary expression must begin with the career of Desiderius Erasmus (c. 1469–1536), the "prince of the Christian humanists." The illegitimate son of a priest, Erasmus was born near Rotterdam in Holland but later, as a result of his wide travels, became in effect a citizen of all northern Europe. Forced into a monastery against his will when he was a teenager, the young Erasmus found there little religion or formal instruction of any kind but plenty of freedom to read what he liked. He devoured all the classics he could get his hands on and the writings of many of the church fathers. When he was

How did the northern and Italian Renaissances differ from one another?

The Renaissance in the North   463

Erasmus, by Hans Holbein the Younger (1497–1543).
This portrait is generally regarded as the most telling visual characterization of the prince of the Christian humanists.

about thirty years of age, he obtained permission to leave the monastery and enroll in the University of Paris, where he completed the requirements for the degree of bachelor of divinity. But Erasmus subsequently rebelled against what he considered the arid learning of Parisian scholasticism. Nor did he ever serve actively as a priest. Instead he made his living from teaching, writing, and the proceeds of various ecclesiastical offices that required no spiritual duties of him. Ever on the lookout for new patrons, he traveled often to England, stayed once for three years in Italy, and resided in several different cities in Germany and the Netherlands before settling finally toward the end of his life in Basel, Switzerland. By means of a voluminous correspondence that he kept up with learned friends he made wherever he went, Erasmus became the leader of a northern European humanist coterie. And through the popularity of his numerous publications, he became the arbiter of northern European cultural tastes during his lifetime.

Erasmus's many-sided intellectual activity may best be appraised from two different points of view: the literary and the doctrinal. As a Latin prose stylist, Erasmus was unequaled since the days of Cicero. Extraordinarily learned and witty, he reveled in tailoring his mode of discourse to fit his subject, creating dazzling verbal effects and coining puns that took on added meaning if the reader knew Greek as well as Latin. Above all, Erasmus excelled in the deft use of irony, poking fun at all and sundry, including himself. For example, in his *Colloquies* (from the Latin for "discussions") he had a fictional character lament the evil signs of the times thus: "kings make war, priests strive to line their pockets, theologians invent syllogisms, monks roam outside their cloisters, the commons riot, and Erasmus writes colloquies."

But although Erasmus's urbane Latin style and wit earned him a wide audience for purely literary reasons, he intended everything he wrote to promote what he called the "philosophy of Christ." Erasmus believed that the entire society of his day was caught up in corruption and immorality because people had lost sight of the simple teachings of the Gospels. Accordingly, he offered to his contemporaries three different categories of publication: clever satires meant to show people the error of their ways, serious moral treatises meant to offer guidance toward proper Christian behavior, and scholarly editions of basic Christian texts.

In the first category belong the works of Erasmus that are still most widely read today—*The Praise of Folly* (1509), in which he pilloried scholastic pedantry and dogmatism as well as the ignorance and superstitious credulity of the masses; and the *Colloquies* (1518), in which he held up contemporary religious practices for examination in a more serious but still pervasively ironic tone. In such works Erasmus let fictional characters do the talking; hence his own views can be determined only by inference. But in his second mode Erasmus did not hesitate to speak clearly in his own voice. The most prominent treatises in this second genre are the quietly eloquent *Handbook of the Christian Knight* (1503), which urged the laity to pursue lives of serene inward piety, and the *Complaint of Peace* (1517), which pleaded movingly for Christian pacifism. Erasmus's pacifism was one of his most deeply held values, and he returned to it again and again in his published works.

Despite the success of his literary works, Erasmus considered his textual scholarship his greatest achievement. Revering the authority of the early Latin fathers Augustine, Jerome, and Ambrose, he brought out reliable editions of all their works. He also used his extraordinary command of Latin and Greek to produce a more accurate edition of the New Testament. After reading Lorenzo Valla's *Notes on the New Testament* in 1504, Erasmus became convinced that nothing was more imperative than divesting the New Testament of the myriad errors in transcription and translation that had piled up during the Middle Ages, for no one could be a good Christian without being certain of exactly what Christ's message really was. Hence he spent ten years studying and comparing all the best early Greek biblical manuscripts he could find in order to establish an authoritative text. When it finally appeared in 1516, Erasmus's Greek New Testament, published together with explanatory notes and his own new Latin translation, was one of the most important landmarks of biblical scholarship of all time. In the hands of Martin Luther, it would play a critical role in the early stages of the Protestant Reformation.

SIR THOMAS MORE

One of Erasmus's closest friends, and a close second to him in distinction among the ranks of the Christian humanists, was the Englishman Sir Thomas More (1478–1535). Following a successful career as a lawyer and as speaker of the House of Commons, in 1529 More was appointed lord chancellor of England. He was not long in this position, however, before he incurred the wrath of King Henry VIII. More, who was loyal to Catholic universalism, opposed the king's design to establish a national church under royal control. Finally, in 1534, when More refused to take an oath acknowledging Henry as head of the Church of England, he was thrown into the Tower of London, and a year later met his death on the scaffold as a Catholic martyr. Much earlier, however, in 1516, long before More had any inkling of how his life was to end, he published the one work for which he will ever be best remembered, *Utopia*. Purporting to describe an ideal community on an imaginary island, the book is really an Erasmian critique of the glaring abuses of the time—poverty undeserved and wealth unearned, drastic punishments, religious persecution, and the senseless slaughter of war. The inhabitants of Utopia hold all their goods in common, work only six hours a day so that all may have leisure for intellectual pursuits, and practice the natural virtues of wisdom, moderation, fortitude, and justice. Iron is the precious metal "because it is useful," war and monasticism do not exist, and toleration is granted to all who recognize the

Sir Thomas More, by Hans Holbein the Younger.

existence of God and the immortality of the soul. Although More advanced no explicit arguments in his *Utopia* in favor of Christianity, he clearly meant to imply that if the Utopians could manage their society so well without the benefit of Christian revelation, Europeans who knew the Gospels ought to be able to do even better.

ULRICH VON HUTTEN

Whereas Erasmus and More were basically conciliatory in their temperaments and preferred to express themselves by means of wry understatement, Erasmus's German disciple Ulrich von Hutten (1488–1523) was of a much more combative disposition. Dedicated to the cause of German cultural nationalism, von Hutten spoke up truculently to defend the "proud and free" German people against foreigners. But his chief claim to fame was his collaboration with another German humanist, Crotus Rubianus, in the authorship of the *Letters of Obscure Men* (1515), one of the most stinging satires in the history of literature. This was written as part of a propaganda war in favor of a scholar named Johann Reuchlin who wished to pursue his study of

HOW DID THE NORTHERN AND ITALIAN RENAISSANCES DIFFER FROM ONE ANOTHER?

THE RENAISSANCE IN THE NORTH   465

Hebrew writings—above all, the Talmud. When scholastic theologians and the German inquisitor general tried to have all Hebrew books in Germany destroyed, Reuchlin and his party strongly opposed the move. After a while it became apparent that direct argument was accomplishing nothing, so Reuchlin's supporters resorted to ridicule. Von Hutten and Rubianus published a series of letters, written in intentionally bad Latin, purportedly by some of Reuchlin's scholastic opponents from the University of Cologne. These opponents, given such ridiculous names as Goatmilker, Baldpate, and Dungspreader, were shown to be learned fools who paraded absurd religious literalism or grotesque erudition. Heinrich Sheep's-mouth, for example, the supposed writer of one of the letters, professed to be worried that he had sinned grievously by eating on Friday an egg that contained the embryo of a chick. The author of another boasted of his "brilliant discovery" that Julius Caesar could not have written Latin histories because he was too busy with his military exploits ever to have learned Latin. Although immediately banned by the church, the letters circulated nonetheless and were widely read, giving ever more currency to the Erasmian proposition that scholastic theology and external religious observances had to be set aside in favor of the most earnest dedication to the simple teachings of the Gospels.

Most Christian humanists tried to remain within the Catholic fold while still espousing their ideal of nonritualistic inward piety. But as time went on, the leaders of Catholicism grew less and less tolerant because lines were hardening in the war with Protestantism.

THE DECLINE OF CHRISTIAN HUMANISM

With Erasmus, More, and von Hutten the list of energetic and eloquent Christian humanists is by no means exhausted, for the Englishman John Colet (c. 1467–1519), the Frenchman Jacques Lefèvre d'Étaples (c. 1455–1536), and the Spaniards Cardinal Francisco Ximénez de Cisneros (1436–1517) and Juan Luís Víves (1492–1540) all made signal contributions to the collective enterprise of editing biblical and early Christian texts and expounding Gospel morality. But despite a host of achievements, the Christian humanist movement, which possessed such an extraordinary degree of international solidarity and vigor from about 1500 to 1525, was thrown into disarray by the rise of Protestantism and subsequently lost its momentum.

The irony here is obvious, for the Christian humanists' emphasis on the literal truth of the Gospels and their devastating criticisms of clerical corruption and religious ceremonialism certainly helped pave the way for the Protestant Reformation initiated by Martin Luther in 1517. But, as we will see in Chapter Thirteen, very few of the older generation of Christian humanists were willing to join Luther in rejecting the fundamental principles on which Catholicism was based, and the few who did became such ardent Protestants that they lost the sense of quiet irony that had been a hallmark of Christian humanist expression. Most Christian humanists tried to remain within the Catholic fold while still espousing their ideal of nonritualistic inward piety. But as time went on, the leaders of Catholicism grew less and less tolerant because lines were hardening in the war with Protestantism. Hence any internal criticism of Catholic religious practices seemed like giving covert aid to the enemy. Erasmus himself, who remained a Catholic, died early enough to escape opprobrium, but several of his less fortunate followers lived on to suffer as victims of the Inquisition.

LITERATURE, ART, AND MUSIC IN THE NORTHERN RENAISSANCE

Yet if Christian humanism faded rapidly after about 1525, the northern Renaissance continued to flourish throughout the sixteenth century in literature and art. In France, Pierre de Ronsard (c. 1524–1585) and Joachim du Bellay (c. 1522–1560) wrote elegant sonnets in the style of Petrarch, and in England the poets Sir Philip Sidney (1554–1586) and Edmund Spenser (c. 1552–1599) drew impressively on Italian literary innovations. Indeed, Spenser's *Faerie Queene*, a long chivalric romance written in the manner of Ariosto's *Orlando Furioso*, communicates as well as any Italian work the gorgeous sensuousness typical of Italian Renaissance culture.

RABELAIS

More original than any of the aforementioned poets was the French prose satirist François Rabelais (*ra-beh-LAY*, c. 1494–1553), probably the best loved of all the great European creative writers of the sixteenth century. Like Erasmus, whom he greatly admired, Rabelais began his career in the clergy, but soon after taking holy orders he left his cloister to study medicine. As a practicing physician Rabelais interspersed his professional activities with literary endeavors, composing almanacs, satires against quacks and astrologers, and burlesques of popular superstitions. But by far his most enduring work was his five volumes of "chronicles" published under the collective title *Gargantua and Pantagruel*.

Rabelais's account of the adventures of Gargantua and Pantagruel, originally the names of legendary medieval giants noted for their fabulous size and gross appetites, served as a vehicle for his lusty humor and his penchant for exuberant narrative as well as for the expression of his philosophy of naturalism. To some degree, Rabelais drew on the precedents of Christian humanism. Thus, like Erasmus, he satirized religious ceremonialism, ridiculed scholasticism, scoffed at superstitions, and pilloried every form of bigotry. But unlike Erasmus, who wrote in a highly cultivated classical Latin style comprehensible to only the most learned readers, Rabelais chose to address a far wider

audience by writing in an extremely down-to-earth French loaded with the crudest vulgarities. Likewise, Rabelais wanted to avoid seeming in any way preachy and therefore eschewed all suggestions of moralism in favor of giving the impression that he wished merely to offer his readers some rollicking good fun. Yet, aside from the critical satire in *Gargantua and Pantagruel*, there runs through all five volumes a common theme of glorifying the human and the natural. For Rabelais, whose robust giants were really life-loving human beings writ very large, every instinct of humanity was healthy, provided it was not directed toward tyranny over others. Thus in his ideal community, the utopian "abbey of Thélème," there was no repressiveness whatsoever, but only a congenial environment for the pursuit of life-affirming, natural human attainments, guided by the single rule of "love and do what thou wouldst."

ARCHITECTURE

Just as Rabelais recounted stories of medieval giants to affirm Renaissance values, so French architects who constructed such splendid Loire châteaux as Amboise,

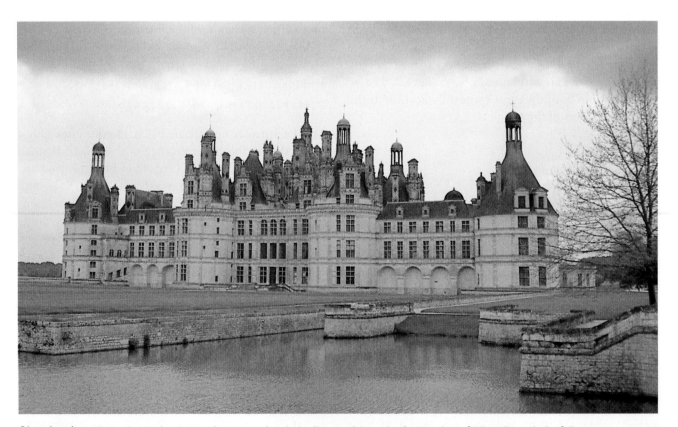

Chambord. Built in the early sixteenth century by an Italian architect in the service of King Francis I of France, this magnificent Loire Valley château combines Gothic and Renaissance architectural traits.

How did the Northern and Italian Renaissances differ from one another?

The Renaissance in the North   467

Chenonceaux, and Chambord combined elements of the late medieval French flamboyant Gothic style with an up-to-date emphasis on classical horizontality to produce some of the most impressively distinctive architectural landmarks ever constructed in France. Yet much closer architectural imitation of Italian models occurred in France as well, for just as Ronsard and du Bellay modeled their poetic style very closely on Petrarch, so Pierre Lescot, the French architect who began work on the new royal palace of the Louvre in Paris in 1546, hewed closely to the classicism of Italian Renaissance masters in constructing a facade that emphasized classical pilasters and pediments.

PAINTING

Northern Renaissance painting is another realm in which we can discern links between thought and art. Certainly the most moving visual embodiments of the ideals of Christian humanism were conceived by the foremost of northern Renaissance artists, the German Albrecht Dürer (1471–1528). Dürer (*DOOR-er*) was the first northerner to master Italian Renaissance techniques of proportion, perspective, and modeling. Dürer also shared with contemporary Italians a fascination with reproducing the manifold works of nature down to the minutest details and a penchant for displaying the human nude in various postures. But whereas Michelangelo portrayed his *David* or *Adam* entirely without covering, Dürer's nudes are seldom lacking their fig leaves, in deference to more restrained northern traditions. Moreover, Dürer consistently refrained from abandoning himself to the pure classicism and sumptuousness of much Italian Renaissance art because he was inspired primarily by the more traditionally Christian ideals of Erasmus. Thus Dürer's serenely radiant engraving of Saint Jerome expresses the sense of accomplishment that Erasmus or any other contemporary Christian humanist may have had while working quietly in his study; and his *Four Apostles* intones a solemn hymn to the dignity and penetrating insight of Dürer's favorite New Testament authors, Saints Paul, John, Peter, and Mark.

Dürer would have loved nothing more than to have immortalized Erasmus in a major painted portrait, but circumstances prevented him from doing this because the paths of the two men crossed only once, and after Dürer started sketching his hero on that occasion his work was interrupted by Erasmus's press of business.

Saint Jerome in His Study, **by Dürer.** Saint Jerome, a hero to both Dürer and Erasmus, represents inspired Christian scholarship. Note how the scene exudes contentment, even down to the sleeping lion, which seems rather like an overgrown tabby cat.

Instead, the accomplishment of capturing Erasmus's pensive spirit in oils was left to another great northern Renaissance artist, the German Hans Holbein the Younger (1497–1543; see p. 463). As good fortune would have it, during a stay in England, Holbein also painted an extraordinarily acute portrait of Erasmus's friend and kindred spirit Sir Thomas More, which enables us to see clearly why a contemporary called More "a man of . . . sad gravity; a man for all seasons" (see p. 464). These two portraits in and of themselves point out a major difference between medieval and Renaissance culture. Whereas the Middle Ages produced no convincing naturalistic likenesses of any leading intellectual figures, Renaissance culture's greater commitment to capturing the essence of human individuality created the environment in which Holbein was able to make Erasmus and More come to life.

MUSIC

Music in western Europe in the fifteenth and sixteenth centuries reached such a high point of development that it constitutes, together with painting and sculpture, one of the most brilliant aspects of Renaissance endeavor. The musical theory of the Renaissance was driven largely by the humanist-inspired but largely fruitless effort to recover and imitate classical musical forms and modes. Musical practice, however, showed much more continuity with medieval musical traditions of number and proportion. At the same time, however, a new expressiveness emerges in Renaissance music, along with a new emphasis on coloration and emotional quality. New musical instruments were also developed, including the lute, the viol, the violin, and a variety of woodwind and keyboard instruments including the harpsichord. New musical forms also emerged: madrigals, motets, and, at the end of the sixteenth century, a new Italian form, the opera. As earlier, musical leadership came from men trained in the service of the church. But the distinction between sacred and profane music was becoming less sharp, and most composers did not restrict their activities to a single field. Music was no longer regarded merely as a diversion or an adjunct to worship but came into its own as a serious independent art.

During the fourteenth century, before or in the early Renaissance period, a musical movement called *ars nova* ("new art") flourished in Italy and France. Its outstanding composers were Francesco Landini (c. 1325–1397) and Guillaume de Machaut (c. 1300–1377). The madrigals, ballads, and other songs composed by the ars nova musicians testify to a rich fourteenth-century tradition of secular music, but the greatest achievement of the period was a highly complicated yet delicate contrapuntal style adapted for ecclesiastical motets. Machaut, moreover, was the first known composer to provide a polyphonic version of the major sections of the Mass.

The fifteenth century ushered in a synthesis of French, Flemish, and Italian elements in the ducal court of Burgundy. This music was melodious and gentle, but in the second half of the century it hardened a little as northern Flemish elements gained in importance. As the sixteenth century opened, Franco-Flemish composers appeared in every important court and cathedral all over Europe, gradually establishing regional-national schools, usually in attractive combinations of Flemish with German, Spanish, and Italian musical cultures. The various genres thus created show a close affinity with Renaissance art and poetry. In the second half of the sixteenth century the leaders of the nationalized Franco-Flemish style were the Fleming Roland de Lassus (1532–1594), the most versatile composer of the age, and the Italian Giovanni Pierluigi da Palestrina (c. 1525–1594), who specialized in highly intricate polyphonic choral music written for Catholic church services under the patronage of the popes in Rome. Music also flourished in sixteenth-century England, where the Tudor monarchs Henry VIII and Elizabeth I were active patrons of the arts. Not only did the Italian madrigal, imported toward the end of the sixteenth century, take on remarkable new life in England, but songs and instrumental music of an original cast anticipated future developments on the Continent. In William Byrd (1543–1623), English music produced a master fully the equal of the great Flemish and Italian composers of the Renaissance period. The general level of musical proficiency seems to have been higher in Queen Elizabeth's day than in ours: the singing of part-songs was a popular pastime in homes

> The madrigals, ballads, and other songs composed by the ars nova musicians testify to a rich fourteenth-century tradition of secular music, but the greatest achievement of the period was a highly complicated yet delicate contrapuntal style adapted for ecclesiastical motets.

CHRONOLOGY

**LIVES OF NORTHERN RENAISSANCE SCHOLARS
AND ARTISTS**

Erasmus	c. 1469–1536
Thomas More	1478–1535
Ulrich von Hutten	1488–1523
Edmund Spenser	c. 1552–1599
François Rabelais	c. 1494–1553
Albrecht Dürer	1471–1528
Hans Holbein the Younger	1497–1543

and at informal social gatherings, and the ability to read a part at sight was expected of the educated elite.

Although accomplishments in counterpoint were already very advanced in the Renaissance period, our modern harmonic system was still in its infancy, and thus there remained much room for experimentation. At the same time we should realize that the music of the Renaissance constitutes not merely a stage in evolution but a magnificent achievement in itself, with masters who rank among the greatest of all time. The composers Lassus, Palestrina, and Byrd are as truly representative of the artistic triumph of the Renaissance as are the painters Leonardo, Raphael, and Michelangelo. Their heritage, long neglected, has within recent years begun to be appreciated, and is now gaining in popularity as interested groups of musicians devote themselves to its revival.

CONCLUSION

The contrasts between the Italian and the northern Renaissance are real, but they must not be exaggerated. The intellectuals of Renaissance Italy were formed in a more secular, more urban educational environment than were the northerners, but they were no less fervent in their Christianity. Petrarch's criticism of scholasticism was not that it was too Christian but, rather, that it was not Christian enough. Petrarch opposed the emotional aridity and stylistic inelegance of scholasticism because he believed they threatened the salvation of Christians. Much the same point might be made about Lorenzo Valla. His critique of the tempo-

ral claims of the papacy sprang not only from the conclusions of his textual scholarship but also from a firm Christian piety. The Platonic Academy might honor Plato as if he were a saint of the church, but these men approached Plato's works in the same spirit with which thirteenth-century scholastic theologians had approached the works of Aristotle. As committed Christians, they were convinced that the conclusions reached by the greatest philosophical minds of classical antiquity must be compatible with Christian truth. It was the task of Christian intellectuals to reveal this compatibility and, by so doing, to strengthen the one true faith.

In considering the contrasts between "civic" and "Christian" humanism, we must also keep in mind the enormous diversity of Renaissance thought. Machiavelli is no more typical an Italian Renaissance thinker than is Ficino, Alberti, or Bruno. In comparing Italian thinkers with northern thinkers, we must therefore be careful to compare like with like. Too often, scholars overdraw the contrasts between Renaissance thought in Italy and northern Europe by choosing Machiavelli, for example, to represent all of Italian humanism and Erasmus to represent northern humanism. Two more different figures can hardly be imagined; but their differences have much more to do with their contrasting presuppositions about human nature than with their allegiances to Italian or northern humanism. A very different picture emerges if we compare, for example, John Colet as a representative of northern humanism with Marsilio Ficino as a representative of Italian humanism or if we compare Petrarch with Sir Thomas More.

Nor should we overdraw the contrasts between the Renaissance and the High Middle Ages. Both Italian and northern humanists shared an optimistic view of human nature as improvable despite the consequences of Adam and Eve's disobedience; but none was more optimistic on this score than was Saint Thomas Aquinas. Both groups emphasized the importance of personal introspection and self-examination; but none took this injunction more seriously than did the Cistercian thinkers of the twelfth century. And finally, both groups shared a belief that the exhortations of intellectuals would lift everyone's morals and conduct them to new heights of virtue. In this regard, High Renaissance intellectual life has a kind of naive optimism that contrasts sharply with the darker, more psychologically complex world of the Middle Ages and with the Reformation era that was about to begin.

KEY TERMS

humanism	*The Prince*	Raphael	Utopia
Medici	Baldassare Castiglione	Michelangelo	Rabelais
Petrarch	Leonardo da Vinci	Erasmus	

SELECTED READINGS

Alberti, Leon Battista. *The Family in Renaissance Florence (Della Famiglia)*. Trans. Renée Neu Watkins. Columbia, S.C., 1969.

Baxandall, Michael. *Painting and Experience in Fifteenth Century Italy.* Oxford, 1972. A classic study of the perceptual world of the Renaissance.

Brucker, Gene. *Florence, the Golden Age, 1138–1737.* Berkeley and Los Angeles, 1998. The standard account by a master historian.

Bruni, Leonardo. *The Humanism of Leonardo Bruni: Selected Texts.* Trans. Gordon Griffiths, James Hankins, and David Thompson. Binghamton, N.Y., 1987. Excellent translations, with introductions, to the Latin works of a key Renaissance humanist.

Burke, Peter. *The Renaissance.* New York, 1997. A brief introduction by an influential modern historian.

Burkhardt, Jacob. *The Civilization of the Renaissance in Italy.* Many editions. The nineteenth-century work that first crystallized an image of the Italian Renaissance with which scholars have been wrestling ever since.

Cassirer, Ernst, et al., eds. *The Renaissance Philosophy of Man.* Chicago, 1948. Important original works by Petrarch, Ficino, and Pico della Mirandola, among others.

Castiglione, Baldassare. *The Book of the Courtier.* Many editions. The translations by C. S. Singleton (New York, 1959) and by George Bull (New York, 1967) are both excellent.

Cellini, Benvenuto. *Autobiography.* Trans. George Bull. Baltimore, 1956. This Florentine goldsmith (1500–1571) is the source for many of the most famous stories about the artists of the Florentine Renaissance.

Cochrane, Eric, and Julius Kirshner, eds. *The Renaissance.* Chicago, 1986. An outstanding collection, from the University of Chicago Readings in Western Civilization series.

Erasmus, Desiderius. *The Praise of Folly.* Trans. J. Wilson. Ann Arbor, Mich., 1958.

Fox, Alistair. *Thomas More: History and Providence.* Oxford, 1982. A balanced account of a man too easily idealized.

Grafton, Anthony, and Lisa Jardine. *From Humanism to the Humanities: Education and the Liberal Arts in Fifteenth- and Sixteenth-Century Europe.* London, 1986. An influential account that presents Renaissance humanism as the elitist cultural program of a self-interested group of pedagogues.

Grendler, Paul, ed. *Encyclopedia of the Renaissance.* New York, 1999. A valuable reference work.

Hale, John R. *The Civilization of Europe in the Renaissance.* New York, 1993. A synthetic volume summarizing the life's work of a major Renaissance historian.

Hankins, James. *Plato in the Italian Renaissance.* Leiden and New York, 1990. A definitive study of the reception and influence of Plato on Renaissance intellectuals.

Hankins, James, ed. *Renaissance Civic Humanism: Reappraisals and Reflections.* Cambridge and New York, 2000. An excellent collection of scholarly essays reassessing republicanism in the Renaissance.

Jardine, Lisa. *Worldly Goods.* London, 1996. A revisionist account that emphasizes the acquisitive materialism of Italian Renaissance society and culture.

Kanter, Laurence, Hilliard T. Goldfarb, and James Hankins. *Botticelli's Witness: Changing Style in a Changing Florence.* Boston, 1997. This catalog for an exhibit of Botticelli's works, at the Gardner Museum in Boston, offers an excellent introduction to the painter and his world.

King, Margaret L. *Women of the Renaissance.* Chicago, 1991. Deals with women in all walks of life and in a variety of roles.

Kristeller, Paul O. *Eight Philosophers of the Italian Renaissance.* Stanford, 1964. An admirably clear and accurate account that fully appreciates the connections between medieval and Renaissance thought.

Kristeller, Paul O. *Renaissance Thought: The Classic, Scholastic, and Humanistic Strains.* New York, 1961. Very helpful in defining the main trends of Renaissance thought.

Lane, Frederic C. *Venice: A Maritime Republic.* Baltimore, 1973. An authoritative account.

Machiavelli, Niccolò. *The Discourses* and *The Prince.* Many editions. These two books must be read together if one is to understand Machiavelli's political ideas properly.

Martines, Lauro. *Power and Imagination: City-States in Renaissance Italy.* New York, 1979. Insightful account of the connections among politics, society, culture, and art.

More, Thomas. *Utopia*. Many editions.

Murray, Linda. *High Renaissance and Mannerism*. London, 1985. The place to start for fifteenth- and sixteenth-century Italian art.

Olson, Roberta, *Italian Renaissance Sculpture*, New York, 1992. The most accessible introduction to the subject.

Perkins, Leeman L. *Music in the Age of the Renaissance*. New York, 1999. A massive new study that nonetheless needs to be read in conjunction with Reese.

Rabelais, François. *Gargantua and Pantagruel*. Trans. J. M. Cohen. Baltimore, Md., 1955. A robust modern translation.

Reese, Gustave. *Music in the Renaissance*, rev. ed. New York, 1959. A great book; still authoritative, despite the more recent work by Perkins, which supplements but does not replace it.

Rice, Eugene F., Jr., and Anthony Grafton. *The Foundations of Early Modern Europe, 1460–1559*, 2d ed. New York, 1994. The best textbook account of its period.

Rowland, Ingrid D. *The Culture of the High Renaissance: Ancients and Moderns in Sixteenth-Century Rome*. Cambridge and New York, 2000. Beautifully written examination of the social, intellectual, and economic foundations of the Renaissance in Rome.

CHAPTER THIRTEEN

REFORMATIONS OF RELIGION

AFTER TWO CENTURIES of economic, social, and political turmoil, Europe in the year 1500 was well on the road to recovery. Population was increasing, the economy was expanding, cities were growing, and the national monarchs of France, England, Spain, Scotland, and Poland were all securely established on their thrones. Throughout Europe, governments at every level were extending and deepening their control over their subjects' lives. After a late-fourteenth-century hiatus, Europe had also resumed its commercial and colonial expansion. Even Catholic Christianity appeared to be going from strength to strength as the sixteenth century dawned. Although the papacy remained mired in territorial wars in Italy, the church itself had weathered the storms that had beset it during the fifteenth century. The Lollards had been suppressed and the Hussites reincorporated into the church. In the struggle over conciliarism, the papacy had successfully won the support of all the major European rulers, reducing the conciliarists to academic isolation at the University of Paris. Meanwhile, at the parish level, the devotion of ordinary Christians to their faith had probably never been higher. To be sure, there were also problems. Although the educational standards of the parish clergy were higher than they had ever been, reformers were quick to note that too many priests were still absent, ignorant, or neglectful of their spiritual duties. Monasticism, by and large, seemed to have lost its spiritual fire; among the populace, religious enthusiasm sometimes led the faithful into gross superstition and doctrinal error. But these were manageable problems. On the whole, the "prospect of Europe" had not looked brighter for several centuries.

No one in 1500 could have predicted that within fifty years Europe's religious unity would be irreparably shattered by a new and powerful Protestant reform movement— or that in the century thereafter an appallingly destructive series of religious wars would shake to their core the foundations of European political life. Yet remarkably, these extraordinary events began with a single German monk named Martin

FOCUS QUESTIONS

• What were the theological premises of Lutheranism?

• Why did Switzerland emerge as such an important center for sixteenth-century Protestantism?

 • How did notions of family and marriage change during the Reformation?

• Why did England become a Protestant country?

• How did the Catholic Reformation differ from the Counter-Reformation?

Luther (1483–1546), whose personal quest for a more certain understanding of sin, grace, and Christian salvation set off a chain reaction throughout Europe, resulting in the secession of millions of Europeans from the Roman Catholic Church and affecting the religious practices of nearly every Christian in Europe, whether Catholic or Protestant. The religious movement that Luther touched off was much larger than Luther himself; nor should Martin Luther's own spiritual journey be seen as an epitome for all of Protestantism. But that said, there is no doubt that the Reformation movement began with Martin Luther—and so must we if we are to understand the extraordinary upheaval this new religious movement brought about.

The Lutheran Upheaval

What were the theological premises of Lutheranism?

To explain the success of the Lutheran revolt in Germany, we must answer three central questions: (1) Why did Luther's theological ideas lead him to break with Rome? (2) Why did large numbers of Germans rally to his cause? (3) Why did so many German princes and towns impose the new religion within their territories? As we shall see, those who followed Luther found his message appealing for different reasons. Many peasants hoped the new religion would free them from the exactions of their lords; towns and princes thought it would allow them to consolidate their political independence; nationalists thought it would liberate Germany from the demands of foreign popes bent on feathering their own nest in central Italy.

What Luther's followers shared, however, was a conviction that their new, Lutheran understanding of Christianity would lead them to heaven, whereas contemporary Catholicism would not. To this degree, *reformation* is a misleading label for the movement Luther initiated. Although Luther himself did begin as a reformer seeking to cleanse contemporary Christianity from its abuses, he quickly developed into an uncompromising opponent of the basic principles of Catholic belief and practice. Many of his followers became even more radical. The religious movement that began with Martin Luther was thus no mere "reformation." It was a frontal assault on the foundations of late medieval religious life.

LUTHER'S QUEST FOR RELIGIOUS CERTAINTY

Although Martin Luther became an inspiration to millions, he was at first a terrible disappointment to his father. The elder Luther was a Thuringian peasant who had prospered by leasing some mines. Eager to see his clever son rise still further, he sent young Luther to the University of Erfurt to study law. In 1505, however, Martin shattered his father's hopes by becoming a monk of the Augustinian order. In some sense, however, Luther always remained faithful to his father's humble roots. Throughout his life, Martin Luther always lived simply and expressed himself in the vigorous, earthy vernacular of the German peasantry.

Like many great figures in the history of religion, Luther arrived at his new understanding of religious truth by a dramatic conversion experience. As a monk, young Luther zealously pursued all the traditional means for achieving his own salvation. Not only did he fast and pray continuously but he confessed so often that his exhausted confessor would sometimes jokingly suggest that if he really wanted to have a rousing confession he should go out and do something dramatic like committing adultery. Yet, try as he might, Luther could find no spiritual peace because he feared that he

Martin Luther. A portrait by Lucas Cranach.

could never perform enough good deeds to deserve so great a gift as salvation. But in 1513 he hit on an insight that granted him relief and changed the course of his life.

Luther's guiding insight pertained to the problem of the justice of God. For years he had worried that it seemed unjust for God to issue commandments that he knew human beings could not observe and then punish them with eternal damnation for not observing them. But after becoming a professor of biblical theology at the University of Wittenberg (many members of his monastic order were expected to teach), Luther was led by his study of the Bible to a new understanding of the problem. Specifically, while meditating on the words in the Psalms "deliver me in thy justice," it suddenly struck him that God's justice had nothing to do with his power to punish but rather with his mercy in saving sinful mortals through faith. As Luther later wrote, "At last, by the mercy of God, I began to understand the justice of God as that by which God makes us just in his mercy and through faith . . . and at this I felt as though I had been born again, and had gone through open gates into paradise." Since this fateful revelation came to Luther in the tower room of his monastery, it is customarily called his "tower experience."

After that, everything seemed to fall into place. Lecturing at Wittenberg in the years immediately following 1513, Luther pondered a passage in Saint Paul's Letter to the Romans (1:17): "[T]he just shall live by faith" until he reached his central doctrine of "justification by faith alone." Luther concluded that God's justice does not demand endless good works and religious rituals for salvation, because humans can never be saved by their own efforts. Rather, humans are saved by God's grace alone, which God offers as an utterly undeserved gift to those whom he has predestined for salvation. Because this grace comes to humans through the gift of faith, from the human perspective men and women are "justified" (i.e., made worthy of salvation) by faith alone. Those whom God has justified through faith will manifest that fact by performing works of piety and charity, but such works are not what saves them. Piety and charity are merely visible signs of each believer's invisible spiritual state, which is known to God alone.

The essence of this doctrine was not original to Luther. It harked back to around the year 400 with the predestinarianism of Saint Augustine (see Chapter Six),

> By the end of the fifteenth century, indulgences were often being granted in return for monetary payments to favored papal causes. To many reformers, this looked like simony: the sin of selling grace in return for cash.

the patron saint of Luther's own monastic order. During the twelfth and thirteenth centuries, however, theologians such as Peter Lombard and Saint Thomas Aquinas had developed a very different understanding of salvation, emphasizing the role that both the church itself (through its sacraments) and the individual believer (through acts of piety and charity) could play in the process of salvation. None of these theologians claimed that a human being could earn his or her way to heaven by good works alone. But the late medieval church unwittingly encouraged such misunderstandings by presenting the process of salvation in increasingly quantitative terms, declaring, for example, that by performing a specific meritorious act (such as a pilgrimage or a pious donation), a believer could reduce the penance she or he owed to God by a specific number of days. From the fourteenth century on, popes claimed to dispense such special grace to the living from the "Treasury of Merits," a storehouse of surplus good works piled up by Christ and the saints in heaven. After 1476, popes also began to assign such excess grace to the dead, to speed their way through purgatory. Most commonly, grace was withdrawn from this treasury and reassigned to needy sinners through indulgences: special remissions of the penitential obligations imposed on Christians by their priests as part of the sacrament of penance. When indulgences began, in the eleventh and twelfth centuries, they could be earned only by demanding spiritual exercises, such as joining a crusade. By the end of the fifteenth century, however, indulgences were often being granted in return for monetary payments to favored papal causes. To many reformers, this looked like simony: the sin of selling grace in return for cash.

Abuses of this sort were widely criticized by early sixteenth-century church reformers such as Erasmus. But Luther's objections to indulgences and prayers for the dead had much more radical consequences, because they rested on a set of Augustinian theological presuppositions that, if taken to their logical conclusion, could result only in dismantling much of contemporary Catholic religious practice. Luther himself may not have realized this when he took the first steps that would lead to his breach with Rome. But as the implications of his ideas became clear, Luther did not withdraw from them. Instead, he pressed on, declaring to his opponents, "Here I stand; God help me, I can do no other."

THE REFORMATION BEGINS

Luther first developed his theological ideas as an academic lecturer, but in 1517 he was goaded into attacking some of the actual practices of the church by a provocation that was too much for him to bear. The story of the indulgence campaign of 1517 in Germany is colorful but unsavory. The worldly Albert of Hohenzollern, youngest brother of the elector of Brandenburg, had sunk himself into enormous debt for several discreditable reasons. In 1513 he had to pay large sums for papal permission to hold the bishoprics of Magdeburg and Halberstadt concurrently, and for assuming these offices, even though at twenty-three he was not old enough to be a bishop at all. Not satisfied, when the prestigious archbishopric of Mainz fell vacant in the next year, Albert gained election to that too, even though he knew this would mean even larger payments to Rome. Obtaining the necessary funds by loans from the German banking firm of the Fuggers, he then struck a bargain with Pope Leo X (1513–1521): Leo authorized the sale of indulgences in Albert's ecclesiastical territories on the understanding that half of the income raised would go to Rome for the building of St. Peter's Basilica, with the other half going to Albert so that he could repay the Fuggers.

Luther did not know the sordid details of Albert's bargain, but he did know that a Dominican friar named Tetzel was soon hawking indulgences throughout much of northern Germany, with Fugger banking agents in his train, and that Tetzel was deliberately giving people the impression that an indulgence was an automatic ticket to heaven for oneself or one's loved ones in purgatory. For Luther, this was doubly offensive: not only was Tetzel violating Luther's conviction that people are saved by faith, not works, he was also misleading people into thinking that if they purchased an indulgence, then they no longer needed to confess their sins to a priest. Tetzel was thus putting their very salvation at risk. So on October 31, 1517, Luther offered to his university colleagues a list of ninety-five theses objecting to Catholic indulgence doctrine, an act conventionally seen as the beginning of the Protestant Reformation.

Luther had not initially intended to publicize his criticisms of Tetzel. He wrote his objections in Latin, not German, and meant them only for academic discussion within the University of Wittenberg. But when some unknown person translated and published Luther's theses, the hitherto obscure monk suddenly gained widespread notoriety. Tetzel and his allies outside the university now demanded that Luther withdraw his theses or defend himself. Rather than backing down, however, Luther became even bolder in his attacks on the church hierarchy. In 1519, in a public disputation held before throngs in Leipzig, Luther defiantly maintained that the pope and all clerics were merely fallible men and that the highest authority for an individual's conscience was the truth of Scripture. Pope Leo X responded by charging Luther with heresy; after that Luther had no alternative but to break with the Catholic Church entirely.

Luther's year of greatest creative activity came in 1520 when, in the midst of the crisis caused by his defiance, he composed a series of pamphlets setting forth his three primary theological premises: justification by faith, the primacy of scripture, and "the priesthood of all believers." We have already examined the meaning of the first premise. By the second he simply meant that the literal meaning of scripture took precedence over church traditions and that beliefs (such as purgatory) or practices (such as prayers to the saints) not explicitly grounded in scripture could be rejected as human inventions. Luther also declared all Christian believers to be spiritually equal before God. Denying

Jacob Fugger "The Rich" (1459–1528). His loans to Albert of Hohenzollern helped to touch off the Protestant Reformation.

Pope Leo X. Raphael's highly realistic portrait shows the pope with his nephews Giulio de' Medici, who would succeed him as pope, and Cardinal de Rossi.

that priests, monks, and nuns had any special spiritual qualities by virtue of their vocations, Luther argued instead for "the priesthood of all believers."

From these premises a host of practical consequences followed. Because works could not lead to salvation, Luther declared fasts, pilgrimages, and the veneration of relics to be spiritually valueless. He also called for the dissolution of all monasteries and convents. He also took steps to demystify the rites of the church, proposing the substitution of German for Latin in church services and reducing the number of sacraments from seven to two (baptism and the Eucharist; in 1520, he also included penance, but he later changed his mind on this). Although Luther continued to believe that Christ was really present in the consecrated bread and wine of the Lord's Supper, he denied that the Mass was a repetition of Christ's sacrifice on the cross and insisted that it was only through the faith of each individual believer that the sacrament could lead anyone to God. To further emphasize that those who presided in churches had no

> Denying that priests, monks, and nuns had any special spiritual qualities by virtue of their vocations, Luther argued instead for "the priesthood of all believers."

supernatural authority, he insisted on calling them ministers or pastors rather than priests. He also proposed to abolish the entire ecclesiastical hierarchy of popes, bishops, and archdeacons. Finally, firm in the belief that no spiritual distinction existed between clergy and laity, Luther argued that ministers could marry, and in 1525 he took a wife himself.

THE BREAK WITH ROME

Widely disseminated by means of the printing press, Luther's brilliant polemical pamphlets of 1520 electrified much of Germany, gaining him passionate popular support and touching off a national religious revolt against the papacy. In highly intemperate colloquial German, Luther declared that "if the pope's court were reduced ninety-nine percent it would still be large enough to give decisions on matters of faith"; that "the cardinals have sucked Italy dry and now turn to Germany"; and that, given Rome's corruption, "the reign of Antichrist could not be worse." As word of Luther's defiance spread, his pamphlets became a publishing sensation. Whereas the average press run of a printed book before 1520 had been 1,000 copies, the first run of *To the Christian Nobility* (1520) was 4,000 which sold out in a few days. Many more thousands of copies quickly followed. Even more popular were woodcut illustrations mocking the papacy and exalting Luther. These sold in the tens of thousands and could be readily understood even by the illiterate.

Luther's denunciations of the papacy reflected widespread public dissatisfaction with recent popes. Pope Alexander VI (1492–1503) had bribed the cardinals to gain the papacy, used the money raised from the jubilee of 1500 to support the military campaigns of his son Cesare, and was so morally corrupt that he was suspected of incest with his own daughter Lucrezia Borgia. Julius II (1503–1513) devoted his reign to enlarging the Papal States through war; a contemporary remarked of him that he would have gained the greatest glory if only he had been a secular prince. Leo X (1513–1521), Luther's opponent, was a member of the Medici family of Florence. Although not spectacularly corrupt or immoral, he was a self-indulgent aesthete who, in the words of a modern Catholic historian, "would not have been deemed fit to be a doorkeeper in the house of the Lord had he lived in the days of the apostles." Nor was criticism of the papacy limited to those who would ultimately become

Pope Alexander VI: "Appearance and Reality." Even before Luther initiated the German Reformation, anonymous critics of the dissolute Alexander VI surreptitiously spread propaganda showing him to be a devil. By lifting a flap one can see Alexander transformed into a monster who proclaims, "I am the pope."

Protestants. In *The Praise of Folly*, first published in 1511 and frequently reprinted, Erasmus declared that if the popes of his day were ever forced to lead Christ-like lives they would be inconsolable. In *Julius Excluded*, published anonymously in Basel in 1517, Erasmus went even further, imagining a conversation at the gates of heaven between Saint Peter and Pope Julius II in which Peter absolutely refused to admit Julius to heaven because he could not believe that the armored, vainglorious figure who stood before him could possibly be the pope.

In Germany, however, resentment of the papacy ran especially high. Because fifteenth-century Germany was so politically fractured, there were no agreements (known as concordats) between pope and emperor limiting papal authority in Germany, as there were with the rulers of Spain, France, and England. As a result, by 1500 the German princes were complaining that papal taxes were so high they were draining the country of its coin. But despite paying such large sums of money to Rome, Germans had almost no influence over papal policy. Frenchmen, Spaniards, and Italians dominated the college of cardinals and the papal bureaucracy, and the popes themselves were invariably Italian (as they would continue to be until 1978). As a result, graduates from the rapidly growing German universities almost never found employment in Rome.

Instead, many joined the throngs of Luther's supporters to become leaders of the new religious movement.

THE DIET OF WORMS

Luther's personal drama was now moving swiftly toward a crisis. Late in 1520, Luther responded to Pope Leo X's bull ordering him to recant by casting not only the bull but all of church law onto a roaring bonfire in front of a huge crowd. Since in the eyes of the church Luther was now a stubborn heretic, he was formally "released" for punishment to his lay overlord, the elector Frederick the Wise of Saxony. Frederick, however, was loath to silence the pope's antagonist. Rather than burning Luther at the stake for heresy, Frederick declared that Luther had not yet received a fair hearing. Early in 1521, he therefore brought him to the city of Worms to be examined by a formal assembly (a "diet") of the princes of the Holy Roman Empire.

At Worms the initiative lay with the presiding officer, the newly elected Holy Roman emperor, Charles V. Charles was not a German; indeed, it is doubtful if he had any national identity at all. As a member of the Habsburg family, he had been born and bred in his ancestral holding of the Netherlands. By 1521, however, through the unpredictable workings of dynastic inheritance, marriage, election, and luck, he had become not only the ruler of the Netherlands, but also king of Germany and Holy Roman emperor, duke of Austria, duke of Milan, and ruler of Franche-Comté. As the grandson of Ferdinand and Isabella on his mother's side, he was also king of Spain; king of Naples, Sicily, and Sardinia; and ruler of all the Spanish possessions in the New World.

Governing such an extraordinary combination of territories posed enormous challenges. Charles's empire

THE EMPIRE OF CHARLES V, c. 1550

Note the dispersed lands Charles V ruled directly through inheritance and marriage; as Holy Roman emperor, he was also the titular ruler of Germany. Which countries and rulers were most threatened by Charles's extraordinary combination of territories? Where might these threatened rulers and countries look for allies against Charles V? How did the threat posed by the Ottoman Empire complicate the political and religious struggles within Christian Europe?

The Emperor Charles V. This view by the Venetian painter Titian depicts the emperor as a sage ruler.

"kidnapping" whereby Luther was spirited off to the elector's castle of the Wartburg and kept out of harm's way for a year.

Thereafter Luther was never again to be in danger of his life. Although the Diet of Worms proclaimed him an outlaw, this edict was never enforced. Instead, Luther went into hiding, and Charles V left Germany to conduct a war with France. In 1522 Luther returned in triumph from the Wartburg to Wittenberg to find that the changes he had called for in ecclesiastical government and worship had already been put into practice by his university supporters. Then, in rapid succession, several German princes formally converted to Lutheranism, bringing their territories with them. By 1530, a considerable part of Germany had thus been brought over to the new faith.

THE GERMAN PRINCES AND THE LUTHERAN REFORMATION

At this point, then, the last of the three major questions regarding the early history of Lutheranism arises: Why did some German princes, secure in their own powers, nonetheless heed Luther's call by establishing Lutheran religious practices within their territories? This is a crucial question, because despite Luther's popular support, his cause surely would have failed had it not been embraced by a number of powerful German princes and free cities. In 1520, Luther was more or less equally popular throughout Germany, but it was only in those territories where rulers formally established Lutheranism (mostly in the German north) that the new religion prevailed. Elsewhere, Luther's sympathizers were forced to flee, face death, or conform to Catholicism.

The power of the princes to determine the religion of their territory reflected developments occuring throughout European society. Everywhere in Europe the major political trend in the years around 1500 was toward dominance by the state in all walks of life, religious as well as secular. Hence rulers sought to control appointments to church offices in their own realms, to restrict the flow of money to Rome, and to limit the independence of church courts. The most powerful rulers in western Europe—primarily the kings of France and Spain—took particular advantage of the continuing struggles between the papacy and the conciliarists (see Chapter Ten) to extract such concessions from the embattled popes. Thus in 1482 Sixtus IV conceded to the Spanish monarchs Ferdinand and Isabella the right to name candidates for all major church offices. In 1487

had no capital and no centralized administrative institutions; it shared no common language, no common culture, and no geographically contiguous borders. It thus stood completely apart from the growing nationalism of late medieval political life. Charles recognized the diversity of his empire and tried wherever possible to rule it through local officials and institutions. But he could not tolerate threats to the two fundamental forces that held his empire together: the emperor himself and Catholicism. Beyond such political calculations, however, Charles was also a faithful and committed Catholic, who was deeply disturbed by the prospect of heresy within his empire. There was therefore little doubt that the Diet of Worms would condemn Martin Luther for heresy. But when Luther refused to back down, even before the emperor himself, Frederick the Wise once more intervened, this time by arranging a

Innocent VIII consented to the establishment of a Spanish Inquisition controlled by the crown, giving the rulers extraordinary powers to dictate religious policies. And in 1516, by the Concordat of Bologna, Leo X granted the choice of bishops and abbots in France to the French king, Francis I, in return for Francis's support against the conciliarists who had gathered at the Fifth Lateran Council (1512–1517). In Germany, however, neither the emperor nor the princes were strong enough to gain such concessions. Hence what they could not achieve by concordats some princes decided to wrest by force.

In this determination they were fully abetted by Luther. As early as 1520 the fiery reformer had recognized that he could never hope to institute new religious practices without the strong arm of the princes behind him, so he implicitly encouraged them to confiscate the wealth of the Catholic Church as an incentive for creating a new order. At first the princes bided their time, but when they realized that Luther had enormous public support and that Charles V would not act swiftly to defend the Catholic faith, several

moved to introduce Lutheranism into their territories. Personal piety surely played a role in individual cases, but political and economic considerations were more generally decisive. By instituting Lutheranism within their territories, Protestant princes could consolidate their authority by naming pastors, cutting off fees to Rome, and curtailing the jurisdiction of church courts. They could also guarantee that the political and religious boundaries of their territories would now coincide. No longer, therefore, would a rival ecclesiastical prince (such as a bishop or archbishop) be able to use his spiritual position to undermine a neighboring secular prince's sovereignty over his territory.

Similar considerations also moved a number of free cities (so called because they were not ruled by territorial princes) to adopt Lutheranism. By adopting the new religion, town councils and guild masters could establish themselves (rather than local aristocrats or bishops) as the supreme governing authority within their towns. Given the added fact that under Lutheranism monasteries and convents could be shut down and their lands appropriated by the newly sovereign secular authorities,

The Seven-Headed Papal Beast. Around 1530 a Lutheran cartoon was circulated in Germany that turned the papacy into the seven-headed beast of the Book of Revelation. The papacy's seven heads consist of pope, cardinals, bishops, and priests; the sign on the cross reads "For money, a sack full of indulgences."

The Seven-Headed Martin Luther. In response, a German Catholic propagandist showed Luther as Revelation's beast. In this cartoon Luther's seven heads show him by turn to be a hypocrite, a fanatic, and Barabbas—the thief who should have been crucified instead of Jesus.

the practical advantages of the new faith were overwhelming, quite apart from any considerations of religious zeal.

Once safely ensconced in Wittenberg under princely protection, Luther began to express ever more vehemently his own profound conservatism in political and social matters. In a treatise of 1523, *On Temporal Authority*, he insisted that "godly" rulers must be obeyed in all things and that even ungodly ones should never be actively resisted since tyranny "is not to be resisted but endured." Then, in 1525, when peasants throughout Germany rebelled against their landlords—in some places encouraged by the religious radical Thomas Müntzer (c. 1490–1525), who urged the use of fire and sword against "ungodly" powers—Luther responded with intense hostility. In his vituperative pamphlet of 1525, *Against the Thievish, Murderous Hordes of Peasants*, he urged all who could to hunt the rebels down like mad dogs, to "strike, strangle, stab secretly or in public, and remember that nothing can be more poisonous than a man in rebellion." After the ruthless suppression of the Peasants' Revolt (which may have cost as many as 100,000 lives), the firm alliance of Lutheranism with state power helped preserve and sanction the existing social order. Never again would there be a mass lower-class uprising in Germany.

As for Luther himself, he concentrated in his last years on debating with younger, more radical religious reformers and on offering spiritual counsel to all who sought it. Never tiring in his amazingly prolific literary activity, he wrote an average of one treatise every two weeks for twenty-five years. To the end Luther was unswerving in his new faith: on his deathbed in 1546 he responded to the question "Will you stand firm in Christ and the doctrine which you have preached?" with a resolute yes.

THE SPREAD OF PROTESTANTISM

Why did Switzerland emerge as such an important center for sixteenth-century Protestantism?

Originating as a term applied to Lutherans who "protested" an action of the German Imperial Diet of 1529, the word *Protestant* was soon applied to a much wider range of European Christians in rebellion against Rome. Lutheranism itself struck lasting roots only in northern Germany and Scandinavia, where it became the state religion of Denmark, Norway, and Sweden during the 1520s. Early Lutheran successes in southern Germany, Poland, and Hungary were eventually rolled back. Elsewhere in Europe, however, competing forms of Protestantism soon emerged from the seeds that Luther had sown. By the 1550s, Protestantism had become a truly international movement; in so doing, however, it also split into a number of competing traditions.

THE REFORMATION IN SWITZERLAND

In the early sixteenth century Switzerland was neither ruled by kings nor dominated by all-powerful territorial princes; instead, prosperous Swiss cities were either independent or on the verge of becoming so. Hence when the leading citizens of a Swiss municipality decided to adopt Protestant reforms no one could stop them, and Protestantism in Switzerland could usually take its own course. Although religious arrangements varied from city to city, three main forms of Protestantism emerged in Switzerland between 1520 to 1550: Zwinglianism, Anabaptism, and Calvinism.

ULRICH ZWINGLI

Zwinglianism, founded by Ulrich Zwingli (*ZWIHNG-lee*, 1484–1531) in Zürich, was the most theologically moderate form of the three. Although Zwingli began his career as a somewhat indifferent Catholic priest,

CHRONOLOGY

ORIGINS OF THE REFORMATION, 1450–1529

Christian humanists call for reforms	1400s–1500s
Growth of German universities	1450–1517
Luther posts the Ninety-five Theses	1517
Luther charged with heresy	1519
Publication of Lutheran theological premises	1520
Diet of Worms declares Luther an outlaw	1521
Peasants' Revolt defeated	1525
Luther's break with Zwingli	1529

WHY DID SWITZERLAND EMERGE AS SUCH AN IMPORTANT CENTER FOR SIXTEENTH-CENTURY PROTESTANTISM?

THE SPREAD OF PROTESTANTISM   483

around 1516 his humanist-inspired study of the Bible convinced him that Catholic theology and practice conflicted with the Gospels. His biblical studies eventually led him also to condemn religious images and hierarchical authority within the church. But he did not speak out publicly until Luther set the precedent. In 1522, however, Zwingli began attacking the authority of the Catholic Church in Zürich. Soon all Zürich and much of northern Switzerland had accepted his religious leadership. Zwingli's reforms closely resembled those of the Lutherans in Germany. Zwingli differed from Luther, however, concerning the theology of the Eucharist: whereas Luther believed in the real presence of Christ's body in the sacrament, for Zwingli the Eucharist conferred no grace at all; it was simply a reminder and communal celebration of Christ's historical sacrifice on the cross. This fundamental disagreement prevented Lutherans and Zwinglians from uniting in a common Protestant front. Fighting independently, Zwingli fell in battle against Catholic forces in 1531. Soon thereafter, his movement was absorbed by the more systematic Protestantism of John Calvin.

ANABAPTISM

Before Calvinism prevailed, however, an even more radical form of Protestantism arose in Switzerland and

Germany. The first Anabaptists were members of Zwingli's circle in Zürich, but they broke with him around 1525 on the issue of infant baptism. Because Anabaptists were convinced that the sacrament of baptism was only effective if administered to willing adults who understood its significance, they rejected infant baptism altogether and required followers who had been baptized as infants to be baptized again as adults (the term *Anabaptism* means "rebaptism"). This doctrine reflected the Anabaptists' fundamental belief that the true church was a small community of believers gathered out of the world (in sociological terms, a sect), whose members had to make a deliberate, inspired decision to join it. No other Protestant groups were prepared to go so far in rejecting the medieval Christian view of the church as a single body to which all members of society belonged from birth. In an age when almost everyone assumed that church and state were inextricably connected, Anabaptism was bound to be anathema to the established powers, both Protestant and Catholic. Yet in its first few years the movement did gain numerous adherents in Switzerland and Germany, above all because it appealed to sincere religious piety in calling for extreme simplicity of worship, pacifism, and strict personal morality.

Disastrously, however, an unrepresentative group of Anabaptist extremists managed to gain control of the

The Anabaptists' Cages, Then and Now. After the three Anabaptist leaders who had reigned in Münster for a year were executed in 1535, their corpses were prominently displayed in cages hung from a tower of the marketplace church. As can be seen from the photo on the right, the bones are now gone but the iron cages remain as a grisly reminder of the horrors of sixteenth-century religious strife.

German city of Münster in 1534. These zealots combined sectarianism with millenarianism, or the belief that God wished to institute a completely new order of justice and spirituality throughout the world before the end of time. Determined to help God bring about this goal, the extremists attempted to turn Münster into a new Jerusalem. A former tailor named John of Leyden assumed the title of "King of the New Temple" and proclaimed himself the successor of the Hebrew king David. Under his leadership Anabaptist religious practices were made obligatory, private property was abolished, the sharing of goods was introduced, and even polygamy was permitted on the grounds of Old Testament precedents. Such practices were deeply shocking to both Protestants and Catholics alike. Münster was besieged and captured by Catholic forces little more than a year after the Anabaptist takeover; and the new David, together with two of his lieutenants, was put to death by excruciating tortures. Thereafter, Anabaptists throughout Europe were ruthlessly persecuted from all sides. Among the few who survived were some who banded together in the Mennonite sect, named for its founder, the Dutchman Menno Simons (c. 1496–1561). This sect, dedicated to pacifism and the simple "religion of the heart" of original Anabaptism, has continued to exist to the present day.

JOHN CALVIN'S REFORMED THEOLOGY

A year after events in Münster sealed the fate of Anabaptism, a twenty-six-year-old French Protestant named John Calvin (1509–1564), who had fled to the Swiss city of Basel to escape religious persecution, published the first version of his *Institutes of the Christian Religion*, the most influential systematic formulation of Protestant theology ever written. Born in Noyon in northern France, Calvin originally had been trained for the law and around 1533 was studying the Greek and Latin classics while living off the income from a church benefice. But then, as he later wrote, while he was "obstinately devoted to the superstitions of Popery," a stroke of light made him feel that God was extricating him from "an abyss of filth." He thereupon became a Protestant theologian and propagandist.

Although some of these details resemble the early career of Luther, the two men were very different figures. Luther was an emotionally volatile personality and a controversialist. He responded to theological problems as they arose or as the impulse struck him, but he never attempted to write systematic theology. Calvin, however, was a coolly analytical legalist, who resolved in

John Calvin. A recently discovered anonymous portrait.

his *Institutes* to set forth all the principles of Protestantism comprehensively, logically, and systematically. As a result, after several revisions and enlargements (the definitive edition appeared in 1559), Calvin's *Institutes* became the most theologically authoritative statement of Protestant beliefs and the nearest Protestant equivalent to Saint Thomas Aquinas's *Summa Theologica*.

Calvin's austere theology started with the omnipotence of God and worked downward. For Calvin the entire universe depends utterly on the will of the Almighty, who created all things for his greater glory. Because of the original fall from grace, all human beings are sinners by nature, bound hand and foot to an evil inheritance they cannot escape. Nevertheless, the Lord for reasons of his own has predestined some for eternal salvation and damned all the rest to the torments of hell. Nothing that human beings may do can alter their fate; their souls are stamped with God's blessing or curse before they are born. Nevertheless, Christians cannot be indifferent to their conduct on earth. If they are among the elect, God will implant in them the desire to live according to his laws. Upright conduct is thus a sign, though not an infallible one, that an individual has been chosen to sit at the throne of glory. Membership in the reformed church (as Calvinist churches are more properly known) is an-

WHY DID SWITZERLAND EMERGE AS SUCH AN IMPORTANT CENTER FOR SIXTEENTH-CENTURY PROTESTANTISM?

THE SPREAD OF PROTESTANTISM   485

other presumptive sign of election to salvation. But most of all, Calvin urged Christians to conceive of themselves as chosen instruments of God, charged to work actively to fulfill God's purposes on earth. Because sin offends God, Christians should do all they can to prevent it, not because their actions will lead to anyone's salvation (they will not), but simply because God's glory is diminished if sin is allowed to flourish unchecked by the efforts of those whom he has chosen for salvation.

Calvin always acknowledged a great theological debt to Luther, but his religious teachings differed from those of the Wittenberg reformer in several essentials. First of all, Luther's attitude toward proper Christian conduct in the world was much more passive than Calvin's. For Luther, a Christian should endure the trials of this life in suffering, whereas for Calvin the world was to be mastered in unceasing labor for God's sake. Calvin's religion was also more legalistic than Luther's. Luther, for example, insisted that his followers attend church on Sunday, but he did not demand that during the remainder of the day they refrain from all pleasure or work. Calvin, on the other hand, issued stern strictures against worldliness of any sort on the Sabbath day of rest and forbade all sorts of minor self-indulgences even on non-Sabbath days.

The two men also differed on fundamental matters of church government and worship. Although Luther broke with the Catholic system of hierarchical church governance, Lutheran district superintendents continued to exercise some of the powers of bishops, including supervision of the parish clergy. Luther also retained many features of traditional worship, including altars, music, ritual, and vestments (special clothing for the clergy). Calvin, however, rejected everything that smacked to him of popery. Thus he argued for the elimination of all traces of nonelective governance within the church. Instead, each congregation should elect its own ministers, and assemblies of ministers and "elders" (laymen responsible for maintaining proper religious conduct among the faithful) were to govern the reformed church as a whole. Calvin also insisted on the utmost simplicity in worship, prohibiting (among much else) vestments, processions, instrumental music, and religious images of any sort, including stained-glass windows. He also dispensed with all remaining vestiges of Catholic sacramental theology by making the sermon,

> Calvin also insisted on the utmost simplicity in worship, prohibiting (among much else) vestments, processions, instrumental music, and religious images of any sort, including stained-glass windows.

rather than the Eucharist, the centerpiece of reformed worship. When these teachings were put into practice, Calvinist services became little more than "four bare walls and a sermon."

CALVINISM IN GENEVA

Consistent with his theological convictions, Calvin was intent on putting his religious teachings into practice. Sensing an opportunity in the French-speaking Swiss city of Geneva, then in the throes of political and religious upheaval, he moved there late in 1536 and began preaching and organizing immediately. In 1538 his activities caused him to be expelled, but in 1541 he returned and the city soon came completely under his sway. Under Calvin's guidance Geneva's government became a theocracy. Supreme authority was vested in a "Consistory" composed of twelve lay elders and between ten and twenty pastors, whose weekly meetings Calvin dominated. Aside from passing legislation

Calvin as Seen by His Enemies. A Catholic caricature in which Calvin's face is a composite made from a fish, a toad, and a chicken.

RELIGIOUS SITUATION IN EUROPE, C. 1560

The religious boundaries of Europe around 1560, roughly thirty years after Martin Luther's movement began, were quite complicated. To what extent did the religious divisions of Europe follow its political boundaries? How would you account for the dispersed areas in which Calvinists predominated? Why did Lutheranism spread north into Scandinavia but not south into Bavaria or west across the Rhine?

proposed to it by a congregation of ministers, the Consistory's main function was to supervise morality, both public and private. To this end, Geneva was divided into districts, and a committee of the Consistory visited every household without warning to check on the behavior of its members. Dancing, card playing, attending the theater, and working or playing on the Sabbath—all were outlawed as works of the devil. Innkeepers were forbidden to allow anyone to consume food or drink without first saying grace or to permit any patron to stay up after nine o'clock. Murder, treason, adultery, witchcraft, blasphemy, and heresy were all capital crimes. Even penalties for lesser crimes were severe. During the first four years after Calvin gained con-

HOW DID NOTIONS OF FAMILY AND MARRIAGE CHANGE DURING THE REFORMATION?

THE DOMESTICATION OF THE REFORMATION, 1525–1560   487

trol in Geneva, there were no fewer than fifty-eight executions out of a total population of only 16,000.

As objectionable as such interference in the private sphere may seem today, in the mid-sixteenth century Calvin's Geneva was a beacon of light to thousands of Protestants throughout Europe. Calvin's disciple John Knox, who brought reformed religion to Scotland, declared Geneva under Calvin "the most perfect school of Christ that ever was on earth since the days of the Apostles." Converts such as Knox flocked to Geneva for refuge or instruction and then returned home to become ardent proselytizers for the new religion. Geneva thus became the center of an international movement dedicated to spreading reformed religion to France and the rest of Europe through organized missionary activity and propaganda.

These missionary efforts were remarkably successful. By the end of the sixteenth century, Calvinists were a majority in Scotland (where they were known as Presbyterians), Holland (where they founded the Dutch Reformed Church), and England (where the Church of England adopted reformed theology but not reformed worship; Calvinists who sought further reforms in worship were known as Puritans). There were also substantial Calvinist minorities in France (where they were called Huguenots), Germany, Hungary, Lithuania, and Poland. God's kingdom on earth had not yet been fully realized; on his deathbed in 1564, Calvin pronounced the Genevans to be still "a perverse and unhappy nation." But an extraordinary revolution had taken place nonetheless in the religious life and practice of Europe.

THE DOMESTICATION OF THE REFORMATION, 1525–1560

How did notions of family and marriage change during the Reformation?

Protestantism had begun as a revolutionary doctrine whose radical claims for the spiritual equality of all true Christian believers had the potential to undermine the social, religious, political, and even gender hierarchies on which European society rested. Luther himself seems not to have anticipated that his ideas might have

such implications, and he was genuinely shocked when the rebellious German peasants and the religious millenarianists at Münster interpreted his teachings in this way. But Luther was by no means solely responsible for the increasing conservatism of Protestant social ideology after 1525. Outside the ranks of the Anabaptists, none of the early Protestant leaders was a social or political radical. To spread their reform message, moreover, Protestant reformers depended on the support of existing social and political leaders: the princes, of course, but no less important, the ruling elites of the German and Swiss towns. As a result, the Reformation movement was speedily "domesticated" in two senses. Not only was the revolutionary potential of Protestantism curbed (Luther rarely spoke about the priesthood of all believers after 1525) but there was also an increasing emphasis within all branches of the burgeoning Protestant movement on the patriarchal family as the central institution of reformed life.

REFORM AND DISCIPLINE

As we saw in Chapter Eleven, efforts to constrain the common people of Europe to lead more strictly disciplined and godly lives had been a frequent feature of the fifteenth-century religious reform movements. Many of these reform efforts were actively embraced and promoted by princes and town councils, most famously perhaps in Florence, where, from 1494 to 1498, the Dominican preacher Girolamo Savonarola led the city on an extraordinary but short-lived campaign of puritanism and moral reform. But there were many other examples of rulers legislating against sin, both before and after Savonarola. When, in 1518, Desiderius Erasmus called on secular rulers to think of themselves as abbots and of their territories as giant monasteries, he was thus sounding for a new century an already-famliar theme.

Protestant rulers, however, took the need to enforce godly discipline on their people with particular seriousness, because the depravity of human nature was a fundamental tenet of their Protestant beliefs. Like Saint Augustine at the end of the fourth century, Protestants believed that people would inevitably turn out badly unless they were compelled to be good. It was, therefore, the responsibility of pastors and magistrates to discipline and control the behavior of their people—not because their good deeds would lead them to heaven but because their evil deeds would anger God and destroy human society.

Protestant godly discipline began with the education of children. Luther himself wrote two catechisms (statements of belief) to teach children the tenets of their faith and the obligations—toward parents, masters, and rulers—that God imposed on them. Luther also insisted that all children, boys and girls alike, should be taught to read the Bible in their own vernacular language. Schooling thus became a characteristically Protestant preoccupation. Even the Protestant family was conceived of as a "school of godliness," in which fathers were expected to instruct and discipline their wives, their children, and their household servants.

But family life in the early sixteenth century still left much to be desired in the eyes of Protestant reformers. Drunkenness, domestic violence, illicit sexual relations, lascivious dancing, and the blasphemous swearing of oaths were commonplace, even among the religiously reformed. Various methods were tried by Protestant congregations to discipline their unruly members, including private counseling, public confessions of wrongdoing, public penances and shamings, exclusion from church services, and even imprisonment. All these efforts met with varying, but generally modest, success. To create godly Protestant families, and to enforce godly discipline on entire communities, was going to require the active cooperation of godly authorities in both church and state.

PROTESTANTISM, GOVERNMENT, AND THE FAMILY

The domestication of the Reformation in this sense took place principally in the free towns of Germany and Switzerland. Here, Protestant attacks on monasticism and clerical celibacy found a receptive audience among townsmen who resented the immunity of monastic houses from taxation, and regarded clerical celibacy as a subterfuge for the seduction of their wives and daughters. Protestant emphasis on the depravity of the human will and the consequent need for that will to be disciplined by godly authority also resonated powerfully with guilds and town governments, which were anxious to maintain and increase the control exercised by town elites (mainly merchants and master craftsmen) over the apprentices and journeymen who made up the majority of the town's male population. By eliminating the competing jurisdictional authority of the Catholic Church, Protestantism also allowed town governments to consolidate all authority within the city into their own hands.

Protestantism reinforced the control of individual craftsmen over their own households by bringing a new emphasis on the family as a "school of godliness," in which an all-powerful father figure was expected to assume responsibility for instructing and disciplining his household according to the precepts of reformed religion. At the same time, Protestantism also introduced a new religious ideal for women. No longer was the celibate nun the exemplar of female holiness; in her place now stood the married and obedient Protestant "goodwife." As one Lutheran prince wrote in 1527: "Those who bear children please God better than all the monks and nuns singing and praying." To this extent, Protestantism resolved the tensions between piety and sexuality that had characterized late medieval Catholicism by declaring firmly in favor of the holiness of marital sexuality.

This did not reflect a newly elevated view of women's spiritual potential, however—quite the contrary. Luther, like his medieval predecessors, continued to regard women as more sexually driven than men and less capable of controlling their sexual desires (although, to be fair, Luther had only a slightly higher view of men's capacity for celibacy). His opposition to convents rested on his belief that, except in extraordinary circumstances, it was impossible for women to remain celibate, so convents simply made illicit sexual behavior inevitable. To control women and prevent sin, it was therefore necessary that all women should be married, preferably at a young age, and so placed under the governance of a godly husband.

For the most part, Protestant town governments were happy to cooperate in shutting down convents. The convent's property went to the town, and most of the nuns were from aristocratic families anyway. But conflicts did arise between Protestant reformers and town fathers over marriage and sexuality, especially over the reformers' insistence that both men and women should marry young as a check on sin. Many German towns were like Augsburg, where men were expected to delay marriage until they had achieved the status of a master craftsman—a requirement that had become increasingly difficult to enforce as guilds sought to restrict the number of journeymen permitted to become masters. In theory, however, apprentices and journeymen were not supposed to marry. Instead, they were expected to frequent the brothels and taverns, a legally recognized world of nonmarital sexuality that town fathers saw as necessary to protect their own wives and daughters from seduction or rape, but that Protestant reformers found morally abhorrent and demanded be abolished.

Towns responded in a variety of ways to these opposing pressures. Some instituted special committees

MARRIAGE AND CELIBACY: TWO VIEWS

These two selections illustrate the strongly contrasting views on the spiritual value of marriage versus celibacy that came to be embraced by Protestant and Catholic religious authorities. The first selection is part of Martin Luther's more general attack on monasticism but emphasizes his view that marriage is the natural and divinely intended state for all human beings. The second selection, from the decrees of the Council of Trent (1545–1563), restates traditional Catholic teaching on the holiness of marriage but also emphasizes the spiritual superiority of virginity to marriage and the necessity of clerical celibacy.

Listen! In all my days I have not heard the confession of a nun, but in the light of Scripture I shall hit upon how matters fare with her and know I shall not be lying. If a girl is not sustained by great and exceptional grace, she can live without a man as little as she can without eating, drinking, sleeping, and other natural necessities. Nor, on the other hand, can a man dispense with a wife. The reason for this is that procreating children is an urge planted as deeply in human nature as eating and drinking. That is why God has given and put into the body the organs, arteries, fluxes, and everything that serves it. Therefore what is he doing who would check this process and keep nature from running its desired and intended course? He is attempting to keep nature from being nature, fire from burning, water from wetting, and a man from eating, drinking, and sleeping.

E. M. Plass, ed., *What Luther Says, vol. 2* (St. Louis, 1959), pp. 888–889.

CANONS ON THE SACRAMENT OF MATRIMONY (1563)

Canon 1. If anyone says that matrimony is not truly and properly one of the seven sacraments . . . instituted by Christ the Lord, but has been devised by men in the Church and does not confer grace, let him be anathema [cursed].

Canon 9. If anyone says that clerics constituted in sacred orders or regulars who have made solemn profession of chastity can contract marriage . . . and that all who feel that they have not the gift of chastity, even though they have made such a vow, can contract marriage, let him be anathema, since God does not refuse that gift to those who ask for it rightly, neither does *he suffer us to be tempted above that which we are able.*

Canon 10: If anyone says that the married state excels the state of virginity or celibacy, and that it is better and happier to be united in matrimony than to remain in virginity or celibacy, let him be anathema.

H. J. Schroeder, *Canons and Decrees of the Council of Trent* (St. Louis and London, 1941), pp. 181–182.

QUESTIONS FOR ANALYSIS

1. Why did Luther believe that the monastic demands for celibacy were impossible to meet? How important an issue was celibacy in the context of sixteenth-century religious conflicts?

to police public morals, of the sort we have seen already in Calvin's Geneva. Some abandoned Protestantism altogether. Others, like Augsburg, flip-flopped back and forth between Protestantism and Catholicism for several decades before finally settling on one religion or the other. But regardless of a town's final choice of religious allegiance, by the end of the sixteenth century a revolution had taken place with respect to town governments' attitudes toward public morality. In their competition with each other, neither Catholics nor Protestants wished to be seen as soft on sin. The result, by 1600, was the abolition of publicly recognized brothels throughout Europe, the illegalization of prostitution, and far stricter governmental supervision of many other aspects of private life in both Catholic and Protestant urban communities.

PROTESTANTISM AND CONTROL OVER MARRIAGE

Protestantism also increased parents' control over their children's choice of marital partners. The medieval Catholic Church defined marriage as a sacrament that did not require the involvement of a priest. The mutual free consent of the two parties, even if given without witnesses or parental approval, was enough to constitute a legally valid marriage in the eyes of the church; at the same time, however, the church would annul a marriage if either of the parties could prove that they had not freely consented to it. Opposition to this doctrine came from many quarters, but especially from parents and other relatives. Because marriage involved rights of inheritance to property, most families regarded it as far too important a matter to be left to the free choice of their children. Instead, parents wanted the power to prevent unsuitable matches and, ideally, to force their children to accept the marriage arrangements their families might negotiate on their behalf. Protestantism offered an opportunity to achieve such control. Luther had declared marriage to be a purely secular matter, not a sacrament at all, that could be regulated however the governing authorities thought best. Calvin largely followed suit, although Calvinist theocracy drew less of a distinction than did Lutheranism between the powers of church and state. Even Catholicism was eventually forced to give way. Although it never entirely abandoned its insistence that both members of the couple must freely consent to their marriage, by the end of the sixteenth century the Catholic

Church required formal public notice of intent to marry and insisted on the presence of a priest at the actual wedding ceremony. Both were efforts to prevent elopements, allowing families time to intervene before an unsuitable marriage was concluded. Individual Catholic countries sometimes went even further in trying to reassert parental control over their children's choice of marital partners. In France, for example, although couples might still marry without parental consent, those who did so now forfeited all of their rights to inherit their families' property. In somewhat different ways, both Protestantism and Catholicism thus moved to strengthen the control that parents could exercise over their children—and, in the case of Protestantism, that husbands could exercise over their wives.

THE ENGLISH REFORMATION

Why did England become a Protestant country?

In England, the Reformation took a rather different course than it did in continental Europe. Although a tradition of popular Lollardy survived into the sixteenth century, the number of Lollards was too small and their influence too limited for Lollardy to have played a significant role in paving the way for the ultimate triumph of Protestantism in England. Nor was England particularly oppressed by the papal exactions and abuses that roiled Germany. English monarchs already exercised close control over church appoint-

---

CHRONOLOGY

SPREAD OF PROTESTANTISM, 1520–1560

Lutheranism becomes state religion in Denmark, Norway, and Sweden	1520s
England breaks with Rome	1534
Geneva adopts theocratic government based on Calvinism	1541
Calvinism spreads to Scotland, England, the Netherlands, and France	1540–1560s
Elizabethan settlement	1559

ments within their kingdom when the sixteenth century began; they also received the lion's share of the papal taxation collected from England. Nor did the church courts inspire any particular resentments. On the contrary, church courts would continue to function in Protestant England until the eighteenth century. Why, then, did sixteenth-century England become a Protestant country at all?

HENRY VIII AND THE BREAK WITH ROME

As is often the case in English history, an answer to this question must begin with the Crown. By 1527 the imperious King Henry VIII had been married for eighteen years to Ferdinand and Isabella's daughter Catherine of Aragon, yet all the offspring of this union had died in infancy, save only Princess Mary. Because Henry needed a male heir to preserve the succession of his Tudor Dynasty and because Catherine was now past childbearing age, Henry had good reasons of state to break his marriage bonds. He also had more personal motives, having become infatuated with a dark-eyed lady-in-waiting named Anne Boleyn. To marry Anne, Henry appealed to Rome to annul his marriage to Catherine, arguing that because Queen Catherine had previously been married to Henry's older brother Arthur (who had died shortly after the ceremony was performed), Henry's marriage to Catherine had been invalid from the beginning. As Henry's representatives pointed out, the Bible pronounced it "an unclean thing" for a man to take his brother's wife and cursed such a marriage with childlessness (Leviticus 20:31). Even a papal dispensation (which Henry and Catherine had obtained for their marriage) could not dispose of such a clear prohibition, as the marriage's childlessness proved.

Henry's suit put Pope Clement VII (1523–1534) in a quandary. Henry was firmly convinced that this scriptural curse had blighted his chances of perpetuating his dynasty; and both Henry and Clement knew that popes in the past had granted annulments to reigning monarchs on far weaker grounds than the ones Henry was alleging. If, however, the pope granted Henry's annulment he would cast doubt on the validity of all papal dispensations. More seriously, however, he would also provoke the wrath of the emperor Charles V, Catherine of Aragon's nephew, whose armies were in firm command of Rome and who at that moment held the pope

himself in captivity. Clement was trapped; all he could do was procrastinate and hope for better days. For two years, he allowed the suit to proceed in England without ever reaching a verdict. Then, suddenly, he transferred the case to Rome, where the legal process began all over again.

Exasperated by these delays, Henry began to increase the pressure on the pope. In 1531 he compelled an assembly of English clergy to declare him "protector and only supreme head" of the church in England. In 1532 he encouraged Parliament to produce an inflammatory list of grievances against the clergy, and used this threat to force the clergy to concede his right as king to approve or disapprove of all church legislation. In January 1533, Henry married Anne Boleyn (already pregnant) even though his marriage to Queen Catherine had still not been annulled. (The new archbishop of Canterbury, Thomas Cranmer, provided the required annulment in May.) In September, Princess Elizabeth was born; her father, disappointed again in his hopes for a son, refused to attend her christening. Nevertheless, Parliament settled the succession to the throne on the children of Henry and Anne, redirected all papal revenues from England into the king's hands,

Henry VIII, by Hans Holbein the Younger.

THE SIX ARTICLES

Although Henry VIII withdrew the Church of England from obedience to the papacy, he continued to lean more toward Catholic than Protestant theology. Some of his advisers, most notably Thomas Cromwell, were committed Protestants; and the king allowed his son and heir, Edward VI, to be raised as a Protestant. But after several years of rapid (and mostly Protestant) change in the English church, in 1539 the king reasserted a set of traditional Catholic doctrines in the Six Articles. These would remain binding on the Church of England until the king's death in 1547.

First, that in the most blessed sacrament of the altar, by the strength and efficacy of Christ's mighty word, it being spoken by the priest, is present really, under the form of bread and wine, the natural body and blood of our Savior Jesus Christ, conceived of the Virgin Mary, and that after the consecration there remains no substance of bread or wine, nor any other substance but the substance of Christ, God and man;

Secondly, that communion in both kinds is not necessary for salvation, by the law of God, to all persons, and that it is to be believed and not doubted . . . that in the flesh, under the form of bread, is the very blood, and with the blood, under the form of wine, is the very flesh, as well apart as though they were both together;

Thirdly, that priests, after the order of priesthood received as afore, may not marry by the law of God;

Fourthly, that vows of chastity or widowhood by man or woman made to God advisedly ought to be observed by the law of God. . . .

Fifthly, that it is right and necessary that private masses be continued and admitted in this the king's English Church and congregation . . . whereby good Christian people . . . do receive both godly and goodly consolations and benefits; and it is agreeable also to God's law;

Sixthly, that oral, private confession is expedient and necessary to be retained and continued, used and frequented in the church of God.

Statutes of the Realm, vol. 3 (London, 1810–1828), p. 739 (modernized).

QUESTIONS FOR ANALYSIS

1. If he leaned more toward Catholicism, then why did Henry VIII allow his son to be raised a Protestant? What does this tell us about the Reformation in England?

prohibited appeals to the papal court, and formally declared "the King's highness to be Supreme Head of the Church of England [having] the authority to redress all errors, heresies, and abuses." In 1536, Henry executed Sir Thomas More for his refusal to endorse this declaration of supremacy and took the first steps toward dissolving England's monasteries. By the end of 1539, the monasteries and convents were gone and their lands and wealth confiscated by the king, who distributed them to his supporters.

These measures broke the bonds that linked the English church to Rome, but they did not make England a Protestant country. Although certain traditional practices (such as pilgrimages and relics) were prohibited, the English church remained overwhelmingly Catholic in organization, doctrine, ritual, and language. The Six Articles promulgated by Parliament in 1539 at Henry VIII's behest left no room for doubt as to official orthodoxy: oral confession to priests, masses for the dead, and clerical celibacy were all confirmed; the Latin Mass continued; and Catholic eucharistic doctrine was not only confirmed but its denial made punishable by death. To most English people, only the disappearance of the monasteries and the king's own continuing matrimonial adventures (he married six wives in all) gave certain evidence that their church was no longer part of the Roman obedience.

Edward VI

For truly committed Protestants, and especially those who had visited Calvin's Geneva, the changes Henry VIII enforced on the English church did not go nearly far enough. In 1547, the accession of the nine-year-old king Edward VI (Henry's son with his third wife, Jane Seymour) gave them their opportunity to finish the task of reformation. Encouraged by the clear Protestant sympathies of the young king himself, Edward's government moved quickly to reform the creeds and ceremonies of the English church. Priests were permitted to marry; English services replaced Latin ones; the veneration of images was abolished, and the images themselves defaced or destroyed; prayers for the dead were abolished, and endowments for such prayers were confiscated; and new articles of belief were drawn up, repudiating all sacraments except baptism and communion and affirming the Protestant doctrine of justification by faith alone. Most important, a new prayer book was published to define precisely how the new, English-language services of the church were to be conducted. Much remained unsettled with respect to both doctrine and worship; but by 1553, when the youthful Edward died, the English church appeared to have become a distinctly Protestant institution.

Encouraged by the clear Protestant sympathies of the young king himself, Edward's government moved quickly to reform the creeds and ceremonies of the English church.

Mary Tudor and the Restoration of Catholicism

Edward's successor, however, was his pious and deeply Catholic sister Mary (1553–1558), Henry VIII's daughter with Catherine of Aragon. Mary speedily reversed her brother's religious policies, restoring the Latin Mass and requiring married priests to give up their wives. She even prevailed on Parliament to vote a return to papal allegiance. Hundreds of Protestants leaders fled abroad, many to Geneva; others, including Archbishop Thomas Cranmer, were burned at the stake for refusing to abjure their Protestantism. News of the martyrdoms spread like wildfire through Protestant Europe. In England, however, Mary's policies sparked relatively little outright resistance at the local level. After two decades of religious upheaval, most English men and women were probably hoping that Mary's reign would bring some stability to their religious lives.

This, however, Mary could not do. The executions she ordered were insufficient to wipe out religious resistance—instead, Protestant propaganda about "Bloody Mary" and the "fires of Smithfield" caused widespread disaffection, even among those who welcomed the return of traditional religious forms. Nor could she do anything to restore monasticism: too many leading families had profited from Henry VIII's dissolution of the monasteries for this to be reversed. Mary's marriage to her cousin Philip, Charles V's son and heir to the Spanish throne, was another miscalculation. Although the marriage treaty stipulated that in the event of Mary's death Philip could not succeed her, her English subjects never trusted him. When the queen allowed herself to be drawn by Philip into a war with France on Spain's behalf in which England lost Calais, its last foothold on the European continent, many English people became highly disaffected. Ultimately, however, what doomed Mary's religious counter-revolution was simply the accidents of biology. Mary was unable to conceive an heir, and when she died after only six years of rule, her throne passed to her Protestant sister, Elizabeth.

The Elizabethan Religious Settlement

The daughter of Henry VIII and Anne Boleyn, and one of the most capable and popular monarchs ever to sit on the English throne, Queen Elizabeth I (1558–1603) was predisposed in favor of Protestantism by the circumstances of her parents' marriage as well as by her upbringing. But Elizabeth was no zealot and wisely recognized that supporting radical Protestantism in England might provoke bitter sectarian strife. Accordingly, she presided over what is customarily known as

Queen Mary and Queen Elizabeth. These two daughters of Henry VIII had strikingly different fates as rulers: the pious Catholic Mary sparked religious division in England and died after only six years on the throne, whereas Elizabeth angled toward the Protestant cause but managed to mediate between the two faiths and become one of England's most popular monarchs.

"the Elizabethan settlement." By a new Act of Supremacy (1559), Elizabeth repealed Mary's Catholic legislation, prohibiting foreign religious powers (i.e., the pope) from exercising any authority within England and declaring herself "supreme governor" of the English church—a more Protestant title than Henry VIII's "supreme head" insofar as most Protestants believed that Christ alone was the head of the church. She also adopted many of the Protestant liturgical reforms instituted by her brother, Edward, including a revised version of the Edwardian prayer book. But she also retained vestiges of Catholic practice, including bishops, church courts, and vestments for the clergy. On most doctrinal matters, including predestination and free will, Elizabeth's Thirty-Nine Articles of Faith (approved in 1562) struck a decidedly Protestant, even Calvinist, tone. But the prayer book was more moderate, and on the critical issue of the Eucharist was deliberately ambiguous. By combining Catholic and Protestant interpretations ("this is my body. . . . Do this in remembrance of me") into a single declaration, the prayer book permitted an enor-

mous latitude for competing interpretations of the service by priests and parishioners alike.

Despite such "latitudinarianism," religious tensions persisted in Elizabethan England, not only between Protestants and Catholics but also between moderate and more extreme Protestants. The queen's artful fudging of these differences was by no means a recipe guaranteed to succeed. Rather, what preserved the Elizabethan religious settlement, and ultimately made England a Protestant country, was the extraordinary length of Queen Elizabeth's reign combined with the fact that for much of that time Protestant England was at war with Catholic Spain. Under Elizabeth, Protestantism and English nationalism gradually fused together into a potent conviction that God himself had chosen England for greatness. After 1588, when English naval forces won an improbable victory over the "invincible" Spanish Armada, Protestantism and Englishness became nearly indistinguishable to most of Queen Elizabeth's subjects. Laws against Catholic recusants became increasingly severe, and although an

How did the Catholic Reformation differ from the Counter-Reformation?

CATHOLICISM TRANSFORMED   495

English Catholic tradition did survive, its adherents were a persecuted minority. Much more alarming was the situation in Ireland, where the vast majority of the population remained Catholic despite the government's efforts to impose Protestantism on them. By 1603, Irishness was as firmly identified with Catholicism as was Englishness with Protestantism; but it was the Protestants who were in the ascendant in both countries.

CATHOLICISM TRANSFORMED

How did the Catholic Reformation differ from the Counter-Reformation?

The historical novelty of Protestantism inevitably casts the spotlight on such religious reformers as Luther and Calvin; but there was also a powerful internal reform movement within the Catholic Church during the sixteenth century. Historians differ about whether to call this movement the "Catholic Reformation" or the "Counter-Reformation." Some prefer the former term because it emphasizes that significant efforts to reform the Catholic Church began before Luther posted his theses and continued long after. Others, however, insist that from the mid-sixteenth century on, most Catholic reformers were inspired primarily by the urgent need to resist the Protestant schism. We will use both terms to refer to two complementary phases of Catholic reform: a Catholic Reformation that came before Luther, and a Counter-Reformation that came after him.

In northern Europe, Christian humanists such as Erasmus and Thomas More also played a role in this Catholic reform movement, not only by criticizing abuses and editing sacred texts, but also by encouraging the laity to lead lives of simple but sincere religious piety.

THE CATHOLIC REFORMATION

The Catholic Reformation began around 1490, and was primarily a movement for moral and institutional reform within the religious orders. Although these efforts received strong support from several secular rulers, the papacy showed little interest in them. As a result, the Catholic Reformation never became a truly international movement. In Spain, reform activities directed by Cardinal Francisco Ximenes de Cisneros (1436–1517) and supported by the monarchy led to the imposition of strict rules of behavior on Franciscan friars and the elimination of abuses prevalent among the diocesan clergy. Ximenes also helped regenerate the spiritual life of the Spanish church. In Italy, earnest clerics labored to make the Italian church more worthy of its calling. Reforming the existing monastic orders was a difficult task, not least because the papal court set such a poor example; but Italian reformers did manage to establish several new religious orders dedicated to high ideals of piety and social service. In northern Europe, Christian humanists such as Erasmus and Thomas More also played a role in this Catholic reform movement, not only by criticizing abuses and editing sacred texts but also by encouraging the laity to lead lives of simple but sincere religious piety.

As a response to the challenges posed by Protestantism, however, the Catholic Reformation proved entirely inadequate. Starting in the 1530s, therefore, a second, more aggressive phase of reform under a new style of vigorous papal leadership began to gather momentum. The leading Counter-Reformation popes—Paul III (1534–1549), Paul IV (1555–1559), Saint Pius V (1566–1572), and Sixtus V (1585–1590)— were collectively the most zealous reforming popes since the High Middle Ages. All led upright personal lives. Some, indeed, were so grimly ascetic that contemporaries wondered whether they were not too holy: as a Spanish councilor wrote of Pius V in 1567, "We should like it even better if the present Holy Father were no longer with us, however great, inexpressible, unparalleled, and extraordinary His Holiness may be." In confronting Protestantism, however, an excessively holy pope was vastly preferable to a self-indulgent one. But these Counter-Reformation popes were not merely holy men. They were also accomplished administrators who reorganized papal finances and filled ecclesiastical offices with bishops and abbots no less renowned for austerity and holiness than were the popes themselves.

These papal reform efforts intensified at the Council of Trent, a general council of the entire church convoked by Paul III in 1545 and which met at intervals thereafter until 1563. The decisions taken at Trent provided the foundations on which a new, Counter-Reformation Catholic Church would be erected. Although the council began by debating

The Council of Trent. This fresco depicts the general council of the entire Catholic Church that met from 1545 and 1563 and produced the foundation for the new Counter-Reformation church.

some form of compromise with Protestantism, Trent ended by reaffirming all of the Catholic doctrinal tenets challenged by Protestant critics. Good works were declared necessary for salvation, and all seven sacraments were declared indispensable means of grace, without which salvation was impossible. Transubstantiation, purgatory, the invocation of saints, and the rule of celibacy for the clergy were all confirmed as essential elements in the Catholic system. The Bible and the traditions of apostolic teaching were held to be of equal authority as sources of Christian truth. Papal supremacy over every bishop and priest was expressly maintained, and the supremacy of the pope over any church council was taken for granted. The Council of Trent even reaffirmed the doctrine of indulgences that had touched off the Lutheran revolt, although it did condemn the worst abuses connected with their sale.

The legislation of Trent was not confined to matters of doctrine. To improve pastoral care of the laity, bishops and priests were forbidden to hold more than one spiritual office. To address the problem of an ignorant priesthood, a theological seminary was to be estab-

lished in every diocese. The council also suppressed a variety of local religious practices and saints' cults, replacing them with new cults authorized and approved by Rome. To prevent heretical ideas from corrupting the faithful, the council also decided to censor or suppress dangerous books. In 1564, a specially appointed commission published the first Index of Prohibited Books, an official list of writings that ought not to be read by faithful Catholics. All of Erasmus's works were immediately placed on the index, even though he had been a chosen Catholic champion against Martin Luther only forty years before. A permanent agency known as the Congregation of the Index was later set up to revise the list, which was revised more than forty times until it was abolished in 1966. The majority of the books condemned have been theological treatises, and probably the effect in retarding the progress of learning has been slight. Nonetheless, the index is a chilling sign of the doctrinal intolerance that characterized sixteenth-century Christianity, both in its Catholic and Protestant varieties.

SAINT IGNATIUS LOYOLA AND THE SOCIETY OF JESUS

In addition to the independent activities of popes and the legislation of the Council of Trent, a third main force propelling the Counter-Reformation was the foundation of the Society of Jesus, commonly known as the Jesuit order, by Saint Ignatius Loyola (1491–1556). In the midst of a youthful career as a worldly soldier, the Spanish nobleman Loyola was wounded in battle in 1521 (the same year in which Luther defied Charles V at Worms). While recuperating, he decided to change his ways and become a spiritual soldier of Christ. For ten months he lived as a hermit in a cave near the Spanish town of Manresa, during which time he experienced ecstatic visions and worked out the principles of his subsequent meditational guide, the *Spiritual Exercises*. This manual, completed in 1535 and first published in 1541, offered practical advice on how to master one's will and serve God through a systematic program of meditations on sin and the life of Christ. Soon made a basic handbook for all Jesuits and widely studied by numerous Catholic laypeople as well, Loyola's *Spiritual Exercises* has had an influence second only to Calvin's *Institutes* among all the religious writings of the sixteenth century.

Nonetheless, Loyola's founding of the Jesuit order itself was certainly his greatest single accomplishment.

How did the Catholic Reformation differ from the Counter-Reformation?

Catholicism Transformed   497

Originating as a small group of six disciples who gathered around Loyola in Paris in 1534 to serve God in poverty, chastity, and missionary work, the Society of Jesus was formally constituted as an order of the church by Pope Paul III in 1540; by the time of Loyola's death it already numbered 1,500 members. The Society of Jesus was by far the most militant of the religious orders fostered by the Catholic reform movements of the sixteenth century. It was not merely a monastic society but a company of soldiers sworn to defend the faith. Their weapons were not to be bullets and spears but eloquence, persuasion, and instruction

The Inspiration of Saint Jerome, by Guido Reni.
In 1546 the Council of Trent declared Saint Jerome's Latin translation of the Bible, known as the Vulgate, to be the official version of the Catholic church; then, in 1592, Pope Clement VIII chose one edition of the Vulgate to be authoritative above all others. Since biblical scholars had known since the early sixteenth century that Saint Jerome's translation contained numerous mistakes, Counter-Reformation defenders of the Vulgate insisted that even his mistakes had been divinely inspired. The point is made visually in Guido Reni's painting of 1635.

in correct doctrines; but the society quickly became accomplished in more worldly methods of exerting influence also. Its organization was patterned after that of a military company, with a general as commander in chief and iron discipline enforced on all members. Individuality was suppressed, and a soldierlike obedience to the general was required from the rank and file. The Jesuit general, sometimes known as the "black pope" (from the color of the order's habit), was elected for life and was not bound to take advice offered by any other member. His sole superior was the pope, to whom all senior Jesuits took a special vow of strict obedience. As a result of this vow, all Jesuits were held to be at the pope's disposal at all times.

The activities of the Jesuits consisted primarily of proselytizing Christians and non-Christians and establishing schools. Originally founded to engage in missionary work abroad, the early Jesuits preached to non-Christians in India, China, and Spanish America. For example, one of Loyola's closest early associates, Saint Francis Xavier (1506–1552), baptized thousands of native people and covered thousands of miles missionizing in South and East Asia. Yet, although Loyola had not at first conceived of his society as comprising shock troops against Protestantism, that is what it primarily became as the Counter-Reformation mounted in intensity. Through preaching and diplomacy—sometimes at the risk of their lives—Jesuits in the second half of the sixteenth century fanned out across Europe in direct confrontation with Calvinists. In many places the Jesuits succeeded in keeping rulers and their subjects loyal to Catholicism, in others they met martyrdom, and in some others—notably Poland and parts of Germany and France—they succeeded in regaining territory previously lost to Protestantism. Wherever they were allowed to settle, the Jesuits set up schools and colleges, for they firmly believed that a vigorous Catholicism depended on widespread literacy and education. Their schools were so well regarded that, after the fires of religious hatred began to subside, upper-class Protestants sometimes sent their children to receive a Jesuit education.

Counter-Reformation Christianity

From the foregoing it should be evident that there is a Counter-Reformation heritage every bit as much as there is a Protestant one. The greatest achievement of these sixteenth-century Catholic reform movements was to

OBEDIENCE AS A JESUIT HALLMARK

The necessity of obedience in the spiritual formation of monks and nuns had been a central theme in Catholic religious thought since the Rule of Saint Benedict. By focusing its demands for obedience specifically on the papacy, however, the Society of Jesus brought a new militancy to this old ideal.

RULES FOR THINKING WITH THE CHURCH

1. Always to be ready to obey with mind and heart, setting aside all judgment of one's own, the true spouse of Jesus Christ, our holy mother, our infallible and orthodox mistress, the Catholic Church, whose authority is exercised over us by the hierarchy.

2. To commend the confession of sins to a priest as it is practised in the Church; the reception of the Holy Eucharist once a year, or better still every week, or at least every month, with the necessary preparation. . . .

4. To have a great esteem for the religious orders, and to give the preference to celibacy or virginity over the married state. . . .

6. To praise relics, the veneration and invocation of Saints: also the stations, and pious pilgrimages, indulgences, jubilees, the custom of lighting candles in the churches, and other such aids to piety and devotion. . . .

9. To uphold especially all the precepts of the Church, and not censure them in any manner; but, on the contrary, to defend them promptly, with reasons drawn from all sources, against those who criticize them.

10. To be eager to commend the decrees, mandates, traditions, rites and customs of the Fathers in the Faith or our superiors. . . .

13. That we may be altogether of the same mind and in conformity with the Church herself, if she shall have defined anything to be black which to our eyes appears to be white, we ought in like manner to pronounce it to be black. For we must undoubt-ingly believe, that the Spirit of our Lord Jesus Christ, and the Spirit of the Orthodox church His Spouse, by which Spirit we are governed and directed to salvation, is the same. . . .

FROM THE CONSTITUTIONS OF THE JESUIT ORDER

Let us with the utmost pains strain every nerve of our strength to exhibit this virtue of obedience, firstly to the Highest Pontiff, then to the Superiors of the Society; so that in all things . . . we may be most ready to obey his voice, just as if it issued from Christ our Lord . . . leaving any work, even a letter, that we have begun and have not yet finished; by directing to this goal all our strength and intention in the Lord, that holy obedience may be made perfect in us in every respect, in performance, in will, in intellect; by submitting to whatever may be enjoined on us with great readiness, with spiritual joy and perseverance; by persuading ourselves that all things [commanded] are just; by rejecting with a kind of blind obedience all opposing opinion or judgment of our own. . . .

Henry Bettenson, ed., *Documents of the Christian Church*, 2d ed. (Oxford, 1967), pp. 259–261.

QUESTIONS FOR ANALYSIS

1. Did total obedience to the church contradict the aspirations of Renaissance humanism?

2. What role did the Jesuits play in the Catholic Reformation? Did the establishment of the Jesuit order somehow serve as a general indictment of the church itself?

THE COUNTER-REFORMATION, 1534–1590

Counter-Reformation popes	1534–1590
Saint Ignatius Loyola founds the Jesuits	1534
Council of Trent convenes	1545–1563
Index of Prohibited Books	1564

Saint Theresa of Avila. She was one of a number of religious women who were honored by Counter-Reformation Catholicism.

defend and revitalize the faith. Had it not been for the determined efforts of these reformers, Catholicism would not have swept over the globe during the seventeenth and eighteenth centuries or reemerged in Europe as the vigorous spiritual force it remains today. But other results stemmed from the Counter-Reformation as well. One was the spread of literacy in Catholic countries due to the educational activities of the Jesuits. Another was the growth of intense concern for acts of charity. Because Counter-Reformation Catholicism continued to emphasize good works as well as faith, charitable activities took on an extremely important role in the revitalized religion. Counter-Reformation spiritual leaders such as Saint Francis de Sales (1567–1622) and Saint Vincent de Paul (1581–1660) urged almsgiving in their sermons and writings, and a wave of founding of orphanages and houses for the poor swept over Catholic Europe.

The Counter-Reformation also brought a new emphasis on the importance of religious women. Counter-Reformation Catholicism did not exalt marriage as a route to holiness for women to the same degree as did Protestantism, but it did foster a distinctive role for a female religious elite—countenancing the mysticism of Saint Teresa of Avila (1515–1582) and establishing new orders of nuns such as the Ursulines and the Sisters of Charity, which had no parallel under Protestantism. Both Protestants and Catholics continued to exclude women from the priesthood or ministry, but Catholic celibate women could pursue religious lives with at least some degree of independence.

The Counter-Reformation did not, however, perpetuate the tolerant Christianity of Erasmus. Instead, Christian humanists lost favor with Counter-Reformation popes, and even natural scientists such as Galileo were sometimes regarded with suspicion (see Chapter Sixteen). But sixteenth-century Protestantism was just as theologically intolerant as sixteenth-century Catholicism, and even more hostile to the cause of rationalism.

Indeed, because Counter-Reformation theologians returned for guidance to the scholasticism of Saint Thomas Aquinas, they tended to be much more committed to the dignity of human reason than were their Protestant counterparts, who emphasized pure scriptural authority and unquestioning faith. It is not entirely coincidental, therefore, that René Descartes, one of the pioneers of seventeenth-century rationalism (and who coined the famous phrase "I think, therefore I am"), was trained as a youth by the Jesuits.

CONCLUSION

Protestantism emerged after the height of the Italian Renaissance and before the scientific revolution and the Enlightenment. It may be tempting, therefore, to think of historical events advancing in an inevitably cumulative way, from the Renaissance to the Reformation to the Enlightenment to the "Triumph of the Modern World." But history is seldom as neat as that. Although scholars continue to disagree on points of detail, most agree that the Protestant Reformation drew relatively little from the civilization of the Renaissance. Indeed, in certain basic respects Protestant principles were completely at odds with the major assumptions of most Renaissance humanists.

Certainly the Renaissance contributed something to the origins of the Protestant Reformation. Criticisms of religious abuses by Christian humanists helped prepare Germany for the Lutheran revolt. Close textual study of the Bible led to the publication of new, more reliable biblical editions used by the Protestant reformers. In this regard a direct line ran from the Italian humanist Lorenzo Valla to Erasmus to Luther: Valla's *Notes on the New Testament* inspired Erasmus to produce his own Greek edition and Latin translation of the New Testament in 1516; Erasmus's New Testament in turn enabled Luther in 1518 to reach some crucial conclusions concerning the literal biblical meaning of penance and became the foundation for Luther's own 1522 translation of the Bible into German. For these and related reasons, Luther addressed Erasmus in 1519 as "our ornament and our hope."

But, in fact, Erasmus quickly showed that he had no sympathy whatsoever with Lutheran principles. Most other Christian humanists followed suit, shunning Protestantism as soon as it became clear to them what Luther and other Protestant reformers were actually teaching. The reasons for this split are clear enough. Most humanists believed in free will, whereas Protestants believed in predestination; humanists tended to think of human nature as basically good, whereas Protestants found it unspeakably corrupt; and most humanists favored urbanity and tolerance, whereas the followers of Luther and Calvin emphasized obedience and conformity.

The Protestant Reformation was not the natural outgrowth of the civilization of the Renaissance. It did, however, contribute to certain traits characteristic of modern European historical development. Foremost among these was the increasing power of Europe's sovereign states. As we have seen, those German princes who converted to Protestantism were moved to do so primarily by the search for sovereignty. The kings of Denmark, Sweden, and England followed suit for much the same reasons. Since Protestant leaders—Calvin as well as Luther—preached absolute obedience to godly rulers, and since the state in Protestant countries assumed direct control of the church, the spread of Protestantism definitely resulted in the growth of state power. But we must not make any simple equation between state power and Protestantism. The power of the state was growing already by 1500, especially in such countries as France and Spain, where Catholic kings already exercised most of the same rights over the church that were forcibly seized by

Lutheran German princes and Henry VIII in the course of their own reformations.

Nationalism too was already a part of this world, as we can see from the way Luther played on it in his appeals during the 1520s. But Luther also did much to foster German cultural nationalism, not least by translating the Bible into vigorous, colloquial German. Until the sixteenth century, Germans from different regions spoke such different dialects of German that they often could not understand each other. Luther's Bible, however, gained such currency that it eventually became the linguistic standard for the entire nation. Protestantism did not unite the German nation politically; instead, Germany soon divided into Protestant and Catholic camps. But elsewhere, as in Holland or parts of central Europe, where Protestants fought successfully against a foreign, Catholic overlord, Protestantism enhanced a sense of national identity. Perhaps the most familiar case of all is that of England, where a sense of nationhood existed long before the advent of Protestantism, but where the new faith lent to that nationalism a new confidence that England was indeed a nation peculiarly favored by God.

Finally, we come to the subject of Protestantism's effects on relationships between the sexes. No consensus among historians exists on this subject. What does seem clear, however, is that Protestant men as individuals could be just as ambivalent about women as their medieval Catholic predecessors had been. John Knox, for example, inveighed against the Catholic regent of Scotland, Mary Stuart, in a treatise called *The First Blast of the Trumpet against the Monstrous Regiment of Women*, yet maintained deeply respectful relationships with women of his own faith. When Queen Mary Tudor required formerly Protestant English priests to give up their wives, many did so with disheartening alacrity. But if one asks how Protestantism as a belief system affected women's social roles, the answer appears to be that it enabled women to become just a shade more equal to men within a framework of continuing subjection. Because Protestantism called on women as well as men to undertake serious study of the Bible, it encouraged primary schooling for both sexes. But Protestant male leaders still insisted that women were naturally inferior to men and should defer to men both within the family and in the larger society. As Calvin himself said, "[L]et the woman be satisfied with her state of subjection and not take it ill that she is made inferior to the more distinguished sex." Both Luther and Calvin appear to have been happily married, but that clearly meant being happily married on their own terms.

KEY TERMS

Martin Luther	Diet of Worms	John Calvin	Elizabeth I
Lutheranism	Ulrich Zwingli	Henry VIII	Council of Trent
Erasmus	Anabaptists	Mary Tudor	Society of Jesus

SELECTED READINGS

Bainton, Roland. *Erasmus of Christendom.* New York, 1969. Still the best biography in English of the Dutch reformer and intellectual.

Bainton, Roland. *Here I Stand: A Life of Martin Luther.* Nashville, Tenn., 1950. Although old and obviously biased in Luther's favor, this remains an absorbing and dramatic introduction to Luther's life and thought.

Benedict, Philip. *Christ's Churches Purely Reformed: A Social History of Calvinism.* New Haven, Conn., 2002. A wide-ranging recent survey of Calvinism in both western and eastern Europe.

Bossy, John. *Christianity in the West, 1400–1700.* Oxford and New York, 1985. A brilliant, challenging picture of the changes that took place in Christian piety and practice as a result of the sixteenth-century reformations.

Bouwsma, William J. *John Calvin: A Sixteenth-Century Portrait.* Oxford and New York, 1988. The best biography of the magisterial reformer.

Collinson, Patrick. *The Religion of Protestants: The Church in English Society, 1559–1625.* Oxford, 1982. A great book by the best contemporary historian of early English Protestantism.

Dillenberger, John. *John Calvin: Selections from His Writings,* Garden City, N.Y., 1971. A judicious selection, drawn mainly from Calvin's *Institutes.*

Dillenberger, John, ed. *Martin Luther: Selections from His Writings.* Garden City, N.Y., 1961. The standard selection, especially good on Luther's theological ideas.

Dixon, C. Scott, ed. *The German Reformation: The Essential Readings.* Oxford, 1999. A collection of important recent articles.

Duffy, Eamon. *The Stripping of the Altars: Traditional Religion in England, c. 1400–c. 1550.* The best study of the hesitant way in which England eventually became a Protestant country.

Hillerbrand, Hans J., ed. *The Protestant Reformation.* New York, 1967. Source selections are particularly good for illuminating the political consequences of Reformation theological ideas.

Loyola, Ignatius. *Personal Writings.* Trans. by Joseph A. Munitiz and Philip Endean. London and New York, 1996. An excellent collection that includes Loyola's autobiography, his spiritual diary, and some of his letters, as well as his *Spiritual Exercises.*

Luebke, David, ed. *The Counter-Reformation: The Essential Readings.* Oxford, 1999. A collection of nine important recent essays.

MacCulloch, Diarmaid. *Reformation: Europe's House Divided, 1490–1700.* London and New York, 2003. A definitive new survey; the best single-volume history of its subject in a generation.

McGrath, Alister E. *Reformation Thought: An Introduction.* Oxford, 1993. A useful explanation, accessible to non-Christians, of the theological ideas of the major Protestant reformers.

Mullett, Michael A. *The Catholic Reformation.* London, 2000. A sympathetic survey of Catholicism from the mid-sixteenth to the eighteenth century that presents the mid-sixteenth-century Council of Trent not as a response to Protestantism but as a continuation of reform efforts dating from the fifteenth century.

Oberman, Heiko A. *Luther: Man between God and the Devil.* Trans. by Eileen Walliser-Schwarzbart. New Haven, Conn., 1989. The best recent biography of Luther, stressing his preoccupations with sin, death, and the devil.

O'Malley, John W. *The First Jesuits.* Cambridge, Mass., 1993. A scholarly account of the origins and early years of the Society of Jesus.

O'Malley, John W. *Trent and All That: Renaming Catholicism in the Early Modern Era.* Cambridge, Mass., 2000. Short, lively, up to date, and with a full bibliography.

Pettegree, Andrew, ed. *The Reformation World.* New York, 2000. An exhaustive multiauthor work representing the most recent thinking about the Reformation.

Pelikan, Jaroslav. *Reformation of Church and Dogma, 1300–1700.* Volume 4: *A History of Christian Dogma.* Chicago, 1984. A masterful synthesis of Reformation theology in its late medieval context.

Roper, Lyndal. *The Holy Household: Women and Morals in Reformation Augsburg.* Oxford, 1989. A pathbreaking study of how Protestantism was adopted and adapted by the town councilors of Augsburg, with special attention to its impact on attitudes toward women, the family, and marriage.

Shagan, Ethan H. *Popular Politics and the English Reformation.* Cambridge, 2002. Argues that the English Reformation reflects an ongoing process of negotiation, resistance, and response between government and people.

Tracy, James D. *Europe's Reformations, 1450–1650.* 2d ed. Lanham, Md., 2006. An outstanding survey, especially strong on Dutch and Swiss developments, but excellent throughout.

Williams, George H. *The Radical Reformation.* 3d ed. Kirksville, Mo., 1992. Originally published in 1962, this is still the best book on Anabaptism and its offshoots.

CHAPTER FOURTEEN

RELIGIOUS WARS AND STATE BUILDING, 1540–1660

S TRANGE AS IT MAY SEEM in retrospect, Martin Luther never intended to fracture the religious unity of Europe. He sincerely believed that once the Bible was available to everyone in an accurate, vernacular translation, then everyone who read the Bible would interpret it in exactly the same way as did he himself. The result, of course, was quite different, as Luther quickly discovered in his bitter disputes with Zwingli and Calvin. Nor did Catholicism crumble in the face of reformed teachings as Luther had believed that it would. Instead, Europe's religious divisions multiplied, speedily crystallizing along political lines. By Luther's death in 1546, a clear pattern had already emerged. With only rare exceptions, Protestantism triumphed in those areas where political authorities supported the reformers. Where rulers remained Catholic, so too did their territories.

This was not the result Martin Luther had intended, but it did faithfully reflect the most basic presumptions of sixteenth-century European life. Anabaptists apart, neither Protestant nor Catholic reformers set out to challenge the standard medieval beliefs about the mutual interdependence of religion and politics—quite the contrary. Sixteenth-century Europeans continued to believe that the proper role of the state was to enforce true religion on its subjects, and sixteenth-century rulers remained convinced that religious pluralism would bring disunion and disloyalty to any state that embraced it. Ultimately, both Catholics and Protestants believed that western Europe had to return to a single religious faith enforced by properly constituted political authorities. What they could not agree on was which faith and which authorities.

The result was a brutal series of religious wars between 1540 and 1660 whose reverberations would continue to be felt until the eighteenth century. Vastly expensive and enormously destructive, these wars affected everyone in Europe, from peasants to princes. They did not arise solely from conflicts over religion. Regionalism, dynasticism, and nationalism were also potent contributors to the chaos into which Europe now plunged. Together, however, these forces of division and disorder brought into question the very survival of the European political order that had emerged since the thirteenth century. Faced with the prospect of political collapse,

FOCUS QUESTIONS

• Why was the period 1540–1660 one of the most turbulent in European history?

• Why did religious conflicts become so deeply entwined with political conflicts during this period?

• What caused the decline of Spain in the seventeenth century?

• Why was this period such a fertile one for political philosophy?

• What was the relationship between the Baroque school and the Counter-Reformation?

Europeans by 1660 were forced to embrace, gradually and grudgingly, a notion that in 1540 had seemed impossible to conceive: that religious toleration, however limited in scope, might be the only way to preserve the political, social, and economic order of the European world.

ECONOMIC, RELIGIOUS, AND POLITICAL TESTS

Why was the period 1540–1660 one of the most turbulent in European history?

The troubles that engulfed Europe during the traumatic century between 1540 and 1660 caught contemporaries unaware. From the mid-fifteenth century on, most of Europe had enjoyed steady economic growth, and the discovery of the New World seemed the basis of greater prosperity to come. Political trends too seemed auspicious, because most western European governments were becoming ever more efficient and providing more internal peace for their subjects. By the middle of the sixteenth century, however, thunderclouds were gathering that would soon burst into terrible storms.

THE PRICE REVOLUTION

Although the causes of these storms were interrelated, we can examine each separately, starting with the great price inflation. Nothing like the upward price trend that affected western Europe in the second half of the sixteenth century had ever happened before. In Flanders the cost of wheat tripled between 1550 and 1600, grain prices in Paris quadrupled, and the overall cost of living in England more than doubled. The twentieth century would see much more dizzying inflations than this, but since the skyrocketing of prices in the later sixteenth century was a novelty, most historians agree on calling it a "price revolution."

Two developments in particular underlay the soaring prices. The first was demographic. Starting in the later fifteenth century, Europe's population began to grow again after the plague-induced falloff: roughly estimated, Europe had about 50 million people around 1450 and 90 million around 1600. Because Europe's food supply remained more or less constant, owing to the lack of any noteworthy breakthroughs in agricultural technology, food prices were driven sharply higher by greater demand. At the same time, wages stagnated or even declined. As a result, workers around 1600 were paying a higher percentage of their wages to buy food than ever before, even though their basic nutritional levels were declining.

Population trends explain much, but since Europe's population did not increase nearly so rapidly in the second half of the sixteenth century as did prices, other explanations for the great inflation are necessary. Foremost among these is the enormous influx of bullion from Spanish America. From 1556 to 1560 roughly 10 million ducats worth of silver passed through the Spanish entry port of Seville. Between 1576 and 1580 that figure doubled, and between 1591 and 1595 it more than quadrupled. Most of this silver was used by the Spanish crown to pay its foreign creditors and its armies abroad; as a result, this bullion quickly circulated throughout Europe, where much of it was minted into coins. This dramatic increase in the volume of money in circulation fueled the spiral of rising prices. "I learned a proverb here," said a French traveler in Spain in 1603, "everything costs much here except silver."

Aggressive entrepreneurs and large-scale farmers profited most from the changed economic circumstances, while the masses of laboring people were hurt the worst. Landlords benefited from the rising prices of agricultural produce and merchants from the increasing demand for luxury goods. But laborers were caught in a squeeze because wages rose far more slowly than prices, owing to the presence of a more than adequate labor supply. Moreover, because the cost of food staples rose at a sharper rate than the cost of most other items of consumption, poor people had to spend an ever greater percentage of their paltry incomes on necessities. When disasters such as wars or poor harvests drove grain prices out of reach, some of the poor literally starved to death. The picture that emerges is one of the rich getting richer and the poor getting poorer—splendid feasts enjoyed amid the most appalling suffering.

The price revolution also placed new pressures on the sovereign states of Europe. Since the inflation depressed the real value of money, fixed incomes from taxes and tolls yielded less and less. Thus merely to keep their incomes constant governments would have been forced to raise taxes. But to compound this problem, most states needed much more real income than previously because they were undertaking more wars;

WHY WAS THE PERIOD 1540–1660 ONE OF THE MOST TURBULENT IN EUROPEAN HISTORY?

ECONOMIC, RELIGIOUS, AND POLITICAL TESTS   505

and warfare, as always, was becoming increasingly expensive. The only recourse, then, was to raise taxes precipitously, but such draconian measures aroused great resentment. Hence governments faced continuous threats of defiance and potential armed resistance.

After 1600 prices rose less rapidly, as population growth slowed and the flood of silver from America began to abate. On the whole, however, the period from 1600 to 1660 was one of economic stagnation rather than growth, even though a few areas—notably Holland— bucked the trend. The rich were usually able to hold their own, but the poor as a group made no advances, because the relationship of prices to wages remained fixed to their disadvantage. Indeed, if anything, the lot of the poor in many places deteriorated because the mid-seventeenth century saw some particularly expensive and destructive wars in which helpless civilians were plundered by rapacious

> On the whole, the period from 1600 to 1660 was one of economic stagnation rather than growth, even though a few areas—notably Holland—bucked the trend.

Peasants Harvesting Wheat, Sixteenth Century. The inflation that swept through Europe in the late 1500s most affected the poor workers, as the abundant labor supply dampened wages while the cost of food rose with poor harvests.

tax collectors or looting soldiers, or sometimes both. The Black Death also returned, wreaking havoc in London and elsewhere during the 1660s.

RELIGIOUS CONFLICTS

It goes without saying that most people would have been far better off had there been fewer wars during this difficult century, but given prevalent attitudes, newly arisen religious rivalries made wars inevitable. Simply stated, until religious passions began to cool toward the end of the period, most Catholics and Protestants viewed each other as minions of Satan who could not be allowed to live. Worse, sovereign states attempted to enforce religious uniformity on the grounds that "crown and altar" offered each other mutual support and in the belief that governments would totter where diversity of faith prevailed. Rulers on both sides felt certain that religious minorities, if allowed to survive in their realms, would inevitably engage in sedition; nor were they far wrong, since militant Calvinists and Jesuits were indeed dedicated to subverting constituted powers in areas where their parties had not yet triumphed. Thus states tried to extirpate all potential religious resistance but, in the process, sometimes provoked civil wars in which each side tended to assume there could be no victory until the other was exterminated. And of course civil wars might become international in scope if foreign powers chose to aid their embattled religious allies elsewhere.

POLITICAL INSTABILITY

Compounding the foregoing problems were the inherent weaknesses of the major European kingdoms. Most of the major states of early modern Europe had grown during the later Middle Ages by absorbing smaller, traditionally autonomous territories, sometimes by conquest, but more often through marriage alliances or inheritance arrangements between their respective ruling families (a policy known as "dynasticism"). At first some degree of provincial autonomy was usually preserved in these newly absorbed territories. But between 1540 and 1660, when governments were making ever greater financial claims on all their subjects or trying to enforce religious uniformity, rulers often rode roughshod over the rights of these traditionally autonomous provinces. The result, once again, was civil war, in which regionalism, economic grievances, and religious animosities were compounded into a volatile and destructive mixture. Nor was that all, since most governments seeking money and/or religious uniformity tried to rule with a firmer hand than before and thus sometimes provoked armed resistance from subjects seeking to preserve their traditional constitutional liberties. Given this bewildering variety of motives for revolt, it is not surprising that the long century between 1540 and 1660 was one of the most turbulent in all of European history.

A CENTURY OF RELIGIOUS WARS

Why did religious conflicts become so deeply entwined with political conflicts during this period?

The greatest single cause of warfare during this period was religious conflict. The wars themselves divide into four phases: a series of German wars from the 1540s to 1555; the French wars of religion from 1562 until 1598; the Dutch wars with Spain between 1566 and 1609; and the Thirty Years' War in Germany between 1618 and 1648.

THE GERMAN WARS OF RELIGION TO 1555

Wars between Catholics and Protestants in Germany began in the 1540s when the Holy Roman emperor Charles V, a devout Catholic, tried to reestablish Catholic unity in Germany by launching a military campaign against several German princes who had instituted Lutheran worship in their territories. Despite several notable victories, Charles's efforts to defeat the Protestant princes failed. Partly this was because he was simultaneously involved in wars against France and so could not devote his entire attention to German affairs. Primarily, however, Charles failed because the Catholic princes of Germany feared that if Charles succeeded in defeating the Protestant princes, he might then suppress their own independence also. As a result, the Catholic princes' support for the foreign-born Charles was only lukewarm; at times, they even joined with the Protestant princes in battle against the

The Emperor Charles V at Muehlberg by Titian. Charles V's attempts to re-create a united Catholic Germany by military means failed. In 1555, he was forced to accept the Peace of Augsburg, which recognized the existence of Protestant and Catholic territories.

emperor. Accordingly, religious warfare sputtered on and off until a compromise settlement was reached in the Peace of Augsburg (1555). This rested on the principle of *cuius regio, eius religio* ("as the ruler, so the religion"), which meant that in those principalities where Lutheran princes ruled, Lutheranism would be the sole state religion; where Catholic princes ruled, their territories would be Catholic also. Although the Peace of Augsburg was a historical milestone inasmuch as Catholic rulers for the first time acknowledged the legality of Protestantism, it boded ill for the future in assuming that no sovereign state larger than a free city (for which it made exceptions) could tolerate religious diversity. Moreover, in excluding Calvinism entirely, it ensured that the German Calvinists would become aggressive opponents of the status quo.

THE FRENCH WARS OF RELIGION

From the 1560s on, Europe's religious wars became far more brutal, partly because the combatants had be-

WHY DID RELIGIOUS AND POLITICAL CONFLICTS BECOME ENTWINED DURING THIS PERIOD?

A CENTURY OF RELIGIOUS WARS 507

come more intransigent (Calvinists and Jesuits customarily took the lead on their respective sides) and partly because the later religious wars were aggravated by regional, political, and dynastic hostilities. Because Geneva bordered on France and because Calvin himself was a Frenchman who longed to convert his mother country, the next act in the tragedy of Europe's confessional warfare was played out on French soil. Calvinist missionaries made considerable headway in France between 1541 (when Calvin took power in Geneva) and the outbreak of religious warfare in 1562. By 1562, Calvinists made up between 10 and 20 percent of France's population, with their numbers swelling daily. Greatly assisting the Calvinist (Huguenot; *HYOO-guh-noh*) cause in France was the conversion of many aristocratic Frenchwomen to Calvinism. Such women often won over their husbands, who in turn maintained large private armies. The foremost example is that of Jeanne d'Albret, queen of the tiny Pyrenean kingdom of Navarre, who brought over to Calvinism her husband, the prominent French aristocrat Antoine de Bourbon, and her brother-in-law, the prince de Condé. Condé took command of the French Huguenot party when civil war broke out in 1562 and was later succeeded in this capacity by Jeanne's son, Henry of Navarre, who came to rule all of France at the end of the century as King Henry IV. But Calvinism in France was also nourished by long-standing regional hosilities within the French kingdom, especially in southern France, where the animosities aroused by the thirteenth-century Albigensian crusade continued to fester.

Until 1562, an uneasy peace continued between the Catholic and the Calvinist forces in France. In 1562, however, the French king died unexpectedly, leaving a young child as his heir. A struggle immediately broke out between the Huguenot Condé and the ultra-Catholic duke of Guise for control of the regency government. And since both Catholics and Protestants assumed that France could have only a single *roi*, *foi*, and *loi* ("king," "faith," and "law"), this political struggle immediately took on a religious aspect. Soon all France was aflame. Rampaging mobs, often incited by members of the clergy, ransacked churches and settled local scores. Although the Huguenots were not strong or numerous enough to gain victory, they were too strong to be defeated, especially in their southern French territorial stronghold. Hence, despite intermittent truces, warfare dragged on at great cost of life until 1572, when a truce was arranged by which the Protestant leader, Henry of Navarre, was to marry the Catholic sister of the reigning French king. At this point, however, the cultivated queen mother, Catherine de' Medici, normally a woman who favored compromise, panicked. Instead of honoring the truce, she plotted with members of the Catholic Guise faction to kill all the Huguenot leaders while they were assembled in Paris for her daugher's wedding to Henry of Navarre. In the early morning of St. Bartholomew's Day (August 24) most of the Huguenot chiefs were murdered in bed, and 2,000 to 3,000 other Protestants were slaughtered in the streets or drowned in the Seine by Catholic mobs. When word of the Parisian massacre spread to the provinces, some 10,000 more Huguenots were killed in a frenzy of blood lust that swept through France. Henry of Navarre escaped, along with his new bride; but after 1572, the conflict entered a new and even more bitter phase.

Only when the politically astute Henry of Navarre succeeded to the French throne as Henry IV (1589–1610), initiating the Bourbon Dynasty that would rule until 1792, did the civil war finally come to an end.

Henry IV. The rule of Henry of Navarre initiated the Bourbon Dynasty in France and ended the bitter civil war.

In 1593 Henry abjured his Protestantism to placate France's Catholic majority, declaring as he did so that "Paris is worth a mass." In 1598, however, he offered limited religious freedom to the Huguenots by the Edict of Nantes. Although the edict recognized Catholicism as the official religion of the kingdom, guaranteeing Catholics the right to practice their religion everywhere in France, Huguenot nobles were now allowed to hold Protestant services privately in their castles; other Huguenots were allowed to worship at specified places (excluding Paris and all cities where bishops and archbishops resided); and the Huguenot party was permitted to fortify some towns, especially in the south and west, for their own military defense. Huguenots were also guaranteed the right to serve in all public offices and to enter the universities and hospitals without hindrance.

Although the Edict of Nantes did not countenance absolute freedom of worship, it nevertheless took a major stride in the direction of toleration. But despite its efforts to create one kingdom with two faiths, the effect of the edict was to divide the French kingdom into separate religious enclaves. In southern and western France, Huguenots came to have their own law courts, staffed by their own judges. They also received substantial powers of self-government, because it was presumed on all sides that the members of one religious group could not be ruled equitably by the adherents of a competing religion. Because of its regional character, Nantes also represented a concession to the long-standing traditions of provincial autonomy within the kingdom of France. In some ways, indeed, the Huguenot areas became a state within a state, thus raising again the perpetual fear in Paris that the kingdom of which it was the capital might once again fly apart into its constituent parts, as had happened during the Hundred Years' War. On its own terms, however, the Edict of Nantes was a success. With religious peace established, France quickly began to recover from decades of devastation, even though Henry IV himself was cut down by the dagger of a Catholic fanatic in 1610.

THE REVOLT OF THE NETHERLANDS

Bitter warfare also broke out between Catholics and Protestants in the Netherlands, where national resentments exacerbated the predictable religious hatreds. For almost a century the Netherlands (or Low Countries), comprising modern-day Holland in the north and Belgium in the south, had been ruled by the Habsburg family of Holy Roman emperors. The southern

Netherlands in particular had prospered greatly from trade and manufacture: southern Netherlanders had the greatest per capita wealth of all Europe, and their metropolis of Antwerp was northern Europe's leading commercial and financial center. Moreover, the half-century-long rule of the Habsburg emperor Charles V (1506–1556) had been popular because Charles, who had been born in the Belgian city of Ghent, felt a sense of rapport with his subjects and allowed them a large degree of local self-government.

But around 1560 the good fortune of the Netherlands began to ebb. When Charles V retired to a monastery in 1556 (dying two years later) he ceded all his vast territories outside of the Holy Roman Empire and Hungary—not only the Netherlands, but Spain, Spanish America, and half of Italy—to his son Philip II

MAP OF THE NETHERLANDS

Why were the southern provinces of the Netherlands more wealthy than the northern ones? How did William the Silent use the geography of the northern Netherlands to his advantage when fighting the Spanish? Why did the north become Calvinist while the south remained Catholic?

WHY DID RELIGIOUS AND POLITICAL CONFLICTS BECOME ENTWINED DURING THIS PERIOD?

A CENTURY OF RELIGIOUS WARS 509

Protestants Ransacking a Catholic Church in the Netherlands. The Protestant fury of 1566 was responsible for the large-scale destruction of religious art and statuary in the Low Countries, provoking the stern repression of Phillip II.

(1556–1598). Unlike Charles, Philip had been born in Spain and, thinking of himself as a Spaniard, made Spain his residence and the focus of his policy. He viewed the Netherlands primarily as a source of income necessary for pursuing Spanish affairs. The better to exploit the region's wealth, Philip tried to tighten his own control over the government of the Netherlands. This aroused the resentment of the local magnates who had dominated the government under Charles V. A religious storm was also brewing. After 1559, when a long war between France and Spain ended, French Calvinists began to stream over the border into the southern Netherlands, making converts wherever they went. Soon there were more Calvinists in Antwerp than in Geneva. To Philip, an ardent supporter of Counter-Reformation Catholicism, this was intolerable. As he declared to the pope on the eve of conflict, "rather than suffer the slightest harm to the true religion and service of God, I would lose all my states and even my life a hundred times over because I am not and will not be the ruler of heretics."

Worried by the growing tensions, a group of local Catholic noblemen led by William of Orange (known as "William the Silent" because he was so successful at hiding his religious and political leanings; in fact he was quite talkative!) appealed to Philip to allow toleration for Calvinists. But before Philip could respond, radical Protestant mobs suddenly began ransacking

Catholic churches throughout the country, desecrating hosts, smashing statuary, and shattering stained-glass windows. Local troops soon brought the situation under control, but Philip II nonetheless decided to dispatch an army of 10,000 Spanish troops, led by the duke of Alva, to wipe out Protestantism in the Netherlands. Alva's rule quickly became a reign of terror. Operating under martial law, his "Council of Blood" examined some 12,000 people on charges of heresy or sedition, of whom 9,000 were convicted and 2,000 to 3,000 executed. William the Silent fled the country, and all hope for a free Netherlands seemed lost.

But the tide turned quickly for two related reasons. First, instead of giving up, William the Silent converted to Protestantism; sought help from Protestants in France, Germany, and England; and organized bands of sea rovers to harass Spanish shipping on the Netherlandish coast. And second, Alva's tyranny helped William's cause, especially when the hated Spanish governor attempted to levy a 10 percent sales tax. With internal disaffection growing, in 1572 William, for tactical military reasons, was able to seize the northern Netherlands even though the north until then had been predominantly Catholic. Thereafter geography played a major role in determining the outcome of the conflict. Spanish armies repeatedly attempted to win back the north, but they were stopped by a combination of impassable rivers and dikes that could be opened to flood out the invaders. Although William the Silent was assassinated by a Catholic in 1584, his son continued to lead the resistance until the Spanish crown finally agreed to a truce in 1609 that implicitly recognized the independence of the northern

CHRONOLOGY

RELIGIOUS WARS, 1540s–1648

German wars	1540s–1555
French wars of religion	1562–1598
Dutch wars with Spain	1566–1609
Thirty Years' War	1618–1648

Dutch Republic. Meanwhile, the pressures of war and persecution had made the whole north Calvinist, whereas the south—which remained under Spanish control—returned to uniform Catholicism.

ENGLAND AND THE DEFEAT OF THE SPANISH ARMADA

Religious strife could spark civil war, as in France, or political rebellions, as in the Netherlands. But it could also provoke warfare between sovereign states, as in the late-sixteenth-century struggle between England and Spain. After persecution by the Catholic queen Mary and her Spanish husband Philip II, English Protestants rejoiced in the rule of Queen Elizabeth I (1558–1603) and naturally harbored great antipathy toward Philip II and the Counter-Reformation. Furthermore, English economic interests were directly opposed to those of the Spanish. A seafaring and trading people, the English in the later sixteenth century were steadily making inroads into Spanish naval and commercial domination and were also determined to resist any Spanish attempt to block England's lucrative trade with the Low Countries. But the greatest source of antagonism lay in the Atlantic, where English privateers, with the tacit consent of Queen Elizabeth, began attacking Spanish treasure ships. Taking as an excuse the Spanish oppression of Protestants in the Netherlands, English admirals or pirates (the terms were really interchangeable) such as Sir Francis Drake and Sir John Hawkins plundered Spanish vessels on the high seas. In a particularly dramatic sailing exploit lasting from 1577 to 1580, prevailing winds and lust for treasure propelled Drake all the way around the world, to return with stolen Spanish treasure worth twice as much as Queen Elizabeth's annual revenue.

All this would have been sufficient provocation for Philip II to retaliate against England, but because he had his hands full in the Netherlands he resolved to invade the island only after the English openly allied with the Dutch rebels in 1585. Even then, Philip moved slowly and made careful plans. Finally, in 1588 he dispatched an enormous fleet, confidently called the "Invincible Armada," to invade insolent Britannia. After an initial standoff in the English Channel, however, the smaller, longer-gunned English warships outmaneuvered the Spanish fleet, while English fireships set some Spanish galleons ablaze and forced the rest to break formation. "Protestant gales" did the rest. After a disastrous circum-

navigation of the British Isles and Ireland, the shattered Spanish flotilla limped home with almost half its ships lost.

The defeat of the Spanish Armada was one of the decisive battles of Western history. Had Spain conquered England, the Spanish might have gone on to crush Holland and perhaps even to destroy Protestantism elsewhere in Europe. But as it was, the Protestant day was saved; and not long afterward Spanish power began to decline, as English and Dutch ships seized command of the seas. In England, patriotic Protestant fervor became especially intense. Popular even before then, "Good Queen Bess" was virtually revered by her subjects until her death in 1603, and England embarked on its golden Elizabethan Age of literary endeavor. War with Spain dragged on inconclusively until 1604, but the fighting never brought England any serious harm and was just lively enough to keep the English people deeply committed to their queen, their country, and the Protestant religion.

> The defeat of the Spanish Armada was one of the decisive battles of Western history.

THE THIRTY YEARS' WAR

With the promulgation of the Edict of Nantes in 1598, the peace between England and Spain of 1604, and the truce between Spain and Holland of 1609, religious warfare in northwestern Europe came briefly to an end. But in 1618 a major new war broke out, this time in Germany. Because this struggle raged more or less unceasingly until 1648 it is known as the Thirty Years' War. Spain and France quickly became engaged in the conflict in Germany and eventually in war with one another. Meanwhile, domestic resentments in Spain, France, and England flared up during the 1640s into concurrent outbreaks of civil war. As an English preacher said in 1643, "these are days of shaking, and this shaking is universal."

The Thirty Years' War began in a welter of religious passions as a war between Catholics and Protestants but ended as an international struggle in which the initial religious dimension was almost entirely forgotten. Between the Peace of Augsburg in 1555 and the outbreak of war in 1618, Calvinists had replaced Lutherans in a few German territories, but the overall balance between Protestants and Catholics within the Holy Roman Empire had remained undisturbed. In 1618, however, war broke out after Ferdinand, the Catholic Habsburg prince of Poland, Austria, and Hungary, was elected king of the Protestant territory of Bohemia. The staunchly Protestant Bohemian nobility had

THE DESTRUCTIVENESS OF THE THIRTY YEARS' WAR

Hans Jakob Christoph von Grimmelshausen (1621–1676) lived through the horrors of the Thirty Years' War. His parents were killed, probably when he was thirteen years of age, and he himself was kidnapped the following year. By age fifteen, he was a soldier. His comic masterpiece, Simplicissimus, *from which this extract is taken, drew heavily on these wartime experiences. Although technically fiction, it portrays with brutal accuracy the cruelty and destructiveness of this war, especially for its peasant victims.*

Although it was not my intention to take the peace-loving reader with these troopers to my dad's house and farm, seeing that matters will go ill therein, yet the course of my history demands that I should leave to kind posterity an account of what manner of cruelties were now and again practised in this our German war: yes, and moreover testify by my own example that such evils must often have been sent to us by the goodness of Almighty God for our profit. For, gentle reader, who would ever have taught me that there was a God in Heaven if these soldiers had not destroyed my dad's house, and by such a deed driven me out among folk who gave me all fitting instruction thereupon? . . .

The first thing these troopers did was, that they stabled their horses: thereafter each fell to his appointed task: which task was neither more nor less than ruin and destruction. For though some began to slaughter and to boil and to roast so that it looked as if there should be a merry banquet forward, yet others there were who did but storm through the house above and below stairs. Others stowed together great parcels of cloth and apparel and all manner of household stuff, as if they would set up a frippery market. All that they had no mind to take with them they cut in pieces. Some thrust their swords through the hay and straw as if they had not enough sheep and swine to slaughter: and some shook the feathers out of the beds and in their stead stuffed in bacon and other dried meat and provisions as if such were better and softer to sleep upon. Others broke the stove and the windows as if they had a never-ending summer to promise. Houseware of copper and tin they beat flat, and packed such vessels, all bent and spoiled, in with the rest. Bed-steads, tables, chairs, and benches they burned, though there lay many cords of dry wood in the yard. Pots and pipkins must all go to pieces, either because they would eat none but roast flesh, or because their purpose was to make there but a single meal.

Our maid was so handled in the stable that she could not come out; which is a shame to tell of. Our man they laid bound upon the ground, thrust a gag into his mouth, and poured a pailful of filthy water into his body: and by this, which they called a Swedish draught, they forced him to lead a party of them to another place where they captured men and beasts, and brought them back to our farm, in which company were my dad, my mother, and our Ursula.

And now they began: first to take the flints out of their pistols and in place of them to jam the peasants' thumbs in and so to torture the poor rogues as if they had been about the burning of witches: for one of them they had taken they thrust into the baking oven and there lit a fire under him, although he had as yet confessed no crime: as for another, they put a cord round his head and so twisted it tight with a piece of wood that the blood gushed from his mouth and nose and ears. In a word each had his own device to torture the peasants, and each peasant his several tortures.

Hans Jakob Christoph von Grimmelshausen, *Simplicissimus*, Trans. S. Goodrich (New York, 1995), pp. 1–3, 8–10, 32–35.

QUESTIONS FOR ANALYSIS

1. Defend the statement that the Thirty Years' War was the first modern war and the Peace of Westphalia was the first modern peace.

The church
Spain
Austria
Brandenburg–Prussia
Boundary of the Holy Roman Empire

RUSSIA

SWEDEN

Stockholm

NORWAY

Christiana

DENMARK

Copenhagen

TEUTONIC ORDER

POLAND

Kiev

Warsaw

Vistula R.

Danzig

EAST PRUSSIA

BALTIC SEA

HUNGARY

Budapest

BLACK SEA

OTTOMAN EMPIRE

Constantinople

AEGEAN SEA

CYPRUS (to Ottoman Empire)

CRETE (to Spain)

MEDITERRANEAN SEA

Danube R.

MECKLEN-BURG

BRANDENBURG

Berlin

SAXONY

HOLY ROMAN EMPIRE

AUSTRIA

Vienna

Elbe R.

HANOVER

Hamburg

HESSE

WÜRTTEM-BERG

BAVARIA

VENICE

(to Venice)

Ragussa

Zara

Cattaro

ADRIATIC SEA

ITALY

PAPAL STATES

Rome

KINGDOM OF THE TWO SICILIES

Naples

NETHERLANDS

Amsterdam

Rhine R.

SPANISH NETH.

LORRAINE

FRANCHE COMTÉ

SWITZ.

MILAN

SAVOY

GENOA

FLORENCE

AVIGNON

PIEDMONT

CORSICA (to Genoa)

SARDINIA (to Spain)

SCOTLAND

Edinburgh

NORTH SEA

Liverpool

ENGLAND

London

IRELAND

Dublin

English Channel

FRANCE

Paris

Seine R.

Loire R.

Bordeaux

Garonne R.

Marseilles

Rhone R.

BALEARIC ISLANDS

ATLANTIC OCEAN

PORTUGAL

Lisbon

ARAGON

CASTILE

Madrid

Tagus R.

SPAIN

Strait of Gibraltar

AFRICA

EUROPE — Area of detail

500 Miles

500 Kilometers

250

250

0

0

EUROPE AT THE END OF THE THIRTY YEARS' WAR

What was at issue in the Thirty Years' War? Why did Catholic France ally with Lutheran Sweden against German and Austrian Catholics? Why did this war, which began as a religious conflict within the Holy Roman Empire, turn into an international struggle? Which European powers stayed out of the war? Why did they do so?

WHAT CAUSED THE DECLINE OF SPAIN IN THE SEVENTEENTH CENTURY?

DIVERGENT PATHS: SPAIN, FRANCE, AND ENGLAND, 1600–1660   513

opposed Ferdinand's election, and when Ferdinand began to suppress Protestantism in Bohemia, they rebelled. German Catholic forces ruthlessly counterattacked, first in Bohemia and then in Germany proper, led by Ferdinand, who in 1619 also became Holy Roman emperor. Within a decade, a German Catholic league seemed close to extirpating Protestantism throughout Germany.

Ferdinand's success raised once again the prospect that an overly powerful Holy Roman emperor might threaten the political autonomy of the German princes, Catholic and Protestant alike. Thus when the Lutheran king of Sweden, Gustavus Adolphus, the "Lion of the North," marched into Germany in 1630 to champion the Protestant cause, he was welcomed by several German Catholic princes who preferred to see the former religious balance restored rather than risk surrendering their sovereignty to Ferdinand II. To make matters still more ironic, Gustavus's Protestant army was secretly subsidized by Catholic France, whose policy was then dictated by a cardinal of the church, Cardinal Richelieu. This was because Habsburg Spain had been fighting in Germany on the side of Habsburg Austria, and Richelieu was determined to prevent France from being surrounded by a strong Habsburg alliance on the north, east, and south. In any event, the military genius Gustavus Adolphus started routing the Habsburgs; but when he fell in battle in 1632, Cardinal Richelieu had little choice but to send ever greater support to the remaining Swedish troops in Germany, until in 1635 French armies entered the war directly on Sweden's side. From then until 1648 the struggle was really one of France and Sweden against Austria and Spain, with Germany a helpless battleground.

Germany suffered more from warfare in the terrible years between 1618 and 1648 than it ever did before or after until the twentieth century. Several German cities were besieged and sacked nine or ten times over, and soldiers from all nations, who often had to sustain themselves by plunder, gave no quarter to defenseless civilians. With plague and disease adding to the toll of outright butchery, some parts of Germany lost more than half their populations, although others went relatively unscathed. Most horrifying was the loss of life in the final four years of the war, when the carnage continued unabated even while peace negotiators had already arrived at broad areas of agreement and were dickering over subsidiary clauses.

Nor did the Peace of Westphalia, which finally ended the Thirty Years' War in 1648, do much to vindicate anyone's death, even though it did establish some abiding landmarks in European history. Above all, from the international perspective, the Peace of Westphalia marked the emergence of France as the predominant power on the continental European scene, replacing Spain. France would hold this position for the next two centuries. The greatest losers in the conflict (aside, of course, from the German people themselves) were the Austrian Habsburgs, who were forced to surrender all the territory they had gained in Germany and to abandon their hopes of using the office of Holy Roman emperor to dominate central Europe. Otherwise, something very close to the German status quo of 1618 was reestablished, with Protestant principalities in the north balancing Catholic ones in the south and Germany so hopelessly divided that it could play no united role in European history until the nineteenth century.

> Above all, from the international perspective, the Peace of Westphalia marked the emergence of France as the predominant power on the continental European scene, replacing Spain.

DIVERGENT PATHS: SPAIN, FRANCE, AND ENGLAND, 1600–1660

What caused the decline of Spain in the seventeenth century?

The long century of war between 1540 and 1660 decisively altered the balance of power among the major kingdoms of western Europe. Germany emerged from the Thirty Years' War a devastated and exhausted land. But after 1600, Spain too was crippled by its unremitting military commitments and exertions. The French monarchy, by contrast, steadily increased its authority over France. By 1660 France had become the most powerful country on the European mainland, decisively eclipsing Spain. In England, meanwhile, a bloody civil war broke out between the king and his critics in Parliament; but after a short-lived experiment in republican rule, England in 1660 returned to its constitutional status as a "mixed" monarchy in which power was shared between king and Parliament.

THE DECLINE OF SPAIN

The story of seventeeth-century Spain's fall from grandeur is almost like a Greek tragedy in its relentless unfolding. Despite the defeat of the Invincible Armada in 1588, in 1600 the Spanish Empire—comprising all of the Iberian Peninsula (including Portugal, which had been annexed by Phillip II in 1580), half of Italy, half of the Netherlands, all of Central and South America, and the Philippine Islands in the Pacific Ocean—was still the mightiest power not just in Europe but in the world. Yet a bare half century later this empire on which the sun never set was beginning to fall apart.

Spain's greatest underlying weakness was economic. At first this may seem odd considering that in 1600, as in the three or four previous decades, huge amounts of American silver were being unloaded on the docks of Seville. Yet as contemporaries themselves recognized, "the new world that Spain had conquered was conquering Spain in turn." Lacking either rich agricultural or mineral resources, Spain desperately needed to develop industries and a balanced trading pattern as its

Atlantic rivals were doing. But the Spanish nobility had prized ideals of chivalry over practical business ever since the days when they were reconquering Christian territory from the Muslims. Thus the Spanish governing class was only too glad to use American silver to buy manufactured goods from other parts of Europe to live in splendor and dedicate itself to military exploits. As a result, few new industries were established; and when the influx of silver began to decline, the Spanish economy was left with nothing except increasing debts.

Nonetheless, the crown, dedicated to supporting the Counter-Reformation and maintaining Spain's international dominance, could not cease fighting abroad. Even in the relatively peaceful year of 1608, about 4 million ducats, out of a total revenue of 7 million, were spent on military expenditures. Thus when Spain became engaged in fighting France during the Thirty Years' War it overextended itself. In 1643 French troops inflicted a stunning defeat on the famed Spanish infantry at Rocroi, the first time that a Spanish army had been overcome in battle since the reign of

The Battle of Rocroi, 1643. Spain's defeat at Rocroi by the French was the first time the Spanish army had lost in battle since the reign of Ferdinand and Isabella, yet another contributing factor to the decline of Spanish power during the Thirty Years' War.

WHAT CAUSED THE DECLINE OF SPAIN IN THE SEVENTEENTH CENTURY?

DIVERGENT PATHS: SPAIN, FRANCE, AND ENGLAND, 1600–1660   515

Ferdinand and Isabella. Worse still was the fact that by then two territories belonging to Spain's European empire were in open revolt.

To understand the causes of these revolts, we must recognize that in the seventeenth century the governing power of Spain lay entirely in Castile. After the marriage of Isabella of Castile and Ferdinand of Aragon in 1469, Castile had emerged as the dominant partner in the Spanish union, becoming even more dominant when it took over Portugal in 1580. In the absence of any great financial hardships, semi-autonomous Catalunya (the most fiercely independent part of Aragon) endured Castilian hegemony. But in 1640, when the strains of warfare induced Castile to limit Catalan liberties to raise more money and men for combat, Catalunya revolted and drove out its Castilian governors. When the Portuguese learned of the Catalan uprising, they revolted as well, followed by southern Italians who rose up against Castilian viceroys in Naples and Sicily in 1647. Only the momentary inability of Spain's greatest external enemies, France and England, to take advantage of its plight saved the Spanish Empire from utter collapse. This gave the Castilian government time to put down the Italian revolts; by 1652 it had also brought Catalunya to heel. But Portugal retained its independence; and by the Peace of the Pyrenees, signed with France in 1659, Spain in effect abandoned its ambition of dominating Europe.

> Having established religious peace in 1598 by the Edict of Nantes, the affable Henry, who declared that there should be a chicken in every French family's pot each Sunday, set out to restore the prosperity of a country devastated by four decades of civil war.

THE GROWING POWER OF FRANCE

A comparison of the fortunes of Spain and France in the first half of the seventeenth century shows some striking similarities between the two countries, but in the end their differences turned out to be most decisive. Spain and France were of almost identical territorial extent, and both countries had been created by the same process of accretion. Just as the Castilian crown had gained Aragon, Catalunya, Granada, and then Portugal, so the kingdom of France had grown by adding such diverse territories as Languedoc, Dauphiné, Provence, Burgundy, and Brittany. Since the inhabitants of all these territories cherished traditions of local independence as much as the Catalans or Portuguese and since the rulers of France, like those of Spain, were determined to govern their provinces ever more firmly—

especially when costs of the Thirty Years' War made ruthless tax collecting urgently necessary—a direct confrontation between the central government and the provinces in France became inevitable, just as in Spain. But France weathered the storm whereas Spain did not, a result largely attributable to France's greater wealth and the greater prestige of the French crown.

In good times most French people, including those from the outlying provinces, tended to revere their king. Certainly they had excellent reason to do so during the reign of Henry IV. Having established religious peace in 1598 by the Edict of Nantes, the affable Henry, who declared that there should be a chicken in every French family's pot each Sunday, set out to restore the prosperity of a country devastated by four decades of civil war. Fortunately, France had enormous economic resiliency, owing primarily to its extremely rich and varied agricultural resources. Unlike Spain, which had to import food, France normally was able to feed itself; and Henry's finance minister, the duke of Sully, quickly saw to it that France could feed itself once more. Among other things, Sully distributed throughout the country free copies of a guide to recommended farming techniques and financed the rebuilding or new construction of roads, bridges, and canals to facilitate the flow of goods. Henry IV also ordered the construction of royal factories to manufacture luxury goods such as crystal, glass, and tapestries and supported the growth of silk, linen, and woolen cloth industries in many different parts of the country. Henry's patronage also allowed the explorer Samuel de Champlain to claim parts of Canada as France's first foothold in the New World. Thus Henry IV's reign certainly must be counted as one of the most benevolent in all French history.

CARDINAL RICHELIEU

Far less benevolent was Henry's de facto successor as ruler of France, Cardinal Richelieu (*RIH-shub-loo*, 1585–1642). The cardinal, of course, was never the real king of France—the actual title was held from 1610 to 1643 by Henry IV's ineffectual son Louis XIII. But as first minister from 1624 to his death in 1642 Richelieu governed as he wished, enhancing centralized royal power at home and expanding French influence in Europe.

CARDINAL RICHELIEU ON THE COMMON PEOPLE OF FRANCE

Armand Jean du Plessis, duke of Richelieu and cardinal of the Roman Catholic church, was the effective ruler of France from 1624 until his death in 1642. His Political Testament *was assembled after his death from historical sketches and memoranda of advice he prepared for King Louis XIII, the ineffectual monarch whom he served. Although the book itself was not published until 1688, there is now little doubt that the writings it contains are indeed Richelieu's own thoughts.*

All students of politics agree that when the common people are too well off it is impossible to keep them peaceable. The explanation for this is that they are less well informed than the members of the other orders in the state, who are much more cultivated and enlightened, and so if not preoccupied with the search for the necessities of existence, find it difficult to remain within the limits imposed by both common sense and the law.

It would not be sound to relieve them of all taxation and similar charges, since in such a case they would lose the mark of their subjection and consequently the awareness of their station. Thus being free from paying tribute, they would consider themselves exempted from obedience. One should compare them with mules, which being accustomed to work, suffer more when long idle than when kept busy. But just as this work should be reasonable, with the burdens placed upon these animals proportionate to their strength, so it is likewise with the burdens placed upon the people. If they are not moderate, even when put to good public use, they are certainly unjust. I realize that when a king undertakes a program of public works it is correct to say that what the people gain from it is returned by paying the *taille* [the most important tax paid to the crown by the French peasantry]. In the same fashion it can be maintained that what a king takes from the people returns to them, and that they advance it to him only to draw upon it for the enjoyment of their leisure and their investments, which would be impossible if they did not contribute to the support of the state.

The Political Testament of Cardinal Richelieu, trans. Henry Bertram Hill (Madison, Wisc., 1961), pp. 31–32.

QUESTIONS FOR ANALYSIS

1. According to Cardinal Richelieu, what does the state need to fear from an educated populace?
2. What theory of the state can be adduced from Richelieu's *Political Testament*?

Accordingly, when Huguenots rebelled against restrictions placed on them by the Edict of Nantes, Richelieu put them down with an iron fist and amended the edict in 1629 by depriving them of their political and military rights. Because his armed campaigns against the Huguenots had been very costly, the cardinal then moved to gain more income for the crown by abolishing the semi-autonomy of Burgundy, Dauphiné, and Provence so that he could introduce direct royal taxation in all three areas. Later, to make sure taxes were efficiently collected, Richelieu instituted a new system of local government by royal officials known as intendants, who were expressly commissioned to ride roughshod over any provincial resistance. By these and

WHAT CAUSED THE DECLINE OF SPAIN IN THE SEVENTEENTH CENTURY?

DIVERGENT PATHS: SPAIN, FRANCE, AND ENGLAND, 1600–1660   517

other methods Richelieu made French government more centralized than ever and managed to double the crown's income during his rule. But since he also engaged in an ambitious foreign policy directed against the Habsburgs of Austria and Spain, resulting in France's costly involvement in the Thirty Years' War, internal pressures mounted in the years after Richelieu's death.

THE FRONDE

A reaction against French governmental centralization manifested itself in a series of revolts between 1648 and 1653 collectively known as "the slingshot tumults," or in French, the *Fronde*. By this time Louis XIII had been succeeded by his son Louis XIV; but because the latter was still a boy, France was governed by a regency consisting of Louis's mother, Anne of Austria, and her paramour Cardinal Mazarin. Both were foreigners (Anne was a Habsburg and Mazarin originally an Italian adventurer named Giulio Mazarini), and many of their subjects, including some extremely powerful nobles, hated them. Popular resentments were greater still because the costs of war, combined with several consecutive years of bad harvests, had brought France temporarily into a grave economic plight. Thus when cliques of nobles expressed their disgust with Mazarin for primarily self-interested reasons, they found much support throughout the country, and uncoordinated revolts against the regency government flared on and off for several years.

France, however, did not come close to falling apart. Above all, the French crown itself, which retained great reservoirs of prestige, owing to a well-established national tradition and the undoubted achievements of Henry IV and Richelieu, was by no means under attack. On the contrary; neither the aristocratic leaders of the Fronde nor the commoners who joined them in revolt claimed to be resisting the young king but only the alleged corruption and mismanagement of Mazarin. Some of the rebels, it is true, insisted that part of Mazarin's fault lay in his pursuit of Richelieu's centralizing, antiprovincial policy. But because most of the aristocrats who led the Fronde were merely "outs" who wanted to be "in," they often squabbled among themselves—sometimes even arranging agreements of convenience with the regency or striking alliances with France's enemy, Spain—and proved completely unable to rally any unified support behind a common program. Thus when Louis XIV began to rule in his own name in 1651 and pretexts for revolt against corrupt ministers

no longer existed, the opposition was soon silenced. As so often happens, the idealists and poor people paid the greatest price for revolt: in 1653 a defeated leader of popular resistance in Bordeaux was broken on the wheel, and not long afterward a massive new round of taxation was proclaimed. Remembering the turbulence of the Fronde for the rest of his life, Louis XIV resolved never to let his aristocracy or his provinces get out of hand again and ruled as the most effective royal absolutist in all of French history.

THE ENGLISH CIVIL WAR

Of all the revolts that shook mid-seventeenth-century Europe, the most radical in its consequences was the English civil war. The causes of this conflict were similar to those that sparked rebellions in Spain and France: constitutional hostilities between the component parts of a composite kingdom; religious animosities between Catholics and Protestants and within the ruling (Protestant) camp itself; struggles for power among competing factions of aristocrats at court; and a fiscal system that could not keep pace even with the increasing costs of government, much less of war. Only in England, however, did these conflicts lead to the deposition and execution of the king (1649), an eleven-year "interregnum" during which England was officially a republic (1649–1660), and ultimately to the restoration of the monarchy under conditions designed to safeguard Parliament's place in government and to guarantee a limited degree of religious toleration for all Protestants.

THE ORIGINS OF THE ENGLISH CIVIL WAR

The chain of events that led to war between king and Parliament in 1642 began in the last decades of Queen Elizabeth's reign (1559–1603). During the 1590s, the expenses of war with Spain together with a rebellion in Ireland, widespread crop failures, and the inadequacies of the antiquated English taxation system drove the queen's government deeply into debt. Factional disputes around the court also became more bitter as courtiers, anticipating the aging queen's death, jockeyed for position under her presumed successor, the Scottish king James Stuart. Only on her deathbed, however, did the queen finally confirm that her throne should go to her Scottish cousin. As a result, neither James nor his new English subjects knew very much about one another when he took the throne at the end of 1603.

The relationship did not begin well. James's English subjects looked down on the Scots whom he brought with him to London. Although English courtiers were pleased to accept their new king's generosity to themselves, they resented the grants he made to his Scottish supporters, whom they blamed, quite unreasonably, for the Crown's indebtedness. James, meanwhile, saw clearly that to resolve his debts he had to have more revenue. But rather than bargain with parliamentary representatives for increased taxation he chose to lecture them on the prerogatives of kingship, comparing kings to gods on earth and declaring: "As it is atheism and blasphemy to dispute what God can do, so it is presumption and high contempt in a subject to dispute what a king can do." When this approach failed to produce the taxation he needed, James made peace with Spain and then took steps to raise revenues without parliamentary approval, imposing new tolls on trade and selling trading monopolies to favored courtiers. These measures aroused further resentments against the king and so made voluntary grants of taxation from Parliament even less likely to be approved. As a result, the king's financial situation steadily worsened.

James I. "The wisest fool in Christendom."

James was more adept with respect to religious policy. Scotland had been a firmly Calvinist country since the 1560s. In England, however, the Elizabethan religious settlement had produced much less theological definition. By 1603 England was clearly a Protestant country, but a significant number of English Protestants continued to hope for a second, or further, reformation that would bring their church more firmly into line with Calvinist principles. Other Protestants resisted such efforts, and labeled those who supported them "Puritans." As king, James was compelled to mediate these conflicts. By and large, he did so successfully. In Scotland, he convinced the reformed church to retain its bishops, and in England, he encouraged Calvinist doctrine while resisting any alterations in the prayer book or the Thirty-Nine Articles of the Faith. Only in Ireland, which remained overwhelmingly Catholic, did James store up future trouble. By encouraging the "plantation" of more than 8,000 Scottish Calvinists in the northern province of Ulster, he undermined the property rights of Irish Catholics and created religious animosities that have lasted until the present day.

The delicate religious balance preserved by James I was shattered in 1625 by the accession of his only surviving son, Charles I. Throwing his father's habitual caution to the winds, Charles immediately launched a new war with Spain, exacerbating his financial problems and alarming his Protestant subjects by proposing to raise Irish Catholic troops for military service in Germany. Protestant alarm was further increased when Charles married Henrietta Maria, the Catholic daughter of King Louis XIII of France. The situation became truly dangerous, however, when Charles, aided by his newly appointed archbishop of Canterbury, William Laud, openly began to favor the most anti-Calvinist elements in the English church and then attempted to impose this religious policy (including a full-fledged system of church government by bishops and a new prayer book) on the forthrightly Calvinist church in Scotland. The Scots rebelled, and in 1640 a Scottish army marched south into England to demand the withdrawal of Charles's Catholicizing religious reforms.

To meet the Scottish threat, Charles was forced to summon the English Parliament for the first time in eleven years. Relations between the king and his parliament had broken down in the late 1620s, when Charles responded to Parliament's refusal to grant him additional funds by demanding forced loans from his subjects and then punishing those who refused to comply by quartering soldiers in their homes or throwing

WHAT CAUSED THE DECLINE OF SPAIN IN THE SEVENTEENTH CENTURY?

DIVERGENT PATHS: SPAIN, FRANCE, AND ENGLAND, 1600–1660   519

Charles I. This portrait by Anthony Van Dyck vividly captures the ill-fated monarch's arrogance.

them into prison without trial. In response, in 1628 Parliament forced the king to accept the Petition of Right, which declared all taxes not voted by Parliament illegal, condemned the quartering of soldiers in private houses, and prohibited arbitrary imprisonment and martial law in time of peace. Angered rather than chastened by the Petition of Right, Charles resolved to rule without Parliament entirely, funding his government during the 1630s with a variety of levies and fines imposed without parliamentary consent.

It was only the Scottish invasion that forced Charles to summon a new Parliament. Once summoned, however, the parliamentarians were determined to impose a series of radical reforms on the king's government before they would even consider granting him funds to raise an army against the Scots. Charles initially cooperated with these reforms, even allowing Parliament to execute his chief minister. But it soon became clear that the parliamentary leaders had no intention of fighting the Scots. Instead, a de facto alliance emerged between them, which was reinforced by their common, Calvinist, religious outlook.

> Angered rather than chastened by the Petition of Right, Charles resolved to rule without Parliament entirely, funding his government during the 1630s with a variety of levies and fines imposed without parliamentary consent.

By 1642, Charles had had enough. Marching his guards into the House of Commons, he tried (but failed) to arrest five of its leaders. Charles then withdrew from London to raise his own army. Parliament responded by summoning its own force and voting the taxation to pay for it. By the end of 1642, open warfare had erupted between king and Parliament.

CIVIL WAR AND COMMONWEALTH

Arrayed on the king's side were most of England's aristocrats and largest landowners, who were almost all loyal to the established Church of England, despite their opposition to some of Charles's own religious innovations. The parliamentary forces were made up of smaller landholders, tradesmen, and artisans, most of whom were Puritans. The king's supporters were commonly known by the aristocratic name of Cavaliers. Their opponents, who cut their hair short in contempt for the fashionable custom of wearing curls, were derisively called Roundheads. At first the royalists, having obvious advantages of military experience, won most of the victories. In 1644, however, the parliamentary army was reorganized, and soon afterward the fortunes of battle shifted. The Cavalier forces were badly beaten, and in 1646 the king was compelled to surrender. Soon thereafter, the episcopate was abolished and a Calvinist-style church was established throughout England.

The struggle might now have ended had not a quarrel developed within the parliamentary party. The majority of its members were ready to restore Charles to the throne as a limited monarch under an arrangement whereby a uniformly Calvinist faith would be imposed on both Scotland and England as the state religion. But a radical minority of Puritans, commonly known as Independents, distrusted Charles and insisted on religious toleration for themselves and all other Protestants. Their leader was Oliver Cromwell (1599–1658), who had risen to command the Roundhead army.

Taking advantage of the dissension within the ranks of his opponents, Charles renewed the war in 1648 but, after a brief campaign, was forced to surrender. Cromwell now resolved to end the life of "that man of blood" and, ejecting all the moderate Protestants from Parliament by force of arms, obliged the "Rump"

DEMOCRACY AND THE ENGLISH CIVIL WAR

The English civil war raised fundamental issues about the political rights and responsibilities of Englishmen. Many of these issues were addressed in a lengthy debate held within the General Council of Cromwell's New Model Army at Putney in October 1647. It is interesting that none of the participants in these debates seems to have recognized the implications their arguments might have for the political rights of women. Only King Charles, speaking moments before his execution in 1649, saw the radical implications of the constitutional experiment on which the parliamentary forces had embarked— but, ironically, it was his own radical assertions of monarchical authority that prompted the rebellion that overthrew him.

THE ARMY DEBATES, 1647

Colonel Rainsborough: Really, I think that the poorest man that is in England has a life to live as the greatest man; and therefore truly, sir, I think it's clear, that every man that is to live under a government ought first by his own consent to put himself under that government; and I do think that the poorest man in England is not at all bound in a strict sense to that government that he has not had a voice to put himself under . . . insomuch that I should doubt whether I was an Englishman or not, that should doubt of these things.

General Ireton: Give me leave to tell you, that if you make this the rule, I think you must fly for refuge to an absolute natural right, and you must deny all civil right; and I am sure it will come to that in the consequence. . . . For my part, I think it is no right at all. I think that no person has a right to an interest or share in the disposing of the affairs of the kingdom, and in determining or choosing those that shall determine what laws we shall be ruled by here, no person has a right to this that has not a permanent fixed interest in this kingdom, and

those persons together are properly the represented of this kingdom who, taken together, and consequently are to make up the represkenters of this kingdom. . . .

We talk of birthright. Truly, birthright there is. . . . [M]en may justly have by birthright, by their very being born in England, that we should not seclude them out of England. That we should not refuse to give them air and place and ground, and the freedom of the highways and other things, to live amongst us, not any man that is born here, though he in birth or by his birth there come nothing at all that is part of the permanent interest of this kingdom to him. That I think is due to a man by birth. But that by a man's being born here he shall have a share in that power that shall dispose of the lands here, and of all things here, I do not think it is a sufficient ground.

Divine Right and Democracy: An Anthology of Political Writing in Stuart England, ed. David Wootton (New York, 1986), pp. 286–287 (language modernized).

CHARLES I ON THE SCAFFOLD, 1649

I think it is my duty, to God first, and to my country, for to clear myself both as an honest man, a good king, and a good Christian.

I shall begin first with my innocence. In truth I think it not very needful for me to insist long upon this, for all the world knows that I never did begin a war with the two Houses of Parliament; and I call God to witness, to whom I must shortly make an account, that I never did intend to incroach upon their privileges. . . .

As for the people—truly I desire their liberty and freedom as much as anybody whatsoever. But I must tell you that their liberty and freedom consists in having of government those laws by which their lives and goods may be most their own. It is not for having share in government. That is nothing pertaining to them. A subject and a sovereign are clean different things, and therefore, until they do that—I mean that you do put the people in that liberty as I say—certainly they will never enjoy themselves.

Sirs, it was for this that now I am come here. If I would have given way to an arbitrary way, for to have all laws changed according to the power of the sword,

I needed not to have come here. And therefore I tell you (and I pray God it be not laid to your charge) that I am the martyr of the people.

Brian Tierney, Donald Kagan, and L. Pearce Williams, eds., *Great Issues in Western Civilization* (New York, 1967), pp. 46–47.

QUESTIONS FOR ANALYSIS

1. What issues did the English civil war raise regarding the rights of freeborn Englishmen? What are the natural rights of man? What are civil rights?
2. For what reasons was Charles I brought to trial and ultimately beheaded? Was Charles truly the "martyr of the people"?

Parliament that remained to vote an end to the monarchy. On January 30, 1649 Charles I was beheaded; a short time later the hereditary House of Lords was abolished, and England became a republic.

But founding a republic was far easier than maintaining one. Officially called a Commonwealth, the new form of government did not last long. Technically the Rump Parliament continued as the legislative body; but Cromwell, with the army at his command, possessed the real power and soon became exasperated by the legislators' attempts to enrich themselves by confiscating their opponents' property. Accordingly, in 1653 he marched a detachment of troops into the Rump Parliament. Declaring "Come, I will put an end to your prating," he ordered the members to disperse. The Commonwealth thus ceased to exist and was soon replaced by the "Protectorate," a thinly disguised

autocracy established under a constitution drafted by officers of the army. Called the Instrument of Government, this text was the nearest approximation to a written constitution England has ever had. Extensive powers were given to Cromwell as lord protector for life, and his office was made hereditary. At first a new Parliament exercised limited authority to make laws and levy taxes, but in 1655 Cromwell abruptly dismissed its members also. Thereafter the government became a virtual dictatorship, with Cromwell wielding a sovereignty more absolute than any Stuart monarch ever dreamed of claiming.

THE RESTORATION OF THE MONARCHY

Given the choice between a Puritan military dictatorship and the old royalist regime, when the occasion arose England unhesitatingly opted for the latter. Years of unpopular Calvinist austerities such as the prohibition of any public recreation on Sundays had discredited the Puritans, making most people long for the milder style of the Elizabethan church. Thus not long after Cromwell's death in 1658, one of his generals seized power and called for elections to a new Parliament, which met in the spring of 1660 and proclaimed as king Charles I's exiled son, Charles II, after Charles first gave the traditional promises of good government and then promised a limited religious toleration for all Protestants.

Charles II (1660–1685) restored bishops to the Church of England, but he did not return to the provocative religious policies of his father. Declaring

CHRONOLOGY

ORIGINS OF THE ENGLISH CIVIL WAR, 1603–1660

Reign of the Stuarts begins	1603
Reign of Charles I	1625–1649
Rule without Parliament	1629–1640
English civil war	1642–1649
Charles I beheaded	1649
Commonwealth	1649–1653
Protectorate	1653–1658
Restoration of the monarchy	1660

with characteristic good humor that he did not wish to "resume his travels," Charles agreed to respect Parliament and observe the Petition of Right. He also accepted all the legislation passed by Parliament immediately before the outbreak of civil war in 1642, including the requirement that Parliament be summoned at least once every three years. After one further test in the late seventeenth century, England thus emerged from its civil war as a limited monarchy, in which power was exercised by "the king in parliament."

THE PROBLEM OF DOUBT AND THE QUEST FOR CERTAINTY

Why was this period such a fertile one for political philosophy?

Between 1540 and 1660, Europeans were forced to confront a world in which all that they had once taken for granted was suddenly cast into doubt. An entirely new world had been discovered in the Americas, populated by millions of people whose very existence compelled Europeans to rethink some of their most basic ideas about humanity and human nature. Equally disorienting, the religious uniformity of Europe, although never absolute, had been shattered to an unprecedented extent by the Reformation and the religious wars that arose from it. In 1540, it was still possible to imagine that these religious divisions might be temporary. By 1660, it was clear they would be permanent. No longer, therefore, could Europeans regard revealed religious faith as an adequate foundation for universal philosophical conclusions, for even Christians now disagreed about the fundamental truths of the faith. Political allegiances were similarly under threat, as intellectuals and common people alike began to assert a right to resist princes with whom they disagreed on matters of religion. Even morality and custom were beginning to seem arbitrary and detached from the natural ordering of the world.

Europeans responded to this pervasive climate of doubt in a variety of ways, ranging from radical skepti-

> Europeans responded to this pervasive climate of doubt in a variety of ways, ranging from radical skepticism to authoritarian assertions of religious fideism and political absolutism.

cism to authoritarian assertions of religious fideism and political absolutism. What united their responses, however, was a sometimes desperate search for new foundations on which to reconstruct some measure of certainty in the face of Europe's new intellectual, religious, and political challenges.

WITCHCRAFT ACCUSATIONS AND THE POWER OF THE STATE

Adding to the fears of Europeans was their conviction that witchcraft was a mortal and increasing threat to their world. Although most people in the Middle Ages believed that certain individuals, usually women, could heal or harm through the practice of magic, it was not until the fifteenth century that learned authorities began to insist that such powers could derive only from some kind of pact made by the witch with the devil. Once this belief became accepted, judicial officers became much more active in seeking out suspected witches for prosecution. In 1484 Pope Innocent VIII ordered papal inquisitors to use all the means at their disposal to detect and eliminate witchcraft, including torture of suspected witches. Predictably, torture increased the number of accused witches who confessed to their alleged crimes; and as more accused witches confessed, more and more witches were "discovered," accused, and executed—even in areas (such as England) where torture was not employed and where the Inquisition did not operate.

In considering the rash of witchcraft persecution that swept early modern Europe, we need to keep two facts in mind. First of all, the witchcraft trials were by no means limited to Catholic countries. Protestant reformers believed in the insidious powers of Satan just as much as Catholics did. Both Luther and Calvin urged that people accused as witches be tried more peremptorily and sentenced with less leniency than ordinary criminals, a recommendation their followers were only too happy to heed. Second, it was only when the efforts of religious authorities to detect witchcraft were backed up by the coercive powers of secular governments to execute them that the fear of witches became truly murderous. Between 1580 and about 1660, however, enthusiasm for catching and killing witches became something like a mania across much of Europe, claiming tens of thou-

WHY WAS THIS PERIOD SUCH A FERTILE ONE FOR POLITICAL PHILOSOPHY?

THE PROBLEM OF DOUBT AND THE QUEST FOR CERTAINTY   523

Supposed Witches Worshiping the Devil in the Form of a Billy Goat. In the background other witches ride bareback on flying demons. This is one of the earliest visual conceptions of witchcraft, dating from around 1460.

sands of victims, of whom at least three quarters were women. The final death toll will never be known, but in the 1620s there was an average of 100 burnings a year in the German cities of Würzburg and Bamberg; around the same time it was said that the town square of Wolfenbüttel "looked like a little forest, so crowded were the stakes." After 1660, accusations of witchcraft gradually diminished; but isolated incidents, such as the one at Salem, Massachusetts, continued to crop up for another half century.

This witch mania reflects the fears that early modern Europeans held not only about the devil but also about the adequacy of traditional remedies (such as prayers, amulets, and holy water) to combat the evils of their world. But it also reflects their growing conviction that only the state, and not the church, had the power to protect them. One of the most striking features of the mania for hunting down witches is the extent to which these prosecutions, in both Catholic and Protestant countries, were state-sponsored affairs, carried out by secular authorities claiming to act as the protectors of society against the spiritual and temporal evils that assailed it. Even in Catholic countries, where witchcraft

prosecutions were sometimes begun in church courts, these cases would be transferred to the state's courts for final judgment and punishment, because church courts were forbidden to impose capital penalties. In Protestant countries, where church courts had been abolished (only England retained church courts), the entire process of detecting, prosecuting, and punishing suspected witches was carried out under the supervision of the state. In both Catholic and Protestant countries, the result of these witchcraft trials was thus a considerable increase in the scope of the state's powers and responsibilities to regulate the lives of its subjects.

THE SEARCH FOR AUTHORITY

The crisis of Europe's iron century (as even contemporaries sometimes called it) was fundamentally a crisis of authority. Attempts to reestablish some foundation for agreed authority took many forms. For the French nobleman Michel de Montaigne (1533–1592), who wrote during the height of the French wars of religion, the result was a searching skepticism about the possibilities of any certain knowledge whatsoever. The son of a Catholic father and a Huguenot mother of Jewish ancestry, the well-to-do Montaigne retired from a legal career at the age of thirty-eight to devote himself to a life of leisured reflection. The *Essays* that resulted were a new literary form originally conceived as "experiments" in writing (the French *essai* simply means "trial"). Because they are extraordinarily well written as well as searchingly reflective, Montaigne's *Essays* are among the most enduring classics of French literature and thought.

Although the range of subjects of the *Essays* is wide, two main themes are dominant. One is a pervasive skepticism. Making his motto *Que sais-je?* ("What do I know?"), Montaigne decided that he knew very little for certain. According to him, "it is folly to measure truth and error by our own capacities" because our capacities are severely limited. Thus, as he maintained in one of his most famous essays, "On Cannibals," what may seem indisputably true and proper to one nation may seem absolutely false to another because "everyone gives the title of barbarism to everything that is not of his usage." From this Montaigne's second main principle followed—the need for moderation. Because all people think they know the perfect religion and the perfect government, yet few agree on what that perfection might be, Montaigne concluded that no religion or government is really perfect and consequently no belief is worth fighting for to the

MONTAIGNE ON SKEPTICISM AND FAITH

Michel de Montaigne's Essays *reflect the curious contradictions of his thought, which in turn mirror the tortured combination of uncertainty and faith that characterized the century in which he lived. Although he begins here by asserting the limits on human knowledge, he ends by concluding that these limits impose on human beings an obligation to accept completely every aspect of the church's religious teachings.*

Perhaps it is not without reason that we attribute facility in belief and conviction to simplicity and ignorance; for . . . the more a mind is empty and without counterpoise, the more easily it gives beneath the weight of the first persuasive argument. That is why children, common people, women, and sick people are most subject to being led by the ears. But then, on the other hand, it is foolish presumption to go around disdaining and condemning as false whatever does not seem likely to us; which is an ordinary vice in those who think they have more than common ability. I used to do so once. . . . But reason has taught me that to condemn a thing thus, dogmatically, as false and impossible, is to assume the advantage of knowing the bounds and limits of God's will and of the power of our mother Nature; and that there is no more notable folly in the world than to reduce these things to the measure of our capacity and competence. . . .

It is a dangerous and fateful presumption, besides the absurd temerity that it implies, to disdain what we do not comprehend. For after you have established, according to your fine understanding, the limits of truth and falsehood, and it turns out that you must necessarily believe things even stranger than those you deny,

you are obliged from then on to abandon these limits. Now what seems to me to bring as much disorder into our consciences as anything, in these religious troubles that we are in, is this partial surrender of their beliefs by Catholics. It seems to them that they are being very moderate and understanding when they yield to their opponents some of the articles in dispute. But, besides the fact that they do not see what an advantage it is to a man charging you for you to begin to give ground and withdraw, and how much that encourages him to pursue his point, those articles which they select as the most trivial are sometimes very important. We must either submit completely to the authority of our ecclesiastical government, or do without it completely. It is not for us to decide what portion of obedience we owe it.

Montaigne: Selections from the Essays, trans. and ed. Donald M. Frame (Arlington Heights, Ill., 1971), pp. 34–38.

QUESTIONS FOR ANALYSIS

1. How does Montaigne reconcile the seemingly contradictory nature of skepticism and faith? How can one be skeptical and maintain faith?

death. Instead, people should accept the teachings of religion on faith, and obey the governments constituted to rule over them, without resorting to fanaticism in either sphere.

Although Montaigne can sound surprisingly modern, he was very much a man of the sixteenth century, believing that "reason does nothing but go astray in everything" and that intellectual curiosity "which

WHY WAS THIS PERIOD SUCH A FERTILE ONE FOR POLITICAL PHILOSOPHY?

THE PROBLEM OF DOUBT AND THE QUEST FOR CERTAINTY   525

prompts us to thrust our noses into everything" is a "scourge of the soul." Montaigne was also a fatalist who thought that in a world governed by unpredictable fortune the best human strategy was to face the good and the bad with steadfastness and dignity. Nonetheless, despite his unheroic and highly personal tone, the wide circulation of Montaigne's *Essays* did help combat fanaticism and religious intolerance in his own and subsequent ages.

Montaigne sought refuge from the trials of his age in skepticism, distance, and resigned dignity. His contemporary the French lawyer Jean Bodin (1530–1596), looked instead to resolve the disorders of the day by reestablishing the powers of the state on new and more secure foundations. Like Montaigne, Bodin was particularly troubled by the upheavals caused by the religious wars in France—he had even witnessed the frightful St. Bartholomew's Day Massacre of 1572 in Paris. But instead of shrugging his shoulders about the bloodshed, he resolved to offer a political plan to make sure turbulence would cease. This he did in his monumental *Six Books of the Commonwealth* (1576), the earliest fully developed statement of absolute governmental sovereignty in Western political thought. According to Bodin, the state arises from the needs of collections of families, but once constituted should brook no opposition, because maintaining order is its paramount duty. For Bodin, sovereignty was "the most high, absolute, and perpetual power over all subjects," consisting principally in the power "to give laws to subjects without their consent." Although Bodin acknowledged the theoretical possibility of government by aristocracy or democracy, he assumed that the nation-states of his day would be ruled by monarchs and insisted that such monarchs could in no way be limited, either by legislative or judicial bodies or even by laws made by their predecessors or themselves. Bodin maintained that every subject must trust in the ruler's "mere and frank good will." Even if the ruler proved a tyrant, Bodin insisted that the subject had no warrant to resist, for any resistance would open the door "to a licentious anarchy which is worse than the harshest tyranny in the world."

Like Bodin, who was moved by the events of St. Bartholomew's Day to formulate a doctrine of political absolutism, Thomas Hobbes (1588–1679) was moved by the turmoil of the English civil war to do the same in his classic of political theory, *Leviathan* (1651). Yet Hobbes differed from Bodin in several respects. For one, whereas Bodin assumed that the absolute sovereign power would be a royal monarch, Hobbes made no such assumption. Any form of government capable of protecting its subjects' lives and property might act as a sovereign (and hence all-powerful) Leviathan. Then too, whereas Bodin defined his state as "the lawful government of families" and hence did not believe that the state could abridge private property rights because families could not exist without property, Hobbes's state existed to rule over atomistic individuals and thus was licensed to trample over both liberty and property if the government's own survival was at stake.

But the most fundamental difference between Bodin and Hobbes lay in the latter's uncompromisingly pessimistic view of human nature. Hobbes posited that the "state of nature" that existed before civil government came into being was a condition of "war of all against all." Because man naturally behaves as "a wolf" toward other men, human life without government is necessarily "solitary, poor, nasty, brutish, and short." To escape such consequences, people therefore surrendered their liberties to a sovereign ruler in exchange for his agreement to keep the peace. Having granted away their liberties, subjects have no right whatsoever to seek them back, and the sovereign could therefore tyrannize as he likes—free to oppress his charges in any way other than to kill them, an act that would negate the very purpose of his rule, which is to preserve his subjects' lives.

Perhaps the most moving attempt to respond to the problem of doubt in seventeenth-century culture was offered by the French moral and religious philosopher Blaise Pascal (1623–1662). Pascal began his career as a mathematician and scientific rationalist. But at age thirty Pascal abandoned science as the result of a conversion experience and became a firm adherent of Jansenism, a puritanical faction within French Catholicism. From then until his death he worked on a highly ambitious philosophical-religious project meant to persuade doubters of the truth of Christianity by appealing simultaneously to their intellects and their emotions. Because of his premature death all that

CHRONOLOGY

THE SEARCH FOR AUTHORITY, 1572–1670

Montaigne's *Essays*	1572–1580
Bodin's *Six Books of the Commonwealth*	1576
Hobbes's *Leviathan*	1651
Pascal's *Pensées*	1670

came of this effort was his *Pensées* (Thoughts), a collection of fragments and short informal pieces about religion written with great literary power. In these he argued that faith alone could show the way to salvation and that "the heart has its reasons of which reason itself knows nothing." Pascal's *Pensées* expresses the author's own terror, anguish, and awe in the face of evil and eternity but presents that awe itself as evidence for the existence of God. Pascal's hope was that on this foundation, some measure of hopefulness about humanity and its capacity for self-knowledge could be re-erected that would avoid both the dogmatism and the extreme skepticism that were so prominent in seventeenth-century society.

LITERATURE AND THE ARTS

What was the relationship between the Baroque school and the Counter-Reformation?

Doubt and the uncertainty of human knowledge were also primary themes in the profusion of literature and art produced during western Europe's iron century. Of course not every poem, play, or painting of the era expressed the same message. During 120 years of extraordinary literary and artistic creativity, works of all genres and sentiments were produced, ranging from the frothiest farces to the darkest tragedies, from the serenest still lifes to the most violent scenes of religious martyrdom. The greatest writers and painters of the period all were moved by a realization of the ambiguities and ironies of human existence not unlike that expressed in different ways by Montaigne and Pascal. They all were fully aware of the horrors of war and human suffering so rampant in their day, but they also sought some measure of redemption for human beings caught up in a world that treated them so cruelly. Out of this tragic balance came some of the greatest works in the entire history of European literature and art.

MIGUEL DE CERVANTES (1547–1616)

Cervantes's masterpiece, the satirical romance *Don Quixote*, recounts the adventures of a Spanish gentleman, Don Quixote of La Mancha, who becomes slightly unbalanced by his constant reading of chivalric epics. His mind filled with all kinds of fantastic

adventures, he sets out at the age of fifty on the slippery road of knight-errantry, imagining windmills to be glowering giants and flocks of sheep to be armies of infidels whom it is his duty to rout with his spear. In his distorted fancy he mistakes inns for castles and serving girls for courtly ladies on fire with love. Set off in contrast to the knight-errant is the figure of his faithful squire, Sancho Panza. The latter represents the ideal of the practical man, with his feet on the ground and content with the modest but substantial pleasures of eating, drinking, and sleeping. Yet Cervantes clearly does not wish to say that the realism of a Sancho Panza is categorically preferable to the "quixotic" idealism of his master. Rather, the two men represent different facets of human nature. Without any doubt, *Don Quixote* is a devastating satire on the anachronistic chivalric mentality that was already hastening Spain's decline. But for all that, the reader's sympathies remain with the protagonist, the man from La Mancha who dares to "dream the impossible dream."

ELIZABETHAN AND JACOBEAN DRAMA

Writing after England's victory over the Spanish Armada, when national pride was at a peak, the dramatists of the so-called English Renaissance exhibited great exuberance without descending into a facile optimism. In fact a strain of reflective seriousness pervades all their best works; and a few, such as the tragedian John Webster (c. 1580–c. 1625), who "saw the skull beneath the skin," were if anything morbid pessimists. Among a bevy of great Elizabethan and Jacobean playwrights, however, the most outstanding were Christopher Marlowe (1564–1593), Ben Jonson (c. 1572–1637), and William Shakespeare (1564–1616). Of the three, the fiery Marlowe, whose life was cut short in a tavern brawl before he reached the age of thirty, was the most popular in his own day. In plays such as *Tamburlaine* and *Doctor Faustus* Marlowe created larger-than-life heroes who seek and come close to conquering everything in their path and feeling every possible sensation. But they meet unhappy ends because, for Marlowe, there are limits on human striving, and wretchedness as well as greatness lies in the human lot. Thus although Faustus asks a reincarnated Helen of Troy, conjured up by Satan, to make him "immortal with a kiss," he dies and is damned in the end because immortality is not awarded by the devil or to be found in earthly kisses.

In contrast to the heroic tragedies of Marlowe, Ben Jonson wrote corrosive comedies that expose human vices and foibles. In the particularly bleak *Volpone* Jonson

WHAT WAS THE RELATIONSHIP BETWEEN THE BAROQUE SCHOOL AND THE COUNTER-REFORMATION?

LITERATURE AND THE ARTS   527

shows people behaving like deceitful and lustful animals, but in the later *Alchemist* he balances an attack on quackery and gullibility with admiration for resourceful lower-class characters who cleverly take advantage of their supposed betters.

The greatest of the Elizabethan dramatists, William Shakespeare, was born into the family of a tradesman in the provincial town of Stratford-on-Avon. Little is known about his early life. He left his native village, having gained a modest education, when he was about twenty, and went to London where he found employment in the theater. How he eventually became an actor and still later a writer of plays is uncertain, but by the age of twenty-eight he had definitely acquired a reputation as an author sufficient to excite the jealousy of his rivals. Before he retired to his native Stratford about 1610 to spend the rest of his days in ease, he had written or collaborated in writing nearly forty plays, over and above 150 sonnets, and two long narrative poems.

Since their author's death, Shakespeare's plays have become a kind of secular Bible wherever the English language is spoken. The reasons lie in the author's unrivaled gift of expression, in his scintillating wit, and most of all in his profound analysis of human character seized by passion and tried by fate. Shakespeare's dramas fall thematically into three groups. Those written during the playwright's early years are characterized by a sense of confidence that, despite human foolishness, the world is fundamentally orderly and just. These include a number of the history plays, which recount England's struggles and glories leading up to the triumph of the Tudor Dynasty; the lyrical romantic tragedy *Romeo and Juliet;* and a number of comedies, including the magical *Midsummer Night's Dream, Twelfth Night, As You Like It,* and *Much Ado about Nothing.* Despite the last-named title, few even of the plays of Shakespeare's early, lightest period are much ado about nothing. Rather, most explore fundamental problems of psychological identity, honor and ambition, love and friendship. Occasionally, they also contain touches of deep seriousness, as in *As You Like It,* when Shakespeare has a character pause to reflect that "all the world's a stage, and all the men and women merely players" who pass through seven "acts" or stages of life.

The plays from Shakespeare's second period are far darker in mood, being characterized by bitterness, pathos, and a troubled searching into the mysteries and meaning of human existence. The series begins with the tragedy of indecisive idealism represented by *Hamlet,* goes on to the cynicism of *Measure for Measure* and *All's Well That Ends Well,* and culminates in the searing tragedies of *Macbeth* and *King Lear,* wherein characters assert that "life's but a walking shadow . . . a tale told by an idiot, full of sound and fury signifying nothing," and that "as flies to wanton boys are we to the gods; they kill us for their sport." Despite their gloom, however, the plays of Shakespeare's second period contain some of the dramatist's greatest flights of poetic grandeur.

Shakespeare ended his dramatic career, however, with a third period characterized by a profound spirit of reconciliation and peace. Of the three plays (all idyllic romances) written during this final period, the last, *The Tempest,* is the widest ranging in its reflections on human nature and the power of art. Ancient animosities are buried and wrongs are righted by a combination of natural and supernatural means, and a wide-eyed, youthful heroine rejoices on first seeing men with the words "O brave new world, that has such people in it!" Here, then, Shakespeare seems to be saying that despite humanity's trials, life is not so bitter after all, and the divine plan of the universe is ultimately benevolent and just.

Though less versatile than Shakespeare, not far behind him in eloquent grandeur stands the Puritan poet John Milton (1608–1674). The leading publicist of Oliver Cromwell's regime, Milton wrote the official defense of the beheading of Charles I as well as a number of treatises justifying Puritan positions in contemporary affairs. But he also loved the Greek and Latin classics at least as much as the Bible and wrote a perfect pastoral elegy, *Lycidas,* mourning in purely classical terms the loss of a dear friend. Later, when forced into retirement by the accession of Charles II, Milton, though now blind, embarked on writing a classical epic, *Paradise Lost,* out of material found in Genesis concerning the creation of the world and the fall of humanity. Setting out to "justify the ways of God to man," Milton in *Paradise Lost* first plays "devil's advocate" by creating the compelling character of Satan, who defies God with boldness and subtlety. But Satan is more than counterbalanced in the end by the real "epic hero" of *Paradise Lost,* Adam, who learns to accept the human lot of moral responsibility and suffering, and is last seen leaving Paradise with Eve, the world "all before them."

> Since their author's death, Shakespeare's plays have become a kind of secular Bible wherever the English language is spoken.

MANNERISM

The ironies and tensions inherent in human existence were also portrayed with eloquence and profundity by several immortal masters of the visual arts who flourished during this tumultuous century. The dominant goal in Italian and Spanish painting during the first half of this period, the years between about 1540 and 1600, was to fascinate the viewer with special effects. This goal, however, was achieved by means of two entirely different styles. (Confusingly, both styles are sometimes referred to as "Mannerism.") The first was based on the style of the Renaissance master Raphael but moved from that painter's gracefulness to a highly self-conscious elegance bordering on the bizarre and surreal. Representatives of this approach were the Florentines Pontormo (1494–1557) and Bronzino (1503–1572). Their sharp-focused portraits are flat and cold, yet strangely riveting.

The other extreme was theatrical in a more conventional sense—highly dramatic and emotionally compelling. Painters who followed this approach were indebted to Michelangelo but went much farther than he did in emphasizing shadowy contrasts, restlessness, and distortion. Of this second group, the two most outstanding were the Venetian Tintoretto (1518–1594) and the Spaniard El Greco (c. 1541–1614). Combining aspects of Michelangelo's style with the traditionally Venetian taste for rich color, Tintoretto produced an enormous number of monumentally large canvases devoted to religious subjects that still inspire awe with their broodingly shimmering light and gripping drama. More emotional still is the work of Tintoretto's disciple, El Greco. Born Domenikos Theotokopoulos on the Greek island of Crete, this extraordinary artist absorbed some of the stylized elongation characteristic of Greco-Byzantine icon painting before traveling to Italy to learn color and drama from Tintoretto. Finally he settled in Spain, where he was called "El Greco"—"the Greek." El Greco's paintings were too strange to be greatly appreciated in his own age, and even now they appear so unbalanced as to seem the work of one almost deranged. Yet such a view slights El Greco's deeply mystical Catholic fervor as well as his technical achievements. Best known today is his transfigured landscape, the *View of Toledo*, with its somber but awesome light breaking where no sun shines. But equally inspiring are his swirling religious scenes and several of his stunning portraits in which gaunt, dignified Spaniards radiate a rare blend of austerity and spiritual insight.

BAROQUE ART AND ARCHITECTURE

The dominant artistic school of southern Europe from about 1600 until the early 1700s was that of the Baroque, a school not only of painting but of sculpture and architecture. The Baroque style retained aspects of the dramatic and the irregular, but it avoided seeming bizarre or overheated and aimed above all to instill a sense of the affirmative. Originating in Rome as an expression of the ideals of the Counter-Reformation papacy and the Jesuit order, Baroque architecture in particular aimed to promote a specifically Catholic worldview. Similarly, Baroque painting often was done in the service of the Counter-Reformation church, which at its high tide around 1620 seemed everywhere to be on the offensive. When Baroque painters were not celebrating Counter-Reformation ideals,

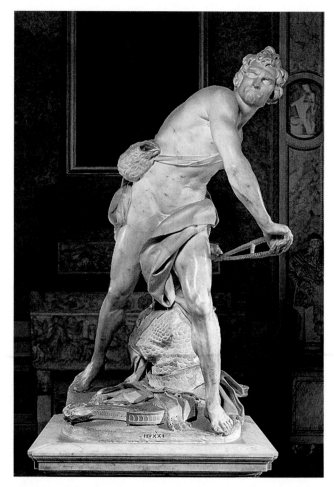

David, by Bernini (1598–1680). Whereas the earlier conceptions of David by the Renaissance sculptors Donatello and Michelangelo were reposeful (see pages 457 and 458), the Baroque sculptor Bernini chose to portray his young hero at the peak of physical exertion.

What was the relationship between the Baroque school and the Counter-Reformation?

Literature and the Arts   529

most of them worked in the service of monarchs who sought their own glorification.

The most imaginative and influential figure of the Roman Baroque was the architect and sculptor Gianlorenzo Bernini (1598–1680), a frequent employee of the papacy who created a magnificent celebration of papal grandeur in the sweeping colonnades leading up to St. Peter's Basilica. Breaking with the serene Renaissance classicism of Palladio, Bernini's architecture retained such classical elements as columns and domes but combined them in ways meant to express both aggressive restlessness and great power. Bernini was also one of the first to experiment with church facades built "in depth"—building frontages not conceived as continuous surfaces but that jutted out at odd angles and seemed to invade the open space in front of them. If the purpose of these innovations was to draw the viewer emotionally into the work of art, the same may be said for Bernini's aims in sculpture. Harking back to the restless motion of Hellenistic statuary—particularly the Laocoön group—and building on tendencies already present in the later sculpture of Michelangelo, Bernini's statuary emphasizes drama and incites the viewer to respond to it rather than serenely to observe.

Because most Italian Baroque painters lacked Bernini's artistic genius, to view the very greatest masterpieces of southern European Baroque painting one must look to Spain and the work of Diego Velázquez (1599–1660). Unlike Bernini, Velázquez, a court painter in Madrid just when Spain hung on the brink of ruin, was not an entirely typical exponent of the Baroque style. Certainly many of his canvases display a characteristically Baroque delight in motion, drama, and power; but Velázquez's best work is characterized by a more restrained thoughtfulness than is usually found in the Baroque. Thus his famous *Surrender of Breda* shows muscular horses and splendid Spanish grandees on the one hand but un-Baroque sympathy for defeated, disarrayed

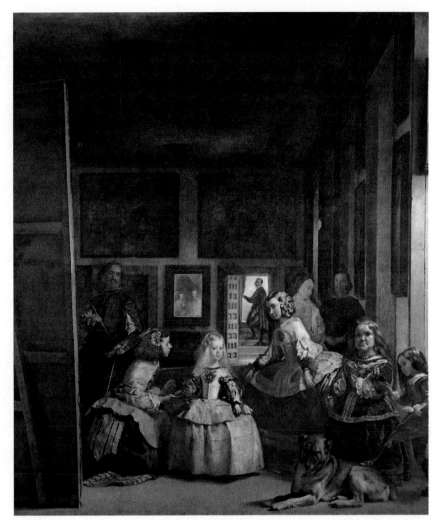

The Maids of Honor, by Diego Velázquez. The artist himself is at work on a double portrait of the king and queen of Spain (who can be seen in the rear mirror), but reality is more obvious in the foreground in the persons of the delicately impish princess, her two maids, and a misshapen dwarf. The twentieth-century Spanish artist Picasso gained great inspiration from this work.

troops on the other. Velázquez's single greatest painting, *The Maids of Honor,* done around 1656 after Spain's collapse, is one of the most thoughtful and probing artistic examinations of illusion and reality ever executed.

DUTCH PAINTING IN THE GOLDEN AGE

Southern Europe's main northern rival for artistic laurels was the Netherlands, where three extremely dissimilar painters all explored the theme of the greatness and wretchedness of man to the fullest. The earliest, Peter Brueghel (c. 1525–1569), worked in a vein related to earlier Netherlandish realism. But unlike his

The Massacre of the Innocents, by Brueghel (c. 1525–1569). This painting shows how effectively art can be used as a means of social commentary. Many art historians believe that Brueghel was tacitly depicting the suffering of the Netherlands at the hands of the Spanish in his own day.

The Horrors of War, by Rubens (1577–1640). The war god Mars here casts aside his mistress, Venus, and threatens humanity with death and destruction. In his old age Rubens took a far more critical view of war than he did for most of his earlier career.

WHAT WAS THE RELATIONSHIP BETWEEN THE BAROQUE SCHOOL AND THE COUNTER-REFORMATION?

LITERATURE AND THE ARTS   531

predecessors, who favored quiet urban scenes, Brueghel exulted in portraying the busy, elemental life of the peasantry. Most famous in this respect are his rollicking *Peasant Wedding* and *Peasant Wedding Dance* and his spacious *Harvesters*, in which guzzling and snoring field hands are taking a well-deserved break from their heavy labors under the noon sun. Such vistas give the impression of uninterrupted rhythms of life, but late in his career Brueghel became appalled by the intolerance and bloodshed he witnessed during the Calvinist riots and the Spanish repression in the Netherlands and expressed his criticism in an understated yet searing manner. In *The Blind Leading the Blind*, for example, we see what happens when ignorant fanatics start showing the way to each other. More powerful still is Brueghel's *Massacre of the Innocents*, which from a distance looks like a snug scene of a Flemish village buried in snow. In fact, however, heartless soldiers are methodically breaking into homes and slaughtering babies, the simple peasant folk are fully at their mercy, and the artist—alluding to a Gospel forgotten by warring Catholics and Protestants alike—seems to be saying "as it happened in the time of Christ, so it happens now."

Vastly different from Brueghel was the Netherlandish Baroque painter Peter Paul Rubens (1577–1640). Since the Baroque was an international movement closely linked to the spread of the Counter-Reformation, it should offer no surprise that Baroque style was extremely well represented in just that part of the Netherlands which, after long warfare, had been retained by Spain. In fact, Rubens of Antwerp was a far more typical Baroque artist than Velázquez of Madrid, painting literally thousands of robust canvases that glorified resurgent Catholicism or exalted second-rate aristocrats by portraying them as epic heroes dressed in bearskins. Even when Rubens's intent was not overtly propagandistic he customarily reveled in the sumptuous extravagance of the Baroque manner, being perhaps most famous today for the pink and rounded flesh of his well-nourished nudes. But unlike a host of lesser Baroque artists, Rubens was not lacking in subtlety and was a man of many moods. His gentle portrait of his son Nicholas catches unaffected childhood in a moment of repose; and though throughout most of his career Rubens had celebrated martial valor, his late *Horrors of War* movingly portrays what he himself called "the grief

Self-Portraits. Self-portraits became common during the sixteenth and seventeenth centuries, reflecting the intense introspection of the period. Left: Rembrandt painted more than sixty self-portraits; this one, dating from around 1660, captures the artist's creativity, theatricality (note the costume), and the honesty of his self-examination. Right: Judith Leyster (1609–1660) was a Dutch contemporary of Rembrandt who pursued a successful career as an artist during her early twenties, before she married. Respected in her own day, she was all but forgotten for centuries thereafter.

of unfortunate Europe, which, for so many years now, has suffered plunder, outrage, and misery."

In some ways a blend of Brueghel and Rubens, the greatest of all Netherlandish painters, Rembrandt van Rijn (1606–1669), defies all attempts at easy characterization. Living across the border from the Spanish Netherlands in staunchly Calvinistic Holland, Rembrandt belonged to a society that was too austere to tolerate the unbuckled realism of a Brueghel or the fleshy Baroque pomposity of a Rubens. Yet Rembrandt managed to put both realistic and Baroque traits to new uses. In his early career he gained fame and fortune as a painter of biblical scenes that lacked the Baroque's fleshiness but retained its grandeur in their swirling forms and stunning experiments with light. Rembrandt was also active as a portrait painter who knew how to flatter his subjects by emphasizing their Calvinistic steadfastness, to the great advantage of his purse. But gradually his prosperity faded, apparently in part because he grew tired of flattering and definitely because he made some bad investments. As personal tragedies mounted in the painter's middle and declining years, his art became more pensive and somber, but it gained in dignity, subtle lyricism, and awesome mystery. Thus his later portraits, including several self-portraits, are imbued with introspective qualities and a suggestion that only half the story is being told. Equally moving are explicitly philosophical paintings such as *Aristotle Contemplating the Bust of Homer*, in which the philosopher seems spellbound by the radiance of the epic poet, and *The Polish Rider*, in which realistic and Baroque elements merge into a higher synthesis portraying a pensive young man setting out fearlessly into a perilous world. Like Shakespeare, Rembrandt knew that life's journey is full of perils, but his most mature paintings suggest that these can be mastered with a courageous awareness of one's human shortcomings.

CONCLUSION

Between 1540 and 1660, Europe was racked by a combination of religious war, political rebellions, and economic crises that undermined confidence in traditional structures of social, religious, and political authority. The result was fear, skepticism, and a search for new, more certain foundations on which to rebuild the social, political, and religious order of Europe. For artists and intellectuals, the period proved to be one of the most creative epochs in the history of Europe. But for common people, the century was one of extraordinary suffering.

After a hundred years of destructive efforts to restore the religious unity of Europe through war, a de facto religious toleration between states was beginning to emerge by 1660 as the only way to preserve the European political order. Within states, toleration was still very limited when this terrible century ended. But in territories where religious rivalries ran too deep to be overcome, rulers were beginning to discover that loyalty to the state was a value that could override even the religious divisions among their subjects. The end result of this century of crises was thus to strengthen Europeans' confidence in the powers of the state to heal their wounds and right their wrongs, with religion relegated more and more to the private sphere of individual conscience. In the following centuries, this new confidence in the state as an autonomous moral agent that acts in accordance with its own "reasons of state," and for its own purposes, would prove a powerful challenge to the traditions of limited consensual government that had emerged out of the Middle Ages.

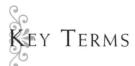

KEY TERMS

Religious Peace of Augsburg	Thirty Years' War	Michel de Montaigne	William Shakespeare
Henry of Navarre	Cardinal Richelieu	*Leviathan*	Rembrandt Van Rijn
Spanish Armada	James I	*Don Quixote*	
	Oliver Cromwell	Baroque	

SELECTED READINGS

Bonney, Richard. *The European Dynastic States, 1494–1660.* Oxford and New York, 1991. An excellent survey of continental Europe during the "long" sixteenth century.

Briggs, Robin. *Early Modern France, 1560–1715,* 2d ed. Oxford and New York, 1997. Updated and authoritative, with new bibliographies.

Briggs, Robin. *Witches and Neighbors: The Social and Cultural Context of European Witchcraft.* New York, 1996. An influential recent account of continental witchcraft.

Cervantes, Miguel de. *Don Quixote.* Trans. Edith Grossman. New York, 2003. A splendid new translation.

Clarke, Stuart. *Thinking with Demons: The Idea of Witchcraft in Early Modern Europe.* Oxford and New York, 1999. By placing demonology into the context of sixteenth- and seventeenth-century intellectual history, Clarke makes sense of it in new and exciting ways.

Cochrane, Eric, Charles M. Gray, and Mark A. Kishlansky. *Early Modern Europe: Crisis of Authority.* Chicago, 1987. An outstanding source collection from the University of Chicago Readings in Western Civilization series.

Held, Julius S., and Donald Posner. *Seventeenth- and Eighteenth-Century Art: Baroque Painting, Sculpture, Architecture.* New York, 1971. The most complete and best-organized introductory review of the subject in English.

Hibbard, Howard. *Bernini.* Baltimore, Md., 1965. The basic study in English of this central figure of Baroque artistic activity.

Hirst, Derek. *England in Conflict, 1603–1660: Kingdom, Community, Commonwealth.* Oxford and New York, 1999. A complete revision of the author's *Authority and Conflict* (1986), this is an up-to-date and balanced account of a period that has been a historical battleground over the past twenty years.

Hobbes, Thomas. *Leviathan.* Ed. Richard Tuck. 2d ed. Cambridge and New York, 1996. The most recent edition, containing the entirety of *Leviathan,* not just the first two parts.

Holt, Mack P. *The French Wars of Religion, 1562–1629.* Cambridge and New York, 1995. A clear account of a confusing time.

Kors, Alan Charles, and Edward Peters. *Witchcraft in Europe, 400–1700: A Documentary History,* 2d ed. Philadelphia, 2000. A superb collection of documents, significantly expanded in the second edition, with up-to-date commentary.

Kingdon, Robert. *Myths about the St. Bartholomew's Day Massacres, 1572–1576.* Cambridge, Mass., 1988. A detailed account of this pivotal moment in the history of France.

Levack, Brian P. *The Witch-Hunt in Early Modern Europe,* 2d ed. London and New York, 1995. The best account of the persecution of suspected witches; coverage extends from Europe in 1450 to America in 1750.

Levin, Carole. *The Heart and Stomach of a King: Elizabeth I and the Politics of Sex and Power.* Philadelphia, 1994. A provocative argument for the importance of Elizabeth's gender for understanding her reign.

Limm, Peter, ed. *The Thirty Years' War.* London, 1984. An outstanding short survey, followed by a selection of primary-source documents.

Lynch, John. *Spain, 1516–1598: From Nation-State to World Empire.* Oxford and Cambridge, Mass., 1991. The best book in English on Spain at the pinnacle of its sixteenth-century power.

MacCaffrey, Wallace. *Elizabeth I.* New York, 1993. An outstanding traditional biography by an excellent scholar.

Martin, Colin, and Geoffrey Parker. *The Spanish Armada.* London, 1988. Incorporates recent discoveries from undersea archaeology with more traditional historical sources.

Martin, John Rupert. *Baroque.* New York, 1977. A thought-provoking, thematic treatment, less a survey than an essay on the painting, sculpture, and architecture of the period.

Mattingly, Garrett. *The Armada.* Boston, 1959. A great narrative history that reads like a novel; for more recent work, however, see Martin and Parker.

Parker, Geoffrey. *The Dutch Revolt,* 2d ed. Ithaca, N.Y., 1989. The standard survey in English on the revolt of the Netherlands.

Parker, Geoffrey. *Philip II.* Boston, 1978. A fine biography by an expert in both the Spanish and the Dutch sources.

Parker, Geoffrey, ed. *The Thirty Years' War,* rev. ed. London and New York, 1987. A wide-ranging collection of essays by scholarly experts.

Pascal, Blaise. *Pensées* (French-English edition). Ed. H. F. Stewart. London, 1950.

Quint, David. *Montaigne and the Quality of Mercy: Ethical and Political Themes in the "Essais."* Princeton, N.J., 1999. A fine treatment that presents Montaigne's thought as a response to the French wars of religion.

Roberts, Michael. *Gustavus Adolphus and the Rise of Sweden.* London, 1973. Still the authoritative English-language account.

Russell, Conrad. *The Causes of the English Civil War.* Oxford, 1990. A penetrating and provocative analysis by one of the leading "revisionist" historians of the period.

Tracy, James D. *Holland under Habsburg Rule, 1506–1566: The Formation of a Body Politic.* Berkeley, Calif., and Los Angeles, 1990. A political history and analysis of the formative years of the Dutch state.

Van Gelderen, Martin. *Political Theory of the Dutch Revolt.* Cambridge, 1995. A fine book on a subject whose importance is too easily overlooked.

PART V
EARLY MODERN EUROPE

SEVENTEENTH- AND EIGHTEENTH-CENTURY European life was shaped by the combined effects of commerce, war, and a steadily growing population. A commercial revolution spurred the development of overseas colonies and trade while opening up new markets for European industry. Agricultural productivity increased, making it possible for Europe to feed a population that had now reached unprecedented levels. Population growth in turn enabled European governments to wage more frequent wars and to employ larger and larger armies.

Although monarchs continued to meet with opposition from the various estates within their realms, they increasingly asserted their power as absolute rulers. Warfare remained the chief instrument of European foreign policy; but slowly the notion of a diplomatic and military balance of power began to displace the pursuit of unrestrained aggrandizement as the primary goal of European state relations.

Profound changes were also occurring in European intellectual life during these centuries. Using new instruments and applying new mathematical techniques, astronomers proved beyond question that the earth was not the center of the universe. Biologists and physicians pioneered a more sophisticated understanding of the nature and processes by which life was created and sustained, and physicists such as Sir Isaac Newton established for the first time a true science of mechanics. During the eighteenth century, these discoveries gave rise to a new confidence in the capacity of human reason alone to understand nature and so to improve human life—a confidence those who held to it declared to be a sign of Enlightenment.

	POLITICS	SOCIETY AND CULTURE	ECONOMY	INTERNATIONAL RELATIONS
1500		Copernicus's *On the Revolutions of the Heavenly Spheres* (1543) Claudio Monteverdi, father of opera (1567–1643) Johannes Kepler (1571–1630) William Harvey (1578–1657)	Enclosure movement (1500–1700s) Demand for sugar escalates in Europe (late 1500s) Widespread crop failure in France (1597–1694)	Sir Francis Drake leads attack on Spanish fleet at Cadíz (1587)
1600		Literacy increases across Europe (1600–1800) Increased urbanization (1600–1750) Smoking spreads in Europe (early 1600s) Over 80,000 leave England for the New World (1607–1650) Galileo's *Starry Messenger* (1610) Bacon's *New Instruments* (1620) Galileo charged with heresy (1632) John Locke (1632–1704) Descartes's *Discourse on Method* (1637)	Mechanically powered saws and calico printing from the Far East (1600s) Dutch East India Company founded (1602)	A total of 11 million Africans forci shipped across the middle passag (1500–1800) English colonists establish Jamestown (1607) *Mayflower* lands in the New World (1620)
	Jean Baptiste Colbert, French finance minister (1619–1683)			
	Reign of Louis XIV, the Sun King (1643–1715) England promulgates Navigation Acts (1651, 1660) Restoration and return of Charles II (1660)	Plague outbreaks (1649–1665) Edmond Halley (1656–1742) Founding of the Royal Society of London and the French Academy of Sciences (1660) Daniel Defoe, author of *Robinson Crusoe* (1660–1731) The Great Fire in London (1666) Johann Sebastian Bach (1685–1750) George Frideric Handel (1685–1759) Newton's *Principia Mathematica* (1687) Locke's *Treatise of Civil Government* and *Essay Concerning Human Understanding* (1690)	French government introduces head tax (c. 1645) Coffee consumption escalates in Europe (1650s) Bank of Sweden founded (1657)	Dutch surrender New Amsterdam to England (1667) Austrian Habsburgs repulse Turks' assault on Vienna (1683) Peace of Augsburg (1686) Portugal regains independence from Spain (1688) William of Orange rules England and Holland (1688) War of the League of Augsburg (1688–1697) Battle of the Boyne, English solidif control of Ireland (1690)
	Louis XIV revokes the Edict of Nantes (1685)			
	Glorious Revolution in England (1688–1689) Reign of Peter the Great of Russia (1689–1725)		Bank of England founded (1694)	
1700		Maize and the potato are introduced in Europe (1700s) Proliferation of salons and coffee-houses (1700s) First daily newspaper in England (1702) Rousseau's *Social Contract* (1762)	Fly shuttle for weaving loom invented (early 1700s) Physiocrats promote concept of laissez-faire (1700s)	War of Spanish Succession (1702–1713) England and Scotland unite to form Great Britain (1707)
	Reign of Charles VI, emperor of Holy Roman Empire (1711–1740) Treaty of Utrecht (1713) Reign of George I, first of Hanoverian dynasty in England (1714–1727) Louis XV (1715–1774) Robert Walpole serves as England's first prime minister (1720–1742)			

POLITICS	SOCIETY AND CULTURE	ECONOMY	INTERNATIONAL RELATIONS	
		German imperial law prohibits journeyman associations (1731) France establishes the Road and Bridge Corps of Engineering (1747)		1731
Reign of Frederick the Great, the "enlightened despot" (1740–1786)	Voltaire's *The Philosophical Letters* (1734) Montesquieu's *Spirit of Laws* (1748) Steady increase in population begins (1750) *Encyclopedia* published by Diderot and d'Alembert (1751–1772) Wolfgang Amadeus Mozart (1756–1791) Beccaria's *On Crimes and Punishment* (1764)		War of Austrian Succession (1740–1748)	
Reign of George III of England (1760–1820) Reign of Catherine the Great of Russia (1762–1796) Maria Theresa and Joseph II of Austria rule jointly (1765–1780)		Antislavery movements emerge in Europe (1760s) James Cook explores Pacific (1768–1779) Abbe Raynal's *Philosophical History of Europeans in the Two Indies* (1770)	Seven Years' War/French and Indian War (1756–1763) Treaty of Paris: France concedes Canada and India to England (1763) French East India Company dissolves (1769) Russo-Turkish War (1769–1792) American Revolution (1775–1783)	
Reign of Louis XVI of France (1774–1792) French Revolution breaks out (1789)	Kant's "What Is Enlightenment?" (1784) Wollstonecraft's *Vindication of the Rights of Woman* (1792) Austen's *Pride and Prejudice* (1813–1817)	Smith's *Inquiry into the Nature and Causes of the Wealth of Nations* (1776)	Russia, Austria, and Prussia fully partition Poland (1795)	1800

CHAPTER FIFTEEN

ABSOLUTISM AND EMPIRE, 1660–1789

THE PERIOD FROM AROUND 1660 (when the English monarchy was restored and Louis XIV of France began his personal rule) to 1789 (when the French Revolution erupted) is traditionally known as the age of absolutism. *Absolutism* was a political theory that encouraged rulers to claim complete sovereignty within their territories. To seventeenth- and eighteenth-century absolutists, complete sovereignty meant that a ruler could make law, dispense justice, create and direct a bureaucracy, declare war, and levy taxation according to his or her own will, without needing the formal approval of any other governing authorities. Frequently, assertions of absolute authority were buttressed by claims that rulers governed their territories by the same divine right that established a father's absolute authority over his household. After the chaos of Europe's "iron century," many Europeans had come to believe that it was only by exalting the sovereignty of such absolute, "patriarchal" rulers that order could be restored to European life.

The age of absolutism was also an age of empire. By 1660, the French, Spanish, Portuguese, English, and Dutch had all established important colonies in the Americas and in Asia. Rivalry among these competing colonial powers was intense and fraught with consequence. In the late seventeenth century, European wars almost always had a colonial aspect. By the middle of the eighteenth century, however, Europe's wars were being driven by colonial considerations and imperial conflicts, as worldwide trade assumed a larger and larger role in the European economy.

Absolutism was not the only political theory according to which European governments sought to rule during this period. England, Scotland, the Dutch Republic, Switzerland, Venice, Sweden, and Poland-Lithuania were all either limited monarchies or republics; in Russia, an extreme autocracy was emerging that ascribed to the tsar

FOCUS QUESTIONS

- What were the aims of absolutist rulers?
- Did John Locke's political principles lie behind the Glorious Revolution in England?
- How did Louis XIV strengthen his control over France?
- What changes lay behind the growing power of Prussia?
- In what ways did Russian absolutism differ from its western European counterparts?

- What factors facilitated the commercial revolution?
- How did the patterns of European colonial settlement in the Americas differ from each other?
- In what ways did eighteenth-century European colonialism differ from seventeenth-century European colonialism?

a degree of control over his subjects' lives and property far beyond anything imagined by western European absolutists. Even in Russia, however, absolutism was never so unlimited in practice as it was in theory. Even the most absolute monarchs of seventeenth- and eighteenth-century Europe could rule effectively only so long as their subjects (and particularly their nobility) were prepared to consent, at least tacitly, to their policies. When serious opposition erupted, even absolutists were forced to back down. And when, in 1789, an outright political revolution occurred, the entire structure of absolutism came crashing to the ground.

THE APPEAL AND JUSTIFICATION OF ABSOLUTISM

What were the aims of absolutist rulers?

Absolutism's promise of stability, prosperity, and order was an appealing alternative to the disorder of the "iron century" that preceded it. This was especially the case for the quintessential absolutist monarch, Louis XIV (1643–1715) of France. The political disturbances of his minority made a lasting impression on the young king. When marauding Parisians entered his bedchamber one night in 1651, Louis saw the intrusion as a horrid affront not only to his own person but to the majesty of the French state he personified. Squabbles among the nobility and criticisms of royal policy by the Paris parlement during his minority convinced him that he must rule assertively and without limitation if France was to survive as a great European state.

Absolutist monarchs sought to gather into their own hands command of the state's armed forces, control over its legal system, and the right to collect and spend the state's financial resources at will. To achieve these goals, they also needed to create an efficient, centralized bureaucracy that owed its allegiance directly to the monarch himself. Creating and sustaining such a bureaucracy was expensive but essential to the larger absolutist goal of weakening the privileged special in-

> Even the most absolute monarchs of seventeenth- and eighteenth-century Europe could rule effectively only so long as their subjects (and particularly their nobility) were prepared to consent, at least tacitly, to their policies.

terests that had hindered the free exercise of royal power in the past. The legally privileged estates of nobility and clergy; the political authority of semi-autonomous regions; and the pretensions of independent-minded representative assemblies such as parliaments, diets, or estates general were all obstacles—in the eyes of absolutists—to strong, centralized monarchical government. The history of abolutism is, as much as anything, a history of attempts by aspiring absolutists to bring such institutions to heel.

In most Protestant countries, the independent power of the church had already been subordinated to the interests of the state when the age of absolutism began. In France, Spain, and Austria, however, where Roman Catholicism had remained the state religion, absolutist monarchs now devoted concerted attention to nationalizing the church and its clergy within their territories. These efforts built on the concordats the French and Spanish monarchies had extracted from the papacy during the fifteenth and sixteenth centuries, but they went much further in consolidating authority over the church into the hands of the monarchy. Even Charles III, the devout Spanish king who ruled from 1759 to 1788, pressed successfully for a papal concordat granting him control over ecclesiastical appointments and the right to nullify any papal bull affecting Spain of which he did not approve.

The most important potential opponents of royal absolutism were not churchmen, however, but nobles. Monarchs dealt with their threat in various ways. Louis XIV deprived the French nobility of political power in the provinces while increasing their social prestige by requiring them to reside at his own lavish court at Versailles. Peter the Great of Russia (1689–1725) forced all his nobles into lifelong government service. Later in the century, Catherine II of Russia (1762–1796) struck a bargain whereby in return for vast estates and a variety of social and economic privileges (including exemption from taxation) the Russian nobility virtually surrendered the administrative and political power of the state into the empress's hands. In Prussia the army was staffed by nobles, as was generally the case in Spain, France, and England also. But in eighteenth-century Austria, the emperor Joseph II (1765–1790) adopted a policy of confrontation rather than accommodation, denying the nobility exemption

ABSOLUTISM AND PATRIARCHY

These selections show how two political theorists justified royal absolutism by deriving it from the absolute authority of a father over his household. Bishop Jacques-Benigne Bossuet (1627–1704) was a famous French preacher who served as tutor to the son of King Louis XIV of France before becoming bishop of Meaux. Sir Robert Filmer (1588–1653) was an English political theorist. Filmer's works attracted particular attention in the 1680s, when John Locke directed the first of his Two Treatises of Government to refuting Filmer's views on the patriarchal nature of royal authority.

BOSSUET ON THE NATURE OF MONARCHICAL AUTHORITY

There are four characteristics or qualities essential to royal authority. First, royal authority is sacred; Secondly, it is paternal; Thirdly, it is absolute; Fourthly, it is subject to reason. . . . All power comes from God. . . . Thus princes act as ministers of God, and his lieutenants on earth. It is through them that he exercises his empire. . . . In this way . . . the royal throne is not the throne of a man, but the throne of God himself. . . .

We have seen that kings hold the place of God, who is the true Father of the human race. We have also seen that the first idea of power that there was among men, is that of paternal power; and that kings were fashioned on the model of fathers. Moreover, all the world agrees that obedience, which is due to public power, is only found . . . in the precept which obliges one to honor his parents. From all this it appears that the name "king" is a father's name, and that goodness is the most natural quality in kings. . . .

Royal authority is absolute. In order to make this term odious and insupportable, many pretend to con-fuse absolute government and arbitrary government. But nothing is more distinct, as we shall make clear when we speak of justice. . . . The prince need account to no one for what he ordains. . . . Without this absolute authority, he can neither do good nor suppress evil: his power must be such that no one can hope to escape him. . . . [T]he sole defense of individuals against the public power must be their innocence. . . .

One must, then, obey princes as if they were justice itself, without which there is neither order nor justice in affairs. They are gods, and share in some way in divine independence. . . . It follows from this that he who does not want to obey the prince . . . is condemned irremissibly to death as an enemy of public peace and of human society. . . . The prince can correct himself when he knows that he has done badly; but against his authority there can be no remedy. . . .

Jacques-Benigne Bossuet, *Politics Drawn from the Very Words of Holy Scripture,* trans. Patrick Riley (Cambridge, 1990), pp. 46–69 and 81–83.

FILMER ON THE PATRIARCHAL ORIGINS OF ROYAL AUTHORITY

The first government in the world was monarchical, in the father of all flesh, Adam being commanded to multiply, and people the earth, and to subdue it, and having dominion given him over all creatures, was thereby the monarch of the whole world; none of his posterity had any right to possess anything, but by his grant or permission, or by succession from him. . . . Adam was the father, king and lord over his family: a son, a subject, and a servant or a slave were one and the same thing at first. . . .

I cannot find any one place or text in the Bible where any power . . . is given to a people either to govern themselves, or to choose themselves governors, or to alter the manner of government at their pleasure. The power of government is settled and fixed by the commandment of "honour thy father"; if there were a higher power than the fatherly, then this commandment could not stand and be observed. . . .

All power on earth is either derived or usurped from the fatherly power, there being no other original to be found of any power whatsoever. For if there should be granted two sorts of power without any subordination of one to the other, they would be in perpetual strife which should be the supreme, for two supremes cannot agree. If the fatherly power be supreme, then the power of the people must be subordinate and depend on it. If the power of the people be supreme, then the fatherly power must submit to it, and cannot be exercised without the licence of the people, which must

quite destroy the frame and course of nature. Even the power which God himself exercises over mankind is by right of fatherhood: he is both the king and father of us all. As God has exalted the dignity of earthly kings . . . by saying they are gods, so . . . he has been pleased . . . [t]o humble himself by assuming the title of a king to express his power, and not the title of any popular government.

Robert Filmer, "Observations upon Aristotle's Politiques" (1652), in *Divine Right and Democracy: An Anthology of Political Writing in Stuart England,* ed. David Wootton (Harmondsworth, UK, 1986), pp. 110–118.

QUESTIONS FOR ANALYSIS

1. Why did some political theorists argue the necessity of absolutism based on the model of the father? Was there an alternative to this model?
2. What would John Locke find so objectionable about the political theory of Robert Filmer? How would Filmer have answered Locke?

from taxation and deliberately blurring the distinctions between nobles and commoners.

Struggles between monarchs and nobles frequently affected relations between local and central government also. In France, the monarch sought to undermine the autonomy of noble-led provincial institutions by requiring the upper nobility to live at his palace. In Spain the monarchy, based in Castile, battled the independent-minded nobles of Aragon and Catalunya. Prussian rulers intruded themselves into the governance of formerly "free" cities by claiming the right to police and tax their inhabitants. The Habsburg emperors tried, unsuccessfully, to suppress the largely autonomous nobility of Hungary. Rarely, however, was the path of confrontation between crown and nobility successful in the long run. The most effective absolutist monarchies of the eighteenth century established a *modus vivendi* with their nobility, in which nobles came to see their own interests as tied to those of the crown. For this reason, cooperation more often characterized the relations between kings and nobles during the eighteenth-century "old regime" (*ancien régime*) than did conflict.

ALTERNATIVES TO ABSOLUTISM

Did John Locke's political principles lie behind the Glorious Revolution in England?

Although absolutism was the dominant model for seventeenth- and eighteenth-century European monarchs, it was by no means the only system by which Europeans governed themselves. In Venice, a republican oligarchy continued to rule the city. In the Netherlands, the territories that had won their independence from Spain during the early seventeenth century combined to form the United Provinces, the only truly new country to take shape in Europe during the early modern era. The Spanish wars created a deep distrust among the Dutch toward monarchs of any stripe. As a result, although Holland dominated the United Provinces, its House of Orange, which had led the wars for independence, never attempted to transform

Did John Locke's political principles lie behind the Glorious Revolution in England?

Alternatives to Absolutism   543

the new country from a republic into a monarchy. Even after 1688, when William of Orange also became King William III of England, the United Provinces remained a republic.

LIMITED MONARCHY: THE CASE OF ENGLAND

At a time when the powers of representative assemblies were being undermined across much of Europe, the English Parliament was the longest-surviving and most highly developed such body in Europe. English political theorists had for centuries seen their government as a mixed monarchy, composed of monarchical, noble, and nonnoble elements. During the seventeenth century, however, these traditions had come under threat, first through Charles I's attempts to rule without Parliament and then during Oliver Cromwell's dictatorial Protectorate. The restoration of the monarchy in 1660 resolved the question of whether England would in future be a republic or a monarchy; but the sort of monarchy England would become remained an open question as the reign of Charles II began.

THE REIGN OF CHARLES II

Despite the fact that he was the son of the beheaded and much-hated Charles I, Charles II (1660–1685) was initially welcomed by most English men and women. On his accession, he declared limited religious toleration for Protestant "dissenters" (Protestants who were not members of the official Church of England). He also promised to observe Magna Carta and the Petition of Right, declaring, with characteristic good humor, that he did not wish to "resume his travels." The unbuttoned moral atmosphere of his court, with its risqué plays, dancing, and sexual licentiousness, reflected a public desire to forget the restraints of the Puritan past. Some critics suggested that Charles, "that known enemy to virginity and chastity," took his role as the father of his country rather too seriously; but in fact he produced no legitimate heir and only a single illegitimate son to vie for the throne.

Having grown up an exile in France, Charles was an admirer of all things French. During the 1670s, however, he began openly to model his kingship on the absolutism of Louis XIV. As a result, the great men of England soon came to be publically divided between Charles's supporters (called by their opponents "Tories," a popular nickname for Irish Catholic bandits) and his

opponents (called by their opponents "Whigs," a nickname for Scottish Presbyterian rebels). Both sides feared absolutism, just as both sides feared a return to the bad old days of the 1640s, when resistance to the Crown had led to civil war and ultimately to republicanism. What they could not agree on was which possibility frightened them more.

Religion also remained a divisive issue. Charles was sympathetic to Roman Catholicism, even to the point of a deathbed conversion in 1685. During the 1670s, he briefly suspended civil penalties against Catholics and Protestant dissenters by asserting his right as king to ignore Parliamentary legislation. The resulting public outcry compelled him to retreat; but this controversy, together with rising opposition to Charles's ardently Catholic brother James as the heir to the throne, led to a series of Whig electoral victories between 1679 and 1681. When a group of radical Whigs attempted to exclude James by law from succeeding his brother on the throne, however, Charles stared the opposition down in the so-called Exclusion Crisis. Thereafter, Charles found that his rising revenues from customs duties, combined with a secret subsidy from Louis XIV, enabled him to govern without relying on Parliament for money. Charles further alarmed Whig politicans by executing several of them on charges of treason and by remodeling local government to make

Charles II.

it more amenable to royal control. Charles died in 1685 with his power enhanced, but he left behind a political and religious legacy that was to be the undoing of his less able and adroit successor.

THE REIGN OF JAMES II

James II was the very opposite of his worldly brother. A zealous Catholic convert, he alienated his Tory supporters, almost all of whom were members of the established Church of England, by suspending the laws preventing Catholics and Protestant dissenters from holding political office. James also flaunted his own Roman Catholicism, openly declaring his wish that all his subjects might be converted and publicly parading papal legates through the streets of London. When, in June 1688, he ordered all Church of England clergymen to read his decree of religious toleration from their pulpits, seven bishops refused and were promptly thrown in prison on charges of seditious libel. At their trial, however, they were declared not guilty, to the enormous satisfaction of the Protestant English populace.

Mary Stuart. Queen Mary and her husband William of Orange became Protestant joint rulers of England in a bloodless coup, taking power from her father, the Catholic James II.

The trial of the bishops was one event that brought matters to a head. The other was the unexpected birth of a son in 1688 to James and his second wife, Mary of Modena. This child, who was to be raised a Catholic, replaced James's much older Protestant daughter Mary Stuart as heir to the thrones of Scotland and England. So unexpected was this birth that there were widespread rumors that the child was not in fact James's son at all but had been smuggled into the royal bedchamber in a warming pan.

With the birth of the "warming-pan baby," events moved swiftly toward a climax. A delegation of Whigs and Tories crossed the channel to Holland to invite Mary Stuart and her Protestant husband, William of Orange, to cross to England with an invading army to preserve Protestantism and English liberties by summoning a new Parliament. As the leader of a continental coalition then at war with France, William also welcomed the opportunity to make England an ally against Louis XIV's expansionist foreign policy.

THE GLORIOUS REVOLUTION

William and Mary's invasion became a bloodless coup (although James is reputed to have suffered a nosebleed at the moment of crisis). Because James fled the country, Parliament was able to declare the throne vacant, clearing the way for William and Mary to accede as joint sovereigns by right of succession. The Bill of Rights, passed by Parliament and accepted by the new king and queen in 1689, reaffirmed English civil liberties such as trial by jury, habeas corpus (a guarantee that no one could be imprisoned unless charged with a crime), and the right to petition the monarch through Parliament for redress of grievances. The Bill of Rights also declared that the monarchy was subject to the law of the land. The Act of Toleration, also passed in 1689, granted Protestant dissenters the right to worship freely, though not to hold political office. And in 1701, the Act of Succession ordained that every future English monarch must be a member of the Church of England. With the childless Queen Mary now dead, this meant that the throne would pass, after King William's death, first to Mary's Protestant sister Anne (1702–1714) and then, if Anne died childless, to George, elector of the German principality of Hanover and the Protestant great-grandson of James I. In 1707, the formal Act of Union between Scotland and England ensured that the Catholic heirs of King James II would in future have no more right to the throne of Scotland than they did to the throne of England.

DID JOHN LOCKE'S POLITICAL PRINCIPLES LIE BEHIND THE GLORIOUS REVOLUTION IN ENGLAND?

ALTERNATIVES TO ABSOLUTISM   545

The English soon referred to the events of 1688 and 1689 as the "Glorious Revolution": glorious because it occurred without bloodshed and also because it firmly established England as a mixed monarchy governed by the "King in Parliament." Although William and Mary and their successors continued to exercise a large measure of executive power, after 1688 no English monarch attempted to govern without Parliament, which has met annually from that time on. Parliament, and especially the House of Commons, also strengthened its control over taxation and expenditure. Protestants in particular celebrated the Glorious Revolution as another sign of God's special favor to England, noting the favorable (Protestant) winds that blew William and Mary so speedily to England and kept King James's fleet from mounting an effective resistance.

Yet 1688 was not all glory. It was a revolution that consolidated the position of large property holders, whose control over local government had been threatened by Charles II and James II. It thus restored the status quo on behalf of a wealthy class of magnates that would soon become even wealthier from government patronage and the profits of war. It also brought misery to the Catholic minority in Scotland and to the Catholic majority in Ireland. After 1690, when King William won a decisive victory over James II's forces at the battle of the Boyne, power in Ireland would lie firmly in the hands of a "Protestant Ascendancy," whose dominance over Irish society would last until modern times.

JOHN LOCKE AND THE CONTRACT THEORY OF GOVERNMENT

The Glorious Revolution was the product of unique political circumstances, but it also reflected anti-absolutist theories of politics that were taking shape in the late seventeenth century in response to the ideas of writers such as Bodin, Hobbes, Filmer, and Bossuet. Chief among these opponents of absolutism was the Englishman John Locke (1632–1704), whose *Two Treatises of Government* were written before the revolution but published for the first time in 1690.

Locke maintained that humans had originally lived in a state of nature characterized by absolute freedom and equality, in which there was no government of any kind. The only law was the law of nature (which Locke equated with the law of reason), by which individuals enforced for themselves their natural rights to life, liberty, and property. Soon, however, humans began to perceive that the inconveniences of the state of nature outweighed its advantages. Accordingly, they agreed first to establish a civil society based on absolute equality and then to set up a government to arbitrate the disputes that might arise within this civil society. But they did not make government's powers absolute. Government was simply the combined power of all members of the society; as such, its authority could "be no more than those persons had in a state of nature before they entered into society, and gave it up to the community." All powers not expressly surrendered to the government were reserved to the people themselves; as a result, governmental authority was both contractual and conditional. If a government exceeded or abused the authority granted to it, society had the right to dissolve it and create another.

Locke condemned absolutism in every form. He denounced absolute monarchy, but he was no less critical of claims for the sovereignty of parliaments. Government, he argued, had been instituted to protect life, liberty, and property; no political authority could infringe an individual's natural rights to preserve these inviolate. The law of nature, which embodied these

> Locke maintained that humans had originally lived in a state of nature characterized by absolute freedom and equality, in which there was no government of any kind.

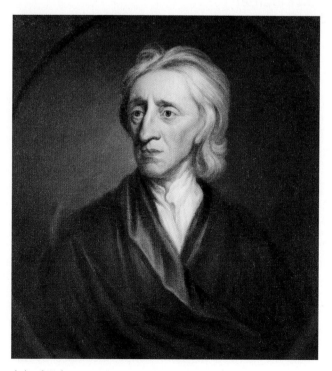

John Locke.

rights, was therefore an automatic and absolute limitation on every branch of government, whether legislative, executive, or judicial.

In the late eighteenth century, Locke's ideas would become an important element in the intellectual background of both the American and French revolutions. Between 1690 and 1720, however, they served a far less radical purpose. The landed magnates who replaced James II with William and Mary read Locke as a defense of their conservative revolution. Rather than protecting their liberty and property, James II had threatened both; hence the magnates were entitled to overthrow the tyranny he had established and replace it with a government that would defend their interests by preserving these natural rights. English government after 1689 would be dominated by Parliament; Parliament in turn was controlled by a landed aristocracy whose common interests far outweighed their incessant competition for office or their occasional disagreements over principle.

royalty. The main facade of the palace was a third of a mile in length. Inside, tapestries and paintings celebrated French military victories and royal triumphs; mirrors reflected shimmering light throughout the building. In the vast gardens outside, statues of the Greek god Apollo, god of the sun, recalled Louis's claim to be the "Sun King" of France. Noblemen vied to attend him when he arose from bed, ate his meals (usually stone cold after having traveled the distance of several city blocks from kitchen to table), strolled in his gardens (even the way the king walked was choreographed by the royal dancing master), or rode to the hunt. As the home of the Sun King, Louis's court was the epicenter of his gleaming royal resplendence. France's leading nobles were required to reside with him at Versailles for a portion of the year; the splendor of Louis's court was deliberately calculated to blind them to the possibility of disobedience while raising their prestige by associating them with himself. Instead of plotting some minor treason on his estate, a

THE ABSOLUTISM OF LOUIS XIV

How did Louis XIV strengthen his control over France?

In Louix XIV's state portrait, it is all but impossible to discern the human being behind the facade of the absolute monarch, dressed in his coronation robes and surrounded by the symbols of his authority. That facade was carefully and artfully constructed by Louis, who recognized, perhaps more fully than any other early modern ruler, the importance of theater to effective kingship. Louis and his successors deliberately staged theatrical demonstrations of their sovereignty to enhance their position as rulers endowed with godlike powers far removed from common humanity.

PERFORMING ROYALTY AT VERSAILLES

Louis's most elaborate exhibitions of his sovereignty took place at his palace at Versailles (*vubr-SY*), the town outside of Paris to which he moved his court. The palace and its grounds became a stage on which Louis mesmerized his nobles into obedience by his performance of the daily rituals and demonstrations of

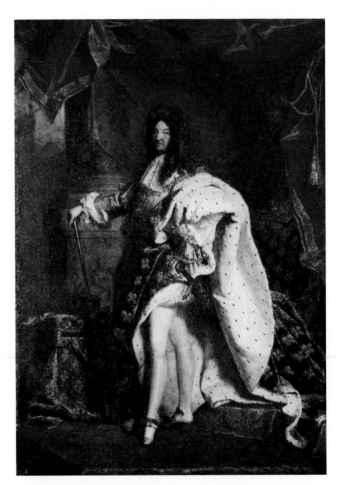

Louis XIV's State Portrait. This portrait by Hyacinthe Rigaud illustrates the degree to which absolute monarchy was defined in terms of studied performance.

The Château of Versailles. Dramatically expanded by Louis XIV in the 1660s from a hunting lodge to the principal royal residence and the seat of government, the château became a monument to the international power and prestige of the grand monarch.

marquis could instead enjoy the pleasure of knowing that on the morrow he would be privileged to engage the king in two or three minutes of conversation as the royal party made its stately progress through the vast palace halls. At the same time, however, the elaborate and almost impossibly detailed rules of etiquette around the court left these privileged nobles in constant suspense, forever fearful of offending the king by committing some trivial violation of proper manners.

Louis understood such theatricality as part of his duty as sovereign, a duty that he took with utmost seriousness. Though far from brilliant, he was hard-working and conscientious. Whether or not he actually remarked *"L'état, c'est moi"* ("I am the state"), he clearly saw himself as serving the interests of the state. As such, he considered himself personally responsible for the well-being of his subjects. "The deference and the respect that we receive from our subjects," he wrote in a memoir he prepared for his son on the art of ruling, "are not a free gift from them but payment for the justice and the protection that they expect from us. Just as they must honor us, we must protect and defend them."

ADMINISTRATION AND CENTRALIZATION

Louis defined his responsibilities in absolutist terms: to concentrate royal power so as to produce domestic tranquillity. While coopting the nobility into his own theater of royalty, he conciliated the upper bourgeoisie by enlisting them as royal administrators and especially as intendants, responsible for administering the thirty-six *generalités* into which France was divided. Intendants usually served outside the region where they were born and were thus unconnected with the local elites over whom they exercised authority. They held office at the king's pleasure and were clearly his men. Other administrators, often from families newly ennobled as a reward for their service, assisted in directing affairs of state from Versailles. These men were not actors in the theater of Louis the Sun King; rather, they were the hardworking assistants of Louis the royal custodian of his country's welfare.

Louis's administrators devoted much of their time and energy to collecting the taxes necessary to finance the large standing army on which his aggressive and highly personal foreign policy depended. These personal elements of early modern absolutism are important to remark. Despite its pretensions to be a political theory, absolutism was fundamentally an approach to government by which ambitious monarchs could increase their own power through conquest and display. As such, it was enormously expensive. In addition to the *taille*, or land tax, which increased throughout the seventeenth century and on which a surtax was levied as well, Louis's government introduced a *capitation* (a head tax) and pressed successfully for the collection of indirect taxes on salt (the *gabelle*), wine, tobacco, and other goods. Because the nobility was exempt from the *taille*, its burden fell most heavily on the peasantry, whose local revolts Louis easily crushed.

Regional opposition was curtailed, but by no means eliminated, during Louis's reign. By removing the provincial nobility to Versailles, Louis cut them off from their local sources of power and influence. To put an end to the obstructive powers of regional parlements, Louis also decreed that members of any parlement that refused to approve and enforce his laws would be summarily exiled. He also crippled the authority of the provincial estates of Brittany, Languedoc, and Franche-Comté. The Estates-General, the national French representative assembly last summoned in 1614, did not meet at all during Louis's reign. It would not meet again until 1789.

> Despite its pretensions to be a political theory, absolutism was fundamentally an approach to government by which ambitious monarchs could increase their own power through conquest and display.

LOUIS XIV'S RELIGIOUS POLICIES

Both for reasons of state and of personal conscience, Louis was determined to impose religious unity on France, regardless of the economic and social costs this entailed. Louis believed firmly that God would favor him in return for such fidelity.

Although the vast majority of the French population was Roman Catholic, French Catholics were divided between Quietists, Jansenists, Jesuits, and Gallicans. Quietists preached retreat into personal mysticism, emphasizing a direct relationship between God and the individual human heart. Such doctrine, dispensing as it did with the intermediary services of the church, was suspect in the eyes of absolutists wedded to the doctrine of *un roi, une loi, une foi* ("one king, one law, one

faith"). Jansenism—a movement named for its founder Cornelius Jansen, a seventeenth-century bishop of Ypres—held to an Augustinian doctrine of predestination that could sound and look surprisingly like a kind of Catholic Calvinism. Louis vigorously persecuted Quietists and Jansenists, offering them the choice of recanting or of prison and exile. Instead, he supported the Jesuits in their efforts to create a Counter-Reformation Catholic Church in France. Louis's support for the Jesuits upset the traditional Gallican Catholics of France, however, who desired a French church independent of papal, Jesuit, and Spanish influence (which they tended to equate). As a result of this dissension among Catholics, the religious aura of Louis's kingship diminished during the course of his reign.

Against the Protestant Huguenots, however, Louis waged unrelenting war. Protestant churches and schools were destroyed, and Protestants were banned from many professions, including medicine and printing. In 1685, Louis revoked the Edict of Nantes, the legal foundation of the toleration Huguenots had enjoyed since 1598. Protestant clerics were exiled, laymen were sent to the galleys as slaves, and their children were forcibly baptized as Catholics. Many families converted, but 200,000 Protestant refugees fled to England, Holland, Germany, and America, bringing with them their professional and artisanal skills. This was an enormous loss to France. Among many other examples, the silk industries of Berlin and London were established by Huguenots fleeing Louis XIV's persecution.

COLBERT AND ROYAL FINANCE

Louis's drive to unify and centralize France depended on a vast increase in royal revenues engineered by Jean Baptiste Colbert, the king's finance minister from 1664 until his death in 1683. Colbert tightened the process of tax collection and eliminated wherever possible the practice of tax farming (which permitted collection agents to retain for themselves a percentage of the taxes they gathered for the king). When Colbert assumed office, only about 25 percent of the taxes collected throughout the kingdom reached the treasury. By the time he died, that figure had risen to 80 percent. Under Colbert's direction, the state sold public

MERCANTILISM AND WAR

Jean-Baptiste Colbert (1619–1683) served as Louis XIV's finance minister from 1664 until his death. He worked assiduously to promote commerce, build up French industry, and increase exports. However much Colbert himself may have seen his economic policies as ends in themselves, to Louis they were always means to the end of waging war. Ultimately, Louis's wars undermined the prosperity that Colbert tried so hard to create. This memorandum, written to Louis in 1670, illustrates clearly the mercantilist presumptions of self-sufficiency on which Colbert operated: every item needed to build up the French navy must ultimately be produced in France, even if it could be acquired at less cost from elsewhere.

And since Your Majesty has wanted to work diligently at reestablishing his naval forces, and since afore that it has been necessary to make very great expenditures, since all merchandise, munitions and manufactured items formerly came from Holland and the countries of the North, it has been absolutely necessary to be especially concerned with finding within the realm, or with establishing in it, everything which might be necessary for this great plan.

To this end, the manufacture of tar was established in Médoc, Auvergne, Dauphiné, and Provence; iron cannons, in Burgundy, Nivernois, Saintonge and Périgord; large anchors in Dauphiné, Nivernois, Brittany, and Rochefort; sailcloth for the Levant, in Dauphiné; coarse muslin, in Auvergne; all the implements for pilots and others, at Dieppe and La Rochelle; the cutting of wood suitable for vessels, in Burgundy, Dauphiné, Brittany, Normandy, Poitou, Saintonge, Provence, Guyenne, and the Pyrenees; masts, of a sort once unknown in this realm, have been found in Provence, Languedoc, Auvergne, Dauphiné, and in the Pyrenees. Iron, which was obtained from Sweden and Biscay, is currently manufactured in the realm. Fine hemp for ropes, which came from Prussia and from Piedmont, is currently obtained in Burgundy,

Mâconnais, Bresse, Dauphiné; and markets for it have since been established in Berry and in Auvergne, which always provides money in these provinces and keeps it within the realm.

In a word, everything serving for the construction of vessels is currently established in the realm, so that Your Majesty can get along without foreigners for the navy and will even, in a short time, be able to supply them and gain their money in this fashion. And it is with this same objective of having everything necessary to provide abundantly for his navy and that of his subjects that he is working at the general reform of all the forests in his realm, which, being as carefully preserved as they are at present, will abundantly produce all the wood necessary for this.

Charles W. Cole, *Colbert and a Century of French Mercantilism*, 2 vols (New York, 1939), p. 320.

QUESTIONS FOR ANALYSIS

1. Could Colbert's economic policies have been used more wisely by Louis XIV? Can mercantilist policies be implemented without resorting to warfare? Is war a necessary component of mercantilism?

offices, including judgeships and mayoralities, and guilds purchased the right to enforce trade regulations. Colbert also tried to increase the nation's income by controlling and regulating its foreign trade. As a confirmed mercantilist (see "Mercantilism and War" on the previous page), Colbert believed that France's wealth would increase if its imports were reduced and its exports increased. He therefore imposed tariffs on foreign goods imported into France while using state money to promote the domestic manufacture of such formerly imported goods as silk, lace, tapestries, and glass. He was especially anxious to create domestic industries capable of producing all the goods France would need for war. To encourage domestic trade, he also improved France's roads, bridges, and waterways.

Despite Colbert's efforts to increase crown revenues, his policies ultimately foundered on the insatiable demands of Louis XIV's wars. Colbert himself foresaw this result when he lectured the king in 1680: "Trade is the source of public finance and public finance is the vital nerve of war. . . . I beg your Majesty to permit me only to say to him that in war as in peace he has never consulted the amount of money available in determining his expenditures." Louis, however, paid him no heed. As a result, by the end of Louis's reign, his aggressive foreign policy lay in ruins and his country's finances had been shattered by the unsustainable costs of war.

The Wars of Louis XIV to 1697

Absolutism was never an end in itself for Louis. It was, rather, a means to an end: glory at home achieved through military victories abroad. From 1661, when Louis began his personal rule, until his death in 1715, Louis kept France on an almost constant war footing. His wars had two main objectives: to lessen the threat posed to France by the Habsburg powers that surrounded it in Spain, the Spanish Netherlands, and the Holy Roman Empire; and to promote the dynastic interests of his own family. Happily for Louis, these two objectives frequently coincided. In 1667–1668 he attacked the Spanish Netherlands, which he claimed on behalf of his wife, capturing the territory of Lille. In 1672, offended by the Dutch role in thwarting his earlier attacks on the Spanish Netherlands and by Dutch propaganda belittling him, Louis attacked Holland and its new leader William of Orange (1672–1702). The great-grandson of the sixteenth-century Protestant champion William the Silent, William of Orange would become the leading figure in Europe resisting Louis's wars of conquest.

The Dutch war ended in 1678–1679 with the Treaty of Nijmegen. Although Louis made little headway in the Low Countries, he did succeed in conquering and holding the eastern territory of Franche-Comté. Thus encouraged, he now turned his attentions eastward, capturing the free city of Strasbourg (1681), Luxembourg (1684), and Cologne (1688). He then pushed across the Rhine to pillage and burn the middle Rhineland, which he claimed on behalf of his unhappy sister-in-law, the daughter of the territory's ruler, the Elector Palatine.

In response to these new aggressions, William of Orange organized the League of Augsburg, which eventually united Holland, England, Spain, Sweden, Bavaria, Saxony, the Rhine Palatinate, and the Austrian Habsburgs against Louis. The resulting Nine Years' War (1689–1697) was extraordinarily destructive. Most of its campaigns were fought in the Low Countries, but the conflict extended from Ireland to India to North America (where it was known as King William's War). Finally, in 1697, the Peace of Ryswick compelled Louis to return most of France's recent gains, except for Strasbourg and its surrounding territory of Alsace. This treaty also recognized William of Orange as the new king of England, thus legitimizing the Glorious Revolution of 1688 that had replaced the Catholic King James II with the Protestant monarchs William and Mary.

The War of the Spanish Succession

The League of Augsburg reflected the emergence of a new diplomatic goal in western and central Europe: the preservation of a balance of power designed to prevent any single country, such as France, from becoming so powerful as to threaten the position of the other major powers within the European state system. This goal

CHRONOLOGY	
THE SPANISH SUCCESSION	
Philip IV	1621–1665
Charles II	1665–1700
Philip V (Philip of Anjou)	1700–1746
Louis XV (of France)	1715–1774

would animate European diplomacy for the next 200 years, until the entire balance-of-power system collapsed in 1914 with the outbreak of World War I. The main proponents of balance-of-power diplomacy were England, the United Provinces, Prussia, and Austria. A balance of power was not, however, a goal to which Louis XIV subscribed. Louis made peace in 1697 with the League of Augsburg because his country was exhausted by war and famine (almost a million people had died in the great French famine of 1693–1694, approximately 5 percent of the entire population). But he was also looking ahead to the real prize: a French claim to succeed to the throne of Spain and so to control the Spanish Empire in the New World, Italy, the Netherlands, and the Philippines.

Louis had married, as his first wife, the elder daughter of King Philip IV of Spain (1621–1665). Philip's younger daughter had married the Holy Roman emperor, Leopold I of Austria (1658–1705). Neither daughter was expected to inherit the Spanish throne. But Philip's only son, King Charles II of Spain (1665–1700), was a mental and physical invalid throughout his life. As it became clear during the 1690s that he would not live much longer, all the major European powers began to concern themselves with the succession to the Spanish throne. The stakes were high. If one of Leopold's sons succeeded, then France would be surrounded on all sides by a united Habsburg power. If Louis XIV's son or grandson succeeded, however, then France would become the preponderant power in Europe and the Americas.

Several schemes to resolve the crisis were floated during the 1690s. One would have given the Spanish succession to the six-year-old prince of Bavaria, a grandnephew of Charles II, but the boy died before the scheme could come to fruition. Another proposal was to give Spain's Italian possessions to Louis XIV and the rest of the Spanish Empire to Leopold; but Leopold blocked this, arguing that the Italian territories should belong to him anyway as Holy Roman emperor and acknowledging, at least tacitly, that Austria lacked the naval capacity to rule Spain's colonial territories in Asia and America.

King Charles II's advisers were not consulted on any of these plans. Their interests were to avoid partition altogether by passing the entire Spanish Empire to a single heir. To achieve this, they arranged for King

> The main proponents of balance-of-power diplomacy were England, the United Provinces, Prussia, and Austria. A balance of power was not, however, a goal to which Louis XIV subscribed.

Charles, in his will, to leave all his possessions to Louis XIV's younger grandson, Philip of Anjou, on two conditions: that Philip renounce his claim to the French throne in favor of his elder brother Louis (who had the first claim by inheritance anyway) and that he keep the Spanish Empire intact. The terms of this will were kept secret but were arranged in consultation with Louis XIV. As soon as Charles II died, Philip V (1700–1746) was therefore proclaimed the new king of Spain, and Louis XIV rushed French troops into the Spanish Netherlands. Louis also sent French merchants into Spanish America and withdrew recognition from William of Orange as king of England.

The resulting war pitted England, the United Provinces, Austria, and Prussia against France, Bavaria, and Spain. William of Orange died in 1702, just as the war began. His role as first general of the coalition passed to two brilliant strategists: the Englishman John Churchill, Duke of Marlborough, and Prince Eugene of Savoy, an upper-class Austrian soldier of fortune. Under their command the allied forces fought a series of fierce battles in the Low Countries and Germany, including an extraordinary march deep into Bavaria, where they inflicted a devastating defeat on the French and their Bavarian allies at Blenheim (1704), killing or capturing 30,000 of the 50,000 troops arrayed against them. Soon thereafter, the English navy captured Gibraltar and the island of Minorca, thus establishing a strategic and commercial foothold in the Mediterranean and opening a new military theater in Spain itself.

By 1709, France was on the verge of defeat. But the allies overreached themselves by demanding that Louis join their war against his own grandson in Spain. The war therefore continued, at enormous cost to both sides. At the battle of Malplaquet (1709), 80,000 French soldiers faced 110,000 allied troops. Marlborough and Eugene forced the French to retreat but suffered 24,000 casualties, twice those of the French. Louis's general wrote to him after the battle, "if God gives us the grace to lose another such battle, Your Majesty may count on his enemies being destroyed."

Queen Anne of England (Mary's sister and William's successor) gradually grew disillusioned with the war and dismissed Marlborough, her most competent general. English and Dutch merchants were also complaining loudly about the damage the war was doing to trade and commerce. A new Tory government in England replaced the Whigs and began sending out peace feelers to France. Meanwhile, the diplomatic situation in Europe was also changing. Leopold I of Austria had died in 1705. When his elder son and successor Joseph I died in 1711, the Austrian monarchy fell to Leopold's younger son, the archduke Charles, who had been the allies' candidate for the throne of Spain. With Charles VI (1711–1740) now the Austrian ruler and the Holy Roman emperor, the prospect of his accession to the Spanish throne threatened to upset the balance of power in Europe all over again.

THE TREATY OF UTRECHT

In 1713 the war finally came to an end with the Treaty of Utrecht. Its terms were reasonably fair to all sides. Philip V, Louis XIV's grandson, remained on the throne of Spain and retained Spain's colonial empire intact; but in return, Louis agreed that France and Spain would never be united under the same ruler. Austria gained territories in the Spanish Netherlands and Italy, including Milan and Naples. The Dutch were guaranteed protection of their borders against

EUROPE AFTER THE TREATY OF UTRECHT (1713)

To what extent did the balance of power within Europe change as a result of the Treaty of Utrecht? Given their geographic location and the extent after 1713, would you expect the Habsburg lands to dominate eighteenth-century Europe? Why or why not?

The Treaty of Utrecht, 1713. This illustration from a French royal almanac depicts the treaty that ended the war of Spanish Succession and reshaped the balance of power in western Europe in favor of Britain and France.

The Treaty of Utrecht reshaped the balance of power in western Europe in fundamental ways. Spain's collapse was already precipitous; by 1713 it was complete. Spain would remain the "sick man of Europe" for the next two centuries. Holland's decline was more gradual, but by 1713 its greatest days were also over. The Dutch would continue to control the Spice Islands, but in the Atlantic world Britain and France were now the dominant powers. They would continue to duel for another half century for control over North America; but at Utrecht the balance of colonial power shifted decisively in Britain's favor. Within Europe, the myth of French military supremacy had been shattered. Britain's navy, not France's army, would rule the new imperial and commercial world of the eighteenth century.

THE REMAKING OF CENTRAL AND EASTERN EUROPE

What changes lay behind the growing power of Prussia?

The decades between 1680 and 1720 were equally decisive in reshaping the balance of power in central and eastern Europe. As Ottoman power waned, the Austro-Hungarian Empire of the Habsburgs emerged as the dominant power in central and southeastern Europe. To the north, Brandenburg-Prussia was also a rising power. The most dramatic changes, however, were occurring in Russia, which would emerge from a long war with Sweden as the dominant power in the Baltic Sea and would soon become a mortal threat to the combined kingdom of Poland-Lithuania.

THE HABSBURG EMPIRE

In 1683, the Ottoman Turks launched their last assault on Vienna. Only the arrival of 70,000 Polish troops saved the Austrian capital from capture. Thereafter, however, Ottoman power in southeastern Europe declined rapidly. By 1699, Austria had reconquered most of Hungary from the Ottomans; by 1718, it controlled all of Hungary and also Transylvania and Serbia. In 1722, Austria acquired the territory of Silesia from Poland. With Hungary now a buffer state between Austria and the Ottomans, Vienna emerged as one of the great cultural and political capitals of eighteenth-century Europe, and

future invasions by France, but the French retained both Lille and Strasbourg. The biggest winner by far was Great Britain (as the combined kingdoms of England and Scotland were known after 1707), which kept Gibraltar and Minorca and also acquired large chunks of French territory in the New World, including Newfoundland, mainland Nova Scotia, the Hudson Bay, and the Caribbean island of St. Kitts. Even more valuable, however, Britain also extracted from Spain the right to transport and sell African slaves in Spanish America. As a result, the British were now poised to become the principal slave merchants and the dominant colonial and commercial power of the eighteenth-century world.

Austria became one of the arbiters of the European balance of power.

Although the Austrian Habsburgs retained their title as Holy Roman emperors and after 1713 also held lands in the Netherlands and Italy, their real power lay in Austria, Bohemia, Moravia, Galicia, and Hungary. These territories were geographically contiguous, but they were deeply divided by ethnicity, religion, and language. Despite the centralizing efforts of a series of Habsburg rulers, their empire would remain a rather loose confederation of highly disparate territories and possessions.

In Bohemia and Moravia, the Habsburgs encouraged landlords to produce crops for export by forcing peasants to provide three days of unpaid work service per week to their lords. In return, the landed elites of these territories permitted the emperors to reduce the political independence of their traditional legislative Estates. In Hungary, however, the powerful and independent nobility resisted such blandishments. Habsburg efforts to administer Hungary through the army and to impose Catholic religious uniformity also met with stiff resistance. As a result, Hungary would remain a semi-autonomous region within the empire whose support the Austrians could never take for granted.

After 1740, the empress Maria Theresa (1740–1780) and her son Joseph II (1765–1790; from 1765 until 1780 the two were co-rulers) pioneered a new style of "enlightened absolutism" within their empire: centralizing the administration in Vienna, increasing taxation, creating a professional standing army, and tightening their control over the church while creating a statewide system of primary education, relaxing censorship, and instituting a new, more liberal criminal code. But in practice, Habsburg absolutism, whether enlightened or not, was always limited by the diversity of its imperial territories and by the weakness of its local governmental institutions.

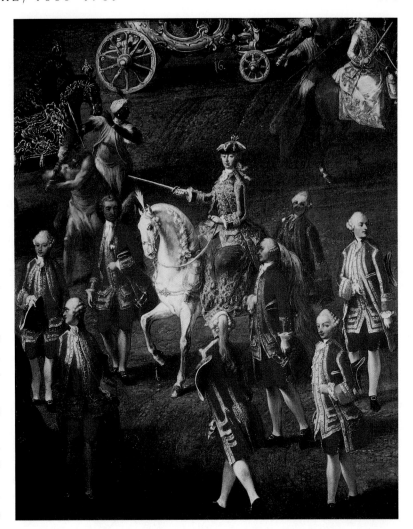

Maria Theresa of Austria. The empress was a formidable monarch and a match for Frederick the Great.

THE RISE OF BRANDENBURG-PRUSSIA

After the Ottoman collapse, the main threat to Austria came from the rising power of Brandenburg-Prussia. Like Austria, Prussia was a composite state made up of several geographically divided territories acquired through inheritance by the Hohenzollern family. Their two main holdings, however, were Brandenburg, centered on its capital city, Berlin, and the duchy of East Prussia. Between these two territories lay Pomerania (claimed by Sweden) and an important part of the kingdom of Poland, including the port of Gdansk (Danzig). The Hohenzollerns' aim was to unite their state by acquiring these intervening territories. Over the course of more than a century of steady state building, they finally succeeded in doing so. In the process, Brandenburg-Prussia became the dominant military power of central Europe and a key player in the balance-of-power diplomacy of the mid-eighteenth century.

The foundations of Prussian greatness were laid by Frederick William, the "Great Elector" (1640–1688). By siding with Poland in a war against Sweden in the late 1650s, he obtained the Polish king's surrender of nominal overlordship of East Prussia. By some crafty diplomatic shuffling during the 1670s, he also protected his western provinces from French attack by returning Pomerania, captured in a recent war, to France's Swedish ally. Behind these diplomatic triumphs, however, lay the Elector's success in building an army and mobilizing the resources to pay for it. By granting to the powerful nobles of his territories (known as *Junkers*) the right to enserf their peasants, by relying on them to staff the officer corps of his army, and by guaranteeing their immunity from taxation, Frederick William gained their support for the effective and highly autocratic taxation system he imposed on the rest of the country. Secure in their control over their own estates and increasingly wealthy from the profits of their grain trade with western Europe, the Junkers were content to surrender management of the Prussian state to a centralized bureaucracy whose most important duty was to increase the size and strength of the Prussian army. In turn, the army became the Great Elector's most important instrument in tightening his own control over the far-flung territories he ruled.

By supporting Austria in the War of the Spanish Succession, the Great Elector's son, Frederick I (1688–

1713), received the right to style himself king of Prussia. (As Holy Roman emperor, the Austrian monarch had the right to create kings.) And by joining the Great Northern War on the side of Russia against Sweden (discussed later in this chapter), Frederick paved the way for Prussia to recover and extend its control over Pomerania. As king, however, his main attention was devoted to developing the cultural life of his new royal capital, Berlin, along the lines laid down by Louis XIV of France.

Frederick William I (1713–1740) returned to the policies of his grandfather. His overriding concern was to build a first-rate army; so single-mindedly did he pursue this goal that he came to be called "the sergeant king." During his reign, the Prussian army grew from 30,000 to 83,000 men, the fourth largest army in Europe after those of France, Russia, and Austria. He also increased the size of the Prussian army in another way by creating a private regiment, the Potsdam Giants, composed exclusively of soldiers over six feet in height. To support his army, Frederick William I increased taxes and streamlined their collection, while shunning the expensive luxuries of court life. So reluctant was he

Prussians Swearing Allegiance to the Great Elector at Königsberg, 1663. The occasion on which the Prussian estates first acknowledged the overlordship of their ruler. This ceremony marked the beginning of the centralization of the Prussian state.

to waste state resources on personal indulgences that it was said he had to invite himself to a nobleman's table to enjoy a good meal. For him, the theater of absolutism was not the palace but the office, where he personally supervised his beloved army and the offices of state that sustained it.

A hard, unimaginative man, Frederick William I had little use for his son Frederick, whose passion was not the army but the flute and who admired French culture as much as his father disdained it. It is not surprising that young Frederick rebelled; in 1730, when he was eighteen, he ran away from court with a friend. Apprehended, the companions were returned to the king, who executed his son's friend before Frederick's eyes. The grisly lesson took. Although Frederick never gave up his love of music and literature, he thereafter bound himself to his royal duties, living in accordance with his own image of himself as "first servant of the state" and earning history's title of Frederick the Great.

Frederick William I had made Prussia a strong state. Frederick the Great (1740–1786) raised his country to the status of a major power. As soon as he became king in 1740, Frederick mobilized the army his father had never taken into battle and occupied the Austrian province of Silesia. Prussia had no conceivable claim to Silesia, but the territory was both rich and poorly defended, and so Frederick seized it with the support of France. The new Habsburg empress Maria Theresa counterattacked; but despite the support of both Britain and Hungary, she was unable to recover Silesia. Emboldened by this early success, Frederick spent the rest of his reign consolidating his gains in Silesia and extending his control over the Polish territories that lay between Prussia and Brandenburg. Through relentless diplomacy and frequent war, Frederick succeeded by 1786 in transforming Prussia into a powerful, contiguous territorial kingdom.

To ensure a united domestic front against Prussia's enemies, Frederick was careful to guarantee the support of the Junkers for his policies. His father had recruited civil servants according to merit rather than birth, but Frederick relied on the nobility to staff the army and his expanding administration. Remarkably, Frederick's strategy worked. His nobility remained loyal, while Frederick fashioned the most highly professional and efficient bureaucracy in Europe.

> Although Frederick never gave up his love of music and literature, he thereafter bound himself to his royal duties, living in accordance with his own image of himself as "first servant of the state" and earning history's title of Frederick the Great.

Frederick showed the same concern for Junker sensibilities in his domestic policies. Like his contemporary Joseph II of Austria, Frederick was an enlightened absolutist who supervised a series of social reforms, prohibited the judicial torture of accused criminals and the bribing of judges, and established a system of elementary schools. Although strongly anti-Semitic, he encouraged religious toleration toward Christians and even declared that he would happily build a mosque in Berlin if he could find enough Muslims to fill it. On his own royal estates he abolished capital punishment, curtailed the forced labor services of his peasantry, and granted them long leases on the land they worked. He also fostered scientific forestry and the cultivation of new crops. He cleared new lands in Silesia and brought in thousands of immigrants to cultivate them. When wars ruined their farms, he supplied his peasants with new livestock and tools. But he never attempted to extend these reforms to the estates of the nobility. To have done so would have alienated the very group on whom Frederick's rule depended.

CHRONOLOGY

ABSOLUTIST RULERS IN CENTRAL EUROPE

France	
Louis XIV	1643–1715
Louis XV	1715–1774
Louis XVI	1774–1792
Brandenburg-Prussia	
Frederick William, The Great Elector	1640–1688
Frederick I	1688–1713
Frederick William I	1713–1740
Frederick the Great	1740–1786
Austria	
Leopold I	1658–1705
Charles VI	1711–1740
Maria Theresa	1740–1780
Joseph II	1765–1790
Russia	
Peter the Great	1689–1725
Catherine the Great	1762–1796

IN WHAT WAYS DID RUSSIAN ABSOLUTISM DIFFER FROM ITS WESTERN EUROPEAN COUNTERPARTS?

AUTOCRACY IN RUSSIA   557

AUTOCRACY IN RUSSIA

In what ways did Russian absolutism differ from its western European counterparts?

An even more dramatic transformation took place in Russia under the dynamic rule of Tsar Peter I (1672–1725). Peter's accomplishments alone would have earned him his title of "Great." But his imposing height—he was six feet eight inches tall—as well as his mercurial personality—jesting one moment, raging the next—certainly added to the outsize impression he made on his contemporaries. Peter was not the first tsar to bring his country into contact with western Europe, but his policies were decisive in making Russia a great European power.

THE EARLY YEARS OF PETER'S REIGN

Since 1613 Russia had been ruled by members of the Romanov Dynasty, who had attempted with some success to restore political stability after the chaotic "time of troubles" that followed the death of the blood-thirsty, half-mad tsar Ivan the Terrible in 1584. But the Romanovs faced a severe threat to their rule between 1667 and 1671, when a Cossack leader (the Russian Cossacks were semi-autonomous bands of peasant cavalrymen) named Stenka Razin led a rebellion in southeastern Russia. This uprising found widespread support, not only from oppressed serfs but also from non-Russian tribes in the lower Volga region who longed to cast off the domination of Moscow. But ultimately Tsar Alexis I (1654–1676) and the Russian nobility were able to defeat Razin's zealous but disorganized bands of rebels, slaughtering more than 100,000 of them in the process.

Like Louis XIV of France, Peter came to the throne as a young boy, and his minority was marked by political dissension and court intrigue. In 1689, however, at the age of seventeen, he overthrew the regency of his half-sister Sophia and assumed personal control of the state. Determined to make Russia into a great military power, the young tsar traveled to Holland and England during the 1690s to study shipbuilding and to recruit skilled foreign workers to help him build a navy. While he was abroad, however, his elite palace guard (the *streltsy*) rebelled, attempting to restore Sophia to the throne. Peter quickly returned home from Vienna and crushed the rebellion with striking savagery. About

1,200 suspected conspirators were summarily executed, many of them gibbeted outside the walls of the Kremlin, where their bodies rotted for months as a graphic reminder of the fate awaiting those who dared challenge the tsar's authority.

THE TRANSFORMATION OF THE TSARIST STATE

Peter is most famous as the tsar who attempted to westernize Russia by imposing a series of social and cultural reforms on the traditional Russian nobility: ordering noblemen to cut off their long beards and flowing sleeves; publishing a book of manners that forbade spitting on the floor and eating with one's fingers; encouraging polite conversation between the sexes; and requiring noblewomen to appear, together with men, in Western garb at weddings, banquets, and other public occasions. The children of Russian nobles were sent to western European courts for their education. Thousands of western European experts were brought to Russia to staff the new schools and academies Peter

Peter the Great. As tsar, Peter I westernized Russia with social and cultural reforms, among them the mandate that traditional nobles cut off their long beards.

built; to design the new buildings he constructed; and to serve in the tsar's army, navy, and administration.

These measures were important, but it is misleading to see them as driven by the tsar's desire to modernize or westernize Russia. Peter's policies transformed Russian life in fundamental ways, but his real goal was to make Russia a great military power, not to remake Russian society. His new taxation system (1724), for example, which assessed taxes on individuals rather than on households, rendered many of the traditional divisions of Russian peasant society obsolete. It was created, however, to raise more money for war. His Table of Ranks, imposed in 1722, had a similar impact on the nobility. By insisting that all nobles must work their way up from the (lower) landlord class to the (higher) administrative class and to the (highest) military class, Peter reversed the traditional hierarchy of Russian noble society, which had valued landlords by birth above administrators and soldiers who had risen by merit. But he also created a powerful new incentive to lure his nobility into administrative and military service to the tsar.

As autocrat of all the Russias, Peter the Great was the absolute master of his empire to a degree unmatched elsewhere in Europe. After 1649, Russian peasants were legally the property of their landlords; by 1750, half were serfs and the other half were state peasants who lived on lands owned by the tsar himself. State peasants could be conscripted to serve as soldiers in the tsar's army, workers in his factories (whose productive capacity increased enormously during Peter's reign), or as forced laborers in his building projects. But serfs too could be taxed by the tsar and summoned for military service, as could their lords. All Russians, of whatever rank, were thus expected to serve the tsar, and all Russia was considered in some sense to belong to him.

To further consolidate his power, Peter replaced the Duma—the nation's rudimentary national assembly— with a hand-picked senate, a group of nine administrators who supervised military and civilian affairs. In religious matters, he took direct control over the Russian Orthodox church by appointing an imperial official to manage its affairs. To cope with the demands of war, he also fashioned a new, larger, and more efficient administration, for which he recruited both nobles and nonnobles. But rank in the new bureaucracy did not de-

> By insisting that all nobles must work their way up from the (lower) landlord class to the (higher) administrative class and to the (highest) military class, Peter reversed the traditional hierarchy of Russian noble society, which had valued landlords by birth above administrators and soldiers who had risen by merit.

pend on birth. One of his principal advisers, Alexander Menshikov, began his career as a cook and finished as a prince. This degree of social mobility would have been impossible in any contemporary western European country. Instead, noble status depended on governmental service, with all nobles expected to participate in Peter's army or administration. Peter was not entirely successful in enforcing this requirement, but the administrative machinery he devised furnished Russia with its ruling class for the next 200 years.

PETER'S FOREIGN POLICY

The goal of Peter's foreign policy was to secure year-round ports for Russia on the Black Sea and the Baltic Sea. In the Black Sea, his enemy was the Ottomans. Here, however, he had little success; although he captured the port of Azov in 1696, he was forced to return it in 1711. Russia would not secure its position in the Black Sea until the end of the eighteenth century. In the north, however, Peter achieved much more. In 1700, he began what would become a twenty-one-year war with Sweden, hitherto the dominant power in the Baltic Sea. By 1703, Peter had secured a foothold on the Gulf of Finland and immediately began to build a new capital city there, which he named St. Petersburg. After 1709, when Russian armies, supported by Prussia, decisively defeated the Swedes at the battle of Poltava, work on Peter's new capital city accelerated. An army of serfs was now conscripted to build the new city, whose centerpiece was a royal palace designed to imitate and rival Louis XIV's Versailles.

The Great Northern War with Sweden ended in 1721 with the Peace of Nystad. This treaty marks a realignment of power in eastern Europe comparable to that effected by the Treaty of Utrecht in the west. Sweden lost its North Sea territories to Hanover and its Baltic German territories to Prussia. Its eastern territories, including the entire Gulf of Finland, Livonia, and Estonia, passed to Russia. Sweden was now a second-rank power in the northern European world. Poland-Lithuania survived but faced the expanding power of Prussia in the west and the expanding power of Russia in the east. It too was a declining power; by

In what ways did Russian absolutism differ from its western European counterparts?

Autocracy in Russia   559

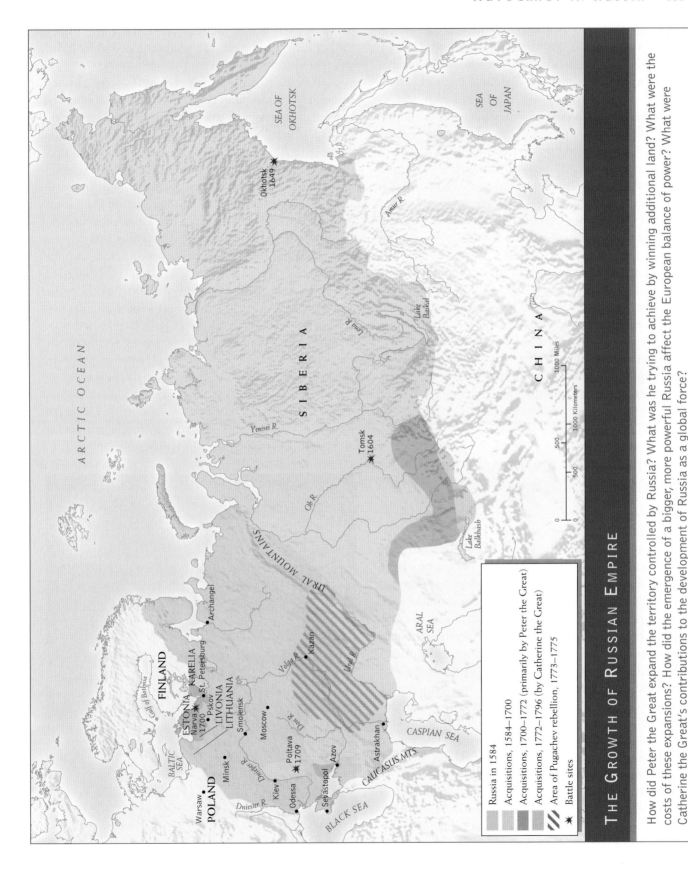

SEA OF OKHOTSK

SEA OF JAPAN

Okhotsk 1649

ARCTIC OCEAN

Amur R.

Lake Baikal

CHINA

S I B E R I A

Lena R.

Yenisei R.

Tomsk 1604

Ob R.

1000 Miles

1000 Kilometers

500

500

0

0

URAL MOUNTAINS

Archangel

Lake Balkhash

ARAL SEA

FINLAND

KARELIA

St. Petersburg

ESTONIA

Narva 1700

Pskov

LIVONIA

LITHUANIA

Smolensk

Moscow

Kazan

Volga R.

Ural R.

Gulf of Bothnia

BALTIC SEA

Minsk

POLAND

Warsaw

Dnieper R.

Kiev

Odessa

Dniester R.

Poltava 1709

Sevastopol

Azov

Don R.

Astrakhan

CASPIAN SEA

CAUCASUS MTS.

BLACK SEA

Russia in 1584
Acquisitions, 1584–1700
Acquisitions, 1700–1772 (primarily by Peter the Great)
Acquisitions, 1772–1796 (by Catherine the Great)
Area of Pugachev rebellion, 1773–1775
✳ Battle sites

The Growth of Russian Empire

How did Peter the Great expand the territory controlled by Russia? What was he trying to achieve by winning additional land? What were the costs of these expansions? How did the emergence of a bigger, more powerful Russia affect the European balance of power? What were Catherine the Great's contributions to the development of Russia as a global force?

the end of the eighteenth century, the kingdom would disappear altogether, its territories swallowed up by its more powerful neighbors. The victors at Nystad were the Prussians and the Russians, both of whom secured their position along the Baltic coast and so positioned themselves to take advantage of the lucrative eastern European grain trade with western Europe.

Peter's victory had come at enormous cost. Direct taxation increased 500 percent during his reign, and his army in the 1720s numbered more than 300,000 men. Peter had made Russia a force to be reckoned with on the European scene; but in so doing, he had also aroused great resentment, especially among his nobility. Peter's only son and heir, Alexis, became the focus for conspiracies against the tsar, until finally Peter had him arrested and executed in 1718. As a result, when Peter died in 1725, he left no son to succeed him. A series of ineffective tsars followed, mostly creatures of the palace guard, under whom the resentful nobles reversed many of Peter the Great's reforms. In 1762, however, the crown passed to Catherine the Great, a ruler whose ambitions and determination were equal to those of her great predecessor.

CATHERINE THE GREAT AND THE PARTITION OF POLAND

Catherine was a German who came to the throne in 1762 on the death of her husband, the weak (and possibly mad) Tsar Peter III, who was deposed and executed in a palace coup that Catherine herself may have helped arrange. Although she cultivated an image of herself as an enlightened ruler (she corresponded with French philosophers, wrote plays, and began to compose a history of Russia), Catherine was determined not to lose the support of the nobility who had placed her on the throne. As a result, her efforts at social reform did not extend much beyond the founding of hospitals and orphanages and the creation of an elementary school system for the children of the provincial nobility. Like her contemporary enlightened absolutists Joseph of Austria and Frederick the Great of Prussia, she too summoned a commission, in 1767, to codify and revise Russian law. But few of its radical proposals (which included the abolition of capital punishment, an end to judicial torture, and prohibitions on the selling of serfs) were ever implemented. Any possibility such measures might have been enforced ended in 1773–1775, when a massive peasant revolt led by a Cossack named Emelyan Pugachev briefly threatened

Moscow itself. Catherine responded to the uprising by further centralizing her own government and by tightening aristocratic control over the peasantry.

Catherine's greatest achievements were gained through war and diplomacy. In 1769, she renewed Peter the Great's push to secure a warm-water port on the Black Sea. In the resulting war with the Ottoman Turks (which ended in 1774), Russia won control over the northern coast of the Black Sea, secured the independence of Crimea (which Russia would annex in 1783), and obtained safe passage for Russian ships through the Bosporus and into the Mediterranean Sea. In the course of this campaign, Russia also won control over several Ottoman provinces along the Danube River.

Russia's gains in the Balkans alarmed Austria, however, which now found itself with the powerful Russian Empire on its southern doorstep. Prussia too was threatening to become involved in the war as an ally of the Ottomans. Frederick the Great's real interests, however, lay much closer to home. To preserve the peace among Russia, Prussia, and Austria, he proposed instead a partition of Poland. Russia would abandon its Danubian conquests and, in return, would acquire the grain fields of eastern Poland, along with a population of 1 to

Catherine the Great.

Dividing the Royal Spoils. A contemporary cartoon showing the monarchs of Europe at work carving up a hapless Poland.

2 million Poles. Austria would take Galicia, acquiring 2.5 million Poles. Prussia, meanwhile, would take the coastal regions of Poland, including the port of Gdansk (Danzig), that separated Brandenburg and Pomerania from East Prussia. As a result of this agreement, finalized in 1772, Poland lost about 30 percent of its territory and about half of its population.

Poland was now paying the price for its political conservatism. Alone among the major central European powers, the Polish nobility had successfully opposed any move toward monarchical centralization as a threat to its liberties, among which was the right of every individual noble to veto any measure proposed in the Polish representative assembly, the Diet. To make matters worse, Polish aristocrats were also quite prepared to accept bribes from foreign powers in return for their vote in elections for the Polish king. In 1764, Catherine the Great had intervened in this way to secure the election of one of her former lovers, Stanislaus Poniatowski, as the new king of Poland. In 1772, King Stanislaus reluctantly accepted the partition of his country because he was too weak to resist it.

In 1788, however, he took advantage of a new Russo-Turkish war to try to strengthen his control over what remained of his kingdom. In May 1791 a new constitution was adopted that established a much stronger monarchy than had previously existed. But it was too late. In January 1792 the Russo-Turkish war ended, and Catherine the Great pounced. Together the Russians and Prussians took two more enormous bites out of Poland in 1793, destroying the new constitution in the process. A final swallow by Russia, Austria, and Prussia in 1795 left nothing of Poland or Lithuania at all.

COMMERCE AND CONSUMPTION

What factors facilitated the commercial revolution?

 Despite the increased military power of Russia, Prussia, and Austria, the balance of power within Europe was shifting steadily toward the west during the eighteenth century. The North Atlantic economies in particular were growing more rapidly than those anywhere else in Europe. As a result, France and Britain were becoming preponderant powers both in Europe and the wider world.

ECONOMIC GROWTH IN EIGHTEENTH-CENTURY EUROPE

The reasons for this rapid economic and demographic growth in northwestern Europe are complex and continue to be disputed by historians. In Britain and Holland, new, more intensive agricultural systems were producing more food per acre than ever before. Combined with improved transportation systems, the new farming methods resulted in fewer famines and a better-nourished population. New crops, especially maize and potatoes (both introduced to Europe from the Americas), also helped increase the supply of food available to feed Europe's growing population. But although famines became less common and less widespread, infectious disease continued to kill half of all Europeans before they reached the age of twenty. Even here, however, some progress was being made. Plague in particular was ceasing to be a major killer, as a degree of immunity (perhaps the result of a genetic mutation) began to emerge within the European population. Together with a better diet, improved sanitation may also have played some role in reducing the infection rates from such killers as typhoid, cholera, smallpox, and measles.

Northwestern Europe was also becoming increasingly urbanized. Across Europe as a whole the total number of urban dwellers did not change markedly between 1600 and 1800. At both dates, approximately 200 cities in Europe had a population of over 10,000. What did change was, first, the fact that these cities were increasingly concentrated in northern and western Europe and, second, the extraordinary growth of the very largest cities. Patterns of trade and commerce had much to do with these shifts. Cities such as Hamburg in Germany, Liverpool in England, Toulon in France, and Cadíz in Spain grew by about 250 percent between 1600 and 1750. Amsterdam, the hub of early modern international commerce, increased from 30,000 in 1530 to 115,000 in 1630 and 200,000 by 1800. Naples, the busy Mediterranean port, went from a population of 300,000 in 1600 to nearly half a million by the late eighteenth century. But even more spectacular population growth occurred in the administrative capitals of Europe. London grew from 674,000 in 1700 to 860,000 a century later. Paris went from 180,000 people in 1600 to more than 500,000 in 1800. Berlin grew from a population of 6,500 in 1661 to 60,000 in 1721 to 140,000 in 1783, of whom approximately 65,000 were state employees or members of their families.

Increased food supplies were needed to feed these burgeoning cities; but to the rising prosperity of northwestern Europe as a whole, developments in trade and manufacturing contributed even more than did agriculture. Spurred by improvements in transportation— better roads and bridges, and new canals—entrepreneurs began to promote the production of textiles in the countryside by distributing ("putting out") wool and flax to rural workers who would card, spin, and weave it into cloth on a piece-rate basis. The entrepreneur would then collect and sell the finished cloth in a market that now extended from local towns to international exporters. For country dwellers, this system (sometimes called *protoindustrialization*) provided welcome employment during otherwise slack seasons of the agricultural year. For the merchant-entrepreneurs

who administered it, the system allowed them to avoid expensive guild restrictions in the towns and to reduce their levels of capital investment, thus reducing their overall costs of production. Urban cloth workers suffered, but the system led nonetheless to markedly increased employment and to much higher levels of industrial production, not only for textiles but also for iron, metalworking, and even toy and clock making.

Despite rural protoindustrialization, the role of cities as manufacturing centers continued to grow during the eighteenth century. In northern France, many of the million or so men and women employed in the textile trade lived and worked in cities such as Amiens, Lille, and Rheims. The rulers of Prussia made it their policy to develop Berlin as a manufacturing center, taking advantage of an influx of French Protestants to establishing a silk-weaving industry there and constructing canals to link the city with Breslau and Hamburg. Most urban manufacturing continued to be carried out in small shops employing anywhere from five to twenty journeymen working under the supervision of a master. But the scale of such enterprise was growing and also becoming more specialized, as workshops began to group together to form a single manufacturing district in which several thousand workers might be employed to produce the same product.

> Increased food supplies were needed to feed these burgeoning cities, but to the rising prosperity of northwestern Europe as a whole, developments in trade and manufacuring contributed even more than did agriculture.

Techniques in some crafts remained much as they had been for centuries. In others, however, inventions changed the pattern of work as well as the nature of the product. Knitting frames, simple devices to speed the manufacture of textile goods, made their appearance in Britain and Holland. Wire-drawing machines and slitting mills, the latter enabling nail makers to convert iron bars into rods, spread from Germany into Britain. Techniques for printing colored designs directly on calico cloth were imported from Asia. New and more efficient printing presses appeared, first in Holland and then elsewhere. The Dutch even invented a machine called a "camel," with which the hulls of ships could be raised in the water so that they could be more easily repaired.

Workers did not readily accept innovations of this kind. Labor-saving machines threw people out of work. Artisans, especially those organized into guilds, were by nature conservative, anxious to protect not only their rights but also their "mysteries," the secrets of their trade. Often, therefore, governments would

POPULATION GROWTH C. 1600

Why did the population of northwestern Europe grow more rapidly? What was the impact of urbanization? How did it affect patterns of life and trade? Why were the largest gains in population on the coasts? How did the expansion of trade and innovations in transportation affect ordinary people in these new urban centers?

intervene to block the widespread use of machines if they threatened to increase unemployment or in some other way to create unrest. The Dutch and some German states, for example, prohibited the use of what was described as a "devilish invention," a ribbon loom capable of weaving sixteen or more ribbons at the same time. But states might also intervene to protect the interests of their powerful commercial and financial backers. On behalf of domestic textile manufacturers and importers of Indian goods, both Britain and France outlawed calico printing for a time. Mercantilist doctrines could also impede innovation. In both Paris and Lyons, for example, the use of indigo dyes was banned because they were manufactured abroad. But

Topsy-Turvy World, **by Jan Steen.** This Dutch painting depicts a household in the throes of the exploding consumer economy that hit Europe in the eighteenth century. Consumer goods ranging from silver and china to clothing and furniture cluttered the houses of ordinary people as never before.

eighteenth-century Britain, the service sector was the fastest-growing part of the economy, outstripping both agriculture and manufacturing. Almost everywhere in urban Europe, the eighteenth century was the golden age of the small shopkeeper. People bought more prepared foods and more ready-made (as opposed to personally tailored) clothing. Advertising became an important part of doing business, helping create demand for new products and shaping popular taste for changing fashions. Even political allegiances could be expressed through consumption when people purchased plates and glasses commemorating favorite rulers or causes.

The result of all these developments was a European economy vastly more complex, more specialized, more integrated, more commercialized, and more productive than anything the world had seen before.

the pressures for economic innovation were irresistable, because behind them lay an insatiable eighteenth-century appetite for goods.

A WORLD OF GOODS

In the eighteenth century, for the first time, a mass market for consumer goods emerged in Europe, and especially in northwestern Europe. Houses became larger, particularly in towns; but even more strikingly, the houses of relatively ordinary people were starting to be crammed with hitherto uncommon luxuries such as sugar, tobacco, tea, coffee, chocolate, newspapers, books, pictures, clocks, toys, china, glassware, pewter, silver plate, soap, razors, furniture (including beds with mattresses, chairs, and chests of drawers), shoes, cotton cloth, and spare clothing. Demand for such products consistently outstripped the supply, causing prices for these items to rise faster than the price of foodstuffs throughout the century. But the demand for them continued unabated. Such goods were indulgences, of course, but they were also repositories of value in which families could invest their surplus cash, knowing that they could pawn them in hard times if cash were needed.

The exploding consumer economy of the eighteenth century spurred demand for manufactured goods of all sorts. But it also encouraged the provision of services. In

COLONIZATION AND TRADE IN THE SEVENTEENTH CENTURY

How did the patterns of European colonial settlement in the Americas differ from each other?

Many of the new consumer goods that propelled the economy of eighteenth-century Europe, including such staples as sugar, tobacco, tea, coffee, chocolate, china, and cotton cloth, were the products of Europe's colonial empires in Asia, Africa, and the Americas. Europe's growing wealth was not simply the result of its colonial possessions, but it is impossible to imagine this prosperity without them. We need, therefore, to examine these European empires and the developing role they played in the economy of the eighteenth-century world. To do so, however, we need to begin by looking at the patterns of seventeenth-century European colonialism.

How did the patterns of European colonial settlement in the Americas differ from each other?

Colonization and Trade in the Seventeenth Century   565

Spanish Colonialism

After the exploits of the conquistadors, the Spanish established colonial governments in Peru and in Mexico, which they controlled from Madrid. In keeping with the doctrines of mercantilism, the Spanish government allowed only Spanish merchants to trade with their American colonies, requiring all colonial exports and imports to pass through a single Spanish port (first Seville, then later the more navigable port of Cadíz), where they were registered at the government-operated customs house. During the sixteenth century, this system worked reasonably well. The Spanish colonial economy was dominated by mining; the lucrative market for silver in East Asia even made it profitable to establish an outpost in Manila, where Spanish merchants exchanged Asian silk for South American bullion. But Spain also took steps to promote farming and ranching in Central and South America and established settlements in Florida and California.

The wealth of Spain's colonial trade tempted the merchants of other countries to win a share of the treasure for themselves. Probably the boldest challengers were the English, whose leading buccaneer was the sea dog Sir Francis Drake. Three times Drake raided the east and west coasts of Spanish America. In 1587 he attacked the Spanish fleet at its anchorage in Cadíz harbor; and in 1588 he played a key role in defeating the Spanish Armada. His career illustrates the mixture of piracy and patriotism that characterized England's early efforts to break into the colonial trade. Until the 1650s, however, the English could only dent the lucrative Spanish trade in bullion, hides, silks, and slaves.

The Spanish colonial economy was dominated by mining; the lucrative market for silver in East Asia even made it profitable to establish an outpost in Manila, where Spanish merchants exchanged Asian silk for South American bullion.

English Colonialism

England's own American colonies had no significant mineral wealth. As a result, English colonists sought profits by establishing agricultural settlements in North America and the Caribbean basin. Their first permanent, though ultimately unsuccessful, colony was founded in 1607 at Jamestown, Virginia. Over the next forty years, 80,000 English emigrants would sail to more than twenty autonomous settlements in the New World. Many of these early settlers were driven by religious motives. The Pilgrims who landed at Plymouth, Massachusetts, in 1620 were one of many dissident groups, both Protestant and Catholic, that sought to escape the English government's attempt to impose religious conformity by emigrating to North America. Strikingly, however, English colonists showed little interest in trying to convert Native American peoples to Christianity. Missionizing played a much larger role in Spanish efforts to colonize Central and South America and French efforts to penetrate the North American hinterlands.

Most of these early English settlements were privately organized. As they began to prosper, however, the governments of both Oliver Cromwell and Charles II began to intervene in their management. Mercantilist-inspired navigation acts, passed in 1651 and 1660 and rigorously enforced thereafter, decreed that all exports from English colonies to the mother country be carried in English ships and forbade the direct exporting of certain "enumerated" products directly from the colonies to continental ports.

The most valuable of those colonial products were sugar and tobacco. Sugar, virtually unknown in Christian Europe during the Middle Ages, became a popular luxury item in the late fifteenth century, when Europeans began to produce it in their Mediterranean and African colonies. Only in the New World, however, did sugar production reach such volumes as to create a mass market for the product. By the middle of the seventeenth century, European demand for sugar had already reached enormous proportions. In the eighteenth century, the sugar England imported from its tiny West Indian colonies of Barbados and Jamaica was worth more than all of its imports from China and India combined.

Sugar, however, could be grown in only a fairly limited geographical and climatic area. Tobacco was much more adaptable. Although tobacco was first imported into Europe by the Spaniards in the mid-sixteenth century, another half century passed before Europeans took up the habit of smoking. At first the plant was believed to possess miraculous healing powers and was referred to as "divine tobacco" and "our holy herb nicotian." (The word *nicotine* derives from the name of the French ambassador to Portugal, Jean Nicot, who brought the tobacco plant to France.) The practice of smoking was first popularized by English explorers, especially by Sir Walter Raleigh, who had learned to smoke while living among the Indians of Virginia. Thereafter, it spread rapidly through all classes of European society. Governments at first joined the

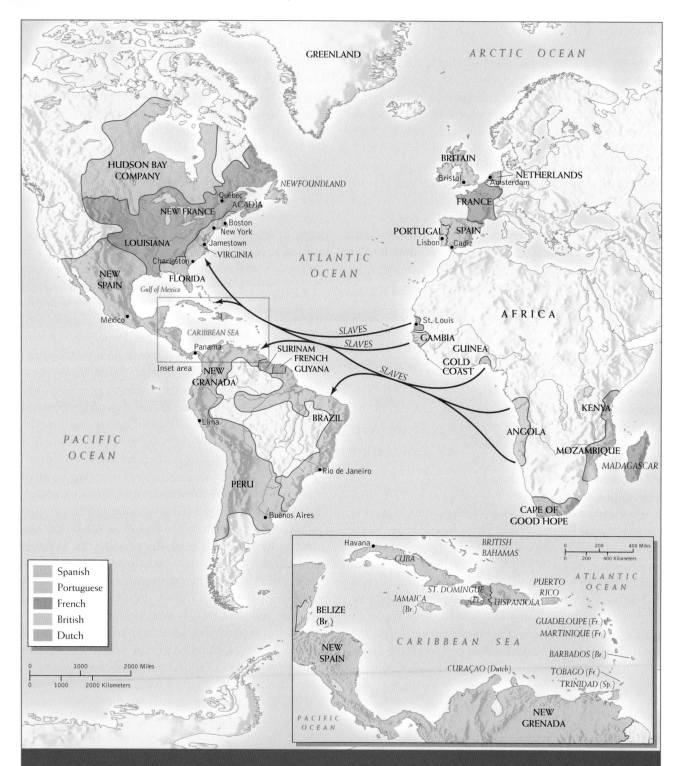

GREENLAND · ARCTIC OCEAN

HUDSON BAY
COMPANY

NEWFOUNDLAND

BRITAIN
Bristol
NETHERLANDS
Amsterdam
FRANCE

Quebec
ACADIA
NEW FRANCE
Boston
New York
LOUISIANA
Jamestown
Charleston
VIRGINIA

PORTUGAL   SPAIN
Lisbon   Cadiz

ATLANTIC
OCEAN

NEW
SPAIN
FLORIDA
Gulf of Mexico

AFRICA

Mexico

CARIBBEAN SEA

St. Louis

SLAVES
SLAVES

GAMBIA   GUINEA
GOLD
COAST

Panama
Inset area   NEW
GRANADA

SURINAM
FRENCH
GUYANA

SLAVES

Lima

BRAZIL

KENYA

PACIFIC
OCEAN

ANGOLA

MOZAMBIQUE

MADAGASCAR

Rio de Janeiro

PERU

Buenos Aires

CAPE OF
GOOD HOPE

Spanish
Portuguese
French
British
Dutch

Havana
CUBA

BRITISH
BAHAMAS

0   200   400 Miles
0   200   400 Kilometers

ATLANTIC
OCEAN

ST. DOMINGUE
(Fr.)
JAMAICA
(Br.)
HISPANIOLA

PUERTO
RICO

BELIZE
(Br.)

GUADELOUPE (Fr.)
MARTINIQUE (Fr.)

CARIBBEAN   SEA

NEW
SPAIN

CURAÇAO (Dutch)

BARBADOS (Br.)

TOBAGO (Fr.)
TRINIDAD (Sp.)

0   1000   2000 Miles
0   1000   2000 Kilometers

PACIFIC
OCEAN

NEW
GRENADA

THE ATLANTIC WORLD

Why were European governments so concerned with closely controlling the means by which certain products traveled from the colonies to European ports? How and why did the financial institutions of the late medieval period thrive on and encourage the economic policies of colonial powers? Why are the trade routes carrying slaves so prominently marked on this map? What does this suggest about the importance of unfree labor to the economic achievements of Europeans in the New World?

HOW DID THE PATTERNS OF EUROPEAN COLONIAL SETTLEMENT IN THE AMERICAS DIFFER FROM EACH OTHER?

COLONIZATION AND TRADE IN THE SEVENTEENTH CENTURY   567

church in condemning the use of tobacco, but by the end of the seventeenth century, having realized the profits to be made from it, they were actively encouraging its production and consumption.

FRENCH COLONIALISM

French colonial policy matured during the administration of Louis XIV's mercantilist finance minister, Jean Baptiste Colbert, who regarded overseas expansion as an integral part of state economic policy. To compete with the English, he encouraged the development of sugar-producing colonies in the West Indies, the largest of which was St. Domingue (present-day Haiti). France also dominated the interior of the North American continent, where French traders bought furs and missionaries preached Christianity to the Indians in a vast territory that stretched from Acadia to Quebec to Louisiana. Yet the financial returns from these lands were never commensurate with their size. Furs, fish, and tobacco were exported to European markets in large quantities but never matched the profits from the Caribbean sugar colonies or from the trading outposts the French maintained in India.

The Dutch East India Company Warehouse and Timber Wharf at Amsterdam. The substantial warehouse, the stockpiles of lumber, and the company ship under construction in the foreground illustrate the degree to which overseas commerce could stimulate the economy of the mother country.

DUTCH COLONIALISM

Until the 1670s, the Dutch controlled the most prosperous commercial empire of the seventeenth century. Although some Dutch settlements were established, including one at the Cape of Good Hope in modern-day South Africa, Dutch colonialism generally followed the "fort and factory" model established by the Portuguese in Asia. In Southeast Asia, the Dutch East India Company, founded in 1602, seized control of Sumatra, Borneo, and the Moluccas (Spice Islands), driving Portuguese traders from an area they had previously dominated and establishing a Dutch monopoly within Europe over pepper, cinnamon, nutmeg, mace, and cloves. The Dutch also secured an

As the primary financiers of seventeenth-century Europe, the Dutch also pioneered new mechanisms for investing in colonial enterprises. One of the most important of these was the joint-stock company, of which the Dutch East India Company was among the first.

exclusive right to trade with Japan and maintained military and trading outposts in China and India as well. In the Western Hemisphere, however, their achievements were less spectacular. After a series of trade wars with England, in 1667 they formally surrendered their colony of New Amsterdam (subsequently renamed New York), retaining only Surinam (off the northern coast of South America) and Curaçao and Tobago (in the West Indies). Although they dominated the seventeenth-century slave trade with Africa, after 1713 the Dutch would lose this position also to the British.

As the primary financiers of seventeenth-century Europe, the Dutch also pioneered new mechanisms for investing in colonial enterprises. One of the most important of these was the joint-stock company, of which the Dutch East India Company was among the first. Such companies raised cash by selling shares in their enterprise to investors. Even though the investors might not take any role in managing the company, they were joint owners of the business and therefore entitled to a share in its profits in proportion with the amount they had invested. Initially, the Dutch East India Company had intended to pay off its investors ten years after its founding, but the directors soon recognized the impossibility of this plan. By 1612, the company's assets—ships, wharves, warehouses, and cargoes—were scattered around the globe. Moreover, its commercial prospects were continuing to improve. The directors therefore urged investors anxious to realize their profits to sell their shares on the Amsterdam stock exchange to other investors, thereby ensuring the continued operation of their enterprise and, in the process, establishing a method of continuous business financing that would soon spread elsewhere in Europe.

CONTRASTING PATTERNS OF COLONIAL SETTLEMENT

Differences in the commercial relationships European countries established with their New World colonies reflected important differences in settlement patterns among these colonies. In Central and South America, a relatively small number of Spaniards had conquered complex, highly populous Native American societies. To rule these new territories, the Spanish quickly replaced native elites with Spanish administrators and churchmen. But by and large they did not attempt to uproot or eliminate existing native cultures. Instead, Spain focused its efforts on controlling and exploiting native labor, so as to extract the maximum possible profit for the crown from the colonies' mineral resources. The native peoples of Spanish America already lived, for the most part, in large, well-organized villages and towns. Spanish colonial policy was to collect tribute from such communities and to convert them to Catholicism but to do so without fundamentally disrupting their existing patterns of life.

The result was widespread cultural assimilation between the Spanish colonizers and the native populace, combined with a relatively high degree of intermarriage between them. Out of this reality emerged a complex and distinctive system of racial and social castes, with pure-blooded Spaniards at the top, peoples of mixed descent in the middle (native, Spanish, and African, in various combinations), and nontribal Indians at the bottom. In theory, these racial categories corresponded with class distinctions; but in practice race and class did not always coincide, and race itself was often a social fiction. Mixed-race individuals who prospered economically often found ways to establish

their "pure" Spanish ancestry by adopting the social practices that characterized elite (i.e., Spanish) status. Spaniards, however, always remained at the top of the social hierarchy, even when they fell into poverty.

Like the Spanish colonies, the French colonies were established and administered as direct crown enterprises. French colonial settlements were conceived mainly as military outposts and trading centers; as a result, they were overwhelmingly populated by men. The elite members of French colonial society were the military officers and administrators sent out from Paris. But below their ranks there was a broad community of interest between the fishermen, fur traders, small farmers, and common soldiers who constituted the bulk of the French settlers of North America. Except in the Caribbean, French colonies depended largely on the fur trade and on fishing; both enterprises relied in turn on cooperative relationships with native peoples. A mutual economic interdependence therefore grew up between these French colonies and the peoples of the surrounding region. Intermarriage, especially between French fur traders and native women, was common. But most French colonies in North America remained dependent on the wages and supplies sent to them from the mother country. Only rarely did they become truly self-sustaining economic enterprises.

The English colonies along the Atlantic seaboard followed a different model. English colonies did not begin as Crown enterprises. Instead they were established either by joint-stock companies (as in Virginia and the Massachusetts Bay colony) or as private, proprietary colonies (such as Maryland and Pennsylvania). Building on their experience in Ireland, English colonists established planned settlements known as plantations, in which they attempted to replicate as many features of English life as possible. Geography also contributed to the resulting concentration of English settlement patterns. The rivers and bays of eastern North America provided the first footholds for English colonists in the New World, and the Atlantic Ocean helped tie these separated settlements together. But aside from the Hudson, there were no great rivers to lead colonists very far inland. Instead, the English colonies clung to the seacoast, and so to each other.

Like the French colonies, the early English colonies relied on fishing and the fur trade for their exports. But primarily, English colonies were agricultural communities, populated by small- and medium-scale landholders for whom control over land was the key to wealth. Partly this was a reflection of the kinds of people whom these privately sponsored colonial enterprises could persuade to immigrate to the New World. But

How did the patterns of European colonial settlement in the Americas differ from each other?

Colonization and Trade in the Seventeenth Century   569

Illinois Indians Trading with French Settlers. This engraving from Nicholas De Fer's 1705 map of the Western Hemisphere illustrates the economic interdependence that developed between early French colonies and the native people of the surrounding region.

this focus on agriculture was also the result of the demographic catastrophe that had struck the native populations of the Atlantic seaboard during the last half of the sixteenth century. European diseases—brought by Spanish armies and by the French, English, and Portuguese fishermen who frequented the rich fishing banks off the New England coast—had already decimated the native peoples of eastern North America even before the first European colonists set foot there. By the early seventeenth century, a great deal of rich agricultural land had been abandoned simply because there were no longer enough native farmers to till it—one reason that many native groups initially welcomed the new arrivals.

Unlike the Spanish, English colonists along the Atlantic seaboard therefore had neither the need nor the opportunity to control a large native labor force. What they wanted, rather, was complete and exclusive control over native lands. To this end, the English colonists soon set out to eliminate, through expulsion and massacre, the indigenous peoples of their colonies. To be sure, there were exceptions. In the Quaker colony of Pennsylvania, colonists and Native Americans maintained friendly relations for more than half a century. In the Carolinas, by contrast, there was widespread enslavement of native people, either for sale to the West Indies or, from the 1690s, to work on the rice plantations along the coast. Elsewhere, however, attempts to enslave the native peoples of North America failed. When English planters looked for bond laborers, they therefore either recruited indentured servants from England (most of whom would be freed after a specified period of service) or else they purchased African captives (who would usually be enslaved for life).

Social relations between the English colonists and native peoples also differed from the patterns we find elsewhere in the New World. In contrast to the Spanish and French colonies, intermarriage between English colonists and natives was rare. Instead, a rigid racial division emerged that distinguished all Europeans, regardless of class, from all Native Americans and Africans. Intermarriage between natives and Africans was relatively common, but between the English and the indigenous peoples of their colonies an unbridgeable gulf soon developed.

> In contrast to the Spanish and French colonies, intermarriage between English colonists and natives was rare. Instead, a rigid racial division emerged that distinguished all Europeans, regardless of class, from all Native Americans and Africans.

COLONIAL RIVALRIES

The fortunes of these colonial empires changed dramatically in the course of the seventeenth and early eighteenth centuries. Spain, mired in persistent economic stagnation and embroiled in a series of expensive wars and domestic rebellions, proved unable to defend its monopoly over colonial trade. In a war with Spain in the 1650s, England captured not only the island of Jamaica but treasure ships lying off the Spanish harbor of Cádiz. Further profit was obtained by bribing Spanish customs officials on a grand scale. During the second half of the century, two thirds of the imported goods sold in Spanish colonies were smuggled in by Dutch, English, and French traders. By 1700, although Spain still possessed a colonial empire, that empire lay at the mercy of its more dynamic rivals. A brief revival of fortunes under more enlightened leadership in the mid-eighteenth century did nothing to prevent its ultimate eclipse.

Portugal, too, found it impossible to prevent foreign penetration of its colonial empire. England in particular worked diligently to win commercial advantages there. In 1703, the English signed a treaty with Portugal allowing English merchants to export woolens duty free into Portugal and allowing Portugal to ship its wines duty free into England. Increasing English trade with Portugal also led to English trade with the Portuguese colony of Brazil, an important sugar producer and the largest of all the New World markets for African slaves. In the eighteenth century, English merchants would dominate these Brazilian trade routes.

COLONIALISM AND EMPIRE

In what ways did eighteenth-century European colonialism differ from seventeenth-century European colonialism?

The 1713 Treaty of Utrecht opened a new era in these colonial rivalries. As we have seen, the biggest losers in these negotiations were the Dutch, who gained only a guarantee of security for their own borders, and the Spanish, who were forced to concede to Britain the right to market slaves in the Spanish colonies. The winners were the British (who acquired large chunks of French territory in North America) and, to a lesser extent, the French, who retained Cape Breton Island, Quebec, the interior portions of North America, and their foothold in India. The eighteenth century would witness a continuing struggle between Britain and France for control over the expanding commerce that now bound the European economy to the Americas and to Asia.

***The Defense of Cadíz against the English,* by Francisco Zurbaran.** The rivalry between European powers that played out over the new colonial possessions further proved the decline of Spain, which lost the island of Jamaica and ships in the harbor of Cádiz to the English in the 1650s.

THE TRIANGULAR TRADE IN SUGAR AND SLAVES

During the eighteenth century, European colonial trade came to be dominated by trans-Atlantic routes that developed in response to the lucrative West Indian sugar industry and to the demand for slaves from Africa to work those Caribbean plantations. In this "triangular" trade, naval superiority gave Britain a decisive

How Slaves Were Stowed aboard Ship during the Middle Passage. Men were "housed" on the right; women on the left; children in the middle. The human cargo was jammed onto platforms six feet wide without sufficient headroom to permit an adult to sit up. This diagram is from evidence gathered by English abolitionists and depicts conditions on the Liverpool slave ship *Brookes.*

advantage over its French, Spanish, Portuguese, and Dutch rivals. Typically, a British ship might begin its voyage from New England with a consignment of rum and sail to Africa, where the rum would be exchanged for a cargo of slaves. From the west coast of Africa the ship would then cross the South Atlantic to the sugar colonies of Jamaica or Barbados, where slaves would be traded for molasses. It would then make the final leg of the journey back to New England, where the molasses would be made into rum. A variant triangle might see cheap manufactured goods move from England to Africa, where they would be traded for slaves. Those slaves would then be shipped to Virginia and exchanged for tobacco, which would be shipped to England and processed there for sale throughout Europe.

The cultivation of New World sugar and tobacco depended on slave labor. As European demand for these products increased, so too did the traffic in enslaved Africans. At the height of the Atlantic slave trade in the eighteenth century, 75,000 to 90,000 Africans were shipped across the Atlantic yearly: at least 6 million in the eighteenth century, out of a total of over 11 million for the entire history of the trade. About 35 percent went to English and French Caribbean plantations; 5 percent (roughly 500,000) to North America; and the rest to the Portuguese colony of Brazil and to the Spanish colonies in Central and South America. By the 1780s, there were more than 500,000 slaves on the largest French plantation island, St. Domingue, and at least 200,000 on its English counterpart, Jamaica.

Although run as a monopoly by various governments in the sixteenth and early seventeenth centuries, the slave trade in the eighteenth century was open to private entrepreneurs who operated ports on the West African coast. These traders exchanged Indian cloth, metal goods, rum, and firearms with African slave merchants in return for their human cargo, who would then be packed by the hundreds into the holds of slave ships for the gruesome Middle Passage across the Atlantic (so called to distinguish it from the slave ship's voyage from Europe to Africa, and then from the colonies back to Europe). Shackled belowdecks without sanitary facilities, the captive men, women, and children suffered horribly. The mortality rate, however, remained at about 10 or 11 percent, not much higher than the rate for a normal sea voyage of 100 days or more. Since traders had to invest as much as £10 per slave in their enterprise, they were generally anxious to ensure that their consignment would reach its destination in good enough shape to be sold for a profit.

THE COMMERCIAL RIVALRY BETWEEN BRITAIN AND FRANCE

British dominance of the slave trade gave it decisive advantages in its colonial struggles with France. As one Englishman wrote in 1749, the slave trade had provided "an unexhastible fund of wealth to this nation." But even apart from the slave trade, the value of colonial commerce was increasing dramatically during the eighteenth century. French colonial trade, valued at 25 million livres in 1716, rose to 263 million livres in 1789. In England, during roughly the same period, foreign trade increased in value from £10 million to £40 million, the latter amount more than twice that for France.

The growing value of colonial commerce tied the interests of governments and transoceanic merchants together in an increasingly tight embrace. Merchants engaged in the colonial trade depended on their governments to protect and defend their overseas investments; but governments depended in turn on merchants and their financial backers to build the ships and sustain the trade on which national power depended. In the eighteenth century, even the ability to wage war rested largely (and increasingly) on a government's ability to borrow the necessary funds from wealthy investors and then to pay back those debts, with interest, over time. As it did in commerce, so too in finance, Britain came to enjoy a decisive advantage in this respect over France. The Bank of England, founded in the 1690s, managed the English national debt with great success, providing the funds required for war by selling shares to investors, then repaying those investors at modcrate rates of interest. In contrast, chronic governmental indebtedness forced the French crown to borrow at ruinously high rates of interest, provoking a series of fiscal crises that in 1789 finally led to the collapse of the French monarchy.

WAR AND EMPIRE IN THE EIGHTEENTH-CENTURY WORLD

After 1713, western Europe remained largely at peace for a generation. In 1740, however, that peace was shattered when Frederick the Great of Prussia took advantage of the accession of a woman, the empress Maria Theresa, to the throne of Austria to seize the Austrian province of Silesia (discussed earlier in this chapter). In the resulting War of the Austrian Succession, France and Spain fought on the side of Prussia, hoping to reverse some of the losses they had suffered in the Treaty of Utrecht. As they had done since the 1690s, Britain and the Dutch Republic sided with Austria. Like those earlier wars, this war quickly spread beyond the frontiers of Europe. In India, the English East India Company lost control over the coastal area of Madras to its French rival; but in North America, British colonists from New England captured the important French fortress of Louisbourg on Cape Breton Island, hoping to put a stop to French interference with their fishing and shipping. When the war finally ended in 1748, Britain recovered Madras and returned Louisbourg to France.

Eight years later, these colonial conflicts reignited when Prussia once again attacked Austria. This time, however, Prussia allied itself with Great Britain. Austria found support from both France and Russia. In Europe, the Seven Years' War (1756–1763) ended in stalemate. In India and North America, however, the war had decisive consequences. In India, mercenary troops employed by the British East India Company joined with native allies to elimate their French competitors. In North America (where the conflict was known as the French and Indian War), British troops captured both Louisbourg and Quebec and also drove French forces from the Ohio River Valley and the Great Lakes. By the Treaty of Paris in 1763, which brought the Seven Years' War to an end, France formally surrendered both Canada and India to the British. Six years later, the French East India Company was dissolved.

THE AMERICAN REVOLUTION

Along the Atlantic seaboard, however, the rapidly growing British colonies were beginning to chafe at rule from London. To recover some of the costs of the Seven Years' War and to pay for the continuing costs of protecting its colonial subjects, the British Parliament imposed a series of new taxes on its American colonies. These taxes were immediately unpopular. Colonists complained that because they had no representatives in Parliament, they were being taxed without their consent—a fundamental violation of their rights as British subjects. They also complained that British restrictions on colonial trade, particularly the requirement that certain goods pass first through British ports

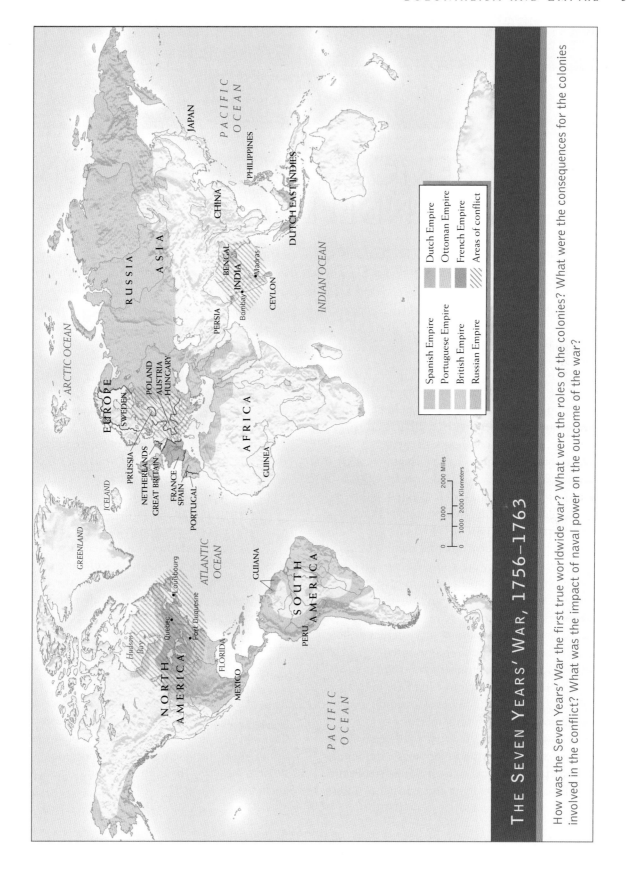

The Seven Years' War, 1756–1763

How was the Seven Years' War the first true worldwide war? What were the roles of the colonies? What were the consequences for the colonies involved in the conflict? What was the impact of naval power on the outcome of the war?

THE AMERICAN DECLARATION OF INDEPENDENCE

The Declaration of Independence, issued from Philadelphia on July 4, 1776, is perhaps the most famous single document of American history. But its familiarity does not lesssen its interest as a piece of political philosophy. The indebtedness of the document's authors to the ideas of John Locke will be obvious from the selections here. But Locke, in turn, drew many of his ideas about the contractual and conditional nature of human government from the conciliarist thinkers of the fifteenth and early sixteenth centuries. The appeal of absolutism notwithstanding, the Declaration shows how vigorous the medieval tradition of contractual, limited government remained at the end of the eighteenth century.

When in the course of human events, it becomes necessary for one people to dissolve the political bonds which have connected them with another, and to assume among the powers of the earth the separate and equal station to which the Laws of Nature and of Nature's God entitle them, a decent respect to the opinions of mankind requires that they should declare the causes which impel them to the separation. . . . We hold these truths to be self-evident, that all men are created equal, that they are endowed by their Creator with certain unalienable rights, that among these are Life, Liberty and the pursuit of Happiness. . . . That to secure these rights, Governments are instituted among men, deriving their just powers from the consent of the governed. . . . That whenever any form of Government becomes destructive of these ends, it is the Right of the People to alter or to abolish it, and to institute new Government, laying its foundation upon such principles and organizing its power in such form, as to them shall seem most likely to effect their Safety and Happiness. Prudence, indeed, will dictate that Governments long established should not be changed for light and transient causes; and accordingly all experience has shown, that mankind are more disposed to suffer, while evils are sufferable, than to right themselves by abolishing the forms to which they are accustomed. But when a long train of abuses and usurpations, pursuing invariably the same Object, evinces a design to reduce them under absolute despotism, it is their right, it is their duty, to throw off such Government, and to provide new Guards for their future security. . . . Such has been the patient sufferance of these Colonies; and such is now the necessity which constrains them to alter their former Systems of Government. . . .

QUESTIONS FOR ANALYSIS

1. In what way was the Declaration of Independence a document that could have been drafted by John Locke? Could the Declaration have been written in the seventeenth rather than the eighteenth century?
2. What is meant by the expression, "life, liberty, and the pursuit of happiness"?

before being transshipped to the Continent, were strangling American livelihoods and so making it impossible to pay even the king's legitimate taxes.

The British government, led since 1760 by the young and inexperienced King George III, responded to these complaints with a badly calculated mixture of vacillation and force. Various taxes were imposed and then withdrawn in the face of colonial resistance. In 1773, however, when East India Company tea was dumped in Boston Harbor by rebellious colonials objecting to the customs duties that had been imposed on it, the British government closed the port of Boston and curtailed the colony's representative institutions. These "Coercive Acts" galvanized the support of the other American colonies for Massachusetts. In 1774, representatives from all the American colonies met at Philadelphia to form the Continental Congress to negotiate with the Crown over their grievances. In April 1775, however, local militiamen at Lexington and Concord clashed with regular British troops sent to disarm them. Soon thereafter, the Continental Congress began raising an army, and an outright rebellion erupted against the British government.

On July 4, 1776, the thirteen colonies formally declared their independence from Great Britain. During the first two years of the war, it seemed unlikely that such independence would ever become a reality. In 1778, however, France, anxious to undermine the colonial hegemony Great Britain had established since 1713, joined the war on the side of the Americans. Spain entered the war in support of France, hoping to recover Gibraltar and Florida (the latter lost in 1763 to Britain). In 1780, Britain also declared war on the Dutch Republic for continuing to trade with the rebellious colonies. Now facing a coalition of its colonial rivals, Great Britain saw the war turn against it. In 1781, combined land and sea operations by French and American troops forced the surrender of the main British army at Yorktown in Virginia. As the defeated British soldiers surrendered their weapons, their band played a song titled "The World Turned Upside Down."

Negotiations for peace began soon after the defeat at Yorktown but were not concluded until September 1783. The Treaty of Paris left Great Britain in control of Canada and Gibraltar. Spain retained its possessions west of the Mississippi River and recovered Florida.

In 1781, combined land and sea operations by French and American troops forced the surrender of the main British army at Yorktown in Virginia. As the defeated British soldiers surrendered their weapons, their band played a song titled "The World Turned Upside Down."

CHRONOLOGY

SEVENTEENTH- AND EIGHTEENTH-CENTURY WARS

Glorious Revolution	1688–1689
War of the League of Augsburg	1689–1697
War of the Spanish Succession	1702–1713
Seven Years' War	1756–1763
American Revolution	1775–1783
The Russo-Turkish War	1787–1792

The United States gained its independence; its western border was fixed on the Mississippi River, and it secured valuable fishing rights off the eastern coast of Canada. France gained only the satisfaction of defeating its colonial rival; but even that satisfaction was short lived. Six years later, the massive debts France had incurred in supporting the American Revolution helped bring about another, very different kind of revolution in France that would permanently alter the history of Europe.

CONCLUSION

Seen in this light, the American War of Independence was the final military conflict in a century-long struggle between Great Britain and France for colonial dominance. But the consequences of Britain's defeat in 1783 were far less significant than might have been expected. Even after American independence, Great Britain would remain the most important trading partner for its former American colonies, while elsewhere around the globe, the commercial dominance Britain had already established would continue to grow. The profits of slavery certainly helped fuel the eighteenth-century British economy; by the end of the century, however, British trade and manufacturing had reached such high levels of productivity that even the abolition of the slave trade (in 1808) and of slavery itself (in 1833) did not impede its continuing growth.

The economic prosperity of late-eighteenth-century Britain was mirrored to some degree throughout northwestern Europe. Improved transportation systems, more reliable food supplies, and growing quantities of consumer goods brought improved standards of living to large numbers of Europeans, even as the overall population of Europe was rising faster after 1750 than it had ever done before. Population growth was especially rapid in the cities, where a new urban middle class was emerging whose tastes drove the market for goods and whose opinions were reshaping the world of ideas.

But the prosperity of late-eighteenth-century Europe remained very unevenly distributed. In the cities, rich and poor lived separate lives in separate neighborhoods. In the countryside, regions bypassed by the developing commercial economy of the period continued to suffer from hunger and famine, just as they had done in the sixteenth and seventeenth centuries. In eastern Europe the contrasts between rich and poor were even more extreme, as many peasants fell into a new style of serfdom that would last until the end of the nineteenth century. War too remained a fact of European life, bringing death and destruction to hundreds of thousands of people across the continent and around the world—yet another consequence of the worldwide reach of these European colonial empires.

Political change was more gradual. Throughout Europe, the powers of governments steadily increased. Administrators became more numerous, more efficient, and more demanding, partly to meet the mounting costs of war but also because governments were starting to take on a much wider range of responsibilities for the welfare of their subjects. Despite the increasing scope of government, however, the structure and principles of government changed relatively little. Apart from Great Britain and the Dutch Republic, the great powers of eighteenth-century Europe were still governed by rulers who styled themselves as absolutist monarchs in the mold of Louis XIV. By 1789, however, the European world was a vastly different place than it had been a century before, when the Sun King had dominated European politics. The full extent of those differences was about to be revealed.

KEY TERMS

balance of power	*Two Treatises on*	Versailles	Catherine the Great
Louis XIV	*Government*	Frederick the Great	Triangular trade
William and Mary	Treaty of Utrecht	Peter the Great	

SELECTED READINGS

Berlin, Ira. *Many Thousands Gone: The First Two Centuries of Slavery in North America.* Cambridge, Mass., 1998. An outstanding synthesis that tells the story from the perspective of the enslaved.

Blanning, T. C. W., ed. *The Eighteenth Century: Europe 1688–1815.* Oxford and New York, 2000. Chapters on political, economic, cultural, and religious developments written by leading experts.

Brewer, John S. *The Sinews of Power: War, Money, and the English State, 1688–1783.* London, 1988; New York, 1989. An extremely influential study of the impact of war on eighteenth-century British government and finance.

Cameron, Euan, ed. *Early Modern Europe: An Oxford History.* Oxford and New York, 1999. A wide-ranging, stimulating, multiauthor survey, topically arranged, that spans the entire period from the Renaissance to the French Revolution.

Campbell, Peter R. *Louis XIV, 1661–1715.* London, 1993. A reliable recent biography; short, with primary source material and a good bibliography.

Collins, James B. *The State in Early Modern France.* Cambridge and New York, 1995. A challenging account of French government and finance between 1620 and 1789.

Doyle, William. *The Old European Order, 1660–1800.* Oxford and New York, 1992. An excellent account of European society during the *ancien régime*, with chapters on population, trade, the social order, and public affairs.

Hufton, Olwen. *The Prospect before Her: A History of Women in Western Europe, 1500–1800.* New York, 1996. A great book by a great social historian.

Hughes, Lindsey. *Russia in the Age of Peter the Great.* New Haven, Conn., 1998. A detailed, scholarly account by the leading British authority on Peter's reign.

Ingrao, Charles. *The Habsburg Monarchy, 1618–1815.* 2d ed. Cambridge and New York, 2000. A recently revised and updated edition of this standard work.

Israel, Jonathan I. *The Dutch Republic: Its Rise, Greatness, and Fall, 1477–1806.* Oxford and New York, 1995. The standard work, especially good on economic developments.

Kishlansky, Mark A. *A Monarchy Transformed: Britain, 1603–1714.* London, 1996. An excellent survey that takes seriously its claims to be a "British" rather than merely an "English" history.

Klein, Herbert S. *The Atlantic Slave Trade.* Cambridge and New York, 1999. An accessible survey by a leading quantitative historian.

Koch, H. W. *A History of Prussia.* London, 1978. Still the best account of its subject.

Lewis, William Roger, gen. ed. *The Oxford History of the British Empire.* Vol. I: *The Origins of Empire: British Overseas Enterprise to the Close of the Seventeenth Century,* ed. Nicholas Canny. Vol. II: *The Eighteenth Century,* ed. Peter J. Marshall. Oxford and New York, 1998. A definitive, multiauthor account.

Locke, John. *Two Treatises of Government.* Ed. Peter Laslett. Rev. ed. Cambridge and New York, 1963. Laslett has revolutionized our understanding of the historical and ideological context of Locke's political writings.

Miller, John, ed. *Absolutism in Seventeenth-Century Europe.* London, 1990. An excellent, multiauthor survey, organized by country.

Monod, Paul K. *The Power of Kings: Monarchy and Religion in Europe, 1589–1715.* New Haven, Conn. 1999. A study of the seventeenth century's declining confidence in the divinity of kings.

Quataert, Donald. *The Ottoman Empire, 1700–1822.* Cambridge and New York, 2000. Well balanced, up to date, and intended to be read by students.

Riasanovsky, Nicholas V., and Steinberg, Mark D. *A History of Russia.* 7th ed. Oxford and New York, 2005. Far and away the best single-volume textbook on Russian history: balanced, comprehensive, intelligent, and with full bibliographies.

Saint-Simon, Louis. *Historical Memoirs.* Many editions. The classic source for life at Louis XIV's Versailles.

Thomas, Hugh. *The Slave Trade: The History of the Atlantic Slave Trade, 1440–1870.* London and New York, 1997. A survey notable for its breadth and depth of coverage and for its attractive prose style.

Tracy, James D. *The Rise of Merchant Empires: Long-Distance Trade in the Early Modern World, 1350–1750.* Cambridge and New York, 1990. Important collection of essays by leading authorities.

White, Richard. *It's Your Misfortune and None of My Own: A History of the American West.* Norman, Okla., 1991. An outstanding textbook with excellent introductory chapters on European colonialism in the Americas.

CHAPTER SIXTEEN

THE NEW SCIENCE OF THE SEVENTEENTH CENTURY

Doubt thou the stars are fire,
Doubt that the sun doth move,
Doubt truth to be a liar,
But never doubt I love.

SHAKESPEARE, *HAMLET*, II.2

"Doubt thou that the stars are fire" and "that the sun doth move." Was Shakespeare alluding to new ideas that might unsettle the ancient understanding of the cosmos? *Hamlet* (c. 1600) was written more than fifty years after Copernicus had suggested, in his treatise *On the Revolutions of the Heavenly Spheres* (1543), that the sun did not move and that the earth did, revolving around the sun. Shakespeare probably knew of such theories, although they circulated only among small groups of learned Europeans, and, as Hamlet's love-torn speech to Ophelia makes clear, they were considered conjecture—or strange mathematical hypotheses. These theories flatly contradicted traditional learning and, just as important, they defied common sense and observation. Learned philosophers, young lovers, shepherds, and sailors alike could watch the sun and the stars move from one horizon to the other each day and night, or so they thought.

Still, a small handful of thinkers did doubt. Shakespeare was born in 1564, the same year as Galileo. By the time the English playwright and the Italian natural philosopher were working, the long process of revising knowledge about the universe, and discovering a new set of rules that explained how the universe worked was under way. By the end of the seventeenth century 100 years later, the building blocks of the new view had been put in place. This intellectual transformation brought sweeping changes to European philosophy and to Western views of the natural world and of humans' place in it.

FOCUS QUESTIONS

• What developments paved the way for the scientific revolution and how?

• How did Copernicus propose to correct the weaknesses in the inherited model of the cosmos?

• To what extent did breakthroughs depend on new observations? To what extent on new theories?

• Was Galileo a success? Why?

• What thinkers and institutions were important in the development of science as a practice?

• What problems did Newton solve?

"Science" entails at least three things: a body of knowledge, a method or system of inquiry, and a community of practitioners and the institutions that support them and their work. The "scientific revolution" of the seventeenth century (usually understood to have begun in the mid-sixteenth century and culminated in 1687 with Newton's *Principia*) involved each of these three realms. As far as the content of knowledge is concerned, the scientific revolution saw the emergence and confirmation of a heliocentric (sun-centered) view of the planetary system, which displaced the earth—and humans—from the center of the universe. Even more fundamental, it brought a new mathematical physics that described and confirmed such a view. Second, the scientific revolution established a method of inquiry for understanding the natural world: a method that emphasized the role of observation, experiment, and the testing of hypotheses. Third, "science" emerged as a distinctive branch of knowledge. During the period covered in this chapter, people referred to the study of matter, motion, optics, or the circulation of blood as natural philosophy (the more theoretical term), experimental philosophy, medicine, and—increasingly—science. The growth of societies and institutions dedicated to what we now commonly call scientific research was central to the changes at issue here. Science required not only brilliant thinkers but patrons, states, and communities of researchers; the scientific revolution was thus embedded in other social, religious, and cultural transformations.

The scientific revolution was not an organized effort. Brilliant theories sometimes led to dead ends, discoveries were often accidental, and artisans grinding lenses for telescopes played a role in the advance of knowledge just as surely as did great abstract thinkers. Old and new worldviews often overlapped as individual thinkers struggled to reconcile their discoveries with their faith or to make their theories (about the earth's movements, for instance) fit with received wisdom. Science was slow to work its way into popular understanding. It did not necessarily undermine religion, and it certainly did not intend to; figures like Isaac Newton thought their work confirmed and deepened their religious beliefs. In short, change came slowly and fitfully. But as the new scientific method began to produce radical new insights into the workings of nature, it eventually came to be accepted well beyond the small circles of experimenters, theologians, and philosophers with whom it began.

"Printing, firearms, and the compass," wrote Francis Bacon, "no empire, sect or star appears to have exercised a greater power and influence on human affairs than these three mechanical discoveries."

THE INTELLECTUAL ORIGINS OF THE SCIENTIFIC REVOLUTION

What developments paved the way for the scientific revolution and how?

The scientific revolution marks one of the decisive breaks between the Middle Ages and the modern world. For all its novelty, however, it was rooted in earlier developments. Medieval artists and intellectuals had been observing and illustrating the natural world with great precision since at least the twelfth century. Medieval sculptors carved plants and vines with extraordinary accuracy, and fifteenth-century painters and sculptors devoted the same careful attention to the human face and form. Nor was the link between observation, experiment, and invention new to the sixteenth century. The magnetic compass had been known in Europe since the thirteenth century; gunpowder since the early fourteenth; printing, which permeated the intellectual life of the period and opened new possibilities—disseminating ideas quickly, collaborating more easily, buying books, and building libraries—since the middle of the fifteenth. "Printing, firearms, and the compass," wrote Francis Bacon, "no empire, sect or star appears to have exercised a greater power and influence on human affairs than these three mechanical discoveries." A fascination with light, which was a powerful symbol of divine illumination for medieval thinkers, encouraged the study of optics and, in turn, new techniques for grinding lenses. Lens grinders laid the groundwork for the seventeenth-century inventions of the telescope and microscope, creating reading glasses along the way. Astrologers were also active in the later Middle Ages, charting the heavens in the firm belief that the stars controlled the fates of human beings.

Behind these efforts to understand the natural world lay a nearly universal conviction that the natural world had been created by God. Religious belief spurred scientific study. One school of thinkers (the Neoplatonists) argued that nature was a book written by its creator to reveal the ways of God to humanity. Convinced that God's perfection must be reflected in

WHAT DEVELOPMENTS PAVED THE WAY FOR THE SCIENTIFIC REVOLUTION AND HOW?

THE INTELLECTUAL ORIGINS OF THE SCIENTIFIC REVOLUTION   581

nature, Neoplatonists searched for the ideal and perfect structures they believed must lie behind the "shadows" of the everyday world. Mathematics, particularly geometry, were important tools in this quest. Johannes Kepler, for example, was deeply influenced by Neoplatonism.

Renaissance humanism also helped prepare the grounds for the scientific revolution. The humanists' educational program placed a low value on natural philosophy, directing attention instead toward the recovery and study of classical antiquity, and humanists revered the authority of the ancients. Yet the energies the humanists poured into recovering, translating, and understanding classical texts (the source of conceptions of the natural world) made many of those important works available for the first time, and to a wider audience. Previously, Arabic sources had provided Europeans with the main route to ancient Greek learning; Greek classics were translated into Arabic and then picked up by late medieval scholars in Spain and Sicily. The humanists' return to the texts themselves—and the fact that the new texts could be more easily printed and circulated—encouraged new study and debate. Islamic scholars knew Ptolemy better than did Europeans until the humanist scholar and printer Johannes Regiomontanus recovered and prepared a new summary of Ptolemy's work. The humanist rediscovery of works by Archimedes—the great Greek mathematician who had proposed that the natural world operated on the basis of mechanical forces, like

> The humanists' return to the texts themselves—and the fact that the new texts could be more easily printed and circulated—encouraged new study and debate.

a great machine, and that these forces could be described mathematically—profoundly impressed important late-sixteenth- and seventeenth-century thinkers, including the Italian scientist Galileo, and shaped mechanical philosophy in the seventeenth century.

The Renaissance also encouraged collaboration between artisans and intellectuals. Twelfth- and thirteenth-century thinkers had observed the natural world, but they rarely tinkered with machines and they had little contact with the artisans who developed expertise in constructing machines for practical use. During the fifteenth century, however, these two worlds began to come together. Renaissance artists such as Leonardo da Vinci were accomplished craftsmen; they investigated the laws of perspective and optics, they worked out geometric methods for supporting the weight of enormous architectural domes, they studied the human body, and they devised new and more effective weapons for war. The Renaissance brought a vogue for alchemy and astrology; wealthy amateurs built observatories and measured the courses of the stars. These social and intellectual developments laid the groundwork for the scientific revolution.

What of the voyages of discovery? Sixteenth-century observers often linked the exploration of the globe to new knowledge of the cosmos. An admirer wrote to Galileo that he had kept the spirit of exploration alive: "The memory of Columbus and Vespucci will be renewed through you, and with even greater nobility, as the sky is more worthy than the earth." The parallel does not work quite so neatly. Columbus had not been driven by an interest in science. Moreover, it took centuries for European thinkers to process the New World's implications for different fields of study, and the links between the voyages of discovery and breakthroughs in science were largely indirect. The discoveries made the most immediate impact in the field of natural history, which was vastly enriched by travelers' detailed accounts of the flora and fauna of the Americas. Finding new lands and cultures in Africa and Asia and the revelation of the Americas, a world unknown to the ancients and unmentioned in the Bible, also laid bare gaps in Europeans' inherited body of knowledge. In this sense, the exploration of the New World dealt a blow to the authority of the ancients.

In sum, the late medieval recovery of ancient texts long thought to have been lost, the expansion of print culture and reading, the turmoil in the church and the

CHRONOLOGY

THE SCIENTIFIC REVOLUTION, 1543–1687

Publication of Copernicus's *On the Revolutions of the Heavenly Spheres*	1543
Tycho Brahe sets up Uranibourg observatory	1576
Kepler sets out his laws in his *Astronomia Nova*	1609
Galileo publishes *The Starry Messenger*	1610
Bacon publishes *Novum Organum*	1620
Galileo publishes *Dialogue Concerning the Two Chief World Systems*	1632
Descartes publishes *Discourse on Method*	1637
Newton publishes *Principia*	1687

fierce wars and political maneuvering that followed the Reformation, and the discovery of a new world across the oceans to explore and exploit, all shook the authority of older ways of thinking. What we call the scientific revolution was part of the intellectual excitement that surrounded these challenges, and, in retrospect, the scientific revolution enhanced and confirmed the importance of these other developments.

THE COPERNICAN REVOLUTION

How did Copernicus propose to correct the weaknesses in the inherited model of the cosmos?

Medieval cosmology (the medieval model of the universe) rested on ancient texts, particularly the work of Aristotle (384–322 B.C.E.), refined and systematized by Ptolemy of Alexandria (100–178 C.E.). Ptolemy himself built on the ideas of earlier Greek astronomers (see Chapter Four). According to this inherited cosmology, the heavens orbited the earth in a carefully organized hierarchy of spheres. Earth and the heavens were fundamentally different, made of different matter and subject to different laws of motion. The sun, moon, stars, and planets were formed of an unchanging (and perfect) quintessence or ether. The earth, by contrast, was composed of four elements (earth, water, fire, and air), and each of these elements had its natural place: the heavy elements (earth and water) toward the center and the lighter ones farther out. The heavens—first the planets, then the stars—traced perfect circular paths around the stationary earth. The motion of these celestial bodies was produced by a prime mover, whom Christians identified as God. The view fit Aristotelian physics, according to which objects could move only if acted on by an external force, and it fit with a belief that each fundamental element of the universe had a natural place. Moreover, the view both followed from and confirmed belief in the purposefulness of God's universe.

By the late Middle Ages astronomers knew that this cosmology, called the "Ptolemaic system," did not correspond exactly to what many had observed. Orbits did not conform to the Aristotelian ideal of perfect circles. Planets, Mars in particular, sometimes appeared

to loop backward before continuing on their paths. Ptolemy had managed to account for these orbital irregularities, but with complicated mathematics. By the early fifteenth century, the efforts to make the observed motions of the planets fit into the model of perfect circles in a geocentric (earth-centered) cosmos had produced astronomical charts that were mazes of complexity. Finally, the Ptolemaic system proved unable to solve serious difficulties with the calendar. That practical crisis precipitated Nicholas Copernicus's intellectual leap forward.

By the early sixteenth century the old Roman calendar was significantly out of alignment with the movement of the heavenly bodies. The major saints' days, Easter, and the other holy days were sometimes weeks off where they should have been according to the stars. Catholic authorities tried to correct this problem, consulting mathematicians and astronomers all over

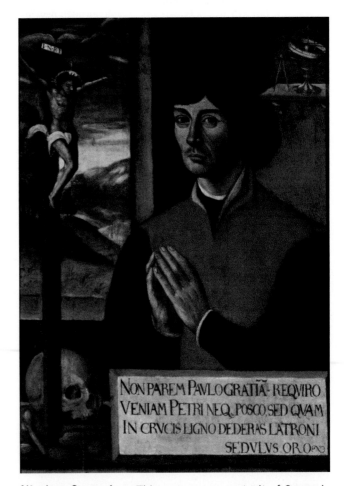

Nicolaus Copernicus. This anonymous portrait of Copernicus characteristically blends his devotion and his scientific achievements. His scholarly work (behind him in the form of an early planetarium) is driven by his faith (as he turns toward the image of Christ triumphant over death).

TO WHAT EXTENT DID BREAKTHROUGHS DEPEND ON NEW OBSERVATIONS? TO WHAT EXTENT ON NEW THEORIES?

TYCHO'S OBSERVATIONS AND KEPLER'S LAWS   583

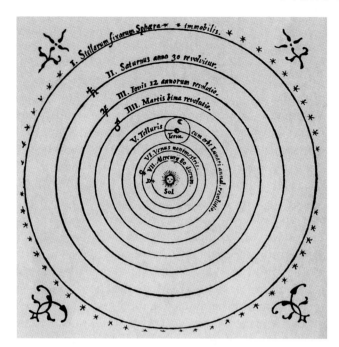

The Copernican Planetary System, 1617. A diagram from a seventeenth-century Dutch treatise depicting the heliocentric structure of the Copernican planetary system.

Europe. One of these was a Polish church official and astronomer, Nicholas Copernicus (1473–1543). Educated in Poland and northern Italy, he was a man of diverse talents. He was trained in astronomy, canon law, and medicine. He read Greek. He was well versed in ancient philosophy. He was also a careful mathematician and a devout Catholic, who did not believe that God's universe could be as messy as the one in Ptolemy's model. His proposed solution, based on mathematical calculations, was simple and radical: Ptolemy was mistaken; the earth was neither stationary nor at the center of the planetary system; the earth rotated on its axis and orbited with the other planets around the sun. Reordering the Ptolemaic system simplified the geometry of astronomy and made the orbits of the planets comprehensible.

Copernicus was in many ways a conservative thinker. He did not consider his work to be a break with either the church or with the authority of ancient texts. He believed, rather, that he had restored a pure understanding of God's design, one that had been lost over the centuries. Still, the implications of his theory troubled him. His ideas contradicted centuries of astronomical thought, and they were hard to reconcile with the observed behavior of objects on earth. If the earth moved, why was that movement imperceptible? Copernicus calculated the distance from the Earth to the Sun to be at least 6 million miles. Even by Coper-

nicus's very low estimate, the Earth was hurtling around the Sun at the dizzying rate of many thousands of miles an hour. How did people and objects remain standing? (The earth is actually about 93 million miles from the sun, moving through space at 67,000 miles an hour and spinning on its axis at about 1,000 miles an hour!)

Copernicus was not a physicist. He tried to refine, rather than overturn, traditional Aristotelian physics, but his effort to reconcile that physics with his new model of a sun-centered universe created new problems and inconsistencies that he could not resolve. These frustrations and complications dogged Copernicus's later years, and he hesitated to publish his findings. Just before his death, he consented to the release of his major treatise, *On the Revolutions of the Heavenly Spheres* (*De Revolutionibus*), in 1543. To fend off scandal, the Lutheran scholar who saw his manuscript through the press added an introduction to the book declaring that Copernicus's system should be understood as an abstraction, a set of mathematical tools for doing astronomy and not a dangerous claim about the nature of heaven and earth. For decades after 1543, Copernicus's ideas were taken in just that sense—as useful but not realistic mathematical hypotheses. In the long run, however, as historian Steven Shapin puts it, Copernicanism represented the first "serious and systematic" challenge to the Ptolemaic conception of the universe.

TYCHO'S OBSERVATIONS AND KEPLER'S LAWS

To what extent did breakthroughs depend on new observations? To what extent on new theories?

Within fifty years, Copernicus's cosmology was revived and modified by two astronomers also critical of the Ptolemaic model of the universe: Tycho Brahe (*TI-koh BRAH-hee*, 1546–1601) and Johannes Kepler (1571–1630). Each was considered the greatest astronomer of his day. Tycho was born into the Danish nobility but he abandoned his family's military and political legacy to pursue his passion for astronomy. He was hot headed as well as talented; at twenty he lost part of his nose in a duel. Like Copernicus he sought to correct the contradictions in traditional astronomy.

Tycho Brahe, 1662. This seventeenth-century tribute shows the master astronomer in his observatory.

Unlike Copernicus, who was a theoretician, Tycho championed observation and believed careful study of the heavens would unlock the secrets of the universe. He first made a name for himself by observing a completely new star, a "nova," that flared into sight in 1572. The Danish king Friedrich II, impressed by Tycho's work, granted him the use of a small island, where he built a castle specially designed to house an observatory. For over twenty years, Tycho meticulously charted the movements of each significant object in the night sky, compiling the finest set of astronomical data in Europe.

Tycho was not a Copernican. He suggested that the planets orbited the sun and the whole system then orbited a stationary earth. This picture of cosmic order, though clumsy, seemed to fit the observed evidence better than the Ptolemaic system, and it avoided the upsetting physical and theological implications of the

Copernican model. In the late 1590s, Tycho moved his work and his huge collection of data to Prague, where he became court astronomer to the Holy Roman emperor Rudolph II. In Prague he was assisted by a young mathematician from a troubled family, Johannes Kepler. Kepler was more impressed with the Copernican model than was Tycho, and Kepler combined study of Copernicus's work with his own interest in mysticism, astrology, and the religious power of mathematics.

Kepler believed that everything in creation, from human souls to the orbits of the planets, had been created according to mathematical laws. Understanding those laws would thus allow humans to share God's wisdom and penetrate the inner secrets of the universe. Mathematics was God's language. Kepler's search for the pattern of mathematical perfection took him through musical harmonies, nested geometric shapes inside the planets' orbits, and numerical formulas. After Tycho's death, Kepler inherited Tycho's position in Prague, as well as his trove of observations and calculations. That data demonstrated to Kepler that two of Copernicus's assumptions abut planetary motion simply

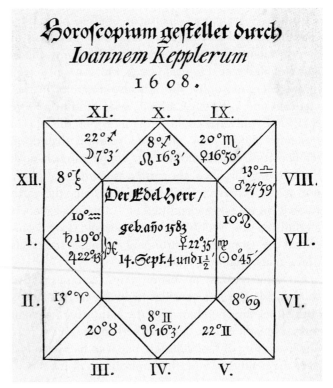

Kepler's Horoscope for von Wallenstein. Kepler, famous for his contribution to modern astronomy, also believed in astrology. He made this horoscope for Eusebius von Wallenstein, who was a general for the Holy Roman Emperor during the Thirty Years' War.

did not match observations. Copernicus, in keeping with Aristotelian notions of perfection, had believed that planetary orbits were circular. Kepler calculated that the planets traveled in elliptical orbits around the sun; this finding became his First Law. Copernicus held that planetary motion was uniform; Kepler's Second Law stated that the speed of the planets varied with their distance from the sun. Kepler also argued that magnetic forces between the sun and the planets kept the planets in orbital motion, an insight that paved the way for Newton's law of universal gravitation formulated nearly eighty years later, at the end of the seventeenth century.

Each of Kepler's works, beginning with *Cosmographic Mystery* in 1596 and continuing with *New Astronomy or Celestial Physics* in 1609 and *The Harmonies of the World* in 1619, revised and augmented Copernicus's theory. His version of Copernicanism fit with remarkable accuracy the best observations of the time (which were Tycho's). Kepler's search for rules of motion that could account for the earth's movements in its new position was also significant. More than Copernicus, Kepler broke down the distinction between the heavens and the earth that had been at the heart of Aristotelian physics.

NEW HEAVENS, NEW EARTH, AND WORLDLY POLITICS: GALILEO

Was Galileo a success? Why?

Kepler had a friend deliver a copy of *Cosmographic Mystery* to the "mathematician named Galileus Galileus," then teaching mathematics and astronomy at Padua, near Venice. Galileo thanked Kepler in a letter that nicely illustrates the Italian's views at the time (1597).

> So far I have only perused the preface of your work, but from this I gained some notion of its intent, and I indeed congratulate myself of having an associate in the study of Truth who is a friend of Truth. . . . I adopted the teaching of Copernicus many years ago, and his point of view enables me to explain many phenomena of nature which certainly remain

inexplicable according to the more current hypotheses. I have written many arguments in support of him and in refutation of the opposite view—which, however, so far I have not dared to bring into the public light. . . . I would certainly dare to publish my reflections at once if more people like you existed; as they don't, I shall refrain from doing so.

Kepler replied, urging Galileo to "come forward!" Galileo did not answer.

At Padua, Galileo couldn't teach what he believed; Ptolemic astronomy and Aristotelian cosmology were the established curriculum. As other opportunities opened up, the ambitious natural philosopher would become less cagey about his views. By the end of his career, Galileo had provided powerful evidence in support of the Copernican model and laid the foundation for a new physics. What was more, he was a witty and persuasive writer, who wrote in the vernacular (Italian) as well as in Latin. Kepler may have been a "friend of Truth," but his work was abstruse and bafflingly mathematical. (So was Copernicus's.) By contrast, Galileo's writings were widely translated and widely read, raising awareness of changes in natural philosophy across Europe. Galileo was a popularizer, and what he popularized was a non-Aristotelian approach to science, with Copernicanism as its centerpiece.

Galileo (1564–1642) was self-assured and contentious—known, as one of his biographers puts it, for his opinions as well as his discoveries. He was impatient with those who opposed him, and his temperament got him into serious and ultimately stifling controversies. He made the case for a new relationship between religion and science, challenging in the process some of the most powerful churchmen of his day. His discoveries made him the most famous scientific figure of his time, but his confidence in his convictions and his penchant for controversy put him on a collision course with Aristotelian philosophy and the authority of the Catholic Church.

Galileo became famous by way of discoveries with the telescope. In 1609 he heard reports from Holland of a lens grinder who had made a spyglass that could magnify very distant objects. Excited, Galileo quickly devised his own telescope; trained it first on earthly objects to demonstrate that it worked; and then, momentously, pointed it at the night sky. The results

By the end of his career, Galileo had provided powerful evidence in support of the Copernican model and laid the foundation for a new physics.

made his career. Galileo studied the moon, finding on it mountains, plains, and other features of an earth-like landscape. His observations suggested that celestial bodies resembled the earth, a view at odds with the conception of the heavens as an unchanging sphere of heavenly perfection, inherently and necessarily different from the earth. He saw moons orbiting Jupiter, evidence that earth was not at the center of all orbits. He saw spots on the sun. Galileo published the results of his observations, first in *The Starry Messenger* (1610) and then in *Letters on Sunspots* in 1613. *The Starry Messenger,* with its amazing reports of Jupiter's moons, was short, aimed to be read by many, and bold. Its frontispiece declared that its pages revealed "great, unusual, and remarkable spectacles, opening these to the consideration of every man, especially of philosophers and astronomers." *The Starry Messenger,* however, only hinted at Galileo's Copernicanism. The *Letters on Sunspots* declared it openly.

A seventeenth-century scientist needed powerful and wealthy patrons. As a professor of mathematics at Padua, Galileo (as he wrote to Kepler) chafed at the power of university authorities. Princely courts offered an inviting alternative. Centers of power and wealth and dispensers of patronage, they were also less subject to church control than the universities. The Medici family of Tuscany, like others, burnished its reputation and bolstered its power by surrounding itself with intellectuals as well as artists. (In the fifteenth century, the Medicis had been patrons of Michelangelo.) Persuaded he would be freer at its court than in Padua, Galileo took a position as tutor to the Medicis and flattered and successfully cultivated the family. He addressed *The Starry Messenger* to them. He named the newly discovered moons of Jupiter "the Medicean stars." He was rewarded with the title of chief mathematician and philosopher to Cosimo de' Medici, the grand duke of Tuscany. Now well positioned in Italy's networks of power and patronage, Galileo was able to pursue his work on astronomy and his conviction that Copernicus's heliocentric (sun-centered) model of the planetary system was correct.

This pursuit, however, was a high-wire act, for he could not afford to antagonize the Catholic Church. Not all churchmen opposed Galileo's work. The great Jesuit astronomers of the day, in fact, accepted his telescopic discoveries. They argued, however, that those discoveries fit perfectly well with Tycho's system and did not require displacing the earth from its position at the center of the universe. Yet politics, intellectual rivalries, Galileo's enthusiastic Copernican friends, and

his own zest for controversy made it hard for Galileo to avoid trouble. In 1614, an ambitious and outspoken Dominican monk denounced Galileo's ideas as dangerous deviations from biblical teachings. Other philosophers and churchmen began to ask Galileo's patrons, the Medicis, whether their court mathematician was teaching heresy.

Disturbed by the murmurings against Copernicanism, Galileo penned a series of letters to defend himself, letters that addressed the relationship between natural philosophy and religion. The best known of these was written in 1615 to the Grand Duchess Christina, mother of Galileo's patron, Cosimo (see next page). Galileo argued that one could be a sincere Copernican and a sincere Catholic. The church, Galileo said, did the sacred work of teaching scripture and saving souls. Accounting for the workings of the physical world was a task better left to natural philosophy, grounded in observation and mathematics. The Bible was a notoriously difficult book, and it was the role of the church's theologians to reconcile its complexity with the new conclusions of natural philosophy. For the church to take a side in controversies over natural science, however, was both needless and risky; to do so might compromise the church's spiritual authority and credibility. Galileo envisioned natural philosophers and theologians as partners in a search for truth, but with very different roles. In a brilliant rhetorical moment, he quoted Cardinal Baronius in suppport of his own argument: the purpose of the Bible was to "teach us how to go to heaven, not how heaven goes."

In spite of Galileo's arguments, the church moved against Copernicanism and against him. In 1616 the Inquisition ruled the propositions that the earth moves and the sun does not "foolish and absurd in philosophy and formally heretical." A decree placed Copernicus's *De Revolutionibus* on the Index of Prohibited Books, and Galileo was warned not to teach Copernicanism.

For a while, he did as he was asked. But when his Florentine friend and admirer Maffeo Barberini was elected pope as Urban VIII in 1623, Galileo believed the door to Copernicanism was (at least half) open. He drafted one of his most famous works, *A Dialogue Concerning the Two Chief World Systems* published in 1632. The *Dialogue* was a hypothetical debate between supporters of the old Ptolemaic system, represented by a character he named Simplicio (simpleton) on the one hand and proponents of the new astronomy on the other. Throughout, Galileo gave the best lines to the Copernicans. At the very end, however, to satisfy the letter

GALILEO ON NATURE, SCRIPTURE, AND TRUTH

One of the clearest statements of Galileo's convictions about religion and science comes from his 1615 letter to the grand duchess Christina, mother of Galileo's patron, Cosimo de' Medici and a powerful figure in her own right. Galileo knew that others objected to his work. The church had warned him that Copernicanism was inaccurate and impious; it could be disproved scientifically, and it contradicted the authority of those who interpreted the Bible. Thoroughly dependent on the Medicis for support, he wrote to the grand duchess to explain his position. In this section of the letter, Galileo sets out his understanding of the parallel but distinct roles of the church and natural philosophers. He walks a fine line between acknowledging the authority of the church and standing firm in his convictions.

Possibly because they are disturbed by the known truth of other propositions of mine which differ from those commonly held, and therefore mistrusting their defense so long as they confine themselves to the field of philosophy, these men have resolved to fabricate a shield for their fallacies out of the mantle of pretended religion and the authority of the Bible. . . .

Copernicus never discusses matters of religion or faith, nor does he use arguments that depend in any way upon the authority of sacred writings which he might have interpreted erroneously. He stands always upon physical conclusions pertaining to the celestial motions, and deals with them by astronomical and geometrical demonstrations, founded primarily upon sense experiences and very exact observations. He did not ignore the Bible, but he knew very well that if his doctrine were proved, then it could not contradict the Scriptures when they were rightly understood. . . .

I think that in discussions of physical problems we ought to begin not from the authority of scriptural passages, but from sense-experiences and necessary demonstrations; for the holy Bible and the phenomena of nature proceed alike from the divine Word, the former as the dictate of the Holy Ghost and the latter as the observant executrix of God's commands. It is necessary for the Bible, in order to be accommodated to the understanding of every man, to speak many things which appear to differ from the absolute truth so far as the bare meaning of the words is concerned. But Nature, on the other hand, is inexorable and immutable; she never transgresses the laws imposed upon her, or cares a whit whether her abstruse reasons and methods of operation are understandable to men. For that reason it appears that nothing physical which sense-experience sets before our eyes, or which necessary demonstrations prove to us, ought to be called in question (much less condemned) upon the testimony of biblical passages which may have some different meaning beneath their words. For the Bible is not chained in every expression to conditions as strict as those which govern all physical effects; nor is God any less excellently revealed in Nature's actions than in the sacred statements of the Bible. . . .

Galileo, "Letter to the Grand Duchess Christina," in *The Discoveries and Opinions of Galileo Galilei*, ed. Stillman Drake (Garden City, N.Y., 1957), pp. 177–183.

QUESTIONS FOR ANALYSIS

1. Why did Galileo need to defend his views in a letter to Christina de' Medici?
2. For Galileo, what is the relationship among God, man, and nature?

of the Inquisition's decree, he had them capitulate to Simplicio.

The Inquisition banned the *Dialogue* and ordered Galileo to stand trial in 1633. Pope Urban, provoked by Galileo's scorn and needing support from church conservatives during a difficult stretch of the Thirty Years' War, refused to protect his former friend. The verdict of the secret trial shocked Europe. Galileo was the most famous scientific figure of his day and the pride of one of the great intellectual centers of Europe. Yet the Inquisition forced Galileo to repent his Copernican position, banned him from working on or even discussing Copernican ideas, and placed him under house arrest for life. According to a story that began to circulate shortly afterward, as he left the court for house arrest he stamped his foot and muttered defiantly, looking down at the earth: "Still, it moves."

The Inquisition could not put Galileo off his life's work. He refined the theories of motion he had begun to develop early in his career. He proposed an early version of the theory of inertia, which held that an object's motion stays the same until an outside force changed it. He calculated that objects of different weights fall at almost the same speed and with a uniform acceleration. He argued that the motion of objects follows regular mathematical laws. The same laws that govern the motions of objects on earth (which could be observed in experiments) could also be observed in the heavens—again a direct contradiction of Aristotelian principles and an important step toward a coherent physics based on a sun-centered model of the universe. Compiled under the title *Two New Sciences* (1638), this work was smuggled out of Italy and published in Protestant Holland.

Galileo provided powerful, though not conclusive, evidence for Copernican cosmology. He also combined discovery, observation, experiment, and mathematics to suggest universal laws of motion. Among his legacies, however, was exactly the rift between religion and science that he had hoped to avoid. Galileo believed that Copernicanism and natural philosophy in general need not subvert theological truths, religious belief, or

Galileo Galilei before the Inquisition by Francois Richard Fleury. This nineteenth-century painting of Galileo before the Holy Office dramatizes the conflict between science and religion and depicts the Italian natural philosopher as defiant. In fact, Galileo submitted, but continued his work under house arrest and published, secretly, in the Netherlands.

WHAT THINKERS AND INSTITUTIONS WERE IMPORTANT IN THE DEVELOPMENT OF SCIENCE AS A PRACTICE?

METHODS FOR A NEW PHILOSOPHY: BACON AND DESCARTES   589

the authority of the church. But his trial seemed to show the contrary, that natural philosophy and church authority could not coexist. Galileo's trial silenced Copernican voices in southern Europe, and the church's leadership retreated into conservative reaction. It was therefore in northwest Europe that the new philosophy Galileo had championed would flourish.

METHODS FOR A NEW PHILOSOPHY: BACON AND DESCARTES

What thinkers and institutions were important in the development of science as a practice?

As the practice of the new sciences became concentrated in Protestant northwest Europe, new thinkers began to spell out standards of practice and evidence. Sir Francis Bacon and René Descartes (*deh-KAHRT*) loomed especially large in this development: setting out methods or the rules that should govern modern science. Bacon (1561–1626) lived at roughly the same time as Kepler and Galileo—and Shakespeare; Descartes (1596–1650) was slightly younger. Both Bacon and Descartes came to believe that theirs was an age of profound change, open to the possibility of astonishing discovery. Both were persuaded that knowledge could take the European moderns beyond the ancient authorities. Both set out to formulate a philosophy to encompass the learning of their age.

"Knowledge is power." The phrase is Bacon's and captures the changing perspective of the seventeenth century and its new confidence in the potential of human thinking. Bacon trained as a lawyer, served in Parliament and, briefly, as lord chancellor to James I of England. His abiding concern was with the assumptions, methods, and practices that he believed should guide natural philosophers and the progress of knowledge. The authority of the ancients should not constrain the ambition of modern thinkers. Deferring to accepted doctrines could block innovation or obstruct understanding. "There is but one course left . . . to try the whole thing anew upon a better plan, and to com-

"Knowledge is power." The phrase is Bacon's and captures the changing perspective of the seventeenth century and its new confidence in the potential of human thinking.

mence a total reconstruction of sciences, arts, and all human knowledge, raised upon the proper foundations." To pursue knowledge did not mean to think abstractly and leap to conclusions; it meant observing, experimenting, confirming ideas, or demonstrating points. If thinkers will be "content to begin with doubts," Bacon wrote, "they shall end with certainties." We thus associate Bacon with the gradual separation of scientific investigation from philosophical argument.

Bacon advocated an *inductive* approach to knowledge: amassing evidence from specific observations to draw general conclusions. In Bacon's view, many philosophical errors arose from beginning with assumed first principles. The traditional view of the cosmos, for instance, rested on the principles of a prime mover and the perfection of circular motion. The inductive method required accumulating data (as Tycho had done, for example) and then, after careful review and experiment, drawing appropriate conclusions. Bacon argued that knowledge was best tested through the cooperative efforts of researchers performing experiments that could be repeated and verified. The knowledge thus gained would be predictable and useful to philosophers and artisans alike, contributing to a wide range of endeavors from astronomy to shipbuilding.

Bacon's vision of science and progress is vividly illustrated by two images. The first, more familiar, is the title page of Bacon's *Great Instauration* (*Instauratio Magna*, 1620) with its bold ships sailing out beyond the Strait of Gibraltar, formerly the limits of the west, into the open sea, in pursuit of unknown but great things to come. The second is Bacon's description of an imagined factory of discovery, "Solomon's house," at end of his utopian *New Atlantis* (1626). Inside the factory, "sifters" would examine and conduct experiments, passing on findings to senior researchers who would draw conclusions and develop practical applications.

Descartes was French, though he lived all over Europe. He was intellectually restless as well; he worked in geometry, cosmology, optics, and physiology—for a while dissecting cow carcasses daily. He was writing a (Copernican) book on physics when he heard of Galileo's condemnation in 1633, a judgement that impressed on him the dangers of "expressing judgements on this world." Descartes's *The Discourse on Method* (1637), for which he is best known, began simply as a preface to three essays on optics, geometry, and

TWO REACTIONS TO THE "NEW PHILOSOPHY"

In his poem "An Anatomie of the World" (1611), the English poet John Donne (1572–1631) summed up the sense of loss and confusion created by the new discoveries in science. "The element of fire" refers to Aristotle's physics. The second selection here is an excerpt from Francis Bacon's Novum Organum *(1620), or "The New Instrument." (The Organon was the name given in the Middle Ages to Aristotle's writings on logic, which became the basic texts of a university education.) Bacon boldly summed up the new learning and new forms of reasoning. Bacon, like Donne, was English. His view of the world, of human knowledge, and of human possibility, however, was very different.*

AN ANATOMIE OF THE WORLD

And new Philosophy calls all in doubt,
The element of Fire is quite put out;
The Sun is lost, and th' Earth, and no man's wit
Can well direct him where to looke for it.
And freely men confesse that this world's spent,
When in the Planets, and the Firmament,
They seeke so many new; they see that this
Is crumbled out againe to his Atomis.
'Tis all in pieces, all cohaerence gone,
All just supply, and all Relation:
Prince, Subject, Father, Sonne, are things forgot,
For every man alone thinkes he hath got
To be a Phoenix, and that then can be
None of that kinde, of which he is, but he.
This is the worlds condition now. . . .

APHORISMS FROM *NOVUM ORGANUM*

XXXI

It is idle to expect any great advancement in science from the superinducing and engrafting of new things upon old. We must begin anew from the very foundations, unless we would revolve forever in a circle with mean and contemptible progress. . . .

XXXVI

One method of delivery alone remains to us which is simply this: we must lead men to the particulars themselves, and their series and order; while men on their side must force themselves for a while to lay their notions by and begin to familiarize themselves with facts. . . .

XLV

The human understanding of its own nature is prone to suppose the existence of more order and regularity in the world than it finds. And though there be many things in nature which are singular and unmatched, yet it devises for them parallels and conjugates and relatives which do not exist. Hence the fiction that all celestial bodies move in perfect circles. . . . Hence too the element of fire with its orb is brought in, to make up the square with the other three which the sense perceives. . . . And so on of other dreams. And these fancies affect not dogmas only, but simple notions also. . . .

XCV

Those who have handled sciences have been either men of experiment or men of dogmas. The men of experiment are like the ant, they only collect and use; the reasoners resemble spiders, who make cobwebs out of their own substance. But the bee takes a middle course: it gathers its material from the flowers of the garden and of the field, but transforms and digests it by a power of its own. Not unlike this is the true business of philosophy; for it neither relies solely or chiefly on the powers of the mind, nor does it take the matter which it gathers from natural history and mechanical experiments and lay it up in the memory whole . . . but lays it up in the understanding altered and digested. Therefore, from a closer and purer league between these two faculties, the experimental and the rational (such as has never yet been made), much may be hoped. . . .

Michael R. Matthews, ed., *The Scientific Background to Modern Philosophy: Selected Readings* (Indianapolis and Cambridge, 1989), pp. 47–48, 50–52.

QUESTIONS FOR ANALYSIS

1. How does Bacon see the relationship between human understanding and science?

meteorology. It is personal, recounting Descartes's dismay at the "strange and unbelievable" theories he encountered in his traditional education. His first response, as he described it, was to systematically doubt everything he had ever known or been taught. Better to clear the slate, he believed, than to build an edifice of knowledge on received assumptions. His first rule was "never to receive anything as a truth which [he] did not clearly know to be such." He took the human ability to think as his point of departure, summed up in his famous and enigmatic, *Je pense, donc je suis,* later translated into Latin as *cogito ergo sum* and in English as "I think, therefore I am." As the phrase suggests, Descartes's doubting led (quickly, by our standards) to self-assurance and truth: the thinking individual existed, reason existed, God existed. For Descartes, then, doubt was a ploy, or a piece that he used in an intellectual chess game to defeat skepticism. Certainty, not doubt, was the centerpiece of the philosophy he bequeathed to his followers.

Descartes, like Bacon, sought a "fresh start for knowledge" or the rules for understanding of the world as it was. Unlike Bacon, Descartes emphasized *deductive* reasoning, proceeding logically from one certainty to another. "So long as we avoid accepting as true what is not so," he wrote in *Discourse on Method,* "and always preserve the right order of deduction of one thing from another, there can be nothing too remote to be reached in the end, or too well hidden to be discovered." For

Descartes, author of *Discourse on Method* (1637), explaining his theories to Queen Kristina of Sweden.

Descartes, mathematical thought expressed the highest standards of reason, and his work contributed greatly to the authority of mathematics as a model for scientific reasoning.

Descartes made a particularly forceful statement for *mechanism*, a view of the world shared by Bacon and Galileo and one that came to dominate seventeenth-century scientific thought. As the name suggested, mechanical philosophy proposed to consider nature as a machine. It rejected the traditional Aristotelian distinction between the works of humans and those of nature and the view that nature, as God's creation, necessarily belonged to a different—and higher—order. In the new picture of the universe that was emerging from the discoveries and writings of the early seventeenth century, it seemed that all matter was composed of the same material and all motion obeyed the same laws. Descartes sought to explain everything, including the human body, mechanically. As he put it firmly, "There is no difference between the machines built by artisans and the diverse bodies that nature alone composes." Nature operated according to regular and predictable laws and was thus accessible to human reason. The belief guided, indeed inspired, much of the scientific experiment and argument of the seventeenth century.

THE POWER OF METHOD AND THE FORCE OF CURIOSITY: SEVENTEENTH-CENTURY EXPERIMENTERS

For nearly a century after Bacon and Descartes, most of England's natural philosophers were Baconian, and most of their colleagues in France, Holland, and elsewhere in northern Europe were Cartesians (followers of Descartes). The English Baconians concentrated on performing experiments in many different fields, producing results that could then be debated and discussed. The Cartesians turned instead toward mathematics and logic. Descartes himself pioneered analytical geometry. Blaise Pascal (1623–1662) worked on probability theory and invented a calculating machine before applying his intellectual skills to theology. The Cartesian thinker Christian Huygens (1629–1695) from Holland combined mathematics with experiments to understand problems of impact and orbital motion. The Dutch Cartesian Baruch Spinoza (1632–1677) applied geometry to ethics and believed he had gone beyond Descartes by proving that the universe was composed of a single substance that was both God and nature.

English experimenters pursued a different course. They began with practical research, putting the alchemist's tool, the laboratory, to new uses. They also sought a different kind of conclusion: empirical laws or provisional generalizations based on evidence rather than absolute statements of deductive truth. Among the many English laboratory scientists of the era were the physician William Harvey (1578–1657), the chemist Robert Boyle (1627–1691), and the inventor and experimenter Robert Hooke (1635–1703).

Harvey's contribution was enormous: he observed and explained that blood circulated through the arteries, heart, and veins. To do this he was willing to dissect living animals (vivisection) and experiment on himself. Boyle performed experiments and established a law (known as Boyle's law) showing that at a constant temperature the volume of a gas decreases in proportion to the pressure placed on it. Hooke introduced the microscope to the experimenter's tool kit. The compound microscope had been invented in Holland early in the seventeenth century. But it was not until the 1660s that Hooke and others demonstrated its potential by using it to study the cellular structure of plants. Like the telescope before it, the microscope revealed an unexpected dimension of material phenom-

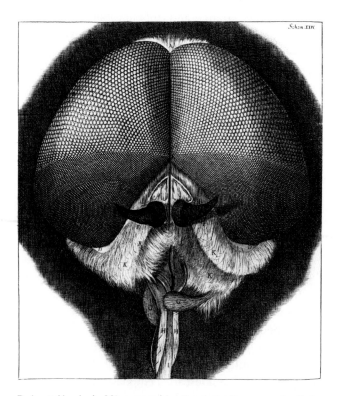

Robert Hooke's *Micrographia*. Hooke's diagram of a fly's eye as seen through a microscope seemed to reveal just the sort of intricate universe the mechanists predicted.

WHAT THINKERS AND INSTITUTIONS WERE IMPORTANT IN THE DEVELOPMENT OF SCIENCE AS A PRACTICE?

METHODS FOR A NEW PHILOSOPHY: BACON AND DESCARTES   593

CHRONOLOGY

MAJOR FIGURES OF THE SCIENTIFIC REVOLUTION

Nicholas Copernicus	1473–1543
Tycho Brahe	1546–1601
Francis Bacon	1561–1626
Galileo Galilei	1564–1642
Johannes Kepler	1571–1630
William Harvey	1578–1657
René Descartes	1596–1650
Blaise Pascal	1623–1662
Robert Boyle	1627–1691
Christian Huygens	1629–1695
Baruch Spinoza	1632–1677
Robert Hooke	1635–1703
Isaac Newton	1642–1727

ena. Examining even the most ordinary objects revealed detailed structures of perfectly connected smaller parts and persuaded many that with improved instruments they would uncover even more of the world's intricacies.

The microscope also provided what many regarded as new evidence of God's existence. The way each minute structure of a living organism, when viewed under a microscope, corresponded to its purpose testified not only to God's existence but to God's wisdom as well. The mechanical philosophy did not exclude God but in fact could be used to confirm his presence. If the universe was a clock, after all, there must be a clockmaker. Hooke himself declared that only imbeciles would believe that what they saw under the microscope was "the production of chance" rather than of God's creation.

The French Academy of Sciences was founded in 1666 and was also tied to seventeenth-century state building, in this case Bourbon absolutism.

SCIENCE, SOCIETY, AND THE STATE

Seventeenth-century state building (see Chapter Fourteen) helped secure the rise of science. In 1660, England's monarchy was restored after two decades of revolution and civil war. The newly crowned King Charles II granted a group of natural philosophers and mathematicians a royal charter (1662) to establish the Royal Society of London, for the "improvement of natural knowledge" and committed to experimentation and collaborative work among natural philosophers. The founders of the Royal Society, in particular Boyle, believed it could serve a political as well as an intellectual purpose. The Royal Society would pursue Bacon's goal of collective research in which members would conduct formal experiments, record the results, and share them with other members. These members would in turn study the methods, reproduce the experiment, and assess the outcome. The enterprise would give England's natural philosophers a common sense of purpose and a system to reach reasoned, gentlemanly agreement on "matters of fact." But by separating systematic scientific research from the dangerous language of politics and religion that had marked the civil war, the Royal Society could also help restore a sense of order and consensus to English intellectual life.

The society's journal, *Philosophical Transactions*, reached out to professional scholars and experimenters throughout Europe. Similar societies began to appear elsewhere. The French Academy of Sciences was founded in 1666 and was also tied to seventeenth-century state building, in this case Bourbon absolutism (see Chapter Fifteen). Royal societies, devoted to natural philosophy as a collective enterprise, provided a state (or princely) sponsored framework for science and an alternative to the important but uncertain patronage of smaller nobles or to the religious (and largely conservative, Aristotelian) universities. Scientific societies reached rough agreement about what constituted legitimate research. They established the modern scientific custom of crediting discoveries to those who were first to publish results. They enabled information and theories to be exchanged more easily across national boundaries, although philosophical differences among Cartesians, Baconians, and traditional Aristotelians remained very difficult to bridge. Science began to take shape as a discipline.

Natural philosophy was, officially, a gentlemanly pursuit. Neither the Royal Society of England nor its French counterpart admitted women. Although women had almost no access to formal education, some could educate themselves by associating with learned men. The aristocratic Margaret Cavendish (1623–1673), for instance, gleaned the information necessary to get her started largely from her family. That observatories were built in private residences enabled some women living in such homes to work their way into the growing field of astronomy. In fact, 14 percent of German astronomers between 1650 and 1710 were women, the most famous of whom was Maria Winkelmann (1670–1720). Winkelmann discovered a comet and prepared calendars for the Berlin Academy of Science but was barred from entering the academy. Gottfried Leibniz, the academy's president explained that, "Already during her husband's lifetime the society was burdened with ridicule because its calendar was prepared by a woman. If she were now to be kept on in such capacity, mouths would gape even wider." Maria Sibylla Merian (1647–1717) also made a career based on observation, in the field of entomology. Merian supported herself and her two daughters by selling exotic insects she collected in the Dutch colony of Surinam. She fought the colony's sweltering climate and malaria to publish her most important scientific work, the *Metamorphosis of the Insects of Surinam,* which details the life cycles of Surinam's insects in sixty ornate illustrations. Merian's *Metamorphosis* was well received in her time; in fact, Peter I of Russia proudly displayed Merian's portrait and books in his study.

Newton Experimenting with Light. Newton showed that what seemed to be a single ray of light could be broken down into many different ones.

"AND ALL WAS LIGHT": ISAAC NEWTON

What problems did Newton solve?

Sir Isaac Newton's work marks the culmination of the scientific revolution. Galileo, peering through his telescope in the early 1600s, had come to believe that the Earth and the heavens were made of the same material. Galileo's experiments with pendulums aimed to discover the laws of motion (and he proposed theories of inertia). It was Newton who articulated those laws and presented a coherent, unified vision of how the universe worked. All bodies in the universe, Newton said, whether on Earth or in the heavens, obeyed the same basic laws. One set of forces and one pattern, which could be expressed mathematically, explained why planets orbited in ellipses and why (and at what speed) apples fell from trees. An

> The man who came to represent the personification of modern science was reclusive, secretive about his findings, and obsessive.

Italian mathematician later commented that Newton was the "greatest and most fortunate of mortals"— because there was only one universe, and he had discovered its laws.

Isaac Newton (1642–1727) was born on Christmas Day to a family of small landowners. His father died before his birth, and it fell to a succession of relatives, family friends, and schoolmasters to spot, then encourage, his genius. In 1661 he entered Trinity College in Cambridge University, where he would remain for the next thirty-five years, first as a student, then as the Lucasian Professor of Mathematics. The man who came to represent the personification of modern science was reclusive, secretive about his findings, and obsessive. During his early work with optics he experimented with his own eyes, pressing them to see how different shapes would change the effects of light and then, intrigued by what he found, inserting a very thick needle "betwixt my eye and the bone as neare to the backside of my eye as I could" to actually curve his eyeball. (Please do not try this at home.)

Newton's first great burst of creativity came at Cambridge, in the years from 1664 to 1666, "the prime of my age for invention." During these years Newton broke new ground in three areas. The first was optics. Descartes believed that color was a secondary quality produced by the speed of particulate rotation but that light itself was white. Newton, using prisms he had purchased at a local fair, showed that white light was composed of different-colored rays. The second area in which Newton produced innovative work during these years was in mathematics. In a series of brilliant insights, he invented both integral calculus and differential calculus, providing mathematical tools to model motion in space. The third area of his creative genius involved his early works on gravity. Newton later told different versions of the same story: the idea about gravity had come to him when he was in a "contemplative mood" and was "occasioned by the fall of an apple." Why did the apple "not go sideways or upwards, but constantly to the earth's center?" "Assuredly the reason is, that the earth draws it. There must be a drawing power in matter." Voltaire, the eighteenth-century French essayist, retold the story to dramatize Newton's simple brilliance. But the theory of gravity rested on mathematical formulations, it was far from simple, and it would not be fully worked out until *Principia*, more than twenty years later.

Newton's work on the composite nature of white light led him to make a reflecting telescope, which used a curved mirror rather than lenses. The telescope earned him election to the Royal Society (in 1672) and drew him out of his sheltered obscurity at Cambridge. Encouraged by the Royal Society's support, he wrote a paper describing his theory of optics and allowed it to be published in *Philosophical Transactions*. Astronomers and scientists across Europe applauded the work. Robert Hooke, the Royal Society's curator of experiments, did not. Hooke was unpersuaded by Newton's mode of argument; he found Newton's claims that science had to be mathematical both dogmatic and high-handed; and he objected—in a series of sharp exchanges with the reclusive genius—that Newton had not provided any physical explanation for his results. Stung by the conflict with Hooke and persuaded

that few natural philosophers could understand his theories, Newton withdrew to Cambridge and long refused to share his work. Only the patient effort of friends and fellow scientists like the astronomer Edmond Halley (1656–1742), already well known for his astronomical observations in the Southern Hemisphere and the person for whom Halley's Comet is named, convinced Newton to publish again.

Newton's *Principia Mathematica* (Mathematical Principles of Natural Philosophy) was published in 1687. It was prompted by a visit from Halley, in which the astronomer asked Newton for his ideas on a question being discussed at the Royal Society: was there a mathematical basis for the elliptical orbits of the planets? Halley's question inspired Newton to expand calculations he had made earlier into an all-encompassing theory of celestial—and terrestrial—dynamics. Halley not only encouraged Newton's work but supervised and financed its publication (though he had less money than Newton); and on several occasions he had to persuade Newton, enraged again by reports of criticism from Hooke and others, to continue with the project and to commit his findings to print.

Newton built on Galileo's work on inertia, Kepler's findings concerning the elliptical orbits of planets, the work of Boyle and Descartes, and even his rival Hooke's work on gravity.

Principia was long and difficult—purposefully so, for Newton said he did not want to be "baited by little smatterers in mathematics". Its central proposition was that gravitation was a universal force and one that could be expressed mathematically. Newton built on Galileo's work on inertia, Kepler's findings concerning the elliptical orbits of planets, the work of Boyle and Descartes, and even his rival Hooke's work on gravity. He once said, "If I have seen further, it is by standing on the shoulders of giants." But Newton's universal theory of gravity, although it drew on work of others before him, formulated something entirely new. His synthesis offered a single, descriptive account of mass and motion. "All bodies whatsoever are endowed with a principle of mutual gravitation." The law of gravitation was stated in a mathematical formula; supported by observation and experience; and, literally, universal.

The scientific elite of Newton's time was not uniformly persuaded. Many mechanical philosophers, particularly Cartesians, objected to the prominence in Newton's theory of forces acting across empty space. Such attractions smacked of mysticism (or the occult); they seemed to lack any driving mechanism. Newton

NEWTON ON THE PURPOSES OF EXPERIMENTAL PHILOSOPHY

When Newton added his General Scholium *to the second edition of* Principia *in 1713, he was seventy-one, president of the Royal Society, and widely revered. Responding to continental critics, he set out his general views on science and its methods, arguing against purely deductive reasoning and reliance on hypotheses about ultimate causes.*

Hitherto we have explained the phenomena of the heavens and of our sea by the power of gravity, but have not yet assigned the cause of this power. This is certain, that it must proceed from a cause that penetrates to the very centres of the sun and planets, without suffering the least diminution of its force; that operates not according to the quantity of the surfaces of the particles on which it acts (as mechanical causes used to do), but according to the quantity of the solid matter which they contain, and propagates its virtue on all sides to immense distances, decreasing always as the inverse square of the distances. . . . [H]itherto I have not been able to discover the cause of those properties of gravity from phenomena, and I frame no hypothesis; for whatever is not deduced from the phenomena is to be called an hypothesis and hypotheses, whether metaphysical or physical, whether of occult qualities or mechanical, have no place in experimental philoso-phy. In this philosophy particular propositions are inferred from the phenomena, and afterwards rendered general by induction. . . . And to us it is enough that gravity does really exist, and acts according to the laws which we have explained, and abundantly serves to account for all the motions of the celestial bodies, and of our sea.

Michael R. Matthews, ed., *The Scientific Background to Modern Philosophy: Selected Readings* (Indianapolis and Cambridge, 1989), p. 152.

QUESTIONS FOR ANALYSIS

1. Why did Isaac Newton declare that "hypotheses, whether metaphysical or physical, whether of occult qualities or mechanical, have no place in experimental philosophy"?

responded to these criticisms in a note added to the next edition of the *Principia* (General Scholium, 1713). He did not know what *caused* gravity, he said, and he did not "feign hypotheses." "For whatever is not deduced from the phenomena must be called hypothesis," he wrote, and has "no place in the experimental philosophy." For Newton, certainty and objectivity lay in the precise mathematical characterization of phenomena —"the mathematization of the universe," as one historian puts it. Science could not, and need not, always uncover causes. It did describe natural phenomena and accurately predict the behavior of objects as confirmed by experimentation.

Other natural philosophers immediately acclaimed Newton's work for solving long-standing puzzles. Thinkers persuaded that the Copernican version of the universe was right had been unable to piece together the physics of a revolving earth. Newton made it possible to do so. Halley provided a poem to accompany the first edition of *Principia*. "No closer to the gods can

Newton and Satire. The English artist and satirist William Hogarth mocking both philosophy and "Newton worship" in 1763. The philosophers' heads are being weighed on a scale that runs from "absolute gravity" to "absolute levity" or "stark fool."

any mortal rise," he wrote, of the man with whom he had worked so patiently. Halley did have a financial as well as an intellectual interest in the book, and he also arranged for it to be publicized and reviewed in influential journals. John Locke (whose own *Essay Concerning Human Understanding* was written at virtually the same time, in 1690) read *Principia* twice and summarized it in French for readers across the Channel. By 1713 pirated editions of *Principia* were being published in Amsterdam for distribution throughout Europe. By the time Newton died, in 1727, he had become an English national hero and was given a funeral at Westminster Abbey. The poet Alexander Pope expressed the awe that Newton inspired in some of his contemporaries in a famous couplet

> Nature and nature's law lay hid in night;
> God said, "Let Newton be!" and all was light.

Voltaire, the French champion of the Enlightenment (discussed in the next chapter), was largely responsible for Newton's reputation in France. In this he was helped by a woman who was a brilliant mathematician in her own right, Emilie du Châtelet. Du Châtelet co-authored a book with Voltaire introducing Newton to a French audience; and she translated *Principia*, a daunting scientific and mathematical task and one well beyond Voltaire's mathematical abilities. Newton's French admirers and publicists disseminated Newton's findings. In their eyes Newton also represented a cultural transformation, a turning point in the history of knowledge.

SCIENCE AND CULTURAL CHANGE

From the seventeenth century on, science stood at the heart of what it meant to be "modern." It also grew increasingly central to the self-understanding of Western culture; indeed, scientific and technological power became one of the justifications for the expansion of Western empires and the subjugation of other peoples. For all these reasons, the revolution in understanding the universe was and often still is presented as a thorough-going break with the past, a moment that recast the architecture of Western culture. But as one historian has written "no house is ever built of entirely virgin materials, according to a plan bearing no resemblance to old patterns, and no body of culture is able to wholly reject its past. Historical change is not like that, and most 'revolutions' effect less sweeping changes than they advertise or than are advertised for them."

To begin with, the transformation we have canvassed in this chapter involved elite knowledge. Ordinary people inhabited a very different cultural world. Second, natural philosophers' discoveries—Tycho's mathematics and Galileo's observations, for instance—did not undo the authority of the ancients in one blow. They did not seek to do so. Third, science did not subvert religion. Even when traditional concepts collapsed in the face of new discoveries, natural philosophers seldom gave up on the project of restoring a picture of a divinely ordered universe. Mechanists argued that the intricate universe revealed by the discoveries of Copernicus, Kepler, Galileo, Newton, and others was evidence of God's guiding presence. Robert Boyle's will provided the funds for a lecture series on the "confutation of atheism" by scientific means. Isaac Newton was happy to have his work contribute to that project. "Nothing," he wrote to one of the lecturers in 1692, "can rejoice me more than to find [*Principia*] usefull for

Establishment of the Academy of Sciences and Foundation of the Observatory, 1667. The 1666 founding of the Academy of Sciences was a measure of the new prestige of science and the potential value of research. Louis XIV sits at the center, surrounded by the religious and scholarly figures who offer the fruits of their knowledge to the French state.

that purpose." The creation of "the Sun and Fixt stars," "the motion which the Planets now have could not spring from any naturall cause alone but were imprest with a divine Agent." Science was thoroughly compatible with belief in God's providential design, at least through the seventeenth century.

The greatest scientific minds were deeply committed to beliefs that do not fit our notion of "modern." Newton, again, is the most striking case in point. The great twentieth-century economist John Maynard Keynes was one of the first to read through Newton's private manuscripts. On the 300th anniversary of Newton's birth (the celebration of which was delayed because of World War II), Keynes offered the following reappraisal of the great scientist:

> I believe that Newton was different from the conventional picture of him. . . .
> In the eighteenth century and since, Newton came to be thought of as the first and greatest of the modern age

> The greatest scientific minds were deeply committed to beliefs that do not fit our notion of "modern."

of scientists, a rationalist, one who taught us to think on the lines of cold and untinctured reason.

> I do not see him in this light. I do not think that any one who has pored over the contents of that box which he packed up when he finally left Cambridge in 1696 and which, though partly dispersed, have come down to us, can see him like that. Newton was not the first of the age of reason. He was the last of the magicians, the last of the Babylonians and Sumerians, the last great mind which looked out on the visible and intellectual world with the same eyes as those who began to build our intellectual inheritance rather less than 10,000 years ago.

Those eyes saw the world as a text, God's message to humanity. Close reading and study would unlock its mysteries. The same impulse led Newton to read about magic, to practice alchemy, and to immerse himself in the writings of the church fathers and in the Bible, which he knew in intimate detail. Newton then, was the last representative of an older tradition, and also, quite unintentionally, the first of a new one.

What, then, did the scientific revolution change? Seventeenth-century natural philosophers had produced new answers to fundamental questions about the physical world. Age-old questions about astronomy and physics had been recast and, to some extent (although it was not yet clear to what extent), answered. In the process there had developed a new approach to amassing, deciphering, and integrating information in a systematic way, an approach that helped yield more insights into the workings of nature as time went on. In this period, too, the most innovative scientific work moved out of the restrictive environment of the church and the universities. Natural philosophers began talking to and working with each other in lay organizations that developed standards of research. England's Royal Society spawned imitators in Florence and Berlin and later in Russia. The French Royal Academy of

Sciences had a particularly direct relationship with the monarchy and the French state. France's statesmen exerted control over the academy and sought to share in the rewards of any discoveries its members made.

New, too, were beliefs about the purpose and methods of science. The practice of breaking a complex problem down into parts made it possible to tackle more and different questions in the physical sciences. Mathematics assumed a more central role in the new science. Finally, rather than simply confirming established truths, the new methods were designed to explore the unknown and provide means to discover new truths. As Kepler wrote to Galileo, "How great a difference there is between theoretical speculation and visual experience, between Ptolemy's discussion of the Antipodes and Columbus's discovery of the New World." Knowledge itself was reconceived. In the

Ramelli, *Le diverse et artificiose* machine (1558). A model of humanist learning, this "book wheel" from the mid-sixteenth century allowed readers to consult several books at a time, cross-referencing, comparing, and immersing themselves in a body of book knowledge.

Bacon, *Instauratio magna* (1620). The new model of learning as discovery. The quotation below reads: "Many shall venture forth and science shall be increased."

older model, to learn was to read: to reason logically, to argue, to compare classical texts, and to absorb a finite body of knowledge. In the newer one, to learn was to discover, and what could be discovered was boundless.

CONCLUSION

The pioneering natural philosophers remained circumspect about their abilities. Some sought to lay bare the workings of the universe; others believed humans could only catalog and describe the regularities observed in nature. By unspoken but seemingly mutual agreement, the question of first causes was left aside. The new science did not say *why*, but *how*. Newton, for one, worked toward explanations that would reveal the logic of creation laid out in mathematics. Yet in the end, he settled for theories explaining motions and relationships that could be observed and tested.

The eighteenth-century heirs to Newton were much more daring. Laboratory science and the work of the scientific societies largely stayed true to the experimenters' rules and limitations. But as we will see in the next chapter, the natural philosophers who began investigating the human sciences cast aside some of their predecessors' caution. Society, technology, government, religion, even the individual human mind seemed to be mechanisms or parts of a larger nature waiting for study. The scientific revolution overturned the natural world as it had been understood for a millennium; it also inspired thinkers more interested in revolutions in society.

KEY TERMS

heliocentric

Aristotelian

Nicholas Copernicus

Galileo Galilei

Discourse on Method

scientific societies

Francis Bacon

SELECTED READINGS

Biagioli, Mario. *Galileo, Courtier.* Chicago, 1993. Emphasizes the importance of patronage and court politics in Galileo's science and career.

Cohen, I. B. *The Birth of a New Physics.* New York, 1985. Emphasizes the mathematical nature of the revolution; unmatched at making the mathematics understandable.

Dear, Peter. *Revolutionizing the Sciences: European Knowledge and Its Ambitions, 1500–1700.* Princeton, N.J., 2001. Among the best short histories.

Drake, Stillman. *Discoveries and Opinions of Galileo.* Garden City, N.Y., 1957. The classic translation of Galileo's most important papers by his most admiring modern biographer.

Feingold, Mardechai, *The Newtonian Moment: Isaac Newton and the Making of Modern Culture.* New York, 2004. An engaging essay on the dissemination of Newton's thought, with excellent visual material.

Gaukroger, Stephen. *Descartes: An Intellectual Biography.* Oxford, 1995. Detailed and sympathetic study of the philosopher.

Gleick, James. *Isaac Newton.* New York, 2003. A vivid and well-documented brief biography.

Grafton, Anthony. *New Worlds, Ancient Texts: The Power of Tradition and the Shock of Discovery.* Cambridge, Mass., 1992. Accessible essay by one of the leading scholars of early modern European thought.

Hall, A. R. *The Revolution in Science, 1500–1750.* New York, 1983. Revised version of a 1954 classic.

Jones, Richard Foster. *Ancients and Moderns: A Study of the Rise of the Scientific Movement in Early Modern England.* Berkeley, Calif., 1961. Still a persuasive study of the scientific revolutionaries' attempts to situate their work in relation to that of the Greeks.

Koestler, Arthur. *The Sleepwalkers: A History of Man's Changing Vision of the Universe.* London, 1958. A readable classic.

Kuhn, Thomas. *The Structure of Scientific Revolutions.* Chicago, 1962. A classic and much-debated study of how scientific thought changes.

Pagden, Anthony, *European Encounters with the New World.* New Haven, Conn., and London, 1993. Subtle and detailed on how European intellectuals thought about the lands they saw for the first time.

Scheibinger, Londa. *The Mind Has No Sex? Women in the Origins of Modern Science*. Cambridge, Mass., 1989. A lively and important recovery of the lost role played by women mathematicians and experimenters.

Shapin, Steven. *The Scientific Revolution*. Chicago, 1996. Engaging, accessible, and brief—organized thematically.

Shapin, Steven, and Simon Schaffer. *Leviathan and the Air Pump*. Princeton, N.J., 1985. A modern classic, on one of the most famous philosophical conflicts in seventeenth-century science.

Stephenson, Bruce. *The Music of the Heavens: Kepler's Harmonic Astronomy*. Princeton, N.J., 1994. An engaging and important explanation of Kepler's otherworldly perspective.

Thoren, Victor. *The Lord of Uranibourg: A Biography of Tycho Brahe*. Cambridge, 1990. A vivid reconstruction of the scientific revolution's most flamboyant astronomer.

Westfall, Richard. *The Construction of Modern Science*. Cambridge, 1977.

Westfall, Richard. *Never at Rest: A Biography of Isaac Newton*. Cambridge, 1980. The standard work.

Wilson, Catherine. *The Invisible World: Early Modern Philosophy and the Invention of the Microscope*. Princeton, N.J., 1995. An important study of how the "microcosmic" world revealed by technology reshaped scientific philosophy and practice.

Zinsser, Judith P. *La Dame d'Esprit: A Biography of the Marquise Du Châtelet*. New York, 2006. An excellent cultural history. To be issued in paper as *Emilie du Châtelet: Daring Genius of the Enlightenment* (2007).

CHAPTER
SEVENTEEN

THE
ENLIGHTENMENT

IN 1762, THE *PARLEMENT* (law court) of Toulouse, in France, convicted
Jean Calas of murdering his son. Calas was Protestant, and Catholic–Protestant
tensions ran high in the region. Witnesses called before the court claimed that
the young Calas had wanted to break with his family and convert to Catholicism,
and they convinced the magistrates that Calas had killed his son rather than let
him fall from the Protestant faith. French law stipulated the punishment. Calas was
tortured twice: first in an attempt to get him to confess and, next, as a formal part
of certain death sentences, to force him to name his alleged accomplices. His arms
and legs were slowly pulled apart, gallons of water were poured down his throat,
and his body was publicly broken on the wheel, which meant that each of his limbs
was smashed with an iron bar. Then the executioner cut off his head. Throughout
the trial, torture, and execution, Calas maintained his innocence. Two years later,
the *Parlement* reversed its verdict, declared Calas not guilty, and offered the family a
payment in compensation.

François Marie Arouet, also known as Voltaire, was one of those appalled by
the verdict and punishment. At the time of the case, Voltaire was the most famous
Enlightenment thinker in Europe. Well connected and a prolific writer, Voltaire took
up his pen to clear Calas' name; he contacted friends, hired lawyers for the family,
and wrote briefs, letters, and essays to bring the case to the public eye. Calas's case
exemplified nearly everything Voltaire opposed in his culture. Intolerance, ignorance,
and what Voltaire throughout his life called religious "fanaticism" and "infamy"
had made a travesty of justice. "Shout everywhere, I beg you, for Calas and against
fanaticism, for it is *l'infame* that has caused their misery," he wrote to his friend Jean
Le Rond d'Alembert, a fellow Enlightenment thinker. Using torture to uncover truth
demonstrated the power of unquestioned and centuries-old practices. Legal procedures
that included secret interrogations, trials behind closed doors, summary judgment
(Calas was executed the day after being convicted, with no review by a higher court),
and barbaric punishments defied reason, morality, and human dignity. Any criminal,

FOCUS QUESTIONS

• What were the common themes and aims of
the Enlightenment writings?

• How did the French *philosophes* challenge the
established order?

• What issues mattered to Enlightenment
thinkers and why?

• Why were colonies and imperial policy important to Enlightenment thinkers?

• Was the Enlightenment revolutionary?

• How did social and cultural change shape the
Enlightenment?

however wretched, "is a man," wrote Voltaire, "and you are accountable for his blood."

Voltaire's comments on the Calas case illustrate the classic concerns of the Enlightenment: the dangers of arbitrary and unchecked authority, the value of religious toleration, and the overriding importance of law, reason, and human dignity in all affairs. He borrowed most of his arguments from others—from his predecessor the baron de Montesquieu and from the Italian writer Cesare Beccaria, whose *On Crimes and Punishments* appeared in 1764. Voltaire's reputation did not rest on his originality as a philosopher. It came from his effectiveness as a writer and advocate, his desire and ability to reach a wide audience. In this, too, he was representative of the Enlightenment project.

THE FOUNDATIONS OF THE ENLIGHTENMENT

What were the common themes and aims of the Enlightenment writings?

The Enlightenment was an eighteenth-century phenomenon, lasting for close to the entire century. Not every important thinker who lived and worked in the eighteenth century rallied to the Enlightenment banner. Some, such as the Italian philosopher of history G. B. Vico (1668–1744), opposed almost everything the Enlightenment stood for; and others, most notably Jean-Jacques Rousseau, accepted certain Enlightenment values but sharply rejected others. Patterns of Enlightenment thought varied from country to country, and they changed in each country over the course of the century. Many eighteenth-century thinkers nonetheless shared the sense of living in an exciting new intellectual environment in which the "party of humanity" would prevail over customary practices and traditional thought.

Enlightenment writings shared several basic characteristics. They were marked, first, by a confidence in the powers of human reason. This self-assurance stemmed from the accomplishments of the scientific revolution. Even when the details of Newton's physics were poorly understood, his methods provided a model for scientific inquiry into other phenomena. Nature operated according to laws that could be grasped by study, observation, and thought. The work of the extraordinary Scottish

writer David Hume (*A Treatise of Human Nature*, 1739–1740, and the *Enquiries Concerning Human Understanding*, 1748) provided the most direct bridge from science to the Enlightenment. Newton had refused hypotheses, or speculation about ultimate causes, arguing for the precise description of natural phenomena (see Chapter Sixteen). Hume took this same rigor and skepticism to the study of morality, the mind, and government, often using Newtonian language or drawing analogies to scientific laws. Hume criticized the "passion for hypotheses and systems" that dominated much philisophical thinking. Experience and careful observation, he argued, usually did not support the premises on which those systems rested. Among Hume's many examples was Thomas Hobbes's theory of human nature, which underpinned the latter's views on government (see Chapter Fourteen).

Human understanding and the exercise of human reason also entailed certain political conditions. "Dare to know!" the German philosopher Immanuel Kant challenged his contemporaries in his classic 1784 essay "What Is Enlightenment?" For Kant, the Enlightenment represented a declaration of intellectual independence. (He also called it an awakening and credited Hume with rousing him from his "dogmatic slumber.") Kant likened the intellectual history of humanity to the growth of a child. Enlightenment, in this view, was an escape from humanity's "self-imposed immaturity" and a long overdue break with humanity's self-imposed parental figure—namely, the Catholic Church. Coming of age meant the "determination and courage to think without the guidance of someone else," as an individual. Reason required autonomy, or freedom from tradition and well-established authorities.

Despite their declarations of independence from the past, Enlightenment thinkers recognized a great debt to their immediate predecessors. Voltaire called Bacon, Newton, and John Locke his "Holy Trinity." Indeed, much of the eighteenth-century Enlightenment consisted of translating, republishing, and thinking through the implications of the great works of the seventeenth century. Enlightenment thinkers drew heavily on Locke's studies of human knowledge, especially his *Essay Concerning Human Understanding* (1690), which was even more influential than his political philosophy. Locke's theories of how humans acquire knowledge gave education and environment a critical role in shaping human character. All knowledge, he argued, originates from sense perception. The human mind at birth is a "blank tablet" (in Latin, *tabula rasa*).

WHAT WERE THE COMMON THEMES AND AIMS OF THE ENLIGHTENMENT WRITINGS?

THE FOUNDATIONS OF THE ENLIGHTENMENT   605

Only when an infant begins to experience things, to perceive the external world with its senses, does anything register in its mind. Locke's starting point, which became a central premise for those who followed, was the goodness and perfectibility of humanity. Building on Locke, eighteenth-century thinkers made education central to their project, because education promised individual moral improvement and social progress. It is worth noting that Locke's theories had potentially more radical implications: education might be able to level hierarchies of status, sex, or race. As we will see, only a few Enlightenment thinkers made such egalitarian arguments. Still, optimism and a belief in universal human progress constituted a second defining feature of nearly all Enlightenment thinking.

Third, Enlightenment thinkers were extraordinarily ambitious and wide ranging. They sought nothing less than the organization of all knowledge. The *scientific*

> Historians have called the Enlightenment a "cultural project," emphasizing Enlightenment thinkers' interest in practical, applied knowledge and their determination to spread knowledge and to promote free public discussion.

method, by which they meant the empirical observation of particular phenomena to arrive at general laws, offered a way to pursue research in all areas—to study human affairs as well as natural ones. Thus they collected evidence to learn the laws governing the rise and fall of nations, and they compared governmental constitutions to arrive at an ideal and universally applicable political system. As the English poet Alexander Pope stated in his *Essay on Man* (1733), "the science of human nature [may be] like all other sciences reduced to a few clear points," and Enlightenment thinkers became determined to learn exactly what those few clear points were. They took up a strikingly wide array of subjects in this systematic manner: knowledge and the mind, natural history, economics, government, religious beliefs, customs of indigenous peoples in the New World, human nature, and sexual (or what we would call gender) and racial differences.

Historians have called the Enlightenment a "cultural project," emphasizing Enlightenment thinkers' interest in practical, applied knowledge and their determination to spread knowledge and to promote free public discussion. They intended, as Denis Diderot (*deed-ROH*) wrote, "to change the common way of thinking" and to advance the cause of "enlightenment" and humanity. Although they shared many of their predecessors' theoretical concerns, they wrote in a very different style and for a much larger audience. Hobbes and Locke had published treatises for small groups of learned seventeenth-century readers. Voltaire, in contrast, wrote plays, essays, and letters; Rousseau composed music, published his *Confessions*, and wrote novels that moved his readers to tears; Hume wrote history for a wide audience. A British aristocrat or a governor in the North American colonies would have read Locke. But a middle-class woman might have read Rousseau's fiction, and shopkeepers and artisans could become familiar with popular Enlightenment-inspired pamphlets. Among the elite, newly formed "academies" sponsored prize essay contests, and well-to-do women and men discussed affairs of state in salons. In other words, the intellectual achievements and goals of the Enlightenment followed from cultural developments in the eighteenth century. Those developments included the expansion of literacy and growing markets for books, new networks of

Voltaire. A brilliant and popular writer, his criticisms of the regime helped establish the international reputation of the *philosophes*.

readers, new forms of intellectual exchange, and the emergence of what some historians call the first "public sphere."

In sum, Enlightenment thinkers confronted their culture, exposing time-worn practices, beliefs, and authority to the shining light of reason. That often meant criticism and satire. They combined an irreverence for custom and tradition with a belief in human perfectibility and progress. They were confident in their ability to understand the world and passionately interested in the relationship between nature and culture, or environment, history, and human character and society. Their program of reform had immediate political implications; in a remarkably short time it changed the premises of government and society throughout the Atlantic world.

THE WORLD OF THE PHILOSOPHES

How did the French *philosophes* challenge the established order?

Enlightenment thought was European in a broad sense, including southern and eastern Europe as well as Europe's colonies in the New World. British thinkers played a—perhaps *the*—key role. France, however, provided the stage for some of the most widely read Enlightenment books and the most closely watched battles. For this reason, Enlightenment thinkers, regardless of where they lived, are often called by the French word *philosophes*. Yet hardly any of the *philosophes*, with the exceptions of David Hume and Immanuel Kant, were philosophers in the sense of being highly original abstract thinkers. Especially in France, Enlightenment thinkers shunned forms of expression that might seem incomprehensible, priding themselves instead on their clarity and style. *Philosophe*, in French, simply meant "a free thinker," a person whose reflections were unhampered by the constraints of religion or dogma in any form.

VOLTAIRE

At the time, the best known of the *philosophes* was Voltaire, born François Marie Arouet (1694–1778). As Erasmus two centuries earlier had embodied Christian

humanism, Voltaire virtually personified the Enlightenment, commenting on an enormous range of subjects in a wide variety of literary forms. Educated by the Jesuits, he emerged quite young as a gifted and sharp-tongued writer. His gusto for provocation landed him in the Bastille (a notorious prison in Paris) for libel and soon afterward in temporary exile in England. In his three years there, Voltaire became an admirer of British political institutions, British culture, and British science; above all, he became an extremely persuasive convert to the ideas of Newton, Bacon, and Locke. His single greatest accomplishment may have been popularizing Newton's work in France and more generally championing the cause of British empiricism and the scientific method against the more Cartesian French.

Voltaire's *Philosophical Letters* (*Letters on the English Nation*), published after his return in 1734, made an immediate sensation. Voltaire's themes were religious and political liberty, and his weapons were comparisons.

Voltaire and Franklin, 1778. Voltaire blesses the grandson of Benjamin Franklin, who stands in the background. The two Enlightenment thinkers met in Paris shortly before Voltaire's death.

His admiration for British culture and politics became a stinging critique of France—and other absolutist countries on the Continent. He praised British open-mindedness and empiricism: the country's respect for scientists and its support for research. He considered the relative weakness of the British aristocracy a sign of Britain's political health. Unlike the French, the British respected commerce and people who engage in it, Voltaire wrote. The British tax system was rational, free of the complicated exemptions for the privileged that were ruining French finances. The British House of Commons represented the middle classes and, in contrast with French absolutism, brought balance to British government and checked arbitrary power. In one of the book's more incendiary passages, he argued that in Britain, violent revolution had actually produced political moderation and stability: "[T]he idol of arbitrary power was drowned in seas of blood. . . . The English nation is the only nation in the world that has succeeded in moderating the power of its kings by resisting them." Of all Britain's reputed virtues, religious toleration loomed largest of all. Britain, Voltaire argued, brought together citizens of different religions in a harmonious and productive culture. In this and other instances, Voltaire oversimplified: British Catholics, Dissenters, and Jews did not have equal civil rights. Yet the British policy of "toleration" did contrast with Louis XIV's intolerance of Protestants. Revoking the Edict of Nantes (1685) had stripped French Protestants of civil rights and had helped create the atmosphere in which Jean Calas—and others—were persecuted.

Voltaire's famous battle cry, "*Écrasez l'infâme*," translates as "crush infamy," and by *infamy* he meant all forms of repression, fanaticism, and bigotry. He wrote the following to an opponent, and it is a statement often cited as the first principle of civil liberty: "I do not agree with a word you say, but I will defend to the death your right to say it." Of all forms of intolerance Voltaire opposed religious bigotry most, and with real passion he denounced religious fraud, faith in miracles, and superstition. "The less superstition, the less fanaticism; and the less fanaticism, the less misery." He did not oppose religion per se; rather he sought to rescue morality, which he believed to come from God, from dogma—elaborate ritual, dietary laws, formulaic prayers—and from a powerful church bureaucracy. He argued for common sense and simplicity, persuaded that these would bring out the goodness in humanity and establish stable authority. "The simpler the laws are, the more the magistrates are respected; the simpler the religion will be, the more one will revere its ministers. Religion can be simple. When enlightened people will announce a single God, rewarder and avenger, no one will laugh, everyone will obey."

Voltaire relished his position as a critic, and it never stopped him from being successful. He was regularly exiled from France and other countries, his books banned and burned. As long as his plays attracted large audiences, however, the French king felt he had to tolerate their author. Voltaire had an attentive international public, including Frederick of Prussia, who invited him to his court at Berlin, and Catherine of Russia, with whom he corresponded about reforms she might introduce in Russia. Voltaire described himself as "contraband," but that seemed only to enhance his value. When he died in 1778, a few months after a triumphant return to Paris, he was possibly the best-known writer in Europe.

Voltaire's famous battle cry, "Écrasez l'infâme," translates as "crush infamy," and by infamy he meant all forms of repression, fanaticism, and bigotry.

MONTESQUIEU

The Baron de Montesquieu (*mahn-tuhs-KYOO*, 1689–1755) was a very different kind of Enlightenment figure. Montesquieu was born to a noble family. He inherited both an estate and, since state offices were property that passed from father to son, a position as magistrate in the *Parlement*, or law court, of Bordeaux. He was not a stylist or a provocateur like Voltaire but a relatively cautious jurist. He did write a satirical novel, *The Persian Letters* (1721), published anonymously (to protect his reputation) in Amsterdam. The novel was composed as letters from two Persian visitors to France. The visitors detailed the odd religious superstitions they witnessed, compared manners at the French court with those in Turkish harems, and likened French absolutism to their own brands of *despotism*, or the abuse of government authority.

Montesquieu's serious treatise *The Spirit of Laws* (1748) may have been the most influential work of the Enlightenment. It was a groundbreaking study in what we would call comparative historical sociology and very Newtonian in its careful, empirical approach. Montesquieu asked about the structures that shaped law. How had different environments, histories, and religious traditions combined to create such a variety of governmental institutions? What were the different forms of government: what spirit characterized each, and what were their respective virtues and shortcomings? Montesquieu proposed a threefold classification of states. A republic was governed by the many—in his view either an elite aristocracy or the people. In the second type, monarchy, a single authority ruled in accordance with the law. Despotism, Montesquieu's most important negative example, allowed a single ruler to govern unchecked by law or other powers, sowing corruption and capriciousness. The soul or spirit of a republic was virtue; of monarchy, honor; of despotism, where no citizen could feel secure and punishment took the place of education, fear. Lest this seem abstract, Montesquieu devoted two chapters to the French monarchy, in which he spelled out what he saw as a dangerous drift toward despotism in his own land. Like other Enlightenment thinkers, Montesquieu admired the British system and its separate and balanced powers—executive, legislative, and judicial—which guaranteed liberty in the sense of freedom from the absolute power of any single governing individual or group. His idealization of "checks and balances" had formative influence on Enlightenment political theorists and members of the governing elites, particularly those who wrote the United States Constitution in 1787.

Montesquieu. The French baron's *Spirit of the Laws* (1748) was probably the most influential single text of the high Enlightenment.

DIDEROT AND THE *ENCYCLOPEDIA*

Voltaire's and Montesquieu's writings represent the themes and style of the French Enlightenment. But the most remarkable French publication of the century was a collective venture: the *Encyclopedia*. The *Encyclopedia* intended to summarize and disseminate all the most advanced contemporary philosophical, scientific, and technical knowledge. In terms of sheer scope, this was the grandest statement of the *philosophes'* goals. It demonstrated how scientific analysis could be applied in nearly all realms of thought. It aimed to reconsider an enormous range of traditions and institutions and to put reason to the task of bringing happiness and progress to humanity. The guiding spirit behind the venture was Denis Diderot. Diderot was helped by the Newtonian mathematician Jean Le Rond d'Alembert (1717–1783) and other leading men of letters, including Voltaire and Montesquieu. The *Encyclopedia* was published, in installments, between 1751 and 1772; by the time it was completed, it ran to seventeen large volumes of text and eleven more of illustrations. A collaborative project, it helped create the *philosophes'* image as the "party of humanity."

The *Encyclopedia* sought to "change the general way of thinking." Diderot commissioned articles that explained recent achievements in science and technology, showing how machines worked and illustrating new industrial processes. The point was to demonstrate how the everyday applications of science could promote progress and alleviate all forms of human misery. Diderot turned the same methods to matters of religion, politics, and the foundations of the social order, including articles on economics, taxes, and the slave trade. Censorship made it difficult to write openly antireligious articles. Diderot, therefore, thumbed his nose at religion in oblique ways; at the entry on the Eucharist, the reader found a terse cross-reference: "See *cannibalism*." Gibes like this aroused storms of controversy when the early volumes of the *Encyclopedia* appeared. The French government revoked permission for the *Encyclopedia* to be published, declaring in 1759 that the encyclopedists were trying to "propagate materialism," which meant atheism, "to destroy Religion, to inspire a spirit of independence, and to nourish the corruption of morals." The volumes sold remarkably well despite such bans and their hefty price. Purchasers belonged to the elite: aristocrats, government officials, prosperous merchants, and a scattering of members of the higher clergy. That elite, though, stretched across Europe, including its overseas colonies.

Technology and Industry. This engraving, from the mining section, is characteristic of Diderot's *Encyclopedia*. The project aimed to detail technological changes, manufacturing processes, and forms of labor—all in the name of advancing human knowledge.

Although the French *philosophes* sparred with the state and the church, they sought political stability and reform. Montesquieu, not surprising in light of his birth and position, hoped that an enlightened aristocracy would press for reforms and defend liberty against a despotic king. Voltaire, persuaded that aristocrats would represent only their particular narrow interests, looked to an enlightened monarch for leadership. Neither was a democrat, and neither conceived of reform from below. Still, their widely read writings were subversive. Their satires of absolutism and, more broadly, arbitrary power, stung. By the 1760s the French critique of despotism provided the language in which many people across Europe articulated their opposition to existing regimes.

INTERNATIONALIZATION OF ENLIGHTENMENT THEMES

What issues mattered to Enlightenment thinkers and why?

The party of humanity was international. French became the lingua franca of much Enlightenment discussion, but "French" books were often published in Switzerland, Germany, and Russia. As we have seen, Enlightenment thinkers admired British institutions

and British scholarship, and they used both as points of reference. Great Britain also produced among the most important Enlightenment thinkers: the historian Edward Gibbon and the Scottish philosophers David Hume and Adam Smith. The *philosophes* considered Thomas Jefferson and Benjamin Franklin part of their group. Despite stiffer resistance from religious authorities, stricter state censors, and smaller networks of educated elites to discuss and support progressive thought, the Enlightenment flourished across central and southern Europe. Frederick II of Prussia housed Voltaire during one of his exiles from France, though the *philosophe* quickly wore out his welcome. Frederick also patronized a small but unusually productive group of Enlightenment thinkers. Northern Italy was an important center of Enlightenment thought. Enlightenment thinkers across Europe raised similar themes: humanitarianism, or the dignity and worth of all individuals; religious toleration; and liberty.

ENLIGHTENMENT THEMES: HUMANITARIANISM AND TOLERATION

Among the most influential writers of the entire Enlightenment was the Italian (Milanese) jurist Cesare Beccaria (1738–1794). Beccaria's *On Crimes and Punishments* (1764) sounded the same general themes as did the French *philosophes*—arbitrary power, reason, and human dignity—and it provided Voltaire with most of his arguments in the Calas case. Beccaria also proposed concrete legal reforms. He attacked the prevalent view that punishments should represent society's vengeance on the criminal. The only legitimate rationale for punishment was to maintain social order and to prevent other crimes. Beccaria argued for the greatest possible leniency compatible with deterrence; respect for individual dignity and humanity dictated that humans should punish other humans no more than is absolutely necessary. Above all, Beccaria's book eloquently opposed torture and the death penalty. The spectacle of public execution, which sought to dramatize the power of the state and the horrors of hell, instead dehumanized the victim, judge, and spectators. In 1766, a few years after the Calas case, another French trial provided an example of what horrified Beccaria and the *philosophes*. A nineteen-year-old French nobleman, convicted of blasphemy, had his tongue cut out and his hand cut off before he was burned at the stake. Since the court discovered the blasphemer had read Voltaire, it ordered the *Philosophical Dictionary* burned along with the body. Sensational cases such as this one helped publicize Beccaria's work, and *On Crimes and Punishments* was quickly translated into a dozen languages. Owing primarily to its influence, most European countries by around 1800 abolished torture, branding, whip-

ping, and various forms of mutilation and reserved the death penalty for capital crimes.

Humanitarianism and reason also counseled religious toleration. Enlightenment thinkers spoke almost as one on the need to end religious warfare and the persecution of heretics and religious minorities. It is important, though, to differentiate between the church as an institution and dogma, against which many Enlightenment thinkers rebelled, and as religious belief, which most accepted. Only the smallest number of Enlightenment thinkers, notably Paul Henri d'Holbach (1723–1789), were atheists, and very few were even avowed agnostics. Many (Voltaire, for instance) were deists, holding a religious outlook that saw God as a "divine clockmaker" who, at the beginning of time, constructed a perfect timepiece and then left it to run with predictable regularity. Enlightenment inquiry proved compatible with very different stances on religion.

> Enlightenment thinkers spoke almost as one on the need to end religious warfare and the persecution of heretics and religious minorities.

Toleration was limited. Most Christians saw Jews as heretics and Christ killers. And although Enlightenment thinkers deplored persecution, they commonly viewed Judaism and Islam as backward religions mired in superstition and obscurantist ritual. One of the few Enlightenment figures to treat Jews sympa-

Instruments of Torture. A man being stretched on the rack (left) and a thumbscrew (right), both from an official Austrian government handbook. By 1800, Beccaria's influence had helped phase out the use of such instruments.

thetically was the German *philosophe* Gotthold Lessing (1729–1781). Lessing's extraordinary play *Nathan the Wise* (1779) takes place in Jerusalem during the Fourth Crusade and begins with a pogrom—or violent, orchestrated attack—in which the wife and children of Nathan, a Jewish merchant, are murdered. Nathan survives to become a sympathetic and wise father figure. He adopts a Christian-born daughter and raises her with three religions: Christianity, Islam, and Judaism. At several points, authorities ask him to choose the single true religion. Nathan shows none exists. The three great monotheistic religions are three versions of the truth. Religion is authentic, or true, only insofar as it makes the believer virtuous.

Lessing modeled his hero on his friend Moses Mendelssohn (1729–1786), a self-educated rabbi and bookkeeper (and the grandfather of the composer Felix Mendelssohn). Moses Mendelssohn moved—though with some difficulty—between the Enlightenment circles of Frederick II and the Jewish community of Berlin. Mendelssohn unsuccessfully tried to avoid religion as a subject. Repeatedly attacked and invited to convert to Christianity, he finally took up the ques-

tion of Jewish identity. In a series of writings, the best-known of which is *On the Religious Authority of Judaism* (1783), he defended Jewish communities against anti-Semitic policies and Jewish religion against Enlightenment criticism. At the same time, he also promoted reform within the Jewish community, arguing that his community had special reason to embrace the broad Enlightenment project: religious faith should be voluntary, states should promote tolerance, humanitarianism would bring progress to all.

ECONOMICS, GOVERNMENT, AND ADMINISTRATION

Enlightenment ideas had a very real currency in affairs of state. The *philosophes* defended reason and knowledge for humanitarian reasons. But they also promised to make nations stronger, more efficient, and more prosperous. Beccaria's proposed legal reforms were a good case in point; he sought to make laws not simply more just but also more effective. In other words, the Enlightenment spoke to individuals but also to states. The *philosophes* addressed issues of liberty and rights but also took up matters of administration, tax collection, and economic policy.

The rising fiscal demands of eighteenth-century states and empires made these issues newly urgent. Which economic resources were most valuable to states? How could governments tap them? Enlightenment economic thinkers such as the physiocrats argued that long-standing mercantilist policies were misguided. By the eighteenth century, *mercantilism* had become a term for a very wide range of policies that shared a belief in government regulation of trade in manufactured goods and precious metals. The physiocrats, most of them French, held that real wealth came from the land and agricultural production. More important, they advocated simplifying the tax system and following a policy of laissez-faire, which comes from the French expression *laissez faire la nature* ("let nature take its course"), letting wealth and goods circulate without government interference.

The now-classic expression of laissez-faire economics, however, came from the Scottish economist Adam Smith (1723–1790), and especially from Smith's landmark treatise *Inquiry into the Nature and Causes of the Wealth of Nations* (1776). Smith disagreed with the physiocrats on the value of agriculture, but he shared their opposition to mercantilism. For Smith, the central issues were the productivity of labor and how labor was used in different sectors of the economy. Mercantile restrictions—such as

Lessing and Mendelssohn. The German philosopher Gotthold Lessing visits his friend Moses Mendelssohn, one of the major Jewish figures of the Enlightenment.

high taxes on imported goods, which was one of the grievances of the colonists throughout the American empires—did not encourage the productive deployment of labor and thus did not create real economic health. For Smith, general prosperity could best be obtained by allowing the famous "invisible hand" to guide economic activity. Individuals, in other words, should pursue their own interests without competition from state-chartered monopolies or legal restraints. As Smith wrote in his earlier *Theory of Moral Sentiments* (1759), self-interested individuals could be "led by an invisible hand . . . without knowing it, without intending it, [to] advance the interest of the society."

The Wealth of Nations spelled out, in more technical and historical detail, the different stages of economic development, how the invisible hand actually worked, and the beneficial aspects of competition. Its perspective owed much to Newton and to the Enlightenment's idealization of both nature and human nature. Smith wanted to follow what he called, in classic Enlightenment terms, the "obvious and simple system of natural liberty." Smith thought of himself as the champion of justice against state-sponsored economic privilege and monopolies. He was a theorist of human feelings as well as of market forces. Smith emerged as the most influential of the new eighteenth-century economic thinkers. In the following century, ironically, his work and his followers became the target of reformers and critics of the new economic world.

EMPIRE AND ENLIGHTENMENT

Why were colonies and imperial policy important to Enlightenment thinkers?

Smith's *Wealth of Nations* formed part of a debate about the economics of empire: *philosophes* and statesmen alike asked how the colonies could be profitable, and to whom. The colonial world loomed large in Enlightenment thinking in several other ways. The new world across the Atlantic offered a foil to the old civilization of Europe, in other words, an often idealized portrait of natural humanity and simplicity, by comparison with which Europe looked decadent or corrupt. Second, Europeans' colonial activities—especially, by the eighteenth century, the slave trade—could not help

but raise pressing issues about humanitarianism, individual rights, and natural law. The effects of colonialism on Europe were a central Enlightenment theme.

Smith wrote in *The Wealth of Nations* that the "discovery of America, and that of a passage to the East Indies by the cape of Good Hope are the two greatest and most important events recorded in the history of mankind. What benefits, or what misfortunes to mankind may herafter result form those great events," he continued, "no human wisdom can foresee." Smith's language was nearly identical to that of a Frenchman, the Abbé Guillaume Thomas François Raynal. Raynal's massive *Philosophical History . . . of Europeans in the Two Indies* (1770), a co-authored work like the *Encyclopedia*, was one of the most widely read works of the Enlightenment, going through twenty printings and at least forty pirated editions. Raynal drew his inspiration from the *Encyclopedia* and aimed at nothing less than a total history of colonization: customs and civilizations of indigenous peoples, natural history, exploration, and commerce in the Atlantic world and India. He also tried to draw up a balance sheet, asking as did Smith, whether colonization had made humanity happier, more peaceful, or better. The question was fully in the spirit of the Enlightenment. So was the answer. Raynal believed that industry and trade brought improvement and progress. Like other Enlightenment writers, however, he and his co-authors considered natural simplicity an antidote to the corruptions of their culture. They sought out and idealized what they considered examples of "natural" humanity, many of them in the New World. For example, they wrote that what Europeans considered savage life might be "a hundred times preferable to that of societies corrupted by despotism" and lamented the loss of humanity's "natural liberty." They condemned the tactics of the Spanish in Mexico and Peru, of the Portuguese in Brazil, and of the British in North America. They echoed Montesquieu's theme that good government required checks and balances against arbitrary authority. In the New World, they argued, Europeans found themselves with virtually unlimited power, which encouraged them to be arrogant, cruel, and despotic. In a later edition, after the outbreak of the American Revolution, the book went even further, drawing parallels between exploitation in the colonial world and inequality at home: "We are mad in the way we act with our colonies, and inhuman and mad in our conduct toward our peasants," asserted one author. Eighteenth-century radicals repeatedly warned that overextended empires sowed seeds of decadence and corruption at home.

THE IMPACT OF THE NEW WORLD ON ENLIGHTENMENT THINKERS

The Abbé Guillaume Thomas François Raynal (1713–1796) was a clergyman and intellectual who moved in the inner circles of the Enlightenment. As a senior cleric he had access to the royal court; as a writer and intellectual he worked with the encyclopedists and other authors who criticized France's institutions, including the Catholic Church of which Raynal himself was a part. Here he tries to offer a perspective on the profound effects of discovering the Americas and ends by asking whether particular historical developments and institutions lead to the betterment of society.

There has never been any event which has had more impact on the human race in general and for Europeans in particular, as that of the discovery of the New World, and the passage to the Indies around the Cape of Good Hope. It was then that a commercial revolution began, a revolution in the balance of power, and in the customs, the industries and the government of every nation. It was through this event that men in the most distant lands were linked by new relationships and new needs. The produce of equatorial regions were consumed in polar climes. The industrial products of the north were transported to the south; the textiles of the Orient became the luxuries of Westerners; and everywhere men mutually exchanged their opinions, their laws, their customs, their illnesses, and their medicines, their virtues and their vices. Everything changed, and will go on changing. But will the changes of the past and those that are to come be useful to humanity? Will they give man one day more peace, more happiness, or more pleasure? Will his condition be better, or will it be simply one of constant change?

Abbé Guillaume Thomas François Raynal, *Philosophical and Political History of European Establishments and Commerce in the Two Indies* (1770), as cited in Dourinda Outram, *The Enlightenment* (Cambridge, 1995), p. 73.

QUESTIONS FOR ANALYSIS

1. Why was the discovery of America of such profound significance for eighteenth-century Europe?
2. Why was Raynal so concerned with people's conduct and happiness?
3. Why does Raynal ask whether historical developments lead to the betterment of society? What is his answer?

SLAVERY AND THE ATLANTIC WORLD

Discussing Europe's colonies and economies inevitably raised the issue of slavery. The sugar islands of the Caribbean were among the most valued possessions of the colonial world and the sugar trade one of the leading sectors of the Western economy. The Atlantic slave trade reached its peak in the eighteenth century. European slave traders sent at least 1 million Africans into New World slavery in the late seventeenth century, and at least 6 million in the eighteenth century. On this topic, however, even thinkers as radical as Raynal and Diderot hesitated, and their hesitations are revealing about the tensions in Enlightenment thought. Enlightenment thinking began with the premise that individuals could reason and govern themselves. Individual moral freedom lay at the heart of what the Enlightenment considered to be a just, stable, and harmonious society.

Slavery defied natural law and natural freedom. Montesquieu, for instance, wrote that civil law created chains, but natural law would always break them. Nearly all Enlightenment thinkers condemned slavery in the metaphorical sense. That the "mind should break free of its chains" and that "despotism enslaved the king's subjects" were phrases that echoed through much eighteenth-century writing. It was common for the central characters of eighteenth-century fiction, such as Voltaire's hero Candide, to meet enslaved people, learning compassion as part of their moral education. Writers dealt more gingerly, however, with the actual enslavement and slave labor of Africans.

Some Enlightenment thinkers skirted the issue of slavery. Others reconciled principle and practice in different ways. Smith condemned slavery as uneconomical. Voltaire, quick to expose his contemporaries' hypocrisy, wondered whether Europeans would look away if Europeans—rather than Africans—were enslaved. Voltaire, however, did not question his belief that Africans were inferior peoples. Montesquieu (who came from Bordeaux, one of the central ports for the Atlantic trade) believed that slavery debased master and slave alike. But he also argued that all societies balanced their systems of labor in accordance with their different needs, and slave labor was one such system. Finally, like many Enlightenment thinkers, Montesquieu defended property rights, including those of slaveholders.

> Nearly all Enlightenment thinkers condemned slavery in the metaphorical sense. That the "mind should break free of its chains" and that "despotism enslaved the king's subjects" were phrases that echoed through much eighteenth-century writing.

The *Encyclopedia*'s article on the slave trade did condemn the slave trade in the clearest possible terms, as a violation of self-government. Humanitarian antislavery movements, which emerged in the 1760s, advanced similar arguments. From deploring slavery to imagining freedom for slaves, however, proved a very long step, and one that few were willing to take. In the end, the Enlightenment's environmental determinism—the belief that environment shaped character—provided a common way of postponing the entire issue. Slavery corrupted its victims, destroyed their natural virtue, and crushed their natural love of liberty. Enslaved people, by this logic, were not ready for freedom. It was characteristic for Warville de Brissot's Society of the Friends of Blacks to call for abolition of the slave trade and to invite Thomas Jefferson, a slaveholder, to join the organization. Only a very few advocated abolishing slavery, and they insisted that emancipation be gradual. Slavery proved one of several realms in which different currents in Enlightenment thought ran toward very different conclusions.

EXPLORATION AND THE PACIFIC WORLD

The Pacific world also figured prominently in Enlightenment thinking. Systematically mapping new sections of the Pacific was among the crucial developments of the age, and one with a tremendous impact on the public imagination. These explorations were also scientific missions, sponsored as part of the Enlightenment project of expanding scientific knowledge. In 1767 the French government sent Louis-Anne de Bougainville (1729–1811) to the South Pacific in search of a new route to China, new lands suitable for colonization, and new spices for the ever lucrative trade. They sent along scientists and artists to record his findings. Like many other explorers, Bougainville found none of what he sought, but his travel accounts—above all his fabulously lush descriptions of the earthly paradise of Nouvelle-Cythère, or Tahiti—captured the attention and imaginations of many at home. The British captain James Cook (1728–1779), who followed Bougainville, made two trips into the South Pacific (1768–1771 and 1772–1775), with impressive results. He charted the coasts of New Zealand and New Holland and added the New Hebrides and Hawaii to European maps. He explored the outer limits of the Antarctic continent, the shores of the Bering Sea, and the Arctic Ocean. The artists and scientists who accompanied Cook and Bougainville vastly expanded the boundaries of European botany, zoology, and geology. Their drawings—such as Sydney Parkinson's extraordinary portraits of the Maori—appealed to a wide public. So did the accounts of dangers overcome and peoples encountered. A misguided attempt to communicate with South Pacific islanders, perhaps with the intention of conveying them to Europe, ended in the grisly deaths of Cook and four royal marines on Hawaii in late January 1779, which surely added to European readers' fascination with his travels. Large numbers of people in Europe avidly read travel accounts of these voyages. When Cook and Bougainville brought Pacific islanders to the metropolis they at-

SLAVERY AND THE ENLIGHTENMENT

The encyclopedists made an exhaustive and deliberate effort to comment on every institution, trade, and custom in Western culture. The project was conceived as an effort to catalog, analyze, and improve each facet of society. Writing in an age of burgeoning maritime trade and expanding overseas empires, they could not, and did not wish to, avoid the subject of slavery. These were their thoughts on plantation slavery, the African slaves who bore its brunt, and broader questions of law and liberty posed by the whole system.

Thus there is not a single one of these hapless souls—who, we maintain, are but slaves—who does not have the right to be declared free, since he has never lost his freedom; since it was impossible for him to lose it; and since neither his ruler nor his father nor anyone else had the right to dispose of his freedom; consequently, the sale of his person is null and void in and of itself: this Negro does not divest himself, indeed cannot under any condition divest himself of his natural rights; he carries them everywhere with him, and he has the right to demand that others allow him to enjoy those rights. Therefore, it is a clear case of inhumanity on the part of the judges in those free countries to which the slave is shipped, not to free the slave instantly by legal declaration, since he is their brother, having a soul like theirs.

From *Encyclopédie*, Vol. 16 (1765), as cited in David Brion Davis, *The Problem of Slavery in Western Culture* (Ithaca, N.Y., 1966), p. 416.

QUESTIONS FOR ANALYSIS

1. What arguments against slavery does the *Encyclopedia* article present? Do you agree with the claim that slavery is legally impossible because no one can sell his or her natural rights? What are natural rights?

2. The enslavement of conquered peoples was historically an ancient and well-established custom, approved by civil and religious authorities. Even some Enlightenment figures, such as Thomas Jefferson, were slave owners. How did some Enlightenment *philosophes* use universal ideas of freedom to argue against custom in regard to slavery and other questions?

---

tracted large crowds. Joshua Reynolds painted portraits of the islanders.

THE IMPACT OF THE SCIENTIFIC MISSIONS

Back in Europe, Enlightenment thinkers drew freely on reports of scientific missions. Since they were already committed to understanding human nature and the origins of society and to studying the effects of the environment on character and culture, stories of new peoples and cultures were immediately fascinating. In

1772 Diderot, one of many eager readers of Bougainville's accounts, published his own reflections on the cultural significance of those accounts, the *Supplément au Voyage de Bougainville*. For Diderot, the Tahitians were the original human beings and, unlike the inhabitants of the New World, were virtually free of European influence. They represented humanity in its natural state, Diderot believed, uninhibited about sexuality and free of religious dogma. Their simplicity exposed the hypocrisy and rigidity of overcivilized Europeans. Others considered the indigenous peoples of the

Maoris in a War Canoe near Lookout Point. This engraving copies an illustration by Sidney Parkinson from James Cook's explorations. Depictions of the exotic Pacific world captured the public's imagination during the Enlightenment.

Pacific akin to the classical civilizations of Greeks and Romans, associating Tahitian women, for instance, with Venus, the Roman goddess of love. All these views said more about Europe and European utopias than about indigenous cultures in the Pacific. Enlightenment thinkers found it impossible to see other peoples as anything other than primitive versions of Europeans. Even these views, however, marked a change from former times. In earlier periods Europeans had understood the world as divided between Christendom and heathen others. In sum, during the eighteenth century a religious understanding of Western identity was giving way to more secular conceptions.

One of the most important scientific explorers of the period was the German scientist Alexander von Humboldt. Humboldt spent five years in Spanish America, aiming to do nothing less than assess the civilization and natural resources of the continent. He went equipped with the most advanced scientific instruments Europe could provide. Between 1814 and 1819, Humboldt produced an impressive multivolume *Personal Narratives of Travels* much like the lavishly illustrated reports by Cook and Bougainville. The expense bankrupted him, sending him to the Prussian court in search of financial support. Humboldt's investigations provide an important link between the Enlightenment and nineteenth-century science. Humboldt, in good Enlightenment fashion, attempted to demonstrate that climate and physical environment determined which forms of life would survive in any given region. These investigations would continue in nineteenth-century discussions of evolutionary change. Charles Darwin referred to Humboldt as "the greatest scientific traveler who ever lived," and the German scientist's writing inspired Darwin's voyage to the Galapagos Islands off the coast of Ecuador.

Thus Europeans who looked outward did so for a variety of reasons and reached very different conclusions. For some Enlightenment thinkers and rulers, scientific reports from overseas fitted into a broad inquiry about civilization and human nature. That inquiry sometimes encouraged self-criticism and at others simply shored up Europeans' sense of their superiority. The late-eighteenth-century revolutions brought this Enlightenment discussion to a close. Yet these themes reemerged during the nineteenth century, when new empires were built and the West's place in the world was reassessed.

THE RADICAL ENLIGHTENMENT

Was the Enlightenment revolutionary?

How revolutionary was the Enlightenment? Enlightenment thought did undermine central tenets of eighteenth-century culture and politics. It did have a wide resonance, well beyond a small group of intellectuals. Yet Enlightenment thinkers did not hold to any single political position. Even the most radical among them disagreed on the implications of their thought. Jean-Jacques Rousseau and Mary Wollstonecraft provide good examples of such radical thinkers.

THE WORLD OF ROUSSEAU

Jean-Jacques Rousseau (roo-SOH, 1712–1778) was an "outsider" who quarreled with the other *philosophes* and contradicted many of their assumptions. He shared the *philosophes'* search for intellectual and political freedom, attacked inherited privilege, and believed in the good of humanity and the possibility of creating a just society. Yet he introduced other strains into Enlightenment thought, especially morality and what was then called "sensibility," or the cult of feeling. He was also considerably more radical than his counterparts, one of the first to talk about popular sovereignty and democracy. He was surely the most

utopian, which made his work popular at the time and has opened it to different interpretations since. In the late eighteenth century he was the most influential and most often cited of the *philosophes*, the thinker who brought the Enlightenment to a larger audience.

Rousseau's milestone and difficult treatise on politics, *The Social Contract,* began with a now famous paradox: "Man was born free, and everywhere he is in chains." How had humans freely forged these chains? To ask this was to reformulate the key questions of seventeenth- and eighteenth-century thought. What were the origins of government? Was government's authority legitimate? If not, Rousseau asked, how could it become so? Rousseau argued that in the state of nature, all men had been equal. (On women, men, and nature, see later in this section.) Social inequality, anchored in private property, profoundly corrupted "the social contract," or the formation of government. Under conditions of inequality, governments and laws represented only the rich and privileged. They became instruments of repression and enslavement. Legitimate governments could be formed, Rousseau argued. "The problem is to find a form of association . . . in which each, while uniting himself with all, may still obey himself alone, and remain as free as before." Freedom did not mean the absence of restraint, it meant that equal citizens obeyed laws they had made themselves. Rousseau hardly imagined any social leveling, and by *equality* he meant only that no one would be "rich enough to buy another, nor poor enough to have to sell oneself."

Rousseau believed that legitimate authority arose from the people alone. His argument has three parts. First, sovereignty should not be divided among different branches of government (as suggested by Montesquieu), and it emphatically could not be usurped by a king. In the late seventeenth century, Locke had spelled out the people's right to rebel against a tyrannical king. Rousseau argued that a king never became sovereign to begin with. Instead, the people themselves acted together as legislators, executives, and judges. Second, exercising sovereignty transformed the nation. Rousseau argued that when individual citizens formed a "body politic," that body became more than just the sum of its parts. He offered what was to many an appealing image of a regenerated and more powerful nation, in which citizens were bound by mutual obligation rather than coercive laws and united in equality rather than divided and weakened by privilege. Third, the national

> Rousseau's milestone and difficult treatise on politics, *The Social Contract,* began with a now famous paradox: "Man was born free, and everywhere he is in chains."

ROUSSEAU'S *SOCIAL CONTRACT* (1762)

Jean-Jacques Rousseau (1712–1778) was one of the most radical Enlightenment thinkers. In his works he suggested that humans needed not only a clearer understanding of natural laws but also a much closer relationship with nature itself and a thorough reorganization of society. He believed that a sovereign society, formed by free association of equal citizens without patrons or factions, was the clearest expression of natural law. This society would make laws and order itself by the genuinely collective wisdom of its citizens. Rousseau sets out the definition of his sovereign society and its authority in the passages reprinted here.

BOOK I, CHAPTER 6

"To find a form of association that defends and protects the person and possessions of each associate with all the common strength, and by means of which each person, joining forces with all, nevertheless obeys only himself, and remains as free as before." Such is the fundamental problem to which the social contract furnishes the solution.

BOOK II, CHAPTER 4

What in fact is an act of sovereignty? It is not an agreement between a superior and an inferior, but an agreement between the body and each of its members, a legitimate agreement, because it is based upon the social contract; equitable, because it is common to all; useful, because it can have no other purpose than the general good; and reliable, because it is guaranteed by the public force and the supreme power. As long as the subjects are only bound by agreements of this sort, they obey no one but their own will, and to ask how far the respective rights of the sovereign and citizens extend is to ask to what point the latter can commit themselves to each other, one towards all and all towards one.

Jean-Jacques Rousseau, *Rousseau's Political Writings*, trans. Julia Conaway Bondanella, ed. Allan Ritter and Julia Conaway Bondanella (New York, 1988), pp. 92. 103.

QUESTIONS FOR ANALYSIS

1. How can one join a political association and yet remain free?
2. If sovereignty is a contract, how long does it last? Can anyone refuse to accept it? Or ignore it?

community would be united by what Rousseau called the "general will." This term is notoriously difficult. Rousseau proposed it as a way to understand the common interest, which rose above particular individual demands. The general will favored equality; that made it general, and in principle at least equality guaranteed that citizens' common interests would be represented in the whole.

Rousseau's lack of concern for balancing private interests against the general will leads some political theorists to consider him authoritarian, coercive, or moralistic. Others interpret the general will as one expression of his utopianism. In the eighteenth century, *The Social Contract* was the least understood of Rousseau's works. Yet it provided influential radical arguments and, more important, extraordinarily powerful images and phrases, which were widely cited during the French Revolution.

Rousseau was better known for his writing on education and moral virtue. His widely read novel *Emile* (1762) tells the story of a young man who learns virtue and moral autonomy in the school of nature rather than in the academy. Rousseau disagreed with other *philosophes'* emphasis on reason, insisting instead that "the first impulses of nature are always right." Children should not be forced to reason early in life. Books, which "teach us only to talk about things we do not know," should not be central to learning until adolescence. Emile's tutor thus walked him through the woods, studying nature and its simple precepts, cultivating his conscience and, above all, his sense of independence. "Nourished in the most absolute liberty, the greatest evil he can imagine is servitude."

Such an education aimed to give men moral autonomy and make them good citizens. Rousseau argued that women should have very different educations. "All education of women must be relative to men, pleasing them, being useful to them, raising them when they are young and caring for them when they are old, advising them, consoling them, making their lives pleasant and agreeable, these have been the duties of women since time began." Women were to be useful socially as mothers and wives. In *Emile*, Rousseau laid out just such an education for Emile's wife-to-be, Sophie. At times, Rousseau seemed convinced that women "naturally" sought out such a role: "Dependence is a natural state for women, girls feel themselves made to obey." At other moments he insisted that girls needed to be disciplined and weaned from their "natural" vices.

Rousseau's conflicting views on female nature provide a good example of the shifting meaning of *nature*, a concept central to Enlightenment thought. Enlightenment thinkers used nature as a yardstick against which to measure society's shortcomings. "Natural" was better, simpler, uncorrupted. What, though, was nature? It could refer to the physical world. It could refer to primitive societies. Often, it was a useful invention.

Rousseau's novels sold exceptionally well, especially among women. *Julie* (subtitled *La nouvelle Héloïse*), published just after *Emile*, went through seventy editions in three decades. *Julie* tells the story of a young woman who falls in love with one man but dutifully obeys her father's order to marry another. At the end, after many travails and twists of the plot, she dies of exposure after rescuing her children from a cold lake—a perfect example of domestic and maternal virtue. One of Rousseau's fellow *philosophes* deemed the tale "hysterical and obscene." What appealed to the public, however, was the love story, the tragedy, and Rousseau's

Enlightenment Education as Illustrated in *Emile*. These colored engravings from Rousseau's influential novel depict Emile's studies in the great outdoors as opposed to the classroom.

conviction that humans were ruled by their hearts as much as their heads, that passion was more important than reason. Rousseau's novels became part of a larger cult of *sensibilité* ("feeling") in middle-class and aristocratic circles, an emphasis on spontaneous expressions of feeling, and a belief that sentiment was an expression of authentic humanity. Thematically, this aspect of Rousseau's work contradicted much of the Enlightenment's cult of reason. It is more closely related to the concerns of nineteenth-century romanticism.

How did Rousseau's ideas fit into Enlightenment views on gender? As we have seen, Enlightenment thinkers considered education key to human progress. Many lamented the poor education of women, especially because, as mothers, governesses, and teachers, many women were charged with raising and teaching children. What kind of education, however, should girls receive? Here, again, Enlightenment thinkers sought to follow the guidance of nature, and they produced scores of essays and books in philosophy, history, literature, and medicine, discussing the nature or character of the sexes. Were men and women different? Were those differences natural, or had they been created by custom and tradition? Humboldt and Diderot wrote essays on the nature of the sexes; scientific travel literature reported on the family structures of indigenous peoples in the Americas, the South Pacific, and China. Histories of civilization by Smith among many others commented on family and gender roles at different stages of history. Montesquieu's *Spirit of the Laws* included an analysis of how the different stages of government affected women. To speculate on the subject, as Rousseau did, was a common Enlightenment exercise.

Some disagreed with his conclusions. Diderot, Voltaire, and the German thinker Theodor Von Hippel, among many others, deplored legal restrictions on women. Rousseau's prescriptions for women's education drew especially sharp criticism. The English writer and historian Catherine Macaulay set out to refute his points. The Marquis de Condorcet argued on the eve of the French Revolution that the Enlightenment promise of progress could not be fulfilled unless women were educated—and Condorcet was virtually alone in asserting that women should be granted political rights.

THE WORLD OF WOLLSTONECRAFT

Rousseau's sharpest critic was the British writer Mary Wollstonecraft (1759–1797). Wollstonecraft published her best known work, *A Vindication of the Rights of Woman*, in 1792, during the French Revolution. Her argument,

however, was anchored in Enlightenment debates and needs to be understood here. Wollstonecraft shared Rousseau's political views and admired his writing and influence. Like Rousseau and her countryman Thomas Paine, a writer who supported the American and French revolutionaries, Wollstonecraft was a republican. She called monarchy "the pestiferous purple which renders the progress of civilization a curse, and warps the understanding." She spoke even more forcefully than Rousseau against inequality and the artificial distinctions of rank, birth, or wealth. Believing that equality laid the basis for virtue, she contended, in classic Enlightenment language, that the society should seek "the perfection of our nature and capability of happiness." She argued more forcefully than any other Enlightenment thinker that (1) women had the same innate capacity for reason and self-government as men, (2) *virtue* should mean the same thing for men and women, and (3) relations between the sexes should be based on equality.

Wollstonecraft did what few of her contemporaries even imagined. She applied the radical Enlightenment critique of monarchy and inequality to the family. The legal inequalities of marriage law, which among other things deprived married women of property rights,

Mary Wollstonecraft. The British writer and radical was one of several Enlightenment thinkers to take up the "woman question."

gave husbands "despotic" power over their wives. Just as kings cultivated their subjects' deference, so culture, she argued, cultivated women's weakness. "Civilized women are . . . so weakened by false refinement, that, respecting morals, their condition is much below what it would be were they left in a state nearer to nature." Middle-class girls learned manners, grace, and seductiveness to win a husband; they were trained to be dependent creatures. "My own sex, I hope, will excuse me, if I treat them like rational creatures instead of flattering their *fascinating* graces, and viewing them as if they were in a state of perpetual childhood, unable to stand alone. I earnestly wish to point out in what true dignity and human happiness consists—I wish to persuade women to endeavor to acquire strength, both of mind and body." A culture that encouraged feminine weakness produced women who were childish, cunning, cruel—and vulnerable. Here Wollstonecraft echoed common eighteenth-century themes. The scheming aristocratic women in Choderlos de Laclos's *Dangerous Liaisons*, written in the 1780s, were meant to illustrate the same points. To Rousseau's specific prescriptions for female education, which included teaching women timidity, chasteness, and modesty, Wollstonecraft replied that Rousseau wanted women to use their reason to "burnish their chains rather than to snap them." Instead, education for women had to promote liberty and self-reliance.

Wollstonecraft was a woman of her time. She argued for the common humanity of men and women but believed that they had different duties and that women's foremost responsibility was mothering and educating children. Like many of her fellow Enlightenment thinkers, Wollstonecraft believed that a natural division of labor existed and that it would ensure social harmony. "Let there be no coercion *established* in society, and the common law of gravity prevailing, the sexes will fall into their proper places." Like others, she wrote about middle-class women, for whom education and property were issues. She was considered scandalously radical for merely hinting that women might have political rights.

The Enlightenment as a whole left a mixed legacy on gender, one that closely paralleled that on slavery. Enlightenment writers developed and popularized arguments about natural rights. They also elevated natural differences to a higher plane by suggesting that nature should dictate different, and quite possibly unequal, social roles. Mary Wollstonecraft and Jean-Jacques Rousseau shared a radical opposition to despotism and slavery, a moralist's vision of a corrupt society, and a concern with virtue and community. Their divergence on gender is characteristic of Enlightenment disagreements about nature and its imperatives and a good example of different directions in which the logic of Enlightenment thinking could lead.

THE ENLIGHTENMENT AND EIGHTEENTH-CENTURY CULTURE

How did social and cultural change shape the Enlightenment?

THE BOOK TRADE

What about the social structures that produced these debates and received these ideas? To begin with, the Enlightenment was bound up in a much larger expansion of printing and print culture. From the early eighteenth century on, book publishing and selling flourished, especially in Britain, France, the Netherlands, and Switzerland. National borders, though, mattered very little. Much of the book trade was both international and clandestine. Readers bought books from stores, by subscription, and by special mail order

CHRONOLOGY	
MAJOR PUBLICATIONS OF THE ENLIGHTENMENT, 1734–1792	
Voltaire, *Philosophical Letters*	1734
Montesquieu, *The Spirit of Laws*	1748
The *Encyclopedia*	1751–1772
Rousseau, *The Social Contract*	1762
Rousseau, *Emile*	1762
Beccaria, *On Crime and Punishments*	1764
Smith, *Inquiry into Nature and Causes of the Wealth of Nations*	1776
Raynal, *Philosophical History*	1770
Wollstonecraft, *A Vindication of the Rights of Woman*	1792

ROUSSEAU AND HIS READERS

Jean-Jacques Rousseau's writings provoked very different responses from eighteenth-century readers—women as well as men. Many women readers loved his fiction and found his views about women's character and prescriptions for their education inspiring. Other women disagreed vehemently with his conclusions. In the first excerpt here, from Rousseau's novel Emile *(1762), the author sets out his views on a woman's education. He argues that her education should fit with what he considers her intellectual capacity and her social role. It should also complement the education and role of a man. The second selection is an admiring response to* Emile *from Anne-Louise-Gennaine Necker, or Madame de Staël (1766–1817), a well-known French writer and literary critic. While she acknowledged that Rousseau sought to keep women from participating in political discussion, she also thought that he had granted women a new role in matters of emotion and domesticity. The third excerpt is from Mary Wollstonecraft, who shared many of Rousseau's philosophical principles but sharply disagreed with his assertion that women and men should have different virtues and values. She believed that women like Madame de Staël were misguided in embracing Rousseau's ideas.*

ROUSSEAU'S *EMILE*

Researches into abstract and speculative truths, the principles and axioms of sciences—in short, everything which tends to generalize our ideas—is not the proper province of women; their studies should be relative to points of practice; it belongs to them to apply those principles which men have discovered. . . . All the ideas of women, which have not the immediate tendency to points of duty, should be directed to the study of men, and to the attainment of those agreeable accomplishments which have taste for their object; for as to works of genius, they are beyond their capacity; neither have they sufficient precision or power of attention to succeed in sciences which require accuracy; and as to physical knowledge, it belongs to those only who are most active, most inquisitive, who comprehend the greatest variety of objects. . . .

She must have the skill to incline us to do everything which her sex will not enable her to do herself, and which is necessary or agreeable to her; therefore she ought to study the mind of man thoroughly, not the mind of man in general, abstractedly, but the dispositions of those men to whom she is subject either by the laws of her country or by the force of opinion.

She should learn to penetrate into the real sentiments from their conversation, their actions, their looks and gestures. She should also have the art, by her own conversation, actions, looks, and gestures, to communicate those sentiments which are agreeable to them without seeming to intend it. Men will argue more philosophically about the human heart; but women will read the heart of men better than they. . . . Women have most wit, men have most genius; women observe, men reason. From the concurrence of both we derive the clearest light and the most perfect knowledge which the human mind is of itself capable of attaining.

Jean-Jacques Rousseau, *Emile* (1762), as cited in Mary Wollstonecraft, *A Vindication of the Rights of Woman* (New York and London, 1992), pp. 124–125.

Madame de Staël

Though Rousseau has endeavoured to prevent women from interfering in public affairs, and acting a brilliant part in the theatre of politics; yet in speaking of them, how much has he done it to their satisfaction! If he wished to deprive them of some rights foreign to their sex, how has he for ever restored to them all those to which it has a claim! And in attempting to diminish their influence over the deliberations of men, how sacredly has he established the empire they have over their happiness! In aiding them to descend from an usurped throne, he has firmly seated them upon that to which they were destined by nature; and though he be full of indignation against them when they endeavour to resemble men, yet when they come before him with all the *charms, weaknesses, virtues,* and *errors* of their sex, his respect for their *persons* amounts almost to adoration.

Cited in Mary Wollstonecraft, *A Vindication of the Rights of Woman* (New York and London, 1992), pp. 203–204.

Mary Wollstonecraft

Rousseau declares that a woman should never, for a moment, feel herself independent, that she should be governed by fear to exercise her *natural* cunning, and made a coquettish slave in order to render her a more alluring object of desire, a *sweeter* companion to man, whenever he chooses to relax himself. He carries the arguments, which he pretends to draw from the indications of nature, still further, and insinuates that truth and fortitude, the corner stones of all human virtue, should be cultivated with certain restrictions, because, with respect to the female character, obedience is the grand lesson which ought to be impressed with unrelenting rigour.

What nonsense! When will a great man arise with sufficient strength of mind to puff away the fumes which pride and sensuality have thus spread over the subject! If women are by nature inferior to men, their virtues must be the same in quality, if not in degree, or virtue is a relative idea; consequently, their conduct should be founded on the same principles, and have the same aim.

Cited in Susan Bell and Karen Offen, eds., *Women, the Family, and Freedom: The Debate in Documents*, Vol. 1, *1750–1880* (Stanford, Calif., 1983), p. 58.

QUESTIONS FOR ANALYSIS

1. How could Rousseau assert that women were unsuited to study the sciences? What evidence did he produce? What arguments might persuade his contemporary readers?
2. According to Rousseau, what would women gain from the "study of men, and the attainment of agreeable accomplishments"?
3. Mary Wollstonecraft thought Rousseau's views on women were nonsense. Why?
4. Why did the two women read Rousseau so differently? Were they misreading?

---

from book distributors abroad. Cheaper printing and better distribution also helped multiply the numbers of journals, some specializing in literary or scientific topics and others quite general. They helped bring daily newspapers, which first appeared in London in 1702, to Moscow, Rome, and cities and towns throughout Europe. By 1780, Britons could read 150 different magazines, and 37 English towns had local newspapers. These changes have been called a "revolution in communication," and they form a crucial part of the larger picture of the Enlightenment.

Governments did little to check this revolutionary transformation. In Britain, the press encountered few restrictions, although the government did use a stamp tax on printed goods to raise the price of newspapers or books and discourage buyers. Elsewhere, laws required publishers to apply in advance for the license or privilege (in the sense of "private right") to print and sell any given work. Some regimes granted more permissions than others. The French government, for instance, alternately banned and tolerated different volumes of the *Encyclopedia*, depending on the subjects covered in the volume, the political climate in the capital, and economic considerations. In practice, publishers frequently printed books without advance permission, hoping that the regime would not notice, but bracing themselves for fines, having their books banned, and finding their privileges temporarily revoked. Russian, Prussian, and Austrian censors tolerated much less dissent; but those governments also sought to stimulate publishing and, to a certain degree, permitted public discussion. Vienna housed an important publishing empire during the reigns of Joseph and Maria Theresa. Catherine of Russia encouraged the development of a small publishing enterprise which, by 1790, was issuing 350 titles a year. In the smaller states of Germany and Italy, governed by many local princes, it was easier to find progressive local patrons, and English and French works also circulated widely through those regions. That governments were patrons as well as censors of new scholarship illustrates the complex relationship between the age of absolutism and the Enlightenment.

As one historian puts it, censorship only made banned books expensive, keeping them out of the hands of the poor. Clandestine booksellers, most near the French border in Switzerland and the Rhineland, smuggled thousands of books across the border to bookstores, distributors, and private customers. What did readers want, and what does this tell us about the reception of the Enlightenment? Many clandestine dealers specialized in what they called "philosophical books," which meant subversive literature of all kinds: stories of languishing in prison, gossipy memoirs of life at the court, pornographic fantasies (often about religious and political figures), and tales of crime and criminals. A book smuggler would have carried several copies of *The Private Lives of Louis XIV* or *The Black Gazette;* Voltaire's comments on *Encyclopedia;* and, less frequently, Rousseau's *Social Contract.* Much of this flourishing eighteenth-century "literary underground," as the historian Robert Darnton calls it, echoed the radical Enlightenment's themes, especially the corruption of the aristocracy and the monarchy's degeneration into despotism. Less explicitly political writings, however, such as Raynal's *History,* Rousseau's novels, travel accounts, biographies, and futuristic fantasies such as Louis Sebastien Mercier's *The Year* 2440 proved equally popular. Even expensive volumes like the *Encyclopedia* sold remarkably well, testifying to a keen public interest. It is worth underscoring that Enlightenment work circulated in popular form, and that Rousseau's novels sold as well as his political theory.

HIGH CULTURE, NEW ELITES, AND THE PUBLIC SPHERE

The Enlightenment was not simply embodied in books; it was produced in networks of readers and new forms of sociability and discussion. Eighteenth-century elite or "high" culture was small in scale but cosmopolitan and very literate, and it took discussion seriously. A new elite joined together members of the nobility and wealthy people from the middle classes. Among the institutions that produced this new elite were learned societies: the American Philosophical Society of Philadelphia, British literary and philosophical societies, and the Select Society of Edinburgh. Such groups organized intellectual life outside of the universities, and they provided libraries, meeting places for discussion, and journals that published members' papers or organized debates on issues from literature and history to economics and ethics. Elites also met in "academies," financed by governments to advance knowledge, whether through research into the natural sciences (the Royal Society of London, and the French Academy of Science, both founded in 1660), promoting the national language (the Académie Française, or French Academy of Literature), or safeguarding traditions in the arts (the various academies of painting). The Berlin Royal Academy, for instance, was founded in 1701 to demonstrate the Prussian state's commitment to learning. Members included scholars in residence, corresponding members in other countries, and honorary associates, so the academy's reach was quite broad; and the Prussian government made a point of bringing in scholars from other countries. Particularly under Frederick II, who was eager to sponsor new research, the Berlin Academy flourished as a center of Enlightenment thinking. The academy's journal published members' papers every year, in French, for a European audience. In France, provincial academies played much the same role. Works such as Rousseau's *Discourse on the Origins of Inequality* were entered in academy-sponsored essay contests. Academy members included government and

CHRONOLOGY	
LIVES OF ENLIGHTENMENT THINKERS	
Baron de Montesquieu	1689–1755
Voltaire	1694–1778
David Hume	1711–1776
Jean-Jacques Rousseau	1712–1778
Guillaume Thomas François Raynal	1713–1796
Denis Diderot	1717–1783
Adam Smith	1723–1790
Mary Wollstonecraft	1759–1797

military officials, wealthy merchants, doctors, noble landowners, and scholars. Learned societies and academies both brought together different social groups (most from the elite); and in so doing, they fostered a sense of common purpose and seriousness.

SALONS

Salons did the same but operated informally. Usually they were organized by well-connected and learned aristocratic women. The prominent role of women distinguished the salons from the academies and universities. Salons brought together men and women of letters with members of the aristocracy for conversation, debate, drink, and food. Rousseau loathed this kind of ritual and viewed salons as a sign of superficiality and vacuity in a privileged and overcivilized world. Thomas Jefferson thought the influence of women in salons had put France in a "desperate state." Some of the salons reveled in parlor games. Others, such as the one organized in Paris by Madame Necker, wife of the future French reform minister, lay quite close to the halls of power and served as testing ground for new policy ideas. Madame Marie-Thérèse Geoffrin, another celebrated French *salonière*, became an important patron of the *Encyclopedia* and exercised influence in placing scholars in academies. Moses Mendelssohn held an open house for intellectuals in Berlin. Salons in London, Vienna, Rome, and Berlin worked the same way; and like academies, they promoted among their participants a sense of belonging to an active, learned elite.

Scores of similar societies emerged in the eighteenth century. Masonic lodges, organizations with elaborate secret rituals whose members pledged themselves to the regeneration of society, attracted a remarkable array of aristocrats and middle-class men. Mozart, Frederick II, and Montesquieu were Masons. Behind their closed doors, the lodges were egalitarian. They pledged themselves to a common project of rational thought and benevolent action, and to banishing religion and social distinction—at least from their ranks.

Other networks of sociability were less exclusive. Coffeehouses multiplied with the colonial trade in sugar, coffee, and tea, and they occupied a central spot in the circulation of ideas. A group of merchants gathering to discuss trade, for instance, could turn to politics; and the many newspapers lying about the café tables provided a ready-to-hand link between their smaller discussions and news and debates elsewhere. The philosopher Immanuel Kant remarked that a sharper public consciousness seemed one of the hall-marks of his time. "If we attend to the course of conversation in mixed companies consisting not merely of scholars and subtle reasoners but also of business people or women, we notice that besides storytelling or jesting they have another entertainment, namely, arguing." The ability to think critically and speak freely, without deferring to religion or tradition, was a point of pride, and not simply for intellectuals. Eighteenth-century cultural changes—the expanding networks of sociability, the flourishing book trade, the new genres of literature, and the circulation of Enlightenment ideas—widened the circles of reading and discussion, expanding what some historians and political theorists call the *public sphere*. That, in turn, began to change politics. Informal deliberations, debates about how to regenerate the nation, discussions of civic virtue, and efforts to forge a consensus played a crucial role in moving politics beyond the confines of the court.

The eighteenth century gave birth to the very idea of public opinion. A French observer described the changes this way: "In the last thirty years alone, a great and important revolution has occurred in our ideas. Today, public opinion has a preponderant force in Europe that cannot be resisted." Few thought the "public" involved more than the elite. Yet by the late eighteenth century, European governments recognized the existence of a civic-minded group that stretched from salons to coffeehouses, academies, and circles of government and to which they needed, in some measure, to respond.

MIDDLE-CLASS CULTURE AND READING

Enlightenment fare constituted only part of the new cultural interests of the eighteenth-century middle classes. Lower down on the social scale, shopkeepers, small merchants, lawyers, and professionals read more and more different kinds of books. Instead of owning one well-thumbed Bible to read aloud, a middle-class family would buy and borrow books to read casually, pass on, and discuss. This literature consisted of science, history, biography, travel literature, and fiction. A great deal of it was aimed at middle-class women, among the fastest-growing groups of readers in the eighteenth century. Etiquette books sold very well; so did how-to manuals for the household. Scores of books about the manners, morals, and education of daughters, popular versions of Enlightenment treatises on education and the mind, illustrate close parallels between the intellectual life of the high Enlightenment and everyday middle-class reading matter.

The rise of a middle-class reading public, much of it female, helps account for the soaring popularity and production of novels, especially in Britain. Novels were the single most popular new form of literature in the eighteenth century. A survey of library borrowing in late-eighteenth-century Britain, Germany, and North America showed that 70 percent of books taken out were novels. For centuries, Europeans had read romances such as tales of the knights of the Round Table. Novels, though, did not treat quasimythical subjects, the writing was less ornate, and the setting and situations were literally closer to home. The novel's more recognizable, nonaristocratic characters seemed more relevant to common middle-class experience. Moreover, examining emotion and inner feeling also linked novel writing with a larger eighteenth-century concern with personhood and humanity. As we have seen, classic Enlightenment writers like Voltaire, Goethe, and Rousseau wrote very successful novels; and those should be understood alongside the *Pamela* or *Clarissa* of Samuel Richardson (1689–1761), the *Moll Flanders* or *Robinson Crusoe* of Daniel Defoe (1660–1731), and the *Tom Jones* of Henry Fielding (1707–1754).

Many historians have noted that women figured prominently among fiction writers. In seventeenth-century France the most widely read authors of romances had been Madeleine de Scudéry and the countess de La Fayette. Later, in England, Fanny Burney (1752–1840), Ann Radcliffe (1764–1823), and Maria Edgeworth (1767–1849) all wrote extremely popular novels. The works of Jane Austen (1775–1817), especially *Pride and Prejudice* and *Emma*, are to many readers the height of a novelist's craft. Women writers, however, were not the only ones to write novels, nor were they alone in paying close attention to the domestic or private sphere. Their work took up central eighteenth-century themes of human nature, morality, virtue, and reputation. Their novels, like much of the nonfiction of the period, explored those themes in domestic as in public settings.

POPULAR CULTURE: URBAN AND RURAL

How much did books and print culture touch the lives of the common people? Literacy rates varied dramatically by gender, social class, and region, but were generally higher in northern than in southern and eastern Europe. It is not surprising that literacy ran highest in cities and towns—higher, in fact, than we might expect. In early eighteenth-century Paris, 85 percent of men and 60 percent of women could read. Well over half the residents of poorer Parisian neighborhoods, especially

A Coffeehouse in London, 1798. Coffeehouses served as centers of social networks and hubs of opinion, contributing to a public consciousness that was new to the Enlightenment. This coffeehouse scene illustrates a mixing of classes, lively debate, and the burgeoning reading culture.

small shopkeepers, domestic servants and valets, and artisans, could read and sign their names. Even the illiterate, however, lived in a culture of print. They saw one-page newspapers and broadsides or flysheets posted on streets and tavern walls and regularly heard them read aloud. Moreover, visual material—inexpensive woodcuts especially, but also prints, drawings, satirical cartoons—figured as prominently as text in much popular reading material. By many measures, then, the circles of reading and discussion were even larger than literacy rates might suggest, especially in cities.

To be sure, poorer households had few books on their shelves, and those tended to be religious texts: an abridged Bible, *The Pilgrim's Progress*, or an illustrated prayer book bought or given on some special occasion and read aloud repeatedly. But popular reading was boosted by the increasing availability of new materials. From the late seventeenth century on, a French firm published a series of inexpensive small paperbacks, the so-called blue books, which itinerant peddlers carried from cities to villages in the countryside for a growing popular market. The blue library included traditional popular literature. That meant short catechisms, quasi-religious tales of miracles, and stories of the lives of the saints, which the church hoped would provide religious instruction. It also included almanacs, books on astrology, and manuals of medical cures for people or farm animals. In the eighteenth century, book peddlers began to carry abridged and simple novels and to sell books on themes popular in the middle classes, such as travel and history. Books provided an incentive to read.

Neither England nor France required any primary schooling, leaving education to haphazard local initiatives. In central Europe, some regimes made efforts to develop state-sponsored education. Catherine of Russia summoned an Austrian consultant to set up a system of primary schools, but by the end of the eighteenth century only 22,000 of a population of 40 million had attended any kind of schools. In the absence of primary schooling, most Europeans were self-taught. The varied texts in the peddler's cart—whether religious, political propaganda, or entertainment—attest to a widespread and rapidly growing popular interest in books and reading.

Like its middle-class counterpart, popular culture rested on networks of sociability. Guild organizations offered discussion and companionship. Street theater

> In early eighteenth-century Paris, 85 percent of men and 60 percent of women could read. Well over half the residents of poorer Parisian neighborhoods, especially small shopkeepers, domestic servants and valets, and artisans, could read and sign their names.

and singers mocking local political figures offered culture to people from different social classes. The difficulties of deciphering popular culture are considerable. Most testimony comes to us from outsiders who regarded the common people as hopelessly superstitious and ignorant. Still, historical research has begun to reveal new insights. It has shown, first, that popular culture did not exist in isolation. Particularly in the countryside, market days and village festivals brought social classes together, and popular entertainments reached a wide social audience. Folktales and traditional songs resist pigeonholing as either elite, middle-class, or popular culture, for they passed from one cultural world to another, being revised and reinterpreted in the process. Second, oral and literate culture overlapped. In other words, even people who could not read often had a great deal of "book knowledge": they argued seriously about points from books and believed that books conferred authority. A group of villagers, for instance, wrote this eulogy to a deceased friend: "he read his life long, and died without ever knowing how to read." The logic and worldview of popular culture needs to be understood on its own terms.

It remains true that the countryside, especially in less economically developed regions, was desperately poor. Life there was far more isolated than in towns. A yawning chasm separated peasants from the world of the high Enlightenment. The *philosophes*, well established in the summits of European society, looked at popular culture with distrust and ignorance. They saw the common people of Europe much as they did indigenous peoples of other continents. They were humanitarians, critical thinkers, and reformers; they were not democrats. The Enlightenment, while well entrenched in eighteenth-century elite culture, nonetheless involved changes that reached well beyond elite society.

EIGHTEENTH-CENTURY MUSIC

European elites sustained other forms of high culture. English gentlemen who read scientific papers aloud in clubs also commissioned architects to design classical revival country houses for the weekends. Royal courts underwrote the academies of painting, which upheld aristocratic taste and aesthetics; Austrian salons that hosted discussions of Voltaire also staged performances of Mozart. We have already noted that the *philosophes'* work crossed genres, from political theory to fiction. Rousseau not only wrote discourses and novels but composed music and wrote an opera. A flourishing musical culture was one of the most important features of the eighteenth century.

BACH AND HANDEL

The early eighteenth century brought the last phase of Baroque music and two of the greatest composers of all time: Johann Sebastian Bach (1685–1750) and George Frideric Handel (1685–1759). Bach was an intensely pious man who remained in the backwaters of provincial Germany all his life. As a church musician in Leipzig for most of his adult career, Bach had to supply music for nearly all Sunday and holiday services, and he combined imagination and brilliance with steely self-discipline and an ability to produce music on demand. He was an ardent Protestant, entirely unaffected by the secularism of the Enlightenment: each one of his church pieces is full of such fervor that the salvation of the world appears to hang on every note. He was also prolific, writing across the entire gamut of contemporary forms (excluding opera), from unaccompanied instrumental pieces to large-scale works for vocal soloists, chorus, and orchestra. Much of his work consists of religious cantatas (over 200 surviving), motets, and Passions, but he also wrote concertos and suites for orchestra, and composed the purest of "pure" music—subtle and complex fugues for keyboard.

As a church musician in Leipzig for most of his adult career, Bach had to supply music for nearly all Sunday and holiday services, and he combined imagination and brilliance with steely self-discipline and an ability to produce music on demand.

Handel, by contrast, was a public-pleasing cosmopolitan, who sought out large, secular audiences. After spending his early years mastering Baroque compositional techniques in Italy, Handel established himself in London. He tried to make a living by composing Italian operas, but after initial success, opera sounded foreign and flowery to British ears. Handel eventually found a more marketable genre, the oratorio: a musical drama to be performed in concert, in English, without staging. Handel's oratorios were usually set to biblical stories but featured very worldly music, replete with ornate instrumentation and frequent flourishes of drums and trumpets. These heroic works succeeded in packing London's halls full of prosperous Britons, who interpreted the victories of the ancient Hebrews in such oratorios as *Israel in Egypt* and *Judas Maccabaeus* as implicit celebrations of Britain's own burgeoning national greatness. Handel's greatest oratorio, *Messiah*, is still sung widely throughout the English-speaking world every Christmas; its stirring "Hallelujah" chorus remains the most popular single choral piece in the entire classical repertoire.

HAYDN AND MOZART

Bach and Handel were among the last and certainly the greatest composers of Baroque music; the Austrians Joseph Haydn (1732–1809) and Wolfgang Amadeus Mozart (1756–1791) were the leading representatives of the Classical style, which swept Europe in the second half of the eighteenth century. Classicism here had nothing to do with imitating music written in classical antiquity. It sought to imitate classical principles of order, clarity, and symmetry—in other words, to sound as a Greek temple looked. The Classical era brought the string quartet and, most impressive, the symphony, sometimes called the novel of music, which has proved to be the most versatile and popular of all Classical musical forms. Composers of the Classical school created music that adhered rigorously to certain structural principles. For example, nearly all Classical symphonies have four movements, and nearly all symphonies open with a first movement in sonata form, characterized by the successive presentation of themes, development, and recapitulation.

Mozart's last three symphonies (out of his total of forty-one) are unequaled in their grace, variety, and technical perfection. But Mozart's short and famously difficult life captures the problems that even prodigiously talented eighteenth-century artists faced. Wolfgang began composing at four, became known as a keyboard virtuoso at six, and wrote his first symphony at nine. Wolfgang's father promoted his son, touring him as a child prodigy (with his very gifted sister) through the courts of Europe: "My boy as an eight-year-old knows as much as what one expects from a man of forty. In short: whoever does not see or hear it cannot believe it." These were the 1760s, the height of the Enlightenment, and Mozart senior grumbled about the climate of skepticism and disbelief. "Nowadays, people ridicule everything that is called a miracle," he wrote. "It was a great pleasure and a great victory for me to hear a Voltairian say to me, 'Now for once in my life I have seen a miracle; this is the first.'" Wolfgang gathered awards and honors from the pope and the Austrian empress Maria Theresa, attracted attention across

Mozart's Last Portrait, 1789. Like the composer's famous *Requiem,* this portrait, painted by Mozart's brother-in-law Joseph Lange, was left unfinished at Mozart's death.

Europe, and became a moneymaker for his family. But once he was no longer a child prodigy, like nearly all eighteenth-century artists and writers he had to rely on patronage. Mozart, a difficult person himself, suffered in the service of the cantankerous Archbishop of Salzburg, a town he hated. He tried to support himself as a freelance composer and keyboard performer in Vienna. Despite his immense productivity and well-known genius, he could barely make ends meet. He lived hand to mouth, borrowing money from his fellow Masons in the Lodge of Beneficence. He was only thirty-five when he died of rheumatic fever. In keeping with eighteenth-century medical practice, his physicians bled him frequently in the last month of his life and may have hastened his death, possibly poisoning his blood with their unsterilized instruments. It is not true that he was buried, unrecognized, in a pauper's grave. His funeral was simple and cheap, in keeping with his poverty, but also with his Masonic principles and Enlightenment opposition to Catholic ritual. His fellow composer Joseph Haydn rued that "we have lost the greatest among us."

The career of Joseph Haydn (1732–1809) provides a revealing contrast. Knowing much better how to take care of himself, he spent most of his life employed by an extremely wealthy Austro-Hungarian aristocratic family that maintained its own private orchestra. But this security entailed the indignity of wearing the Esterházy uniform, like any common butler. Only toward the end of his life, in 1791, did Haydn, then famous, strike out on his own by traveling to London, where for five years (excluding a brief interval) he supported himself handsomely by writing for a paying public rather than for private patrons. Eighteenth-century London was one of the rare places with a commercial market for culture. In this regard London was the wave of the future, for in the nineteenth century serious music would leave the aristocratic salon for urban concert halls all over Europe. In deeply aristocratic Austria, Haydn had been obliged to wear servants' livery; in London he was greeted as a creative genius, one of the earliest composers to be regarded as such. Haydn's "Miracle" symphony, written for performance in a London concert hall, is called that because during one performance a chandelier came crashing down, narrowly missing the crowd gathered to see the genius conduct. Although not the first writer of symphonies, Haydn is often termed the "father of the symphony." In over 100 works in the symphonic form—especially his last 12 symphonies, which he composed in London—Haydn formulated the most enduring techniques of symphonic composition and demonstrated the symphony's enormous creative potential.

Opera

Finally, opera flourished in the eighteenth century. Opera was a seventeenth-century creation, developed most significantly by the Italian Baroque composer Claudio Monteverdi (1567–1643), who combined music with theater for greater dramatic intensity. Monteverdi's new form of opera appealed immediately: within one generation operas were performed in all the leading cities of Italy, and by the eighteenth century they had captured attention across Europe. Staged within magnificent settings and calling on the talents of singers, musicians, dramatists, and stage designers, opera expressed as clearly as any art form Baroque artists' dedication to grandeur, drama, and display. In the Classical period, opera's popularity was boosted by Christoph Willibald von Gluck (1714–1787). Gluck, who came to Paris from Austria as the musical tutor of the young Marie Antoinette, insisted that the texts be as important as the music. He simplified arias, emphasized dramatic action, and produced high-end entertainment for the French court. Mozart, however, was the greatest operatic composer of the Classical era. *The Marriage of Figaro, Don Giovanni,* and *The Magic Flute* remain among the best-loved operas of all time.

Eighteenth-century musicians, like eighteenth-century writers, found their careers and art shaped by changing structures of culture. Despite a trend toward secularism, the church continued to provide support for much everyday music. In a very few cases—Haydn's in London is one—composers could be supported by the market. Aristocratic and court patronage, however, remained the pillars of support for musicians. And musicians, like Enlightenment writers, had an ambivalent relationship with their patrons and culture. Rousseau, in his role as a composer, railed at the way in which the aristocracy set the tone of opera productions in his time. He deplored pretentious staging and emotional inauthenticity. In his own opera he tried to bring different themes—nature, simplicity, and virtue—to the stage. The British writer Samuel Johnson called patrons "insolent wretches." Mozart relied on the overbearing Archbishop of Salzburg to commission work and, just as important, ensure that it would be performed; but he resented his position: "I did not know that I was a valet." One of Mozart's most popular operas—*The Marriage of Figaro,* based on a French play—circled around just these themes: relations between masters and servants, the abuses of privilege, and the presumptuousness of the European nobility.

The Marriage of Figaro, indeed, followed a classic eighteenth-century path to popularity. The author of the play was born Pierre Caron, the son of a watchmaker. Caron rose to become watchmaker to the king,

The Magic Flute, 1793. Mozart's opera opened in 1791, just before the extraordinary young composer died.

bought a noble office, married well, took the name Pierre Augustin de Beaumarchais, and wrote several comedies in an Enlightenment tone satirizing the French nobility. *Figaro* ran into trouble with French censors, but like so many other banned works, the play sold well. It was translated into Italian, was set to music by Mozart (who was a Mason), and played to appreciative elite audiences from Paris to Prague. Satire, self-criticism, the criticism of hierarchy, optimism and social mobility, and a cosmopolitan outlook supported by what was in many ways a traditional society—all of these are key to understanding eighteenth-century culture as well as the Enlightenment.

CONCLUSION

The Enlightenment arose from the scientific revolution, from the new sense of power and possibility that science created, and from the rush of enthusiasm for new forms of inquiry. Together, the Enlightenment and the scientific revolution created science as a form of knowledge. Eighteenth-century thinkers scrutinized a remarkably wide range of topics: human nature, reason and the processes of understanding, religion, belief, law, the origins of government authority, economics, and social practices. Whether well-known *philosophes* or underground journalists, they raised problems that made regimes, their contemporaries, and even themselves uncomfortable. Ideas circulated in popular forms from plays and operas to journalism. Intellectual changes went hand in hand with social and cultural ones: government efforts to put their states on a new footing, the emergence of a new elite, and the expansion of the public sphere.

The Atlantic revolutions (the American Revolution of 1776, the French Revolution of 1789, and the Latin American upheavals of the 1830s) were steeped in the language of the Enlightenment. The constitutions of the new nations formed by these revolutions followed the basic ideas of Enlightenment liberalism: neither religion nor the state could impede individual freedom of conscience; government authority could not be arbitrary; equality and freedom were natural; humans sought happiness, prosperity, and the expansion of their potential. These arguments had been made, tentatively, earlier. But when the North American colonists declared their independence from Britain in 1776, they called these ideas "self-evident truths." That bold declaration marked both the distance traveled since the late seventeenth century and the self-confidence that was the Enlightenment's hallmark.

KEY TERMS

reason	humanitarianism	salons
Voltaire	Adam Smith	Wolfgang Amadeus Mozart
The *Encyclopedia*	Jean-Jacques Rousseau	

SELECTED READINGS

Baker, Keith. *Condorcet: From Natural Philosophy to Social Mathematics.* Chicago, 1975. An important reinterpretation of Condorcet as a social scientist.

Bell, Susan, and Karen Offen, eds. *Women, the Family, and Freedom: The Debate in Documents.* Vol. 1, *1750–1880.* Stanford, Calif., 1983. An excellent introduction to Enlightenment debates about gender and women.

Blum, Carol. *Rousseau and the Republic of Virtue: The Language of Politics in the French Revolution.* Ithaca and London, 1986. Fascinating account of how eighteenth-century readers interpreted Rousseau.

Buchan, James. *The Authentic Adam Smith: His Life and Ideas.* New York, 2006.

Calhoun, Craig, ed. *Habermas and the Public Sphere.* Cambridge, Mass., 1992. Calhoun's introduction is a good starting point for Habermas's argument.

Cassirer, E. *The Philosophy of the Enlightenment.* Princeton, N.J., 1951.

Chartier, Roger. *The Cultural Origins of the French Revolution.* Durham, N.C., 1991. Looks at topics from religion to violence in everyday life and culture.

Darnton, Robert. *The Business of Enlightenment: A Publishing History of the* Encyclopédie, *1775–1800.* Cambridge, Mass., 1979. Darnton's work on the Enlightenment offers a fascinating blend of intellectual, social, and economic history. See his other books as well: *The Literary Underground of the Old Regime* (Cambridge, Mass., 1982); *The Great Cat Massacre and Other Episodes in French Cultural History* (New York, 1984); and *The Forbidden Best Sellers of Revolutionary France* (New York and London, 1996).

Davis, David Brion. *The Problem of Slavery in Western Culture.* New York, 1988. A Pulitzer Prize–winning examination of a central issue as well as a brilliant analysis of different strands of Enlightenment thought.

Gay, Peter. *The Enlightenment: An Interpretation.* Vol. 1, *The Rise of Modern Paganism.* Vol. 2, *The Science of Freedom.* New York, 1966–1969. Combines an overview with an interpretation. Emphasizes the *philosophes'* sense of identification with the classical world and takes a generally positive view of their accomplishments. Includes extensive annotated bibliographies.

Gray, Peter. *Mozart.* New York, 1999. Brilliant short study.

Goodman, Dena. *The Republic of Letters: A Cultural History of the French Enlightenment.* Ithaca, N.Y., 1994. Important in its attention to the role of literary women.

Hazard, Paul. *The European Mind: The Critical Years (1680–1715).* New Haven, Conn., 1953. A basic and indispensable account of the changing climate of opinion that preceded the Enlightenment.

Hildesheimer, Wolfgang. *Mozart.* New York, 1982. An exceptionally literate and thought-provoking biography.

Israel, Jonathan Irvine. *Radical Enlightenment: Philosophy and the Making of Modernity, 1650–1750.* New York, 2001. Massive and erudite, a fresh look at the international movement of ideas.

Israel, Jonathan Irvine. *Enlightenment Contested: Philosophy, Modernity, and the Emancipation of Man, 1670–1752.* New York, 2006. Massive and erudite, a fresh look at the international movement of ideas.

Munck, Thomas. *The Enlightenment: A Comparative Social History 1721–1794.* London, 2000. An excellent recent survey, especially good on social history.

Outram, Dorinda. *The Enlightenment.* Cambridge, 1995. An excellent short introduction and a good example of new historical approaches.

Porter, Roy. *The Creation of the Modern World: The Untold Story of the British Enlightenment.* New York, 2000.

Rendall, Jane. *The Origins of Modern Feminism: Women in Britain, France and the United States, 1780–1860.* New York, 1984. A very basic survey.

Sapiro, Virginia. *A Vindication of Political Virtue: The Political Theory of Mary Wollstonecraft.* Chicago, 1992. A subtle and intelligent analysis for more advanced readers.

Shklar, Judith. *Men and Citizens: A Study of Rousseau's Social Theory.* London, 1969.

Shklar, Judith. *Montesquieu.* Oxford, 1987. Shklar's studies are brilliant and accessible.

Taylor, Barbara. *Mary Wollstonecraft and the Feminist Imagination.* Cambridge and New York, 2003. Fascinating study that sets Wollstonecraft in the radical circles of eighteenth century England.

Venturi, Franco. *The End of the Old Regime in Europe, 1768–1776: The First Crisis.* Trans. R. Burr Litchfield. Princeton, N.J., 1989.

Venturi, Franco. *The End of the Old Regime in Europe, 1776–1789.* Princeton, N.J. 1991. Both detailed and wide-ranging, particularly important on international developments.

Watt, Ian P. *The Rise of the Novel.* London, 1957. The basic work on the innovative qualities of the novel in eighteenth-century England.

PART VI
THE AGE OF REVOLUTION

IN THE CENTURIES AFTER 1492, the West took on a new form, as Europe built empires extending out over the Atlantic. These Atlantic empires had enormous ramifications. They had made Europe a global power. They had become a source of wealth, trade, and economic development. They spurred thought, pushing Europeans to reflect on issues ranging from cosmology, physics, and navigation to history and how Europeans fit into the history of humanity. The Atlantic empires offered a new arena of conflict between European powers: imperial rivalry and colonial concerns increasingly assumed center stage in European wars. Finally, in the late eighteenth century, they became the staging ground for revolution.

What historians call the "age of revolution" lasted from the 1770s through at least half of the nineteenth century. It opened in the North American colonies, with a revolt against the British Empire. It became a crisis that shook eighteenth-century Europe and the Atlantic world, bringing revolutionary movements to the British Empire, France and her empire in the Caribbean, Belgium, and the Netherlands and then to the Spanish and Portugese empires in Central and South America. Repressed, or contained, by Europe's powerful states, revolutions nonetheless broke out again across Europe in 1848, reaching into the Austrian and Prussian empires in central Europe.

At the same time, a longer and slower but no less dramatic revolution in industry restructured the economies of the West. The Industrial Revolution took place in approximately the same period of time and affected many of the same people—though in different ways and to varying degrees. The major developments of the nineteenth and early twentieth centuries—the decline of landed aristocracies and the rise of new social groups, the emergence of dramatically new forms of politics, changes in political and social thought, industrial expansion, and the reorientation of European empires—all had their roots in these two revolutions. Together the revolutions toppled absolutism, mercantilism, and what was left of feudalism. They produced the theory and practice of economic individualism and political liberalism. The wrenching changes they wrought polarized Europe for several generations.

	POLITICS	SOCIETY AND CULTURE	ECONOMY	INTERNATIONAL RELATIONS
1750		Johann Wolfgang von Goethe (1749–1852)	British export production increases 80 percent (1750–1770)	
		William Blake (1757–1827)	British Parliament increases enclosures (1750–1860)	
	Reign of Catherine the Great of Russia (1762–1796)	William Wordsworth (1770–1850)	Spinning jenny, water frame, and spinning mule invented (1764–1799)	Poland partitioned by Russia, Austria, and Prussia (1772, 1793, 1795)
	American Revolution (1774–1782)	Goethe's *Faust* (1790)	James Watt patents improved steam engine (1769)	
			Industrial Revolution (1780–1880)	
	Louis XVI calls Assembly of Notables (1788)			
	The French Revolution breaks out (1789)	Jeremy Bentham's *Introduction to the Principles of Morals and Legislation* (1789)		
	Great Fear in the French countryside (1789)			
	Declaration of the Rights of Man and of the Citizen (1789)			
	French National Assembly abolishes feudal rights and privileges (1789)			
1790	Slave revolt in St. Domingue (1791)	Edmund Burke's *Reflections on the Revolution in France* (1790)		Slave rebellion in St. Domingue sparks British and Spanish invasion (1791)
	Louis XVI of France overthrown and French Republic declared (1792)	Thomas Paine's *Rights of Man* (1791)		France declares war on Austria and Prussia (1792)
	Reign of Terror (1793–1794)		Eli Whitney invents cotton gin (1793)	England enters war against France (1793)
	French Convention abolishes slavery and primogeniture (1793–1794)			Revolutionary France occupies Low Countries, Rhineland, and parts of Spain and Italy (1794–1796)
	Maximilien Robespierre executed (1794)			
		Heinrich Heine, German poet (1797–1856)		
		Wordsworth's and Coleridge's *Lyrical Ballads* (1798)		
		Thomas Malthus's *Essay on the Principle of Population* (1798)		
		Eugène Delacroix, French painter (1799–1837)		
	Napoleon Bonaparte is declared temporary consul (1799)	Honoré de Balzac, French novelist (1799–1850)		
1800	President Thomas Jefferson (1800–1808)	Emergence of Romanticism (early 1800s)	Women make up 50 percent of British textile workforce (c. 1800)	Peace of Amiens temporarily halts war between Britain and France (1801)
	Bonaparte's Concordat with the pope (1801)	Continental population doubles (1800–1850)		Napoleon unsuccessfully tries to restore slavery in St. Domingue (1801–1803)
	Bonaparte elected Consul for Life by plebiscite (1802)			Louisiana Purchase (1803)
	Bonaparte crowns himself Emperor Napoleon I (1804)	Napoleonic Code (1804)		Independent state of Haiti (formerly St. Domingue) (1804)
		George Sand, novelist (1804–1876)		Nelson's victory at Trafalgar breaks French naval power (1805)
				Napoleon defeats Austria and Russia at battle of Austerlitz (1805)
			Napoleon's Continental System imposed (1806)	
			Serfdom abolished in Prussia (1807)	
1808	Prussian reform era begins (1808)	Johann Gottlieb Fichte's *Addresses to the German Nation* (1808)		Napoleon invades Spain (1808)

POLITICS	SOCIETY AND CULTURE	ECONOMY	INTERNATIONAL RELATIONS	
			Napoleon marries Mary Louise of the Habsburgs (1809)	1809
	Grimm's *Fairy Tales* by the Brothers Grimm (1813)		Napoleon's Russian campaign (1812)	
Bourbon monarchy restored in France (1815)			Napoleon exiled to Elba (1814) Congress of Vienna (1814–1815) Napoleon defeated at Waterloo (1815) German Confederation created by Congress of Vienna (1815)	
	Gustav Courbet, French painter (1819–1877)	Prussian Zollverein (customs union) founded (1818)	Quintuple Alliance formed (1818) Greek war of independence (1821–1827) Monroe Doctrine (1823)	
Decembrist Revolt in Russia (1825)			Serbia emerges from within Ottoman Empire (1828)	
Revolution in France, Belgium (1830) Mazzini founds Young Italy society (1831) Electoral Reform Act in England (1832) Poor Laws Reform in England (1834) Reign of Queen Victoria (1837–1901) British Chartist movement (1838–1848)	Alexis de Tocqueville's *Democracy in America* (1835–1840) *The Economist* is founded (1838) Emergence of Realism in art and literature (1840s) Great Famine in Ireland (1845–1849)	First railway to carry passengers (1830) Rail transport spreads across Continent (1840s) Zollverein expands to include nearly all German states (1840s) Poor harvests contribute to economic crisis across Europe (1845) Great Irish Famine (1845–1849)		
Repression of revolutionary movements in central and eastern Europe (1848–1850)	Seneca Falls Convention (1848)		Treaty of Guadalupe Hidalgo ends war between United States and Mexico (1848) United States buys western territory, including California, for $15 million (1848)	
Louis-Napoleon Bonaparte overthrows Second Republic (1851)	Florence Nightingale's medical reforms (1850s) Great Exhibit of the Works of Industry in All Nations, London (1851)	California gold rush (1849) Serfdom abolished in southern and eastern Europe (1850) Great Exhibition of the Works of Industry in All Nations, London (1851) Britain exports half of world's iron (1852) Cotton accounts for 40 percent of domestic exports from Britain (1852)		1850
	Charles Darwin's *On the Origin of Species* (1859) John Stuart Mill's *On Liberty* (1859)	Agricultural laborers still largest workforce in Britain (1860) Britain and France sign free-trade agreement (1860) Emancipation of serfs in Russia (1861)	Crimean War (1854–1856) Sardinia takes Lombardy, Papal States, and various duchies (1859)	
Reign of Kaiser Wilhelm I (1861–1888) Civil War in the United States (1861–1865) Otto von Bismarck appointed prime minister of Germany (1862)	Victor Hugo's *Les Misérables* (1862)		Victor Emmanuel II claims title of king of Italy (1861–1878)	
Reform Bill of 1867 in England (1867)	Fyodor Dostoyevsky's *Crime and Punishment* (1866) Mill's *Subjection of Women* (1869)	Slavery abolished in United States (1865) Railroad connects Mississippi Valley with Pacific coast (1869)	Seven Weeks' War; Prussia takes Schleswig-Holstein (1866) Canada gains independence (1867)	
			Franco-Prussian War (1870–1871) Italians take Rome from Napoleon III's protection (1870) German Empire proclaimed (1871)	1870

CHAPTER EIGHTEEN

THE FRENCH REVOLUTION

IN 1789, ONE EUROPEAN out of every five lived in France. Many Europeans considered France the center of European culture. It followed that a revolution in France would immediately command the attention of Europe and assume international significance. Yet the French Revolution attracted and disturbed men and women for much more important reasons. Both its philosophical ideals and its political realities mirrored attitudes, concerns, and conflicts that had occupied the minds of educated Europeans for decades.

The revolutionaries raised issues that resonated across Europe. Absolutism was increasingly the bane of a wide spectrum of thoughtful opinion. Aristocrats across Europe and the colonies resented monarchical inroads on their ancient freedoms. Members of the middle class, many of whom were very successful, chafed under a system of official privilege that they increasingly considered outmoded. Peasants fiercely resented what seemed to them the never-ceasing demands of central government on their limited resources. Nor were resentments focused exclusively on absolutist monarchs. Tensions existed as well between country and city dwellers, between rich and poor, overprivileged and underprivileged, slave and free. The French Revolution of 1789 was the most dramatic, most tumultuous expression of all these conflicts.

The age of revolution opened in the North American colonies. The American Revolution of 1776 had been a crisis of the British Empire. It had been one of the last in a series of conflicts between England and France over colonial control of the New World. It became one of the first crises of the old regime in France. "The New World was where the fears and aspirations . . . were first dramatized, where extra-legal associations of common citizens defied acts of a sovereign power, where

FOCUS QUESTIONS

• How were the French and American Revolutions different?

• What were the causes of the French Revolution?

• How did a fiscal crisis become a political crisis?

 • Why did the French Revolution become more radical?

• How did Bonaparte come to power?

• How did Napoleon centralize his authority?

• What led to Napoleon's downfall?

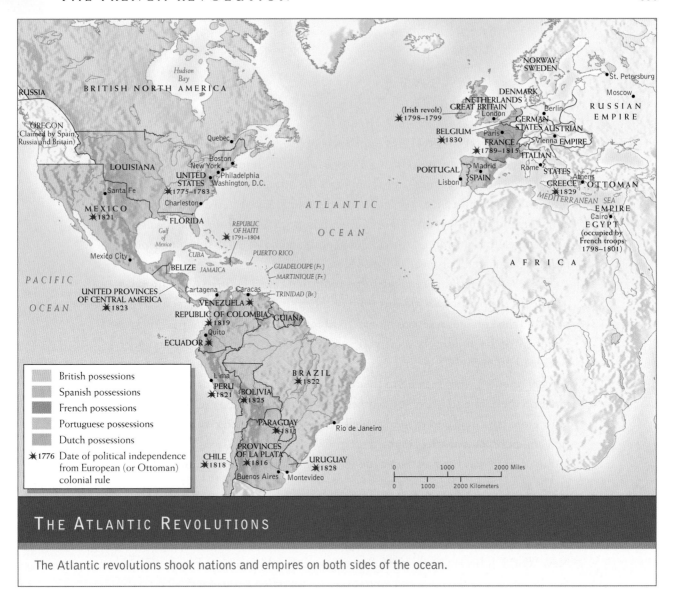

THE ATLANTIC REVOLUTIONS

The Atlantic revolutions shook nations and empires on both sides of the ocean.

abstract ideals of political philosophy were substantiated in the actions of ordinary men," as one historian says. Among "enlightened" Europeans, the success with which citizens of the new nation had thrown off British rule and formed a republic based on Enlightenment principles was the source of tremendous optimism. Change would come, many believed. Reform was possible. The costs would be modest.

If the American Revolution first dramatized Europeans' aspirations, the French Revolution deepened their fears. The French Revolution proved a more radical project, though it did not necessarily begin that way. It became immeasurably more costly—protracted, complex, and violent. It aroused much greater hopes and consequently, in many cases, bitter disillusionment. It raised issues that would not be settled for half a century.

THE FRENCH REVOLUTION: AN OVERVIEW

How were the French and American revolutions different?

In Charles Dickens's *Tale of Two Cities* (1859), the source of many popular images of revolution, the French upheaval blurs into a frightening picture of bloodthirsty crowds watching a guillotine. The picture is memorable but misleading. The term *French Revolution* is a shorthand for a complex series of events between 1789 and 1799. (Napoleon ruled from 1799 to 1814–1815.)

To simplify, those events can be divided into four stages. In the first stage, running from 1788 to 1792, the struggle was constitutional and relatively peaceful. An increasingly bold elite articulated its grievances against the king. Like the American revolutionaries, French elites refused taxation without representation; attacked despotism, or arbitrary authority; and offered an Enlightenment-inspired program to rejuvenate the nation. Reforms, many of them breathtakingly wide ranging, were instituted—some accepted or even offered by the king, and others passed over his objections. The peaceful, constitutional phase did not last. Unlike the American Revolution, the French Revolution did not stabilize around one constitution or one set of political leaders, for many reasons.

Reforms met with resistance, dividing the country. The threat of dramatic change within one of the most powerful countries in Europe created international tensions. In 1792, these tensions exploded into war; and the crises of war, in turn, spelled the end of the Bourbon monarchy and the beginning of the republic. The second stage of the revolution, which lasted from 1792 to 1794, was one of acute crisis, consolidation, and repression. A ruthlessly centralized government mobilized all the country's resources to fight the foreign enemy as well as counterrevolutionaries at home, to destroy traitors and the vestiges of the Old Regime.

The Terror, as this policy was called, did save the republic, but it exhausted itself in factions and recriminations and collapsed in 1794. In the third phase, from 1794 to 1799, the government drifted. France remained a republic. It continued to fight with Europe. Undermined by corruption and division, the state fell prey to the ambitions of a military leader, in this case Napoleon Bonaparte. Napoleon's rule, punctuated by astonishing victories and catastrophes, stretched from 1799 to 1815. It began as a republic, became an empire, and ended—after a last hurrah—in the muddy fields outside the Belgian village of Waterloo. After Napoleon's final defeat, the other European monarchs restored the Bourbons to the throne. That Restoration, however, would be short lived, and the cycle of revolution and reaction continued into the nineteenth century.

THE COMING OF THE REVOLUTION

What were the causes of the French Revolution?

What were the long-term causes of the revolution in France? Historians long ago argued that the causes and outcomes should be understood in terms of class conflict. According to this interpretation, a rising bourgeoisie, or middle class, inspired by Enlightenment ideas and by its own self-interest, overthrew what was left of the aristocratic order. This interpretation drew on the writings of the nineteenth-century philosopher Karl Marx and on much twentieth-century sociology.

Historians have substantially modified this bold thesis. To be sure, the origins of the revolution lie in eighteenth-century French society. Yet that society was not simply divided between a bourgeois class and the aristocracy. Instead, it was increasingly dominated by a new elite or social group that brought together aristocrats, officeholders, professionals, and—to a lesser degree—merchants and businessmen. To understand the revolution, we need to understand this new social group and its conflicts with the government of Louis XVI.

French society was divided into Three Estates. (An individual's *estate* marked his standing, or status, and it determined legal rights, taxes, and so on.) The First Estate comprised all the clergy; the Second Estate, the nobility. The Third Estate, by far the largest, included everyone else, from wealthy lawyers and businessmen to urban laborers and poor peasants. Within the political and social elite of the country, a small but powerful group, these legal distinctions often seemed artificial. To begin with, in the upper reaches of society, the social boundaries between nobles and wealthy commoners were ill-defined. Noble title was accessible

CHRONOLOGY

PERIODS OF THE FRENCH REVOLUTION ERA, 1789–1815

1. The First French Revolution	July 1789–August 1792
2. The Second French Revolution	August 1792–July 1794
3. The Directory	1794–1799
4. The Napoleonic era	1799–1815

to those who could afford to buy an ennobling office. For example, close to 50,000 new nobles were created between 1700 and 1789. The nobility depended for its vigor on a constant infusion of talent and economic power from the wealthy social groups of the Third Estate.

The case of the family of the revolutionary figure Honoré Gabriel Riqueti, the comte de Mirabeau (*mihr-ab-BOH*), illustrates the changes. Mirabeau's sixteenth-century ancestors had been merchants. In 1570, however, one of them had purchased the seigneury (land that conferred noble title) of Mirabeau. In the following century another bought himself the title of marquis. Mirabeau, a lawyer, also held a commission in the cavalry that his grandfather once commanded. Aristocrats spoke of a distinction between the nobility of the sword and of the robe, the former supposedly of a more ancient and distinguished lineage derived from military service, the latter aristocrats because they had purchased administrative or judicial office (hence the robe). As the example of the Mirabeau family shows, even that distinction could be illusory.

Wealth did not take predictable forms. Most noble wealth was proprietary—that is, tied to land, urban properties, purchased offices, and the like. Yet noble families did not disdain trade or commerce, as historians long thought. In fact, noblemen financed most industry, and they also invested heavily in banking and such enterprises as ship owning, the slave trade,

mining, and metallurgy. Moreover, the very wealthy members of the Third Estate also preferred to invest in secure, proprietary holdings. Thus, throughout the century, much bourgeois wealth was transformed into noble wealth, and a significant number of rich bourgeois became noblemen. Wealthy members of the bourgeoisie themselves did not see themselves as a separate class. They thought of themselves as different from—and often opposed to—the common people, who worked with their hands. But they identified with the values of a nobility to which they frequently aspired.

There were, nonetheless, important social tensions. Less prosperous lawyers—and there were an increasing number of them—were jealous of the privileged position of a favored few in their profession. Over the course of the century the price of offices rose, making it more difficult to buy one's way into the nobility, and creating tensions between middling members of the Third Estate and the very rich in trade and commerce who, by and large, were the only group able to afford to climb the social ladder. Less wealthy nobles resented the success of rich, upstart commoners whose income allowed them the luxury of life in the grand style that they could not have themselves. In sum, several fault lines ran through the elite and the middle classes. All these social groups could nonetheless join in attacking a government and an economy that were not serving their interests.

Prerevolutionary Propaganda, 1788–1789. These prints illustrate the popular view that the Third Estate (commoners) were carrying the burden of national taxation on its shoulders while doing the productive work of the nation.

The Enlightenment had changed public debate (see Chapter Seventeen). Although ideas did not cause the revolution, they played a critical role in articulating grievances. The political theories of Locke, Voltaire, and Montesquieu could appeal to both discontented nobles and members of the middle class. Voltaire was popular because of his attacks on noble privileges; Locke and Montesquieu gained widespread followings because of their defense of private property and limited sovereignty. Montesquieu's ideas appealed to the noble lawyers and officeholders who dominated France's powerful law courts, the *parlements*. They read his doctrine of checks and balances as a defense of parlements as the governmental bodies that would provide a check to the despotism of the king's government. When conflicts arose, noble leaders presented themselves as defenders of a national political community threatened by the king and his ministers.

The campaign for change was also fueled by economic reformers. The "physiocrats," as they were called in France, urged the government to simplify the tax system and free the economy from mercantilist regulations. They urged the government to lift its controls on the price of grain, for example, which had been imposed to keep the cost of bread low but, they argued, had interfered with the natural workings of the market.

In the countryside, peasants were caught in a web of obligations to landlords, church and state: a tithe, or levy, on farm produce owed to the church; fees for the use of a landlord's mill or wine press; fees to the landlord; and fees when land changed hands. In addition, peasants paid a disproportionate share of both direct and indirect taxes—the most onerous of which was the salt tax—levied by the government. (For some time the production of salt had been a state monopoly; every individual was required to buy at least seven pounds a year from the government works. The result was a commodity whose cost was often as much as fifty or sixty times its actual value.) Further grievances stemmed from the requirement to maintain public roads (the corvée) and from the hunting privileges that nobles for centuries had regarded as the distinctive badge of their order.

Social and economic conditions deteriorated on the eye of the revolution. A general price increase during much of the eighteenth century, which permitted the French economy to expand by providing capital for investment, created hardship for the peasantry and for urban tradesmen and laborers. Their plight deteriorated further at the end of the 1780s, when poor harvests sent bread prices sharply higher. In 1788 families found themselves spending more than 50 percent of their income on bread, which made up the bulk of their diet. The following year the figure rose to as much as 80 percent. Poor harvests reduced demand for manufactured goods, and contracting markets in turn created unemployment. Many peasants left the countryside for the cities, hoping to find work there—only to discover that urban unemployment was far worse than that in rural areas. Evidence indicates that between 1787 and 1789 the unemployment rate in many parts of urban France was as high as 50 percent.

> Evidence indicates that between 1787 and 1789 the unemployment rate in many parts of urban France was as high as 50 percent.

CHRONOLOGY

ORIGINS OF THE FRENCH REVOLUTION, 1788–1789

Failure of fiscal reform	1787–1788
Louis XVI summons the Estates General	May 1788
Bread riots across France	Spring 1789
Estates General convenes in Paris	May 1789
Third Estate declares itself the National Assembly	May 1789
Oath of the Tennis Court	June 1789
Fall of the Bastille	July 14, 1789

FAILURE AND REFORM

An inefficient tax system further weakened the country's financial position. Not only was taxation tied to differing social standings but it varied as well from region to region—some areas, for example, were subject to a much higher rate than others. Special circumstances and exemptions made the task of collectors more difficult. The financial system, already burdened by debts incurred under Louis XIV, all but broke down completely under the increased expenses brought on by French participation in the American Revolution. The cost of servicing the national debt of approximately 4 billion livres in the 1780s consumed 50 percent of the nation's budget.

Louis XVI. Louis inherited both absolutism and challenges to it.

Problems with the economy reflected weaknesses in France's administrative structure, ultimately the responsibility of the country's absolutist monarch, Louis XVI (1774–1792). Anxious to serve his people in "enlightened" ways, Louis wished to improve the lot of the poor, to abolish torture, and to shift the burden of taxation onto the richer classes. Yet he lacked the ability to put these reforms into effect. His well-intentioned attempts at reform ultimately undermined his own authority. He appointed such reformers as Anne-Robert-Jacques Turgot, a philosopher, physiocrat, and former provincial intendant, and Jacques Necker, a Swiss Protestant banker, as finance ministers, only to arouse opposition among traditionalist factions within the court. He allowed his wife, the young but strong-willed Marie Antoinette—daughter of Austria's Maria Theresa—a free hand to dispense patronage among her friends. The result was constant intrigue and frequently reshuffled alliances at Versailles.

Wrangling between the central government and the provincial parlements also slowed reform. As we have noted, the parlements had reasserted their independence during the early years of the reign of Louis XV. Throughout the century they had grown increasingly insistent on what they began to call their "constitutional" rights, or privileges. When Louis XVI pressed for new taxes to be paid by the nobility as well as the rest of the community after the expensive Seven Years' War, the parlements successfully defended the nobility's right to be exempt from major national taxes. In the mid-1770s this episode was reenacted when Turgot, Louis XVI's principal financial minister, proposed reducing the debt by curtailing court expenses, replacing the labor requirements with a small tax on landowners, and abolishing certain guild restrictions to stimulate manufacturing. The Paris parlement steadfastly opposed such innovations, claiming that Turgot was trampling on ancient prerogatives and privileges—and he was.

In the end, however, the plan failed because the king withdrew his support of Turgot. Although the parlements were jealous of their prerogatives, they could not indefinitely inhibit the reforms of a determined monarch. Louis XVI, however, was not determined. By 1788, a weak monarch, together with a chaotic financial situation and severe social tensions, brought absolutist France to the edge of political disaster.

THE DESTRUCTION OF THE OLD REGIME

How did a fiscal crisis become a political crisis?

The fiscal crisis precipitated the revolution. In 1787 and 1788 the king's principal ministers, Charles de Calonne and Loménie de Brienne, attempted to institute a series of reforms to stave off bankruptcy. To meet the mounting deficit, they proposed new taxes, notably a stamp duty and a direct tax on the annual produce of the land.

Hoping to persuade the nobility to agree to these reforms, the king summoned an Assembly of Notables from among the aristocracy. This group used the financial emergency to attempt major constitutional reforms. Most important, they insisted that any new tax scheme must be approved by the Estates General, the

WHAT IS THE THIRD ESTATE? (1789)

The Abbé Emmanuel-Joseph Sieyès (1748–1836) was, by virtue of his office, a member of the First Estate of the Estates General. Nevertheless, his political savvy led him to be elected as a representative of the Third Estate from the district of Chartres. Sieyès was a formidable politician as well as a writer. His career during the Revolution, which he ended by assisting Napoleon's seizure of power, began with one of the most important radical pamphlets of 1789. In What Is the Third Estate?, *Sieyès posed fundamental questions about the rights of the estate, which represented the great majority of the population and helped provoke its secession from the Estates General.*

The plan of this book is fairly simple. We must ask ourselves three questions.

1. What is the Third Estate? *Everything.*
2. What has it been until now in the political order? *Nothing.*
3. What does it want to be? *Something.*

It suffices to have made the point that the so-called usefulness of a privileged order to the public service is a fallacy; that without help from this order, all the arduous tasks in the service are performed by the Third Estate; that without this order the higher posts could be infinitely better filled; that they ought to be the natural prize and reward of recognized ability and service; and that if the privileged have succeeded in usurping all well-paid and honorific posts, this is both a hateful iniquity towards the generality of citizens and an act of treason to the commonwealth.

Who is bold enough to maintain that the Third Estate does not contain within itself everything needful to constitute a complete nation? It is like a strong and robust man with one arm still in chains. If the privileged order were removed, the nation would not be something less but something more. What then is the Third Estate? All; but an "all" that is fettered and oppressed. What would it be without the privileged order? It would be all; but free and flourishing. Nothing will go well without the Third Estate; everything would go considerably better without the two others.

Emmanuel-Joseph Sieyès, *What is the Third Estate?* trans. M. Blondel, ed. S. E. Finer (London, 1964), pp. 53–63.

QUESTIONS FOR ANALYSIS

1. How might such a pamphlet change a political debate?
2. What images or arguments would have been persuasive?

representative body of the Three Estates of the realm, and that the king had no legal authority to arrest and imprison arbitrarily. In this, they echoed the English aristocrats of 1688 and the American revolutionaries of 1776.

Faced with economic hardship and financial chaos, Louis XVI summoned the Estates General (which had not met since 1614) to meet in 1789. His action appeared to many as the only solution to France's deepening problems. Long-term grievances and short-term hardships had produced bread riots across the country in the spring of 1789. Looting in Brittany, Flanders, Provence, and elsewhere was accompanied by demands that the king take measures to make bread affordable. Fear that the forces of law and order were collapsing and that the common people might take matters into their own hands spurred the Estates General. Each of the three orders elected its own

The Tennis Court Oath, by Jacques Louis David (1748–1825). In June 1789, in the hall where royalty played a game known as *jeu de paume* (similar to tennis), leaders of the revolution swore to draft a constitution. In the center of this painting, standing on the table, is Jean Bailly, president of the National Assembly. Seated at the table below him is the Abbé Sieyès. Mirabeau stands in the right foreground with a hat in his left hand.

deputies—the Third Estate indirectly through local assemblies. These assemblies were charged as well with the responsibility of drawing up lists of grievances (*cahiers des doléances*) further heightening expectations for fundamental reform.

The delegates of the Third Estate, though elected by assemblies chosen in turn by artisans and peasants, represented the outlook of the elite. Only 13 percent were men of business. About 25 percent were lawyers; 43 percent were government officeholders of some sort.

By tradition, each estate met and voted as a body. In the past, this had generally meant that the First Estate (the clergy) had combined with the Second (the nobility) to defeat the Third. Now the Third Estate made it clear it would not tolerate such an arrangement. The Third's interests were articulated most memorably by the Abbé Emmanuel Sieyès, a radical member of the clergy. "What Is the Third Estate?" asked Sieyès, in his famous pamphlet of January 1789. Everything, he answered, and pointed to eighteenth-century social changes to bolster his point. In early 1789, Sieyès's

views were still unusually radical. But the leaders of the Third Estate agreed that the three orders should sit together and vote as individuals. More important, they insisted that the Third Estate should have twice as many members as the First and Second.

The king first opposed "doubling the Third" and then changed his position. His unwillingness to take a strong stand on voting procedures cost him support he might otherwise have obtained from the Third Estate. Shortly after the Estates General opened at Versailles in May 1789, the Third Estate, angered by the king's attitude, took the revolutionary step of leaving the body and declaring itself the National Assembly. Locked out of the Estates General meeting hall on June 20, the Third Estate and a handful of sympathetic nobles and clergymen moved to a nearby indoor tennis court.

Here, under the leadership of the volatile, maverick aristocrat Mirabeau and the radical clergyman Sieyès, they bound themselves by a solemn oath not to separate until they had drafted a constitution for France. This Oath of the Tennis Court, sworn on June 20,

1789, can be seen as the beginning of the French Revolution. By claiming the authority to remake the government in the name of the people, the National Assembly was not merely protesting against the rule of Louis XVI but asserting its right to act as the highest sovereign power in the nation. On June 27 the king virtually conceded this right by ordering all the delegates to join the National Assembly.

FIRST STAGES OF THE FRENCH REVOLUTION

The first stage of the French Revolution extended from June 1789 to August 1792. In the main, this stage was moderate, its actions dominated by the leadership of liberal nobles and men of the Third Estate. Yet three events in the summer and fall of 1789 furnished evidence that their leadership would be challenged.

POPULAR REVOLTS

From the beginning of the political crisis, public attention was high. It was roused not merely by interest in political reform but also by the economic crisis that, as we have seen, brought the price of bread to astronomical heights. Many believed that the aristocracy and the

king were conspiring to punish the Third Estate by encouraging scarcity and high prices. Rumors circulated in Paris during the latter days of June 1789 that the king's troops were mobilizing to march on the city. The electors of Paris (those who had voted for the Third Estate—workshop masters, artisans, and shopkeepers) feared not only the king but also the Parisian poor, who had been parading through the streets and threatening violence. The common people would soon be referred to as sans-culottes (sahn koo-LAWTS). The term, which translates to "without breeches," was an antiaristocratic badge of pride: a man of the people wore full-length trousers rather than aristocratic breeches with stockings and gold-buckled shoes. Led by the electors, the people formed a provisional municipal government and organized a militia of volunteers to maintain order. Determined to obtain arms, they made their way on July 14 to the Bastille, an ancient fortress where guns and ammunition were stored. Built in the Middle Ages, the Bastille had served as a prison for many years but was no longer much used. Nevertheless, it symbolized hated royal authority. When crowds demanded arms from its governor, he procrastinated and then, fearing a frontal assault, opened fire, killing ninety-eight of the attackers. The crowd took revenge, capturing the fortress (which held only seven prisoners—five common criminals and

Women of Paris Leaving for Versailles, October 1789. A crowd of women, accompanied by Lafayette and the National Guard, marched to Versailles to confront the king about shortages and rising prices in Paris.

two people confined for mental incapacity) and decapitating the governor. Similar groups took control in other cities across France. The fall of the Bastille was the first instance of the people's role in revolutionary change.

The second popular revolt occurred in the countryside. Peasants, too, expected and feared a monarchical and aristocratic counterrevolution. Rumors flew that the king's armies were on their way, that Austrians, Prussians, or "brigands" were invading. Frightened and uncertain, peasants and villagers organized militias; others attacked and burned manor houses, sometimes to look for grain but usually to find and destroy records of manorial dues. This "Great Fear," as historians have labeled it, compounded the confusion in rural areas. The news, when it reached Paris, convinced deputies at Versailles that the administration of rural France had simply collapsed.

The third instance of popular uprising, the "October Days of 1789," was brought on by economic crisis. This time Parisian women from the market district, angered by the soaring price of bread and fired by rumors of the king's continuing unwillingness to cooperate with the assembly, marched to Versailles on October 5 and demanded to be heard. Not satisfied with its reception by the assembly, the crowd broke through the gates to the palace, calling for the king to return to Paris from Versailles. On the afternoon of the following day the king yielded. The National Guard, sympathetic to the agitators, led the crowd back to Paris, the procession headed by a soldier holding aloft a loaf of bread on his bayonet.

Each of these popular uprisings shaped the political events unfolding at Versailles. The storming of the Bastille persuaded the king and nobles to agree to the creation of the National Assembly. The Great Fear compelled the most sweeping changes of the entire revolutionary period. In an effort to quell rural disorder, on the night of August 4 the assembly took a giant step toward abolishing all forms of privilege. It eliminated the church tithe (tax on the harvest), the labor requirement known as the corvée, the nobility's hunting privileges, and a wide variety of tax exemptions and monopolies. In effect, these reforms obliterated the remnants of feudalism. One week later, the assembly abolished the sale of offices, thereby sweeping away one of the fundamental institutions of the Old Regime. The king's return to Paris during the October Days of 1789 undercut his ability to resist further changes.

THE NATIONAL ASSEMBLY AND THE RIGHTS OF MAN

The assembly issued its charter of liberties, the Declaration of the Rights of Man and of the Citizen, in September 1789. It declared property to be a natural right, along with liberty, security, and "resistance to oppression." It declared freedom of speech, religious toleration, and liberty of the press inviolable. All citizens were to be treated equally before the law. No one was to be imprisoned or punished without due process of law. Sovereignty resided in the people, who could depose officers of the government if they abused their powers. These were not new ideas; they represented the outcome of Enlightenment discussions and revolutionary debates and deliberations. The Declaration became the preamble to the new constitution, which the assembly finished in 1791.

> The assembly issued its charter of liberties, the Declaration of the Rights of Man and of the Citizen, in September 1789. It declared property to be a natural right, along with liberty, security, and "resistance to oppression." It declared freedom of speech, religious toleration, and liberty of the press inviolable.

Whom did the Declaration mean by "man and the citizen"? The revolutionaries distinguished between "passive" citizens, guaranteed rights under law, and "active" citizens, who paid a certain amount in taxes and could thus vote and hold office. About half the adult males in France qualified as active citizens. Even their power was curtailed, because they could vote only for "electors," men whose property ownership qualified them to hold office. Later in the revolution, the more radical republic abolished the distinction between active and passive, and the conservative regimes reinstated it. Which men could be trusted to participate in politics and on what terms was a hotly contested issue.

So, to a certain extent, were the rights of religious minorities. The revolution gave full civil rights to Protestants, though in areas long divided by religious conflict those rights were challenged by Catholics. The revolution did, hesitantly, give civil rights to Jews, a measure that sparked protest in areas of eastern France. Religious toleration, a central theme of the Enlightenment, meant ending persecution; it did not mean that the regime was prepared to accommodate

DECLARATION OF THE RIGHTS OF MAN AND OF THE CITIZEN

One of the first important pronouncements of the National Assembly after the Tennis Court Oath was the Declaration of the Rights of Man and of the Citizen. The authors drew inspiration from the American Declaration of Independence, but the language is even more heavily influenced by the ideals of French Enlightenment philosophers, particularly Rousseau. Following are the Declaration's preamble and some of its most important principles.

The representatives of the French people, constituted as the National Assembly, considering that ignorance, disregard, or contempt for the rights of man are the sole causes of public misfortunes and the corruption of governments, have resolved to set forth, in a solemn declaration, the natural, inalienable, and sacred rights of man, so that the constant presence of this declaration may ceaselessly remind all members of the social body of their rights and duties; so that the acts of legislative power and those of the executive power may be more respected . . . and so that the demands of the citizens, grounded henceforth on simple and incontestable principles, may always be directed to the maintenance of the constitution and to the welfare of all. . . .

Article 1. Men are born and remain free and equal in rights. Social distinctions can be based only on public utility.

Article 2. The aim of every political association is the preservation of the natural and imprescriptible rights of man. These rights are liberty, property, security, and resistance to oppression.

Article 3. The source of all sovereignty resides essentially in the nation. No body, no individual can exercise authority that does not explicitly proceed from it.

Article 4. Liberty consists in being able to do anything that does not injure another; thus the only limits upon each man's exercise of his natural laws are those that guarantee enjoyment of these same rights to the other members of society.

Article 5. The law has the right to forbid only actions harmful to society. No action may be prevented that is not forbidden by law, and no one may be constrained to do what the law does not order.

Article 6. The law is the expression of the general will. All citizens have the right to participate personally, or through representatives, in its formation. It must be the same for all, whether it protects or punishes. All citizens, being equal in its eyes, are equally admissable to all public dignities, positions, and employments, according to their ability, and on the basis of no other distinction than that of their virtues and talents. . . .

Article 16. A society in which the guarantee of rights is not secured, or the separation of powers is not clearly established, has no constitution.

Declaration of the Rights of Man and of the Citizen, as cited in K. M. Baker, ed., *The Old Regime and the French Revolution* (Chicago; 1987), pp. 238–239.

QUESTIONS FOR ANALYSIS

1. How could a group of deputies elected to advise Louis XVI on constitutional reforms proclaim themselves a National Assembly? Why was the creation of the National Assembly a truly revolutionary act?

2. In what ways was the Declaration of the Rights of Man a moral document? What is it about the style or tone of the Declaration that identifies it as a peculiarly eighteenth-century document?

religious difference. The assembly abolished serfdom and banned slavery in continental France. It remained silent on colonial slavery; and although delegations pressed the assembly on political rights for free people of color, the assembly exempted the colonies from the constitution's provisions. Events in the Caribbean, as we will see, later forced the issue.

The rights and roles of women became the focus of sharp debate: not politics but working women's guilds or trade organizations, marriage and divorce, poor relief, and education. The Englishwoman Mary Wollstonecraft's milestone book *A Vindication of the Rights of Woman* (see Chapter Seventeen) was penned during the revolutionary debate over national education. Should girls be educated? To what end? Wollstonecraft, as we have seen, argued strongly that reforming education required forging a new concept of independent and equal womanhood. Even Wollstonecraft, however, only hinted at political representation, aware that such an idea would "excite laughter."

Only a handful of thinkers broached the subject of women in politics: the aristocratic Enlightenment thinker the Marquis de Condorcet and, from another shore, Marie Gouze, the self-educated daughter of a butcher. Gouze became an intellectual and playwright and renamed herself Olympe de Gouges. Like many "ordinary" people, she found in the explosion of revolutionary activity the opportunity to address the public by writing speeches, pamphlets, or newspapers. She composed her own manifesto, the *Declaration of the Rights of Woman and the Citizen* (1791). Beginning with the proposition that "social distinctions can only be based on the common utility," she declared that women had the same rights as men, including resistance to authority, participation in government, and naming the fathers of illegitimate children, and that last demand offers a glimpse of the shame, isolation, and hardship faced by a unmarried woman.

De Gouges's demand for equal rights was very unusual. Still, women fully participated in the everyday activities of the revolution, joining clubs, demonstrations, and debates; women artisans' organizations had a well-established role in municipal life and argued, forcefully, for their rights to produce and sell goods; market women were familiar public figures, often central to the circulation of news and spontaneous popular demonstrations (the October Days are a good example). The regime celebrated the support of women "citizens," and female figures were favorite allegories for liberty, prudence, and the bounty of nature. Those were abstractions. Real women were increasingly expected to contribute to the revolution as supportive mothers, educators, and tenders of the private sphere, not to be involved in public. When the revolution radicalized, the regime prohibited women's clubs entirely.

THE NATIONAL ASSEMBLY AND THE CHURCH

One of the central issues to confront the assembly involved religion, especially the organization of the church. In November 1789 the National Assembly resolved to confiscate the lands of the church and to use them as collateral for the issue of assignats, interest-bearing notes that eventually circulated as paper money. The assembly hoped—vainly, as it turned out—that this device would resolve the country's inflationary crisis. In July of the following year it enacted the Civil Constitution of the Clergy, which provided that all bishops and priests should be subject to the authority of the state. Their salaries were to be paid out of the public treasury, and they were required to swear allegiance to the new state, making it clear they served France rather than Rome. The assembly's aim was to make the Catholic Church of France a truly national and civil institution.

Reforming the church turned into a bitterly divisive matter; it polarized large sections of France. The church's privileged position during the Old Regime, including its vast monastic land holdings, had earned it the resentment of many. On the other hand, the practice of centuries had made the parish church an institution of enormous importance in the small towns and villages of France. In rural areas, the local priest not only baptized, married, and buried people but helped

CHRONOLOGY

THE FIRST FRENCH REVOLUTION, 1789–1792

Fall of the Bastille	July 14, 1789
The Great Fear	summer 1789
Declaration of the Rights of Man and of the Citizen	August 1789
The October Days	1789
National Assembly enacts the Civil Constitution of the Clergy	July 1790
Royal family tries to escape Paris	June 1791
National Assembly declares war on Austria and Prussia	April 1792

SOCIAL GRIEVANCES ON THE EVE OF THE REVOLUTION (1789)

During the elections to the Estates General, communities drew up "notebooks of grievances" to be presented the government. The following comes from a rural community, Lignère la Doucelle.

For a long time now, the inhabitants have been crushed beneath the excessive burden of the multiplicity of taxes that they have been obliged to pay. Their parish is large and spread out, but it is a hard land with many uncultivated areas, almost all of it divided into small parcels. There is not one single farm of appreciable size, and these small properties are occupied either by the poor or by people who are doing so poorly that they go without bread every other day. They buy bread or grain nine months of the year. No industries operate in this parish, and from the time they began complaining, no one has ever listened. The cry of anguish echoed all to the way to the ministry after having fruitlessly worn out their intendants. They have always seen their legitimate claims being continuously denied, so may the fortunate moment of equality revive them.

* * *

That all lords, country gentlemen, and others of the privileged class who, either directly or through their proxies, desire to make a profit on their wealth, regardless of the nature of that wealth, pay the same taxes as the common people.

* * *

That the seigneur's mills not be obligatory, allowing everyone to choose where he would like to mill his grain.

* * *

That the children of common people living on a par with nobles be admitted for military service, as the nobility is.

That the king not bestow noble titles upon someone and their family line, but that titles be bestowed only upon those deserving it.

That nobility not be available for purchase or by any fashion other than by the bearing of arms or other service rendered to the State.

* * *

That church members be only able to take advantage of one position. That those who are enjoying more than one be made to choose within a fixed time period.

That future abbeys all be placed into the hands of the king, that His Majesty benefit from their revenue as the head abbots have been able to.

That in towns where there are several convents belonging to the same order, there be only one, and the goods and revenue of those that are to be abolished go to the profit of the crown.

That the convents where there are not normally twelve residents be abolished.

That no tenth of black wheat be paid to parish priests, priors or other beneficiaries, since this grain is only used to prepare the soil for the sowing of rye.

That they also not be paid any tenths of hemp, wool, or lamb. That in the countryside they be required to conduct burials and funerals free of charge. That the ten sous for audit books, insinuations, and the 100 [sous] collected for the parish be abolished.

* * *

That grain be taxed in the realm at a fixed price, or rather that its exportation abroad be forbidden except in the case where it would be sold at a low price.

Armand Bellée, ed., Cahiers de plaintes & doléances des paroisses de la province du Maine pour les Etats-généraux de 1789, vol. 2 (Le Mans, 1881–1892), pp. 578–582.

QUESTIONS FOR ANALYSIS

1. What, according to the petition, are the most significant problems the community faces? How are these problems explained?

2. What measures do the people expect the king to enact?

3. In what ways did the revolutionaries deal with these grievances?

with any written documents. The church provided poor relief and other services. In many areas peasants relied on and respected the local clergy. The dramatic changes enacted by the Civil Constitution of the Clergy thus sparked fierce resistance in some parts of rural France—resistance fueled by a combination of religious feeling and desire for local autonomy. When the pope threatened to excommunicate priests who signed the Civil Constitution, he raised the stakes: signing an oath of allegiance to the new French state now meant damnation later. When the government insisted, it drove many people, especially peasants in the deeply Catholic areas of western France into open counterrevolt, the rebel priests among them.

The National Assembly made a series of economic and governmental changes with lasting effects. To raise money, it sold off church lands, although few of the genuinely needy could afford to buy them. To encourage the growth of economic enterprise, it abolished guilds. To rid the country of local aristocratic power, it reorganized local governments, dividing France into eighty-three equal departments. These measures aimed to defend individual liberty and freedom from customary privilege. Their principal beneficiaries were, for the most part, members of the elite, people on their way up under the previous regime who were able to take advantage of the opportunities, such as buying land or being elected to office, that the new one offered. In this realm as elsewhere, the social changes of the revolution endorsed changes already under way in the eighteenth century.

> Though the constitution of 1791 declared France a monarchy, after Varennes, Louis was little more than a prisoner of the assembly.

A NEW STAGE: POPULAR REVOLUTION

Why did the French Revolution become more radical?

In the summer of 1792, the revolution entered a second stage. The moderate leaders were toppled and replaced by republicans, who repudiated the monarchy and claimed to rule on behalf of a sovereign people. Why this abrupt and drastic change? Was the revolution blown off course? These are among the most difficult questions about the French Revolution. Answers need to begin by taking account of (at least) three factors: changes in popular politics, a crisis of leadership, and international polarization.

First, the revolution politicized the common people, especially in cities. Newspapers filled with political and social commentary multiplied, freed from restrictions on printing. From 1789 forward, a wide variety of political clubs became part of daily political life. Some were formal, almost like political parties, gathering members of the elite to debate issues facing the country and influence decisions in the assembly. Other clubs opened their doors to those excluded from formal politics, and they read aloud from newspapers and discussed the options facing the country, from the provisions of the constitution to the trustworthiness of the king and his ministers. This political awareness was heightened by nearly constant shortages and fluctuating prices. Prices particularly exasperated the working people of Paris who had demanded changes in 1789 and had eagerly awaited change since then. Urban demonstrations, often led by women, demanded cheaper bread; political leaders in clubs and newspapers called for the government to control rising inflation. Club leaders spoke for men and women who felt cheated by the constitution.

A second major reason for the change of course was a lack of effective national leadership. Louis XVI remained a weak, vacillating monarch. He was forced to support measures personally distasteful to him, in particular the Civil Constitution of the Clergy. He was thus sympathetic to the plottings of the queen, who was in contact with her brother Leopold II of Austria. Urged on by Marie Antoinette, Louis agreed to attempt an escape from France in June 1791, hoping to rally foreign support for counterrevolution. The members of the royal family managed to slip past their palace guards in Paris, but they were apprehended near the border at Varennes and brought back to the capital. Though the constitution of 1791 declared France a monarchy, after Varennes, Louis was little more than a prisoner of the assembly.

THE COUNTERREVOLUTION

The third major reason for the dramatic turn of affairs was war. From the outset of the revolution, men and women across Europe had been compelled, by the very intensity of events in France, to take sides in the conflict. In the years immediately after 1789, the revolution in France won the enthusiastic support of a wide range of thinkers. The British poet William Wordsworth, who later became disillusioned, recalled his initial mood: "Bliss was it in that dawn to be alive." His sentiments were echoed across the Continent by poets and philosophers, including the German Johann Gottfried von Herder, who declared the revolution the most important historical moment since the Reformation. Political societies in Britain proclaimed their allegiance to the principles of the new revolution, often quite incorrectly, seeing it as nothing more than a French version of the events of 1688. In the Low Countries, western Germany, and Italy, "patriots" organized.

Others opposed the course of the revolution from the start. Exiled nobles, who had fled France for sympathetic royal courts in Germany and elsewhere, did all they could to stir up counterrevolutionary sentiment. In Britain the conservative cause was strengthened by the publication in 1790 of Edmund Burke's *Reflections on the Revolution* in France. A Whig politician who had sympathized with the American revolutionaries, Burke deemed the revolution in France a monstrous crime against the social order (see page 652).

Burke's famous book aroused some sympathy for the counterrevolutionary cause. That sympathy only slowly turned to active opposition. The first European states to express public concern about events in revolutionary France were Austria and Prussia, declaring in 1791 that order and the rights of the monarch of France were matters of "common interest to all sovereigns of Europe." The leaders of the French assembly pronounced the declaration an affront to national sovereignty. Nobles who had fled France played into their hands with plots and pronouncements against the government. Oddly, perhaps, almost all of the political factions in France believed war would serve their cause. The assembly's leaders expected an aggressive policy to shore up the people's loyalty and bring freedom to the rest of Europe. Counterrevolutionaries hoped the intervention of Austria and Prussia would undo all that had happened since 1789. Radicals, suspicious of aristocratic leaders and the king, believed that war would expose traitors with misgivings about the revolution and flush out those who sympathized with the king and European tyrants. On April 20, 1792, the assembly declared war against Austria and Prussia. Thus began the war that would keep the Continent in arms for a generation.

As the radicals expected, the French forces met serious reverses. By August 1792 the allied armies of Austria and Prussia had crossed the frontier and were threatening to capture Paris. Many, including soldiers, believed that the military disasters were evidence of

Playing Cards from the French Revolution. Revolutionaries tried to create entirely new images of politics and virtue; these were the cultural accompaniment to political transformation. The cards depict, from left to right, a Sans Culotte (note the long trousers), Jean-Jacques Rousseau, and Justice.

DEBATING THE FRENCH REVOLUTION: EDMUND BURKE AND THOMAS PAINE

The best-known debate on the French Revolution set the Irish-born conservative Edmund Burke against the British radical Thomas Paine. Burke opposed the French Revolution from the beginning. His Reflections on the Revolution in France was published early, in 1790, when the French king was still securely on the throne. Burke disagreed with the premises of the revolution. Rights, he argued, were not abstract and "natural" but the results of specific historical traditions. Remodeling the French government without reference to the past and failing to pay proper respect to tradition and custom had, in his eyes, destroyed the fabric of French civilization.

Thomas Paine was one of many to respond to Burke. The Rights of Man (1791–1792) defended the revolution and, more generally, conceptions of human rights. In the polarized atmosphere of the revolutionary wars, simply possessing Paine's pamphlet was cause for imprisonment in Britain.

EDMUND BURKE

You will observe, that from the Magna Charta to the Declaration of Rights, it has been the uniform policy of our constitution to claim and assert our liberties, as an entailed inheritance derived to us from our forefathers. . . . We have an inheritable crown; an inheritable peerage; and a house of commons and a people inheriting privileges, franchises, and liberties, from a long line of ancestors. . . .

You had all these advantages in your ancient states, but you chose to act as if you had never been moulded into civil society, and had every thing to begin anew. You began ill, because you began by despising every thing that belonged to you. . . . If the last generations of your country appeared without much luster in your eyes, you might have passed them by, and derived your claims from a more early race of ancestors. . . . Respecting your forefathers, you would have been taught to respect yourselves. You would not have chosen to consider the French as a people of yesterday, as a nation of low-born servile wretches until the emancipating year of 1789. . . . [Y]ou would not have been content to be represented as a gang of Maroon slaves, suddenly broke loose from the house of bondage, and therefore to be pardoned for your abuse of liberty to which you were not accustomed and ill fitted. . . .

. . . The fresh ruins of France, which shock our feelings wherever we can turn our eyes, are not the devastation of civil war; they are the sad but instructive monuments of rash and ignorant councel in time of profound peace. They are the display of inconsiderate and presumptuous, because unresisted and irresistible authority. . . .

Nothing is more certain, than that of our manners, our civilization, and all the good things which are connected with manners, and with civilization, have, in this European world of ours, depended upon two principles; and were indeed the result of both combined; I mean the spirit of a gentleman, and the spirit of religion. The nobility and the clergy, the one by profession, the other by patronage, kept learning in existance, even in the midst of arms and confusions. . . . Learning paid back what it received to nobility and priesthood. . . . Happy if they had all continued to know their indissoluble union, and their proper place. Happy if learning, not debauched by ambition, had been satisfied to continue the instructor, and not aspired to be the master! Along with its natural protectors and guardians, learning will be cast into the mire, and trodden down under the hoofs of a swinish multitude.

Edmund Burke, *Reflections on the Revolution in France* (1790) (New York, 1973), pp. 45, 48, 49, 52, 92.

THOMAS PAINE

Mr. Burke, with his usual outrage, abuses the *Declaration of the Rights of Man*. . . . Does Mr. Burke mean to deny that man has any rights? If he does, then he must mean that there are no such things as rights any where, and that he has none himself; for who is there in the world but man? But if Mr. Burke means to admit that man has rights, the question will then be, what are those rights, and how came man by them originally?

The error of those who reason by precedents drawn from antiquity, respecting the rights of man, is that they do not go far enough into antiquity. They stop in some of the intermediate stages of an hundred or a thousand years, and produce what was then a rule for the present day. This is no authority at all. . . .

To possess ourselves of a clear idea of what government is, or ought to be, we must trace its origin. In doing this, we shall easily discover that governments must have arisen either *out* of the people, or *over* the people. Mr. Burke has made no distinction. . . .

What were formerly called revolutions, were little more than a change of persons, or an alteration of local circumstances. They rose and fell like things of course, and had nothing in their existance or their fate that could influence beyond the spot that produced them. But what we now see in the world, from the revolutions of America and France, is a renovation of the natural order of things, a system of principles as universal as truth and the existance of man, and combining moral with political happiness and national prosperity.

Thomas Paine, *The Rights of Man* (New York, 1973), pp. 302, 308, 383.

QUESTIONS FOR ANALYSIS

1. What are the most significant points of disagreement between the two men?
2. What does each of them think has happened in France?
3. What images and language does each use to make his case? Why?

---

the king's treason. On August 10, Parisian crowds, organized by their radical leaders, attacked the royal palace. The king was imprisoned and a second and far more radical revolution began.

THE FRENCH REPUBLIC

From this point, the country's leadership passed into the hands of the more egalitarian leaders of the Third Estate. These new leaders were known as Jacobins, the name of the political club to which they belonged. Although their headquarters were in Paris, their membership extended throughout France. Their members included large numbers of professionals, government officeholders, and lawyers; but they proclaimed themselves spokesmen for the people and the nation. An increasing number of artisans joined Jacobin clubs as the movement grew, and other, more democratic clubs expanded as well.

The National Convention, elected by free white men, became the effective governing body of the country for the next three years. It was elected in September 1792, at a time when enemy troops were advancing, spreading panic. Rumors flew that prisoners in Paris were plotting to aid the enemy. They were hauled from their cells, dragged before hastily convened tribunals, and killed.

The "September Massacres" killed more than 1,000 "enemies of the Revolution" in less than a week. Similar riots engulfed Lyons, Orléans, and other French cities.

The newly elected convention was far more radical than its predecessor, and its leadership was determined to end the monarchy. On September 21, the convention declared France a republic. In December it placed the king on trial, and in January 1793 he was condemned to death by a narrow margin. The heir to the grand tradition of French absolutism met his end bravely as "citizen Louis Capet," beheaded by the guillotine. Introduced as a swifter and more humane form of execution, the frightful mechanical headsman came to symbolize revolutionary fervor.

The convention took other radical measures. It confiscated the property of enemies of the revolution, breaking up some large estates and selling them on easier terms to less-wealthy citizens. It abruptly canceled the policy of compensating nobles for their lost privileges. It repealed primogeniture, so that property would not be inherited exclusively by the oldest son but would be divided in substantially equal portions among all immediate heirs. It abolished slavery in French colonies (discussed later). It set maximum prices for grain and other necessities. In an astonishing effort to root out Christianity from everyday life, the convention adopted a new calendar. The calendar year began with the birth of the republic (September 22, 1792) and divided months in such a way as to eliminate the Catholic Sunday.

Most of this program was a hastily improvised response to crisis and political pressure from the common people in the cities and their leaders, by now a popular movement. In the three years after 1790, prices had risen staggeringly: wheat by 27 percent, beef by 136 percent, potatoes by 700 percent. While the government imposed its maximums in Paris, small vigilante militias, representing the sans-culottes, attacked those they considered hoarders and profiteers.

The convention also reorganized its armies, with astonishing success. By February 1793, Britain, Holland, Spain, and Austria were in the field against the French. Britain came into the war for strategic and economic reasons. The British feared French penetration into the Low Countries directly across the Channel and, more generally, France's threat to Britain's growing global power. The allied coalition, though united only in its desire to contain France, was nevertheless a formidable force. To counter it, the revolutionary government mustered all men capable of bearing arms. The revolution flung fourteen hastily drafted armies into battle under the leadership of newly promoted, young, and inexperienced officers. What they lacked in training and discipline they made up for in organization, mobility, flexibility, courage, and morale. (In the navy, however, where skill was of paramount importance, the revolutionary French never succeeded in matching the performance of the British.) In 1793–1794, the French armies preserved their homeland. In 1794–1795, they occupied the Low Countries; the Rhineland; and parts of Spain, Switzerland, and Savoy. In 1796, they invaded and occupied key parts of Italy and broke the coalition that had arrayed itself against them.

THE REIGN OF TERROR

In 1793, however, those victories lay in a hard-to-imagine future. France was in crisis. In 1793, the convention drafted a new democratic constitution based on male suffrage. That constitution never took effect—suspended indefinitely by wartime emergency. Instead, the convention prolonged its own life year after year

The Execution of Louis XVI. A revolutionary displays the king's head moments after his execution in January 1793.

and increasingly delegated its responsibilities to a group of twelve leaders, or the Committee of Public Safety. The committee's ruthlessness had two purposes: to seize control of the revolution and to prosecute all the revolution's enemies—"to make terror the order of the day." The Terror lasted less than two years but left a bloody and authoritarian legacy.

Perhaps the three best-known leaders of the radical revolution were Jean Paul Marat, Georges Jacques Danton, and Maximilien Robespierre, the latter two members of the Committee of Public Safety. Marat was educated as a physician and by 1789 had already earned enough distinction in that profession to be awarded an honorary degree by St. Andrews University in Scotland. Marat opposed nearly all of his moderate colleagues' assumptions, including their admiration for Great Britain, which Marat considered corrupt and despotic. Soon made a victim of persecution and forced to take refuge in unsanitary sewers and dungeons, he persevered as the editor of the popular

news sheet *The Friend of the People*. Exposure to infection left him with a chronic and painful skin disease, from which baths provided the only relief. In the summer of 1793, at the height of the crisis of the revolution, he was stabbed in his bath by Charlotte Corday, a young royalist, and thus became a revolutionary martyr.

Danton, like Marat, was a popular political leader, well known in the more plebian clubs of Paris. Elected a member of the Committee of Public Safety in 1793, he had much to do with organizing the Terror. As time went on, however, he wearied of ruthlessness and displayed a tendency to compromise, which gave his opponents in the convention their opportunity. In April 1794, Danton was sent to the guillotine. On mounting the scaffold he is reported to have said, "Show my head to the people; they do not see the like every day."

The most famous of the radical leaders was Maximilien Robespierre. Born of a family reputed to be of Irish descent, Robespierre trained in law and quickly became a modestly successful lawyer. His eloquence and his consistent, or ruthless, insistence that leaders respect the "will of the people" eventually won him a following in the Jacobin club. Later, he became president of the National Convention and a member of the Committee of Public Safety. Though he had little to

Robespierre Guillotining the Executioner. The original caption for this 1783 engraving read, "Robespierre guillotines the executioner after having had all the French guillotined." This caricature cost the engraver his life.

The Death of Robespierre. Robespierre being guillotined himself after his fall from power.

defeated the counterrevolutionaries, and launched murderous campaigns of pacification—torching villages, farms, and fields and killing all who dared oppose them and many who did not.

During the period of the Terror, from September 1793 to July 1794, the most reliable estimates place the number of executions as high as 25,000 to 30,000 in France as a whole, fewer than 20,000 of whom were condemned by the courts. Approximately 500,000 were incarcerated between March 1793 and August 1794. These numbers, however, do not include the

The Death of Marat. This painting by the French artist David immortalized Marat. The note in the slain leader's hand is from Charlotte Corday, his assassin.

do with starting the Terror, he was nevertheless responsible for enlarging its scope. "The Incorruptible," he came to represent ruthlessness justified as virtue and necessary to revolutionary progress.

The two years of the Terror brought dictatorship, centralization, suspension of any liberties, and war. The committee faced foreign enemies and opposition from both the political right and left at home. In June 1793, responding to an escalating crisis, leaders of the "Mountain," a party of radicals allied with Parisian artisans, purged moderates from the convention. Rebellions broke out in the provincial cities of Lyons, Bordeaux, and Marseilles, mercilessly repressed by the committee and its local representatives. The government also faced counterrevolution in the west, where movements enlisted peasants and artisans, who believed their local areas were being invaded and who fought for their local priest or against the summons from the revolutionaries' conscription boards. By the summer, the forces in the west posed a serious threat to the convention. Determined to stabilize France, whatever the cost, the committee redeployed its forces,

French Republic, 1792
Annexed to France, 1792–1795
Sister republics

FRANCE AND ITS SISTER REPUBLICS

The French revolutionaries, fighting against the conservative monarchs of Europe, conquered and annexed large sections of Italy, the Austrian Netherlands, and Switzerland. Napoleon did not begin these wars, though he continued and greatly expanded them.

pacification of the west and rebellious cities in the Rhone Valley, which took more than 100,000 lives. Few victims of the Terror were aristocrats. Many more were peasants or laborers accused of hoarding, treason, or counterrevolutionary activity. Anyone who appeared to threaten the republic, no matter what his or her social or economic position, was at risk. When some time later the Abbé Sieyès was asked what he had done to distinguish himself during the Terror, he responded dryly, "I lived."

THE LEGACY OF THE SECOND FRENCH REVOLUTION

Several points need to be made concerning this "second" French Revolution. First, for a time, revolutionary enthusiasm affected the everyday life of French men, women, and children in a remarkably direct way. Workers' trousers replaced the breeches that had been a sartorial badge of the middle classes and the nobility. A red cap, said to symbolize freedom from slavery, became popular headgear, wigs vanished. Men and women addressed each other as "citizen" or "citizeness." Public life was marked by ceremonies designed to dramatize the break with the Old Regime and celebrate new forms of fraternity. In the early stages of the revolution, these festivals seem to have captured genuine popular enthusiasm for new ways of living and thinking. Under the Committee of Public Safety, they became didactic and hollow.

Patriotic Women's Club. The members of this patriotic club wear constitutional bonnets to show their support for the revolution and the reforms of the convention.

CHRONOLOGY	
THE SECOND FRENCH REVOLUTION, 1792–1794	
First Republic established	summer 1792
National Convention elected	September 1792
Execution of the king	January 1793
War between Britain, Holland, Spain, and France	February 1793
Reign of Terror	September 1793–July 1794
Purge of the Jacobins	July 27, 1794
Execution of Robespierre	July 28, 1794

Second, the radical revolution of 1792–1793 dramatically reversed the trend toward decentralization and democracy. The assembly replaced local officials, some of them still royalist in sympathy, with "deputies on mission," whose task was to conscript troops and generate patriotic fervor. When these deputies appeared too eager to act independently, they were replaced by "national agents," with instructions to report directly to the committee. In another effort to stabilize authority, the assembly closed down all the women's political clubs, decreeing them a political and social danger. Ironically, those who claimed to govern in the name of the people found the popular movement threatening.

Third, the revolution eroded the strength of those traditional institutions—church, guild, parish—that had for centuries given people a common bond. In their place now stood patriotic organizations and a culture that insisted on loyalty to one national cause. Those organizations had first emerged with the election campaigns, meetings, and pamphlet wars of 1788 and the interest they heightened. They included the political clubs and local assemblies, which at the height of the revolution (1792–1793) met every day of the week and offered an apprenticeship in politics. The army of the republic become the premier national institution.

It is true that the revolution divided France, mobilizing counterrevolutionaries as well as revolutionaries. At the same time, the revolution, war, and culture of citizenly sacrifice forged new bonds. The sense that the rest of Europe, carrying what the verses of the *Marseillaise*, the most famous anthem of the revolution, called the "blood-stained flag of tyranny," would crush the new nation and its citizens unquestionably strengthened French national identity.

FROM THE TERROR TO BONAPARTE: THE DIRECTORY

How did Bonaparte come to power?

The Committee of Public Safety might have saved France from enemy armies but could not save itself. Inflation became catastrophic. The long string of military victories convinced growing numbers that the committee's demands for continuing self-sacrifice and Terror were no longer justified. By July 1794, the committee was virtually without allies. On July 27 (9 Thermidor, according to the new calendar), Robespierre was shouted down while attempting to speak on the floor of the convention. The following day, along with twenty-one other conspirators, he met his death by guillotine.

Ending the Terror did not immediately bring moderation. Vigilante groups of royalists hunted down Jacobins. The repeal of the maximum, or price controls, combined with the worst winter in a century caused widespread misery. Other measures that had constituted the Terror were gradually repealed. In 1795 the National Convention adopted a new and more conservative constitution. It granted suffrage to all adult male citizens who could read and write. Yet it set up indirect elections: citizens voted for electors, who in turn chose the legislative body. Wealthy citizens thus held authority. Eager to avoid personal dictatorship, it vested executive authority in a board of five men known as the Directory, chosen by the legislative body. The new constitution included not only a bill of rights but also a declaration of the duties of the citizen.

The Directory lasted longer than its revolutionary predecessors. It still faced discontent on both the radical left and the conservative right. On the left, the Directory repressed radical movements to abolish private property and parliamentary-style government, including one led by the radical "Gracchus Babeuf." Dispatching threats from the right proved more challenging. In 1797 the first free elections held in France as a republic returned a large number of monarchists to the councils of government, alarming politicians who had voted to execute Louis XVI. Backed by the army, the Directory annulled most of the election results. After two years of more uprisings and purges, and with the country still plagued by severe inflation, the Directors grew desperate. This time they called the brilliant young general Napoleon Bonaparte to their assistance.

Bonaparte's first military victory had come in 1793, with the recapture of Toulon from royalist and British forces, and had earned him promotion from captain to brigadier general at the age of twenty-four. He had also been a supremely political general and was briefly arrested for his Jacobin associations. But he won the Directory's gratitude. In October 1795, he delivered what he called a "whiff of grapeshot," which saved the convention from attack by opponents of the new constitution. He won a string of victories in Italy, forcing Austria to withdrawal (temporarily) from the war. He attempted to defeat Britain by attacking British forces in Egypt and the Near East, a campaign that went well on land but ran into trouble at sea, where the French fleet was defeated by Admiral Horatio Nelson (Abukir Bay, 1798). Bonaparte found himself trapped in Egypt by the British and unable to win a decisive victory.

It was at this point that the call came from the Directory. Bonaparte slipped away from Egypt and appeared in Paris, already having agreed to participate in a coup d'état with the leading Director, that former revolutionary champion of the Third Estate, the Abbé Sieyès. On November 9, 1799 (18 Brumaire), Bonaparte was declared a "temporary consul." He was the answer to the Directory's prayers: a strong, popular leader who was not a king. Sieyès declared that Bonaparte would provide "Confidence from below, authority from above." With those words Sieyès pronounced the end of the revolutionary period.

> On November 9, 1799 (18 Brumaire), Bonaparte was declared a "temporary consul." He was the answer to the prayers of the Directory: a strong, popular leader who was not a king.

NAPOLEON AND IMPERIAL FRANCE

How did Napoleon centralize his authority?

Few figures in Western history have compelled the attention of the world as Napoleon Bonaparte did during the fifteen years of his rule in France. Few men lived on with such persistence as myth, not just in their own countries, but across the West. Why? For the great majority of ordinary Europeans, memories of the French

Revolution were dominated by those of the Napoleonic wars, which devastated Europe, convulsed its politics, and traumatized its peoples for a generation. What began as political revolution and popular revolt continued in war and ended in an effort to create a new kind of European empire. To many observers, that entire drama seemed embodied in the career of one man. From the onset of war in 1792, France's revolutionaries had turned to France's armies for defense and survival. It seemed all too natural that the future of the revolution should be bound up with the successes of its greatest general, Napoleon Bonaparte.

Bonaparte's relationship to the revolution was not simple. His regime consolidated some of the revolution's political and social changes but sharply repudiated others. He presented himself as the son of the revolution, but he also borrowed freely from very different regimes, fashioning himself as the heir to Charlemagne, or to the Roman Empire. His regime remade revolutionary politics and the French state; offered stunning examples of the new kinds of warfare; and left a legacy of conflict and legends of French glory that lingered in the dreams, or nightmares, of Europe's statesmen and citizens for more than a century.

CONSOLIDATING AUTHORITY: 1799–1804

Bonaparte's early career reinforced the claim that the revolution rewarded the efforts of able men. The son of a provincial Corsican nobleman, he attended the École Militaire in Paris. In prerevolutionary France he would have been unable to rise beyond the rank of major, which required buying a regimental command. The revolution, however, had abolished the purchase of military office, and Bonaparte quickly became a general. Here, then, was a man who had risen from obscurity because of his own gifts, which he lent happily to the service of France's revolution. His character seemed to suit the age of Enlightenment as well, and his early admirers noted his wide range of talents and intellectual interests, including history, law, and mathematics. He took ideas seriously. He read—and wrote—constantly, even when on his military campaigns. His strengths as a leader were remarkable. He created financial, legal, and military plans and mastered their every detail. He worked endlessly and slept little. He inspired others, even those initially opposed to him. And he believed he was the destined savior of France. That last conviction made him a charismatic leader—and eventually led to his undoing.

In the first five years of his reign, Bonaparte quickly consolidated personal power. After he overthrew the government in 1799, he assumed the title of "first consul" and governed in the name of the republic. A new constitution established universal white male suffrage and set up two legislative bodies. Elections, however, were indirect, and the power of the legislative bodies sharply curbed. "The government?" said one observer. "There is Bonaparte." Bonaparte instituted what has since become a common authoritarian device, the plebiscite, which put a question directly to popular vote. This allows the head of state to bypass politicians or legislative bodies who might disagree with him—as well as permitting local officials to tamper with ballot boxes. In 1802, flush with victory abroad, he asked the legislature to proclaim him consul for life. When the senate refused to do so, Bonaparte's Council of State stepped in, offered him the title, and had it ratified by plebiscite. Throughout, his regime retained the appearance of consulting with the people, but its most important feature was the centralization of authority.

That authority came from reorganizing the state, and on this score Bonaparte's accomplishments were extraordinary and lasting. Bonaparte's regime confirmed the abolition of privilege, thereby promising "careers open to talent." Centralizing administrative departments, he accomplished what no recent French regime had yet achieved: an orderly and generally fair system of taxation. More efficient tax collection and fiscal management also helped halt the inflationary spiral that had crippled the revolutionary governments, although Bonaparte's regime relied heavily on resources from areas he had conquered to fund his military ventures. As we have seen, earlier revolutionary regimes began to reorganize France's administration—abolishing the ancient fiefdoms with their separate governments, legal codes, privileges, and customs—setting up a uniform system of departments. Bonaparte continued that work, pressing it further and putting an accent on centralization. He replaced elected officials and local self-government with centrally appointed prefects and subprefects, who answered directly to the Council of State in Paris. The prefects wielded considerable power, much more than any elected representative: they were in charge of everything from collecting statistics and reporting on the economy and the population to education, roads, and public works. Fifty years later, under the Second Empire of Napoleon's nephew, the prefect of Paris would mastermind a massive rebuilding of the French capital, which bears a Napoleonic stamp to this day. The state recruited civil servants according to talent, not title (though the elite remained dominant). With more integrated administration, in which the different branches were coordinated (and supervised from above), a more professional bureaucracy, and more rational and efficient taxation (though the demands of war strained the system), Napoleon's state marked the transition from Bourbon absolutism to the modern state.

LAW, EDUCATION, AND A NEW ELITE

Napoleon's most significant contribution to modern state building, and one exported to the areas he conquered, was the promulgation of a new legal code in 1804. Each revolutionary regime had taken up the daunting task of modernizing the laws; each had run out of time. Napoleon tolerated no delays, and threw himself into the project, pressing his own ideas and supervising half the meetings. The Napoleonic Code, as the civil code came to be called, bore the imprint of his philosophy and ambitions. The code pivoted on two principles that had remained significant through all the constitutional changes since 1789: uniformity and individualism. It cleared through the thicket of different and contradictory legal traditions that governed the ancient provinces of France, creating one uniform law. It confirmed the abolition of feudal privileges of all kinds: not only noble and clerical privileges but the special rights of craft guilds, municipalities, and so on. It set the conditions for exercising property rights: the drafting of contracts, leases, and stock companies. The code's provisions on the family, which Napoleon developed personally, insisted on the importance of paternal authority and the subordination of women and children. In 1793, during the most radical period of the revolution, men and women had been declared "equal in marriage"; now Napoleon's code affirmed the "natural supremacy" of the husband. Married women could not sell property, run a business, or have a profession without their husbands' permission. Fathers had the sole right to control their children's financial affairs, consent to their marriages, and (under the ancient right to correction) to imprison them for up to six months without showing cause. Divorce remained legal, but under unequal conditions; a man could sue for divorce on the grounds of adultery, but a woman could do so only if her husband moved his "concubine" into the family's house. Most important to the common people, the code prohibited paternity suits for illegitimate children.

In all, Napoleon developed seven legal codes covering commercial law, civil law and procedures, crime, and punishment. Like the civil code, the new criminal code consolidated some of the gains of the revolution,

treating citizens as equals before the law and outlawing arbitrary arrest and imprisonment. Yet it, too, reinstated brutal measures that the revolutionaries had abolished, such as branding and cutting off the hands of parricides. The Napoleonic legal regime was more egalitarian than law under the Old Regime but no less concerned with authority.

Napoleon also rationalized the educational system. He ordered the establishment of *lycées* (high schools) in every major town to train civil servants and army officers and a school in Paris to train teachers. To supplement these changes, Napoleon brought the military and technical schools under state control and founded a national university to supervise the entire system. It is not surprising that he built up a new military academy. He reorganized and established solid financing for the premier schools of higher education: the polytechnic (for engineers) and the normal (for teachers), to which students would be admitted based on examinations and from which would issue the technical, educational, and political elites of the country. Like almost all his reforms, this one reinforced reforms introduced during the revolution, and it intended to abolish privilege and create "careers open to talent." Napoleon also embraced the burgeoning social and physical sciences of the Enlightenment. He sponsored the Institute of France, divided into four sections, or academies: fine arts, sciences, humanities, and language (the famous Academie Française). These academies dated back to the age of absolutism—now they were coordinated and put on a new footing. They acquired under Napoleon the character that they have preserved to this day: centralized, meritocratic, and geared to serving the state.

Who benefited from these changes? Like Bonaparte's other new institutions, the new schools helped confirm the power of a new elite. The new elite included businessmen, bankers, and merchants but was still composed primarily of powerful landowners. What was more, at least half of the fellowships to the high schools went to the sons of military officers and high civil servants. Finally, like most of Bonaparte's reforms, changes in education aimed to strengthen the empire: "My object in establishing a teaching corps is to have a means of directing political and moral opinion," Napoleon said bluntly.

Bonaparte's early measures were ambitious. To win support for them, he made allies without regard for their past political affiliations. He admitted back into the country exiles of all political stripes. His two fellow consuls were a regicide of the Terror and a bureaucrat of the Old Regime. His minister of police had been an extreme radical republican; his minister of foreign affairs was the aristocrat and opportunist Charles Talleyrand. The most remarkable act of political reconciliation came in 1801, with Bonaparte's concordat with the pope, an agreement that put an end to more than a decade of hostility between the French state and the Catholic Church. Although it shocked anti-clerical revolutionaries, Napoleon, ever the pragmatist, believed that reconciliation would create domestic harmony and international solidarity. The agreement gave the pope the right to depose French bishops and to discipline the French clergy. In return, the Vatican agreed to forgo any claims to church lands expropriated by the revolution. That property would remain in the hands of its new middle-class rural and urban proprietors. The concordat did not revoke the principle of religious freedom established by the revolution, but it did win Napoleon the support of conservatives who had feared for France's future as a godless state.

Such political balancing acts increased Bonaparte's general popularity. Combined with early military successes (peace with Austria in 1801 and with Britain in 1802), they muffled any opposition to his personal ambitions. He had married Josephine de Beauharnais, a Creole from Martinique and an influential mistress of the revolutionary period. Josephine had given the Corsican soldier-politician legitimacy and access among the revolutionary elite early in his career. Neither Bonaparte nor his ambitious wife were content to be first among equals, however; and in December of 1804, he finally cast aside any traces of republicanism. In a ceremony that evoked the splendor of medieval kingship and Bourbon absolutism, he crowned himself Emperor Napoleon I in the Cathedral of Notre Dame in Paris. Napoleon did much to create the modern state, but he did not hesitate to proclaim his links to the past.

IN EUROPE AS IN FRANCE: NAPOLEON'S EMPIRE

The nations of Europe had looked on—some in admiration, others in horror, all in astonishment—at the phenomenon that was Napoleon. A coalition of European powers led by Austria, Prussia, and Britain had fought France from 1792 until 1795, in hopes of maintaining European stability. This first coalition collapsed in disarray, defeated by the French armies and by financial exhaustion. The coalition was revived in 1798, at Britain's behest, but in the end it fared no better than the first effort. Despite Napoleon's debacle in Egypt, French victories in Europe split the alliance. Russia and

Austria withdrew from the fray in 1801, and even the intransigent British were forced to make peace the following year.

That peace lasted a year; and by 1805 the Russians, Prussians, Austrians, and Swedes had joined the British in an attempt to contain France. Their efforts were to no avail. Napoleon's military superiority led to defeats, in turn, of all three continental allies. Napoleon was a master of well-timed, well-directed shock attacks on the battlefield: movement, regrouping, and pressing his advantage. He led an army that had transformed European warfare; first raised as a revolutionary militia, it was now a trained conscript army, loyal, well supplied by a nation whose economy was committed to serving the war effort, and led by generals promoted largely on the basis of talent. This new kind of army, directed with Napoleon's lethal flair, inflicted crushing defeats on his enemies. The battle of Austerlitz, in December 1805, was a triumph for the French against the combined forces of Austria and Russia and became a symbol of the emperor's apparent invincibility. His subsequent victory against the Russians at Friedland in 1807 only added to his reputation.

Out of these victories Napoleon created his new empire and affiliated states. To the southeast, the empire included Rome and the pope's dominions, Tuscany, and the Dalmatian territories of Austria (now the coastline of Croatia). To the east Napoleon's rule extended over a federation of German states known as the Confederation of the Rhine and a section of Poland. These new states were presented as France's gift of independence to patriots elsewhere in Europe, but in practice they served as a military buffer against renewed expansion by Austria. The empire itself was ringed by the allied kingdoms of Italy, Naples, Spain, and Holland, whose thrones were occupied by Napoleon's brothers, brothers-in-law, and trusted generals. "If only Father could see us now!" one of the siblings is supposed to have exclaimed.

The empire brought the French Revolution's practical consequences—a powerful, centralizing state and an end to old systems of privilege—to Europe's doorstep, applying to the empire principles that had already transformed France. Administrative modernization, which meant overhauling the procedures, codes, and practices of the state, was the most powerful feature of changes introduced. The empire changed the terms of government service (careers open to talent), handing out new titles and recruiting new men for the civil service and the judiciary. It ended the nobility's monopoly on the officer corps. The new branches of government hired engineers, mapmakers, surveyors, and legal consultants. Public works and education were reorganized.

Prefects in the outer reaches of the empire, as in France, built roads, bridges, dikes (in Holland), hospitals, and prisons; they reorganized universities and built observatories. In the empire and some of the satellite kingdoms tariffs were eliminated, feudal dues abolished, new tax districts formed, and plentiful new taxes collected to support the new state.

In the realm of liberty and law, Napoleon's rule eliminated feudal and church courts and created a single legal system. The Napoleonic Code was often introduced, but not always or entirely. (In southern Italy measures against the Catholic Church were deemed too controversial.) Reforms eliminated many inequalities and legal privileges. The Duchy of Warsaw in Poland ended serfdom but offered no land reform, so former serfs became impoverished tenants. In most areas, the empire gave civil rights to Protestants and Jews. In Rome, the conquering French opened the gates of the Jewish ghetto—and made Jews subject to conscription. In some areas, Catholic monasteries, convents, and other landholdings were broken up and sold, almost always to wealthy buyers. In the empire as in France, and under Napoleon as during the revolution, those who benefited were the elite: people and groups already on their way up and with the resources to take advantage of opportunities.

In government, the regime sought a combination of legal equality (for men) and stronger state authority. The French and local authorities created new electoral districts, expanded the suffrage, and wrote constitutions, but newly elected representative bodies were dismissed if they failed to cooperate, few constitutions were ever fully applied, and political freedoms were often fleeting. Napoleon's regime referred to revolutionary principles to anchor its legitimacy, but authority remained its guiding light. All governmental direction emanated from Paris and therefore from Napoleon.

Finally, in the empire as in France, Napoleon displayed his signature passions. The first of these was an Enlightenment zeal for accumulating useful knowledge. The empire gathered statistics as never before, for it was important to know the resources—including population—that a state had at its disposal. That spirit had been evident already in Bonaparte's extraordinary 1798 excursion into Egypt. He took hundreds of scholars and artists along with the army, founded the Egyptian institute in Cairo, and sent researchers off to make a systematic inventory of the country (its geology, rivers, minerals, antiquities, animal life) and to conduct archaeological expeditions to Upper Egypt, where they sketched the pyramids and excavated what would turn out to be the Rosetta stone (see Chapter

Twenty). Napoleon's second passion was cultivating his relationship to imperial glories of the past. He poured time and energy into (literally) cementing his image for posterity. The Arc de Triomphe in Paris, designed to imitate the Arc of Constantine in Rome, is the best example; but Napoleon also ordered work to be undertaken to restore ruins in Rome, to make the Prado Palace in Madrid a museum, and to renovate and preserve the Alhambra in Granada.

Such were Napoleon's visions of his legacy and himself. How did others see him? Europe offered no single reaction. Some countries and social groups collaborated enthusiastically, some negotiated, some resisted. Napoleon's image as a military hero genuinely inspired young men from the elite, raised in a culture that prized military honor. By contrast, Catholic peasants in Spain fought him from the beginning. In many small principalities previously ruled by princes—the patchwork states of Germany, for example, and the repressive kingdom of Naples—reforms that provided for more efficient, less corrupt administration, a workable tax structure, and an end to customary privilege were welcomed by most of the local population. Yet the

Napoleon on Horseback at the St. Bernard Pass, by Jacques Louis David, 1801. David painted many episodes of the revolution: the Tennis Court Oath, the death of Marat, and the rise and rule of Napoleon. Here, Napoleon heroically leads his troops over the Alps into Italy to attack Austrian troops.

Napoleonic presence proved a mixed blessing. Vassal states contributed heavily to the maintenance of the emperor's military power. The French levied taxes, drafted men, and required states to support occupying armies. In Italy, the policy was called "liberty and requisitions"; and the Italians, Germans, and Dutch paid an especially high price for reforms—in terms of economic cost and numbers of men recruited. From the point of view of the common people, the local lord and priest had been replaced by the French tax collector and army recruiting board.

The demands of war and empire slowly but irretrievably cost Napoleon the support of revolutionaries, former Enlightenment thinkers, and liberals across the Continent. The German composer Ludwig van Beethoven originally planned to dedicate his Third Symphony, the *Eroica*, to Napoleon. Like so many European idealists, Beethoven at first hoped that Bonaparte would bring liberty to the whole continent. But Napoleon's empire building and his self-coronation in 1804 forced a swift and bitter change of judgment. Beethoven revoked the dedication to Bonaparte, declaring, "Now he, too, will trample on all the rights of man and indulge only his ambition."

Beethoven's words, however, were not the last verdict. It is telling that even Napoleon's enemies came to believe that the upstart emperor represented the wave of the future, particularly in regard to the reorganization of the state. Though they fought Napoleon, Prussian and Austrian administrators set about instituting reforms that resembled his: changing rules of promotion and recruitment, remodeling bureaucracies, redrawing districts, eliminating some privileges, and so on. Many who came of age under Napoleon's empire believed that, for better or worse, his empire was modern.

THE RETURN TO WAR AND NAPOLEON'S DEFEAT: 1806–1815

What led to Napoleon's downfall?

Napoleon's boldest attempt at consolidation, a policy banning British goods from the Continent, was a dangerous failure. Britain had bitterly opposed each of France's revolutionary regimes since the death of Louis XVI; now it tried to rally Europe against Napoleon with promises of generous financial loans and trade. The Continental System, established in 1806, sought to starve Britain's trade and force its surrender. The system failed for several reasons. Throughout the war Britain retained control of the seas. The British naval blockade of the Continent, begun in 1807, effectively countered Napoleon's system. While the French Empire strained to transport goods and raw materials overland to avoid the British blockade, the British successfully developed a lively trade with South America. A second reason for the failure of the system was its internal tariffs. Europe divided into economic camps, at odds with each other as they tried to subsist on what the Continent alone could produce and manufacture. Finally, the system hurt the Continent more than Britain. Stagnant trade in Europe's ports and unemployment in its manufacturing centers eroded public faith in Napoleon's dream of a working European empire.

The Continental System was Napoleon's first serious mistake. This ambition to create a European empire, modeled on Rome and ruled from Paris, was to become a second cause of his decline. The symbols of his empire—reflected in painting, architecture, and the design of furniture and clothing—were deliberately Roman in origin. This was not a novelty; the early revolutionaries, Jacobins in particular, harked back to the Roman republic as their model for political virtue, drawing on its imagery in art and political rhetoric. But the triumphal columns and arches Napoleon had erected to commemorate his victories recalled the ostentatious monuments of the Roman emperors. He made his brothers and sisters the monarchs of his newly created kingdoms. In 1809 he divorced the empress Josephine and ensured himself a successor of royal blood by marrying a Habsburg princess, Marie Louise—the great-niece of Marie-Antionette. As we have seen, the overextended empire could change quickly from a strength to a vulnerability.

Over time, the bitter tonic of defeat began to have an effect on Napoleon's enemies, who changed their own approach to waging war. After the Prussian army was humiliated at Jena in 1806 and forced out of the war, a whole generation of younger Prussian officers reformed their military and their state by demanding rigorous practical training for commanders and a genuinely national army made up of patriotic Prussian citizens rather than well-drilled mercenaries.

The myth of Napoleon's invincibility worked against him as well, as he took ever greater risks with France's military and national fortunes. Russian numbers and Austrian artillery inflicted horrendous losses on the French at Wagram in 1809, although these difficulties were forgotten in the glow of victory. Napoleon's allies and supporters shrugged off the British admiral Horatio Nelson's victory at Trafalgar in 1805 as no more than a temporary check to the emperor's ambitions. But Trafalgar broke French naval power in the Mediterranean and led to a rift with Spain, which had been France's equal partner in the battle and suffered equally in the defeat. In the Caribbean, too, Napoleon was forced to cut growing losses (see page 669).

A crucial moment in Napoleon's undoing came with his invasion of Spain in 1808. The invasion aimed, eventually, toward the conquest of Portugal, which had remained a stalwart ally of the British. Napoleon overthrew the Spanish king, installed his own brother on the throne, and then imposed a series of reforms similar to those he had instituted elsewhere in Europe. Napoleon's blow against the Spanish monarchy weakened its hold on its colonies across the Atlantic, and the Spanish crown never fully regained its grip (see Chapter Twenty). But in Spain itself, Napoleon reckoned without two factors that led to the ultimate failure

of his mission: the presence of British forces under Sir Arthur Wellesley (later the Duke of Wellington) and the determined resistance of the Spanish people. They particularly detested Napoleon's interference in the affairs of the church. The peninsular wars, as the Spanish conflicts were called, were long and bitter. The smaller British force learned how to concentrate a devastating volume of gunfire on the French pinpoint attacks on the open battlefield and laid siege to French garrison towns. The Spanish quickly began to wear down French numbers, supplies, and morale through guerrilla warfare. Terrible atrocities were committed by both sides; the French military's torture and execution of Spanish guerrillas and civilians was immortalized by the Spanish artist Francisco Goya (1746–1828) with sickening accuracy in his prints and paintings. Though at one point Napoleon himself took charge of his army, he could not achieve anything more than temporary victory. The Spanish campaign was the first indication that Napoleon could be beaten, and it encouraged resistance elsewhere.

Napoleon on the Battlefield of Eylau. Amid bitter cold and snow, Napoleon engaged with the Russian army in February 1807. Although technically a victory for the French, it was only barely that, with the French losing at least 10,000 men and the Russians twice as many. This painting, characteristic of Bonaparte propaganda, emphasizes not the losses but the emperor's saintlike clemency—even enemy soldiers reach up toward him.

The second, and most dramatic stage in Napoleon's downfall began with the disruption of his alliance with Russia. As an agricultural country, Russia had suffered a severe economic crisis when it was no longer able to trade its surplus grain for British manufactures. The consequence was that Tsar Alexander I began to wink at trade with Britain and to ignore or evade the protests from Paris. By 1811 Napoleon decided that he could no longer endure this flouting of their agreement. He collected an army of 600,000 and set out for Russia in the spring of 1812. Only a third of the soldiers in this "Grande Armée" were French; nearly as many were Polish or German, joined by soldiers and adventurers from the rest of France's client states. It was the grandest of Napoleon's imperial expeditions, an army raised from across Europe and sent to punish the autocratic tsar. The invasion ended in disaster. The Russians refused to make a stand, drawing the French farther and farther into the heart of their country. Just before Napoleon reached the ancient Russian capital of Moscow, the Russian army drew the French forces into a bloody, seemingly pointless battle in the narrow streets of a town called Borodino, where both sides suffered terrible losses of men and supplies, harder on the French who were now so far from home. After the battle, the Russians permitted Napoleon to occupy Moscow. But on the night of his entry, Russian partisans put the city to the torch, leaving little but the blackened walls of the Kremlin palaces to shelter the French troops.

Hoping that the tsar would eventually surrender, Napoleon lingered amid the ruins for more than a month. On October 19 he finally ordered the homeward march. The delay was a fatal blunder. Long before he had reached the border, the terrible Russian winter was on his troops. Frozen streams, mountainous drifts of snow, and bottomless mud slowed the retreat almost to a halt. To add to the miseries of frostbite, disease, and starvation, mounted Cossacks rode out of the blizzard to harry the exhausted army. Each morning the miserable remnant that pushed on left behind circles of corpses around the campfires of the night before. Temperatures dropped to −27°F. On December 13 a few thousand broken soldiers crossed the frontier into Germany—a fragment of the once proud Grande Armée. Nearly 300,000 of its soldiers and untold thousands of Russians lost their lives in Napoleon's Russian adventure.

After the retreat from Russia, the anti-Napoleonic forces took renewed hope. United by a belief that they might finally succeed in defeating the emperor, Prussia, Russia, Austria, Sweden, and Britain renewed their attack. Citizens of many German states in particular saw this as a war of liberation, and indeed most of the fighting took place in Germany. The climax of the

The 3rd of May, 1808, by **Francisco Goya.** This painting of the execution of Spanish rebels by Napoleon's army as it marched through Spain is one of the most memorable depictions of a nation's martyrdom.

campaign occurred in October 1813 when, at what was thereafter known as the Battle of the Nations, fought near Leipzig, the allies dealt the French a resounding defeat. Meanwhile, allied armies won significant victories in the Low Countries and Spain. By the beginning of 1814, they had crossed the Rhine into France. Left with an army of inexperienced youths, Napoleon retreated to Paris, urging the French people to resist despite constant setbacks at the hands of the larger invading armies. On March 31, Tsar Alexander I of Russia and King Frederick William III of Prussia made their triumphant entry into Paris. Napoleon was forced to abdicate unconditionally and was sent into exile on the island of Elba, off the Italian coast.

Napoleon was back on French soil in less than a year. In the interim the allies had restored the Bourbon dynasty to the throne, in the person of Louis XVIII, brother of Louis XVI. Despite his administrative abilities, Louis could not fill the void left by Napoleon's abdication. It was no surprise that, when the former emperor staged his escape from Elba, his fellow countrymen once more rallied to his side. By the time Napoleon reached Paris, he had generated enough support to cause Louis to flee the country. The allies, meeting in Vienna to conclude peace treaties with the French, were stunned by the news of Napoleon's return. They dispatched a hastily organized army to meet the emperor's typically bold offensive push into

NAPOLEON'S EUROPEAN EMPIRE AT ITS HEIGHT

What did Napoleon want from the rest of Europe? Where was he successful; where did he fail, and why? Where did his rule leave the most lasting impact? Could he have maintained his empire?

TWO LETTERS FROM NAPOLEON

Napoleon placed his brothers on the thrones of different vassal states in conquered territories throughout Europe. The first excerpt here is from a letter to his brother Eugène, head of one of the new Italian states, in which Napoleon explains how Italy's lucrative silk trade was to be diverted to damage English commercial interests and bolster the French Empire. It provides a revealing glimpse of Napoleon's vision of a united Europe, with the other countries' futures tied to France's.

On March 1, 1815, Napoleon landed in the south of France, having escaped from his exile on the island of Elba. The restored Bourbon king abdicated, and Napoleon ruled for 100 more days, until his defeat at the battle of Waterloo in June. The second selection is excerpted from a proclamation, addressed to the sovereigns of Europe, explaining the emperor's return. It is an excellent illustration of Napoleon's self-image, his rhetoric, and his belief that he represented the force of history itself.

LETTER TO PRINCE EUGÈNE, AUGUST 23, 1810

I have received your letter of August 14. All the raw silk from the Kingdom of Italy goes to England, for there are no silk factories in Germany. It is therefore quite natural that I should wish to divert it from this route to the advantage of my French manufacturers: otherwise my silk factories, one of the chief supports of French commerce, would suffer substantial losses. I cannot agree with your observations. My principle is *France first.* You must never lose sight of the fact that, if English commerce is supreme on the high seas, it is due to her sea power: it is therefore to be expected that, as France is the strongest land power, she should claim commercial supremacy on the continent: it is indeed our only hope. And isn't it better for Italy to come to the help of France, in such an important matter as this, than to be covered with Customs Houses? For it would be short-sighted not to recognise that Italy owes her independence to France; that it was won by French blood and French victories; that it must not be misused; and that nothing could be more unreasonable than to start calculating what commercial advantages France gets out of it.

Piedmont and Parma produce silk too; and there also I have prohibited its export to any country except France. It is no use for Italy to make plans that leave French prosperity out of account; she must face the fact that the interests of the two countries hang together. Above all, she must be careful not to give France any reason for annexing her; for if it paid France to do this, who could stop her? So make this your motto too—*France first.*

CIRCULAR LETTER TO THE SOVEREIGNS OF EUROPE, APRIL 4, 1815

Monsieur, My Brother,

You will have learnt, during the course of last month, of my landing again in France, of my entry into Paris, and of the departure of the Bourbon family. Your Majesty must by now be aware of the real nature of these events. They are the work of an irresistible power, of the unanimous will of a great nation conscious of its duties and of its rights. A dynasty forcibly reimposed upon the French people was no longer suitable for it: the Bourbons refused to associate themselves with the natural feelings or the national customs; and France was forced to abandon them. The popular voice called for a liberator. The expectation which had decided me to make the supreme sacrifice was in vain. I returned; and from the place where my foot first touched the shore I was carried by the affection of my subjects into the bosom of my capital.

My first and heartfelt anxiety is to repay so much affection by the maintenance of an honourable peace. The re-establishment of the Imperial throne was necessary for the happiness of Frenchmen: my dearest hope is that it may also secure repose for the whole of Europe. Each national flag in turn has had its gleam of glory: often enough, by some turn of fortune, great victories have been followed by great defeats. . . . I have provided the world in the past with a programme of great contests; it will please me better in future to acknowledge no rivalry but that of the advocates of peace, and no combat but a crusade for the felicity of mankind. It is France's pleasure to make a frank avowal of this

noble ideal. Jealous of her independence, she will always base her policy upon an unqualified respect for the independence of other peoples. . . .

> *Monsieur* my Brother,
> Your good Brother,
>   Napoleon

K. M. Baker, ed., *The Old Regime and the French Revolution* (Chicago, 1987), pp. 419–420, 426–427.

QUESTIONS FOR ANALYSIS

1. How does Napoleon see his empire?
2. Can the different views be reconciled?
3. Do you think Napoleon was sincere?

the Low Countries. At the battle of Waterloo, fought over three bloody days from June 15 to 18, 1815, Napoleon was stopped by the forces of his two most persistent enemies, Britain and Prussia, and suffered his final defeat. This time the allies took no chances and shipped their prisoner off to the bleak island of St. Helena in the South Atlantic. The once-mighty emperor, now the exile Bonaparte, lived out a dreary existence writing self-serving memoirs until his death in 1821.

LIBERTY, POLITICS, AND SLAVERY: THE HAITIAN REVOLUTION

In the French colonies across the Atlantic, the revolution took a different course, with wide-ranging ramifications. The Caribbean islands of Guadeloupe, Martinique, and St. Domingue occupied a central role in the eighteenth-century French economy because of the sugar trade. Their planter elites had powerful influence in Paris. The French National Assembly (like its American counterpart) declined to discuss the matter of slavery in the colonies, unwilling to encroach on the property rights of slave owners and fearful of losing the lucrative sugar islands to their British or Spanish rivals should discontented slave owners talk of independence from France. (Competition between the European powers for the islands of the Caribbean was intense; that islands would change hands was a real possibility.) French men in the National Assembly also had to consider the question of rights for free men of color, a group that included a significant number of wealthy owners of property (and slaves).

St. Domingue had about 40,000 whites of different social classes, 30,000 free people of color, and 500,000 slaves, most of them recently enslaved in West Africa. In 1790, free people of color from St. Domingue sent a delegation to Paris, asking to be seated by the assembly, underscoring that they were men of property and, in many cases, of European ancestry. The assembly refused. Their refusal sparked a rebellion among free people of color in St. Domingue. The French colonial authorities repressed the movement quickly—and brutally. They captured Vincent Ogé, a member of the delegation to Paris and one of the leaders of the rebellion, and publicly executed him and his allies by breaking on the wheel and decapitation. Radical deputies, in Paris, including Robespierre, expressed outrage but could do little to change the assembly's policy.

In August 1791 the largest slave rebellion in history broke out in St. Domingue. How much that rebellion owed to revolutionary propaganda is unclear; like many rebellions during the period, it had its own roots. The British and the Spanish invaded, confident they could crush the rebellion and take the island. In the spring of 1792, the French government, on the verge of collapse and war with Europe, scrambled to win allies in St. Domingue by making free men of color citizens. A few months later (after the revolution of August 1792), the new French Republic dispatched commissioners to St. Domingue with troops and instructions to hold the island. There they faced a combination of different forces: Spanish and British troops, defiant St. Domingue planters, and slaves in rebellion. In this context, the local French commissioners reconsidered their commitment to slavery; in 1793 they promised freedom to slaves who would join the French. A year later, the assembly in Paris extended to all the colonies what had already been accomplished in St. Domingue, essentially by a slave rebellion.

Emancipation and war brought new leaders to the fore, chief among them a former slave, Toussaint Bréda, later Toussaint L'Ouverture (*too-SAN LOO-vehr-tur*), meaning "the one who opened the way." Over the course of the next five years, Toussaint and his soldiers, now allied with the French army, emerged victorious over the French planters, the British (in 1798), and the Spanish (in 1801). Toussaint also broke the power of his rival generals in both the mulatto and former slave armies, becoming the statesman of the revolution. In 1801, Toussaint set up a constitution, swearing allegiance to France but denying France any right to interfere in St. Domingue affairs. The constitution abolished slavery, reorganized the military, established Christianity as the state religion (this entailed a rejection of vodoun, a blend of Christian and various West and Central African traditions), and made Toussaint governor for life. It was an extraordinary moment in the revolutionary period: the formation of an authoritarian society but also an utterly unexpected symbol of the universal potential of revolutionary ideas.

Toussaint's accomplishments, however, put him on a collision course with the other French general he admired and whose career was remarkably like his own: Napoleon Bonaparte. St. Domingue stood at the center of Bonaparte's vision of an expanded empire in the New World, an empire that would recoup North American territories France had lost under the Old Regime and pivot around the lucrative combination of the Mississippi, French Louisiana, and the sugar and slave colonies of the Caribbean. In January 1802, Bonaparte dispatched 20,000 troops to bring the island under control. Toussaint, captured when he arrived for discussions with the French, was shipped under heavy guard to a prison in the mountains of eastern France, where he died in 1803. Fighting continued in St. Domingue, however, with fires now fueled by Bonaparte's decree reestablishing slavery where the convention had abolished it. The war turned into a nightmare for the French. Yellow fever killed thousands of French troops, including one of Napoleon's best generals and brother-in-law. Armies on both sides committed atrocities. By December 1803, the French army had collapsed. Napoleon scaled back his vision of an American empire and sold the Louisiana territories to Thomas Jefferson. "I know the value of what I abandon . . . I renounce it with the greatest regret," he told an aide. In St. Domingue, a general in the army of former slaves, Jean-Jacques Dessalines, declared the independent state of Haiti in 1804.

The Haitian revolution remained, in significant ways, an anomaly. It was the only successful slave revolution in history and by far the most radical of the revolutions that occurred in this age. It suggested that the emancipatory ideas of the revolution and Enlightenment might apply to non-Europeans and enslaved peoples—a suggestion that residents of Europe attempted to ignore but one that struck home with planter elites in North and South America. Combined with later rebellions in the British colonies, it contributed to the British decision to end slavery in 1838. And it cast a long shadow over nineteenth-century slave societies from the southern United States to Brazil. The Napoleonic episode, then, had wide-ranging effects across the Atlantic: in North America, the Louisiana purchase; in the Caribbean, the Haitian revolution; in Latin America, the weakening of Spain and Portugal's colonial empires.

Toussaint L'Ouverture. A portrait of L'Ouverture, leader of what would become the Haitian revolution, as a general.

CHRONOLOGY

REIGN OF NAPOLEON, 1799–1815

Napoleon becomes first consul	1799
Concordat with the pope	1801
Napoleon becomes consul for life	1802
Napoleon abolishes the republic and crowns himself emperor	1804
Napoleonic Code	1804
The Continental System	1806
Napoleon invades Spain	1808
Invasion of Russia	1812
Abdication of Napoleon	1814
Return and final exile of Napoleon	1815

CONCLUSION

The tumultuous events in France formed part of a broad pattern of late-eighteenth-century democratic upheaval. The French Revolution was the most violent, protracted, and contentious of the revolutions of the era; but the dynamics of revolution were much the same everywhere. One of the most important developments of the French Revolution was the emergence of a popular movement, which included political clubs representing people previously excluded from politics, newspapers read by and to the common people, and political leaders who spoke for the sans-culottes. In the French Revolution as in other revolutions, the popular movement challenged the early and moderate revolutionary leadership, pressing for more radical and democratic measures. And as in other revolutions, the popular movement in France was defeated, and authority was reestablished by a quasi-military figure. Likewise, the revolutionary ideas of liberty, equality, and fraternity were not specifically French; their roots lay in the social structures of the eighteenth century and in the ideas and culture of the Enlightenment. Yet French armies brought them, literally, to the doorsteps of many Europeans.

What was the larger impact of the revolution and the Napoleonic era? Its legacy is partly summed up in three key concepts: liberty, equality, and nation. Liberty meant individual rights and responsibilities and, more specifically, freedom from arbitrary authority. By equality, as we have seen, the revolutionaries meant the abolition of legal distinctions of rank among European men. Though their concept of equality was limited, it became a powerful mobilizing force in the nineteenth century. The most important legacy of the revolution may have been the new term *nation*. Nationhood was a political concept. A nation was formed of citizens, not a king's subjects; it was ruled by law and treated citizens as equal before the law; sovereignty did not lie in dynasties or historic fiefdoms but in the nation of citizens. This new form of nation gained legitimacy when citizen armies repelled attacks against their newly won freedoms; the victories of "citizens in arms" lived on in myth and history and provided the most powerful images of the period. As the war continued, military nationhood began to overshadow its political cousin. By the Napoleonic period, this shift became decisive; a new political body of freely associated citizens was most powerfully embodied in a centralized state, its army, its greatest general turned emperor of the French, and a kind of citizenship defined by individual commitment to the needs of the nation at war.

The French did not hesitate to champion their principles abroad. Some of those principles were revolutionary; others, imperial. In the German and Italian principalities the domination of an alien emperor and his unwelcome agents helped forge opposition and a national identity of their own.

When the revolutionary period closed, the three concepts of liberty, equality, and nationality were no longer merely ideas. They had taken shape in new communities and institutions. They had created new alliances among countries. They also polarized Europe and much of the world, giving rise to debates, grievances, and conflict that would shape the nineteenth century.

KEY TERMS

The Three Estates

Declaration of the Rights of Man and of the Citizen

fall of the Bastille

abolition of feudalism

bourgeoisie

Committee of Public Safety

Civil Constitution of the Clergy

fall and execution of the king

plebiscite

Napoleonic Code

SELECTED READINGS

Applewhite, Harriet B., and Darline G. Levy, eds. *Women and Politics in the Age of the Democratic Revolution.* Ann Arbor, Mich., 1990. Essays on France, Britain, the Netherlands, and the United States.

Bell, David A. *The First Total War: Napoleon's Europe and the Birth of Warfare as We Know It.* Boston and New York, 2007. Lively and concise study of the "cataclysmic intensification" of warfare.

Blackburn, Robin. *The Overthrow of Colonial Slavery.* London and New York, 1988. A longer view of slavery and its abolition.

Blanning, T. C. W. *The French Revolutionary Wars, 1787–1802.* Oxford, 1996. On the revolution and war.

Blum, Carol. *Rousseau and the Republic of Virtue: The Language of Politics in the French Revolution.* Ithaca, N.Y., 1986. Excellent on how Rousseau was read by the revolutionaries.

Cobb, Richard. *The People's Armies.* New Haven, Conn., 1987. Brilliant and detailed analysis of the popular militias.

Connelly, Owen. *The French Revolution and Napoleonic Era.* 3rd ed., New York, 2000. Accessible, lively, one-volume survey.

Darnton, Robert, *The Forbidden Best-Sellers of Pre-Revolutionary France.* New York, 1995. One of Darnton's many imaginative studies of subversive opinion and books on the eve of the revolution.

Doyle, William. *Origins of the French Revolution.* New York, 1988. A revisionist historian surveys recent research on the political and social origins of the revolution and identifies a new consensus.

Doyle, William. *Oxford History of the French Revolution.* New York, 1989.

Dubois, Laurent. *Avengers of the New World. The Story of the Haitian Revolution.* Cambridge, Mass., 2004. Now the best and most accessible study.

Dubois, Laurent, and John D. Garrigus. *Slave Revolution in the Caribbean, 1789–1804: A Brief History with Documents.* New York, 2006. A particularly good collection.

Englund, Steven. *Napoleon, A Political Life.* Cambridge, Mass., 2004. Prize-winning biography, both dramatic and insightful.

Forrest, Alan. *The French Revolution and the Poor.* New York, 1981. A moving and detailed social history of the poor, who fared little better under revolutionary governments than under the Old Regime.

Furet, Francois. *Revolutionary France, 1770–1880.* Trans. Antonia Nerill. Cambridge, Mass., 1992. Overview by the leading revisionist.

Geyl, Pieter. *Napoleon: For and Against.* Rev. ed. New Haven, Conn., 1964. The ways in which Napoleon was interpreted by French historians and political figures.

Hunt, Lynn. *The French Revolution and Human Rights.* Boston, 1996. A collection of documents.

Hunt, Lynn. *Politics, Culture, and Class in the French Revolution.* Berkeley, Calif., 1984. An analysis of the new culture of democracy and republicanism.

Hunt, Lynn, and Jack R. Censer. *Liberty, Equality, Fraternity: Exploring the French Revolution.* University Park, Pa., 2001. Two leading historians of the revolution have written a lively, accessible study, with excellent documents and visual material.

Landes, Joan B. *Women and the Public Sphere in the Age of the French Revolution.* Ithaca, N.Y., 1988. On gender and politics.

Lefebvre, Georges. *The Coming of the French Revolution.* Princeton, N.J., 1947. The classic Marxist analysis.

Lewis, G., and C. Lucas. *Beyond the Terror: Essays in French Regional and Social History, 1794–1815.* New York, 1983. Shifts focus to the understudied period after the Terror.

O'Brien, Connor Cruise. *The Great Melody: A Thematic Biography of Edmund Burke.* Chicago, 1992. Passionate, partisan, and brilliant study of Burke's thoughts about Ireland, India, America, and France.

Palmer, R. R. *The Age of the Democratic Revolution: A Political History of Europe and America, 1760–1800.* 2 vols. Princeton, N.J., 1964. Impressive for its scope; places the French Revolution in the larger context of a worldwide revolutionary movement.

Palmer, R. R., and Isser Woloch. *Twelve Who Ruled: The Year of the Terror in the French Revolution.* Princeton, N.J. 2005. The terrific collective biography of the Committee of Public Safety, now updated.

Schama, Simon. *Citizens: A Chronicle of the French Revolution.* New York, 1989. Particularly good on art, culture, and politics.

Soboul, Albert. *The Sans-Culottes: The Popular Movement and Revolutionary Government, 1793–1794.* Garden City, N.Y., 1972. Dated, but a classic.

Sutherland, D. M. G. *France, 1789–1815: Revolution and Counterrevolution.* Oxford, 1986. An important synthesis of work on the revolution, especially in social history.

Thompson, J. M. *Robespierre and the French Revolution.* London, 1953. An excellent short biography.

Tocqueville, Alexis de. *The Old Regime and the French Revolution.* Garden City, N.Y., 1955. Originally written in 1856, this remains a provocative analysis of the revolution's legacy.

Trouillot, Michel Rolph. *Silencing the Past.* Boston, 1995. Essays on the Haitian revolution.

Woloch, Isser. *The New Regime: Transformations of the French Civic Order, 1789–1820.* New York, 1994. The fate of revolutionary civic reform.

Woolf, Stuart. *Napoleon's Integration of Europe.* New York, 1991. Technical but very thorough.

Chapter NINETEEN

CHAPTER CONTENTS

The Industrial Revolution and Nineteenth-Century Society

THE FRENCH REVOLUTION TRANSFORMED the political and diplomatic landscape of Europe suddenly and dramatically. The transformation of industry came more gradually. By the 1830s or 1840s, however, writers and social thinkers were increasingly aware of unexpected and extraordinary changes in their economic world. They spoke of an "industrial revolution," one that seemed to parallel the ongoing revolution in politics. The term has stayed with us. The Industrial Revolution spanned the hundred years after 1780. It represented the first breakthrough from an agricultural, artisanal, and overwhelmingly rural economy to one characterized by larger-scale manufacturing, more capital-intensive enterprises, and urbanization. It involved new sources of energy and power, faster transportation, mechanization, higher productivity, and new ways of organizing human labor. It triggered social changes with revolutionary consequences for the West and its relationship with the world.

Of all the changes, perhaps the most revolutionary came at the very root of human endeavor: new forms of energy. Over the space of two or three generations, a society and an economy that had drawn on water, wind, and wood for most of its energy needs came to depend on steam engines and coal. In 1800, the world produced 10 million tons of coal. In 1900, it produced 1 billion: 100 times more. The Industrial Revolution brought the beginning of the fossil-fuel age. It shattered the constraints of previous times, it opened an era of unprecedented economic growth, and it began to alter irrevocably the balance of humanity and the environment. Within a few more generations, by the end of the nineteenth century, the new energy regime would include oil and electricity—but historians refer to that period as the second industrial revolution.

Machines gripped contemporaries' imaginations, dazzling some observers and disturbing others. The novelist Charles Dickens, for instance, compared the piston of the steam engine working "monotonously up and down" to "the head of an elephant in a state of melancholy madness." Mechanization made possible enormous gains in productivity in some sectors; in so doing it shifted the basis of the economy, in some

FOCUS QUESTIONS

• Why did the Industrial Revolution first take hold in Britain?

• What specific changes did the Industrial Revolution bring?

• How was the Industrial Revolution different on the Continent?

• What were the long- and short-term consequences of industrialization?

• Who were the new middle classes?

cases creating entirely new livelihoods and industrial regions while rendering others obsolete. Yet to focus on mechanization can be misleading. Especially at the outset, mechanization was limited to a few sectors of the economy and did not always lead to a dramatic break with techniques used in the past. Above all, technology did not dispense with human toil. Historians emphasize that the Industrial Revolution intensified human labor—carrying water or iron rails, digging trenches, harvesting cotton, sewing by hand, or pounding hides—much more often than it eased it.

One historian suggests we speak of an "industrious revolution." The "revolution" did not lie in machines themselves. Instead, it lay in the mushrooming growth of new economic system based on mobilizing capital and labor on a much larger scale. Its sweeping effects redistributed wealth, influence, and power. It created new social classes and produced new social tensions.

> The "revolution" did not lie in machines themselves. Instead, it lay in the mushrooming growth of new economic system based on mobilizing capital and labor on a much larger scale.

It also prompted deep-seated cultural shifts. The English cultural critic Raymond Williams has pointed out that in the eighteenth century, *industry* referred to a human quality: a hardworking woman was "industrious"; an ambitious clerk showed "industry." By the middle of the nineteenth century, *industry* had come to mean an economic system, one that followed its own inner logic and worked on its own—seemingly independent of humans. This is our modern understanding of the term, and it was born during the early nineteenth century. As the Industrial Revolution altered the foundations of the economy, it also changed the very assumptions with which people approached economics and the ways in which they regarded the role of human beings in the economy. These new assumptions could foster a sense of power but also anxieties about powerlessness.

Living as we do in the early twenty-first century, an age of economic and technological transformations, we may identify with the 1840s' sense of extraordinary, far-reaching, and little-understood change. We feel the economic and social world shifting but are unable to grasp the effects, and the changes are simultaneously exhilarating and unsettling. The cascading effects of new technologies, new forms of communication, and new economic imperatives make it difficult to differentiate results from causes. Are new technologies the driving force of change, or are they the effects of other structural transformations? What sectors of the econ-omy and which kinds of employment will expand and which will become obsolete? Will dizzying rises in productivity benefit workers? Will all social groups share in economic growth? These questions and others that haunt us today arose during the first Industrial Revolution. Only in retrospect can we piece together the answers.

The dramatic changes of the late eighteenth and early nineteenth centuries built on developments in earlier times. Overseas commercial exploration and development had opened new territories to European trade. The continents of India, Africa, and North and South America had been woven into the pattern of European economic expansion. Expanding networks of trade and finance created new markets for goods and sources for raw materials; and they made it easier to mobilize capital for investment. All these developments paved the way for industrialization. The seventeenth and eighteenth centuries had seen significant "proto-industrialization," or the spread of manufacturing in rural areas in specific regions (see Chapter Fifteen). Especially in England, as we will see, it had also brought changes in agriculture and property holding with far-reaching ramifications. Population growth, which began in the eighteenth century, was also a key factor. Last, more elusive social and cultural developments, such as more secure property rights or new forms of social mobility, played an essential role in the revolution that created the modern industrial world.

The industrial revolution itself began in northern England and western Scotland during the late eighteenth century and from there moved slowly and unevenly across continental Europe. Various factors (supplies of labor, resources, and capital) and important developments (technological innovations, the emergence of new economic institutions, government subsidies, and legal changes) came together in different ways at different moments. For that reason, industrialization did not follow any single path across the various regions of Europe. Nor did it sweep aside older forms of production. New machines coexisted with intensive, old-fashioned hand labor. Manufacturing regions developed alongside vast areas of seemingly unchanged subsistence agriculture within the same nation. We begin with early industrialization in Great Britain and then turn to the more diverse changes that came later elsewhere.

WHY DID THE INDUSTRIAL REVOLUTION FIRST TAKE HOLD IN BRITAIN?

THE INDUSTRIAL REVOLUTION IN BRITAIN, 1760–1850   675

THE INDUSTRIAL REVOLUTION IN BRITAIN, 1760–1850

Why did the Industrial Revolution first take hold in Britain?

Great Britain in the eighteenth century had a fortunate combination of natural, economic, and cultural resources. It was a small and secure island nation with a robust empire and control over crucial lanes across the oceans. It had ample supplies of coal, rivers, and a well-developed network of canals—all of which proved important at different stages of early industrialization.

Industrialization's roots lay in agriculture. By the middle of the eighteenth century, agriculture in Britain was more thoroughly commercialized than it was elsewhere. British agriculture had been transformed by a combination of new techniques, new crops, and changes in patterns of property holding, especially the "enclosure" of fields and pastures, which turned small holdings, and in many cases commonly held lands, into large fenced tracts that were privately owned and individually managed by commercial landlords. The British Parliament encouraged enclosure with a series of bills in the second half of the eighteenth century. Commercialized agriculture was more productive and yielded more food for a growing and increasingly urban population. The concentration of property in fewer hands drove small farmers off the land, sending them to look for work in other sectors of the economy. Last, commercialized agriculture produced higher profits and more wealth for a class of landed investors, wealth that would be invested in industry.

A key precondition for industrialization was Britain's growing supply of available capital, in the forms of private wealth and well-developed banking and credit institutions. London had become the leading center for international trade, and the city was a headquarters for the transfer of raw material, capital, and manufactured products throughout the world. Portugal alone channeled as much as £50,000 in Brazilian gold per week

into London. Nor was banking limited to London; it was well established in the provinces as well. British merchants and financiers had accumulated substantial and well-organized resources, and they had established relatively secure banking. This made capital more readily available to underwrite new economic enterprises and eased the transfer of money and goods—importing, for instance, silks from the East or Egyptian and North American cottons.

Social and cultural conditions also encouraged investment in enterprises. In Britain far more than on the Continent, the pursuit of wealth was perceived to be a worthy goal. Since the Renaissance the nobility of Europe had cultivated the notion of gentlemanly conduct, in part to hold the line against those moving up from below. British aristocrats, whose ancient privileges were meager when compared with those of continental nobles, respected commoners with a talent for making money and did not hesitate to invest themselves. Their scramble to enclose their lands reflected a keen interest in commercialization and investment. Outside the aristocracy, an even lower barrier separated merchants from the rural gentry. Indeed, many of the entrepreneurs of the early Industrial Revolution came from the small gentry or independent (yeoman) farmer class. Eighteenth-century Britain was not by any means free of social snobbery: lords looked down on bankers and bankers looked down on craft workers. But a lord's disdain might well be tempered by the fact that his own grandfather had worked in the counting house.

Growing domestic and international markets made eighteenth-century Britain prosperous. The British were voracious consumers. The court elite followed and bought up yearly fashions, and so did most of Britain's landed and professional society. "Nature may be satisfied with little," one London entrepreneur declared. "But it is the wants of fashion and the desire of novelties that causes trade." The country's small size and the fact that it was an island encouraged the development of a well-integrated domestic market. Unlike continental Europe, Britain did not have a system of internal tolls and tariffs, so goods could be moved freely to wherever they might fetch the best price. A constantly improving transportation system boosted that freedom of movement. So did a favorable political climate. Some members of Parliament were

> Unlike continental Europe, Britain did not have a system of internal tolls and tariffs, so goods could be moved freely to wherever they might fetch the best price. A constantly improving transportation system boosted that freedom of movement. So did a favorable political climate.

businessmen themselves; others were investors. And both groups were eager to encourage by legislation the construction of canals, the establishment of banks, and the enclosure of common lands. In the late eighteenth century Parliament passed acts to finance turnpike building at the rate of forty roads per year, to construct canals, and to open up harbors and navigable streams.

Foreign markets promised even greater returns than domestic ones, though with greater risks. British foreign policy responded to its commercial needs. At the end of every major eighteenth-century war, Britain wrested overseas territories from its enemies. At the same time, Britain was penetrating hitherto unexploited territories, such as India and South America, in search of further potential markets and resources. In 1759, over one third of all British exports went to the colonies; by 1784, if we include the former colonies in North America, that figure had increased to one half. Production for export rose by 80 percent between 1750 and 1770; production for domestic consumption gained just 7 percent over the same period. The British possessed a merchant marine capable of transporting goods around the world and a navy practiced in the art of protecting its commercial fleets. By the 1780s, Britain's markets, together with its fleet and its established position at the center of world commerce, gave

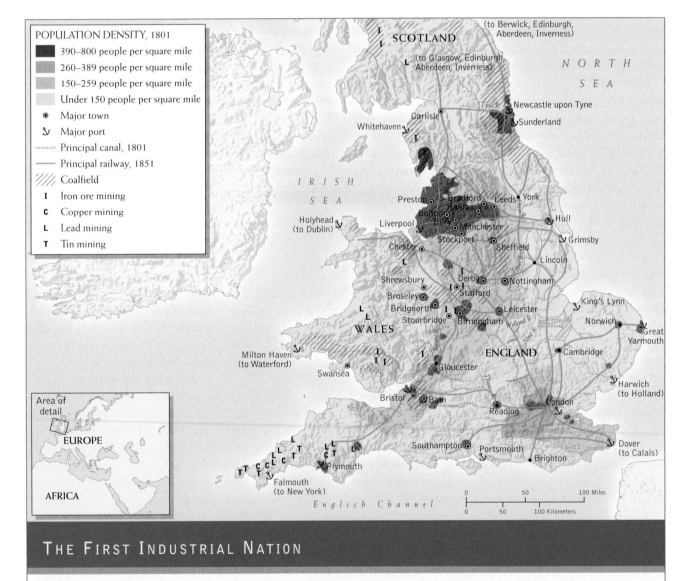

POPULATION DENSITY, 1801

- 390–800 people per square mile
- 260–389 people per square mile
- 150–259 people per square mile
- Under 150 people per square mile
- ⊙ Major town
- ⚓ Major port
- ⊶⊶ Principal canal, 1801
- —— Principal railway, 1851
- ▨ Coalfield
- I Iron ore mining
- C Copper mining
- L Lead mining
- T Tin mining

THE FIRST INDUSTRIAL NATION

The Industrial Revolution first took hold in Great Britain. How did its size and status as an island affect industrialization? Why did Great Britain build its first railroad between Durham and Darlington? Why did the railroad system expand more quickly in Great Britain than on the Continent?

WHY DID THE INDUSTRIAL REVOLUTION FIRST TAKE HOLD IN BRITAIN?

THE INDUSTRIAL REVOLUTION IN BRITAIN, 1760–1850   677

its entrepreneurs unrivaled opportunities for trade and profit. These factors enabled Britain to experience the first great changes that would become an industrial revolution.

INNOVATION IN THE TEXTILE INDUSTRIES

The Industrial Revolution began with dramatic technological leaps in a few well-placed industries, the first of which was cotton textiles. The industry was already long established. Tariffs prohibiting imports of East Indian cottons, which Parliament had imposed to protect British woolen goods, had spurred the manufacture of British cotton. British textile manufacturers imported raw materials from India and the American South and borrowed patterns from Indian spinners and weavers. What, then, were the revolutionary breakthroughs?

In 1733, John Kay's invention of the flying shuttle speeded the process of weaving. The task of spinning thread, however, had not kept up. A series of com-

Cotton Spinning, 1861. An illustration from a series showing spinning at Walter Evans and Company, cotton manufacturers in Derby, England.

paratively simple mechanical devices eliminated this spinning-to-weaving bottleneck. The most important device was the spinning jenny, invented by James Hargreaves, a carpenter and hand-loom weaver, in 1764 (patented 1770). The spinning jenny, named after the inventor's wife, was a compound spinning wheel capable of producing sixteen threads at once—though the threads were not strong enough to be used for the longitudinal fibers, or warp, of cotton cloth. The invention of the water frame by Richard Arkwright, a barber, in 1769, made it possible to produce both warp and woof (latitudinal fibers) in great quantity. In 1799 Samuel Compton invented the spinning mule, which combined the features of both the jenny and the frame. All of these important technological changes were accomplished by the end of the eighteenth century.

The water frame and the spinning mule had enormous advantages over the spinning wheel. A jenny could spin from 6 to 24 times more yarn than a hand spinner. By the end of the eighteenth century, a mule could produce 200 to 300 times more. Just as important, the new machines made better-quality—stronger and finer—thread. These machines revolutionized production across the textile industry. Last, the cotton gin, invented by the American Eli Whitney in 1793, mechanized the process of separating cotton seeds from the fiber, thereby speeding up the production of cotton and reducing its price. The supply of cotton fibers could now expand to keep pace with rising demand from cotton cloth manufacturers. This cotton gin had many effects, including, paradoxically, changing the economics of slavery in the United States. The cotton-producing slave plantations in the American South became significantly more profitable, their labor now enmeshed in the very brisk and lucrative trade with merchant exporters of raw cotton and manufacturers who produced cotton textiles in the northern United States and England.

The first textile machines were inexpensive enough to be used by spinners in their own cottages. But as machines grew in size and complexity, they were housed instead in workshops or mills located near water that could be used to power the machines. Eventually, the further development of steam-driven equipment allowed manufacturers to build mills wherever they could be used. Frequently, those mills went up in towns and cities in the north of England, away from the older commercial and seafaring centers, but where local politicians were interested in textile manufacturing and the money and growth it brought in its wake. From 1780 on, British cotton textiles flooded the

THE FACTORY SYSTEM, SCIENCE, AND MORALITY: TWO VIEWS

Reactions to the Industrial Revolution and the factory system it produced ranged from celebration to horror. Dr. Andrew Ure, a Scottish professor of chemistry, was fascinated with these nineteenth-century applications of Enlightenment science. He believed that the new machinery and its products would create a new society of wealth, abundance, and, ultimately, stability through the useful regimentation of production.

Friedrich Engels (1820–1895) was one of the many socialists to criticize Dr. Ure as shortsighted and complacent in his outlook. Engels was himself part of a factory-owning family and so was able to examine the new industrial cities at close range. He provides a classic nineteenth-century analysis of industrialization. The Condition of the Working Class in England *is compellingly written, angry, and revealing about middle-class concerns of the time, including female labor.*

DR. ANDREW URE (1835)

This island [Britain] is preeminent among civilized nations for the prodigious development of its factory wealth, and has been therefore long viewed with a jealous admiration by foreign powers. This very pre-eminence, however, has been contemplated in a very different light by many influential members of our own community, and has even been denounced by them as the certain origin of innumerable evils to the people, and of revolutionary convulsions to the state. . . .

The blessings which physico-mechanical science has bestowed on society, and the means it has still in store for ameliorating the lot of mankind, has been too little dwelt upon; while, on the other hand, it has been accused of lending itself to the rich capitalists as an instrument for harassing the poor, and of exacting from the operative an accelerated rate of work. It has been said, for example, that the steam-engine now drives the power-looms with such velocity as to urge on their attendant weavers at the same rapid pace; but that the hand-weaver, not being subjected to

this restless agent, can throw his shuttle and move his treddles at his convenience. There is, however, this difference in the two cases, that in the factory, every member of the loom is so adjusted, that the driving force leaves the attendant nearly nothing at all to do, certainly no muscular fatigue to sustain, while it produces for him good, unfailing wages, besides a healthy workshop *gratis:* whereas the non-factory weaver, having everything to execute by muscular exertion, finds the labour irksome, makes in consequence innumerable short pauses, separately of little account, but great when added together; earns therefore proportionally low wages, while he loses his health by poor diet and the dampness of his hovel.

Andrew Ure, *The Philosophy of Manufacturers: Or, An Exposition of the Scientific, Moral and Commercial Economy of the Factory System of Great Britain,* 1835, as cited in J. T. Ward, *The Factory System,* vol. 1 (New York, 1970), pp. 140–141.

FRIEDRICH ENGELS (1844)

Histories of the modern development of the cotton industry, such as those of Ure, Baines, and others, tell on every page of technical innovations. . . . In a well-ordered society such improvements would indeed be welcome, but social war rages unchecked and the benefits derived from these improvements are ruthlessly monopolized by a few persons. . . . Every improvement in machinery leads to unemployment, and the greater the technical improvement the greater the unemployment. Every improvement in machinery affects a number of workers in the same way as a commercial crisis and leads to want, distress, and crime. . . .

Let us examine a little more closely the process whereby machine-labour continually supesedes hand-labour. When spinning or weaving machinery is installed practically all that is left to be done by the hand is the piecing together of broken threads, and the machine does the rest. This task calls for nimble fingers rather than muscular strength. The labour of grown men is not merely unnecessary but actually unsuitable. . . . The greater the degree to which physical labour is displaced by the introduction of machines worked by water- or steam-power, the fewer grown men need be employed. In any case women and children will work for lower wages than men and, as has already been ob-

served, they are more skillful at piecing than grown men. Consequently it is women and children who are employed to do this work. . . . When women work in factories, the most important result is the dissolution of family ties. If a woman works for twelve or thirteen hours a day in a factory and her husband is employed either in the same establishment or in some other works, what is the fate of the children? They lack parental care and control. . . . It is not difficult to imagine that they are left to run wild.

Friedrich Engels, *The Condition of the Working Class in England in 1844*, trans. and ed. W. O. Henderson and W. H. Chaloner (New York, 1958), pp. 150–151, 158, 160.

QUESTIONS FOR ANALYSIS

1. According to Andre Ure, why was industrialization good for Britain? How can the blessings of "physicomechanical science" lead to the improvement of humanity?
2. What criticism did Engels level at Ure and other optimists on industrialization? Why did Engels think conditions for workers were getting worse instead of better?
3. Why do these two writers disagree about the effects of technological change?

world market. Numbers testify to the revolutionary changes in the expanding industry. Between 1760 and 1800, British exports of cotton goods grew from £250,000 worth a year to £5 million. In 1760, Britain imported 2.5 million pounds of raw cotton; in 1787, 22 million pounds; in 1837, 366 million pounds. By 1815, the export of cotton textiles amounted to 40 percent of the value of all domestic goods exported from Great Britain. Although the price of manufactured cotton goods fell dramatically, the market expanded so rapidly that profits continued to increase.

Behind these statistics lay a revolution in clothing. Cotton in the form of muslins and calicos was fine enough to appeal to wealthy consumers. Cotton was also light and washable. For the first time, ordinary people could have sheets, table linens, curtains, and underwear. (Wool was too scratchy.) As one writer commented in 1846, the revolution in textiles had ushered in a "brilliant transformation" in dress. "Every woman used to wear a blue or black dress that she kept

ten years without washing it for fear that it would fall to pieces. Today her husband can cover her in flower-printed cotton for the price of a day's wages."

The explosive growth of textiles also prompted a debate about the benefits and tyranny of the new industries. The British Romantic poet William Blake famously wrote in biblical terms of the textile mills' blight on the English countryside.

> And did the Countenance Divine
> Shine forth upon our clouded hills?
> And was Jerusalem builded here
> Among these dark Satanic mills?

By the 1830s, the British House of Commons was holding hearings on employment and working conditions in factories, recording testimony about working days that stretched from 3:00 A.M. to 10:00 P.M., the employment of very small children, and workers who lost hair and fingers in the mills' machinery. Women

Resisting Industrialization. A crowd attacks a spinning jenny, a symbol of the costs of industrial transformation.

and children counted for roughly two thirds of the labor force in textiles. The principle of regulating any labor (and emphatically that of adult men), however, was controversial. Only gradually did a series of factory acts prohibit hiring children under age nine and limit the labor of workers under age eighteen to ten hours a day.

COAL AND IRON

Meanwhile, decisive changes were transforming the production of iron. As in the textile industry, many important technological changes came during the eighteenth century. A series of innovations (coke smelting, rolling, and puddling) enabled the British to substitute coal (which they had in abundance) for wood (which was scarce and inefficient) to heat molten metal and make iron. The new "pig iron" was higher quality and could be used in building an enormous variety of iron products: machines, engines, railway tracks, agricultural implements, and hardware. Those iron products became, literally, the infrastructure of industrialization. Britain found itself able to export both coal and iron to rapidly expanding markets around the industrializing regions of the world. Between 1814 and 1852, exports of British iron doubled, rising to over 1 million tons of iron, more than half of the world's total production.

Rising demand for coal required mining deeper veins. In 1711, Thomas Newcomen had devised a

cumbersome but remarkably effective steam engine for pumping water from mines. Though it was immensely valuable to the coal industry, its usefulness in other industries was limited by the amount of fuel it consumed. In 1763, James Watt, who made scientific instruments at the University of Glasgow, was asked to repair a model of the Newcomen engine. While tinkering with the machine, he hit on a way to improve it: adding a separate chamber to condense the steam eliminated the need to cool the cylinder. Watt patented his first engine incorporating this device in 1769. Watt's genius as an inventor far surpassed his ability as a businessman. He admitted that he would "rather face a loaded cannon than settle a disputed account or make a bargain." As a consequence, he fell into debt in attempting to place his machines on the market. He was rescued by Matthew Boulton, a wealthy hardware manufacturer from Birmingham. The two men formed a partnership, with Boulton providing the capital. By 1800 the firm had sold 289 engines for use in factories and mines. Watt and Boulton made their fortune from their invention's efficiency; they earned a regular percentage of the increased profits from each mine that operated an engine.

Steam power was still energy consuming and expensive and so only slowly replaced traditional water power. A series of improvements over the course of the nineteenth century made steam engines vastly more powerful than they had been in Watt's day. Even in its early form, however, the steam engine decisively transformed the nineteenth-century world with one application: the steam-driven locomotive. Railroads revolutionized industry, markets, public and private financing, and ordinary people's conceptions of space and time.

CHRONOLOGY

THE INDUSTRIAL REVOLUTION IN GREAT BRITAIN, 1733–1825

Invention of the fly shuttle	1733
Invention of the spinning jenny	1764
Invention of the water frame	1769
Invention of the steam engine	1769
Invention of the spinning mule	1779
Invention of the cotton gin	1793
First railroad built	1825

WHY DID THE INDUSTRIAL REVOLUTION FIRST TAKE HOLD IN BRITAIN?

THE INDUSTRIAL REVOLUTION IN BRITAIN, 1760–1850   681

Child Labor in the Mines. This engraving of a young worker pulling a coal cart up through the narrow shaft of a mine accompanied a British Parliamentary report on child labor.

THE COMING OF RAILWAYS

Transportation had improved during the years before 1830, but moving heavy materials, particularly coal, remained a problem. It is significant that the first modern railway, built in England in 1825, ran from the Durham coal field of Stockton to Darlington, near the coast. Coal had traditionally been hauled short distances via tramways, or tracks along which horses pulled coal carts. The Stockton-to-Darlington railway was a logical extension of a tramway, designed to answer the transportation needs produced by constantly expanding industrialization. The man primarily responsible for the design of the first steam railway was George Stephenson, a self-educated engineer who had not learned to read until he was seventeen. The locomotives on the Stockton-Darlington line traveled at fifteen miles per hour, the fastest rate at which machines had yet moved goods overland. Soon they would move people as well, transforming transportation in the process.

Building railways became a massive enterprise and a risky but potentially profitable opportunity for investment. No sooner did the first combined passenger and goods service open in 1830, operating between Liverpool and Manchester, England, than plans were formulated and money pledged to extend rail systems throughout Europe, the Americas, and beyond. In 1830, there were no more than a few dozen miles of railway in the world. By 1840, there were over 4,500 miles; by

1850, over 23,000. British engineers, industrialists, and investors were quick to realize the global opportunities available in constructing railways overseas; a large part of Britain's industrial success in the later nineteenth century came through building other nations' infrastructures. The English contractor Thomas Brassey, for instance, built railways in Italy, Canada, Argentina, India, and Australia.

Throughout the world, a veritable army of construction workers built the railways. In Britain, they were called "navvies," derived from *navigator*, a term first used for the construction workers on Britain's

Manchester to Liverpool, late nineteenth century. Lower class passengers, physically separated from their social superiors, are packed into the rear of the train.

eighteenth-century canals. Navvies were a rough lot, living with a few women in temporary encampments as they migrated across the countryside. Often they were immigrant workers and faced local hostility. A sign posted by local residents outside a mine in Scotland in 1845 warned the Irish navvies to get "off the ground and out of the country" in a week or else be driven out "by the strength of our armes and a good pick shaft." Later in the century railway building projects in Africa and the Americas were lined with camps of immigrant Indian and Chinese laborers, who also became targets of nativist (a term that means "opposed to foreigners") anger.

The magnitude of the navvies' accomplishment was extraordinary. In Britain and in much of the rest of the world, mid-nineteenth-century railways were constructed almost entirely without the aid of machinery. An assistant engineer on the London-to-Birmingham line calculated that the labor involved was the equivalent of lifting 25 billion cubic feet of earth and stone 1 foot high. He compared this feat with building the Great Pyramid, a task he estimated had involved the hoisting of some 16 billion tons. The building of

the pyramid, however, had required over 200,000 men and had taken twenty years. The construction of the London-to-Birmingham railway was accomplished by 20,000 men in less than five years. If we translated this into individual terms, a navvy was expected to move an average of 20 tons of earth per day. Railways were produced by toil as much as by technology, by human labor as much as by engineering; they illustrate why some historians prefer to use the term *industrious* revolution.

Steam engines, textile machines, new ways of making iron, and railways—all these were interconnected. Changes in one area endorsed changes in another. Pumps run by steam engines made it possible to mine deeper veins of coal; steam-powered railways made it possible to transport coal. Mechanization fueled the production of iron for machines and the mining of coal to run steam engines. The railway boom multiplied the demand for iron products: rails, locomotives, carriages, signals, switches, and the iron to make all of these. Building railroads called for engineering expertise: scaling mountains, designing bridges and tunnels. Railway construction, which required capital

Navvies and the Steam Excavation Machine. Despite help from new construction technology, much of the work on mid-nineteenth-century railways was manual labor done by navvies, many of whom were immigrant workers.

investment beyond the capacity of any single individual, forged new kinds of public and private financing. The scale of production expanded and the tempo of economic activity quickened, spurring the search for more coal, the production of more iron, the mobilization of more capital, and the recruitment of more labor. Steam and speed were becoming the foundation of the economy and of a new way of life.

THE INDUSTRIAL REVOLUTION ON THE CONTINENT

How was the Industrial Revolution different on the Continent?

Continental Europe, with its different natural, economic, and political resources, followed a different path. Eighteenth-century France, Belgium, and Germany did have manufacturing districts in regions with raw materials, access to markets, and long-standing traditions of craft and skill. Yet for a variety of reasons, changes along the lines seen in Britain did not occur until the 1830s. Britain's transportation system was highly developed; those of France and Germany were not. France was far larger than England: its rivers more difficult to navigate; its seaports, cities, and coal deposits farther apart. Much of central Europe was divided into small principalities, each with its own set of tolls and tariffs, which complicated the transportation of raw materials or manufactured goods over any considerable distance. The Continent had fewer raw materials, coal in particular, than Britain. The abundance and cheapness of wood discouraged exploration that might have resulted in new discoveries of coal. It also meant that high-energy-consuming, coal-run steam engines were less economical on the Continent. Capital, too, was less readily available. Early British industrialization was underwritten by private wealth; this was less feasible elsewhere. Different patterns of landholding formed obstacles to the commercialization of agricul-

ture. In the east, serfdom was a powerful disincentive to labor-saving innovations. In the west, especially in France, the large number of small peasants, or farmers, stayed put on the land.

The wars of the French Revolution and Napoleon did hasten legal changes and the consolidation of state power, but they disrupted economies. During the eighteenth century, the population had grown and mechanization had begun in a few key industries. The ensuing political upheaval, the financial strains of warfare, and the thundering hooves of armies, however, did virtually nothing to help economic development. Napoleon's Continental System and British destruction of French merchant shipping hurt commerce badly. The ban on British-shipped cotton stalled the growth of cotton textiles for decades, though the armies' greater demand for woolen cloth kept that sector of textiles humming. Iron processing increased to satisfy the military's rising needs, but techniques for making iron remained largely unchanged. Probably the revolutionary change most beneficial to industrial advance in Europe was the removal of previous restraints on the movement of capital and labor—for example, the abolition of craft guilds and the reduction of tariff barriers across the Continent.

After 1815, a number of factors combined to change the economic climate. In those regions with a well-established commercial and industrial base—the northeast of France, Belgium, and swaths of territory across the Rhineland, Saxony, Silesa, and northern Bohemia (see map on page 686)—population growth further boosted economic development. Rising population did not by itself produce industrialization, however: in Ireland, where other necessary factors were absent, more people meant less food.

Transportation improved. The Austrian Empire added over 30,000 miles of roads between 1830 and 1847; Belgium almost doubled its road network in the same period; France built not only new roads but 2,000 miles of canals. These improvements, combined with the construction of railroads in the 1830s and 1840s, opened up new markets and encouraged new methods of manufacturing. In many of the Continent's manufacturing regions, however, industrialists could long continue to tap large pools of skilled but inexpensive labor. Thus older methods of putting out

> In many of the Continent's manufacturing regions, however, industrialists could long continue to tap large pools of skilled but inexpensive labor. Thus older methods of putting out industry and handwork persisted alongside new-model factories.

industry and handwork persisted alongside new-model factories.

In what other ways was the continental model of industrialization different? Governments played a considerably more direct role in industrialization. France and Prussia, for instance, granted considerable subsidies to private companies that built railroads. After 1849, the Prussian state took on the task itself, as did Belgium and, later, Russia—an undertaking that required importing material and expertise but that often yielded significant profits. In Prussia, the state also operated a large proportion of that country's mines. Governments on the Continent provided incentives for and laws favorable to industrialization. Limited-liability laws, to take the most important example, allowed investors to own shares in a corporation or company without becoming liable for the company's debts—and they enabled enterprises to recruit many small investors to put together the capital for massive investments in railroads, other forms of industry, and commerce.

Mobilizing capital for industry was one of the challenges of the century. In Great Britain, overseas trade had created well-organized financial markets; on the Continent, capital was dispersed and in short supply. New joint-stock investment banks, unlike private banks, could sell bonds to and take deposits from individuals and smaller companies. They could offer start-up capital in the form of long-term, low-interest commercial loans to aspiring entrepreneurs. The Belgian Société Générale dated from the 1830s, the Austrian Creditanstalt and the French Crédit Mobilier from the 1850s. The Crédit Mobilier, for instance, founded in 1852 by the wealthy and well-connected Périere brothers, assembled enough capital to finance insurance companies; the Parisian bus system; six municipal gas companies; transatlantic shipping; enterprises in other European countries; and, with the patronage of the state, the massive railroad-building spree of the 1850s. The Périeres' success earned them reputations as upstart speculators, and the Crédit Mobilier collapsed in scandal, but the revolution in banking was well under way.

Finally, continental Europeans actively promoted invention and technological development. They were willing for the state to establish educational systems whose aim, among others, was to produce a well-trained elite capable of assisting in the development of industrial technology. In sum, what Britain had produced almost by chance, the Europeans began to reproduce by design.

INDUSTRIALIZATION AFTER 1850

Until 1850 Britain remained the preeminent industrial power. Individual British factories were small by the standards set later in the century, let alone those of modern times. Still, their output was tremendous and their ability to sell to home and foreign markets was unrivaled. Between 1850 and 1870, however, France, Germany, Belgium, and the United States emerged as challengers to the power and place of British manufacturers. The British iron industry remained the largest in the world (in 1870 Britain still produced half the world's pig iron), but it grew more slowly than did its counterparts in France or Germany. Most of continental Europe's gains came as a result of continuing changes in those areas we recognize as important for sustained industrial growth: transport, commerce, and government policy. The spread of railways encouraged the free movement of goods. International monetary unions were established and restrictions removed on international waterways such as the Danube. Free trade went hand in hand with removing guild barriers to entering trades and ending restrictions on practicing business. Guild control over artisanal production was abolished in Austria in 1859 and in most of Germany by the mid-1860s. Laws against usury,

Silk Weavers of Lyons, 1850. The first significant working-class uprisings in nineteenth-century France occurred in Lyons in 1831 and 1834. Note the domestic character of the working conditions.

most of which had ceased to be enforced, were officially abandoned in Britain, Holland, Belgium, and in many parts of Germany. Governmental regulation of mining was surrendered by the Prussian state in the 1850s, freeing entrepreneurs to develop resources as they saw fit. Investment banks continued to form, encouraged by an increase in the money supply and an easing of credit after the California gold fields opened in 1849.

The first phase of the industrial revolution, one economic historian reminds us, was confined to a narrow set of industries and can be summed up rather simply: "cheaper and better clothes (mainly made of cotton), cheaper and better metals (pig iron, wrought iron, and steel) and faster travel (mainly by rail)." The second half of the century brought changes farther afield and in areas where Great Britain's early advantages were no longer decisive. Transatlantic cable (starting in 1865) and the telephone (invented in 1876) laid the ground for a revolution in communications. New chemical processes, dyestuffs, and pharmaceuticals emerged. So did new sources of energy: electricity, in which the United States and Germany led both invention and commercial development; and oil, which was being refined in the 1850s and widely used by 1900. Among the early exploiters of Russian oil discoveries were the Swedish Nobel brothers and the French Rothschilds. The developments that eventually converged to make the automobile came primarily from Germany and France. The internal combustion engine, important because it was small, efficient, and could be used in a very wide variety of situations, was developed by Carl Benz and Gottlieb Daimler in the 1880s. The removable pneumatic tire was patented in 1891 by Edouard Michelin, a painter who had joined with his engineer brother in running the family's small agricultural-equipment business. These developments are discussed fully in Chapter Twenty-three, but their pioneers' familiar names illustrate how industry and invention had diversified over the course of the century.

In eastern Europe, the nineteenth century brought different patterns of economic development. Spurred by the ever-growing demand for food and grain, large sections of eastern Europe developed into concentrated, commercialized agriculture regions that played the specific role of exporting food to the west. Many of those large agricultural enterprises were based on

As machines were introduced in some sectors to do specific tasks, they usually intensified the tempo of handwork in other sectors. Thus, even in the industrialized regions, much work was still accomplished in tiny workshops—or at home.

serfdom and remained so, in the face of increasing pressure for reform, until 1850. Peasant protest and liberal demands for reform only gradually chipped away at the nobility's determination to hold onto its privilege and system of labor. Serfdom was abolished in most parts of eastern and southern Europe by 1850 and in Poland and Russia in the 1860s.

Although industry continued to take a back seat to agriculture, eastern Europe had several important manufacturing regions. By the 1880s, the number of men and women employed in the cotton industry in the Austrian province of Bohemia exceeded that in the German state of Saxony. In the Czech region, textile industries, developed in the eighteenth century, continued to thrive. By the 1830s, there were machine-powered Czech cotton mills and iron works. In Russia, a factory industry producing coarse textiles—mostly linens—had grown up around Moscow. At mid-century, Russia was purchasing 24 percent of the total British machinery exports to mechanize its own mills. Many who labored in Russian industry actually remained serfs until the 1860s—about 40 percent of them employed in mines. Of the over 800,000 Russians engaged in manufacturing by 1860, however, most were employed in small workshops of about forty persons.

By 1870, then, the core industrial nations of Europe included Great Britain, France, Germany, Italy, the Netherlands, and Switzerland. Austria stood at the margins. Russia, Spain, Bulgaria, Greece, Hungary, Romania, and Serbia formed the industrial periphery—and some regions of these nations seemed virtually untouched by the advance of industry. What was more, even in Great Britain, the most fully industrialized nation, agricultural laborers still constituted the single largest occupational category in 1860 (although they formed only 9 percent of the overall population). In Belgium, the Netherlands, Switzerland, Germany, France, Scandinavia, and Ireland, 25 to 50 percent of the population still worked on the land. In Russia, the number was 80 percent. *Industrial*, moreover, did not mean automation or machine production, which long remained confined to a few sectors of the economy. As machines were introduced in some sectors to do specific tasks, they usually intensified the tempo of handwork in other sectors. Thus even in the industrialized regions, much work was still accomplished in tiny workshops—or at home.

Moscow

RUSSIAN EMPIRE

St. Petersburg

BLACK SEA

OTTOMAN EMPIRE

Uppsala
Stockholm

SWEDEN

NORWAY

DENMARK

Copenhagen

BALTIC SEA

Warsaw

Lemberg

Cracow

SILESIA

Posen

Lodz

Breslau

AUSTRIAN EMPIRE

Budapest

Vienna

Prague

Pilsen

Steyr

NORTH SEA

NETHERLANDS

Amsterdam

Hamburg

GERMAN EMPIRE

Bremen

Berlin

Hanover

RUHR

Essen

Cologne

Kassel

Leipzig

Dresden

Zwickau

Chemnitz

Eisenach

Frankfurt

Nuremberg

Munich

MEDITERRANEAN SEA

Naples

Rome

Florence

ITALY

Milan

Turin

Livorno

SWITZ.

Zurich

Basel

Avignon

Lyons

Marseilles

Barcelona

Brussels

BELGIUM

Lille

Liège

Karlsruhe

SAAR

Strasbourg

Mulhouse

Stuttgart

Le Havre

Amiens

Paris

Orleans

Tours

FRANCE

Limoges

Nantes

Gijon

Santander

Bilbao

Oviedo

Madrid

Granada

Seville

Jerez

Lisbon

Glasgow

Darlington

Leeds

Sheffield

UNITED KINGDOM

Liverpool

Manchester

Birmingham

Cardiff

London

Dublin

ATLANTIC OCEAN

AFRICA

Area of detail

EUROPE

PERCENT OF POPULATION LIVING IN CITIES OF 100,000 OR MORE

5 percent or less
6 to 10 percent
20 percent or more

Railroads in 1850
Centers of industry
Iron ore deposits
Coal and lignite deposits

30C Miles

100 200 300 Kilometers

0   100   200   300

THE INDUSTRIAL REVOLUTION

Why were the effects of the Industrial Revolution more rapidly apparent in Great Britain and in north central Europe? How did an extensive railroad system help accelerate industrialization? What effects did the Industrial Revolution have on urban population densities?

INDUSTRY AND EMPIRE

From an international perspective, nineteenth-century Europe was the most industrial region of the world. Europeans, particularly the British, jealously guarded their international advantages. They preferred to do so through financial leverage. Britain, France, and other European nations gained control of the national debts of China, the Ottoman Empire, Egypt, Brazil, Argentina, and other non-European powers. They also supplied large loans to other states, which bound those nations to their European investors. If the debtor nations expressed discontent, as Egypt did in the 1830s when it attempted to establish its own cotton textile industry, they confronted financial pressure and shows of force. Coercion, however, was not always necessary or even one sided. Social change in other empires—China, Persia, and the Mughal Empire of India, for example—made those empires newly vulnerable and created new opportunities for the European powers and their local partners. Ambitious local elites often reached agreements with Western governments or groups such as the British East India Company. These trade agreements transformed regional economies on terms that

sent the greatest profits to Europe after a substantial gratuity to the Europeans' local partners. Where agreements could not be made, force prevailed, and Europe took territory and trade by conquest.

Industrialization tightened global links between Europe and the rest of the world, creating new networks of trade and interdependence. To a certain extent, the world economy divided between the producers of manufactured goods—Europe itself—and suppliers of the necessary raw materials and buyers of finished goods—everyone else. Cotton growers in the southern United States, sugar growers in the Caribbean, and wheat growers in Ukraine accepted their arrangements with the industrialized West and typically profited by them. If there were disputes, however, those suppliers often found that Europe could look elsewhere for the same goods or dictate the terms of trade down the business end of a bank ledger or a cannon barrel.

In 1811 Britain imported 3 percent of the wheat it consumed. By 1891, that portion had risen to 79 percent. Why? In an increasingly urban society, fewer people lived off the land. The commercialization of agriculture, which began early in Britain, had taken even firmer hold elsewhere, turning new regions—

British Clipper Ships in Calcutta Harbor, 1860. Calcutta, a long-established city on the eastern coast of India, was one of the hubs of the British Empire—a center for trade in cotton, jute, opium, and tea. The dazzling new clipper ships, first built in the 1830s and 1840s, were very fast and were central to the global economy of the nineteenth century.

Australia, Argentina, and North America (Canada and the United States)—into centers of grain and wheat production. New forms of transportation, finance, and communication made it easier to shuttle commodities and capital through international networks. Those simple percentages, in other words, dramatize the new interdependence of the nineteenth century; they illustrate as well as any statistics can how ordinary Britons' lives—like their counterparts' in other nations—were embedded in an increasingly global economy.

THE SOCIAL CONSEQUENCES OF INDUSTRIALIZATION

What were the long- and short-term consequences of industrialization?

We have mentioned population growth as one factor in industrial development, but it deserves treatment on its own terms. By any measure, the nineteenth century constituted a turning point in European demographic history. In 1800 the population of Europe as a whole was estimated roughly at 205 million. By 1850, it had risen to 274 million; by 1900, 414 million; on the eve of World War I it was 480 million. (Over the same span of time, world population went from about 900 million to 1.6 billion.) Britain, with its comparatively high standard of living, saw its population rise from 16 to 27 million. Increases, however, came in the largely rural regions as well. In Russia, the population rose from 39 to 60 million during the same period.

POPULATION

How do historians explain this population explosion? Some speculate that the cyclical potency of microbes made certain fatal diseases less virulent. From 1796 on, Edward Jenner's technique of vaccinating for smallpox gradually gained acceptance and made the disease less fatal. Improved sanitation helped curb cholera, though not until much later in the nineteenth century. Governments were better able and more determined to monitor and improve the lives of their people. Less expensive foods of high nutritional value—most notably the potato—and the ability to transport foodstuffs cheaply by railroad meant that many European populations were better nourished and so less susceptible to debilitating illness. But real changes in mortality and life expectancy came only late in the nineteenth or the beginning of the twentieth century. In 1880, the average male life expectancy in the city of Berlin was no more than 30 years, and in rural districts nearby it was 43. Historians now attribute the population growth of the nineteenth century to rising fertility rather than to falling mortality. Men and women married earlier, which raised fertility (the number of births per woman) and family size. Peasants tended to set up households at a younger age. The spread of rural manufacturing allowed couples in the countryside to marry and set up households—even before they inherited any land. Not only did the age of marriage fall but more people married. Population growth has its own dynamic, increasing the number of young and fertile people, thus raising significantly the ratio of births to total population.

LIFE ON THE LAND: THE PEASANTRY

Even as the West grew more industrial, the majority of people continued to live on the land. Conditions in the countryside were harsh. Peasants—as farmers of humble origin were called in Europe—still did most of their sowing and harvesting by hand. Millions of tiny farms produced, at most, a bare subsistence living, and families wove, spun, made knives, and sold butter to make ends meet. The average daily diet for an entire family in a good year might amount to no more than two or three pounds of bread—a total of about 3,000 calories daily. By many measures, living conditions for rural inhabitants of many areas in Europe grew worse in the first half of the nineteenth century, a fact of considerable political importance in the 1840s. Rising population put more pressure on the land. Small holdings and indebtedness were chronic problems in regions where peasants scraped by on their own lands. The uncertainties of the market compounded the unpredictability of the weather and the harvest. Over the course of the century some 37 million people—most of them peasants—left Europe, eloquent testimony to the bleakness of rural life. They

> By many measures, living conditions for rural inhabitants of many areas in Europe grew worse in the first half of the nineteenth century, a fact of considerable political importance in the 1840s.

THOMAS MALTHUS ON POPULATION AND POVERTY

Thomas Malthus's enormously influential Essay on the Principle of Population (1798) marked a shift away from Enlightenment optimism about the "perfectibility of society" and a break with a long tradition of considering a large population to be a sign of economic strength. The English cleric (1766–1834) argued that hopes for prosperity ran up against a simple and grim law of nature: population grew more rapidly than food supply. Famine, disease, poverty, infant malnutrition—Malthus considered all of these inevitable, indeed "positive," checks on population. Governments could do nothing to alleviate poverty, he argued; instead the poor had to exercise "moral restraint," postpone marriage, and have fewer children.

I say, that the power of population is indefinitely greater than the power in the earth to produce subsistence for man.

Population, when unchecked, increases in a geometrical ratio. Subsistence increases only in an arithmetical ratio. A slight acquaintance with numbers will shew the immensity of the first power in comparison of the second.

By that law of our nature which makes food necessary to the life of man, the effects of these two unequal powers must be kept equal.

This implies a strong and constantly operating check on population from the difficulty of subsistence. This difficulty must fall somewhere and must necessarily be severely felt by a large portion of mankind.

Through the animal and vegetable kingdoms, nature has scattered the seeds of life abroad with the most profuse and liberal hand. She has been comparatively sparing in the room and the nourishment necessary to rear them. The germs of existence contained in this spot of earth, with ample food, and ample room to expand in, would fill millions of worlds in the course of a few thousand years. Necessity, that imperious all pervading law of nature, restrains them within the prescribed bounds. The race of plants and the race of animals shrink under this great restrictive law. And the race of man cannot, by any efforts of reason, escape from it. Among plants and animals its effects are waste of seed, sickness, and premature death. Among mankind, misery and vice. The former, misery, is an absolutely necessary consequence of it. Vice is a highly probable consequence, and we therefore see it

abundantly prevail, but it ought not, perhaps, to be called an absolutely necessary consequence. The ordeal of virtue is to resist all temptation to evil.

This natural inequality of the two powers of population and of production in the earth, and that great law of our nature which must constantly keep their effects equal, form the great difficulty that to me appears insurmountable in the way to the perfectibility of society. All other arguments are of slight and subordinate consideration in comparison of this. I see no way by which man can escape from the weight of this law which pervades all animated nature. No fancied equality, no agrarian regulations in their utmost extent, could remove the pressure of it even for a single century. And it appears, therefore, to be decisive against the possible existence of a society, all the members of which should live in ease, happiness, and comparative leisure; and feel no anxiety about providing the means of subsistence for themselves and families.

Consequently, if the premises are just, the argument is conclusive against the perfectibility of the mass of mankind.

Thomas Malthus, *An Essay on the Principle of Population*, ed. Philip Appleman, Norton Critical Edition, 2nd ed. (New York, 2004), pp. 19–20.

QUESTIONS FOR ANALYSIS

1. How does Malthus's conception of *nature* differ from that of Enlightenment thinkers?
2. Can you detect Malthus's influence in the documents on p. 691 concerning the 1846 Irish famine?

settled where land was plentiful and inexpensive: the vast majority in the United States and others in places from South America, northern Africa, New Zealand, and Australia to Siberia. In many cases, governments encouraged emigration to ease overcrowding.

The most tragic combination of famine, poverty, and population in the nineteenth century came to Ireland in the Great Famine of 1845–1849. Potatoes, which had come to Europe from the New World, fundamentally transformed the diets of European peasants, providing much more nutrition for less money than corn and grain. They also grew more densely, an enormous advantage for peasants scraping a living from small plots of land. Nowhere did they become more important than in Ireland, where the climate and soil made growing grain difficult and both overpopulation and poverty were rising. When a fungus hit the potato crop—first in 1845 and again, fatally, in 1846 and 1847—no alternate foods were at hand. At least 1 million Irish died of starvation; of dysentery from spoiled foods; or of fever, which spread through villages and the overcrowded poorhouses. Before the famine, tens of thousands of Irish were already crossing the Atlantic to North America; they accounted for one third of all voluntary migration to the New World. In the ten years after 1845, 1.5 people million left Ireland for

> When a fungus hit the potato crop—first in 1845 and again, fatally, in 1846 and 1847—no alternate foods were at hand. At least 1 million Irish died of starvation; of dysentery from spoiled foods; or of fever, which spread through villages and the overcrowded poorhouses.

good. The potato blight also struck in Germany, Scotland, and the Netherlands, but with less catastrophic results. Europe had known deadly famines for centuries. The tragic Irish famine came late, however, at a time when many thought that starvation was receding into the past, and it illustrated just how vulnerable the nineteenth-century countryside remained to bad harvests and shortages.

Changes in the land depended partly on particular governments. States that were more sympathetic to commercialized agriculture passed legislation making it simpler to transfer and reorganize land, encouraging the elimination of small farms and the creation of larger, more efficient units of production. In Britain, over half the total area of the country, excluding wasteland, was composed of estates of 1,000 acres or more. In Spain, the fortunes of large-scale commercial agriculture fluctuated with changes in the political regime: in 1820, the liberal regime passed legislation encouraging the free transfer of land; when absolutism was restored in 1823 the law was repealed. In Russia land was worked in vast blocks; some of the largest landowners possessed over half a million acres. Until the emancipation of the serfs in the 1860s, landowners claimed the labor of dependent peasant populations for as much as several days per week. But the system of serfdom gave

Potato Fields. A scene from the Irish countryside in the late eighteenth century showing potatoes densely planted on a hillside.

THE IRISH FAMINE:
INTERPRETATIONS AND RESPONSES

When the potato blight appeared for the second year in a row in 1846, famine came to Ireland. The first letter excerpted here is from Father Theobald Mathew, a local priest, to Charles Edward Trevelyan, the English official in charge of Irish relief. While Father Mathew attributes the potato blight to "divine providence," he also worries that businessmen opposed to government intervention in a free market will let the Irish starve.

The second and third excerpts are from letters that Trevelyan wrote to other British officials concerned with the crisis. Trevelyan makes clear that, although he does not want the government to bear responsibility for starving its people, he believes that the famine will work to correct "social evils" in Ireland, by which he means everything from families having too many children to farmers failing to plant the right crops. In the nineteenth century, reactions to food crises were reshaped by the rise of new economic doctrines, changing social assumptions, and the shifting relationship between religion and government. These letters provide good examples of those changes and how they affected government officials.

THE REVEREND THEOBALD MATHEW TO TREVELYAN

Cork, 7 August 1846.

Divine providence, in its inscrutable ways, has again poured out upon us the viol [*sic*] of its wrath. A blot more destructive than the simoom of the desert has passed over the land, and the hopes of the poor potato-cultivators are totally blighted, and the food of a whole nation has perished. On the 27th of last month I passed from Cork to Dublin, and this doomed plant bloomed in all the luxuriance of an abundant harvest. Returning on the 3rd instant, I beheld, with sorrow, one wide waste of putrefying vegetation. In many places the wretched people were seated on the fences of their decaying gardens, wringing their hands and wailing bitterly the destruction that had left them foodless.

It is not to harrow your benevolent feelings, dear Mr. Trevelyan, I tell this tale of woe. No, but to excite your sympathy in behalf of our miserable peasantry. It is rumoured that the capitalists in the corn and flour trade are endeavoring to induce government not to protect the people from famine, but to leave them at their mercy. I consider this a cruel and unjustifiable interference.

TREVELYAN TO ROUTH

Treasury, 3 February 1846.

That indirect permanent advantages will accrue to Ireland from the scarcity and the measures taken for its relief, I entertain no doubt; but if we were to pursue these incidental objects to the neglect of any of the precautions immediately required to save the people from actual starvation, our responsibility would be fearful indeed. Besides, the greatest improvement of all which could take place in Ireland would be to teach the people to depend upon themselves for developing the resources of their country, instead of having recourse to the assistance of the government on every occasion. Much has been done of late years to put this important matter on its proper footing; but if a firm stand is not made against the prevailing disposition to take advantage of this crisis to break down all barriers, the true permanent interest of the country will, I am convinced, suffer in a manner which will be irreparable in our time.

TREVELYAN TO LORD MONTEAGLE

To the Right Hon. Lord Monteagle.

My Dear Lord,

I need not remind your lordship that the ability even of the most powerful government is extremely limited in dealing with a social evil of this description. It forms no part of the functions of government to provide supplies of food or to increase the productive powers of the land. In the great institution of the business of society, it falls to the share of government to protect the merchant and the agriculturist in the free exercise of their respective employments; but not itself to carry on those employments; and the condition of a community depends upon the result of the efforts which each member of it makes in his private and individual capacity. . . .

I must give expression to my feelings by saying that I think I see a bright light shining in the distance through the dark cloud which at present hangs over Ireland. A remedy has been already applied to that portion of the maladies of Ireland which was traceable to political causes, and the morbid habits which still to a certain extent survive are gradually giving way to a more healthy action. The deep and inveterate root of social evil remains, and I hope I am not guilty of irreverence in thinking that, this being altogether beyond the power of man, the cure has been applied by the direct stroke of an all-wise providence in a manner as unexpected and unthought of as it is likely to be effectual. God grant that we may rightly perform our part and not turn into a curse what was intended for a blessing. The ministers of religion and especially the pastors of the Roman Catholic Church, who possess the largest share of influence over the people of Ireland, have well performed their part; and although few indications appear from any proceedings which have yet come before the public that the landed proprietors have even taken the first step of preparing for the conversion of the land now laid down to potatoes to grain cultivation, I do not despair of seeing this class in society still taking the lead which their position requires of them, and preventing the social revolution from being so extensive as it otherwise must become.

Believe me, my dear lord, yours very sincerely,

C. E. Trevelyan. Treasury, 9 October 1846.

Noel Kissane, *The Irish Famine: A Documentary History* (Dublin, 1995), pp. 17, 47, 50–51.

QUESTIONS FOR ANALYSIS

1. Would you agree with Trevelyan that dealing with "social evil" was beyond the function of government? What actions could or should governments take in times of famine?
2. In what ways did new economic doctrines, changing assumptions about society, and a shift in the relationship between religion and government affect British government officials?
3. What, concretely, does each of these individuals propose to do about the famine?

---

neither landowners nor serfs much incentive to improve farming or land-management techniques.

European serfdom, which bound hundreds of thousands of men, women, and children to particular estates for generations, made it difficult to buy and sell land freely and created an obstacle to the commercialization and consolidation of agriculture. Yet the opposite was also the case. In France, peasant landholders who had benefited from the the French Revolution's sale of lands and laws on inheritance stayed in the countryside, continuing to work their small farms. Although French peasants were poor, they could sustain themselves on the land. This had important consequences. France suffered less agricultural distress, even in the 1840s, than did other European countries; migration from country to city was slower than in the other nations; far fewer peasants left France for other countries.

Industrialization came to the countryside in other forms. Improved communication networks not only afforded rural populations a keener sense of events and opportunities elsewhere but also made it possible for governments to intrude into the lives of these men and women to a degree previously impossible. Central bureaucracies now found it easier to collect taxes from the peasantry and to conscript sons of peasant families into armies. Some rural cottage industries faced direct competition from factory-produced goods, which meant less work or lower piece rates and falling incomes for families, especially during winter months. In other sectors of the economy, industry spread out

WHAT WERE THE LONG- AND SHORT-TERM CONSEQUENCES OF INDUSTRIALIZATION?

THE SOCIAL CONSEQUENCES OF INDUSTRIALIZATION   693

into the countryside, making whole regions producers of shoes, shirts, ribbons, cutlery, and so on in small shops and workers' homes. Changes in the market could usher in prosperity, or they could bring entire regions to the verge of starvation.

Vulnerability often led to political violence. Rural rebellions were common in the early nineteenth century. In southern England in the late 1820s, small farmers and day laborers joined forces to burn barns and haystacks, protesting the introduction of threshing machines, a symbol of the new agricultural capitalism. They masked and otherwise disguised themselves, riding out at night under the banner of their mythical leader, "Captain Swing." Their raids were preceded by anonymous threats, such as the one received by a large-scale farmer in the county of Kent: "Pull down your threshing machine or else [expect] fire without delay. We are five thousand men [a highly inflated figure] and will not be stopped." In the southwest of France, peasants, at night and in disguise, attacked local authorities who had barred them from collecting wood in the forests. Since forest wood was in demand for new furnaces, the peasants' traditional gleaning rights had come to an end. Similar rural disturbances broke out across Europe in the 1830s and 1840s: insurrections against landlords; against tithes, or taxes to the church; against laws curtailing customary rights; against unresponsive governments. In Russia, serf uprisings were a reaction to continued bad harvests and exploitation.

Many onlookers considered the nineteenth-century cities dangerous seedbeds of sedition. Yet conditions in the countryside and frequent flareups of rural protest remained the greatest source of trouble for governments, and rural politics exploded, as we will see, in the 1840s. Peasants were land poor, deep in debt, and precariously dependent on markets. More important, however, a government's inability to contend with rural misery made it look autocratic, indifferent, or inept—all political failings.

THE URBAN LANDSCAPE

The growth of cities was one of the most important facts of nineteenth-century social history, and one with significant cultural reverberations. Over the course of the nineteenth century, as we have seen, the overall population of Europe doubled. The percentage of that population living in cities tripled—that is, urban populations rose sixfold. Like industrialization, urbanization generally moved from the northwest of Europe to the southeast, but it also followed very specific demands for resources, labor, and transportation. In mining and manufacturing areas or along newly built railway lines, it sometimes seemed that cities (like Manchester, Birmingham, and Essen) sprang up from nowhere. Industrialization swelled the size of port cities such as Danzig (modern Gdansk), Le Havre, and Rotterdam. Most striking to contemporaries was the very rapid expansion of Europe's old cities. Sometimes the rates of growth were dizzying. Between 1750 and 1850, London (Europe's largest city) grew from 676,000 to 2.3 million. The population of Paris went from 560,000 to 1.3 million, adding 120,000 new residents between 1841 and 1846 alone! Berlin, which like Paris became the hub of a rapidly expanding railway system, nearly tripled in size during the first half of the century alone. Such rapid expansion was almost necessarily unplanned, and the combination of unregulated growth and the pressure of numbers brought in its wake new social problems.

Almost all nineteenth-century cities were overcrowded and unhealthy, their largely medieval infrastructures strained by the

Agricultural Disturbances. Violence erupted in southern England in 1830 in protest against the introduction of threshing machines.

burden of new population and the demands of industry. Construction lagged far behind population growth, especially in the working-class districts of the city. In many of the larger cities, old and new, working men and women who had left families behind in the country lived in temporary lodging houses. The poorest workers dwelt in wretched basement or attic rooms, often without any light or drainage. A local committee appointed to investigate conditions in the British manufacturing town of Huddersfield—by no means the worst of that country's urban centers—reported that there were large areas without paving, sewers, or drains, "where garbage and filth of every description are left on the surface to ferment and rot; where pools of stagnant water are almost constant; where dwellings adjoining are thus necessarily caused to be of an inferior and even filthy description; thus where disease is engendered, and the health of the whole town perilled."

Governments gradually adopted measures in an attempt to cure the worst of these ills, if only to prevent the spread of catastrophic epidemics. Legislation was designed to rid cities of their worst slums by tearing them down and to improve sanitary conditions by supplying both water and drainage. Yet by 1850, these projects had only just begun. Paris, perhaps better supplied with water than any other European city, had enough for no more than two baths per person per year; in London, human waste remained uncollected in 250,000 domestic cesspools; in Manchester, fewer than a third of the dwellings were equipped with toilets of any sort.

INDUSTRY AND ENVIRONMENT IN THE NINETEENTH CENTURY

The Industrial Revolution began many of the environmental changes of the modern period. Nowhere were those changes more visible than in the burgeoning cities. Dickens's description of the choking air and polluted water of "Coketown," the fictional city in *Hard Times* (1854) is deservedly well known:

> It was a town of red brick, or of brick that would have been red if the smoke and ashes had allowed it. . . . It was a town of machines and tall chimneys, out of which interminable serpents of smoke trailed themselves forever and ever, and never got uncoiled. It had a black canal in it, and a river that ran purple with ill-smelling dye, and vast piles of building full of windows where there was a rattling and a trembling all day long.

Wood-fired manufacturing and heating for home had long spewed smoke across the skies, but the new concentration of industrial activity and the transition to coal made the air measurably worse. In London especially, where even homes switched to coal early, smoke from factories, railroads, and domestic chimneys hung heavily over the city; and the last third of the century brought the most intense pollution in its history. Over all of England, air pollution took an enormous toll on health, contributing to the bronchitis and tuberculosis that accounted for 25 percent of British deaths. The coal-rich and industrial regions of North America (especially Pittsburgh) and central Europe were other concentrations of pollution; the Ruhr in particular by the end of the century had the most polluted air in Europe.

Toxic water—produced by industrial pollution and human waste—posed the second critical environmenal hazard in urban areas. London and Paris led the way in building municipal sewage systems, though those emptied into the Thames and the Seine. Cholera, typhus, and tuberculosis were natural predators in areas without adequate sewage facilities or fresh water. The Rhine River, which flowed through central Europe's industrial heartland and intersected with the Ruhr, was thick with detritus from coal mining, iron processing, and the chemical industry. Spurred by several epidemics of cholera, in the late nineteenth century the major cities began to purify their water supplies; but conditions in the air, rivers, and land continued to worsen until at least the mid-twentieth century.

SEX IN THE CITY

Prostitution flourished in nineteenth-century cities; in fact it offers a microsom of the nineteenth-century urban economy. At mid-century the number of prostitutes in Vienna was estimated to be 15,000; in Paris, where prostitution was a licensed trade, 50,000; in London, 80,000. London newspaper reports of the 1850s cataloged the elaborate hierarchies of the vast underworld of prostitutes and their customers. Those included entrepreneurs with names like Swindling Sal who ran lodging houses; the pimps and "fancy men" who managed the trade of prostitutes on the street; and the relatively few "prima donnas" or courtesans who enjoyed the protection of rich, upper-middle-class lovers, who entertained lavishly and whose wealth allowed them to move on the fringes of more respectable high society. The heroines of Alexandre Dumas's novel *La Dame aux Camélias* and of Giuseppe

WHAT WERE THE LONG- AND SHORT-TERM CONSEQUENCES OF INDUSTRIALIZATION?

THE SOCIAL CONSEQUENCES OF INDUSTRIALIZATION   695

View of London with Saint Paul's Cathedral in the Distance, by William Henry Crome. Despite the smog-filled skies and intense pollution, many entrepreneurs and politicians celebrated the new prosperity of the Industrial Revolution. As W. P. Rend, a Chicago businessman, wrote in 1892, "Smoke is the incense burning on the altars of industry. It is beautiful to me. It shows that men are changing the merely potential forces of nature into articles of comfort for humanity."

Verdi's opera *La Traviata* (The Lost One) were modeled on these women. Yet the vast majority of prostitutes were not courtesans but rather women (and some men) who worked long and dangerous hours in port districts of cities or at lodging houses in the overwhelmingly male working-class neighborhoods. Most prostitutes were young women who had just arrived in the city or working women trying to manage during a period of unemployment.

THE SOCIAL QUESTION

Against the backdrop of the French Revolution of 1789 and subsequent revolutions in the nineteenth century (as we will see in the following chapters), the new "shock" cities of the nineteenth century and their swelling multitudes posed urgent questions. Political leaders, social scientists, and public health officials across all of Europe issued thousands of reports—many of them several volumes long—on criminality, water supply, sewers, prostitution, tuberculosis and cholera, alcoholism, wet nursing, wages, and unemployment. Radicals and reformers grouped all these issues under a broad heading known as "the social question." Governments, pressed by reformers and by the omnipresent rumblings of unrest, felt they had to address these issues before complaints swelled into revolution. They did so, in the first social engineering: police forces, public health, sewers and new water supplies, inoculations, elementary schools, Factory Acts (regulating work hours), poor laws (outlining the conditions of receiving relief), and new urban regulation and city planning. Central Paris, for instance, would be almost entirely redesigned in the ninteenth century—the crowded, medieval, and revolutionary poor neighborhoods gutted; markets rebuilt; streets widened and lit (see Chapter Twenty-One). From the 1820s on, the social question hung over Europe like a cloud, and it formed part of the backdrop to the revolutions of 1848 (discussed in Chapter Twenty-One). Surveys and studies, early social science, provided direct inspiration for novelists such as Honoré de Balzac, Charles Dickens, and Victor Hugo. In his novel *Les Misérables* (1862), Hugo even used the sewers of Paris as a central metaphor for the general condition of urban existence. Both Hugo and Dickens wrote sympathetically of the poor, of juvenile delinquency, and of child labor; revolution was never far from their minds. The French writer Balzac had little sympathy for the poor, but he shared his fellow writers' views on the corruption of modern life. His *Human Comedy* (1829–1855) was a series of ninety-five novels and stories, including *Eugenie Grandet, Old Goriot, Lost Illusions,* and *A Harlot High and Low.* Balzac was biting in his observations about ruthless and self-promoting young men and about the cold calculations behind romantic liaisons. And he was but one of many writers to use prostitution as a metaphor for what he considered the deplorable materialism and desperation of his time.

THE MIDDLE CLASSES

Who were the new middle classes?

Balzac's many novels aimed to be a sweeping portrait of middle-class society in the early to mid-nineteenth century. They are peopled with characters from all walks of life—journalists, courtesans, small-town mayors, mill owners, shopkeepers, and students. Balzac's main argument throughout is clear: he believed the political changes of the French Revolution and the social changes of industrialization had done no more than replace an older aristocracy (for which Balzac was nostalgic) with a new and materialistic middle class (which he disdained). Older hierarchies expressed as rank, status, and privilege, he believed, had given way to gradations based on wealth, or social class. It is not surprising that Balzac

The middle class was not one homogeneous unit, in terms of occupation or income. Movement within middle-class ranks was often possible in the course of one or two generations.

(although he was deeply conservative) was Karl Marx's favorite novelist. Balzac's point was echoed by many others: by Dickens, whose middle-class characters are often heartless, rigid, and obtuse; by the French artist Honoré Daumier, whose famous caricatures of early nineteenth-century lawyers are veritable portraits of power and arrogance; and by the British novelist William Makepeace Thackeray in his similarly panoramic *Vanity Fair* (1847–1848). One of Thackeray's characters observes caustically that "Ours is a ready-money society. We live among bankers and city big-wigs . . . and every man, as he talks to you, is jingling his guineas in his pocket." Works of literature need to be approached cautiously, for their characters express their authors' points of view. Still, literature and art offer an extraordinary source of social historical detail and insight. And we can safely say that the rising visibility of the middle classes and their new political and social power—lamented by some writers but hailed by others—were central facts of nineteenth-century society.

Who were the middle classes? (Another common term for this social group, the *bourgeoisie,* originally meant city [*bourg*] dweller.) The middle class was not one homogeneous unit, in terms of occupation or income. Movement within middle-class ranks was often possible in the course of one or two generations. Very few, however, moved from the working class into the middle class. Most middle-class success stories began in the middle class itself, with the children of relatively well-off farmers, skilled artisans, or professionals. Upward mobility was almost impossible without education, and education was a rare, though not unattainable, luxury for working-class children. Careers open to talents, that goal achieved by the French Revolution, frequently meant opening jobs to middle-class young men who could pass exams. The examination system was an important path upward within government bureaucracies.

The journey from middle class to aristocratic, landed society was equally difficult. In Britain, mobility of this sort was easier to achieve than on the Continent. Sons from wealthy upper-middle-class families, if they were sent to elite schools and universities and if they left the commercial or industrial world for a career in politics, might actually move up. William Gladstone, son of a Liverpool merchant, attended the exclusive educational preserves of Eton (a private boarding school) and Oxford University, married into the aristocratic Grenville family, and became prime

The Legislative Belly, by Honore Daumier, 1834. Daumier's caricatures of bourgeois politicians prefigure George Grosz's acerbic drawings and paintings of the twentieth century.

minister of England. Yet Gladstone was an exception to the rule, even in Britain, and most upward mobility was much less spectacular.

Nevertheless, the European middle class helped sustain itself with the belief that it was possible to get ahead by means of intelligence, pluck, and serious devotion to work. The Englishman Samuel Smiles, in his extraordinarily successful how-to-succeed book *Self-Help* (1859), preached a gospel dear to the middle class. "The spirit of self-help is the root of all genuine growth in the individual," Smiles wrote. "Exhibited in the lives of many, it constitutes the true source of national vigor and strength." As Smiles also suggested, those who suceeded were obliged to follow middle-class notions of respectability. The middle-classes' claim to political power and cultural influence rested on arguments that they constituted a new and deserving social elite, superior to the common people yet sharply different from the older aristocracy, and the rightful custodians of the nation's future. Thus middle-class respectability, like a code, stood for many values. It meant financial independence, providing responsibly for one's family, avoiding gambling and debt. It suggested merit and character as opposed to aristo-cratic privilege and hard work as opposed to living off noble estates. Respectable middle-class gentlemen might be wealthy, but they should live modestly and soberly, avoiding conspicuous consumption, lavish dress, womanizing, and other forms of dandyish be-havior associated with the aristocracy. We need to emphasize that these were aspira-tions and codes, not social realities. They nonetheless remained key to the middle-class sense of self and understanding of the world.

PRIVATE LIFE AND MIDDLE-CLASS IDENTITY

Family and home played a central role in forming middle-class identity. Few themes were more common in nineteenth-century fiction than men and women pursuing mobility and status by or through marriage. Fami-lies served intensely practical pur-poses: sons, nephews, and cousins were expected to assume responsibil-ity in family firms when it came their turn; wives managed accounts; and parents-in-law provided business connections, credit, inheritance, and so on. The family's role in middle-class thought, however, did not arise only from these practical considerations; family was part of a larger worldview. A well-governed household offered a coun-terpoint to the business and confusion of the world, and families offered continuity and tradition in a time of rapid change.

GENDER AND THE CULT OF DOMESTICITY

There was no single type of middle-class family or home. Yet many people held powerful convictions about how a respectable home should be run and about the rituals, hierarchies, and distinctions that should prevail therein. According to advice manuals, poetry, and middle-class journals, wives and mothers were supposed to occupy a "separate sphere" of life, in which they lived in subordination to their spouses. "Man for the field and woman for the hearth; man for the sword and for the needle she. . . . All else confu-sion," wrote the British poet Alfred Lord Tennyson in 1847. These prescriptions were directly applied to young people. Boys were educated in secondary schools; girls at home. This nineteenth-century con-ception of separate spheres needs to be understood in relation to much longer-standing traditions of paternal authority, which were codified in law. Throughout

Europe, laws subjected women to their husbands' authority. The Napoleonic Code, a model for other countries after 1815, classified women, children, and the mentally ill together as legally incompetent. In Britain, a woman transferred all her property rights to her husband on marriage. Although unmarried women did enjoy a degree of legal independence in France and Austria, laws generally assigned them to the "protection" of their fathers. Gender relations in the nineteenth century rested on this foundation of legal inequality. Yet the idea or doctrine of separate spheres was meant to underscore that men's and women's spheres complemented each other. Thus, for instance, middle-class writings were full of references to spiritual equality between men and women; and middle-class people wrote, proudly, of marriages in which the wife was a "companion" and "helpmate."

It is helpful to recall that members of the middle class articulated their values in opposition to aristocratic customs on the one hand and the lives of the common people on the other. They argued, for instance, that middle-class marriages did not aim to found aristocratic dynasties and were not arranged to accumulate power and privilege; instead they were to be based on mutual respect and division of responsibilities. A respectable middle-class woman should be free from the unrelenting toil that was the lot of a woman of the people. Called in Victorian Britain the "angel in the house," the middle-class woman was responsible for the moral education of her children. It was understood that being a good wife and mother was a demanding task, requiring an elevated character. This belief, sometimes called the "cult of domesticity," was central to middle-class Victorian thinking about women. Home life, and by extension the woman's role in that life, were infused with new meaning. As one young woman put it after reading a popular book on female education, "What an important sphere a woman fills! How thoroughly she ought to be qualified for it—I think hers the more honourable employment than a man's." In sum, the early nineteenth century brought a general reassessment of femininity. The roots of this reassessment lay in early-nineteenth-century religion and efforts to moralize society, largely to guard against the disorders of the French and Industrial Revolutions.

As a housewife, a middle-class woman had the task of keeping the household functioning smoothly and harmoniously. She maintained the accounts and directed the activities of the servants. Having at least one ser-

> Called in Victorian Britain the "angel in the house," the middle-class woman was responsible for the moral education of her children.

vant was a mark of middle-class status; and in wealthier families governesses and nannies cared for children, idealized views of motherhood notwithstanding. The middle classes, however, included many gradations of wealth, from a well-housed banker with a governess and five servants to a village preacher with one. Moreover, the work of running and maintaining a home was enormous. Linens and clothes had to be made and mended. Only the wealthy had the luxury of running water, and others had to carry and heat water for cooking, laundry, and cleaning. Heating with coal and lighting with kerosene involved hours of cleaning, and so on. If the "angel in the house" was a cultural ideal, it was partly because she had real economic value.

Outside the home, women had very few respectable options for earning a living. Unmarried women might act as companions or governesses—the British novelist Charlotte Brontë's heroine Jane Eyre did so and led a generally miserable life until "rescued" by marriage to her difficult employer. But nineteenth-century convictions about women's moral nature, combined as they were with middle-class aspirations to political leadership, encouraged middle-class wives to undertake voluntary charitable work or to campaign for social reform. In Britain and the United States, women

Illustration from a Victorian Book on Manners. Advice books such as this were very popular in the nineteenth century—a mark, perhaps, of preoccupation with status and the emergence of new social groups.

played an important role in the struggle to abolish the slave trade and slavery in the British Empire. Many of these movements also drew on the energies of religious, especially Protestant, organizations, committed to the eradication of social evils and moral improvement. Throughout Europe, a wide range of movements to improve conditions for the poor in schools and hospitals, for temperance, against prostitution, or for legislation on factory hours were often run by women. Florence Nightingale, who went to the Crimean Peninsula in Russia to nurse British soldiers fighting there in the 1850s, remains the most famous of those women, whose determination to right social wrongs compelled them to defy conventional notions of woman's "proper" sphere. Equally famous—or infamous, at the time—was the French female novelist George Sand (1804–1876), whose real name was Amandine Aurore Dupin Dudevant. Sand dressed like a man and smoked cigars, and her novels often told the tales of independent women thwarted by convention and unhappy marriage.

Queen Victoria, who came to the British throne in 1837, labored to make her solemn public image reflect contemporary feminine virtues of moral probity and dutiful domesticity. Her court was eminently proper, a marked contrast to that of her uncle George IV, whose cavalier ways had set the style for high life a generation before. Though possessing a bad temper, Victoria trained herself to curb it in deference to her ministers and her public-spirited, ultrarespectable husband, Prince Albert of Saxe-Coburg. She was a successful queen because she embodied the traits important to the middle class, whose triumph she seemed to epitomize and whose habits of mind we have come to call Victorian. Nineteenth-century ideas about gender had an impact on masculinity as well femininity. Soon after the revolutionary and Napoleonic period, men began to dress in sober, practical clothing—and to see as effeminate or dandyish the wigs, ruffled collars, and tight breeches that had earlier been the pride of aristocratic masculinity.

"PASSIONLESSNESS": GENDER AND SEXUALITY

Victorian ideas about sexuality are among the most remarked-on features of nineteenth-century culture. They have become virtually synonymous with anxiety, prudishness, and ignorance. An English mother counseling her daughter about her wedding night is said to have told her to "lie back and think of the Empire."

Etiquette apparently required that piano legs be covered. Many of these anxieties and prohibitions, however, have been caricatured. More recently, historians have tried to disentangle the teachings or prescriptions of etiquette books and marriage manuals from the actual beliefs of men and women. Equally important, they have sought to understand each on its own terms. Beliefs about sexuality followed from convictions, described earlier, concerning separate spheres. Indeed, one of the defining aspects of nineteenth-century ideas about men and women is the extent to which they rested on scientific arguments about nature. Codes of morality and methods of science combined to reinforce the certainty that specific characteristics were inherent to each sex. Men and women had different social roles, and those differences were rooted in their bodies. The French social thinker Auguste Comte provides a good example: "Biological philosophy teaches us that, through the whole animal scale, and while the specific type is preserved, radical differences, physical and moral, distinguish the sexes." Comte also spelled out the implications of biological difference: "[T]he equality of the sexes, of which so much is said, is incompatible with all social existence. . . . The economy of the human family could never be inverted without an entire change in our cerebral organism." Women were unsuited for higher education because their brains were smaller or because their bodies were fragile. "Fifteen or 20 days of 28 (we may say nearly always) a woman is not only an invalid, but a wounded one. She ceaselessly suffers from love's eternal wound," wrote the well-known French author Jules Michelet about menstruation.

Finally, scientists and doctors considered women's alleged moral superiority to be literally embodied in an absence of sexual feeling, or "passionlessness." Scientists and doctors considered male sexual desire natural, if not admirable—an unruly force that had to be channeled. Many governments legalized and regulated prostitution—which included the compulsory examination of women for venereal disease—precisely because it provided an outlet for male sexual desire. Doctors disagreed about female sexuality, but the British doctor William Acton stood among those who asserted that women functioned differently:

I have taken pains to obtain and compare abundant evidence on this subject, and the result of my inquiries I may briefly epitomize as follows:—I should say that the majority of women (happily for society) are not very much troubled with sexual feeling of any kind. What men are habitually, women are only exceptionally.

MARRIAGE, SEXUALITY, AND THE FACTS OF LIFE

In the nineteenth century sexuality became the subject of much anxious debate, largely because it raised other issues: the roles of men and women, morality, and social respectability. Doctors threw themselves into the discussion, offering their expert opinions on the health (including the sexual lives) of the population. Yet doctors did not dictate people's private lives. Nineteenth-century men and women responded to what they experienced as the facts of life more than to expert advice. The first document provides an example of medical knowledge and opinion in 1870. The second offers a glimpse of the daily realities of family life in 1830.

A FRENCH DOCTOR DENOUNCES CONTRACEPTION

One of the most powerful instincts nature has placed in the heart of man is that which has for its object the perpetuation of the human race. But this instinct, this inclination, so active, which attracts one sex towards the other, is liable to be perverted, to deviate from the path nature has laid out. From this arises a number of fatal aberrations which exercise a deplorable influence upon the individual, upon the family and upon society. . . .

We hear constantly that marriages are less fruitful, that the increase of population does not follow its former ratio. I believe that this is mainly attributable to genesiac frauds. It might naturally be supposed that these odious calculations of egotism, these shameful refinements of debauchery, are met with almost entirely in large cities, and among the luxurious classes, and that small towns and country places yet preserve that simplicity of manners attributed to primitive society, when the *pater familias* was proud of exhibiting his numerous offspring. Such, however, is not the case, and I shall show that those who have an unlimited confidence in the patriarchal habits of our country people are deeply in error. At the present time frauds are practiced by all classes. . . .

The laboring classes are generally satisfied with the practice of Onan [withdrawal]. . . . They are seldom familiar with the sheath invented by Dr. Condom, and bearing his name.

Among the wealthy, on the other hand, the use of this preservative is generally known. It favors frauds by rendering them easier; but it does not afford complete security. . . .

Case X.—This couple belongs to two respectable families of vintners. They are both pale, emaciated, downcast, sickly. . . .

They have been married for ten years; they first had two children, one immediately after the other, but in order to avoid an increase of family, they have had recourse to conjugal frauds. Being both very amorous, they have found this practice very convenient to satisfy their inclinations. They have employed it to such an extent, that up to a few months ago, when their health began to fail, the husband had intercourse with his wife habitually two and three times in twenty-four hours.

The following is the condition of the woman: She complains of continual pains in the lower part of the abdomen and kidneys. These pains disturb the functions of the stomach and render her nervous. . . . By the touch we find a very intense heat, great sensibility to pressure, and all the signs of a chronic metritis. The patient attributes positively her present state to the too frequent approaches of her husband.

The husband does not attempt to exculpate himself, as he also is in a state of extreme suffering. It is not in the genital organs, however, that we find his disorder, but in the whole general nervous system; his history will find its place in the part of this work relative to general disturbances. . . .

Louis-François-Etienne Bergeret. The Preventive Obstacle, or Conjugal Onanism, tr. P. de Marmon (New York, 1870), pp. 3–4, 12, 20–22, 25, 56–57, 100–101, 111–113. Originally published in Paris in 1868.

Death in Childbirth (1830)

Mrs. Ann B. Pettigrew was taken in Labour after returning from a walk in the garden, at 7 o'clock in the evening of June 30, 1830. At 40 minutes after 11 o'clock, she was delivered of a daughter. A short time after, I was informed that the Placenta was not removed, and, at 10 minutes after 12 was asked into the room. I advanced to my dear wife, and kissing her, asked her how she was, to which she replied, I feel very badly. I went out of the room, and sent for Dr. Warren.

I then returned, and inquired if there was much hemorrhage, and was answered that there was. I then asked the midwife (Mrs. Brickhouse) if she ever used manual exertion to remove the placenta. She said she had more than fifty times. I then, fearing the consequences of hemorrhage, observed, Do, my dear sweet wife, permit Mrs. Brickhouse to remove it: To which she assented. . . . After the second unsuccessful attempt, I desired the midwife to desist. In these two efforts, my dear Nancy suffered exceedingly and frequently exclaimed: "O Mrs Brickhouse you will kill me," and to me, "O I shall die, send for the Doctor." To which I replied, "I have sent."

After this, my feelings were so agonizing that I had to retire from the room and lay down, or fall. Shortly after which, the midwife came to me and, falling upon her knees, prayed most fervently to God and to me to forgive her for saying that she could do what she could not. . . .

The placenta did not come away, and the hemorrhage continued with unabated violence until five o'clock in the morning, when the dear woman breathed her last 20 minutes before the Doctor arrived.

So agonizing a scene as that from one o'clock, I have no words to describe. O My God, My God! have mercy on me. I am undone forever. . . .

Cited in Erna Olafson Hellerstein, Leslie Parker Hume, and Karen M. Offen, eds. *Victorian Women: A Documentary Account of Women's Lives in Nineteenth-Century England, France, and the United States*. (Stanford: Stanford University Press, 1981) pp. 193–94, 219–20.

QUESTIONS FOR ANALYSIS

1. The French doctor believed that an increasing population was a sign of a healthy state. Sex was lawful within marriage for procreation, he argued, and artificial birth control interfered with nature. How and why does he describe the birth control methods as "conjugal frauds"?
2. What happened to a "very amorous" couple that practiced birth control? Why did the French doctor think excessive sexual indulgence led to physical and mental deterioration?
3. What problem or problems concern the French doctor? Why?
4. What might be the effects of the conditions described in the second document?

Like other nineteenth-century men and women, Acton also believed that more open expressions of sexuality were disreputable and, also, that working-class women were less "feminine."

Convictions like these reveal a great deal about Victorian science and medicine, but they did not necessarily dictate people's intimate lives. As far as sexuality was concerned, the absence of any reliable contraception mattered more in people's experiences and feelings than sociologists' or doctors' opinions. Abstinence and withdrawal were the only common techniques for preventing pregnancy. Their effectiveness was limited, since until the 1880s doctors continued to believe that a woman was most fertile during and around her menstrual period. Midwives and prostitutes knew of other forms of contraception and abortifacients (all of them dangerous and most ineffective), and surely some middle-class women did as well, but such information was not respectable middle-class fare. Concretely, then, sexual intercourse was directly related to the very

real dangers of frequent pregnancies. In England, 1 in 100 childbirths ended in the death of the mother; at a time when a woman might become pregnant eight or nine times in her life, this was a sobering prospect. Those dangers varied with social class, but even among wealthy and better-cared-for women, they took a real toll. It is not surprising that middle-class women's diaries and letters are full of their anticipations of childbirth, both joyful and anxious. Queen Victoria, who bore nine children, declared that childbirth was the "shadow side" of marriage—and she was a pioneer in using anesthesia!

MIDDLE-CLASS LIFE IN PUBLIC

The public life of middle-class families literally reshaped the nineteenth-century landscape. Houses and their furnishings were powerful symbols of material security. Solidly built, heavily decorated, they proclaimed the financial worth and social respectability of those who dwelt within. In provincial cities they were often freestanding villas. In London, Paris, Berlin, and Vienna, they might be in rows of five- or six-story townhouses or large apartments. Whatever particular shape they took, they were built to last a long time. The rooms were certain to be crowded with furniture, art objects, carpets, and wall hangings. The size of the rooms, the elegance of the furniture, the number of servants—all depended, of course, on the extent of one's income. A bank clerk did not live as elegantly as a bank director. Yet they shared many standards and aspirations, and those common values helped bind them to the same class, despite the differences in their material way of life.

As cities grew, they became increasingly segregated. Middle-class people lived far from the unpleasant sights and smells of industrialization. Their residential areas, usually built to the west of the cities, out of the path of the prevailing breeze and therefore of industrial pollution, were havens from congestion. The public buildings in the center, many constructed during the nineteenth century, were celebrated as signs of development and prosperity. The middle classes increasingly managed their cities' affairs, although members of the aristocracy retained considerable power, especially in central Europe. And it was these new middle-class civic leaders who provided new industrial cities with many of their architectural landmarks: city halls, stock exchanges, museums, opera houses, outdoor concert halls, and department stores. One historian has called these buildings the new cathedrals of the industrial age; projects intended to express the community's values and represent public culture, they were monuments to social change.

The suburbs changed as well. The advent of the railways made outings to concerts, parks, and bathing spots popular. They made it possible for families of relatively moderate means to take one- or two-week-long trips to the mountains or to the seashore. New resorts opened, offering racetracks, mineral springs baths, and cabanas on the beach. Mass tourism would not come until the twentieth century. But the now familiar Impressionist paintings of the 1870s and 1880s testify to something that was dramatically new in the nineteenth century: a new range of middle-class leisures.

WORKING-CLASS LIFE

Like the middle class, the working class was divided into various subgroups and categories, determined in this case by skill, wages, gender, and workplace. Workers'

experiences varied, depending on where they worked, where they lived, and, above all, how much they earned. A skilled textile worker lived a life far different from that of a ditch digger, the former able to afford the food, shelter, and clothing necessary for a decent existence, the latter barely able to scrape by.

Some movement from the ranks of the unskilled to the skilled was possible, if children were provided, or provided themselves, with at least a rudimentary education. Yet education was considered by many parents a luxury, especially since children could be put to work at an early age to supplement a family's meager earnings. Downward mobility from skilled to unskilled was also possible, as technological change—the introduction of the power loom, for example—drove highly paid workers into the ranks of the unskilled and destitute.

Working-class housing was unhealthy and unregulated. In older cities single-family dwellings were

Apartment Living in Paris. This print shows that on the Continent rich and poor often lived in the same buildings, the rich on the lower floors, the poor at the top. This sort of residential mixing was less common in Britain.

broken up into apartments, often of no more than one room per family. In new manufacturing centers, rows of tiny houses, located close by smoking factories, were built back to back, thereby eliminating any cross-ventilation or space for gardens. Crowding was commonplace. A newspaper account from the 1840s noted that in Leeds, a textile center in northern Britain, an ordinary worker's house contained no more than 150 square feet, and that in most cases those houses were "crammed almost to suffocation with human beings both day and night."

Household routines, demanding in the middle classes, were grinding for the poor. The family remained a survival network, in which everyone played a crucial role. In addition to working for wages, wives were expected to house, feed, and clothe the family on the very little money different members of the family earned. A good wife was able to make ends meet even in bad times. Working women's daily lives involved constant rounds of carrying and boiling water, cleaning, cooking, and doing laundry—in one- and two-room crowded, unventilated, poorly lit apartments. Families could not rely on their own gardens to help supply them with food. City markets catered to their needs for cheap goods, but these were regularly stale, nearly rotten, or dangerously adulterated. Formaldehyde was added to milk to prevent spoilage. Pounded rice was mixed into sugar. Fine brown earth was introduced into cocoa.

WORKING WOMEN IN THE INDUSTRIAL LANDSCAPE

Few figures raised more public anxiety and outcry in the nineteenth century than the working woman. Contemporaries worried out loud about the "promiscuous mixing of the sexes" in crowded and humid workshops. Nineteenth-century writers, starting in England and France, chronicled what they considered to be the economic and moral horrors of female labor: unattended children running in the streets, small children caught in accidents at the mills or the mines, pregnant women hauling coal, or women laboring alongside men in shops.

Women's work was not new. Industrialization made it more visible. Women and children formed nearly half the labor force in some of the most modern industries, such as textiles. Women workers were paid less

and were considered less likely to make trouble; manufacturers sought to recruit women mill hands from neighboring villages, paying good wages by comparison with other jobs open to women; in some cases they asked poor-law officials to find "needy and suitable families" for the mills. Most began to work at the age of ten or eleven years old; and once they had children they either put their children out to wet nurses, brought them to the mills, or continued to earn wages doing piecework (paid by the piece rather than by the hour) at home. One of the common causes of labor protest during the period was the introduction of women workers to do jobs considered the property of men.

Still, most women did not work in factories, and the gender division of labor remained remarkably unchanged. Most women labored at home or in small workshops—"sweatshops," as they came to be called—for notoriously low wages, paid not by the hour but by the piece for each shirt stitched or each matchbox glued. And by far the greatest number of unmarried working-class women worked, less visibly, in domestic service, a job that brought low wages and, to judge by the testimony of many women, coercive sexual relationships with male employers or their sons. Domestic service, however, provided room and board. In a time when a single woman simply could not survive on her own wages, a young woman who had just arrived in the city had few choices: marriage, which was unlikely to happen right away; renting a room in a boardinghouse, many of which were often centers of prostitution; domestic service; or living with someone. How women balanced the demands for money and the time for household work varied with the number and age of their children. Mothers were actually more likely to work when their children were very small, for there were more mouths to feed and the children were not yet old enough to earn wages.

Poverty, the absence of privacy, and the particular vulnerabilities of working-class women made working-class sexuality very different from its middle-class counterpart. Illegitimacy rose dramatically between 1750 and 1850. In Frankfurt, Germany, for example, where the illegitimacy rate had been a mere 2 percent in the early 1700s, it reached 25 percent in 1850. In Bordeaux, France, in 1840, one third of the recorded births were illegitimate. Reasons for this increase are

> Most women labored at home or in small workshops—"sweatshops," as they came to be called—for notoriously low wages, paid not by the hour but by the piece for each shirt stitched or each matchbox glued.

difficult to establish. Greater mobility and urbanization meant weaker family ties, more opportunities for young men and women, and more vulnerabilities. Premarital sex was an accepted practice in preindustrial villages, but because of the social controls that dominated village life, it was almost always followed by marriage. These controls were weaker in the far more anonymous setting of a factory town or commercial city. The economic uncertainties of the early industrial age meant that a young workingman's promise of marriage based on his expectation of a job might frequently be difficult to fulfill. Economic vulnerability drove many single women into temporary relationships that produced children and a continuing cycle of poverty and abandonment. Historians have shown, however, that in the city as in the countryside, many of these temporary relationships became enduring ones: the parents of illegitimate children would marry later. Again, nineteenth-century writers dramatized what they considered the disreputable sexuality of the "dangerous classes" in the cities. Some of them attributed illegitimacy, prostitution, and so on to the moral weakness of working-class

people, others to the systematic changes wrought by industrialization. Both sides, however, overstated the collapse of the family and the destruction of traditional morality. Working-class families transmitted expectations about gender roles and sexual behavior: girls should expect to work, daughters were responsible for caring for their younger siblings as well as for earning wages, sexuality was a fact of life, midwives could help desperate pregnant girls, marriage was an avenue to respectability, and so on. The gulf that separated these expectations and codes from those of middle-class women was one of the most important factors in the development of nineteenth-century class identity.

A LIFE APART: "CLASS" CONSCIOUSNESS

The new demands of factory life also created common experiences and difficulties. The factory system, emphasizing as it did standard rather than individual work patterns, denied skilled laborers the pride in craft they

Capital and Labour. In its earliest years, the British magazine *Punch,* though primarily a humorous weekly, manifested a strong social conscience. This 1843 cartoon shows the capitalists enjoying the rewards of their investments while the workers shiver in cold and hunger.

had previously enjoyed. Many workers found themselves stripped of the protections of guilds and formal apprenticeships that had bound their predecessors to a particular trade or place and that were outlawed or sharply curtailed by legislation in France, Germany, and Britain in the first half of the nineteenth century. Factory hours were long; before 1850 workdays were usually twelve to fourteen hours long. Textile mills remained unventilated, so that minute particles of material lodged in workers' lungs. Machines were unfenced and posed a particular danger to child workers, often hired, because of their supposed agility, to clean under and around the moving parts. Surveys by British physicians in the 1840s cataloged the toll that long factory hours and harsh working conditions were taking, particularly on young workers, such as spinal curvature and other bone malformations that resulted from standing hour after hour in unnatural positions at machines. And what was true of factories was true as well of mines, in which over 50,000 children and young people were employed in Britain in 1841. Children were used to haul coal to underground tramways or shafts. The youngest were set to work—often for as long as twelve hours at a stretch—operating doors that regulated the ventilation in the mines. When they fell asleep during long shifts they jeopardized the safety of the entire workforce.

Factories also imposed new routines and disciplines. Artisans in earlier times worked very long hours for very little pay. But at least to some degree, they could set their own hours and structure their own activities, moving from their home workshops to their small garden plots and back again as they wished. In a factory, all "hands" learned the discipline of the whistle. To function efficiently, a factory demanded that all employees begin and end work at the same time. Most workers could not tell time; fewer possessed clocks. None was accustomed to the relentless pace of the machine. To increase production, the factory system encouraged the breaking down of the manufacturing process into specialized steps, each with its own assigned time, an innovation that upset workers accustomed to completing a task at their own pace. Workers began to see machinery itself as the tyrant that had changed their lives and bound them to a kind of industrial slavery. A radical working-class song written in Britain in the 1840s expressed the feeling:

> "There is a king and a ruthless king; / Not a king of the poet's dream; / But a tyrant fell, white slaves know well, / And that ruthless king is steam."

Yet the defining feature of working-class life was vulnerability—to unemployment, sickness, accidents in dangerous jobs, family problems, and spikes in the prices of food. Seasonal unemployment, high in almost all trades, made it impossible to collect regular wages. Markets for manufactured goods were small and unstable, producing cyclical economic depressions; when those came, thousands of workers found themselves laid off with no system of unemployment insurance to sustain them. The early decades of industrialization were also marked by several severe agricultural depressions and economic crises. During the crisis years of the 1840s, half the working population of Britain's industrial cities was unemployed. In Paris, 85,000 went on relief in 1840. Families survived by working several small jobs, pawning their possessions, and getting credit from local wineshops and grocery stores. The chronic insecurity of working-class life helped fuel the creation of workers' self-help societies, fraternal associations, and early socialist organizations. It also meant that economic crises could have explosive consequences (see Chapter Twenty).

By mid-century, various experiences were beginning to make working people conscious of themselves as different from and in opposition to the middle classes. Changes in the workplace—whether the introduction of machines and factory labor, speedups, subcontracting to cheap labor, or the loss of guild protections—were part of the picture. The social segregation of the rapidly expanding nineteenth-century cities also contributed to the sense that working people lived a life apart. Class differences seemed embedded in a very wide array of everyday experiences and beliefs: work, private life, expectations for children, the roles of men and women, and definitions of respectability. Over the course of the nineteenth century all of these different experiences gave concrete, specific meaning to the word *class*.

CONCLUSION

Between 1800 and 1900, the population of Europe doubled. Over that same period, Europe's gross national product more than doubled. Yet even startling statistics on growth only begin to suggest how profoundly Europe's economics, politics, and culture were transformed. The Industrial Revolution was one of the turning points in the history of the world. It did not happen overnight and it did not happen evenly. In

1900 agriculture was still the largest single sector of employment. Villages and farms in vast stretches of Europe could seem virtually untouched by industry. Landowners still exercised enormous political and social clout, even when they had to share power with new elites. Yet the changes were by any measure extraordinary; they reached across the globe and into the private lives of ordinary people. Family structures changed. Industry changed the European landscape and, even more fundamental, humanity's relationship to the environment. As we will see in later chapters, the revolutionary transformations in communication, transportation, and economics had among their many effects the expansion of national states and bureaucracies. Europe's economic surge forward also decisively altered the global balance of power, tilting the scales toward an increasingly industrialized West. Economic development became a new yardstick of value, tech-nology a measure of progress. Increasingly, the West came to be associated with—or even defined as—those nations with advanced industrial economies.

Industrialization created new forms of wealth along-side new kinds of poverty. It also fostered an acute awareness of the disparity between social groups. In the eighteenth century, that disparity would have been described in terms of birth, rank, or privilege. In the nineteenth century, it was increasingly seen in terms of class. Champions and critics of the new order alike spoke of a "class society," and new class identities were another key feature of the period. They were embodied in the growing and overcrowded working-class districts of the new cities, in the daily experiences of work, in new conceptions of respectability, and in middle-class homes. Those new identities would be sharpened in the political events to which we now turn.

KEY TERMS

enclosure	Charles Dickens	sweatshops
spinning jenny	*Human Comedy*	the social question
Irish potato famine	cult of domesticity	

SELECTED READINGS

Berg, Maxine. *The Age of Manufactures: Industry, Innovation, and Work in Britain, 1700–1820*. Oxford, 1985. Good on new scholar-ship and on women.

Bridenthal, Renate, Claudia Koonz, and Susan Stuard, eds. *Becoming Visible: Women in European History*, 2d ed. Boston, 1987. Excellent, wide-ranging introduction.

Briggs, Asa. *Victorian Cities*. New York, 1963. A survey of British cities, stressing middle-class attitudes toward the new urban environment.

Cameron, R. E. *France and the Industrial Development of Europe*. Princeton, 1968. Valuable material on the Industrial Revo-lution outside Britain.

Chevalier, Louis. *Laboring Classes and Dangerous Classes during the First Half of the Nineteenth Century*. New York, 1973. An im-portant, though controversial, account of crime, class, and middle-class perceptions of life in Paris.

Cipolla, Carlo M., ed. *The Industrial Revolution, 1700–1914*. New York, 1976. A collection of essays that emphasizes the wide range of industrializing experiences in Europe.

Cott, Nancy. *The Bonds of Womanhood: "Woman's Sphere" in New England, 1780–1935*. New Haven, Conn., and London, 1977. One of the most influential studies of the para-doxes of domesticity.

Davidoff, Leonore, and Catherine Hall. *Family Fortunes: Men and Women of the English Middle Class, 1780–1850*. Chicago, 1985. A brilliant and detailed study of the lives and ambitions of several English families.

Ferguson, Niall. *The Cash Nexus: Money and Power in the Modern World, 1700–2000* (New York, 2001). A very stimulating and fresh overview of the period.

Ferguson, Niall. "The European Economy, 1815–1914." In *The Nineteenth Century*, ed. T. C. W. Blanning. Oxford and New York, 2000. A very useful short essay.

Gay, Peter. *The Bourgeois Experience: Victoria to Freud*. New York, 1984. A multivolume, path-breaking study of middle-class life in all its dimensions.

Gay, Peter. *Schnitzler's Century: The Making of Middle-Class Culture, 1815–1914*. New York and London, 2002. A synthesis of some of the arguments presented in *The Bourgeois Experience*.

Hellerstein, Erna, Leslie Hume, and Karen Offen, eds. *Victorian Women: A Documentary Account*. Stanford, Calif., 1981. Good collection of documents, with excellent introductory essays.

Hobsbawm, Eric J. *The Age of Capital, 1848–1875.* London, 1975. Among the best introductions.

Hobsbawm, Eric J. *The Age of Revolution, 1789–1848.* London, 1962.

Hobsbawm, Eric, and George Rudé. *Captain Swing: A Social History of the Great English Agricultural Uprising of 1830.* New York, 1975. Analyzes rural protest and politics.

Kemp, Tom. *Industrialization in Nineteenth-Century Europe.* London, 1985. Good general study.

Kindelberger, Charles. *A Financial History of Western Europe.* London, 1984. Emphasis on finance.

Landes, David S. *The Unbound Prometheus: Technological Change and Industrial Development in Western Europe from 1750 to the Present.* London, 1969. Excellent and thorough on technological change and its social and economic context.

Langer, William L. *Political and Social Upheaval, 1832–1852.* New York, 1969. Comprehensive and detailed survey.

McNeill, J. R. *Something New under the Sun: An Environmental History of the Twentieth-Century World.* New York and London, 2000. Short section on the nineteenth century.

Mokyr, Joel. *The Lever of Riches: Technological Creativity and Economic Progress.* New York, 1992. A world history, from antiquity through the nineteenth century

O'Gráda, Cormac. *Black '47 and Beyond: The Great Irish Famine.* Princeton, N.J., 1999.

O'Gráda, Cormac. *The Great Irish Famine.* Cambridge, 1989. A fascinating and recent assessment of scholarship on the famine.

Rendall, Jane. *The Origins of Modern Feminism: Women in Britain, France and the United States, 1780–1860.* New York, 1984. Helpful overview.

Rose, Sonya O. *Limited Livelihoods: Gender and Class in Nineteenth-Century England.* Berkeley, Calif., 1992. On the intersection of culture and economics.

Sabean, David Warren. *Property, Production, and Family Neckarhausen, 1700–1870.* New York, 1990. Brilliant and very detailed study of gender roles and family.

Sabel, Charles, and Jonathan Zeitlin. "Historical Alternatives to Mass Production." *Past and Present* 108 (August 1985): 133–176. On the many forms of modern industry.

Schivelbusch, Wolfgang. *Disenchanted Night: The Instrialization of Light in the Nineteenth Century.* Berkeley, Calif., 1988.

Schivelbusch, Wolfgang. *The Railway Journey.* Berkeley, 1986. Schivelbusch's imaginative studies are among the best ways to understand how the transformations of the nineteenth century changed daily experiences.

Thompson, E. P. *The Making of the English Working Class.* London, 1963. Shows how the French and Industrial Revolutions fostered the growth of working-class consciousness. A brilliant and important work.

Tilly, Louise, and Joan Scott. *Women, Work and the Family.* New York, 1978. Now the classic study.

Valenze, Deborah. *The First Industrial Woman.* New York, 1995. Excellent and readable on industrialization and economic change in general.

Williams, Raymond. *Keywords: A Vocabulary of Culture and Society.* New York, 1976. Brilliant and indispensable for students of culture, and now updated as *New Keywords: A Revised Vocabulary of Culture and Society* (2005), by Lawrence Grossberg and Meaghan Morris.

Zeldin, Theodore. *France, 1848–1945,* 2 vols. Oxford, 1973–1977. Eclectic and wide-ranging social history.

CHAPTER TWENTY

FROM RESTORATION TO REVOLUTION, 1815–1848

WHEN NAPOLEON LEFT THE FIELD OF BATTLE at Waterloo on June 18, 1815, headed back to his Elysée palace and, eventually, to exile on the rocky shore of St. Helena in the South Atlantic, his victorious opponents hoped the age of revolution had ended. The Austrian foreign minister Klemens von Metternich, perhaps the most influential conservative diplomat of the early nineteenth century, called revolution a "sickness," "plague," and "cancer," and with his allies set out to inoculate Europe against any further outbreaks. As Metternich and others saw it, revolution produced war. Peace, therefore, rested on avoiding political turmoil and keeping a firm grip on domestic affairs in all the countries of Europe.

Within Metternich's lifetime, however, waves of revolution would again sweep across Europe—in the 1820s, 1830s, and again in 1848. Conservative efforts to restore the old order succeeded only in part. Why? To begin with, the developments of the eighteenth century proved impossible to reverse. The expansion of an informed public, a development that went back to the Enlightenment, continued. The word *citizen* (and the political rights that it implied) was controversial in the tumultuous aftermath of the French Revolution, but it was difficult to banish the term from the West's vocabulary. More people thought about and participated in politics. New political ideologies and new political groups and allegiances made the early nineteenth century very different from the world that conservatives sought to retrieve. Second, industrialization and the far-reaching changes we surveyed in the last chapter eroded the foundations of the conservative order. Steam presses transformed printing; railroads changed the speed at which newspapers traveled. Cities became centers of political activity. Above all, social changes created new antagonisms and conflicts.

This is not to say that the revolutionaries carried the day. Many of the revolutions failed or were repressed. And although the old order was not restored, conservatism, renewed and adapted, gained a new foothold. This period offers a fascinating case study in sudden changes, vaulting hopes, partial successes, unintended consequences, and political adaptation—for revolutionaries and conservatives alike.

FOCUS QUESTIONS

• What principles guided the Congress of Vienna?

• What were the new political ideologies of the nineteenth century?

• What were the themes of Romanticism as an artistic movement? Did Romanticism have political implications?

• How did the events of 1830 bring the Restoration to an end?

In culture as well as in politics, imagination and a sense of possibility were among the defining characteristics of the first half of the century. Romanticism broke with what many artists considered the cold Classicism and formality of eighteenth-century art. The Enlightenment had championed reason; the Romantics prized subjectivity, feeling, and spontaneity. Their revolt against eighteenth-century conventions had ramifications far beyond literature and painting. The Romantics had no single political creed: some were fervent revolutionaries and others fervent traditionalists who looked to the past, to religion or history for inspiration. Their sensibility, however, infused politics and culture. And to look ahead, their collective search for new means of expression sent nineteenth-century art off in a new direction.

BACK TO THE FUTURE: RESTORING ORDER, 1815–1830

What principles guided the Congress of Vienna?

In 1814 the victorious European powers met at the Congress of Vienna. The peace settlement aimed high, seeking to satisfy the great powers' territorial ambitions and guarantee international tranquility. The congress became a long affair and produced two peace treaties: one in 1814 and another in 1815, after Napoleon's startling escape from exile and his final defeat at Waterloo. Thus conservatives had months to celebrate the defeat of the upstart revolutionary emperor, holding expensive banquets with elaborate aristocratic etiquette, where dignitaries and relieved members of European royalty and nobility jockeyed for positions at the table.

THE CONGRESS OF VIENNA AND THE RESTORATION

The central cast at the congress were the major powers, with Tsar Alexander I (1801–1825) and the Austrian diplomat Klemens von Metternich (1773–1859) in dominant roles. In the wake of Napoleon's fall Russia had emerged as the most powerful continental state. The Russian tsar Alexander, raised in the court of

Catherine the Great, had taken in both Enlightenment doctrines from his French tutor and notions of absolutist authority from his autocratic father, Tsar Paul. In 1801 he succeeded his murdered father, and during the Napoleonic Wars he presented himself as the "liberator" of Europe. Many feared that he would substitute an all-powerful Russia for an all-powerful France. The French prince Charles Maurice de Talleyrand (1754–1838) had a surprisingly strong supporting role, considering that he represented the defeated nation. Talleyrand had been a bishop and a revolutionary, had survived the Terror by going into exile in the United States, and had returned to serve as Napoleon's foreign minister before turning on the emperor and becoming foreign minister to the restored Louis XVIII. That he was present at Vienna testified to his diplomatic skill— or opportunism.

Metternich, the architect of the peace, grew up the son of an Austrian diplomat in the unstable patchwork of the small German states. As a student at the University of Strasbourg, the young Metternich had witnessed popular violence connected with the French Revolution and to this he attributed his lifelong hatred of political change. He had tried to upset the 1807 alliance between Napoleon and Tsar Alexander in the interest of Austria and had played some part in arranging the marriage of Napoleon to the Austrian archduchess Marie Louise. Metternich once said he admired spiders, "always busy arranging their houses with the greatest of neatness in the world." At the Congress of Vienna, he attempted at every turn to arrange international affairs with equal neatness to suit his own diplomatic designs. His central concerns, nearly obsessions, were checking Russian expansionism and preventing political and social change. He feared that Tsar Alexander might provoke revolution to establish Russian supremacy in Europe. For this reason he favored treating the defeated French with moderation. Indeed, at one point he was ready to restore Napoleon as emperor of the French—under the protection and supervision of the Habsburg monarchy. Metternich was an archconservative who readily resorted to harsh repressive tactics, including secret police and spying. Yet the peace he crafted was enormously significant and helped to prevent a major European war until 1914.

The congress sought to restore order and "legitimate" authority. It recognized Louis XVIII as the legitimate sovereign of France and confirmed the restoration of Bourbon rulers in Spain and the two Sicilies. The other monarchs of Europe had no interest in undermining the French restoration: Louis XVIII was their bulwark against revolution. But after Napoleon's Hundred Days in 1815, when the French people seemed to welcome the former emperor back from exile, the allies became sterner; France was compelled to pay an indemnity of 700 million francs and to support an allied army of occupation for five years. Its boundaries were to remain essentially the same as in 1789, more restricted than the "greater France" of the revolutionary years, but the boundaries were not so punitive as they might have been.

The peace built strong barriers against any renewed French expansion. Here the guiding principle was the balance of power, according to which no country should be powerful enough to destabilize international relations. The Dutch Republic, conquered by the French in 1795, was restored as the kingdom of the

THE CONGRESS OF VIENNA

Note how the borders of European nations were established after the final defeat of Napoleon. How had Napoleon's conquests changed the political geography of Europe? Did the delegates at Vienna build on some of Napoleon's ideas for organizing his own empire? Was the settlement reached at Vienna a success? What were the major social and political concerns of the diplomats, and how did they try to address them?

Netherlands. Its territory now reached into Belgium, formerly the Austrian Netherlands. This now substantial power would secure the French border. For the same reason, the allies ceded the German left bank of the Rhine to Prussia. Austria expanded its empire in northern Italy, regaining the territories lost to Napoleon.

The peace of 1815 had especially important consequences for Germany and Poland. Napoleon had reorganized the German states into the Confederation of the Rhine. At Vienna the great powers reduced the number of German states and principalities from over 300 to 39 and linked them with Prussia into a loose German Confederation under the honorary presidency of Austria. This confederation would later become the basis for German unification, but such was not the intent of the peacemakers. To check possible Russian aggression, the other European nations supported the German Confederation and maintained the independent kingdoms of Bavaria, Wurttemburg, and Saxony. Poland, which had been partitioned out of existence by Russia, Austria, and Prussia in the 1790s, became a bone of contention and an object of the great powers' territorial ambitions. In the end, the parties compromised. They created a nominally independent kingdom of Poland but gave control over it to Tsar Alexander. Sections of Poland also went to Prussia and Austria. Prussia took a part of Saxony. Like the other victorious powers, Britain demanded compensation for long years at war and received territories that had been under French dominion in South Africa and South America as well as the island of Ceylon. Britain's military successes in the Napoleonic Wars helped secure her growing commercial empire (see Chapter Nineteen).

The Congress of Vienna also called for a Concert of Europe to secure the peace and create permanent stability. Britain, Austria, Prussia, and Russia formed the Quadruple Alliance (renamed the Quintuple Alliance when France was admitted in 1818). Its members pledged to meet regularly and to cooperate in the suppression of any disturbances—either attempts to overthrow legitimate governments or to change international boundaries. Tsar Alexander I persuaded the allies to join him in the declaration of a Holy Alliance dedicated to establishing justice, Christian charity, and peace. The Holy Alliance only made Europe's leaders suspicious of Alexander's intentions. Many of

> King Leopold of the Belgians, placed on his throne by the allies, observed that war now threatened to become "a conflict of principles"—a conflict sparked by revolutionary ideas and setting "peoples" against emperors.

the aristocratic statesmen gathered at Vienna were steeped in the values of the Enlightenment and wary of crusading. Many might have shared the British foreign minister's belief that the Holy Alliance was "a piece of sublime mysticism and nonsense." In any event, they attempted to forge a different conception of authority, centered on legitimacy. What made a ruler "legitimate" and reinforced his power was not divine right but international treaties, support, and a series of guarantees.

King Leopold of the Belgians, placed on his throne by the allies, observed that war now threatened to become "a conflict of principles"—a conflict sparked by revolutionary ideas, and setting "peoples" against emperors. "From what I know of Europe," he continued, "such a conflict would change her form and overthrow her whole structure." Metternich and many of his fellow diplomats at Vienna dedicated the rest of their lives to seeing that such a conflict would never take place.

REVOLT AGAINST RESTORATION

From the beginning, the restoration met opposition. Much of the early resistance was clandestine, centered in secret organizations driven underground by repressive tactics. In Metternich's own backyard, for instance, the Italian Carbonari (a group that took its name from the charcoal with which members blackened their faces) vowed to oppose the government in Vienna and its conservative allies, whose power extended down into the Italian peninsula. The Carbonari's influence spread through southern Europe and France during the 1820s. Members of the organization identified one another through obscure rituals and met in hiding. Their political views were murky. Some Carbonari called for constitutions, political representation, and other liberal reforms. Others sang the praises of Bonaparte. The former emperor, indeed, became more popular in exile— where he became a mythologized alternative to the restored Bourbons—than he had been during his war-torn reign. Veterans of the Napoleonic armies helped create what came to be called the Napoleonic legend, and military officers were prominent among the ranks of the Carbonari.

In Naples and Piedmont on the Italian peninsula, and especially in Spain and the Spanish Empire, opposition to the restoration turned to revolt. In both cases, restored monarchs who had pledged to respect constitutional reforms abandoned their promises, attempting to squelch elections and reinstate privileges. Alarmed at the threat to Austrian power on the Italian peninsula but determined to have international support, Metternich summoned Austrian, Prussian, and Russian representatives to a meeting. They issued the Troppau memorandum (1820), declaring that they would aid each other in suppressing revolution. France and Britain declined to sign. Although they agreed that any revolution threatened international stability, they did not want their hands tied by treaties. Metternich felt he had diplomatic permission to suppress the uprisings in Italy, forcing the rebels into prison or exile. The French took on the Spanish revolution. They sent 200,000 troops to the Iberian Peninsula in 1823. This force crushed the Spanish revolutionaries and restored the beleaguered King Ferdinand's authority. Ferdinand tortured and publicly executed hundreds of rebels.

REVOLUTION IN LATIN AMERICA

King Ferdinand's empire in Latin America, however, would not be restored. Napoleon's earlier conquest of Spain (1807) had shaken the foundations of Spain's once vast colonial rule. Elites in the Spanish colonies had long chafed under imperial control. They resented taxes, restrictive trade policies, and privileges granted to *peninsulares* (people born in Spain). With the king under house arrest, guarded by French troops, they saw an opportunity for self-government—an opportunity that made them unlikely to accept the restoration of Ferdinand's authority after the French had been driven out. From 1810 on, independence movements gathered momentum, beginning in Río de la Plata (now Argentina), which declared its independence in 1816. The general of the Río de la Plata forces, José de San Martín (1778–1850), led an extraordinary march across the Andes to confront royalist forces and liberate Chile and Peru. The other key military and political figure of the South American revolutions, Simón Bolívar (1783–1830), led a series of uprisings from Venezuela across to Bolivia, eventually joining forces with San Martín. The two men had very different visions of postrevolutionary government. San Martín was a monarchist. Bolívar, however, was a republican, willing to mobilize free people of color and slaves (who made up around one quarter of those fighting the Spanish) as well as Indians to fight against Spanish rule. He aimed to create a large pan-American republic on the continent along the lines of the United States

or the France of Napoleon, whom he admired. Neither leader realized his ambitions. Political revolt unleashed conflict and in many cases violent civil war. On the one hand were elites who aimed only to free themselves from Spain and, on the other, more radical groups that wanted land reform, an end to slavery, or the dismantling of social and racial hierarchies. In the end, the radical movements were repressed, and the newly independent nations were dominated by an alliance of conservative landowners and military officers.

Metternich and his conservative allies would have preferred to prevent the Latin American revolutions. But they ran up against two forces: the newly ambitious United States and Britain. In 1823 the American president James Monroe issued the Monroe Doctrine, warning Europe's great powers that he would regard any effort to intervene in the affairs of the New World as an unfriendly act. The new U.S. doctrine would

Secret Meeting of the Carbonari. Not all resistance took the form of open protest. The Carbonari, an Italian organization named for the charcoal that obscured the faces of its members, was an underground expression of opposition to the restoration.

ATLANTIC OCEAN

MEXICO (1821)

Gulf of Mexico

Mexico City •

CUBA (Spanish)

SANTO DOMINGO (1821)

BRITISH HONDURAS

HAITI (1804)

PUERTO RICO (Spanish)

CARIBBEAN SEA

UNITED PROVINCES OF CENTRAL AMERICA (1823)

• Caracas

GUIANA (British)
SURINAME (Dutch)
GUIANA (French)

VENEZUELA (1830)

• Bogotá

COLOMBIA (1819)

ECUADOR (1822)   Quito •

BRAZIL (1822)

PERU (1824)

• Lima

PACIFIC OCEAN

BOLIVIA (1825)

PARAGUAY (1811)

São Paulo •
Rio de Janeiro •

Asunción •

CHILE (1818)

ARGENTINA (1816)

URUGUAY (1828)

Santiago •

Buenos Aires •   Montevideo •

ATLANTIC OCEAN

0   500   1000 Miles
0   500   1000 Kilometers

NEW NATIONS OF LATIN AMERICA

After Haiti became the Western Hemisphere's second independent nation, many areas of Central and South America also broke away from colonial rule. Whereas the North American colonists had revolted against a vibrant and powerful empire, many of the Latin American revolutionaries took advantage of the disorder created by the Napoleonic Wars. How did Napoleon's grab for the Spanish and Portuguese crowns facilitate the independence movement in South America? How do these revolutions fit into a pattern of Atlantic revolutions established in the late eighteenth century?

have remained a dead letter, however, without British support. Britain was ready to recognize the independence of the South American republics to gain new trading partners and used its navy to keep Spain from intervening. By the middle of the 1820s, then, the once enormous Spanish Empire in the New World had vanished. Portugal's colonial foothold in Latin America also ended when Brazil declared independence in 1822. These revolutions, which brought sweeping changes to the entire continent, arguably marked the end of an age that had opened in 1492. They also dramatized the global significance of the French Revolution of 1789, which reached well beyond the core states of Europe and remade states across a significant portion of the Atlantic world and the Americas.

Russia: The Decembrists

Revolt also broke out in Russia, the heart of the conservative alliance. In 1825, Tsar Alexander died, and uncertainty about his heir sparked an uprising among a group of army officers. Many of the Decembrists, as they were called, came from noble families and were members of elite regiments. Many of them had served in the tsarist armies that drove Napoleon back to France and had been posted there during the years while the peace was being settled. Young and idealistic, they took seriously Tsar Alexander's claim that Russia was the liberator of Europe. If Russia was to assume that kind of "moral greatness," though, it needed to reform. Serfdom contradicted the promise of liberation, and so did the autocratic tsar's monopoly on political power. Not only were Russian peasants enslaved, they argued, but Russian nobles were "slaves to the tsar."

The Decembrists had no single political program. They ranged from constitutional monarchists to Jacobin republicans. The rebels hoped to persuade Alexander's liberal-minded brother Constantine to assume the throne and guarantee a constitution. The attempt failed. Constantine was unwilling to usurp power from the rightful heir, a third brother, Nicholas. The officers themselves failed to attract support from the rank-and-file peasant soldiers, and without such support were doomed to fail. This does not mean that repression was easy. The new tsar, Nicholas I (1825–1855), ruthlessly interrogated hundreds of mutinous soldiers, sentencing many to hard labor and exile. The five leaders, sentenced to death, were more troublesome. Young members of the elite, they were the cream of the crop and attractive candidates for martyrdom. The tsar ordered them hanged at dawn inside the walls of the Peter and Paul Fortress in

St. Petersburg and buried in secret graves, so that neither their funerals nor their gravesites could provide occasions for unrest.

Nicholas went on to rule in the manner of his predecessor. Among his most autocratic acts was the creation of the Third Section, a political police force, to prevent further domestic disorder. Like the secret police of so many conservative powers, it was overstretched and undermanned, but its very existence contributed to a culture of fear and suspicion. Nicholas became perhaps Europe's most uncompromising conservative.

Russia nonetheless showed signs of change. Bureaucracy became more centralized, more efficient, and less dependent on the nobility for political support and everyday operation. The government systematically codified laws in 1832. Rising demand for Russian grain encouraged large landowners to reorganize their estates for more effective production and the state to build railways to transport grain to western markets. Other opponents of the regime, like Alexander Herzen, who admired the Decembrists, would carry on the Decembrists' unresolved political legacy.

Southeastern Europe: Greece and Serbia

The conservative European powers were more open to rebellion when it was directed against rival empires. Such was the case in Greece and Serbia, both provinces in the Balkan region of the sprawling and once powerful Ottoman Empire, where local movements began to demand autonomy and to ask the Europeans to sponsor their struggles. The first Greek uprising of 1821 was led by Alexander Ypsilantis, a former officer in the Russian army who enjoyed close relations with Tsar Alexander. Alexander refused to intervene. A second rising, however, drew not only support from the British government but also hundreds of volunteers from Europe.

Of all the revolts of the early nineteenth century, none captured more attention and sympathy than the Greek war for independence (1821–1827). Why was this conflict significant? The answer has little to do with realities in the Balkans; it lies instead in conceptions of European identity. Christians in Europe cast the rebellion as a part of an ongoing struggle between Christianity and Islam. From a secular point of view, the Greeks' battle could be interpreted as both a crusade for liberty and a struggle to preserve the ancient classical heritage of the land. Increasingly Europeans spoke of Greece as the birthplace of the West. "We are all Greeks," wrote Percy Shelley, the Romantic poet. "Our laws, our literature, our religion, our arts have their roots in Greece. But for Greece . . . we might still have been savages and idolators." George Gordon, better known as Lord Byron (1788–1824), another Romantic poet, fought in Greece. The French Romantic painter Eugène Delacroix memorialized the Greek struggle in his *Massacre at Chios* (1824). "Philhellenic" (devoted to classical Greece) committees in cities across Europe raised money and sent volunteers; men and women in Paris wore blue and white ribbons to show that they had given to the Greek cause. Celebrating the Greeks went hand in hand with demonizing the Turks and reviving the theme of "Turkish despotism," which had figured prominently in the Enlightenment. A British official remarked, "Almost the whole extent of European Turkey presents a dreadful picture of anarchy, rebellion, and barbarism." Europeans of different political persuasions sought to identify themselves with a Greek heritage, which they contrasted with images of Eastern or Islamic tyranny. Europeans, in short, saw the struggle through their own lens.

On the ground in Greece, both sides were ruthless. On several occasions Greek forces besieged Turkish towns and killed the inhabitants. In March 1822, Greeks invaded and proclaimed the independence of the island of Chios, then inhabited by Turks and Greeks who remained loyal to the Ottomans. When Ottoman troops arrived to retake the island, the Greek invaders killed their Turkish prisoners and fled. The Turks took their revenge by slaughtering thousands of Greeks and selling 40,000 more into slavery. Delacroix's *Massacre at Chios*, characteristically, depicted only Turkish brutality.

Ultimately, Greek independence depended on great-power politics. In 1827, British, French, and, now, Russian troops went in against the Turks. (Tsar Alexander's successor, Nicholas, favored intervention.) Two London Protocols, in 1829 and 1830, established Greek independence from the Ottoman Empire, although one year later the allies put the son of the king of Bavaria on the Greek throne.

The struggle between the European powers and the Ottomans similarly helped create the independent nation of Serbia in 1828. With Russian encouragement and aid, Serbia became semi-independent: an Orthodox Christian principality (with significant minority populations) under Ottoman rule. Serbia went on to press for more territory, claiming territories held by another power in the region, the Austrian Empire, a struggle that would escalate at the end of the nineteenth century.

In sum, when the leaders of independence movements could take advantage of conflict between the great powers, or, when those movements fell in line with Europe's ongoing struggle against the Ottoman

The Massacre at Chios, by Eugène Delacroix (1798–1863). Delacroix was a Romantic painter of dramatic and emotional scenes. Here he put his brush to work for the cause of liberty, eulogizing the more than 20,000 Greeks slain by the Turks during the Greek war of independence in 1822. The painting illustrates the fusion of Romanticism and nationalism so characteristic of the period.

CHRONOLOGY

CONCERT OF EUROPE, 1815–1830

Congress of Vienna	1814–1815
Quintuple Alliance	1818
France restores King Ferdinand in Spain	1823
South American revolutions	1810–1825
Decembrist revolt in Russia	1825
Greek war of independence	1821–1827
Serbian independence	1828

WHAT WERE THE NEW POLITICAL IDEOLOGIES OF THE NINETEENTH CENTURY?

TAKING SIDES: NEW IDEOLOGIES IN POLITICS   717

Empire, as in Greece and Serbia, they were more likely to succeed. Both of those new nations, however, were small and fragile. Only 800,000 Greeks actually lived in the new Greek state. Serbia's existence was protected by the great powers until 1856. Moreover, neither of the new nations broke their close links with the Ottomans. Greek and Serbian overseas merchants, bankers, and administrators were still well ensconced in the Ottoman Empire. The region, then, remained one of the borderlands of the West, a multiethnic and multireligious meeting point between Europe and the Ottoman Empire, a region whose peoples alternated between tolerant coexistence and bitter conflict.

TAKING SIDES: NEW IDEOLOGIES IN POLITICS

What were the new political ideologies of the nineteenth century?

These rebellions made it clear that issues raised by the French Revolution were very much alive. Early nineteenth-century politics did not have parties as we know them today. But more clearly defined groups and competing doctrines, or ideologies, took shape during this time. An ideology may be defined as a coherent system of thought regarding the social and politcal order, one that consciously competes with other views of how the world is or should be. The major political ideologies of modern times—conservatism, liberalism, socialism, and nationalism—were first articulated in this period. Their roots lay in earlier times, but ongoing political battles brought them to the fore. So did the Industrial Revolution (see Chapter Nineteen) and the social changes that accompanied it, which proved a tremendous spur to political and social thought. Would the advance of industry yield progress or misery? What were the "rights of man," and who would enjoy them? Did equality necessarily go hand in hand with liberty? This exceptionally fertile period cast up several different responses to these questions. A brief survey of the political horizon will show how alternatives were taking shape and will dramatize how the ground had shifted since the eighteenth century.

Conservatives believed that change had to be slow, incremental, and managed to strengthen the structures of authority. Conserving the past and cultivating tradition would ensure an orderly future.

PRINCIPLES OF CONSERVATISM

At the Congress of Vienna and in the Restoration generally, the most important guiding concept was legitimacy. Legitimacy had broad appeal as a general antirevolutionary policy. It might be best understood as a code word for a new political order. Conservatives aimed to make legitimate—and thus to solidify—both the monarchy's authority and a hierarchical social order. The most thoughtful conservatives of the period did not believe that the old order would survive completely intact or that time could be reversed, especially after the events of the 1820s made it clear that the Restoration would be challenged. They did believe, however, that the monarchy guaranteed political stability, that the nobility were the rightful leaders of the nation, and that both needed to play active and effective roles in public life. They insisted that, as a matter of strategy, the nobility and the Crown shared a common interest, despite their disagreements in the past. Conservatives believed that change had to be slow, incremental, and managed to strengthen the structures of authority. Conserving the past and cultivating tradition would ensure an orderly future.

Edmund Burke's writings became a point of reference for nineteenth-century conservatives. His *Reflections on the Revolution in France* was more influential in this new context than it had been during the 1790s, when it was first published. Burke did not oppose all change; he had argued, for instance, that the British should let the North American colonies go. But he opposed talk of natural rights, which he considered dangerous abstractions. He believed enthusiasm for constitutions to be misguided and the Enlightenment's emphasis on what he called the "conquering power of reason" to be dangerous. Instead, Burke counseled deference to experience, tradition, and history. Other conservatives, such as the French writers Joseph de Maistre (1753–1821) and Louis-Gabriel-Ambroise Bonald (1754–1840), penned carefully elaborated defenses of absolute monarchy and its main pillar of support, the Catholic Church. De Maistre, for instance, blamed the Enlightenment's critique of the Catholic Church for the French Revolution, and he assailed Enlightenment individualism for ignoring the bonds and collective institutions (the church, for instance, or family) that he believed held society together. As conservatives saw it, monarchy, aristocracy, and the church were the mainstays of the social and political order. Those institutions needed to stand together in face of the challenges of the new century.

Conservatism was not simply the province of intellectuals. A more broadly based revival of religion in the early nineteenth century also expressed a popular reaction against revolution and an emphasis on order, discipline, and tradition. What was more, conservative thinkers also exercised influence well beyond their immediate circle. Their emphasis on history, on the untidy and unpredictable ways in which history unfolded, and their awareness of the past became increasingly central to social thought and artistic visions of the first half of the century.

LIBERALISM

Liberalism's core was a commitment to individual liberties, or rights. Liberals believed that the most important function of government was to protect liberties and that doing so would benefit all, promoting justice, knowledge, progress, and prosperity. Liberalism had three components. First, liberalism called for equality before the law, which meant ending traditional privileges and the restrictive power of rank and hereditary authority. Second, liberalism held that government needed to be based on political rights and the consent of the governed. Third, in economics, liberalism meant a belief in the benefits of unfettered economic activity, or economic individualism.

The roots of legal and political liberalism lay in the late seventeenth century, in the work of John Locke, who had defended the English Parliament's rebellion against absolutism and the "inalienable" rights of the British people (see Chapter Fifteen). Liberalism had been developed by the Enlightenment writers of the eighteenth century and, especially, the founding texts of the American and French Revolutions (the Declaration of Independence and the Declaration of the Rights of Man). Freedom from arbitrary authority, imprisonment, and censorship; freedom of the press; the right to assemble and deliberate: these principles were the starting points for nineteenth-century liberalism. Liberals believed in individual rights, that those rights were inalienable, and that they should be guaranteed in written constitutions. (Conservatives, as we saw earlier, considered constitutions abstract and dangerous.) Most liberals called for constitutional as opposed to hereditary monarchy; all agreed that a monarch who abused power could legitimately be overthrown.

Liberals advocated direct representation in government—at least for those who had the property and public standing to be trusted with the responsibilities of power. Liberalism by no means required democracy. To the contrary, who should have the right to vote was a hotly debated issue. Nineteenth-century liberals, with fresh memories of the French Revolution of 1789, were torn between their belief in rights and their fears of political turmoil. They considered property and education essential prerequisites for participation in politics. Wealthy liberals opposed extending the vote to the common people. To demand universal male suffrage was radical indeed, and to speak of enfranchising women or people of color even more so. As far as slavery was concerned, nineteenth-century liberalism inherited the contradictions of the Enlightenment. Belief in individual liberty collided with vested economic interests, determination to preserve order and property, and increasingly "scientific" theories of racial inequality (see Chapter Nineteen).

Economic liberalism was newer. Its founding text was Adam Smith's *Wealth of Nations* (1776), which attacked mercantilism (the government practice of regulating manufacturing and trade in order to raise revenues) in the name of free markets. Smith's argument that the economy should be based on a "system of natural liberty" was reinforced by a second generation of economists and popularized in journals such as the *Economist*, founded in 1838. The economists (or political economists, as they were called) sought to identify basic economic laws: the law of supply and demand, the balance of trade, the law of diminishing returns, and so on. They argued that economic policy had to begin by recognizing these laws. David Ricardo (1772–1823) of Britain, for example, set out laws of wages and of rents, trying to determine the long-run outcomes of fluctuations in each. The political economists believed that economic activity should be unregulated. Labor should be contracted freely, unhampered by guilds or unions. Property should be unencumbered by feudal restrictions. Goods should circulate freely, which meant, concretely, an end to government-granted monopolies and traditional practices of regulating markets, especially in valuable commodities such as grain, flour, or corn. At the time of the Irish famine, for instance, their writings played a role in hardening opposition to government intervention or relief (see Chapter Nineteen). The functions of the state should be kept to a minimum. Government's role was to preserve order and protect property but not to interfere with the natural play of economic forces, a doctrine known as *laissez-faire*, which

WHAT WERE THE NEW POLITICAL IDEOLOGIES OF THE NINETEENTH CENTURY?

TAKING SIDES: NEW IDEOLOGIES IN POLITICS   719

translates, roughly, as "leave things to go on their own." This strict opposition to government intervention makes nineteenth-century liberalism significantly different from liberalism as we know it today.

Liberty and freedom meant different things in different countries. In lands occupied by other powers, liberal parties demanded freedom from foreign rule. The colonies of Latin America demanded liberty from Spain, and similar struggles set Greece and Serbia against the Ottoman Empire, northern Italy against the Austrians, Poland against Russian rule, and so on. In central and southeastern Europe, liberty meant eliminating feudal privilege and allowing at least the educated elite access to political power, more rights for local parliaments, and creating representative national political institutions. Some cited the British system of government as a model; others the French Declaration

Adam Smith pointing to his book *The Wealth of Nations* (1776). Smith was an Enlightenment thinker whose work was popularized in the nineteenth century, and he helped to establish "political economy," or economics.

of the Rights of Man. Most shied away from the radicalism of the French Revolution. The issue was constitutional, representative government. In such countries as Russia, Prussia, and France under the restored Bourbon monarchy, liberty meant political freedoms, such as the right to vote, assemble, and print political opinions without censorship.

In Great Britain, where political freedoms were relatively well established, liberals focused on expanding the franchise, on laissez-faire economics and free trade, and on reforms aimed at creating limited and efficient government. In this respect, one of the most influential British liberals was Jeremy Bentham (1748–1832). Bentham's major work, *The Principles of Morals and Legislation* (1789), illustrates how nineteenth-century liberalism continued the Enlightenment legacy and also transformed it. Unlike, for instance, Smith, Bentham did not believe that human interests were naturally harmonious or that a stable social order could emerge naturally from a body of self-interested individuals. Instead he proposed that society adopt the organizing principle of utilitarianism. Social institutions and laws (an electoral system, for instance, or a tariff) should be measured according to their social usefulness—according to whether they produced the "greatest happiness of the greatest number." If a law passed this test, it could remain on the books; if it failed, it should be jettisoned. Utilitarians acknowledged the importance of the individual. Each individual best understood his or her own interests and was, therefore, best left free, whenever possible, to pursue those interests as he or she saw fit. Only when an individual's interests conflicted with the interests—the happiness—of the greatest number was individual freedom to be curtailed. The intensely practical spirit of utilitarianism enhanced its influence as a creed for reform.

RADICALISM, REPUBLICANISM, AND EARLY SOCIALISM

The liberals were flanked on their left by two radical groups: republicans and socialists. Whereas liberals advocated a constitutional monarchy (in the name of stability and keeping power in hands of men of property), republicans, as their name implies, pressed further, demanding a government by the people, an expanded franchise, and democratic participation in politics. Where liberals called for individualism and laissez-faire, socialists put the accent on equality. To put it in the terms that were used at the time, socialists raised the "social question." How could growing social inequality and the miseries of working people be remedied? The social question, they insisted, was an urgent political matter. Socialists offered varied responses to this question and different ways of redistributing economic and social power. These solutions ranged from cooperation and new ways of organizing everyday life to collective ownership of the means of production; some were speculative, others very concrete.

Socialism was a nineteenth-century system of thought and a response in large measure to the visible problems ushered in by industrialization: the intensification of labor, the poverty of working-class neighborhoods in industrial cities, and the widespread perception that a hierarchy based on rank and privilege had been replaced by one based on social class. For the socialists, the problems of industrial society were not incidental; they arose from the core principles of competition, individualism, and private property. The socialists did not oppose in-

> To put it in the terms that were used at the time, socialists raised the "social question." How could growing social inequality and the miseries of working people be remedied?

dustry and economic development. On the contrary, what they took from the Enlightenment was a commitment to reason and human progress. They believed society could be both industrial and humane.

These radical thinkers were often explicitly utopian. Robert Owen, a wealthy industrialist turned reformer, bought a large cotton factory at New Lanark in Scotland and proceeded to organize the mill and the surrounding town according to the principles of cooperation rather than those of profitability. New Lanark organized good housing and sanitation, good working conditions, child care, free schooling, and a system of social security for the factory's workers. Owen advocated a general reorganization of society on the basis of cooperation and mutual respect, and he tried to persuade other manufacturers of the rightness of his cause. The Frenchman Charles Fourier, too, tried to organize utopian communities based on the abolition of the wage system, the division of work accord-

Quadrille Dancing at Lanark, Robert Owen's Model Community. Owen's Scottish experiment with cooperative production and community building, including schooling for infants, was only one of many utopian ventures in early-nineteenth-century Europe and North America.

WHAT WERE THE NEW POLITICAL IDEOLOGIES OF THE NINETEENTH CENTURY?

TAKING SIDES: NEW IDEOLOGIES IN POLITICS   721

ing to people's natural inclinations, the complete equality of the sexes, and collectively organized child care and household labor. The charismatic socialist Flora Tristan (1803–1844) toured France speaking to workers about the principles of cooperation and the equality of men and women. Numerous men and women followed like-minded leaders into experimental communities. That so many took utopian visions seriously is a measure of people's unhappiness with early industrialization and of their conviction that society could be organized along radically different lines.

Other socialists proposed simpler, practical reforms. Louis Blanc, a French politician and journalist, campaigned for universal male suffrage with an eye to giving working-class men control of the state. Instead of protecting private property and the manufacturing class, the transformed state would become "banker of the poor," extending credit to those who needed it and establishing "associations of production," a series of workshops governed by laborers that would guarantee jobs and security for all. Such workshops were established, fleetingly, during the French Revolution of 1848. So were clubs promoting women's rights. Pierre-Joseph Proudhon (1809–1865) also proposed establishing producers' cooperatives that would sell goods at a price workers could afford, working-class credit unions, and so on. Proudhon's "What Is Property?"— to which the famous answer was "property is theft"— became one of the most widely read socialist pamphlets, familiar to artisans, laborers, and middle-class intellectuals, including Karl Marx. As we will see, a period of economic depression and widespread immiseration in the 1840s brought the socialists many more working-class followers.

KARL MARX'S SOCIALISM

The father of modern socialism, Karl Marx (1818–1883), was barely known in the early nineteenth century. His reputation rose later, after 1848, when a wave of revolutions and violent confrontation seemed to confirm his distinctive theory of history and make earlier socialists' emphasis on cooperation, setting up experimental communities, and peaceful reorganization of industrial society seem naive.

Marx grew up in Trier, in the western section of Germany, in a region and a family keenly interested in the political debates and movements of the revolutionary era. His family was Jewish, but his father had converted to Protestantism to be able to work as a lawyer. Marx studied law briefly at the University of Berlin before turning instead to philosophy and particularly the ideas of Georg Wilhelm Friedrich Hegel. With the so-called Young Hegelians, a group of rebellious students who chafed under the narrow thinking of a deeply conservative Prussian university system, Marx appropriated Hegel's concepts for his radical politics. His radicalism (and atheism, for he repudiated all his family's religious affiliations) made it impossible for him to get a post in the university. He became a journalist, writing now-famous articles on, for instance, peasants "stealing" wood from forests that used to be common land. From 1842 to 1843 he edited the *Rhineland Gazette* (*Rheinische Zeitung*). The paper's criticism of legal privilege and political repression put it on a collision course with the Prussian government, which closed it down and sent Marx into exile—first in Paris, then Brussels, and eventually London.

While in Paris Marx studied early socialist theory, economics, and the history of the French Revolution. He also began a lifelong intellectual and political partnership with Friedrich Engels (1820–1895). Engels was the son of a textile manufacturer from the German Rhineland and had been sent to learn business with a merchant firm in Manchester, one of the heartlands of England's Industrial Revolution (see Chapter Nineteen). Rather than follow in his father's footsteps, however, Engels took up his pen to denounce the miserable working and living conditions in Manchester and what he saw as the systematic inequalities of capitalism (*The Condition of the Working Classes in England*, 1844). Marx and Engels joined a small international group of radical artisans called the League of the Just, in 1847 renamed the Communist League. The league asked Marx to draft a statement of its principles, published in 1848 as the *Communist Manifesto*.

The *Communist Manifesto* laid out Marx's theory of history in short form. World history had passed through three major stages, each characterized by conflict between social groups: master and slave in ancient slavery, lord and serf in feudalism, and bourgeois and proletariat in capitalism. According to Marx's theory, the stage of feudal or aristocratic property relations had ended in 1789, when the French Revolution overthrew the old order, ushering in bourgeois political power and industrial capitalism. In the *Communist Manifesto*, Marx and Engels admired the revolutionary accomplishments of capitalism, saying that the bourgeoisie had "created more impressive and more colossal productive forces than had all preceding generations together." But, they argued, the revolutionary character of capitalism would also undermine the bourgeois economic order.

As capital became more concentrated in the hand of the few, a growing army of wage workers would become increasingly aware of its economic and political disenfranchisement; struggle between these classes was central to industrial capitalism itself. Eventually, the *Communist Manifesto* predicted, recurring economic crises, caused by capitalism's unending need for new markets and the cyclical instability of overproduction, would bring capitalism to collapse. Workers would seize the state, reorganize the means of production, abolish private property, and eventually create a communist society.

What was distinctive about Marx's version of socialism? It took up the disparity between public proclamations of progress and workers' daily experiences in a systematic, scholarly manner. Marx was an inexhaustible reader and thinker, with a extraordinarily broad range. He took insights where he found them: in British economics, French history, and German philosophy. He wove others' ideas that labor was the source

of value and that property was expropriation into a new theory of history that was also a thoroughgoing critique of nineteenth-century liberalism.

From Hegel Marx imported the view of history as a dynamic process, with an inner logic, moving toward human freedom. (This is a good example of the larger influence of conservative historical thinking.) In Hegel's view, the historical process did not unfold in any simple and predictable way. Instead history proceeded "dialectically" or through conflict. Hegel saw the conflict as one between ideas: a "thesis" produced an "anti-thesis," and the clash between the two created a distinctive and new "synthesis." Marx applied Hegel's notions to the specifics of history. He did not begin with ideas, as Hegel had, but rather with the material (social and economic) forces that he believed drove history. Hence the term *dialectical materialism*, which is used to describe Marxist thought.

Marx synthesized international cross-currents of European thought and politics in the 1840s. His concerns with the relationship between economics and politics were characteristic of his time. Like other radicals, he addressed the gap between liberal demands for freedom and liberal silence on social equality. He was only one of many socialists, however, and before the revolutions of 1848 one of the least well known. Those revolutions erupted the same year the *Communist Manifesto* was published but well before it had any effect. Only in the second half of the century would Marxism become the leading socialist doctrine.

CITIZENSHIP AND COMMUNITY: NATIONALISM

Of all the political ideologies of the early nineteenth century, nationalism is most difficult to grasp. Its premises are elusive. What, exactly, counted as a nation? Who demanded a nation, and what did their demand mean? In the early nineteenth century, nationalism was usually aligned with liberalism. As the century progressed, however, it became increasingly clear that nationalism could be molded to fit any doctrine.

The meaning of *nation* has changed over time. The term comes from the Latin verb *nasci*, "to be born," and suggests "common birth." In sixteenth-century England, the nation designated the aristocracy, or those who shared noble birthright. The French nobility also referred to itself as the nation. Those earlier and unfamiliar usages are important. They highlight the most significant development of the late eighteenth and

Karl Marx, 1882. Despite the unusual smile in this portrait, Marx was near the end of his life, attempting to recuperate in Algeria from sickness and the deaths of his wife and daughter.

WHAT WERE THE NEW POLITICAL IDEOLOGIES OF THE NINETEENTH CENTURY?

TAKING SIDES: NEW IDEOLOGIES IN POLITICS   723

early nineteenth centuries: the French Revolution re-defined nation to mean the people, or the sovereign people. The revolutionaries of 1789 boldly claimed that the nation, and no longer the king, was the sovereign power. *Vive la nation*, or "long live the nation"—a phrase found everywhere, from government decrees to revolutionary festivals, engravings, and memorabilia—celebrated a new political community, not a territory or an ethnicity. Philosophically, the French revolutionaries and the others who developed their views took from Jean-Jacques Rousseau the argument that a regenerated nation, based on the equality of its members (on the limits of that equality, see Chapter Eighteen), was not only more just but also more powerful. On a more concrete level, the revolutionaries built a national state, army, and legal system whose jurisdiction trumped the older regional powers of the nobility, a national system of law, and a national army. In the aftermath of the French Revolution of 1789, the nation became what one historian calls "the collective image of modern citizenry."

In the early nineteenth century, then, *nation* symbolized legal equality, constitutional government, and unity, or an end to feudal privileges and divisions. Conservatives disliked the term. National unity and the creation of national political institutions threatened to erode the local power of aristocratic elites. New nations rested on constitutions, which, as we have seen, conservatives considered dangerous abstractions. Nationalism became an important rallying cry for liberals across Europe in the early nineteenth century precisely because it was associated with political transformation. It celebrated the achievements and political awakening of the common people.

Nationalism also went hand in hand with liberal demands for economic modernity. Economists, such as the influential German Friedrich List (1789–1846), sought to develop national economies and national infrastructures: larger, stronger, better integrated, and more effective systems of banking, trade, transportation, production, and distribution. List linked ending the territorial fragmentation of the German states and the development of manufacturing to "culture, prosperity, and liberty."

Nationalism, however, could easily undermine other liberal values. When liberals insisted on the value and importance of individual liberties, those committed to

building nations replied that their vital task might require the sacrifice of some measure of each citizen's freedom. The Napoleonic army, a particularly powerful symbol of nationhood, appealed to conservative proponents of military strength and authority as well as to liberals who wanted an army of citizens.

Nineteenth-century nationalists wrote as if national feeling were natural, inscribed in the movement of history. They waxed poetic about the sudden awakening of feelings slumbering within the collective consciousness of a "German," an "Italian," a "French," or a "British" people. This is misleading. National identity (like religious, gender, or ethnic identities) developed and changed historically. It rested on specific nineteenth-century political and economic developments; on rising literacy; on the creation of national institutions such as schools or the military; and on the new importance of national rituals, from voting to holidays and village festivals. Nineteenth-century governments sought to develop national feeling, to link their peoples more closely to their states. State-supported educational systems taught a "national" language, fighting the centrifugal forces of traditional dialects. Italian became the official language of the Italian nation, despite the fact that only 2.5 percent of the population spoke it. In other words, even a minority could define a national culture. Textbooks and self-consciously nationalist theater, poetry, and painting helped elaborate and sometimes "invent" a national heritage.

> Nationalism became an important rallying cry for liberals across Europe in the early nineteenth century precisely because it was associated with political transformation. It celebrated the achievements and political awakening of the common people.

Political leaders associated the nation with specific causes. But ordinary activities, such as reading a daily newspaper in the morning, helped people imagine and identify with their fellow citizens. As one influential historian puts it, "[A]ll communities larger than primordial villages of face-to-face contact (and perhaps even these) are imagined." The nation is imagined as "limited," "sovereign", and "finally, it is imagined as a community, because regardless of the actual inequality and exploitation that may prevail . . . , the nation is always conceived as a deep, horizontal comradeship." The different meanings of *nationhood*, the various political beliefs it evoked, and the powerful emotions it tapped made nationalism exceptionally unpredictable.

These were the principal political ideologies of the early nineteenth century. They were rooted in the

MAJOR EUROPEAN LANGUAGE GROUPS, c. 1850

Examine the distribution of language groups throughout Europe. What is the relationship between language and nationalism? How did states encourage the development of a national identity? Why would the divisions between language groups have created problems for the European empires?

eighteenth century but brought to the forefront by the political turmoil of the early nineteenth century. Some nineteenth-century ideologies were continuations of the French revolutionary trio: liberty (from arbitrary authority), equality (or the end of legal privi-

lege), and fraternity (the creation of new communities of citizens). Others, like conservatism, were reactions against the French Revolution. All could be reinterpreted. All became increasingly common points of reference as the century unfolded.

WHAT WERE THE THEMES OF ROMANTICISM AS AN ARTISTIC MOVEMENT?

CULTURAL REVOLT: ROMANTICISM   725

CULTURAL REVOLT: ROMANTICISM

What were the themes of Romanticism as an artistic movement? Did Romanticism have political implications?

Romanticism, the most significant cultural movement of the early nineteenth century, also took form in the polarized aftermath of Enlightenment and revolution. An exceptionally diverse intellectual movement, it touched all the arts and permeated politics as well. Put most simply, it marked a reaction against the Classicism of the eighteenth century and against many of the values of the Enlightenment. Eighteenth-century Classical art had aspired to reason, discipline, and harmony. Romanticism, in contrast, stressed emotion, freedom, and imagination. Romantic artists prized the individual, individuality, and subjective experience; many were personally rebellious and sought out intense experiences. In contrast to Enlightenment thinkers, they considered intuition, emotion, and feelings better guides to truth—and to human happiness—than reason and logic.

BRITISH ROMANTIC POETRY

Romanticism developed earliest in England and Germany, where it arose as part of a reaction against the Enlightenment and French classicism; it came later to France. Like any intellectual or artistic movement, Romanticism did not completely break with its predecessors. Indeed, the early Romantics developed themes first raised by dissenting figures of the Enlightenment, especially Jean-Jacques Rousseau (see Chapter Seventeen). Rousseau's key themes—nature, simplicity, and feeling—ran through the very influential *Lyrical Ballads* (1798) of William Wordsworth (1770–1850) and Samuel Taylor Coleridge (1772–1834). Wordsworth considered emotions, or soul, the core of humanity; for him, poetry was "the spontaneous overflow of powerful feelings." Like Rousseau, Wordsworth also emphasized the ties of compassion and feeling that bind all of humankind, regardless of social class. "We have all of us one human heart," he wrote; "men who do not wear fine clothes can feel deeply." Like Rousseau, Wordsworth considered nature to be humanity's most trustworthy teacher, and he considered the experience of nature the source of true feeling. Poetic insights could be inspired by landscapes and the memories those evoked—in Wordsworth's case the wild hills and tumbledown cottages of England's Lake District. At the head of his poem "The Ruined Cottage," Wordsworth quoted from the Scottish Romantic poet Robert Burns:

> Give me a spark of Nature's fire,
> 'Tis the best learning I desire . . .
> My muse, though homely in attire,
> May touch the heart.

The Lake Poets, as Wordsworth and Coleridge were sometimes called, offered one key theme of nineteenth-century Romanticism: a view of nature that rejected the abstract mechanism of eighteenth-century thought. Nature was not a system whose operations were to be observed with a critical eye. Instead, humanity was immersed in nature; the human soul needed to be opened to nature's sublime (literally, inspiring wonder and awe) power.

Like Wordsworth, the poet William Blake (1757–1827) championed the individual imagination and poetic vision and saw both as transcending the narrow limits of the material world. Blake was a fierce and brilliant critic of industrial society and its daily corruptions, of the factories (which he called the "dark satanic mills") that blighted the English landscape, and of the values of a market culture in which everything was for sale. For Blake, imagination did not just lead to poetry. Imagination could awaken human sensibilities and sustain belief in different values, breaking humanity's "mind-forged manacles," or constraints of the contemporary world. In this, Blake's poetry paralleled early socialist efforts to imagine a better world. And like many Romantics, Blake looked back to a past in which he thought society had been more organic, united, and humane.

English Romanticism reached its height with the next generation of English romantic poets—George Gordon, Lord Byron (1788–1824), Percy Bysshe Shelley (1792–1822), and John Keats (1795–1821). Some of these poets' lives and loves appealed as much as their writing, for their adventures seemed to personify their poetic themes. Lord Byron, for instance, took the Romantic emphasis on creativity, imagination, and spontaneity to new levels. Poetry, he wrote, was the "lava of the imagination, whose eruption prevents an earthquake." Byron was also an aristocrat, well known as rich, handsome, and defiant of nineteenth-century English conventions. His countless love affairs

Newton, by William Blake, 1795. Blake was also a brilliant graphic artist. Here he depicts Sir Isaac Newton shrouded in darkness, distracted by his scientific calculations from the higher sphere of the imagination. Blake's image is a romantic critique of Enlightenment science, for which Newton had become a hero.

helped create the association between Romanticism and rebellion against conformity and inhibition. Those affairs were hardly carefree. Byron entered into an ill-starred marriage with an unhappy woman, whom he treated cruelly and drove away after a year. The powerful images in his poetry offer glimpses of his excruciating inner turmoil. Byron also rebelled against political convention; his Romanticism was inseparable from liberal politics. He assailed British political leaders as corrupt, narrow minded, and repressive; defended working-class movements in the name of liberty; and sailed off to fight in the Greek movement for independence from the Ottoman Turks. When he died in Greece (of tuberculosis, not in battle), he seemed to epitomize the liberal Romantic hero. Byron's close friend Percy Shelley continued to take Romantic poetry and politics to new heights. The subject of Shelley's *Prometheus Unbound* (1820) virtually defines Romantic heroism and its cult of individual audacity. Prometheus, defying Zeus, had stolen fire for humanity and as punishment found himself chained to a rock while an eagle tore out his heart.

WOMEN WRITERS, GENDER, AND ROMANTICISM

Perhaps the best-known work of Romantic fiction, however, is Mary Godwin Shelley's *Frankenstein* (1818).

Mary was the daughter of two radical literary "celebrities": the philosopher William Godwin and the feminist Mary Wollstonecraft (see Chapter Seventeen), who died as her daughter was born. Mary Godwin met Shelley when she was sixteen, had three children by him before they married, and published *Frankenstein* when she was twenty. The novel captures especially well the Romantic critique of Enlightenment reason and early nineteenth-century ambivalence about science. Shelley herself was fascinated with scientific developments of her times—from electricity to mesmerism—and with their dangers as well as their promise. The story turns around a madly ambitious and eccentric Swiss scientist determined to find the secret of human life. Along the way he prowls through charnel houses where the dead were kept before burial, studying corpses, the parts of the body, and stages of decomposition. (Shelley said she was often asked how a young girl "came to think of, and to dilate upon, so very hideous an idea.") Dr. Frankenstein finally does produce life, in the form of a freakish monster. Though the monster is artificially made, he has human feelings, and when he finds himself spurned by his horrified creator, he becomes consumed by loneliness, longing, and murderous self-hatred, wreaking havoc on all. Shelley cast the novel in characteristically Romantic fashion, as a twisted creation myth, a story of individual genius gone wrong, and a study of agonizingly powerful feeling.

WHAT WERE THE THEMES OF ROMANTICISM AS AN ARTISTIC MOVEMENT?

CULTURAL REVOLT: ROMANTICISM   727

For all these reasons, the novel became a point of reference in Western culture. Dr. Frankenstein, forced to acknowledge that he "had been the author of unalterable evils," became one of its most memorable characterizations of the limits of reason and the impossibility of controlling nature.

First, then, Romanticism stressed the limits of reason and the power of emotion. Second, it insisted on the uniqueness and subjectivity of individual experience. The mind was not a blank tablet on which one's senses imprinted knowledge, which was John Locke's image and central to most Enlightenment philosophy. Instead, Romantics regarded the mind as a source of imagination and creativity. The Romantics' belief in individuality and creativity led in several directions. It became a cult of artistic genius—of the "inexplicably and uniquely creative individual" who was able to see things that others could not. It led artists—and ordinary people—to seek out experiences that would elicit intense emotions and spark leaps of imagination and creativity, experiences that could range from traveling to exotic lands to using opium. The Romantic style encouraged the daring to defy conventionality, as did Lord Byron, the Shelleys, or the French women writers Germaine de Staël and George Sand (Amandine Aurore Lucile Dupin, 1804–1876). Sand, like Lord Byron, cultivated a persona. In her case this meant earning a living as a woman writer, taking lovers as she liked, and wearing men's clothing—all in rebellion against middle-class moral codes.

Women played an important role in Romantic letters, and Romanticism stimulated new thinking about gender and artistic creativity. In the eighteenth and nineteenth centuries it was common to assert that men were rational and women emotional, or intuitive. Romanticism, though, valued the emotional and intuitive as creative. Madame de Staël (1766–1817), who emigrated from France to Germany during the

Mary Shelley's *Frankenstein*. Perhaps the best-known work of Romantic fiction, *Frankenstein* joined the Romantic critique of Enlightenment reason with early-nineteenth-century ambivalence about science to create a striking horror story. Shelley (pictured at left at age nineteen, around the time she published *Frankenstein*) was the daughter of the philosopher William Godwin and the feminist Mary Wollstonecraft; she married the poet Percy Shelley. On the right is an engraving from the first illustrated edition of the work (1831) by Theodore Von Holst.

revolutionary period, played a key part in popularizing German Romanticism in France in her *De l'Allemagne* (Germany, 1810) and wrote many books of history. The language of Romanticism helped Madame de Staël describe herself as a genius. Claiming the role of artist-genius became a way for some women to subvert social norms. Romanticism also suggested that men could be emotional and that men and women shared a common human nature. Last, and perhaps most important to literate middle-class people, by emphasizing the search for individuality and valuing emotion and the soul as well as sensuality, the Romantics forged new ways of writing—and indeed thinking—about love. Some historians have called Romanticism a "cultural style," and as such it reached well beyond small circles of artists, into the everyday writing and thoughts of men and women.

ROMANTIC PAINTING

Painters of the early nineteenth century carried the Romantic interest in subjectivity and imagination onto their canvases. In Great Britain, romantic painting was best represented by John Constable (1776–1837) and J. M. W. Turner (1775–1851). Both British painters tried to develop more emotional and poetic approaches to nature. "It is the soul that sees," wrote Constable, echoing Wordsworth. Constable pored over Isaac Newton's prisms, studying the properties of light, but with an eye to capturing the "poetry" of a rainbow. His landscapes emphasized the artist's individual technique and way of seeing. Turner's intensely subjective, personal, and imaginative paintings were even more unconventional. Turner experimented with brush strokes and color to produce some of the most remarkable

The Slave Ship, by Joseph Mallord William Turner, 1840. The atmospheric turmoil of the mise-en-scène in Turner's painting both heightens and obscures the tragedy occurring in the foreground—drowning slaves cast into the sea by a slave ship. The looming typhoon suggests that the guilty may not escape Nature's justice.

WHAT WERE THE THEMES OF ROMANTICISM AS AN ARTISTIC MOVEMENT?

CULTURAL REVOLT: ROMANTICISM   729

Weymouth Bay, by John Constable. "It is the soul that sees," wrote Constable. Like other Romantic artists, Constable explored new forms of feeling and perception.

paintings of his time. Critics assailed the paintings, saying they were too abstract, incomprehensible. "I did not paint it to be understood," Turner retorted on one occasion. Turner's concerns were those of his contemporaries: imagination, the creativity of the artist, and the force of nature. Yet his technique took Romantic painting to a new level.

In France the leading Romantic painters were Théodore Géricault (1791–1824) and Eugène Delacroix (1799–1863). Delacroix's paintings look very different from Turner's. But Delacroix's ideas about subjectivity and the creative process, which he set out in detailed diaries, shared much with Turner's. The poet Charles Baudelaire, who represents the last stages of French Romanticism, credited Delacroix with showing him new ways to see: "The whole visible universe is but a storehouse of images and signs. . . . All the faculties of the

human soul must be subordinated to the imagination." Romanticism opened new ways of visualizing the world and pointed the way toward experiments, later in the century, that launched modernism.

ROMANTIC POLITICS: LIBERTY, HISTORY, AND NATION

Romanticism had many dimensions, and Romantic artists championed contradictory causes. "Romanticism, so often ill-defined, is only . . . liberalism in literature. Liberty in Art, Liberty in Society, behold the double banner that rallies the intelligence." So wrote Victor Hugo (1802–1885), whose poetry, plays, and immensely influential historical novels focused sympathetically on the experience of the common people.

Nôtre Dame de Paris (1831) and *Les Misérables* (1862) are the most famous. Delacroix's *Liberty Leading the People* represented revolutionary Romanticism (see page 733). So did the poetry of Shelley and Byron.

Yet Romantics could be ardently conservative. The French conservative François Chateaubriand's *Genius of Christianity* (1802) argued that the religious experiences of the national past were woven into the present and could not be unraveled without destroying the fabric of culture. In characteristically Romantic terms, Chateaubriand put the accent on religious emotion, feeling, and subjectivity. Artistic and literary interest in religion had much wider resonance, and the period witnessed a broad and popular religious revival. It also renewed interest in medieval literature, art, and architecture. Romanticism cut across political lines, providing imagery for both conservatives and liberals.

Early-nineteenth-century nationalism was suffused with Romantic imagery. The Romantic emphasis on individuality was easily transmuted into an insistence on the uniqueness of cultures. Among the most influential nationalist thinkers was the German Johann von Herder, a Protestant pastor and theologian and author of *Ideas for a Philosophy of Human History.* For Herder, civilization did not arise from a learned, cultivated, and international elite—here, as elsewhere, Romantic thinkers took their distance from the Enlightenment *philosophes.* Instead, Herder argued, civilization sprang from the culture of the common people, in German the *Volk.* Each culture had to express its own unique historical character, or *Volksgeist,* the spirit (genius) of the people. Whereas some Romantics prized individual genius, Herder extolled the particular genius of a people and insisted that each nation must be true to its own particular heritage, in Germany's case its culture and language.

The Romantics' keen interest in historical development and destiny also sealed their place in the nationalist tradition. The brothers Grimm, editors of the famous collection of fairy tales (1812–1815), traveled across Germany to study native dialects and collected folktales, which were published as part of a national heritage. The poet Friedrich Schiller retold the drama of the Swiss hero William Tell (1804) to make it a rallying cry for German national consciousness, though ironically, the Italian composer Gioacchino Rossini

The twenty-three-volume, lavishly illustrated *Description of Egypt,* published in French between 1809 and 1828, became an intellectual event in Europe, heightening the soaring interest in Eastern languages and history. "We are now all orientalists," wrote Victor Hugo in 1829.

turned Schiller's poem into an opera that promoted Italian nationalism. In Britain, Sir Walter Scott retold in many of his novels the popular history of Scotland; Wordsworth's *Lyrical Ballads* sought to evoke the simplicity and virtue of the English people. The Pole Adam Mickiewicz wrote the national epic *Pan Tadeusz* (Lord Thaddeus) as a vision of a recently lost way of life.

ORIENTALISM

The same cultural currents—a passion for grand theories of cultures, their distinctive characteristics, and their historical development—also created a wave of interest in the "Orient." Napoleon had invaded Egypt in 1798, seeking military advantage against the British but also, and perhaps more important in the long run, knowledge, cultural splendor, and imperial glory. "This Europe of ours is a molehill," Napoleon wrote in his characteristic style. "Only in the East, where 600 million human beings live, is it possible to found great empires and realize great revolutions." The dozens of scholars who accompanied Napoleon's Army of the Orient established the Egyptian Institute, charged with systematically collecting facts about Egyptian natural history, culture, and industry. Other discoveries during the same period opened a new world of knowledge. Among the many artifacts the French took from Egypt was the soon to be famous Rosetta stone, a block with what scholars discovered to be versions of the same text in three different languages and scripts: hieroglyphic writing (pictorial script), demotic (a version of early alphabetic script), and Greek, which, since it was familiar, enabled scholars to begin deciphering the first two. Egyptian obelisks, with their now readable hieroglyphic inscriptions, yielded more clues about ancient Egypt. The twenty-three-volume, lavishly illustrated *Description of Egypt,* published in French between 1809 and 1828, became an intellectual event in Europe, heightening the soaring interest in Eastern languages and history. "We are now all orientalists," wrote Victor Hugo in 1829. Great-power rivalries in Egypt, the British incursions into India, the Greek civil war, the French invasion of Algeria in 1830: all these developments raised Europeans' interests in the region and were the political accompaniment to the "Oriental renaissance."

WHAT WERE THE THEMES OF ROMANTICISM AS AN ARTISTIC MOVEMENT?

CULTURAL REVOLT: ROMANTICISM   731

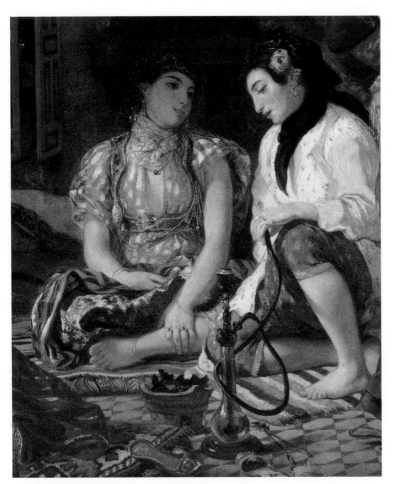

Women of Algiers, **by Eugène Delacroix.** This is one of many paintings done during Delacroix's trips through North Africa and a good example of the Romantics' Orientalism.

Nineteenth-century Europeans cast the Orient in a specific political and cultural role. In the words of one scholar, "[T]he Orient has helped to define Europe (or the West) as its contrasting image, idea, personality, experience." We saw earlier that during the 1820s Greek rebellion against the Ottoman Turks, Europeans sought to identify themselves with a Greek heritage and against what they insisted was "Oriental" or Islamic cruelty and despotism. Rebelling against the rules of eighteenth-century Classicism, social conventions, and Enlightenment rationalism, European artists and intellectuals were not only fascinated with ethnography and eager to explore new regions but also quick to classify the East as the land of bold color, sensuality, mystery, and irrationality. Delacroix's and, later, Renoir's paintings of women in Algeria are good examples of this viewpoint. The religious revival of the period had similar effects; scholars and artists looking for the roots of Christianity hoped to find them in what they thought of as the "unchanged habits of the East." Fascination with medieval history

and religion also fired up images of medieval crusades—important subjects for such Romantics as Scott and Chateaubriand. The "Oriental" renaissance supplied a rich imagery for nineteenth-century Western painting, literature, and scholarship. It also helped create what would become well-established habits of mind. Europeans built up oversimplified images of the differences between the West and the "Orient."

GOETHE AND BEETHOVEN

Many artists of the turn of the century are hard to classify. Johann Wolfgang von Goethe (1749–1832) had an enormous influence on the Romantic movement and on German writers trying to cast off the French style and develop their own language and voice. His early novel *The Sorrows of Young Werther* (1774), a story of a young man's yearnings and restless love, captivated readers all over Europe. Yet Goethe backed away from what he came to consider the excessiveness of Romanticism: its cult of feeling over restraint and order, which Goethe considered self-indulgent and "morbid." In 1790 Goethe published the first part of his masterpiece, *Faust,* a drama in verse, which he finished one year before he died in 1832. The play retold the German legend of the man who sold his soul to the devil in return for eternal youth and universal knowledge. It was more Classical in its tone than other works of the Romantic era, though it still reflected a Romantic concern with spiritual freedom and humanity's daring.

The composer Ludwig van Beethoven (1770–1827) considered himself a Classicist and was steeped in the principles of the eighteenth century. The glorification of nature and Romantic individuality ring clearly through his work, and his insistence that instrumental music (without vocal accompaniment) could become more poetic and expressive of emotion made him the key figure for later Romantic composers. "Music is a more sublime revelation than all wisdom and all philosophy," he wrote, "[and] it is the wine that inspires and leads to fresh creations." His musical achievements did indeed raise the standing of music as an art form and placed it at the center of the Romantic movement. Beethoven's life and politics also became part of his legacy. Like many of his contemporaries he was caught up in a burst of enthusiasm for the French Revolution of 1789. Disillusionment set in when Napoleon, whom he had admired as a revolutionary and for whom he had originally named the *Eroica* symphony, crowned himself emperor and repudiated his principles; and Beethoven's disappointment continued through the Napoleonic Wars. At the same time, by the age of thirty-two, Beethoven knew that he was losing his hearing. He hoped the problem could be cured, but it slowly put an end to his career as a virtuoso pianist; by 1819 he was completely deaf. As his condition worsened and his disenchantment deepened, he withdrew into composing, his solitude a powerful symbol of alienation and extraordinary creativity.

Beethoven and Goethe were transitional figures between the eighteenth and nineteenth centuries. They also illustrate the elusiveness of a simple definition of Romanticism. The Romantic movement was composed of many different currents that sometimes cut across each other: a critique of eighteenth-century Classicism; a quasi-mystical view of nature; a return to history, a cult of individual heroism, defiance, and creativity; and a search for a new way of seeing. At Romanticism's core lay an insistence that the arts needed to find a new way of expressing emotion and feeling, a search that sent nineteenth-century art in a new direction.

REFORM AND REVOLUTION

How did the events of 1830 bring the Restoration to an end?

In the 1820s, the conservative Restoration faced scattered opposition. The most decisive blow against it came in 1830 in France. There, the Congress of Vienna had returned a Bourbon monarch to the throne. Louis XVIII was the oldest of the former king's surviving brothers. Louis claimed absolute power, but in the name of reconciliation he granted a "charter" and conceded some important rights: legal equality, careers open to talent, and a two-chamber parliamentary government. Voting rights excluded most citizens from government. This narrowly based rule, combined with the sting of military defeat, nostalgia for a glorious Napoleonic past and, for some, memories of the revolution, undermined the Restoration in France.

THE 1830 REVOLUTION IN FRANCE

In 1824, Louis was succeeded by his far less conciliatory brother Charles X (1824–1830), who was determined to reverse the legacies of the revolutionary and Napoleonic eras. At Charles' direction the French assembly voted to compensate members of the nobility whose land had been confiscated and sold during the revolution. Doing so appeased the ultraroyalists, as the extreme right wing was called, but it antagonized property holders who had benefited from the revolution. Charles's regime also restored the Catholic Church to its traditional place in French classrooms. These policies provoked widespread discontent, several votes of no confidence in the monarch, and a series of elections that brought liberal opponents of the regime to the French Chamber of Deputies. The rising tide of liberal public opinion was also swollen by economic hard times. In Paris and the provinces, worried police reports flagged the extent of unemployment, hunger, and anger. Confronted with alarming evidence of the regime's unpopularity, Charles and his ministers called new elections; and when those went against them, the king tried, essentially, to overthrow the parliamentary regime. The so-called July Ordinances of 1830 dissolved the newly elected chamber before it had even met; imposed strict censorship on the press; further restricted suffrage so as to exclude almost completely anyone outside the nobility; and called for new elections.

In return for these measures, Charles got revolution. Parisians—especially workers, artisans, students, and writers—took to the streets. Three days of intense street battles followed in which the revolutionaries, fighting behind hastily constructed barricades, defied the army and the police, neither of which was willing to fire into the crowds. Aware that his support had evaporated, Charles abdicated. Many of the revolutionaries on the barricades wanted a republic. But other leaders of the movement wanted to avoid the domestic and international turmoil of the revolution of 1789. They ushered in the Duke of Orléans as King Louis Philippe (1830–1848), promoting him as a constitutional monarch accountable to the people: king of the French, not king of France. The new regime, called the July Monarchy, doubled the number of eligible voters. Yet voting was still a privilege, not a right, and was still based on steep requirements of property ownership. The major beneficiaries of the revolution were the propertied classes. Still, the revolution of 1830 brought the common people back into politics, reviving the memories of the revolution of 1789, and it spurred movements elsewhere.

For opponents of the Restoration across Europe, 1830 assumed enormous importance. It suggested that history was moving in a new direction and that the political landscape had changed, opening up new possibilities.

BELGIUM AND POLAND IN 1830

In 1815, the Congress of Vienna had agreed to join Belgium (then called the Austrian Netherlands) to Holland, forming one large state as a buffer against France. The union had never been popular in Belgium, and news of the July revolution in France catalyzed Belgian opposition. The city of Brussels rebelled; the Dutch king sent in troops; faced with barricades and intense street fighting, the troops withdrew. The great powers, preoccupied with other matters and unwilling to allow one of the group to intervene, agreed to guarantee Belgian neutrality—a provision that remained in force in 1914.

Revolt also spread to Poland, where it faced the far more formidable forces of the Russian Empire. Poland was not an independent state; by the provisions of the Congress of Vienna it was under Russian governance. It did, however, have its own parliament (or *diet*), a relatively broad electorate, a constitution, and guarantees of basic liberties of speech and the press—guarantees that were increasingly ignored by the Russian-imposed head of state, the tsar's brother Constantine. In Poland as in Belgium, news of the French Revolution of 1830

Liberty Leading the People, by Eugene Delacroix. This painting is among the best-known images of the revolutions of 1830. Delacroix is the same artist who had mourned the extinction of liberty in his painting of the *Massacre at Chios* in Greece (see page 716). The allegorical female figure of liberty leads representatives of the united people: a middle-class man (identified by his top hat), a worker, and a boy of the streets wielding a pistol. Neither middle-class people nor children fought on the barricades, and the image of revolutionary unity was romanticized. But optimistic images of what the French called the Three Glorious Days of July 1830 were widespread.

POPULAR UNREST IN PARIS, 1828

Throughout Europe the police regularly reported on the mood of the common people. This police report, filed in Paris in 1828, captures the rising anger of citizens in the capital. Poor grain harvests in the years before had helped drive up prices. In the working-class districts of Paris, the economic crisis fueled criticism of the regime. The report also reflects the anxieties of the police, who were not persuaded they could enforce order.

A handwritten placard has been put up at the corner of the rue Saint-Nicolas in the quartier des Quinze-Vingts: "Long live Napoleon! War to the death against Charles X and the priests who are starving us to death!" Several workers cheered, saying that "they would make an end of it, if die they must, since there was no work for them. . . ." Similar leaflets have been distributed in the rue de Charenton and the rue de Charonne in the faubourg Saint-Marceau and the faubourg Saint-Martin. . . . People are saying in the wine shops and workshops that the people must assemble and march on the Tuileries to demand work and bread and that they do not fear the soldiery, since many of them have been won over. This exasperation on the part of the workers has been noted ever since the recent rise in prices, and professional agitators (there are plenty of them in the faubourgs) are trying to exploit it to incite the workers to indulge in excesses. Circumstances are favorable. A great many workers have been suffering for a long time and the price of bread is driving them to utter despair. . . . I have begged the Prefect of Police to get some digging and similar work started from which they can earn at least a pittance.

Louis Chevalier, *Laboring Classes and Dangerous Classes in Paris during the First Half of the Nineteenth Century* (Princeton, N.J., 1973), p. 266.

QUESTIONS FOR ANALYSIS

1. What does this report tell us about the sources of unrest?
2. What does it tell us about those who wrote it—namely the police?

---

tipped the country into revolt. The revolutionaries— an initially well-organized coalition of Polish aristocrats defending their autonomy and students, military officers, and middle-class people demanding political reforms—drove Constantine out. Within less than a year, however, Russian forces retook Warsaw. The fiercely conservative tsar Nicholas crushed the Polish revolt with the same heavy hand that he had just used on the Decembrists at home and put Poland under military rule.

REFORM IN GREAT BRITAIN

Why was there no revolution in England? One answer is that there almost was. After an era of political conservatism that paralleled that on the Continent, British politics took a different direction, and Britain became one of the most liberal nations in Europe.

The end of the Napoleonic Wars brought with it a major agricultural depression in Britain, and the combination of low wages, unemployment, and bad harvests provoked regular social unrest. In the new industrial towns of the north, where economic conditions were especially bad, radical members of the middle class joined with workers to demand increased representation in Parliament. In 1819 a crowd of 60,000 gathered to demonstrate for political reform in St. Peter's Field in Manchester. The militia and some soldiers on horseback charged the crowd, killing 11 and injuring 400, including 113 women. British radicals condemned what they called "Peterloo," a domestic Waterloo, in which the nation's army had turned against its own citizens. Parliament quickly passed the Six Acts (1819), which outlawed "seditious and blasphemous" literature, increased the stamp tax on newspapers, allowed the searching of houses for arms, and restricted the rights of public meeting.

Prodded by pressure from below, British political leaders reversed their opposition to reform. Ironically, reforms began under the conservative Tory Party. British foreign policy became less conservative, and Catholics and dissenting Protestants (non-Anglicans, such as Baptists, Congregationalists, and Methodists) were allowed to participate in public political life. Tories, however, refused to reform political representation in the House of Commons. For centuries Parliament had represented the interests of the major propertied class. About two thirds of the members of the House of Commons were either directly nominated by or indirectly owed their election to the patronage of the richest titled landowners in the country. Many of the parliamentary electoral districts, or boroughs, which returned members to the House of Commons, were controlled by landowners who used their power to return candidates sympathetic to their interests. These were the "rotten" or "pocket" boroughs, so called because they were said to be in the pockets of those men who controlled them. Defenders of the system argued that Parliament looked after the interests of the nation at large, which they perceived to coincide with the interests of landed property.

Liberals in the opposing Whig Party, the new industrial middle class, and radical artisans argued passionately for reform. Liberals in particular were not proponents of democracy; they wanted to enfranchise only responsible citizens. Yet they made common cause with well-organized middle- and working-class radicals to intensify the push for reform. A Birmingham banker named Thomas Attwood, for instance, organized the Political Union of the Lower and Middle Classes of the People. By July 1830, similar organizations had arisen in several provincial cities, some willing to engage in

bloody clashes with army units and police. Middle-class shopkeepers announced they would withhold taxes and, if necessary, form a national guard. Also plagued by an outbreak of cholera, the country appeared to be on the verge of serious general disorder, if not outright revolution. Lord Grey, head of the Whig Party, seized the opportunity to press through reform.

The Reform Bill of 1832 eliminated the rotten boroughs from Parliament. It reallocated 143 parliamentary seats, most of them from the rural south, to the industrial north. It expanded the franchise, but with property qualifications only one in six men could vote. Produced by nearly revolutionary conditions, the bill ended as a relatively modest measure. It reduced but did not destroy the political strength of landed aristocratic interests. It admitted British liberals, including some of the industrial middle classes, into a junior partnership with the landed elite that had ruled Britain for centuries and was to rule it for at least one more generation.

What changes did the new regime bring? It abolished slavery in the British colonies, effective in 1838 (this is considered in a broader context in the following chapter). The most striking example of middle-class power came with the repeal of the Corn Laws in 1846. The Corn Laws (the British term for *wheat* is "corn") protected British landlords and grain farmers from foreign competition. Although those laws had been modified in the 1820s, they continued to keep the price of bread artificially high. More important, the industrial middle classes increasingly viewed them as special protections for the aristocracy. The campaign to accomplish repeal was superbly orchestrated and relentless, combining the support of those who believed, in principle, in reform and free trade and those who had a direct economic stake in a new system. The Anti–Corn Law League, which drew surprisingly broad support, held large meetings throughout the north of England and lobbied members of Parliament. In the end the league achieved a crucial victory, persuading Prime Minister Sir Robert Peel that repealing the Corn Laws was both inevitable and necessary for Britain's economic health and global power. The free trade policy inaugurated in 1846 endured until the 1920s.

BRITISH RADICALISM AND THE CHARTIST MOVEMENT

Disappointment with the narrow gains of the 1832 reform focused attention on farther-reaching political change, in the form of what was called the "People's Charter." This document, circulated across the country by committees of Chartists, as they were known, and signed by millions, contained six demands: universal white male suffrage, institution of the secret ballot, abolition of property qualifications for membership in the House of Commons, annual parliamentary elections, payment of salaries to members of the House of Commons, and equal electoral districts.

As economic conditions deteriorated in the 1840s, Chartism spread. The movement also tapped into local traditions of worker self-help and organization. Chartists disagreed about tactics and goals. Should immigrant Irish Catholics in England be included in the movement or excluded as dangerous competitors for scarce jobs? Should the franchise be extended only to working men, representing their families as respectable, interested members of society, or to women as well? Three examples illustrate the range of Chartist positions. The Chartist William Lovett, a cabinetmaker, was as fervent a believer in self-improvement as any member of the middle class. He advocated a union of educated workers to acquire their fair share of the nation's increasing industrial bounty. The Chartist Feargus O'Connor, a member of a minor Anglo-Irish landholding family but a political radical, appealed to the more impoverished and desperate class of workers. He attacked industrialization and the resettlement of the poor on agricultural allotments. Another Chartist, Bronterre O'Brien, openly admired Robespierre and shocked crowds by attacking "the big-bellied, little-brained, numbskull aristocracy." Chartism comprised many smaller movements with different emphases, but its goal was political democracy as a means to social justice.

Democracy was a very radical demand in the 1840s. It is not surprising that Chartists faced fierce opposition. They persisted. Committees presented massive petitions for the Charter to Parliament in 1839 and 1842; on both occasions they were summarily rejected. In the north of England, political demands took shape against a backdrop of strikes, trade-union demonstrations, and attacks on factories and manufacturers, who imposed low wages and long hours or who harassed unionists. The combination of political and social radicalism did not sway the government; conservatives saw anarchy, and liberals repudiated any interest in revolution. The movement peaked in April 1848. Partly inspired by revolution in continental Europe, Chartist leaders planned a major demonstration and show of force in London. A procession of 25,000 workers as-

sembled and carried to Parliament a petition containing 6 million signatures demanding the six points. Confronted once again with the specter of open class conflict, special constables and contingents of the regular army were marshaled under the now aged Duke of Wellington, hero of the battle of Waterloo, to resist this threat to order. In the end, only a small delegation of leaders presented the petition to Parliament. Rain, poor management, and unwillingness on the part of many to do battle with the well-armed constabulary put an end to the Chartists' campaign. A relieved liberal observer, Harriet Martineau, observed, "From that day it was a settled matter that England was safe from revolution."

THE HUNGRY FORTIES

The economic and political conditions that sowed unrest in England produced revolution on the Continent. Poor harvests began in the early 1840s. In 1845–1846, the crisis became acute. For two years in a row, the grain harvest failed completely. The potato blight struck, bringing starvation to Ireland (see page 691) and hunger to Germany, another potato-growing region. By 1846–1847, food prices had, on average, doubled. Bread riots broke out across Europe. City and village dwellers attacked carts carrying grain, either refusing to let merchants take it to other markets or simply taking the grain and selling it at what they considered a fair price. Compounding the problem was a cyclical industrial slowdown across Europe, which threw thousands of workers into unemployment. Starving peasants and unemployed laborers swamped public-relief organizations. The years 1846 and 1847 were "probably the worst of the entire century in terms of want and human suffering," and the decade has earned the name "the Hungry Forties."

C H R O N O L O G Y	
REFORM IN GREAT BRITAIN, 1832–1867	
Electoral Reform Bill	1832
Slavery abolished in British West Indies	1838
Chartist Movement	1840s
Corn Laws repealed	1846
Great Reform Bill	1867
Woman suffrage movement grows	1860s

WOMEN IN THE ANTI–CORN LAW LEAGUE, 1842

The campaign to repeal the Corn Laws enlisted many middle-class women in its ranks. For many such women, the anti–Corn Law campaign led to other causes, such as women's suffrage. This article, hostile to the reform campaign, deplores women's participation in the endeavor.

We find that the council of the Manchester Anti-Corn-Law Association had invited the inhabitants to 'an *anti-Corn-law tea-party*, to be held on the 20th of May, 1841—gentlemen's tickets, 2s.; ladies 1s. 6d.' . . . [L]adies were advertised as *stewardesses* of this assembly. So now the names of about 300 Ladies were pompously advertised as the *Patroness* and *Committee* of the *National Bazaar*. We exceedingly wonder and regret that the members of the Association . . . and still more that anybody else, should have chosen to exhibit their wives and daughters in the character of political agitators; and we most regret that so many ladies—modest, excellent, and amiable persons we have no doubt in their domestic circles—should have been persuaded to allow their names to be *placarded* on such occasions—for be it remembered, this Bazaar and these *Tea-parties* did not even pretend to be for any *charitable* object, but entirely for the purposes of *political agitation*. . . .

We have before us a letter from Mrs. Secretary Woolley to one body of workmen. . . . She 'appeals to them to stand forth and denounce as *unholy*, unjust, and cruel all restrictions on the food of the people'.

She acquaints them that 'the ladies are resolved to perform *their* arduous part in the attempt to *destroy a monopoly* which, for *selfishness* and its *deadly* effects, has no parallel in the history of the world'. 'We therefore', she adds, 'ask you for contributions. . . .'

Now surely . . . not only should the *poorer classes* have been exempt from such unreasonable solicitations, but whatever subscriptions might be obtainable from the wealthier orders should have been applied, not to *political agitation* throughout England, but to charitable relief at home.

J. Croker, "Anti–Corn Law Legislation," *Quarterly Review* (December, 1842), as cited in Patricia Hollis, ed., *Women in Public: The Women's Movement 1850–1900* (London, 1979), p. 287.

QUESTIONS FOR ANALYSIS

1. What do we learn about characteristically Victorian objections to women's participation in politics?
2. What does the document tell us about the reformers' arguments and tactics?

Hunger itself does not cause revolution. It does, however, test governments' abilities and their legitimacy. When the inadequate public relief systems in France foundered, when troops moved to repress potato riots in Berlin, and when regimes armed middle-class citizens to protect themselves against the poor, governments looked both authoritarian and inept. Under those circumstances, states lost the confidence of their supporters, starting a wave of revolution that swept across Europe, breaking first in France.

THE FRENCH REVOLUTION OF 1848

The French monarchy installed after the July revolution of 1830 seemed to differ little from its predecessor. The new king, Louis Philippe, gathered around him representatives of the banking and industrial elite. The regime often gave the impression of complacency. When confronted with demands to enfranchise more of the middle class, the prime minister quipped that everyone was free to rise into the ranks of the wealthy. "Enrich yourselves," he counseled. Construction projects and the expansion of the railway system presented ample opportunities for graft. The regime disappointed the high hopes that it had inspired. Republican societies proliferated, especially in such cities as Paris and Lyons, where worker and artisans associations had long political traditions. In 1834, the government declared radical political organizations illegal. Rebellions broke out in Lyons and Paris, bringing two days of repression, death, and arrests. The government's authoritarian image and refusal to expand the franchise drove even moderates into opposition. By 1847, the opposition had organized a campaign for electoral reform throughout France. Since political meetings were outlawed, the opposition organized political "banquets," where opponents of the regime drank toasts to reform—though not to outright revolution. Defying the king's threats, the opposition called a final, giant banquet for February 22, 1848. When the government banned the meeting, revolution broke out. In a surprisingly short time, Louis Philippe abdicated the throne.

The provisional government of the new republic was a remarkable group, consisting of a combination of liberals, republicans, and—for the first time—socialists. It set about making a new constitution, with elections based on universal male suffrage. Yet tensions between middle-class republicans and socialists, which had momentarily dissolved in opposition to Louis Philippe, now reemerged. Among working men and women, the most widely supported demand was the "right to work," which meant the ability to earn a living wage, to be able to support oneself. The provisional

The Great Chartist Rally of April 10, 1848. The year 1848 brought revolution to continental Europe and militant protest to England. This photo shows the April rally in support of the Chartists' six points, which included expanding the franchise, abolishing property qualifications for representatives, and instituting a secret ballot.

government cautiously supported this demand, creating what were called National Workshops, a program of public works in and around Paris. Initial plans called for the employment of no more than 10,000 or 12,000 individuals. But with unemployment running as high as 65 percent in the construction trades and 51 percent in textiles and clothing, workers streamed in, as many as 66,000 by April and 120,000 by June 1848.

Popular politics flourished in 1848. The provisional government lifted restrictions on freedom of speech and political activity. About 170 new journals and more than 200 clubs formed within weeks. Delegations claiming to represent the oppressed of all European countries—Chartists, Hungarians, Poles—moved freely about the city, attracting attention, if not devoted followings. Women's clubs and newspapers appeared, with names like *The Voice of Women* or *The Opinion of Women* and demands ranging from real, universal suffrage to living wages. This revival of popular poli-tics, though, convinced rising numbers of middle-class onlookers that stern measures were needed. Elections reinforced the concern for order. Universal male suffrage by no means guaranteed radical victory, and rural voters, worried about revolutionary Paris, elected moderate republicans and monarchists.

By late spring 1848, a majority of the French assembly believed that the workshop system had become a financial drain and, worse, a serious threat to social order. At the end of May, the government closed the workshops to new enrollment, excluded anyone who had resided in Paris for less than six months, and sent all members between the ages of eighteen and twenty-five to the army. On June 21, the government simply ended the program, repudiating any responsibility for the social question. The reaction brought some of the bloodiest conflict of the period. Laborers, journeymen, the unemployed, traditional manual laborers, social-

The Revolution of 1848 in France. A contemporary engraving celebrating the triumph of the people. Note the themes borrowed from Delacroix's painting of 1830 (see page 733).

ists, and some republican leaders once more built barricades across Paris. For four days, June 23–26, they defended themselves in an ultimately hopeless military battle against armed forces recruited, in part, from willing provincials eager enough to assist in the repression of the urban working class. The repression itself was ferocious, shocking many observers. About 3,000 were killed and 12,000 more arrested, the majority of whom were deported to Algerian labor camps.

In the aftermath of the June Days, the French government moved quickly to bring order to the country. Assembly members hoped a strong leader would bring dissidents to heel. Four candidates ran for president of the republic: Alphonse de Lamartine, the moderate republican; General Louis Eugène Cavaignac, who had comanded the troops in June; Alexandre August Ledru-Rollin, a socialist; and Louis Napoleon Bonaparte, nephew of the former emperor, who polled more than twice as many votes as the other three candidates combined.

"All facts and personages of great importance in world history occur twice . . . the first time as tragedy, the second as farce." This was how Karl Marx (no admirer of Napoleon I) summarized the relationship of Louis Napoleon to his uncle. The upstart, rumored by other detractors to be illegitimate, had spent most of

Defying the king's threats, the opposition called a final, giant banquet for February 22, 1848. When the government banned the meeting, revolution broke out.

TWO VIEWS OF THE JUNE DAYS, FRANCE, 1848

These two passages make for an interesting comparison. The socialist Karl Marx reported on the events of 1848 in France as a journalist for a German newspaper. For Marx, the bloodshed of the June Days shattered the "fraternal illusions" of February 1848, when the king had been overthrown and the provisional government established. That bloodshed also symbolized a new stage in history: one of acute class conflict.

The French liberal politician Alexis de Tocqueville also wrote about his impressions of the revolution. (Tocqueville's account, however, is retrospective, for he wrote his memoirs well after 1848.) For Marx, a socialist observer, the June Days represented a turning point: "the working class was knocking on the gates of history." For Tocqueville, a member of the government, the actions of the crowd sparked fear and conservative reaction.

KARL MARX'S JOURNALISM

The last official remnant of the February Revolution, the Executive Commission, has melted away, like an apparition, before the seriousness of events. The fireworks of Lamartine [French Romantic poet and member of the provisional government] have turned into the war rockets of Cavaignac [French general, in charge of putting down the workers' insurrection]. *Fraternité,* the fraternity of antagonistic classes of which one exploits the other, this *fraternité,* proclaimed in February, on every prison, on every barracks—its true, unadulterated, its prosaic expression is civil war, civil war in its most fearful form, the war of labor and capital. This fraternity flamed in front of all the windows of Paris on the evening of June 25, when the Paris of the bourgeoisie was illuminated, whilst the Paris of the proletariat [Marxist term for the working people] burnt, bled, moaned. . . . The February Revolution was the beautiful revolution, the revolution of universal sympathy, because the antagonisms, which had flared up in it against the monarchy, slumbered peacefully side by side, still undeveloped, because the social struggle which formed its background had won only a joyous existence, an existence of phrases, of words. The June revolution is the ugly revolution, the repulsive revolution, because things have taken the place of phrases, because the republic uncovered the head of the monster itself, by striking off the crown that shielded and concealed it.— Order! was the battle cry of Guizot . . . Order! shouts Cavaignac, the brutal echo of the French National Assembly and of the republican bourgeoisie. Order! thundered his grape-shot, as it ripped up the body of the proletariat. None of the numerous revolutions of the French bourgeoisie since 1789 was an attack on order; for they allowed the rule of the class, they allowed the slavery of the workers, they allowed the bourgeois order to endure, however often the political form of this rule and of this slavery changed. June has attacked this order. Woe to June!"

Neue Rheinische Zeitung (New Rhineland Gazette), June 29, 1848; from Karl Marx, *The Class Struggles in France* (New York, 1964), pp. 57–58.

ALEXIS DE TOCQUEVILLE REMEMBERS THE JUNE DAYS (1893)

Now at last I have come to that insurrection in June which was the greatest and the strangest that had ever taken place in our history, or perhaps in that of any other nation: the greatest because for four days more than a hundred thousand men took part in it, and there were five generals killed; the strangest, because the insurgents were fighting without a battle cry, leaders, or flag, and yet they showed wonderful powers of coordination and a military expertise that astonished the most experienced officers.

Another point that distinguished it from all other events of the same type during the last sixty years was that its object was not to change the form of government, but to alter the organization of society. In truth it was not a political struggle (in the sense in which we have used the word "political" up to now), but a class struggle, a sort of "Servile War." . . . One should not see it only as a brutal and a blind, but as a powerful effort of the workers to escape from the necessities of their condition, which had been depicted to them as an illegitimate depression, and by the sword to open up a road towards that imaginary well-being that had been shown to them in the distance as a right. It was this mixture of greedy desires and false theories that engendered the insurrection and made it so formidable. These poor people had been assured that the goods of the wealthy were in some way the result of a theft committed against themselves. They had been assured that inequalities of fortune were as much opposed to morality and the interests of society as to nature. This obscure and mistaken conception of right, combined with brute force, imparted to it an energy, tenacity and strength it would never have had on its own.

From Alexis de Tocqueville, *Recollections: The French Revolution of 1848*, ed. J. P. Mayer and A. P. Kerr, trans. George Lawrence (New Brunswick, N.J., 1987), pp. 436–437.

QUESTIONS FOR ANALYSIS

1. Was Tocqueville sympathetic to the revolutionaries of June?
2. Did Tocqueville think the events were historically significant?
3. Where did Tocqueville agree and disagree with Marx?

---

his life in exile. His name gave him a wide and suitably vague appeal. Conservatives believed he would protect property and order. Some people on the left had heard of his book *The Extinction of Pauperism* or of his correspondence with important socialists. "Napoleon" evoked glory and greatness. Whatever his origins, as one historian puts it, "he was very precisely the son of the Napoleonic myth." His role as an "an all-purpose personage" helped secure his electoral victory. As one old peasant expressed it, "How could I help voting for this gentleman—I whose nose was frozen at Moscow?"

It is not surprising that Louis Napoleon used his position to consolidate his power. He enlisted the support of the Catholics by restoring the Church's role in education and by sending an expedition to Rome in 1849 to rescue the pope from revolutionaries. (The Italian revolutions are discussed in the next chapter.) The regime hastened to demobilize radicals across the country, banning meetings, workers' associations, and so on. In 1851 he invited the people to grant him the power to draw up a new constitution. A plebiscite shortly thereafter authorized his actions. After one year Louis Napoleon Bonaparte ordered another plebiscite and, with the approval of over 95 percent of the voters, established the Second Empire and assumed the title of Napoleon III (1852–1870), emperor of the French.

Why was the French Revolution of 1848 significant? First, its dynamics would be repeated elsewhere. The middle classes played a pivotal political role. Louis Philippe's regime had been proudly bourgeois but ended up alienating many of its supporters. Denied a direct political voice, key groups of the middle class swung to the opposition, allying themselves with radicals who never would have toppled the regime alone. Yet demands for reform soon ran up against fears of disorder and desire for a strong state. This familiar dynamic led to the collapse of the republic and to the rule of Louis Napoleon Bonaparte. Second, many contemporaries saw the June Days as simply naked class

Barricade in the rue de la Mortellerie, June, 1848, by Ernest Meissonier (1815–1891). A very different view of 1848, a depiction of the June Days.

struggle. The violence of the June Days shattered many of the liberal aspirations of the earlier period. The romantic image of revolutionary unity captured in Delacroix's *Liberty Leading the People* now seemed naive. In the aftermath of 1848, the interests and politics of middle- and working-class people were more sharply differentiated and more directly at odds. Socialism would come into its own as an independent political force.

CONCLUSION

The French Revolution of 1789 had polarized Europe; in its aftermath new political identities formed and new political ideologies were spelled out. The Congress of Vienna, or peace settlement of 1815, had aimed to establish a new international system and to inoculate Europe against revolution. It succeeded in the first aim, but only partially in the second. The combination of new politics with industrialization and rapid social change undermined the conservative order. From the 1820s through the 1840s, social grievances and political disappointments created powerful movements for change, first in Latin America and the Balkans, then in western Europe and Great Britain.

The French Revolution of 1848 (the second since the defeat of Napoleon) became the opening act of a much larger drama. In southern and central Europe, as we will see in the next chapter, the issues were framed differently. Still, the dynamics of revolution in France foreshadowed the turn of events in other lands: exhilarating revolutionary successes were followed by the unraveling of revolutionary alliances and the emergence of new forms of conservative government. Throughout the West, the mid-century crisis of 1848 became a turning point. In its aftermath, the kinds of broad revolutionary alliances that had produced revolution were vanquished by class politics, and utopian socialism gave way to Marxism. In culture as in politics Romanticism faded, its expansive sense of possibility replaced by the more biting viewpoint of realism. Economies and states changed. Conservatism, liberalism, and socialism adapted to new political conditions. How this happened and the explosive role of nationalism in the process are the subjects of the next chapter.

KEY TERMS

Congress of Vienna and Restoration
Greek civil war
conservatism
liberalism

The Wealth of Nations
socialism
The Communist Manifesto
nationalism

Romanticism
Chartist movement
French Revolutions of 1830
     and 1848

SELECTED READINGS

Agulhon, Maurice. *The Republican Experiment, 1848–1852.* New York, 1983. A full treatment of the revolution in France.

Anderson, Benedict. *Imagined Communities: Reflections on the Origin and Spread of Nationalism.* London, 1983. The most influential recent study of the subject, highly recommended for further reading.

Briggs, Asa. *The Age of Improvement, 1783–1867.* New York, 1979. A survey of England from 1780 to 1870, particularly strong on Victorian attitudes.

Colley, Linda. *Britons: Forging the Nation, 1707–1837.* New Haven, Conn., 1992. An important analysis of Britain's emerging national consciousness in the eighteenth and early nineteenth centuries.

Furet, François. *Revolutionary France, 1770–1880.* New York, 1970. An excellent and fresh overview by one of the preeminent historians of the revolution of 1789.

Gilbert, Sandra M., and Susan Gubar. *The Madwoman in the Attic: The Woman Writer and the Nineteenth-Century Literary Imagination.* New Haven, Conn., and London, 1970. A study of the history of women writers and on examination of women writers as historians of their time.

Hobsbawm, Eric. *The Age of Revolution: Europe 1789 to 1848.* New York, 1970. A classic, and still very useful, account of the period.

Kramer, Lloyd. *Nationalism: Political Cultures in Europe and America, 1775-1865.* London, 1998. Excellent recent overview.

Langer, William. *Political and Social Upheaval, 1832–1851.* New York, 1969. Long the standard and still the most comprehensive survey.

Laven, David, and Lucy Riall. *Napoleon's Legacy: Problems of Government in Restoration Europe.* London, 2002. A recent collection of essays.

Levinger, Matthew. *Enlightened Nationalism: The Transformation of Prussian Political Culture 1806–1848.* New York, 2000. A recent and nuanced study of Prussian conservatism, with implications for the rest of Europe.

Macfie, A. L. *Orientalism.* London, 2002. Introductory but very clear.

Merriman, John M., ed. *1830 in France.* New York, 1975. Emphasizes the nature of revolution and examines events outside Paris.

Pinkney, David. *The French Revolution of 1830.* Princeton, N.J., 1972. A reinterpretation, now the best history of the revolution.

Porter, Roy, and Mikulas Teich, eds. *Romanticism in National Context.* Cambridge, 1988.

Raeff, Marc. *The Decembrist Movement.* New York, 1966. A study of the Russian uprising with documents.

Sahlins, Peter. *Forest Rites: The War of the Demoiselles in Nineteenth-Century France.* Cambridge, Mass., 1994. A fascinating study of relations among peasant communities, the forests, and the state.

Said, Edward W. *Orientalism.* New York, 1979. A brilliant and biting study of the imaginative hold of the Orient on European intellectuals.

Saville, John. *1848: The British State and the Chartist Movement.* New York, 1987. A detailed account of the movement's limited successes and ultimate failure.

Schroeder, Paul. *The Transformation of European Politics, 1763–1848.* Oxford and New York, 1994. For those interested in international relations and diplomacy; massively researched and a fresh look at the period. Especially good on the Congress of Vienna.

Sewell, William H. *Work and Revolution in France: The Language of Labor from the Old Regime to 1848.* Cambridge, 1980. A very influential study of French radicalism and its larger implications.

Smith, Bonnie. *The Gender of History: Men, Women, and Historical Practice.* Cambridge, Mass., 1998. On Romanticism and the historical imagination.

Wordsworth, Jonathan, Michael C. Jaye, and Robert Woof. *William Wordsworth and the Age of English Romanticism.* New Brunswick, N.J., 1987. Wide ranging and beautifully illustrated, a good picture of the age.

CHAPTER TWENTY-ONE

WHAT IS A NATION?
TERRITORIES, STATES,
AND CITIZENS,
1848–1871

EIGHTEEN FORTY-EIGHT WAS A TUMULTUOUS YEAR. From Berlin to Budapest to Rome, insurgents rushed to hastily built barricades, forcing kings and princes to beat an equally hasty—though only temporary—retreat. Across the Atlantic, the treaty of Guadalupe Hidalgo ended the war between Mexico and the United States with a massive territorial transaction: for a sum of $15 million, the United States acquired half a million square miles of western territory, including California. The exchange nearly completed U.S. continental expansion, but it also ushered in conflicts that led to the American Civil War. In July 1848, the Seneca Falls Convention marked the emergence of an organized movement for woman suffrage in the United States, which was paralleled in Europe. The New York *Herald* detected a disturbing connection among the year's events and commented nervously that "To whatever part of the world the attention is directed, the political and social fabric is crumbling. . . . [T]he work of revolution is no longer confined to the Old World, nor to the masculine gender." It was in 1848, too, that miners struck gold in California, launching an event with transatlantic resonance, the gold rush. When news of California gold reached Paris in the fall of 1848 after a summer of bitter social conflict, Karl Marx acidly remarked that "golden dreams were to supplant the socialist dreams of the Paris workers."

Territorial expansion, regime change, economic development, and debates about who deserved citizenship: all these were issues in 1848, and all were part of the process of nationalism and nation building. The upheavals of 1848 marked the high point of the age of revolution, and their failure signaled the end of that age. The era of nation-states, however, was coming into full form. *Nationalism,* as defined in the last chapter, is the sense of belonging to a community that shares historical, geographic, cultural, or political traditions. As historians point out, this sense is both powerful and diffuse and so could be—and was—cultivated by intellectuals, revolutionaries, and governments for different purposes. Nationalism could serve liberal or conservative politics and goals. During the first part of the nineteenth century, nationalism was usually linked to liberal goals; by the end of the century it had

FOCUS QUESTIONS

- Did nationalism fuel the revolutions of 1848 or did it undermine them?

- Why did the efforts to unify Italy and Germany succeed during the 1860s?

- What were the similarities between slavery and serfdom? Where did slavery survive and why?

- Why was the Crimean War significant?

been given a conservative meaning. The year 1848 was an important moment in this larger sea change. *Nation building* refers to the process of creating new states and reconstructing older ones, a process in which the nineteenth century marked a crucial stage. Territorial changes, such as the treaty of Guadalupe Hidalgo, which dramatically transformed the boundaries of the United States, were significant. But so were political reforms and new state structures that changed how governments worked and how they related to their citizens. The American Civil War, the unification of Italy, and the creation of a single Germany involved wrenching political change as well as territory. All three had far-reaching ramifications for the international order. France, Britain, Russia, and Austria were also rebuilt during this period—their bureaucracies overhauled and their electorates expanded; relations among ethnic groups reorganized; Russian serfdom, like American slavery, abolished. Changing relations among states and those they governed lay at the heart of nation building. And these changes were hastened by reactions against the revolutionary upheavals of 1848.

NATIONALISM AND REVOLUTION IN 1848

Did nationalism fuel the revolutions of 1848 or did it undermine them?

In central and eastern Europe, the spring of 1848 brought a dizzying sequence of revolution and repression. The roots of revolution lay in social antagonisms, economic crisis, and political grievances. But these revolutions were also shaped decisively by nationalism. To be sure, reformers and revolutionaries had liberal goals: representative government, an end to privilege, economic development, and so on. They also sought some form of national unity. Indeed, reformers in Germany, Italy, Poland, and the Austrian Empire believed that their liberal goals might be realized only in a vigorous, "modern" nation-state. The fate of the 1848 revolutions in these regions demonstrated nationalism's power to mobilize opponents of the regime but also its potential to splinter revolutionary alliances and to override other allegiances and values entirely.

WHO MAKES A NATION? GERMANY IN 1848

In 1815, there was no "Germany." The Congress of Vienna had created the German Confederation, a loose organization of thirty-eight states, including Austria and Prussia but not their non-German territories in sections of Poland and Hungary. The confederation was intended to provide only common defense. It had no real executive power. As a practical matter, Prussia was, with Austria, the great power in the area and would play a central role in German politics.

In 1806, Prussia had been defeated by the French under Napoleon. Many Prussians considered the defeat an indictment of the country's inertia since the reign of Frederick the Great (1740–1786). Aiming to revive "patriotism and a national honor and independence," they passed a series of aggressive reforms, imposed from above. Prussian reformers reconstituted the army, following the Napoleonic example. Officers were recruited and promoted on the basis of merit rather than birth, although the large majority continued to come from the Junker (*YUN-kur*; aristocratic) class. Other reforms modernized training at the royal cadet school in Berlin and encouraged the middle class to take a more active role in the civil service. In 1807, serfdom and the estate system were abolished. A year later, in a conscious attempt to increase middle-class Germans' sense of themselves as citizens, cities and towns were allowed to elect their councilmen and handle their own finances. (Justice and security continued to be administered by the central government in Berlin.) The Prussian reformers expanded facilities for both primary and secondary education and founded the University of Berlin, which numbered among its faculty several ardent nationalists.

Prussia aimed to establish itself as the leading German state and a counter to Austrian power in the region. Prussia's most significant victory in this respect came with the Zollverein, or customs union, in 1834, which established free trade among the German states and a uniform tariff against the rest of the world—an openly protectionist policy advocated by the economist Friedrich List. By the 1840s, the union included almost all of the German states except German Austria and offered manufacturers a market of almost 34 million people. The spread of the railways after 1835 accelerated exchange within this expanded internal market.

During the 1840s, in both Prussia and the smaller German states, political clubs of students and other

DID NATIONALISM FUEL THE REVOLUTIONS OF 1848 OR DID IT UNDERMINE THEM?

NATIONALISM AND REVOLUTION IN 1848   747

radicals joined with middle-class groups of lawyers, doctors, and businessmen to press new demands for representative government and reform. Newspapers multiplied, defying censorship. Liberal reformers resented both Prussian domination of the German Confederation and the conservatism of the Habsburgs, who ruled the Austrian Empire. They attacked the combination of autocracy and bureaucratic authority that stifled political life in Prussia and Austria. German

nationhood, they reasoned, would break Austrian or Prussian domination and end the sectional fragmentation that made reform so difficult.

When Frederick William IV (1840–1861) succeeded to the Prussian throne in 1840, hopes ran high. The new kaiser did gesture toward liberalizing reforms. When economic troubles hit in the 1840s, however, the regime reverted to authoritarianism. Frederick William sent the army to crush a revolt among the textile

GERMAN CONFEDERATION, 1815

Compare this map with the one on page 764. What helped bring the various states of the German Confederation together? What was their relationship with German-speaking Prussia? What factors prevented a more formally unified German state at this time?

weavers of Silesia, who were protesting British imports and, more generally, unemployment, falling wages, and hunger. The brutality of the regime's response shocked many. The kaiser also opposed constitutionalism and any representative participation in issues of legislation and budgets.

As in France, liberals and radicals in Prussia and the German states continued their reform campaigns. And when revolution came to France in the spring of 1848, unrest spread across the Rhine. In the smaller German states, kings and princes yielded surprisingly quickly to revolutionary movements. The governments promised freedom of the press, elections, expanded suffrage, jury trials, and other liberal reforms. In Prussia, Frederick William, shaken by unrest in the countryside and stunned by a showdown in Berlin between the army and revolutionaries in which 250 were killed, finally capitulated.

THE FRANKFURT ASSEMBLY AND GERMAN NATIONHOOD

The second and most idealistic stage of the revolution began with the election of delegates to an all-German assembly in Frankfurt, where representatives from Prussia, Austria, and the small German states met to discuss creating a unified German nation. Most of the delegates came from the professional classes—lawyers, professors, administrators—and most were moderate liberals. Many had assumed that the Frankfurt Assembly would draft a constitution for a liberal, unified Germany, much as an assembly of Frenchmen had done for their country in 1789. The comparison was mistaken. In 1789 a French nation-state and a centralized sovereign power already existed, to be reformed and redirected by the assembled French delegates. By contrast, the Frankfurt Assembly had no resources, no sovereign power to take, no single legal code. It did not even have a suitable meeting place: for eleven months the delegates worked in a single public room in an old church with terrible acoustics—no place to debate and decide on legislation. Although the assembly benefited from the energy, idealism, and devotion of the delegates, it faced enormous obstacles; and at times it teetered on the brink of chaos.

Procession of the German Assembly. This procession opened the assembly's first session at Saint Paul's Church in Frankfurt, May 1848.

On the assembly floor, questions of nationality proved contentious and destructive. Which Germans would be in the new state? A majority of the assembly's delegates argued that Germans were all those who, by language, culture, or geography, felt themselves bound to the enterprise of unification. They believed the German nation should include as many Germans as possible—a position encouraged by the spectacle of disintegration in the Habsburg Empire. This was the "Great German" position. It was countered by a minority who called for a "Small Germany," one that left out all lands of the Habsburg Empire, including German Austria. Great Germans had a majority but were stymied by other nationalities unwilling to be included in their fold. The Czechs in Bohemia, for instance, wanted no part of Great Germany. After a long and difficult debate, and when the Austrian Emperor

> The Prussian monarch wanted both the crown and a larger German state, but on his own terms. After a brief protest, summarily suppressed by the military, the delegates went home, disillusioned by their experience and convinced that their liberal and nationalist goals were incompatible.

FREDERICK WILLIAM IV REFUSES THE THRONE

In March 1849, after months of deliberation and constitution making, the Frankfurt Assembly offered the throne of its proposed German state to the Prussian monarch Frederick William IV, who quickly turned it down. He had already reflected on the matter. In an earlier (December 1848) letter to one of his advisers, the diplomat Christian von Bunsen, he had set out his reasoning as follows.

I want the princes' approval of neither *this* election nor *this* crown. Do you understand the words emphasized here? For you I want to shed light on this as briefly and brightly as possible. First, *this* crown is no crown. The crown which a Hohenzoller [the Prussian royal house] could accept, *if* circumstances *permitted*, is not one *made* by an assembly sprung from a revolutionary seed in the genre of the crown of cobble stones of Louis Philippe—even if this assembly was established with the sanction of princes . . . but one which bears the stamp of God, one which makes [the individual] on whom it [the crown] is placed, after his anointment, a "divine right" monarch—just as it has elevated more than 34 princes to Kings of the Germans by divine right and just as it bonds the last of these to his predecessors. The crown worn by Ottonians, Staufens [earlier German royal houses], Habsburgs can of course also be worn by a Hohenzoller; it honors him overwhelmingly with the luster of a thousand years. But *this* one, to which you regrettably refer, overwhelmingly dishonors [its bearer] with its smell of the gunpowder of the 1848 revolution—the silliest, dumbest, worst,

though—thank God!—not the most evil of this century. Such an imaginary headband, baked out of dirt and the letters of the alphabet, is supposed to be welcome to a legitimate divine right king: to put it more precisely, to the King of Prussia who is blessed with a crown which may not be the oldest but, of all those which have never been stolen, is the most noble? . . . I will tell you outright: if the thousand-year-old crown of the German nation . . . should be bestowed again, it will be *I* and my equals who will bestow it. And woe to those who assume [powers] to which they have no title.

Ralph Menning, *The Art of the Possible: Documents on Great Power Diplomacy, 1814–1914* (New York, 1996), p. 82.

QUESTIONS FOR ANALYSIS

1. On what grounds does Frederick William refuse the crown?
2. What does he mean by "the crown of cobble stones"?

withdrew his support, the assembly retreated to the Small German solution and in April 1849 offered the crown of the new German nation to Frederick William IV.

Frederick William refused the offer. The assembly's proposed constitution, he argued, was too liberal and to owe his crown to a parliament would be demeaning. The Prussian monarch wanted both the crown

CHRONOLOGY

NATION BUILDING IN GERMANY, 1800–1850

Napoleon defeats Prussia	1806
Edict abolishing serfdom	1807
Municipal Ordinance of 1808	
Creation of the Zollverein	1834
Liberal protests	1820s–1840s
Revolution of 1848	
Frankfurt Assembly meets	1848
Frederick Willam grants Prussian constitution	1850

and a larger German state, but on his own terms. After a brief protest, summarily suppressed by the military, the delegates went home, disillusioned by their experience and convinced that their liberal and nationalist goals were incompatible. Some fled repression by emigrating to the United States. Others convinced themselves to sacrifice their liberal views for the seemingly realistic goal of nationhood. In Prussia itself, the army dispatched what remained of the revolutionary forces.

Elsewhere, though, popular revolution was taking its own course. Peasants ransacked tax offices and burned castles; workers smashed machines. In towns and cities, citizen militias formed. New daily newspapers multiplied. So did political clubs. For the first time, many of these clubs admitted women (although they denied them the right to speak), and newly founded women's clubs demanded political rights. This torrent of popular unrest made moderate reformers uneasy; they considered universal manhood suffrage too radical. While peasant and worker protests had forced the king to make concessions in the early spring of 1848, moderate reformers now found those protests threatening.

For those moderates, national unification increasingly appealed as a way to mantain order. "In order to realize our ideas of freedom and equality, we want above all a strong and powerful government," claimed one candidate during the election campaigns for the Frankfurt Assembly. Popular sovereignty, he continued, "strengthened by the authority of a hereditary monarchy, will be able to repress with an iron hand any disorder and any violation of the law." In this context, nationhood stood for a new constitution and political community but also for a sternly enforced rule of law.

PEOPLES AGAINST EMPIRE: THE HABSBURG LANDS

In the sprawling Habsburg (Austrian) Empire, nationalism played a different, centrifugal role. The empire was a shadow of its former self. In the sixteenth century, under Charles V, it had included Spain, parts of Burgundy, and the Netherlands. In the nineteenth century the Habsburgs still ruled over a wide array of ethnic and language groups: Germans, Czechs, Magyars, Poles, Slovaks, Serbs, and Italians, to name only the most prominent. In some areas of the empire, these groups lived in relative separation and isolation. Elsewhere they coexisted, though not always harmoniously. The Habsburgs found it increasingly difficult to hold their empire together as these groups' varying national demands escalated after 1815.

In the Polish territories of the empire, nationalist sentiment was strongest among aristocrats, who were especially conscious of their historic role as leaders of the Polish nation. Here, the Habsburg Empire successfully set Polish serfs against Polish lords, ensuring that social grievances dampened ethnic nationalism. In the Hungarian region, national claims were likewise advanced by the relatively small Magyar aristocracy. (*Hungarian* is a political term; *Magyar*, which was often used, refers to the Hungarians' non-Slavic language.) Yet they gained an audience under the gifted and influential leadership of Lajos (Louis) Kossuth (*KAW-shut*). A member of the lower nobility, Kossuth was by turns a lawyer, publicist, newspaper editor, and political leader. To protest the closed-door policy of the empire's barely representative Diet (parliament), Kossuth published transcripts of parliamentary debates and distributed them to a broader public. He campaigned for independence and a separate Hungarian parliament, but he also (and more influentially) brought politics to the people. Kossuth staged political "banquets" like those in France, at which local and national personalities made speeches in the form of toasts and interested citizens could eat, drink, and participate in politics. The Hungarian political leader combined aristocratic style with rabble-rousing politics: a delicate balancing act but one that, when it worked, catapulted him to the center of Habsburg politics. He was as well known in the Habsburg capital of Vienna as he was in Pressburg and Budapest.

The other major nationalist movement that troubled the Habsburg Empire was pan-Slavism. Slavs included Russians, Poles, Ukrainians, Czechs, Slovaks, Slovenes,

DID NATIONALISM FUEL THE REVOLUTIONS OF 1848 OR DID IT UNDERMINE THEM?

NATIONALISM AND REVOLUTION IN 1848   751

Croats, Serbs, Macedonians, and Bulgarians. Before 1848 pan-Slavism was primarily a cultural movement united by a general pro-Slavic sentiment. It was internally divided, however, by the competing claims of different Slavic languages and traditions. Pan-Slavism inspired the works of the Czech historian and political leader, František Palacký, author of the *History of the Bohemian People*, and the Slovak Jan Kollár, whose book *Salvy Dcera* (Slava's daughter) mourned the loss of identity among Slavs in the Germanic world. The movement also influenced the Polish Romantic poet Adam Mickiewicz (*mihtz-KYAY-vihch*), who sought to rekindle Polish nationhood against foreign oppression.

The fact that Russia and Austria were rivals in Eastern Europe made pan-Slavism a volatile and unpredictable political force in the regions of Eastern Europe where the two nations vied for power and influence. Tsar Nicholas of Russia sought to use pan-Slavism to his advantage, making arguments about "Slavic" uniqueness part of his "autocracy, orthodoxy, nationality" ideology after 1825. Yet the tsar's Russian-sponsored pan-Slavism alienated Western-oriented Slavs who resented Russia's ambitions. Here, as elsewhere, nationalism created a tangled web of alliances and antagonisms.

AUSTRIA AND HUNGARY IN 1848: SPRINGTIME OF PEOPLES AND THE AUTUMN OF EMPIRE

The empire's combination of political, social, and ethnic tensions came to the point of explosion in 1848. The Habsburgs faced multiple challenges to their authority from the east, the south, and within. The opening salvo came from the Hungarians. Emboldened by uprisings in France and Germany, Kossuth stepped up his reform campaigns, pillorying the "Metternich system" of Habsburg autocracy and control, demanding representative institutions throughout the empire and autonomy for the Hungarian Magyar nation. The Hungarian Diet prepared to draft its own constitution. In Vienna, the seat of Habsburg power, a popular movement of students and artisans demanding political and social reforms built barricades and attacked the imperial palace. A Central Committee of Citizens took shape, as did a middle-class militia, or national guard, determined at

> The paradox of nationalism in central Europe was that no cultural or ethnic majority could declare independence in a given region without prompting rebellion from other minority groups that inhabited the same area.

once to maintain order and to press demands for reform. The Habsburg regime tried to shut the movement down by closing the university, but that only unleashed more popular anger. The regime found itself forced to retreat almost entirely. Metternich, whose political system had weathered so many storms, fled to Britain in disguise—a good indication of the political turmoil—leaving the emperor Ferdinand I in Vienna. The government conceded to radical demands for male suffrage and a single house of representatives. It agreed to withdraw troops from Vienna and to put forced labor and serfdom on a path to abolition. The government also yielded to Czech demands in Bohemia, granting that kingdom its own constitution. To the south, Italian liberals and nationalists attacked the empire's territories in Naples and Venice. In Milan, the forces of King Charles Albert of Piedmont routed the Austrians, raising hopes of victory. As what would be called "the springtime of peoples" unfolded, Habsburg control of its various provinces seemed to be coming apart.

Yet the explosion of national sentiment that shook the empire later allowed it to recoup its fortunes. The paradox of nationalism in central Europe was that no cultural or ethnic majority could declare independence in a given region without prompting rebellion from other minority groups that inhabited the same area. In Bohemia, for instance, Czechs and Germans who lived side by side had worked together to pass reforms scuttling feudalism. Within a month, however, nationalism began to fracture their alliance. German Bohemians set off to attend the all-important Frankfurt Assembly, but the Czech majority refused to send representatives and indeed countered by convening a confederation of Slavs in Prague. What did the delegates at the Slav confederation want? Some were hostile to what the Russian anarchist Mikhail Bakunin called the "monstrous Austrian empire." But the majority of delegates preferred to be ruled by the Habsburgs (though with some autonomy) than to be dominated by either the Germans or the Russians.

This bundle of animosities allowed the Austrians to divide and conquer. In May 1848, during the Slav Congress, a student- and worker-led insurrection broke out in Prague. On the orders of the newly installed liberal government, Austrian troops entered the city to restore

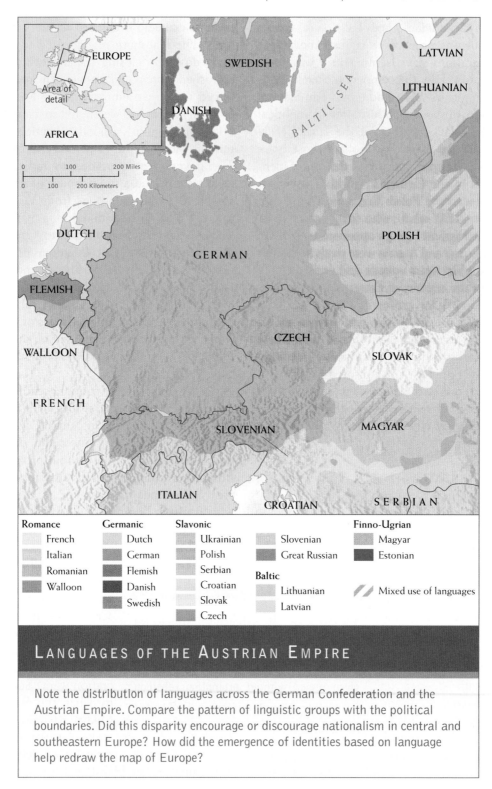

LANGUAGES OF THE AUSTRIAN EMPIRE

Romance
- French
- Italian
- Romanian
- Walloon

Germanic
- Dutch
- German
- Flemish
- Danish
- Swedish

Slavonic
- Ukrainian
- Polish
- Serbian
- Croatian
- Slovak
- Czech
- Slovenian
- Great Russian

Baltic
- Lithuanian
- Latvian

Finno-Ugrian
- Magyar
- Estonian

/// Mixed use of languages

Note the distribution of languages across the German Confederation and the Austrian Empire. Compare the pattern of linguistic groups with the political boundaries. Did this disparity encourage or discourage nationalism in central and southeastern Europe? How did the emergence of identities based on language help redraw the map of Europe?

order, sent the Slav Congress packing, and reasserted control in Bohemia. For economic as well as political reasons, the new government was determined to keep the empire intact. The regime also sent troops to regain control in the Italian provinces of Lombardy and

Venetia, and quarrels among the Italians helped the Austrians succeed.

Nationalism and counternationalism in Hungary set the stage for the final act of the drama. The Hungarian parliament had passed a series of laws including new

DID NATIONALISM FUEL THE REVOLUTIONS OF 1848 OR DID IT UNDERMINE THEM?

NATIONALISM AND REVOLUTION IN 1848   753

Hungarian revolutionary Lajos Kossuth, 1851. A leader of the Hungarian nationalist movement who combined aristocratic style with rabble-rousing politics, Kossuth almost succeeded in an attempt to separate Hungary from Austria in 1849.

provisions for the union of Hungary and Austria. In the heat of 1848 Ferdinand I had little choice but to accept them. The Hungarian parliament abolished serfdom and ended noble privilege to prevent a peasant insurrection. It also established freedom of the press and of religion and changed the suffrage requirements, enfranchising small property holders. Many of these measures (called the March laws) were hailed by Hungarian peasants, Jewish communities, and liberals. But other provisions—particularly the extension of Magyar control—provoked opposition from the Croats, Serbs, and Romanians within Hungary. The Austrian government took advantage of these divisions. It appointed the anti-Hungarian Josip Jelacic as governor of the breakaway province of Croatia. Encouraged by the Austrians, Jelacic first broke off links with Hungary and then launched an attack. In response, Kossuth rallied the Hungarian forces and turned the tide in their favor. On April 14, 1848, Kossuth upped the ante, severing all ties between Hungary and Austria. The new Austrian emperor, Franz Josef, now played his last card: he asked for military support from Nicholas I

of Russia. The Habsburgs were unable to win their "holy struggle against anarchy," but the Russian army of over 300,000 found it an easier task. By mid-August 1849, the Hungarian revolt was crushed.

In the city of Vienna itself, the revolutionary movement had lost ground. When economic crisis and unemployment helped spark a second popular uprising, the emperor's forces, with Russian support, descended on the capital. On October 31, the liberal government capitulated. The regime reestablished censorship, disbanded the national guard and student organizations, and put twenty-five revolutionary leaders to death in front of a firing squad. Kossuth went into hiding and lived the rest of his life in exile.

THE EARLY STAGES OF ITALIAN UNIFICATION IN 1848

The Italian penninsula had not been united since the Roman Empire. At the beginning of the nineteenth century it was a patchwork of small states. Austria occupied the northernmost states of Lombardy and Venetia, which were also the most urban and industrial. Habsburg dependents also ruled Tuscany, Parma, and Modena, extending Austria's influence over the north of the penninsula. The independent Italian states included the southern kingdom of the Two Sicilies, governed by members of the Bourbon family; the Papal States, ruled by Pope Gregory XVI (1831–1846); and most important, Piedmont-Sardinia, ruled by the reform-minded monarch Charles Albert (1831–1849) of the House of Savoy. Charles Albert had no particular commitment to creating an Italian national state, but by virtue of Piedmont-Sardinia's economic power, geographical location, and long tradition of opposition to the Habsburgs, Charles Albert's state played a central role in nationalist and anti-Austrian politics.

The leading Italian nationalist in this period—one whose republican politics Charles Albert disliked—was Giuseppe Mazzini (1805–1872) from the city of Genoa, in Piedmont. Mazzini began his political career as a member of the Carbonari (see Chapter Twenty), an underground society pledged to resisting Austrian control of the region and establishing constitutional rule. In 1831 Mazzini founded his own society, Young Italy, which was anti-Austrian and in favor of constitutional reforms but also dedicated to Italian unification. Charismatic and persuasive, Mazzini was one of the best-known nationalists of his time. He spoke in characteristically Romantic tones of the awakening of the Italian people and of the common people's mission to bring republicanism to the world. Under his leadership Young Italy clubs multiplied. Yet the organization's favored tactics, plotting mutinies and armed rebellions, proved ineffective. In 1834, Mazzini launched an invasion of the kingdom of Sardinia. Without sufficient support, it fizzled, driving Mazzini into exile in England.

Mazzini's republican vision of a united Italy clashed with the goals of his potential allies. Many liberals shared his commitment to creating a single Italian state but not his enthusiasm for the people and popular movements. They hoped instead to merge existing governments into a some form of constitutional monarchy or, in a few cases, for a government under the pope. Mazzini's insistence on a democratic republic committed to social and political transformation struck pragmatic liberals as utopian and well-to-do members of the middle classes as dangerous.

The turmoil that swept across Europe in 1848 raised hopes for political and social change and put Italian unification on the agenda. Popular revolts forced the

> Charismatic and persuasive, Mazzini was one of the best-known nationalists of his time. He spoke in characteristically Romantic tones of the awakening of the Italian people and of the common people's mission to bring republicanism to the world.

conservative, independent kingdoms on the peninsula to grant civil liberties and parliamentary government. In the north, the provinces of Venetia and Lombardy rebelled against the Austrian occupation. Charles Albert of Piedmont-Sardinia provided them with military support and took up the banner of Italian nationalism, although many charged that he was primarily interested in expanding his own power. In Rome, a popular uprising challenged the power of the pope and established a republic, with Mazzini as its head. These movements were neither coordinated nor ultimately successful. Within a year, the Austrians had regained the upper hand in the north. French forces under Louis Napoleon intervened in the Papal States; and although they met fierce resistance from the Roman republicans joined by Giuseppe Garibaldi (discussed later in this chapter), they nonetheless restored the pope's power. Like most of the radical movements of 1848, these uprisings failed. Still, they raised the hopes of nationalists who spoke of a *risorgimento*, or Italian resurgence, that would restore the nation to the position of leadership it had held in Roman times and during the Renaissance.

Giuseppe Mazzini.

BUILDING THE NATION-STATE

Why did the efforts to unify Italy and Germany succeed during the 1860s?

In the wake of the revolutions of 1848, new nation-states were built—often, ironically, by former critics of nationalism. Since the French Revolution of 1789, conservative politicians had associated nationhood with liberalism: constitutions, reforms, new political communities. Nationalism evoked memories of popular movements clashing with authoritarian governments. During the second half of the century, however, the political ground shifted dramatically. States and governments took the national initiative. Alarmed by revolutionary ferment, they promoted economic development, pressed social and political reforms, and sought to shore up their base of support. Rather than

Why did the efforts to unify Italy and Germany succeed during the 1860s?

Building the Nation-State 755

allow popular nationalist movements to emerge from below, statesmen consolidated their governments' powers and built nations from above.

France under Napoleon III

Napoleon III, like his uncle, believed in personal rule and the development of a centralized state. His constitution, modeled on that of the first French empire, gave control of finance, the army, and foreign affairs exclusively to the emperor. The assembly, elected by universal male suffrage, held virtually no power and could only approve legislation drafted at the emperor's direction by the Council of State. Through bureaucratic expansion, the regime aimed to put the countryside under the political and administrative thumb of the modern state, undermining traditional elites and cultivating a new relationship with the people. "The confidence of our rough peasants can be won by an energetic authority," as one of the regime's representatives put it.

Napoleon III and his government also took steps to develop the economy, harboring a near-utopian faith in the ability of industrial expansion to bring prosperity, political support, and national glory. An adviser to the emperor expressed it this way: "I see in industry, machinery and credit the indispensable auxiliaries of humanity's moral and material progress." The government thus encouraged a variety of progressive economic developments, including credit and other new forms of financing. It passed new limited-liability laws to spur growth and signed a free-trade treaty with Britain in

Paris Rebuilt. Baron Haussmann, Prefect of Paris under Napoleon III, presided over the wholesale rebuilding of the city, with effects we still see today. The Arc de Triomphe became the center of an *etoile* (star) pattern, with the wide boulevards named after Napoleon I's famous generals. (Photograph from the 1960s.)

1860. The government also supported the founding of the Crédit Mobilier, an investment banking institution that sold shares publicly and financed such enterprises as railroads, insurance and gas companies, the coal and construction industries, and the building of the Suez Canal (see Chapter Twenty-two). In a different vein, Napoleon III also reluctantly permitted the existence of trade unions and the legalization of strikes. By appealing to both workers and the middle class, he sought to symbolize his country's reemergence as a leading world power.

Perhaps the best illustration of the Second Empire's policies was the transformation of the nation's capital. In Paris, as in other nineteenth-century cities, the medieval infrastructure was buckling under the weight of industrial development. Cholera epidemics had killed 20,000 in 1832 and 19,000 in 1849. In 1850, only one house in five had running water. Economic and public-health incentives to rebuild were multiplied by political concerns, for such "unhealthy conditions" bred not only disease but also crime—and revolution. The massive rebuilding, financed by the Crédit Mobilier among other investment institutions, razed much of the medieval center of the city and erected 34,000 new buildings, including elegant new hotels with the first elevators. The construction installed new water pipes and sewer lines (a popular attraction at the 1867 International Exposition), laid out 200 kilometers of new streets, and rationalized the traffic flow (perhaps unsuccessfully) around the Arc de Triomphe. Wide new boulevards, many named for Napoleon I's most famous generals, radiated outward from the Arc. This wholesale renovation did not benefit everyone. Although the regime built model worker residences, demolitions and rising rents drove working people out of the city center into the increasingly segregated suburbs. Baron Haussmann, the Prefect of Paris who presided over the project, considered the new city a monument to "cleanliness and order." Others called Haussmann an "artist of demolition." For centuries monarchs had taken on massive building projects, but this was different—an unprecedented and conscious state effort to change what contemporaries conceived of as the "mechanics" or "system" of modern urban life.

Napoleon III pursued an aggressive foreign policy, with a similar intent on grandeur but with catastrophic consequences. First came mixed results against Russia in the Crimea, then success against the Austrians in Italy, then an adventurous expedition to Mexico, where his attempt to help establish another empire met with costly failure. Finally and most disastrous, the emperor was drawn into a war with Prussia that brought the collapse of his regime in 1870.

VICTORIAN BRITAIN AND THE SECOND REFORM BILL (1867)

Less roiled by the revolutionary wave of 1848, Great Britain was more willing and able to chart a course of significant social and political reform, continuing a process that had begun in 1832 with the First Reform Bill. The government faced mounting demands to extend the franchise beyond the middle classes. Industrial expansion sustained a growing stratum of highly skilled and relatively well paid workers (almost exclusively male). These workers, concentrated for the most part within the building, engineering, and textile industries, turned away from the tradition of militant radicalism that had characterized the "Hungry Forties." Instead they favored collective self-help through cooperative societies or trade unions, whose major role was to accumulate funds for insurance against old age and unemployment. They saw education as a tool for advancement and patronized the mechanics' institutes and similar institutions founded by them or on their behalf. These prosperous workers created real pressure for electoral reform.

Some argued for the vote in the name of democracy. Others borrowed arguments from earlier middle-class campaigns for electoral reform: they were responsible workers, respectable and upstanding members of society, with strong religious convictions and patriotic feelings. Unquestionably loyal to the state, they deserved the vote and direct representation just as much as the middle class. These workers were joined in their campaign by many middle-class dissenting reformers in the Liberal Party, whose religious beliefs (as dissenters from the Church of England) linked them to the workers' campaigns for reform. Dissenters had long been discriminated against. They were denied posts in the civil service and the military, which liberals felt should be open to talent, and for centuries had been excluded from the nation's premier universities, Oxford and Cambridge, unless they renounced their faith and subscribed to the articles of the Anglican church. Moreover, they resented paying taxes to support the Church of England, which was largely staffed by sons of the gentry and run in the interests of landed society. The fact that the community of dissent crossed class lines was vital to Liberal Party politics and the campaign for reforming the vote.

WHY DID THE EFFORTS TO UNIFY ITALY AND GERMANY SUCCEED DURING THE 1860S?

BUILDING THE NATION-STATE   757

MILL'S LOGIC, OR FRANCHISE FOR FEMALES
"Pray clear the way, there, for these—ah—persons."

John Stuart Mill and Suffragettes. Cartoon published in 1860, by which time Mill had established a reputation as a liberal political philosopher and supporter of woman suffrage. Mill argued that women's enfranchisement was essential to personal liberty, to expanding humanity's potential, and to social progress.

suffrage movement, building on women's remarkable participation in earlier reform campaigns, especially the Anti–Corn Law League and the movement to abolish slavery. Their cause found a passionate supporter in John Stuart Mill, perhaps the century's most brilliant, committed, and influential defender of personal liberty. Mill's father had worked closely with the Utilitarian philosopher Jeremy Bentham, and the young Mill had been a convinced Utilitarian himself (see Chapter Twenty). He went on, however, to develop much more expansive notions of human freedom. In 1859, Mill wrote *On Liberty*, which many consider the classic defense of individual freedom in the face of the state and the "tyranny of the majority." During the same period he coauthored—with his lover and eventual wife, Harriet Taylor—essays on women's political rights, the law of marriage, and divorce. At the time, Taylor was trapped in an unhappy marriage and divorce required an act of Parliament. Taylor's relationship with Mill thus added a measure of personal scandal to their political views, which contemporaries considered scandalous enough. His *The Subjection of Women* (1869), published after Harriet died, argued what few could even contemplate: that women had to be considered individuals on the same plane as men and that women's freedom was a measure of social progress. *Subjection* was an international success and with *On Liberty* became one of the defining texts of Western liberalism. Mill's arguments, however, did not carry the day. Only militant suffrage movements and the crisis of World War I brought women the vote.

The decade or so following the passage of the Reform Bill of 1867 marked the high point of British liberalism. By opening the doors to political participation, liberalism had accomplished a peaceful restructuring of political institutions and social life. It did so under considerable pressure from below, however; and in Britain as elsewhere, liberal leaders made it clear that these doors were unquestionably not open to

Working-class leaders and middle-class dissidents joined in a countrywide campaign for a new reform bill and a House of Commons responsive to their interests. They were backed by some shrewd Conservatives, such as Benjamin Disraeli (1804–1881), who argued that political life would be improved, not disrupted, by including the "aristocrats of labor." In actuality, Disraeli was betting that the newly enfranchised demographic would vote Conservative; and in 1867, he steered through Parliament a bill that reached farther than anything proposed by his political opponents. The 1867 Reform Bill doubled the franchise by extending the vote to any men who paid poor rates or rent of £10 or more a year in urban areas (this meant, in general, skilled workers) and to rural tenants paying rent of £12 or more. As in 1832, the bill redistributed seats, with large northern cities gaining representation at the expense of the rural south. The responsible working class had been deemed worthy to participate in the affairs of state.

The reform bill was silent on women; but an important minority insisted that liberalism should include women's enfranchisement. These advocates mobilized a woman everyone. Their opposition to woman suffrage is interesting for what it reveals about their views on male and female nature. They insisted that female individuality (expressed in voting, education, or wage earning) would destabilize family life. Yet their opposition to woman suffrage also reflected conception of the vote: casting a ballot was a specific privilege granted only to specific social groups in return for their contributions to and vested interest in society. Men of property might champion the rule of law and representative government, but they balked at the prospect of a truly democratic politics and did not shy from heavy-handed, law-and-order politics. Expanding the franchise created new constituencies with new ambitions and paved the way for socialist and labor politics in the last quarter of the century. Tensions within liberalism remained and forecast conflicts in the future.

ITALIAN UNIFICATION: CAVOUR AND GARIBALDI

The failed efforts to unify Italy in 1848 left behind two different visions of Italian statehood. The first was most closely associated with Mazzini, who, as we have seen, believed in a republican Italy, built by the people. Mazzini's cause was taken up by the colorful figure Giuseppe Garibaldi. No political theorist, Garibaldi was a guerrilla fighter who had been exiled twice: first in Latin America, where he fought along with independence movements, and again in the United States. Like Mazzini, Garibaldi was committed to achieving national unification through a popular movement.

A decidedly different route to unification—a constitutional monarchy—was favored by more moderate nationalists, who sought economic and political reforms but intended to steer clear of democracy and the forces it might unleash. Rather than arousing popular movements, these moderates pinned their hopes on the kingdom of Piedmont-Sardinia, whose king, Charles Albert, had taken up the anti-Austrian cause in 1848. Though Charles Albert had been defeated and died in exile, his son Victor Emmanuel II (1849–1861) brought a man into his government who would embody the conservative vision of nationhood: the shrewd Sardinian nobleman Count Camillo Benso

Giuseppe Garibaldi.

di Cavour (1810–1861). "In Italy a democratic movement has almost no chance of success," Cavour declared. He instead pursued ambitious but pragmatic reforms guided by the state. First as minister of commerce and agriculture and then as prime minister, he promoted economic expansion, encouraged the construction of a modern transportation infrastructure, reformed the currency, and sought to raise Piedmont-Sardinia's profile in international relations. Garibaldi and Cavour thus represented two different routes to Italian unification: Garibaldi stood for unification from below, Cavour for unification guided from above.

Cavour's plan depended on diplomacy. Since Piedmont-Sardinia did not have the military capacity to counter the Austrians in northern Italy, Cavour skillfully cultivated an alliance with one of Austria's traditional rivals: Napoleonic France. In 1858 Cavour held a secret

> No political theorist, Garibaldi was a guerrilla fighter who had been exiled twice: first in Latin America, where he fought along with independence movements, and again in the United States.

WHY DID THE EFFORTS TO UNIFY ITALY AND GERMANY SUCCEED DURING THE 1860s?

BUILDING THE NATION-STATE   759

meeting with Napoleon III, who agreed to cooperate in driving the Austrians from Italy if Piedmont would cede Savoy and Nice to France. A war with Austria was duly provoked in 1859, and for a time all went well for the Franco-Italian allies. After the conquest of Lombardy, however, Napoleon III suddenly withdrew, concerned that he might either lose the battle or antagonize French Catholics, who were alienated by Cavour's hostility to the pope. Deserted by the French, Piedmont could not expel the Austrians from Venetia. Yet the campaign made extensive gains. Piedmont-Sardinia annexed Lombardy. The duchies of Tuscany, Parma, and Modena

THE UNIFICATION OF ITALY

Why did the Austrian von Metternich call Italy nothing but a "geographic expression" at midcentury? Why did Cavour see French support and sympathy as crucial to the cause of unification? Why did leadership of the unification movement fall to the Piedmont? Why did the Papal States oppose the unification of Italy?

BUILDING THE ITALIAN NATION: THREE VIEWS

The charismatic revolutionary Giuseppe Mazzini left more than fifty volumes of memoirs and writings. In the first excerpt, he sets out his vision of the "regeneration" of the Italian nation and the three Romes: ancient Rome, the Rome of the popes, and (in the future) the Rome of the people, which would emancipate the peoples of Europe. Mazzini's conception of Italian nationalism was Romantic in its interpretation of Italy's distinctive history and destiny and revolutionary in its emphasis on the Italian people rather than on statesmen.

The National Society was formed in 1857 to support Italian unification. By the 1860s, the society had over 5,000 members. It was especially strong in the Piedmont, where it was formed, and central Italy. Giuseppe la Farina was a tenacious organizer; he drafted the society's political creed and had it printed and sold throughout Italy.

The unification of Italy owed as much to Cavour's hard-nosed diplomacy as it did to middle-class movements for unification. In 1862, one of Cavour's contemporaries offered an assessment of the count and how he had found "an opening in the complicated fabric of European politics," reprinted in the third piece here.

MAZZINI AND ROMANTIC NATIONALISM

I saw regenerate Italy becoming at one bound the missionary of a religion of progress and fraternity. . . .

The worship of Rome was a part of my being. The great Unity, the One Life of the world, had twice been elaborated within her walls. Other peoples—their brief mission fulfilled—disappeared for ever. To none save to her had it been given twice to guide and direct the world. . . . There, upon the vestiges of an epoch of civilization anterior to the Grecian, which had had its seat in Italy . . . the Rome of the Republic, concluded by the Caesars, had arisen to consign the former world to oblivion, and borne her eagles over the known world, carrying with them the idea of right, the source of liberty.

In later days . . . she had again arisen, greater than before, and at once constituted herself, through her Popes—the accepted center of a new Unity. . . .

Why should not a new Rome, the Rome of the Italian people . . . arise to create a third and still vaster Unity; to link together and harmonize earth and heaven, right [law] and duty; and utter, not to individuals but to peoples, the great word Association—to make known to free men and equal their mission here below?

Giuseppe Mazzini, *The Life and Writings of Joseph Mazzini* (London, 1964), as cited in Denis Mack Smith, *The Making of Italy, 1796–1870* (New York, 1968), pp. 48–49.

THE POLITICAL CREED OF THE NATIONAL SOCIETY, FEBRUARY 1858

Italian independence should be the aim of every man of spirit and intelligence. Neither our educational system in Italy, nor our commerce and industry, can ever be flourishing or properly modernized while Austria keeps one foot on our neck. . . . What good is it to be

born in the most fertile and beautiful country in the world, to lie midway between East and West with magnificent ports in both the Adriatic and Mediterranean, to be descended from the Genoese, the Pisans, the men of Amalfi, Sicily and Venice? What use is it to have invented the compass, to have discovered the New World and been the progenitor of two civilizations? . . .

To obtain political liberty we must expel the Austrians who keep us enslaved. To win freedom of conscience we must expel the Austrians who keep us slaves of the Pope. To create a national literature we must chase away the Austrians who keep us uneducated. . . .

Italy must become not only independent but politically united. Political unity alone can reconcile various interests and laws, can mobilize credit and put out collective energies to speeding up communications. Only thus will we find sufficient capital for large-scale industry. Only thus will we create new markets, suppress internal obstacles to the free flow of commerce, and find the strength and reputation needed for traffic in distant lands. . . .

Everything points irresistibly to political unification. Science, industry, commerce, and the arts all need it. No great enterprise is possible any longer if we do not first put together the skill, knowledge, capital and labor of the whole of our great nation. The spirit of the age is moving toward concentration, and woe betide any nation that holds back!

A. Franchi, ed., *Scritti politici di Giuseppe La Farina*, vol. 2 (Milan, 1870), as cited in Denis Mack Smith, *The Making of Italy, 1796–1870* (New York, 1968), pp. 224–225.

COUNT CAVOUR AS A LEADER

Count Cavour undeniably ranks as third among European statesmen after Lord Palmerston [British prime minister 1885–1858, 1859–1865] and the Emperor Napoleon. . . . Count Cavour's strength does not lie in his principles; for he has none that are altogether inflexible. But he has a clear, precise aim, one whose greatness would—ten years ago—have made any other man reel: that of creating a unified and independent Italy. Men, means, circumstances were and still are matters of indifference to him. He walks straight ahead, always firm, often alone, sacrificing his friends, his sympathies, sometimes his heart, and often his conscience. Nothing is too difficult for him. . . .

Count Cavour . . . always has the talent to assess a situation and the possibilities of exploiting it. And it is this wonderful faculty that has contributed to form the Italy of today. As minister of a fourth-rate power, he could not create situations like Napoleon III, nor has he possessed the support of a great nation like Palmerston.

Count Cavour had to seek out an opening in the complicated fabric of European politics; he had to wriggle his way in, conceal himself, lay a mine, and cause an explosion. And it was by these means that he defeated Austria and won the help of France and England. Where other statesmen would have drawn back, Cavour plunged in headlong—as soon as he had sounded the precipice and calculated the possible profit and loss. The Crimean expeditionary force . . . the cession of Nice, the invasion of the Papal States last autumn [i.e., in 1860], were all the outcome of his vigorous stamina of mind.

There in brief you have the man of foreign affairs. He is strong; he is a match for the situation, for the politicians of his time or indeed of any time.

F. Petruccelli della Gattina, *I moribundi del Palazzo Carignano* (Milan, 1862), as cited in Denis Mack Smith, *The Making of Italy, 1796–1870* (New York, 1968), pp. 181–182.

QUESTIONS FOR ANALYSIS

1. In what ways was Mazzini's vision Romantic?
2. How did the National Society's practical nationalism differ from Mazzini's Romantic vision?
3. What was Cavour's strategy?

agreed by plebiscite to join the new state. By the end of this process in 1860, Piedmont-Sardinia had grown to more than twice its original size and was by far the most powerful state in Italy.

As Cavour consolidated the northern and central states, events in the southern states seemed to put those areas up for grabs as well. The unpopular Bourbon king of the Two Sicilies, Francis II (1859–1860), faced a fast-spreading peasant revolt that rekindled the hopes of earlier insurrections of the 1820s and 1840s. That revolt, in turn, got a much needed boost from Garibaldi, who landed in Sicily in May of 1860. "The Thousand,"

CHRONOLOGY

UNIFICATION OF ITALY, 1848–1870

Revolutions of 1848	
Italian war with Austria	1859
Conquest of the kingdom of Two Sicilies	1860
Austria cedes Venetia	1866
Occupation of Rome	1870
Law of Papal Guaranties enacted	1870

as Garibaldi's volunteer fighters called themselves, embodied the widespread support for Italian unification: they came from the north as well as from the south and counted among them members of the middle class as well as workers and artisans. Garibaldi's troops took Sicily in the name of Victor Emmanuel (though Garibaldi insisted that Sicily keep its autonomy), and then continued on to the mainland. By November 1860, Garibaldi's forces, alongside local insurgents, had taken Naples and toppled the kingdom of Francis II. Emboldened by success, Garibaldi looked to Rome, where French troops guarded the pope.

Garibaldi's rising popularity put him on a collision course with Cavour. "Now what will happen? It is impossible to forsee," the prime minister wrote a friend as he contemplated developments in the south. Cavour worried that Garibaldi's forces would bring French or Austrian intervention, with unknown consequences. He feared Garibaldi's "irresistible" prestige. Above all Cavour preferred that Italian unification happen quickly, under Piedmont-Sardinia's stewardship, without domestic turmoil or messy, unpredictable negotiations with other Italian states. "As long as he [Garibaldi] is faithful to his flag, one has to march along with him," Cavor wrote. "This does not alter the fact that it would be eminently desirable for the revolution . . . to be accomplished without him." Determined to recoup the initiative, Cavour dispatched Victor Emmanuel and his army to Rome. Flush with success, the king ordered Garibaldi to cede him military authority, and Garibaldi obeyed. Most of the peninsula was united under a single rule, and Victor Emmanuel assumed the title of king of Italy (1861–1878). Cavour's vision of Italian nationhood had won the day.

The final steps of Italy's territorial nation building came indirectly. Venetia remained in the hands of the Austrians until 1866, when Austria was defeated by Prussia and forced to relinquish their last Italian stronghold.

Rome had resisted conquest largely because of the military protection that Napoleon III accorded the pope. But in 1870 the outbreak of the Franco-Prussian War compelled Napoleon to withdraw his troops. That September, Italian soldiers occupied Rome; and in July 1871, Rome became capital of the united Italian kingdom.

What of the pope's authority? The Italian parliament passed the Law of Papal Guaranties to define and limit the pope's status—an act promptly defied by the reigning pontiff, Pius IX, who refused to have anything to do with a disrespectful secular government. His successors continued to close themselves off in the Vatican until 1929, when a series of agreements between the Italian government and Pius XI settled the dispute.

In 1871 Italy was a state, but nation building was hardly over. A minority of the "Italian" population spoke Italian; the rest used local and regional dialects so diverse that schoolteachers sent from Rome to Sicily were mistaken for foreigners. As one politician remarked, "We have made Italy; now we must make Italians." The task did not prove easy. The gap between an increasingly industrialized north and a poor and rural south remained wide. Cavour and those who succeeded him as prime minister had to contend with those economic and social inequalities, with rising tensions beween landlords and agricultural workers in rural regions, and with lingering resentments of the centralized northern-oriented state. Banditry in the territory of the former kingdom of the Two Sicilies compelled the central administration to dispatch troops to quell serious uprisings, killing more people than in the war of unification. Regional differences and social tensions, then, made building the Italian nation an ongoing process.

THE UNIFICATION OF GERMANY: REALPOLITIK

In 1853, the former revolutionary August Ludwig von Rochau wrote a short book with a long title: *The Principles of Realpolitik Applied to the Conditions of Germany.* Rochau banished the idealism and revolutionary fervor of his youth. "The question of who ought to rule . . . belongs in the realm of philosophical speculation," he wrote. "Practical politics has to do with the simple fact that it is power alone than can rule." In Rochau's view, power would not accrue to those with a "just" cause— those who supported constitutions and Enlightenment conceptions of rights. Instead power came indirectly, through diverse forms such as the expansion of the economy and social institutions. In several important

WHY DID THE EFFORTS TO UNIFY ITALY AND GERMANY SUCCEED DURING THE 1860S?

BUILDING THE NATION-STATE   763

ways, Rochau's views captured the changing outlook of broad sections of the German middle classes. *Realpolitik* became the watchword of the 1850s and 1860s and was most closely associated with the deeply conservative and pragmatic Otto von Bismarck, whose skillful diplomacy and power politics played such an important role in German unification. Yet the German nation was not built by one statesman's efforts. It was the product of the growth of national feeling, recalculations of middle-class interests, diplomacy, war, and struggles between the regime and its opponents.

Despite its decisive defeat in 1848, German liberalism had revived within a decade, in the face of considerable odds. The staunchly antirevolutionary King Frederick William had granted a Prussian constitution that established a bicameral (two-house) parliament, with the lower lower house elected by universal male suffrage. A series of edicts, however, modified the electoral system to reinforce hierarchies of wealth and power. The new provisions divided voters into three classes based on the amount of taxes they paid, and their votes were apportioned accordingly. (This new system was considered an improvement over the traditional practice of representation by estates, which had been dismantled in France in 1789.) Thus the relatively few wealthy voters who together paid one third of the country's taxes elected one third of the legislators, meaning a large landowner or industrialist exercised nearly a hundred times the voting power of a common workingman. In 1858 William I, who had led troops against the revolutionaries of 1848 in his youth, became prince regent of Prussia. (William became king in 1861 and ruled until 1888.) Although a notoriously conservative state, Prussia was not a monolith. A decade of industrial growth had expanded the size and confidence of the middle class. By the late 1850s, Prussia had an active liberal intelligensia, a thoughtful and engaged press, and a liberal civil service dedicated to political and economic modernization. These changes helped forge a liberal political movement that won a majority in elections to the lower house and could confidently confront the king.

The particular bone of contention (though hardly the only issue) between liberals and the king was military spending. William wanted to expand the standing army, reduce the role of reserve forces (a more middle-class group), and, above all, ensure that military matters were

> Yet the German nation was not built by one statesman's efforts. It was the product of the growth of national feeling, recalculations of middle-class interests, diplomacy, war, and struggles between the regime and its opponents.

not subject to parliamentary control. Opponents in Parliament suspected the king of making the military his own private force, or a state within a state. Between 1859 and 1862 relations deteriorated; and when liberals' protests went unanswered, they refused to approve the regular budget. Faced with a crisis, in 1862 William named Otto von Bismarck minister-president of Prussia. (A prime minister answers to Parliament; Bismarck did not.) This crucial moment in Prussian domestic politics became a decisive turning point in the history of German nationhood.

Born into the Junker class of conservative, land-owning aristocrats, Bismarck not only supported the monarchy during the revolutionary period of 1848–1849 but had fiercely opposed the liberal movement. He was not a nationalist. He was before all else a Prussian. He did not institute domestic reforms because he favored the rights of a particular group but because he thought that these policies would unify and strengthen Prussia. When he maneuvered to bring other German states under Prussian domination, he did so not in pursuit of a grand German design but because he believed that union in some form was inevitable and that Prussia had to seize the initiative. Bismarck happily acknowledged that he admired power and that he considered himself destined for greatness. At one point he had considered a career in the military, a common choice for someone with aristocratic origins, and he later regretted that he was compelled to serve his country from behind a desk rather than at the front. Whatever his post, he intended to command and to turn opportunities to his advantage. "I want to play the tune the way it sounds good to me or not at all," he declared. He had a reputation for cynicism, arrogance, and uninhibited frankness in expressing his views. Yet the Latin phrase he fondly quoted distills his more careful assessment of politics and of the relationship between even masterful individuals and history: "Man cannot create or control the tide of time, he can only move in the same direction and try to direct it."

In Prussia, Bismarck defied parliamentary opposition. When the liberal majority refused to levy taxes, he dissolved Parliament and collected them anyway, claiming that the constitution, whatever its purposes, had not been designed to subvert the state. His most decisive actions, however, were in foreign policy. Once opposed to nationalism, Bismarck skillfully played the national card to preempt his liberal opponents at home and to make German nation building an accomplishment—and an extension—of Prussian authority.

The other "German" power was Austria, which wielded considerable influence within the German Confederation and especially over the largely Catholic regions in the south. Bismarck saw a stark contrast between Austrian and Prussian interests, believed that the confederation had outlived its usefulness, and skillfully exploited Austria's economic disadvantages and the Habsburgs' internal ethnic struggles. He inflamed a long-smoldering

TOWARD THE UNIFICATION OF GERMANY

Note the stages leading to the unification of the German state. How did the German state of Prussia expand at the expense of Poland and the Austrian Empire? How did the nineteenth-century wars with France strengthen the emergent Prussian state? Examine closely the fragmented states of the region. What challenges did Bismarck face in building a unified Germany? What cultural and historical factors could he use to his advantage?

WHY DID THE EFFORTS TO UNIFY ITALY AND GERMANY SUCCEED DURING THE 1860S?

BUILDING THE NATION-STATE   765

dispute with Denmark over Schleswig (SHLAYS-vihg) and Holstein, two provinces peopled by Germans and Danes and claimed by both the German Confederation and Denmark. Liberal-nationalist feeling about the provinces ran high in the German Confederation, and a German liberal noble who claimed to be the rightful heir to Schleswig-Holstein became a minor public hero. In 1864, the Danish king attempted to annex the provinces, prompting a German nationalist outcry. Bismarck cast the conflict as a Prussian matter and persuaded Austria to join Prussia in a war against Denmark. The war was short, and it forced the Danish ruler to cede the two provinces to Austria and Prussia. As Bismarck hoped, the victorious alliance promptly fell apart. In 1866 casting Prussia as the defender of larger German interests, he declared war on Austria. The conflict, known as the Seven Weeks' War, ended in Prussian victory. Austria gave up all claims to Schleswig and Holstein, surrendered Venetia to the Italians, and agreed to dissolve the German Confederation. In its place Bismarck created the North German Confederation, a union of all the German states north of the Main River.

Bismarck "played power politics with an eye to public opinion." Both wars had strong public support, and Prussian victories weakened liberal opposition to the king and his president-minister. In the aftermath of the Austrian defeat, Prussian liberals gave up their battle over budgets, the military, and constitutional provisions. Bismarck also neutralized his opponents by other means. He admired Napoleon III's use of plebiscites to strengthen his regime and, like the French emperor, sought support among the masses. He understood that Germans did not necessarily support business elites, the bureaucracies of their own small states, or the Austrian Habsburgs. The constitution of the North German Confederation gave the appearance of a more liberal political body, with a bicameral legislature, freedom of the press, and universal male suffrage in the lower house. Its structure, however, gave Prussia and the conservative emperor a decisive advantage in the North German Confederation—and in the soon to be expanded empire.

The final step in the completion of German unity was the Franco-Prussian War of 1870–1871. Bismarck hoped that a conflict with France would arouse German nationalism in Bavaria, Württemberg, and other southern states still outside the confederation and overcome their historic wariness of Prussia. A diplo-

matic tempest concerning the right of the Hohenzollerns (Prussia's ruling family) to occupy the Spanish throne created an opportunity to foment a Franco-German misunderstanding. King William agreed to meet with the French ambassador at the resort spa of Ems in Prussia to discuss the Spanish succession. William initially acquiesced to French demands, but when the French blundered by asking for "perpetual exclusion" of the Hohenzollern family from the Spanish throne, Bismarck seized his opportunity. He edited a telegraph from the kaiser and released portions of it to the press so as to make it appear that King William had rebuffed the ambassador. Once the redacted report reached France, the nation reacted with calls for war. Prussia echoed the call, and Bismarck published evidence that he claimed proved French designs on the Rhineland.

As soon as war was declared, the south German states rallied to Prussia's side. The conflict was quickly over. No European powers came to France's aid. Austria, the most likely candidate, remained weakened by its recent war with Prussia. The Hungarians welcomed a strengthened Prussia, for the weaker Austria was as a German power, the stronger would be the Magyar claims to power sharing in the empire. In the battlefield, France could not match Prussia's professionally trained and superbly equipped forces. The war began in July and ended in September with the defeat of the French and the capture of Napoleon III at Sedan in France. Insurrectionary forces in Paris continued to hold out against the Germans through the winter of 1870–1871, but the French imperial government collapsed.

On January 18, 1871, in the Hall of Mirrors at Versailles, symbol of the powerful past of French absolutism, the German Empire was proclaimed. All the German states that had not already been absorbed

> On January 18, 1871, in the Hall of Mirrors at Versailles, symbol of the powerful past of French absolutism, the German Empire was proclaimed.

CHRONOLOGY

UNIFICATION OF GERMANY, 1854–1871

Crimean War	1854–1856
Bismarck becomes prime minister	1862
Danish War	1864
Seven Weeks' War	1866
Franco-Prussian War	1870–1871

Actualité.   N°28.

Lith Pinot et Sagaire édité à Epinal   Déposé.

Voici encore Bismarck avec son grand balai qui houspille et ramasse tous les allemands récalcitrants.

Allons! allons donc morbleu!... plus vite que ça! ou les français vont manger votre choucroute!!

Bismarck Sweeping away the Stubborn Germans.
Bismarck helped provoke the Franco-Prussian War of
1870–1871 by cultivating the perception that France
was a threat to Germany. This caricature reads "Here is
Bismarck, still with his big broom, who scolds and picks
up all of the recalcitrant Germans. Let's go! Go or die!
Faster than that! Or the French will eat your sauerkraut!"

into the Prussian fold, except Austria, declared their
allegiance to William I, henceforth emperor or kaiser.
Four months later, at Frankfurt, a treaty between the
French and the Germans ceded the border region of
Alsace to the new German Empire and forced the
French to pay an indemnity of 5 billion francs. Prussia
accounted for 60 percent of the new state's territory
and population. The Prussian kaiser, prime minister,
army, and most of the bureaucracy remained intact,
now reconfigured as the German nation-state. This
was not the new nation for which Prussian liberals
had hoped. It marked a "revolution from above"
rather than from below. Still, the more optimistic
believed that the German Empire would evolve in a
different political direction and that they could eventually "extend freedom through unity."

THE STATE AND NATIONALITY: CENTRIFUGAL FORCES IN THE AUSTRIAN EMPIRE

Germany emerged from the 1860s a stronger, unified
nation. The Habsburg Empire faced a very different
situation, with different resources, and emerged a weakened, precariously balanced, multiethnic dual monarchy, also called Austria-Hungary.

As we have seen, ethnic nationalism was a powerful
force in the Habsburg monarchy in 1848. Yet the
Habsburg state, with a combination of military repression and tactics that divided its enemies, had proved
more powerful. It abolished serfdom but made few
other concessions to its opponents. The Hungarians,
who had nearly won independence in the spring of
1848, were essentially reconquered. The Imperial
Council, which developed into a House of Lords,
nominally accommodated representatives of the nationalities. Other developments were also intended to
strengthen the Habsburg state. Administrative reforms
created a new and more uniform legal system, rationalized taxation, and imposed a single-language policy
that favored German. The issue of managing ethnic relations, however, only grew more difficult. Through
the 1850s and 1860s the subject nationalities, as they
were often called, bitterly protested the powerlessness
of their local Diets (parliaments), military repression,
cultural disenfranchisement, and electoral districts that
reduced their representation. The Czechs in Bohemia,
for instance, grew increasingly alienated by policies
that favored the German minority of the province and
increasingly insistent on their Slavic identity—a movement welcomed by Russia, willing enough to become
the sponsor of a broad pan-Slavism. The Hungarians,
or Magyars, the most powerful of the subject nationalities, sought to reclaim the autonomy they had
glimpsed in 1848.

In this context, Austria's damaging defeats at the
hands of Piedmont-Sardinia in 1859 and Prussia in
1866 became especially significant. The 1866 war in
particular forced the emperor Francis Joseph to renegotiate the very structure of the empire. To stave off a
revolution by the Hungarians, Francis Joseph agreed to
a new federal structure in the form of the Dual Monarchy. Austria-Hungary had a common system of taxation, a common army, and made foreign and military
policy together. Francis Joseph was emperor of Austria
and king of Hungary. But internal and constitutional
affairs were separated. The Ausgleich, or Settlement,

WHAT WERE THE SIMILARITIES BETWEEN SLAVERY AND SERFDOM? WHERE DID SLAVERY SURVIVE AND WHY?

NATION AND STATE BUILDING IN RUSSIA, THE UNITED STATES, AND CANADA   767

allowed the Hungarians to establish their own constitution, their own legislature, and their own capital, combining the cities of Buda and Pest.

What of the other nationalities? The official policy of the Dual Monarchy stated that they were not to be discriminated against and that they could use their own languages. Official policy was only loosely enforced. More important, elevating the Hungarians and conferring on them alone the benefits of political nationhood could only worsen relations with other groups. On the Austrian side of the Dual Monarchy, minority nationalities such as the Poles, Czechs, and Slovenes resented their second-class status. On the Hungarian side, the regime embarked on a project of Magyarization, attempting to make the state, the civil service, and the schools more thoroughly Hungarian—an effort that did not sit well with Serbs and Croats.

It was impossible, then, to speak of national unification in the Habsburg lands. The Austrian emperor remained deeply opposed to nationalism, considering it, rightly, a centrifugal force that would destroy his kingdom. Unlike the governments of France, England, Italy, or Germany, the Habsburgs did not seek to build a nation-state based on a common cultural identity. It tried instead to build a state and administrative structure strong enough to keep the pieces from spinning off, playing different minorities off against each other, and conceding autonomy only when essential. As the nineteenth century unfolded, subject nationalities would appeal to other powers—Serbia, Russia, the Ottomans—and this balancing act would become more difficult.

NATION AND STATE BUILDING IN RUSSIA, THE UNITED STATES, AND CANADA

What were the similarities between slavery and serfdom? Where did slavery survive and why?

The challenges of nationalism and nation building also occupied Russia, the United States, and Canada. In all three countries, nation building entailed territorial and economic expansion, the incorporation of new peoples, and—in Russia and the United States—contending with the enormous problems of slavery and serfdom.

TERRITORY, THE STATE, AND SERFDOM: RUSSIA

Serfdom in Russia, which had been legally formalized in 1649, had begun to draw significant protest from the intelligentsia under the reign of Catherine the Great (1762–1796). After 1789, and especially after 1848, the abolition of serfdom elsewhere in Europe made the issue more urgent. Abolishing serfdom became part of the larger project of building Russia as a modern nation. How that should happen was the subject of much debate. Two schools of thought emerged. The "Slavophiles," or Romantic nationalists, sought to preserve Russia's distinctive features. They idealized traditional Russian culture and the peasant commune, rejecting Western secularism, urban commercialism, and bourgeois culture. In contrast, the "westernizers" wished to see Russia adopt European developments in science, technology, and education, which they believed to be the foundation for Western liberalism and the protection of individual rights. Both groups agreed that serfdom must be abolished. The Russian nobility, however, tenaciously opposed emancipation. Tangled debates about how lords would be compensated for the loss of "their" serfs, and how emancipated serfs would survive without full-scale land redistribution, also checked progress on the issue. The Crimean War (discussed later in this chapter) broke the impasse. In its aftermath, Alexander II (1855–1881) forced the issue. Worried that the persistence of serfdom had sapped Russian strength and contributed to its defeat in the war, and persuaded that serfdom would only continue to prompt violent conflict, he ended serfdom by decree in 1861.

The emancipation decree of 1861 was a reform of massive scope; but paradoxically, it produced limited change. It granted legal rights to some 22 million serfs and authorized their title to a portion of the land they had worked. It also required the state to compensate landowners for the properties they relinquished. Large-scale landowners vastly inflated their compensation claims, however, and managed to retain much of the most profitable acreage for themselves. As a result, the land granted to peasants was often of poor quality and insufficient to sustain themselves and their families. Moreover, the newly liberated serfs had to

THE ABOLITION OF SERFDOM IN RUSSIA

The abolition of serfdom was central to Tsar Alexander II's program of modernization and reform after the Crimean War. Emancipated serfs were now allowed to own their land, ending centuries of bondage. The decree, however, emphasized the tsar's benevolence and the nobility's generosity—not peasant rights. The government did not want emancipation to bring revolution to the countryside; it sought to reinforce the state's authority, the landowners' power, and the peasants' obligations. After spelling out the detailed provisions for emancipation, the decree added the paragraphs reprinted here.

Emancipation did not solve problems in the Russian countryside. On the contrary, it unleashed a torrent of protest, including complaints from peasants that nobles were undermining attempts to reform. These petitions in the second section detail the struggles that came in the wake of emancipation in two villages.

TSAR ALEXANDER II'S DECREE EMANCIPATING THE SERFS, 1861

And We place Our hope in the good sense of Our people.

When word of the Government's plan to abolish the law of bondage [serfdom] reached peasants unprepared for it, there arose a partial misunderstanding. Some [peasants] thought about freedom and forgot about obligations. But the general good sense [of the people] was not disturbed in the conviction that anyone freely enjoying the goods of society correspondingly owes it to the common good to fulfill certain obligations, [a conviction held] both by natural reason and by Christian law, according to which "every soul must be subject to the governing authorities." . . .

Rights legally acquired by the landlords cannot be taken from them without a decent return or [their] voluntary concession; and that it would be contrary to all justice to make use of the lords' land without bearing the corresponding obligation.

And now We hopefully expect that the bonded people, as a new future opens before them, will understand and accept with gratitude the important sacrifice made by the Well-born Nobility for the improvement of their lives.

James Cracraft, ed., *Major Problems in the History of Imperial Russia* (Lexington, Mass., 1994), pp. 340–344.

EMANCIPATION: THE VIEW FROM BELOW

PETITION FROM PEASANTS IN PODOSINOVKA (VORONEZH PROVINCE) TO ALEXANDER II, MAY 1863

The most merciful manifesto of Your Imperial Majesty from 19 February 1861, with the published rules, put a limit to the enslavement of the people in blessed Russia. But some former serfowners—who desire not to improve the peasants' life, but to oppress and ruin them—apportion land contrary to the laws, choose the best land from all the fields for themselves, and give the poor peasants . . . the worst and least usable lands.

To this group of squires must be counted our own, Anna Mikhailovna Raevskaia. . . . Of our fields and resources, she chose the best places from amidst our strips, and, like a cooking ring in a hearth, carved off

300 dessiatines [measures of land] for herself. . . . But our community refused to accept so ruinous an allotment and requested that we be given an allotment in accordance with the local Statute. . . . The peace arbitrator . . . and the police chief . . . slandered us before the governor, alleging that we were rioting and that it is impossible for them to enter our village.

The provincial governor believed this lie and sent 1,200 soldiers of the penal command to our village. . . . Without any cause, our village priest Father Peter—rather than give an uplifting pastoral exhortation to stop the spilling of innocent blood—joined these reptiles, with the unanimous incitement of the authorities. . . . They summoned nine township heads and their aides from other townships. . . . In their presence, the provincial governor—without making any investigation and without interrogating a single person—ordered that the birch rods be brought and that the punishment commence, which was carried out with

cruelty and mercilessness. They punished up to 200 men and women; 80 people were at four levels (with 500, 400, 300 and 200 blows); some received lesser punishment . . . and when the inhuman punishment of these innocent people had ended, the provincial governor said: "If you find the land unsuitable, I do not forbid you to file petitions wherever you please," and then left. . . .

We dare to implore you, Orthodox emperor and our merciful father, not to reject the petition of a community with 600 souls, including wives and children. Order with your tsarist word that our community be allotted land . . . as the law dictates without selecting the best sections of fields and meadows, but in straight lines. . . . [Order that] the meadows and haylands along the river Elan be left to our community without any restriction; these will enable us to feed our cattle and smaller livestock, which are necessary for our existence.

PETITION FROM PEASANTS IN BALASHOV DISTRICT TO GRAND DUKE CONSTANTIN NIKOLAEVICH, JANUARY 25, 1862

Your Imperial Excellency! Most gracious sire! Grand Duke Konstantin Nikolaevich! . . .

After being informed of the Imperial manifesto on the emancipation of peasants from serfdom on 1861 . . . we received this [news] with jubilation. . . . But from this moment, our squire ordered that the land be cut off from the entire township. But this is absolutely intolerable for us: it not only denies us profit, but threatens us with a catastrophic future. He began to hold repeated meetings and [tried to] force us to sign that we agreed to accept the above land allotment. But, upon seeing so unexpected a change, and bearing in mind the gracious manifesto, we refused. . . . After assembling the entire township, they tried to force us into making illegal signatures accepting the land cut-offs. But when they saw that this did not succeed, they had a company of soldiers sent in. . . . Then [Colonel] Globbe came from

their midst, threatened us with exile to Siberia, and ordered the soldiers to strip the peasants and to punish seven people by flogging in the most inhuman manner. They still have not regained consciousness.

Gregory L. Freeze, ed., *From Supplication to Revolution: A Documentary Social History of Imperial Russia* (New York, 1988), pp. 170–173.

QUESTIONS FOR ANALYSIS

1. What were Tsar Alexander II's warnings and to whom were they addressed?
2. From a peasant's perspective, what issue mattered most?
3. What do these remarkable documents reveal about events after emancipation?

pay in installments for their land, which was not in fact granted to them individually, but rather to a village commune that collected their payments. As a result, the pattern of rural life in Russia did not change drastically. The system of payment kept peasants in the villages—not as free-standing farmers but as agricultural laborers for their former masters.

While the Russian state undertook reforms, it also expanded its territory. After midcentury, the Russians pressed east and south. They invaded and conquered several independent Islamic kingdoms along the former Silk Road and expanded into Siberia in search of natural resources. Russian diplomacy wrung various commercial concessions from the Chinese that led to

The Emancipation of the Serfs. This engraving depicts officials delivering the formal decree liberating serfs. A massive reform granting legal rights to millions of people, emancipation was undermined by the payments serfs owed to their former owners.

the founding of the Siberian city of Vladivostok in 1860. Racial, ethnic, and religious differences made governing a daunting task. In most cases, the Russian state did not try to assimilate the populations of the new territories: an acceptance of ethnic particularity was a pragmatic response to the difficulties of governing such a heterogeneous population. When the state did attempt to impose Russian culture, the results were disastrous. Whether power was wielded by the nineteenth-century tsars or, later, by the Soviet Union, powerful centrifugal forces pulled against genuine unification. Expansion helped Russia create a vast empire that was geographically of one piece, but by no means one nation.

TERRITORY AND THE NATION: THE UNITED STATES

The American Revolution had bequeathed to the United States a loose union of slave and free states,

tied together in part by a commitment to territorial expansion. The so-called Jeffersonian Revolution combined democratic aspirations with a drive to expand the nation's boundaries. Leaders of the movement, under the Democratic-Republican president Thomas Jefferson (1801–1809), campaigned to add the Bill of Rights to the Constitution and were almost exclusively responsible for its success. Though they supported, in principle, the separation of powers, they believed in the supremacy of the people's representatives and viewed with alarm attempts of the executive and judicial branches to increase their power. They supported a political system based on an aristocracy of "virtue and talent," in which respect for personal liberty would be the guiding principle. They opposed the establishment of a national religion and special privilege, whether of birth or of wealth. Yet the Jeffersonian vision of the republic rested on the independence of yeomen farmers, and the independence and prosperity of those farmers depended on the availability of new lands. This made territorial expansion, as exemplified

WHAT WERE THE SIMILARITIES BETWEEN SLAVERY AND SERFDOM? WHERE DID SLAVERY SURVIVE AND WHY?

NATION AND STATE BUILDING IN RUSSIA, THE UNITED STATES, AND CANADA   771

by the Louisiana Purchase in 1803, central to Jeffersonian America. Expansion brought complications. While it did provide land for many yeomen farmers in the north and south, it also added millions of acres of prime cotton land, thus extending the empire of slavery. The purchase of the port of New Orleans made lands in the south well worth developing but led the American republic forcibly to remove Native Americans from the Old South west of the Mississippi River. This process of expansion and expropriation stretched from Jefferson's administration through the age of Jackson, or the 1840s.

Under Andrew Jackson (1829–1837), the Democrats (as some of the Democratic-Republicans were now called) transformed the circumscribed liberalism of the Jeffersonians. They campaigned to extend the suffrage to all white males; they argued that all office-holders should be elected rather than appointed; and they sought the frequent rotation of men in positions of political power—a doctrine that permitted politicians to use patronage to build national political parties. Moreover, the Jacksonian vision of democracy and nationhood carried over into a crusade to incorporate more territories into the republic. It was the United States' "Manifest Destiny," wrote a New York editor, "to overspread the continent allotted by Providence for the free development of our yearly multiplying millions." That "overspreading" brought

AMERICAN EXPANSION IN THE EARLY NINETEENTH CENTURY

A crucial turning point in American westward expansion came in 1803, when the Louisiana Purchase transferred a vast expanse of land from Napoleon I's France to the United States. Napoleon had failed to reconquer Saint-Domingue and restore slavery there, and he urgently needed to regroup his forces for war in Europe. Both factors persuaded him to give up visions of a North American empire. How did the withdrawal of a major colonial power reshape American attitudes about the western frontier? What further issues did the Louisiana Purchase raise?

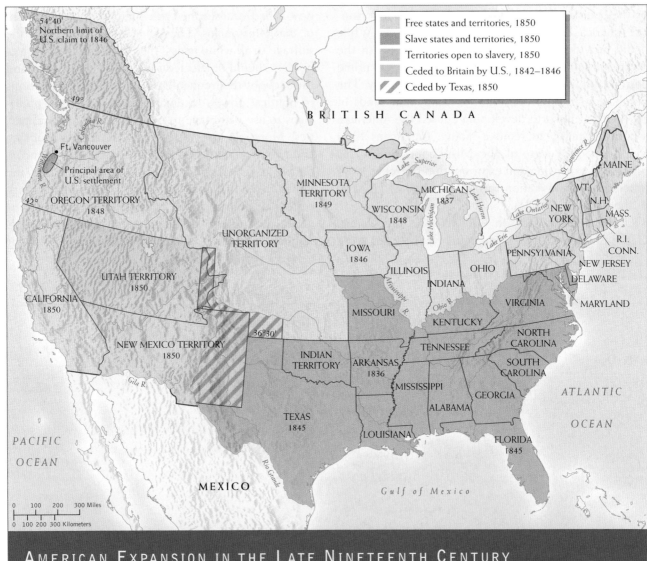

Free states and territories, 1850
Slave states and territories, 1850
Territories open to slavery, 1850
Ceded to Britain by U.S., 1842–1846
Ceded by Texas, 1850

AMERICAN EXPANSION IN THE LATE NINETEENTH CENTURY

Note the stages by which American settlement progressed across the North American continent and the organization of newly acquired territory by the American government. How was American expansion different from European colonialism? How was it similar? Why were the Utah and New Mexico territories opened to slavery even though the west and southwest had previously been considered free? What role did California statehood play in such considerations?

Oregon and Washington into the Union through a compromise with the British and brought Arizona, Texas, New Mexico, Utah, Nevada, and California through war with Mexico—all of which led to the wholesale expropriation of Native American lands. Territorial expansion was key to nation building, but it was built on increasingly impossible conflict over slavery.

THE POLITICS OF SLAVERY IN THE WEST

When the age of revolution opened in the 1770s, slavery was legal everywhere in the Americas. By the point we have reached, the close of the age of revolution, slavery remained legal only in the southern United States,

WHAT WERE THE SIMILARITIES BETWEEN SLAVERY AND SERFDOM? WHERE DID SLAVERY SURVIVE AND WHY?

NATION AND STATE BUILDING IN RUSSIA, THE UNITED STATES, AND CANADA   773

Brazil, and Cuba. (It endured, too, in most of Africa and parts of India and the Islamic world.) Why? There are two ways to approach this issue. The first is to ask why slavery lasted so long in these areas. The second, perhaps more appropriate, requires setting aside our assumption that the moral arc of history leads toward freedom, to borrow a phrase from Martin Luther King Jr.. How and why was slavery, which had been embedded for centuries in economies and culture, abolished elsewhere in the West?

The revolutions of the eighteenth century by no means brought emancipation in their wake. Eighteenth-century Enlightenment thinkers had persuaded many Europeans that slavery contradicted natural law and natural freedom (see Chapter Seventeen). As one historian trenchantly puts it, however, "slavery became a metaphor for everything that was bad—except the institution of slavery itself." Thus Virginia planters who helped lead the

CHRONOLOGY

SLAVE RESISTANCE AND ABOLITION IN THE NEW WORLD, 1791–1888

Slave rebellion in Saint Domingue becomes Haitian Revolution	1791–1804
African slave trade banned by Great Britain and United States	1808
Missouri Compromise	1818–1821
Major slave rebellion in Jamaica	1831
British emancipates 800,000 slaves (effective 1838)	1833
United States annexes Texas as a slave state	1845
France and Denmark abolish slavery	1848
Treaty of Guadaloupe Hidalgo	1848
Dred Scott decision	1857
American Civil War	1861–1865
Spain begins gradual emancipation	1870
Brazilian Emancipation	1871–1888

This poster, created by northern African American abolitionists, exhorts fellow blacks to fight in the American Civil War.

American Revolution angrily refused to be "slaves" to the English king while defending plantation slavery. The planters' success in throwing off the British king expanded their power and strengthened slavery. Likewise, the French revolutionaries denounced the tyranny of a king who would "enslave" them but refused to admit free people of color to the revolutionary assembly for fear of alienating the planters in the lucrative colonies of Martinique, Guadeloupe, and Saint Domingue. Only a slave rebellion in Saint Domingue in 1791 forced the French revolutionaries, eventually, to contend with the contradictions of revolutionary policy. Napoleon's failure to repress that rebellion allowed for the emergence of Haiti in 1804 (see Chapter Eighteen). The Haitian revolution sent shock waves through the Americas, alarming slave owners and offering hope to slaves and former slaves. In the words of a free black sailmaker in Philadelphia, the Haitian nation signaled that black people "could not always be detained in their present bondage." Yet the Haitian revolution had other, contradictory consequences. The "loss" of slave-based sugar production in the former Saint Domingue created an opportunity for its expansion elsewhere, in the U.S. south, and in Brazil, where slavery expanded in the production of sugar, gold, and coffee. Finally, slavery remained intact in the French, British, and Spanish colonial islands in the Caribbean, backed by the Congress of Vienna in 1815.

An abolitionist movement did emerge, in England. The country that ruled the seas was "the world's leading purchaser and transporter of African slaves," and the movement aimed to abolish that trade. From the 1780s on, pamphlets and books (the best known is *The Interesting Narrative of the Life of Olaudah Equiano*, 1789) detailed the horrors of the slave ships to an increasingly sympathetic audience. Abolitionist leaders like William Wilberforce believed that the slave trade was immoral and hoped that banning it would improve conditions for the enslaved, though like most abolitionists Wilberforce did not want to foment revolt. In 1807 the reform movement compelled Parliament to pass a bill declaring the "African Slave Trade to be contrary to the principles of justice, humanity and sound policy" and prohibiting British ships from participating in it, effective 1808. The United States joined in the agreement; ten years later the Portugese agreed to a limited ban on traffic north of the equator. More treaties followed, which slowed but did not stop the trade.

What roots did abolitionism tap? Some historians argue that slavery was becoming less profitable and that its decline made humanitarian concern easier to accept. Others argue that slavery was expanding: among other things, ships carried 2.5 million slaves to markets in the Americas in the four decades *after* the abolition of slave trade. Some historians believe economic factors undermined slavery. Adam Smith and his followers argued that free labor, like free trade, was more efficient. This was not necessarily the case, but such arguments still had an effect. Critics claimed slavery was wasteful as well as cruel. Economic calculations, however, did less to activate abolitionism than a belief that the slave trade and slavery itself represented the arrogance and callousness of wealthy British traders, their planter allies, and the British elite in general. In a culture with high literacy and political traditions of activism, calls for "British liberty" mobilized many. In England, and especially in the United States, religious revivals supplied much of the energy for the abolitionist movement. The hymn "Amazing Grace" was written by a former slave trader turned minister, John Newton, to describe his conversion experience and salvation. The moral and religious dimensions of the struggle made it acceptable for women, who would move from antislavery to the Anti–Corn Law League and, later, to woman suffrage. Finally, the issue spoke to working people whose sometimes brutal working conditions and sharply limited political rights we have discussed in the previous chapters. To oppose slavery and to insist that labor should be dignified, honorable, and minimally free resonated broadly in the social classes accustomed to being treated as "servile." The issue, then cut across material interests and class politics, and antislavery petitions were signed by millions in the 1820s and 1830s.

Slave rebellions and conspiracies to rebel also shook opinion. The year 1800 brought a slave rebellion in Virginia; 1811, an uprising in Louisiana; 1822, an alleged conspiracy in South Carolina. The British colonies saw significant rebellions in the Barbados (1816); Demerara, just east of Venezuela (1823); and most important, the month-long insurrection in Jamaica (1831). All of these were ferociously repressed. Slave rebellions had virtually no chance of succeeding and usually erupted only when some crack in the system opened up: divisions within the white elite or the (perceived) presence of a sympathetic outsider. Still, especially against the backdrop of the Haitian revolution and the rise of abolitionism, these rebellions had important consequences. They increased slaveholders' sense of vulnerability and isolation. They polarized debate. Outsiders (in England or New England) often recoiled at the brutality of repression. Slave owners responded to antislavery sentiment much as Russian serf owners had responded to their critics, by insisting that slavery was vital to their survival, that emancipation of inferior peoples would sow chaos, and that abolitionists were dangerously playing with fire.

In Great Britain, the force of abolitionism wore down the defense of slavery. In the aftermath of the great Reform Bill of 1832, Great Britain emancipated 800,000 slaves in its colonies—effective in 1838, after four years of "apprenticeship." In France, republicans took the strongest antislavery stance, and emancipation came to the French colonies when the revolution of 1848 brought republicans, however briefly, to power.

In Latin America, slavery's fate was determined by demographics, economics, and the politics of breaking away from the Spanish and Portugese empires. In most of mainland Spanish America (in other words, not Cuba or Brazil), slavery had been of secondary importance, due to the relative ease of escape and the presence of other sources of labor. As the struggles for independence escalated, nationalist leaders recruited slaves and free people of color to fight against the Spanish, promising emancipation in return. Simon de Bolívar's 1817 campaign to liberate Venezuela was fought in part by slaves, ex-slaves, and 6,000 troops from Haiti. The new nations in Spanish America passed emancipation measures in stages but had eliminated slavery by the middle of the century.

Cuba was starkly different: with 40 percent of its population enslaved, the Spanish island colony had almost as many slaves as all of mainland Spanish America together. A Cuban independence movement would have detonated a slave revolution, a fact that provided a powerful incentive for Cuba to remain under the Spanish crown. Spain, for its part, needed the immensely profitable sugar industry and could not afford to alienate Cuban planters pushing for an end to slavery. Only a combination of slave rebellion in Cuba and liberal revolution in Spain brought abolition, beginning in the 1870s. Brazil, too, was 40 percent enslaved and, like Cuba, had a large population of free people of color. Unlike Cuba, Brazil won national independence, breaking away from Portugal with relative ease (1822). Like the American south, Brazil came through the revolution for independence with slavery not only intact but expanding, and slavery endured in Brazil until 1888.

THE AMERICAN CIVIL WAR, 1861–1865

The politics of slavery, then, were by no means unique to the United States, but in the United States the combination of a growing abolitionist movement, a slave-owning class that feared the economic power of the north, and territorial expansion created deadlock and crisis. As the country expanded west, North and South engaged in a protracted tug of war about whether new states were to be "free" or "slave." In the North, territorial expansion heightened calls for free labor; in the South it deepened whites' commitment to an economy and society based on plantation slavery. Ultimately, the changes pushed southern political leaders toward secession. The failure of a series of elaborate compromises led to the outbreak of the Civil War in 1861.

The protracted and costly struggle proved a first experience of the horrors of modern war and prefigured World War I. It also decisively transformed the nation. First, it abolished slavery. Second, it established the preeminence of the national government over states' rights. The Fourteenth Amendment to the Constitution stated specifically that all Americans were citizens of the United States and not of an individual state or territory. In declaring that no citizen was to be deprived of life, liberty, or property without due process of law, it established that "due process" was to be defined by the

national, not the state or territorial, government. Third, in the aftermath of the Civil War, the U.S. economy expanded with stunning rapidity. In 1865, there were 35,000 miles of railroad track in the United States; by 1900, there were almost 200,000. Industrial and agricultural production rose, putting the United States in a position to compete with Great Britain. As we will see later on, American industrialists, bankers, and retailers introduced innovations in assembly-line manufacturing, corporate organization, and advertising that startled their European counterparts and gave the United States new power in world politics. These developments were all part of the process of nation building. They did not overcome deep racial, regional, or class divides. Though the war brought the South back into the Union, the rise of northern capitalism magnified the backwardness of the South as an underdeveloped agricultural region whose wealth was extracted by northern industrialists. The railroad corporations, which pieced together the national infrastructure, became the classic foe of labor and agrarian reformers. In these ways, the Civil War laid the foundations for the modern American nation-state.

"EASTERN QUESTIONS": INTERNATIONAL RELATIONS AND THE DECLINE OF OTTOMAN POWER

Why was the Crimean War significant?

During the nineteenth century, questions of national identity and international power were inextricable from contests over territory. War and diplomacy drew and redrew boundaries as European nations groped toward a sustainable balance of power. The rise of new powers, principally the German Empire, posed one set of challenges to Continental order. The waning power of older regimes posed another. The Crimean War, which lasted from 1854 to 1856, was a particularly gruesome attempt to cope with the most serious such collapse. As the Ottoman Empire lost its grip on its provinces in southeastern Europe, the "Eastern Question" of who would benefit from Ottoman weakness drew Europe into war. At stake were not only territorial gains but also strategic interests, alliances, and the balance of power in Europe.

And though the war occurred before the unification of the German and Italian states, it structured the system of Great Power politics that guided Europe until (and indeed toward) World War I.

THE CRIMEAN WAR, 1854–1856

The root causes of the war lay in the Eastern Question and the decline of the Ottoman Empire. The crisis that provoked it, however, involved religion—namely French and Russian claims to protect religious minorities and the Holy Places of Jerusalem within the Muslim Ottoman Empire. In 1853 a three-way quarrel among France (on behalf of Roman Catholics), Russia (representing Eastern Orthodox Christians), and Turkey devolved into a Russian confrontation with the Turkish sultan. Confident that Turkey would be unable to resist, concerned that other powers might take advantage of Turkish weakness, and persuaded (mistakenly) that they had British support, the Russians moved troops into the Ottoman-governed territories of Moldavia and Walachia. (These territories lie north and west of the point at which the Danube River meets the Black Sea.) In October 1853 Turkey, also persuaded they would be supported by the British, declared war on Russia. The war became a disaster for the Turks, who lost their fleet at the battle of Sinope in November. But Russia's success alarmed the British and the French, who considered Russian expansion a threat to their interests in the Balkans; the eastern Mediterranean; and, for the British, the route to India. Determined to check that expansion, France and Britain each declared war on Russia in March 1854. In September they landed on the Russian peninsula of Crimea and headed for the Russian naval base at Sevastopol, to which they laid siege. France, Britain, and the Ottomans were joined in 1855 by the small but ambitious Italian state of Piedmont-Sardinia, all fighting against the Russians. This was the closest Europe had come to a general war since 1815.

The war was relatively short, but its conduct was devastating. Conditions on the Crimean peninsula were dire, and the disastrous mismanagement of supplies and hygiene by the British and French led to epidemics among the troops. At least as many soldiers died from typhus or cholera as in combat. The fighting was bitter, marked by such notoriously inept strategies as the British "charge of the Light Brigade," in which a British cavalry unit was slaughtered by massed Russian artillery. Vast battles pitted tens of thousands of British and French troops against Russian formations, combat that was often settled with bayonets. Despite the disciplined toughness of the British and French troops, and despite their nations' dominance of the seas around Crimea, the Russians denied them a clear victory. Sevastopol, under siege for nearly a year, did not fall until September 1855. The bitter, unsatisfying conflict was ended by treaty in 1856.

For the French and Sardinians, the bravery of their soldiers bolstered positive national sentiments at home; for the British and Russians, however, the poorly managed war provoked waves of intense criticism. As far as international relations were concerned, the peace settlement dealt a blow to Russia, whose influence in the Balkans was drastically curbed. The provinces of Moldavia and Walachia were united as Romania, and became an independent nation. Austria's refusal to come to the aid of Russia cost her the support of her powerful former ally. The Crimean War embarrassed France and

Captain Dames of the Royal Artillery, 1855. Roger Fenton studied painting in London and then Paris, where he learned about and started to experiment with photography. He developed a mobile darkroom and ventured into the English countryside. in 1855, he went to the Crimea, subsidized by the British government. Photographs of movement and troops in battle were still impossible, and political restraint kept him from photographing the horrors of the increasingly unpopular Crimean War. Still, his were the first war photographs.

THE CRIMEAN WAR

Note the theater of operations and the major assaults of the Crimean War. Why did the Crimean War erupt? Who fought whom, and why? Did the allies achieve their objectives? In what ways was the Crimean War the first modern war?

left Russia and Austria considerably weaker, opening an advantage for Bismarck in the 1860s, as we saw earlier.

The Crimean War was important in other ways as well. Though fought largely with the same methods and mentalities employed in the Napoleonic Wars forty years earlier, the war brought innovations that forecast the direction of modern warfare. It saw the first significant use of rifled muskets, underwater mines, and trench warfare as well as the first tactical use of railroads and telegraphs.

In addition, the war was covered by the first modern war correspondents and photojournalists, making it the most public war to date. Reports from the theater of war were sent "live" by telegraph to Britain and France with objective and sobering detail; the (London) *Times* reporter William Howard Russell, for instance, heaped criticism on the government for the deplorable conditions British soldiers endured. The care and supply of the troops became national scandals in the popular press, prompting dramatic changes in the military's administrative and logistical systems and making heroes of individual doctors and nurses such as Florence Nightingale. The British government and commercial publishers both sent photographers to document the war's progress and perhaps also to counter charges that troops were undersupplied and malnourished. Roger Fenton, the most prominent and prolific of these war photographers, employed the new medium to capture the grim realities of camp life. Technological limitations and political considerations kept him from photographing the more gruesome carnage of the battlefield, but Fenton's photographs introduced a new level of realism and immediacy to the public's conception of war.

REALISM: "DEMOCRACY IN ART"

The journalistic reporting from the Crimean War was remarkable because it avoided the heroic and bombastic language to which nineteenth-century readers were accustomed. In this way, it reflected a dominant cultural trend of the mid-nineteenth century: the rise of the artistic movement known as realism. In both painting and literature, realism signaled a strict rejection of artistic conventions and ready-made formulas in favor of what artists saw as more honest, objective, and authentic representations of the world. Whereas Romanticism had sought higher truths, with an emphasis on emotion and imagination, realism trained its gaze on empirical reality. As the French painter Gustave Courbet (*corBAY;* 1819–1877) claimed, "[T]he art of painting can only consist of the representation of objects which are visible and tangible for the artist."

The Stone Breakers by Gustave Courbet, 1849. Courbet was a French realist painter who depicted everyday men and women in an honest and unromantic manner. Considered one of his most important works, this painting of two ordinary peasants building a road was destroyed in Dresden during World War II.

Realism's focus on the material world owed much to the ideals of nineteenth-century science, which seemed to cut through traditional moral and philosophical concerns in pursuit of empirical facts. The French novelist Émile Zola (1840–1902), who along with Honoré de Balzac and Gustave Flaubert was among the most prominent realist writers, aimed for an exact, scientific presentation of society. He read Darwin's theories of evolution and often grimly cast his characters as victims of heredity and social circumstance. Like many realists, Zola was also motivated by a powerful sympathy for common people and a desire for social justice. His novels confronted the many social problems of working-class industrial life—alcoholism, poverty, hunger, strikes—as did the famous works of Charles Dickens, which included vivid descriptions of urban squalor, tempered by a humanitarian spirit. Realist painters also shared this sympathy for the common people, and they shocked refined sensibilities by making beggars, miners, laundry women, railroad workers, prostitutes, and peasants the subjects of their work.

The realists' sympathy for the poor and dispossessed meant a sharp critique of contemporary society. Artists and writers called for "democracy in art," in Courbet's words, paralleling demands for the democratization of politics and society. Born in the wake of the 1848 upheavals, realism was often considered a direct manifestation of the revolutionary spirit, and indeed many of its proponents were self-conscious political radicals. Critics scornfully noted that "the vile multitude, chased out of politics, [was] reappearing in painting." Yet realism was also marked by the disillusionment that characterized the post-revolutionary era of conservative reaction. The movement's politics were ambivalent. What united the realists was a belief that the lower classes had a right to literary and artistic representation, and that this required a meticulous observation of characters and their environment.

In Russia, writers felt similarly compelled to take on social and political issues such as poverty, crime, and gender roles; but they joined those topics to larger philosophical themes, creating a distinctive hybrid of realism and Romanticism. Ivan Turgenev, who spent much of his life in France, was the first Russian novelist to become well known to western Europe. His brooding novel *Fathers and Sons* (1861), which condemned the existing social order, inspired a group of young Russian intellectuals who sought to reform society by abandoning their parents' emphasis on status, wealth, and leisure, turning instead to serve "the people." Feodor Dostoevsky (1821–1911), whose nov-

Author Leo Tolstoy. Although a wealthy landowner, Tolstoy often dressed as a peasant. He became increasingly ascetic, casting off the corruptions of the world, and pacifist. In this picture he is leaving his home for a hermitage.

els mirrored his harrowing personal life, explored the psychology of anguished minds with sympathy and morbid intensity. The third outstanding novelist of the late nineteenth century, Leo Tolstoy, examined Russian society in such epic novels as *War and Peace* (1862–1869), which focused on the fate of individuals caught up in powerful movements of history.

CONCLUSION

The twenty years between 1850 and 1870 brought intense nation building in the Western world. The unification of Germany and Italy changed the map of Europe, with important consequences for the balance of power. The emergence of the United States as a major power also had international ramifications. For old as well as new nation-states, economic development and political transformation—often on a very large scale—were important means of increasing and securing the state's power. Yet demands for more representative government, the abolition of privilege, and land reform had to be reckoned with, as did the systems of slavery and serfdom. Trailing the banner of nationhood was an explosive set of questions about how to balance the power and interests of minorities and majorities, of the wealthy and poor, of the powerful and the dispossessed. Nation building not only changed states, it transformed relations between states and their citizens.

These transformations were anything but predictable. Nationalism showed itself to be a volatile, erratic, and malleable force during the mid-nineteenth century. It provided much of the fuel for revolutionary movements in 1848, but it also helped tear their movements apart, undermining revolutionary gains. Those who had linked their democratic goals to the rise of new nation-states were sorely disappointed. In the aftermath of the defeated revolutions, most nation building took a conservative tack. Nationalism came to serve the needs of statesmen and bureaucrats who did not seek an "awakening of peoples" and who had serious reservations about popular sovereignty. For them, nations simply represented modern, organized, and stronger states.

The upshot of this fit of nation building was a period of remarkable stability on the Continent, which ushered in an era of unprecedented capitalist and imperial expansion. The antagonisms unleashed by German unification and the crumbling of the Ottoman Empire would reemerge, however, in the Great Power politics that precipitated World War I.

KEY TERMS

nationalism and nation building	pan-Slavism	Giuseppe Garibaldi	realism
	Giuseppe Mazzini	Otto von Bismarck	
Frankfurt Assembly	John Stuart Mill	Crimean War	

SELECTED READINGS

Beales, Derek. *The Risorgimento and the Unification of Italy.* New York, 1971. Objective, concise survey of Italian unification.

Blackbourn, David. *The Long Nineteenth Century: A History of Germany, 1780–1918.* New York, 1998. Recent and excellent.

Blackburn, Robin. *The Overthrow of Colonial Slavery.* London, 1988. Brilliant and detailed overview of the social history of slavery and antislavery movements.

Brophy, James M. *Capitalism, Politics, and Railroads in Prussia, 1830–1870.* Columbus, Ohio, 1998. Important, clear, and helpful.

Coppa, Frank. *The Origins of the Italian Wars of Independence.* London, 1992. Lively narrative.

Craig, Gordon. *Germany, 1866–1945.* New York, 1978. An excellent and thorough synthesis.

Davis, David Brian. *Inhuman Bondage: The Rise and Fall of Slavery in the New World.* New York, 2006. As one reviewer aptly puts it, "A gracefully fashioned masterpiece."

Deak, Istvan. *The Lawful Revolution: Louis Kossuth and the Hungarians, 1848–1849.* New York, 1979. The best on the subject.

Eyck, Erich. *Bismarck and the German Empire.* 3d ed. London, 1968. The best one-volume study of Bismarck.

Hamerow, Theodore S. *The Birth of a New Europe: State and Society in the Nineteenth Century.* Chapel Hill, N.C., 1983. A discussion of political and social change, and their relationship to industrialization and the increase in state power.

Hamerow, Theodore S. *The Social Foundations of German Unification, 1858–1871.* 2 vols. Princeton, N.J., 1969–1972. Concentrates on economic factors that determined the solution to the unification question. An impressive synthesis.

Higonnet, Patrice. *Paris: Capital of the World.* London, 2002. Fascinating and imaginative study of Paris as "capital of the nineteenth century."

Hobsbawm, Eric J. *Nations and Nationalism since 1870: Programme, Myth, Reality.* 2d ed. Cambridge, 1992. A clear, concise analysis of the historical and cultural manifestations of nationalism.

Howard, Michael. *The Franco-Prussian War.* New York, 1981. The war's effect on society.

Hutchinson, John, and Anthony Smith, eds. *Nationalism.* New York, 1994. A collection of articles, not particularly historical, but with the merit of discussing non-European nationalisms.

Johnson, Susan. *Roaring Camp.* New York, 2000. A history of one mining camp in California and a micro-history of the larger forces changing the West and the world.

Kolchin, Peter. *Unfree Labor: American Slavery and Russian Serfdom.* Cambridge, Mass., 1987. Pioneering comparative study.

Mack Smith, Denis. *Cavour and Garibaldi.* New York, 1968.

Mack Smith, Denis. *The Making of Italy, 1796–1870.* New York, 1968. A narrative with documents.

Nochlin, Linda. *Realism.* New York, 1971. Now a classic.

Pflanze, Otto. *Bismarck and the Development of Germany.* 2d ed. 3 vols. Princeton, N.J., 1990. Extremely detailed analysis of Bismarck's aims and policies.

Pinkney, David. *Napoleon III and the Rebuilding of Paris.* Princeton, N.J., 1972. An interesting account of the creation of modern Paris during the Second Empire.

Robertson, Priscilla. *Revolutions of 1848: A Social History.* Princeton, N.J., 1952. Old-fashioned narrative, but very readable.

Sammons, Jeffrey L. *Heinrich Heine: A Modern Biography.* Princeton, N.J., 1979. An excellent historical biography as well as a study of culture and politics.

Sheehan, James J. *German Liberalism in the Nineteenth Century.* Chicago, 1978. Fresh and important synthesis.

Sperber, Jonathan. *The European Revolutions, 1848–1851.* New York, 1994. Now the best single volume on the period, with bibliography.

Sperber, Jonathan. *Rhineland Radicals: The Democratic Movement and the Revolution of 1848–1849.* Princeton, N.J., 1993. A detailed study of Germany, by the author of an overview of the revolutions of 1848.

Stearns, Peter N. *1848: The Revolutionary Tide in Europe.* New York, 1974. Stresses the social background of the revolutions.

Zeldin, Theodore. *The Political System of Napoleon III.* Compact and readable, by one of the major scholars of the period.

PART VII

THE WEST AT THE WORLD'S CENTER

THE YEARS BETWEEN 1870 and 1945 have been called the "European era." Three developments run through this period. The first is the rapid and dramatic expansion of European empires. The industrial development of western Europe and the United States gave those nations unprecedented global power. That newfound power produced both confidence and crisis. Although the economic might of the Western nations enabled them to dominate the less-developed quarters of the globe, it also created new and dangerous competition among them. The second development, slower and more uneven, was the emergence of "mass" politics and culture: the expansion of suffrage and of liberal and parliamentary democracy, new techniques for mobilizing (or manipulating) citizens, and modern cultural forms ranging from mass-market newspapers and advertising to radio and movies. The third theme to consider involves the wrenching transformations brought by war. Twice during the period, in 1914 and 1939, international and domestic pressures exploded a fragile peace. Twice during the period, war proved shockingly different from what citizens, soldiers, or political leaders expected. And twice during the period, in 1918 and 1945, Europeans awoke to a world they barely recognized. The two world wars had far reaching consequences, among them the fracturing of the European empires and the transformation of Europe's place in the world.

	POLITICS	SOCIETY AND CULTURE	ECONOMY	INTERNATIONAL RELATIONS
			Britain monopolizes opium trade in China (1830s)	British expand foothold in India (1797–1818)
				Opium Wars (1839–1842)
				Treaty of Nanjing (1842)
			Production of steel alloys revolution-ized (1850–1870s)	
		Karl Marx and Friedrich Engels publish *Communist Manifesto* (1848)		
	Reign of Alexander II (1855–1881)	Gustave Flaubert's *Madame Bovary* (1856)		
	Sepoy Rebellion in India (1857–1858)			
1860		Darwin's *On the Origin of Species* (1859)		
	American Civil War (1861–1864)			
	Emancipation of serfs in Russia (1861)	Leo Tolstoy's *War and Peace* (1862–1869)		
	Otto von Bismarck unifies Germany (1862–1871)	Fyodor Dostoyevsky's *Crime and Punishment* (1866)		
	Reform Bill of 1867 in England (1867)			
	Pope Pius IX's pronouncement of papal infallibility (1869)		Limited liability laws change invest-ment strategies (1870)	Franco-Prussian War (1870–1871)
	Bismarck's Kulturkampf (1871–1878)	First Impressionist salon with Claude Monet and others (1874)	Birth of vertical and horizontal monopolies (1870)	European scramble for Africa (1870–1900)
	Repression of Paris Commune (1871)			Britain gains control of Suez Canal (1875)
	Third French Republic (1875)		Electricity demand rises (1880s)	Congress of Berlin redraws Balkan states (1878)
1880	The progressive movement in the United States (1880 1914)		Rockefeller's Standard Oil Company controls over 90 percent of U.S. oil (1880s)	British occupation of Egypt begins (1882)
	Alexander III and the Counter Reforms (1881–1894)		Russia launches industrialization program (1880–1890s)	France moves into Vietnam, Laos, and Cambodia (1883–1893)
	Bismarck's health and social legislation (1883–1884)	Friedrich Nietzsche's *Thus Spoke Zarathustra* (1883)	Sherman Anti-Trust Act in the United States (1890)	Berlin West Africa Conference (1884–85)
	Reform Bill expands male suffrage in Britain (1884)	Émile Zola's *Germinal* (1885)		
	Kaiser Wilhelm II ascends throne (1888)	Completion of the Eiffel Tower (1889)		
		Anti-Semitic League founded in Paris (1889)		
		Vincent Van Gogh's *The Starry Night* (1889)	Birth of the department store (1890s)	Sino-Japanese War (1894–1905)
	Bismarck resigns (1890)			Italian forces defeated by Ethiopians (1896)
				Fashoda Crisis (1898)
				Boer War (1898–1901)
	The Dreyfus Affair (1894–1899)			Spanish-American War (1898)
				United States annexes Puerto Rico and makes Cuba a Protectorate (1898)
1900	Boxer Rebellion in China (1900)	Sigmund Freud publishes *The Interpreta-tion of Dreams* (1899)	Discovery of oil fields in Russia, Bor-neo, Persia, and Texas (1900)	London Pan-African Conference (1900)
	Sinn Fein Party forms in Ireland (1900)			
	French laws separate church and state (1901–1905)			
	Labour Party established in Britain (1901)			
	Vladimir Lenin's "What Is to Be Done?" (1902)			
	Russian Marxists split into Bolsheviks and Mensheviks (1903)			United States occupies Panama (1903)
	British House of Lords loses veto power (1911)			First and Second Balkan Wars (1912–1913)
				World War I (1914–1918)
				Battle of the Marne (1914)
		Albert Einstein proposes Theory of General Relativity (1915)		*Lusitania* sunk by German U-boat (1915)
				Battles of Verdun and the Somme (1916)
	Russian Revolution in February and October (1917)		Bread riots and strikes against wartime shortages in Britain (1917)	United States enters World War I (1917)

POLITICS	SOCIETY AND CULTURE	ECONOMY	INTERNATIONAL RELATIONS	
		Vladimir Lenin's *Imperialism: The Highest Stage of Capitalism* (1917)	Treaty of Brest-Litovsk (1918)	**1917**
ssian Civil War (1918–1920)				
tain extends vote to men and women over age thirty (1918)				
rman (Weimar) Republic declared 1918)				
neteenth Amendment gives American women vote (1919)	Dadaist and Surrealist artistic movements flourish (1920–1940)	Hyperinflation in Weimar Republic (1920–1924)	Treaty of Versailles (1919–1920)	
parate parliaments for north and outh Ireland (1920)	Marie Stopes opens birth control clinic in London (1921)	Beginning of New Economic Policy in Soviet Union (1921)		
ussolini's fascists march on Rome 1922)	T. S. Eliot's *The Waste Land* (1922)			
	Hitler writes *Mein Kampf* in prison (1924)			
seph Stalin's Revolution from above (1927–1928)		Joseph Stalin's First Five-Year Plan for modernization of Russian economy (1928–1932)	Kellogg-Briand Pact (1928)	
		American stock market crash (1929)		
		Great Depression (1929–1933)		
	James Chadwick discovers the neutron (1932)	Britain abandons gold standard (1931)	Japan invades Manchuria (1931)	**1930**
itler appointed chancellor of Germany, proclaims the Third Reich 1933)	German laws exclude Jews from public office (1933)	United States abandons gold standard (1933)		
oncentration camp for political prisners opens at Dachau (1933)	Leni Riefenstahl's *Triumph of the Will* (1934)	One third of American workers unemployed (1933)		
pular Front government formed by eon Blum (1936)		President Franklin Roosevelt announces the New Deal (1933)	Italy conquers Ethiopia (1935–1936)	
anish Civil War (1936–1939)			Germany and Italy form Axis (1935)	
eat Terror of Stalin (1937–1938)				
azis begin deporting Jews in occuied territories to ghettos (1939)	Otto Hahn and Fritz Strassman split the atom (1939)		Germany annexes Austria (1938)	
			Hitler invades Czechoslovakia (1939)	
			Soviet Union signs nonaggression pact with Germany (1939)	
			Soviets and Germans invade Poland (1939)	
			Britain and France declare war on Germany (1939)	
inston Churchill becomes prime minister of England (1940)	Charlie Chaplin's *The Great Dictator* (1940)	Winston Churchill brokers Lend-Lease program with Franklin Roosevelt (1940)	France surrenders to Germany (1940)	**1940**
			Battle of Britain (1940–1941)	
			Germany invades the Soviet Union (1941)	
			Japan strikes Pearl Harbor; United States enters World War II (1941)	
			Japan invades Philippines (1941)	
	Enrico Fermi stages first controlled nuclear chain reaction (1942)		American island-hopping campaigns in the Pacific (1942)	
			Rommel and the Afrika Korps defeated in Tunisia (1942)	
			Warsaw ghetto uprising (1943)	
			D-Day: Allies land at Normandy (1944)	
			Germany surrenders (1945)	**1945**
			United States detonates nuclear bombs over Hiroshima and Nagasaki in August (1945)	
			Conferences at Potsdam and Yalta (1945)	
			Nuremberg trials (1945)	
			United Nations founded (1945)	

CHAPTER TWENTY-TWO

IMPERIALISM AND COLONIALISM, 1870–1914

I N 1869, THE SUEZ CANAL opened with a grandiose celebration. The imperial yacht *Eagle*, Empress Eugénie of France on board, entered the canal on November 17, followed by sixty-eight steamships carrying the rest of the party—the emperor of Austria, the crown prince of Prussia, the grand duke of Russia, and scores of other dignitaries. Flowery speeches flowed freely, as did the champagne. The ceremony cost a staggering £1.3 million. Even so, the size of the celebration paled in comparison to the canal itself. The largest project of its kind, and a masterful feat of engineering, the canal sliced through 100 miles of Egyptian desert to link the Mediterranean and Red seas, which cut the trip from London to Bombay in half. As a fast, cheap, and efficient route to the East, the canal had instant strategic importance. Moreover, the canal dramatically showcased—and to many Europeans, justified—the abilities of Western power and technology to transform the globe.

The building of the canal was the result of half a century of France and Britain's increasingly pervasive commercial, financial, and political involvement in Egypt. French troops under Napoleon I led the way, but Britain's bankers soon followed. European financial interests developed a close relationship with those who governed Egypt as a semi-independent state inside the Ottoman Empire. By 1875 the canal itself had come under the control of Britain, which had purchased 44 percent of the shares in the canal from the khedive (viceroy) of Egypt when he was threatened with bankruptcy. By the late 1870s, these economic and political relationships had produced debt and instability in Egypt and consternation among European investors who wanted returns on their loans. In a bid to produce both an independent state and an Egyptian nation—not so different from the European model—free of foreign "interference," a group of Egyptian army officers, led by 'Urabi Pasha, took control of Egypt's government in 1882.

After much debate, the British government decided to intervene. They did not believe Suez to be at risk, but they were determined to protect their investments by controlling the budget and enforcing a debt settlement. The Royal Navy shelled Egyptian forts along the canal into rubble. A special task force of troops led by Britain's most successful colonial general, "Garnet" Wolseley, landed along the shore

FOCUS QUESTIONS

- What were the causes of the new imperialism?
- How did the British reorganize their rule in India?
- How did trade relationships change between Europe and China?
- What was the "civilizing mission"?
- What events set off the "scramble for Africa"?
- How did imperialism enter into European culture?
- Which nations clashed at the turn of the century and why?

of the canal near 'Urabi Pasha's central base. Wolseley planned his attack down to the last detail—the order of maneuvers looked very much like a railway timetable—and overwhelmed the Egyptian lines just before dawn, at bayonet point. This striking success rallied immediate popular support at home, but the political consequences ran much deeper and lasted for more than seventy years. Britain took over effective control of the province of Egypt. Lord Evelyn Baring (immediately nicknamed "Over" Baring by British anticolonialists) assumed the role of proconsul in a power-sharing relationship with Egyptian authorities—a relationship in which all the real power rested with Britain. Britain put conditions on the repayment of loans owed by the former Egyptian government and regulated the trade in

Egyptian cotton that helped supply Britain's textile mills. Most important, intervention secured the route to India and the markets of the East.

The convergence of technology, money, and politics involved in the Suez Canal epitomizes the interplay of economics and empire in late-nineteenth-century Europe. The years 1870 to 1914 brought both rapid industrialization throughout the West and the stunningly rapid expansion of Western power abroad. The "new imperialism" of the late nineteenth century was distinguished by its scope, intensity, and long-range consequences. It transformed cultures, economies, and states. Projects such as the Suez Canal changed—literally—the landscape and map of the world. They not only brought together newly made money and fresh desires

The Inauguration of the Suez Canal. This allegory illustrates the union of the Mediterranean and Red Seas attended by Ismail Pasha, the khedive of Egypt, Abdul Aziz, sultan of the Ottoman Empire, Ferdinand de Lesseps, president of the Suez Canal Company, Empress Eugenie of France, and several mermaids. It also represents the nineteenth-century vision of imperialism as a bearer of global progress, promoting technological advance and breaking down barriers between the Orient and the West.

for power, they also represented an ideology: the belief in technology and in Western superiority. Physically and imaginatively, the opening of the Suez Canal undermined notions of an "Orient" divided from the West. In the minds of imperialists, the elimination of geographic barriers had opened the entire world, its lands and peoples, to the administrative power of the West.

The new imperialism, however, was not a one-way street, nor did it allow the West simply to conquer vast territories and dictate its terms to the rest of the world. The new political and economic relationships between colonies and dependent states on the one hand and the "metropole" (the colonizing power) on the other ran both ways, bringing changes to the both parties. Fierce competition among nations upset the balance of power. The new imperialism was an expression of European strength, but it was also profoundly destabilizing.

IMPERIALISM

What were the causes of the new imperialism?

Imperialism is the process of extending one state's control over another—a process that takes many forms. Historians begin by distinguishing between formal and informal imperialism. *Formal imperialism*, or colonialism, was sometimes exercised by direct rule: the colonizing nations annexed territories outright and established new governments to subjugate and administer other states and peoples. Sometimes colonialism worked through indirect rule: the conquering Europeans reached agreements with indigenous leaders and governed them. There was no single technique of colonial management; as we will see, resistance forced colonial powers to shift strategies frequently.

Informal imperialism refers to a more subtle and less visible exercise of power, in which the stronger state allowed the weaker state to maintain its independence while reducing its sovereignty. Informal imperialism took the form of carving out zones of European sovereignty and privilege, such as treaty ports, within other states. It could mean using European economic, political, and cultural power to get advantageous treaties or terms of trade. Informal imperialism was not only common but played an even more fundamental role in shaping global power relations.

Both formal and informal imperialism expanded dramatically in the nineteenth century. The "scramble for Africa" was the most sudden and startling case of formal imperialism: from 1875 to 1902 Europeans seized up to 90 percent of the continent. The overall picture is no less remarkable: between 1870 and 1900, a small group of Western states (France, Britain, Germany, the Netherlands, Russia, and the United States) colonized about one quarter of the world's land surface. In addition to these activities, Western states extended informal empire in sections of China and Turkey, across South and East Asia, and into Central and South America. So striking was this expansion of European power and sovereignty that by the late nineteenth century contemporaries were speaking of the "new imperialism."

Imperialism was not new. It is more helpful to think of nineteenth-century developments as a new stage of European empire building. The "second European empires" took hold after the first empires, especially those in the New World, had by and large collapsed. The British Empire in North America was shattered in 1776 by the American Revolution. French imperial ambitions across the Atlantic were toppled along with Napoleon. Spanish and Portuguese domination of Central and South America ended with the Latin American revolutions of the early nineteenth century. In what ways were the second, nineteenth-century European empires different?

The nineteenth-century empires rose against the backdrop of developments we considered in the preceding chapters: industrialization, liberal revolutions, and the rise of nation-states. These developments changed Europe, and they changed European imperialism. First, industrialization created new economic needs for raw materials. Second, industrialization, liberalism, and science forged a new view of the world, history, and the future. A distinguishing feature of nineteenth-century imperialism lay in Europeans' conviction that economic development and technological advances would inevitably bring progress to the rest of the world. Third, especially in the case of Britain and France, the nineteenth-century imperial powers were also in principle democratic nations, where government authority rested on consent and on the equality of most citizens. This made conquest and subjugation more difficult to justify and raised increasingly thorny questions about the status of colonized peoples. Nineteenth-century imperialists sought to distance themselves from earlier histories of conquest. They spoke not of winning souls for the church or subjects for the king but rather of building railroads and harbors, encouraging social reform, and fulfilling Europe's secular mission to bring civilization to the world.

The "new" aspects of nineteenth-century imperialism, however, resulted equally from changes and events outside Europe. Resistance, rebellion, and recognition of colonial failures obliged Europeans to develop new strategies of rule. The Haitian revolution of 1804, echoed by slave rebellions in the early nineteenth century, compelled the British and French, slowly, to end the slave trade and slavery in their colonies in the 1830s and 1840s, although new systems of forced labor cropped up to take their places. The example of the American Revolution encouraged the British to grant self-government to white settler states in Canada (1867), Australia (1901), and New Zealand (1912). In India, as we will see, the British responded to rebellion by taking the area away from the East India Company and putting it under control of the Crown, by requiring civil servants to undergo more training, and by much more careful policing of indigenous peoples. Almost everywhere, nineteenth-century empires established carefully codified racial hierarchies to organize relationships between Europeans and different indigenous groups. (Apartheid in South Africa is but one example.) In general, nineteenth-century imperialism involved less independent entrepreneurial activity by merchants and traders (such as the East India Company) and more "settlement and discipline." This meant that empire became a vast project, involving legions of administrators, schoolteachers, and engineers. Nineteenth-century imperialism, then, arose from new motives. It produced new forms of government and management in the colonies. Last, it created new kinds of interactions between Europeans and indigenous peoples.

> The "new" aspects of nineteenth-century imperialism resulted equally from changes and events outside Europe. Resistance, rebellion, and recognition of colonial failures obliged Europeans to develop new strategies of rule.

THE NEW IMPERIALISM AND ITS CAUSES

All historical events have many causes. The causes of a development with the scope, intensity, and long-range importance of the new imperialism inevitably provoke heated controversy. The most influential and long-standing interpretation points to the economic dynamics of imperialism. As early as 1902, the British writer J. A. Hobson charged that what he named the "scramble for Africa" had been driven by the interests of a small group of wealthy financiers. British taxpayers subsidized armies of conquest and occupation, and journalists whipped up the public's "spectatorial lust of jingoism," but Hobson believed that the core interests behind imperialism were those of international capitalists. At a time when fierce economic competition was producing protectionism and monopolies, he argued, and when western Europe did not provide the markets that industry needed, investors sought out secure investment opportunities overseas, in colonies. Hobson saw investors and international bankers as the central players: "large savings are made which cannot find any profitable investment in this country; they must find employment elsewhere." Yet investors were not alone. Their interests matched those of manufacturers involved in colonial trade, the military, and the armaments industry. Hobson was a reformer and social critic. His point was that international finance and business had distorted conceptions of England's real national interests. He hoped that genuine democracy would be an antidote to the country's imperial tendencies.

Hobson's analysis, still widely read, inspired the most influential Marxist critique of imperialism, which came from the Russian socialist and revolutionary leader Vladimir Ilich Lenin (see Chapter Twenty-One). Like Hobson, Lenin underscored the economics of imperialism. Unlike Hobson, he considered imperialism to be an integral part of late-nineteenth-century capitalism. Competition and the monopolies that it produced had lowered domestic profits. Capitalists, Lenin argued, could enlarge their markets at home only by raising workers' wages, which would have the effect of further reducing profits. Thus the "internal contradictions" of capitalism produced imperialism, compelling capitalists to invest and to search for new markets overseas. If this were the case, it followed that Hobson's hopes for democratic reform were misplaced; only overthrowing capitalism itself could check imperialist expansion, conflict, and violence. Lenin published his book *Imperialism: The Highest Stage of Capitalism* (1917) at the height of World War I, a war many considered imperialist. The timing gave real urgency to his argument that revolution alone could topple capitalism, imperialism, and the forces that had brought the world to the brink of disaster.

Historians now would agree that economic pressures were one, though only one, important cause of imperialism. In the case of Great Britain, roughly half its total of

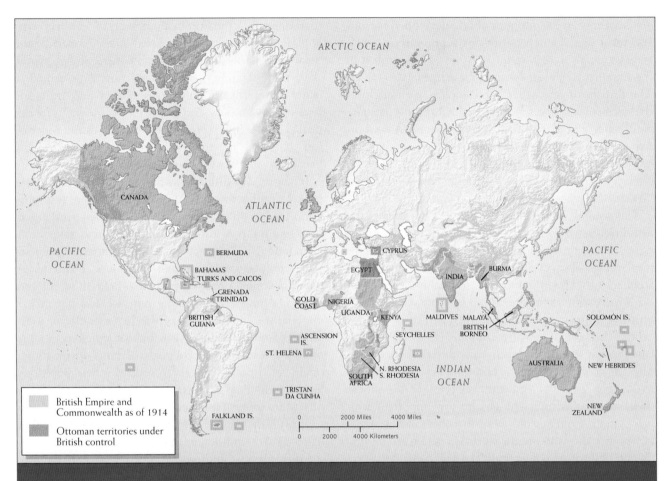

THE BRITISH EMPIRE IN 1914

What made India the center of the British Empire? Why did Britain intervene in Egyptian politics in 1882 and take control of the country? What were the political motivations for the British to expand their empire? According to Hobson, how did industrialization and capitalism drive nineteenth century imperialism? What were some of the cultural justifications for imperialism?

£4 billion in foreign investments was at work within its empire. As Hobson, Lenin, and their contemporaries correctly noted, late-nineteenth-century London was rapidly becoming the banker of the world. In all western European countries, demand for raw materials made colonies seem a necessary investment and helped persuade governments that imperialism was a worthwhile policy. Rubber, tin, and minerals from the colonies supplied European industries; foods, coffee, sugar, tea, wool, and grain supplied European consumers.

Yet the economic explanation has limits. Colonial markets were generally too poor to meet the needs of European manufacturers. Africa, the continent over which Europeans frantically scrambled, was the poorest and least profitable to investors. Regarding overseas investment, before 1914 only a very small portion of German capital was invested in German colonies.

Only one fifth of French capital was so invested; indeed, the French had more capital invested in Russia, hoping to stabilize that ally against the Germans, than in all their colonial possessions. Yet some of these calculations are clear only in retrospect. Many nineteenth-century Europeans expected the colonies to produce profits. French newspapers, for instance, reported that the Congo was "rich, vigorous, and fertile virgin territory," with "fabulous quantities" of gold, copper, ivory, and rubber. Such hopes certainly contributed to expansionism, even if the profits of empire did not match Europeans' expectations.

A second interpretation of imperialism emphasizes strategic and nationalist motives more than economic interests. International rivalries reinforced the belief that vital national interests were at stake and made European powers more determined to control both the governments and economies of less-developed nations and territories. French politicians supported imperialism as a means to restore the prestige and honor lost in the humiliating defeat by the Prussians in 1870–1871. The British, on the other hand, looked with alarm at the accelerating pace of industrialization in Germany and France and feared losing their existing and potential world markets. The Germans, recently unified in a modern nation, viewed overseas empire as a national birthright and as a way of entering the club of Great Powers.

This second, noneconomic, interpretation stresses the new links between imperialism and nineteenth-century state and nation building. That nations should be empires was not always self-evident. Otto von Bismarck, the architect of German unification, long considered colonialism overseas a distraction from far more serious issues on the continent of Europe. By the last decades of the century, however, Germany had joined France and England in what seemed an urgent race for territories. Advocates of colonialism—from businessmen and explorers to writers (such as Rudyard Kipling) and political theorists—spelled out why empire was important to a new nation. Colonies did more than demonstrate military power; they showed the vigor of a nation's economy, the strength of its convictions, the will of its citizenry, the force of its laws, and the power of its culture. A strong national community could assimilate others, bring progress to new lands and new peoples. One German proponent of expansion called colonialism the "national continuation of the German desire for unity." Lobby groups such as the German Colonial Society, the French Colonial Party, and the Royal Colonial Institute argued for empire in similar terms, as did newspapers, which also recognized the attractions of sensational stories of overseas conquest. Presented in this way, as part of nation building, imperialism seemed to rise above particular interests or mundane cost–benefit analysis. Culture, law, religion, and industry were vital national products, and their value rose as they were exported and defended abroad.

Third, imperialism had important cultural dimensions. A French diplomat once described the British imperial adventurer Cecil Rhodes as "a force cast in an idea"; the same might be said of imperialism itself. Imperialism as an idea excited such explorers as the Scottish missionary David Livingston, who believed that the British conquest of Africa would put an end to the East African slave trade and "introduce the Negro family into the body of corporate nations." Rudyard Kipling, the British poet and novelist, wrote of the "white man's burden" (see page 812), a notorious phrase

that referred to the European mission to "civilize" what Kipling and others considered the "barbaric" and "heathen" quarters of the globe. Taking arms against the slave trade, famine, disorder, and illiteracy seemed to many Europeans not only a reason to invade Africa and Asia but also a duty and proof of a somehow superior civilization. These convictions did not cause imperialism, but they illustrate how central empire building became to the West's self-image.

In short, it is difficult to disentangle the economic, political, and strategic causes of imperialism. It is more important to understand how the motives overlapped. Strategic interests often persuaded policy makers that economic issues were at stake. Different constituencies—the military, international financiers, missionaries, colonial lobby groups at home—held different and often clashing visions of the purpose and benefits of imperialism. Imperial policy was less a matter of long-range planning than of a series of quick responses, often improvised, to particular situations. International rivalries led policy makers to redefine their ambitions. So did individual explorers, entrepreneurs, and groups of settlers who established claims to hitherto unknown territories that home governments then felt compelled to recognize and defend. Finally, Europeans were not the only players on the stage. Their goals and practices were shaped by social changes in the countries in which they became involved; by the independent interests of local peoples; and by resistance, which, as often as not, they found themselves unable to understand and powerless to stop.

Is there any reason to call nineteenth-century imperialism *new*? Economic integration, or developing lines of investment and trade to the advantage of the Europeans, was not new. The informal and subterranean exercise

C H R O N O L O G Y

MAJOR IMPERIAL CONFLICTS, 1839–1905

First Opium War, China	1839–1842
Great Mutiny, India	1857–1858
Siege of Khartoum, Sudan	1884–1885
Italian invasion of Ethiopa	1896
Crisis of Fashoda, Sudan	1898
Spanish-American War	1898
Boer War, South Africa	1899–1902
Boxer Rebellion, China	1900
Russo-Japanese War	1904–1905

of European power at work in Latin America, China, and the Ottoman Empire was a much more long-term process. This kind of power expanded more or less continuously through the modern period. But nineteenth-century imperialism did have new aspects or specific features stamped on it by developments within Europe and by indigenous resistance to Europeans.

Imperialism in South Asia

How did the British reorganize their rule in India?

India was the center of the British Empire, the jewel of the British Crown. It was also an inheritance from eighteenth-century empire building, secured well before the period of the new imperialism. The conquest of most of the subcontinent began in the 1750s and quickened during the age of revolution. Conquering India helped compensate for "losing" North America. General Cornwallis, defeated at Yorktown, went on to a brilliant career in India. By the mid-nineteenth century, India had become the focal point of Britain's newly expanded global power, which reached from southern Africa across South Asia and to Australia. Keeping this region involved changing tactics and forms of rule.

Until the mid-nineteenth century, British territories in the subcontinent were under the control of the British East India Company. The company had its own military, divided into European and (far larger) Indian divisions. The company held the right to collect taxes on land from Indian peasants. Until the early nineteenth century, the company had legal monopolies over trade in all goods, including indigo, textiles, salt, minerals, and—most lucrative of all—opium. The British government had granted trade monopolies in its northern American colonies. Unlike North America, however, India never became a settler state. In the 1830s Europeans were a tiny minority, numbering 45,000 in an Indian population of 150 million. The company's rule was repressive and enforced by the military. Soldiers collected taxes; civil servants wore military uniforms; British troops brashly commandeered peasants' oxen and carts for their own purposes. Typically, though, the company could not enforce its rule

uniformly. It governed some areas directly, others through making alliances with local leaders, and others still by simply controlling goods and money. Indirect rule, here as in other empires, meant finding indigenous collaborators and maintaining their good will. Thus the British cultivated groups that had provided administrators in earlier regimes: the Rajputs and Bhumihars of North India, whom they considered especially effective soldiers, and merchants of big cities such as Calcutta. They offered economic privileges, state offices, or military posts to either groups or entire nations that agreed to ally with the British against others.

British policy shifted between two poles: one group wanted to "westernize" India, another believed it safer, and more practical, to defer to local culture. Christian missionaries, whose numbers rose as occupation expanded, were determined to replace "blind superstition" with the "genial influence of Christian light and truth." Indignant at such practices as child marriage and *sati* (in which a widow immolated herself on her husband's funeral pyre), they sought support in England for a wide-ranging assault on Hindu culture. Secular reformers, many of them liberal, considered "Hindoos" and "Mahommedans" susceptible to forms of despotism—in both the family and in the state. They turned their reforming zeal to legal and political change. But other company and British administrators warned their countrymen not to meddle with Indian institutions and practices. "Englishmen are as great fanatics in politics as Mahommedans in religion. They suppose that no country can be saved without English institutions," said one British administrator. Indirect rule, they argued, would only work with the cooperation of local powers. Conflicts such as these meant that the British never agreed on any single cultural policy.

By the mid-nineteenth century, India had become the focal point of Britain's newly expanded global power, which reached from southern Africa across South Asia and to Australia. Keeping this region involved changing tactics and forms of rule.

From Mutiny to Rebellion

The company's rule often met resistance and protest. In 1857–1858, it was particularly badly shaken by what the British called the "Sepoy [soldiers'] Rebellion," now known in India as the Great Mutiny of 1857. The uprising began near Delhi, when the military disciplined a regiment of *sepoys* (the traditional term for Indian soldiers employed by the British) for refusing to use rifle cartridges greased with pork fat—unacceptable to either Hindus or Muslims. Yet as the British prime minister

Disraeli later observed, "The decline and fall of empires are not affairs of greased cartridges." The causes of the mutiny were much deeper and involved social, economic, and political grievances. Indian peasants attacked law courts and burned tax rolls, protesting debt and corruption. In areas such as Oudh, which had recently been annexed, rebels defended their traditional leaders, who had been summarily ousted by the British. Army officers from privileged castes resented arbitrary treatment at the hands of the British; they were first promoted as loyal allies and then forced to serve without what they considered titles and honors. The mutiny spread through large areas of northwest India. European troops, which counted for fewer than one fifth of those in arms, found themselves losing control. Religious leaders, both Hindu and Muslim, seized the occasion to denounce Christian missionaries sent in by the British and their assault on local traditions and practices.

At first the British were faced with a desperate situation, with areas under British control cut off from one another and pro-British cities under siege. Loyal Indian troops were brought south from the frontiers, and British troops, fresh from the Crimean War, were shipped directly from Britain to suppress the rebellion. The fighting lasted more than a year, and the British matched the rebels' early massacres and vandalism with a systematic campaign of repression. Whole rebel units were either killed rather than being allowed to surrender or else tried on the spot and executed. Towns and villages that supported the rebels were burned, just as the rebels had burned European homes and outposts. Yet the defeat of the rebellion caught the British public's imagination. After the bloody, inconclusive mess of Crimea, the terrifying threat to British India and the heroic rescue of European hostages and British territory by British troops were electrifying news. Pictures of the Scottish highland regiments (wearing wool kilts in the sweltering heat of India) liberating besieged white women and children went up in homes across the United Kingdom. At a political level, British leaders were stunned by how close the revolt had brought them to disaster and were determined never to repeat the same mistakes.

At a political level, British leaders were stunned by how close the revolt had brought them to disaster and were determined never to repeat the same mistakes.

After the mutiny, the British were compelled to reorganize their Indian empire, developing new strategies of rule. The East India Company was abolished, replaced by the British Crown. The British *raj* (or rule) was governed directly, though the British also sought out collaborators and cooperative interest groups. Princely India was left to the indigenous princes, who were subject to British advisers. The British also reorganized the military and tried to change relations among soldiers. Indigenous troops were separated from each other to avoid the kind of fraternization that proved subversive. As one British officer put it, "If one regiment mutinies I should like to have the next so alien that it would fire into it." Even more than before, the British sought to rule through the Indian upper classes rather than in opposition to them. Queen Victoria, now empress of India, set out the

British Executing Leaders of Indian Rebellion of 1857. The British were determined to make an example of the rebel Indian soldiers of the Great Mutiny. This engraving shows executions in which the condemned were blown apart by cannons.

INDIA: POLITICAL DIVISIONS AND MUTINY

How and why did the British become involved in India, and why did India soon become central to the foreign policy and economic interests of Great Britain? Why did the British decide to annex directly the various parts of India, and what political conditions made the advance of British control easier? Why did formal, direct British rule—with the appointment of a viceroy—come only in 1861?

principles of indirect rule: "We shall respect the rights, dignity and honour of native princes as our own, and we desire that they, as well as our own subjects, should enjoy that prosperity and that social advancement which can only be secured by internal peace and good government." Civil-service reform opened up new positions to members of the Indian upper classes. The British had to reconsider their relationship to Indian cultures. Missionary activity was subdued, and the British channeled their reforming impulses into the more secular projects of economic development, railways, roads, irrigation, and so on. Still, consensus on effective colonial strategies was elusive. Some administrators counseled more reform and change; others sought to give the princes more support. The British tried both, in fits and starts, until the end of British rule in 1947.

In India, the most prominent representative of the new imperialism was Lord Curzon, a prominent conservative and the viceroy of India from 1898 to 1905. Curzon deepened British commitments to the region. Concerned about the British position in the world, he warned of the need to fortify India's borders against Russia. He urged continued economic investment. Curzon worried out loud that the British would be worn down by resistance to the raj and that, confronted with their apparent inability to transform Indian culture, they would become cynical, get "lethargic and think only of home." In the same way that Rudyard Kipling urged the British and the Americans to "take up the white man's burden" (see page 812), Curzon pleaded with his countrymen to see how central India was to the greatness of Britain.

What did India provide to Great Britain? By the eve of World War I, India was Britain's largest export market. One tenth of all the British Empire's trade passed through India's port cities of Madras, Bombay, and Calcutta. India mattered enormously to Britain's balance of payments; surpluses earned there compensated for deficits with Europe and the United States. Equally important to Great Britain were the human resources of India. Indian laborers worked on tea plantations in Assam, near Burma, and they built railways and dams in southern Africa and Egypt. British rule cast an enormous diaspora of Indian workers throughout the empire. Over a million indentured Indian servants left their country in the second half of the century. India also provided the British Empire with highly trained engineers, land surveyors, clerks, bureaucrats, schoolteachers, and merchants. The nationalist leader Mohandas Gandhi, for instance, first came into the

public eye as a young lawyer in Pretoria, South Africa, where he worked for an Indian law firm. The British deployed Indian troops across the empire. (They would later call up roughly 1.2 million troops in World War I.) For all these reasons, men such as Curzon found it impossible to imagine their empire, or even their nation, without India.

How did the British raj shape Indian society? The British practice of indirect rule sought to create an Indian elite that would serve British interests, a group "who may be the interpreters between us and the millions whom we govern—a class of persons Indian in colour and blood, but English in tastes, in opinion, in morals, and in intellect," as one British writer put it. Eventually, this practice created a large social group of British-educated Indian civil servants and businessmen, well trained for government and skeptical about British

British Imperialism. This cartoon, "The Execution of 'John Company,'" appeared in *Punch* magazine in 1857. It celebrates the end of the British East India Company's corrupt rule. Note the reference to executions such as the ones on page 794.

LORD CURZON ON THE IMPORTANCE OF INDIA AND INDIANS TO THE BRITISH EMPIRE

Lord George Nathaniel Curzon (1859–1925) served as viceroy of India from 1898 to 1905 and as foreign secretary from 1919 to 1924. He made his reputation in India, and as a prominent Tory politician he became among the most vocal proponents of the new imperialism. In this speech Curzon spells out the benefits of empire and underscores British dependence on India.

If you want to save your Colony of Natal from being over-run by a formidable enemy, you ask India for help, and she gives it; if you want to rescue the white men's legations from massacres at Peking, and the need is urgent, you request the Government of India to despatch an expedition, and they despatch it; if you are fighting the Mad Mullah in Somaliland, you soon discover that Indian troops and an Indian general are best qualified for the task, and you ask the Government of India to send them; if you desire to defend any of your extreme out-posts or coaling stations of the Empire, Aden, Mauritius, Singapore, Hong-Kong, even Tien-tsin or Shan-hai-kwan, it is to the Indian Army that you turn; if you want to build a railway to Uganda or in the Soudan, you apply for Indian labour. When the late Mr. Rhodes was engaged in developing your recent acquisition of Rhodesia, he came to me for assistance. It is with Indian coolie labor that you exploit the plantations equally of Demerara and Natal; with Indian trained officers that you irrigate and dam the Nile; with Indian forest officers that you tap the re- sources of Central Africa and Siam; with Indian survey- ors that you explore all the hidden places of the earth. . . . [Moreover,] India is a country where there will be much larger openings for the in- vestment of capital in the future than has hitherto been the case, and where a great work of industrial and commercial exploita- tion lies before us.

Andrew Porter, ed., *The Oxford History of the British Empire*. Vol. 3: *The Nineteenth Century* (Oxford, 1999), p. 403.

QUESTIONS FOR ANALYSIS

1. Curzon not only served as viceroy of India and foreign minister but also had extensive knowledge of Afghanistan and Persia. Drawing on his expertise, what did he think was the greatest value of India to the British Empire?
2. How did British adventurers and merchants get rich in India, a country regarded as poor today? Was India rich or poor in Curzon's time?

claims that they brought progress to the subcontinent. This group provided the leadership for the nationalist movement that challenged British rule in India. At the same time, this group became increasingly distant from the rest of the nation. The overwhelming majority of Indians remained either desperately poor peasants struggling to subsist on diminishing plots of land and, in many cases, in debt to British landlords, or villagers working in the textile trade beaten down by imports of cheap manufactured goods from England.

IMPERIALISM IN CHINA

How did trade relations change between
Europe and China?

In China, too, European imperialism escalated early, well before the period of the new imperialism. Yet there it took a different form. Europeans did not conquer and annex whole regions. Instead, they forced favorable trade agreements at gunpoint, set up treaty ports where Europeans lived and worked under their own jurisdiction, and established outposts of European missionary activity—all with such dispatch that the Chinese spoke of their country as being "carved up like a melon."

Since the seventeenth century European trade with China—in coveted luxuries such as silk, porcelain, art objects, and tea—had run up against resistance from the Chinese government, which was determined to keep foreign traders, and foreign influence in general, at bay. By the early nineteenth century, however, Britain's global ambitions and rising power were setting the stage for a confrontation. Freed from the task of fighting Napoleon, the British set their sights on improving the terms of the China trade, demanding the rights to come into open harbors and to have special trading privileges. The other source of constant friction involved the harsh treatment of British subjects by Chinese law courts— including the summary execution of several Britons convicted of crimes. And by the 1830s, these diplomatic conflicts had been intensified by the opium trade.

THE OPIUM TRADE

Opium provided a direct link among Britain, British India, and China. Since the sixteenth century, the drug had been produced in India and carried by Dutch and, later, British traders. In fact, opium (derived from the poppy plant) was one of the very few commodities that Europeans could sell in China, and for this reason it became crucial to the balance of East–West

trade. When the British conquered northeast India, they also annexed one of the richest opium-growing areas and became deeply involved in the trade—so much so that historians do not shy from calling East India Company rule a "narco-military empire." British agencies designated specific poppy-growing regions and gave cash advances to Indian peasants who cultivated the crop. Producing opium was a labor-intensive process: peasant cultivators collected sap from the poppy seeds, others cleaned the sap and formed it into opium balls, which were dried before being weighed and shipped out. In the opium-producing areas northwest of Calcutta, "factories" employed as many as 1,000 Indian workers who formed and cured the opium as well as young boys, whose job it was to turn the opium balls every four days.

From India, the East India Company sold the opium to "country traders"—small fleets of British, Dutch, and Chinese shippers who carried the drug to Southeast Asia and China. Silver paid for the opium came back to the East India Company, which used it, in turn, to buy Chinese goods for the European market. The trade, therefore, was not only profitable, it was key to a triangular European-Indian-Chinese economic relationship. Production and export rose dramatically in

An Opium Factory in Patna, India, c. 1851. Balls of opium dry in a huge warehouse before being shipped to Calcutta for export to China and elsewhere.

the early nineteenth century. By the 1830s, when the British-Chinese confrontation was taking shape, opium provided British India with more revenues than any other source except taxes on land.

People all over the world consumed opium, for medicinal reasons as well as for pleasure. The Chinese market was especially lucrative. Eighteenth-century China had witnessed a craze for tobacco smoking that taught users how to smoke opium. A large, wealthy Chinese elite of merchants and government officials provided much of the market, but opium smoking also became popular among soldiers, students, and Chinese laborers. In the nineteenth century opium imports followed Chinese labor all over the world—to Southeast Asia and San Francisco. In an effort to control the problem, the Chinese government banned opium imports, prohibited domestic production, criminalized smoking, and in the 1830s began a full-scale campaign to purge the drug from China. That campaign set the Chinese emperor on a collision course with British opium traders. In one confrontation the Chinese drug commissioner Lin confiscated 3 million pounds of raw opium from the

> In the nineteenth century opium imports followed Chinese labor all over the world—to Southeast Asia and San Francisco.

British and washed it out to sea. In another the Chinese authorities blockaded British ships in port, and local citizens demonstrated angrily in front of British residences.

The Opium Wars

In 1839, these simmering conflicts broke into what was called the first Opium War. Drugs were not the core of the matter. They highlighted larger issues of sovereignty and economic status: the Europeans' "rights" to trade with whomever they pleased, bypassing Chinese monopolies; to set up zones of European residence in defiance of Chinese sovereignty; and to proselytize and open schools. War flared up several times over the course of the century. After the first war of 1839–1842, in which British steam vessels and guns overpowered the Chinese fleet, the Treaty of Nanking (1842) compelled the Chinese to give the British trading privileges, the right to reside in five cities, and the port of Hong Kong "in perpetuity." After a second war, the British secured yet more treaty ports

The Opium Trade, 1880s. A European merchant examines opium.

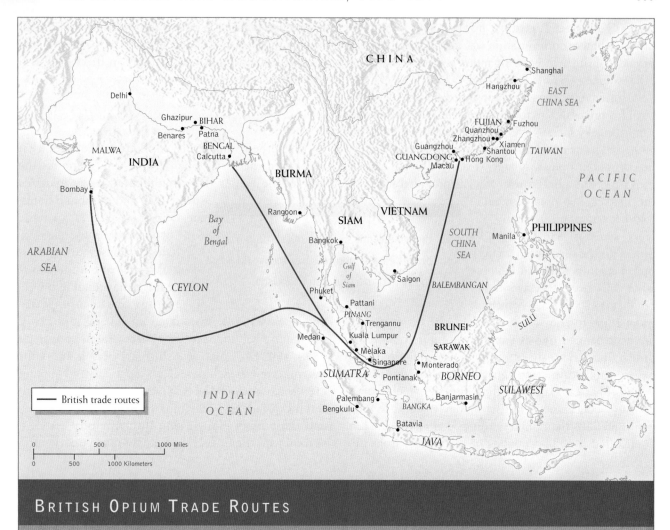

BRITISH OPIUM TRADE ROUTES

Note the major trade routes used by the British in the shipment of opium in Asia. How did opium come to play such an important role? How did the intensification of the opium trade affect the British position in this part of the world? What social and political problems did it create?

and privileges, including the right to send in missionaries. In the aftermath of those agreements between the Chinese and the British, other countries demanded similar rights and economic opportunities. By the end of the nineteenth century—during the period of the new imperialism—the French, Germans, and Russians had claimed mining rights and permission to build railroads, to begin manufacturing with cheap Chinese labor, and to arm and police European communities in Chinese cities. In Shanghai, for instance, 17,000 foreigners lived with their own courts, schools, churches, and utilities. The United States, not wanting to be shouldered aside, demanded its own Open Door Policy. Japan was an equally active imperialist power in the Pacific, and the Sino-Japanese war of

1894–1895 was a decisive moment in the history of the region. The Japanese victory forced China to concede trading privileges, the independence of Korea, and the Liaotung Peninsula in Manchuria. It opened a scramble for spheres of influence and for mining and railway concessions. The demand for reparations forced the Chinese government to levy greater taxes. All these measures heightened resentment and destabilized the regime.

Surrendering privileges to Europeans and the Japanese seriously undermined the authority of the Chinese Qing (Ching) emperor at home and only heightened popular hostility to foreign intruders. Authority at the imperial center had been eroding for more than a century by 1900, hastened by the Opium

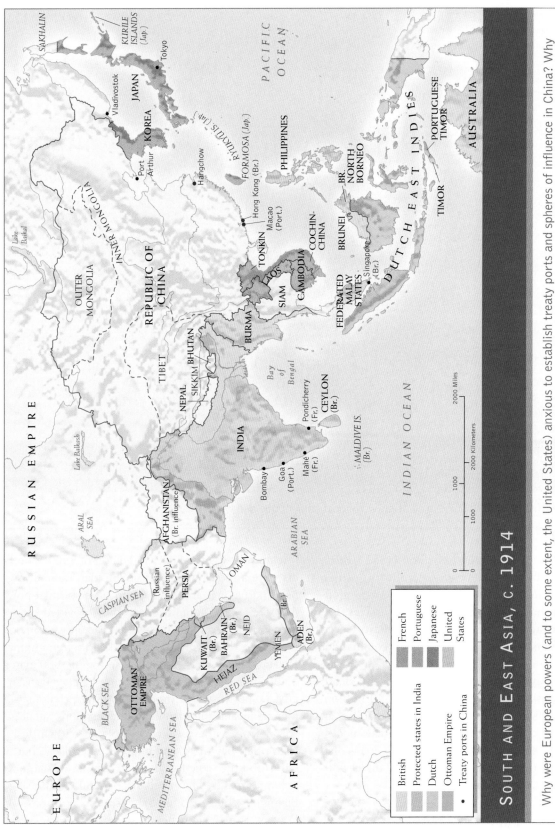

SOUTH AND EAST ASIA, c. 1914

Why were European powers (and to some extent, the United States) anxious to establish treaty ports and spheres of influence in China? Why was control of Chinese markets particularly crucial to British economic interests? What was the relationship among colonial powers, capitalist investors, and the Chinese government? How did the Boxer Rebellion and the effects of the Open Door Policy encourage more intensive exploitation in other parts of Southeast Asia?

Russian Empire, 1795
Russian acquisitions, 1795–1855
Russian acquisitions, 1855–1914
Russian sphere of influence
Occupied by Russia

BUILDING THE RUSSIAN EMPIRE

What drove Russian expansion? Which areas were most contentious and why?

Wars and by the vast Taiping Rebellion (1852–1864), an enormous, bitter, and deadly conflict in which radical Christian rebels in south-central China challenged the authority of the emperors themselves. On the defensive against the rebels, the dynasty hired foreign generals, including the British commander Charles Gordon, to lead its forces. The war devastated China's agricultural heartland; and the death toll, never confirmed, may have reached 20 million. This ruinous disorder and the increasing inability of the emperor to keep order and collect the taxes necessary to stabilize trade and repay foreign loans, led European countries to take more and more direct control of their side of the China trade.

THE BOXER REBELLION

From a Western perspective, the most important of the nineteenth-century rebellions against the corruptions of

foreign rule was the Boxer Rebellion of 1900. The Boxers were a secret society of young men trained in Chinese martial arts and believed to have spiritual powers. Antiforeign and antimissionary, they provided the spark for a loosely organized but widespread uprising in northern China. Bands of Boxers attacked foreign engineers, tore up railway lines, and in the spring of 1900 marched on Beijing. They laid siege to the foreign legations in the city, home to several thousand Western diplomats and merchants and their families. The legations' small garrison defended their walled compound with little more than rifles, bayonets, and improvised artillery; but they withstood the siege for fifty-five days until a large relief column arrived. The rebellion, particularly the siege at Beijing, mobilized a global response. Europe's Great Powers, rivals everywhere else in the world, drew together in response to this crisis to tear China apart. An expedition numbering 20,000 troops—combining the forces of Britain, France, the United States, Germany, Italy, Japan, and Russia—ferociously repressed the Boxer movement. The outside powers then demanded indemnities, new trading concessions, and reassurances from the Chinese government.

The Boxer Rebellion was one of several anti-imperialist movements at the end of the nineteenth century. The rebellion testified to the vulnerability of Europeans' imperial power. It dramatized the resources Europeans would have to devote to maintaining their far-flung influence. In the process of repression, the Europeans became committed to propping up corrupt and fragile governments to protect their agreements and interests, and they were drawn into putting down popular uprisings against local inequalities and foreign rule.

In China the age of the new imperialism capped a century of conflict and expansion. By 1900, virtually all of Asia had been divided up among the European powers. Japan, an active imperial power in its own right, maintained its independence. British rule extended from India across Burma, Malaya, Australia, and New Zealand. The Dutch, Britain's longstanding trade rivals, secured Indonesia. Thailand remained independent. During the 1880s, the French moved into Indochina. Imperial rivalries (among Britain, France, and Russia, China and Japan, Russia and Japan) caused the struggle for influence and economic advantage in Asia; that struggle, in turn exacerbated nationalist feeling. Imperial expansion, the expression of European power, was showing its destabilizing effects.

> The maneuvering, spying, and support of friendly puppet governments by Russia and Britain became known as the "Great Game" and foreshadowed Western countries' jockeying for the region's oil resources in the twentieth century.

RUSSIAN IMPERIALISM

Russia was a persistently imperialist power throughout the nineteenth century. Its rulers championed a policy of annexation—by conquest, treaty, or both—of lands bordering on the existing Russian state. Beginning in 1801, with the acquisition of Georgia after a war with Persia, the tsars continued to pursue their expansionist dream. Bessarabia and Turkestan (taken from the Turks) and Armenia (from the Persians) vastly increased the empire's size. This southward colonization brought the Russians close to war with the British twice: first in 1881, when Russian troops occupied territories in the trans-Caspian region, and again in 1884–1887, when the tsar's forces advanced to the frontier of Afghanistan. In both cases the British feared incursions into areas they deemed within their sphere of influence in the Middle East. They were concerned, as well, about a possible threat to India. The maneuvering, spying, and support of friendly puppet governments by Russia and Britain became known as the "Great Game" and foreshadowed Western countries' jockeying for the region's oil resources in the twentieth century.

Russian expansion also moved east. In 1875, the Japanese traded the southern half of Sakhalin Island for the previously Russian Kurile Islands. The tsars' eastward advance was finally halted in 1904. Russian expansion in Mongolia and Manchuria came up against Japanese expansion, and the two powers went to war. Russia's huge imperial army more than met its match in a savage, bloody conflict. Russia's navy was sent halfway round the world to reinforce the beleaguered Russian troops but was ambushed and sunk by the better-trained and -equipped Japanese fleet. This national humiliation helped provoke a revolt in Russia and led to an American-brokered peace treaty in 1905 (see Chapter Twenty-Three). The defeat shook the already unsteady regime of the tsar and proved that

An American caricature of the Boxer Rebellion. Uncle Sam (to the obstreperous Boxer) "I occasionally do a little boxing myself."

European nations were not the only ones who could play the imperial game successfully.

THE FRENCH EMPIRE AND THE CIVILIZING MISSION

What was the "civilizing mission"?

Like British expansion into India, French colonialism in Northern Africa began before the so-called new imperialism of the late nineteenth century. By the 1830s, the French had created a general government of their possessions in Algeria, the most important of which were cities along the Mediterranean coast. From the outset the Algerian conquest was different from most other colonial ventures: Algeria became a settler state, one of the few apart from South Africa. Some of the early settlers were utopian socialists, out to create ideal communities; some were workers the French government deported after the revolution of 1848 to be "resettled" safely as farmers; some were winegrowers whose vines at home had been destroyed by an insect infestation. The settlers were by no means all French; they included Italian, Spanish, and Maltese merchants and shopkeepers of modest means, laborers, and peasants. By the 1870s, in several of the coastal cities, this new creole community outnumbered indigenous Algerians, and within it, other Europeans outnumbered the French. With the French military's help, the settlers appropriated land, and French business concerns took cork forests and established mining in copper, lead, and iron. Economic activity was for European benefit. The first railroads, for instance, did not even carry passengers; they took iron ore to the coast for export to France, where it would be smelted and sold.

The settlers and the French government did not necessarily pursue common goals. In the 1870s, the new and still fragile Third Republic (founded after Napoleon III was defeated in 1870; see Chapter Twenty-One), in an effort to ensure the settlers' loyalty, made the colony a department of France. This gave the French settlers the full rights of republican citizenship. It also gave them the power to pass laws in Algeria that consolidated their privileges and community (naturalizing all Europeans, for instance) and further disenfranchised indigenous populations, who had no voting rights at all. French politicians in Paris occasionally objected to the settlers' contemptuous treatment of indigenous peoples, arguing that it subverted the project of "lifting up" the natives. The French settlers in Algeria had little interest in such a project; although they paid lip service to republican ideals, they wanted the advantages of Frenchness for themselves. Colonial administrators and social scientists differentiated the "good" mountain-dwelling Berbers, who could be brought into French society, from the "bad" Arabs, whose religion made them supposedly inassimilable. In Algeria, then, colonialism was at the very least a three-way relationship and illustrates the dynamics that made colonialism in general a contradictory enterprise.

Before the 1870s, colonial activities aroused relatively little interest among the French at home. But after the humiliating defeat in the Franco-Prussian War (1870–1871) and the establishment of the Third

Surrender of the Berber People to the French. In Algeria French colonialism created a settler state; by the 1870s, to secure European settlers' loyalty, the colony was made a department of France.

Republic, colonial lobby groups and, gradually, the government became increasingly adamant about the benefits of colonialism. These benefits were not simply economic. Taking on the "civilizing mission" would reinforce the purpose of the French republic and the prestige of the French people. It was France's duty "to contribute to this work of civilization." Jules Ferry, a republican political leader, successfully argued for expanding the French presence in Indochina, saying, "We must believe that if Providence deigned to confer upon us a mission by making us masters of the earth, this mission consists not of attempting an impossible fusion of the races but of simply spreading or awakening among the other races the superior notions of which we are the guardians." Those "superior notions" included a commitment to economic and technological progress and to liberation from slavery, political oppression, poverty, and disease. In what Ferry ironically considered an attack on the racism of his contemporaries, he argued that "the superior races have a right vis-à-vis the inferior races . . . they have a right to civilize them."

Under Ferry, the French acquired Tunisia (1881), northern and central Vietnam (Tonkin and Annam; 1883), and Laos and Cambodia (1893). They also carried this civilizing mission into their colonies in West Africa. European and Atlantic trade with the west coast of Africa—in slaves, gold, and ivory—had been well established for centuries. In the late nineteenth century, trade gave way to formal administration. The year 1895 saw the establishment of a Federation of French West Africa, a loosely organized administration to govern an area nine times the size of France, including Guinea, Senegal, and the Ivory Coast. Even with reforms and centralization in 1902, French control remained uneven. Despite military campaigns of pacification, resistance remained, and the French dealt gingerly with tribal leaders, at some times deferring to their authority and at others trying to break their power. They established French courts and law only in cities, leaving Islamic or tribal courts to run other areas. The federation aimed to rationalize the economic exploitation of the area, and to replace "booty capitalism" with a more careful management and development of resources. The French called this "enhancing the value" of the region, which was part of the civilizing mission of the modern republic. The federation embarked on an ambitious program of public works. Engineers rebuilt the huge harbor at Dakar, the most important on the coast, to accommodate rising exports. With some utopian zeal they redesigned older cities, tried to improve sanitation and health, improved water systems, and so on. The French republic was justifiably proud of the Pasteur Institute for bacteriological research, which opened in France in 1888; overseas institutes became part of the colonial enterprise. One plan called for a large-scale West African railroad network to lace through the region. A public-school program built free schools in villages not controlled by missionaries. Education, though, was not compulsory and was usually for boys.

Slaves in Chains, 1896. In Africa, native labor was exploited by Europeans and by other Africans, as here.

Such programs plainly served French interests. "Officially this process is called civilizing, and after all, the term is apt, since the undertaking serves to increase the degree of prosperity of our civilization," remarked one Frenchman who opposed the colonial enterprise. None of these measures aimed to give indigenous peoples political rights. As one historian puts it, "the French Government General was in the business not of making citizens, but of civilizing its subjects." More telling, however, the French project was not often successful. The French government did not have the resources to carry out its plans, which proved much more expensive and complicated than anyone imagined. Transportation costs ran very high. Labor posed the largest problems. Here as elsewhere, Europeans faced massive resistance from the African peasants, whom they wanted to do everything from building railroads to working mines and carrying rubber. The Europeans resorted to forced labor, signing agreements with local tribal leaders to deliver workers, and they turned a blind eye to the continuing use of slave labor in the interior. For all of these reasons, the colonial project did not produce the profits some expected. In important respects, however, the French investment in colonialism was cultural. Railroads, schools, and projects such as the Dakar harbor were, like the Eiffel Tower (1889), symbols of the French nation's modernity, power, and world leadership.

THE "SCRAMBLE FOR AFRICA" AND THE CONGO

What events set off the "scramble for Africa"?

French expansion into West Africa was but one instance of Europe's voracity on the African continent. The scope and speed with which the major European powers conquered and colonized, asserting formal control was astonishing. The effects were profound. In 1875, 11 percent of the continent was in European hands. By 1902, the figure was 90 percent. European powers mastered logical problems of transport and communication; they learned how to keep diseases at bay. They also had new weapons. The Maxim gun, adopted by the British army in 1889 and first used by British colonial troops, pelted out as many as 500 rounds a minute; it turned encounters with indigenous forces into bloodbaths and made armed resistance virtually impossible.

THE CONGO FREE STATE

In the 1870s, the British had formed new imperial relationships in the north and west of Africa and along the southern and eastern coasts. A new phase of European involvement struck right at the heart of the continent. Until the latter part of the nineteenth century this territory had been out of bounds for Europeans. The rapids downstream on such strategic rivers as the Congo and the Zambezi made it difficult to move inland, and tropical diseases against which Europeans had little or no resistance were lethal to most explor-

ers. But during the 1870s, a new drive into central Africa produced results. The target was the fertile valleys around the river Congo, and the European colonizers were a privately financed group of Belgians paid by their king, Leopold II (1865–1909). They followed in the footsteps of Henry Morton Stanley, an American newspaperman and explorer who later became a British subject and a knight of the realm. Stanley hacked his way through thick canopy jungle and territory where no European had previously set foot. His "scientific" journeys inspired the creation of a society of researchers and students of African culture in Brussels, in reality a front organization for the commercial company set up by Leopold. The ambitiously named International Association for the Exploration and Civilization of the Congo was set up in 1876 and soon set about signing treaties with local elites, which opened the whole Congo River basin to commercial exploitation. The vast resources of palm oil and natural rubber and the promise of minerals (including diamonds) were now within Europeans' reach.

The strongest resistance that Leopold's company faced came from other colonial powers, particularly Portugal, which objected to this new drive for occupation. In 1884, a conference was called in Berlin to settle the matter of control over the Congo River basin. It was chaired by the master of European power politics, Otto von Bismarck, and attended by all the leading colonial nations as well as by the United States. The conference established ground rules for a new phase of European economic and political expansion. Europe's two great overseas empires, Britain and France, and the strongest emerging power inside Europe, Germany, joined forces and settled the Congo issue. Their dictates seemed to be perfectly in line with nineteenth-century liberalism. The Congo valleys would be open to free trade and commerce; a slave trade still run by some of the Islamic kingdoms in the region would be suppressed in favor of free labor; and a Congo Free State would be set up, denying the region to the formal control of any single European country.

In reality the Congo Free State was run by Leopold's private company, and the region was opened up to unrestricted exploitation by a series of large European corporations. The older slave trade was suppressed, but the European companies took the "free" African labor guaranteed in Berlin and placed workers in equally bad conditions. Huge tracts of land, larger than whole European countries, became diamond

ATROCITIES IN THE CONGO

George Washington Williams (1849–1891), an African American pastor, journalist, and historian, was among a handful of international observers who went to the Congo in the 1890s to explore and report back on conditions. He wrote several reports: one for the U.S. government, another that he presented at an international antislavery conference, several newspaper columns, and an open letter to King Leopold, from which the following is excerpted.

Good and Great Friend,

I have the honour to submit for your Majesty's consideration some reflections respecting the Independent State of Congo, based upon a careful study and inspection of the country and character of the personal Government you have established upon the African Continent. . . .

I was led to regard your enterprise as the rising of the Star of Hope for the Dark Continent, so long the habitation of cruelties. . . . When I arrived in the Congo, I naturally sought for the results of the brilliant programme:— *"fostering care," "benevolent enterprise,"* an *"honest and practical effort"* to increase the knowledge of the natives *"and secure their welfare."* . . .

I was doomed to bitter disappointment. Instead of the natives of the Congo "adopting the fostering care" of your Majesty's Government, they everywhere complain that their land has been taken from them by force; that the Government is cruel and arbitrary, and declare that they neither love nor respect the Government and its flag. Your Majesty's Government has sequestered their land, burned their towns, stolen their property, enslaved their women and children, and committed other crimes too numerous to mention in detail. It is natural that they everywhere shrink from *"the fostering care"* your Majesty's Government so eagerly proffers them.

There has been, to my absolute knowledge, no *"honest and practical effort made to increase their knowledge and secure their welfare."* Your Majesty's Government has never spent one franc for educational purposes, nor instituted any practical system of industrialism. Indeed the most unpractical measures have been adopted *against* the natives in nearly every respect; and in the capital of your Majesty's Government at Boma there is not a native employed. The labour system is radically unpractical. . . . [R]ecruits are transported under circumstances more cruel than cattle in European countries. They eat their rice twice a day by the use of their fingers; they often thirst for water when the season is dry; they are exposed to the heat and rain, and sleep upon the damp and filthy decks of the vessels often so closely crowded as to lie in human ordure. And, of course, many die. . . .

All the crimes perpetrated in the Congo have been done in *your* name, and *you* must answer at the bar if Public Sentiment for the misgovernment of a people, whose lives and fortunes were entrusted to you by the august Conference of Berlin, 1884–1885. . . .

George Washington Williams, "An Open Letter to His Serene Majesty Leopold II, King of the Belgians, and Sovereign of the Independent State of Congo, July 1890," in *George Washington Williams: A Biography*, ed. John Hope Franklin (Chicago, 1985), pp. 243–254.

QUESTION FOR ANALYSIS

1. What were Williams's concerns and to what extent were they shared by others?

ATLANTIC

OCEAN

Algiers (Fr.)
Ceuta (Sp.) Melilla (Sp.)
MEDITERRANEAN SEA
ALGIERS   TUNIS
MOROCCO

TRIPOLI

EGYPT
British occupied
(nominally Turkish
suzerainty)

RIO DE ORO

RED SEA

SENEGAL

MAHDIST
STATE   ERITREA

GAMBIA   TUKOLOR
EMPIRE   DAHOMEY   Lake Chad   OBOCK (Fr.)

BORNU
SOKOTO   ABYSSINIAN
PORT.   SAMORI'S   CALIPHATE   EMPIRE
GUINEA   STATE   (ETHIOPIA)   BRITISH
ASHANTI   SOMALILAND
SIERRA
LEONE   LIBERIA   ROYAL NIGER
IVORY COAST   COY. SPHERE
GOLD COAST   Porto
Novo   CAMEROON   BUNYORO
TOGO   (Fr.)
LAGOS   BUGANDA KINGDOM
OIL RIVERS   Lake Victoria
FERNANDO PO (Sp.)   FRENCH   CONGO   Witu (Ger.)
SÃO THOMÉ (Port.)   CONGO   FREE   BRITISH EAST AFRICA SPHERE
RIO MUNI (Sp.)   STATE
SULTANATE OF
ZANZIBAR
ATLANTIC
Lake
KATANGA   Tanganyika   GERMAN EAST AFRICA
OCEAN   CODEPENDENCY SPHERE

ANGOLA   Lake
TEKE   Nyasa

MOZAMBIQUE   MADAGASCAR
SOUTH-   MATABELE
WEST   LAND   INDIAN
AFRICA   HERERO
OCEAN
WALVIS BAY (Br.)   NAMA
TRANSVAAL
REPUBLIC   SWAZILAND
BECHUANALAND   ZULULAND
PROTECTORATE   NATAL
BRITISH
BECHUANALAND   CAPE   BASUTOLAND
COLONY
ORANGE FREE STATE

Legend:
- Indigenous power
- Turkish suzerainty
- Portuguese
- British
- King Leopold's State
- German
- Boer
- French
- Italian
- Spanish

0   500   1000 Miles
0   500   1000 Kilometers

AFRICA, C. 1886

Who were the winners and losers in the scramble for Africa before World War I? Although the French claim was
the largest, why were the British imperial gains more impressive? Given their late arrival as a unified nation and
colonial power, how did Germany fare in the race for colonial possessions? Why did Italy, despite an advantageous

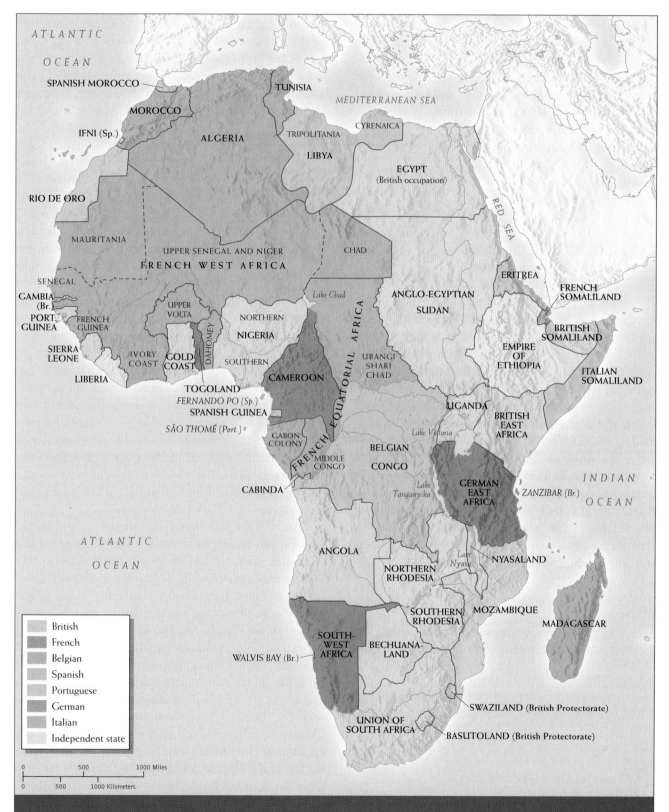

AFRICA, C. 1914

Legend:
- British
- French
- Belgian
- Spanish
- Portuguese
- German
- Italian
- Independent state

geographical relationship to Africa, fare so poorly in carving out an African empire? What does the result of the scramble for Africa suggest about how European powers regarded each other and why they felt maintaining economic and material resources was so important?

mines or plantations for the extraction of palm oil, rubber, or cocoa. African workers labored in appalling conditions, with no real medicine or sanitation, too little food, and according to production schedules that made European factory labor look mild by comparison. Hundreds of thousands of African workers died from disease and overwork. Because European managers did not respect the different cycle of seasons in central Africa, whole crop years were lost, leading to famines. Laborers working in the heat of the dry season often carried individual loads on their backs that would have been handled by heavy machinery in a European factory. Thousands of Africans were pressed into work harvesting goods Europe wanted. They did so for little or no pay, under the threat of beatings and mutilation for dozens of petty offenses against the plantation companies, who made the laws of the Free State. Eventually the scandal of the Congo became too great to go on unquestioned. A whole generation of authors and journalists, most famously Joseph Conrad in his *Heart of Darkness*, publicized the arbitrary brutality and the vast scale of suffering. In 1908 Belgium was forced to take direct control of the Congo, turning it into a Belgian colony. A few restrictions at least were imposed on the activities of the great plantation companies that had brought a vast new store of raw materials to European industry by using slavery in all but name.

Eventually the scandal of the Congo became too great to go on unquestioned. A whole generation of authors and journalists, most famously Joseph Conrad in his *Heart of Darkness,* publicized the arbitrary brutality and the vast scale of suffering.

The Partition of Africa

The occupation of Congo, and its promise of great material wealth, pressured other colonial powers into expanding their holdings. By the 1880s, the "scramble for Africa" was well under way, hastened by stories of rubber forests or diamond mines in other parts of central and southern Africa. The guarantees made at the 1884 Berlin conference allowed the Europeans to take further steps. The French and Portugese increased their holdings. Italy moved into territories along the Red Sea, beside British-held land and the independent kingdom of Ethiopia.

Germany came relatively late to empire overseas. Bismarck was reluctant to engage in an enterprise that he believed would yield few economic or political advantages. Yet he did not want either Britain or France to dominate Africa, and Germany seized colonies in strategic locations. The German colonies in Cameroon and most of modern Tanzania separated the territories of older, more established powers. Though the Germans were not the most enthusiastic colonialists, they were still fascinated by the imperial adventure and jealous of their territories. When the Herero people of German Southwest Africa (now Namibia) rebelled in the early 1900s, the Germans responded with a vicious campaign of village burning and ethnic killing that nearly annihilated the Herero.

Great Britain and France had their own ambitions. The French aimed to move west to east across the continent, an important reason for the French expedition to Fashoda (in the Sudan) in 1898 (discussed later). Britain's part in the "scramble" took place largely in southern and eastern Africa and was encapsulated in the dreams and career of one man: the diamond tycoon, colonial politician, and imperial visionary Cecil Rhodes. Rhodes, who made a fortune from the South African diamond mines in the 1870s and 1880s and founded the diamond-mining company DeBeers, became prime minister of Britain's Cape Colony in 1890. (He left part of this fortune for the creation of the Rhodes scholarships to educate future leaders of the empire at Oxford.) In an uneasy alliance with the Boer settlers in their independent republics and with varying levels of support from London, Rhodes pursued two great personal and imperial goals. The personal goal was to build a southern African empire that was founded on diamonds. "Rhodesia" would fly the Union Jack out of pride but send its profits into Rhodes's own companies. Through bribery, double

CHRONOLOGY	
The "Scramble for Africa," 1870–1908	
European drive into central Africa	1870s
French acquire Tunisia	1881
Berlin Congress	1884
Germany colonizes Cameroon and Tanzania	1884
Federation of French West Africa	1895
Congo becomes a Belgian colony	1908

Left: "The Rhodes Colossus." This cartoon, which appeared in *Punch* magazine, satirized the ambitions of Cecil Rhodes, the driving force behind British imperialism in South Africa. **Right: "Now We Shant Be Long to Cairo."** So read the banner across Engine No. 1, taking the first train from Umtali to Salisbury, Rhodesia. In Cecil Rhodes's vision, the Capetown-to-Cairo railway symbolized British domination of the African continent.

dealing, careful coalition politics with the British and Boer settlers, warfare, and outright theft, Rhodes helped carve out territories occupying the modern nations of Zambia, Zimbabwe, Malawi, and Botswana—most of the savannah of southern Africa. Rhodes had a broader imperial vision, one that he shared with the new British colonial secretary in the late 1890s, Joseph Chamberlain. The first part of that vision was a British presence along the whole of eastern Africa, symbolized by the goal of a Cape-to-Cairo railway. The second was that the empire should make Britain self-sufficient, with British industry able to run on the goods and raw materials shipped in from its colonies, then exporting many finished products back to those lands. Once the territories of Zambeziland and Rhodesia were taken, Rhodes found himself turning against the European settlers in the region, a conflict that led to outright war in 1899 (discussed later in this chapter).

This battle over strategic advantage, diamonds, and European pride was symbolic of the scramble. As each European power sought its "place in the sun," in the famous phrase of the German kaiser William II, they brought more and more of Africa under direct colonial control. It created a whole new scale of plunder as companies were designed and managed to strip the continent of its resources, and African peoples faced a combination of direct European control and indirect rule, which allowed local elites friendly to European interests literally to lord over those who resisted. The partition of Africa was the most striking instance of the new imperialism, with international and domestic repercussions.

IMPERIAL CULTURE

How did imperialism enter into European culture?

The relationship between the metropole and the colonies was not carried on at a distance; imperialism was thoroughly anchored in late nineteenth-century Western culture. Images of empire were everywhere in the metropole. They were not just in the propagandist literature distributed by the proponents of colonial expansion but on tins of tea and boxes of cocoa, as background themes in posters advertising everything from

RUDYARD KIPLING AND HIS CRITICS

Rudyard Kipling (1865–1936) remains one of the most famous propagandists of empire. His novels, short stories, and poetry about the British imperial experience in India were defining texts for the cause in which he believed. Kipling's poem, was—and continues to be—widely read, analyzed, attacked, and praised. His immediate goal was to influence American public opinion during the Spanish–American War, but he also wanted to celebrate the moral and religious values of European imperialism in general.

THE WHITE MAN'S BURDEN

Take up the Whi̶̶̶̶̶̶̶̶̶̶—
    Send forth th̶̶̶̶
Go, bind your ̶̶̶̶
    To serve yo̶̶̶
To wait, in h̶̶̶
    On flutte̶̶̶
Your new-̶̶̶̶
    Half devil an̶̶̶

Take up the White Man's b̶̶̶
    In patience to abide,
To veil the threat of terror
    And check the show of pride;
By open speech and simple,
    An hundred times made plain,
To seek another's profit
    And work another's gain.

Take up the White Man's burden—
    The savage wars of peace—
Fill full the mouth of Famine,
    And bid the sickness cease;
And when your goal is nearest
    (The end for others sought)
Watch sloth and heathen folly
    Bring all your hope to nought.

Take up the White Man's burden—
    No iron rule of kings,
But toil of serf and sweeper—
    The tale of common things.
The ports ye shall not enter,
    The roads ye shall not tread,

Go, make them with your living
    And mark them with your dead.

Take up the White Man's burden,
    And reap his old reward—
The blame of those ye better
    The hate of those ye guard—
The cry of hosts ye humour
    (Ah, slowly!) toward the light:—
"Why brought ye us from bondage,
    Our loved Egyptian night?"

Take up the White Man's burden—
    Ye dare not stoop to less—
Nor call too loud on Freedom
    To cloak your weariness.
By all ye will or whisper,
    By all ye leave or do,
The silent sullen peoples
    Shall weigh your God and you.

Take up the White Man's burden!
    Have done with childish days—
The lightly-proffered laurel,
    The easy ungrudged praise:
Comes now, to search your manhood
    Through all the thankless years,
Cold, edged with dear-bought wisdom,
    The judgment of your peers.

Rudyard Kipling, "The White Man's Burden," *McClure's Magazine* 12 (Feb. 1899).

TO THE EDITOR OF *THE NATION*

Sir: The cable informs us that "Kipling's stirring verses, the 'Call to America,' have created a . . . profound impression" on your side. What that impression may be, we can only conjecture. There is something almost sickening in this "imperial" talk of assuming and bearing burdens for the good of others. They are never assumed or held where they are not found to be of material advantage or ministering to honor or glory. Wherever empire (I speak of the United Kingdom) is extended, and the climate suits the white man, the aborigines are, for the benefit of the white man, cleared off or held in degradation for his benefit. . . .

Taking India as a test, no one moves a foot in her government that is not well paid and pensioned at her cost. No appointments are more eagerly contended for than those in the Indian service. A young man is made for life when he secures one. The tone of that service is by no means one "bound to exile," "to serve . . . captives' need," "to wait in heavy harness," or in any degree as expressed in Mr. Kipling's highfalutin lines. It is entirely the contrary: "You are requested not to beat the servants" is a not uncommon notice in Indian hotels. . . . So anxious are we, where good pay is concerned, to save Indians the heavy burden of enjoying them, that, while our sons can study and pass at home for Indian appointments, her sons must study and pass in England; and even in India itself whites are afforded chances closed to natives. . . .

There never was a fostered trade and revenue in more disastrous consequences to humanity than the opium trade and revenue. There never was a more grinding and debilitating tax than that on salt. . . .

Alfred Webb, "Mr. Kipling's Call to America," *The Nation* 68 (Feb. 23, 1899).

QUESTIONS FOR ANALYSIS

1. What benefits did Kipling think imperialism brought, and to whom?
2. What, exactly, was the "burden"?
3. What were Webb's arguments against Kipling? Why did he think that imperial talk was "almost sickening"? Did Europeans really suffer in their colonial outposts? In British India, with its well-established civil service, Webb thought not. Why did he mention the opium trade and the salt tax?

---

dance halls to sewing machines. Museums and world's fairs displayed the products of empire and introduced spectators to "exotic peoples" who were now benefiting from European education. Music halls rang to the sound of imperialist songs. Empire was almost always present in novels of the period, sometimes appearing as a faraway setting for fantasy, adventure, or stories of self-discovery. Sometimes imperial themes and peoples were presented as a subtly menacing presence at home. Even in the tales of Sherlock Holmes, which were set in London and not overtly imperialist, the furnishings of empire provided instantly recognizable signs of opulence and decadence. In *The Sign of Four*, Holmes visits a gentleman in a lavish apartment: "Two great tiger-skins thrown athwart [the carpet] increased the suggestion of Eastern luxury, as did a huge hookah which stood upon a mat in the corner." In *The Man with the Twisted Lip*, Watson wanders into one of the supposed opium dens in the East End of London and is waited on by a "sallow Malay attendant." The dens themselves were largely an invention; police records of the time show very few locations in London that supplied the drug. As a realm of fantasy, overseas empires and "exotic" cultures became part of the century's sexual culture. Photos and postcards of North African harems and unveiled Arab women were common in European pornography, as were colonial memoirs that chronicled the sexual adventures of their authors.

Empire, however, was not simply background; it played an important part in establishing European identity. In the case of France, the "civilizing mission" demonstrated to French citizens the grandeur of their nation. Building railroads and "bringing progress to other lands" illustrated the vigor of the French republic. Many British writers spoke in similar tones. One called the British empire "the greatest secular agency for good known to the world." Another, using more religious language, argued, "The British race may safely be called a missionary race. The command to go and teach all nations is one that the British people have, whether rightly or wrongly, regarded as specially laid upon themselves." The sense of high moral purpose was not restricted to male writers or authority figures. In England, the United States, Germany, and France, the speeches and projects of women's reform movements were full of references to empire and the civilizing mission. Britain's woman suffrage movement, for instance, was fiercely critical of the British government but often equally nationalist and imperialist. Asking that women be brought into British politics seemed to involve calling on them to take on imperial, as well as civic, responsibilities. British women reformers wrote about the oppression of Indian women by child marriage and sati and saw themselves shouldering the "white woman's burden" of reform. The French suffragist Hubertine Auclert wrote a book titled *Arab Women in Algeria* (1900), which angrily indicted both French colonial administrators for their indifference to the condition of women in their domains and the French republic for shrugging off the claims of women at home. Her arguments stung precisely because they rested on the assumption that European culture should be enlightened. Arab women were "victims of Muslim debauchery," wrote Auclert, and polygamy led to "intellectual degeneracy." The image of women languishing in the colonies not only dramatized the need for reform, it enabled European women in their home countries to see themselves as bearers of progress. The liberal writer and political theorist John Stuart Mill (see Chapter Twenty) regularly used the colonial world as a foil. When he wanted to drive home a point about freedom of speech or religion, he pointed to India as a counterexample, trading in stereotypes about Hindu or Muslim "obscurantism," and appealing to British convictions that theirs was the superior civilization. This contrast between colonial backwardness or moral degeneration and European civility and stability shaped Western culture and political debate.

Imperial culture also gave new prominence to theories of race. In the 1850s, Count Arthur de Gobineau (*GOH-bih-noh*; 1816–1882) had written a massive tome, *The Inequality of the Races*, but the book sparked little interest until the period of the new imperialism, when it was translated into English and widely discussed. For Gobineau, race offered the "master key" to understanding problems in the modern world. He ar-

gued, "The racial question overshadows all other problems of history . . . the inequality of the races from whose fusion a people is formed is enough to explain the whole course of its destiny." Some of Gobineau's ideas followed from earlier Enlightenment projects that compared and examined different cultures and governments. Unlike his Enlightenment predecessors, however, Gobineau did not believe that environment had any effect on politics, culture, or morals. Race was all. He argued that a people degenerated when it no longer had "the same blood in its veins, continual adulteration having gradually affected the quality of that blood." Enlightenment thinkers often argued that slavery made its victims unable to understand liberty. Gobineau, by contrast, asserted that slavery proved its victims' racial inferiority.

Houston Stewart Chamberlain (1855–1927), the son of a British admiral, tried to improve Gobineau's theories and make them more scientific. That meant tying racial theories to the new scientific writing about evolution, Charles Darwin's natural science, and Herbert Spencer's views about the evolution of societies. (On Darwin and Spencer, see Chapter Twenty-Three.) Like other European thinkers concerned with race, Chamberlain used the concept of evolutionary change to show that races changed over time. Chamberlain's books proved extremely popular, selling tens of thousands of copies in England and Germany. Francis Galton (1822–1911), a British scientist who studied evolution, similarly explored how hereditary traits were communicated from generation to generation. In 1883, Galton first used the term *eugenics* to refer to the science of improving the "racial qualities" of humanity through selective breeding of "superior types." Karl Pearson (1857–1936), who did pioneering work in the use of statistics, turned his systematic analysis to studies of intelligence and genius, sharing Galton's worries that only new policies of racial management would check Europe's impending decline. These theories did not, by themselves, produce an imperialist mindset, and they were closely linked with other developments in European culture, particularly renewed antagonism about social class and a fresh wave of European anti-Semitism (see Chapter Twenty-Three). Yet the increasingly scientific racism of late-nineteenth-century Europe made it easier for many to reconcile the rhetoric of progress, individual freedom, and the civilizing mission with

> Empire, however, was not simply background; it played an important part in establishing European identity.

"The Face of Crime." Francis Galton combined sets of twelve photographs to form an "ideal type" for criminals. Galton believed that if a man resembled one of the photographs shown here, one could tell he would be a criminal.

contempt for other peoples. It also provided a rationale for imperial conquest and a justification for the bloodshed that imperialism brought, for instance, in Africa.

Still, Europeans disagreed on these issues. Politicians and writers who championed imperialism, or offered racial justifications for it, met with opposition. Such thinkers as Hobson and Lenin condemned the entire imperial enterprise as an act of greed and antidemocratic arrogance. Writers such as Conrad, who shared many of their contemporaries' racism, nevertheless believed that imperialism signaled deeply rooted pathologies in European culture. In short, one result of imperialism was serious debate about its effects and causes. Many of the anti-imperialists were men and women from the colonies themselves, who brought their case to the metropole. The British Committee of the Indian National Congress, for instance, gathered together many members of London's Indian community determined to educate British public opinion about the exploitation of Indian peoples and resources. This work involved speaking tours, demonstrations, and meetings with potentially sympathetic British radicals and socialists.

Perhaps the most defiant of all anti-imperialist actions was the London Pan-African conference of 1900, staged at the height of the "scramble for Africa" and during the Boer War (discussed next). The conference grew out of an international tradition of African American, British, and American antislavery movements, and out of groups like the African Association (founded in 1897), which brought the rhetoric used earlier to abolish slavery to bear on the tactics of European imperialism. They protested forced labor in the mining compounds of South Africa as akin to slavery and asked in very moderate tones for some autonomy and representation for native African peoples. The Pan-African Conference of 1900 was small, but it drew delegates from the Caribbean, West Africa, and North America, including the thirty-two-year-old Harvard Ph.D. and leading African American intellectual W. E. B. Du Bois (1868–1963). The conference issued a proclamation "To the Nations of the World," with a famous introduction written by Du Bois. "The Problem of the twentieth century is the problem of the color line. . . . In the metropolis of the modern world, in this the closing year of the nineteenth century," the proclamation read, "there has been assembled a congress of men and women of African blood, to deliberate solemnly the present situation and outlook of the darker races of mankind." The British government ignored the conference completely. Yet Pan-Africanism, like Indian nationalism, grew by sudden (and, for imperialists, disturbing) leaps after World War I.

In recent years historians have become increasingly interested in colonial cultures, or the results of the imperial encounter across the world. Cities such as Bombay, Calcutta, and Shanghai boomed in the period, more than tripling in size. Hong Kong and other treaty ports, run as outposts of European commerce and culture, were transformed as Europeans built banks, shipping enterprises, schools, and military academies, and engaged in missionary activities. The variety of national experiences makes generalization very difficult, but we can underscore a few points. First, colonialism created new, hybrid cultures. Both European and indigenous institutions and practices, especially religion, were transformed by their contact with each other. Second, although Europeans often considered the areas they annexed "laboratories" for creating well-disciplined and orderly societies, the social changes Europeans brought in their wake confounded such plans. In both western and southern Africa, European demands for labor brought men out of their villages, leaving their families behind, and crowded them by the thousands into the shantytowns bordering sprawling new cities. Enterprising locals set up all manner of illegal businesses catering to transitory male workers, disconcerting European authorities in the process. Hopes that European rule would create a well-disciplined labor force and well-patrolled cities were quickly dashed.

Third, authorities on both sides of the colonial encounter worried enormously about preserving national traditions and identity in the face of an inevitably hybrid and constantly changing colonial culture. Especially in China and India, debates about whether education should be Westernized or continue on traditional lines set off fierce debates. Chinese elites, already divided over such customs as foot binding and concubinage (the legal practice of maintaining formal sexual partners for men outside their marriage), found their dilemmas heightened as imperialism became a more powerful force. Uncertain whether such practices should be repudiated or defended, they wrestled with great anguish over the ways in which their own culture had been changed by the corruption of colonialism. Proponents of reform and change in China or India had to sort through their stance toward modern Western culture, the culture of the colonizers, and traditional popular culture. For their part, British, French, and Dutch colonial authorities fretted that too much familiarity between colonized and colonizer would weaken European traditions and undermine European power. In Phnom Penh, Cambodia (then part of French Indochina), where French citizens lived in neighborhoods separated from the rest of the city by a moat, colonial authorities nonetheless required "dressing appropriately and keeping a distance from the natives." Scandalized by what he considered the absence of decorum among the French in the city, a French journalist asserted that a French woman should never be seen in the public market. "The Asians cannot understand such a fall." European women were to uphold European standards and prestige.

It is not surprising that sexual relations provoked the most anxiety and also the most contradictory responses. "In this hot climate, passions run higher" wrote a French administrator in Algeria. "The French soldiers seek out Arab women due to their strangeness and newness." "It was common practice for unmarried Englishmen resident in China to keep a Chinese girl, and I did as others did," reported a British man stationed in Shanghai. But when he followed convention and married an English woman, he sent his Chinese mistress and their three children to England to avoid any awkwardness. European administrators fitfully tried to prohibit liaisons between European men and indigenous women, labeling such affairs as "corrupting" and "nearly always disastrous." They grew increasingly hostile to the children of such unions. But such prohibitions only drove relations underground, increasing the gap between the public facade of colonial rule and the private

reality of colonial lives. In this and other spheres, colonial culture forced a series of compromises about "acceptability" and created changing, sometimes subtle, ethnic hierarchies. And such local and personal dramas were no less complex than the Great Powers' clashes over territories.

CRISES OF EMPIRE AT THE TURN OF THE TWENTIETH CENTURY

Which nations clashed at the turn of the century, and why?

The turn of the twentieth century brought a series of crises to the Western empires. Those crises did not end European rule. They did, however, create sharp tensions among Western nations. The crises also drove imperial nations to expand their economic and military commitments in territories overseas. They shook Western confidence. In all of these ways, they became central to Western culture in the years before World War I.

FASHODA

The first crisis, in the fall of 1898, pitted Britain against France at Fashoda, in the Egyptian Sudan. Britain's establishment of a protectorate in Egypt after the 1880s Suez Canal confrontation had several important effects. It changed British strategy in east Africa, encouraging Rhodes's Cape-to-Cairo ideas. It also opened up the archaeological and cultural treasures of Egypt's past to British adventurers and academics, keen students—and self-aggrandizing editors—of history. It seemed that the most ancient civilization was now linked to the most successful modern one, and British explorers could trace the source of the Nile by traveling up waters that were governed under a British flag.

Explorers were not the only Britons to venture farther up the Nile. In the name of protecting the new, pro-British ruler, Britain intervened in an Islamic uprising in the Sudan. An Anglo-Egyptian force was sent to the Sudanese capital, Khartoum, led by the most flamboyant—and perhaps least sensible—of Britain's colonial generals, Charles "Chinese" Gordon, well known for his role in suppressing the Taiping Rebellion in China. The Sudanese rebels, led by

Mahdi (a religious leader who claimed to be the successor to the prophet Muhammad), besieged Gordon. British forces were ill prepared to move south on the Nile in strength; Gordon ended up dying a "hero's death" as the rebels stormed Khartoum. Avenging Gordon occupied officials in Egypt and the British popular imagination for more than a decade. In 1898, a second large-scale rebellion provided the opportunity. An Anglo-Egyptian army commanded by a methodical and ambitious engineer, General Horatio Kitchener, sailed south up the Nile and attacked Khartoum. Using modern rifles, artillery, and machine guns, they massacred the Mahdi's army at the town of Omdurman and retook Khartoum. Gordon's body was disinterred and reburied with pomp and circumstance as the British public celebrated a famous and easy victory.

That victory brought complications, however. France, which held territories in central Africa next door to the Sudan, saw the British presence along the eastern side of Africa as a prelude to Britain's dominance of the whole continent. A French expedition was sent to the Sudanese town of Fashoda (now Kodok) to challenge British claims to the southernmost part of the territory. The French faced off with troops from Kitchener's army. For a few weeks in September 1898 the situation teetered on the brink of war. The matter was resolved, however, when Britain not only called France's bluff but also provided guarantees against further expansion by cementing borders for the new Anglo-Egyptian Sudan, an even greater extension of the political control that had begun with the Suez Canal.

ETHIOPIA

Traditional methods of imperial rule and notions of European military and moral superiority faced other challenges at the turn of the century. The Boxer Rebellion in China was one of a number of indigenous revolts against Western imperial methods and its consequences. The Russo-Japanese War was a dangerously large conflict between two imperial powers that challenged notions of inherent European superiority over all the peoples of the world.

Other complications for European powers arose as well. During the 1880s and 1890s Italy had been developing a small empire of its own along the shores of the Red Sea. Italy annexed Eritrea and parts of Somalia, and shortly after the death of Gordon at Khartoum defeated an invasion of its new colonies by the Mahdi's forces. These first colonial successes encouraged Italian politicians, still trying to build a modern

industrial nation, to mount a much more ambitious imperial project. In 1896, an expedition was sent to conquer Ethiopia. Ethiopia was a mountainous, inland empire, the last major independent African kingdom. Its emperor, Menelik II, was a savvy politician and shrewd military commander. His subjects were largely Christian, and the empire's trade had allowed Menelik to invest in the latest European artillery to guard his vast holdings. The expedition, which consisted of a few thousand professional Italian soldiers and many more Somali conscripts, marched into the mountain passes of Ethiopia. Menelik let them come, knowing that by keeping to the roads the Italian commanders would have to divide their forces. Menelik's own huge army moved over the mountains themselves; and as the disorganized Italian command tried to regroup near the town of Adowa in March 1896, the Ethiopian army set on the separate columns and destroyed them completely, killing 6,000. Adowa

Emperor Menelik II. Ethiopia was the last independent African kingdom, its prosperity a counter to the European opinion of African cultures. Menelik soundly defeated the Italian attempt to conquer his kingdom in 1896.

was a national humiliation for Italy and an important symbol for African political radicals and reformers during the early twentieth century. Menelik's prosperous kingdom seemed a puzzling and perhaps dangerous exception to European judgments about African cultures generally.

SOUTH AFRICA: THE BOER WAR

Elsewhere in Africa vaulting ambitions led to an even more troubling kind of conflict: Europeans fighting European settlers. The Afrikaners, also called Boers (an appropriation of the Dutch word for "farmer"), were settlers from the Netherlands and Switzerland who had arrived in South Africa with the Dutch East India Company in the early 1800s and who had a long and troubled relationship with their imperial neighbor, Great Britain. Over the course of the nineteenth century the Afrikaners trekked inland from the Cape, setting up two independent republics away from the influence of Britain: the Transvaal and the Orange Free State. In the mid-1880s, gold reserves were discovered in the Transvaal. As a British diamond magnate and imperialist, Rhodes had actually tried to provoke war between Britain and the Boers in hopes of adding the Afrikaners' prosperous diamond mines and pastureland to his own territory of Rhodesia. In 1899, as the result of a series of disputes, Britain did go to war with the Afrikaners. Despite the recent British victory in the Sudan, the British army was woefully unprepared for the war: supplies, communications, and medicine for the army in South Africa were a shambles. These initial problems were followed by several humiliating defeats as British columns were shot to pieces by Afrikaner forces who knew the terrain. British garrisons at the towns of Ladysmith and Mafeking were besieged. Angered and embarrassed by these early failures the British government, particularly the colonial secretary Chamberlain, refused any compromise. The new British commander, Sir Robert Roberts, used superior British resources and the railroads built to service the diamond mines to his advantage. British forces steamrolled the Boers, relieved the besieged British garrisons, and took the Afrikaner capital at Pretoria. There were celebrations in London and hopes that the war was now over.

The Afrikaners, however, were determined never to surrender. Supplied by other European nations, particularly Germany and the Netherlands, the Afrikaners took to the wilderness in commandos (small raiding parties) and fought a guerrilla war that dragged on for another three years. British losses due to the commandos and disease led British generals to take most of the comprehensive and brutal steps to which later Western armies would frequently resort in the face of guerrilla warfare. Armored blockhouses were set up to guard strategic locations, shooting at anything that moved. Special cavalry units—often using Irish or Australian horsemen fighting for the mother country, Britain—were sent in to fight the guerrillas on their own terms, each side committing its share of atrocities. Black Africans, despised by both sides, suffered the effects of famine and disease as the war destroyed valuable farmland. The British also instituted *concentration camps*—the

LA GUERRE AU TRANSVAAL
Les camps de reconcentration

An English Concentration Camp during the Boer War. In an attempt to block support to guerrilla fighters, the English restricted Afrikaner civilians to camps where appalling conditions led to the death of nearly 20,000 people over two years. This illustration appeared in *Le Petit Journal* in 1901.

first use of the term—where Afrikaner civilians were rounded up and forced to live in appalling conditions so that they would be unable to lend aid to the guerrillas. Nearly 20,000 civilians died due to disease and poor sanitation over the course of two years. These measures provoked an international backlash. European and American newspapers lambasted the British as imperial bullies. The concentration camps bred opposition in Britain itself, where protesters, labeled "pro-Boers" by the conservative press, campaigned against these violations of white Europeans' rights while saying very little about the fate of native Africans in the conflict. In the end, the Afrikaners acquiesced. Afrikaner politicians signed their old republics over to a new British Union of South Africa that gave them a share of political power. The settlement created an uneasy alliance between English settlers and Afrikaners; politicians for both parties preserved their high standards of living by relying on cheap African labor and, eventually, a system of racial segregation known as apartheid.

U.S. IMPERIALISM

Finally, imperialism brought Spain and the United States to blows in the Spanish–American War of 1898. American imperialism reached back at least fifty years and was closely bound up with nation building: the conquest of new territories, the expansion of state power, and the defeat of the North American Indians (see Chapter Twenty-One). The United States had come to blows with Mexico in the 1840s. Weakened by debt, Mexico was increasingly unable to exert its authority over the large, sparsely populated, and farflung territories that included Texas and California. Those lands thus beckoned to the American government and to white North Americans eager for land. By 1845, the roughly 7,000 Mexicans in California had been joined by 1,000 white Americans. The American president tried, unsuccessfully, to purchase California and then provoked Mexico into war. Mexico's defeat and the treaty of Guadalupe Hidalgo in 1848 (see page 745) enabled the United States to acquire the southwest, an enormous territorial gain and one that would make the issue of slavery more acute.

The U.S. conflict with Spain in the late nineteenth century followed a similar pattern. Spain's imperial authority had frayed; in the 1880s and 1890s it faced regular rebellions in its Caribbean and Pacific colonies. The American popular press talked up the

Three generations of Afrikaner, or Boer, soldiers.

cause of the rebels. American economic interests worried about their considerable investments in Cuba, and when an American battleship accidentally exploded in port at Havana, Cuba, advocates of empire and much of the press clamored for revenge. American opinion was not unanimous. President William McKinley was extremely wary of going to war, but he also understood its political necessity. The United States stepped in to protect its economic interests, to guarantee the maritime security of trade routes in the American and the Pacific, and to demonstrate the power of the newly built-up American navy. It declared war on Spain in 1898 and swiftly won.

In Spain, the Spanish-American War provoked an entire generation of writers, politicians, and intellectuals to national soul searching. It also had long-term consequences. Spain's defeat undermined the Spanish monarchy, which fell in 1912. The political tensions that toppled the monarchy, however, did not disappear; they eventually resurfaced in the violence of the Spanish Civil War of the 1930s, an important episode in the origins of World War II.

In the United States, the "splendid little war" against Spain was followed by the annexation of Puerto Rico, a protectorate over Cuba, and by a short but brutal war against Philippine rebels who liked American no better than Spanish colonialism. In the Americas, the United States continued its interventions. When the Colombian province of Panama threatened to rebel in 1903, the United States quickly backed the rebels, recognized Panama as a republic, and granted that republic protection—while building the Panama Canal on land leased from the new government. The Panama Canal (which opened officially in 1914), like Britain's canal at Suez, cemented American dominance of the seas in the Western Hemisphere and the eastern Pacific. Interventions in Hawaii and, later, Santo Domingo were further evidence of U.S. imperial power.

In the United States, as in Great Britain, the last decade of the century brought a rush of missionary activity, spurred by the same civilizing mission, or conviction that such activity carried culture, prosperity, and progress to backward lands. China particularly captured American missionaries' imaginations. In some cases, Americans self-consciously imitated the British Empire and imperial spirit. In others, they shied away from officially embracing colonialism. The decision to annex the Philippines, for example, was controversial and followed a very close vote in Congress. British writer Kipling called on the rapidly rising American nation to take up the burden of empire, but his summons met with a divided response.

CONCLUSION

In the last quarter of the nineteenth century, the long-standing relationship between Western nations and the rest of the world entered a new stage. That stage was distinguished by the stunningly rapid extension of formal Western control and by new patterns of discipline and settlement. It was driven by the rising economic needs of the industrial West; by territorial conflict; and by nationalism, which by the late nineteenth century linked nationhood to empire. Among its immediate results was the creation of a self-consciously imperial culture in the West. At the same time, however, it plainly created unease and contributed powerfully to the sense of crisis that swept through the late-nineteenth-century West.

For all its force, this Western expansion was never unchallenged. Imperialism provoked resistance and required constantly changing strategies of rule. During World War I, mobilizing the resources of empire would become crucial to victory. In the aftermath, reimposing the conditions of the late nineteenth century would become nearly impossible. And over the longer term, the political structures, economic developments, and patterns of race relations established in this period would be contested throughout the twentieth century.

KEY TERMS

new imperialism	Boxer Rebellion	eugenics	Spanish–American War
Indian Rebellion of 1857	Leopold II	Pan-African Conference	
Opium Wars	Arthur de Gobineau	Boer War	

SELECTED READINGS

Adas, Michael. *Machines as the Measure of Man: Science, Technology, and Ideologies of Western Dominance.* Ithaca, N.Y., and London, 1989. An important study of Europeans' changing perceptions of themselves and others during the period of industrialization.

Bayly, C. A. *Indian Society and the Making of the British Empire.* Cambridge, 1988. A good introduction, and one that bridges eighteenth- and nineteenth-century imperialisms.

Burton, Antoinette. *Burdens of History: British Feminists, Indian Women, and Imperial Culture, 1865–1915.* Chapel Hill, N.C.,

1994. On the ways in which women and feminists came to support British imperialism.

Cain, P. J., and A. G. Hopkins. *British Imperialism, 1688–2000.* London, 2002. A new edition of one of the most influential studies. Excellent overview and exceptionally good on economics.

Clancy Smith, Julia, and Frances Gouda. *Domesticating the Empire: Race, Gender, and Family Life in French and Dutch Colonialism.* Charlottesville, Va., and London, 1998. A particularly good collection of essays that both breaks new historical ground and is accessible to nonspecialists. Essays cover daily life and private life in new colonial cultures.

Conklin, Alice. *A Mission to Civilize: The Republican idea of Empire in France and West Africa, 1895–1930.* Stanford, Calif., 1997. One of the best studies of how the French reconciled imperialism with their vision of the Republic.

Cooper, Frederick, and Ann Laura Stoler. *Tensions of Empire: Colonial Cultures in a Bourgeois World.* Berkeley, Calif., 1997. New approaches, combining anthropology and history, with an excellent bibliography.

Headrick, Daniel R. *The Tools of Empire: Technology and European Imperialism in the Nineteenth Century.* Oxford, 1981. A study of the relationship between technological innovation and imperialism.

Hobsbawm, Eric. *The Age of Empire, 1875–1914.* New York, 1987. Surveys the European scene at a time of apparent stability and real decline.

Hochschild, Adam. *King Leopold's Ghost: A Story of Greed, Terror, and Heroism in Colonial Africa.* Boston, 1998. Reads like a great novel.

Lorcin, Patricia. *Imperial Identities: Stereotyping, Prejudice and Race in Colonial Algeria.* New York, 1999.

Louis, William Roger. *The Oxford History of the British Empire.* 5 vols. Oxford, 1998. Excellent and wide-ranging collection of the latest research.

Metcalf, Thomas. *Ideologies of the Raj.* Cambridge, 1995.

Pakenham, Thomas. *The Scramble for Africa, 1876–1912.* London, 1991. A well-written narrative of the European scramble for Africa in the late nineteenth century.

Prochaska, David. *Making Algeria French: Colonialism in Bône, 1870–1920.* Cambridge, 1990. One of the few social histories of European settlement in Algeria in English.

Robinson, Ronald, and J. Gallagher. *Africa and the Victorians: The Official Mind of Imperialism.* London, 1961. A classic.

Said, Edward. *Culture and Imperialism.* New York, 1993. A collection of brilliant, sometimes controversial, essays.

Sangari, Kumkum, and Sudesh Vaid. *Recasting Women: Essays in Colonial History.* New Delhi, 1989. A collection of essays on women in India.

Schneer, Jonathan. *London 1900: The Imperial Metropolis.* New Haven, Conn., 1999. Excellent study of the empire—and opposition to empire—in the metropole.

Spence, Jonathan. *The Search for Modern China.* New York, 1990. An excellent and readable introduction to modern Chinese history.

Chapter
TWENTY-THREE

MODERN INDUSTRY
AND MASS POLITICS,
1870–1914

"WE ARE ON THE EXTREME PROMONTORY OF AGES!"
decreed the Italian poet and literary editor F. T. Marinetti in
1909. In a bombastic manifesto—a self-described "inflamma-
tory declaration" printed on the front page of a Paris newspaper—Marinetti introduced Europe to an aggressive art movement called futurism. Revolting against what
he considered the tired and impotent conservatism of Italian culture, Marinetti
called for a radical renewal of civilization through "courage, audacity, and revolt."
Enamored with the raw power of modern machinery, with the dynamic bustle of
urban life, he trumpeted "a new form of beauty, the beauty of speed." Most notable,
Marinetti celebrated the heroic violence of warfare and disparaged the moral and
cultural traditions that formed the bedrock of nineteenth-century liberalism.

At the time Marinetti issued his manifesto, five years before World War I, people
across Europe indeed felt themselves to be living in a radically new world. A series
of explosive developments in the years since 1870 accounted for this change. A second industrial revolution spurred enormous growth in the scope and scale of industry and changed the lives of ordinary people. Mass politics became a fact of life.
New blocs of voters brought new demands to the political arena, and national governments struggled to maintain order and legitimacy. Socialists mobilized growing
numbers of industrial workers, while suffragists demanded the franchise for women.
In the arts and sciences, new theories challenged age-old notions of nature, society,
truth, and beauty. Challenges, however, are not always welcome. Few Europeans
embraced the modern era with the unflinching abandon of the futurists.

FOCUS QUESTIONS

• What developments sparked the second
industrial revolution?

• Why did working-class movements grow so
dramatically during this period?

• What rights did women claim, and why were
they so controversial?

• What are "mass politics" and how did nation-
states respond to them?

• What impact did new scientific theories have
on culture?

New Technologies and Global Transformations

What developments sparked the second industrial revolution?

In the last third of the nineteenth century, new technologies transformed the face of manufacturing in Europe, leading to new levels of economic growth and complex realignments among industry, labor, and national governments. Like Europe's first Industrial Revolution, which began in the late eighteenth century and centered on coal, steam, and iron, this second industrial revolution relied on innovation in three key areas: steel, electricity, and chemicals.

Harder, stronger, and more malleable than iron, steel had long been prized as a construction material. But until the mid-nineteenth century, producing steel cheaply and in large quantities was impossible. That changed between the 1850s and 1870s, as three different processes for refining and mass-producing alloy steel revolutionized the metallurgical industry—one by the Englishman Henry Bessemer, the others in tandem between the German Siemen brothers and the French engineer Pierre Martin. Although iron did not disappear overnight, it was soon eclipsed by soaring steel production. Britain's shipbuilders made a quick and profitable switch to steel construction and thus kept their lead in the industry. Germany and America, however, dominated the rest of the steel industry. By 1901 Germany was producing almost half again as much steel as Britain, allowing Germany to build a massive national and industrial infrastructure.

Annual Output of Steel (in millions of metric tons)

Year	Britain	Germany	France	Russia
1875–1879	0.90	—	0.26	0.08
1880–1884	1.82	0.99	0.46	0.25
1885–1889	2.86	1.65	0.54	0.23
1890–1894	3.19	2.89	0.77	0.54
1895–1899	4.33	5.08	1.26	1.32
1900–1904	5.04	7.71	1.70	2.35
1905–1909	6.09	11.30	2.65	2.63
1910–1913	6.93	16.24	4.09	4.20

Carlo Cipolla, *The Fontana Economic History of Europe*, vol. 3(2) (London, 1976), p. 775.

Like steel, electricity had been discovered earlier, and its advantages were similarly well known. Easily transmitted over long distances to be converted into heat, light, and other types of energy, electricity was finally made available for commercial and domestic use by another set of nineteenth-century innovations. In 1800, the Italian Alessandro Volta invented the chemical battery. In 1831, the English scientist Michael Faraday discovered electromagnetic induction, which led to the first electromagnetic generator in 1866. By the 1880s, engineers and technicians had developed alternators and transformers capable of producing high-voltage alternating current. By century's end, large power stations, which often used cheap water power, could send electric current over vast distances. In 1879 Thomas Edison and his associates invented the incandescent-filament lamp and changed electricity into light. The demand for electricity skyrocketed, and soon entire metropolitan areas were electrified. As a leading sector in the new economy, electrification powered subways, tramways, and, eventually, long-distance railroads; it made possible new techniques in the chemical and metallurgical industries; and gradually, it dramatically altered living habits in ordinary households.

The chemical industry was a third sector of important new technologies. The efficient production of alkali and sulfuric acid transformed the manufacture of such consumer goods as paper, soaps, textiles, and fertilizer. Britain and particularly Germany became leaders in the field. The British led the way in the production of hand soap and household cleaners. Heightened concerns for household hygiene and new techniques in mass marketing enabled the British entrepreneur Harold Lever to market his soaps and cleansers around the world. German production, on the other hand, focused on industrial use, such as developing synthetic dyes and methods for refining petroleum, and came to control roughly 90 percent of the world's chemical market.

Other innovations contributed to the second industrial revolution. For instance, the growing demand for efficient power spurred the invention of the liquid-fuel internal combustion engine. Already, improved steam turbines had engines running at record speeds, but internal combustion engines offered two major advantages: they were more efficient and did not require stoking, as did steam engines. By 1914 most navies had converted from coal to oil, as had domestic steamship companies. The new engines' dependence on crude petroleum and distilled gasoline at first threatened

The Second Industrial Revolution. A German electrical engineering works illustrates the scale of production during the second industrial revolution.

their general application, but the discovery of oil fields in Russia, Borneo, Persia, and Texas around 1900 allayed fears. Protecting these oil reserves thus became a vital state prerogative. The adoption of oil-powered machinery had another important consequence: industrialists who had previously depended on nearby rivers or coal mines for power were free to take their enterprises to regions bereft of natural resources. The potential for worldwide industrialization was in place. Of course, the internal combustible engine would bring even more radical changes to twentieth-century transportation in the future, but the automobile and the airplane were both still in their infancies before 1914.

CHANGES IN SCOPE AND SCALE

These technological changes were part of a much larger process—impressive increases in the scope and scale of industry. Technologies were both causes and consequences of the race toward a bigger, faster, cheaper, and more efficient world. At the end of the

nineteenth century, size mattered. The rise of heavy industry and mass marketing had factories and cities growing hand in hand, while advances in media and mobility spurred the creation of national mass cultures. For the first time, ordinary people followed the news on national and global levels. They watched as European powers divided the globe, enlarging their empires with prodigious feats of engineering mastery; railroads, dams, canals, and harbors grew to monumental proportions. Such projects embodied the ideals of modern European industry. They also generated enormous income for builders, investors, bankers, entrepreneurs, and, of course, makers of steel and concrete. Canals in central Europe, railroads in the Andes, and telegraph cables spanning the ocean floors: these "tentacles of empire," as one historian dubs them, stretched across the globe.

Yet industrialization also brought profound, if less spectacular, changes in Europe. The population grew constantly, particularly in central and eastern Europe. Russia's population increased by nearly a quarter and

Industrial Concentration
- Cities
- Areas

Mining
- Low-grade coal
- High-grade coal
- Iron ore
- Petroleum

- Steel
- Engineering
- Chemicals
- Electrical industry
- Oil production

Railroad Development
- Lines completed by 1848
- Area of main railroad completed by 1870
- Lines after 1870

THE INDUSTRIAL REGIONS OF EUROPE

This map shows the distribution of mineral resources, rail lines, and industrial activity. What nations enjoyed advantages in the development of industry and why? What resources were most important for industrial growth in the second half of the nineteenth century?

Population Growth in Major States between 1871 and 1911
(population in millions)

	About 1871	*About 1911*	*Percent Increase*
German Empire	41.1	64.9	57.8
France	36.1	39.6	9.7
Austria-Hungary*	35.8	49.5	38.3
Great Britain	31.8	45.4	42.8
Italy	26.8	34.7	29.5
Spain	16.0	19.2	20.0

*Not including Bosnia-Herzegovina.
Colin Dyer, *Population and Society in Twentieth Century France* (New York, 1978), p. 5.

Germany's by half in the space of a generation. Britain's population, too, grew by nearly one third between 1881 and 1911. Thanks to improvements in both crop yields and shipping, food shortages declined, which rendered entire populations less susceptible to illness and high infant mortality. Advances in medicine, nutrition, and personal hygiene diminished the prevalence of dangerous diseases such as cholera and typhus, and improved conditions in housing and public sanitation transformed the urban environment.

CREDIT AND CONSUMERISM

Changes in scope and scale not only transformed production but also altered consumption. Indeed it was during this period that consumption began to shift, slowly, to the center of economic activity and theory. The era in which economists would worry about consumer confidence and experts could systematically track the public's buying habits did not begin until the middle of the twentieth century, but developments pointed toward that horizon. Department stores offering both practical and luxury goods to the middle class were one mark of the times—of urbanization, economic expansion, and the new importance attached to merchandising. Advertising took off as well. The lavishly illustrated posters of the late nineteenth century that advertised concert halls, soaps, bicycles, and sewing machines were only one sign of underlying economic changes. Even more significant, by the 1880s new stores sought to attract working-class people by introducing the all-important innovation of credit payment. In earlier times, working-class families pawned watches, mattresses, or furniture to borrow money; now they began to buy on credit, a change that would eventually have seismic effects on both households and national economies.

Poster for *Motocycles Comiot*, 1899. The rise of consumer spending in the middle class created a new industry and a new art: advertising. This advertisement, like many from the period, contrasted new with old, leisure with toil, and speed, or freedom, with inertia.

These new, late-nineteenth-century patterns of consumption, however, were largely urban. In the countryside, peasants continued to save money under mattresses; pass down a few pieces of furniture for generations; make, launder, and mend their own clothes and linens; and offer a kilo of sugar as a generous household gift. Only slowly did retailers whittle away at these traditional habits. Mass consumption remained difficult to imagine in what was still a deeply stratified society.

THE RISE OF THE CORPORATION

Economic growth and the demands of mass consumption spurred reorganization, consolidation, and regulation of capitalist institutions. Although capitalist enterprises had been financed by individual investors through the joint-stock principle at least since the

THE DANGERS OF
CONSUMER CULTURE

By 1880 the Bon Marché in Paris, the world's first department store, was turning over the astronomical sum of 80 million francs annually and came to embody the new rhythm and tempo of mass consumer culture. The vast scale of selling sparked debate about the decline of the family store, the recreation of browsing and window shopping, and, above all, the "moral disaster" of women's limitless desire for goods. In writing the novel The Ladies' Paradise *(1883), Émile Zola noted he wanted to "write the poem of modern activity." The passage here captures the fascination for Denise, a clerk in her uncle's fabric shop, of the fictitious department store the Ladies' Paradise.*

But what fascinated Denise was the Ladies' Paradise on the other side of the street, for she could see the shop-windows through the open door. The sky was still overcast, but the mildness brought by rain was warming the air in spite of the season; and in the clear light, dusted with sunshine, the great shop was coming to life, and business was in full swing.

Denise felt that she was watching a machine working at high pressure; its dynamism seemed to reach to the display windows themselves. They were no longer the cold windows she had seen in the morning; now they seemed to be warm and vibrating with the activity within. A crowd was looking at them, groups of women were crushing each other in front of them, a real mob, made brutal by covetousness. And these passions in the street were giving life to the materials: the laces shivered, then drooped again, concealing the depths of the shop with an exciting air of mystery; even the lengths of cloth, thick and square, were breathing, exuding a tempting odour, while the overcoats were throwing back their shoulders still more on the dummies, which were acquiring souls, and the huge velvet coat was billowing out, supple and warm, as if on shoulders of flesh and blood, with heaving breast and quivering hips. But the furnace-like heat with which the shop was ablaze came above all from the selling, from the bustle at the counters, which could be felt behind the walls. There was the continuous roar of the machine at work, of customers crowding into the departments, dazzled by the merchandise, then propelled towards the cash-desk. And it was all regulated and organized with the remorselessness of a machine: the vast horde of women were as if caught in the wheels of an inevitable force. . . .

Émile Zola, *The Ladies' Paradise*, trans. Brian Nelson (New York, 1995), pp. 15–16.

QUESTIONS FOR ANALYSIS

1. What did Zola find significant in large-scale commerce?
2. The first Industrial Revolution faced the challenge of production. In what ways was consumption the challenge of the late nineteenth century? What obstacles did merchants confront when encouraging people to consume?

sixteenth century, it was during the late nineteenth century that the modern corporation came into its own. To mobilize the enormous funds needed for large-scale enterprises, entrepreneurs needed to offer better guarantees on investors' money. To provide such protection, most European countries enacted or improved their limited-liability laws, which ensured that stockholders could lose only the value of their shares in the event of bankruptcy. Insured in this way, many thousands of middle-class men and women now considered corporate investment a promising venture. After 1870, stock markets ceased to be primarily a clearinghouse for state paper and railroad bonds, and instead attracted new commercial and industrial ventures.

Limited liability was one part of a larger trend of incorporation. Whereas most firms had been small or middle size, companies now incorporated to attain the necessary size for survival. In doing so, they tended to shift control from company founders and local directors to distant bankers and financiers. Because financial institutions represented the interests of investors whose primary concern was the bottom line, bankers' control over industrial growth encouraged an ethos of impersonal finance capital.

Equally important, the second industrial revolution created a strong demand for technical expertise, which undercut traditional forms of family management. University degrees in engineering and chemistry became more valuable than on-the-job apprenticeships. The emergence of a white-collar class (middle-level salaried managers who were neither owners nor laborers) marked a significant change in work life and for society's evolving class structure.

The drive toward larger business enterprises was spurred by a desire for increased profits. It was also encouraged by a belief that consolidation protected society against the hazards of boom-and-bust economic fluctuations and against the wasteful inefficiencies of unbridled, "ruinous" competition. Some industries combined vertically, attempting to control every step of production from the acquisition of raw materials to the distribution of finished products. Andrew Carnegie's steel company in Pittsburgh controlled costs by owning the iron and coal mines necessary for steel production as well as by acquiring its own fleet of steamships and railways to transport ore to the mills. A second form of corporate self-protection was horizontal alignment. Organizing into cartels, companies in the same industry would band together to fix prices and control competition, if not eliminate it outright. Coal, oil, and steel companies were especially suited to the organization of cartels, since only a few major players could afford the huge expense of building, equipping, and running mines, refineries, and foundries. In 1894, for example, German entrepreneurs organized the Rhenish-Westphalian Coal Syndicate, which captured 98 percent of Germany's coal

market by using ruthless tactics against small competitiors, who could join the syndicate or face ruin. Through similar tactics, both legal and illegal, John D. Rockefeller's Standard Oil Company came to control the refined petroleum market in the United States, producing over 90 percent of the country's oil by the 1880s. The monopoly was sustained through the Standard Oil Trust, a legal innovation that enabled Rockefeller to control and manage assets of allied companies through the government. Cartels were particularly strong in Germany and America but less so in Britain, where dedication to free-trade policies made price fixing difficult, and in France, where family firms and laborers both opposed cartels and where there was also less heavy industry.

Though governments sometimes tried to stem the burgeoning power of cartels (in the United States, for instance, where the "trust-buster" president Theodore Roosevelt put teeth into earlier antitrust laws), the dominant trend of this period was increased cooperation between governments and industry. Contrary to the laissez-faire mentality of early capitalism, corporations developed close relationships with the states in the West—most noticeably in colonial industrial projects, such as the construction of railroads, harbors, and seafaring steamships. These efforts were so costly, or so unprofitable, that private enterprise would not have undertaken them alone. But because they served larger political and strategic interests, governments funded them willingly. Such interdependence was underscored by the appearance of businessmen and financiers as officers of state. The German banker Bernhard Dernburg was the German secretary of state for colonies. Joseph Chamberlain, the British manufacturer and mayoral boss of industrial Birmingham, also served as the colonial secretary. And in France, Charles Jonnart, president of the Suez Canal Company and the Saint-Étienne steel works, was later governor general of Algeria. Tied to imperial interests, the rise of modern corporations had an impact around the globe.

> Coal, oil, and steel companies were especially suited to the organization of cartels, since only a few major players could afford the huge expense of building, equipping, and running mines, refineries, and foundries.

GLOBAL ECONOMICS

From the 1870s on, the rapid spread of industrialization heightened competition among nations. The search for markets, goods, and influence fueled much of the imperial expansion and, consequently, often put countries at odds with each other. Trade barriers arose again to protect home markets. All nations except Britain raised tariffs, arguing that the needs of the nation-state trumped laissez-faire doctrine. Yet changes in international economics fueled the continuing growth of an interlocking, worldwide system of manufacturing, trade, and finance. For example, the near universal adoption of the gold standard in currency exchange greatly facilitated world trade. Pegging the value of currencies, particularly Britain's powerful pound sterling, against the value of gold meant that currencies could be readily exchanged. The common standard also allowed nations to use a third country to mediate trade and exchange to mitigate trade imbalances—a common problem for the industrializing West. Almost all European countries, dependent on vast supplies of raw materials to sustain their rate of industrial production, imported more than they exported. To avoid the mounting deficits that this practice would otherwise incur, European economies relied on "invisible" exports: shipping, insurance, and banking services. The extent of Britain's exports in these areas was far greater than that of any other country. London was the money market of the world, to which would-be borrowers looked for assistance before turning elsewhere. By 1914, Britain had $20 billion invested overseas, compared with $8.7 billion for France and $6 billion for Germany. Britain also used its invisible trade to secure relationships with food-producing nations, becoming the major overseas buyer for the wheat of the United States and Canada, the beef of Argentina, and the mutton (lamb) of Australia. These goods, shipped cheaply aboard refrigerated vessels, kept down food prices for working-class families and eased the demand for increased wages.

During this period the relationship between European manufacturing nations and the overseas sources of their materials—whether colonies or not—was transformed, as detailed in the last chapter. Those changes, in turn, reshaped economies and cultures on both sides of the imperial divide. Europeans came to expect certain foods on their tables; whole regions of Africa, Latin America, and Asia geared toward producing for the European market. This international push toward mass manufacturing and commodity production necessarily involved changes in deep-seated patterns in consumption and in production. It altered the landscape and habits of India as well as those of Britain. It brought new rhythms of life to women work-

ing in clothing factories in Germany, to porters carrying supplies to build railways in Senegal, to workers dredging the harbor of Dakar.

LABOR POLITICS, MASS MOVEMENTS

Why did working-class movements grow so dramatically during this period?

The rapid expansion of late-nineteenth-century industry brought a parallel growth in the size, cohesion, and activism of Europe's working classes. The men and women who worked as wage laborers resented corporate power—resentment fostered not only by the exploitation and inequalities they experienced on the job but also by living "a life apart" in Europe's expanding cities (see Chapter Nineteen). Corporations had devised new methods of protecting and promoting their interests, and workers did the same. Labor unions, which were traditionally limited to skilled male workers in small-scale enterprises, grew during the late nineteenth century into mass, centralized, nationwide organizations. This "new unionism" emphasized organization across entire industries and, for the first time, brought unskilled workers into the ranks, increasing power to negotiate wages and job conditions. More important, though, the creation of national unions provided a framework for a new type of political movement: the socialist mass party.

Why did socialism develop in Europe after 1870? Changing national political structures provide part of the answer. Parliamentary constitutional governments opened the political process to new participants, including socialists. Now part of the legislative process, socialists in Parliament led efforts to expand voting rights in the 1860s and 1870s. Their success created new constituencies of working-class men. At the same time, traditional struggles between labor and management moved up to the national level; governments aligned with business interests, and legislators countered working-class agitation with antilabor and antisocialist laws. To radical leaders, the organization of

Now part of the legislative process, socialists in Parliament led efforts to expand the franchise in the 1860s and 1870s. Their successful efforts created new constituencies of working-class men.

WHY DID WORKING-CLASS MOVEMENTS GROW SO DRAMATICALLY DURING THIS PERIOD?

LABOR POLITICS, MASS MOVEMENTS   831

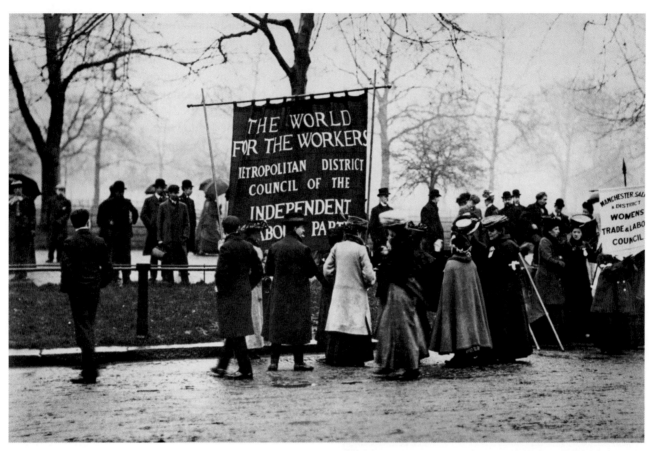

Independent Labor Party Demonstration in England, c. 1893. Activism among workers swelled in the late nineteenth century. Increasingly powerful labor unions had a profound impact on politics.

national mass political movements seemed the only effective way to counter industrialists' political strength. Thus, during this period, socialist movements abandoned their earlier revolutionary traditions (exemplified by the romantic image of barricaded streets) in favor of legal, public competition within Europe's parliamentary systems.

This shift to popular mass politics, and the accompanying success of labor movements, owed as much to ideas as to social changes. The most influential radical thinker was Karl Marx, whose early career was discussed in Chapter Twenty. Since the 1840s Marx and his collaborator Fredrick Engels had been intellectuals and activists, writing pamphlets and participating in the organization of fledgling socialist movements. Then, in 1867, Marx published the first of three volumes of *Capital*, a work he believed was his greatest contribution to the struggle for human emancipation. It provided historical materialism with a theoretical foundation, and it also attacked capitalism on the battlefield of economics. In the spirit of nineteenth-century science, Marx claimed to offer a systematic analysis of how capitalism

forced workers to exchange their labor for subsistence wages while enabling owners of the means of production to amass both wealth and power. Splicing together the scholarly study of economics with calls for revolutionary politics, the book became the preeminent socialist critique of capitalism.

For a variety of reasons, Marxism's explosive synthesis of thought and action appealed to workers and intellectuals across the West. First, Marxism made some of the most radical, insistent arguments for democracy and political inclusion of the period. Throughout Europe, though particularly in the western nations, Marxist socialism provided a crucial foundation for building a democratic mass politics. Few other groups pushed so strongly to secure civil liberties, expand conceptions of citizenship, or build a welfare state. As a theoretical matter, Marxism also made powerful claims for gender equality, though in practice woman suffrage took a back seat to class politics. Marxist utopianism was a crucial element, too, for its powerful promise of a better and attainable future for laborers rallied large numbers of workers to the cause.

Socialist Party Pamphlet, c. 1895. Socialism emerged as a powerful political force throughout Europe in the late nineteenth century, although appearing in different forms depending on the region. This German pamphlet quotes from the *Communist Manifesto* of 1848, calling for workers of the world to unite.

Not all working-class movements, however, were Marxist. Even as Marxist thought was taken up in various political and labor organizations, differences among the philosophies, objectives, and methods of various left-wing groups remained strong. Such differences were amplified across industries, occupation, regions, and nations; there was no homogenous workers' movement. The most divisive issues were the role of violence and whether socialists should cooperate with liberal, or bourgeois governments—and if so, to what end. Some "gradualists," particularly in Britain, were willing to work with liberals for piecemeal reform, while more radical socialists sought parliamentary power as a way to hasten the overthrow of capitalism. Anarchists and syndicalists rejected parliamentary politics altogether. This first pivotal debate over this issue

occurred at the International Working Men's Association, or First International, which was founded in 1864 to promote coordinated labor activity throughout Europe. Marx and his supporters argued fiercely in favor of political mass movements; anarchists such as Mikhail Bakunin rejected centralized organizations of all kinds (whether nation-states or socialist parties) and called instead for terror and violence.

THE SPREAD OF SOCIALIST PARTIES— AND ALTERNATIVES

Marxism spread through a number of socialist and social democratic parties founded between 1875 and 1905 in Germany, Belgium, France, Austria, and Russia. These parties were disciplined, politicized workers' organizations aimed at seizing control of the state for revolutionary change. The model among them was the SPD, the German Social Democratic Party. Formed in 1875, the SPD first aimed for political change within Germany's parliamentary political system; but after an era of oppressive antisocialist laws, it adopted an explicitly Marxist platform—preparing a politically conscious proletariat for the imminent collapse of capitalism. By the outbreak of World War I, the Social Democrats were the largest, best organized workers' party in the world. Several key factors made Germany particularly receptive to social democracy: rapid and extensive industrialization, a large urban working class, a new parliamentary constitution, a national government hostile to organized labor, and no tradition of liberal reform.

The importance of this last factor is most evident when we consider the case of Britain, which was the world's first—and most—industrialized country, yet that had a much smaller, and more moderate, socialist presence than other European nations. Through the end of the nineteenth century, much of the socialist agenda was advanced by radical Liberals in Britain, which forestalled the growth of an independent socialist party. Even when a separate Labour Party was formed in 1901, it remained distinctively moderate, committed to reform of the capitalist system and to measures such as public housing, welfare benefits, and improved wages, rather than a complete overhaul. For the range of political activists who belonged to the Labour Party, and for Britain's many trade unions as well, Parliament remained a legitimate vehicle for effecting social change, limiting the appeal of revolutionary Marxism.

WHY DID WORKING-CLASS MOVEMENTS GROW SO DRAMATICALLY DURING THIS PERIOD?

LABOR POLITICS, MASS MOVEMENTS   833

Left: Anarchism. Anarchists, with their reliance on violence, stood at the radical end of the socialist spectrum. Anarchists committed several high-profile political assassinations, such as the assassination of French president Marie François Carnot in 1894. **Right: Syndicalism.** Syndicalists, also on the radical side of the socialist spectrum, favored massive movements of direct action, such as the general strike depicted in this poster.

Parliamentary reform provided one popular alternative to the Marxist program; anarchism provided another. Anarchists were opposed to centrally organized economies and politics and to the very existence of state authority, and they advocated individual sovereignty and small-scale, localized democracy. They shared an underlying set of values with the Marxists but differed radically on how to advance them. Renouncing parties, unions, and any form of modern mass organization, anarchists fell back on the tradition of conspiratorial violence, which Marx had so forcefully opposed. Consequently, one of anarchism's defining characteristics was its reliance on terrorism, or what the Italian anarchists called "propaganda by the deed." Though not all adopted such methods, anarchists became notorious by assassinating Tsar Alexander II in 1881 and five other heads of state in the following years. Influential anarchists such as Peter Kropotkin and Mikhail Bakunin believed that "exemplary terror" could spark popular revolt. Revealing the vulnerability of powerful political leaders, they thought, would create chaos and embolden the people. Though anarchism (perhaps inherently) made no substantial gains as a movement, it kept alive a radical, violent alternative to Marxism's emphasis on parliamentary politics.

Another type of socialist movement, known as syndicalism, gained popularity around the turn of the century, particularly among agricultural laborers in France, Italy, and Spain. Following socialist principles, syndicalism demanded that workers share ownership and control of the means of production and that the capitalist state be overthrown and replaced by workers' syndicates, or trade associations. Although often elided with anarchism (as in the term *anarcho-syndicalism*), syndicalism was a distinct doctrine that did not call for terror but rather for direct action, including strikes and sabotage. The most widely read theorist of syndicalism, the French intellectual Georges Sorel, argued that a general strike of all industrial workers would do more to bring down the state than would electoral politics. When Sorel later moved to the extreme right, however, more popular and practical leaders emerged in France, where they joined with other French union leaders in 1895 to create the General Confederation of Labor. Committed to working outside the legally constituted framework of French politics, the confederation and other syndicalist organizations helped spur radicalism among socialists—especially after the attempted revolution in Russia in 1905—but did not build a lasting presence in European politics.

THE LIMITS OF SUCCESS

By the turn of the century, popular socialist movements had made impressive gains all across Europe: in 1895, seven socialist parties had captured between a quarter and a third of the votes in their countries. But just as socialists gained a permanent foothold in national politics, they were also straining under limitations and internal conflicts that had hindered their parties from the outset. Working-class movements, in fact, had never gained anywhere near full worker support. Although some workers remained loyal to older liberal traditions or to religious parties, many others were excluded from socialist politics by its narrow definition of who constituted the working class—that is, only male industrial workers. In terms of elections at least, socialist parties were running up against a wall that they themselves had constructed.

At the same time, the enduring conflict between revolutionaries and reformers, between casting votes and throwing stones, erupted with renewed intensity after 1900. On one side, committed socialists began to question Marx's core assumptions about the inevitability of workers' impoverishment and the collapse of the bourgeois order. A German group of so-called revisionists, led by Eduard Bernstein, challenged Marxist doctrine and called for a shift to moderate reform. Though Bernstein's faction failed to win a majority of votes at either domestic or international congresses, his pragmatism appealed to socialists and workers across the Continent. At the other end of the spectrum, however, were advocates of increased radicalism and direct action. Inspired by the unexpected (and unsuccessful) revolutionary uprising in Russia in 1905, German Marxists such as Rosa Luxembourg called for mass strikes, hoping to seize the moment and ignite a widespread proletarian revolution.

Conflicts over strategy peaked just before World War I, as moderates, reformists, and orthodox Marxists debated about how to respond to the threat of international conflict. Yet these divisions did not diminish the strength and appeal of turn-of-the-century socialism. Indeed, on the eve of the war, governments discreetly consulted with labor leaders about rank-and-file workers' willingness to enlist and fight. Having built impressive organizational and political strength since the 1870s, working-class parties now affected the ability of nation-states to wage war. In short, they had come of age.

DEMANDING EQUALITY: SUFFRAGE AND THE WOMEN'S MOVEMENT

What rights did women claim, and why were they so controversial?

Since the 1860s, the combination of working-class activism and liberal constitutionalism had expanded male suffrage rights across Europe: by 1884, Germany, France, and Britain had enfranchised most men. But nowhere did women have the right to vote. Nineteenth-century political ideology relegated women to the status of second-class citizens, and even egalitarian-minded socialists seldom challenged this entrenched hierarchy. Excluded from the workings of parliamentary and mass party politics, women pressed their interests through independent organizations and through forms of direct action. The new women's movement won some crucial legal reforms during this period; and after the turn of the century, its militant campaign for suffrage fed the growing sense of political crisis, most notably in Britain.

> The new women's movement won some crucial legal reforms during this period; and after the turn of the century, its militant campaign for suffrage fed the growing sense of political crisis, most notably in Britain.

Women's organizations, such as the General German Women's Association, pressed first for educational and legal reforms. In Britain, women's colleges were established at the same time that women won the right to control their own property. (Previously women surrendered their property, including wages, to their husbands.) Laws in 1884 and 1910 gave Frenchwomen the same right and the ability to divorce their husbands. German women, too, won more favorable divorce laws by 1870, and in 1900 they were granted full legal rights.

After these important changes in women's status, suffrage crystallized as the next logical goal. Indeed, votes became *the* symbol for women's ability to attain full personhood. As the suffragists saw it, enfranchisement meant not merely political progress but economic, spiritual, and moral advancement as well. By the last third of the century, middle-class women throughout western Europe had founded clubs, published journals, organized petitions, sponsored assemblies, and initiated other public activities to press for the vote. The number of middle-class women's societies rapidly multiplied; some, such as the German League of Women's Voting

WHAT RIGHTS DID WOMEN CLAIM, AND WHY WERE THEY SO CONTROVERSIAL?

DEMANDING EQUALITY: SUFFRAGE AND THE WOMEN'S MOVEMENT   835

Militant Martyrdom for Woman Suffrage. Emily Davison throwing herself under the king's horse at the derby in 1913.

unaccustomed to such kinds of violence from women. The intensity of suffragists' moral claims was dramatically embodied by the 1913 martyrdom of Emily Wilding Davison who, wearing a "Votes for Women" sash, threw herself in front of the king's horse on Derby Day and was trampled to death.

REDEFINING WOMANHOOD

The campaign for woman suffrage was perhaps the most visible and inflammatory aspect of a larger cultural shift, in which traditional Victorian gender roles were redefined. In the last third of the nineteenth century, economic, political, and social changes were undermining the view that men and women should occupy distinctly different spheres. Women became increasingly visible in the workforce as growing numbers of them took up a greater variety of jobs. Some working-class women joined the new factories and workshops in an effort to stave off their families' poverty, in spite of some working-class men's insistence that stable families required women at home. In addition, the expansion of government and corporate bureaucracies, coupled with a scarcity of male labor due to industrial growth, brought middle-class women to the workforce as social workers and clerks. The increase in hospital services and the advent of national compulsory education required more nurses and teachers. Again, a shortage of male workers and a need to fill so many new jobs as cheaply as possible made women a logical choice. Thus women, who had campaigned vigorously for access to education, began to see doors opening to them. Swiss universities and medical schools began to admit women in the 1860s. In the 1870s and 1880s, British women established their own colleges at Cambridge and Oxford. Parts of the professional world began to look dramatically different: in Prussia, for instance, 14,600 full-time women teachers were staffing schools by 1896. These changes in women's employment began to deflate the myth of female domesticity.

Rights, established in 1902, were founded solely to advocate votes. To the left of middle-class movements were organizations of feminist socialists, women such as Clara Zetkin and Lily Braun who believed that only a socialist revolution would free women from economic as well as political exploitation.

In Britain, woman suffrage campaigns exploded in violence. Millicent Fawcett, a distinguished middle-class woman with connections to the political establishment, brought together sixteen different organizations into the National Union of Women's Suffrage Societies (1897), committed to peaceful, constitutional reform. But the movement lacked the political or economic clout to sway a male legislature. They became increasingly exasperated by their inability to win over either the Liberal or Conservative Party, each of which feared that female suffrage would benefit the other. For this reason Emmeline Pankhurst founded the Women's Social and Political Union (WSPU) in 1903, which adopted tactics of militancy and civil disobedience. WSPU women chained themselves to the visitors' gallery in the House of Commons, slashed paintings in museums, inscribed "Votes for Women" in acid on the greens of golf courses, disrupted political meetings, burned politicians' houses, and smashed department-store windows. The government countered violence with repression. When arrested women went on hunger strikes in prisons, wardens fed them by force—tying them down, holding their mouths open with wooden and metal clamps, and running tubes down their throats. In 1910 the suffragists' attempt to enter the House of Commons set off a six-hour riot with policemen and bystanders, shocking and outraging a nation

Women became more active in politics—an area previously termed off limits. This is not to say that female political activity was unprecedented; in important ways, the groundwork for women's new political participation had been laid earlier in the century. Reform movements of the early nineteenth century depended on women and raised women's standing in public. First with charity work in religious associations and later with hundreds of

Changes in White-Collar Work. Clerical work was primarily male until the end of the nineteenth century, when cadres of women workers and the emergence of new industries and bureaucracies transformed employment.

classes, and widened the scope of possibilities for later generations.

These changes in women's roles were paralleled by the emergence of a new social type, dubbed the "new woman." A new woman demanded education and a job; she refused to be escorted by chaperones when she went out; she rejected the restrictive corsets of mid-century fashion. In other words, she claimed the right to a physically and intellectually active life and refused to conform to the norms that defined nineteenth-century womanhood. The new woman was an image—in part the creation of artists and journalists, who filled newspapers, magazines, and advertising billboards with pictures of women riding bicycles in bloomers (voluminous trousers with a short skirt); smoking cigarettes; and enjoying the cafés, dance halls, tonic waters, soaps, and other emblems of consumption. Very few women actually fitted this image: among other things, most were too poor. Still, middle- and working-class women demanded more social freedom and redefined gender norms in the process. For some onlookers, women's newfound independence amounted to shirking domestic responsibilities, and they attacked women who defied convention as ugly "half-men," unfit and unable to marry. For supporters, though, these new women symbolized a welcome era of social emancipation.

secular associations, women throughout Europe directed their energies toward poor relief, prison reform, Sunday school, temperance, ending slavery and prostitution, and expanding educational opportunities for women. Reform groups brought women together outside the home, encouraging them to speak their minds as free-thinking equals and to pursue political goals—a right denied them as individual females. And while some women in reform groups supported political emancipation, many others were drawn into reform politics by appeals to the belief that they had a special moral mission: they saw their public activities as merely an extension of feminine domestic duties. Nonetheless, nineteenth-century reform movements had opened up the world beyond the home, particularly for the middle

Opposition to these changes was intense, sometimes violent, and not exclusively male. Men scorned the women who threatened their elite preserves in universities, clubs, and public offices; but a wide array of female antisuffragists also denounced the movement. Conservatives such as Mrs. Humphrey Ward maintained that bringing women into the political arena would sap the virility of the British Empire. Octavia Hill, a noted social worker, stated that women should refrain from politics and in so doing, "temper this wild struggle for place and power." Christian commentators criticized suffragists for bringing moral decay through selfish individualism. Still others believed feminism would dissolve the family, a theme that fed into a larger discussion on the decline

WHAT ARE "MASS POLITICS," AND HOW DID NATION-STATES RESPOND TO THEM?

LIBERALISM AND ITS DISCONTENTS: NATIONAL POLITICS AT THE TURN OF THE CENTURY   837

Organized Antifeminism. Male students demonstrate against opening some universities to women.

of the West amid a growing sense of cultural crisis. Indeed, the struggle for women's rights provided a flashpoint for an array of European anxieties over labor, politics, gender, and biology—all of which suggested that an orderly political consensus, so ardently desired by middle-class society, was slipping from reach.

LIBERALISM AND ITS DISCONTENTS: NATIONAL POLITICS AT THE TURN OF THE CENTURY

What are "mass politics," and how did nation-states respond to them?

Having championed doctrines of individual rights throughout the nineteenth century, middle-class liberals found themselves on the defensive after 1870. Previously, political power had rested on a balance between middle-class interests and traditional elites. The landed aristocracy shared power with industrial magnates; monarchical rule coexisted with constitutional freedoms. During the late nineteenth century, the rise of mass politics upset this balance. An expanding franchise and rising expectations brought newcomers to the political stage. As we have seen, trade unions, socialists, and feminists all challenged Europe's governing classes by demanding that political participation be open to all. Governments responded in turn, with a mix of conciliatory and repressive measures. As the twentieth century approached, political struggles became increasingly fierce, and, by World War I, the foundation of traditional parliamentary politics was crumbling. For both the left and the right, for both insiders and outsiders, negotiating this unfamiliar terrain required the creation of new and distinctly modern forms of mass politics.

FRANCE: THE THIRD REPUBLIC AND THE PARIS COMMUNE

The Franco-Prussian War of 1870, which completed the unification of the victorious Germany, was a bruising defeat for France. The government of the Second Empire folded. In its wake, the French proclaimed a republic whose legitimacy was contested from the start. Crafting a durable republican system proved difficult. The new constitution of the Third Republic, which was finally instituted in 1875, signaled a triumph of democratic and parliamentary principles. Establishing democracy, however, was a volatile process, and the Third Republic faced class conflicts, scandals and the rise of new forms of right-wing politics that would poison politics for decades to come.

No sooner had the government surrendered than it faced a crisis that pitted the nation's representatives against the radical city of Paris. During the war, the city had appointed its own municipal government, the Commune. Paris not only refused to surrender to the Germans but proclaimed itself the true government of France. The city had been besieged by the Germans for four months; most people who could afford to flee had done so; and the rest, hungry and radicalized, defied the French government sitting in Versailles and negotiating the terms of an armistice with the Germans. The armistice signed, the French government turned its attention to the city. After long and fruitless negotiations, in March 1871 the government sent troops to disarm the capital. Since the Commune's strongest support came from the workers of Paris, the conflict became a class war. For a week, the "communards" battled against the government's troops, building barricades to stop the invaders, taking and shooting hostages, and retreating very slowly into the northern working-class neighborhoods of the city. The French government's repression was brutal. At least 25,000 Parisians were executed, killed in fighting, or consumed in the fires that raged through the city; thousands more were deported to the penal colony of New Caledonia in the South Pacific. The Paris Commune was a brief episode, but it cast a long shadow and reopened old political wounds. For Marx, who wrote about the Commune, and for other socialists, it illustrated the futility of an older insurrectionary tradition on the left and the need for more mass-based democratic politics.

THE DREYFUS AFFAIR AND ANTI-SEMITISM AS POLITICS

On the other side of the French political spectrum, new forms of radical right-wing politics emerged that would foreshadow developments elsewhere. As the age-old foundations of conservative politics, the Catholic Church and the landed nobility, slipped, more radical right-wing politics took shape. Stung by the defeat of 1870 and critical of the republic and its premises, the new right was nationalist, antiparliamentary, and anti-

liberal (in the sense of commitment to individual liberties). Maurice Barrès, for instance, elected deputy in 1889, declared that parliamentary government had sown "impotence and corruption" and was too weak to defend the nation. During the first half of the nineteenth century, nationalism had been associated with the left (see Chapter Twenty). Now it was more often invoked by the right and linked to xenophobia (fear of foreigners) in general and anti-Semitism in particular.

Édouard Drumont's career provides a case in point. Drumont was an extraordinarily successful anti-Semitic journalist who attributed all of late-nineteenth-century France's problems to the baneful influence of an international Jewish conspiracy and labeled all of the right wing's enemies "Jewish." Drumont merged three strands of anti-Semitism: (1) long-standing Christian anti-Semitism, which damned the Jewish people as Christ killers; (2) economic anti-Semitism, which insisted that the wealthy banking family of Rothschild was representative of all Jews; and (3) late-nineteenth-century racial thinking, which opposed the Aryan (Indo-European) race to the (inferior) Semitic race. Drumont packed these themes into a powerful ideology of hatred. Jews in the army subverted the national interest; financial scandals came from international conspiracies; mass culture, the women's movement, dance halls, and all the developments that were supposedly corrupting French culture simply demonstrated the strength of "cosmopolitan and international Jewish interests"; "wealthy Jewish bankers" and "greedy Jewish socialists and trade unionists" preyed on the peasants and small shopkeepers of France. Drumont pounded at these themes in his newspaper, *La Libre Parole* (Free Speech) founded in 1892, through his Anti-Semitic League, and in his 500-page bestseller, *Jewish France* (1886), which sold 100,000 copies in the first two months.

This politicized anti-Semitism exploded with the Dreyfus Affair, a pivotal political moment in the life of the French Republic. In 1894 a group of monarchist officers in the French army accused Alfred Dreyfus, a Jewish captain on the French general staff, of selling military secrets to Germany. Tried by court-martial, Dreyfus was convicted, stripped of his rank, and deported for life to Devil's Island, a ghastly prison in the Atlantic Ocean. In 1896 Colonel Georges

The Dreyfus Affair. The January 1, 1895, edition of *Le Petit Journal* depicts the military degradation of Alfred Dreyfus.

ANTI-SEMITISM IN LATE-NINETEENTH-CENTURY FRANCE

Over the course of the nineteenth century, European (though not Russian) Jewish people slowly gained more legal and political rights: access to occupations from which they had been barred, the right to vote and hold political office, the right to marry non-Jews, and so on. France, the land of the revolution of 1789, appeared to many European Jews the beacon of liberty. But in the late nineteenth century, France also proved the birthplace of new forms of anti-Semitism. This excerpt from Édouard Drumont's best-selling Jewish France *(1885) illustrates some themes of that ideology: the effort to displace economic grievances; conservative hatred of the republic, parliamentary government; the legacy of 1789; and conservative nationalism.*

The only one who has benefitted from the Revolution [of 1789] is the Jew. Everything comes from the Jew; everything returns to the Jew.

We have here a veritable conquest, an entire nation returned to serfdom by a minute but cohesive minority, just as the Saxons were forced into serfdom by William the Conqueror's 60,000 Normans.

The methods are different, the result is the same. One can recognize all the characteristics of a conquest: an entire population working for another population, which appropriates, through a vast system of financial exploitation, all of the profits of the other. Immense Jewish fortunes, castles, Jewish townhouses, are not the fruit of any actual labor, of any production: they are the booty taken from an enslaved race by a dominant race.

It is certain, for example, that the Rothchild family, whose French branch alone possesses a declared fortune of three billion [francs], did not have that money when it arrived in France; it has invented nothing, it has discovered no mine, it has tilled no ground. It has therefore appropriated these three billion francs from the French without giving them anything in exchange. . . .

Thanks to the Jews' cunning exploitation of the principles of '89, France was collapsing into dissolution. Jews had monopolized all of the public wealth, had invaded everything, except the army. The representatives of the old [French] families, whether noble or bourgeois . . . gave themselves up to pleasure, and were corrupted by the Jewish prostitutes they had taken as mistresses or were ruined by the horse-sellers and money-lenders, also Jews, who aided the prostitutes. . . .

The fatherland, in the sense that we attach to that word, has no meaning for the Semite. The Jew . . . is characterized by an *inexorable universalism*.

I can see no reason for reproaching the Jews for thinking this way. What does the word "Fatherland" mean? Land of the fathers. One's feelings for the Fatherland are engraved in one's heart in the same way that a name carved in a tree is driven deeper into the bark with each passing year, so that the tree and the name eventually become one. You can't become a patriot through improvization; you are a patriot in your blood, in your marrow.

Can the Semite, a perpetual nomad, ever experience such enduring impressions? . . .

Édouard Drumont, *La France juive. Essai d'histoire contemporaine* (Paris, 1885), excerpt trans. Cat Nilan, 1997.

QUESTIONS FOR ANALYSIS

1. What legal and political rights did Jewish communities in Europe gain over the course of the nineteenth century? Why?
2. Drumont tries to elicit several anxieties. What does he think his readers should fear, and why? What does he mean by "inexorable universalism"?
3. In what ways was anti-Semitism an ideology?

Picquart, the new head of the Intelligence Division, questioned the verdict and, after an initial probe, announced that the trial documents were forgeries.

When the War Department denied Dreyfus a new trial, the "case" became an "affair," polarizing the country. Republicans, socialists, liberals, and such figures as the writer Émile Zola backed Dreyfus. As the Dreyfusards, as they were called, saw it, they stood for progress and justice against reaction and prejudice, and the survival of the Republic lay in the balance. Zola, for instance, blasted the French establishment in a provocative newspaper essay "J'accuse!" that accused the government, the courts, and the military of falsifying documents, covering up treason, and blatantly ignoring basic issues of justice. On the other side, the anti-Dreyfusards included other socialists, who considered the affair a distraction from more important economic issues, monarchists, militarists, and some clergy. One Catholic newspaper insisted that the question was not whether Dreyfus was guilty or innocent but whether Jews and unbelievers were not the "secret masters of France."

After six years of bitter controversy, an executive order in 1899 set Dreyfus free. In 1906, the supreme court cleared him of all guilt, reinstating him in the army as a major and inducting him into the Legion of Honor.

Despite Jewish emancipation, or the granting of civil rights, Herzl came to believe Jewish people might never be assimilated into Western culture and that staking the Jewish community's hopes on acceptance and tolerance was dangerous folly.

Among the affair's many consequences was the separation of church and state in France. Republicans were convinced that the church and the army were hostile to the Republic. Laws passed between 1901 and 1905 prohibited religious orders in France not authorized by the state, forbade clerics to teach in schools, and, finally, dissolved the union of the Catholic Church and the state.

The Third Republic emerged stronger in the first decade of the new century. At the same time, the radical right and anti-Semitism were plainly political forces across Europe. The mayor of Vienna in 1897 was elected on an anti-Semitic platform. The Russian secret police forged and published a book called *The Protocols of the Learned Elders of Zion* (1903 and 1905), which imagined a Jewish plot to dominate the world. The Russian state also helped frame Mendel Beiless, a Jewish clerk from Ukraine who was arrested in 1911, convicted of murder, and kept in prison two years before being cleared. Political anti-Semitism as theorized by Drumont and practiced by others across Europe, in-timately linked to late-nineteenth-century nationalism, insistently cast social and political issues as racial ones.

ZIONISM

Among the many people to watch with alarm as the Dreyfus Affair unfolded was Theodor Herzl (1860–1904), a Hungarian-born journalist working in Paris. The rise of virulent anti-Semitism in the land of the French Revolution troubled Herzl deeply. He considered the Dreyfus Affair "only the dramatic expression of a much more fundamental malaise." Despite Jewish emancipation, or the granting of civil rights, Herzl came to believe Jewish people might never be assimilated into Western culture and that staking the Jewish community's hopes on acceptance and tolerance was dangerous folly. Herzl endorsed the different strategy of Zionism, the building a separate Jewish homeland outside of Europe (though not necessarily in Palestine). A small movement of Jewish settlers, mainly refugees from Russia, had already begun to establish settlements outside of Europe. Herzl was not the first to voice these goals, but he was the most effective advocate of political Zionism. He argued that Zionism should be recognized as a modern nationalist movement, capable of negotiating with other states. In 1896 Herzl published *The State of the Jews* (1896); a year later he convened the first Zionist Congress in Switzerland. Throughout he was involved in high politics, meeting with British and Ottoman heads of state. Herzl's vision of a Jewish homeland had strong utopian elements, for he believed that building a new state had to be based on a new and transformed society, eliminating inequality and establishing rights. Although Herzl's writings met with much skepticism, they received an enthusiastic reception in areas of eastern Europe where anti-Semitism was especially violent. During the turmoil of World War I, specific wartime needs prompted the British to become involved in the issue, embroiling Zionism in international diplomacy (see Chapter Twenty-Four).

GERMANY'S SEARCH FOR IMPERIAL UNITY

Through deft foreign policy, three short wars, and a groundswell of national sentiment, Otto von Bismarck

What are "Mass Politics," and how did Nation-States respond to them?

Liberalism and Its Discontents: National Politics at the Turn of the Century   841

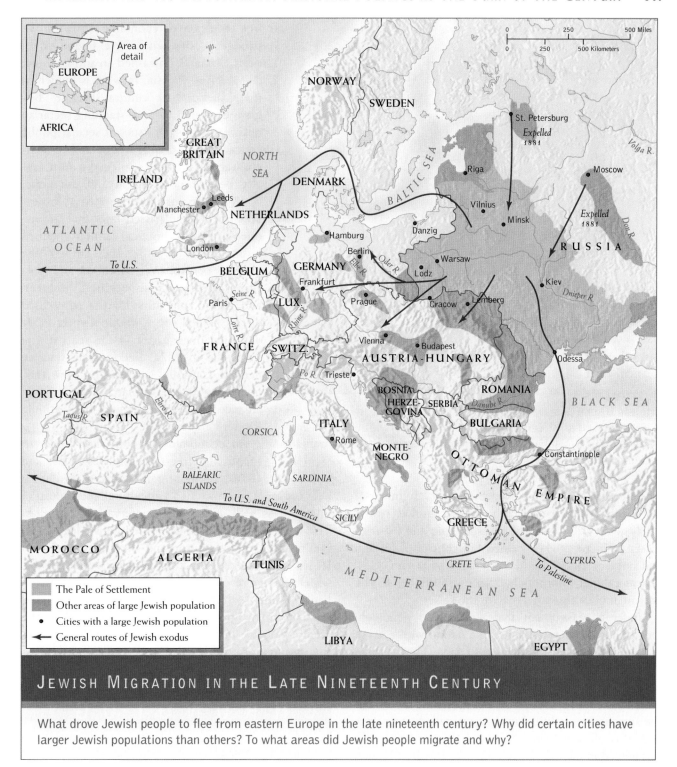

JEWISH MIGRATION IN THE LATE NINETEENTH CENTURY

What drove Jewish people to flee from eastern Europe in the late nineteenth century? Why did certain cities have larger Jewish populations than others? To what areas did Jewish people migrate and why?

united Germany under the banner of Prussian conservatism during the years 1864 to 1871. In constructing a federal political system, Bismarck sought to create the centralizing institutions of a modern nation-state while safeguarding the privileges of Germany's traditional elites, including a dominant role for Prussia. Bismarck's

constitution assigned administrative, educational, and juridical roles to local state governments and established a bicameral parliament to oversee Germany's national interests. The appointed delegates of the upper house (the Bundesrat) served as a conservative counterbalance to the more democratic lower house

Otto von Bismarck leaves office, 1890. This political cartoon shows Bismarck resigning as Kaiser Wilhelm II childishly plays with "Socialism," a doll made of dynamite. Germany anxiously watches the scene from the background.

(the Reichstag), which was elected through universal male suffrage. In the executive branch, power rested solely with Wilhelm I, the Prussian king and German kaiser (emperor), who wielded full control of foreign and military affairs. Unlike in France or Britain, Germany's cabinet ministers had no responsibility to the parliament but answered only to the kaiser.

Under a government that was neither genuinely federal nor democratic, building a nation with a sense of common purpose was no easy task. The German government successfully created imperial agencies for banking, coinage, federal courts, and railroads, all of which fostered administrative and economic union. But the question of political unity remained. Many states had, after all, sided with Austria in 1866 and had only acquiesced in German unity under the threat of French conquest. Three fault lines in Germany's political landscape especially threatened to crack the national framework: the divide between Catholics and Protestants; the growing Social Democratic Party; and the potentially divisive economic interests of agriculture and industry.

Between 1866 and 1876, Bismarck governed principally with liberal factions interested in promoting free trade and economic growth. To strengthen ties with these liberal coalitions, Bismarck unleashed an anti-Catholic campaign in Prussia. In what is known as the *Kulturkampf*, or "cultural struggle," Bismark appealed to long-standing sectarian tensions over such issues as secular public education and civil marriage and to anxieties about Catholics' allegedly torn loyalty between the nation and the pope. With the support of a majority of Protestant liberals, he passed laws that imprisoned priests for political sermons, banned Jesuits from Prussia, and curbed the church's control over education and marriage. The campaign backfired, however, and public sympathy for the persecuted clergy helped the Catholic Center Party win fully one quarter of the seats in the Reichstag in 1874. Recognizing that he needed Catholic support for new economic legislation, Bismarck negotiated an alliance of convenience with the Catholic Center Party in 1878.

An economic downturn had undercut support for free trade policies in the late 1870s, prompting Bismarck to fashion a new coalition that included agricultural and industrial interests, as well as socially conservative Catholics. This new alliance passed protectionist legislation (grain tariffs, duties on iron and steel) that riled both laissez-faire liberals and the German working class, which was represented by the SPD. Just as Bismarck had used anti-Catholic sentiments to solidify his previous alliance, he now turned against a new enemy of the empire—Social Democrats—and couched his protectionist and antisocial legislation in terms of defending

CHRONOLOGY

GERMANY'S QUEST FOR POLITICAL UNITY, 1871–1890

Bismarck's Kulturkampf	1871–1878
Conciliation with the Vatican	1878
Bismarck's antisocialist legislation	1878–1884
Bismarck launches social legislation	1883–1890
Bismarck resigns	1890

WHAT ARE "MASS POLITICS," AND HOW DID NATION-STATES RESPOND TO THEM?

LIBERALISM AND ITS DISCONTENTS: NATIONAL POLITICS AT THE TURN OF THE CENTURY   843

a "Christian moral order." In 1878, after two separate attempts on the life of the emperor, Bismarck declared a national crisis to push through a series of antisocialist laws that forbade Social Democrats to assemble or distribute their literature. Additional legislation further expelled socialists from major cities. In effect, these laws obliged the Social Democratic Party to become a clandestine organization, fostering a subculture of workers who increasingly viewed socialism as the sole answer to their political needs.

Having made the stick to beat down organized-labor politics, Bismarck now offered a carrot to German workers with an array of social reforms. Workers were guaranteed sickness and accident insurance, rigorous factory inspection, limited working hours for women and children, a maximum workday for men, public employment agencies, and old-age pensions. By 1890, Germany had put together a raft of social legislation, with the exception of unemployment insurance, that became a prototype for the majority of Western nations in the decades to come. Yet it is significant that the laws failed to achieve Bismarck's short-term political goal of winning workers' loyalty. In spite of all legal hindrances, votes for the SPD more than quadrupled between 1881 and 1890, the year that Bismarck resigned.

> By 1912, the Social Democrats polled a third of the votes cast and elected the largest single bloc to the Reichstag; yet the kaiser refused to allow any meaningful political participation beyond a tight-knit circle of elites.

The embittered atmosphere created by Bismarck's domestic politics prompted the new kaiser, Wilhelm II, to move in a new direction. He dramatically suspended the antisocialist legislation in 1890, legalizing the SPD. By 1912, the Social Democrats polled a third of the votes cast and elected the largest single bloc to the Reichstag, yet the kaiser refused to allow any meaningful political participation beyond a tight-knit circle of elites. Meanwhile, commercial, industrial, and agriculture interests deadlocked over tariffs. Any conclusion to this volatile standoff was preempted by the outbreak of World War I.

BRITAIN: FROM MODERATION TO MILITANCE

During the half century before 1914, the British prided themselves on what they believed to be an orderly and workable system of government. After the passage of the Second Reform Bill in 1867, which extended suffrage to more than a third of the nation's adult males, the two major political parties, Liberal and Conservative, vied with each other to win the support of this growing voting bloc. Parliament responded to new voters' concerns with laws that recognized the legality of trade unions, commissioned the rebuilding of large urban areas, provided elementary education for all children, and permitted male religious dissenters to attend the elite universities of Oxford and Cambridge. In 1884, suffrage expanded to include more than three fourths of adult males.

Two central figures, the Conservative Benjamin Disraeli and the Liberal William Gladstone, dominated the new parliamentary politics. Disraeli, a converted Jew and best-selling novelist, was eminently pragmatic, whereas Gladstone, a devout Anglican and moral reformer, viewed politics as "morality writ large." Despite their opposing sensibilities and bitter parliamentary clashes, the two men led parties that, in retrospect, seem to share largely similar outlooks. Managed by cabinet ministers drawn from the upper middle class and the landed gentry, both Liberals and Conservatives offered moderate programs that appealed to the widening electorate. Cabinet ministers prepared legislation but acknowledged the ultimate authority of the House of Commons, which could remove a governing cabinet with a vote of no confidence. Steered by men whose similar education and outlooks promised middling solutions, the British political system was stable and "reasonable."

Even Britain's working-class movements were notably moderate until the turn of the century, when at last new trade unions and middle-class socialist societies combined to create the independent Labour Party in 1901. Pressed from the left, the Liberal ministry that took office in 1906 passed sickness, accident, old-age, and unemployment insurance acts, along with other concessions to trade unions. To pay for the new welfare programs—and for a larger navy to counter the German buildup—the chancellor of the exchequer (finance minister), David Lloyd George, proposed an explosively controversial budget in 1909, which included progressive income and inheritance taxes, designed to make the wealthy pay at higher rates. The bill provoked a rancorous showdown with the House of Lords, which was forced not only to pass the budget but also to surrender permanently its power to veto legislation passed by the Commons. The acrimony of this debate pointed to an increasingly militant tenor in British politics, which to many seemed headed for chaos.

Indeed, after 1900, Britain's liberal parliamentary framework, which had so successfully channeled the rising demands of mass society since the 1860s, began to buckle, as an array of groups rejected legislative activity in favor of radical action. Industrial militants launched enormous labor protests, including nationwide strikes of coal and rail workers and citywide transportation strikes in London and Dublin. Woman suffragists adopted violent forms of direct action (discussed earlier). Meanwhile, in Ireland, radical nationalists began to favor armed revolution as the simplest solution to the parliamentary wrangling over the details of Irish home rule, or self-government.

Ireland had been put under the direct government of the British Parliament in 1800, and various political and military efforts to regain Irish sovereignty over the course of the nineteenth century had failed. By the 1880s, a modern nationalist party (the Irish Parliamentary Party) had begun to make substantial political gains through the legislative process, but as with other reform-minded groups (such as woman suffrage), its agenda was increasingly eclipsed toward the turn of the century by more radical organizers. These proponents of "new nationalism" disdained the party's representatives as ineffectual and out of touch. New groups revived interest in Irish history and culture and provided organizational support to the radical movement, as did such militant political organizations as Sinn Féin and the Irish Republican Brotherhood. In 1913, as a Liberal plan to grant home rule was once again on the table (prompting panic in Ulster, the Protestant-majority counties of northern Ireland, which feared Catholic rule) Irish nationalists called a number of paramilitary groups into action. Already awash in domestic crises, Britain now seemed on the verge of a civil war—a prospect delayed only by the outbreak of World War I in Europe.

RUSSIA: THE ROAD TO REVOLUTION

The industrial and social changes that swept Europe proved especially unsettling in Russia. An autocratic political system was ill equipped to handle conflict and the pressures of modern society. Western industrialization challenged Russia's military might. Western political doctrines—liberalism, democracy, socialism—threatened its internal political stability. Like other nations, tsarist Russia negotiated these challenges with a combination of repression and reform.

In the 1880s and 1890s Russia launched a program of industrialization that made it the world's fifth largest economy by the early twentieth century. The state largely directed this industrial development, for despite the creation of a mobile workforce after the emancipation of the serfs in 1861, no independent middle class capable of raising capital and stewarding industrial enterprises emerged. In fact, the Russian state financed more domestic industrial development than any other major European government during the nineteenth century.

Rapid industrialization heightened social tensions. The transition from country to city life was sudden and harsh. Men and women left agriculture for factory work, straining the fabric of village life and rural culture. In the industrial areas, workers lived in large barracks and were marched, military style, to and from the factories, where working conditions were among the worst in Europe. They coped by leaving their villages only temporarily and returning to their farms for planting or the harvest. Social change strained Russia's legal system, which did not recognize trade unions or employers' associations. Laws still distinguished among nobles, peasants, clergy, and town dwellers, categories that did not correspond to an industrializing society. Outdated banking and financial laws failed to serve the needs of a modern economy.

Real legal reform, however, would threaten the regime's stability. Alexander II (1855–1881), "the Tsar Liberator" (emancipator of the serfs), had grown wary of change. Instead of loosening restrictions, he tightened them. The regime set up a system of provincial and county assemblies, or zemstvos, elected by all social classes (though dominated by the nobility) in 1864, only to curtail their rights and ability to discuss politics. It extended censorship to the press and schools as well. When the tsar was killed by a radical assassin in 1881, his successor, Alexander III (1881–1894), steered the country sharply to the right. Russia had nothing in common with western Europe, Alexander III claimed; his people had been nurtured on mystical piety for centuries and would be utterly lost without a strong autocratic system. This principle guided stern repression. The regime curtailed all powers of the zemstvos, increased the authority of the secret police, and subjected villages to the governmental authority of nobles appointed by the state.

Nicholas II (1894–1917) continued these Counter Reforms. Like his father, he ardently advocated Russifi-

WHAT ARE "MASS POLITICS," AND HOW DID NATION-STATES RESPOND TO THEM?

LIBERALISM AND ITS DISCONTENTS: NATIONAL POLITICS AT THE TURN OF THE CENTURY   845

cation, or government programs to extend the language, religion, and culture of greater Russia over the empire's non-Russian subjects. Russification amounted to coercion, expropriation, and physical oppression: Finns lost their constitution, Poles studied their own literature in Russian translation, and Jews perished in pogroms. (*Pogrom* is a Russian term for violent attacks on civilians, which in the late nineteenth century were usually aimed at Jewish communities.) The Russian government did not organize pogroms, but it was openly anti-Semitic and made a point of looking the other way when villagers massacred Jews and destroyed their homes, businesses, and synagogues. Other groups whose repression by the state led to long-lasting undercurrents of anti-Russian nationalism included the Georgians, Armenians, and Azerbaijanis of the Caucasus Mountains.

The most important radical political group in late-nineteenth-century Russia was a large, loosely knit group of men and women who called themselves populists. Populists believed that Russia needed to modernize on its own terms, not the West's. They envisioned an egalitarian Russia based on the ancient institution of the village commune (*mir*). Advocates of populism sprang primarily from the middle class; many of its adherents

were young students, and women made up about 15 percent—a significantly large proportion for the period. They formed secret bands, plotting the overthrow of tsarism through anarchy and insurrection. They dedicated their lives to "the people," attempting wherever possible to live among common laborers so as to understand and express the popular will. Populism's historical importance lies less in what it accomplished, which was little, than in what it promised for the future. It acted as a seedbed of organized agitation in Russia, which would in time produce revolution. Populists read Marx's *Capital* and revised his ideas to produce a doctrine suited to Russia. Populists' emphasis on peasant socialism influenced the Social Revolutionary Party, formed in 1901, which also concentrated on increasing the political power of the peasant and building a socialist society based on the agrarian communalism of the mir.

The emergence of industrial capitalism and a new, desperately poor working class created Russian Marxism. Organized as the Social Democratic Party, Russian Marxists concentrated their efforts on behalf of urban workers and saw themselves as part of the international working-class movement. They made little headway in a peasant-dominated Russia before World War I, but they provided disaffected urban factory workers and

Execution of the Conspirators against Alexander II. Known as the liberator of the serfs, Tsar Alexander II grew increasingly restrictive and unpopular late in his reign and was assassinated in 1881 by radicals. Six were ultimately hanged for the crime, although the execution of the woman at the center was delayed because she was pregnant.

CHRONOLOGY

THE RUSSIAN ROAD TO REVOLUTION, 1861–1905

Emancipation of the serfs	1861
State-directed industrialization begins	1880s–1890s
Alexander II assassinated	1881
Alexander III launches counterreforms	1881–1894
Nicholas II continues Russification policies	1894–1905
Russo-Japanese War	1904–1905
The first Russian revolution: Bloody Sunday and October Manifesto	1905

intellectuals alike with a powerful ideology that stressed the necessity of overthrowing the tsarist regime and the inevitability of a better future. Autocracy would give way to capitalism and capitalism to an egalitarian, classless society. Russian Marxism blended radical, activist opposition with a rational, scientific approach to history, furnishing revolutionaries with a set of concepts with which to understand the upheavals of the young twentieth century.

In 1903 the leadership of the Social Democratic Party split over an important disagreement on revolutionary strategy. One group, temporarily in the majority and quick to name itself the Bolsheviks (majority group), believed that the Russian situation called for a strongly centralized party of active revolutionaries. The Bolsheviks also insisted that the rapid industrialization of Russia meant that they did not have to follow Marx's model for the West. Instead of working for liberal capitalist reforms, Russian revolutionaries could skip a stage and immediately begin to build a socialist state. The Mensheviks (which means minority) were more cautious or "gradualist," seeking slow changes and reluctant to depart from Marxist orthodoxy. When the Mensheviks regained control of the Social Democratic Party, the Bolsheviks formed a splinter party under the leadership of the young, dedicated revolutionary Vladimir Ilyich Ulanov, who lived in political exile in western Europe between 1900 and 1917. He wrote under the pseudonym of Lenin, from the Lena River in Siberia, where he had been exiled earlier.

Lenin's theoretical abilities and organizational energy commanded respect, enabling him to remain the leader of the Bolsheviks even while living abroad. From exile Lenin preached unrelenting class struggle; the need for a coordinated revolutionary socialist movement throughout Europe; and, most important, the belief that Russia was passing into an economic stage that made it ripe for revolution. It was the Bolsheviks' responsibility to organize a revolutionary party on behalf of workers, for without the party's discipline, workers could not effect change. Lenin's treatise *What Is to Be Done?* (1902) set out his vision of Russia's special destiny, and it denounced gradualists who had urged collaboration with moderate parties. Lenin considered revolution the only answer to Russia's problems, and he argued that organizing for revolution needed to be done, soon, by vanguard agents of the party acting in the name of the working class.

THE FIRST RUSSIAN REVOLUTION

The revolution that came in 1905, however, took all of these radical movements by surprise. Its unexpected occurrence resulted from Russia's resounding defeat in the Russo-Japanese War of 1904–1905. But the revolution had deeper roots. Rapid industrialization had transformed Russia unevenly; certain regions were heavily industrial, while others were less integrated into the market economy. The economic boom of the 1880s and 1890s turned to bust in the early 1900s, as demand for goods tapered off, prices plummeted, and the nascent working class suffered high levels of unemployment. At the same time, low grain prices resulted in a series of peasant uprisings, which, combined with students' energetic radical organizing, became overtly political.

As dispatches reported the defeats of the tsar's army and navy, the Russian people grasped the full extent of the regime's inefficiency. Hitherto apolitical middle-class subjects clamored for change, and radical workers organized strikes and held demonstrations in every important city. Trust in the benevolence of the tsar was severely shaken on January 22, 1905—"Bloody Sunday"—when a group of 200,000 workers and their families, led by a priest, Father Gapon, went to demonstrate their grievances at the tsar's winter palace in St. Petersburg. When guard troops killed 130 demonstrators and

> From exile Lenin preached unrelenting class struggle; the need for a coordinated revolutionary socialist movement throughout Europe; and, most important, the belief that Russia was passing into an economic stage that made it ripe for revolution.

LENIN'S VIEW OF A REVOLUTIONARY PARTY

At the turn of the century, Russian revolutionaries debated political strategy. How could Russian autocracy be defeated? Should revolutionaries follow the programs of their counterparts in the West? Or did the Russian situation require different tactics? In What Is to Be Done? *(1902) Lenin (Vladimir Ilyich Ulyanov, 1870–1924) argued that Russian socialists needed to revise the traditional Marxist view, according to which a large and politically conscious working class would make revolution. In Russia, Lenin argued, revolution required a small but dedicated group of revolutionaries to lead the working class. Lenin's vision was important, for it shaped the tactics and strategies of the Bolsheviks in 1917 and beyond.*

[T]he national tasks of Russian Social-Democracy are such as have never confronted any other socialist party in the world. We shall have occasion further on to deal with the political and organisational duties which the task of emancipating the whole people from the yoke of autocracy imposes upon us. At this point, we wish to state only that the *role of vanguard fighter can be fulfilled only by a party that is guided by the most advanced theory.* . . .

I assert: (1) that no revolutionary movement can endure without a stable organisation of leaders maintaining continuity; (2) that the broader the popular mass drawn spontaneously into the struggle, which forms the basis of the movement and participates in it, the more urgent the need for such an organisation, and the more solid this organisation must be (for it is much easier for all sorts of demagogues to side-track the more backward sections of the masses); (3) that such an organisation must consist chiefly of people professionally engaged in revolutionary activity; (4) that in an autocratic state, the more we *confine* the membership of such an organisation to people who are professionally engaged in revolutionary activity and who have been professionally trained in the art of combating the political police, the more difficult will it be to unearth the organisation; and (5) the *greater* will be the number of people from the working class and from the other social classes who will be able to join the movement and perform active work in it. . . .

Social-Democracy leads the struggle of the working class, not only for better terms for the sale of labour-power, but for the abolition of the social system that compels the property-less to sell themselves to the rich. Social-Democracy represents the working class, not in its relation to a given group of employers alone, but in its relation to all classes of modern society and to the state as an organised political force. Hence, it follows that not only must Social-Democrats not confine themselves exclusively to the economic struggle. . . . We must take up actively the political education of the working class and the development of its political consciousness.

Vladimir Lenin, *What Is to Be Done?* in *Collected Works of V. I. Lenin*, vol. 5 (Moscow, 1964), pp. 369–70, 373, 375.

QUESTIONS FOR ANALYSIS

1. What were the key features of Lenin's thought?
2. Here Lenin more or less set down the rules for the revolutionary vanguard. What historical experiences and political theories shaped his thinking? In what ways was the Russian experience unique?

Bloody Sunday. Demonstrating workers who sought to bring their grievances to the attention of the tsar were met and gunned down by government troops, January 1905.

wounded several hundred, the government seemed not only ineffective but arbitrary and brutal.

Over the course of 1905 general protest grew. Merchants closed their stores, factory owners shut down their plants, lawyers refused to plead cases in court. The autocracy lost control of entire rural towns and regions as local authorities were ejected and often killed by enraged peasants. Forced to yield, Tsar Nicholas II issued the October Manifesto, pledging guarantees of individual liberties, a moderately liberal franchise for the election of a Duma, and genuine legislative veto powers for the Duma. Although the 1905 revolution brought the tsarist system perilously close to collapse, it failed to convince the tsar that fundamental political change was necessary. Between 1905 and 1907 Nicholas revoked most of the promises made in the October Manifesto. Above all, he deprived the Duma of its principal powers and decreed that it be elected indirectly on a class basis, which ensured a legislative body of obedient followers.

Nonetheless, the revolt of 1905 persuaded the tsar's more perceptive advisers that reform was urgent. The agrarian programs sponsored by the government's leading minister, Peter Stolypin, were especially significant. Between 1906 and 1911 the Stolypin reforms provided for the sale of 5 million acres of royal land to peasants, granted permission to peasants to withdraw from the mir and form independent farms, and canceled peasant property debts. Further decrees legalized labor unions, reduced the working day (to ten hours in most cases),

and established sickness and accident insurance. Liberals could reasonably hope that Russia was on the way to becoming a progressive nation on the Western model, yet the tsar remained stubbornly autocratic. Russian agriculture remained suspended between an emerging capitalist system and the traditional peasant commune; Russian industry, though powerful enough to allow Russia to maintain its status as a world power, had hardly created a modern, industrial society capable of withstanding the enormous strains that Russia would face during World War I.

NATIONALISM AND IMPERIAL POLITICS: THE BALKANS

In southeastern Europe rising nationalism continued to divide the disintegrating Ottoman Empire. Before 1829 the entire Balkan peninsula, bounded by the Aegean, Black, and Adriatic Seas, was controlled by the Turks. Over the course of the next eighty-five years, however, the Turkish empire ceded territories to rival European powers, especially Russia and Austria, as well as to nationalist revolts by the empire's Christian subjects. Once a formidable world power, the Ottoman Empire was now dubbed the "sick man of Europe." In 1829, at the conclusion of a war between Russia and Turkey, Sultan Abdul Hamid II (1876–1909) acknowledged the independence of Greece and granted autonomy to both Serbia and the provinces that later became Romania. As the years passed, resentment against Ottoman rule spread through other Balkan territories. In 1875–1876 there were uprisings in Bosnia, Herzegovina, and Bulgaria, which the sultan suppressed with effective ferocity. Reports of atrocities against Christians gave Russia an excuse to renew its long-standing struggle for domination of the Balkans. In this Russo-Turkish War (1877–1878), the armies of the tsar won a smashing victory. The Treaty of San Stefano, which terminated the conflict, forced the sultan to surrender nearly all of his territory in Europe, except for a remnant around Constantinople. But at this juncture the Great Powers intervened. Austria and Great Britain were especially opposed to granting Russia jurisdiction over so large a portion of the Near East. In 1878 a congress of the Great Powers, meeting in Berlin, transferred Bessarabia to Russia, Thessaly to Greece, and Bosnia and Herzegovina to the control of Austria. Montenegro, Serbia,

The Decline of the Ottoman Empire, 1699–1912

How do you explain the slow decline of Ottoman power in relationship to Europe and the emerging global economy? What were European interests in the areas controlled by the Ottomans? How did they advance those interests? The decline of Ottoman power had enormous significance for relations among European nations themselves. Why?

Map labels:

EUROPE
FRANCE
SWITZERLAND
ITALY
SPAIN
Madrid
Bay of Biscay
Rome
AUSTRIA
Vienna
Turks defeated 1683
Budapest
HUNGARY 1699
1699
1716
1699
1812
BOSNIA 1878
SERBIA 1878
MONTENEGRO
ROMANIA 1878
BULGARIA 1878
1888
TURKEY IN EUROPE
GREECE 1830
Athens
Navarino
CRETE
AEGEAN SEA
IONIAN SEA
ADRIATIC SEA
TYRRHENIAN SEA
MEDITERRANEAN SEA
Algiers
Oran
ALGERIA 1830
TUNISIA 1881
Tunis
Tripoli
LIBYA Conquered by Italy 1912
CYRENAICA
Bengasi
AFRICA
SUDAN

RUSSIAN EMPIRE
ARAL SEA
CASPIAN SEA
SEA OF AZOV
1739
1783
1784
1783
1784
1791
Odessa
Sevastopol
BLACK SEA
Kutchuk Kainardji
Constantinople
Angora
TURKEY
GEORGIA 1859
1878
Tiflis
ARMENIA 1878
Kars
1703
Batum
PERSIA
Teheran
MESOPOTAMIA
Baghdad
Basra
Tigris R
Euphrates R
Damascus
Acre
HOLY LAND
Jerusalem
Suez Canal
SINAI
Tel-el-Kebir
Cairo
EGYPT 1882
Nile R
RED SEA
ARABIA
HEJAZ
Mecca
Persian Gulf
ADEN
INDIAN OCEAN
CYPRUS 1878

Legend:
Boundary of Ottoman Empire 1699
Austria
Russia
Britain
France
Independent States (with date of independence)
Ottoman Empire 1912

Scale:
0   250   500 Miles
0   250   500 Kilometers

and Romania also became independent states, thus launching the modern era of Balkan nationalism. Seven years later the Bulgars, who had been granted some degree of autonomy by the Congress of Berlin, seized the province of Eastern Rumelia from Turkey. In 1908 they established the independent kingdom of Bulgaria. In 1908 Austria annexed the provinces of Bosnia and

Herzegovina, which it had administered since 1878, and in 1911–1912 Italy entered into war with Turkey. The power vacuum in the Orient significantly strained Europe's imperial balance of power.

A nationalist movement also emerged in Turkey itself. For some time informed Turks had grown increasingly impatient with the sultan's weakness and his

NEW NATIONS IN THE BALKANS

Consider the dates at which these nations won or were granted their independence. How did they become sovereign? What larger powers had interests in their survival? What problems did the emergence of these new nations solve? What new problems did it create?

government's incompetence. Those who had been educated in European universities advocated national rejuvenation through the introduction of Western science and democratic reforms. Invoking a Western liberal variant of nationalism, these reformers called themselves "Young Turks" and in 1908 successfully forced the sultan to establish a constitutional government. The following year, in the face of a reactionary movement, they deposed Sultan Abdul Hamid II and placed on the throne his brother, Mohammed V (1909–1918). The real powers of government were now entrusted to a grand vizier and ministers responsible to an elected parliament. The new representative government did not, however, extend liberties to the empire's non-Turkish inhabitants. On the contrary, the Young Turks launched a vigorous effort to "Ottomanize" all their imperial subjects, trying to bring both Christian and Muslim communities under more centralized control and to spread Turkish culture. That effort, intended to compensate for the loss of territories in Europe, undercut the popularity of the new reformist regime.

THE SCIENCE AND SOUL OF THE MODERN AGE

What impact did new scientific theories have on culture?

Ninteenth-century liberals believed in individualism, progress, and science. Not only did science deliver technological and material rewards but it also confirmed liberals' faith in the power of human reason to uncover and command the laws of nature. Toward the end of the century, however, scientific developments defied these expectations. Darwin's theory of evolution, psychology, and social science all introduced visions of humanity that were sharply at odds with conventional wisdom. At the same time, artists and intellectuals mounted their own revolt against nineteenth-century conventions. Morals, manners, institutions, traditions: all established values and assumptions were under question, as a generation of self-consciously avant-garde artists called for a radical break with the past. These upheavals in the world of ideas unsettled older conceptions of individuality, culture, and consciousness. The modern individual no longer seemed the free and ratio-

nal agent of Enlightenment thought, but rather the product of irrational inner drives and uncontrollable external circumstances. As Georg Simmel, one of the founders of modern sociology, wrote in 1902: "The deepest problems of modern life derive from the claim of the individual to preseve the autonomy and individuality of his existence in the face of overwhelming social forces, of historical heritage, of external culture, and of the technique of life."

DARWIN'S REVOLUTIONARY THEORY

If Marx changed conceptions of society, Charles Darwin did him one better, perhaps, for his theory of organic evolution by natural selection transformed conceptions of nature itself. As both a scientific explanation and an imaginative metaphor for political and social change, Darwin's theory of evolution introduced an unsettling new picture of human biology, behavior, and society. As with Marxism, its core concepts were embraced by some and abhorred by others, and were interpreted and deployed in a variety of unexpected, often conflicting, ways that profoundly shaped the late nineteenth and early twentieth centuries.

Theories of evolution did not originate with Darwin but none of the earlier theories had gained widespread scientific or popular currency. Geologists and other scientists in the nineteenth century had challenged the biblical account of creation with evidence that the world was formed by natural processes over millions of years. The nature of those processes remained unknown, however, particularly the question of how different species arose. One important attempt at an answer was proposed in the early nineteenth century by the French biologist Jean Lamarck, who argued that behavioral changes could alter an animal's physical characteristics within a single generation, and that these new traits would be passed on to offspring. (In a famous example, Lamarck believed that giraffes' long necks resulted from generations of giraffes reaching for ever higher leaves.) Over time, Lamarck suggested, the inheritance of acquired characteristics produced new species of animals. Though widely attacked, Lamarck's hypothesis had its adherents, and absent an understanding of genetic inheritance, it persisted as a popular conception of evolution into the twentieth century.

A more convincing hypothesis of organic evolution appeared in 1859, however, with the publication of the *Origin of Species* by British naturalist Charles Darwin. The son of a small-town physician, Darwin had spent five years in the 1830s as an unpaid naturalist aboard

DARWIN AND HIS READERS

Charles Darwin's Origin of Species *(1859) and his theory of natural selection transformed Western knowledge of natural history. The impact of Darwin's work, however, extended well beyond scientific circles. It assumed a cultural importance that exceeded even Darwin's scholarly contribution. How Darwinism was popularized is a complex question, for writers and readers could mold Darwin's ideas to fit a variety of political and cultural purposes. The first excerpt comes from the conclusion to* The Origin of Species *itself, and it sets out the different laws that Darwin thought governed the natural world. The second excerpt, comes from the autobiography of Nicholas Osterroth (1875–1933), a clay miner from western Germany. Osterroth was ambitious and self-educated. The passage recounts his reaction to hearing about Darwin and conveys his enthusiasm for late-nineteenth-century science.*

ORIGIN OF SPECIES

The natural system is a genealogical arrangement, in which we have to discover the lines of descent by the most permanent characters, however slight their vital importance may be.

The framework of bones being the same in the hand of a man, wing of a bat, fin of the porpoise, and leg of the horse,—the same number of vertebrae forming the neck of the giraffe and of the elephant,—and innumerable other such facts, at once explain themselves on the theory of descent with slow and slight successive modifications. The similarity of pattern in the wing and leg of a bat, though used for such different purposes,—in the jaws and legs of a crab,—in the petals, stamens, and pistils of a flower, is likewise intelligible on the view of the gradual modification of parts or organs, which were alike in the early progenitor of each class. . . .

It is interesting to contemplate an entangled bank, clothed with many plants of many kinds, with birds singing on the bushes, with various insects flitting about, and with worms crawling through the damp earth, and to reflect that these elaborately constructed forms, so different from each other, and dependent on each other in so complex a manner, have all been produced by laws acting around us. These laws, taken in the largest sense, being Growth with Reproduction; Inheritance which is almost implied by reproduction; Variability from the indirect and direct action of the external conditions of life, and from use and disuse; a Ratio of Increase so high as to lead to a Struggle for Life, and as a consequence to Natural Selection, entailing Divergence of Character and the Extinction of less-improved forms. Thus, from the war of nature, from famine and death, the most exalted object which we are capable of conceiving, namely, the production of the higher animals, directly follows. There is grandeur in this view of life, with its several powers, having been originally breathed into a few forms or into one; and that, whilst this planet has gone cycling on according to the fixed law of gravity, from so simple a beginning endless forms most beautiful and most wonderful have been, and are being, evolved.

Charles Darwin, *The Origin of Species* (Harmondsworth, UK, 1968), pp. 450–451, 458–460.

NICHOLAS OSTERROTH: A MINER'S REACTION

The book was called *Moses or Darwin?* . . . Written in a very popular style, it compared the Mosaic story of creation with the natural evolutionary history, illuminated the contradictions of the biblical story, and gave a concise description of the evolution of organic and inorganic nature, interwoven with plenty of striking proofs.

What particularly impressed me was a fact that now became clear to me: that evolutionary natural history was monopolized by the institutions of higher learning; that Newton, Laplace, Kant, Darwin, and Haeckel brought enlightenment only to the students of the upper social classes; and that for the common people in the grammar school the old Moses with his six-day creation of the world still was the authoritative world view. For the upper classes there was evolution, for us creation; for them productive liberating knowledge, for us rigid faith; bread for those favored by fate, stones for those who hungered for truth!

Why do the people need science? Why do they need a so-called Weltanschauung [world view]? The people must keep Moses, must keep religion; religion is the poor man's philosophy. Where would we end up if every miner and every farmhand had the opportunity to stick his nose into astronomy, geology, biology, and anatomy? Does it serve any purpose for the divine world order of the possessing and privileged classes to tell the worker that the Ptolemaic heavens have long since collapsed; that out there in the universe there is an eternal process of creation and destruction; that in the universe at large, as on our tiny earth, everything is in the grip of eternal evolution; that this evolution takes place according to inalterable natural laws that defy even the omnipotence of the old Mosaic Jehovah; . . . Why tell the dumb people that Copernicus and his followers have overturned the old Mosaic creator, and that Darwin and modern science have dug the very ground out from under his feet of clay?

That would be suicide! Yes, the old religion is so convenient for the divine world order of the ruling class! As long as the worker hopes faithfully for the beyond, he won't think of plucking the blooming roses in this world. . . .

The possessing classes of all civilized nations need servants to make possible their godlike existence. So they cannot allow the servant to eat from the tree of knowledge.

Alfred Kelly, ed., *The German Worker: Working-Class Autobiographies from the Age of Industrialization* (Berkeley, Calif., 1987), pp. 185–186.

QUESTIONS FOR ANALYSIS

1. Was the theory of evolution revolutionary? If so, how? Would it be fair to say that Darwin did for the nineteenth century what Newton did for the seventeenth and eighteenth centuries?
2. Why did people think the natural world was governed by laws? Was this a religious belief or a scientific fact?
3. What aspects of Darwin appealed to Osterroth and why?

the H.M.S. *Beagle,* a ship that had been chartered for scientific exploration on a trip around the world. The voyage gave Darwin an unparalleled opportunity to observe the manifold variations of animal life. He contrasted island-dwelling species with related animals on nearby continents and compared the traits of living creatures with those of fossilized remains. From a familiarity with pigeon breeding (a popular Victorian hobby), Darwin knew that particular traits could be artificially selected by means of controlled mating. Was a similar process of "selection" at work in nature?

Darwin's revolutionary answer was yes. He theorized that variations within a population (such as longer beaks or protective coloring) made certain individual organisms better equipped for survival, increasing their chances of breeding and thus passing their advantageous traits to the next generation. To reach this conclusion, Darwin drew on the ideas of the economist and demographer Thomas Malthus, who earlier argued that in nature many more individuals are born than can survive and that, consequently, the weaker ones must perish in the struggle for food. In Darwin's explanation, this Malthusian competition led to adaptation and, if adaptation was successful, to survival. The environment, he argued, "selects" those variants among offspring that are best able to survive and reproduce while eliminating other, less "fit" biological traits.

Darwin used this theory of variation and natural selection to explain the origin of new species. He believed that individual plants and animals with favorable characteristics would transmit their inherited qualities to their descendants over generations and that successive eliminations of the least fit would eventually produce a new species. Darwin applied his concept of evolution not only to plant and animal species but also to humans. In his view, the human race had evolved from an apelike ancestor, long since extinct, but probably a common precursor of the existing anthropoid apes and humans. Darwin introduced this unsettling idea in his second great work, *The Descent of Man* (1871). At least since Newton, science had inspired faith in human ability to understand and master the natural world; the Darwinian revolution seemed to put such faith in jeopardy.

DARWINIAN THEORY AND RELIGION

The implications of Darwin's writings went far beyond the domain of the evolutionary sciences. Most notably, they challenged the basis of deeply held religious beliefs, sparking a public discussion on the existence and knowability of God. Although popular critics denounced Darwin for contradicting literal interpretations of the Bible, those contradictions were not what made religious middle-class readers uncomfortable. The work of prominent theologians, such as David Friedrich Strauss, had already helped Christians adapt their faith to biblical inaccuracies and inconsistencies. They did not need to abandon either Christianity or faith simply because Darwin showed (or argued) that the world and its life forms had developed over millions of years rather than six days. What religious readers in the nineteenth century found difficult to accept was Darwin's challenge to their belief in a benevolent God and a morally guided universe. By Darwin's account, the world was governed not by order, harmony, and divine will, but by random chance and constant, undirected struggle. Moreover, the Darwinian worldview seemed to redefine notions of good and bad only in terms of an ability to survive, thus robbing humanity of critical moral certainties. Darwin himself was able to reconcile his theory with a belief in God, but others latched on his work to fiercely attack Christian orthodoxy. One such figure was the philosopher Thomas Henry Huxley, who earned himself the nickname of "Darwin's bulldog" by inveighing against Christians who were appalled by the implications of Darwinian theory. Huxley called himself an agnostic (from the Greek *agnostos*, or "unknowable"), a person who believed that neither the existence nor the nature of God

could be known, and asserted that "there is no evidence of the existence of such a being as the God of the theologians." Opposed to all forms of dogma, Huxley argued that the thinking person should simply follow reason "as far as it can take you" and recognize that the ultimate character of the universe lay beyond his or her grasp.

SOCIAL DARWINISM

The theory of natural selection also influenced the social sciences, which were just developing at the end of the nineteenth century. New disciplines such as sociology, psychology, anthropology, and economics aimed to apply scientific methods to the analysis of society and introduced new ways of quantifying, measuring, and interpreting human experience. Under the authoritative banner of "science," these disciplines exerted a powerful influence on society, oftentimes to improve the health and well-being of European men and women. But, as we will see with the impact of Social Darwinism, the social sciences could also provide justification for forms of economic, imperial, and racial dominance.

The so-called Social Darwinists, whose most famous proponent was the English philosopher Herbert Spencer (1820–1903), adapted Darwinian thought in a way that would have shocked Darwin himself, by applying his concept of individual competition and survival to relationships among classes, races, and nations. Spencer, who coined the phrase *survival of the fittest,* used evolutionary theory to expound the virtues of free competition and attack state welfare programs. As a champion of individualism, Spencer condemned all forms of collectivism as primitive and counterproductive, relics of an earlier stage of social evolution. Government attempts to relieve economic and social hardships—or to place constraints on big business—were, in Spencer's view, hindrances to the vigorous advancement of civilization, which could occur only through individual adaptation and competition. Particularly in America, such claims earned Spencer high praise from some wealthy industrialists, who were no doubt glad to be counted among the fittest.

Unlike the science of biological evolution, a popularized Social Darwinism was easy to comprehend, and its concepts (centering on a struggle for survival) were soon integrated into the political vocabulary of the day. Proponents of laissez-faire capitalism and opponents of socialism used Darwinist rhetoric to justify marketplace competition and the "natural order" of

Cephalograph. This illustration from Herbert Spencer's autobiography shows a device designed to measure skulls. He believed that the size of one's skull determined brain capacity and applied the idea of "survival of the fittest" to justify theories of white racial superiority.

rich and poor. Nationalists embraced Social Darwinism to rationalize imperialist expansion and warfare. Spencer's doctrine also became closely tied to theories of racial hierarchy and white superiority, which claimed that the white race had reached the height of evolutionary development and had thus earned the right to dominate and rule other races (see Chapter Twenty-Five). Ironically, some progressive middle-class reformers relied on a similar set of racial assumptions: their campaigns to improve the health and welfare of society played to fears that Europe, though dominant, could move down the evolutionary ladder. Despite its unsettling potential, Darwinism was used to advance a range of political objectives and to shore up an array of ingrained prejudices.

EARLY PSYCHOLOGY: PAVLOV AND FREUD

Although the new social scientists self-consciously relied on the use of rational, scientific principles, their findings often stressed the opposite: the irrational, even animalistic nature of human experience. Darwin had already called into question the notion that humanity was fundamentally superior to the rest of the animal kingdom, and similarly discomfitting conclusions came from the new field of psychology. Physiological experiments, which could establish connections between body and mind, promised an entirely new way to comprehend the mental makeup of humans. For instance, the work of the Russian physician Ivan Pavlov (1849–1936) explained a type of behavior called "classical conditioning," in which a random stimulus can be made to produce a (sometimes unintended) physical reflex reaction. Pavlov's famous experiment showed that if dogs were fed after they heard the ringing of a bell, the animals would eventually salivate at the sound of the bell alone, exactly as if they smelled and saw food. Moreover, Pavlov insisted that such conditioning constituted a significant part of human behavior as well. Known as "behaviorism," this type of physiological psychology avoided vague concepts such as mind and consciousness, concentrating instead on the reaction of muscles, nerves, glands, and visceral organs. Rather than being governed by reason, human activity was recast by behaviorists as a bundle of physiological responses to stimuli in the environment.

Like behavorism, a second major school of psychology also suggested that human behavior was largely motivated by unconcious and irrational forces. Founded by the Austrian physician Sigmund Freud (1856–1939), the discipline of psychoanalysis posited a new, dynamic, and unsettling theory of the mind, in which a variety of unconscious drives and desires conflict with a rational and moral conscience. Developed over many years of treating patients with nervous ailments, Freud's model of the psyche contained three elements: (1) the id, or undisciplined desires for pleasure, sexual gratification, aggression, and so on; (2) the superego, or conscience, which registers the prohibitions of morality and culture; and (3) the ego, the arena in which the conflict between id and super-ego works itself out. Freud believed that most cases of mental disorder result from an irreconcilable tension between natural drives and cultural restraints. Freud believed that by studying such disorders, as well as dreams and slips of the tongue, scientists could glimpse the submerged areas of consciousness and thus understand seemingly irrational behavior. Indeed, Freud's seach for an all-encompassing theory of the mind was deeply grounded in the tenets of nineteenth-century science. By stressing the irrational, however, Freud's theories fed a growing anxiety about the value and limits of human reason. Likewise, they brought to fore a powerful critique of the constraints imposed by the moral and social codes of Western civilization.

NIETZSCHE'S ATTACK ON TRADITION

No one provided a more sweeping or more influential assault on Western values than the German philosopher Friedrich Nietzsche (*NEE-chuh*; 1844–1900). Nietzsche skewered the moral certainties of the nineteenth century. Like Freud, Nietzsche had observed a middle-class culture that he believed to be dominated by illusions and self-deceptions, and he sought to unmask them. In a series of works that rejected rational argumentation in favor of an elliptical, suggestive prose style, Nietzsche presented his critque of Western culture. Essentially, he argued that bourgeois faith in such concepts as science, progress, democracy, and religion represented a futile, and thus reprehensible, search for security and truth. Nietzsche categorically denied the possibility of knowing truth or reality, since all knowlege comes filtered through linguistic, scientific, or artistic systems of representation. He famously ridiculed Judeo-Christian morality for instilling a repressive conformity that drained civilization of its vitality. Though Nietzsche's philosophy did not offer any concrete political or social objectives, it resounded with themes of personal liberation, especially freedom from the stranglehold of history and tradition. Indeed, Nietzsche's ideal individual, or "supcrman," was onc who abandoned the burdens of cultural conformity and created an independent set of values based on artistic vision and strength of character. Only through individual struggle against the chaotic universe did Nietzsche forecast salvation for Western civilization. His publications, including *Thus Spake Zarathustra* (1883), *Beyond Good and Evil* (1886), and *On the Genealogy of Morals* (1887), achieved widespread fame beginning in the 1890s, just when the strains of modernization were beginning to crack the foundations of European society.

> Though Nietzsche's philosophy did not offer any concrete political or social objectives, it resounded with themes of personal liberation, especially freedom from the stranglehold of history and tradition.

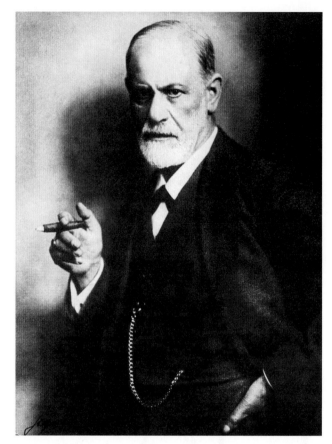

Sigmund Freud. Freud's theory of the mind and the unconscious broke with many of the basic assumptions about human nature during his time. He remained, however, a committed nineteenth-century scientist and believed he had uncovered new laws that governed culture as well as individuals.

RELIGION AND ITS CRITICS

Faced with these various scientific and philosophical challenges, the institutions responsible for the maintenance of traditional faith found themselves on the defensive. The Roman Catholic Church responded to the encroachments of secular society by appealing to its dogma and venerated traditions. In 1864 Pope Pius IX issued a Syllabus of Errors, condemning what he regarded as the principal religious and philosophical errors of the time. Among them were materialism, free thought, and indifferentism (the idea that one religion is as good as another). The pope also convoked the first church council since the Catholic Reformation, which in 1871 pronounced the dogma of papal infallibility.

This meant that in his capacity "as pastor and doctor of all Christians," the pope was infallible in regard to all matters of faith and morals. Though generally accepted by pious Catholics, the claim of papal infallibility provoked a storm of protest and was denounced by the governments of several Catholic countries, including France, Spain, and Italy. The death of Pius IX in 1878 and the accession of Pope Leo XIII, however, brought a more accommodating climate to the church. The new pope acknowledged that there was good as well as evil in modern civilization. He added a scientific staff to the Vatican and opened archives and observatories, but made no further concessions to liberalism in the political sphere.

Protestants were also compelled to respond to a modernizing world. Since they were taught to understand God with the aid of little more than the Bible and a willing conscience, Protestants, unlike Catholics, had little in the way of doctrine to help them defend their faith. Some fundamentalists chose to ignore the implications of scientific and philosophical inquiry altogether and continued to believe in the literal truth of the Bible. Others were willing to agree with the school of American philosophers known as pragmatists (principally Charles S. Peirce and William James), who taught that "truth" was whatever produced useful, practical results; by their logic, if belief in God provided mental peace or spiritual satisfaction, then the belief was true. Other Protestants sought solace from reli-

gious doubt in founding missions, laboring among the poor, and other good works. Many adherents to this social gospel were also modernists who accepted the ethical teachings of Christianity but discarded beliefs in miracles and original sin.

NEW READERS AND THE POPULAR PRESS

The effect of various scientific and philosophical challenges on the men and women who lived at the end of the nineteenth century cannot be measured precisely. Millions undoubtedly went about the business of life untroubled by the implications of evolutionary theory, content to believe as they had believed before. Certainly, for most members of the middle class, the challenge of socialism was understood as "real" in a way that the challenges of science and philosophy probably were not. Socialism threatened specific interests. The theories of Darwin and Freud, though in the air and troubling, did not matter to the same degree. Men and women could postpone thoughts about their origins and ultimate destiny. Furthermore, as we have seen, many religious men and women could reconcile faith and religion with the new science. Yet the changes we have been discussing eventually had a profound impact. Darwin's theory was not too complicated to be popularized. If educated men and women

The New Power of the Press. With the spread of literacy, newspapers adapted to the needs and desires of the new mass audience. Here British railway passengers scramble for the latest edition.

had neither the time nor inclination to read the *Origin of Species*, they read magazines and newspapers that summarized (not always correctly) its implications. They encountered some of its central concepts in other places, from political speeches to novels and crime reports.

The diffusion of these new ideas was facilitated by rising literacy rates and by new forms of printed mass culture. Between 1750 and 1870, readership had expanded from the aristocracy to include middle-class circles and, thereafter, to an increasingly literate general population. In 1850 approximately half the population of Europe was literate. In subsequent decades, country after country introduced state-financed elementary and secondary education to provide opportunities for social advancement, to diffuse technical and scientific knowledge, and to inculcate civic and national pride. Britain instituted elementary education in 1870, Switzerland in 1874, Italy in 1877. France expanded its existing system between 1878 and 1881. After 1871 Germany instituted a state system modeled on Prussia's. By 1900, approximately 85 percent of the population in Britain, France, Belgium, the Netherlands, Scandinavia, and Germany could read. The era of mass readership had arrived. Elsewhere, however, the percentages were far lower, ranging between 30 and 60 percent.

In those countries where literacy rates were highest, commercial publishers such as Alfred Harmsworth in Britain and William Randolph Hearst in the United States hastened to serve the new reading public. Middle-class readers had for some time been well supplied with newspapers catering to their interests and point of view. The *Times* of London had a readership of well over 50,000 by 1850; the *Presse* and the *Siècle* in France, a circulation of 70,000. By 1900, however, other newspapers were appealing to the newly literate, and doing so by means of sensational journalism and spicy, easy-to-read serials. Advertisements drastically lowered the costs of the mass-market newspapers, enabling even workers to purchase one or two newspapers a day. The yellow journalism of the penny presses merged entertainment and sensationalism with the news, aiming to increase circulation and thus secure more lucrative advertising sales. Publishers and marketing men weren't the only ones eager to reach this emerging mass market, however. As the new century progressed, artists, activists, politicians—and above all, governments—would become increasingly preoccupied with communicating their messages to the masses.

THE FIRST MODERNS: INNOVATIONS IN ART

In the crucible of late-nineteenth-century Europe—bubbling with scientific, technological, and social transformations—artists across the Continent began critically and systematically to reexamine the nature of art in the modern world. New generations of painters, poets, writers, and composers began to question the moral and cultural values of liberal, middle-class society. Some did so with grave hesitation, others with heedless abandon. In a dizzying array of experiments, innovations, ephemeral art movements, and bombastic manifestos, the pioneers of what would later be termed "modernism" developed the artistic forms and aesthetic values that came to dominate much of the twentieth century.

Like all such terms, *modernism* is notoriously difficult to define: it encompassed a diverse and often contradictory set of theories and practices that spanned the entire range of cultural production—from painting, sculpture, literature, and architecture to theater, dance, and musical composition. Despite such diversity, however, modernist movements did share certain key characteristics: first, a sense that the world had radically changed and that change should be embraced (hence the modernists' interest in science and technology); second, a belief that traditional values and assumptions were outdated; and third, a new conception of what art could do, one that stressed expression over representation and insisted on experiment and freedom.

In addition to these trends, early modernism was distinguished by a new understanding of the relationship between art and society. Though some artists and writers did indeed turn inward, toward investigations of purely aesthetic questions, many others embraced the notion that art could effect profound social and spiritual change. The abstract painter Wassily Kandinsky (1866–1944), for instance, who was a devotee of occult mysticism (especially popular around the turn of the century), believed that visionary artists would

> Despite such diversity, however, modernist movements did share certain key characteristics: first, a self-conscious sense of rupture from history and tradition; second, a rejection of established values and assumptions; and third, a radical insistence on expressive and experimental freedom.

Black Lines by Wassily Kandinsky, 1913.
Kandinsky broke from the traditional
representational approach of nineteenth-
century painting with his abstractions and
was one of a generation of turn-of-the-
century artists who reexamined and experimented with their art forms.

carry society from "the soulless-material life of the nineteenth century" toward "the psychic-spiritual life of the twentieth century." Notions that contemporary society was materialistic and morally bankrupt figured prominently in modernist critiques of European culture. And while artists like Kandinsky pointed to salvation in a utopian future, others used their art to examine the present unflinchingly, probing the psychological and social pathologies of urban industrial society. In the political arena, modernist hostility toward conventional values sometimes translated into support for antiliberal movements at the political peripheries—radical anarchism on the left and proto-fascism on the right. This push toward the ideological edges mirrored the modernists' aesthetic tendencies. In the words of one scholar: "After the nineteenth century had established a remarkably safe, intimate center where the artist and the audience could dwell, the modernist age reached out to the freakish circumferences of art."

THE REVOLT ON CANVAS

Like most artistic movements, modernism defined itself in opposition to a set of earlier principles. For painters in particular, this meant a rejection both of mainstream academic art, which affirmed the chaste and moral outlook of museumgoers, and of the socially conscious realist tradition (see Chapter Twenty), which strove for rigorous, even scientific exactitude in representing material reality. The rebellion of modern artists went even further, however, by discarding altogether the centuries-old tradition of representation, or what French painter Paul Gauguin (1848–1903) called the "shackles of verisimilitude." Since the Renaissance, Western art had sought to accurately depict three-dimensional visual reality; paintings were considered to be "mirrors," or "windows" on the world. But during the late nineteenth century, artists turned their backs to the visual world, focusing instead on subjective, psychologically oriented, intensely emotional forms of self-expression. As the Norwegian painter Edvard Munch claimed: "Art is the opposite of nature. A work of art can come only from the interior of man."

Though challenges to the tradition of representational art occurred earlier in the nineteenth century, the first significant breaks emerged with the French impressionists, who came to prominence as young artists in the 1870s. Strictly speaking, the impressionists were realists. Steeped in scientific theories about sensory perception, they attempted to record natural phenomena objectively. Instead of painting objects themselves, they captured the transitory play of light on surfaces, giving their works a sketchy, ephemeral quality that differed sharply from realist art. And though subsequent artists revolted against what they deemed the sterile objectivity of this scientific approach, the impressionist painters, most famously Claude Monet (*moh-NAY;* 1840–1926) and Pierre-Auguste Renoir (1841–1919), left two important legacies to the European avant-garde. First, by developing new techniques without reference to past styles, the impressionists paved the way for younger artists to experiment more freely. Second, because the official salons rejected their work, the impressionists organized their own independent exhibitions from 1874 to 1886. These shows effectively undermined the French Academy's centuries-old monopoly on artistic display and aesthetic standards, and they established a tradition of autonomous outsider exhibits, which figures prominently in the history of modernism.

In the wake of impressionism, a handful of innovative artists working at the end of the nineteenth century laid the groundwork for an explosion of creative experimentation after 1900. Chief among them was the Frenchman Paul Cézanne (1839–1906), whose efforts to "make of Impressionism something solid and durable" entailed a reduction of natural forms to their geometric equivalents, a rejection of traditional perspective, and (most important) an emphasis on the subjective arrangement of

color and form. Perhaps more so than anyone, Cézanne shattered the window of representational art. Instead of a reflection of the world, painting became a vehicle for an artist's self-expression. The Dutchman Vincent van Gogh also explored art's expressive potential, with greater emotion and subjectivity. For Van Gogh, painting was a labor of faith, a way to channel his violent passions. For Paul Gauguin, who fled to the Pacific islands in 1891, art promised a utopian refuge from the corruption of Europe. Gauguin in particular was influenced by the symbolist movement around the turn of the century. The symbolists were a group of artists and writers who were deeply suspicious of material reality, and who sought transcendental truth though imagination, personal feelings, and psychological perceptions.

Especially in Germany, avant-garde artists expressed a wrenching disillusionment with modern society. Emil Nolde (1867–1956) railed against the "irresponsible voraciousness" with which European empires "annihilated peoples and races—and always under the hypocritical pretext of the best intentions." Emphasizing the parallel

Self Portrait, Study for *Ermiten,* Egon Schiele, 1912.
The Viennese artist Schiele represents another side of early modernism which, instead of moving towards abstraction, sought to portray raw psychological expression.

Portrait of Ambroise Vollard, **Pablo Picasso, 1909.** In the early twentieth century, Picasso and George Braque radically transformed painting with their cubist constructions, breaking the depiction of reality into fragmented planes. Vollard, an important art dealer of the period, loses recognizable form as his figure descends.

corruption of artistic culture, Nolde's contemporary James Ensor (1860–1949) later wrote that "All the rules, all the canons of art vomit death exactly like their bronze-mouthed brothers of the battlefield." Collectively referred to as expressionists, these painters turned to acid colors, violent figural distortions, and crude depictions of sexuality that shocked middle-class viewers. Inspired by the psychological dramas of his compatriot Henrik Ibsen, Edvard Munch (1863–1944) sought to express the interior consciousness of the human mind. The Austrian Egon Schiele (1890–1918) explored sexuality and the body with disturbingly raw, graphic imagery.

After the turn of the century, a diverse crop of avant-garde movements flowered across Europe. In bohemian

Paris, the Frenchman Henri Matisse (1869–1954) and Pablo Picasso (1881–1973), a Catalan Spaniard, pursued their groundbreaking aesthetic experiments in relative quiet. Clamoring for attention, on the other hand, were groups of artists who reveled in the energetic dynamism of modern life. The cubists in Paris, vorticists in Britain, and futurists in Italy all embraced a hard, angular aesthetic of the machine age. While other modernists sought an antidote to fin-de-siècle malaise by looking backward to so-called primitive cultures, these new movements embraced the future in all its uncertainty—often with the kind of aggressive, hypermasculine language that later emerged as a hallmark of fascism. In the futurist *Manifesto*, for instance, F. T. Marinetti proclaimed: "We will glorify war—the only true hygiene of the world—militarism, patriotism, the destructive gesture of anarchist, the beautiful Ideas which kill." In Russia and Holland, meanwhile, a few intensely idealistic painters made perhaps the most revolutionary aesthetic leap of early modernism, into totally abstract, or "object-less" painting.

The breadth and diversity of modern art defy simple categories and explanations. The profound changes that swept the visual arts were paralleled across the cultural spectrum (developments discussed in Chapter Twenty-Eight). And though they remained the province of a small group of artists and intellectuals before 1914, these radical revisions of artistic values entered the cultural mainstream soon after World War I.

ONCLUSION

Many Europeans who had grown up in the period from 1870 to 1914, but lived through the hardships of World War I, looked back on the prewar period as a golden age of European civilization. In one sense this retrospective view is apt. After all, the continental powers had successfully avoided major wars, enabling a second phase of industrialization to provide better living standards for the growing populations of mass society. An overall spirit of confidence and purpose fueled Europe's perceived mission to exercise political, economic, and cultural dominion in the far reaches of the world. Yet European politics and culture also registered the presence of powerful—and destabilizing—forces of change. Industrial expansion, relative abundance, and rising literacy produced a political climate of rising expectations. As the age of mass politics arrived, democrats, socialists, and feminists clamored for access to political life, threatening violence, strikes, and revolution. Marxist socialism especially changed radical politics, redefining the terms of debate for the next century. Western science, literature, and the arts explored new perspectives on the individual, undermining some of the cherished beliefs of nineteenth-century liberals. The competition and violence central to Darwin's theory of evolution, the subconscious urges that Freud found in human behavior, and the rebellion against representation in the arts all pointed in new and baffling directions. These experiments, hypotheses, and nagging questions accompanied Europe into the Great War of 1914. They would help shape Europeans' responses to the devastation of that war. After the war, the political changes and cultural unease of the period from 1870 to 1914 would reemerge in the form of mass movements and artistic developments that would define the twentieth century.

KEY TERMS

second industrial revolution	woman suffrage	Bloody Sunday	Sigmund Freud
anarchism	Dreyfus Affair	Young Turks	Friedrich Nietzsche
	Irish home rule	Charles Darwin	modernism

SELECTED READINGS

Berlanstein, Lenard. *The Working People of Paris, 1871–1914.* Baltimore, Md. 1984. A social history of the workplace and its impact on working men and women.

Berlin, Isaiah. *Karl Marx: His Life and Environment.* 4th ed. New York, 1996. An excellent short account.

Blackbourn, David. *The Long Nineteenth Century: A History of Germany, 1780–1918.* New York, 1998. Among the best surveys of German society and politics.

Bowler, Peter J. *Evolution: The History of an Idea.* Berkeley, Calif., 1984. One of the author's several excellent studies of evolution of Darwinism.

Bredin, Jean-Denis. *The Affair: The Case of Alfred Dreyfus.* New York, 1986. Detailed and readable.

Burns, Michael. *Dreyfus: A Family Affair.* New York, 1992. Follows the story Dreyfus through the next generations.

Chipp, Herschel B. *Theories of Modern Art: A Source Book by Artists and Critics.* Berkeley, Calif., 1968.

Clark, T. J. *The Painting of Modern Life: Paris in the Art of Manet and His Followers.* New York, 1985. Argues for seeing impressionism as a critique of French society.

Eley, Geoff. *Forging Democracy.* Oxford, 2002. Wide-ranging and multinational account of European radicalism from 1848 to the present.

Frank, Stephen. *Crime, Cultural Conflict, and Justice in Rural Russia, 1856–1914.* Berkeley, Calif., 1999. A revealing study of social relations from the ground up.

Gay, Peter. *The Bourgeois Experience: Victoria to Freud,* 5 vols. New York, 1984–2000. Imaginative and brilliant study of private life and middle class culture.

Gay, Peter. *Freud: A Life of Our Time.* New York, 1988. Beautifully written and lucid about difficult concepts; now the best biography.

Herbert, Robert L. *Impressionism: Art, Leisure, and Parisian Society.* New Haven, 1988. An accessible and important study of the impressionists and the world they painted.

Hughes, H. Stuart. *Consciousness and Society.* New York, 1958. A classic study on late-nineteenth-century European thought.

Jelavich, Peter. *Munich and Theatrical Modernism: Politics, Playwriting, and Performance, 1890–1914.* Cambridge, Mass., 1985. On modernism as a revolt against nineteenth-century conventions.

Jones, Gareth Stedman. *Outcast London.* Oxford, 1971. Studies the breakdown in class relationships during the second half of the nineteenth century.

Joyce, Patrick. *Visions of the People: Industrial England and the Question of Class, 1848–1914.* New York, 1991. A social history of the workplace.

Kelly, Alfred. *The German Worker: Autobiographies from the Age of Industrialization.* Berkeley, Calif., 1987. Excerpts from workers' autobiographies provide fresh perspective on labor history.

Kern, Stephen. *The Culture of Time and Space.* Cambridge, Mass., 1983. A cultural history of the late nineteenth century.

Landes, David. *The Unbound Prometheus: Technological Change and Industrial Development in Western Europe from 1750 to the Present.* New York, 1969. Includes a first-rate analysis of the second industrial revolution.

Lidtke, Vernon. *The Alternative Culture: Socialist Labor in Imperial Germany.* New York, 1985. A probing study of working-class culture.

Marrus, Michael Robert. *The Politics of Assimilation: A Study of the French Jewish Community at the Time of the Dreyfus Affair.* Oxford, 1971. Excellent social history.

Micale, Mark S. *Approaching Hysteria: Disease and Its Interpretations.* Princeton, N.J., 1995. Important study of the history of psychiatry before Freud.

Rupp, Leila J. *Worlds of Women: The Making of an International Women's Movement.* Princeton, N.J., 1997.

Schivelbusch, Wolfgang. *Disenchanted Night: The Industrialization of Light in the Nineteenth Century.* Berkeley, Calif., 1995. Imaginative study of how electricity transformed everyday life.

Showalter, Elaine. *The Female Malady: Women, Madness, and English Culture, 1890–1980.* New York, 1985. Brilliant and readable on Darwin, Freud, gender, and World War I.

Silverman, Deborah L. *Art Nouveau in Fin-de-Siècle France: Politics, Psychology, and Style.* Berkeley, 1989. A study of the relationship between psychological and artistic change.

Smith, Bonnie. *Changing Lives: Women in European History since 1700.* New York, 1988. A useful overview of European women's history.

Tickner, Lisa. *The Spectacle of Women: Imagery of the Suffrage Campaign, 1907–14.* Chicago, 1988. A very engaging study of British suffragism.

Verner, Andrew. *The Crisis of Russian Autocracy: Nicholas II and the 1905 Revolution.* Princeton, N.J., 1990. A detailed study of this important event.

Vital, David. *A People Apart: A Political History of the Jews in Europe, 1789-1939.* Oxford and New York, 1999. Comprehensive and extremely helpful.

Weber, Eugen. *Peasants into Frenchmen: The Modernization of Rural France, 1870–1914.* Stanford, 1976. A study of how France's peasantry was assimilated into the Third Republic.

CHAPTER TWENTY-FOUR

CHAPTER CONTENTS

THE FIRST
WORLD WAR

IN SEVERAL CRUCIAL RESPECTS, the twentieth century began in August 1914, with the outbreak of the World War I—a four-year conflict that dealt a lethal blow to many nineteenth-century ideals and institutions. Soldiers marched into battle with the confidence and ambition bred by imperial successes. The leading nations of Europe were at the height of their power. Europe was the center of the world economy and commanded far-flung empires. Many Europeans entered the war with faith in modernity, persuaded the future promised prosperity, peace, and progress—all the advantages of "civilization."

Despite those expectations, many people harbored fears about the future. The war justified that quiet dread. The "Great War" introduced the ugly face of industrial warfare and the grim capacities of the modern world. It caught Europeans unprepared not only militarily but also economically and politically. In a catastrophic combination of old mentalities and new technologies, the war left 9 million dead soldiers in its wake. Soldiers were not the only casualties. World War I was waged against entire nations and had profound economic and political ramifications for the people of Europe. Four years of fighting destroyed many of the institutions and assumptions of the previous century, from monarchies and empires to European economic hegemony. The war strained relations between classes and generations. It disillusioned many, even citizens of the victorious nations. As the British writer Virginia Woolf put it, "It was a shock—to see the faces of our rulers in the light of shell-fire." The war eroded the foundations of nineteenth-century economies and unleashed social upheaval. It banished older forms of authoritarianism and ushered in new ones that bore the distinctive mark of the twentieth century. Finally, the war proved nearly impossible to settle; antagonisms bred in battle only intensified in the war's aftermath and would eventually lead to the World War II. Postwar Europe faced more problems than peace could manage.

FOCUS QUESTIONS

- What were the causes of World War I?
- Why did German war plans fail?
- Why did the war become a stalemate?
- Why did the Allies persist with an offensive strategy?

 • What was the role of empire in World War I?
- What social changes did the war bring?
- What caused the Russian revolutions, and what role did the war play in their outcomes?
- How and why did the Allies win the war?

THE JULY CRISIS

What were the causes of World War I?

In the decades before 1914 Europe had built a seemingly stable peace. Through the complex negotiations of Great Power geopolitics, Europe had settled into two systems of alliance: the Triple Entente (later the Allied Powers) of Britain, France, and Russia rivaled the Triple Alliance (later the Central Powers) of Germany, Austria-Hungary, and Italy. Within this balance of power, the nations of Europe challenged one another for economic, military, and imperial advantage. The scramble for colonies abroad accompanied a fierce arms race at home, where military leaders assumed that superior technology and larger armies would result in a quick victory in a European war. Indeed the prevailing atmosphere of international suspicion made such a war seem likely to many of Europe's political and military elites. Yet none of the diplomats, spies, military planners, or cabinet ministers of Europe—nor any of their critics—predicted the war they eventually got. Nor did many expect that the Balkan crisis of July 1914 would touch off that conflict, engulfing all of Europe in just over a month's time.

The Great Powers had long been involved in the affairs of southeast Europe. The Balkans lay between two long-standing but increasingly vulnerable empires:

the Austro-Hungarian and the Ottoman. The region was also home to newly formed states under the sway of ambitious nationalist movements, pan-Slavic ethnic crusaders, and local power brokers. Balkan politics were a traditional focus for Russian intervention in European affairs and also for German and British diplomacy. Despite these entanglements, the Great Powers tried to avoid direct intervention, seeking instead to bring the new Balkan states into the web of alliances. In 1912 the independent states of Serbia, Greece, Bulgaria, and Montenegro launched the First Balkan War against the Ottomans; in 1913, the Second Balkan War was fought over the spoils of the first. Through reasonable diplomacy, the Great Powers steered clear of entanglement, and these wars remained localized. If diplomacy failed, as it ultimately did in the summer of 1914, the Great Powers' system of alliances would actually hasten the outbreak of a wider war.

The link between Balkan conflict and continental war would be the Austro-Hungarian Empire, which was struggling to survive amid increasing nationalist ambitions. The "dual monarchy," as it was called after reforms in 1867, had frustrated many ethnic groups excluded from the arrangement. Czechs and Slovenes protested their second-class status in the German half of the empire; Poles, Croats, and ethnic Romanians chafed at Hungarian rule. The province of Bosnia was particularly volatile, home to Serbs, Croats, Bosnian Muslims, and other ethnic groups and formerly part of the Ottoman Empire. In 1878, Austria-Hungary had occupied and then annexed Bosnia, drawing hatred and resistance from most of Bosnia's ethnic groups. Bosnian Serbs, in particular, had hoped to secede and join the independent kingdom of Serbia. But now the Austrians blocked their plans. So with the support of Serbia, the Bosnian Serbs began an underground war against the empire to achieve their goals. Bosnia would become the crucible of European conflict.

On June 28, 1914, Franz Ferdinand (1889–1914), archduke of Austria and heir to the Austro-Hungarian Empire, paraded through Sarajevo, the capital of Bosnia. As a hotbed of Serb resistance, Sarajevo was an admittedly dangerous place for the head of the hated empire to parade in public. The archduke had escaped an assassination attempt earlier in the day, with a

Franz Ferdinand and His Wife, Sophie. The Austrian archduke and archduchess, in Sarajevo on June 28, 1914, approaching their car before they were assassinated.

bomb barely missing his automobile. That afternoon, when the archduke's car made a wrong turn and stopped to back up, a nineteen-year-old Bosnian student named Gavrilo Princip shot Ferdinand and his wife at point-blank range. Princip was a member of the Young Bosnian Society, a national liberation group with close links to Serbia. He considered the assassination part of a struggle for his people's independence. It became the start of World War I.

Shocked by Ferdinand's death, the Austrians treated the assassination as a direct attack by the Serbian government. Eager for retribution, Austria issued an ultimatum

EUROPEAN ALLIANCES ON THE EVE OF WORLD WAR I

The Triple Alliance, among Germany, Austria-Hungary, and Italy dated back to 1882. Italy's attachment to that alliance was weak, and she had a secret agreement with France. In 1915 she entered World War I on the British and French side. The Triple Entente (or understanding) among France, Great Britain, and Russia was more recent. Economic ties between France and Russia had helped ally those powers in 1892. An escalating naval arms race between Germany and Great Britain pushed the British to settle their colonial disputes with France, formerly their bitter rival in Africa, in 1904. An Anglo-Russian agreement in 1907 completed the three way understanding. The Triple Entente also threatened to "encircle" Germany. How did the Germans react? How did the alliance system shape nations' actions and strategic calculations during the summer of 1914?

to Serbia three weeks later, demanding that the Serbian government denounce the aims and activities of the Bosnian Serbs; prohibit further propaganda and subversion; and, perhaps most provocative, allow Austro-Hungarian officials to prosecute and punish Serbian officials who the Austrians believed were involved in the assassination. The demands were deliberately unreasonable. Austria wanted war, a punitive campaign to restore order in Bosnia and crush Serbia. The Serbs recognized

the provocation and mobilized their army three hours before sending a reply, which nonetheless agreed to all but the most important Austrian demands. Austria responded with its own mobilization and declared war three days later, on July 28, 1914.

For a brief moment, it seemed possible to avoid a wider war. At first diplomats and politicians hoped to write the confrontation off as another crisis in the Balkans. Austria's steady escalation, coupled with

THE BALKAN CRISIS, 1878–1914

For background, reconsider the maps on pages 849 and 850 on the decline of Ottoman power and its effects. What problems did nationalism create in the area? What were Serbia's aims? Why was Bosnia-Herzegovina particularly volatile? Why did the Austro-Hungarian Empire care about the region? What other European powers were interested, and why?

Russia's traditional ties to Serbia, ultimately made that impossible. (Many historians also fault Germany here, for failing to coax allied Austria back from the brink.) For Austria, the conflict was a matter of prestige and power politics—a chance to reassert the fraying empire's authority in the face of the rising nationalism of its peoples. For Russia, too, the emerging conflict was an opportunity to regain some of the tsar's authority by standing up for the rights of "brother Slavs." Initially, Russia planned to respond to Austria's threat with a partial mobilization, but when the orders came down on July 30, Russia mobilized fully—its troops were readied to fight both Austria and Germany.

The crisis spread, and the Germans were prepared. Sitting in the most precarious geographic position, Germany necessarily had the most detailed war plans. Its military planners were among those who considered war inevitable and an opportunity to settle the nation's future in continental Europe. As Russia began to mobilize, Kaiser William II (1888–1918) sent an ultimatum to St. Petersburg demanding that Russian mobilization cease within twelve hours; the Russians refused. Meanwhile, the German ministers demanded to know France's intentions. Premier René Viviani (1914–1915) replied that France would act "in accordance with her interests"—which meant an immediate mobilization against Germany. Finally facing the dual threat it had long anticipated, Germany mobilized on August 1 and declared war on Russia—and two days later, on France. The next day, the German army invaded Belgium on its way to take Paris.

The invasion of neutral Belgium provided a rallying cry for the British generals and diplomats who wanted Britain to join the nascent continental conflict. Despite Britain's secret pacts with France and despite its public guarantee of Belgium's neutrality, British entry into the Great War was not a foregone conclusion. The Liberal government opposed entry and acquiesced primarily for fear of being turned out of office. Indeed, one historian has recently suggested (rather controversially) that Germany's war aims and imperial ambitions did not in fact pose a substanital threat to Britain's empire, and that the United Kingdom's best interest was to remain neutral in 1914. Proponents of war, however, could resort to an irrefutable tenet of British foreign policy: that to maintain the balance of power, no single nation should be allowed to dominate the Continent. Thus, on August 4, Britain entered the war against Germany.

Other nations were quickly drawn into the struggle. On August 7 the Montenegrins joined the Serbs in fighting Austria. Two weeks later the Japanese declared war on Germany, mainly to attack German possessions in the Far East. On August 1 Turkey allied with Germany, and in October began the bombardment of Russian ports on the Black Sea. Italy had been allied with Germany and Austria before the war; but at the outbreak of hostilities, the Italians cited a strict interpretation of their obligations and declared neutrality. They insisted that since Germany had invaded neutral Belgium, they owed Germany no protection.

The diplomatic maneuvers during the five weeks that followed the assassination at Sarajevo have been characterized as "a tragedy of miscalculation." Diplomats' hands were tied, however, by the strategic thinking and rigid timetables set by military leaders. Generals considered speed of prime importance. To them, once war seemed certain, time spent on diplomacy was time lost on the battlefield. A number of other factors also contributed to the outbreak of war when it came. For instance, while Austria negotiated about its ultimatum for three weeks, during the delay both Russia and Germany felt obliged to make shows of strength. Reasoned debate about the problem never occurred. During the crisis government officials had little contact with each other, and even less with the diplomats and ambassadors of other countries. Several heads of state, including the kaiser and the president of France, along with many of their ministers, spent most of July on vacation; they returned to find their generals holding orders for mobilization, waiting for signature. Austria's mismanagement of the crisis and Russia's inability to find a way to intervene without mobilizing its army contributed greatly to the spiraling confrontation. It is clear, however, that powerful German officials were arguing that war was inevitable. They insisted that Germany should fight before Russia recovered from its 1905 loss to Japan, and before the French army could benefit from its new three-year

CHRONOLOGY

WORLD WAR I BEGINS

Assassination of Archduke Franz Ferdinand of Austria	June 28, 1914
Austria and Russia mobilize for war	July 28, 1914
Germany declares war on Russia and France	August 1–3, 1914
Britain enters war against Germany	August 4, 1914

TOWARD WORLD WAR I: DIPLOMACY IN THE SUMMER OF 1914

The assassination of Franz Ferdinand in Sarajevo on June 28, 1914, set off an increasingly desperate round of diplomatic negotiations. As the following exchanges show, diplomats and political leaders on both sides swung from trying to provoke war to attempting to avert or, at least, contain it. A week after his nephew, the heir to the throne, was shot, Franz Joseph set out his interpretation of the long-standing conflict with Serbia and its larger implications—reprinted here.

The second selection comes from an account of a meeting of the Council of Ministers of the Austro-Hungarian Empire on July 7, 1914. The ministers disagreed sharply about diplomatic strategies and about how crucial decisions should be made.

The British foreign secretary Sir Edward Grey, for one, was shocked by Austria's demands, especially its insistence that Austrian officials would participate in Serbian judicial proceedings. The Serbian government's response was more conciliatory than most diplomats expected, but diplomatic efforts to avert war still failed. The Austrians' ultimatum to Serbia included the following demands given in the final extract here.

EMPEROR FRANZ JOSEPH OF AUSTRIA-HUNGARY TO KAISER WILLIAM II OF GERMANY, JULY 5, 1914

The plot against my poor nephew was the direct result of an agitation carried on by the Russian and Serb Pan-Slavs, an agitation whose sole object is the weakening of the Triple Alliance and the destruction of my realm.

So far, all investigations have shown that the Sarajevo murder was not perpetrated by one individual, but grew out of a well-organized conspiracy, the threads of which can be traced to Belgrade. Even though it will probably be impossible to prove the complicity of the Serb government, there can be no doubt that its policy, aiming as it does at the unification of all Southern Slavs under the Serb banner,

encourages such crimes, and that the continuation of such conditions constitutes a permanent threat to my dynasty and my lands. . . .

This will only be possible if Serbia, which is at present the pivot of Pan-Slav policies, is put out of action as a factor of political power in the Balkans.

You too are [surely] convinced after the recent frightful occurrence in Bosnia that it is no longer possible to contemplate a reconciliation of the antagonism between us and Serbia and that the [efforts] of all European monarchs to pursue policies that preserve the peace will be threatened if the nest of criminal activity in Belgrade remains unpunished.

AUSTRO-HUNGARIAN DISAGREEMENTS OVER STRATEGY

[Count Leopold Berchtold, foreign minister of Austria-Hungary] . . . both Emperor Wilhelm and [chancellor] Bethmann Hollweg had assured us emphatically of Germany's unconditional support in the event of military complications with Serbia. . . . It was clear to him that a military conflict with Serbia might bring about war with Russia. . . .

[Count Istvan Tisza, prime minister of Hungary] . . . We should decide what our demands on Serbia will be [but] should only present an ultimatum if Serbia rejected them. These demands must be hard but not so that they cannot be complied with. If Serbia accepted them, we could register a noteworthy diplomatic success and our prestige in the Balkans would be enhanced. If Serbia rejected our demands, then he too would favor military action. But he would already now go on record that we could aim at the downsizing but not the complete annihilation of Serbia because, first, this would provoke Russia to fight to the death and, second, he—as Hungarian premier—could never consent to the monarchy's annexation of a part of Serbia. Whether or not we ought to go to war with Serbia was not a matter for Germany to decide. . . .

[Count Berchtold] remarked that the history of the past years showed that diplomatic successes against Serbia might enhance the prestige of the monarchy temporarily, but that in reality the tension in our relations with Serbia had only increased.

[Count Karl Stürgkh, prime minister of Austria] . . . agreed with the Royal Hungarian Prime Minister that we and not the German government had to determine whether a war was necessary or not . . . [but] Count Tisza should take into account that in pursuing a hesitant and weak policy, we run the risk of not being so sure of Germany's unconditional support. . . .

[Leo von Bilinsky, Austro-Hungarian finance minister] . . . The Serb understands only force; a diplomatic success would make no impression at all in Bosnia and would be harmful rather than beneficial. . . .

AUSTRO-HUNGARY'S ULTIMATUM TO SERBIA

The Royal Serb Government will publish the following declaration on the first page of its official *journal* of 26/13 July:

"The Royal Serb Government condemns the propaganda directed against Austria-Hungary, and regrets sincerely the horrible consequences of these criminal ambitions.

"The Royal Serb Government regrets that Serb officers and officials have taken part in the propaganda above-mentioned and thereby imperiled friendly and neighbourly relations.

"The Royal Government . . . considers it a duty to warn officers, officials and indeed all the inhabitants of the kingdom [of Serbia], that it will in future use great severity against such persons who may be guilty of similar doings.

The Royal Serb Government will moreover pledge itself to the following:

1. to suppress every publication likely to inspire hatred and contempt against the Monarchy;

2. to begin immediately dissolving the society called *Narodna Odbrana;** to seize all its means of propaganda and to act in the same way against all the societies and associations in Serbia, which are busy with the propaganda against Austria-Hungary.

3. to eliminate without delay from public instruction everything that serves or might serve the propaganda against Austria-Hungary, both where teachers or books are concerned;

4. to remove from military service and from the administration all officers and officials who are guilty of having taken part in the propaganda against Austria-Hungary, whose names and proof of whose guilt the I. and R. Government [Imperial and Royal, that is, the Austro-Hungarian empire] will communicate to the Royal Government;

5. to consent to the cooperation of I. and R. officials in Serbia in suppressing the subversive movement directed against the territorial integrity of the Monarchy;

6. to open a judicial inquest [*enquête judiciaire*] against all those who took part in the plot of 28 June, if they are to be found on Serbian territory; the I. and R. Government will delegate officials who will take an active part in these and associated inquiries;

The I. and R. Government expects the answer of the Royal government to reach it not later than Saturday, the 25th, at six in the afternoon. . . .

*Narodna Odbrana, or National Defense, was pro-Serbian and anti-Austrian but nonviolent. The Society of the Black Hand, to which Franz Ferdinand's assassin belonged, considered Narodna Odbrana too moderate.

Ralph Menning, *The Art of the Possible: Documents on Great Power Diplomacy, 1814–1914* (New York, 1996), pp. 400, 402–403, and 414–415 (source for all three excerpts).

QUESTIONS FOR ANALYSIS

1. Emperor Franz Joseph's letter to Kaiser Wilhelm II tells of the Austrian investigation into the assassination of Archduke Franz Ferdinand. What did Franz seek from his German ally? What did the emperors understand by the phrase, "if Serbia . . . is put out of action as a factor of political power in the Balkans"? Why might the Germans support a war against Serb-sponsored terrorism?

2. Could the Serbians have accepted the Austrian ultimatum without total loss of face and sacrifice of their independence? British and Russian foreign ministers were shocked by the demands on Serbia. Others thought the Austrians were justified, and that Britain would act similarly if threatened by terrorism. If, as Leo von Bilinsky said, "The Serb understands only force," why didn't Austria declare war without an ultimatum?

conscription law, which would put more men in uniform. The same sense of urgency characterized the strategies of all combatant countries. The lure of a bold, successful strike against one's enemies, and the fear that too much was at stake to risk losing the advantage, created a rolling tide of military mobilization that carried Europe into battle.

THE MARNE AND ITS CONSEQUENCES

Why did German war plans fail?

Declarations of war were met with a mix of public fanfare and private concern. Though saber-rattling romantics envisioned a war of national glory and spiritual renewal, plenty of Europeans recognized that a continental war put decades of progress and prosperity at risk. Bankers and financiers, who might have hoped to profit from increased wartime production or

from captured colonial markets, were among those most opposed to the war. They correctly predicted that a major war would create financial chaos. Many young men, however, enlisted with excitement. On the Continent, volunteer soldiers added to the strength of conscript armies, while in Britain (where conscription wasn't introduced until 1916) over 700,000 men joined the army in the first eight weeks alone. Like many a war enthusiast, these men expected the war to be over by Christmas.

If less idealistic, the expectations of the politicians and generals in charge were also soon to be disproved. Military planners foresaw a short, limited, and decisive war—a tool to be used where diplomacy failed. They thought that a modern economy simply could not function amid a sustained war effort and that modern weaponry made protracted war impossible. They placed their bets on size and speed: bigger armies, more powerful weapons, and faster offensives would win the war. But for all of their planning, they were unable to respond to the uncertainty and confusion of the battlefield.

The Germans based their offensive on what is often called the Schlieffen plan, named for Count Alfred von

THE SCHLIEFFEN PLAN AND THE GERMAN OFFENSIVE

The map on the left details the offensive strategy developed (and modified several times) by Alfred Schlieffen, chief of the German General Staff, and Helmuth von Moltke, his successor in the decade after 1890. What strategy did they propose, and why? The map on the right shows the German offensive. How was the plan modified, and why? With what consequences?

Schlieffen (*SHLEE-fen*), chief of the German General Staff from 1890 to 1905. Schlieffen and his successor, Helmuth von Moltke the younger, modified plans several times in order to suit Germany's efficient, well-equipped, but increasingly outnumbered army. They called for attacking France first to secure a quick victory that would neutralize the Western Front and free the German army to fight Russia in the east. With France expecting an attack through Alsace-Lorraine, the Germans would instead invade through Belgium and sweep down through northwestern France to fight a decisive battle near Paris. For over a month, the German army advanced swiftly. Yet as Moltke's uncle, the celebrated Prussian general, had once observed, no plan survives first contact with the enemy. What was more, the plan overestimated the army's physical and logistical capabilities. The speed of the operation—advancing twenty to twenty-five miles a day—was simply too much for soldiers and supply lines to keep up with. They were also slowed by the resistance of the poorly armed but determined Belgian army and by the intervention of Britain's small but highly professional field army, whose trained marksmen caused terrible losses among the advancing Germans. Plans changed. First, fearing the Russians would move faster than expected, German commanders altered the offensive plan by dispatching some troops to the east instead of committing them all to the assault on France. Second, they chose to attack Paris from the northeast instead of circling to the southwest.

Nevertheless, German plans seemed to be working during August. French counterattacks into Alsace-Lorraine failed, and casualties mounted as the French lines retreated toward Paris. Yet German successes began to erode. The Belgian and British defense collapsed the German front into a single major thrust toward Paris. The French commander, Jules Joffre, who was immensely calm under pressure and almost callously indifferent to casualties, reorganized his armies and slowly drew the Germans into a trap. In September, with the Germans just thirty miles outside of the capital, Britain and France launched a successful counteroffensive at the battle of the Marne. The German line retreated to the Aisne River, and what remained of the Schlieffen Plan was dead.

After the Marne, unable to advance, the armies tried to outflank one another to the north, racing to the sea. After four months of swift charges across open ground,

> Politicians and generals began a continual search for ways to break the stalemate and to bring the war out of trenches, seeking new allies, new theaters, and new weapons. But they also remained committed to offensive tactics on the Western Front.

Germany set up a fortified, defensive position that the Allies could not break. Along an immovable front, stretching over 400 miles from the northern border of Switzerland to the English Channel, the Great Powers literally dug in for a protracted battle. By Christmas, trench warfare was born, and the war had just begun.

The Marne proved to be the most strategically important battle of the entire war. This single battle upended Europe's expectations of war and dashed hopes that it would quickly finish. The war of movement had stopped dead in its tracks, where it would remain for four years. The war would prove long, costly, and deadly. Politicians and generals began a continual search for ways to break the stalemate and to bring the war out of trenches, seeking new allies, new theaters, and new weapons. But they also remained committed to offensive tactics on the Western Front. Whether through ignorance, stubbornness, callousness, or desperation, military leaders continued to order their men to go "over the top."

Allied sucess at the Marne resulted in part from an unexpectedly strong Russian assault in eastern Prussia, which pulled some German units away from the attack on the west. But Russia's initial gains were obliterated at the battle of Tannenberg, August 26–30. Plagued with an array of problems, the Russian army was tired

Russian Prisoners in Late August 1914, after the Battle of Tannenberg. The German army, under Paul von Hindenburg and Erich Ludendorff, crushed the Russians and took 92,000 prisoners. The Russians continued to fight, but the photograph highlights the weakness of even a massive army and the scale of the combat.

and half-starved; the Germans devastated it, taking 100,000 prisoners and virtually destroying the Russian Second Army. The Russian general killed himself on the battlefield. Two weeks later, the Germans won another decisive victory at the battle of the Masurian Lakes, forcing the Russians to retreat from German territory. Despite this, Russian forces were able to defeat Austrian attacks to their south, inflicting terrible losses and thereby forcing the Germans to commit more troops to Russia. Through 1915 and 1916, the Eastern Front remained bloody and indecisive, with neither side able to capitalize on its gains.

STALEMATE, 1915

Why did the war become a stalemate?

In the search for new points of attack, both the Allies and the Central Powers added new partners. The Ottoman Empire (Turkey) joined Germany and Austria at the end of 1914. In May 1915, Italy joined the Allies, persuaded by the popular support of its citizens and lured by land and money. The Treaty of London of April 1915 promised Italy financial reparations, parts of Austrian territory, and pieces of Germany's African colonies when (and if) the Allies won the war. Bulgaria also hoped to gain territory in the Balkans and joined the war on the side of the Central Powers a few months later. The entry of these new belligerents expanded the geography of the war and introduced the possibility of breaking the stalemate in the west by waging offensives on other fronts.

GALLIPOLI AND NAVAL WARFARE

Turkey's involvement, in particular, altered the dynamics of the war, for it threatened Russia's supply lines and endangered Britain's control of the Suez Canal. To defeat Turkey quickly—and in hopes of bypassing the western front—the British first lord of the admiralty, Winston Churchill (1911–1915), argued for a naval offensive in the Dardanelles, the narrow strait separating Europe and Asia Minor. Under particularly incompetent leadership, however, the Royal Navy lacked adequate planning, supply lines, and maps to mount a successful campaign. The Allied attack began with a series of ineffective naval bombardments and mine sweeps, resulting in the loss or damage of six Allied

ships. The Allies then attempted a land invasion of the Gallipoli peninsula, beginning in April 1915. The combined force of French, British, Australian, and New Zealand troops made little headway. The Turks defended the narrow coast from positions high on fortified cliffs, and the shores were covered with nearly impenetrable barbed wire. During the disastrous landing, a British officer recalled, "the sea behind was absolutely crimson, and you could hear the groans through the rattle of musketry." The battle became entrenched on the beaches at Gallipoli, and the casualties mounted for seven months before the Allied commanders admitted defeat and ordered a withdrawal in December. The Gallipoli campaign—the first large-scale amphibious attack in history—was a major defeat for the Allies. It brought death into London's neighborhoods and the cities of Britain's industrial north. Casualties were particularly devastating in the "white dominions"—practically every town and hamlet in Australia, New Zealand, and Canada lost young men, sometimes all the sons of a single family. The campaign cost the Allies 200,000 soldiers and did little to shift the war's focus away from the deadlocked Western Front. In fact, the failure of "going around" simply reinforced the logic of fighting in the trenches.

By 1915 both sides realized that fighting this prolonged and costly "modern" war would require countries to mobilize all of their resources. As one captain put it in a letter home, "It is absolutely certainly a war of 'attrition,' as somebody said here the other day, and we have got to stick it out longer than the other side and go on producing men, money, and material until they cry quits, and that's about it, as far as I can see."

The Allies started to wage war on the economic front. Germany was vulnerable, dependent as it was on imports for at least one third of its food supply. The Allies' naval blockade against all of central Europe aimed to slowly drain their opponents of food and raw materials. Germany responded with a submarine blockade, threatening to attack any vessel in the seas around Great Britain. On May 7, 1915, the German submarine *U-20*, without warning, torpedoed the passenger liner *Lusitania*, which was secretly carrying war supplies. The attack killed 1,198 people, including 128 Americans. The attack provoked the animosity of the United States, and Germany was forced to promise that it would no longer fire without warning. (This promise proved only temporary: in 1917 Germany would again declare unrestricted submarine warfare, drawing America into the war.) Although the German blockade against Britain destroyed more tonnage, the blockade

Lusitania, **Drawing by Claus Bergen, 1915.** Despite German threats against any British or Allied vessels in the zones of war, the passenger liner *Lusitania* left New York for Liverpool at the end of April 1915. The liner was attacked and sunk as she neared the end of her trip. Bergen's drawing emphasizes the magnitude of the disaster, with civilians pitched into the water or huddled on lifeboats. It is an excellent example of the angry reaction from the Allied countries, as well as from the United States.

against Germany was more devastating in the long run, as the continued war effort placed increasing demands on the national economy.

TRENCH WARFARE

While the war escalated economically and politically, life in the trenches—the "lousy scratch holes," as a soldier called them—remained largely the same: a cramped and miserable existence of daily routines and continual killing. Indeed, some 25,000 miles of trenches snaked along the Western Front, normally in three lines on each side of "No Man's Land." The front line was the attack trench, lying anywhere from fifty yards to a mile away from the enemy. Behind the front lay a maze of connecting trenches and lines. Here is how the preeminent historian of warfare describes the scene behind the front line, where the army faced the enemy:

[H]olding it down on to, even dragging it back along that path, was a densely woven net of what staff officers call rear link—to divisional dumps, water-points, telephone exchanges, railhead, ammunitions parks, ordnance depots—whose function was to extend the reach of the army by whose effect, centripetal rather than centrifugal, was to attract it backwards towards its own base. These links were in theory elastic, but they were to prove notably rigid whenever the strain of an advance was thrown upon them, while the points to which they were anchored—corps and army bases, field parks, headquarters, forage and shell dumps, hospitals— were virtually immovable; it would take month of peace, in 1918–1919, to prise them loose form the subsoil.

The common assertion that railroads, the central symbol of an industrial age, made war more mobile, is misleading. Trains might take men to the front, but mobility ended there. Machine guns and barbed wire rendered sending men over the top a nightmare; and as the passage just cited shows, logistics too, stymied generals' efforts to regain a war of movement.

The British and French trenches were wet, cold, and filthy. Rain turned the dusty corridors into squalid mud pits and flooded the floors up to waist level. "Hell is not fire," was the grim observation of a French soldiers' paper, "the real hell is the mud." Soldiers lived with lice and large black rats, which fed on the dead soldiers and horses that cast their stench over everything. Cadavers could go unburied for months and were often just embedded in the trench walls. It was little wonder that soldiers were rotated out of the front lines frequently—after only three to seven days—to be relieved from what one soldier called "this present, ever-present, eternally present misery, this stinking world of sticky, trickling earth ceilinged by a strip of threatening sky." Indeed, the threat of enemy fire was constant: 7,000 British men were killed or wounded daily. This "wastage," as it was called, was part of the routine, along with the inspections, rotations, and mundane duties of life on the Western Front. Despite this danger, the trenches were a relatively reliable means of protection, especially compared to the casualty rates of going on the offensive.

As the war progressed, new weapons added to the frightening dimensions of daily warfare. Besides artillery, machine guns, and barbed wire, the instruments of war now included exploding bullets, liquid fire, and poison gas. Gas, in particular, brought visible change to the battlefront. First used effectively by the Germans in April 1915 at the second battle of Ypres, poison gas was not only physically devastating—especially in its later forms—but also psychologically disturbing. The deadly cloud frequently hung over the trenches, although the quick appearance of gas masks limited its effectiveness. Like other new weapons, poison gas solidified the lines and took more lives but could not end the stalemate. The war dragged through its second year, bloody and stagnant. Soldiers grew accustomed to the stalemate, while their leaders plotted ways to end it.

SLAUGHTER IN THE TRENCHES: THE GREAT BATTLES, 1916–1917

Why did the Allies persist with an offensive strategy?

War: Old and New. Chlorine gas entered the war at the first battle of Ypres in 1915; mustard gas, which burned eyes and skin, came soon after. Gas did not tilt the military balance, but it was frightening, and pictures like this added to the surreal image of World War I.

The bloodiest battles of all—those that epitomize World War I—occurred in 1916–1917. Massive campaigns in the war of attrition, these assaults produced hundreds of thousands of casualties and only minor territorial gains. These battles encapsulated the military tragedy of the war: a strategy of soldiers in cloth uniforms marching against machine guns. The result, of course, was carnage. The common response to these staggering losses was to replace the generals in charge. But though commanders changed, commands did not. Military planners continued to believe that their original strategies were the right ones and that their plans had simply been frustrated by bad luck and German determination. The "cult of the offensive" insisted that a breakthrough was possible with enough troops and enough weapons.

But the manpower needed could not be moved efficiently or protected adequately. Unprotected soldiers armed with rifles, grenades, and bayonets were simply no match for machine guns and deep trenches. Another major problem of military strategy—and another explanation for the continued slaughter—was the lack of effective communication between the front lines and general headquarters. If something went wrong at the front (which happened frequently) it was impossible for the leaders to know in time to make meaningful corrections. As the great battles of the Great War illustrate, firepower had outpaced mobility, and the Allied generals simply did not know how to respond.

VERDUN

The first of these major battles began with a German attack on the French stronghold of Verdun, near France's eastern border, in February 1916. Verdun had little strategic importance, but it quickly became a symbol of France's strength and was defended at all costs. Germany's goal was not necessarily to take the city but rather to break French morale—France's "remarkable devotion"—at a moment of critical weakness. As the German general Erich von Falkenhayn (1914–1916) said, the offensive would "compel the French to throw in every man they have. If they do so the forces of France will bleed to death." One million shells were fired on the first day of battle, inaugurating a ten-month struggle of back-and-forth fighting offensives and counteroffensives of intense ferocity at enormous cost and zero gain. Led by General Henri Pétain (1914–1918), the French pounded the Germans with artillery and received heavy bombardment in return. The Germans relied on large teams of horses, 7,000 of which were killed in a single day, to drag their guns through the muddy, cratered

> By the end of June, over 400,000 French and German soldiers were dead. "Verdun," writes one historian, "had become a place of terror and death that could not yield victory."

terrain. The French moved supplies and troops into Verdun continually. Approximately 12,000 delivery trucks were employed for service. So were 259 out of the 330 regiments of the French army. Neither side could gain a real advantage—one small village on the front changed hands thirteen times in one month alone—but both sides incurred devastating losses of life. By the end of June, over 400,000 French and German soldiers were dead. "Verdun," writes one historian, "had become a place of terror and death that could not yield victory." In the end, the advantage fell to the French, who survived and who bled the Germans as badly as they suffered themselves.

THE SOMME

Meanwhile, the British opened their own offensive against Germany farther west, beginning the battle of the Somme on June 24, 1916. The Allied attack began with a fierce five-day bombardment, blasting the German lines with a massive amount of artillery. Over 1,400 guns delivered nearly 3 million shells; the blasts could be heard all the way across the English Channel. The British assumed that this preliminary attack would break the mesh of German wire, destroy Germany's trenches, and clear the way for Allied troops to advance forward. They were tragically wrong. The shells the British used were designed for surface combat, not to penetrate the deep, reinforced trenches dug by the Germans. The wire and trenches withstood the bombardment. When

Poison Gas. Troops run through a cloud of toxic gas during a fight in Flanders, September 1917.

the British soldiers were ordered over the top toward enemy lines, they found themselves snared in wire and facing fully operational German machine guns. Each man carried sixty pounds of supplies that were to be used during the expected fighting in the German trenches. A few British commanders who had disobeyed orders and brought their men forward before the shelling ended were able to break through German lines. Elsewhere it was hardly a battle; whole British divisions were simply mowed down. Those who made it to the enemy trenches faced bitter hand-to-hand combat with pistols, grenades, knives, bayonets, and bare hands. On the first day of battle alone, a stunning 20,000 British soldiers died, and another 40,000 were wounded. The carnage continued from July until mid-November, resulting in massive casualties on both sides: 500,000 German, 400,000 British, and 200,000 French. The losses were unimaginable, and the outcome was equally hard to fathom: for all their sacrifices, neither side made any real gains. The first lesson of the Somme was offered later, by a war veteran: "Neither side had won, nor could win, the War. The War had won, and would go on winning." The futility of offensive war was not lost on the soldiers, yet morale remained surprisingly strong. Although mutinies and desertions occurred on both sides, they were rare; and surrenders became an important factor only in the final months of the war.

With willing armies and fresh recruits, military commanders maintained their strategy and pushed for victories on the Western Front again in 1917. The French general Robert Nivelle (1914–1917) promised to break through the German lines with overwhelming manpower, but the "Nivelle Offensive" (April–May 1917) failed immediately, with first-day casualties like those at the Somme. The British also reprised the Somme at the third battle of Ypres (July–October 1917), in which a half million casualties earned Great Britain only insignificant gains—and no breakthrough. The one weapon with the potential to break the stalemate, the tank, was finally introduced into battle in 1916, but with such reluctance by tradition-bound commanders that its half-hearted employment made almost no difference. Other innovations were equally indecisive. Airplanes were used almost exclusively for reconnaissance, though occasional "dogfights" did occur between German and Allied pilots. And though the Germans sent zeppelins to raid London, they did little significant damage.

Off the Western Front, fighting produced further stalemate. The Austrians continued to fend off attacks in Italy and Macedonia, while the Russians mounted a successful offensive against them on the Eastern Front. The initial Russian success brought Romania into the war on Russia's side, but the Central Powers quickly retaliated and knocked the Romanians out of the war within a few months.

The Lines of Battle on the Western Front. A British reconnaissance photo showing three lines of German trenches (right), No Man's Land (the black strip in the center), and the British trenches (partially visible to the left). The upper right hand quadrant of the photo shows communications trenches linking the front to the safe area.

Ypres. Entrenched in craters, the 16th Canadian machine-gun company endures the mud after the Third Battle of Ypres, usually called the Battle of Passchendaele (July-November, 1917). ("Passiondale" in the British pronunciation.) Ypres, along the Yperlee river near the Belgian coast, was the object of three major battles during the war. The third, an Allied offensive, aimed to attack German submarine bases and to strengthen the Allied position if Russia withdrew from the war.

The war at sea was equally indecisive, with neither side willing to risk the loss of enormously expensive battleships. The British and German navies fought only one major naval battle early in 1916, which ended in stalemate. Afterward they used their fleets primarily in the economic war of blockades.

As a year of great bloodshed and growing disillusionment, 1916 showed that not even the superbly organized Germans had the mobility or fast-paced communications to win the western ground war. Increasingly, warfare would be turned against entire nations, including civilian populations on the home front and in the far reaches of the European empires.

WAR OF EMPIRES

What was the role of empire in World War I?

Coming as it did at the height of European imperialism, the Great War quickly became a war of empires, with far-reaching repercussions. As the demands of warfare rose, Europe's colonies provided soldiers and material support. Britain, in particular, benefited from its vast network of colonial dominions and dependencies, bringing in soldiers from Canada, Australia, New Zealand, India, and South Africa. Nearly 1.5 million Indian troops served as British forces, some on the Western Front and many more in the Middle East, fighting in Mesopotamia and Persia against the Turks. The French empire, especially North and West Africa, sent 607,000 soldiers to fight with the Allies; 31,000 of them died in Europe. Colonial recruits were also employed in industry. In France, where even some French conscripts were put to work in factories, the international labor force numbered over 250,000, including workers from China, Vietnam, Egypt, India, the West Indies, and South Africa.

As the war stalled in Europe, colonial areas also became strategically important theaters for armed engagement. Although the campaign against Turkey began poorly for Britain with the debacle at Gallipoli, beginning in 1916 Allied forces won a series of battles, pushing the Turks out of Egypt and eventually capturing Baghdad, Jerusalem, Beirut, and other cities throughout the Middle East. The British commander in Egypt and Palestine was Edmund Allenby (1919–1925), who led a multinational army against the Turks. Allenby was a shrewd general and an excellent manager of men and supplies in desert conditions, but in his campaigns the support of different Arab peoples seeking independence from the Turks proved crucial. Allenby allied himself to the successful Bedouin (nomadic peoples speaking Arabic) revolts that split the Ottoman Empire; the British officer T. E. Lawrence (1914–1918) popularized the Arabs' guerrilla actions. When one of the senior Bedouin aristocrats, the emir Abdullah, captured the strategic port of Aqaba in July 1917, Lawrence took credit and entered popular mythology as "Lawrence of Arabia."

Britain encouraged Arab nationalism for its own strategic purposes, offering a qualified acknowledgment of Arab political aspirations. At the same time, for similar but conflicting strategic reasons, the British declared their support of "the establishment in Palestine of a national home for the Jewish people." Britain's foreign secretary, Arthur Balfour, made the pledge. European Zionists, who were seeking a Jewish homeland, took the Balfour Declaration very seriously. The conflicting pledges to Bedouin leaders and Zionists sowed the seeds of the future Arab-Israeli conflict. First the war and then the promise of oil drew Europe more deeply into the Middle East, where conflicting dependencies and commitments created numerous postwar problems.

1914–1915

— Fronts, end of 1914
--- Fronts, end of 1915

JAPAN
(Aug. 23, 1914)

NORWAY

SWEDEN

NORTH SEA

DENMARK

BALTIC SEA

Riga

KURLAND

British Blockade, Nov. 1914

RUSSIA
(Aug. 1, 1914)

GREAT BRITAIN
(Aug. 4, 1914)

Kiel

Hamburg

× Masurian Lakes Sept. 1914

Tannenberg Aug. 27–30, 1914 ×

POLAND

Warsaw   Brest-Litovsk

Kiev

London

NETH.

The Hague

GERMANY
(Aug. 1, 1914)

Berlin

ATLANTIC OCEAN

BEL.
(Aug. 4, 1914)

LUX.

Invasion, Aug. 1914

GALICIA

Prague

Limit of German Advance, 1915

Battle of the Marne Sept. 1915

Paris

Allied Offensive Sept.–Nov. 1915

FRANCE
(Aug. 3, 1914)

SWITZER-LAND

Munich

Vienna

Budapest

AUSTRIA-HUNGARY
(July 28, 1914)

ROMANIA

BLACK SEA

Bordeaux

Milan

SAN MARINO
(June 3, 1915)

Bucharest

Belgrade

Marseilles

ADRIATIC SEA

Sarajevo

SERBIA
(July 28, 1914)

BULGARIA
(Oct. 14, 1914)

Sofia

Constantinople

ITALY
(May 23, 1915)

Rome

MONTE-NEGRO
(Aug. 5, 1914)

ALBANIA

GREECE

Gallipoli

Salonika

Dardanelles

OTTOMAN EMPIRE
(Nov. 2, 1914)

Allied Offensive Feb. 1915– Jan. 1916

THE FIRST WORLD WAR

Allied Powers   Central Powers

Neutral nations

Dates of entry into the war: (Aug. 1, 1914)

EUROPE

Area of detail

AFRICA

NORWAY

SWEDEN

Jutland May–June 1916 ×

NORTH SEA

DENMARK

BALTIC SEA

Riga

KURLAND

RUSSIA

GREAT BRITAIN

Kiel

Hamburg

POLAND
Independent, Nov. 5, 1916

Warsaw   Brest-Litovsk

The Hague

NETH.

Berlin

Russian Offensive June–Dec. 1916

London

GERMANY

ATLANTIC OCEAN

BEL.

Somme, June–Nov. 1916 ×

LUX.

GALICIA

Prague

CARPATHIAN MTS.

Paris

Verdun, July–Dec. 1916

Munich

Vienna

Budapest

AUSTRIA-HUNGARY

ROMANIA
(Aug. 27, 1916)

BLACK SEA

FRANCE

SWITZER-LAND

Milan

Belgrade

Bucharest

PORTUGAL
(Mar. 9, 1916)

Marseilles

ADRIATIC SEA

MONTENEGRO
Surrender, Jan. 1916

SERBIA

BULGARIA

Sofia

Constantinople

SPAIN

ITALY

Rome

ALBANIA

GREECE
(Oct. 18, 1916)

Salonika

OTTOMAN EMPIRE

1916

— Fronts, Aug. 31, 1916
--- Fronts, Dec. 31, 1916

MEDITERRANEAN   SEA

A. THE GREAT WAR, 1914–1916

What were the most important developments of these years? At which point did the Western Front become stalemated, and what were the consequences? What happened on the Eastern Front?

B. THE GREAT WAR, 1917–1918

What were the key events of 1917, and how did they change the course of the war? Consider the map of 1918. Why might many German people have believed they nearly won the war? Why were developments in the Middle East significant in the war's aftermath?

IRISH REVOLT

The Ottoman Empire was vulnerable; so was the British. The demands of war strained precarious bonds to the breaking point. Before the war, long-standing tensions between Irish Catholics and the Protestant British government had reached fever pitch, and civil war was likely. The Sinn Féin (Ourselves Alone) Party had formed in 1900 to fight for Irish independence, and a home rule bill had passed Parliament in 1912. But with the outbreak of war in 1914, national interests took precedence over domestic politics: the "Irish question" was tabled, and 200,000 Irishmen volunteered for the British army. The problem festered, however, and on Easter Sunday 1916, a group of nationalists revolted in Dublin. The insurgents' plan to smuggle in arms from Germany failed, and they had few delusions of achieving victory. The British army arrived with artillery and machine guns; they shelled parts of Dublin and crushed the uprising within a week.

The revolt was a military disaster but a striking political success. Britain shocked the Irish public by executing the rebel leaders. Even the British prime minister David Lloyd George (1916–1922) thought the military governor in Dublin exceeded his authority with these executions. The martyrdom of the "Easter Rebels" seriously damaged Britain's relationship with its Irish Catholic subjects. The deaths galvanized the cause of Irish nationalism and touched off guerrilla violence that kept Ireland in turmoil for years. Finally, a new home rule bill was enacted in 1920, establishing separate parliaments for the Catholic south of Ireland and for Ulster, the northeastern counties where the majority population was Protestant. The leaders of the so-called Dáil Éireann (Irish Assembly), which had proclaimed an Irish Republic in 1918 and therefore been outlawed by Britain, rejected the bill but accepted a treaty that granted dominion status to Catholic Ireland in 1921. Dominion was followed almost immediately by civil war between those who abided by the treaty and those who wanted to absorb Ulster, but the con-

British Repression of Easter Rebellion, Dublin, 1916. British troops line up behind a moveable barricade made up of household furniture during their repression of the Irish revolt. The military action did not prevent further conflict.

flict ended in an uneasy compromise. The Irish Free State was established, and British sovereignty was partially abolished in 1937. Full status as a republic came, with some American pressure and Britain's exhausted indifference, in 1945.

THE HOME FRONT

What social changes did the war bring?

When the war of attrition began in 1915, the belligerent governments were unprepared for the strains of sustained warfare. The costs of war—in both money and manpower—were staggering. In 1914 the war cost Germany 36 million marks per day (five times the cost of the war of 1870), and by 1918 the cost had skyrocketed to 146 million marks per day. Great Britain had estimated it would need 100,000 soldiers but ended up mobilizing 3 million. The enormous task of feeding, clothing, and equipping the army became as much of a challenge as breaking through enemy lines; civilian populations were increasingly asked—or forced—to support these efforts. Bureaucrats and industrialists led the effort to mobilize the home front, focusing all parts of society on the single goal of military victory. The term *total war* was introduced to describe this intense mobilization of society. Goverment propagandists insisted that civilians were as important to the war effort as soldiers, and in many ways they were. As workers, taxpayers, and consumers, civilians were vital parts of the war economy. They produced munitions; purchased war bonds; and shouldered the burden of tax hikes, inflation, and material privations.

The demands of industrial warfare led first to a transition from general industrial manufacturing to munitions production and then to increased state control of all aspects of production and distribution. The governments of Britain and France managed to direct the economy politically, without serious detriment to the standard of living in their countries. Germany, meanwhile, put its economy in the hands of army and industry; under the Hindenburg Plan, named for Paul von Hindenburg (1916–1919), the chief of the imperial staff of the German army, pricing and profit margins were set by individual industrialists.

Largely because of the immediate postwar collapse of the German economy, historians have characterized Germany's wartime economy as a chaotic, ultimately

Women at Work.
The all-out war effort combined with a manpower shortage at home brought women into factories across Europe in unparalleled numbers. In this photo men and women work side by side in a British shell factory.

disastrous system governed by personal interest. New research, however, suggests that this was not the case: Germany's systems of war finance and commodity distribution, however flawed, were not decisively worse than those of Britain or France.

WOMEN IN THE WAR

As Europe's adult men left farms and factories to become soldiers, the composition of the workforce changed: thousands of women were recruited into fields that had previously excluded them. Young people, foreigners, and unskilled workers were also pressed into newly important tasks; in the case of colonial workers, their experiences had equally critical repercussions. But because they were more visible, it was women who became symbolic of many of the changes brought by the Great War. In Germany, one third of the labor force in heavy industry was female by the end of the war; and in France, 684,000 women worked in the munitions industry alone. In England the "munitionettes," as they were dubbed, numbered nearly a million. Women also entered the clerical and service sectors. In the villages of France, England, and Germany, women became mayors, school principals, and mail carriers. Hundreds of thousands of women worked with the army as nurses and ambulance drivers, jobs that brought them very close to the front lines. With minimal supplies and under squalid conditions, they worked to save lives or patch bodies together.

In some cases, war offered new opportunities. Middle-class women often said that the war broke down the restrictions on their lives; those in nursing learned to drive and acquired rudimentary medical knowledge. At home they could now ride the train, walk the street, or go out to dinner without an older woman present to chaperone them. In terms of gender roles, an enormous gulf sometimes seemed to separate the wartime world from nineteenth-century Victorian society. In one of the most famous autobiographies of the war, *Testament of Youth*, author Vera Brittain (1896–1970) recorded the dramatic new social norms that she and others forged during the rapid changes of wartime. "As a generation of women we were now sophisticated to an extent which was revolutionary when compared with the romantic ignorance of 1914. Where we had once spoken with polite evasion of 'a certain condition,' or 'a certain profession,' we now unblushingly used the words 'pregnancy' and 'prostitution.'" For every Vera Brittain who celebrated the changes, however, journalists, novelists, and other observers grumbled that women were now smoking, refusing to wear

the corsets that gave Victorian dresses their hourglass shape, or cutting their hair into the new fashionable bobs. The "new woman" became a symbol of profound and disconcerting cultural transformation.

How long lasting were these changes? In the aftermath of the war, governments and employers scurried to send women workers home, in part to give jobs to veterans, in part to deal with male workers' complaints that women were undercutting their wages. Efforts to demobilize women faced real barriers. Many women wage earners—widowed, charged with caring for relatives, or faced with inflation and soaring costs— needed their earnings more than ever. It was also difficult to persuade women workers who had grown accustomed to the relatively higher wages in heavy industry to return to their poorly paid traditional sectors of employment: the textile and garment industries and

SAMMELT ausgekämmtes Frauenhaar!
Unsere Industrie braucht es für Treibriemen.
Annahme:

Deutsche Frauenhaar-Sammlung vom Roten Kreuz, Sitz Magdeburg

German Poster, 1918. "Collect women's hair that has been combed out. Our industry needs it for drive belts." This poster calls on women to donate their hair, which was used to replace leather and hemp, to the war effort.

ONE WOMAN'S WAR

Vera Brittain (1893–1970) was talented, ambitious, and privileged. She was among the few women to attend Oxford University the year before the war. When war broke out, her fiancé enlisted in the British army. Brittain later joined the Voluntary Aid Detachment and served as a nurse in Europe and in the Mediterranean. In this excerpt from her memoir, Testament of Youth, Brittain writes home to her family from France in 1917, worrying about morale on the home front. She also reflects on women's different and often conflicting duties and on what the war meant to her as a sheltered girl from a well-to-do family.

"Conditions . . . certainly seem very bad," I wrote to my family on January 10th [1917] . . . "But do if you can," I implored, "try to carry on without being too despondent and make other people do the same . . . for the great fear in the Army and all its appurtenances out here is not that it will ever give up itself, but that the civil population at home will fail us by losing heart—and so of course morale—just at the most critical time. . . .

This despondency at home was certainly making many of us in France quite alarmed; because we were women we feared perpetually that, just as our work was reaching its climax, our families would need our youth and vitality for their own support. One of my cousins, the daughter of an aunt, had already been summoned home from her canteen work in Boulogne; she was only one of many, for as the War continued to wear out strength and spirits, the middle-aged generation, having irrevocably yielded up its sons, began to lean with increasing weight upon its daughters. . . .

What exhausts women in wartime is not the strenuous and unfamiliar tasks that fall upon them, nor even the hourly dread of death for husbands or lovers or brothers or sons; it is the incessant conflict between personal and national claims which wears out their energy and breaks their spirit. . . .

When I was a girl . . . I imagined that life was individual, one's own affair; that the events happening in the world outside were important enough in their own way, but were personally quite irrelevant. Now, like the rest of my generation, I have had to learn again and again . . . about the invasion of personal preoccupations by the larger destinies of mankind, and at last to recognise that no life is really private, or isolated, or self-sufficient. People's lives were entirely their own, perhaps . . . when the world seemed enormous, and all its comings and goings were slow and deliberate. But this is so no longer, and never will be again, since man's inventions have eliminated so much of distance and time; for better, for worse, we are now each of us part of the surge and swell of great economic and political movements, and whatever we do, as individuals or as nations, deeply affects everyone else.

Vera Brittain, *Testament of Youth: An Autobiographical Study of the Years 1900–1925* (London, 1989), pp. 401, 422–423, 471–472.

QUESTIONS FOR ANALYSIS

1. Keeping up morale on the home front was a serious issue for the countries at war. Besides demands for able workers to replace men in uniform and care for the casualties, Britain had to deal with labor disputes and an uprising in Ireland. France faced inflation and mutinies, which were kept secret. Germany and Russia suffered from severe shortages of munitions, supplies, and food. Yet these problems also provided women with opportunities to serve. What were the resulting social and political effects?

2. How did Brittain explain women's responses to conflicting personal and national claims during wartime? Was there "a loss of innocence" among women at home as well as among men at the front?

domestic service. The demobilization of women after the war, in other words, created as many dilemmas as had their mobilization. Governments passed "natalist" policies to encourage women to go home, marry, and—most important—have children. These policies did make maternity benefits—time off, medical care, and some allowances for the poor—available to women for the first time. Nonetheless, birth rates had been falling across Europe by the early twentieth century, and they continued to do so after the war. One upshot of the war was the increased availability of birth control—Marie Stopes (1880–1958) opened a birth-control clinic in London in 1921—and a combination of economic hardship, increased knowledge, and the demand for freedom made men and women more likely to use it. Universal suffrage, and the vote for all adult men and women, and for women in particular, had been one of the most controversial issues in European politics before the war. At the end of the fighting it came in a legislative rush. Britain was first off the mark, granting the vote to all men and women over thirty with the Representation of the People Act in 1918; the United States gave women the vote with the Nineteenth Amendment the following year. Germany's new republic and the Soviet Union did likewise. France was much slower to offer woman suffrage (1945) but did provide rewards and incentives for the national effort.

MOBILIZING RESOURCES

Along with mobilizing the labor front, the wartime governments had to mobilize men and money. All the belligerent countries had conscription laws before the war, except for Great Britain. Military service was seen as a duty, not an option. Bolstered by widespread public support for the war, this belief brought millions of young Europeans into recruitment offices in 1914. The French began the war with about 4.5 million trained soldiers, but by the end of 1914—just four months into the war—300,000 were dead and 600,000 injured. Conscripting citizens and mustering colonial troops became increasingly important. Eventually, France called up 8 million citizens: almost two thirds of Frenchmen aged eighteen to forty. In 1916, the British finally introduced conscription, dealing a serious blow to civilian morale; by the summer of 1918, half its army was under the age of nineteen.

American Propaganda Poster, World War I. The mad beast, meant to represent Germany, with *militarism* on his helmet, threatens American civilization with a club of *Kultur* (culture). All the warring countries produced similar propaganda.

In 1916, the British finally introduced conscription, dealing a serious blow to civilian morale; by the summer of 1918, half its army was under the age of nineteen.

Government propaganda, while part of a larger effort to sustain both soldier and civilian morale, was also important to the recruitment effort. From the outset, the war had been sold to the people on both sides of the conflict as a moral and righteous crusade. In 1914, the French president Raymond Poincaré (1913–1920) assured his fellow citizens that France had no other purpose than to stand "before the universe for Liberty, Justice and Reason." Germans were presented with the task of defending their superior *Kultur* (culture) against the wicked encirclement policy of the Allied nations: "May God punish England!" was practically a greeting in 1914. By the middle of the war, massive propaganda campaigns were under way. Film, posters, postcards, newspapers—all forms of media proclaimed the strength of the cause, the evil of the enemy, and the absolute necessity of total victory. The success of these campaigns is difficult to determine, but it is clear that they had at least one painful effect—they made it more difficult for any country to accept a fair, nonpunitive peace settlement.

Financing the war was another heavy obstacle. Military spending accounted for 3 to 5 percent of government expenditure in the combatant countries before 1914 but soared to perhaps half of each nation's budget during the war. Governments had to borrow money or print more of it. The Allied nations borrowed heavily from the British, who borrowed even more from the United States. American capital flowed across the Atlantic long before the United States entered the war. And though economic aid from the United States was a decisive factor in the Allies' victory, it left Britain with a $4.2 billion debt and hobbled the United Kingdom as a financial power after the war. The situation was far worse for Germany, which faced a total blockade of money and goods. In an effort to get around this predicament, and lacking an outside source of cash, the German government funded its war effort largely by increasing the money supply. The amount of paper money in circulation increased by over 1,000 percent during the war, triggering a dramatic rise in inflation. During the war, prices in Germany rose about 400 percent, double the inflation in Britain and France. For middle-class people living on pensions or fixed incomes, these price hikes were a push into poverty.

Desperation on the German Home Front, 1918. A German photograph of women digging through garbage in search of food. The last year of the war brought starvation to cities in Germany and Austria-Hungary, sending many people into the countryside to forage for provisions.

THE STRAINS OF WAR, 1917

The demands of total war worsened as the conflict dragged into 1917. On the front lines, morale fell as war-weary soldiers began to see the futility of their commanders' strategies. After the debacle of the Nivelle Offensive, the French army recorded acts of mutiny in two thirds of its divisions; similar resistance arose in nearly all major armies in 1917. Military leaders portrayed the mutineers as part of a dangerous pacifist movement, but most were nonpolitical. As one soldier put it: "All we wanted was to call the government's attention to us, make it see that we are men, and not beasts for the slaughterhouse." Resistance within the Germany army was never organized or widespread but existed in subtler forms. Self-mutilation rescued some soldiers from the horror of the trenches; many more were released because of various emotional disorders. Over 600,000 cases of "war neuroses" were reported among German troops—an indication, if not of intentional disobedience, of the severe physical and psychological trauma that caused the mutinies.

The war's toll also mounted for civilians, who often suffered from the same shortages of basic supplies that afflicted the men at the front. In 1916–1917, the lack of clothing, food, and fuel was aggravated in central Europe by abnormally cold, wet weather. These strains provoked rising discontent on the home front. Although governments attempted to solve the problem with tighter controls on the economy, their policies often provoked further hostilities from civilians. "The population has lost all confidence in promises from the authorities," a German official reported in 1917, "particularly in view of earlier experiences with promises made in the administration of food."

In urban areas, where undernourishment was worst, people stood in lines for hours to get food and fuel rations that scarcely met their most basic needs. The price of bread and potatoes—still the central staples of working-class meals—soared. Prices were even higher in the thriving black market that emerged in cities. Consumers worried aloud that speculators were hoarding supplies and creating artificial shortages, selling tainted goods, and profiting from others' miseries. They decried the government's "reckless inattention" to families. Governments, however, were concentrated on the war effort and faced difficult decisions about who needed supplies the most—soldiers at the front, workers in the munitions industry, or hungry and cold families.

Like other nations, Germany moved from encouraging citizens to restrain themselves—"those who stuff themselves full, those who push out their paunches in all directions, are traitors to the Fatherland"—to direct control, issuing ration cards in 1915. Britain was the last to institute control, rationing bread only in 1917 when Germany's submarines sank an average of 630,000 tons per month and brought British food reserves within two weeks of starvation level. But rations indicated only what was allowed, not what was available. Hunger continued despite mass bureaucratic control. Governments regulated not only food but also working hours and wages; and unhappy workers directed their anger at the state, adding a political dimension to labor disputes and household needs. The bread lines, filled mainly by women, were flash points of political dissent, petty violence, even large-scale riots. Likewise, the class conflicts of prewar Europe had been briefly muffled by the outbreak of war and mobilization along patriotic lines, but as the war ground on, political tensions reemerged with new intensity. Thousands of strikes erupted throughout Europe, involving millions of frustrated workers. In April 1917, 300,000 in Berlin went on strike to protest ration cuts. In May, a strike of Parisian seamstresses touched off a massive work stoppage that included even white-collar employees and munitions workers. Shipbuilders and steelworkers in Glasgow went on strike as well, and the British government replied by sending armored cars to "Red Glasgow." Stagnation had given way to crisis on both sides. The strains of total war and the resulting social upheavals threatened political regimes throughout Europe. Governments were pushed to their limits. The Russian Revolution, which resulted in the overthrow of the tsar and the rise of Bolshevism, was only the most dramatic response to widespread social problems.

THE RUSSIAN REVOLUTIONS OF 1917

What caused the Russian revolutions, and what role did the war play in their outcomes?

The first country to break under the strain of total war was tsarist Russia. The outbreak of war temporarily united Russian society against a common enemy, but Russia's military effort quickly turned sour. All levels of Russian society became disillusioned with Tsar Nicholas II who was unable to provide leadership was but nonetheless unwilling to open government to those who could. The political and social strains of war brought two revolutions in 1917. The first, in February, overthrew the tsar and established a transitional government. The second, in October, was a communist revolution that marked the emergence of the Soviet Union.

WORLD WAR I AND THE FEBRUARY REVOLUTION

Like the other participants in World War I, Russia entered the war with the assumption that it would be over quickly. Autocratic Russia, plagued by internal difficulties before 1914 (see Chapter Twenty-Five), could not sustain the political strains of extended warfare. In all the warring countries success depended on leaders' ability not only to command but also to maintain social and political cooperation. Tsar Nicholas II's political authority had been shaky for many years, undermined by his unpopular actions following the October Revolution of 1905 and his efforts to erode the minimal political power he had grudgingly granted to the Duma, Russia's parliament. Corruption in the royal court further tarnished the tsar's image. The best Nicholas's supporters could say about him was that he was morally upright and devoted to his family. Once war broke out the tsar insisted on personally commanding Russian troops, leaving the government in the hands of his court, especially his wife, Alexandra, and her eccentric spiritual mentor and faith healer, Grigorii Rasputin (1872?–1916). Rasputin won the tsarina's sympathy by treating her hemophiliac son, and he used his influence to operate corrupt and self-aggrandizing schemes. His presence only added to

WHAT CAUSED THE RUSSIAN REVOLUTIONS, AND WHAT ROLE DID THE WAR PLAY IN THEIR OUTCOMES?

THE RUSSIAN REVOLUTIONS OF 1917   889

Grigorii Rasputin. Rasputin won the trust of the Russian Tsar's family by presenting himself as a faith healer, and one who could help the Tsar's son, Alexei, who suffered from hemophilia. The rising influence of the "holy man" heightened perceptions that the Tsar was mired in the past and unable to lead Russia to the future.

the image of a court mired in decadence, incompetent to face the modern world.

In 1914, the Russians advanced against the Austrians into Galicia in the south, but during 1914 and 1915 Russia suffered terrible defeats. All of Poland and substantial territory in the Baltics fell to the Germans at the cost of a million Russian casualties. Although the Russian army was the largest in Europe, it was poorly trained and, at the beginning of the war, undersupplied and inadequately equipped. In the first battles of 1914, generals sent soldiers to the front without rifles or shoes, instructing them to scavenge supplies from fallen comrades. By 1915, to the surprise of many, Russia was producing enough food, clothing, and ammunition, but political problems blocked the supply effort. The tsarist government distrusted public

> By 1915, to the surprise of many, Russia was producing enough food, clothing, and ammunition, but political problems blocked the supply effort.

initiatives and tried to direct all provisioning itself. Tsarist officials insisted on making crucial decisions about the allocation of supplies without any consultation. Another major offensive in the summer of 1916 brought hope for success but turned into a humiliating retreat. Demoralized and poorly supplied, the hastily trained peasants in the Russian armies found their will to fight disappearing fast. When word came that the government was requisitioning grain from the countryside to feed the cities, peasants began to desert en masse, returning to their farms to guard their families' holdings. By the end of 1916, a combination of political ineptitude and military defeat brought the Russian state to the verge of collapse.

The same problems that hampered the Russian war effort also crippled the tsar's ability to override domestic discontent and resistance. As the war dragged on, the government faced not only liberal opposition in the Duma, soldiers unwilling to fight, and an increasingly militant labor movement but also a rebellious urban population. City dwellers were impatient with inflation and shortages of food and fuel. In February 1917, these forces came together in Petrograd (now St. Petersburg). The revolt began on International Women's Day, February 23, an occasion for a loosely organized march of women—workers, mothers, wives, and consumers—demanding food, fuel, and political reform. The march was the latest in a wave of demonstrations and strikes that had swept through the country during the winter months. This time, within a few days the unrest spiraled into a mass strike of 300,000 people. Nicholas II sent in police and military forces to quell the disorder. When nearly 60,000 troops in Petrograd mutinied and joined the revolt, what was left of the tsar's power evaporated. Nicholas II abdicated the throne on March 2. This abrupt decision brought a century-long struggle over Russian autocracy to a sudden end.

After the collapse of the monarchy, two parallel centers of power emerged. Each had its own objectives and policies. The first was the provisional government, organized by leaders in the Duma and composed mainly of middle-class liberals. The new government hoped to establish a democratic system under constitutional rule. Its main task was to set up a national election for a constituent assembly, and it also acted to grant and secure civil liberties, release political prisoners, and redirect power into the hands of local officials. The other center of power lay with the

Russian soldiers in retreat, July 1917.

soviets, a Russian term for local councils elected by workers and soldiers. Since 1905, socialists had been active in organizing these councils, which claimed to be the true democratic representatives of the people. A soviet, organized during the 1905 revolution and led by the well-known socialist Leon Trotsky, reemerged after February 1917 and asserted claim to be the legitimate political power in Russia. The increasingly powerful soviets pressed for social reform, the redistribution of land, and a negotiated settlement with Germany and Austria. Yet the provisional government refused to concede military defeat. Continuing the war effort made domestic reform impossible and cost valuable popular support. More fighting during 1917 was just as disastrous as before, and this time the provisional government paid the price. By autumn desertion in the army was rampant, administering the country was nearly impossible, and Russian politics teetered on the edge of chaos.

THE BOLSHEVIKS AND THE OCTOBER REVOLUTION

The Bolsheviks, a branch of the Russian social democratic movement, had little to do with the events of February 1917. Over the course of the next seven months, however, they became enough of a force to

overthrow the provisional government. The chain of events leading to the October revolution surprised most contemporary observers, including the Bolsheviks themselves. Marxism had been quite weak in late-nineteenth-century Russia, although it made small but rapid inroads during the 1880s and 1890s. In 1903 the leadership of the Russian Social Democrats split over revolutionary strategy and the steps to socialism. One group, which won a temporary majority (and chose to call itself the Bolsheviks, or "members of the majority"), favored a centralized party of active revolutionaries. They believed that revolution alone would lead directly to a socialist regime. The Mensheviks (members of the minority), like most European socialists, wanted to move toward socialism gradually, supporting bourgeois or liberal revolution in the short term. Because peasants constituted 80 to 85 percent of the population, the Mensheviks also reasoned that a proletarian revolution was premature and that Russia needed to complete its capitalist development first. The Mensheviks regained control of the party, but the Bolshevik splinter party survived under the leadership of the young, dedicated revolutionary Vladimir Ilyich Ulyanov, who adopted the pseudonym Lenin.

Lenin was a member of the middle class; his father had been an inspector of schools and a minor political functionary. Lenin himself had been expelled from university for engaging in radical activity after his elder brother was executed for involvement in a plot to assassinate Tsar Alexander III. Lenin spent three years as a political prisoner in Siberia. After that, from 1900 until 1917, he lived and wrote as an exile in western Europe.

Lenin believed that the development of Russian capitalism made socialist revolution possible. To bring revolution, he argued, the Bolsheviks needed to organize on behalf of the new class of industrial workers. Without the party's disciplined leadership, Russia's factory workers could not accomplish change on the necessary scale. Lenin's Bolsheviks remained a minority among Social Democrats well into 1917 and industrial workers, a small part of the population. But the Bolsheviks' dedication to the singular goal of revolution and their tight, almost conspiratorial organization gave them tactical advantages over larger and more loosely organized

WHAT CAUSED THE RUSSIAN REVOLUTIONS, AND WHAT ROLE DID THE WAR PLAY IN THEIR OUTCOMES?

THE RUSSIAN REVOLUTIONS OF 1917   891

Russian Revolution. Russian demonstrators scatter as tsarist troops shoot into the crowd during the February Revolution, 1917.

workers, into organizing a Bolshevik attack on the provisional government on October 24–25, 1917. On October 25, Lenin appeared from hiding to announce to a stunned meeting of Soviet representatives that "all power had passed to the Soviets." The head of the provisional government fled to rally support at the front lines, and the Bolsheviks took over the Winter Palace, the seat of the provisional government. The initial stage of the revolution was quick and relatively bloodless. In fact, many observers believed they had seen nothing more than a coup d'état, one that might quickly be reversed. Life in Petrograd went on as normal.

opposition parties. The Bolsheviks merged a peculiarly Russian tradition of revolutionary zeal with Western Marxism and endowed the mix with a sense that their goals could be achieved immediately. Lenin and his followers created a party capable of seizing the moment that history presented when the tsar left the scene.

Throughout 1917 the Bolsheviks consistently demanded an end to the war, improvement in working and living conditions for workers, and redistribution of aristocratic land to the peasantry. Popular discontent with the provisional government shot up after the government's disastrous military offensives against the Germans. The provisional government tried to enlist a conservative military leader, General Lavr Kornilov, to bring order to Petrograd by military force. While the provisional government struggled to hold together the Russian war effort, Lenin led the Bolsheviks on a bolder course, shunning any collaboration with the "bourgeois" government and condemning its imperialist war policies. Even most Bolsheviks considered Lenin's approach too radical. Yet as conditions in Russia deteriorated, his uncompromising calls for "Peace, Land, and Bread, Now" and "All Power to the Soviets" won the Bolsheviks support from workers, soldiers, and peasants. As many ordinary people saw it, the other parties could not govern, win the war, or achieve an honorable peace. While unemployment continued to climb and starvation and chaos reigned in the cities, the Bolsheviks' power and credibility were rising fast.

In October 1917, Lenin convinced his party to act. He goaded Trotsky, who was better known among

The Bolsheviks took the opportunity to rapidly consolidate their position. First, they moved against all political competition, beginning with the soviets. They immediately expelled parties that disagreed with their actions, creating a new government in the soviets composed entirely of Bolsheviks. Trotsky, sneering at moderate socialists who walked out to protest what they saw as an illegal seizure of power, scoffed: "You are a mere handful, miserable, bankrupt; your role is finished, and you may go where you belong—to the garbage heap of history." The Bolsheviks did follow through on the provisional government's promise to elect a Constituent Assembly. But when they did not win a majority in the elections, they refused to let the assembly reconvene. From that point on, Lenin's Bolsheviks ruled socialist Russia, and later the Soviet Union, as a one-party dictatorship.

In the countryside, the new Bolshevik regime did little more than ratify a revolution that had been going on since the summer of 1917. When peasant soldiers at the front heard that a revolution had occurred, they streamed home to take land they had worked for generations and believed was rightfully theirs. The provisional government had set up commissions to deal methodically with the legal issues surrounding the redistribution of land, a process that threatened to become as complex as the emancipation of the serfs in 1861. The Bolsheviks simply approved the spontaneous redistribution of the nobles' land to peasants without compensation to former owners. They nationalized banks and gave workers control of factories.

TOWARD THE OCTOBER REVOLUTION: LENIN TO THE BOLSHEVIKS

In the fall of 1917, Lenin was virtually the only Bolshevik leader who believed that an insurrection should be launched immediately. As the provisional government faltered, he attempted to convince his fellow Bolsheviks that the time for revolution had arrived.

Having obtained a majority in the Soviets of Workers' and Soldiers' Deputies of both capitals, the Bolsheviks can and *must* take power into their hands.

They can do so because the active majority of the revolutionary elements of the people of both capitals is sufficient to attract the masses, to overcome the resistance of the adversary, to vanquish him, to conquer power and to retain it. For, in offering immediately a democratic peace, in giving the land immediately to the peasants, in re-establishing the democratic institutions and liberties which have been mangled and crushed by Kerensky [leader of the provisional government], the Bolsheviks will form a government which *nobody* will overthrow. . . .

The majority of the people is *with* us. . . .[T]he majority in the Soviets of the capitals is the *result* of the people's progress *to our side*. The vacillation of the Socialist-Revolutionaries and Mensheviks . . . is proof of the same thing . . .

To "wait" for the Constituent Assembly would be wrong. . . . Only our party, having assumed power, can secure the convocation of the Constituent Assembly; and, after assuming power, it could blame the other parties for delaying it and could substantiate its accusations. . . .

It would be naive to wait for a "formal" majority on the side of the Bolsheviks; no revolution ever waits for this. . . . History will not forgive us if we do not assume power now.

No apparatus? There is an apparatus: the Soviets and democratic organisations. The international situation *just now*, on the *eve* of a separate peace between the English and the Germans, is *in our favour*. It is precisely now that to offer peace to the peoples means to *win*.

Assume power *at once* in Moscow and in Petrograd . . . ; we will win *absolutely and unquestionably*.

Vladimir Ilyich Lenin, *Bol'sheviki dolzhny vzyat'vlast'* (The Bolsheviks *must seize power*), cited in Richard Sakwa, *The Rise and Fall of the Soviet Union, 1917–1991* (New York and London, 1999), p. 45.

QUESTIONS FOR ANALYSIS

1. Lenin was surprised by the sudden collapse of the tsarist regime in the February Revolution of 1917. Why did he think the Bolsheviks could seize power? What were the key elements of his strategy for winning the necessary popular support?
2. Convinced he was right, Lenin returned to Petrograd in disguise and personally presented his arguments for an armed takeover to the Bolshevik Central Committee. What did he mean by saying that "it would be naive to wait for a 'formal' majority on the side of the Bolsheviks; no revolution ever waits for *this*"?

Most important, the new government sought to take Russia out of the war. It eventually negotiated a separate treaty with Germany, signed at Brest-Litovsk in March 1918. The Bolsheviks surrendered vast Russian territories: the rich agricultural region of Ukraine, Georgia, Finland, Russia's Polish territories, the Baltic states, and more. However humiliating, the treaty ended Russia's role in the fighting and saved the fledgling communist regime from almost certain military defeat at the hands of the Germans. The treaty enraged Lenin's political enemies, both moderates and reactionaries, who were still a force to be reckoned with—

and who were prepared to wage a civil war rather than accept the revolution. Withdrawing from Europe's war only plunged the country into a vicious civil conflict (see Chapter Twenty-Eight).

Russian autocracy had fended off opposition for the better part of a century. After a long struggle, the regime, weakened by the war, had collapsed with little resistance. By the middle of 1917, Russia was not suffering a crisis of government but rather an absence of government. In June, at the First All-Russian Congress of Soviets, a prominent Menshevik declared, "At the present moment, there is not a political party in Russia that would say: Hand the power over to us, resign, and we will take your place. Such a party does not exist in Russia." Lenin shouted back from the audience, "It does exist!" Indeed, seizing power had been easy for the Bolsheviks, but building the new state proved vastly more difficult.

John Reed, an American journalist covering the Russian Revolution, called the events of October "ten days that shook the world." What had been shaken? First, the Allies, for the revolution allowed the Germans to win the war on the Eastern Front. Second, conservative governments, which in the aftermath of the war worried about a wave of revolution sweeping away other regimes. Third, the expectations of many socialists, startled to see a socialist regime gain and hold power in what many considered a backward country. Over the long run, 1917 was to the twentieth century what the French Revolution had been to the nineteenth century. It was a political transformation, it set the agenda for future revolutionary struggles, and it created the frames of mind on the right and the left for the century that followed.

THE ROAD TO GERMAN DEFEAT, 1918

How and why did the Allies win the war?

Russia's withdrawal dealt an immediate strategic and psychological blow to the Allies. Germany could soothe domestic discontent by claiming victory on the Eastern Front, and it could now concentrate its entire army in the west. The Allies feared that Germany would win the war before the United States, which entered the conflict in April 1917, could make a difference. It almost happened. With striking results, Germany shifted its offensive strategy to infiltration by small groups under flexible command. On March 21, Germany initiated a major assault on the west and quickly broke through the Allied lines. The British were hit hardest. Some units, surrounded, fought to the death with bayonets and grenades, but most recognized their plight and surrendered, putting tens of thousands of prisoners in German hands. The British were in retreat everywhere and their commander, Sir Douglas Haig, issued a famous order warning that British troops "now fight with our backs to the wall." The Germans advanced to within fifty miles of Paris by early April. Yet the British—and especially troops from the overseas empire—did just as they were asked and stemmed the tide. As German forces turned southeast instead, the French, who had refused to participate in the foolish attacks over the top, showed stubborn courage on the defensive, where they bogged down in heat, mud, and casualties. It had been a last great try by the well-organized German army; exhausted, it now waited for the Allies to mount their own attack.

When it came in July and August, the Allied counterattack was devastating and quickly gathered steam. New offensive techniques had finally materialized. The Allies improved their use of tanks and the "creeping barrage," in which infantry marched close behind a rolling wall of shells to overwhelm their targets. In

Vladimir Ilyich Lenin. Lenin speaking in Moscow in 1918, at the first anniversary of the October revolution. A forceful speaker and personality, Lenin was the single most powerful politician in Russia between October 1917 and his death in 1924.

another of the war's ironies these new tactics were pioneered by the conservative British, who launched a crushing counterattack in July, relying on the survivors of the armies of the Somme reinforced by troops from Australia, Canada, and India. The French made use of the burgeoning numbers of American troops, whose generals attacked the Germans with the same harrowing indifference to casualties shown in 1914. Despite their lack of experience, the American troops were tough and resilient. When combined with more experienced French and Australian forces, they punched several large holes through German lines, crossing into the "lost provinces" of Alsace and Lorraine by October. At the beginning of November, the sweeping British offensive had joined up with the small Belgian army and was pressing toward Brussels.

The Allies finally brought their material advantage to bear on the Germans, who were suffering acutely by the spring of 1918. This was not only because of the continued effectiveness of the Allied blockade but also because of growing domestic conflict over war aims. On the front lines, German soldiers were exhausted. Following the lead of their distraught generals, the troops let morale sink, and many surrendered. Facing one shattering blow after another, the German army was pushed deep into Belgium. Popular discontent mounted, and the government, which was now largely in the hands of the military, seemed unable either to win the war or to meet basic household needs.

Germany's network of allies was also coming undone. By the end of September, the Central Powers were headed for defeat. In the Middle East, Allenby's army, which combined Bedouin guerrillas, Indian sepoys, Scottish highlanders, and Australian light cavalry, decisively defeated Ottoman forces in Syria and Iraq. In the Balkans, France's capable battlefield commander, Louis Franchet d'Esperey (1914–1921), completely reorganized the Allied war effort. He transformed the Allied expedition that had been sent to Greece and with the help of sympathetic Greek politicians drew that country into the war. The results were remarkable. In September, a three-week offensive by the Greek and Allied forces knocked Bulgaria out of the war. Franchet d'Esperey's army, which included many exiled Serbs, pushed on to defeat Austrian forces and a number of exhausted German divisions. Austria-Hungary faced disaster on all sides, collapsing in Italy as well as the Balkans. Czech and Polish representatives in the Austrian government began pressing for self-government. Croat and Serb politicians proposed a "kingdom of Southern Slavs" (soon known as Yugoslavia). When Hungary joined the chorus for independence the emperor, Karl I, accepted reality and sued for peace. The empire that had started the conflict surrendered on November 3, 1918, and disintegrated soon after.

Germany was now left with the impossible task of carrying on the struggle alone. By the fall of 1918, the country was starving and on the verge of civil war. German forces in Belgium stemmed the British attack short of Brussels but were still reeling from French and American attacks to the south. A plan to use the German surface fleet to attack the combined British and American navies only produced a mutiny among German sailors at the start of November. Revolutionary tremors swelled into an earthquake. On November 8 a republic was proclaimed in Bavaria, and the next day nearly all of Germany was in the throes of revolution. The kaiser's abdication was announced in Berlin on November 9; he fled to Holland early the next morning. Control of the German government fell to a provisional council headed by Friedrich Ebert (1912–1923), the socialist leader in the Reichstag. Ebert and his colleagues immediately took steps to negotiate an armistice. The Germans could do nothing but accept the Allies' terms, so at five o'clock in the morning of November 11, 1918, two German delegates met with the Allied army commander in the Compiègne forest and signed papers officially ending the war. Six hours later the order for cease fire was given across the Western Front. That night thousands of people danced through the streets of London, Paris, and Rome, engulfed in a different delirium from that four years before, a joyous burst of exhausted relief.

Casualty of War. A German soldier killed during the Allies' October 1917 offensive.

The United States as a World Power

The final turning point of the war had been the entry of the United States in April 1917. Although America had supported the Allies financially throughout the war, its official intervention undeniably tipped the scales. The United States created a fast and efficient wartime bureaucracy, instituting conscription in May 1917. About 10 million men were registered, and by the next year, 300,000 soldiers a month were being shipped "over there." Large amounts of food and supplies also crossed the Atlantic, under the armed protection of the U.S. Navy. This system of convoys effectively neutralized the threat of German submarines to Allied merchant ships: the number of ships sunk fell from 25 to 4 percent. America's entry—though not immediately decisive—gave a quick, colossal boost to British and French morale, while severely undermining Germany's.

Soldiers in the American Expedition Forces wearing gas masks.

The direct cause of America's entry into the war was the German U-boat. Germany had gambled that unrestricted submarine warfare would cripple Britain's supply lines and win the war. But by attacking neutral and unarmed American ships, Germany only provoked an opponent it could not afford to fight. Germany correctly suspected that the British were clandestinely receiving war supplies from U.S. passenger ships; and on February 1, 1917, the kaiser's ministers announced that they would sink all ships on sight, without warning. The American public was further outraged by an intercepted telegram from Germany's foreign minister, Arthur Zimmerman (1916–1917), stating that Germany would support a Mexican attempt to capture American territory if the United States entered the war. The United States cut off diplomatic relations with Berlin, and on April 6 President Woodrow Wilson (1913–1921) requested and received a declaration of war by Congress.

Wilson vowed that America would fight to "make the world safe for democracy," to banish autocracy and militarism, and to establish a league or society of nations in place of the old diplomatic maneuvering. The Americans' primary interest was maintaining the international balance of power. For years, U.S. diplomats and military leaders believed that American security depended on the equilibrium of strength in Europe. As long as Britain could prevent any one nation from achieving supremacy on the Continent, the United States was safe. But now Germany threatened not only the British navy—which had come to be seen as the shield of American security—but also the international balance of power. American involvement stemmed those threats in 1918, but the monumental task of establishing peace still lay ahead.

Total War

The search for peace was spurred by shock at the murderousness of the war. As early as 1915 contemporaries were speaking of "the Great War"; the transformations were there for all to see. The changing technologies of warfare altered strategic calculations. New artillery was heavier, with a longer range and more deadly results: German mobile howitzers, such as "Big Bertha," could fire shells of over 1,000 pounds at a targets nine miles and even farther away. (One shelled Paris from seventy-five miles out.) Most innovations, however, favored defense. Offensive movement became increasingly difficult, and sending men over the top cost more in lives than it gained in territory. Communications lagged behind firepower. Although communications worked relatively well in the trenches, as soon as men advanced, they were in communications no-man's land, where even the best-laid plans (and most were not) became chaotic. In 1918 wireless sets made a difference; until then armies relied on runners. This was modern, industrialized warfare, first glimpsed in the American Civil

C H R O N O L O G Y

MAJOR EVENTS OF WORLD WAR I AND ITS AFTERMATH, 1914–1920

Battle of the Marne	September 1914
Gallipoli campaign	April–December 1915
Sinking of the *Lusitania*	May 1915
Battle of Verdun	February–July 1916
Battle of the Somme	July–November 1916
Russian revolutions	
Tsar Nicholas II overthrown	February 1917
Communist Revolution	October 1917
Treaty of Brest-Litovsk	March 1918
Russian Civil War	1918–1920
United States enters the war	April 1917
Final offensives	March–November 1918
Germany surrenders	November 11, 1918
Paris negotiations	1919–1920

War but now more advanced and on a much larger scale. It still deployed cloth-uniformed men, heartbreakingly unprotected against the newly destructive weapons. And it still required human intelligence, speed, brute force—or courage—on a massive scale. The statistics and what they imply still strain the imagination: 74 million soldiers were mobilized on both sides; 6,000 people were killed each day for more than 1,500 days.

The warring nations, Europe's new industrial powerhouses, were also empires. Hence the "world" war. Historian Jay Winter describes the war as a gigantic and deadly whirlwind; when it stalled, deadlocked, on the Western Front, "more human and material resources were drawn inexorably into its vortex." Those resources came from all over the globe. Mobilization also reached more deeply into civilian society. Economies bent to military priorities. Propaganda escalated to sustain the effort, fanning old hatreds and creating new ones. Atrocities against civilians came in its wake. Europe had known brutal wars against civilians before, and guerilla war during the time of Napoleon, but World War I vastly magnified the violence and multiplied the streams of refugees. Minorities who lived in the crumbling Russian, Austro-Hungarian, or Ottoman Empires were especially vulnerable. Jewish populations in Russia had lived in fear of pogroms before 1914; now they were attacked by Russian soldiers who accused them of encouraging the enemy. Austria-Hungary, like-

wise, summarily executed minorities suspected of Russian sympathies. The worst atrocities came against the Armenian community in Turkey. Attacked by the Allies at Gallipoli (although, as we saw earlier, the 1915 Allied landing turned into an Allied catastrophe) and at war with the Russians to the north, the Turkish government turned on its Armenian subjects, labeling them a security risk. Orders came down for "relocation," and relocation became genocide. Armenian leaders were arrested; Armenian men were shot; and entire Armenian villages were force marched to the south, robbed, and beaten to death along the way. Over the course of the war, a million Armenians died.

All of these developments—military, economic, and psychological mobilization; a war that tested the powers of a state and its economy; violence against civilians—were the component parts of total war and foreshadowed the conflict to be unleashed in 1939.

TRANSFORMATION: THE PEACE SETTLEMENT

 The Paris Peace Conference, which opened in January 1919, was an extraordinary moment, one that dramatized just how much the world had been transformed by the war and the decades that preceded it. Gone were the Russian, Austro-Hungarian, and German Empires. That the American president Woodrow Wilson played such a prominent role marked the rise of the United States as a world power. The United States' new status was rooted in the economic development of the second industrial revolution during the nineteenth century. In mass production and technological innovation, it had rivaled the largest European powers (England and Germany) before the war. During the war, American intervention (although it came late) had decisively broken the military-economic deadlock. And in the war's aftermath American industrial culture, engineering, and financial networks loomed very large on the European Continent. Wilson and his entourage spent several months in Paris at the conference—a first for an American president while in office and European leaders, first extended encounter with an American head of state.

American prominence was far from the only sign of global change. Some thirty nations sent delegates to the peace conference, a reflection of three factors: the scope of the war, heightened national sentiment and aspiration, and the tightening of international communication and economic ties in the latter part of the nineteenth century. The world in 1900 was vastly more globalized than it had been fifty years earlier. Many more countries had political, economic, and human investments in the war and its settlement. A belief that peace would secure and be secured by free peoples in sovereign nations represented the full flowering of nineteenth-century liberal nationalism. Delegates came to work for Irish home rule, for a Jewish state in Palestine and for nations in Poland, Ukraine, and Yugoslavia. Europe's colonies, which had been key to the war effort and were increasingly impatient with their status, sent delegates to negotiate for self-determination. As we will see, however, the western European leaders' commitment to the principle of national self-determination was hedged by their imperial assumptions. Non-state actors —in other words international groups asking for women's suffrage, civil rights, minimum wages, or maximum hours—came to the Paris Peace Conference as well, for these were now seen as international issues. Last, reporters from all over the world wired news home from Paris, a sign of vastly improved communications, transatlantic cables, and the mushrooming of the mass press.

"Long Live Wilson!" Paris crowds greet President Wilson after the war. Despite public demonstrations of this sort, Wilson's attempt to shape the peace was a failure.

Making peace was easier said than done. Conflicting ambitions and interests complicated the process. Although many attended, the conference was largely controlled by the so-called Big Four: the U.S. president Woodrow Wilson, the British prime minister David Lloyd George (1916–1922), the French premier Georges Clemenceau (1917–1920), and the Italian premier Vittorio Orlando (1917–1919). In total, five separate treaties were signed, one with each of the defeated nations: Germany, Austria, Hungary, Turkey, and Bulgaria. The settlement with Germany was called the Treaty of Versailles, after the town in which it was signed.

Wilson's widely publicized Fourteen Points represented the spirit of idealism. Wilson had proposed the Fourteen Points before the war ended, as the foundation of a permanent peace. Based on the principle of "open covenants of peace, openly arrived at," they called for an end to secret diplomacy, freedom of the seas, removal of international tariffs, and reduction of national armaments "to the lowest point consistent with safety." They also called for the "self-determination of peoples"

and for the establishment of the League of Nations to settle international conflicts. Thousands of copies of the Fourteen Points had been scattered by Allied planes over the German trenches and behind the lines in an attempt to convince both soldiers and civilians that the Allied nations were striving for a just and durable peace. They shaped the expectations that Germans brought to the peace talks. "The day of conquest and aggrandizement is gone by; so is also the day of secret covenants entered into in the interest of particular governments," Wilson had said. "It is this happy fact . . . which makes it possible for every nation whose purposes are consistent with justice and the peace of the world to avow now or at any other time the objects it has in view."

Idealism, however, was undermined by other imperatives. Throughout the war, Allied propaganda led soldiers and civilians to believe that their sacrifices to the war effort would be compensated by payments extracted from the enemy. Total war demanded total victory. Lloyd George had campaigned during the British election of 1918 on the slogan "Hang the Kaiser!" Clemenceau had twice in his long lifetime seen France invaded and its existence imperiled. With the tables turned, he believed that the French should take full advantage of their opportunity to place Germany under strict control. The devastation of the war and the fiction that Germany could be made to pay for it made compromise impossible. The settlement with Germany reflected this desire for punishment.

The Versailles treaty required Germany to surrender the "lost provinces" of Alsace and Lorraine to France and to give up territories in the north to Denmark and a large part of Prussia to the new state of Poland. The treaty gave Germany's coal mines in the Saar basin to France for fifteen years, at which point the German government could buy them back. Germany's province of East Prussia was cut off from the rest of its territory. The port of Danzig, where the majority of the population was German, was put under the administrative control of the League of Nations and the economic domination of Poland. The treaty disarmed Germany, forbid a German air force, and reduced its navy to a token force to match an army capped at 100,000 volunteers. To protect France and Belgium, all German soldiers and fortifications were to be removed from the Rhine Valley.

The most important part of the Versailles treaty, and one of the parts at odds with Wilson's original plan, was the "war-guilt" provision in Article 231. Versailles held Germany and its allies responsible for the loss and damage suffered by the Allied governments and their citizens "as a consequence of the war imposed upon them by the aggression of Germany and her allies." Germany would be forced to pay massive reparations. The exact amount was left to a Reparations Commission, which set the total at $33 billion in 1921. The Germans deeply resented these harsh demands, but others outside of Germany also warned of the dangers of punitive reparations. In *The Economic Consequences of the Peace*, the noted British economist John Maynard Keynes (1883–1946) argued that reparations would undermine Europe's most important task: repairing the world economy.

The other treaties at the Paris Peace Conference were based partly on the Allies' strategic interests, partly on the principle of national self-determination. The experience of the prewar years convinced leaders that they should draw nations' boundaries to conform to the ethnic, linguistic, and historical traditions of the people they were to contain. Wilson's idealism about freedom and equal representation confirmed these aims. Thus representatives of Yugoslavia were granted a state. Czechoslovakia was created, Poland reestablished, Hungary separated from Austria, and the Baltic states made independent (see the map on page 899). These national boundaries did not, indeed in most cases could not, follow ethnic divisions; they were created according to facts on the ground, hasty compromises, and political dictates—such as insulating western

Europe from the communist threat of the Soviet Union. The peacemakers carved new nations from older, multiethnic empires, especially the Austro-Hungarian Empire, whose fragility had helped spark the war and whose structure had collapsed with the conflict. Creating nations, however, almost invariably created new minorities within those nations. The architects of the new Europe wrestled, briefly, with the problem of minorities, but did not resolve it. The issue would return, and undermine European stability in the 1930s.

The Ottoman Empire ended as well, with two results: the creation of the modern Turkish state and a new structure for British and French colonial rule. As territories were taken form the Ottomans, Greece chose to seize some by force. The effort was successful at first, but the Turks counterattacked, driving out Greek forces by 1923 and creating the modern state of Turkey under the charismatic leadership of General Mustafa Kemal Attaturk (1923–1938). Ottoman territories placed under French and British control became part of the colonial "mandate system," which legitimized Europe's dominance over territories in the Middle East, Africa, and the Pacific. Territories were divided into groups on the basis of their location and their "level of development," or how far, in European eyes, they would have to travel to earn self-government. Choice pieces of land became mandates held, in principle, by the League of Nations but administered by Britain (Transjordan, Iraq, and Palestine) and France (Lebanon and Syria). The British and French empires, then, expanded after the war, although those territories held trouble ahead—the British faced revolt in Iraq and escalating tensions in Palestine, where they tried to juggle promises made to Zionist settlers and claims of indigenous arab communities. Arab leaders, accompanied by their advocate T. E. Lawrence, attended the Versailles conference and listened as their hopes for independence were strictly circumscribed.

The peoples of the Allies' existing colonies were less fortunate. Ho Chi Minh, a young student from Indochina attending a Parisian university, was one of many colonial activists who attended the conference to protest conditions in the colonies and to ask that the rights of nations be extended to their homelands. Well-organized delegations from French West Africa and from the Congress Party of India, which favored dominion status in return for the wartime efforts of millions of Indian soldiers who had fought for the British Empire, were also snubbed. The peacemakers' belief in democracy and self-determination collided with their baseline assumptions—inherited from the nineteenth century—about Western superiority; those assumptions justified imperial rule. Although the European powers

Legend

- 1914 boundaries
- New boundaries as a result of postwar treaties
  - To Great Britain
  - To France
  - To Italy
  - To Rumania
  - To Denmark
  - To Yugoslavia (Serbia and Montenegro)
  - To Belgium
  - To Greece
  - Became independent

TERRITORIAL CHANGES IN EUROPE AND THE NEAR EAST AFTER WORLD WAR I

Note the changes in geography as a result of World War I. What areas were most affected by the changes within Europe, and why? Can you see any obvious difficulties created by the redrawing of the map of Europe? What historical circumstances and/or new threats guided the victors to create such geopolitical anomalies?

spoke about reforming colonialism, little was done. Many nationalists in the colonies who had favored moderate legislative change decided that active struggle might be the only answer to the injustices of colonialism.

Each of the five peace treaties incorporated the Covenant of the League of Nations, an organization envisioned as the arbiter of world peace, but it never achieved the idealistic aims of its founders. The League was handicapped from the start by a number of changes to its original design. The arms-reduction requirement was watered down, and the League's power to enforce it was rendered almost nonexistent. Japan would not join unless it was allowed to keep former German concessions in China. France demanded that both Germany and Russia be excluded from the League. This contradicted Wilson's goals but had already been legitimized in Paris, where neither Soviet Russia nor the defeated Central Powers were allowed at the talks. The League received an even more debilitating blow when the U.S. Congress, citing the long-standing national preference for isolation, refused to approve U.S. membership in the League. Hobbled from the start, the international organization had little potential to avert conflicts.

The League began as a utopian response to global conflict and registered the urgency of reorganizing world governance. Its history, however, reflected the larger problems of power politics that emerged after the war.

CONCLUSION

Europe fought World War I on every front possible—military, political, social, and economic. Consequently, the war's effects extended far beyond the devastated landscapes of the Western Front. Statistics can only hint at the enormous loss of human life: of the 70 million men who were mobilized, nearly 9 million were killed. Russia, Germany, France, and Hungary recorded the highest number of deaths, but the smaller countries of southeast Europe had the highest percentages of soldiers killed. Almost 40 percent of Serbia's soldiers died in battle. With the addition of war-related deaths caused by privation and disease, Serbia lost 15 percent of its population. In comparison, Britain, France, and Germany lost only 2 to 3 percent of their populations. But the percentages are much more telling if we focus on the young men of the war generation. Germany lost one third of men aged nineteen to twenty-two in 1914. France and Britain sustained similar losses, with mortal-ity among young men reaching eight to ten times the normal rate. This was the "lost generation."

The war planted seeds of political and social discontent around the globe. Relations between Russia and western Europe grew sour and suspicious. The Allies had attempted to overthrow the Bolsheviks during the war and had excluded them from the negotiations afterward; these actions instilled in the Soviets a mistrust of the West that lasted for generations. The Allied nations feared that Russia would dominate the new states of eastern Europe, building a "Red Bridge" across the continent. Elsewhere, the conflicting demands of colonialism and nationalism struck only a temporary balance, while the redrawn maps left ethnic and linguistic minorities in every country. The fires of discontent raged most fiercely in Germany, where the Treaty of Versailles was decried as outrageously unjust. Nearly all national governments agreed that it would eventually have to be revised. Neither war nor peace had ended the rivalries that caused the Great War.

The war also had powerful and permanent economic consequences. Beset by inflation, debt, and the difficult task of industrial rebuilding, Europe found itself displaced from the center of the world economy. The war had accelerated the decentralization of money and markets. Many Asian, African, and South American nations benefited financially as their economies became less dependent on Europe, and they were better able to profit from Europe's need for their natural resources. The United States and Japan reaped the biggest gains and emerged as leaders in the new world economy.

The war's most powerful cultural legacy was disillusionment. A generation of men had been sacrificed to no apparent end. Surviving soldiers—many of them permanently injured, both physically and psychologically—were sickened by their participation in such useless slaughter. They were disgusted by the greedy abandonment of principles by the politicians at Versailles. In the postwar period many younger men and women mistrusted the "old men" who had dragged the world into the war. These feelings of loss and alienation were voiced in the vastly popular genre of war literature—memoirs and fiction that commemorated the experience of soldiers on the front lines. The German writer and ex-soldier Erich Maria Remarque captured the disillusion of a generation in his novel *All Quiet on the Western Front:* "Through the years our business has been killing;—it was our first calling in life. Our knowledge of life is limited to death. What will happen afterwards? And what shall come out of us?"

That was the main question facing postwar Europe. The German novelist Thomas Mann recognized that

1918 had brought "an end of an epoch, revolution and the dawn of a new age," and that he and his fellow Germans were "living in a new and unfamiliar world." The struggle to define this new world would increasingly be conceived in terms of rival ideologies—democracy, communism, and fascism—competing for the future of Europe. The eastern autocracies had fallen with the war, but liberal democracy was soon on the decline as well. While militarism and nationalism remained strong, calls for major social reforms gained force during worldwide depression. Entire populations had been mobilized during the war, and they would remain so afterward—active participants in the age of mass politics. Europe was about to embark on two turbulent decades of rejecting and reinventing its social and political institutions. As Tomas Masaryk, the first president of newly formed Czechoslovakia, described it, postwar Europe was "a laboratory atop a graveyard."

KEY TERMS

Allied Powers	Battle of the Marne	Sinn Féin	Vladimir Lenin
Central Powers	trench warfare	*Testament of Youth*	Peace of Paris
Franz Ferdinand	*Lusitania*	February and October Revolutions	mandate system

SELECTED READINGS

Chickering, Roger. *Imperial Germany and the Great War, 1914–1918.* New York, 1998. An excellent synthesis.

Eksteins, Modris. *Rites of Spring: The Great War and the Birth of the Modern Age.* New York, 1989. Fascinating, though impressionistic, on war, art, and culture.

Ferguson, Niall. *The Pity of War.* London, 1998. A fresh look at the war, including strategic issues, international relations, and economics.

Ferro, Marc. *The Great War, 1914–1918.* London, 1973. Very concise overview.

Figes, Orlando. *A People's Tragedy: A History of the Russian Revolution.* New York, 1997. Excellent, detailed narrative.

Fischer, Fritz. *War of Illusions.* New York, 1975. Deals with Germany within the context of internal social and economic trends.

Fitzpatrick, Sheila. *The Russian Revolution, 1917–1932.* New York and Oxford, 1982. Concise overview.

Fussell, Paul. *The Great War and Modern Memory.* New York, 1975. A brilliant examination of British intellectuals' attitudes toward the war.

Higonnet, Margaret Randolph, et al., eds. *Behind the Lines: Gender and the Two World Wars.* New Haven, Conn., 1987. A collection of essays.

Hynes, Samuel. *A War Imagined: The First World War and English Culture.* New York, 1991. The war as perceived on the home front.

Jelavich, Barbara. *History of the Balkans: Twentieth Century.* New York, 1983. Useful for an understanding of the continuing conflict in eastern Europe.

Joll, James. *The Origins of the First World War.* London, 1984. Comprehensive and very useful.

Keegan, John. *The First World War.* London, 1998. The best overall military history.

Macmillan, Margaret, and Richard Holbrooke. *Paris 1919: Six Months That Changed the World.* New York, 2003. Fascinating fresh look at the peace conference.

Mazower, Mark. *Dark Continent: Europe's Twentieth Century.* New York, 1999. An excellent survey, particularly good on nations and minorities in the Balkans and eastern Europe.

Rabinowitch, Alexander. *The Bolsheviks Come to Power.* New York, 1976. A well-researched and carefully documented account.

Roberts, Mary Louise. *Civilization without Sexes: Reconstructing Gender in Postwar France, 1917–1927.* Chicago, 1994. A prize-winning study of the issues raised by the "new woman."

Schivelbusch, Wolfgang. *The Culture of Defeat: On National Trauma, Mourning, and Recovery.* New York, 2001. Fascinating if impressionistic comparative study.

Smith, Leonard. *Between Mutiny and Obedience: The Case of the French Fifth Infantry Division during World War I.* Princeton, N.J., 1994. An account of mutiny and the reasons behind it.

Stevenson, David. *Cataclysm: The First World War as Political Tragedy.* New York, 2003. Detailed and comprehensive, now one of the best single-volume studies.

Stites, Richard. *Revolutionary Dreams: Utopian Visions and Experimental Life in the Russian Revolution.* New York, 1989. The influence of utopian thinking on the revolution.

Williams, John. *The Home Fronts: Britain, France and Germany, 1914–1918.* London, 1972. A survey of life away from the battlefield and the impact of the war on domestic life.

Winter, J. M. *The Experience of World War I.* New York, 1989. Comprehensive illustrated history viewing the war from different perspectives.

CHAPTER TWENTY-FIVE

CHAPTER CONTENTS

TURMOIL BETWEEN THE WARS

THE GREAT WAR TOPPLED four empires and left 9 million dead in its wake. Death reached across borders, ideologies, classes, and generations; it touched ancient mansions, industrial cities, towns, and farmsteads across Europe and its overseas dominions. It destroyed lives and futures, shook cherished standards and pillars of stability, and produced haunting revelations of brutality. Coming to terms with the war's incalculable losses produced a wide range of reactions, from dogged efforts to return to prewar "normalcy" to repudiations of the past, cultural experimentation, and idealistic attempts to build new nations. Among the most striking developments of the interwar period was the near collapse of democracy. By the late 1930s, few Western democracies remained. Even in those that did, most notably Great Britain, France, and the United States, regimes were frayed by the same pressures and strains that in other countries wrecked democratic governments entirely.

The reasons for the decline of democracy varied according to particular national circumstances. We can, however, identify some general causes. The foremost was a series of continuing disruptions in the world economy. These came first in the wake of World War I and, later, with the Great Depression of 1929–1933. A second source of crisis lay in increased social conflict. Across the West, the strains of war deepened long-standing social rifts, and the disappointments of the postwar period polarized politics. Many expected the peace to bring change. After the sacrifices of the war years, most citizens had been rewarded with the vote. It was far from clear, however, that their votes counted, or that the traditional elites who dominated the economy and seemed to hold the reins of politics had lost any of their power. Broad swathes of the electorate became increasingly attracted to political parties, many of them extremist, that promised to transform nations and their cultures. Finally, nationalism, which had been sharpened by the war, proved a key source of discontent in its aftermath. In Italy and Germany frustrated nationalist sentiment turned against governments. In new countries such as Czechoslovakia, and across eastern and southern Europe, friction among national minorities posed enormous problems for relatively fragile democratic regimes.

FOCUS QUESTIONS

- What did socialism come to mean in the Soviet Union after the revolution?
- What were the components of Italian fascism?
- Was the Weimar republic vulnerable?
- How did the Nazis come to power?
- How did the Western democracies deal with the Great Depression?
- How did artists respond to political and cultural polarization?

The most dramatic instance of democracy's decline came with the rise of new authoritarian dictatorships, especially in the Soviet Union, Italy, and Germany. As we shall see, the experiences of those three countries differed significantly as a result of varying historical circumstances and personalities. Yet in each case, many citizens allowed themselves to be persuaded that only drastic measures could bring order from chaos. Those measures, including the elimination of parliamentary government, strict restrictions on political freedom, and increasingly virulent repression of the "enemies" of the state were implemented with a combination of violence, intimidation, and propaganda. That so many citizens seemed willing to sacrifice their freedoms was a measure of their alienation, impatience, or desperation.

THE SOVIET UNION UNDER LENIN AND STALIN

What did socialism come to mean in the Soviet Union after the revolution?

THE RUSSIAN CIVIL WAR

The Bolsheviks seized power in October 1917. They signed a separate peace with Germany in March, 1918 (the Treaty of Brest Litovsk) and then turned to consolidating their own position. The October revolution and withdrawing from the war, however, had divided Russian society, igniting a war that turned out to be far more costly than conflict with Germany. Fury at the terms of Brest Litovsk mobilized the Bolsheviks' enemies, especially those associated with the ousted tsarist regime, who began to attack the new government from the periphery of the old empire. Known collectively as "Whites," the Bolsheviks' opponents were a varied lot, only loosely bound by their common goal of removing the "Reds" from power. Their military force came mainly from supporters of the old regime, including tsarist military officers, reactionary monarchists, the former nobility, and disaffected liberal supporters of the monarchy. The Whites were joined by groups as diverse as liberal supporters of the provisional government, Mensheviks, Social Revolutionaries, and anarchist peasant bands known as "Greens" who opposed all central state power. The Bolsheviks also faced insurrections from strong nationalist movements in some parts of the former Rus-

sian Empire: Ukraine, Georgia, and the north Caucasus regions. Finally, several foreign powers, including the United States, Great Britain, and Japan, launched small but threatening interventions on the periphery of the old empire. Outside support for the Whites proved to be an insignificant threat to the Bolsheviks, but it served as a propaganda device; the Bolsheviks claimed that the Whites were intriguing with foreign powers that wanted to invade Russia. The intervention also heightened Bolshevik mistrust of the capitalist world which, in the Marxists' view, would naturally oppose the existence of the world's first "socialist" state.

The Bolsheviks eventually won the civil war because they gained greater support—or at least tacit acceptance—from the majority of the population and because they were better organized for the war effort itself. At the beginning of the war, the Bolsheviks mobilized quickly, foregoing many of their radical concerns about egalitarianism and political self-determination in favor of strong bureaucratic and military structures. Leon Trotsky, the revolutionary hero of 1905 and 1917, became the new commissar of war and created a hierarchical, disciplined military machine that grew to some 5 million men by 1920. Trotsky's Red Army triumphed over the White armies by the end of 1920, although fighting continued into 1922. The Bolsheviks also

Lenin and Stalin. Under Stalin this picture was used to show his close relationship with Lenin. In fact, the photograph has been doctored.

WHAT DID SOCIALISM COME TO MEAN IN THE SOVIET UNION AFTER THE REVOLUTION?

THE SOVIET UNION UNDER LENIN AND STALIN   905

invaded Poland and nearly reached Warsaw before being thrown back.

When the civil war was over, the country had suffered some 1 million combat casualties, several million deaths from hunger and disease caused by the war, and 100,000 to 300,000 executions of non-combatants as part of Red and White terror. The barbarism of the war engendered lasting hatreds within the emerging Soviet nation, especially among ethnic minorities, and it brutalized the fledgling society that came into existence under the new Bolshevik regime.

The civil war also shaped the Bolsheviks' approach to economic aspects of socialism. On taking power in 1917, Lenin expected to create, for the short term at least, a state-capitalist system that resembled the successful European wartime economies. The new government took control of large-scale industry, banking, and all other major capitalist concerns while allowing small-scale private economic activity, including agriculture, to continue. The civil war pushed the new government toward a more radical economic stance known as "war communism." The Bolsheviks began to requisition grain from the peasantry, and they outlawed private trade in consumer goods as "speculation," militarized production facilities, and abolished money. Most of these innovations were improvised responses to deteriorating economic conditions beyond the regime's control. The idea of war communism, however, was attractive to radical Bolsheviks. Indeed, many believed that war communism would replace the capitalist system that had collapsed in 1917.

Such hopes were largely unfounded. War communism sustained the Bolshevik military effort, but further disrupted the already war-ravaged economy. The civil war devastated Russian industry and emptied major cities. The population of Moscow fell by 50 percent between 1917 and 1920. Kiev's population fell by 25 percent. The masses of urban workers, who had strongly supported the Bolshevik revolution, melted back into the countryside; only 1.5 million of the 3.5 million workers employed in major industries before 1917 remained on the job by the end of 1920. Industrial output had fallen by 1920–1921 to only 20 percent of prewar levels. Most devastating were the effects of war communism on agriculture. On the one hand, the civil war had solved the "land question" to the benefit of peasants, who spontaneously seized and redistributed noble lands. By 1919 peasants held almost 97 percent of the land in small plots, generally

fewer than twenty acres. Nonetheless, the agricultural system was severely disrupted by the civil war, by the grain requisitioning of war communism, and by the outlawing of all private trade in grain. Large-scale famine resulted in 1921 and claimed some 5 million lives.

As the civil war came to a close, urban workers and soldiers became increasingly impatient with the Bolshevik regime, which had promised socialism and workers' control but had delivered something more akin to a military dictatorship. Large-scale strikes and protests broke out in late 1920, but the Bolsheviks moved swiftly and effectively to subdue the "popular revolts." In crushing dissent, the Bolshevik regime that emerged from the civil war made a clear statement that internal competition would not be tolerated.

> In crushing dissent, the Bolshevik regime that emerged from the civil war made a clear statement that internal competition would not be tolerated.

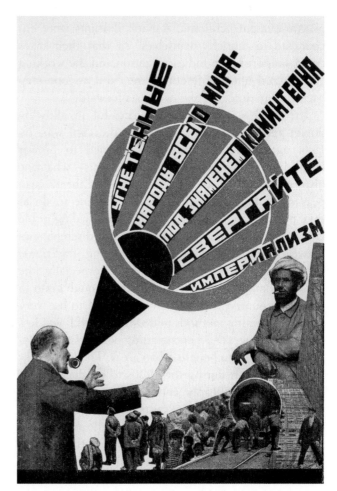

The Young Guard. In the years following 1917, many within the Russian avant-garde wished to aid the revolution with their work. This literary magazine, which here has a constructivist-style cover, promoted Bolshevik values.

THE NEP PERIOD

In response to these political and economic difficulties, the Bolsheviks abandoned war communism and in March 1921 embarked on a radically different course known as the New Economic Policy (NEP). The NEP reverted to the state capitalism that had been tried immediately after the revolution. The state was to continue to own all major industry and financial concerns (which Lenin called the "commanding heights" of the economic system), while individuals were to be allowed to own private property, trade freely within limits, and—most important—farm their land for their own benefit. Fixed taxes on the peasantry replaced grain requisitioning; what peasants grew beyond the tax requirements was theirs to do with as they saw fit. The Bolshevik most identified with the NEP was Nikolai Bukharin (1888–1938), a young and brilliant Marxist theoretician who argued that the Bolsheviks could best industrialize the Soviet Union by taxing private peasant economic activity. Peasants were encouraged to "enrich themselves" so that their taxes could support urban industrialization and the working class. Lenin himself described the NEP as "one step backward in order to take two steps forward."

The NEP was undeniably successful in allowing Soviet agriculture to recover from the civil war; by 1924 agricultural harvests had returned to prewar levels. It was a prosperous time for peasants—what one historian describes as the "golden age of the Russian peasantry." Peasants were largely left alone to do as they pleased, and they responded by redividing noble lands among themselves to level wealth discrepancies between rich and poor, by reinforcing traditional social structures in the countryside (especially the peasant commune), and by producing enough grain to feed the country, though they continued to use very primitive farming methods to do so. The NEP was less successful, however, in encouraging peasants to participate in markets to benefit urban areas. The Bolsheviks found it difficult during the 1920s to produce manufactured goods cheaply enough to get peasants to trade their grain for them. Peasants responded to these difficulties by simply abstaining from the market and keeping excess grain, their livestock, or their illegal moonshine for themselves. The result was a series of shortages in grain deliveries to cities, a situation that prompted many Bolsheviks to call for revival of the radical economic practices of war communism. The fate of these radical proposals, however, was tied to the fate of the man who would, contrary to all expectations, replace Lenin as the leader of the USSR and become one of the most notorious dictators of all time: Joseph Stalin.

STALIN AND THE "REVOLUTION FROM ABOVE"

Stalin's rise was swift and unpredicted. His political success was rooted in intraparty conflicts in the 1920s, but it was also closely tied to the abrupt end of the NEP period in the late 1920s and to the beginning of a massive program of social and economic modernization. This "revolution from above," as many call it, was the most rapid social and economic transformation any nation has seen in modern history. It was carried out, however, at unprecedented human cost.

Stalin (1879–1953) was a Bolshevik from the Caucasus nation of Georgia; his real name was Iosep Jughashvili. The son of a poor shoemaker, Stalin, at his mother's insistence, originally studied at an Orthodox seminary to become a priest. Rejecting the priesthood, he participated in revolutionary activity in the Caucasus and spent many years in Siberian exile before the revolution. He was an important member of the Bolshevik Party before and during the Russian Revolution. Yet Stalin was not one of the central figures of the early Bolshevik Party, and he was certainly not a front runner for party leadership. The question of Lenin's successor arose with the leader's poor health after 1922 and his death in 1924, but the civil war hero Leon Trotsky was widely assumed to be the best candidate for Lenin's position. Other top Bolsheviks, however, also aspired to a leading role.

CHRONOLOGY

THE EARLY SOVIET UNION, 1917–1929

Bolsheviks seize power	October 1917
Treaty of Brest-Litovsk	March 1918
Russian Civil War	1918–1920
Bolsheviks suppress nationalist rebellions	1920–1921
Launch of the NEP	1921
Lenin dies	1924
Stalin, Trotsky, Bukharin vie for power	1924–1928
Stalin seizes full power	1928–1929

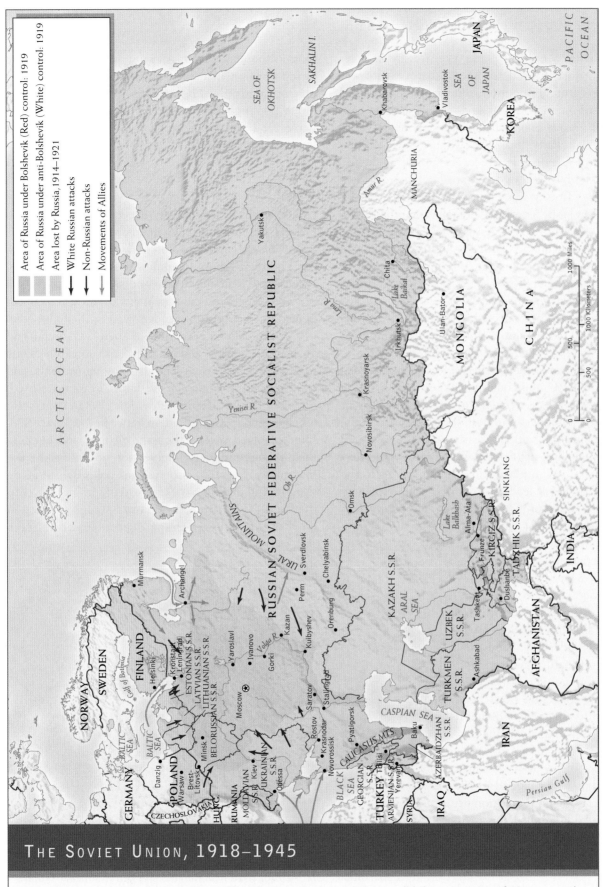

Area of Russia under Bolshevik (Red) control: 1919
Area of Russia under anti-Bolshevik (White) control: 1919
Area lost by Russia, 1914–1921
White Russian attacks
Non-Russian attacks
Movements of Allies

PACIFIC OCEAN

JAPAN

SEA OF JAPAN

KOREA

Vladivostok

SAKHALIN I.

SEA OF OKHOTSK

Khabarovsk

MANCHURIA

Amur R.

CHINA

MONGOLIA

Ulan-Bator

Chita

Lake Baikal

Irkutsk

SINKIANG

Lake Balkhash

Alma-Ata

Frunze

KIRGIZ S.S.R.

TADZHIK S.S.R.

Dushanbe

Yakutsk

Lena R.

Krasnoyarsk

Novosibirsk

RUSSIAN SOVIET FEDERATIVE SOCIALIST REPUBLIC

Yenisei R.

Ob. R.

URAL MOUNTAINS

Omsk

KAZAKH S.S.R.

ARAL SEA

UZBEK S.S.R.

Tashkent

INDIA

AFGHANISTAN

TURKMEN S.S.R.

Ashkabad

ARCTIC OCEAN

Murmansk

Archangel

NORWAY

SWEDEN

FINLAND

Helsinki

Gulf of Bothnia

BALTIC SEA

Kronstadt

Leningrad

ESTONIAN S.S.R.

LATVIAN S.S.R.

LITHUANIAN S.S.R.

Minsk

BELORUSSIAN S.S.R.

Danzig

GERMANY

POLAND

Warsaw

Brest-Litovsk

CZECHOSLOVAKIA

HUNG.

RUMANIA

MOLDAVIAN S.S.R.

UKRAINIAN S.S.R.

Kiev

Odessa

BLACK SEA

Sverdlovsk

Perm

Chelyabinsk

Orenburg

Kazan

Kuibyshev

Volga R.

Yaroslavl

Ivanovo

Gorki

Moscow

Saratov

Stalingrad

Rostov

Krasnodar

Novorossisk

Pyatigorsk

CAUCASUS MTS.

Tbilisi

GEORGIAN S.S.R.

ARMENIAN S.S.R.

Yerevan

TURKEY

SYRIA

IRAQ

AZERBAIDZHAN S.S.R.

Baku

CASPIAN SEA

IRAN

Persian Gulf

1000 Miles
1000 Kilometers
500
500
0
0

THE SOVIET UNION, 1918–1945

How did the civil war of 1917–1920 affect the new Soviet state? How did the possession of Moscow and Leningrad (St. Petersburg) aid the Bolsheviks in their victory over the Whites? How was Stalin's dictatorship instrumental in modernizing and uniting the Soviet Union's vast and diverse landscape?

Though not a brilliant orator like Trotsky or a respected Marxist theoretician like Bukharin, Stalin was nonetheless a master political strategist, and he played the game of internal party politics almost without fault after Lenin's death. Stalin sidelined his opponents within the Bolshevik Party, many of whom supported the Leninist principle of collective leadership within the top ruling circle, by isolating and expelling each of them successively. Trotsky was the first to go, driven out of top party circles by a coalition of Stalin and others who, ironically, feared Trotsky's desire to take control of the party himself. Stalin then turned on his former allies and removed them in turn, culminating in the removal of Bukharin from the Politburo in 1928–1929.

Stalin's campaign against Bukharin was not just political. It was also connected to Stalin's desire to discard the NEP system and to launch an all-out industrialization drive. By the late 1920s, Stalin had begun to agree with those critics of the NEP who had argued that the Soviet Union could not hope to industrialize by relying on taxes generated from small-scale peasant agriculture. Stalin began to push for an increase in the tempo of industrialization as early as 1927, prompted by fears of falling behind the West and by the perceived threat of another world war. Almost all of the top-level Bolshevik leaders supported Stalin's plan to step up the tempo of industrialization. But hardly anybody supported what happened next: an abrupt turn toward forced industrialization and collectivization of agriculture.

In 1927 a poor harvest caused yet another crisis in the grain-collection system. Low prices for agricultural goods and high prices for scarce industrial goods led peasants to hoard grain, resulting in food shortages in cities and difficulties in collecting taxes from the peasantry. In early 1928 Stalin ordered local officials in the distant Urals and Siberian areas, which were alleged to have bumper crops but to be behind in tax payments, to begin requisitioning grain. He soon applied this revival of war communism to the entire country. In 1929 the upper echelons of the party abruptly reversed the course set by NEP and embarked on the complete collectivization of agriculture, begin-

ning in the major grain-growing areas. Peasants there were to be convinced, by force if necessary, to give up private farmlands. They would either join collective farms, pooling resources and giving a set portion of the harvest to the state, or work on state farms, where they were paid as laborers.

COLLECTIVIZATION

Collectivization was initially expected to be a gradual process, but in late 1929 Stalin embarked on collectivization of agriculture by force. Within a few months, the Politburo (short for political bureau, which governed the Communist Party and state) began to issue orders to use force against peasants who resisted collectivization, though those orders were at first shrouded in secrecy. The process that ensued was brutal and chaotic. Local party and police officials forced peasants to give up their private land, farming implements, and livestock and to join collective farms. Peasants resisted, often violently. There were some 1,600 large-scale rebellions in the Soviet Union between 1929 and 1933; some involved several thousand people, and quelling them required military intervention, including the use of artillery. Peasants also resisted collectivization by slaughtering their livestock instead of turning it over to the farms, a loss that hampered agricultural production for years to follow. Sensing a possible crisis, Stalin

Winter Deportations, 1929–1930. Ukrainian families charged with being "kulaks" were deported from their homes because of their refusal to join Stalin's "collective farming" plan. Many of the evicted families were shipped north by train to the Arctic where they perished due to the lack of adequate food and shelter.

WHAT DID SOCIALISM COME TO MEAN IN THE SOVIET UNION AFTER THE REVOLUTION?

THE SOVIET UNION UNDER LENIN AND STALIN   909

called the process to a temporary halt in early 1930, but soon thereafter ordered the process to proceed more gradually, and by 1935 collectivization of agriculture was complete in most areas of the Soviet Union.

To facilitate collectivization, Stalin also launched an all-out attack on peasants designated as *kulaks* (a derogatory term for well-to-do farmers, literally meaning "tight-fisted ones"). Most kulaks, though, were not any better off than their neighbors, and the word became one of many terms for peasants hostile to collectivization. Between 1929 and 1933, some 1.5 million peasants were uprooted, dispossessed of their property, and resettled from their farmlands to either inhospitable reaches of the Soviet east and north or to poor farmland closer to their original homes. The land and possessions of these unfortunate

> Between 1929 and 1933, some 1.5 million peasants were uprooted, dispossessed of their property, and resettled from their farmlands to either inhospitable reaches of the Soviet east and north or to poor farmland closer to their original homes.

peasants were distributed to collective farms or, just as often, to the local officials and peasants participating in the liquidation process. The liquidation of kulaks as a class magnified the disruptive effects of agricultural collectivization, and the two together produced one of the most devastating famines in modern European history. Peasants who were forced into collective farms had little incentive to produce extra food, and exiling many of the most productive peasants not surprisingly weakened the agricultural system. In 1932–1933, famine spread across the southern region of the Soviet Union. This was the most productive agricultural area in the country, and the famine that struck there was thus particularly senseless. The 1933 famine cost some 3 to 5 million lives. During the famine, the Bolsheviks maintained substantial grain reserves in other parts of the country, enough to save many hundreds of thousands of lives at a minimum, but they refused to send this grain to the affected areas, preferring instead to seal off famine-stricken regions and allow people to starve. Grain reserves were instead sold overseas for hard currency and stockpiled in case of war. After 1935 there would never again be any large-scale resistance to Soviet power in the countryside. Yet resistance had forced the state to cede small private plots of land to peasant families; this land provided as much as 50 percent of the nation's produce from a tiny fraction of the land.

THE FIVE-YEAR PLANS

In Stalin's view, collectivization provided the resources for the other major aspect of his revolution from above: a rapid campaign of forced industrialization. The road map for this industrialization process was the first Five-Year Plan (1928–1932), an ambitious set of goals that Stalin and his cohorts drew up in 1927 and continued to revise upward. The plan called for truly herculean industrialization efforts, and its results rank as one of the most stunning periods of economic growth the modern world has ever seen. The industrial output of the Soviet Union increased by 50 percent in five years; the annual rate of growth during the first Five-Year Plan was between 15 and 22 percent. This rate of growth seemed even more impressive in the context of the economic depression that was shaking

"We Smite the Lazy Workers!" This Russian propaganda poster was used to mobilize workers to the "Five-Year Plan."

STALIN'S INDUSTRIALIZATION OF THE SOVIET UNION

How did the Soviet people experience Stalin's industrialization drive? New archives have helped historians glimpse what the common people lived through and how they responded. The letters in the second selection come from several hundred that workers and peasants sent to Soviet newspapers and authorities recounting their experiences and offering their opinions. Both of the ones printed here were sent to the Soviet paper Pravda.

The first excerpt is a speech Stalin gave at a Conference of Managers of Socialist Industry in 1931. In his usual style, he invoked fears of Soviet backwardness and Russian nationalism while summoning all to take up the task of industrial production.

"THE TASKS OF BUSINESS EXECUTIVES"

It is sometimes asked whether it is not possible to slow down the tempo somewhat, to put a check on the movement. No, comrades, it is not possible! The tempo must not be reduced! On the contrary, we must increase it as much as is within our powers and possibilities. This is dictated to us by our obligations to the workers and peasants of the USSR. This is dictated to us by our obligations to the working class of the whole world.

To slacken the tempo would mean falling behind. And those who fall behind get beaten. But we do not want to be beaten. No, we refuse to be beaten! One feature of the history of old Russia was the continual beatings she suffered because of her backwardness. She was beaten by the Mongol khans. She was beaten by the Turkish beys. . . . She was beaten by the British and French capitalists. She was beaten by the Japanese barons. All beat her—for her backwardness: for military backwardness, for cultural backwardness, for political backwardness, for industrial backwardness, for agricultural backwardness. . . .

We are fifty or a hundred years behind the advanced countries. We must make good this distance in ten years. Either we do it, or we shall be crushed. . . .

In ten years at most we must make good the distance which separates us from the advanced capitalist countries. We have all the 'objective' possibilities for this. The only thing lacking is the ability to take proper advantage of these possibilities. And that depends on us. *Only* on us! . . . It is time to put an end to the rotten policy of non-interference in production. It is time to adopt a new policy, a policy adapted to the present times—the policy of interfering in everything. If you are a factory manager, then interfere in all the affairs of the factory, look into everything, let nothing escape you, learn and learn again. Bolsheviks must master technique. It is time Bolsheviks themselves became experts. . . .

There are no fortresses which Bolsheviks cannot capture. We have assumed power. We have built up a huge socialist industry. We have swung the middle peasants to the path of socialism. . . . What remains to be done is not so much: to study technique, to master science. And when we have done that we will develop a tempo of which we dare not even dream at present.

Joseph Stalin, "The Tasks of Business Executives," [speech given at the First All-Union Conference of Managers of Socialist Industry, February 4, 1931], as cited in Richard Sakwa, *The Rise and Fall of the Soviet Union, 1917–1991* (New York, 1999), pp. 187–188.

STALIN'S INDUSTRIAL DEVELOPMENT: THE VIEW FROM BELOW

It should not be forgotten that many millions of workers are participating in the building of socialism. A horse with its own strength can drag seventy-five poods,[*] but its owner has loaded it with a hundred poods, and in addition he's fed it poorly. No matter how much he uses the whip, it still won't be able to move the cart.

This is also true for the working class. They've loaded it with socialist competition, shock work, overfulfilling the industrial and financial plan, and so forth. A worker toils seven hours, not ever leaving his post, and this is not all he does. Afterward he sits in meetings or else attends classes for an hour and a half or two in order to increase his skill level, and if he doesn't do these things, then he's doing things at home. And what does he live on? One hundred fifty grams of salted mutton, he will make soup without any of the usual additives, neither carrots, beets, flour, nor salt pork. What kind of soup do you get from this? Mere "dishwater."

—B.N. Kniazev, Tula, Sept. 1930.

Comrade Editor, Please give me an answer. Do the local authorities have the right to forcibly take away the only cow of industrial and office workers? What is more, they demand a receipt showing that the cow was handed over voluntarily and they threaten you by saying if you don't do this, they will put you in prison for failure to fulfill the meat procurement. How can you live when the cooperative distributes only black bread, and at the market goods have the prices of 1919 and 1920? Lice have eaten us to death, and soap is given only to railroad workers. From hunger and filth we have a massive outbreak of spotted fever.

—Anonymous, from
Aktybinsk, Kazakhstan

[*]A pood is a Russian unit of weight, equal to 36.11 pounds.

Lewis Siegelbaum and Andrei Sokolov, *Stalinism as a Way of Life: A Narrative in Documents* (New Haven, Conn., and London: 2000), pp. 39–41.

QUESTIONS FOR ANALYSIS

1. What are Stalin's priorities?
2. What images does Stalin use to capture his audience's attention?
3. How did the Soviet people experience Stalin's industrialization drive?

---

the foundations of Western economies in the late 1920s and early 1930s. The Bolsheviks built entirely new industries in entirely new cities. The factory town of Magnitogorsk, for example, emerged from absolutely barren, uninhabited steppes in 1929 to become a steel-producing factory town of some 250,000 residents in 1932; at least in scale, it rivaled anything that the West had built. The industrialization drive transformed the nation's landscape and population as well. Cities such as Moscow and Leningrad doubled in size in the early 1930s, while new cities sprang up across the country. In 1926, only one fifth of the population lived in towns. Fifteen years later, in 1939, roughly a third did. The urban population had grown from 26 million to 56 million in under fifteen years. The Soviet Union was well on its way to becoming an urban, industrial society.

This rapid industrialization came, however, at enormous human cost. Many large-scale projects were carried out with prison labor, especially in the timber and mining industries. The labor camp system, known as the *gulag*, became a central part of the Stalinist economic system. People were arrested and sent to camps on a bewildering array of charges, ranging from petty criminal infractions to contact with foreigners to having the ill fortune to be born of bourgeois or kulak parents. The camp system spread throughout the USSR in the 1930s: by the end of the decade, roughly 3.6 million people were incarcerated by the regime. This army of prisoners was used to complete the most arduous and dangerous industrialization tasks, such as the construction of the Moscow–White Sea canal. To save money, the canal connecting Moscow to the seaports of the north was constructed without the use of any machinery. It was literally dug by hand, with human labor used to power everything from conveyor belts to pile drivers. Tens of thousands of individuals lost their lives during construction. One of Stalin's pet projects, it never functioned properly, was too shallow, and froze over in winter. It was bombed early in World War II.

"Imperialists Cannot Stop the Success of the Five-Year Plan!"

The economic system created during this revolution from above was also fraught with structural problems that would plague the Soviet Union for its entire history. The command economy, with each year's production levels entirely planned in advance in Moscow, never functioned in a rational way. Heavy industry was always favored over light industry, and the emphasis on quantity made quality practically meaningless. A factory that was charged with producing a certain number of pairs of shoes, for example, could cut costs by producing all one style and size. The consumer would be left with useless goods, but the producer would fulfill the plan. Stalin's industrialization drive did transform the country from an agrarian nation to a world industrial power in the space of a few short years, but in the longer run, the system would become an economic disaster.

The Stalin revolution also produced fundamental cultural and economic changes. The revolution from above altered the face of Soviet cities and the working class populating them. New cities were largely made up of first-generation peasants who brought their rural traditions to the cities with them, changing the fragile urban culture that had existed during the 1920s. Women, too, entered the urban workforce in increasing numbers in the 1930s—women went from 20 percent to almost 40 percent of the workforce in one decade, and in light industry they made up two thirds of the labor force by 1940.

At the same time, Stalin promoted a sharply conservative shift in all areas of culture and society. In art, the radical modernism of the 1920s was crushed by socialist realism, a deadening aesthetic that celebrated the drive toward socialism and left no room for experimentation. Family policy and gender roles underwent a similar reversal. Early Bolshevik activists had promoted a utopian attempt to rebuild one of the basic structures of prerevolutionary society—the family—and to create a genuinely new proletarian social structure. The Bolsheviks in the 1920s legalized divorce, expelled the Orthodox Church from marriage ceremonies, and legalized abortion. Stalin abandoned these ideas of communist familial relations in favor of efforts to strengthen traditional family ties: divorce became more difficult, abortion was outlawed in 1936 except in cases that threatened the life of the mother, and homosexuality was declared a criminal offense. State subsidies and support for mothers, which were progressive for the time, could not change the reality that Soviet women were increasingly forced to carry the double burden of familial and wage labor to support Stalin's version of Soviet society. All areas of Soviet cultural and social policy experienced similar reversals.

THE GREAT TERROR

The apogee of Stalinist repression came with the "Great Terror" of 1937–1938, which left nearly a million people dead and as many as 1.5 million more in labor camps. As Stalin consolidated his personal dictatorship over the country, he eliminated enemies—real and imagined—along with individuals and groups he considered superfluous to the new Soviet society. As we have seen, repression was central to the Stalinist system from the early 1930s, yet the years 1937–1938 brought a qualitative and quantitative change—a whirlwind of mass repression unprecedented in scale.

The Terror was aimed at various categories of internal "enemies," from the top to the very bottom of Soviet society. Former and current political elites were perhaps the most visible victims. The top level of the Bolshevik party itself was purged almost completely; some 100,000 party members were removed, most facing prison sentences or execution. Many top party officials including Bukharin were condemned at carefully staged show trials and then shot. The purge also struck—with particular ferocity—nonparty elites, industrial managers, and intellectuals. Between 1937 and 1938, Stalin purged the military of people he deemed potential threats, arresting some 40,000 officers and shooting at least 10,000. These purges disrupted the government and the economy but allowed Stalin to promote a new, young cadre of officials who had no experience in the pre-Stalinist era and who owed their careers, if not their lives, to Stalin personally. Whole ethnic groups were viewed with suspicion, including Poles, Ukrainians, Lithuanians, Latvians, Koreans, and others with supposed cross-border ties that, in Stalin's mind, represented a national security threat. From the bottom, some 200,000 to 300,000 "dekulakized" peasants, petty criminals, and other social misfits were arrested, and many shot.

The Great Terror remains one of the most puzzling aspects of Stalin's path to dictatorial power. The Terror succeeded, with a certain twisted kind of logic, in solidifying Stalin's personal control over all aspects of social and political life in the Soviet Union, but it did so by destroying the most talented elements in Soviet society. The Terror was to some extent the result of Stalin's personal paranoia, but it was also a fitting end to the "Stalin revolution" that began in 1927–1928 with the end of the NEP.

The results of the Stalin revolution were profound. No other regime in the history of western Europe had ever attempted to reorder completely the politics, economy, and society of a major nation. The Soviets had done so in a mere ten years. By 1939 private manufacturing and trade had been almost entirely abolished. Factories, mines, railroads, and public utilities were exclusively owned by the state. Stores were either government enterprises or cooperatives in which consumers owned shares. Agriculture had been almost completely socialized. The decade was not entirely grim, however. There were advances, especially in the area of social reform. Illiteracy was reduced from nearly 50 percent to about 20 percent, and higher education was made available to increasingly large numbers. Government assistance for working mothers and free hospitalization did a great deal to raise the national standard of health. The society that emerged from this terrible decade was industrial, more urban

CHRONOLOGY

THE STALINIST REVOLUTION, 1927–1938

Launch of collectivization	1927
Launch of the first Five-Year Plan	1928
Stalin breaks with the NEP	1929
Stalin pauses collectivization	1930
Liquidation of the kulaks	1929–1933
The Great Terror	1937–1938

than rural, and more modern than traditional. But it was a society badly pummeled in the process, one in which many of the most productive peasants, gifted intellectuals, and experienced economic and social elites were purged from society in the name of total dictatorial power. The USSR that emerged from this tumultuous period would barely be able to withstand the immense strains placed on it when the Germans struck less than three years after the end of the Terror.

THE EMERGENCE OF FASCISM IN ITALY

What were the components of Italian fascism?

Like many European nations, Italy emerged from World War I as a democracy in distress. Italy was on the winning side and had been among the Big Four nations (with France, Great Britain, and the United States) that put together the postwar settlement. Yet the war had cost Italy nearly 700,000 lives and over $15 billion. These sacrifices were no greater than those of France or Britain but were hard to bear for a much poorer nation. Moreover, Italy had received secret promises of specific territorial gains during the war, only to find those promises withdrawn when they conflicted with principles of self-determination. Italian claims to the west coast of the Adriatic, for instance, were bitterly disputed and in the end denied by Yugoslavia. Italy received most of the Austrian territories it demanded, but many maintained that these were inadequate rewards for their sacrifices. Groups of militant nationalists seized Fiume, a port city on the Adriatic, and held it for a year before being disbanded by the Italian army. At first the nationalists blamed the "mutilated victory" on President Wilson, but after a short time they turned on their own rulers and what they considered the weaknesses of parliamentary democracy.

Italy had long-standing problems that were made worse by the war. Since unification, the Italian nation had been rent by an unhealthy economic split—divided into a prosperous industrialized north and a poor agrarian south. Social conflict over land, wages, and local power caused friction in the countryside as well as in urban centers. Governments were often seen as corrupt, indecisive, and defeatist. This was the background for the more immediate problems that Italy faced after the war.

Inflation and unemployment were perhaps the most destructive effects of the war. Inflation produced high prices, speculation, and profiteering. And though normally wages would have risen also, the postwar labor market was glutted by returning soldiers. Furthermore, business elites were shaken by strikes, which became increasingly large and frequent, and by the closing of foreign markets. The parliamentary government that was set up after the war failed to ease these dire conditions, and Italians wanted radical reforms. For the working class, this meant socialism. In 1919, the socialists won about a third of the seats in the Chamber of Deputies. The movement grew increasingly radical: in 1920, the socialist and anarchist workers seized scores of factories, most in the metallurgy sector, and tried to run them for the benefit of the workers themselves. In the countryside, most peasants were land poor, and many had no land at all, but instead worked for wages as rural laborers on large estates. Demands for land reform grew more militant. In some rural areas, so-called Red Leagues tried to break up large estates and force landlords to reduce their rents. In all these actions, the model of the Russian Revolution, although it was only vaguely understood, encouraged the development of local radicalism. In large numbers, voters abandoned the poorly organized parties of the center and the moderate left. They supported two more radical groups: the Socialists and the Catholic People's Party (newly formed with the pope's blessing), which appealed to the common people, especially in the countryside. Neither party preached revolution, yet both urged wide-ranging social and economic reforms.

Members of the fasci were young idealists, fanatical nationalists. After the war, these groups formed the base of Mussolini's fascist movement.

The rising radical tide, especially seen against the backdrop of the Bolshevik revolution, worried other social groups. Industrialists and landowners feared for their property. Small shopkeepers and white-collar workers—social groups that did not think the working-class movement supported their interests—found themselves alienated by business elites on the one hand and by apparently revolutionary radicals on the other. The threat from the left provoked a strong surge to the right. Fascism appeared in the form of vigilante groups breaking up strikes, fighting with workers in the streets, or ousting the Red Leagues from lands occupied in the countryside.

THE RISE OF MUSSOLINI

"I am fascism," said Benito Mussolini, and indeed, the success of the Italian fascist movement depended heavily on his leadership. Mussolini (1883–1945) was the son of a socialist blacksmith. His mother was a schoolteacher, and he deferentially followed in her footsteps. But he was restless and dissatisfied, soon leaving Italy for further study in Switzerland. There he gave part of his time to his books and the rest to writing articles for socialist newspapers. Expelled from the country for fomenting strikes, he returned to Italy, where he became a journalist and eventually the editor of *Avanti,* the leading socialist daily.

Mussolini did not hold to any particular doctrine, and he reversed himself at several points. When war broke out in August 1914, Mussolini insisted that Italy should remain neutral. He had scarcely adopted this position when he began urging participation on the Allied side. Deprived of his position as the editor of *Avanti,* he founded a new paper, *Il Popolo d'Italia,* and dedicated its columns to arousing enthusiasm for war. He regarded the Italian government's decision the following spring to go in on the side of the Allies as a personal victory.

As early as October 1914, Mussolini had organized groups, called fasci, to help drum up support for the war. Members of the fasci were young idealists, fanatical nationalists. After the war, these groups formed the base of Mussolini's fascist movement. (The word *fascism* derives from the Latin *fasces:* an ax surrounded by a bundle of sticks that represented the authority of the Roman state. The Italian *fascio* means "group" or "band.") In 1919 Mussolini drafted the original platform of the Fascist Party. It had several surprising elements, including universal (including woman) suffrage, an eight-hour workday, and a tax on inheritances. A new platform, adopted in 1920, abandoned all references to economic reforms. Neither platform earned the fascists much political success.

What the fascists lacked in political support, they made up for in aggressive determination. They gained the respect of the middle class and landowners, and intimidated many others, by forcefully repressing radical movements of industrial workers and peasants. They attacked socialists, often physically, and succeeded in taking over some local governments. As the national regime weakened, Mussolini's coercive politics made him look like a solution to the absence of leadership. In September 1922, he began to negotiate with other

EUROPE IN 1923

Which countries lost territories after World War I, and with what consequences? How did the Russian revolution change European politics? What problems arose in the Central and Eastern European nations created after World War I?

parties and the king for fascist participation in government. On October 28 an army of about 50,000 fascist militia, in black-shirted uniforms, marched into Rome and occupied the capital. The premier resigned, and the following day the king, Victor Emmanuel III, reluctantly invited Mussolini to form a cabinet. Without firing a shot the Black Shirts had gained control of the Italian government. The explanation of their success is to be found less in the strength of the fascist movement itself than in the Italian disappointments after the war and the weakness of the older governing classes.

The parliamentary system had folded under pressure. And though Mussolini had "legally" been granted his power, he immediately began to establish a one-party dictatorship. The doctrines of Italian fascism had three components. The first was statism. The state was declared to incorporate every interest and every loyalty of its members. There was to be "nothing above the state, nothing outside the state, nothing against the state." The second was nationalism. Nationhood was the highest form of society, with a life and a soul of its own, transcending the individuals who composed it. The third was militarism. Nations that did not expand would eventually wither and die. Fascists believed that war ennobled man and regenerated sluggish and decadent peoples.

Mussolini began to rebuild Italy in accordance with these principles. The first step was to change electoral laws so they granted his party solid parliamentary majorities and to intimidate the opposition. He then moved to close down parliamentary government and other parties entirely. He abolished the cabinet system and all but extinguished the powers of the Parliament. He made the Fascist Party an integral part of the Italian constitution. Mussolini assumed the dual position of prime minister and party leader (*duce*), and he used the party's militia to eliminate his enemies by violent means. Mussolini's government also controlled the police, muzzled the press, and censored academic activity.

Meanwhile, Mussolini preached the end of class conflict and its replacement by national unity. He began to reorganize the economy and labor, taking away the power of the country's labor movement. The Italian economy was placed under the management of twenty-two corporations, each responsible for a major industrial enterprise. In each corporation were representatives of trade unions, whose members were organized by the Fascist Party, the employers, and the government. Together, the members of these corporations were given the task of determining working conditions, wages, and prices. It is not surprising, however, that the decisions of these bodies were closely supervised by the government and favored the position of management. Indeed, the government quickly aligned with big business, creating more of a corrupt bureaucracy than a revolutionary economy.

Mussolini secured some working-class assent with state-sponsored programs, including massive public-works projects, library building, paid vacations for workers, and social security. In 1929, he settled Italy's sixty-year-old conflict with the Roman Catholic Church. He signed a treaty granting independence to the papal residence in the Vatican City and promising restitution for expropriations that occurred during Italian unification. The treaty also established Roman Catholicism as the official religion of the state, guaranteed religious education in the nation's schools, and made religious marriage ceremonies mandatory. The agreement with the church was part of Mussolini's campaign to "normalize" relations with other Italian institutions—army, industry, church, monarchy—to maintain stability.

In fact, Mussolini's regime did much to maintain the status quo. Party officers exercised some political supervision over bureaucrats, yet did not infiltrate the bureaucracy in significant numbers. Moreover, Mussolini remained on

Mussolini Reviews a Fascist Youth Parade. Mobilizing youth was central to fascism and Nazism; it demonstrated the vigor of the movements.

friendly terms with the elites who had assisted his rise to power. Whatever he might proclaim about the distinctions between fascism and capitalism, the economy of Italy remained dependent on private enterprise.

The Italian dictator boasted that fascism had pulled the country back from economic chaos. Like other European economies, the Italian economy did improve in the late 1920s. The regime created the appearance of efficiency, and Mussolini's admirers famously claimed that he had at last "made the trains run on time." Fascism, however, did little to lessen Italy's plight during the worldwide depression of the 1930s.

Like Nazism later, fascism had contradictory elements. It sought to restore traditional authority and, at the same time, mobilize all of Italian society for economic and nationalist purposes—a process that inevitably undercut older authorities. It created new authoritarian organizations and activities that comported with these goals: exercise programs to make the young fit and mobilized, youth camps, awards to mothers of large families, political rallies, and parades in small towns in the countryside. Activities like these offered people a feeling of political involvement though they no longer enjoyed political rights. This mobilized but essentially passive citizenship was a hallmark of fascism.

WEIMAR GERMANY

Was the Weimar Republic vulnerable?

On November 9, 1918—two days before the armistice ending World War I—thousands of Germans swarmed the streets of Berlin in a nearly bloodless overthrow of the imperial government. A massive and largely unexpected uprising, the demonstration converged on the Reichstag in the city center, where a member of the Social Democratic Party (SPD) announced the birth of the new German republic. The kaiser had abdicated only hours before, turning the government over to the Social Democratic leader Friedrich Ebert. The revolution spread quickly through the war-ravaged country; councils of workers and soldiers controlled most major cities within a couple of days, and hundreds of cities by month's end.

The "November Revolution" was fast and far reaching, though not as revolutionary as many middle- and upper-class conservatives feared. The majority of socialists steered a cautious, democratic course: they wanted reforms but were willing to leave much of the existing imperial bureaucracy intact. Above all, they wanted a popularly elected national assembly to draft a constitution for the new republic.

Two months passed, however, before elections could be held—a period of crisis that verged on civil war. Once in control, the Social Democratic leadership made order its top priority. The revolutionary movement that had brought the SPD to power now threatened it. Independent socialists and a nascent Communist Party wanted radical reforms, and in December 1918 and January 1919, they staged armed uprisings in the streets of Berlin. Fearful of a Bolshevik-style revolution, the Social Democratic government turned against its former allies and sent militant bands of workers and volunteers to crush the uprisings. During the conflict, the government's fighters murdered Rosa Luxemburg and Karl Liebknecht—two German communist leaders who became instant martyrs. Violence continued into 1920, creating a lasting bitterness among groups on the left.

More important, the revolutionary aftermath of the war gave rise to bands of militant counterrevolutionaries. Veterans and other young nationalists joined so-called *Freikorps* (free corps). Such groups developed throughout the country, drawing as many as several hundred thousand members. Former army officers who led these militias continued their war experience by fighting against Bolsheviks, Poles, and communists. The politics of the Freikorps were fiercely right wing. Anti-Marxist, anti-Semitic, and antiliberal, they openly opposed the new German republic and its parliamentary democracy. Many of the early Nazi leaders had fought in World War I and participated in Freikorps units.

Germany's new government—known as the Weimar Republic (*VY-mahr*) for the city in which its constitution was drafted—rested on a coalition of socialists, Catholic centrists, and liberal democrats, a necessary compromise since no single party won a majority of the votes in the January 1919 election. The Weimar constitution was based on the values of parliamentary liberalism and set up an open, pluralistic framework for German democracy. Through a series of compromises,

> The politics of the Freikorps were fiercely right wing. Anti-Marxist, anti-Semitic, and antiliberal, they openly opposed the new German republic and its parliamentary democracy.

the constitution established universal suffrage (for both women and men) and a bill of rights that guaranteed not only civil liberties but also a range of social entitlements. On paper, at least, the revolutionary movement had succeeded.

Yet the Weimar government lasted just over a decade. By 1930 it was in crisis, and in 1933 it collapsed. What happened? The failure of German democracy was not a foregone conclusion. It resulted from a combination of social, political, and economic crises that were singly manageable but collectively disastrous.

Many of Weimar's problems were born from Germany's defeat in World War I, which was not only devastating but also humiliating. The ignominious loss to the Allies shocked many Germans, who soon latched onto rumors that the army hadn't actually been defeated in battle but instead had been stabbed in the back by socialists and Jewish leaders in the German government. Army officers cultivated this story even before the war was over; and though untrue, it helped salve the wounded pride of German patriots. In the next decade, those in search of a scapegoat also blamed the seemingly lax republican regime, epitomized by what they considered the modern decadence of 1920s Berlin. What was needed, many critics argued, was authoritative leadership to guide the nation and regain the world's respect.

The Treaty of Versailles magnified Germany's sense of dishonor. Germany was forced to cede a tenth of its territory, accept responsibility for the war, and slash the size of its army to a mere 100,000 men—a punishment that riled the politically powerful corps of officers. Most important, the treaty saddled Germany with punitive reparations. Negotiating the $33 billion debt created problems for all the governments involved; provoked anger from the German public; and, in a global economy, had unintended effects on the recipients as well as the debtors. Some opponents of the reparations settlement urged an obstructionist policy of nonpayment, arguing that the enormous sum would doom Germany's economy for the foreseeable future. Indeed, by one estimate, the debt would not have been paid off until 1987. In 1924 Germany accepted a new schedule of reparations designed by an international committee headed by the American financier Charles G. Dawes and the German chancellor Gustav Stresemann had moved Germany toward a foreign policy of cooperation and rapprochement that lasted throughout the 1920s. Many German people, however, continued to resent reparations, Versailles, and the government that refused to repudiate the treaty.

Hyperinflation. German children use stacks of money as toys. In July 1922, the American dollar was worth 670 German marks; in November 1923 it was worth 4,210,500,000,000.

Major economic crises also played a central role in Weimar's collapse. The first period of emergency occurred in the early 1920s. Still reeling from wartime inflation, the government was hard pressed for revenues. Funding postwar demobilization programs, social welfare, and reparations forced the government to continue to print money. Inflation became nearly unstoppable. By 1923, as one historian writes, the economic situation had "acquired an almost surrealistic quality." A pound of potatoes cost about nine marks in January, 40 million marks by October. Beef went for almost 2 trillion marks per pound. The government finally took drastic measures to stabilize the currency in 1924, but millions of Germans had already been ruined. For those on fixed incomes, such as pensioners and stockholders, savings and security had vanished. Middle-class employees, farmers, and workers were all hard hit by the economic crisis, and many of them abandoned the traditional political parties in protest. In their eyes, the parties that claimed to represent the middle classes had created the problems and proved incapable of fixing them.

Beginning in 1925, however, Germany's economy and government seemed to be recovering. By borrowing money, the country was able to make its scaled-down reparations payments and to earn money by selling cheap exports. In large cities, socialist municipal governments sponsored building projects that included schools, hospitals, and low-cost worker housing. But such economic and political stability was misleading. The economy remained dependent on large infusions of capital from the United States set up by the Dawes plan as part of the effort to settle reparations. That dependence made the German economy especially vulnerable to American economic developments. When the U.S. stock market crashed in 1929, beginning the Great Depression (discussed later in this chapter), capital flow to Germany virtually stopped.

The Great Depression pushed Weimar's political system to the breaking point. In 1929, there were 2 million unemployed; in 1932, 6 million. In those three years production dropped by 44 percent. Artisans and small shopkeepers lost both status and income. Farmers fared even worse, having never recovered from the crisis of the early 1920s. Peasants staged mass demonstrations against the government's agricultural policies even before the depression hit. For white-collar and civil service employees, the depression meant lower salaries, poor working conditions, and a constant threat of unemployment. The government drifted toward crisis itself, facing opposition from all sides. Burdened with plummeting tax revenues and spiraling numbers of Germans in need of relief, the government repeatedly cut welfare benefits, which further demoralized the electorate. Finally, the crisis created an opportunity for Weimar's opponents. Many leading industrialists supported a return to authoritarian government, and they were allied with equally conservative landowners, united by a desire for protective economic policies to stimulate the sale of domestic goods and foodstuffs. Those conservative forces wielded considerable power in Germany, beyond the control of the government. So too did the army and the civil service, which were staffed with opponents of the republic—men who rejected the principles of parliamentary democracy and international cooperation that Weimar represented.

The Great Depression pushed Weimar's political system to the breaking point. In 1929, there were 2 million unemployed; in 1932, 6 million. In those three years production dropped by 44 percent.

Hitler and the National Socialists

How did the Nazis come to power?

Adolf Hitler was born in 1889 in Austria, not Germany. The son of a petty customs official in the Austrian civil service, Hitler dropped out of school and went to Vienna in 1909 to become an artist. That failed. He was rejected by the academy and forced to eke out a dismal existence doing manual labor and painting cheap watercolors in Vienna. Meanwhile he developed the violent political prejudices that would become the guiding principles of the Nazi regime. He ardently admired the Austrian politicians preaching anti-Semitism, anti-Marxism, and Pan-Germanism. When war broke out in 1914, Hitler was among the jubilant crowds in the streets of Munich; and though he was an Austrian citizen, he enlisted in the German army, where he claimed to have finally found meaning in his life. After the war, he joined the newly formed German Workers' Party, whose name changed in 1920 to the National Socialist Workers' Party (abbreviated in popular usage to Nazi). The Nazis were but one among many small, militant groups of disaffected Germans devoted to racial nationalism and to the overthrow of the Weimar Republic. They grew out of the political milieu that refused to accept the defeat or the November Revolution and that blamed both on socialists and Jews.

Ambitious and outspoken, Hitler quickly moved up the rather short ladder of party leadership as a talented stump orator. By 1921 he was the *Führer*—the leader—to his followers in Bavaria. The wider public saw him as a "vulgar demagogue"—if they noticed him at all. In November 1923, during the worst days of the inflation crisis, the Nazis made a failed attempt (the Beer Hall Putsch in Munich) at overthrowing the state government of Bavaria. Hitler spent the next seven months in prison, where he wrote his autobiography and political manifesto *Mein Kampf* (*myn KAHMPF*) (My struggle) in 1924. Combining anti-Semitism with anticommunism, the book set out at great length the popular theory that Germany had been betrayed by its enemies and that the country needed strong leadership to regain international prominence. The failed 1923 putsch proved an eye-opening experience for Hitler; he recognized that the Nazis would have to play politics if they wanted to gain power. Released from prison in 1924, Hitler resumed leadership of the party. In the next five years, he consolidated his power over a growing membership of ardent supporters. Actively cultivating the image of the Nazi movement as a crusade against (Jewish) Marxism and capitalism, he portrayed himself as the heroic savior of the German people.

An equally important factor in Hitler's rise to power was the Nazis' ambitious and unprecedented campaign program. In the "inflation election" of 1924, the Nazis polled 6.6 percent of the vote as a protest party at the radical fringe. With the economic stabilization of the mid-1920s, their meager share dropped to below 3 percent. But during this time of seeming decline, the Nazis were building an extensive organization of party activists that helped lay the foundation for the party's electoral gains later.

The 1928 election was a pivotal moment for both Weimar and for the Nazis for two reasons. First, from this point on, politics became polarized between right and left, making it virtually impossible to put together a coalition that would support the continuation of Weimar democracy. Second, it was apparent that alienated voters, especially peasants, were deserting their traditional political parties and voting for other interest-group organizations that would voice their grievances and push their demands. The Nazis quickly learned how to benefit from this splintering of the electorate. Previously they had tried, with little success, to win the large German working-class vote away from the left. Now, guided by its chief propagandist, Joseph Goebbels, the party stepped up its efforts to attract members of the urban and rural middle classes. The party's most consistent message, hammered home in propaganda, speeches, and rallies, was that the Nazis opposed everything about Weimar: the political system, economic organizations, the left and the labor movement, the more liberal moral codes, women wearing "decadent" flapper fashions, and "cosmopolitan" movies such as *All Quiet on the Western Front.* (Nazi gangs started a street riot outside the first showing of the film in Berlin; Goebbels broke up a later showing by tossing stench bombs and mice into the theater.) The answers to Germany's problems, the Nazis argued, could be found only by breaking with Weimar. Presenting itself

> Other segments of the middle class—notably pensioners, the elderly, and war widows—came to support the Nazis during the economic crisis, when they feared reduction of insurance or pension benefits and when the older conservative parties failed to meet their needs.

as young and dynamic, the party built a national profile as an alternative to the parties of middle-class conservatives. In 1930, bolstered by the economic crisis, the Nazis were better funded and better organized than ever, and they won 18.3 percent of the vote.

Who voted for the Nazis? Recent analysis of election results and campaign materials suggests that different groups supported the Nazis at varying times and for varying reasons. The Nazis polled highly with small property holders and the rural middle class long before the depression. The Nazis offered these voters economic protection and renewed social status. Other segments of the middle class—notably pensioners, the elderly, and war widows—came to support the Nazis during the economic crisis, when they feared reduction of insurance or pension benefits and when the older conservative parties failed to meet their needs. The Nazis also courted the traditionally elitist civil service. And though they failed to win votes from industrial workers, the Nazis found some of their strongest support among workers in handicrafts and small-scale manufacturing.

In 1930, the Nazi Party won 107 of 577 seats in the Reichstag, second only to the Social Democrats, who controlled 143. No party could gain a majority. No governing coalition was possible without Nazi support. And the Nazis refused to join any cabinet that was not headed by Hitler. The chancellor, Heinrich Brüning of the Catholic Center Party, continued to govern by emergency decrees, but his deflationary economic policies were disastrous. Industrial production

CHRONOLOGY

THE RISE OF NAZISM, 1920–1934

National Socialist Workers' Party founded	1920
Beer Hall Putsch in Munich	1923
Hitler writes *Mein Kampf* in prison	1924
Hitler consolidates power	1924–1929
Hitler loses presidential election	1932
Hitler appointed chancellor of Germany	1933
Nazi Party rules Germany	1933
Night of Long Knives	1934

Nazism and the Rural Myth. To stress the rural roots of Aryan Germany, Hitler appeared in lederhosen in the 1920s.

continued to crash and unemployment continued to climb. In 1932, Hitler ran for president and narrowly lost, although he staged an unprecedented campaign by airplane, visiting twenty-one cities in six days. When another parliamentary election was called in July 1932, the Nazis won 37.4 percent of the vote, which, though not a majority, was a significant plurality. The Nazis could claim that they were the party able to draw support across class, geographic, and generational lines. They benefited from their position as outsiders, untainted by involvement in unpopular parliamentary coalitions. Indeed, the failure of the traditional parties was key to the success of the Nazis.

Despite its electoral success in 1932, the Nazi Party had not won a majority; Hitler was not in power. Instead, Hitler was appointed chancellor in January 1933 by President Hindenburg, who hoped to create a conservative coalition government by bringing the Nazis into line with the less radical parties. Hindenburg and others in the government had underestimated the Nazis' power and popularity. Legally installed in office, Hitler immediately made the most of it. When a Dutch anarchist with links to the Communist Party set fire to the Reichstag on

the night of February 27, Hitler seized the opportunity to suspend civil rights "as a defensive measure against communist acts of violence." He convinced Hindenburg to dissolve the Reichstag and to order a new election on March 5, 1933. Under Hitler's sway, the new parliament legally granted him unlimited powers for the next four years. Hitler proclaimed his new government the Third Reich. (The first Reich was the German Empire of the Middle Ages; the second was that of the kaisers.)

Nazi Germany

By the fall of 1933, Germany had become a one-party state. The socialist and communist left was crushed by the new regime. Almost all non-Nazi organizations had been either abolished or forced to become part of the Nazi system. Nazi Party leaders took over various government departments; party *Gauleiters*, or regional directors, assumed administrative responsibility throughout the country. Party propaganda sought to impress citizens with the regime's "monolithic efficiency." But in fact, the Nazi government was a tangled bureaucratic maze, with both agencies and individuals vying fiercely for Hitler's favor.

Ironically, at the end of the party's first year in power, the most serious challenges to Hitler came from within the party. Hitler's paramilitary Nazi storm troopers (the SA) had been formed to maintain discipline within the party and impose order in society. SA membership soared after 1933, and many in the SA hailed Hitler's appointment as the beginning of a genuinely Nazi revolution. Such radicalism was alarming to the more traditional conservative groups that had helped make Hitler chancellor. If Hitler was to maintain power, then, he needed to tame the SA. On the night of June 30, 1934, more than a thousand high-ranking SA officials, including several of Hitler's oldest associates, were executed in a bloody purge known as the Night of Long Knives. The purge cleared the way for a second paramilitary organization, the *Schutzstaffel* ("bodyguard"), or SS. Headed by the fanatical Heinrich Himmler, the SS became the most dreaded arm of Nazi terror. As Himmler saw it, the mission of the SS was to fight political and racial enemies of the regime, which included building the system of concentration camps. The first camp, at Dachau, opened in March 1933. The secret state police, known as the Gestapo, were responsible for the arrest, incarceration in camps, and murder of thousands of Germans. But the police force was generally understaffed and deluged with paperwork—as one historian has shown, the Gestapo was not "omniscient, omnipotent, and omnipresent." In fact, the majority of arrests was based on voluntary denunciations made by ordinary citizens against each other, often as petty personal attacks. It was not lost on the Gestapo leadership that these denunciations created a level of control that the Gestapo itself could never achieve.

Despite—or perhaps because of—these efforts to quash opposition, Hitler and the Nazis enjoyed a sizable amount of popular support. Many Germans approved of Hitler's use of violence against the left. The Nazis could play on deep-seated fears of communism, and they spoke a language of intense national pride and unity that had broad appeal. Many Germans saw Hitler as a symbol of a strong, revitalized Germany. Propagandists fostered a Führer cult, depicting Hitler as a charismatic leader with the magnetic energy to bring people to their knees. Hitler's appeal also rested on his ability to give the German people what they wanted: jobs for workers, a productive economy for industrialists, a bulwark against communism for those who feared the wave of revolution. His appeal lay not so much in the programs he championed, many of which were ill conceived or contradictory, but in his revolt against politics as they had been practiced in Germany. Finally, he promised to lead Germany back to national greatness and to "overthrow" the Versailles settlement, and through the 1930s he seemed to be doing so with a series of bloodless diplomatic triumphs.

Hitler's plans for national recovery called for full-scale rearmament and economic self-sufficiency. With policies similar to those of other Western nations, the Nazis made massive public investments, set strict market controls to stop inflation and stabilize the currency, and sealed Germany off from the world economy. The regime launched state financed construction projects—highways, public housing, reforestation. Late in the decade, as the Nazis rebuilt the entire German military complex, unemployment dropped from over 6 million to under 200,000. The German economy looked better than any other in Europe. Hitler claimed this as his "economic miracle." Such improvements were significant, especially in the eyes of Germans who had lived through the continual turmoil of war, inflation, political instability, and economic crisis.

Like Mussolini, Hitler moved to abolish class conflict by stripping working-class institutions of their power. He outlawed trade unions and strikes, froze wages, and organized workers and employers into a National Labor Front. At the same time, the Nazis increased workers' welfare benefits, generally in line with the other Western nations. Class distinctions were somewhat blurred by the regime's attempts to infuse a new national "spirit" into the entire society. Popular organizations cut across class lines, especially among the youth. The Hitler Youth, a club modeled on the Boy Scouts, was highly successful at teaching children the values of Hitler's Reich; the National Labor Service drafted students for a term to work on state-sponsored building and reclamation projects. Government policy encouraged women to withdraw from the labor force, both to ease unemployment and to conform to Nazi notions of a woman's proper role. "Can woman," one propagandist asked, "conceive of anything more beautiful than to sit with her husband in her cozy home and listen inwardly to the loom of time weaving the weft and warp of motherhood?"

NAZI RACISM

At the core of Nazi ideology lay a particularly virulent racism. Much of this racism was not new. Hitler and the Nazis drew on a revived and especially violent form of nineteenth-century social Darwinism, according to which nations and people struggled for survival, with the superior peoples strengthening themselves in the process. By the early twentieth century, the rise of the social sciences had taken nineteenth-century prejudices and racial thinking into new terrain. Just as medical science had cured bodily ills, doctors, criminologists, and social workers sought ways to cure social ills. Across the West, scientists and intellectuals worked to purify the body politic, improve the human race, and eliminate the "unfit." Even progressive-minded individuals sometimes subscribed to eugenics, a program of racial engineering to improve either personal or public fitness. Eugenic policies in the Third Reich began with a 1933 law for the compulsory sterilization of "innumerable inferior and hereditarily tainted" people. This "social-hygienic racism" later became the systematic murder of mentally and physically ill patients. Social policy was governed by a basic division between those who possessed "value" and those who did not, with the aim of creating a racial utopia.

The centerpiece of Nazi racism was anti-Semitism. This centuries-old phenomenon was part of Christian society from the Middle Ages on. By the nineteenth century, traditional Christian anti-Semitism was joined by a current of nationalist anti-Jewish theory. A great many of the theorists of European nationalism saw the Jewish people as permanent outsiders who could only be assimilated and become citizens if they denied their Jewish

NAZI PROPAGANDA

The Nazis promised many things to many people. As the document by Goebbels shows, anti-Semitism allowed them to blend their racial nationalism, vaguely defined (and anti-Marxist) socialism, and disgust with the state of German culture and politics. Joseph Goebbels, one of the early members of the party, became director of propaganda for the party in 1928. Later Hitler appointed him head of the National Ministry for Public Enlightenment and Propaganda. The Nazis worked hard to win the rural vote, as evidenced by the Nazi campaign pamphlet reprinted in the second excerpt. The Nazis tried to appeal to farmers' economic grievances, their fears of socialism on the one hand and big business on the other, and their more general hostility to urban life and culture.

JOSEPH GOEBBELS, "WHY ARE WE ENEMIES OF THE JEWS?"

We are NATIONALISTS because we see in the NATION the only possibility for the protection and the furtherance of our existence.

The NATION is the organic bond of a people for the protection and defense of their lives. He is nationally minded who understands this IN WORD AND IN DEED. . . .

Young nationalism has its unconditional demands, BELIEF IN THE NATION is a matter of all the people, not for individuals of rank, a class, or an industrial clique. The eternal must be separated from the contemporary. The maintenance of a rotten industrial system has nothing to do with nationalism. I can love Germany and hate capitalism; not only CAN I do it, I also MUST do it. The germ of the rebirth of our people LIES ONLY IN THE DESTRUCTION OF THE SYSTEM OF PLUNDERING THE HEALTHY POWER OF THE PEOPLE.

WE ARE NATIONALISTS BECAUSE WE, AS GERMANS, LOVE GERMANY. And because we love Germany, we demand the protection of its national spirit and we battle against its destroyers.

WHY ARE WE SOCIALISTS?

We are SOCIALISTS because we see in SOCIALISM the only possibility for maintaining our racial existence and through it the reconquest of our political freedom and the rebirth of the German state. SOCIALISM has its peculiar form first of all through its comradeship in arms with the forward-driving energy of a newly awakened nationalism. Without nationalism it is nothing, a phantom, a theory, a vision of air, a book. With it, it is everything, THE FUTURE, FREEDOM, FATHERLAND! . . .

WHY DO WE OPPOSE THE JEWS?

We are ENEMIES OF THE JEWS, because we are fighters for the freedom of the German people. THE JEW IS THE CAUSE AND THE BENEFICIARY OF OUR MISERY. He has used the social difficulties of the broad masses of our people to deepen the unholy split between Right and Left among our people. He has made two halves of Germany. He is the real cause for our loss of the Great War.

The Jew has no interest in the solution of Germany's fateful problems. He CANNOT have any. FOR HE LIVES ON THE FACT THAT THERE HAS BEEN NO SOLUTION. If we would make the German people a unified community and give them freedom before the world, then the Jew can have no place among us. He has the best trumps in his hands when a people lives in inner and outer slavery. THE JEW IS RESPONSIBLE FOR OUR MISERY AND HE LIVES ON IT.

That is the reason why we, AS NATIONALISTS and AS SOCIALISTS, oppose the Jew. HE HAS CORRUPTED OUR RACE, FOULED OUR MORALS, UNDERMINED OUR CUSTOMS, AND BROKEN OUR POWER.

NATIONAL SOCIALIST CAMPAIGN PAMPHLET, 1932

GERMAN FARMER YOU BELONG TO HITLER! WHY?

The German farmer stands between two great dangers today:

The one danger is the American economic system—Big capitalism!

it means "world economic crisis"

it means "eternal interest slavery" . . .

it means that the world is nothing more than a bag of booty for Jewish finance in Wall Street, New York, and Paris

it enslaves man under the slogans of progress, technology, rationalization, standardization, etc.

it knows only profit and dividends

it wants to make the world into a giant trust

it puts the machine over man

it annihilates the independent, earth-rooted farmer, and its final aim is the world dictatorship of Jewry [. . .]

it achieves this in the political sphere through parliament and the swindle of democracy. In the economic sphere, through the control of credit, the mortgaging of land, the stock exchange and the market principle [. . .]

The farmer's leagues, the Landvolk and the Bavarian Farmers' League all pay homage to this system.

The other danger is the Marxist economic system of bolshevism:

it knows only the state economy

it knows only one class, the proletariat

it brings in the controlled economy

it doesn't just annihilate the self-sufficient farmer economically—it roots him out [. . .]

it brings the rule of the tractor

it nationalizes the land and creates mammoth factory-farms

it uproots and destroys man's soul, making him the powerless tool of the communist idea—or kills him

it destroys the family, belief, and customs [. . .]

it is anti-Christ, it desecrates the churches [. . .]

its final aim is the world dictatorship of the proletariat, that means ultimately the world dictatorship of Jewry, for the Jew controls this powerless proletariat and uses it for his dark plans

Big capitalism and bolshevism work hand in hand; they are born of Jewish thought and serve the master plan of world Jewry.

Who alone can rescue the farmer from these dangers?

NATIONAL SOCIALISM!

Anton Kaes, Matin Jay, and Edward Dimendberg, *The Weimar Republic Sourcebook* (Los Angeles, 1994), pp. 137–38, 142 (source for both documents).

QUESTIONS FOR ANALYSIS

1. How did Goebbels use metaphors of illness and health, growth and decay? Do the metaphors suggest what the Nazis would try to do to cure the ills of Germany if they took power?

2. How does Goebels's anti-Semitism differ from the nineteenth-century French anti-Semitism documented on page 839?

3. The Nazi campaign pamphlet of 1932 targeted German farmers. How did the pamphlet play on their fears of market manipulation by American big business and Bolshevik demands for collectivization and seizure of private land? How did the Nazis identify themselves with Christianity and traditional values, sincerely or not?

4. How, specifically, does the party proposed to deal with the "two great dangers of today"?

identity. At the end of the nineteenth century, during the Dreyfus affair in France (see Chapter Twenty-three), French and European anti-Semites launched a barrage of propaganda against Jews—scores of books, pamphlets, and magazines blamed Jews for all the troubles of modernity, from socialism to international banks and mass culture. The late nineteenth century also brought a wave of pogroms—violent assaults on Jewish communities—

especially in Russia. Racial anti-Semitism drew the line between Jews and non-Jews on the basis of erroneous biology. Religious conversion, which traditional Christian anti-Semites encouraged, would not change biology. Nor would assimilation, which was counseled by more secular nationalist thinkers.

It is important not to generalize, but anti-Semitism in these different forms was a well-established and open political force in most of the West. By attacking Jews, anti-Semites attacked modern institutions—from socialist parties and the mass press to international banking—as part of a "international Jewish conspiracy" to undermine traditional authority and nationality. Conservative Party leaders told shopkeepers and workers that "Jewish capitalists" were responsible for the demise of small businesses, for the rise of giant department stores, and for precarious economic swings that threatened their livelihoods. In Vienna, middle-class voters supported the openly anti-Semitic Christian Democrats. In Germany, in 1893, sixteen avowed anti-Semites were elected to the Reichstag, and the Conservative party made anti-Semitism part of its official program. Hitler gave this anti-Semitism an especially murderous twist by tying it to doctrines of war and social-hygienic racism.

To what extent was the Nazis' virulent anti-Semitism shared? Although the "Jewish Question" was clearly Hitler's primary obsession during the early 1920s, he made the theme less central in campaign appearances as the Nazi movement entered mainstream politics, shifting instead to attacks on Marxism and the Weimar democracy. Moreover, anti-Semitic beliefs would not have distinguished the Nazi from any other party on the political right; it was likely of only secondary importance to people's opinions of the Nazis. Soon after Hitler came to power, though, German Jews faced discrimination, exclusion from rights as citizens, and violence. Racial laws excluded Jews from public office as early as April 1933. The Nazis encouraged a boycott of Jewish merchants, while the SA created a constant threat of random violence. In 1935, the Nuremberg Decrees deprived Jews (defined by bloodline) of their German citizenship and prohibited marriage between Jews and other Germans. Violence escalated. In November 1938, the SA attacked some 7,500 Jewish stores, burned nearly 200 synagogues, killed ninety-one Jews, and beat up thousands more in a campaign of terror known as *Kristallnacht*, the Night of Broken Glass. Violence like this did raise some opposition from ordinary Germans. Legal persecution, however, met only silent acquiescence. And from the perspective of Jewish people, *Kristallnacht* made it plain that there was no safe place for them in Germany. Unfortunately, only one year remained before the outbreak of war made it impossible for Jews to escape.

What did national socialism and fascism have in common? Both arose in the interwar period as responses to World War I and the Russian Revolution. Both were violently antisocialist and anti-communist, determined to "rescue" their nations from the threat of Bolshevism. Both were intensely nationalistic; they believed that national solidarity came before all other allegiances and superseded all other rights. Both opposed parliamentary government and democracy as cumbersome and divisive. Both found their power in mass-based authoritarian politics. Similar movements existed in all the countries of the West, but only in a few cases did they actually form regimes. Nazism, however, distinguished itself by making a racially pure state central to its vision, a vision that would lead to global struggle and mass murder.

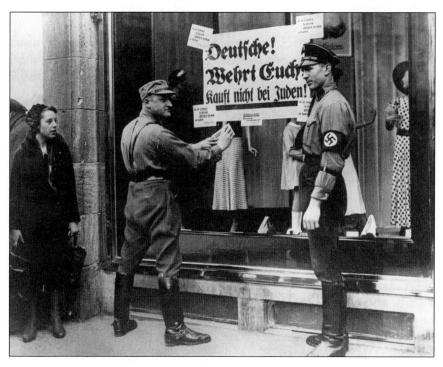

Nazi boycott of Jewish shops in Berlin, 1933. Nazis stand in front of a Jewish-owned clothing store. "Germans! Buy nothing from the Jews!"

THE GREAT DEPRESSION IN THE DEMOCRACIES

How did the Western democracies deal with the Great Depression?

The histories of the three major Western democracies—Great Britain, France, and the United States—run roughly parallel during the years after World War I. In all three countries governments put their trust in prewar policies and assumptions until the Great Depression forced them to make major social and economic reforms, reforms that would lay the foundations of the modern welfare state. These nations weathered the upheavals of the interwar years, but they did not do so easily.

France continued to fear Germany and took every opportunity to keep the Germans as weak as possible. Under the leadership of the moderate conservative Raymond Poincaré during the 1920s, France tried to keep the price of manufactured goods low by restraining wages. This policy of deflation kept businessmen happy but put a heavy burden on the working class. Édouard Herriot interrupted Poincaré's service as premier, serving for two years in the mid-1920s. A radical socialist by affiliation, Herriot was a spokesman for small-business owners, farmers, and the lower middle class. Herriot said he supported social reform, but he refused to raise taxes to pay for it. Meanwhile, class conflict simmered just below the surface. As industries prospered, employers refused to bargain with labor unions. A period of major strikes immediately after the war was followed by a sharp decline in union activity. And even though the government passed a modified social insurance program in 1930—insuring against sickness, old age, and death—workers remained dissatisfied.

Social conflict flared in Britain as well. Anxious to regain its position as the major industrial and financial power in the world, Britain also pursued a policy of deflation, hoping to make its manufactured goods cheaper and more attractive on the world market. The result was a reduction in wages that undermined the standard of living of many British workers. Their resentment helped elect the first Labour Party government in 1924, and a second in 1929. The Labour Party accomplished little, however, because of its minority position in Parliament. Besides, its leader, Prime Minister J. Ramsay MacDonald, was a rather timid socialist. The Conservative government returned to power in 1925 under Stanley Baldwin and refused to abandon its deflationary policy, which continued to drive down wages. British trade unions grew increasingly militant in response, and in 1926, the unions staged a nationwide general strike. The strike's only appreciable effect was to heighten middle-class antipathy toward workers.

The United States was the bastion of conservatism among the democracies. The presidents elected in the 1920s—Warren G. Harding, Calvin Coolidge, and Herbert Hoover—upheld a social philosophy formulated by the barons of big business in the nineteenth century. The Supreme Court used its power of judicial review to nullify progressive legislation enacted by state governments and occasionally by Congress.

The conservative economic and social policies of the prewar period were dealt their deathblow by the Great Depression of 1929. This worldwide depression peaked during the years 1929–1933, but its effects lasted a decade. For those who went through it, the depression was perhaps the formative experience of their lives and the decisive crisis of the interwar period. It was an important factor in the rise of Nazism; but in fact, it forced every country to forge new economic policies and to deal with unprecedented economic turmoil.

THE ORIGINS OF THE GREAT DEPRESSION

What caused the Great Depression? Its deepest roots lay in the instability of national currencies, and in the interdependence of national economies. Throughout the 1920s, Europeans had seen a sluggish growth rate. A major drop in world agricultural prices hurt the countries of southern and eastern Europe, where agriculture was small in scale and high in cost. Unable to make a profit on the international market, these agricultural countries bought fewer manufactured goods from the more industrial sectors of northern Europe, causing a widespread drop in industrial productivity. Restrictions on free trade crippled the economy even more. Although debtor nations needed open markets to sell their goods, most nations were raising high trade barriers to protect domestic manufacturers from foreign competition.

Then in October of 1929, prices on the New York Stock Exchange collapsed. On October 24, "Black Thursday," 12 million shares were traded amid unprecedented chaos. Even more surprising, the market kept falling. Black Thursday was followed by Black

How did the Western democracies deal with the Great Depression?

The Great Depression in the Democracies   927

Monday and then Black Tuesday: falling prices, combined with an enormously high number of trades, made for the worst day in the history of the stock exchange to that point. The rise of the United States as an international creditor during the Great War meant that the crash had immediate, disastrous consequences in Europe. When the value of stocks dropped, banks found themselves short of capital and then, when not rescued by the government, forced to close. International investors called in their debts. A series of banking houses shut their doors, among them Credit Anstalt, the biggest bank in Austria and one with significant interests in two thirds of Austrian industry. Workers lost their jobs, indeed manufacturers laid off virtually entire workforces. In 1930, 4 million Americans were unemployed, in 1933, 13 million—nearly a third of the workforce. By then, per capita income in the United States had fallen 48 percent. In Germany, too, the drop was brutal. In 1929, 2 million were unemployed; in 1932, 6 million. Production dropped 44 percent in Germany, 47 percent in the United States. The stock-market collapse led to widespread bank failure and brought the economy virtually to a standstill.

The governments of the West initially responded to the depression with monetary measures. In 1931 Great Britain abandoned the gold standard; the United States followed suit in 1933. By no longer pegging their currencies to the price of gold, these countries hoped to make money cheaper and thus more available for economic recovery programs. This action was the forerunner of a broad program of currency management, which became an important element in a general policy of economic nationalism. In another important move, Great Britain abandoned its time-honored policy of free trade in 1932, raising protective tariffs as high as 100 percent. But monetary policy alone could not end the hardships of ordinary families. Governments were increasingly forced to address their concerns with a wide range of social reforms.

Britain was the most cautious in its relief efforts. A national government composed of Conservative, Liberal, and Labour Party members came to power in 1931. To underwrite effective programs of public assistance, however, the government would have to spend beyond its income—something it was reluctant to do. France, on the other hand, adopted the most advanced set of policies to combat the effects of the

> Black Thursday was followed by Black Monday and then Black Tuesday: falling prices, combined with an enormously high number of trades, made for the worst day in the history of the stock exchange to that point.

depression. In 1936, responding to a threat from ultraconservatives to overthrow the republic, a Popular Front government under the leadership of the socialist Léon Blum was formed by the Radical, Radical Socialist, and Communist Parties, and lasted for two years. The Popular Front nationalized the munitions industry and reorganized the Bank of France to break the largest stockholders' monopolistic control over credit. The government also decreed a forty-hour week for all urban workers and initiated a program of public works. For the benefit of the farmers it established a wheat office to fix the price and regulate the distribution of grain. Although the Popular Front temporarily quelled the threat from the political right, conservatives were generally uncooperative and unimpressed by the attempts to aid the French working class. Both a socialist and Jewish, Blum faced fierce anti-Semitism in France. Fearing that Blum was the forerunner of a French Lenin, conservatives declared, "Better Hitler than Blum." They got their wish before the decade was out.

The most dramatic response to the depression came in the United States for two reasons. First, the United States had clung longest to nineteenth-century economic philosophy. Before the depression, the business classes adhered firmly to the creed of freedom of contract. Industrialists insisted on their right to form monopolies, and they used the government as a tool to frustrate the demands of both workers and consumers. Second, the depression was more severe in the United States than in the European democracies. America had survived World War I unscathed—and indeed, had benefited enormously—but now its economy was ravaged even more than Europe's. In 1933, Franklin D. Roosevelt succeeded Herbert Hoover as president and announced the New Deal, a program of reform and reconstruction to rescue the country.

The New Deal aimed to get the country back on its feet without destroying the capitalist system. The government would manage the economy, sponsor relief programs, and fund public-works projects to increase mass purchasing power. These policies were shaped by the theories of the British economist John Maynard Keynes, who had already proved influential during the 1919 treaty meetings at Paris. Keynes argued that capitalism could create a just and efficient society if governments played a part in its management. First, Keynes abandoned the sacred cow of balanced budgets. Without advocating continuous deficit financing, he would have the government deliberately operate in the red whenever private investments weren't enough. Keynes also favored the creation of large amounts of venture capital —money for high-risk, high-reward investments—which he saw as the only socially productive form of capital. Finally, he recommended monetary control to promote prosperity and full employment.

Along with Social Security and other programs, the United States adopted a Keynesian program of "currency management," regulating the value of the dollar according to the needs of the economy. The New Deal helped both individuals and the country recover, but it left the crucial problem of unemployment unsolved. In 1939, after six years of the New Deal, the United States still had more than 9 million jobless workers—a figure that exceeded the combined unemployment of the rest of the world. Only with the outbreak of a new world war—which required millions of soldiers and armament workers—did the United States reach the full recovery that the New Deal had failed to deliver.

U.S. Farmers on Their Way West in the 1930s. Forced from their land by depression, debts, and drought, thousands of farmers and their families headed to California, Oregon, and Washington in search of employment.

INTERWAR CULTURE: ARTISTS AND INTELLECTUALS

How did artists respond to political and cultural polarization?

We have seen how governments and their citizens responded to social, political, and economic crises. The interwar period brought equally dramatic upheavals in the arts and sciences. Revolutionary artistic forms that were pioneered at the turn of the century moved from the margins to the mainstream. Artists, writers, architects, and composers rejected traditional aesthetic values and experimented with new forms of expression.

Scientists and psychologists challenged deeply held beliefs about the universe and about human nature. Finally, mass culture, in the form of radio, movies, and advertising, sharpened many anxieties, and stood as a stark example of the promise and peril of modern times.

INTERWAR INTELLECTUALS

Like many other people, novelists, poets, and dramatists were disillusioned by the brute facts of world war and by the failure of victory to fulfill its promises. Much of the literature of the interwar period reflected themes of frustration, cynicism, and disenchantment; but many writers were also fascinated by revolutionary developments in science, including the probing of psychoanalysts into the hidden secrets of the mind. The works of several writers came to represent the mood of the era: the early novels of the American Ernest Hemingway, for example, along with the poetry of the Anglo-American T. S. Eliot and the plays of the German Bertolt Brecht. In *The Sun Also Rises* (1926), Hemingway gave the public a powerful description of the so-called lost generation, a pattern followed by other writers, such as the American F. Scott Fitzgerald. In his monumental poem *The Waste Land* (1922), Eliot presented a philosophy that was close to despair: life is a living death, to be endured as boredom and frustration. Eliot's themes were echoed by William Butler Yeats, an Irish nationalist poet who, like Eliot, deplored the superficiality of modern life. In plays written for the working-class patrons of cabarets, Brecht decried the corruption of the state and the pointlessness of war. Like many artists, he rebelled against high culture and bourgeois values, but he also protested against the pretentious elitism of his contemporaries.

> In his monumental poem *The Waste Land* (1922), Eliot presented a philosophy that was close to despair: life is a living death, to be endured as boredom and frustration.

Other writers focused their attention on consciousness and inner life, often experimenting with new forms of prose. The Irish writer James Joyce was much renowned for his experiments with language and literacy forms—especially the "stream of consciousness," a technique he perfected in *Ulysses* (1922). The same was true, though to a lesser extent, of the novels of the Frenchman Marcel Proust and the Englishwoman Virginia Woolf (1882–1941). Woolf's essays and novels, among them *Mrs. Dalloway* (1925), *To the Lighthouse* (1927), and *A Room of One's Own* (1929), offered an eloquent and biting critique of Britain's elite institutions, from the universities that isolated women in separate, underfunded colleges to the suffocating decorum of middle-class families and relationships.

The depression of the 1930s forced many writers to reexamine the style and purpose of their work. Amid threats of economic devastation, totalitarianism, and war, literature became increasingly politicized. Authors felt themselves called to indict injustice and cruelty and to point the way to a better society. Moreover, they no longer directed their work to fellow intellectuals alone but to ordinary men and women as well. In *The Grapes of Wrath* (1939), for example, the American writer John Steinbeck depicted the plight of impoverished farmers fleeing from the Dust Bowl to California only to find that all the land had been monopolized by companies that exploited their workers. Young British writers such as W. H. Auden, Stephen Spender, and Christopher Isherwood were communist sympathizers who believed that it was their duty as artists to politicize their work to support the revolution. They rejected the pessimism of their immediate literary forebears in favor of optimistic commitment to their cause.

INTERWAR ARTISTS

Trends in visual art tended to parallel those in literature. The innovations of the prewar avant-garde thrived in the postwar period and, in fact, continued to dominate art throughout much of the twentieth century. Artists continued to focus on subjective experiences, multiplicities of meaning, and personal expression. Numerous and varied styles emerged, though all were characteristically modern in their rejection of traditional forms and values. Visual art responded to the rapid transformations of twentieth-century society— changes brought about by new technologies, scientific discoveries, the abandonment of traditional beliefs, and the influence of non-Western cultures. Like writers of the period, visual artists pushed the boundaries of aesthetics, moving far from the conventional tastes of average men and women.

Pablo Picasso followed his particular genius as it led him further into cubist variations and inventions. A group known as "expressionists" argued that color and line express inherent psychological qualities all by themselves, and so a painting need not have a representational subject at all. The Russian Wassily Kandinsky carried this position to its logical conclusion by calling his untitled paintings "improvisations" and insisting that they meant nothing. A second group of expressionists rejected these intellectual experiments in favor of what they called "objectivity," by which they meant a candid appraisal of the state of humanity. They were frequent attackers of the greed and decadence of postwar Europe. Chief among this group was the German George Grosz (*grohz*), whose cruel, satiric line has been likened to a "razor lancing a carbuncle." His scathing cartoon-like images became the most popular portraits of the despised Weimar government.

Another school rebelled against the very idea of aesthetic principle. Principles were based on reason, their argument went, and the world had proved beyond all

Marcel Duchamp. In these photos Duchamp used shaving cream to transform his appearance. Much of Duchamp's artwork showed his questioning of the role of the artist, as in this photo which he arranged, but which was actually taken by his fellow artist, Man Ray.

doubt—by fighting itself to death—that reason did not exist. Calling themselves dadaists (allegedly after a name picked at random from the dictionary), these artists were led by the Frenchman Marcel Duchamp, the German Max Ernst, and the Alsatian Jean (Hans) Arp. Rejecting all formal artistic conventions, dadaists concocted haphazard "fabrications" from cutouts and juxtapositions of wood, glass, and metal, and gave them bizarre names, for example, *The Bride Stripped Bare by Her Bachelors, Even* (Duchamp). The artists claimed their works were meaningless and playful; but critics thought otherwise, seeing them instead as expressions of the subconscious. Dadaism influenced surrealist artists such as the Italian Giorgio de Chirico and the Spaniard Salvador Dali, who explored the interior of the mind and produced irrational, fantastic, and generally melancholy paintings. Dadaism also took on political undertones, especially in Germany, by offering a nihilistic social critique that bordered on anarchism. Extending their attacks on rationalism to theater and print, these artists challenged the very basis of national culture.

Some artists responded to the sense of international crisis much as writers did.

During the 1930s, their paintings expressed pain and outrage directly to a mass audience. The most important members of this new movement were the Mexican muralists Diego Rivera and José Clemente Orozco, and the Americans Thomas Hart Benton and Reginald Marsh. These men sought to depict the social conditions of the modern world, presenting in graphic detail the hopes and struggles of ordinary people. Though they broke with the conventions of the past, there was nothing unintelligible about their work. It was art intended for everyone. Much of it bore the sting of social satire. Orozco, in particular, delighted in pillorying the hypocrisy of the church and the greed and cruelty of plutocrats and plunderers.

Architects, too, rejected sentimentality and tradition. Between 1880 and 1890 designers in Europe and America announced that the prevailing architectural styles were out of harmony with the needs of modern civilization. Modern architects pioneered a style known as "functionalism"; this group included Otto Wagner in Austria, Charles Édouard Jeanneret (known as Le Corbusier) in France, and Louis Sullivan and Frank Lloyd Wright in the United States. The basic principle of functionalism was that the appearance of a

Architectural Style in Germany between the Wars. The Bauhaus, by Walter Gropius (1883–1969). This school in Dessau, Germany, is a starkly functional prototype of the interwar "international style."

building should proclaim its actual use and purpose. "Form ever follows function" was Sullivan's maxim. Ornamentation was designed to reflect an age of science and machines. A leading European practitioner of functionalism was the German Walter Gropius, who in 1919 established a school—the Bauhaus—in Dessau to serve as a center for the theory and practice of modern architecture. Gropius and his followers declared that their style of design, which in time came to be called "international," was the only one that permitted an honest application of new materials—chromium, glass, steel, and concrete.

Interwar Scientific Developments

One powerful influence on the artists and intellectuals of the day was neither social nor political, but scientific. The pioneering work of the German physicist Albert Einstein revolutionized not only the entire structure of physical science but also challenged ordinary people's most basic beliefs about the universe. Quickly recognized as one of the greatest intellects of all time, Einstein began to question the very foundations of traditional physics early in the twentieth century. By 1915, he had proposed entirely new ways of thinking about space, matter, time, and gravity. His most famous theory, the principle of relativity, states that space and motion are relative to each other instead of being absolute. To the familiar three dimensions, Einstein added a fourth—time—and represented all four as fused in the space–time continuum. This meant that mass depends on motion, so that bodies in motion (especially at very high velocities) have a different shape and mass than they would at rest.

Einstein's theories paved the way for another revolutionary development in physics—the splitting of the atom. As early as 1905 Einstein became convinced of the equivalence of mass and energy and worked out a formula for the conversion of one into the other. Expressed as $E = mc^2$, the equation states that the amount of energy locked within the atom is equal to the mass multiplied by the square of the velocity of light. The formula had no practical application for years. Then in 1932, when the Englishman Sir James Chadwick discovered the neutron, which carries no electric charge, scientists had an ideal weapon for bombarding the atom—that is, a way to split it. In 1939 two German physicists, Otto Hahn and Fritz Strassman, successfully split atoms of uranium by bombarding them with neutrons. The initial reaction produced a chain of reactions: each atom that was split shot off more neutrons, which split even more atoms. Scientists in Germany,

Great Britain, and the United States were spurred on by governments anxious to turn these discoveries into weapons during World War II. American scientists soon prepared an atomic bomb, the most destructive weapon ever created. The legacy was ironic for Einstein, a man who devoted much of his life to promoting pacifism, liberalism, and social justice.

Another important contribution to physics that quickly entered popular culture was the "uncertainty principle" posited by the German physicist Werner Heisenberg in 1927. Heisenberg, who was strongly influenced by Einstein, showed that it is impossible—even in theory—to measure both the position and the speed of an object at the same time. The theory was of consequence only when dealing with atoms or subatomic particles, because of the interconnected nature of waves and particles on such a small scale. Though the public had little to no understanding of these ground-breaking scientific concepts, metaphorical invocations of relativity and the uncertainty principle fitted the ambiguities of the modern world. For many people, nothing was definite, everything was changing—and science seemed to be proving it.

Mass Culture and Its Possibilities

Cultural change, however, extended far beyond circles of artistic and intellectual elites. The explosive rise of mass media in the interwar years transformed popular culture and the lives of ordinary people. New mass media—especially radio and films—reached audiences of unprecedented size. Political life incorporated many of these new media, setting off worries that the common people, increasingly referred to as the "masses," could be manipulated by demagogues and propaganda. In 1918, mass politics was rapidly becoming a fact of life: that meant nearly universal suffrage (varying by country), well-organized political parties reaching out to voters, and in general, more participation in political life. Mass politics was accompanied by the rise of mass culture: books, newspapers, films, and fashions were produced in large numbers and standardized formats, which were less expensive and more accessible, appealing not only to more, but to more kinds of people. Older forms of popular culture were often local and class specific; mass culture, at least in principle, cut across lines of class and ethnicity, and even nationality. The term, however, can easily become misleading. The world of culture did not suddenly become homogenous. No more than half the population read newspapers regularly. Not everyone listened to the radio, and those who did certainly did not believe everything they heard. The pace of cultural change, however, did quicken perceptibly. And in the interwar years, mass culture showed that it held both democratic and authoritarian potential.

The expansion of mass culture rested on widespread applications of existing technologies. Wireless communication, for instance, was invented before the turn of the twentieth century and saw limited use in World War I. With major financial investment in the 1920s, though, the radio industry boomed. Three out of four British families had a radio by the end of the 1930s; and in Germany, the ratio was even higher. In every European country, broadcasting rights were controlled by the government; in the United States, radio was managed by corporations. The radio broadcast soon became the national soapbox for politicians, and it played no small role in creating new kinds of political language. President Franklin Roosevelt's reassuring "fireside chats" took advantage of the way that radio bridged the public world of politics with the private world of the home. Hitler cultivated a different kind of radio personality, barking his fierce invectives; he made some fifty addresses in 1933 alone. In Germany, Nazi propagandists beamed their messages into homes or blared them through loudspeakers in town squares, constant and repetitive. Broadcasting created new rituals of

> Older forms of popular culture were often local and class specific; mass culture, at least in principle, cut across lines of class and ethnicity, and even nationality.

political life—and new means of communication and persuasion.

So did advertising. Advertising was not new, but it was newly prominent. Businesses spent vastly more on advertising than they had before. Hard-hitting visual images replaced older ads that simply announced products, prices, and brand names. Many observers considered advertising the most "modern" of art forms. Why? It was efficient communication, streamlined and standardized, producing images that would appeal to all. It was scientific, drawing on modern psychology; advertising agencies claimed to have a science of selling to people. In a world remade by mass politics, and at a moment when the purchasing power of the common people was beginning to rise, however slowly, the high stakes in advertising (as in much of mass culture) were apparent to many.

The most dramatic changes came on movie screens. The technology of moving pictures came earlier; the 1890s were the era of nickelodeons and short action pictures. And in that period, France and Italy had strong film industries. Further popularized by news shorts during the war, film boomed in the war's aftermath. When sound was added to movies in 1927, costs soared, competition intensified, and audiences grew rapidly. By the 1930s, an estimated 40 percent of British adults went to the movies once a week, a strik-

Voice of the People, Voice of God (1920) by George Grosz. Industrialization, World War I, and political change combined to make early-twentieth-century Berlin a center of mass culture and communication. In this drawing, the radical artist and social critic George Grosz, deplores the newspapers' power over public opinion. That public opinion could be manipulated was a common theme for many who wrote about early-twentieth-century democracy.

ingly high figure. Many went more often than that. The U.S. film industry gained a competitive edge in Europe, buoyed by the size of its home market, by huge investments in equipment and distribution, by aggressive marketing, and by Hollywood's star system of long-term contracts with well-known actors who, in a sense, standardized the product and guaranteed a film's success.

Germany, too, was home to a particularly talented group of directors, writers, and actors, and to a major production company, UFA (Universum Film AG), which ran the largest and best-equipped studios in Europe. The UFA's history paralleled the country's: it was run by the government during World War I, devastated by the economic crisis of the early 1920s, rescued by wealthy German nationalists in the late

A poster advertising the Chermin de Fer du Nord, a rail transport company that connected Paris to the English Channel.

1920s, and finally taken over by the Nazis. During the Weimar years, UFA produced some of the most remarkable films of the period, including *Der letzte mann* (*The Last Man;* released as *The Last Laugh* in English), a universally acclaimed film directed by F. W. Murnau, one of the two great masters of German expressionism. Fritz Lang was the other, directing such masterpieces as the science-fiction film *Metropolis* (1926) and his most famous German film, *M* (1931). After Hitler's rise to power, the Nazis took control of UFA, placing it under the control of Joseph Goebbels and the Ministry of Propaganda. Though production continued unabated during the Third Reich, many of the industry's most talented members fled from the oppressive regime, ending the golden age of German cinema.

Many found the new mass culture disturbing. As they perceived it, the threat came straight from the United States, which deluged Europe with cultural exports after the war. Hollywood westerns, cheap dime novels, and jazz music—which became increasingly popular in the 1920s—introduced Europe to new ways of life. Advertising, comedies, and romances disseminated new and often disconcerting images of femininity. With bobbed haircuts and short dresses, "new women" seemed assertive, flirtatious, capricious, and materialistic. The Wild West genre was popular with teenage boys, much to the dismay of their parents and teachers, who saw westerns as an inappropriate, lower-class form of entertainment. In Europe, the cross-class appeal of American popular culture grated against long-standing social hierarchies. Conservative critics abhorred the fact that "the parson's wife sat nearby his maid at Sunday matinees, equally rapt in the gaze of Hollywood stars." American critics expressed many of the same concerns. Yet the United States enjoyed more social and political stability than Europe. War and revolution had shaken Europe's economies and cultures, and in that context "Americanization" seemed a handy shorthand for economic as well as cultural change. One critic expressed a common concern: "America is the source of that terrible wave of uniformity that gives everyone the same [*sic*]: the same overalls on the skin, the same book in the hand, the same pen between the fingers, the same conversation on the lips, and the same automobile instead of feet."

Authoritarian governments, in particular, decried these developments as decadent threats to national culture. Fascist, communist, and Nazi governments alike tried to control not only popular culture but also high culture and modernism, which were typically out

CINEMA: FRITZ LANG ON THE FUTURE OF THE FEATURE FILM IN GERMANY, 1926

Fritz Lang (1890–1976) came from Austria to Berlin after World War I and became one of the German Weimar Republic's most brilliant movie directors, best known for Metropolis *(1926) and* M *(1931). In this essay, Lang reflects on the technological, artistic, and human potential of film. Like many European filmmakers he was fascinated by American movies. In 1932 Joseph Goebbels, dazzled by Lang's work, asked him to work on movies for the Nazis. Lang immediately left Germany for Paris and, from there, for the United States where he continued to make films in Hollywood.*

There has perhaps never before been a time so determined as ours in its search for new forms of expression. Fundamental revolutions in painting, sculpture, architecture, and music speak eloquently of the fact that people of today are seeking and finding their own means of lending artistic form to their sentiments. . . .

The speed with which film has developed in the last five years makes all predictions about it appear dangerous, for it will probably exceed each one by leaps and bounds. Film knows no rest. What was invented yesterday is already obsolete today. This uninterrupted drive for new modes of expression, this intellectual experimentation, along with the joy Germans characteristically take in overexertion, appear to me to fortify my contention that film as art will first find its form in Germany. . . .

Germany has never had, and never will have, the gigantic human and financial reserves of the American film industry at its disposal. To its good fortune. For that is exactly what forces us to compensate a purely material imbalance through an intellectual superiority. . . .

The first important gift for which we have film to thank was in a certain sense *the rediscovery of the human face.* Film has revealed to us the human face with unexampled clarity in its tragic as well as grotesque, threatening as well as blessed expression.

The second gift is that of visual empathy: in the purest sense the expressionistic representation of thought processes. No longer will we take part purely externally in the workings of the soul of the characters in film. We will no longer limit ourselves to seeing the effects of feelings, but will experience them in our own souls, from the instant of their inception on, from the first flash of a thought through to the logical last conclusion of the idea. . . .

The internationalism of filmic language will become the strongest instrument available for the mutual understanding of peoples, who otherwise have such difficulty understanding each other in all too many languages. To bestow upon film the double gift of ideas and soul is the task that lies before us. . . .

Anton Kaes, Matin Jay, and Edward Dimendberg, *The Weimar Republic Sourcebook* (Los Angeles, 1994), pp. 622–623.

QUESTIONS FOR ANALYSIS

1. Why does Lang suggest that his own time is in search of "new forms of expression"? Do artists always search for new forms, or might this be a specifically twentieth-century phenomena?

2. What did Lang mean by calling "the rediscovery of the human face" and "visual empathy" gifts of film? Did television, video, and electronic media have comparable effects on how we see the world and other beings in it?

3. How does Lang see the technological, artistic, and human potential of film?

Fritz Lang's *M*. In this film Peter Lorre, a Jewish actor, played the role of a child murderer, who maintains that he should not be punished for his crimes. Lorre's speech at the end of the film was used in the Nazi propaganda film "The Eternal Jew" as proof that Jews were innate criminals who showed no remorse for their actions.

of line with the designs of the dictators. Stalin much preferred socialist realism to the new Soviet avant-garde. Mussolini had a penchant for classical kitsch, though he was far more accepting of modern art than Hitler, who despised its decadence. Nazism had its own cultural aesthetic, promoting "Aryan" art and architecture and rejecting the modern, international style they associated with the "international Jewish conspiracy." Modernism, functionalism, and atonality were banned: the hallmarks of Weimar Germany's cultural preeminence were replaced by a state-sponsored revival of an alleged mystical and heroic past. Walter Gropius's acclaimed experiments in modernist architecture, for example, stood as monuments to everything the Nazis hated. The Bauhaus school was closed

in 1933, and Hitler hired Albert Speer as his personal architect, commissioning him to design grandiose neo-classical buildings, including an extravagant plan to rebuild the entire city of Berlin.

The Nazis, like other authoritarian governments, used mass media as efficient means of indoctrination and control. Movies became part of the Nazis' pioneering use of "spectacular politics." Media campaigns, mass rallies, parades and ceremonies: all were designed to display the strength and glory of the Reich and to impress and intimidate spectators. In 1934 Hitler commissioned the filmmaker Leni Riefenstahl to record a political rally staged by herself and Albert Speer in Nuremberg. The film, titled *Triumph of the Will*, was a visual hymn to the Nordic race and the Nazi regime. Everything in the film was on a huge scale: masses of bodies stood in parade formation, flags rose and fell in unison; the film invited viewers to surrender to the power of grand ritual and symbolism. The comedian Charlie Chaplin riposted in his celebrated lampoon *The Great Dictator* (1940), an enormously successful parody of Nazi pomposities.

The Nazis also tried to eliminate the influences of American popular culture, which even before 1933 had been decried as an example of biological and cultural degeneracy. For instance, critics associated American dances and jazz (which were increasingly popular in German cities) with what the Nazis deemed "racially inferior" blacks and Jews. With culture, however, the Nazis were forced to strike a balance between party propaganda and popular entertainment. The regime allowed many cultural imports, including Hollywood films, to continue, while consciously cultivating German alternatives to American cinema, music, fashions, and even dances. Joseph Goebbels, the minister of propaganda who controlled most film production, placed a high value on economic viability. During the Third Reich, the German film industry turned out comedies, escapist fantasies, and sentimental romances. It developed its own star system and tried to keep audiences happy; meanwhile it became a major competitor internationally. For domestic consumption, the industry also produced vicious anti-Semitic films, such as *The Eternal Jew* (1940) and *Jew Süss* (1940), a fictional tale of a Jewish moneylender who brings the city of Württemberg to ruin in the eighteenth century. In the final scene of the film, the town expels the entire Jewish community from its midst, asking that "posterity honor this law." Goebbels reported that the entire Reich cabinet had viewed the film and considered it "an incredible success."

CONCLUSION

The strains of World War I created a world that few recognized—transformed by revolution, mass mobilization, and loss. In retrospect, it is hard not to see the period that followed as a succession of failures. Capitalism foundered in the Great Depression, democracies collapsed in the face of authoritarianism, and the Treaty of Versailles proved hollow. Yet we better understand the experiences and outlooks of ordinary people if we do not treat the failures of the interwar period as inevitable. By the late 1920s, many were cautiously optimistic that the Great War's legacy could be overcome and that problems were being solved. The Great Depression wrecked these hopes, bringing economic chaos and political paralysis. Paralysis and chaos, in turn, created new audiences for political leaders offering authoritarian solutions and brought more voters to their political parties. Finally, economic troubles and political turmoil made contending with rising international tensions, to which we now turn, vastly more difficult. By the 1930s, even cautious optimism about international relations had given way to apprehension and dread.

KEY TERMS

Bolsheviks	fascism	*Kristallnacht*	UFA
Joseph Stalin	Nazism	Great Depression	
collectivization	Weimar Republic	New Deal	
Great Terror	Adolf Hitler	Albert Einstein	

SELECTED READINGS

Carr, E. H. *The Bolshevik Revolution, 1917–1923.* London and New York, 1950–1953. One of the classics.

Cohen, Stephen F. *Bukharin and the Bolshevik Revolution: A Political Biography, 1888–1938.* New York, 1973. Excellent study of one of the early Bolshevik leaders and of the significance of the revolution as a whole.

Conquest, Robert. *The Great Terror: A Reassessment.* New York, 1990. One of the first histories of the Terror, should be read in conjunction with others in this list.

Crew, David F., ed. *Nazism and German Society, 1933–1945.* New York, 1994. An excellent and accessible collection of essays.

Degrazia, Victoria. *Irresistible Empire: America's Advance through 20th-Century Europe.* Cambridge, Mass., 2005. Brilliant analysis of "Americanization" in many forms, including business practices, movie studios, and models of gender relations.

Figes, Orlando. *Peasant Russia Civil War: The Volga Countryside in Revolution, 1917–1921.* Oxford, 1989. Detailed and sophisticated but readable. Study of the region from the eve of the revolution through the civil war.

Fitzpatrick, Shelia. *Everyday Stalinism: Ordinary Life in Extraordinary Times: Soviet Russia in the 1930s.* Oxford and New York, 1999. Gripping on how ordinary people dealt with famine, repression, and chaos.

Friedlander, Saul. *Nazi Germany and the Jews: The Years of Persecution. 1933–1939.* Rev. ed. New York, 2007. Excellent; the first of a two-volume study.

Gay, Peter. *Weimar Culture.* New York, 1968. Concise and elegant overview.

Getty, J. Arch, and Oleg V. Naumov. *The Road to Terror: Stalin and the Self-Destruction of the Bolsheviks, 1932–1939.* New Haven, Conn., 1999. Combines analysis with documents made public for the first time.

Goldman, Wendy Z. *Women, the State, and Revolution: Soviet Family Policy and Social Life, 1917–1936.* New York, 1993. On the Bolshevik attempts to transform gender and family.

Kershaw, Ian. *Hitler.* 2 vols: *1889–1936 Hubris,* New York, 1999; *1936–1945: Nemesis,* New York, 2001. Now the best biography: insightful about politics, culture, and society as well as the man.

Kershaw, Ian. *The Hitler Myth: Image and Reality in the Third Reich.* New York, 1987. Brilliant study of how Nazi propagandists sold the myth of the Fuhrer and why many Germans bought it.

Klemperer, Victor. *I Will Bear Witness: A Diary of the Nazi Years, 1933–1941*. New York, 1999. *I Will Bear Witness: A Diary of the Nazi Years, 1942–1945*. New York, 2001. Certain to be a classic.

Lewin, Moshe. *The Making of the Soviet System: Essays in the Social History of Interwar Russia*. New York, 1985. One of the best to offer a view from below.

McDermott, Kevin. *Stalin: Revolutionary in an Era of War*. Basingstoke, UK, and New York, 2006. Useful, short, and recent.

Montefior, Simon Sebag. *Stalin: The Court of the Red Tsar*. London, 2004. On the relations among the top Bolsheviks, an interesting personal portrait. Takes you inside the inner circle.

Orwell, George. *The Road to Wigan Pier*. London, 1937. On unemployment and life in the coal mining districts of England, by one of the great British writers of the twentieth century.

Orwell, George. *Homage to Catalonia*. London, 1938. A firsthand account of the Spanish Civil War.

Rentschler, Eric. *The Ministry of Illusion: Nazi Cinema and Its Afterlife*. Cambridge, Mass., 1996. For the more advanced student.

Service, Robert. *Stalin: A Biography*. London, 2004. Updates Tucker.

Suny, Ronald Grigor. *The Revenge of the Past: Nationalism, Revolution, and the Collapse of the Soviet Union*. Stanford, Calif., 1993. Path-breaking study of the issues of nationalism and ethnicity form the revolution to the end of the Soviet Union.

Tucker, Robert C. *Stalin as Revolutionary, 1879–1929*. New York, 1973.

Tucker, Robert C. *Stalin in Power: The Revolution from Above, 1928–1941*. New York, 1990. With *Stalin as Revolutionary* emphasizes Stalin's purpose and method and sets him in the tradition of Russian dictators.

CHAPTER TWENTY-SIX

CHAPTER CONTENTS

THE SECOND
WORLD WAR

IN SEPTEMBER 1939, Europe was consumed by another world war. The Second World War was not simply a continuation of the first. Both were triggered by threats to the European balance of power. Yet even more than the Great War, World War II was a conflict among nations, whole peoples, and fiercely opposing ideals. The methods of warfare in World War II had little in common with those of the first. In 1914, military firepower had outmatched mobility, resulting in four years of static, mud-sodden slaughter. In 1939, mobility was joined to firepower on a massive scale. The results were terrifying. On the battlefield, the tactics of high-speed armored warfare (*Blitzkrieg*), aircraft carriers sinking ships far below the horizon, and submarines used in vast numbers to dominate shipping lanes changed the scope and the pace of fighting. This was not a war of trenches and barbed wire but a war of motion, dramatic conquests, and terrible destructive power. The devastation of 1914–1918 paled in comparison to this new, global conflict.

The other great change involved not tactics, but targets. Much of the unprecedented killing power now available was aimed directly at civilians. Cities were laid waste by artillery and aerial bombing. Whole regions were put to the torch, while towns and villages were systematically cordoned off and leveled. Whole populations were targeted as well, in ways that continue to appall. The Nazi regime's systematic murder of gypsies, homosexuals, and other "deviants," along with the effort to exterminate the Jewish people completely, made World War II a horrifyingly unique event. So did the United States' use of a weapon whose existence would dominate politics and society for the next fifty years: the atomic bomb. The naive enthusiasm that had marked the outbreak of the Great War was absent from the start. Terrible memories of the first conflict lingered. Yet those who fought against the Axis Powers (and many of those who fought for them) found that their determination to fight and win grew as the war went on. Unlike the seemingly meaningless killing of the Great War, World War II was cast as a war of absolutes, of good and evil, of national and global survival. Nevertheless the scale of destruction brought with it a profound weariness. It also provoked deep-seated questions about the value of Western "civilization" and the terms on which it, and the rest of the world, might live peaceably in the future.

FOCUS QUESTIONS

• What were the long-term causes of World War II?

• What was the policy of appeasement?

• What accounts for the early German successes in World War II?

• What made World War II a global war?

 • How were the Nazis able to rule over a continental empire?

• In what ways was World War II a "racial war"?

• How did the war transform the home fronts?

• How did the Soviets defeat the Germans?

THE CAUSES OF THE WAR: UNSETTLED QUARRELS, ECONOMIC FALLOUT, AND NATIONALISM

What were the long-term causes of World War II?

The causes of World War II were rooted in the peace settlement of 1919–1920. The peace had created as many problems as it had solved. The senior Allied heads of state yielded to demands that involved annexing German territory and creating satellite states out of the eastern European empires. In doing so, the peacemakers created fresh bitterness and conflict. The Versailles treaty and its champions, such as President Woodrow Wilson, proclaimed the principle of self-determination for the peoples of eastern and southern Europe. Yet the new states created by the treaty crossed ethnic boundaries, created new minorities without protecting them, involved political compromises, and frustrated many of the expectations they had raised. The unsteady new boundaries would be redrawn by force in the 1930s. The Allied powers also kept up the naval blockade against Germany after the end of the fighting. This forced the new German government to accept harsh terms that deprived Germany of its political power in Europe and saddled the German economy with the bill for the conflict in a "war guilt" clause. The blockade and its consequences created grievances that many angry, humiliated Germans considered legitimate.

Power politics persisted after the peace conference. Although Woodrow Wilson and other sponsors of the League of Nations acclaimed the League as a means to eliminate power struggles, it did nothing of the sort. The signatures on the peace treaties were hardly dry when the victors began carving out new alliances to maintain their supremacy, interfering in the new central European states and the mandate territories added to the British and French empires in the Middle East. Even the League itself was fundamentally an alliance of the victors against the vanquished. It is not surprising that politicians feared international relations would be undermined by this imbalance of power.

A second cause of World War II was the failure to create lasting, binding standards for peace and security. Diplomats spent the ten years after Versailles trying to restore such standards. Some put their faith in the legal and moral authority of the League. Others saw disarmament as the most promising means of guaranteeing peace. Throughout the 1920s, a number of important European statesmen—the German and French foreign ministers Gustav Stresemann and Aristide Briand and the British prime ministers Stanley Baldwin and Ramsay MacDonald—tried to reach a set of agreements that would stabilize the peace and prevent rearmament. In 1925 an effort was made to secure the frontiers on the Rhine established at Versailles. In 1928, the Kellogg-Briand Pact attempted to make war an international crime. Despite the good faith of many of the statesmen involved, none of these pacts carried any real weight. Each nation tried to include special provisions and exceptions for "vital interests," and these efforts compromised the treaties from the start. Had the League of Nations been better organized, it might have relieved some of the tensions or at least prevented clashes between nations. But the League was never a league of all nations. Essential members were absent, since Germany and the Soviet Union were excluded for most of the interwar period and the United States never joined.

Economic conditions were a third important cause of renewed conflict. The huge reparations imposed on the Germans and France's occupation of much of Germany's industrial heartland helped slow Germany's recovery. German and French stubbornness about the pace of repayments combined disastrously to bring on the German inflation of the early 1920s. The spiraling inflation made German money nearly worthless, damaging the stability and credibility of Germany's young republic almost beyond repair.

The depression of the 1930s contributed to the coming of the war in several ways. It intensified economic nationalism. Baffled by problems of unemployment and business stagnation, governments imposed high tariffs in an effort to preserve the home market for their own producers. The collapse of investment and terrible domestic unemployment caused the United States to withdraw even further from world affairs. Although France suffered less than some other countries, the depression still inflamed tensions between management and labor. This conflict exacerbated political battles between left and right, making it difficult for either side to govern France. Britain turned to its empire, raising tariffs for the first time and guarding its financial investments jealously.

In Germany, the Great Depression was the last blow to the Weimar Republic. In 1933 power passed to the Nazis, who promised a total program of national renewal. In the fascist states (and, exceptionally, the United States), public works projects of one kind or another were prescribed as an answer to mass unemployment. This produced highways, bridges, and railroads; it also produced a new arms race.

Despite the misgivings of many inside the governments of Britain and France, Germany was allowed to ignore the terms of the peace treaties and rearm. Armaments expansion on a large scale first began in Germany in 1935, with the result that unemployment was reduced and the effects of the depression eased. Other nations followed the German example, not simply as a way to boost their economies but in response to growing Nazi military power. In the Pacific, the decline of Japanese exports meant that the nation did not have enough foreign currency to pay for vital raw materials from overseas. This played into the hands of Japan's military regime. Japanese national ambitions and Japanese leaders' perception of the political and cultural inferiority of the Chinese led Japan to fresh imperial adventures in the name of establishing economic stability in East Asia. They began in 1931 with the invasion of Manchuria and moved from there to create a "Greater Pacific Co-Prosperity Sphere," which involved seizing other territories as Japanese colonies. Raw materials could then be bought with Japanese money and more of Asia would serve the needs of Japan's empire.

Imperial success could serve as consolation when economic methods failed. As the depression dragged on in fascist Italy, Mussolini tried to distract his public with national conquests overseas, culminating in the invasion of Ethiopia in 1935.

In sum, the tremendous economic hardship of the depression, a contested peace treaty, and political weakness undermined international stability. But the decisive factor in the crises of the 1930s and the trigger for another world war lay in a blend of violent nationalism and modern ideologies that glorified the nation and national destiny. This blend, particularly in the forms of fascism and militarism, appeared around the world in many countries. By the middle of the 1930s, recognizing common interests, fascist Italy and Nazi Germany formed an Axis, an alliance binding their goals of national glory and international power. They were later joined by Japan's military regime. In Spain, the ultranationalist forces that tried to overthrow the Spanish Republic, setting off the Spanish Civil War (discussed later), believed they were reviving the stability, authority, and morality of the nation. Fascist or semifascist regimes spread in eastern Europe, in Yugoslavia, Hungary, and Romania. One exception to this sobering trend toward authoritarianism was Czechoslovakia. Czechoslovakia boasted no ethnic majority. Although the Czechs practiced an enlightened policy of minority self-government and although their government was remarkably stable, questions of nationality remained a potential source of friction. Those questions became a key factor as international tensions mounted in the late 1930s.

THE 1930S: CHALLENGES TO THE PEACE, APPEASEMENT, AND THE "DISHONEST DECADE"

What was the policy of appeasement?

The 1930s brought the tensions and failures caused by the treaties of 1919–1920 to a head, creating a global crisis. Fascist and nationalist governments flouted the League of Nations by launching new conquests and efforts at national expansion. With the memories of 1914–1918 still fresh, these new crises created an atmosphere of deepening fear and apprehension. Each new conflict seemed to warn that another, much wider war would follow unless it could somehow be averted. Ordinary people, particularly in Britain, France, and the United States, were divided. Some saw the actions of the aggressors as a direct challenge to civilization, one that had to be met with force if necessary. Others hoped to avoid premature or unnecessary conflict. Their governments tried instead at several points to negotiate with the fascists and keep a tenuous peace. Writers, intellectuals, and politicians on the left vilified these efforts. Many saw the period as a series of missed opportunities to prevent renewed warfare. In 1939, on the first day of World War II, the British poet and leftist W. H. Auden condemned the behavior of Western governments, calling the 1930s "a low, dishonest decade."

The object of Auden's venom was the policy of "appeasement" pursued by Western governments in the face of German, Italian, and Japanese aggression. Appeasement was neither simple power politics nor pure cowardice. It was grounded in three deeply held assumptions. The first assumption was that doing anything to provoke another war was unthinkable. With the memory of the slaughter of 1914–1918 fresh in their minds, many in the West embraced pacifism, or at any rate adopted an attitude that kept them from facing up to the uncompromising aggression of the fascist governments, especially Nazi Germany. Second, many in Britain and the United States argued that Germany had been mistreated by the Versailles treaty and harbored legitimate grievances that should be acknowledged and resolved. Finally, many appeasers were staunch anticommunists. They believed that the fascist states in Germany and Italy were an essential bulwark against the advance of Soviet communism and that division among the major European states only played into the hands of the USSR. Yet this last point divided the appeasers. All were concerned with maintaining Europe's balance of power. One group, however, believed that the Soviets posed the greater threat and that accommodating Hitler might create a common interest against a common enemy. The other faction believed that Nazi Germany presented the true threat to European stability. Nevertheless, they believed, Hitler would have to be placated until Britain and France finished rearming. At that point, they hoped, their greater military power would deter Hitler or Mussolini from risking a general European war. It took most of the 1930s for the debate among appeasers to come to a head. Meanwhile, the League of Nations faced more immediate and pressing challenges.

The 1930s brought three crucial tests for the League: crises in China, Ethiopia, and Spain. In China, the Japanese invasion of Manchuria in 1931 turned into an invasion of the whole country. Chinese forces were driven before the Japanese advance, and the Japanese deliberately targeted civilians to break the Chinese will to fight. In 1937, the Japanese laid siege to the strategic city of Nanjing. Their orders on taking the city were simple: "kill all, burn all, destroy all." More than 200,000 Chinese citizens were slaughtered in what came to be known as the "Rape of Nanjing." The League voiced shock and disapproval but did nothing. In 1935 Mussolini began his efforts to make the Mediterranean an Italian empire by returning to Ethiopia to avenge the defeat of 1896. This time the Italians came with tanks, bombers, and poison gas. The

> With the memory of the slaughter of 1914–1918 fresh in their minds, many in the West embraced pacifism, or at any rate adopted an attitude that kept them from facing up to the uncompromising aggression of the fascist governments, especially Nazi Germany.

Ethiopians fought bravely but hopelessly, and this imperial massacre aroused world opinion. The League attempted to impose sanctions on Italy and condemned Japan. But for two reasons, no enforcement followed. The first was British and French fear of communism and their hope that Italy and Japan would act as counterweights to the Soviets. The second reason was practical. Enforcing sanctions would involve challenging Japan's powerful fleet or Mussolini's newly built battleships. Britain and France were unwilling, and dangerously close to unable, to use their navies to those ends.

THE SPANISH CIVIL WAR

The third challenge came closer to home. In 1936 civil war broke out in Spain. A series of weak republican governments, committed to large-scale social reforms, could not overcome opposition to those measures and political polarization. War broke out as extreme right-wing military officers rebelled. Although Hitler and Mussolini had signed a pact of nonintervention with the other Western powers, both leaders sent troops and equipment to assist the rebel commander, Francisco Franco (1939–1975). The Soviet Union countered with aid to communist troops serving under the banner of the Spanish Republic. Again, Britain and France failed to act decisively. Thousands of volunteers from England, France, and the United States—including many working-class socialists and writers such as George Orwell and Ernest Hemingway—took up arms as private soldiers for the Republican government. They saw the war as a test of the West's determination to resist fascism and military dictatorships. Their governments were much more hesitant. For the British, Franco was anticommunist at least, just like Mussolini and the Japanese. The French prime minister Léon Blum, a committed antifascist, stood at the head of a Popular Front government—an alliance of socialists, communists, and republicans. The Popular Front had been elected on a program of social reform and opposition to Hitler abroad and fascism in France. Yet Blum's margin of support was limited. He feared that intervening in Spain would further polarize his country, bring down his government, and make it impossible to follow through on any commitment to the conflict. In Spain, despite some heroic fighting, the Republican camp degenerated into a hornet's nest of

Guernica (1937), by Pablo Picasso. One of Picasso's most influential paintings, *Guernica* was painted as a mural for the Spanish republican government as it fought for survival in the Spanish Civil War. The Basque town of Guernica had been bombed by German fighters just a few months earlier, in April 1937. Near the center a horse writhes in agony; to the left a distraught woman holds her dead child.

competing factions: republican, socialist, communist, and anarchist.

The Spanish Civil War was brutal. Both the German and the Soviet "advisers" saw Spain as a "dress rehearsal" for a later war between the two powers. They each brought in their newest weapons and practiced their skills in destroying civilian targets from the air. In April 1937, a raid by German dive bombers utterly destroyed the town of Guernica in northern Spain in an effort to cut off Republican supply lines and terrorize civilians. It shocked public opinion and was commemorated by Pablo Picasso in one of the most famous paintings of the twentieth century. Both sides committed atrocities. The Spanish Civil War lasted three years, ending with a complete victory for Franco in 1939. In the aftermath, Britain and France proved reluctant to admit Spanish Republicans as refugees, even though Republicans faced recriminations from Franco's regime.

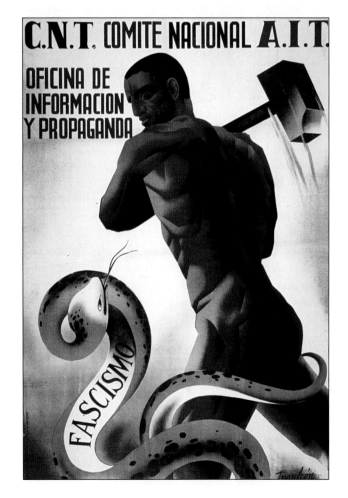

Propaganda Posters. Such posters provide some of the most lasting documentation of the Spanish Civil War. Business owners were encouraged to fill every available space with them, and bombed out ruins were covered over with posters, all in the hopes of keeping the people in favor of the war.

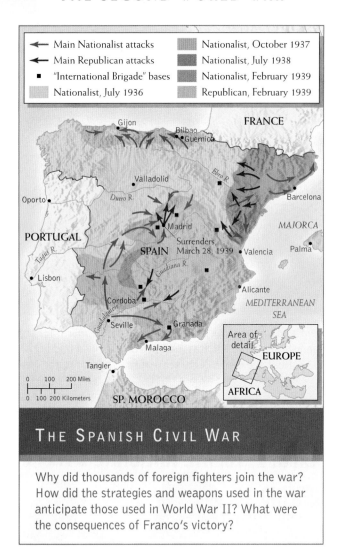

← Main Nationalist attacks		Nationalist, October 1937	
← Main Republican attacks		Nationalist, July 1938	
■ "International Brigade" bases		Nationalist, February 1939	
Nationalist, July 1936		Republican, February 1939	

THE SPANISH CIVIL WAR

Why did thousands of foreign fighters join the war? How did the strategies and weapons used in the war anticipate those used in World War II? What were the consequences of Franco's victory?

he removed Germany from the League of Nations, to which it had finally been admitted in 1926. In 1935 he defied the disarmament provisions of the Treaty of Versailles and revived conscription and universal military training. Hitler's stated goals were the restoration of Germany's power and dignity inside Europe and the unification of all ethnic Germans inside his Third German Reich. As the first step in this process, Germany reoccupied the Rhineland in 1936. It was a risky move, chancing war with the much more powerful French army. But France and Britain did not mount a military response. In retrospect, this was an important turning point; the balance of power tipped in Germany's favor. While the Rhineland remained demilitarized and German industry in the Ruhr valley was unprotected, France held the upper hand. After 1936, it no longer did so.

In March 1938, Hitler annexed Austria, reaffirming his intention to bring all Germans into his Reich. Once more, no official reaction came from the West.

John Heartfield, *Have No Fear—He's a Vegetarian.*
Heartfield (born Helmut Herzfeld) was a German radical associated with the Dada movement and communism. This photomontage appeared in a French magazine in 1936, as Hitler's warlike intentions became clear. Pierre Laval, then prime minister of France and later architect of French collaboration with the Nazis, whispers reassuringly to a rooster, a symbol for France, as Hitler sharpens his knife.

Franco sent 1 million of his Republican enemies to prison or concentration camps.

Hitler drew two lessons from Spain. The first was that if Britain, France, and the Soviet Union ever tried to contain fascism, they would have a hard time coordinating their efforts. The second was that Britain and France were deeply averse to fighting another European war. This meant that the Nazis could use every means short of war to achieve their goals.

GERMAN REARMAMENT AND THE POLITICS OF APPEASEMENT

Hitler took advantage of this combination of international tolerance and war weariness to advance his ambitions. As Germany rearmed, Hitler played on Germans' sense of shame and betrayal, proclaiming their right to regain their former power in the world. In 1933,

The Nazis' next target was the Sudetenland in Czechoslovakia, a region with a large ethnic German population. With Austria now a part of Germany, Czechoslovakia was almost entirely surrounded by its hostile neighbor. Hitler declared that the Sudetenland was a natural part of the Reich and that he intended to occupy it. The Czechs did not want to give way. Hitler's generals were wary of this gamble. Czechoslovakia had a strong, well-equipped army and a line of fortifications along the border. Many in the French and Polish governments were willing to come to the Czechs' aid. According to plans already being laid for a wider European war, Germany would not be ready for another three to four years. But Hitler gambled, and the British prime minister, Neville Chamberlain, obliged him. Chamberlain decided to take charge of international talks about the Sudetenland and agreed to Hitler's terms. Chamberlain's logic was that this dispute was about the balance of power in Europe. If Hitler were allowed to unify all Germans in one state, he reasoned, then German ambitions would be satisfied. Chamberlain also believed that his country could not commit to a sustained war. Finally, defending eastern European boundaries against Germany ranked low on Great Britain's list of priorities, at least in comparison to ensuring free trade in western Europe and protecting the strategic centers of the British Empire.

On September 29, 1938, Hitler met with Chamberlain, Premier Édouard Daladier (1938–1940) of France, and Mussolini in a four-power conference in Munich. The result was another capitulation by France and Britain. The four negotiators bargained away a major slice of Czechoslovakia, while Czech representatives were left to await their fate outside the conference room. Chamberlain returned to London proclaiming "peace in our time." Hitler soon proved that boast hollow. In March 1939 Germany invaded what was left of Czechoslovakia and established a puppet regime in its capital, Prague. This was Germany's first conquest of non-German territory, and it sent shock waves across Europe. It convinced public and political opinion outside Germany of the futility of appeasement. Chamberlain was forced to shift his policies completely. British and French rearmament sped up dramatically. Together with France, Britain guaranteed the sovereignty of the two states now directly in Hitler's path, Poland and Romania.

Meanwhile, the politics of appeasement had fueled Stalin's fears that the Western democracies might strike a deal with Germany at Soviet expense, thus diverting Nazi expansion eastward. The Soviet Union had not been invited to the Munich conference, and, suspicious that Britain and France were unreliable allies, Stalin became convinced that he should look elsewhere for security. Tempted by the traditional Soviet desire for territory in Poland, Stalin was promised a share of Poland, Finland, the Baltic states, and Bessarabia by Hitler's representatives. In a cynical reversal of their anti-Nazi proclamations that stunned many, the Soviets signed a nonaggression pact with

The Munich Conference, 1938. Prime Minister Chamberlain of Britain and Hitler during the Munich conference.

CHRONOLOGY

THE ROAD TO WORLD WAR II, 1931–1940

Japanese invasion of Manchuria	1931
Germany leaves the League of Nations	1933
Germany begins remilitarization	March 1935
Germany reoccupies the Rhineland	March 1936
Spanish Civil War	April 1936–April 1939
Germany annexes Austria	March 1938
Munich Conference	September 1938
Nazi–Soviet Pact	August 1939
Germany invades Poland	September 1939
Germany invades the Low Countries and France	May 1940

Germany

German advances
- Reoccupied Rhineland, March 1936
- Annexed Austria, March 1938
- Annexed Sudetenland, October 1938
- Annexed Bohemia and Moravia, March 1939
- Annexed Memel, March 1939

Italy
- Annexed Albania, April 1939

Poland and Hungary
- Annexed Czech territory, 1938 and 1939

( ) Former independent nations: Albania, Austria, and Czechoslovakia

GERMAN AND ITALIAN EXPANSION, 1936–1939

What were Hitler's first steps to unify all the ethnic Germans in Europe? How did he use these initial gains to annex territory from the Czechs? What were the official reactions from Britain, France, and the Soviet Union? After winning Czechoslovakia, why did Hitler choose to invade Poland? How were the Germans able to conquer Poland and France so quickly?

WHAT ACCOUNTS FOR THE EARLY GERMAN SUCCESSES IN WORLD WAR II?

THE OUTBREAK OF HOSTILITIES AND THE FALL OF FRANCE   947

the Nazis in August 1939. By going to Munich, Britain and France had put their interests first; the Soviet Union would now look after its own.

THE OUTBREAK OF HOSTILITIES AND THE FALL OF FRANCE

What accounts for the early German successes in World War II?

After his success in Czechoslovakia, Hitler demanded the abolition of the Polish Corridor. This was a narrow strip of land connecting Poland with the Baltic Sea. The corridor also divided East Prussia from the rest of Germany, separating yet another large German population from union with the Reich. Judging Britain and France by past performance, Hitler believed their pledges to Poland were worthless. With the Soviets now in his camp, he expected that Poland would consent and the Western allies would back down again. When Poland stood firm instead, Hitler attacked. On September 1, 1939, German troops crossed the Polish border. Britain and France sent a joint warning to Germany to withdraw. There was no reply. On September 3, Britain and France declared war.

The conquest of Poland was shockingly quick. It demanded great resources—Germany committed nearly all of its combat troops and planes to the invasion—but the results were remarkable. Well-coordinated attacks by German panzers (tanks) and armored vehicles, supported by devastating air power, cut the large but slow-moving Polish army to pieces. German infantry still moved on foot or via horse-drawn transport, but their disciplined advance followed the devastating work of the panzers. The Poles fought doggedly but were so stunned and disorganized that they had little hope of mounting an effective defense. The "lightning war" (*Blitzkrieg*) for which the German officer corps had trained so long was a complete success. Within three weeks German troops were laying siege to Warsaw. German terror bombing, designed to destroy the heart of Warsaw from the air and frighten the population into surrender, was successful. Poland, a large country with a large army, was dismembered in four weeks.

In accordance with its agreement with Nazi Germany, the Soviet Union also invaded Poland from the east, taking their share of Polish territory and using Stalin's signature methods to deal with the enemy: rounding up millions to be deported, imprisoned, or executed. Wary that German aggression would turn on them, the Soviets also hastened to shore up their position to the north, on the Russo-Finnish border. Since at least 1938 the Soviets had demanded from Finland various arrangements to protect Leningrad, from access to strategic locations and permission to build fortifications in Finland to the outright ceding of territory—all of which the Finns had refused. Shortly after the invasion of Poland, then, the Soviets attacked Finland. Despite the Soviets' overwhelming superiority in numbers and material, the Finns fought back tenaciously. The Soviets faced a very difficult campaign—an alarming demonstration of the damaging effects of Stalin's terror on the Soviet military. Although the Soviet Union concluded the undeclared four-month Winter War with a precarious victory in March 1940, Hitler and the rest of the world had made note of Stalin's weaknesses.

After the fall of Poland the conflict became an ominous "phony war" or "sitzkrieg," as it was sometimes called. The fighting in Poland was followed by a winter of anxious nonactivity with occasional headlines about naval skirmishes. In the spring of 1940 that calm was broken by a terrible storm. The Germans struck first in Scandinavia, taking Denmark in a day and invading Norway. Britain and France tried to aid the Norwegian defense and sank a large number of German ships, but the Allied expedition failed. Then the real blow was struck. On May 10, German forces swarmed through Belgium and the Netherlands on their way to France. The two nations were conquered in short order. When the Dutch succeeded in flooding canals that protected their major cities and defended that line with hard-fighting marines, Hitler ordered his air force to bomb the city of Rotterdam. More than 800 Dutch civilians died, and the Netherlands surrendered the next day. The Belgians' stubborn and effective defense of their nation was cut short when King Albert suddenly surrendered after two weeks of fighting, fearing similar destruction. In turn Albert stayed on as a figurehead for the Nazis, reviled by Belgians who found other ways to carry on the fight against Germany.

The large French army was carved up by the *Blitzkrieg* (blitz-KREEG). Its divisions were isolated, outflanked, and overwhelmed by German aircraft and armored columns working according to an exacting plan. French units either fought fierce battles until they were hopelessly surrounded or simply collapsed. The French army and French artillery, much of it better built than its German equivalent, were poorly

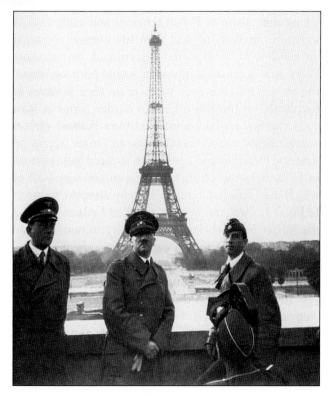

June 23, 1940. Hitler and Nazi architect Albert Speer pose across the river from the Eiffel Tower after capturing Paris.

organized and rendered useless in the face of rapid German maneuvers. The defeat turned quickly into a rout. Hundreds of thousands of civilians, each carrying a few precious possessions loaded on carts, fled south. They were joined by thousands of Allied soldiers without weapons, and these columns of refugees were attacked constantly by German dive bombers. The disorganized British made a desperate retreat to the port of Dunkirk on the English Channel, where many of Britain's best troops were sacrificed holding off the panzers. At the beginning of June 1940, despite heavy German air attacks, Britain's Royal Navy evacuated more than 300,000 British and French troops, with the help of commercial and pleasure boats that had been pressed into emergency service.

After Dunkirk, the conflict was bitter but the outcome inevitable. French reservists fought, as their commanders asked, "to the last cartridge," killing thousands of Germans. Without proper organization and more firepower, however, this bravery was useless. The Germans swept through the northwest and the heart of the country, reaching Paris in mid-June 1940. The political will of France's government collapsed along with its armies. Rather than withdrawing to Britain or French colonies in North Africa, the French surren-

dered on June 22. The armistice cut the country in two. The Germans occupied all of northern France, including Paris and the Channel ports. The south, and French territories in North Africa, lay under the jurisdiction of a deeply conservative government formed at the spa town of Vichy (*VIH-shee*) under the leadership of an elderly World War I hero, Marshal Henri Philippe Pétain. France had fallen. One of Germany's historic enemies, the victor of the previous war, an imperial power and nation of almost 60 million citizens, was reduced to chaos and enemy occupation in forty days.

The penalties exacted on France did not end with defeat. Many liberals within France, and most of the Free French movement quickly established in London, soon felt they had two enemies to fight: Germany and Pétain's regime. The Vichy government proposed to collaborate with the Germans in return for retaining a small measure of sovereignty, or so it believed. The regime also instituted its own National Revolution, which came very close to fascism. Vichy repudiated the republic, accusing it of sapping France's strength. The state proceeded to reorganize French life and political institutions, strengthening the authority of the Catholic Church and the family and helping the Germans crush any resistance. "Work, Family, and Country"— this was Vichy's call to order.

NOT ALONE: THE BATTLE OF BRITAIN AND THE BEGINNINGS OF A GLOBAL WAR

What made World War II a global war?

Before launching an invasion across the Channel, the Nazis attempted to establish superiority in the air. From July 1940 to June 1941, in the Battle of Britain, thousands of planes dropped millions of tons of bombs on British targets: first aircraft and airfields and then, as the focus shifted to breaking Britain's will, civilian targets such as London. More than 40,000 British civilians died. Yet the British stood firm. This was possible in part because of a German mistake. After a daring British bombing raid on Berlin, Hitler angrily told his generals to concentrate on civilian targets. This spared

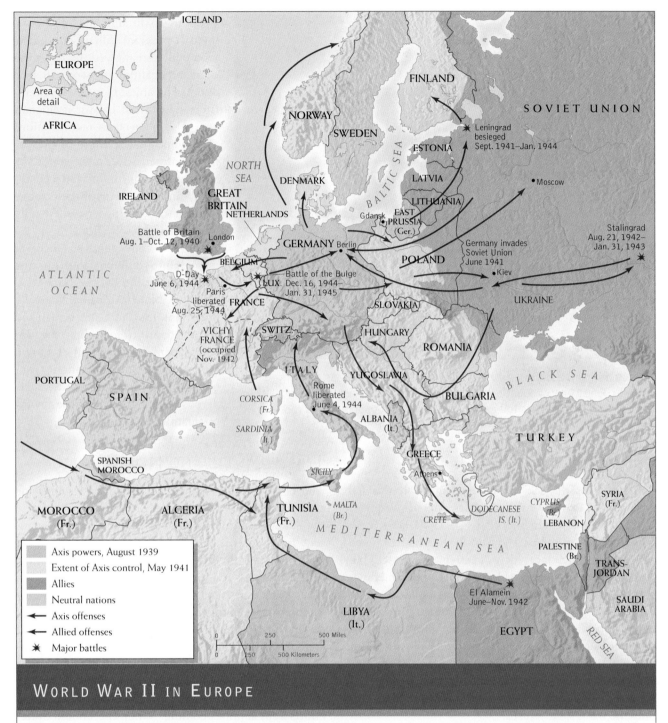

WORLD WAR II IN EUROPE

Note the alliance systems and major offensives of the European Theater in World War II. What explains the rapid expansion of Axis control until May 1941? In what ways did geography both aid and potentially hinder the Axis effort to conquer Europe? How did Adolf Hitler hope to neutralize either the Soviet Union or Great Britain early in the war? How did the sieges at Leningrad and Stalingrad prove instrumental in sustaining the Allied effort?

the Royal Air Force, whose bases had been steadily devastated up to that point. Given the chance to keep fighting, the R.A.F. forced a costly stalemate in the air. Hitler scrapped the invasion plans, turning his attention east toward Russia.

Another important reason for the determined British resistance was a change of political leadership. In May 1940, Chamberlain's catalog of failures finished his career. He was toppled by a coalition government that brought together Conservative, Liberal, and Labour

London during the Battle of Britain. German air raids that lasted from August 1940 to June 1941 wrought destruction but did not achieve Hitler's goal of breaking the British. The Holland House Library in London lost its roof but managed to engage in business as usual.

politicians for the sake of national unity. It was led by the most unlikely of the choices offered to replace him: Winston Churchill (1940–1945, 1951–1955). Churchill was a political maverick who had changed parties more than once. He was extremely talented, but also arrogant. He had a sharp temper and sometimes seemed unstable, and before 1939 his political career was judged to be over. As prime minister he was not much of an administrator, constantly proposing wild schemes, but he had two genuine gifts. The first was language. Churchill spoke extraordinary words of courage and defiance just when the British public wanted and needed to hear them. He was utterly committed to winning the war.

"You ask what is our policy," Churchill said in his first speech as prime minister in May of 1940, before the Battle of Britain began. "I will say, it is to wage war with all our might, with all the strength that God can give us, to wage war against a monstrous tyranny never surpassed in the dark, lamentable catalogue of human crime."

The second was personal diplomacy. He convinced the American president Franklin Roosevelt (1933–1945), who supported the Allies, to break with American neutrality and send massive amounts of aid and weapons to Britain free of charge, under a program called Lend-Lease. Churchill also allowed the new government coalition to work to best effect. The ablest Conservative ministers stayed, but Labour politicians were also allowed to take positions of genuine power. Most of the Labour representatives turned out to be excellent administrators and were directly in touch with Britain's huge working class, which now felt fully included in the war effort.

With Britain's survival, the war moved into different theatres: the Atlantic (a battle over sea lanes and supplies), North Africa (strategically important for the Suez Canal and access to oil), the Pacific (the war with Japan), and the Soviet Union (where Hitler's determination to annihilate Stalin merged with his murderous campaign against the Jewish populations of Europe).

THE ATLANTIC AND NORTH AFRICA

The Battle of the Atlantic, launched as a submarine campaign to starve out the British, was a dire threat to the Allies. Learning from World War I, the Germans sent hundreds of submarines (U-boats) out in "wolf packs" to stalk the major sea lanes to Britain. German submarines sank millions of tons of merchant shipping, as far away as the coasts of Brazil and Florida. Britain's supplies of weapons, raw materials, and food hung in the balance. The British devoted a huge naval effort and great technical resourcefulness to saving their convoys. They developed modern sonar and new systems of aerial reconnaissance and cracked the Germans' codes for communicating with the wolf packs. These efforts kept supplies coming. When the United States entered the war in December, 1941 (see next section), the British supplied the experience and technology and the Americans the numbers and firepower to sink many more U-boats. By late 1942 the threat receded.

The war in North Africa began because Britain had to protect the Suez Canal, but Britain was soon drawn into a larger conflict. Indian, South African, and West African troops fighting for the British drove the Italians from Ethiopia in May 1941. The Soviets and the British invaded Iran to keep its shah (ruler) from making a deal with Germany over Iranian oil and held the country until 1946. A small, well-led British army in Egypt humiliated a much larger Italian invasion force. The British nearly captured Italy's colony of Libya, and this forced Germany to intervene. An elite armored force called the Afrika Korps, led by Germany's most daring tank commander, Erwin Rommel, drove the British back in the spring of 1941 and started a grudging two-year war in the desert. The British fielded an international army, which included as many Australians, Indians, and New Zealanders as it did Britons, pitted against the Germans and Italians. The fighting swung back and forth for eighteen months, with the British taking the worst of it. Then the momentum shifted. Despite heavy losses from German planes and submarines, the British defeated the Italian navy and took control of the Mediterranean. They also established domination in the air over the desert. When Rommel tried to invade Egypt, his forces were stopped and badly defeated near the town of El Alamein in the autumn of 1942, then driven back toward Tunisia. "This is not the end," said Winston Churchill in his inimitable style, after the British victory at El Alamein. "It is not even the beginning of the end. But it is, perhaps, the end of the beginning."

> "This is not the end," said Winston Churchill in his inimitable style, after the British victory at El Alamein. "It is not even the beginning of the end. But it is, perhaps, the end of the beginning."

The United States intervened in November 1942, landing in the French territories of Algeria and Morocco. A conference was held at Casablanca, Morocco, among the Allied powers to discuss the future course of the war and the fate of French territories in North Africa. French administrators in Algeria and Morocco, who had supported Vichy, at least in public, surrendered peacefully or joined the Allied side. Rommel still defended Tunisia against the Allies for four months, but a joint offensive broke the German lines in March 1943, ending the fighting.

THE ALLIES AND JAPAN IN THE PACIFIC

The war became truly global when Japan struck the American naval base at Pearl Harbor, Hawaii, on the morning of December 7, 1941. The Japanese had been involved in a costly war in China since the 1930s. To win and to establish a Japanese empire throughout Asia, they would have to destroy America's Pacific fleet and seize the colonies of the British, Dutch, and French empires. Like Germany, Japan began with lightning blows. The attack on Pearl Harbor was a brilliant act of surprise that devastated the American fleet and shocked the American public. It was

"A date which will live in infamy," December 7, 1941. The U.S.S. *West Virginia* was one of eight battleships sunk during the Japanese surprise attack targeting Battleship Row at the American naval base at Pearl Harbor. More than 2,000 people were killed, but most of the American fleet, en route to or from other locations in the Pacific, was spared.

not, however, the success that the Japanese wanted. Eight U.S. battleships were sunk and more than 2,000 lives lost; but much of the American fleet—including its aircraft carriers, submarines, and many smaller ships— were safely at sea on the day of the strike. The unpro- voked attack galvanized American public opinion in a way the war in Europe had not. When Germany rashly declared war on the United States as well, America declared itself ready to take on all comers and joined the Allies.

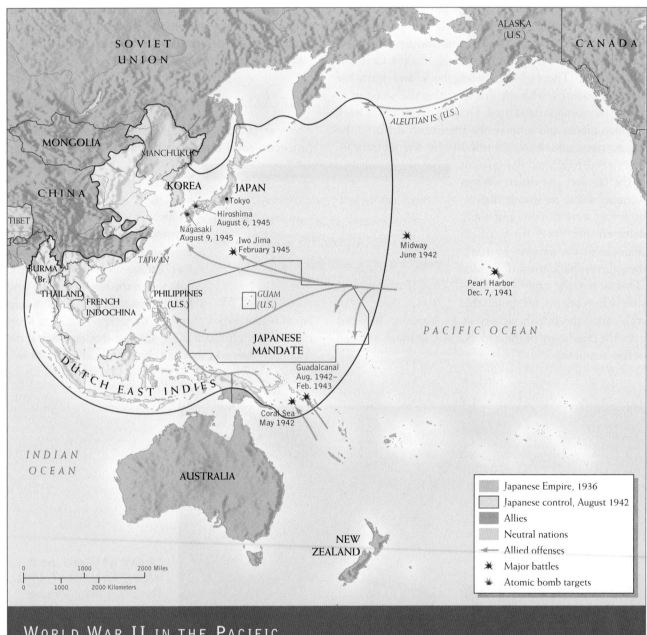

WORLD WAR II IN THE PACIFIC

Note the major operations and important geographical features of the Pacific Theater during World War II. Why did the Japanese strategy depend on destroying the American Pacific fleet at the time Japan attacked the Philip- pines, Dutch East Indies, and Southeast Asia? How did the fact that American aircraft carriers were not at Pearl Harbor affect the next major battles of the war in the Pacific: Coral Sea and Midway? What factors led the Amer- icans to decide that the dropping of atomic bombs on Hiroshima and Nagasaki was the most expeditious way to end the war?

Despite the mixed results at Pearl Harbor the Japanese enjoyed other, stunning successes. For the European colonial powers, Japan's entry into the war was a catastrophe. Japanese troops swept through the British protectorate of Malaya in weeks, sinking the Pacific squadrons of both the British and Dutch navies in the swift attacks. Britain's fortified island port at Singapore, the keystone of British defenses in the Pacific, fell at the end of December 1941. The shock of the loss nearly took Churchill's government with it. Thousands of British and Australian troops were captured and sent off to four years of torture, forced labor, and starvation in Japanese prison camps. The Japanese also invaded the Philippines in December; and while American soldiers and marines held out on the island of Corregidor for some time, they too were forced to surrender. Some took to the hills to fight as guerrillas; the rest were forced on a death march to Japanese labor camps. The Dutch East Indies fell next, and it seemed there would be no stopping Japanese ships and soldiers before they reached Australia.

Reeling from Japan's blows, the Allies finally reorganized during 1942. After taking Singapore, Japanese troops pressed on into Burma. Several famous British generals tried and failed to defend Burma, with disastrous losses of men and matériel. After these failures, command fell to an obscure Indian Army officer, William Slim. For a British officer, Slim had quite humble origins. He was a career soldier, a minor hero in World War I, and perhaps the best strategist in the British Army. Even more important, the millions of non-white imperial troops from India and Africa who were under his command liked and respected him as an honest, unprejudiced man. He reorganized imperial defenses, and a joint force of British and Indian troops defeated an attempted Japanese invasion of India at the border near the end of 1942. After that, with an army drawn from around the world, Slim began to push the Japanese back. In New Guinea, Australian troops fresh from North Africa were first to defeat the Japanese on land in bitter hand-to-hand fighting and staged a counterattack through the high mountain jungles. At sea, America's navy benefited from a rapidly increased production schedule that turned out new ships and planes to outnumber the Japanese, and two gifted admirals, Chester Nimitz and William Halsey, who outfought them. In 1942 the United States won crucial victories in the Coral Sea and at Midway, a battle fought at sea, but won and lost by aircraft flown from each side's carriers. American marines landed on the island of Guadalcanal in early 1942 and captured this strategic Japanese base after months of bitter fighting. Their success began a

campaign of island hopping as the marines destroyed Japan's network of island bases throughout the Pacific. This was brutal warfare, often settled with grenades and bayonets. Each side considered the other racially inferior. The Japanese often refused to surrender; the Americans and Australians also took few prisoners. By 1943, the Japanese victories had been halted, the Japanese navy had lost most of its capital ships, and the Allies began a slow march to Singapore and the Philippines.

The Rise and Ruin of Nations: Germany's War in the East and the Occupation of Europe

How were the Nazis able to rule over a continental empire?

While battles ebbed and flowed in the Atlantic and the North African desert, Germany moved southeast into the Balkans. In 1941 Germany took over Yugoslavia almost without a fight. The Germans split Yugoslavia's ethnic patchwork by establishing a Croatian puppet state, pitting Croats against their Serb neighbors who were ruled directly by the Nazis. Romania, Hungary, and Bulgaria joined the Nazis' cause as allies. The Greeks, who had dealt a crushing defeat to an Italian invasion, were suddenly confronted with a massive German force that overran the country. The Greeks stubbornly refused to surrender. An unexpected combination of Greek, British, and New Zealand troops nearly defeated the German paratroopers sent to capture the island of Crete in June of 1941. Many Greeks also took to the mountains as guerrillas, but in the end the country fell. By the summer of 1941, with the exceptions of Sweden and Switzerland, the whole European continent was either allied with the Nazis or subject to their rule. These victories, and the economy of plunder that enriched Germany with forced labor and other nations' money, won Hitler considerable popularity at home. But these were only the first steps in a larger plan.

Hitler's ultimate goals, and his conception of Germany's national destiny, lay to the east. Hitler had always seen the nonaggression pact with the Soviet Union as an act of convenience, to last only until

Germany was ready for this final conflict. By the summer of 1941, it seemed Germany was ready. On June 22, 1941, Hitler began Operation Barbarossa, the invasion of the Soviet Union. The elite of the German army led the way, defeating all the forces the Russians could put in front of them. Stalin's purges of the 1930s had exiled or executed many of his most capable army officers, and the effects showed in Russian disorganization and disaffection in the face of the panzers. Hundreds of thousands of prisoners were taken as German forces pressed deep into Byelorussia (modern Belarus), the Baltic states, and Ukraine. Like Napoleon, the Germans led a multinational army; it included Italians, Hungarians, most of the Romanian army, and freelance soldiers from the Baltics and Ukraine who bore grudges against Stalin's authoritarian regime. During the fall of 1941, the Nazis destroyed much of the Red Army's fighting strength and vigorously pursued their two goals: the destruction of communism and racial purification.

The war against the Soviets was a war of ideologies and of racial hatred. The advancing Nazi forces left burning fields and towns in their wake and methodically wiped the occupied territories clean of "undesirable elements." When Russian guerrillas counterattacked with sniping and sabotage, German forces shot or hanged hundreds of innocent hostages at a time in reprisal, often torturing their victims first. The Russian guerrillas quickly chose to deliver the same punishment to any captured Germans. By the end of 1941 it was clear that the war in the East was a war of destruction and that both sides believed that only one side would be allowed to survive. In 1941, it seemed the victors would be German. Their forces were on the march toward the capital at Moscow. On orders from Berlin, however, German forces pushing toward Moscow were diverted south to attack Russia's industrial heartland in an effort to destroy the Soviets' ability to resist before the Russian winter set in. This left the Soviet capital free, and the Russian population, its leaders, and its armies, began to organize a much more determined resistance.

Hitler nonetheless managed to piece together an empire that stretched across the entire continent of Europe. "We come as the heralds of a New Order and a new justice," his regime announced. Hitler specifically compared his rule to a "new Indian empire," and claimed to have studied British imperial techniques. Much of the

"Cultural Terror," 1944. Produced in Nazi-occupied Holland, this cultural Frankenstein warns of the looming destruction of European identity with the advance of American troops.

> By the end of 1941 it was clear that the war in the East was a war of destruction and that both sides believed that only one side would be allowed to survive.

New Order was improvised and rested on a patchwork of provisional regimes: military government in Poland and Ukraine, collaborators in France, allied fascists in Hungary, and so on. The clearest principle was German supremacy. "The emphatic German decision to organize Europe hierarchically, like a pyramid with Germany at the top, is known to all," said an Italian diplomat at the time. The empire was meant to feed German citizens and maintain their morale and support for the war, which would prevent the "stab in the back" that Hitler believed had thwarted a German victory in 1914–1918. Occupied countries paid inflated "occupation costs" in taxes, food, industrial production, and manpower. More than 2 million foreign workers were brought into Germany in 1942–1943 from France, Belgium, Holland, and the Soviet Union. As they conscripted workers, the Nazis spoke of uniting Europe to

AXIS EUROPE, 1941

How had Hitler and Mussolini come to dominate the bulk of mainland Europe by the eve of the German invasion of the Soviet Union? Why did Hitler choose to annex certain territories to Germany but settle for occupation in others?

save it from the "Red Menace" of communism. This propaganda seems to have had little effect. To the contrary, at least in France, deporting citizens to labor in Germany did more than any other policy to drive individuals into the resistance.

The demands of enemy occupation and the political and moral questions of collaboration and resistance, were issues across occupied Europe. The Nazis set up puppet regimes in a number of occupied territories. Both Norway and the Netherlands were deeply divided by the occupation. In each country a relatively small but dedicated party of Nazis governed in the name of the Germans, while at the same time well-organized and determined resistance movements gathered information for the Allies and carried out acts of sabotage. In Denmark, the population was much more united against their German occupiers, engaging in regular acts of passive resistance that infuriated German administrators. They also banded together as private citizens to smuggle most of the country's Jewish population out to safety in neutral Sweden.

Elsewhere the relationship between collaboration, resistance, and self-interested indifference was more complex. In France, collaboration ranged from simple survival tactics under occupation to active support for Nazi ideals and goals. The worst example of this was the Vichy regime's active anti-Semitism and the aid given by French authorities in isolating, criminalizing, and deporting Jews in France to the concentration camps. Living with the German conquerors forced citizens in France (and elsewhere) to make choices. Many chose to protect their own interests by sacrificing those of others, particularly such "undesirables" as Jews and communists. At the same time, communist activists, some members of the military, and ordinary citizens—such as the people of France's central mountains, who had a long tradition of smuggling and resisting government—became active guerrillas (maquis) and saboteurs. They established links with the Free French movement in London, led by the charismatic, stiff-necked general Charles de Gaulle, and supplied important intelligence to the Allies. In eastern Europe, resistance movements provoked both open warfare against the fascists and civil war within their own countries. The Germans' system of occupation in Yugoslavia pitted a fascist Croat regime against most Serbs; the Croatian fascist guard, the Ustasha, massa-cred hundreds of thousands of Orthodox Catholic Serbs. Ironically, a Croat, Josip Broz (Tito), emerged as the leader of the most powerful Yugoslavian resistance movement—militarily the most significant resistance in the war. Tito's troops were communists and strong enough to form a guerrilla army. They fought Germans, Italians, and Croat fascists, and they gained support and supplies from the Allies.

Perhaps the most important moral issue facing citizens of occupied Europe was not their national allegiance but rather their personal attitude to the fate of the Nazis' sworn enemies: Jews, communists, gypsies, homosexuals, and political "undesirables." Some French Jews along the Riviera found the Italian Catholic army officers who occupied the area more willing to save them from deportation than their fellow Frenchmen. This deeply personal dilemma—whether to risk family, friends, and careers to aid the deportees or simply to look the other way and allow mass murder—was one of the most powerful of the war.

> Perhaps the most important moral issue facing citizens of occupied Europe was not their national allegiance but rather their personal attitude to the fate of the Nazis' sworn enemies: Jews, communists, gypsies, homosexuals, and political "undesirables."

RACIAL WAR, ETHNIC CLEANSING, AND THE HOLOCAUST

In what ways was World War II a "racial war"?

From the beginning, the Nazis had seen the conflict as a racial war. In *Mein Kampf* Hitler had already outlined his view that war against the *Untermenschen*, or "subhuman" Jews, Gypsies, and Slavs, was natural and necessary. Not only would it purify the German people, but it would also conquer territory for their expansion. Thus as soon as the war broke out, the Nazis began to implement ambitious plans for redrawing the racial map of the Reich, or what is now called ethnic cleansing. In the fall of 1939, with Poland conquered, Heinrich Himmler directed the SS to begin massive population transfers. Ethnic Germans were moved from elsewhere into the borders of the Reich, while Poles and Jews were de-

Polish Jews, Evicted from the Warsaw Ghetto, Being Deported. Most of the trains led to death camps.

cording to the war's rhythms and Hitler's wildly changing moods. Between 1938 and 1941 Nazi plans had no single focus. Plans ranged from forcing German Jews to emigrate to deporting all Europe's Jews to Madagascar, a former French colony off the southern coast of Africa. All these schemes took shape against the background of daily terror and frequent massacres, especially in Poland. It is certain, however, that the invasion of the Soviet Union in June 1941 marked a turning point in the deadly path to the Holocaust. Operation Barbarossa, as the invasion was called, brought several changes. First, it was animated by the Nazis' intense ideological and racial hatreds, directed against Slavs, Jews, and Marxists. Goebbels, for example, called the Russians "not a people but an agglomeration of animals." The invasion of Poland had been vicious. The invasion of the Soviet Union was openly a "war of extermination." Second, the invading German army succeeded more quickly than it expected. The huge gains created euphoria in the Nazi hierarchy; Hitler seemed very close to realizing his dreams of an eastern empire. But success also bred fear or worry at the prospect of controlling the millions of Soviet prisoners, Soviet civilians, and Soviet Jews who had now fallen into Nazi hands. The combination of elation and anxiety was deadly. It led, quickly, from systematic brutality to atrocities, and then to murder on a scale few could have imagined.

As the Nazi army swept into the Soviet Union in 1941, captured communist officials, political agitators, and any hostile civilians were imprisoned, tortured, or shot. About 5.5 million military prisoners were taken and marched to camps. Over half of them died of starvation or were executed. Poles from regions that had been under Soviet rule, Jews, and Russians were deported to Germany to work as slave labor in German factories. On the heels of the army came special battalions of *Einsatzgruppen*, or "death squads." Joined by 11,000 extra SS troops, they stormed through Jewish villages and towns with Russian or Polish populations identified as "difficult." The men of the villages were shot; the women and children either deported to labor camps or massacred along with the men. By September 1941, the *Einsatzgruppen* reported that in their efforts at

ported to specially designated areas in the east. Over 200,000 ethnic Germans from the Baltic states were resettled in Western Prussia. Welcoming these ethnic Germans went hand in hand with a brutal campaign of terror against the Poles, especially Polish Jews. The Nazis sought to root out all sources of potential resistance. Professors at the University of Cracow, considered dangerous intellectuals, were deported to concentration camps, where they died. The SS shot "undesirables," such as the inmates of Polish mental asylums, partly to allow SS troops to occupy the asylums' barracks. Poles were deported to forced labor camps. The Nazis began to transport Jews by the thousands to the region of Lublin, south of Warsaw. Special death squads also began to shoot Jews in the streets and in front of synagogues. These Polish campaigns took 100,000 Jewish lives in 1940.

The elimination of European Jewry stood at the center of the Nazis' *Rassenkampf*, or "racial struggle." We have seen the role of anti-Semitism in Hitler's rise to power and the escalating campaign of terror against the Jewish community inside Germany in the 1930s, including the Night of the Broken Glass (see Chapter Twenty-Five). The war radicalized that campaign. Historians disagree about whether or not the Nazis had a blueprint for the extermination of Europe's Jews. Most now emphasize that Nazi priorities shifted ac-

THE HOLOCAUST: MASSACRES IN UKRAINE

The following account of a mass shooting in Ukraine comes from a German engineer testifying at the Nuremberg trials in 1946. Events like these happened so often that his is but one of many such descriptions. Note that the SS allowed him to witness these events.

From September 1941 until January 1944, I was the manager and chief engineer of a branch of the construction firm, Josef Jung of Solingen with its headquarters in Sdolbunow, Ukraine. In this capacity I had to visit the firm's building sites. The firm was contracted by an Army construction office to build grain silos on the former air field near Dubno in the Ukraine.

When I visited the site office on 5 October 1942 my foreman, Hubert Moennikes of Hamburg–Harburg, Aussenmühlenweg 21, told me that Jews from Dubno had been shot near the site in three large ditches which were about thirty metres long and three metres deep. Approximately 1,500 people a day had been killed. All of the approximately 5,000 Jews who had been living in Dubno up to the action were going to be killed. Since the shootings had taken place in his presence he was still very upset.

Whereupon I accompanied Moennikes to the building site and near it saw large mounds of earth about thirty metres long and two metres high. A few lorries were parked in front of the mounds from which people were being driven by armed Ukrainian militia under the supervision of an SS man. The militia provided the guards on the lorries and drove them to and from the ditch. All these people wore the prescribed yellow patches on the front and back of their clothing so that they were identifiable as Jews.

Moennikes and I went straight to the ditches. We were not prevented from doing so. I could now hear a series of rifle shots from behind the mounds. The peo-

ple who had got off the lorries—men, women, and children of all ages—had to undress on the orders of an SS man who was carrying a riding or dog whip in his hand. They had to place their clothing on separate piles for shoes, clothing and underwear. I saw a pile of shoes containing approximately 800–1,000 pairs, and great heaps of underwear and clothing.

Without weeping or crying out these people undressed and stood together in family groups, embracing each other and saying good-bye while waiting for a sign from another SS man who stood on the edge of the ditch and also had a whip. During the quarter of an hour in which I stood near the ditch, I did not hear a single complaint or a plea for mercy. . . .

I walked round the mound and stood in front of the huge grave. The bodies were lying so tightly packed together that only their heads showed, from almost all of which blood ran down over their shoulders. Some were still moving. Others raised their hands and turned their heads to show they were still alive. The ditch was already three quarters full. I estimate that it already held about a thousand bodies. I turned my eyes towards the man doing the shooting. He was an SS man; he sat, legs swinging, on the edge of the ditch. He had an automatic rifle resting on his knees and was smoking a cigarette. The people, completely naked, climbed down steps which had been cut into the clay wall of the ditch, stumbled over the heads of those lying there and stopped at the spot indicated by the SS man. They lay down on top of the dead or wounded; some stroked those still living and spoke quietly to them. Then I heard a series of rifle shots. I looked into the ditch and saw the bodies contorting or, the heads already inert, sinking on the corpses beneath. Blood flowed from the nape of their necks. I was surprised not to be ordered away, but I noticed three postmen in uniform standing nearby. Then the next batch came up, climbed down into the ditch, laid themselves next to the previous victims and were shot.

On the way back, as I rounded the mound, I saw another lorry load of people which had just arrived. This one included the sick and infirm. An old and very emaciated woman with frightfully thin legs was being undressed by others, already naked. She was being supported by two people and seemed paralysed. The naked people carried the woman round the mound. I left the place with Moennikes and went back to Dubno by car. . . .

I am making the above statement in Wiesbaden, Germany on 10 November 1945. I swear to God that it is the whole truth.

Fred. Gräbe

J. Noakes and G. Pridham, *Nazism: A History in Document and Eyewitness Accounts, 1919–1945*, Vol. 2 (New York, 1988), pp. 1100–1101.

QUESTIONS FOR ANALYSIS

1. Who was Gräbe, and how did he come to witness these events?
2. This document is unusual in providing information on victims, perpetrators, and bystanders. What do we learn about each?
3. Why did Gräbe talk about what he saw at Dubno, when others kept silent?

---

pacification they had killed 85,000 people, most of them Jews. By April 1942, the number was 500,000. This killing began before the gas chambers had gone into operation and continued through the campaigns on the eastern front. As of 1943, the death squads had killed roughly 2.2 million Jews.

As Operation Barbarossa progressed, German administrations of occupied areas herded local Jewish populations even more tightly into the ghettos some Jewish communities had occupied for centuries: Warsaw and Lodz in Poland were the largest. There, Nazi administrators, accusing Jewish people in the ghettos of hoarding supplies, refused to allow food to go in. The ghettos became centers of starvation and disease. Those who left the ghetto were shot rather than returned. A German doctor summarized the regime's logic about killing this way: "One must, I can say it quite openly in this circle, be clear about it. There are only two ways. We sentence the Jews in the ghetto to death by hunger or we shoot them. Even if the end result is the same, the latter is more intimidating." In other words, the point was not simply death, but terror.

Through the late summer and fall of 1941, Nazi officials discussed and put together plans for mass killings in death camps. The ghettos had already been sealed; now

> By September 1941, the *Einsatzgruppen* reported that in their efforts at pacification they had killed 85,000 people, most of them Jews. By April 1942, the number was 500,000.

orders came down that no Jews were to leave any occupied areas. That summer the Nazis had experimented with vans equipped with poison gas, which could kill thirty to fifty people at a time. Those experiments and the gas chambers were designed with the help of scientists from the T-4 euthanasia program, which had already killed 80,000 racially, mentally, or physically "unfit" individuals in Germany. By October 1941, the SS was building camps with gas chambers and deporting people to them. Auschwitz-Birkenau (*OWSH-vihts BIHR-kuh-now*), which had been built to hold Polish prisoners, was built up to be the largest of the camps. Auschwitz eventually held many different types of prisoners—"undesirables" like Jehovah's Witnesses and homosexuals, Poles, Russians, and even some British POWs—but Jews and gypsies were the ones systematically annihilated there. Between the spring of 1942 and the fall of 1944 over 1 million people were killed at Auschwitz-Birkenau alone. The opening of the death camps set off the greatest wave of slaughter from 1942 to 1943. Freight cars hauled Jewish people to the camps, first from the ghettos of Poland, then from France, Holland, Belgium, Austria, the Balkans, and later from Hungary and Greece. Bodies were buried in pits dug by prisoners or burned in crematoria.

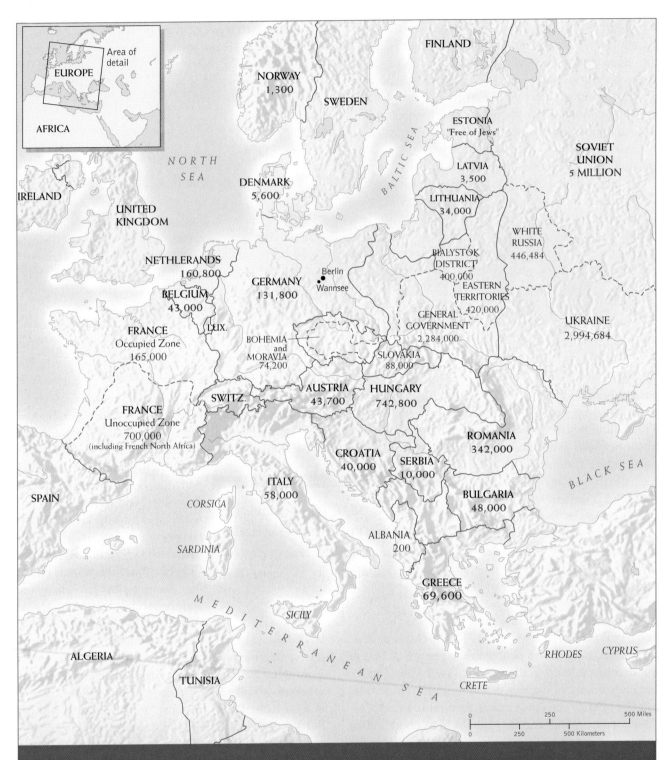

Map labels:

EUROPE
Area of detail
AFRICA

FINLAND

NORWAY
1,300

SWEDEN

ESTONIA
"Free of Jews"

SOVIET UNION
5 MILLION

NORTH SEA

IRELAND

DENMARK
5,600

LATVIA
3,500

LITHUANIA
34,000

UNITED KINGDOM

WHITE RUSSIA
446,484

NETHLERANDS
160,800

GERMANY
131,800

Berlin
Wannsee

BIALYSTOK DISTRICT
400,000

EASTERN TERRITORIES
420,000

BELGIUM
43,000

FRANCE
Occupied Zone
165,000

LUX.

BOHEMIA and MORAVIA
74,200

GENERAL GOVERNMENT
2,284,000

UKRAINE
2,994,684

SLOVAKIA
88,000

FRANCE
Unoccupied Zone
700,000
(including French North Africa)

SWITZ.

AUSTRIA
43,700

HUNGARY
742,800

ROMANIA
342,000

CROATIA
40,000

SERBIA
10,000

BLACK SEA

SPAIN

ITALY
58,000

CORSICA

ALBANIA
200

BULGARIA
48,000

SARDINIA

GREECE
69,600

MEDITERRANEAN SEA

SICILY

RHODES

CYPRUS

ALGERIA

TUNISIA

CRETE

0   250   500 Miles
0   250   500 Kilometers

HITLER'S "FINAL SOLUTION": JEWS MARKED FOR DEATH

On January 20, 1942, German officials met at Wannsee (just outside Berlin) to discuss the "final solution" to the Jewish problem. They also discussed what they believed to be the remaining number of Jewish people in territories they controlled or soon hoped to control. Examine these figures closely. How many millions of innocent people did the Nazis propose to slaughter?

The Holocaust. These German civilians were compelled to view the bodies of concentration camp victims at the Landesburg camp in 1945.

The death camps have come to symbolize the horrors of Nazism as a system of modern mass murder. Yet it is worth emphasizing that much of the slaughter was not anonymous, industrialized, or routine and that it took place in face-to-face encounters outside the camps. Jews and other victims were not simply killed. They were tortured, beaten, and executed publicly while soldiers and other onlookers recorded the executions with cameras—and sent photos home to their families. During the last phases of the war, inmates still in the concentration camps were taken on death marches whose sole purpose was suffering and death. Nor was the killing done by the specially indoctrinated SS and *Einsatzgruppen*. The Nazi regime called up groups of conscripts, such as Reserve Police Battalion 101, from duty in its home city of Hamburg and sent it into occupied territories. Once there, the unit of middle-aged policemen received and obeyed orders to kill, in one day, 1,500 Jewish men, women, and children in one village. The commander offered to excuse men who did not feel they could carry out this assignment; only a few asked for a different task. In one Polish town, occupied first by the Soviets and then retaken by the Nazis, the Polish villagers themselves, with minimal guidance or help from German soldiers, turned on their Jewish neighbors and killed hundreds in a day.

How many people knew of the extent of the Holocaust? No operation of this scale could be carried out without the cooperation or knowledge of many: the Nazi hierarchy; architects who helped build the camps; engineers who designed the gas chambers and crematoria; municipal officials of cities from which people were deported; train drivers; residents of villages near the camps, who reported the smell of bodies burning; and so on. It is not surprising that most who suspected the worst were terrified and powerless. It is also not surprising that many people did not want to know and did their best to ignore evidence and carry on with their lives. Many who continued to support the Nazis did so for other reasons, out of personal opportunism or because they opposed communism and wanted order restored. Yet mere popular indifference does not provide a satisfactory explanation for the Nazis' ability to accomplish the murder of so many people. Many Europeans—German, French, Dutch, Polish, Swiss, and Russian—had come to believe that there was a "Jewish problem" that had to be "solved." The Nazis tried to conceal the death camps. Yet they knew they could count on vocal support for requiring Jews to be specially identified, for restrictions on marriage and property ownership, and for other kinds of discrimination. For reasons

"Jewish Couple in Budapest," Evgeny Khaldei (1945). Khaldei, a Soviet photographer and journalist who traveled with the Red Army, left a remarkable and moving account of his encounter with this woman and man. "There was a Jewish couple wearing Stars of David. They were afraid of me. There was still fighting going on in the city, and they thought I might be an SS soldier. So I said *Sholem Aleichem* [hello] to them, and the woman began to cry. After I'd taken the picture, I pulled their stars off and said, 'The fascists are beaten. It's terrible to be marked like that. . . .'"

THE HOLOCAUST:
TWO PERSPECTIVES FROM THE SS

An SS officer charged with inspecting the death camps wrote the first account here of his visit to Belzec, a camp in occupied Poland, near the former Russian border. He opposed the regime. Shortly after leaving this description, in 1945, he committed suicide.

Heinrich Himmler (1900–1945), one of the founding members of the Nazi Party and head of the SS, became one of the most powerful members of the Nazi government. He directed the purge of the rebellious SA in 1934, expanded the SS, supervised the network of death camps, and by 1943—when the speech reprinted here was given—had become minister of the interior for the administration of the Reich. Few represent better the combination of ambition, ideology, and ruthlessness that characterized Nazi leaders. Himmler committed suicide when captured by Allied troops in 1945.

THE DEATH CAMPS

Next morning, shortly before seven, I was told: 'the first transport will arrive in ten minutes'. And, in fact, after a few minutes, the first train arrived from the direction of Lemberg (Lvov). 45 wagons with 6,700 people, of whom 1,450 were already dead on arrival. Behind the barred hatches stared the horribly pale and frightened faces of children, their eyes full of the fear of death. Men and women were there too. . . .

The chambers fill up. 'Pack them in'—that is what Captain Wirth has ordered. People are treading on each others' toes. 700–800 in an area of twenty-five square metres, in forty-five cubic metres! The SS push them in as far as possible. The doors shut; in the meantime, the others are waiting outside in the open, naked. 'It is the same in winter', I was told. 'But they could catch their death of cold', I say. 'But that's just what they are there for', replied an SS man in dialect. Now at last I understood why the whole apparatus is called the Heckenholt Foundation. Heckenholt is the driver of the diesel engine, a little technician who constructed the installation. The people are going to be killed by the diesel exhaust gases. But the diesel engine won't start! Captain Wirth arrives. He is clearly embarrassed that this should happen just on the day when I am here. Yes indeed, I can see the whole thing. And I wait. My stop watch faithfully records it all. Fifty minutes, 70 seconds [*sic!*]. Still the diesel won't start. The people wait in their gas chambers. In vain. One can hear them crying, sobbing. . . . Captain Wirth hits the Ukrainian who is responsible for helping *Unterscharführer* Heckenholt with the diesel engine twelve or thirteen times in the face with his riding whip. After two hours forty-nine minutes—the stop watch has recorded it all—the engine starts. Up to this moment, the people have been living in these four chambers, four times 750 people in four times forty-five cubic metres. A further twenty-five minutes pass. That's right, many are now dead. One can see through the little peepholes when the electric light illuminates the chambers for a moment. After twenty-eight minutes, only a few are still alive. At last, after thirty-two minutes, they are all dead. . . .

HIMMLER'S INSTRUCTIONS TO THE SS

I also want to talk to you quite frankly about a very grave matter. We can talk about it quite frankly among ourselves and yet we will never speak of it publicly. Just as we did not hesitate on 30 June 1934 to do our duty as we were bidden, and to stand comrades who had lapsed up against the wall and shoot them, so we have never spoken about it and will never speak of it. It appalled everyone, and yet everyone was certain that he would do it the next time if such orders should be issued and it should be necessary.

I am referring to the Jewish evacuation programme, the extermination of the Jewish people. It is one of those things which are easy to talk about. 'The Jewish people will be exterminated', says every party comrade, 'It's clear, it's in our programme. Elimination of the Jews, extermination and we'll do it.' And then they come along, the worthy eighty million Germans, and each one of them produces his decent Jew. It's clear the others are swine, but this one is a fine Jew. Not one of those who talk like that has watched it happening, not one of them has been through it. Most of you will know what it means when a hundred corpses are lying side by side, or five hundred or a thousand are lying there. To have stuck it out and—apart from a few exceptions due to human weakness—to have remained decent, that is what has made us tough. This is a glorious page in our history and one that has never been written and can never be written. For we know how difficult we would have made it for ourselves if, on top of the bombing raids, the burdens and the de-

privations of war, we still had Jews today in every town as secret saboteurs, agitators and troublemakers. We would now probably have reached the 1916–17 stage when the Jews were still part of the body of the German nation.

We have taken from them what wealth they had. I have issued a strict order, which SS *Obergruppenführer* Pohl has carried out, that this wealth should, as a matter of course, be handed over to the Reich without reserve. We have taken none of it for ourselves. . . . All in all, we can say that we have fulfilled this most difficult duty for the love of our people. And our spirit, our soul, our character has not suffered injury from it. . . .

J. Noakes and G. Pridham, *Nazism: A History in Document and Eyewitness Accounts, 1919–1945*, Vol. 2 (New York, 1988), pp. 1151–1152, 1199–1200 (Source for both documents).

QUESTIONS FOR ANALYSIS

1. "This is a glorious page in our history," says Himmler, but one that "can never be written." How does he reconcile that contradiction? What was glorious? To what extent did the Nazis try to conceal what they were doing?

2. What does Himmler's speech suggest about the psychology of Nazism, or about the ways in which members of the SS were persuaded to become murderers?

that had to do with both traditional Christian anti-Semitism and modern, racialized nationalism, many Europeans had come to see Jewish Europeans as "foreign," no longer members of their national communities.

What of other governments? Their level of cooperation with the Nazis' plans varied. The French Vichy regime, on its own initiative, passed laws that required Jews to wear identifying stars and strictly limited their movements and activities. When the German government demanded roundups and deportations of Jews,

> For reasons that had to do with both traditional Christian anti-Semitism and modern, racialized nationalism, many Europeans had come to see Jewish Europeans as "foreign," no longer members of their national communities.

Vichy cooperated. On the other hand, Italy, though a fascist country, participated less actively. Not until the Germans occupied the north of Italy in 1943 were drastic anti-Semitic measures implemented. The Hungarian government, also fascist and allied with the Nazis, persecuted Jews but dragged its heels about deportations. Thus the Hungarian Jewish community survived—until March 1944, when Germans, disgusted with their Hungarian collaborators, took direct control and immediately began mass deportations. So determined were the Nazis to carry out their

DEPORTATION RAILWAYS

Between March 1942 and November 1944, Jews are known to have been deported from every location on this map—as well as from numerous other locales—to Auschwitz, where most were killed. Note the effort made by the Nazis to transport Jews from the very frontiers of the empire at the height of a two-front war. Consider what this says about the Nazi regime in particular and about other states willing to collaborate with the Nazis.

"final solution" that they killed up to 12,000 Hungarian Jews a day at Auschwitz in May 1944, contributing to a total death toll of 600,000.

In the face of this Nazi determination, little resistance was possible. The concentration camps were designed to numb and incapacitate their inmates, making them acquiesce in their own slow deaths even if they were not killed right away. In his famous account, the survivor Primo Levi writes: "Our language lacks words to express this offence, the demolition of a man. . . . It is not possible to sink lower than this; no human condition is more miserable than this, nor could it conceivably be so. Nothing belongs to us any more; they have taken away our clothes, our shoes, even our hair; if we speak, they will not listen to us, and if they listen, they will not understand." A few rebellions in Auschwitz and Treblinka were repressed with savage efficiency. In the villages of Poland, Ukraine, and elsewhere, people rounded up to be deported or shot had to make split-second decisions to escape. Saving oneself nearly always meant abandoning one's children or parents, which very few could—or would—do. The countryside offered no shelter; local populations were usually either hostile or too terrified to help. Reprisals horrified all. Families of Jews and gypsies were ordinary people whose lives could not have prepared them for the kind of violence that rolled over them.

The largest Jewish resistance came in the Warsaw ghetto, in the spring of 1943. The previous summer, the Nazis had deported 80 percent of the ghetto's residents to the camps, making it clear that those left behind had little hope of survival. Those in the ghetto had virtually no resources, yet, when deportations started again, a small Jewish underground movement—1,000 fighters, perhaps, in a community of 70,000—took on the Nazis with a tiny arsenal of gasoline bombs, pistols, and ten rifles. The Nazis responded by burning the ghetto to the ground and executing and deporting to the camps nearly everyone who was left. Some 56,000 Jews died. "The Warsaw Ghetto is no more," reported the SS commander at the end. Word of the rising did spread, but the repression made it clear that the targets of Nazi extermination could choose only between death in the streets or death in the camps. Sustained resistance, as one person remarked, would have required "the prospect of victory."

The Holocaust claimed between 4.1 and 5.7 million Jewish lives. Even those numbers do not register the nearly total destruction of some cultures. In the Baltic states (Latvia and Lithuania), Germany, Czechoslovakia, Yugoslavia, and Poland, well over 80 percent of the long-established Jewish communities were annihilated. Elsewhere, the figures were closer to 50 percent. The Holocaust was unique. It was part of a racial war and of an even longer period of ethnically motivated mass murder. Through both world wars and afterward ethnic and religious groups—Armenians, Poles, Serbian Orthodox, ethnic Germans—were hunted, massacred, and legally deported en masse. Hitler's government had planned to build a "new Europe," safe for ethnic Germans and their allies and secure against communism, on the graveyards of whole cultures.

TOTAL WAR: HOME FRONTS, THE WAR OF PRODUCTION, BOMBING, AND THE BOMB

How did the war transform the home fronts?

World War II was a "total war." Even more than World War I, it involved the combined efforts of whole populations. Larger armed forces were moving much more swiftly across territory, locked in constant battle with equally well-armed opponents. This demanded massive resources and national commitment to industry, drawing in the whole economies of the combatants. Standards of living changed around the world. In the neutral nations of Latin America, which supplied vast amounts of raw materials to the Allies, wartime profits led to a wave of prosperity known as the "dance of the millions." In the lands occupied by Germany or Japan, economies of forced extraction robbed local areas of resources, workers, and even food. In East Asia deprivations caused rising resentment of the Japanese, who had been seen initially as liberators ending the rule of the old colonial powers. In the United States, Detroit produced no new models of car or truck between 1940 and 1945. Work schedules were grueling. Women and the elderly, pressed back into wage work or

> In the Baltic states (Latvia and Lithuania), Germany, Czechoslovakia, Yugoslavia, and Poland, well over 80 percent of the long-established Jewish communities were annihilated.

working for the first time, put in long shifts (in Britain and Russia these sometimes ran over twelve hours) before returning home to cook, clean, and care for families and neighbors also affected by enemy bombing and wartime shortages. Diets changed. Though Germany lived comfortably off the farmlands of Europe for several years and the United States could lean on its huge agricultural base, food, gasoline, and basic household goods were still rationed. In occupied Europe and the Soviet Union rations were just above starvation level and sometimes fell below in areas near the fighting. Britain, dependent on its empire and other overseas sources for food and raw materials, ran a comprehensive rationing system that kept up production and ensured a drab but consistent diet on the table.

Production—the industrial ability to churn out more tanks, tents, planes, bombs, and uniforms than the other side—was essential to winning the war. Britain, the Soviet Union, and America each launched comprehensive, well-designed propaganda campaigns that encouraged the production of war equipment on an unmatched scale. Appeals to patriotism, to communal interests, and to a common stake in winning the war struck a chord. The Allied societies proved willing to regulate themselves and commit to the effort. Despite strikes and disputes with government officials, the Allied powers devoted more of their economies to war production, more efficiently, than any nations in history. Not only did they build tanks, ships, and planes capable of competing with advanced German and Japanese designs but they built them by the tens of thousands, swamping the enemy with constant reinforcements and superior firepower. Japan nearly reached comparable levels of production but then slowly declined, as Allied advances on land and American submarines cut off overseas sources of vital supplies. Germany, despite its reputation for efficiency and its access to vast supplies of slave labor, was less efficient in its use of workers and materials than the Allied nations. The Germans' ability to produce devastatingly successful weapons led to a damaging side effect—vast amounts of money and time spent developing the pet projects of high-ranking Nazi officials or trying to make unsuccessful designs work. Rather than losing time and resources pursuing perfection, the Allies developed working, standard designs and produced them in overwhelming numbers.

Because industry was essential to winning the war, centers of industry became vital military targets. The Allies began bombing German ports and factories almost as soon as the Germans started their own campaigns. Over time, American and British planners became equally ruthless on an even larger scale. Both of these Allied nations made a major commitment to strategic bombing, developing new planes and technology that allowed them to put thousands of bombers in the air both night and day over occupied Europe. As the war wore on and Germany kept fighting, the Allies expanded their campaign. They moved from pinpoint bombing of the military and industry in Germany to striking such targets across all of occupied Europe and bombing Germany's civilian population in earnest. For the British, despite a public debate about the morality of bombing, it was a war of retribution; for the Americans, it was an effort to grind the Germans down without sacrificing too many Allied lives. The Allies killed tens of thousands of German civilians as they struck Berlin, ports such as Hamburg, and the industrial cities of the Ruhr, but German war production persisted. At the

"Just a Good Afternoon's Work!" A British poster mobilizing women for part-time factory work.

same time German fighter planes shot down hundreds of Allied bombers, causing heavy losses. After the Allied invasion of Europe, bombing expanded well beyond targets of military value. The German city of Dresden, a center of culture and education that lacked heavy industry, was firebombed with a horrifying death toll. This gave Allied generals and politicians pause, but strategic bombing continued. German industry was slowly degraded, but the German will to keep fighting, like Britain's or the Soviet Union's, remained intact.

THE RACE TO BUILD THE BOMB

While the Allies carried out their bombing campaigns over Germany and Japan, Allied scientists in America were at work on the most powerful bomb ever designed. It was an unlikely weapon suggested from an obscure scientific field: atomic physics. British physicists—who, along with German scientists, led the field—believed that it would be possible to split the structure of an atom. The process, called fission, would split the subatomic particles apart in a huge burst of energy. The British scientists believed that, given the resources, they could stage a chain reaction, causing the fission of one atom to trigger splits in others, as though unraveling a thread in the structure of the universe. This would produce an explosion of extraordinary scope and power. British scientists began work on the idea but lacked the resources and enough radioactive material to stage a controlled chain reaction. The United States had those resources; and as America entered the war, the British passed on their theories and technical information to American scientists. A group of physicists, some native-born Americans, many refugees from the fascist regimes of Europe, were set to work creating a chain reaction. Enrico Fermi, an Italian physicist and a dedicated antifascist, was put in charge of designing the world's first nuclear reactor, built on the campus of the University of Chicago. In December 1942 Fermi staged the first controlled chain reaction at the site.

Meanwhile, the governments of the United States and Germany were both racing toward a military application of fission. The Germans were hampered in their efforts from the start. Many of their best specialists were Jewish or anti-Nazi refugees now working for the Americans. The Germans also lacked crucial bits of technical information and had fewer resources. When specially trained Norwegian commandos destroyed the Germans' heavy water facility (used to separate out

the uranium needed for the bomb) at Telemark, Norway, the German project went with it. Yet American officials feared that it had not been destroyed, and they also sensed the enormous power of the new weapon. A government project, code-named "Manhattan," had already been set up to manage an all-out effort at building an American atomic bomb. The project went on under the tightest security of the war; most of President Roosevelt's cabinet and the U.S. Congress did not know the real purpose of Manhattan.

In 1943 a laboratory was established at Los Alamos, New Mexico, bringing together the most capable nuclear physicists in the country, citizens and immigrants, old and young, to come up with a working design for a bomb. The physicist J. Robert Oppenheimer was placed in charge of the project, along with a U.S. Army Air Corps supervisor. After nearly two years they came up with a working design whose prototype would be dropped by plane and detonated in midair above the target, for maximum effect. The first test of the device was held on July 16, 1945, near Los Alamos. The wave of heat and the roar of the explosion were indescribable. The test tower was vaporized. The ball of fire that rose in a mushroom shape overhead was the physical expression of a blast equal to 20,000 tons of dynamite. Manhattan was a success. America now possessed the most destructive weapon ever devised. After watching the blast, Oppenheimer was moved to recite a phrase from an ancient Hindu text, a bitter commentary on his own work: "I am become Death, and the destroyer of worlds."

THE ALLIED COUNTERATTACK AND THE DROPPING OF THE ATOMIC BOMB

How did the Soviets defeat the Germans?

Hitler had invaded the Soviet Union in June 1941. Within two years the war in the east had become his undoing; within four years it brought about his destruction.

The early successes of the German-led invasion were crippling. Nearly 90 percent of the Soviets' tanks,

Prisoners of War. Over 90,000 captured German troops were forced to march through the streets of Stalingrad after a defeat by the Soviet forces. The combination of the battle and the Russian winter resulted in the German loss of over 300,000 men.

most of their aircraft, and huge stores of supplies were destroyed or captured. Nazi forces penetrated deep into European Russia. The Soviets fought regardless. By late 1941 German and Finnish forces had cut off and besieged Leningrad (St. Petersburg). Yet the city held out for 844 days—through three winters, massive destruction by artillery and aircraft, and periods of starvation—until a large relief force broke the siege. Russian partisans stepped up their campaigns of ambush and terrorism, and many of the Germans' former allies in Ukraine and elsewhere turned against them in reaction to Nazi pacification efforts.

> The crucial year on the Russian front came in 1943, as German efforts to break the back of Soviet industry resulted in the largest, most destructive battles the world has ever seen.

THE EASTERN FRONT

Most important, the character of the war on the eastern front changed. What had begun as a struggle between Nazi invaders and Stalin's regime became a war to save the *rodina*, the Russian motherland, as Russians fought for their own homes and families. Stalin, a shrewd politician, understood this; the message of Soviet propaganda changed to include a healthy dose of praise for Mother Russia. After surviving the winter of 1941–1942, the Russian public became convinced that they could indeed survive the war and became committed to driving the Germans from their homeland, whatever the cost. The second change in the war was a Russian victory won by what Stalin called "General Winter." Successive winters, followed by

hot, muddy summers, took a steady toll in Nazi lives and supplies, sapping German morale. The third change was the astonishing recovery of Soviet industry. The Soviets received some American and British aid, delivered at great risk over Arctic routes, but most of their achievement was self-sufficient. Whole industries were rebuilt behind the safety of the Ural Mountains, and entire populations of cities were displaced to work in them, turning out tanks, fighter planes, machine guns, and ammunition. Once the Russians achieved the same aerial stalemate that existed over Britain, their seemingly endless labor reserves were backed with boundless reserves of equipment. The fourth change in the war had to do with the Germans, who became victims of their own success. The *Blitzkrieg*, at first a brilliantly inventive way of fighting a war, became a predictable set of maneuvers run according to a checklist. The Russians were eager students of that routine. They learned each stage of the process well, exploited its weaknesses, and became particularly good at lulling the Germans into a false sense of success before overwhelming them from unexpected angles.

The crucial year on the Russian front came in 1943, as German efforts to break the back of Soviet industry resulted in the largest, most destructive battles the world has ever seen. The first of these began in 1942, with a massive German-led offensive in the Volga River Valley, aimed at the city of Stalingrad. The Germans hoped to split Soviet forces and destroy valuable factories. But once German, Romanian, and Italian troops entered the suburbs of the city they were drawn into bitter house-to-house fighting by Russian defenders. The outnumbered Soviet forces fought beyond the last cartridge,

CHRONOLOGY

THE EASTERN FRONT

Germans invade Soviet Union	June 1941
Siege of Leningrad	September 1941–January 1942
Battle of Stalingrad	September 1942–January 1943
Battle of Kursk	July 1943
Soviet forces reach Berlin	April 1945
Germany surrenders	May 1945

using rocks and knives when they had to. Germany's panzers were rendered useless by grenades and fire-bombs in the narrow streets. The city was reduced to rubble, which sometimes gave the Russians cover to surprise German and Romanian units. Russian forces were pushed back to the Volga River as winter came on, but the Nazis' supplies began to run low. In November 1942 large Russian armies encircled the enemy forces inside the city itself. The attackers were now besieged, in a battle that went on through a cruel winter.

Infuriated, Hitler demanded that his commanders relieve the embattled troops. Every attempt to break through was defeated, and at the end of January 1943 the German commander in Stalingrad defied orders and surrendered the haggard survivors of his army. More than a quarter of a million German, Romanian, and Italian bodies were dragged from the wrecked city. Two times that many German troops died in the whole course of the battle. The Russians suffered up to a million casualties, including 100,000 civilians. Despite the unparalleled casualties—the battle dwarfed even Verdun in the Great War or the fighting between China and Japan—the Russians had won a crucial victory. After Stalingrad, Hitler appeared less and less often in public, and his worst tendencies to gloom and paranoia grew as the Russian front turned against his dreams.

After Stalingrad, the Soviets mounted a series of offensives that turned German forces back from the heart of Russia. In the summer of 1943 German tank commanders launched a massive counterattack near the city of Kursk in the center of the front lines. Their early victories were a baited trap; several Russian armies were waiting, with masses of men and the newest Russian tanks, specially designed to destroy the panzers. The result may have been the largest battle ever fought, lasting six weeks and involving over 6,000 tanks and more than 2 million men between the two sides. Bogged down amid snipers and minefields and raked by Russian artillery and rocket launchers, the German army group, nearly a million strong, was crushed. The Russians, led by their commander at Stalingrad and the shrewdest opponent of the *Blitzkrieg*, Grigorii Zhukov, then launched a major offensive into Ukraine. By the spring of 1944 Ukraine was back in Soviet hands. With the relief of Leningrad and attacks into Byelorussia that reached the Polish border, the Russians turned the tables. Romania was knocked out of the war during 1944, and Soviet armies poured into the Balkans, eventually meeting up with Tito's victori-

ous partisans in Yugoslavia. Zhukov, who had taken charge of most of the Soviet armies, ground down German resistance in Poland during the winter of 1944. Several German armies collapsed, and Soviet forces, joined by communist partisans from the eastern European countries, retook large parts of Czechoslovakia. It was these battles, along with the fighting in Italy and Yugoslavia, that destroyed the German army. Hitler's most ambitious goal had brought the downfall of the Nazi regime and death to a generation of German soldiers.

THE WESTERN FRONT

During the campaigns in the East, Stalin continually pressured his allies to open a second front in the West. The American-led attack on Italy was a response to that pressure. Allied forces first invaded Sicily and then the Italian mainland. Italy's government deposed Mussolini and surrendered in the summer of 1943. A civil war ensued, because most Italians, especially communist partisans, sided with the Allies, while dedicated fascists continued to fight for their exiled leader. Italy was invaded by both sides; large Allied armies and more than a dozen elite German divisions occupied the country. The result was eighteen months of bitter fighting on Italy's muddy hillsides, in high mountains and bombed-out towns,

> The most important "second front" was opened on June 6, 1944, with the massive Allied landings in Normandy.

Storming "fortress Europe." American troops landing on Omaha beach June 6, 1944. In the three months that followed, the Allies poured more than 2 million men, almost half a million vehicles, and 4 million tons of supplies onto the continent—a measure of how firmly the Germans were established.

Evgeny Khaldei, "Raising the Red Flag Over the Reichstag," May 1, 1945. Khaldei was one of several Soviet Jewish photographers to document Nazi atrocities and (in this case) Soviet heroism on the Eastern front. In this photograph, which became the best-known image of Soviet victory, a Soviet soldier raises a flag over the Reichstag in Berlin.

consuming vast resources and tens of thousands of lives on each side. Nevertheless, the fighting in Italy cost Germany much more than it did the Allies, who liberated all the major Italian cities and entered Austria by the spring of 1945.

The most important "second front" was opened on June 6, 1944, with the massive Allied landings in Normandy. Though deadly in places, the landings were a masterpiece of planning and deception. The Germans fiercely defended the dense hedgerows of Normandy, but Allied air superiority and a vast buildup of men and matériel led to a breakthrough. An American landing on the Riviera in August had much more immediate success, aided by the French

CHRONOLOGY

THE WESTERN FRONT

Germany invades the Low Countries	May 1940
French surrender	June 1940
Battle of Britain	July 1940–June 1941
D-Day invasion	June 1944
Liberation of Paris	August 1944
Battle of the Bulge	December 1944
Allies invade Germany	April 1945
Germany surrenders	May 1945

resistance. In late July and August the Allies swept through France, liberating Paris on August 14 and pushing into Belgium. After that it was rough going. Allied commanders in the West were gifted organizers, but their skills as strategists were mixed. A British airborne invasion of the Netherlands and an American thrust into the forests of the Rhineland were bloody failures. The Germans mounted their own devastating attack in December 1944, under cover of winter storms, in the Battle of the Bulge. It was a last effort with their best men and equipment; they captured thousands of prisoners and nearly broke through Allied lines. Nevertheless, several elite American units beat off much larger German forces at key points until the snow cleared and the Allies mounted a crushing counterattack. Over the winter they destroyed German forces in the Rhineland and Holland. In April 1945, the Allies crossed the Rhine—in one of the war's ironies, French troops were the first to do so. The Germans collapsed. American tanks swept south, British and Canadian forces north. The Allies had learned the tactics of the *Blitzkrieg* on the receiving end, and now the Americans used them to overwhelm resistance. This genuine military success was helped by the fact that most Germans preferred to surrender to Americans or Britons than face the Russians to the east.

At the same time, those Soviet troops were approaching fast. By late April they had taken Prague and Vienna. On April 21, 1945, Zhukov's forces hammered their way into the suburbs of Berlin. During the next ten days a savage battle raged amid the ruins and heaps of rubble. More than 100,000 Russians and Germans died. Adolf Hitler killed himself in a bomb-proof shelter beneath the Chancellery on April 30. On May 2 the heart of the city was captured, and the Soviets' red banner flew from the Brandenburg Gate. On May 7 the German high command signed a document of unconditional surrender. By the next day the war in Europe was over.

THE WAR IN THE PACIFIC

The war in the Pacific came to an end four months later. The Japanese were rolled back on all fronts. Slim's international army in Burma had waged a wily campaign to drive out the Japanese. British, Indian, and Nepalese troops liberated the Burmese capital, Rangoon; at the same time the Germans were surrendering in the West. That same spring, Australian forces recaptured the Dutch East Indies, while an Anglo-Australian attack on Singapore was planned for the autumn. The U.S. Navy had won one of its greatest victories the previous fall, when William Halsey's task force destroyed most of Japan's surviving surface ships in the gulfs of the Philippine islands. American forces landed and within weeks the Philippine capital of Manila fell, taken house by house in bloody fighting. The remaining battles—amphibious assaults on a series of islands running toward the Japanese mainland—were just as brutal. Japanese pilots, hopelessly outnumbered in the air, mounted suicide attacks on American ships, while American marines and Japanese soldiers fought over every inch of the shell-blasted rocks in the middle of the Pacific. In June 1945, the Japanese island of Okinawa fell to American forces after eighty-two days of desperate fighting. American forces now had a foothold less than 500 miles from the Japanese home islands. Chinese forces, Nationalist and communist alike, combined to force the Japanese back on Hong Kong. The Soviets chose this moment to enter the fray. Their forces marched rapidly through Manchuria and into

CHRONOLOGY	
THE WAR IN THE PACIFIC	
Japanese bomb Pearl Harbor	December 1941
Singapore falls to Japan	December 1941
Battles of Midway, Coral Sea, and	
Guadalcanal	1942
Invasion of the Philippines	Fall 1944
Battle of Okinawa	June 1945
Soviets invade Manchuria and	
Korea	June–July 1945
Atomic bombs dropped on	
Hiroshima and Nagasaki	August 6 and 9, 1945
Japan surrenders	August 14, 1945

the colonial territory of Korea. The government in Tokyo awaited an invasion and called on its citizens for supreme endeavors to meet the crisis.

On July 26 the heads of the U.S, British, and Chinese governments issued a joint proclamation calling on Japan to surrender or be destroyed. The United States had already begun that process of destruction by using its most advanced bomber, the B-29, which could fly above Japanese efforts to shoot it down, in the systematic bombing of Japanese cities. Many of the wooden Japanese cities were hit with firebombs, which created storms of flame and killed hundreds of thousands of civilians. Yet the Japanese refused to surrender. In the absence of that surrender, the United States planned to increase the pace of destruction. They chose to use the atomic bomb.

Many senior military and naval officers argued that use of the bomb was not necessary, on the assumption that Japan was already beaten. Some of the scientists involved, who had done their part hoping to counter the Nazis, believed that using the bomb for political ends would set a deadly precedent. Harry Truman, who had succeeded Roosevelt after the latter's death in April 1945, decided otherwise. On August 6, a single atomic bomb was dropped on Hiroshima, obliterating about 60 percent of the city. Three days later a second bomb was dropped on Nagasaki. President Truman warned that the United States would use as many atom bombs as necessary to bring Japan to its knees. On August 14, Japan surrendered unconditionally.

The decision to drop the bomb, and its consequences, was extraordinary. It did not greatly alter the

The Atom Bomb. A mushroom cloud hovers over Nagasaki after the city was bombed August 9, 1945. Hiroshima had been bombed three days earlier.

THE ATOMIC BOMB AND ITS IMPLICATIONS

In July 1945, scientists associated with the Manhattan Project became involved in debates about how the atomic bomb could be deployed. Members of the Scientific Panel of the secretary of war's Interim Advisory Committee agreed that a bomb could be used militarily but disagreed about whether it could be used without prior warning and demonstration. Other groups of scientists secretly began to circulate petitions, such as the one reprinted here, in which they set out their views. The petitions never reached the president, but they raised issues that did emerge in the postwar period.

In the section of his memoirs reprinted here, President Harry S Truman sets out the views of other scientists on the secretary of war's advisory committee. He explains the logic of his decision to use the atomic bomb against Hiroshima (August 6, 1945) and Nagasaki (August 9, 1945) and the events as they unfolded.

A PETITION TO THE PRESIDENT OF THE UNITED STATES

July 17, 1945

A PETITION TO THE PRESIDENT OF THE UNITED STATES

We, the undersigned scientists, have been working in the field of atomic power. Until recently we have had to fear that the United States might be attacked by atomic bombs during this war and that her only defense might lie in a counterattack by the same means. Today, with the defeat of Germany, this danger is averted and we feel impelled to say what follows:

The war has to be brought speedily to a successful conclusion and attacks by atomic bombs may very well be an effective method of warfare. We feel, however, that such attacks on Japan could not be justified, at least not unless the terms which will be imposed after the war on Japan were made public in detail and Japan were given an opportunity to surrender. . . .

[I]f Japan still refused to surrender our nation might then, in certain circumstances, find itself forced to resort to the use of atomic bombs. Such a step, however, ought not to be made at any time without seriously considering the moral responsibilities which are involved.

The development of atomic power will provide the nations with new means of destruction. The atomic bombs at our disposal represent only the first step in this direction, and there is almost no limit to the destructive power which will become available in the course of their future development. Thus a nation which sets the precedent of using these newly liberated forces of nature for purposes of destruction may

have to bear the responsibility of opening the door to an era of devastation on an unimaginable scale.

If after this war a situation is allowed to develop in the world which permits rival powers to be in uncontrolled possession of these new means of destruction, the cities of the United States as well as the cities of other nations will be in continuous danger of sudden annihilation. . . .

The added material strength which this lead [in the field of atomic power] gives to the United States brings with it the obligation of restraint and if we were to violate this obligation our moral position would be weakened in the eyes of the world and in our own eyes. It would then be more difficult for us to live up to our responsibility of bringing the unloosened forces of destruction under control.

In view of the foregoing, we, the undersigned, respectfully petition: first, that you exercise your power as Commander-in-Chief, to rule that the United States shall not resort to the use of atomic bombs in this war unless the terms which will be imposed upon Japan have been made public in detail and Japan knowing these terms has refused to surrender; second, that in such an event the question of whether or not to use atomic bombs be decided by you in the light of the considerations presented in this petition as well as all the other moral responsibilities which are involved.

Michael B. Stoff, Jonathan F. Fanton, and R. Hal Williams, eds., *The Manhattan Project: A Documentary Introduction to the Atomic Age* (New York, 2000), p. 173.

PRESIDENT TRUMAN'S MEMOIRS

I had realized, of course, that an atomic bomb explosion would inflict damage and casualties beyond imagination. On the other hand, the scientific advisers of the committee reported, "We can propose no technical demonstration likely to bring an end to the war; we see no acceptable alternative to direct military use." It was their conclusion that no technical demonstration they might propose, such as over a deserted island, would be likely to bring the war to an end. It had to be used against an enemy target.

The final decision of where and when to use the atomic bomb was up to me. Let there be no mistake about it. I regarded the bomb as a military weapon and never had any doubt that it should be used. The top military advisers to the President recommended its use, and when I talked to Churchill he unhesitatingly told me that he favored the use of the atomic bomb if it might aid to end the war.

In deciding to use this bomb I wanted to make sure that it would be used as a weapon of war in the manner prescribed by the laws of war. That meant that I wanted it dropped on a military target. I had told Stimson that the bomb should be dropped as nearly as possibly upon a war production center of prime military importance.

Stimson's staff had prepared a list of cities in Japan that might serve as targets. Kyoto, though favored by General Arnold as a center of military activity, was eliminated when Secretary Stimson pointed out that it was a cultural and religious shrine of the Japanese.

Four cities were finally recommended as targets: Hiroshima, Kokura, Niigata, and Nagasaki. They were listed in that order as targets for the first attack. The order of selection was in accordance with the military importance of these cities, but allowance would be given for weather conditions at the time of the bombing. Before the selected targets were approved as proper for military purposes, I personally went over them in detail with Stimson, Marshall, and Arnold, and we discussed the matter of timing and the final choice of the first target. . . .

On August 6, the fourth day of the journey home from Potsdam, came the historic news that shook the world. I was eating lunch with members of the *Augusta's* crew when Captain Frank Graham, White House Map Room watch officer, handed me the following message:

> TO THE PRESIDENT
> FROM THE SECRETARY OF WAR
>
> Big bomb dropped on Hiroshima August 5 at 7:15 P.M. Washington time. First reports indicate complete success which was even more conspicuous than earlier test.

I was greatly moved. I telephoned Byrnes aboard ship to give him the news and then said to the group of sailors around me, "This is the greatest thing in history. It's time for us to get home."

Harry S Truman, *Memoirs*, Vol. 1 (Garden City, NY, 1955), pp. 419–421.

QUESTIONS FOR ANALYSIS

1. To express their fears about how the atomic bomb would be used, scientists circulated petitions. Look at the outcomes the scientists proposed. Which came closest to subsequent events? Which was the most prudent? The most honest?

2. Is it appropriate for scientists to propose how new weapons should be used? Are they overreaching in trying to give advice in foreign affairs and military strategy? Or are they obligated to voice moral qualms?

scope of or the plans for the American destruction of Japan. Many more Japanese died in the earlier fire bombings than in the two atomic blasts. Yet the bomb was an entirely new kind of weapon, built with untried technology; some of its designers feared that the test blast might split *every* atom in the universe. It was one of the most terrifying results of the new relationship between science and political power. The nature of the bomb mattered as well. The instant, total devastation of the blasts, along with the cancerous radiation that lingered for years and claimed victims decades later, was something terribly new. The world now had a weapon that could destroy not just cities and peoples, but humanity itself.

Nuremberg. The city had been seen as a center of the Nazi regime. The destruction of this city was a visible sign to Allied troops of the victory over the Nazis.

CONCLUSION

After World War I, many Europeans awoke to find a world they no longer recognized. In 1945 many Europeans came out from shelters or began the long trips back to their homes, faced with a world that hardly existed at all. The products of industry—tanks, submarines, strategic bombing—had destroyed the structures of industrial society—factories, ports, and railroads. The tools of mass culture—fascist and communist appeals, patriotism proclaimed via radios and movie screens, mobilization of mass armies and industry—had been put to full use. In the aftermath, much of Europe lay destroyed and, as we will see, vulnerable to the rivalry of the postwar superpowers: the United States and the Soviet Union.

The two world wars profoundly affected Western empires. Nineteenth-century imperialism had made twentieth-century war a global matter. In both conflicts the warring nations had used the resources of empire to their fullest. Key campaigns, in North Africa, Burma, Ethiopia, the Pacific, were fought in and over colonial territories. Hundreds of thousands of colonial troops—sepoys and Gurkhas from India and Nepal, Britain's King's African Rifles, French from Algeria and West Africa—served in armies on both sides of the conflict. After two massive mobilizations, many anticolonial leaders found renewed confidence in their own peoples' courage and resourcefulness, and they seized the op-

portunity of European weakness to press for independence. In many areas that had been under European or Japanese imperial control, from sections of China, to Korea, Indochina, Indonesia, and Palestine—the end of World War II only paved the way for a new round of conflict. This time, the issue was when imperial control would be ended, and by whom.

World War II also carried on the Great War's legacy of massive killing. Historians estimate that nearly 50 million people died. The killing fields of the east took the highest tolls: 25 million Soviet lives. Of those, 8.5 million were in the military, and the rest civilians; 20 percent of the Polish population and nearly 90 percent of the Polish Jewish community; 1 million Yugoslavs, including militias of all sides; 4 million German soldiers and 500,000 German civilians, not including the hundreds of thousands of ethnic Germans who died while being deported west at the end of the war, in one of the many acts of ethnic cleansing that ran through the period. Even the United States, shielded from the full horrors of total war by two vast oceans, lost 292,000 soldiers in battle and more to accidents or disease.

Why was the war so murderous? The advanced technology of modern industrial war and the openly genocidal ambitions of the Nazis offer part of the answer. The global reach of the conflict offers another. Finally World War II overlapped with, and eventually devolved into, a series of smaller, no less bitter conflicts: a civil war in Greece; conflicts between Orthodox, Catholics, and Muslims in Yugoslavia; and political battles for control of the French resistance. Even when those struggles claimed fewer lives, they left deep political scars. So did memories of the war. Hitler's empire could not have lasted as long as it did without active collaboration or passive acquiescence from many, a fact that produced bitterness and recrimination for years.

In this and many other ways, the war haunted the second half of the century. Fifty years after the battle of Stalingrad, the journalist Timothy Rybeck discovered that hundreds of skeletons still lay, in the open, on the fields outside the city. Many bodies had never been buried. Others had been left in shallow mass graves. As wind and water eroded the soil, farmers plowed the fields, and teenagers dug for medals and helmets to sell as curiosities, more bones kept rising to the surface. One of the supervisors charged with finding permanent graves and building memorials to the fallen contemplated the task with more than simple weariness. "This job of reburying the dead," he said, "will never be done."

KEY TERMS

Blitzkreig	Dunkirk	Operation Barbarossa	Hiroshima
appeasement	Winston Churchill	Auschwitz-Birkenau	
Guernica	Pearl Harbor	Manhattan Project	

SELECTED READINGS

The U.S. Holocaust Memorial Museum has an extraordinary collection of articles, photographs, and maps. See www.ushmm.org.

Bartov, Omer. *Hitler's Army: Soldiers, Nazis, and War in the Third Reich*. New York, 1991. A Study of the radicalization of the German army on the Russian front.

Braithwaite, Rodric. *Moscow. 1941: A City and Its People at War*. London, 2006. Readable account of one of the turning points of the war.

Browning, Christopher R. *The Path to Genocide: Essays on Launching the Final Solution*. Cambridge, 1992. Discusses changing interpretations and case studies. See also the author's *Ordinary Men: Reserve Police Battalion 101 and the Final Solution in Poland*.

Burrin, Philippe. *France under the Germans: Collaboration and Compromise*. New York, 1996. Comprehensive on occupation and collaboration.

Carr, Raymond. *The Spanish Tragedy: The Civil War in Perspective*. London, 1977. A thoughtful introduction to the Spanish Civil War and the evolution of Franco's Spain.

Dawidowicz, Lucy S. *The War against the Jews, 1933–1945*. New York, 1975. A full account of the Holocaust.

Divine, Robert A. *Roosevelt and World War II*. Baltimore, Md., 1969. A diplomatic history.

Djilas, Milovan. *Wartime*. New York, 1977. An insider's account of the partisans' fighting in Yugoslavia and a good example of civil war within the war.

Gellately, Robert, and Ben Kiernan, eds. *The Specter of Genocide: Mass Murder in Historical Perspective*. New York, 2003. A particularly thoughtful collection of essays.

Gilbert, Martin. *The Appeasers*. Boston, 1963. Excellent study of British pro-German sentiment in the 1930s.

Graham, Helen. *The Spanish Civil War: A Very Short Introduction*. Oxford and New York, 2005. Excellent and very concise, based on the author's new interpretation in the more detailed *The Spanish Republic at War, 1936–1939*. Cambridge, 2002.

Hilberg, Raul. *The Destruction of the European Jews*. 2nd ed. 3 vols. New York, 1985. An excellent treatment of the Holocaust, its origins, and its consequences.

Kedward, Roderick. *In Search of the Maquis: Rural Resistance in Southern France, 1942–1944*. Oxford, 1993. An engaging study of French guerilla resistance.

Keegan, John. *The Second World War*. New York, 1990. By one of the great military historians of our time.

Mann, Michael. *The Dark Side of Democracy: Explaining Ethnic Cleansing*. New York, 2005. Brilliant and theoretical as well as historical.

Marrus, Michael R. *The Holocaust in History*. Hanover, N.H., 1987. Thoughtful analysis of central issues.

Mawdsley, Evan. *Thunder in the East: The Nazi-Soviet War, 1941–1945*. New York, 2005.

Megargee, Geoffrey. *War of Annihilation: Combat and Genocide on the Eastern War, 1941*. Lanham, Md., 2006. Represents some of the new historical work on the eastern front.

Merridale, Catherine. *Ivan's War: Life and Death in the Red Army, 1939–1945*. New York, 2006. Raises many new questions and insights.

Michel, Henri. *The Shadow War: The European Resistance, 1939–1945*. New York, 1972. Compelling reading.

Milward, Alan S. *War, Economy, and Society, 1939–1945*. Berkeley, Calif., 1977. On the economic impact of the war and the strategic impact of the economy.

Noakes, Jeremy, and Geoffrey Pridham. *Nazism: A History in Documents and Eyewitness Accounts, 1919–1945*. New York, 1975. An excellent combination of analysis and documentation.

Overy, Richard. *Russia's War*. New York, 1998. A very readable account that accompanies the PBS series by the same title.

Overy, Richard. *Why the Allies Won*. New York, 1995. Excellent analysis; succint.

Paxton, Robert O. *Vichy France: Old Guard and New Order, 1940–1944*. New York, 1982. Brilliant on collaboration and Vichy's National Revolution.

Stoff, Michael B. *The Manhattan Project: A Documentary Introduction to the Atomic Age*. New York, 1991. Political, scientific, and historical; excellent documents and commentary.

Weinberg, Gerhard L. *A Global History of World War II*. New York, 1995. Now the most comprehensive history.

Wilkinson, James D. *The Intellectual Resistance in Europe*. Cambridge, Mass., 1981. A comparative study of the movement throughout Europe.

PART VIII

THE WEST AND
THE WORLD

THE SECOND WORLD WAR was the great watershed of the twentieth
century. Its legacies were many and pervasive. The "hot war" between the
Allies and the Axis was superseded by a rivalry between the most powerful of
the Allies: the United States and the Soviet Union. The superpowers possessed
nuclear weapons, global reach, and networks of alliances that gave them the
authority of empires. The "cold war" between these powers dominated the
recovery from the world war, and global politics in general, for four decades.
The rise and fall of cold-war politics is a fundamental theme in twentieth-
century history; it is one of the two historical trends followed here.

While the cold war seemed to centralize the political, cultural, and economic
life of the world around the twin poles of the superpowers, the other key theme
of the later twentieth century involves the decentralizing effects of globalization.
This began with the breaking apart of Europe's old colonial empires and the
emergence of new nations. New forms of politics and protest emerged as well,
based on social movements of women, ethnic minorities, and peoples denied
a political voice in the age of imperialism. The Western European empires
were not the only ones to collapse. With the end of the cold war, the unofficial
empire of the Soviet Union collapsed as well, producing new nations and new
hopes. These events seemed to leave the United States as the world's leading
power, but the rest of the world would not simply become an American empire
by default or consent to being "Americanized" on the United States' terms.
As the twentieth century came to an end, it was clear that the west operated
in a much tighter network of world civilizations. The circumstances in which
this globalized world emerged are the focus of this last section.

	POLITICS	SOCIETY AND CULTURE	ECONOMY	INTERNATIONAL RELATIONS
				Mohandas Gandhi (1869–1948)
	Malcolm X (1925–1965)	Alexander Fleming discovers first antibiotic, penicillin (1928)		
	Martin Luther King Jr. (1929–1968)			
1940		Albert Camus, *The Stranger* (1942)		Gandhi leads independence movement in India (1940s)
				Soviet Union draws Iron Curtain over eastern Europe (1945–1948)
				Chinese Communist Revolution (1945–1949)
				India gains independence; formation of Pakistan (1947)
				Truman Doctrine (1947)
				Vietnam War, French phase (1947–1954)
	Germany divided; Berlin airlift (1948–1949)		Marshall Plan (1948)	Civil war in Greece (1948)
				Josip Tito declares Yugoslavia independent of Soviet Union (1948)
				State of Israel formed (1948)
	Konrad Adenauer, chancellor of West Germany (1949–1963)	George Orwell, *1984* (1949)		Formation of NATO (1949)
1950	Mao Zedong's Great Leap Forward (1950s)	Simone de Beauvoir, *The Second Sex* (1949)	European Coal and Steel Community created (1951)	Korean War (1950–1953)
				Abdel Nasser becomes president of Egypt (1952)
	Joseph Stalin dies (1953)	Samuel Beckett, *Waiting for Godot* (1953)		United States and Soviet Union test hydrogen bombs (1953)
	Khrushchev's regime (1953–1964)	Francis Crick and James Watson discover structure of DNA (1953)		Algerian war ends with Algerian independence (1954–1962)
		Jonas Salk develops polio vaccine (1953)		Formation of Warsaw Pact (1955)
				Vietnam War, U.S. phase (1955–1975)
	Nikita Khrushchev begins de-Stalinization (1956)	Boris Pasternak, *Dr. Zhivago* (1957)		Suez Crisis (1956)
				Hungarian rebellion repressed by Soviets (1956)
	Charles de Gaulle forms Fifth Republic in France (1958)		European Economic Community (EEC, Common Market) formed (1958)	
1960	Cultural Revolution in China (1960s)	Günter Grass, *The Tin Drum* (1959)	Inflation rates rise across western Europe (late 1960s–1970s)	Cuban revolution (1959)
	John F. Kennedy, president (1961–1963)	Joseph Heller, *Catch-22* (1961)		
		Frantz Fanon, *The Wretched of the Earth* (1961)		
	Berlin Wall built (1961)	Rachel Carson, *Silent Spring* (1962)		Cuban Missile Crisis (1962)
	Martin Luther King Jr. leads March on Washington (1963)	Betty Friedan, *The Feminine Mystique* (1963)		Vietnam War (1963–1975)
	Leonid Brezhnev leads Soviet Union (1964–1982)	Herbert Marcuse, *One-Dimensional Man* (1964)		
		The Beatles play in New York (1964)		
		Birth control pill becomes available (mid-1960s)		Six-Day War between Israel and Arab nations (1967)
	Student protests and worker strikes in Paris (1968)			
	Czech revolt; Prague Spring (1968)			
1970	Willy Brandt, chancellor of West Germany (1970–1974)			SALT treaties (1970s and early 1980s)
				Gradual détente between Soviet Union and Western powers (1970s)
	Watergate scandal (1972–1974); President Richard Nixon resigns		Western European citizens elect representatives to EEC parliament (1972)	Nixon visits China (1972)

POLITICS	SOCIETY AND CULTURE	ECONOMY	INTERNATIONAL RELATIONS	
		Oil prices rise steadily, worsening widespread recession (1973–1980s)	OPEC embargo against Western powers (1973) Arab-Israeli War (1973) Camp David Accords (1978) Soviet military intervention in Afghanistan (1979–1989)	1973
Margaret Thatcher, prime minister of England (1979–1990) Polish Solidarity workers movement organizes strikes (1980) Ronald Reagan, president (1980–1988) Helmut Kohl becomes chancellor of West Germany (1982) Mikhail Gorbachev, leader of Communist party (1985–1991) Renewed Solidarity strikes in Poland, demonstrations across Eastern bloc (1988) Break-up of Soviet power in eastern Europe (1989) Berlin Wall falls (1989) Tiananmen Square massacre (1989) Germany reunifies (1990) Boris Yeltsin elected president of Russian Federation (1990) Soviet Union dissolved (1992)	Asian population reaches 3 billion (1986) Nuclear reactor accident at Chernobyl (1986)	Computer revolution begins (1980s)		1980
Nelson Mandela elected president of South Africa; end of apartheid (1994)		Eastern European economies in crisis (1990s) Internet revolution begins (1990s) NAFTA signed by Canada, Mexico, and United States (1993)	Persian Gulf War (1991) Yugoslavian civil wars (1991–1992, 1992–1995) Genocide in Rwanda (1994) Russia's war with Chechnya begins (1994) Pakistan and India test nuclear weapons (late 1990s) War in Kosovo (1999)	1990
	Scientists in Scotland clone a sheep (1997) Global population exceeds 6 billion (2001)		United States declares war on terrorism (2001)	2001

CHAPTER TWENTY-SEVEN

THE COLD WAR WORLD: GLOBAL POLITICS, ECONOMIC RECOVERY, AND CULTURAL CHANGE

THE WAR ENDED THE WAY a passage through a tunnel ends," wrote Heda Kovály, a Czech woman who survived the concentration camps. "From far away you could see the light ahead, a gleam that kept growing, and its brilliance seemed ever more dazzling to you huddled there in the dark the longer it took to reach it. But when at last the train burst out into the glorious sunshine, all you saw was a wasteland." The war left Europe a land of wreckage and confusion. Millions of refugees trekked hundreds or thousands of miles on foot to return to their homes while others were forcibly displaced from their lands. In some areas housing was practically nonexistent, with no available means to build anew. Food remained in dangerously short supply; a year after the war, roughly 100 million people in Europe still lived on less than 1,500 calories per day. Families scraped vegetables from their gardens or traded smuggled goods on the black market. Governments continued to ration food, and without rationing a large portion of the Continent's population would have starved. During the winter of 1945–1946, many regions had little or no fuel for heat. What coal there was—less than half the prewar supply—could not be transported to the areas that needed it most. The brutality of international war, civil war, and occupation had divided countries against themselves, shredding relations among ethnic groups and fellow citizens. Ordinary people's intense relief at liberation often went hand in hand with recriminations over their neighbors' wartime betrayal, collaboration, or simple opportunism.

How does a nation, a region, or a civilization recover from a catastrophe on the scale of World War II? Nations had to do much more than deliver food and rebuild economic infrastructures. They had to restore—or create—government authority, functioning bureaucracies, and legitimate legal systems. They had to rebuild bonds of trust and civility between citizens, steering a course between demands for justice on the one hand and the overwhelming desire to bury memories of the past on the other. On the contrary, rebuilding entailed a commitment to renewing democracy—to creating democratic institutions that could withstand threats such as those the West had experienced in the 1930s. Some aspects of this process were extraordinarily successful, more so than even the most optimistic forecaster might have thought possible in 1945. Others failed or were deferred until later in the century.

FOCUS QUESTIONS

• What were the causes of the cold war?

• How did Western Europe recover from World War II?

 • What were the links between decolonization, World War II, and the cold war?

• What themes defined postwar culture?

The war's devastating effects brought two dramatic changes in the international balance of power. The first change was the emergence of the so-called superpowers, the United States and the Soviet Union, and the swift development of a "cold war" between them. The cold war divided Europe, with Eastern Europe occupied by Soviet troops, and Western Europe dominated by the military and economic presence of the United States. The second great change came with the dismantling of the European empires that had once stretched worldwide. The collapse of empires and the creation of newly emancipated nations raised the stakes in the cold war and brought superpower rivalry to far-flung sections of the globe. Those events, which shaped the postwar recovery and necessarily created a new understanding of what "the West" meant, are the subject of this chapter.

THE COLD WAR AND A DIVIDED CONTINENT

What were the causes of the cold war?

No peace treaty ended World War II. Instead, as the war drew to a close, relations between the Allied powers began to fray over issues of power and influence in Central and Eastern Europe. After the war, they descended from mistrust to open conflict. The United States and Soviet Union rapidly formed the centers of two imperial blocs. Their rivalry, which came to be known as the cold war, pitted against each other two military powers, two sets of state interests, and two ideologies: capitalism and communism. The cold war's manifold repercussions reached well beyond Europe, for anticolonial movements, sensing the weakness of European colonial powers, turned to the Soviets for help in their struggles for independence. The cold war thus structured the peace, shaped international relations for four decades, and affected governments and peoples across the globe who depended on either of the superpowers.

THE IRON CURTAIN

The Soviet Union had insisted during the wartime negotiations at Tehran (1943) and Yalta (1945) that it had a legitimate claim to control Eastern Europe, a claim that some Western leaders accepted as the price

of defeating Hitler and others ignored so as to avoid a dangerous confrontation. When visiting Moscow in 1944, Churchill and Stalin quietly bargained over their respective spheres of influence, offering each other "percentages" of the countries that were being liberated. The Declaration of Principles of Liberated Europe issued at Yalta in 1945 guaranteed free elections, but Stalin believed that the framework of allied cooperation gave him a free hand in Eastern Europe. Stalin's siege mentality pervaded his authoritarian regime and cast nearly everyone at home or abroad as a potential threat or enemy of the state. Yet Soviet policy did not rest on personal paranoia alone. The country's catastrophic wartime losses made the Soviets determined to maintain political, economic, and military control of the lands they had liberated from Nazi rule. For the Soviets, Eastern Europe served as both "a sphere and a shield." When their former allies resisted their demands, the Soviets became suspicious, defensive, and aggressive.

In Eastern Europe, the Soviet Union used a combination of diplomatic pressure, political infiltration, and military power to create "people's republics" sympathetic to Moscow. In country after country, the same process unfolded: first, states set up coalition governments that excluded former Nazi sympathizers; next came coalitions dominated by communists; finally, one party took hold of all the key positions of power. This was the process that prompted Winston Churchill, speaking at a college graduation in Fulton, Missouri, in 1946, to say that "an Iron Curtain" had "descended across Europe." In 1948, the Soviets crushed a Czechoslovakian coalition government headed by the liberal leaders Eduard Beneš and Jan Masaryk—a break with Yalta's guarantee of democratic elections that shocked many. By that year, governments dependent on Moscow had also been established in Poland, Hungary, Romania, and Bulgaria. Together these states were referred to as the Eastern bloc.

The Soviet campaign to control Eastern Europe did not go unchallenged. The Yugoslavian communist and resistance leader Marshal Tito (Josip Broz, 1892–1980) fought to keep his government independent of Moscow. Unlike most Eastern European communist leaders, Tito came to power on his own during the war. He drew on support from Serbs, Croats, and Muslims in Yugoslavia—thanks to his wartime record, which gave him political authority rooted in his own country. Moscow charged that Yugoslavia had "taken the road to nationalism," or become a "colony of the imperialist nations" and expelled the country from the communist countries' economic and military pacts. Determined to

Legend:

Allied occupation of Germany and Austria, 1945–1955

Territory lost by Germany

Territory gained by Soviet Union

Postwar national boundaries, to 1989

"Iron Curtain" to 1989

1945 Year Communist control of government was gained

NORTH
SEA

NORWAY

Oslo

SWEDEN

Stockholm

FINLAND

From
Finland,
1940–1956

Helsinki

Leningrad

DENMARK

Copenhagen

BALTIC SEA

ESTONIA
To U.S.S.R.,
1940

LATVIA
To U.S.S.R.,
1940

NETHERLANDS

Amsterdam

U.S.
Zone

Elbe R.

Bremen

British
Zone

Incorporated into
U.S.S.R., 1945

Gdansk
(Danzig)

LITHUANIA
To U.S.S.R.,
1940

BELGIUM

Brussels

Rhine R.

Soviet
Zone

Berlin

EAST
GERMANY
(1949)

Bonn

Incorporated into
Poland, 1945

Oder R.

Warsaw

WHITE
RUSSIA

Brest

From Poland,
1940–1947

WEST
GERMANY

French
Zone

U.S.
Zone

POLAND
(1947)

UKRAINE

LUXEMBOURG

Prague

CZECHOSLOVAKIA
(1948)

From
Czechoslovakia,
1945–1947

Munich

Vienna

U.S.
Zone

Soviet Zone

Bern

French Zone

AUSTRIA

British
Zone

Budapest

From Romania,
1940–1947

BESSARABIA

SWITZERLAND

Milan

HUNGARY
(1949)

Po R.

From Italy,
1945

ROMANIA
(1947)

CRIMEA

Yalta

ADRIATIC SEA

YUGOSLAVIA
(1945)

Bucharest

Danube R.

BLACK SEA

From Romania,
1940–1947

CORSICA
(Fr.)

ITALY

Rome

BULGARIA
(1946)

Sofia

Istanbul

SARDINIA
(It.)

Tirane

ALBANIA
(1944)

TURKEY

GREECE

SICILY
(It.)

Athens

MEDITERRANEAN

CRETE

CYPRUS

SEA

0   200   400 Miles
0   200   400 Kilometers

Inset (East Germany / Berlin):

EAST GERMANY

French
Sector

WEST

British
Sector

BERLIN

U.S. Sector

EAST

Soviet
Sector

BERLIN

Potsdam

Berlin Wall (1961–1989)

0   10 Miles
0   10 Kilometers

SOVIET UNION
(1917)

Inset (locator):

EUROPE

Area of
detail

AFRICA

TERRITORIAL CHANGES IN EUROPE AFTER WORLD WAR II

At the end of World War II, the Soviet Union annexed territory in Eastern Europe to create a buffer between it and Western Europe. At the same time, the United States established a series of military alliances in Western Europe to stifle the spread of communism in Europe. How did these new territorial boundaries aggravate the tensions between Soviet Union and the United States?

reassert control elsewhere, the Soviets demanded purges in the parties and administrations of various satellite governments. These began in the Balkans and extended through Czechoslovakia, East Germany, and Poland. The fact that democratic institutions had been shattered before the war made it easier to establish dictatorships in its aftermath. The purges succeeded by playing on fears and festering hatreds; in several areas those purging the governments attacked their opponents as Jewish. Anti-Semitism, far from being crushed, remained a potent political force—as Heda Kovály explained, it became common to blame Jews for bringing the horrors of war.

> "[N]ot since Rome and Carthage had there been such a polarization of power on this earth."

The end of war did not mean peace. In Greece, as in Yugoslavia and through much of the Balkans, war's end brought a local communist-led resistance to the verge of seizing power. The British and the Americans, however, were determined to keep Greece in their sphere of influence, as per informal agreements with the Soviets. Only large infusions of aid to the anticommunist monarchy allowed them to do so. The bloody civil war that lasted until 1949 took a higher toll than the wartime occupation. Greece's bloodletting became one of the first crises of the cold war and a touchstone for the United States' escalating fear of communist expansion. "Like apples in a barrel infected by the corruption of one rotten one, the corruption of Greece would infect Iran and all to the East . . . Africa . . . Italy and France," warned Dean Acheson in 1947, then deputy head of America's State Department. "[N]ot since Rome and Carthage had there been such a polarization of power on this earth."

Defeated Germany lay at the heart of these two polarizing power blocs and soon became the front line of their conflict. The Allies had divided Germany into four zones of occupation. Although the city of Berlin was deep in Soviet territory, it too was divided. The occupation zones were intended to be temporary, pending an official peace settlement. But the Soviets and the French, British, and Americans quarreled over reparations and policies for the economic development of Germany. Administrative conflicts among the Western powers were almost as intense as their disagreements with the Soviets; Britain and the United States nearly had a serious falling out over food supply and trade in their zones. Yet the quickening cold war put those arguments on hold, and in 1948 the three Western allies began to create a single government for their territories. They passed reforms to ease the economic crisis and introduced a new currency—a powerful symbol of economic unity. The Soviets retaliated by cutting all road, train, and river access from the western zone to West Berlin, but the Western allies refused to cede control over the capital. For eleven months they airlifted supplies over Soviet territory to the besieged western zone of Berlin, a total of 12,000 tons of supplies carried by hundreds of flights every day. The Berlin blockade lasted nearly a year, from June 1948 to May 1949. It ended with the creation of two Germanies: the Federal Republic in the west and the German Democratic Republic in the former Soviet zone. Within a few short years both countries looked strikingly like armed camps.

THE MARSHALL PLAN

The United States countered the expansion of Soviet power and locally based communist movements with massive programs of economic and military aid to Western Europe. In a 1947 speech to Con-

The Remains of Dresden, 1947. Dresden was devastated by a controversial Allied bombing in February, 1945. Kurt Vonnegut dramatically portrayed its destruction and the aftermath in his novel *Slaughterhouse-Five.*

Rubble surrounds the bombed-out Reichstag in Berlin, 1948.

gress arguing for military assistance to anticommunists in Greece, President Harry Truman set out what would come to be called the Truman Doctrine, a pledge to support the resistance of "free peoples" to communism. The Truman Doctrine, however, also tied the contest for political power to economics. The American president declared the Soviet–American conflict to be a choice between "two ways of life." A few months later, Secretary of State George Marshall outlined an ambitious plan of economic aid to Europe including, initially, the Eastern European states: the European Recovery Program. The Marshall Plan provided $13 billion of aid over four years (beginning in 1948), targeted to industrial redevelopment. The plan supplied American tractors, locomotive engines, food, technical equipment, and capital to participating states. Unlike a relief plan, however, the Marshall Plan encouraged the participating states to diagnose their own economic problems and to develop their own solutions. The Marshall Plan also encouraged coordination between European countries, partly out of idealism (some spoke of a "United States of Europe") and partly to dissuade France from asking for reparations and trying to dismantle the German economy. With a series of other economic agreements the Marshall Plan became one of the building blocks of European economic unity. The American program, however, required measures such as decontrol of prices, restraints on wages, and balanced budgets. The Americans encouraged opposition to left-leaning politicians and movements that might be sympathetic to communism.

The United States also hastened to shore up military defenses. In April 1949, Canada, the United States, and representatives of Western European states signed an agreement establishing the North Atlantic Treaty Organization (NATO). Greece, Turkey, and West Germany were later added as members. An armed attack against any one of the NATO members would now be regarded as an attack against all and bring a united military response. NATO established a joint military command in 1950, with Dwight Eisenhower, the wartime commander

GERMANY DIVIDED AND THE BERLIN AIRLIFT

In the summer of 1948, the Soviet Union blocked routes through the German Democratic Republic to the Western Allies zone of Berlin. The blockade exacerbated tensions between the Soviet Union and the United States and forced the Allies to airlift supplies to West Berlin. At one point, planes landed in Berlin every three minutes.

of Allied forces in the West, as its senior military officer. NATO's ground forces began with thirty divisions in 1950, and by 1953 had nearly sixty—including, perhaps most surprising, a dozen divisions from the young state of West Germany. West German rearmament had been the subject of agonizing debate, particularly in Britain and France, but American pressure and a sense of strategic necessity led to its acceptance within Western Europe. Among the most striking aspects of World War II's aftermath was how rapidly Germany was reintegrated into Europe. In the new cold war world, *the West* quickly came to mean anticommunism. Potentially reliable allies, whatever their past, were not to be punished or excluded.

> In the new cold war world, *the West* quickly came to mean anticommunism. Potentially reliable allies, whatever their past, were not to be punished or excluded.

NATO's preparations for another European war depended heavily on air power, a new generation of jet bombers that would field the ultimate weapon of the age, the atomic bomb. Thus any conflict that broke out along the new German frontier threatened to dwarf the slaughter that had so recently passed.

TWO WORLDS AND THE RACE FOR THE BOMB

The Soviets viewed NATO, the Marshall Plan, and especially the United States' surprising involvement in Europe's affairs with mounting alarm. Rejecting an original offer of Marshall Plan aid, they established an Eastern European version of the plan, the Council for Mutual Economic Assistance, or Comecon. In 1947 the Soviets organized an international political arm, the Cominform (Communist Information Bureau), responsible for coordinating worldwide communist policy and programs. They responded to NATO with the establishment of their own military alliances, confirmed by the Warsaw Pact of 1955. This agreement set up a joint command among the states of Albania, Bulgaria, Czechoslovakia, Hungary, Poland, Romania, and East Germany, and guaranteed the continued presence of Soviet troops in all those countries.

All these conflicts were darkened by the shadow of the nuclear arms race. In 1949, the Soviet Union surprised American intelligence by testing its first atom bomb (modeled on the plutonium bomb that Americans had tested in 1945). In 1953 both superpowers demonstrated a new weapon, the hydrogen or "super" bomb, which was a thousand times more powerful than the bomb dropped on Hiroshima. Within a few

years both countries developed smaller bombs and systems of delivery that made them usable. Intercontinental missiles were built that could field first one and then several nuclear warheads, fired from land or from a new generation of atomic-powered submarines that roamed the seas at all times ready to act. J. Robert Oppenheimer warned that the H-bomb so dramatically raised the ability to make war against civilians that it could become a "weapon of genocide." Beyond the grim warnings that nuclear war would wipe out human civilization, the bomb had

The Arms Race: A Soviet View. *Nyet!* (No!) An arm raised in protest and fear against the backdrop of a bomb exploding.

more specific strategic consequences. The nuclearization of warfare fed into the polarizing effect of the cold war, for countries without nuclear arms found it difficult to avoid joining either the Soviet or American pact. Over the long term, it encouraged a disparity between two groups of nations: on the one hand, the superpowers, with their enormous military budgets, and on the other nations that came to rely on agreements and international law. It changed the nature of face-to-face warfare as well, encouraging "proxy wars" between clients of the superpowers and raising fears that local conflicts might trigger general war.

The hydrogen bomb quickly took on enormous cultural significance as the single most compelling symbol of the age. It seemed to confirm both humanity's power and its vulnerability. The leaps in knowledge that it represented boosted contemporaries' confidence in science and progress. At the same time, weapons of mass destruction and humanity's emerging power to obliterate itself raised gnawing questions about whether that confidence was misplaced.

Was the cold war inevitable? Could the Americans and the Soviets have negotiated their disagreements? On the Soviet side, Stalin's personal suspiciousness, ruthlessness, and autocratic ambitions combined with genuine security concerns to fuel the cold war mentality. U.S. leaders, for their part, believed that the devastation of the Continent gave the Soviets an opportunity to establish communist regimes in Western as well as Eastern Europe. Western Europeans alone could not respond effectively to multiplying postwar crises in Germany, Greece, and elsewhere. The United States, too, was unwilling to give up the military, economic, and political power it had acquired during the war. As it turned away from its traditional isolationism, the U.S. thus articulated new strategic interests with global consequences, including access to European industry and far-flung military bases. These interests played into Soviet fears. In this context, trust became all but impossible.

A new international balance of power quickly produced new international policies. In 1946 George Kennan argued that the United States needed to make containing the Soviet threat a priority. The Soviets had not embarked on world revolution, Kennan said. Thus the United States needed to respond, not with "histrionics: with threats or blustering or superfluous gestures of outward toughness" but rather "by the adroit and vigilant application of counter-force at a series of constantly shifting geographical and political points." Containment became the point of reference for U.S. foreign policy for the next forty years.

At its height, the cold war had a chilling effect on domestic politics in both countries. In the Soviet Union writers and artists were attacked for deviation from the party line. The party disciplined economists for suggesting that Western European industry might recover from the damage it had sustained. The radio blared news that Czech or Hungarian leaders had been exposed as traitors. In the United States, congressional committees launched campaigns to root out "communists" everywhere.
On both sides of the Iron Curtain, the cold war intensified everyday anxiety, bringing air-raid drills, spy trials, warnings that a way of life was at stake, and appeals to defend family and home against the menacing "other."

> On both sides of the Iron Curtain, the cold war intensified everyday anxiety, bringing air-raid drills, spy trials, a belief that a way of life was at stake, and appeals to defend family and home against the menacing "other."

KHRUSHCHEV AND THE THAW

Stalin died in 1953. Nikita Khrushchev's slow accession to power, not secure until 1956, signaled a change of direction. Khrushchev possessed a kind of earthy directness that, despite his hostility to the West, helped for a time to ease tensions. Stalin had secluded himself in the Kremlin; Khrushchev traveled throughout the world. On a visit to the United States in 1959, he traded quips with Iowa farmers and was entertained at Disneyland. Khrushchev was a shrewd politician, switching quickly between angry anti-American rhetoric and diplomatic reconciliation. Showing his desire to reduce international conflict, Khrushchev soon agreed to a summit meeting with the leaders of Britain, France, and the United States. This summit led to a series of understandings that eased the frictions in heavily armed Europe and produced a ban on testing nuclear weapons above ground in the early 1960s.

Khrushchev's other change of direction came with his famous "secret speech" of 1956, in which he acknowledged (behind the closed doors of the Twentieth Party Congress) the excesses of Stalin's era. Though the speech was secret, Krushchev's accusations were widely discussed. The harshness of Stalin's regime had generated popular discontent and demands for a shift from the production of heavy machinery and armaments to the manufacture of consumer goods, for a measure of freedom in the arts, for an end to police

C H R O N O L O G Y

THE EARLY COLD WAR IN EUROPE, 1946–1961

Churchill's "Iron Curtain" speech	1946
Truman Doctrine	1947
Soviets launch Cominform and COMECON	1947
Eastern bloc established	1948
Marshall Plan	1948
Berlin blockade	1948–1949
Formation of NATO	1949
Stalin dies	1953
Formation of the Warsaw Pact	1955
Revolts in East Germany, Poland, and Hungary	1953–1956
Khrushchev visits the United States	1959
Building of the Berlin Wall	1961

Nikita Khrushchev. Premier (1958–1964) and First Secretary of the Communist Party (1953–1964) of the Soviet Union, Khrushchev visited the United States in 1959. Here he is shown joking with an Iowa farmer.

repression. How, under these circumstances, could the regime keep de-Stalinization within safe limits? The thaw did unleash forces that proved difficult to control. Between 1956 and 1958, the Soviet prison camps released thousands of prisoners. Soviet citizens besieged the regime with requests to rehabilitate relatives who had been executed or imprisoned under Stalin, partly to make themselves again eligible for certain privileges of citizenship, such as housing. In the new cultural climate, private life—family issues, the shortage of men after the war, and the problem of orphans—became a legitimate subject of concern and discussion.

The thaw provided a brief window of opportunity for some of the Soviet Union's most important writers. In 1957, Boris Pasternak's novel *Doctor Zhivago* could not be published in the Soviet Union, and Pasternak was barred from receiving his Nobel Prize. That Aleksandr Solzhenitsyn's (*suhl-zhih-NYEE-tsihn*) first novel, *One Day in the Life of Ivan Denisovich*, could be published in 1962 marked the relative cultural freedom of the thaw. *Ivan Denisovich* was based on Solzhenitsyn's own experiences in the camps, where he had spent eight years for criticizing Stalin in a letter, and was a powerful literary testimony to the repression Khrushchev had acknowledged. By 1964, however, Khrushchev had fallen and the thaw ended, driving criticism and writers such as Solzhenitsyn underground. *The First Circle* (1968), also autobiographical, told the story of a group of imprisoned scientists doing research for the secret police. Sol-

zhenitsyn kept working on what would become *The Gulag Archipelago*, the first massive historical and literary study of the Stalinist camps (gulags). He secretly collected memoirs and personal testimony from prisoners, kept notes on cigarette rolling papers, and buried drafts of chapters behind his house. The Soviet secret police found a copy of the manuscript in a taxicab just when Solzhenitsyn had finished it. *The Gulag Archipelago* was published nonetheless in 1973 in Paris, but one year later the regime arrested Solzhenitsyn on charges of treason and sent him into exile. The most celebrated Soviet dissident was neither a democrat nor pro-Western. He was an idealist and a moralist, with roots among nineteenth-century Russian authors and philosophers. From exile Solzhenitsyn attacked the corruptions of American commercialism as well as Soviet repressiveness.

REPRESSION IN EASTERN EUROPE

The year of Stalin's death, tensions had exploded in Eastern Europe. The East German government, burdened by reparations payments to the Soviet Union, faced an economic crisis. The government's awareness of West German economic success made matters

THE COLD WAR: SOVIET AND AMERICAN VIEWS

The first excerpt is from a speech titled "The Sinews of Peace" that was delivered by Winston Churchill at Westminster College in Fulton, Missouri, in early 1946. In it, he coined the phrase Iron Curtain, warning of the rising power of the Soviet Union in Eastern Europe.

The next excerpt is from an address by Nikita Khrushchev, who became first secretary of the Communist Party in 1953. Three years later, his power secure, he began publicly to repudiate the crimes of Joseph Stalin. Khrushchev presided over a short-lived thaw in Soviet–American relations. Yet, as can be seen in his address, Khrushchev shared Churchill's conception of the world divided into two mutually antagonistic camps.

WINSTON CHURCHILL'S "IRON CURTAIN" SPEECH

A shadow has fallen upon the scenes so lately lighted by the Allied victory. Nobody knows what Soviet Russia and its Communist international organization intend to do in the immediate future, or what are the limits, if any, to their expansive and proselytizing tendencies. I have a strong admiration and regard for the valiant Russian people and for my wartime comrade, Marshal Stalin. There is deep sympathy and goodwill in Britain . . . towards the people of all the Russias and a resolve to persevere through many differences and rebuffs in establishing lasting friendships. We understand the Russian need to be secure on her western frontiers by the removal of all possibility of German aggression. We welcome Russia to her rightful place among the leading nations of the world. We welcome her flag upon the seas. Above all, we welcome constant, frequent and growing contacts between the Russian people and our own people on both sides of the Atlantic. It is my duty however . . . to place before you certain facts about the present position in Europe.

From Stettin in the Baltic to Trieste in the Adriatic, an iron curtain has descended across the Continent. Behind that line lie all the capitals of the ancient states of Central and Eastern Europe. Warsaw, Berlin, Prague, Vienna, Budapest, Belgrade, Bucharest and Sofia, all these famous cities and the populations around them lie in what I must call the Soviet sphere, and all are subject in one form or another, not only to Soviet influence but to a very high and, in many cases, increasing measure of control from Moscow. . . .

From what I have seen of our Russian friends and Allies during the war, I am convinced that there is nothing they admire so much as strength, and there is nothing for which they have less respect than for weakness, especially military weakness. For that reason the old doctrine of a balance of power is unsound. We cannot afford, if we can help it, to work on narrow margins, offering temptations to a triad of strength. If the Western Democracies stand together in strict adherence to the principles of the United Nations Charter, their influences for furthering those principles will be immense and no one is likely to molest them. If however they become divided or falter in their duty and if these all-important years are allowed to slip away then indeed catastrophe may overwhelm us all.

Winston Churchill, *Winston S. Churchill: His Complete Speeches, 1897–1963*, vol. 7, 1943–1949, ed. Robert Rhodes James (New York, 1983), pp. 7290–7291.

Nikita Khrushchev, "Report to the Communist Party Congress (1961)"

Comrades! The competition of the two world social systems, the socialist and the capitalist, has been the chief content of the period since the 20th party Congress. It has become the pivot, the foundation of world development at the present historical stage. Two lines, two historical trends, have manifested themselves more and more clearly in social development. One is the line of social progress, peace and constructive activity. The other is the line of reaction, oppression and war.

In the course of the peaceful competition of the two systems capitalism has suffered a profound moral defeat in the eyes of all peoples. The common people are daily convinced that capitalism is incapable of solving a single one of the urgent problems confronting mankind. It becomes more and more obvious that only on the paths to socialism can a solution to these problems be found. Faith in the capitalist system and the capitalist path of development is dwindling. Monopoly capital, losing its influence, resorts more and more to intimidating and suppressing the masses of the people, to methods of open dictatorship in carrying out its domestic policy and to aggressive acts against other countries. But the masses of the people offer increasing resistance to reaction's acts.

It is no secret to anyone that the methods of intimidation and threat are not a sign of strength but evidence of the weakening of capitalism, the deepening of its general crisis. As the saying goes, if you can't hang on by the mane, you won't hang on by the tail! Reaction is still capable of dissolving parliaments in some countries in violation of their constitutions, of casting the best representatives of the people into prison, of sending cruisers and marines to subdue the "unruly." All this can put off for a time the approach of the fatal hour for the rule of capitalism. The imperialists are sawing away at the branch on which they sit. There is no force in the world capable of stopping man's advance along the road of progress.

Current Soviet Policies IV, ed. Charlotte Saikowski and Leo Gruliow, from trans. *Current Digest of the Soviet Press*, Joint Committee on Slavic Studies (1962, pp. 42–45).

QUESTIONS FOR ANALYSIS

1. Whom did Churchill blame for building the Iron Curtain between the Soviet sphere and the Western sphere?
2. Was the Soviet Union actively trying to create international communism? Was the United States trying to spread the Western way of life on a global scale?

---

worse. The illegal exodus of East German citizens to the West rose sharply: 58,000 left in March 1953 alone. In June, when the government demanded hefty increases in industrial productivity, strikes broke out in East Berlin. Unrest spread throughout the country. The Soviet army put down the uprising, and hundreds were executed in the subsequent purge. In the aftermath, the East German government, under the leadership of Walter Ulbricht, used fears of disorder to solidify one-party rule.

In 1956, emboldened by Khrushchev's de-Stalinization, Poland and Hungary rebelled, demanding more independence in the management of their domestic affairs. Striking workers led the opposition in Poland. The government wavered, responding first with military repression and then with a promise of liberalization. Eventually the anti-Stalinist Polish leader Wladyslaw Gomulka won Soviet permission for his country to pursue its own "ways of Socialist development" by pledging Poland's loyalty to the terms of the Warsaw Pact.

Events in Hungary turned out very differently. The charismatic leader of Hungary's communist government, Imre Nagy, was as much a Hungarian nationalist as a communist. Under his government, protests against Moscow's policies developed into a much broader anticommunist struggle and, even more important, attempted secession from the Warsaw Pact. Khrushchev might contemplate looser ties between Eastern Europe and Moscow, but he would not tolerate an end to the pact. On November 4, 1956, Soviet troops occupied Budapest, arresting and executing leaders of the Hungarian rebellion. The Hungarians took up arms, and street fighting continued for several weeks. The Hungarians had hoped for Western aid, but Dwight Eisenhower, newly elected to a second term as president, steered clear of giving support. Soviet forces installed a new government under the staunchly communist Janos Kadar, the repression continued, and tens of thousands of Hungarian refugees fled for the West. Khrushchev's efforts at presenting a gentler, more conciliatory Soviet Union to the West had been shattered by revolt and repression.

Khrushchev's policy of "peaceful coexistence" with the West did not reduce his determination to stave off any military threat to Eastern Europe. By the mid-1950s, NATO's policy of putting battlefield nuclear weapons in West Germany seemed evidence of just such a threat. What was more, East Germans continued to flee the country via West Berlin. Between 1949 and 1961, 2.7 million East Germans left, blunt evidence of the unpopularity of the regime. Attempting to stem the tide, Khrushchev demanded that the West recognize the permanent division of Germany with a free city in Berlin. When that demand was refused, in 1961 the East German government built a ten-foot wall separating the two sectors of the city. The wall brought a dangerous show of force on both sides, as the Soviets and Americans mobilized reservists for war. The newly elected American president, John F. Kennedy, marked Berlin's contested status with a visit when he proclaimed that "all free men" were fellow citizens of noncommunist West Berlin. For almost thirty years, until 1989, the Berlin Wall remained a monument to how the hot war had gone cold, and mirrored, darkly, the division of Germany and Europe as a whole.

The Berlin Wall, 1961. Thirteen years after the blockade, the East German government built a wall between East and West Berlin to stop the flow of escapees to the West. This manifestation of the Iron Curtain was dismantled in 1989.

Economic Renaissance

How did Western Europe recover from World War II?

Despite the ongoing tensions of a global superpower rivalry, the postwar period brought a remarkable recovery in Western Europe: the economic "miracle." Economists still debate its causes. Some factors resulted directly from the war, which encouraged a variety of technological innovations that could be applied in peacetime: improved communications (the invention of radar, for example), the development of synthetic materials, the increasing use of aluminum and alloy steels, and advances in the techniques of prefabrication. Wartime manufacturing had added significantly to nations' productive capacity. The Marshall Plan seems to have been less central than many claimed at the time, but it solved immediate problems having to do with the balance of payments and a shortage of American dollars to buy American goods. This boom was fueled by a third set of factors: high consumer demand and, consequently, very high levels of employment throughout the 1950s and 1960s. Brisk domestic and foreign consumption encouraged expansion, continued capital investment, and technological innovation. Rising demand for Europe's goods hastened agreements that encouraged the free flow of international trade and currencies (discussed later).

It was now assumed that states would do much more economic management—directing investment, making decisions about what to modernize, coordinating policies between industries and countries—than before. This, too, was a legacy of wartime. As one British official observed, "We are all planners now." Government tactics for steering the economy varied. West Germany provided tax breaks to encourage business investment; Britain and Italy offered investment allowances to their steel and petroleum industries. France, Britain, Italy, and Austria led the way in experiments with nationalizing industry and services in an effort to raise productivity. The result was a series of "mixed" economies combining public and private ownership. In France, where public ownership was already well advanced in the 1930s, railways, electricity and gas, banking, radio and television, and a large segment of the automobile industry were brought under state management. In Britain, the list was equally long: coal and utilities; road, railroad, and air transport; and banking. Though nationalization was less common in West Germany, the railway system (state owned since the late nineteenth century); some electrical, chemical, and metallurgical concerns; and the Volkswagen company—the remnant of Hitler's attempt to produce a "people's car"—were all in state hands, though the latter was largely returned to the private sector in 1963.

These government policies and programs contributed to astonishing growth rates. Between 1945 and 1963 the average yearly growth of West Germany's gross domestic product (gross national product [GNP] minus income received from abroad) was 7.6 percent; in Austria, 5.8 percent; in Italy, 6 percent; in the Netherlands, 4.7 percent; and so on. Not only did the economies recover from the war but they reversed prewar economic patterns of slack demand, overproduction, and insufficient investment. Production facilities were hard pressed to keep up with soaring demand.

West Germany's recovery was particularly spectacular, and particularly important to the rest of Europe. Production increased sixfold between 1948 and 1964. Unemployment fell to record lows, reaching 0.4 percent in 1965, when there were six jobs for every unemployed person. The contrast with the catastrophic unemployment of the Great Depression heightened the impression of a miracle. Prices rose but then leveled off, and many citizens could plunge into a domestic buying spree that caused production to soar. In the 1950s, the state and private industry built half a million new housing units each year, to accommodate citizens whose homes had been destroyed; new resident refugees from East Germany and Eastern Europe; and transient workers from Italy, Spain, Greece, and elsewhere drawn by West Germany's high demand for labor. German cars, specialized mechanical goods, optics, and chemicals returned to their former role leading world markets. West German women were included in the process: during the 1950s, German politicians encouraged women to take up a role as "citizen consumers," as active but prudent buyers of goods that would keep the German economy humming.

Under the direction of a minister for planning, Jean Monnet, the French government played a direct role in industrial reform, contributing not only capital but expert advice, and facilitating shifts in the national labor pool to place workers where they were most needed.

> Not only did the economies recover from the war but they reversed prewar economic patterns of slack demand, overproduction, and insufficient investment. Production facilities were hard pressed to keep up with soaring demand.

The plan gave priority to basic industries; the production of electricity doubled, the steel industry was thoroughly modernized, and the French railway system became the fastest and most efficient on the Continent. Italy's industrial "miracle" came later but was even more impressive. Stimulated by infusions of capital from the government and from the Marshall Plan, Italian companies soon began to compete with other European international giants. The products of Olivetti, Fiat, and Pirelli became familiar in households around the world to an extent that no Italian goods had in the past. Electric power production doubled between 1938 and 1953. By 1954 real wages were 50 percent higher than they had been in 1938.

European nations with little in common in terms of political traditions or industrial patterns all shared in the general prosperity. Rising GNPs, however, did not level the differences among and within states. In southern Italy, illiteracy remained high and land continued to be held by a few rich families; the per capita GNP in Sweden was almost ten times that of Turkey. Britain remained a special case. The Conservative prime minister, Harold Macmillan, campaigned successfully for reelection in 1959 with the slogan "You've never had it so good"—an accurate enough boast. British growth was respectable when compared with past performance. Yet the British economy remained sluggish. The country was burdened with obsolete factories and methods, the legacy of its early industrialization, and by an unwillingness to adopt new techniques in old industries or invest in more successful new ones. It was plagued as well by a series of balance-of-payments crises precipitated by an inability to sell more goods abroad than it imported.

EUROPEAN ECONOMIC INTEGRATION

The Western European renaissance was a collective effort. From the Marshall Plan on, a series of international economic organizations began to bind the Western European countries together. The first of these was the European Coal and Steel Community (ECSC), founded in 1951 to coordinate trade in, and the management of, Europe's most crucial resources. Coal was still king in mid-twentieth-century Europe; it fueled everything from steel manufacturing and trains to household heating, and counted for 82 percent of Europe's primary energy consumption. It was also key to relations between West Germany, with abundant coal mines, and France, with its coal-hungry steel mills. The ECSC joint High Authority, which consisted of experts from each of the participating countries, had power to regulate prices, to increase or limit production, and to impose administrative fees. In 1957, the Treaty of Rome transformed France, West Germany, Italy, Belgium, Holland, and Luxembourg—into the European Economic Community (EEC), or Common Market. The EEC aimed to abolish trade barriers among its members. Moreover, the organization pledged itself to common external tariffs, to the free movement of labor and capital among the member nations, and to building uniform wage structures and social security systems to create similar working conditions throughout the Common Market. A commission headquartered in Brussels administered the program; by 1962, Brussels had more than 3,000 "Eurocrats."

Integration did not proceed smoothly. Great Britain stayed away, fearing the effects of the ECSC on its declining coal industry and on its long-time trading relationship with Australia, New Zealand, and Canada. Britain did not share France's need for raw materials and the others' need for markets; it continued to rely on its economic relations with the Empire and Commonwealth. One of the few victors in World War II, Britain assumed that it could hold its global economic position in the postwar world. In the other countries, domestic opposition to EEC provisions on wages or agricultural prices often threatened to scuttle agreements. The French and other countries insisted on protecting agriculture, sensitive to the importance of the peasantry to political stability and invested in the countryside's place in national identity.

The seismic shifts that began to make oil and atomic power more important than coal (see Chapter Twenty-Eight) made the ECSC less effective. Still, the European Economic Community was a remarkable success. By 1963, it had become the world's largest importer. Its steel production was second only to that of the United States, and total industrial production was over 70 percent higher than it had been in 1950. Last, it established a new long-term political trend: individual countries sought to Europeanize solutions to their problems.

Likewise, crucial agreements reached in Bretton Woods, New Hampshire, in July 1944 aimed to coordinate the movements of the global economy and to internationalize solutions to economic crises, avoiding catastrophes such as those that plagued the 1930s. Bretton Woods created the International Monetary Fund and the World Bank, both designed to establish pre-dictable and stable exchange rates, prevent speculation, and enable currencies—and consequently trade—to move freely. All other currencies were pegged to the dollar, which both reflected and enhanced the United States' role as the foremost financial power. The new international system was formed with the American–European sphere in mind, but these organizations soon began to play a role in economic development in what came to be known as the Third World. The postwar period, then, quickened global economic integration, largely on American terms.

ECONOMIC DEVELOPMENT IN THE EAST

Although economic development in Eastern Europe was not nearly so dramatic as that in the West, significant advances occurred there as well. National incomes rose and output increased. Poland and Hungary, in particular, strengthened their economic connections with the West, primarily with France and West Germany. By the late 1970s, about 30 percent of Eastern Europe's trade was conducted outside the Soviet bloc. Nevertheless, the Soviet Union required its satellites to design their economic policies to serve more than their own national interests. Regulations governing COMECON, the Eastern European equivalent of the Common Market, ensured that the Soviet Union could sell its exports at prices well above the world level and compelled other members to trade with the Soviet Union to their disadvantage. Emphasis initially was on heavy industry and collectivized agriculture, though political tension in countries such as Hungary and Poland forced the Soviets eventually to moderate their policies so as to permit the manufacture of more consumer goods and the development of a modest trade with the West.

THE WELFARE STATE

Economic growth became one of the watchwords of the postwar era. Social welfare was another. The roots of the new legislation extended back to the insurance plans for old age, sickness, and disability introduced by Bismarck in Germany in the late 1880s. But economic expansion allowed postwar European states to fund more comprehensive social programs, and commitments to putting democracy on a stronger footing provided the political motivation. Clement Atlee, a socialist and the leader of the British Labour Party, coined the term *welfare state*; his government, in power until 1951, led the way in enacting legislation that provided free medical care to all through the National Health Service, assistance to families, and guaranteed secondary education of some kind. The welfare state also rested on the assumption that governments could and should try to support popular purchasing power, generate demand, and provide either employment or unemployment insurance, assumptions spelled out earlier by John Maynard Keynes (*General Theory*, 1936) or William Beveridge's important 1943 report on full employment. Although the British Labour Party and continental socialist parties pressed these measures, welfare was a consensus issue, backed by the moderate coalitions that governed most postwar Western European states.

Understood in this way, welfare was not poor relief, but an entitlement. Thus it marked a break with centuries-old ways of thinking about poverty and citizenship. In 1950, the British sociologist T. H. Marshall outlined a short but extremely influential history of states, citizenship, and rights. The late seventeenth and eighteenth centuries had brought civil rights, Marshall argued—the Lockean freedoms of religion, property, and contract. The nineteenth century brought political rights. The twentieth century would bring the "whole range [of social rights] from the right to a mod-

> Although the British Labour Party and continental socialist parties pressed these measures, welfare was a consensus issue, backed by the moderate coalitions that governed most postwar Western European states.

icum of economic welfare and security to the right to share to the full in the social heritage and to live the life of a civilized being according to the standards prevailing in the society." It is worth noting that Marshall's short history did not explain why the history of women's rights was so different; not only did women get *civil* and *political* rights late but they gained social rights only insofar as they were family members or mothers. Still, Marshall's theory best expressed the ideas behind the political current of social democracy: the growing conviction that democracy and social welfare went hand in hand, that all citizens deserved the same "social heritage," in Marshall's words, and that diminishing the sharp inequalities of class society was crucial to fortifying democratic culture.

EUROPEAN POLITICS

Postwar political leaders were overwhelmingly pragmatic. Konrad Adenauer, the West German chancellor from 1949 to 1963, despised German militarism and blamed that tradition for Hitler's rise to power. Still, he was apprehensive about German parliamentary democracy and governed in a paternalistic, sometimes authoritarian, manner. His determination to end the centuries-old hostility between France and Germany contributed significantly to the movement toward economic union. Alcide De Gasperi, the Italian premier from 1948 to 1953, was also centrist. Among postwar French leaders, the most colorful was the Resistance hero General Charles de Gaulle. De Gaulle had retired from politics in 1946 when French voters refused to accept his proposals for strengthening the executive branch of the government. In 1958, faced with civil turmoil caused by the Algerian war (see page 1006) and an abortive coup attempt by a group of right-wing army officers, France's government collapsed and de Gaulle was invited to return. De Gaulle accepted but insisted on a new constitution. That constitution, which created the Fifth Republic in 1958, strengthened the executive branch of the government in an effort to avoid the parliamentary deadlocks that had weakened the country earlier. De Gaulle used his

Charles de Gaulle Presenting His Plan to Strengthen the Executive Branch of the Government in 1946. When voters rejected his ideas, he retired, only to return in 1958 to outline a new constitution.

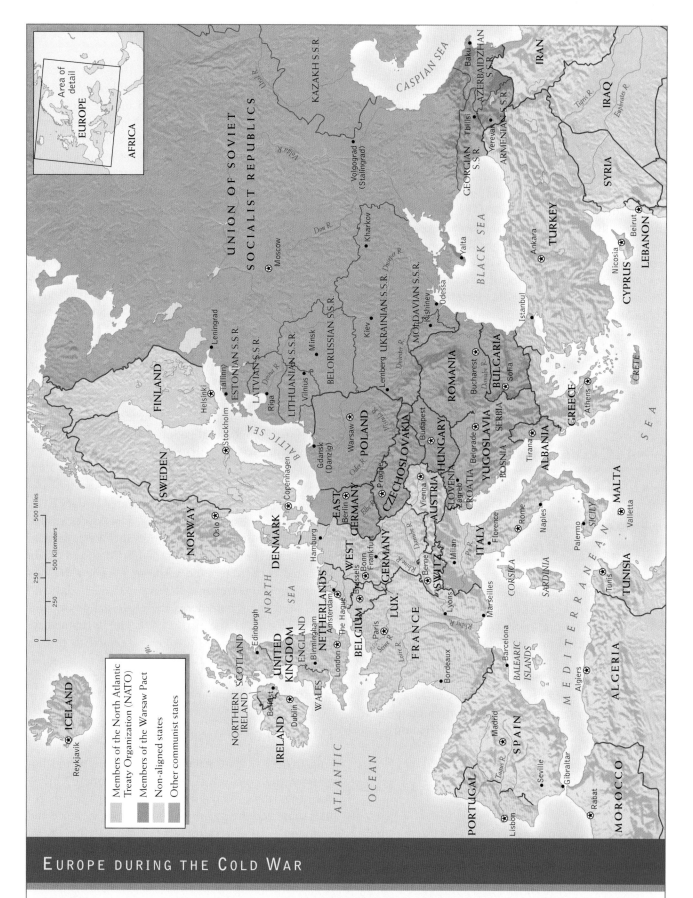

EUROPE DURING THE COLD WAR

Examine the membership of NATO and the Warsaw Pact, respectively. What type of government characterized the member states of each? Why did the membership of each alliance stay relatively stable for nearly half a century? Why did certain socialist governments (Sweden, Finland) and federal democracies (Switzerland) remain neutral rather than join either pact? Why did Yugoslavia, under a communist government, not join the Warsaw Pact?

new authority to restore France's power and prestige. "France is not really herself unless in the front rank," he wrote in his memoirs. "France cannot be France without greatness." Greatness, for de Gaulle, involved reorienting foreign policy, which included an end to France's grip on Algeria. Resisting U.S. influence in Europe, he pulled French forces out of NATO in 1966. He cultivated better relations with the Soviet Union and with West Germany. Finally, he accelerated French economic and industrial expansion by building a modern military establishment, complete with atomic weapons. Like his counterparts, de Gaulle was not, by nature, a democrat. He steered a centrist course, working hard to produce practical solutions to political problems and thereby undermine radicalism in any form. Most other Western European nations did the same.

REVOLUTION, ANTICOLONIALISM, AND THE COLD WAR

What were the links between decolonization, World War II, and the cold war?

In the colonial world as in Europe, the end of war unleashed new conflicts. Those conflicts became closely bound up with Europe's political and economic recovery, they had an enormous if delayed effect on Western culture, and they complicated the cold war. The cold war, as we have seen, created two powerful centers of gravity for world politics. But the wave of anticolonial independence movements that swept through postwar Asia and Africa created a new group of nations that would attempt to avoid aligning with one or the other bloc, and would call itself the "Third World."

THE CHINESE REVOLUTION

The first in this wave of movements was also the single most radical change in the developing world after World War II: the Chinese Revolution. A civil war had raged in China since 1926, when Nationalist forces under Jiang Jeishi (Chiang Kai-shek, 1887–1975) had fought first in the south, then in the north, against communist insurgents under the leadership of Mao

Zedong (*mow zeh*-DOONG; 1893–1976). A truce in 1937 brought the warring sides together to face the Japanese. When Japan was defeated and the occupation ended, the communists, still led by Mao, refused to surrender the northern provinces they controlled. Civil war broke out again. The United States intervened, first to mediate and then with massive military support for the Nationalists. But the Nationalists, corrupt and unrepresentative, were defeated in the field and surrendered in 1949.

Even more than the Russian Revolution, the Chinese Revolution was the act of a nation of peasants. With a program that emphasized radical reform in the countryside (reducing rents, providing health care and education, and reforming marriage), peasant mobilization, and autonomy from Western colonial powers, Mao adapted Marxism to conditions very different from those imagined by its founders. And as in Russia, communism in China provided a model—not necessarily successful—for economic development. The new leaders of the "great people's revolution" set about turning the country into a modern, industrial nation within a generation, at huge human cost and with very mixed results.

As a successful peasant revolt, the Chinese Revolution stood as a model to anticolonial activists the world over. To colonial powers, it represented a dangerous possible outcome of decolonization. The "loss of China" provoked fear and consternation in the West, particularly in the United States. Although Mao and Stalin distrusted each other, and relations between the two largest communist countries were extremely difficult, the United States considered these two nations a communist bloc until the early 1970s. In its immediate aftermath, the Chinese Revolution seemed to tip the balance in a standoff between communism and capitalism, and it intensified Western military and diplomatic anxiety about governments throughout Asia.

THE KOREAN WAR

This anxiety helped make Korea into one of the hot spots of the cold war. Effectively a Japanese colony since the 1890s, Korea suffered as its Japanese occupiers subjected the country to horrendous violence and exploited its resources for generations. At the end of World War II the Soviet Union's eastern offensive forced the Japanese out; Korea was then divided between those Russian troops in the north and their American counterparts in the south. As in Germany, two new states were established: communist North Korea, run by the Soviet client Kim Jong II, and South

WHAT WERE THE LINKS BETWEEN DECOLONIZATION, WORLD WAR II, AND THE COLD WAR?

REVOLUTION, ANTICOLONIALISM, AND THE COLD WAR   997

A Red Guard Demonstration. Middle-school students display their solidarity with Mao Zedong's revolution by waving copies of a book of his quotations. The slogan proclaims, "Not only are we able to destroy the old world, we are able to build a new world instead—Mao Zedong."

Korea, run by the anticommunist autocrat Syngman Rhee. North Korea's government soon decided that this arrangement should not last. In June 1950, communist North Korean troops attacked across the border, crushing resistance in the south and forcing noncommunist forces and a small American garrison to retreat to the far end of the peninsula. The United States took advantage of a temporary Russian boycott of the United Nations and brought the invasion before the Security Council. The council passed a resolution permitting an American-led "police action" to defend South Korea and counter the communists.

That action fell to General Douglas MacArthur, a hero of World War II and the military governor of occupied Japan. He mounted an audacious amphibious attack behind North Korean lines and cut northern forces to pieces. MacArthur drove the Korean communists to the Chinese border and pressed for the authority to attack them as they retreated into China, hoping to punish China and help reverse the Chinese Revolution. President Harry S Truman (1945–1953) denied this rash request and relieved MacArthur of command for exceeding his authority. The price had already been paid, however; more than a million Chinese troops flooded across the border in support of the North Koreans. The international troops aiding South Korea were forced into a bloody, headlong retreat in the dead of winter. During that difficult winter the able and patient American general Matthew Ridgeway took over from MacArthur and stemmed the retreat. The war, however, became a stalemate. Chinese and North Korean troops dug in against the UN force, composed largely of American and South Korean troops but drawn from around the world—small contingents from Britain, Australia, Ethiopia, the Netherlands, and Turkey distinguished themselves in the fighting. The conflict dragged on for two years as peace talks began. It was a bitter war of artillery battles, hand-to-hand fighting, attacks up well-defended hillsides, and punishing cold. The end, decreed in June 1953, was inconclusive. Korea remained divided roughly along the original line drawn in 1945, no longer at war but not at peace. With 53,000 Americans and over 1 million Koreans and Chinese dead, South Korea had not been "lost," but neither had China or the United States won a decisive victory. As in Germany, the inability of major powers to achieve their ultimate goals resulted in a divisive settlement and a divided nation.

DECOLONIZATION

The Chinese Revolution proved the start of a larger wave. Between 1947 and 1960 the sprawling European empires built during the nineteenth century disintegrated. Imperialism had always provoked resistance. Opposition to colonial rule had stiffened after World War I, forcing war-weakened European states to renegotiate the terms of empire. After World War II, older forms of empire quickly became untenable. In some regions, European states simply sought to cut their losses and withdraw, their financial, political, and human resources depleted. In others, well-organized and tenacious nationalist movements successfully demanded new constitutional arrangements and independence. In a third set of cases, European powers were drawn into complicated, multifaceted, and extremely violent struggles between different movements of indigenous peoples and European settler communities—conflicts the European states had helped create.

THE BRITISH EMPIRE UNRAVELS

India was the first and largest of the colonies to win self-government after the war. As we have seen, rebellions such as the Sepoy Mutiny challenged the representatives of Britain in India throughout the nineteenth century (see Chapter Twenty-Five). During the early stages of World War II, the Indian National Congress (founded 1885), the umbrella party for the independence movement, called on Britain to "quit India." The extraordinary Indian nationalist Mohandas K. (Mahatma) Gandhi (1869–1948) had been at work in India since the 1920s and had pioneered anticolonial ideas and tactics that echoed the world over. In the

CHRONOLOGY

MAJOR DEVELOPMENTS IN ASIA, 1947–1997

India gains independence	1947
Chinese Communist Revolution	1949
Korean War	1950–1953
Vietnamese defeat the French	1954
Chinese Cultural Revolution	1960s
Vietnam War (United States)	1964–1975
United States recognizes Communist China	1972
Tiananmen Square	1989
Hong Kong reverts to Chinese control	1997

face of colonial domination, Gandhi advocated not violence but *swaraj*, or self-rule, urging Indians individually and collectively to develop their own resources and to withdraw from the imperial economy—by going on strike, refusing to pay taxes, or boycotting imported textiles and wearing homespun. By 1947 Gandhi and his fellow nationalist Jawaharlal Nehru (1889–1964, prime minister 1947–1964), the leader of the proindependence Congress Party, had gained such widespread support that the British found it impossible to continue in power. The Labour Party government elected in Britain in 1945 had always favored Indian independence. Now that independence became a British political necessity.

While talks established the procedures for independence, however, India was torn by ethnic and religious conflict. A Muslim League, led by Mohammed Ali Jinnah (1876–1948), wanted autonomy in largely Muslim areas and feared the predominantly Hindu Congress party's authority in a single united state. Cycles of rioting broke out between the two religious communities. In June 1947, British India was partitioned into the nations of India (majority Hindu) and Pakistan (majority Muslim). The process of partition brought brutal religious and ethnic warfare. More than 1 million Hindus and Muslims died, and an estimated 12 million became refugees, evicted from their lands or fleeing the fighting. Throughout the chaos Gandhi, now eighty, continued to protest violence and to focus attention on overcoming the legacy of colonialism. He argued that "[R]eal freedom will come when we free ourselves of the dominance of western education, western culture, and western way of living which have been ingrained in us." In January 1948, he was assassinated by a Hindu zealot. Conflict continued between the independent states of India and Pakistan. Nehru, who became first prime minister of India, embarked on a program of industrialization and modernization—not at all what Gandhi would have counseled. Nehru proved particularly adept at maneuvering in the cold war world, steering a course of nonalignment with either of the blocs, getting aid for industry from the Soviet Union and food imports from the United States.

PALESTINE

The year 1948 brought more crises for the British Empire, including an end to the British mandate in Palestine. During World War I, British diplomats had encouraged Arab nationalist revolts against the Ottoman Empire. With the 1917 Balfour Declaration, they had also promised a "Jewish homeland" in Palestine for

MOHANDAS GANDHI AND NONVIOLENT ANTICOLONIALISM

After leading a campaign for Indian rights in South Africa between 1894 and 1914, Mohandas K. Gandhi (1869–1948), known as Mahatma ("great-souled") Gandhi, became a leader in the long battle for home rule in India. This battle was finally won in 1947 and brought with it the partition of India and the creation of Pakistan. Gandhi's insistence on the power of nonviolent noncooperation brought him to the forefront of Indian politics and provided a model for many later liberation struggles, including the American civil rights movement. Gandhi argued that only nonviolent resistance, which dramatized the injustice of colonial rule and colonial law, had the spiritual force to unite a community and end colonialism.

Passive resistance is a method of securing rights by personal suffering; it is the reverse of resistance by arms. When I refuse to do a thing that is repugnant to my conscience, I use soul-force. For instance, the Government of the day has passed a law which is applicable to me. I do not like it. If by using violence I force the Government to repeal the law, I am employing what may be termed body-force. If I do not obey the law and accept the penalty for its breach, I use soul-force. It involves sacrifice of self.

Everybody admits that sacrifice of self is infinitely superior to sacrifice of others. Moreover, if this kind of force is used in a cause that is unjust, only the person using it suffers. He does not make others suffer for his mistakes. Men have before now done many things which were subsequently found to have been wrong. . . . It is therefore meet that he should not do that which he knows to be wrong, and suffer the consequence whatever it may be. This is the key to the use of soul-force. . . .

It is contrary to our manhood if we obey laws repugnant to our conscience. Such teaching is opposed to religion and means slavery. If the Government were to ask us to go about without any clothing, should we do so? If I were a passive resister, I would say to them that I would have nothing to do with their law. But we have so forgotten ourselves and become so compliant that we do not mind any degrading law.

A man who has realized his manhood, who fears only God, will fear no one else. Man-made laws are not necessarily binding on him. Even the Government does not expect any such thing from us. They do not say: "You must do such and such a thing." But they say: "If you do not do it, we will punish you." We are sunk so low that we fancy that it is our duty and our religion to do what the law lays down. If man will only realize that it is unmanly to obey laws that are unjust, no man's tyranny will enslave him. This is the key to self-rule or home-rule.

M. K. Gandhi, "Indian Home Rule (1909)," in *The Gandhi Reader: A Source Book of His Life and Writings*, ed. Homer A. Jack (Bloomington, Ind., 1956), pp. 104–121.

QUESTIONS FOR ANALYSIS

1. Why did Gandhi believe that "sacrifice of self" was superior to "sacrifice of others"?
2. What did Gandhi mean when he said that "it is contrary to our manhood if we obey laws repugnant to our conscience"?

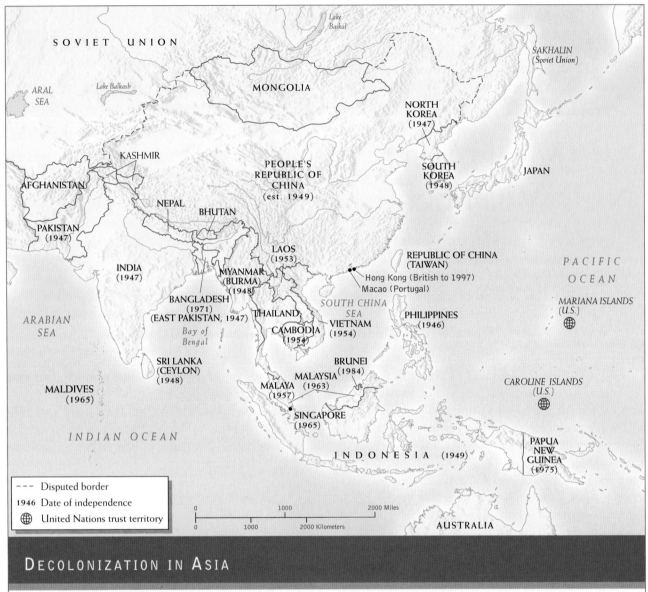

SOVIET UNION

Lake Baikal

SAKHALIN (Soviet Union)

ARAL SEA

Lake Balkash

MONGOLIA

NORTH KOREA (1947)

KASHMIR

PEOPLE'S REPUBLIC OF CHINA (est. 1949)

SOUTH KOREA (1948)

JAPAN

AFGHANISTAN

NEPAL

BHUTAN

PAKISTAN (1947)

INDIA (1947)

LAOS (1953)

REPUBLIC OF CHINA (TAIWAN)

PACIFIC OCEAN

MYANMAR (BURMA) (1948)

Hong Kong (British to 1997)
Macao (Portugal)

BANGLADESH (1971) (EAST PAKISTAN, 1947)

THAILAND

SOUTH CHINA SEA

PHILIPPINES (1946)

MARIANA ISLANDS (U.S.)

ARABIAN SEA

Bay of Bengal

CAMBODIA (1954)

VIETNAM (1954)

SRI LANKA (CEYLON) (1948)

BRUNEI (1984)

CAROLINE ISLANDS (U.S.)

MALDIVES (1965)

MALAYSIA (1963)
MALAYA (1957)

SINGAPORE (1965)

INDIAN OCEAN

INDONESIA   (1949)

PAPUA NEW GUINEA (1975)

--- Disputed border
1946 Date of independence
🌐 United Nations trust territory

0   1000   2000 Miles
0   1000   2000 Kilometers

AUSTRALIA

DECOLONIZATION IN ASIA

Britain and the United States facilitated relatively peaceful transitions to independence for their possessions in Asia. France fought hard to hold Indochina but left after major military defeats. Cold war tensions in Asia led to both the Korean War and the Vietnam War.

European Zionists. Contradictory promises and the flight of European Jews from Nazi Germany contributed to rising conflict between Jewish settlers and Arabs in Palestine during the 1930s and provoked an Arab revolt bloodily suppressed by the British. At the same time, the newly important oil concessions in the Middle East were multiplying Britain's strategic interests in the Suez Canal, Egypt, and the Arab nations generally. Mediating local conflicts and balancing their own interests proved an impossible task. In 1939, in the name of regional stability, the British strictly limited further Jewish immigration. They tried to

maintain that limit after the war, but now they faced pressure from tens of thousands of Jewish refugees from Europe. The conflict quickly became a three-way war: among Palestinian Arabs fighting for what they considered their land and their independence, Jewish settlers and Zionist militants determined to defy British restrictions, and British administrators with divided sympathies, embarrassed and shocked by the plight of Jewish refugees and committed to maintaining good Anglo-Arab relations. The British responded militarily. By 1947, there was one British soldier for every eighteen inhabitants of the Mandate. The years

WHAT WERE THE LINKS BETWEEN DECOLONIZATION, WORLD WAR II, AND THE COLD WAR?

REVOLUTION, ANTICOLONIALISM, AND THE COLD WAR   1001

of fighting, however, with terrorist tactics on all sides, persuaded the British to leave. The United Nations voted (by a narrow margin) to partition the territory into two states. Neither Jewish settlers nor Palestinian Arabs found the partition satisfactory and both began to fight for territory even before British troops withdrew. No sooner did Israel declare its independence in May 1948 than five neighboring states invaded. The new but well-organized Israeli nation survived the war and extended its boundaries. On the losing side a million Palestinian Arabs who fled or were expelled found themselves clustered in refugee camps in the Gaza Strip and on the West Bank of the Jordan River, which the armistice granted to an enlarged state of Jordan. It is remarkable that the conflict did not become a cold war confrontation at the start. For their own reasons, both Soviets and Americans recognized Israel. The new nation, however, marked a permanent change to the culture and balance of power in the region.

AFRICA

A number of West African colonies established assertive independence movements before and during the 1950s, and the British government moved hesitantly to meet their demands. By the middle of the 1950s, Britain agreed to a variety of terms for independence in these territories, leaving them with written constitutions and a British legal system but little else in terms of modern infrastructure or economic support. Defenders of British colonialism claimed that these formal institutions would give advantages to the independent states, but without other resources, even the most promising foundered. Ghana, known formerly as the Gold Coast and the first of these colonies to gain independence, was seen in the early 1960s as a model for free African nations. Its politics soon degenerated, however, and its president, Kwame Nkrumah, became the first of several African leaders driven from office for corruption and autocratic behavior.

Belgium and France also withdrew from their holdings. By 1965 virtually all of the former African colonies had become independent, and virtually none of them possessed the means to redress losses from colonialism to make that independence work. As Belgian authorities raced out of the Congo in 1960, they left crumbling railways and fewer than two dozen indigenous people with college educations.

The process of decolonization was relatively peaceful—except where large populations of European settlers complicated European withdrawal. In the north, settler resistance made the French exit from Algeria wrenching and complex (discussed later). In the east, in Kenya, the majority Kikuyu population revolted against British rule and against a small group of settlers. The uprising, which came to be known as the Mau Mau rebellion, soon turned bloody. British troops fired freely at targets in rebel-occupied areas, sometimes killing civilians. Internment camps set up by colonial security forces became sites of atrocities that

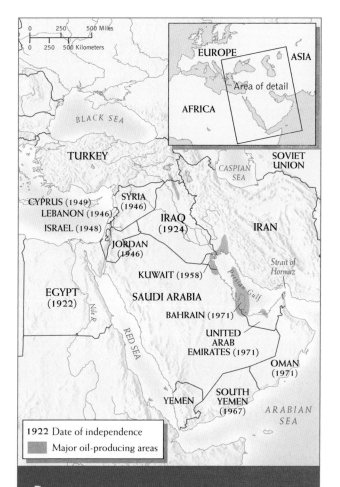

DECOLONIZATION IN THE MIDDLE EAST

Under the control of the Ottoman Empire before World War I, much of the Middle East was ruled directly or indirectly by the British and French after the war. Britain, the main colonial power, granted independence to most of its holdings in the first years after World War II, although it did maintain control of small states in the Persian Gulf and Arabian Sea region until 1971.

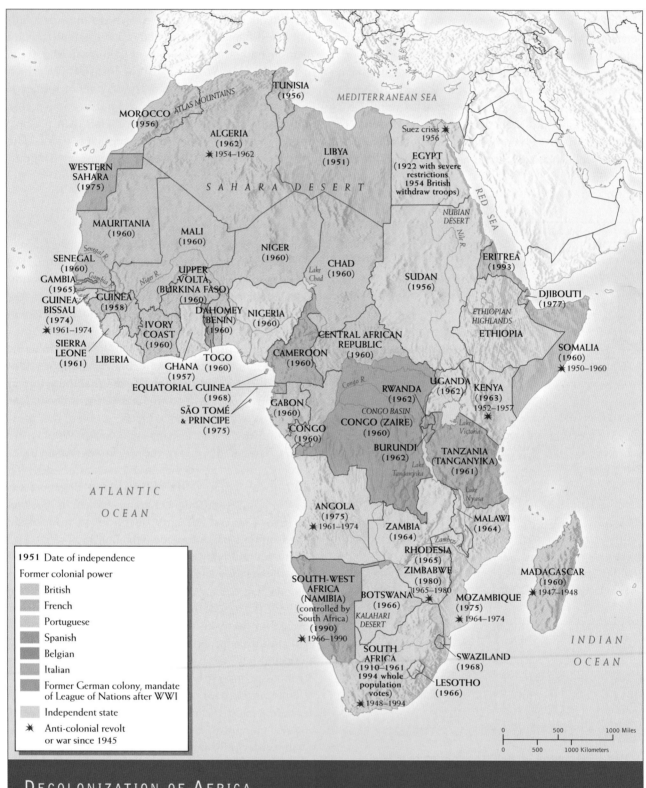

TUNISIA
(1956)

MEDITERRANEAN SEA

MOROCCO (ATLAS MOUNTAINS)
(1956)

ALGERIA
(1962)
✳ 1954–1962

LIBYA
(1951)

Suez crisis ✳
1956

EGYPT
(1922 with severe
restrictions
1954 British
withdraw troops)

WESTERN
SAHARA
(1975)

SAHARA DESERT

NUBIAN
DESERT

Nile R.

RED SEA

MAURITANIA
(1960)

MALI
(1960)

NIGER
(1960)

CHAD
(1960)

Lake
Chad

SUDAN
(1956)

ERITREA
(1993)

SENEGAL
(1960)

Senegal R.

DJIBOUTI
(1977)

GAMBIA
(1965)

Gambia

Niger R.

UPPER
VOLTA
(BURKINA FASO)
(1960)

GUINEA
BISSAU
(1974)
✳ 1961–1974

GUINEA
(1958)

DAHOMEY
(BENIN)
(1960)

NIGERIA
(1960)

ETHIOPIAN
HIGHLANDS

IVORY
COAST
(1960)

CENTRAL AFRICAN
REPUBLIC
(1960)

ETHIOPIA

SIERRA
LEONE
(1961)

LIBERIA

GHANA
(1957)

TOGO
(1960)

CAMEROON
(1960)

SOMALIA
(1960)
✳ 1950–1960

EQUATORIAL GUINEA
(1968)

Congo R.

UGANDA
(1962)

RWANDA
(1962)

KENYA
(1963)
1952–1957

SÃO TOMÉ
& PRINCIPE
(1975)

GABON
(1960)

CONGO BASIN

CONGO (ZAIRE)
(1960)

Lake
Victoria

CONGO
(1960)

BURUNDI
(1962)

TANZANIA
(TANGANYIKA)
(1961)

Lake
Tanganyika

ATLANTIC

OCEAN

Lake
Nyasa

ANGOLA
(1975)
✳ 1961–1974

ZAMBIA
(1964)

MALAWI
(1964)

Zambezi

RHODESIA
(1965)

MADAGASCAR
(1960)
✳ 1947–1948

ZIMBABWE
(1980)
1965–1980

SOUTH-WEST
AFRICA
(NAMIBIA)
(controlled by
South Africa)
(1990)
✳ 1966–1990

BOTSWANA
(1966)

MOZAMBIQUE
(1975)
✳ 1964–1974

KALAHARI
DESERT

INDIAN

OCEAN

SOUTH
AFRICA
(1910–1961
1994 whole
population
votes)
✳ 1948–1994

SWAZILAND
(1968)

LESOTHO
(1966)

1951 Date of independence

Former colonial power

British

French

Portuguese

Spanish

Belgian

Italian

Former German colony, mandate
of League of Nations after WWI

Independent state

✳   Anti-colonial revolt
or war since 1945

0   500   1000 Miles

0   500   1000 Kilometers

DECOLONIZATION OF AFRICA

What were the forces behind decolonization in Africa? How did they vary from one region to another?

WHAT WERE THE LINKS BETWEEN DECOLONIZATION, WORLD WAR II, AND THE COLD WAR?

REVOLUTION, ANTICOLONIALISM, AND THE COLD WAR   1003

drew public investigations and condemnation by even the most conservative British politicians and army officers. In 1963, a decade after the rebellion began, the British conceded Kenyan independence.

In the late 1950s, the British prime minister Harold Macmillan endorsed independence for a number of Britain's African colonies as a response to powerful winds of change. In southern Africa, the exceptionally large and wealthy population of European settlers set their sails against those winds, a resistance that continued on for decades. These settlers, a mixture of English migrants and the Franco-Dutch Afrikaners who traced their arrival to the eighteenth century, controlled huge tracts of fertile farmland along with some of the most lucrative gold and diamond mines on earth. This was especially true in South Africa. There, during the late 1940s, Britain's Labour government set aside its deep dislike of Afrikaner racism in a fateful political bargain. In return for guarantees that South African gold would be used carefully to support Britain's global financial power, Britain tolerated the introduction of apartheid in South Africa. Even by other standards of segregation, apartheid was especially harsh. Under its terms, Africans, Indians, and colored persons of mixed descent lost all political rights. All the institutions of social life, including marriage and schools, were segregated. What was more, the government tried to block the dramatic social consequences of the expansion of mining and industrialization in general, especially African migration to cities and a new wave of labor militancy in the mines. Apartheid required Africans to live in designated "homelands," forbade them to travel without specific permits, and created elaborate government bureaus to manage the labor essential to the economy. The government also banned any political protest. These measures made Western powers uncomfortable with the segregationist regime, but white South Africans held on to American support by presenting themselves as a bulwark against communism.

To the north, in the territories of Rhodesia, the British government encouraged a large federation, controlled by white settlers but with the opportunity for majority rule in the future. By the early 1960s, however, the federation was on the verge of collapse; the majority-rule state of Malawi was allowed to exit the federation in 1964, and Rhodesia split on northern and southern lines. In the north, the premier relented and accepted majority government under the black populist Kenneth Kaunda. In the south, angry Afrikaners backed by 200,000 right-wing English migrants who had arrived since 1945 refused to accept majority rule. When the British government attempted to force their hand, the settlers unilaterally declared independence in 1965 and began a bloody civil war against southern Rhodesia's black population that lasted half a generation.

CRISIS IN SUEZ AND THE END OF AN ERA

For postwar Britain, empire was not only politically complicated but cost too much. Britain began to withdraw from naval and air bases around the world because they had become too expensive to maintain. The Labour government did try to maintain British power and prestige in the postwar world. In Malaya, British forces repressed a revolt by ethnic Chinese communists and then helped support the independent states of Singapore and Malaysia, maintaining British companies' and banks' ties with Malaysia's lucrative rubber and oil reserves. Labour also launched carefully targeted efforts at "colonial development" to tap local natural resources Britain hoped to sell on world markets. "Development," however, was underfunded and largely disregarded in favor of fulfilling cold war commitments elsewhere. In the Middle East, the British government protected several oil-rich states with its military and helped overthrow a nationalist government in Iran to ensure that the oil states invested their money in British financial markets.

In Egypt, however, the British refused to yield a traditional point of imperial pride. In 1951 nationalists compelled the British to agree to withdraw their troops from Egyptian territory within three years. In 1952 a group of nationalist army officers deposed Egypt's King Farouk, who had close ties to Britain, and proclaimed a republic. Shortly after the final British withdrawal an Egyptian colonel, Gamal Abdel Nasser (1918–1970), became president of the country (1956–1970). His first major public act as president was to nationalize the Suez Canal Company. So doing would help finance the construction of the Aswan Dam on the Nile, and both the dam and nationalizing the canal represented economic independence and Egyptian national pride. Nasser also helped develop the anticolonial ideology of pan-Arabism, proposing

> Nasser also helped develop the anticolonial ideology of pan-Arabism, proposing that Arab nationalists throughout the Islamic world should create an alliance of modern nations, no longer beholden to the West.

that Arab nationalists throughout the Islamic world should create an alliance of modern nations, no longer beholden to the West. Finally, Nasser was also willing to take aid and support from the Soviets to achieve that goal, which made the canal into a cold war issue.

Three nations found Nasser and his pan-Arab ideals threatening. Israel, surrounded on all sides by un-friendly neighbors, was looking for an opportunity to seize the strategic Sinai Peninsula and create a buffer against Egypt. France, already fighting a war against Al-gerian nationalists, hoped to destroy what it considered the Egyptian source of Arab nationalism. Britain de-pended on the canal as a route to its strategic bases and was stung by this blow to imperial dignity. Though the British were reluctant to intervene, they were urged on by their prime minister, Sir Anthony Eden; Eden had developed a deep personal hatred of Nasser. In the autumn of 1956, the three nations colluded in an attack on Egypt. Israel occupied the Sinai while British and French jets destroyed Egypt's air force on the ground. The former colonial powers landed troops at the mouth of the canal but lacked the resources to push on in strength toward Cairo. As a result the war left Nasser in power and made him a hero to the Egyptian public for holding the imperialists at bay. The attack was con-demned around the world. The United States angrily called its allies' bluff, inflicting severe financial penalties on Britain and France. Both countries were forced to withdraw their expeditions. For policy makers in Great Britain and France, the failure at Suez marked the end of an era.

FRENCH DECOLONIZATION

In two particular cases, France's experience of decolo-nization was bloodier, more difficult, and more dam-aging to French prestige and domestic politics than any in Britain's experience, with the possible exception of Northern Ireland. The first was Indochina, where French efforts to restore imperial authority after losing it in World War II only resulted in military defeat and further humiliation. The second case, Algeria, became not only a violent colonial war but also a struggle with serious political ramifications at home.

THE FIRST VIETNAM WAR, 1946–1954

Indochina was one of France's last major imperial ac-quisitions in the nineteenth century. Here, as else-where, the two world wars had helped galvanize first nationalist and then, also, communist independence movements. In Indonesia, nationalist forces rebelled against Dutch efforts to restore colonialism, and the country became independent in 1949. In Indochina, the communist resistance became particularly effective under the leadership of Ho Chi Minh. Ho was French educated and, his expectations raised by the Wilsonian principles of self-determination, had hoped his coun-try might win independence at Versailles in 1919 (see Chapter Twenty-Four). He read Marx and Lenin and absorbed the Chinese communists' lessons about orga-nizing peasants around social and agrarian as well as national issues. During World War II, Ho's movement fought first the Vichy government of the colony and later Japanese occupiers and provided intelligence re-ports for the Allies. In 1945, however, the United States and Britain repudiated their relationship with Ho's independence movement and allowed the French to reclaim their colonies throughout Southeast Asia. The Vietnamese communists, who were fierce nation-alists as well as Marxists, renewed their guerrilla war against the French.

The fighting was protracted and bloody; France saw in it a chance to redeem its national pride. After one of France's most capable generals, Jean de Lattre de Tassigny, finally achieved a military advantage against the rebels in 1951, the French government might have decolonized on favorable terms. Instead, it decided to press on for total victory, sending troops deep into Vietnamese territory to root out the rebels. One major base was established in a valley bordering modern Laos, at a hamlet called Dien Bien Phu. Ringed by high mountains, this vulnerable spot became a base for thousands of elite French paratroopers and colonial soldiers from Algeria and West Africa—the best of France's troops. The rebels besieged the base. Tens of thousands of Vietnamese nationalist fighters hauled heavy artillery by hand up the mountainsides and

CHRONOLOGY

MAJOR DEVELOPMENTS IN AFRICA, 1952–PRESENT

Egypt gains independence	1952
Congo gains independence	1960
Algeria gains independence	1962
Rhodesia gains independence	1965
Massive economic decline	1970s–1990s
Apartheid ends in South Africa	1992–1994
AIDS epidemic in sub-Saharan Africa	1980s–present

THE VIETNAM WAR: AMERICAN ANALYSIS OF THE FRENCH SITUATION

At the end of World War II, the French government sought to recoup its prestige and empire by reasserting control of the former colony of Indochina. The French faced fierce resistance from nationalist forces under the French-educated leader Ho Chi Minh. Within a few years, American advisers were beginning to shore up the faltering French army. Cold war ideology, anxiety about China and Korea, and a conviction that they could do what the French could not combined to draw the Americans more deeply into the war. In 1950, the Central Intelligence Agency drew up this analysis of the strategic situation.

For more than three years, an intense conflict has been in progress in Indochina in which nationalistic Vietnamese forces under the leadership of the Moscow-trained revolutionist, Ho Chi Minh, have opposed the reimposition of French authority. Within Vietnam . . . a precarious military balance exists between the French and their Vietnamese followers on the one hand and Ho's resistance forces on the other. Thus far, French progress toward both political and military objectives has been substantially less than is necessary to eliminate the threat to French tenure posed by the resistance.

The French position and Bao Dai's [emperor of Vietnam since 1926] prospects have recently been further weakened: politically by Chinese Communist and Soviet recognition of Ho Chi Minh, and militarily by the ability of the Chinese Communist forces to make military supplies available to Ho's forces. Unless the French and Bao Dai receive substantial outside assistance, this combined political and military pressure may accelerate a French withdrawal from all or most of Indochina which, previous to the Chinese Communist and Soviet recognition of Ho, had been estimated as probably occurring within two years. . . .

The fighting in Indochina constitutes a progressive drain on French military resources which is weakening France as a partner in the Western alliance. If France is driven from Indochina, the resulting emergence of an indigenous Communist-oriented regime in Vietnam, in combination with the pressures which will be exerted by the new government of China and the Soviet Union, can be expected to cause adjacent Thailand and Burma to yield to this Communist advance. Under these conditions Malaya and Indonesia would also become highly vulnerable.

The French are trying to halt the present unfavorable trend by according certain aspects of sovereignty to Emperor Bao Dai. . . . The French political aim is to attract non-Communist nationalists from the leadership of Ho Chi Minh to that of Bao Dai.

Meanwhile, Soviet and Chinese Communist recognition of Ho's regime has made it clear that the Kremlin is now prepared to exert greater pressure to achieve its objective of installing a Communist regime in Indochina. France alone is incapable of preventing such a development and can turn only to the US for assistance in thwarting this Communist strategy. Having already publicly proclaimed support of Bao Dai, the US is now faced with the choice of bolstering his weak and vulnerable position or of abandoning him and accepting the far-reaching consequences of Communist control of Indochina.

National Archives, College Park, Md. Record Group 263 (Records of the Central Intelligence Agency), *Estimates of the Office of Research Evaluation, 1946–1950*, box 4.

QUESTIONS FOR ANALYSIS

1. Explain how the author of this CIA report has used George Kennan's policy of containment. What would happen if the French military forces withdrew? Why was Southeast Asia such a hot spot in the decade following World War II?

2. Did the French or American military, just coming off a European theater of war, have any idea what it would be like to wage war in a place like Southeast Asia?

bombarded the network of forts set up by the French. The siege lasted for months, becoming a protracted national crisis in France.

When Dien Bien Phu fell in May 1954, the French government began peace talks in Geneva. The Geneva Accords, drawn up by the French, Vietnamese politicians including the communists, the British, and the Americans, divided Indochina into three countries: Laos, Cambodia, and Vietnam, which was partitioned into two states. North Vietnam was taken over by Ho Chi Minh's party; South Vietnam by a succession of Western-supported politicians. Corruption, repression, and instability in the south, coupled with Ho Chi Minh's nationalist desire to unite Vietnam, guaranteed that the war would continue. The U.S. government, which had provided military and financial aid to the French, began to send aid to the South Vietnamese regime. The Americans saw the conflict through the prism of the cold war: their project was not to restore colonialism but to contain communism and prevent it from spreading through Southeast Asia. The limits of this policy would not become clear until the mid-1960s.

"Dien-Bien-Phu: . . . They Sacrificed Themselves for Liberty." The sentiments expressed in this poster, which was intended to commemorate the French soldiers who died at Dien Bien Phu in May 1954, helped to deepen French commitments to colonial control in Algeria.

ALGERIA

Still reeling from the humiliation of Dien Bien Phu, France faced a complex colonial problem closer to home, in Algeria. Since the 1830s, the colony had evolved into a settler society of three social groups. First, in addition to a small class of French soldiers and administrators, there were also one million European settlers. They typically owned farms and vineyards near the major cities, or formed the working-class and merchant communities inside those cities. All of them were citizens of the three administrative districts of Algeria, which were legally part of France. The community produced some of France's best-known writers and intellectuals: Albert Camus, Jacques Derrida, and Pierre Bourdieu, among others. In the small towns and villages of Algeria lived a second group of (largely Muslim) Berbers, whose long history of service in the French army entitled them to certain formal and informal privileges within the colony. Finally, there were millions of Muslim Arabs, some living in the desert south but most crowded into impoverished neighborhoods in the cities. The Arabs were the largest and most deprived group in Algerian society. Between the world wars the French government had offered small reforms to increase their rights and representation, and

WHAT WERE THE LINKS BETWEEN DECOLONIZATION, WORLD WAR II, AND THE COLD WAR?

REVOLUTION, ANTICOLONIALISM, AND THE COLD WAR   1007

An Algerian POW imprisoned by the French in a cellar for animals during the Algerian War of Independence, 1961.

it had hoped to meld the three groups into a common Algerian society. Reforms came too late and were also undercut by European settlers anxious to maintain their privileges.

At the end of World War II, Algerian nationalists called on the Allies to recognize Algeria's independence in return for good service during the war. Public demonstrations became frequent, and in several cases turned into attacks on settler-landowners. In one rural town, Setif, celebrations of the defeat of Germany flared into violence against settlers. French repression was harsh and immediate: security forces killed several thousand Arabs. After the war the French government approved a provincial assembly for all of Algeria, elected by two pools of voters, one made up of settlers and mostly Berber Muslims, the other of Arabs. This very limited enfranchisement gave Arab Algerians no political power. The more important changes were economic. All of Algeria suffered in the difficulties after the war. Many Arab Algerians felt they had to emigrate; several hundred thousand went to work in France. While citizens of mainland France read their papers and frowned over the war in Indochina, the situation in Algeria grew more serious. By the middle of the 1950s, a younger generation of Arab activists, unhappy with the leadership of the moderates, had taken charge of a movement dedicated to independence by force. The National Liberation Front (FLN) was organized, which leaned toward socialism and demanded equal citizenship for all.

The war in Algeria became a war on three fronts. The first was a guerrilla war between the regular French Army and the FLN, fought in the mountains and deserts of the country. This war continued for years, a clear military defeat for the FLN but never a clear-cut victory for the French. The second war,

fought out in Algeria's cities, began with an FLN campaign of bombing and terrorism. European civilians were killed, and the French administration retaliated with its own campaign. French paratroopers hunted down and destroyed the networks of FLN bombers. The information that allowed the French to break the FLN network was extracted through systematic torture conducted by French security forces. The torture became an international scandal, bringing waves of protest in France. This third front of the Algerian war divided France, brought down the government, and ushered de Gaulle back into power.

De Gaulle visited Algiers to wild cheering from settlers and declared that Algeria would always be French. After another year of violence, he and his advisers had changed their minds. By 1962 talks had produced a formula for independence: a referendum would be held, voted on by the whole population of Algeria. On July 1, 1962, the referendum passed by a landslide vote. Arab political groups and guerrillas from the FLN entered Algiers in triumph. Settlers and Berbers who had fought for the French army fled Algeria for France by the hundreds of thousands. Later, these refugees were joined in France by another influx of Arab economic migrants.

Algeria illustrated the dramatic domestic impact of decolonization. The war cut deep divides through French society, largely because the very identity of France seemed at stake. Withdrawing from Algeria

Ben Cherif, a commander in the FLN, handcuffed in 1961.

meant reorienting French views of what it meant to be a modern power. De Gaulle summed up the trade-off in his memoirs: to stay in Algeria would "keep France politically, financially, and militarily bogged down in a bottomless quagmire when, in fact, she needed her hands free to bring about the domestic transformation necessitated by the twentieth century and to exercise her influence abroad unencumbered." In France and other imperial powers, the conclusions seemed clear. Traditional forms of colonial rule could not withstand the demands of postwar politics and culture; the leading European nations, once distinguished by their empires, would have to look for new forms of influence. The domestic transformation of which de Gaulle spoke—recovery from the war, economic restructuring, and political renewal—had to take place on a radically changed global stage.

POSTWAR CULTURE AND THOUGHT

What themes defined postwar culture?

The postwar period brought a remarkable burst of cultural production. Writers and artists did not hesitate to take up big issues: freedom, civilization, and the human condition itself. The search for democratic renewal gave this literature urgency; the moral dilemmas of war, occupation, and resistance gave it resonance and popular appeal. The process of decolonization, too, forced the issues of race, culture, and colonialism to center stage in Western debates.

THE BLACK PRESENCE

The journal *Présence Africaine* (African presence), founded in Paris in 1947, was only one in a chorus of new cultural voices. *Présence Africaine* published such writers as Aimé Césaire (b. 1913), the surrealist poet from Martinique, and Léopold Senghor of Senegal (1906–2001). Césaire and Senghor were brilliant students, educated in the most elite French universities, and elected to the French National Assembly. Césaire became an important political figure in the former French Caribbean colony and (after 1946) Department of Martinique; in 1960 Senghor was elected the first president of Senegal. Both men, in important respects

models of Frenchness, became the most influential exponents of *Négritude*, which could be translated as "black consciousness" or "black pride." Senghor wrote:

> Assimilation was a failure. We could assimilate mathematics of the French language, but we could never strip off our black skins or root out black souls. And so we set out on a fervent quest for . . . our collective soul. Negritude is the whole complex of civilized values—cultural, economic, social and political—which characterize the black people.

Césaire's early work took its lead from surrealism and the exploration of consciousness. Later, his work became more political. *Discourse on Colonialism* (1950) was a powerful indictment of the material and spiritual squalor of colonialism, which, he argued, not only dehumanized colonial subjects but degraded the colonizers themselves.

Césaire's student Frantz Fanon (1925–1961), also from Martinique, went further. He argued that withdrawing into an insular black culture (as he interpreted Negritude) was not an effective response to racism. People of color, he believed, needed a theory of radical social change. Fanon trained in psychiatry and worked in Algeria, where he became a member of the National Liberation Front. In *Black Skin, White Masks* (1952) he examined the effects of colonialism and racism from the point of view of a radical psychiatrist. *The Wretched of the Earth* (1961) became one of the most influential revolutionary manifestos of the period. More than Césaire, and bluntly rejecting Gandhi's theories and practice, Fanon argued that violence was rooted in colonialism and, therefore, in anticolonial movements. But he also believed that many anticolonial leaders would be corrupted by their ambition and by collaboration with former colonial powers. Revolutionary change, he believed, could come only from poor peasants, or those who "have found no bone to gnaw in the colonial system."

How did these writers fit into postwar culture? Western intellectuals sought to revive humanism and democratic values after the atrocities of World War II. Fanon and others pointed out that the struggles over colonialism made that project more difficult; the violent repression of anticolonial movements in places such as Algeria seemed to be a relapse into brutality. They pointed to the ironies of Europe's "civilizing mission" and demanded a reevaluation of blackness as a central concept in Western culture. The West's postwar recovery would entail eventually facing this challenge to the universal claims of its culture.

ANTICOLONIALISM AND VIOLENCE

Born in the French Caribbean colony of Martinique, Frantz Fanon (1925–1961) studied psychiatry in France before moving on to work in Algeria in the early 1950s. Fanon became a member of the Algerian revolutionary National Liberation Front (FLN) and an ardent advocate of decolonization. Black Skin, White Masks, published in 1952 with a preface by Jean-Paul Sartre, was a study of the psychological effects of colonialism and racism on black culture and individuals. The Wretched of the Earth (1961) was a revolutionary manifesto, one of the most influential of the period. Fanon attacked nationalist leaders for their ambition and corruption. He believed that revolutionary change could come only from poor peasants, those who "have found no bone to gnaw in the colonial system." Diagnosed with leukemia, Fanon sought treatment in the Soviet Union and then in Washington, D.C., where he died.

In decolonization, there is therefore the need of a complete calling in question of the colonial situation. If we wish to describe it precisely, we might find it in the well-known words: "The last shall be first and the first last." Decolonization is the putting into practice of this sentence. . . .

The naked truth of decolonization evokes for us the searing bullets and bloodstained knives which emanate from it. For if the last shall be first, this will only come to pass after a murderous and decisive struggle between the two protagonists. That affirmed intention to place the last at the head of things, and to make them climb at a pace (too quickly, some say) the well-known steps which characterize an organized society, can only triumph if we use all means to turn the scale, including, of course, that of violence.

You do not turn any society, however primitive it may be, upside down with such a program if you have not decided from the very beginning, that is to say from the actual formation of that program, to overcome all the obstacles that you will come across in so doing. The native who decides to put the program into practice, and to become its moving force, is ready for violence at all time. From birth it is clear to him that this narrow world, strewn with prohibitions, can only be called in question by absolute violence.

Frantz Fanon, *The Wretched of the Earth*, trans. Constance Farrington (New York, 1963), pp. 35–37.

QUESTIONS FOR ANALYSIS

1. Why did Fanon believe that violence lay at the heart of both the colonial relationship and anticolonial movements?

2. What arguments would he offer to counter Gandhi?

EXISTENTIALISM

The French existentialist writers, most prominently Jean-Paul Sartre (SAHR-truh; 1905–1980) and Albert Camus (KAM-oo; 1913–1960), put the themes of individuality, commitment, and choice at center stage. The existentialists took themes from Nietzsche, Heidegger, and Kierkegaard, reworking them in the new context of war-torn Europe. Their starting point was that "existence precedes essence." In other words, meaning in life is not given, but created. Thus individuals were "condemned to be free" and to give their lives meaning by making choices and accepting responsibility. To deny one's freedom or responsibility was to act in "bad faith." War, collaboration and resistance, genocide, and the development of

Simone de Beauvoir.

weapons of mass destruction all provided specific points of reference and gave these abstractions new meaning. The existentialists' writing was also clear and accessible, which contributed to their enormous popularity. Although Sartre wrote philosophical treatises, he also published plays and short stories. Camus's own experience in the resistance gave him tremendous moral authority—he became the symbol of a new generation. His novels—including *The Stranger* (1942), *The Plague* (1947), and *The Fall* (1956)—often revolved around metaphors for the war, showing that people were responsible for their own dilemmas and, through a series of antiheroes, exploring the limited ability of men and women to help each other.

Existentialist insights opened other doors. The existentialist approach to race, for instance, emphasized that no meaning inhered in skin color; instead race derived meaning from a lived experience or situation. As Frantz Fanon wrote, white and black exist "only insofar as they create one another." The same approach could be applied to gender. In her famous introduction to *The Second Sex* (1949), Simone de Beauvoir (*duh bohv-WAHR;* 1908–1986) argued that "One is not born a woman, one becomes one." Women, like men, were condemned to be free. Beauvoir went on to ask why women seemed to accept their secondary status or why, in her words, they "dreamed the dreams of men." The scope and ambition of *The Second Sex* helped make

it enormously influential; it was virtually encyclopedic, analyzing history, myth, biology, and psychology, bringing the insights of Marx and Freud to bear on the "woman question." Beauvoir's life also contributed to the book's high profile. A brilliant student from a strict middle-class background, she had a lifelong affair with Sartre but did not marry him, leading many to romanticize her as a liberated and accomplished woman intellectual. She had little to do with feminism, however, until the late 1960s. When *The Second Sex* was published, it was associated with existentialism; only later would it become a key text of the women's movement (see Chapter Twenty-Eight).

MEMORY AND AMNESIA: THE AFTERMATH OF WAR

The theme of individual helplessness in the face of state power ran through countless works of the period, beginning, most famously, with George Orwell's *Animal Farm* (1946) and *1984* (1949). The American Joseph Heller's wildly popular *Catch-22* (1961) represented a form of popular existentialism, concerned with the absurdity of war and offering a biting commentary on regimentation and its toll on individual freedom. The Czech author Milan Kundera, who fled the repressive Czech government to live in Paris, eloquently captured the bittersweet efforts to resist senseless bureaucracy. Some writers expressed their despair by escaping into the absurd and fantastic. In Samuel Beckett's deeply pessimistic *Waiting for Godot* (1953, by an Irishman in French) and in the Briton Harold Pinter's *Caretaker* (1960) and *Homecoming* (1965) nothing happens. Characters speak in banalities, paralyzed by the absurdity of modern times.

Other authors ventured into the realms of hallucination, science fiction, and fantasy. The novels of the Americans William Burroughs and Kurt Vonnegut carry readers from interior fantasies to outer space. One of the most popular books of the period was *The Lord of the Rings* (1954–1955), written before and during World War II by the Briton J. R. R. Tolkien. Set in the fantasy world of Middle Earth, Professor Tolkien's tribute to the ancient Celtic and Scandinavian languages he studied and the power of human myths was seized on by a generation of young romantics who rebelled against postwar Western culture for their own reasons.

Questions of terror and dictatorship haunted social and political thought of the postwar era, and especially the work of émigrés from Europe. Representatives of the "Frankfurt school" of German Marxism, by wartime refugees in the United States, sought to understand how fascism and Nazism had taken root in Western culture and politics. Theodor Adorno joined Max Horkheimer in a series of essays, *Dialectic of Enlightenment* (1947), the best known of which indicted the "culture industry" for depoliticizing the masses and crippling democracy. Adorno also co-authored *The Authoritarian Personality* (1950), which used social surveys in an effort to discover how people become receptive to racism, prejudice, and dictatorship. Whatever the specific roots of German Nazism, the Frankfurt school suggested, there were also more general tendencies in modern societies that should give cause for concern.

Hannah Arendt (1906–1975), a Jewish refugee from Germany, was the first to propose that both Nazism and Stalinism should be understood as forms of a novel, twentieth-century form of government: totalitarianism (*The Origins of Totalitarianism*, 1951). Unlike earlier forms of tyranny or despotism, totalitarianism worked by mobilizing mass support. It used terror to crush resistance, break down political and social institutions, and atomize the public. Totalitarianism, Arendt argued, also forged new ideologies. Totalitarian regimes did not concern themselves with whether killing was justified by law; they justified camps and extermination by pointing to the objective laws of history or racial struggle. By unleashing destruction and eliminating entire populations, totalitarian politics made collective resistance virtually impossible. Arendt returned to the same theme in a provocative and disturbing essay on the trial of a Nazi leader, *Eichmann in Jerusalem* (1963). To many readers' distress, she pointedly refused to demonize Nazism. Instead she explored what she termed "the banality of evil": how the rise of new forms of state power and terror had created in a world in which Nazis such as Adolf Eichmann could implement genocide as simply one more policy. The crisis of totalitarianism, Arendt argued, was the moral collapse of society, for it destroyed human feeling and the power of resistance in executioners and victims—"tormentors and the tormented"—alike.

Discussions of the war and its legacy, however, were limited. Some memoirs and novels dealing directly with the war and its brutal aftermath did reach a large international public: Jerzy Kosinski's novel about a boy in wartime Poland, *The Painted Bird*; Czeslaw Milosz's memoir of intellectual collaboration in Eastern Europe, *The Captive Mind* (1951); the German

> Questions of terror and dictatorship haunted social and political thought of the postwar era, and especially the work of émigrés from Europe.

Günter Grass's *Tin Drum* (1959), which portrayed the Nazi and war experience in a semi-autobiographical genre and earned Grass recognition as "the conscience of his generation." Of all the memoirs, *The Diary of a Young Girl* by Anne Frank, published in 1947, was undoubtedly the most widely read. Yet the main current in postwar culture ran in a different direction, toward repressing painful issues and bad memories. Postwar governments could not or would not purge all those implicated in war crimes. In France, the courts sentenced 2,640 to death and executed 791; in Austria 13,000 were convicted of war crimes and 30 executed. Those who called for justice grew demoralized and cynical. Others responded by mythologizing the Resistance and exaggerating participation in it and by avoiding discussion of collaboration. For ten years French television considered *The Sorrow and the Pity* (1969), Marcel Ophüls's brilliant and unsparing documentary on a French town under Vichy, too controversial for broadcast. Most Jewish survivors, wherever they lived, found that few editors were interested in publishing their stories. In 1947, only a small publishing house would take on the Italian survivor Primo Levi's *Survival in Auschwitz*; the book and Levi's other writings did not find a wide audience until later.

The cold war was an important factor in burying and distorting memories. West of the Iron Curtain, the eagerness to embrace West Germany as an ally, the single-minded emphasis on economic development, and ardent anticommunism blurred views of the past. One example involved Klaus Barbie, an agent for the Gestapo in occupied France who among other things arrested and personally tortured members of the Resistance and deported thousands, including Jewish children, to concentration camps. After the war American intelligence services recruited Barbie for his anticommunist skills and paid to smuggle him out of Europe, beyond the reach of those who wanted to prosecute him for war crimes. He was finally extradited from Bolivia in 1983, tried in France for crimes against humanity, and convicted. In the Eastern bloc, regimes declared fascism to be a thing of the past and did not scrutinize that past or seek out the many who collaborated with the Nazis. Thus, reckoning with history was postponed until the fall of the Soviet Union. On both sides of the Iron Curtain, the vast majority of people turned inward, cherishing their domestic lives, relieved to have privacy.

THE WAR THAT REFUSES TO BE FORGOTTEN

Heda Margolis Kovály was born in Prague and returned to her city after surviving the concentration camps. Like many refugees and survivors, she received an uncertain welcome home. In Czechoslovakia and elsewhere, the Nazi occupation left a legacy of bitterness and division that persisted for decades. Survivors reminded other Europeans of the war and made them defensive. Paradoxically, as Kovály shows, it was common to blame the victims for the war's troubles.

And so ended that horrible long war that refuses to be forgotten. Life went on. It went on despite both the dead and the living, because this was a war that no one had quite survived. Something very important and precious had been killed by it or, perhaps, it had just died of horror, of starvation, or simply of disgust— who knows? We tried to bury it quickly, the earth settled over it, and we turned our backs on it impatiently. After all, our real life was now beginning and what to make of it was up to us.

People came crawling out of their hide-outs. They came back from the forests, from the prisons, and from the concentration camps, and all they could think was, "It's over; it's all over." . . . Some people came back silent, and some talked incessantly as though talking about a thing would make it vanish. . . . While some voices spoke of death and flames, of blood and gallows, in the background, a chorus of thousands repeated tirelessly, "You know, we also suffered. . . . [N]othing but skimmed milk. . . . No butter on our bread. . . ."

Sometimes a bedraggled and barefoot concentration camp survivor plucked up his courage and knocked on the door of prewar friends to ask, "Excuse me, do you by any chance still have some of the stuff we left with you for safekeeping?" And the friends would say, "You must be mistaken, you didn't leave anything with us, but come in anyway!" And they would seat him in their parlor where his carpet lay on the floor and pour herb tea into antique cups that had belonged to his grandmother. . . . He would say to himself, "What does it matter? As long as we're alive? What does it matter?" . . .

It would also happen that a survivor might need a lawyer to retrieve lost documents and he would remember the name of one who had once represented large Jewish companies. He would go to see him and sit in an empire chair in a corner of an elegant waiting room, enjoying all that good taste and luxury, watching pretty secretaries rushing about. Until one of the pretty girls forgot to close a door behind her, and the lawyer's sonorous voice would boom through the crack, "You would have thought we'd be rid of them finally, but no, they're impossible to kill off—not even Hitler could manage it. Every day there're more of them crawling back, like rats. . . ." And the survivor would quietly get up from his chair and slip out of the waiting room, this time not laughing. On his way down the stairs his eyes would mist over as if with the smoke of the furnaces at Auschwitz.

Heda Margolis Kovály, *Under a Cruel Star: A Life in Prague 1941–1968*, trans. Franci Epstein and Helen Epstein with the author (Cambridge, Mass., 1986), pp. 45–46.

QUESTIONS FOR ANALYSIS

1. What did Kovály mean when she remarked that World War II was "a war that no one had quite survived"? Can such an argument be made about all wars? In what ways was World War II distinctive?
2. Kovály describes individual encounters. Do her stories illuminate larger social and cultural developments?

CONCLUSION

One of the last serious and most dramatic confrontations of the cold war came in 1962, in Cuba. A revolution in 1958 had brought the charismatic communist Fidel Castro to power. Immediately after, the United States began to work with exiled Cubans, supporting among other ventures a bungled attempt to invade via the Bay of Pigs in 1961. Castro not only aligned himself with the Soviets but invited them to base nuclear missiles on Cuban soil, only a few minutes' flying time from Florida. When American spy planes identified the missiles and related military equipment in 1962, Kennedy confronted Khrushchev. After deliberating about the repercussions of an air strike, Kennedy ordered a naval blockade of Cuba. On October 22, he appeared on television, visibly tired and without makeup, announced the grave situation to the public,

The Cold War in Everyday Life. A Soviet matchbook label, 1960, depicts a Soviet fist destroying a U.S. plane.

and challenged Khrushchev to withdraw the weapons and "move the world back from the abyss of destruction." Terrified of the looming threat of nuclear war, Americans fled urban areas, prepared for a cramped and uncomfortable existence in fallout shelters, and bought firearms. After three nerve wracking weeks, the Soviets agreed to withdraw and to remove the bombers and missiles already on Cuban soil. But citizens of both countries spent many anxious hours in their bomb shelters, and onlookers the world over wrestled with their rising fears that a nuclear Armageddon was upon them.

The Cuban missile crisis provided one inspiration for Stanley Kubrick's classic *Dr. Strangelove* (1964), a devastating and dark comedy with many cold war themes. The story concerns an "accidental" nuclear attack and the demented characters responsible for it. It also concerns the repression of memory and the sudden reversals of alliances brought about by the cold war. The wildly eccentric German scientist Dr. Strangelove shuttles between his present life working for the Americans and his barely repressed past as an enthusiastic follower of Hitler. The screenplay was based on the British writer Peter Bryant's *Two Hours to Doom* (1958), one of many 1950s novels with an apocalyptic scenario. The Cuban missile crisis brought the plot so close to home that when the film came out Columbia Pictures felt compelled to issue a disclaimer: "It is the stated position of the United States Air Force that their safeguards would prevent the occurrence of such events as are depicted in this film." Black humor seemed to be a common cultural mechanism for dealing with the terrible possibility of world annihilation. The protagonist of Bob Dylan's 1963 "Talkin' World War III Blues" playfully narrates an apocalyptic dream in which he drives an abandoned Cadillac ("a good car to drive after a war"), approaches the inhabitants of a bunker for a TV dinner, and lights a cigarette on a radioactive parking meter.

The cold war reached deep into postwar culture, and it dominated postwar politics. It decisively shaped the development of both the Soviet and American states. In his farewell address, President Eisenhower warned that a "military-industrial complex" had taken shape and that its "total influence—economic, political, even spiritual—is felt in every city, every statehouse, every office of the federal government." Yet other, equally important developments marked the period. The nation-state expanded in nonmilitary realms, taking on new roles in economic planning and management, in educating citizens, and in ensuring social welfare. Those changes were driven by a search

Bay of Pigs, 1961. American President John F. Kennedy brandishes the combat flag of the Cuban landing brigade.

for democracy and stability. Former colonies became nations. In the long run the formation of the Third World mattered as much, if not more, than the bipolar divisions established by the cold war. Global and regional economic integration quickened. Economic growth helped all the Western nations (in different measures) recover from the devastation of war, though whether Europe would regain its former global power was doubtful. Finally, economic growth had unintended consequences. By the 1960s, social and cultural changes were beginning to undermine the cold war settlement.

Key Terms

Marshall Plan	Mohandas K.	Algerian war	ECSC
NATO	(Mahatma) Gandhi	Berlin Wall	social democracy
Khrushchev	Ho Chi Minh	Berlin blockade	existentialism

Selected Readings

Aron, Raymond. *The Imperial Republic: The United States and the World, 1945–1973*. Lanham, Md., 1974. An early analysis by a leading French political theorist.

Carter, Erica. *How German Is She? Postwar West German Reconstruction and the Consuming Woman*. Ann Arbor, Mich., 1997. A thoughtful examination of gender and the reconstruction of the family in West Germany during the 1950s.

Clayton, Anthony. *The Wars of French Decolonization*. London, 1994. Good survey.

Connelly, Matthew. *A Diplomatic Revolution: Algeria's Fight for Independence and the Origins of the Post–Cold War Era*. New York and Oxford, 2003. An international history.

Cooper, Frederick, and Ann Laura Stoler, eds. *Tensions of Empire: Colonial Cultures in a Bourgeois World*. Berkeley, Calif., 1997. Collection of new essays, among the best.

Darwin, John. *Britain and Decolonization: The Retreat from Empire in the Postwar World*. New York, 1988. Best overall survey.

Deák, István, Jan T. Gross, and Tony Judt, eds. *The Politics of Retribution in Europe: World War II and Its Aftermath*. Princeton, N.J., 2000. Collection focusing on the attempt to come to terms with World War II in Eastern and Western Europe.

Farmer, Sarah. *Martyred Village: Commemorating the 1944 Massacre at Oradour-sur-Glane*. Berkeley, Calif., 1999. Gripping story of French attempts to come to terms with collaboration and complicity in atrocities.

Holland, R. F. *European Decolonization 1918–1981: An Introductory Survey*. New York, 1985. Sprightly narrative and analysis.

Jarausch, Konrad Hugo, ed. *Dictatorship as Experience: Towards a Socio-Cultural History of the GDR*. Trans. Eve Duffy. New York, 1999. Surveys recent research on the former East Germany.

Judt, Tony. *The Burden of Responsibility: Blum, Camus, and the French Twentieth Century*. Chicago and London, 1998. Also on French intellectuals.

Judt, Tony. *A Grand Illusion? An Essay on Europe.* New York, 1996. Short and brilliant.

Judt, Tony. *Past Imperfect: French Intellectuals, 1944–1956.* Berkeley, Calif., 1992. Very readable, on French intellectuals, who loomed large during this period.

Judt, Tony. *Postwar. A History of Europe Since 1945.* London, 2005. Detailed, comprehensive, and ground breaking, this single volume surpasses any other account of the entire postwar period.

Koven, Seth, and Sonya Michel. *Mothers of a New World: Maternalist Politics and the Origins of Welfare States.* New York, 1993. Excellent essays on the long history of welfare politics.

LaFeber, Walter. *America, Russia, and the Cold War.* New York, 1967. A classic, now in its ninth edition.

Large, David Clay. *Berlin.* New York, 2000. Accessible and engaging.

Leffler, Melvyn P. *A Preponderance of Power: National Security, the Truman Administration, and the Cold War.* Stanford, Calif., 1992. Solid political study.

Louis, William Roger. *The Ends of British Imperialism: The Scramble for Empire, Suez, and Decolonization.* London, 2006. Comprehensive and wide ranging.

Macey, David. *Frantz Fanon.* New York, 2000. Comprehensive recent biography.

Medvedev, Roy. *Khrushchev.* New York, 1983. A perceptive biography of the Soviet leader by a Soviet historian.

Milward, Alan S. *The Reconstruction of Western Europe, 1945–1951.* Berkeley, Calif., 1984. A good discussion of the "economic miracle."

Moeller, Robert G. *War Stories: The Search for a Usable Past in the Federal Republic of Germany.* Berkeley, Calif., 2001. Revealing analyses of postwar culture and politics.

Reynolds, David. *One World Divisible: A Global History Since 1945.* New York, 2000. Fresh approach, comprehensive, and very readable survey.

Rousso, Henri. *The Vichy Syndrome: History and Memory in France since 1944.* Cambridge, Mass., 1991. First in a series of books by one of the preeminent French historians.

Schissler, Hanna, ed. *The Miracle Years: A Cultural History of West Germany, 1949–1968.* Princeton, N.J., 2001. The cultural effects of the economic miracle.

Schneider, Peter. *The Wall Jumper: A Berlin Story.* Chicago, 1998. A fascinating novel about life in divided Berlin.

Shepard, Todd. *The Invention of Decolonization: The Algerian War and the Remaking of France.* Ithaca, N.Y., 2006. Excellent and original: a study of the deeply wrenching war's many ramifications.

Trachtenberg, Mark. *A Constructed Peace: The Making of the European Settlement, 1945–1963.* Princeton, N.J., 1999. A detailed study of international relations that moves beyond the Cold War framework.

Wilder, Gary. *The French Imperial Nation-State: Negritude and Colonial Humanism between the Two World Wars.* Chicago, 2005. Fascinating new study of the Negritude thinkers in their context.

Yergin, Daniel. *Shattered Peace: The Origins of the Cold War.* New York, 1977. Rev. ed. 1990. Dramatic and readable.

Young, Marilyn B. *The Vietnam Wars, 1945–1990.* New York, 1991. Excellent account of the different stages of the war and its repercussions.

CHAPTER TWENTY-EIGHT

RED FLAGS
AND VELVET
REVOLUTIONS:
THE END OF
THE COLD WAR,
1960–1990

consequences of sweeping changes in Western sexual life. Such measures were ineffective as well as unjust, they argued. French feminists dramatized the point by publishing the names of 343 well-known women, including Beauvoir, who admitted to having had illegal abortions. A similar petition came out in Germany the following year and was followed by petitions from doctors and tens of thousands of supporters. In sum, the legal changes followed from political demands, and those in turn reflected a quiet or subterranean rebellion of many women (and men)—one with longer-term causes. Mass consumption, mass culture, and startlingly rapid transformations in public and private life were all intimately related.

SOCIAL MOVEMENTS DURING THE 1960S

What spurred the social movements of the 1960s?

The social unrest of the 1960s was international. Its roots lay in the political struggles and social transformations of the postwar period. Of these, the most important were anticolonial and civil rights movements. The successful anticolonial movements (see Chapter Twenty-Seven) reflected a growing racial consciousness and also helped encourage that consciousness. Newly independent African and Caribbean nations remained wary about revivals of colonialism and the continuing economic hegemony of Western Europe and America. Black and Asian immigration into those nations produced tension and frequent violence. In the West, particularly in the United States, people of color identified with these social and economic grievances.

THE CIVIL RIGHTS MOVEMENT

The emergence of new black nations in Africa and the Caribbean was paralleled by growing African American insurgency. World War II increased African American migration from the American South to

northern cities, intensifying a drive for rights, dignity, and independence that began in the prewar era with organizations such as the National Association for the Advancement of Colored People (NAACP) and the National Urban League. By 1960, various civil rights groups, led by the Congress of Racial Equality (CORE), had started to organize boycotts and demonstrations directed at private businesses and public services that discriminated against blacks in the South. The preeminent figure in the civil rights movement in the United States during the 1960s was Martin Luther King Jr. (1929–1968). A Baptist minister, King embraced the philosophy of nonviolence promoted by the Indian social and political activist Mohandas K. Gandhi. King's personal participation in countless demonstrations, his willingness to go to jail for a cause that he believed to be just, and his ability as an orator to arouse both blacks and whites with his message led to his position as the most highly regarded—and most widely feared—defender of black rights. His inspiring career was tragically ended by assassination in 1968.

King and organizations such as CORE aspired to a fully integrated nation. Other charismatic and important black leaders sought complete independence from white society, fearing that integration would leave African Americans without the spiritual or material resources necessary for a community's pride, dignity, and autonomy. The most influential of the black nationalists

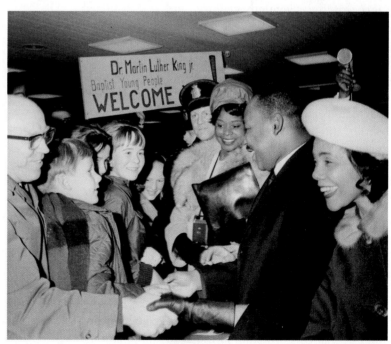

Martin Luther King Jr., 1964. The African American civil rights leader is welcomed in Oslo, Norway, on a trip to accept the Nobel Peace Prize. He would be assassinated four years later.

was Malcolm X (1925–1965), who assumed the "X" after having discarded his "white" surname (Little). For most of his adult life a spokesman for the Black Muslim movement, Malcolm X urged blacks to renew their commitment to their own heritage; to establish black businesses for economic autonomy; and to fortify economic, political, and psychological defenses against white domination. Like King he was assassinated, in 1965 while addressing a rally in Harlem.

Civil rights laws passed under President Lyndon B. Johnson (1963–1969) in the 1960s did bring African Americans some measure of equality with regard to voting rights—and, to a much lesser degree, school desegregation. In other areas, such as housing and job opportunities, white racism continued. Economic development passed by many African American communities, and subsequent administrations pulled back from the innovative programs of the Johnson era.

These problems were not confined to the United States. West Indian, Indian, and Pakistani immigrants in Britain met with discrimination in jobs, housing, and everyday interaction with the authorities—producing frequent racial disturbances in major British cities. France witnessed hostility toward Algerian immigration, Germany toward the importation of Turkish labor. In Western Europe, as in the United States, struggles for racial and ethnic integration became central to the postcolonial world.

The civil rights movement had enormous significance for the twentieth century, and it galvanized other movements as well. It dramatized as perhaps no other movement could the chasm between the egalitarian promises of American democracy and the real inequalities at the core of the American social and political life—a chasm that could be found in other Western nations as well. African American claims were morally and politically compelling, and the civil rights movement sharpened others' criticisms of what they saw as a complacent, narrowly individualistic, materialist culture.

THE ANTIWAR MOVEMENT

The United States' escalating war in Vietnam became a lightning rod for discontent. In 1961, President John F. Kennedy (1917–1963) promised to "bear any burden" necessary to fight communism and to ensure the victory of American models of representative government and free-market economics in the developing nations. Kennedy's plan entailed massive increases in foreign aid, much of it in weapons. It provided the impetus for

THE WAR IN VIETNAM AND SOUTHEAST ASIA

The 1954 Geneva Accords divided Vietnam at the seventeenth parallel. The north went to Ho Chi Minh, the communist leader, and the south was controlled by Ngo Dinh Diem, an ally of the United States. In 1956, South Vietnam refused to hold the elections mandated in the Geneva Accords. Ho Chi Minh mobilized a guerrilla army, the Viet Cong, and the Vietnam War began. How did the Viet Cong use the proximity of Cambodia and Laos to their strategic advantage? Why did the United States choose to get involved?

humanitarian institutions such as the Peace Corps, intended to improve local conditions and show Americans' benevolence and good intentions. Bearing burdens, however, also meant fighting guerrillas who turned to the Soviets for aid. This involved covert interventions in Latin America, the Congo, and, most important, Vietnam.

By the time of Kennedy's death in 1963, nearly 15,000 American "advisers" were on the ground alongside South Vietnamese troops. Kennedy's successor, Lyndon Johnson, began the strategic bombing of North Vietnam and rapidly drew hundreds of thousands of American troops into combat in South Vietnam. The rebels in the south, known as the Viet Cong, were solidly entrenched, highly experienced guerrilla fighters, and were backed by the professional, well-equipped North Vietnamese army under Ho Chi Minh. The South Vietnamese government resisted efforts at reform, losing popular support. Massive efforts by the United States produced only stalemate, mounting American casualties, and rising discontent.

Vietnam did much to cause the political turmoil of the 1960s in the United States. As Martin Luther King Jr. pointed out, the war—which relied on a disproportionate number of black soldiers to conduct a war against a small nation of color—echoed and magnified racial inequality at home. Exasperated by troubles in the field, American planners continued to escalate military commitments, with no effect. Peace talks in Paris stalled while the death toll on all sides increased. The involuntary draft of young American men expanded and polarized the public. In 1968 criticism forced President Johnson to abandon his plans to run for a second term. Johnson's successor, Richard M. Nixon, who won a narrow victory on the basis of promises to end the war, expanded it instead. Student protests against the war frequently ended in violence. The government brought criminal conspiracy charges against Benjamin Spock, the nation's leading pediatrician, and William Sloane Coffin, the chaplain of Yale University, for encouraging young people to resist the draft. Avoiding the draft became so widespread that the system was changed in 1970. And from other countries' points of view, the Vietnam War became a spectacle: one in which the most powerful, wealthiest nation of the world seemed intent on destroying a land of poor

> The student movement itself can be seen as a consequence of postwar developments: a growing cohort of young people with more time and wealth than in the past; generational consciousness heightened, in part, by the marketing of mass youth culture; and educational institutions unable to deal with rising numbers and expectations.

peasants in the name of anticommunism, democracy, and freedom. The tarnished image of Western values stood at the center of 1960s protest movements in the United States and Western Europe.

THE STUDENT MOVEMENT

The student movement itself can be seen as a consequence of postwar developments: a growing cohort of young people with more time and wealth than in the past; generational consciousness heightened, in part, by the marketing of mass youth culture; and educational institutions unable to deal with rising numbers and expectations. In France, the number of students in high school rose from 400,000 in 1949 to 2 million in 1969; in universities, over the same period, enrollments skyrocketed, from 100,000 to 600,000. The same was true in Italy, Britain, and West Germany. Universities, which had been created to educate a small elite, found both their teaching staffs and their facilities overwhelmed. Lecture halls were packed, university bureaucracies did not respond to requests, and thousands of students took exams at the same time. More philosophically, students raised questions about the role and meaning of elite education in a democratic society and about the relationships among the university as a "knowledge factory," consumer culture, and neocolonial ventures such as the Vietnam War and—for the French—the Algerian wars. Conservative traditions made intellectual reform difficult. In addition, student demands for fewer restrictions on personal life—for instance, permission to have a member of the opposite sex in a dormitory room—provoked authoritarian reactions from university representatives. Waves of student protest were not confined to the United States and Western Europe. They swept across Poland and Czechoslovakia where students protested one-party bureaucratic rule, stifling intellectual life, and authoritarianism, and helped sustain networks of dissidents. By the mid-1960s, simmering anger in Eastern Europe had once again reached a dangerous point.

1968

Nineteen sixty-eight was an extraordinary year, quite similar to 1848 with its wave of revolution (see Chapter

Twenty). It was even more intensely international, a reflection of tightening global ties. International youth culture fostered a sense of collective identity. The new media relayed images of civil rights protest in the United States to Europe, and broadcast news footage of the Vietnam War on television screens from West Virginia to West Germany. The wave of unrest shook both the Eastern and Western blocs. Protest movements assailed bureaucracy and the human costs of the cold war: on the Soviet side, bureaucracy, authoritarianism, and indifference to civilians; on the Western side, bias and monopolies in the news media, the military-industrial complex, and American imperialism. The Soviet regime, as we have seen, responded with repression. In the United States and Western Europe, traditional political parties had little idea what to make of these new movements and those who participated in them. In both cases, events rapidly overwhelmed political systems.

PARIS

The most serious outbreak of student unrest in Europe came in Paris in the spring of 1968. The French Republic had been shaken by conflicts over the Algerian war in the early 1960s. Even more important, the economic boom had undermined the foundations of the regime and de Gaulle's traditional style of rule. French students at the University of Paris demanded reforms that would modernize their university. Protest first peaked at Nanterre, a new branch of the university built on a former air force depot. Nanterre was in a poor and poorly served neighborhood, starved for funds, and overcrowded with students. Petitions, demonstrations, and confrontations with university authorities traveled

The Press Is Poison. Criticizing the official media was central to the politics of May 1968.

quickly from Nanterre to the Sorbonne, in central Paris. In the face of growing disorder, the University of Paris shut down—sending students into the streets and into uglier confrontations with the police. The police reacted with repression and violence, which startled onlookers and television audiences and backfired on the regime. Sympathy with the students' cause expanded rapidly, bringing in other opponents of President de Gaulle's regime. Massive trade-union strikes broke out. Workers in the automobile industry, technical workers, and public-sector employees—from gas and electricity utilities to the mail system to radio and television—went on strike. By mid-May, an astonishing 10 million French workers had walked off their jobs. De Gaulle had no sympathy for the students: "Reform, yes—bed wetting, no," he reportedly declared at the height of the confrontation. At one point, it looked as if the government would fall. The regime, however, was able to satisfy the strikers with wage increases and to appeal to public demand for order. The student movements, isolated, gradually petered out and students agreed to resume university life. The regime did recover, but the events of 1968 helped weaken de Gaulle's position as president and contributed to his retirement from office the following year.

There had been protest and rebelliousness in the 1950s, but the scale of events in 1968 was astonishing. Paris was not the only city to explode in 1968. Student protest broke out in West Berlin, targeting the government's close ties to the autocratic shah of Iran and the power of media corporations. Clashes with the police turned violent. In Italian cities, undergraduates staged several demonstrations to draw attention to university overcrowding. Twenty-six universities were closed. The London School of Economics was nearly shut down by protest. In Mexico City a confrontation with the police ended with the deaths of hundreds of protesters, most of them students—on the eve of the 1968 Olympics, hosted by the Mexican government. Those Olympics reflected the political contests of the period: African nations threatened to boycott if South Africa, with its apartheid regime, participated. Two African American medalists raised their hands in a black power salute during an awards ceremony—and the Olympic Committee promptly sent them home. In Vietnam, the Viet Cong defied American claims to have turned the tide by launching a new offensive. The Tet offensive, named for the Vietnamese new year, brought the highest casualty rates to date in the Vietnam War and an explosion of protest. Antiwar demonstrations and student rebellions spread across the country. President Johnson, battered by the effects of Tet and already worn down by

1960s POLITICS: THE SITUATIONISTS

In 1957, a small group of European artists and writers formed a group called the Situationist International. The movement combined the artistic traditions of dada and surrealism with anarchism and Marxism. Unlike traditional Marxists, the situationists did not focus on the workplace. Instead they developed a broad critique of everyday life, protesting the stifling of art, creativity, and imagination in contemporary society. They denounced the "tyranny" of consumer culture, which constantly invented new needs and desires to fuel consumption. Capitalism, they said, had "colonized" everyday life. The situationists' ideas and especially their unorthodox, surrealist style, became influential during the events of May 1968 in France. All around Paris students painted situationist slogans such as those printed here.

The social movements of 1968 cut across cold war boundaries, attacking Western consumerism as well as Soviet authoritarianism. A group of students and situationists sent a telegram (second excerpt) to the Politburo of the Communist Party of the Soviet Union in May 1968.

SITUATIONIST ANTICAPITALISM, 1968

OCCUPY THE FACTORIES

POWER TO THE WORKERS COUNCILS

ABOLISH CLASS SOCIETY

DOWN WITH THE
SPECTACLE-COMMODITY SOCIETY

ABOLISH ALIENATION

ABOLISH THE UNIVERSITY

HUMANITY WON'T BE HAPPY TILL THE
LAST BUREAUCRAT IS HUNG WITH THE GUTS
OF THE LAST CAPITALIST

DEATH TO THE COPS

FREE ALSO THE 4 GUYS CONVICTED FOR
LOOTING DURING THE 6 MAY RIOT

—OCCUPATION COMMITTEE OF THE
AUTONOMOUS AND POPULAR
SORBONNE UNIVERSITY

SITUATIONIST ANTICOMMUNIST SLOGANS, 1968

17 MAY 1968 / To the Politburo of the Communist party of the USSR the Kremlin Moscow / Shake in your shoes bureaucrats. The international power of the workers councils will soon wipe you out. Humanity won't be happy till the last bureaucrat is hung with the guts of the last capitalist. Long live the struggle of the Kronstadt sailors and of the Makhnovshchina against Trostky and Lenin. Long live the 1956 Councilist insurrection of Budapest • Down with the state • Long live revolutionary Marxism. Occupation committee of the Autonomous and Popular Sorbonne

"Slogans to Be Spread Now by Every Means," in *Situationist International Anthology,* ed. and trans. Ken Knabb (Berkeley, Calif., 1981), pp. 334–345.

QUESTIONS FOR ANALYSIS

1. Are there any common themes in these sets of slogans?
2. Why has 1968 often been called "the year of the barricades"?

Anti-government protests in Mexico City, 1968.

often the case, party members were divided between proponents of reform and those fearful that reform would unleash revolution. The reformers, however, also gained support from outside the party, from student organizations, the press, and networks of dissidents. As in Western Europe and the United States, the protest movement overflowed traditional party politics.

In the Soviet Union, Khrushchev had fallen in 1964, and the reins of Soviet power passed to Leonid Brezhnev as secretary of the Communist Party. Brezhnev was more conservative than Khrushchev, less inclined to bargain with the West, and prone to defensive actions to safeguard the Soviet sphere of influence. Initially, the Soviets tolerated Dubček as a political eccentric. The events of 1968 raised their fears. Most Eastern European communist leaders denounced Czech reformism, but student demonstrations of support broke out in Poland and Yugoslavia, calling for an end to one-party rule, less censorship, and reform of the judicial system. In addition, Josip Broz Tito of Yugoslavia and Nicolae Ceausescu (*chow-SHEHS-koo*) of Romania —two of the more stubbornly independent communists in Eastern Europe—visited Dubček. To Soviet eyes these activities looked as if they were directed against the Warsaw Pact and Soviet security; they also saw American intervention in Vietnam as evidence of heightened anticommunist activities around the world. When Dubček attempted to democratize the Communist Party and did not attend a meeting of members of the Warsaw Pact, the Soviets sent tanks and troops into Prague in August 1968. Again the world watched as streams of Czech refugees left the country and a repressive government, picked by Soviet security forces, took charge. Dubček and his allies were subjected to imprisonment or "internal exile." Twenty percent of the members of the Czech Communist Party

the war, chose not to run for reelection. The year 1968 also saw damage and trauma for the country's political future, because of the assassinations of Martin Luther King Jr. (April 4, 1968) and presidential candidate Robert F. Kennedy (June 5, 1968). King's assassination was followed by a wave of rioting in more than fifty cities across the United States, followed in late summer by street battles between police and student protesters at the Democratic National Convention in Chicago. Some saw the flowering of protest as another "springtime of peoples." Others saw it as a long nightmare.

PRAGUE

The student movement in the United States and Western Europe also took inspiration from one of the most significant challenges to Soviet authority since the Hungarian revolt of 1956 (see Chapter Twenty-Seven): the "Prague spring" of 1968. The events began with the emergence of a liberal communist government in Czechoslovakia, led by the Slovak Alexander Dubček (*DOOB-chehk*). Dubček had outmaneuvered the more traditional, authoritarian party leaders. He advocated "socialism with a human face"; he encouraged debate within the party, academic and artistic freedom, and less censorship. As was

> When Dubček attempted to democratize the Communist Party and did not attend a meeting of members of the Warsaw Pact, the Soviets sent tanks and troops into Prague in August 1968.

LUDVÍK VACULÍK, "TWO THOUSAND WORDS" (1968)

During the Prague spring of 1968, a group of Czech intellectuals published a document titled "Two Thousand Words That Belong to Workers, Farmers, Officials, Scientists, Artists, and Everybody" that has become known simply as the "Two Thousand Words." This manifesto called for further reform, including increased freedom of the press. Seen as a direct affront by Moscow, the manifesto heightened Soviet-Czech tensions. In August 1968, Warsaw Pact tanks rolled into Prague, overthrowing the reformist government of Alexander Dubček.

Most of the nation welcomed the socialist program with high hopes. But it fell into the hands of the wrong people. It would not have mattered so much that they lacked adequate experience in affairs of state, factual knowledge, or philosophical education, if only they had enough common prudence and decency to listen to the opinion of others and agree to being gradually replaced by more able people. . . .

The chief sin and deception of these rulers was to have explained their own whims as the "will of the workers." Were we to accept this pretense, we would have to blame the workers today for the decline of our economy, for crimes committed against the innocent, and for the introduction of censorship to prevent anyone writing about these things. The workers would be to blame for misconceived investments, for losses suffered in foreign trade, and for the housing shortage. Obviously no sensible person will hold the working class responsible for such things. We all know, and every worker knows especially, that they had virtually no say in deciding anything. . . .

Since the beginning of this year we have been experiencing a regenerative process of democratization. . . .

Let us demand the departure of people who abused their power, damaged public property, and acted dishonorably or brutally. Ways must be found to compel them to resign. To mention a few: public criticism, resolutions, demonstrations, demonstrative work brigades, collections to buy presents for them on their retirement, strikes, and picketing at their front doors. But we should reject any illegal, indecent, or boorish methods. . . . Let us convert the district and local newspapers, which have mostly degenerated to the level of official mouthpieces, into a platform for all the forward-looking elements in politics; let us demand that editorial boards be formed of National Front representatives, or else let us start new papers. Let us form committees for the defense of free speech. . . .

There has been great alarm recently over the possibility that foreign forces will intervene in our development. Whatever superior forces may face us, all we can do is stick to our own positions, behave decently, and initiate nothing ourselves. We can show our government that we will stand by it, with weapons if need be, if it will do what we give it a mandate to do. . . .

The spring is over and will never return. By winter we will know all.

Jaromir Navratil, *The Prague Spring 1968*, trans. Mark Kramer, Joy Moss, and Ruth Tosek (Budapest, 1998), pp. 177–181.

QUESTIONS FOR ANALYSIS

1. Where, according to the authors of this document, did socialism go wrong?
2. What specific reforms do they demand?

A Russian tank attacked during the Prague Spring, 1968.

were expelled in a series of purges. After the destruction of the Prague spring, Soviet diplomats consolidated their position according to the new Brezhnev Doctrine. The doctrine stated that no socialist state could adopt policies endangering the interests of international socialism, and that the Soviet Union could intervene in the domestic affairs of any Soviet bloc nation if communist rule was threatened. In other words, the repressive rules applied to Hungary in 1956 would not change.

What were the effects of 1968? De Gaulle's government recovered. The Republican Richard M. Nixon won the U.S. election of 1968. From 1972 to 1975 the United States withdrew from Vietnam; in the wake of that war came a refugee crisis and a new series of horrific regional conflicts. In Prague, Warsaw Pact tanks put down the uprising, and in the Brezhnev Doctrine the Soviet regime reasserted its right to control its satellites. Serious cold war confrontations rippled along Czechoslovakia's western border as refugees fled west, and in the Korean peninsula after North Korea's seizure of an eavesdropping ship from the U.S. Navy. Over the long term, however, the protesters' and dissidents' demands

> In Eastern Europe and the Soviet Union, dissent was defeated but not eliminated. The crushing of the Czech rebellion proved thoroughly disillusioning, and in important respects the events of 1968 prefigured the collapse of Soviet control in 1989.

proved more difficult to contain. In Eastern Europe and the Soviet Union, dissent was defeated but not eliminated. The crushing of the Czech rebellion proved thoroughly disillusioning, and in important respects the events of 1968 prefigured the collapse of Soviet control in 1989. In Western Europe and the United States, the student movement subsided but its issues and the kinds of politics that it pioneered proved more enduring. Feminism (or, more accurately, second-wave feminism) really came into its own after 1968, its numbers expanded by women a generation younger than Simone de Beauvoir and Betty Friedan. They had been in student political organizations in the 1960s and their impatience with traditional political parties and, often, their male student allies, sent them into separate groups, where they championed equality in sexual relationships and in the family. In a phrase that captured some of the changes of the 1950s and 1960s, they insisted that "the personal is political." As one English woman said, "We wanted to redefine the meaning of politics to include an analysis of our daily lives," which meant sexuality, health, child care, cultural images of women, and so on. The antiwar movement took up the issue of nuclear weapons—a particularly volatile issue in Europe. Finally, the environmental movement took hold—concerned not only with pollution and the world's dwindling resources but also with mushrooming urbanization and the kind of unrestrained economic growth that had given rise to the 1960s. Over the long term, in both Europe and the United States, voters' loyalties to traditional political parties became less reliable and smaller parties multiplied; in this way, new social movements eventually became part of a very different political landscape.

ECONOMIC STAGNATION: THE PRICE OF SUCCESS

What caused the economic stagnation of the 1970s and 1980s?

Economic as well as social problems plagued Europe during the 1970s and 1980s, but these problems had begun earlier. By the middle of the 1960s, for example, the West German growth rate had slowed. Demand for manufactured goods fell, and in 1966 the country suffered its first postwar recession. Volkswagen, the symbol of the German miracle, introduced a shortened work week; almost 700,000 West Germans were thrown out of work altogether. In France a persistent housing shortage increased the cost of living. Though new industries continued to prosper, the basic industries—coal, steel, and railways—began to run up deficits. Unemployment was rising in tandem with prices. Prime Minister Harold Wilson's pledge to revive Britain's economy by introducing new technology foundered on crises in the foreign-exchange value of the pound, which were compounded by continued low levels of growth. The Common Market—expanded in 1973 to include Britain, Ireland, and Denmark, and again in the early 1980s to admit Greece, Spain, and Portugal—struggled to overcome problems stemming from the conflict between the domestic economic regulations characteristic of many European states and the free-market policies that prevailed within what would become the European Economic Community (EEC) countries.

Oil prices spiked for the first time in the early 1970s, compounding these difficulties. In 1973, the Arab-dominated Organization of Petroleum Exporting Countries (OPEC) instituted an oil embargo against the Western powers. In 1973, a barrel of oil cost $1.73; in 1975, it cost $10.46; by the early 1980s, the price had risen to over $30. This increase produced an inflationary spiral; interest rates rose and with them the price of almost everything else Western consumers were used to buying. Rising costs produced wage demands and strikes. The calm industrial relations of the 1950s and early 1960s were a thing of the past. At the same time, European manufacturers encountered serious competition, not only from such highly developed countries as Japan but also from the increasingly active economies of Asia and Africa, in which the West had invested capital eagerly in the previous decades. By 1980 Japan had captured 10 percent of the automobile market in West Germany and 25 percent in Belgium. In 1984, unemployment in Western Europe reached about 19 million. The lean years had arrived.

Economies in the Soviet bloc also stalled. The expansion of heavy industry had helped recovery in the postwar period, but by the 1970s, those sectors no longer provided growth or innovation. The Soviet Communist Party proclaimed in 1961 that by 1970 the USSR would exceed the United States in per capita production. By the end of the 1970s, however, Soviet per capita production was not much higher than in the less industrialized countries of southern Europe. The Soviets were also overcommitted to military defense industries that had become inefficient, though lucrative for the party members who ran them. The Soviet economy did get a boost from the OPEC oil price hikes of 1973 and 1979. (OPEC was founded in 1961; the Soviet Union did not belong, but as the world's largest producer of oil, it benefited from rising prices.) Without this boost, the situation would have been far grimmer.

Following an impressive economic performance during the early 1970s, the Eastern European nations encountered serious financial difficulties. Their success had rested in part on capital borrowed from the West. By 1980 those debts weighed heavily on their national economies. Poland's hard-currency indebtedness to Western countries, for example, was almost four times greater than its annual exports. The solution to this problem, attempted in Poland and elsewhere, was to cut back on production for domestic consumption in order to increase exports. Yet this policy encountered strong popular opposition. Although there was virtually no unemployment in Eastern Europe, men and women were by no means happy with their economic situation. Working hours were longer than in Western Europe, and goods and services, even in prosperous times, were scarce.

Unemployment Demonstration, 1974. A crowd of workers in Rome, Italy, gathered to protest inflation and unemployment, in a strike that lasted twenty-four hours.

Western governments struggled for effective reactions to the abrupt change in their economic circumstances. The new leader of the British Conservative Party, Margaret Thatcher, was elected prime minister in 1979—and reelected in 1983 and 1987—on a program of curbing trade-union power, cutting taxes to stimulate the economy, and privatizing publicly owned enterprises. The economy remained weak, with close to 15 percent of the workforce unemployed by 1986. In West Germany, a series of Social Democratic governments attempted to combat economic recession with job-training programs and tax incentives, both financed by higher taxes. These programs did little to assist economic recovery, and the country shifted to the right.

The fact that governments of right and left were unable to recreate Europe's unprecedented postwar prosperity suggests the degree to which economic forces remain outside the control of individual states. The continuing economic malaise renewed efforts to Europeanize common problems. By the end of the 1980s, the EEC embarked on an ambitious program of integration. Long-term goals, agreed on when the EU (European Union) was formed in 1991, included a monetary union—with a central European bank and a single currency—and unified social policies to reduce poverty and unemployment. As the twenty-first century opened, the European member states had begun to institute several of these steps. It remained unclear whether that new European "federal" state would over-

C H R O N O L O G Y

**DEVELOPMENT OF THE EUROPEAN
ECONOMIC COMMUNITY**

European coal and steel community founded	1951
Rome treaty forms EEC	1957
European community expanded	1985
Treaty of Maastricht creates European union	1991

come its members' claims of national sovereignty or whether it would develop the economic and political strength to counter the global domination of the United States.

SOLIDARITY IN POLAND

In 1980, unrest again peaked in Eastern Europe, this time with the Polish labor movement Solidarity. Polish workers organized strikes that brought the government of the country to a standstill. The workers formulated several key demands. First, they objected to working conditions imposed by the government to combat a severe economic crisis. Second, they protested high prices and, especially shortages, both of which had roots in government policy and priorities. Above all, though, the Polish workers in Solidarity demanded truly independent labor unions instead of labor organizations sponsored by the government. Their belief that society had the right to organize itself and, by implication, create its own government, stood at the core of the movement. The strikers were led by an electrician from the Gdansk shipyards, Lech Walesa. Walesa's charismatic personality appealed not only to the Polish citizenry but to sympathizers in the West. Again, however, the Soviets assisted a military regime in reimposing authoritarian rule. The Polish president, General Wojciech Jaruzelski, had learned from Hungary and Czechoslovakia and played a delicate game of diplomacy to maintain the Polish government's freedom of action while repressing Solidarity itself. But the implied Soviet threat remained.

EUROPE RECAST: THE COLLAPSE OF COMMUNISM AND THE END OF THE SOVIET UNION

What caused the collapse of communism?

One of history's fascinations is its unpredictability. There has been no more telling example of this in recent times than the sudden collapse of the Eastern European communist regimes in 1989, the dramatic end to the cold war, and the subsequent disintegration of the once-powerful Soviet Union.

GORBACHEV AND SOVIET REFORM

This sudden collapse flowed, unintended, from a new wave of reform begun in the mid-1980s. In 1985 a new generation of officials began taking charge of the Soviet Communist Party, a change heralded by Mikhail Gorbachev's appointment to the party leadership. In his mid-fifties, Gorbachev was significantly younger than his immediate predecessors and less prey to the habits of mind that had shaped Soviet domestic and foreign affairs. He was frankly critical of the repressive aspects of communist society as well as its sluggish economy, and he did not hesitate to voice those criticisms openly. His twin policies of *glasnost* (intellectual openness) and *perestroika* (economic restructuring) held out hope for a freer, more prosperous Soviet Union. Under Gorbachev, a number of imprisoned dissidents were freed, among them Andrei Sakharov, the scientist known as the "father of the Soviet hydrogen bomb," and later a fierce critic of the cold war arms race.

The policies of perestroika took aim at the privileges of the political elite and the immobility of the state bureaucracy by instituting competitive elections to official positions and limiting terms of office. Gorbachev's program of perestroika called for a shift from the centrally planned economy instituted by Stalin to a mixed economy combining planning with the operation of market forces. In agriculture, perestroika accelerated the move away from cooperative production and instituted incentives for the achievement of production targets. Gorbachev planned to integrate the Soviet Union into the international economy by participating in organizations such as the International Monetary Fund.

Even these dramatic reforms, however, were too little too late. Ethnic unrest, a legacy of Russia's nineteenth-century imperialism, threatened to split the Soviet Union apart, while secession movements gathered steam in the Baltic republics and elsewhere. From 1988 onward, fighting between Armenians and Azerbaijanis over an ethnically Azerbaijani region located inside Armenia threatened to escalate into a border dispute with Iran. Only Soviet troops patrolling the border and Gorbachev's willingness to suppress a separatist revolt in Azerbaijan by force temporarily quelled the conflict.

Spurred on by these events in the Soviet Union, the countries of Eastern Europe began to agitate for independence from Moscow. Gorbachev encouraged open discussion—glasnost—not only in his own country but also in the satellite nations. He revoked the Brezhnev Doctrine's insistence on single-party socialist governments

Gorbachev in Poland at the Height of his Power in 1986.
Perestroika aimed at the privileges of the political elite
and would eventually lead to his fall from power.

and made frequent and inspiring trips to the capitals of
neighboring satellites.

Glasnost rekindled the flame of opposition in
Poland, where Solidarity had been defeated but not
destroyed by the government in 1981. In 1988 the
union launched a new series of strikes. These disturbances culminated in an agreement between the government and Solidarity that legalized the union and
promised open elections. The results, in June 1989, astonished the world: virtually all of the government's
candidates lost; the Citizen's Committee, affiliated
with Solidarity, won a sizable majority in the Polish
parliament.

In Hungary and Czechoslovakia, events followed a
similar course during 1988 and 1989. Janos Kadar, the
Hungarian leader since the Soviet crackdown of 1956,
resigned in the face of continuing demonstrations in
May 1988 and was replaced by the reformist government of the Hungarian Socialist Workers' Party. By the
spring of 1989 the Hungarian regime had been purged
of Communist Party supporters. The government also
began to dismantle its security fences along the Austrian border. A year later the Hungarian Democratic
Forum, pledging it would reinstate full civil rights and

restructure the economy, secured a plurality of seats in
the National Assembly.

The Czechs, too, staged demonstrations against Soviet domination in late 1988. Brutal beatings of student
demonstrators by the police in 1989 radicalized the
nations' workers and provoked mass demonstrations.
Civic Forum, an opposition coalition, called for the installation of a coalition government to include non-
communists, for free elections, and for the resignation
of the country's communist leadership. It reinforced its
demands with continuing mass demonstrations and
threats of a general strike that resulted in the toppling
of the old regime and the election of the playwright
and Civic Forum leader Václav Havel as president.

FALL OF THE BERLIN WALL

The most significant political change in Eastern Europe
during the late 1980s was the collapse of communism in
East Germany and the unification of East and West Germany. Although long considered the most prosperous
of the Soviet satellite countries, East Germany suffered
from severe economic stagnation and environmental
degradation. Waves of East Germans registered their
discontent with worsening conditions by massive illegal
emigration to the West. This exodus combined with
evidence of widespread official corruption to force the
resignation of East Germany's long-time, hard-line premier, Erich Honecker. His successor, Egon Krenz,
promised reforms, but he was nevertheless faced with
continuing protests and continuing mass emigration.

On November 4, 1989, the government, in a move
that acknowledged its powerlessness to hold its citizens
captive, opened its border with Czechoslovakia. This
move effectively freed East Germans to travel to the
West. In a matter of days, the Berlin Wall—the embodi-
ment of the cold war, the Iron Curtain, and the division
of East from West—was demolished by groups of ordinary citizens. Jubilant throngs from both sides walked
through the gaping holes that now permitted men,
women, and children to take the few steps that symbolized the return to freedom and a chance for national
unity. Free elections were held throughout Germany in
March 1990, resulting in a victory for the Alliance for
Germany, a coalition allied with the West German
chancellor Helmut Kohl's Christian Democratic Union.
With heavy emigration continuing, reunification talks
quickly culminated in the formal proclamation of a
united Germany on October 3, 1990.

The public mood, in Eastern Europe and perhaps
worldwide, was swept up with the jubilation of these

peaceful "velvet revolutions" during the autumn of 1989. Yet the end of one-party rule in Eastern Europe was not accomplished without violence. The single most repressive government in the old Eastern bloc, Nicolae Ceaucescu's outright dictatorship in Romania, came apart with much more bloodshed. By December, faced with the wave of popular revolts in surrounding countries and riots by the ethnic Hungarian minority in Transylvania, a number of party officials and army officers in Romania tried to hold on to their own positions by deposing Ceaucescu. His extensive secret police, however, organized resistance to the coup; the result was nearly two weeks of bloody street fighting in the capital Bucharest. Individual snipers loyal to Ceaucescu were still killing passing civilians from rooftops, forcing dangerous efforts to root them out, while the rest of Eastern Europe celebrated Christmas and the new year with new political systems. Ceaucescu himself and his wife were seized by populist army units and executed; images of their bloodstained bodies flashed worldwide by satellite television.

Throughout the rest of Eastern Europe, single-party governments in the countries behind what was left of the tattered Iron Curtain—Albania, Bulgaria, and Yugoslavia—collapsed in the face of democratic pressure for change. Meanwhile, in the Soviet Union itself, inspired by events in Eastern Europe, the Baltic republics of Lithuania and Latvia strained to free themselves from Soviet rule. In 1990 they unilaterally proclaimed their independence from the Soviet Union, throwing into sharp relief the tension between "union" and "republics." Gorbachev reacted with an uncertain mixture of armed intervention and promises of greater local autonomy. In the fall of 1991 Lithuania and Latvia, along with the third Baltic state of Estonia, won international recognition as independent republics.

THE COLLAPSE OF THE SOVIET UNION

While Soviet influence eroded in Eastern Europe, at home the unproductive Soviet economy continued to fuel widespread ire. With the failure of perestroika—largely the result of a lack of resources and an inability to increase production—came the rise of a powerful political rival to Gorbachev, his erstwhile ally Boris Yeltsin. The reforming mayor of Moscow, Yeltsin was elected president of the Russian Federation—the largest Soviet republic—on an anti-Gorbachev platform in 1990. Pressure from the Yeltsin camp weakened Gorbachev's ability to maneuver independent of reactionary factions in the Politburo and the military, undermining his reform program and his ability to remain in power.

The Soviet Union's increasingly severe domestic problems led to mounting protests in 1991, when Gorbachev's policies failed to improve—indeed diminished—the living standard of the Soviet people. Demands increased that the bloated government bureaucracy respond with a dramatic cure for the country's continuing economic stagnation. Gorbachev appeared to lose his political nerve, having first ordered and then canceled a radical "five-hundred-day" economic reform plan, at the same time agreeing to negotiations with the increasingly disaffected republics within the union, now clamoring for independence. Sensing their political lives to be in jeopardy, a group of highly placed hard-line Communist Party officials staged an abortive coup in August 1991. They made Gorbachev and his wife prisoners in their summer villa, then declared a return to party-line orthodoxy in an effort to salvage what remained of the Soviet Union's global leverage and the Communist Party's domestic power. The Soviet citizenry, especially in large cities like Moscow and Leningrad, defied their self-proclaimed saviors.

Reagan at the Berlin Wall.

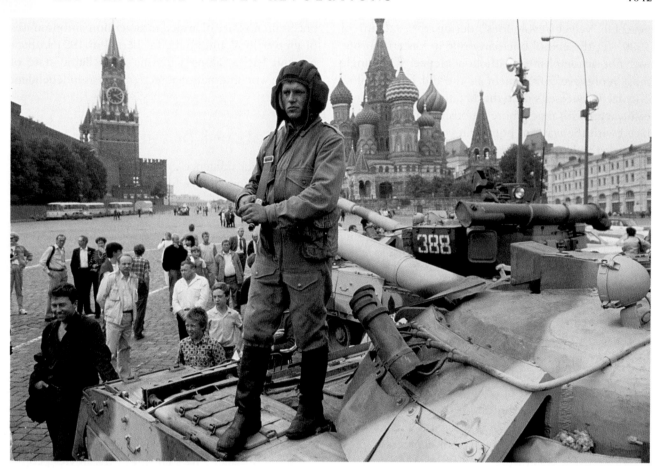

Russian tanks in Red Square near the Kremlin.

Led by Boris Yeltsin, who at one point mounted a tank in a Moscow street to rally the people, they gathered support among the Soviet republics and the military and successfully called the plotters' bluff. Within two weeks, Gorbachev was back in power and the coup leaders were in prison.

Ironically, this people's counterrevolution returned Gorbachev to office while destroying the power of the Soviet state he led. Throughout the fall of 1991, as Gorbachev struggled to hold the union together, Yeltsin joined the presidents of the other large republics to capitalize on the discontent. On December 8, 1991, the presidents of the republics of Russia, Ukraine, and Byelorussia (now called Belarus) declared that the Soviet Union was no more: "The USSR as a subject of international law and geopolitical reality is ceasing to exist." Though the prose was flat, the message was momentous. The once-mighty Soviet Union, founded seventy-five years before in a burst of revolutionary fervor and violence, had evaporated nearly overnight, leaving in its wake a collection of eleven far from powerful nations loosely joined together as the Commonwealth of Independent States. On December 25, 1991, Gorbachev resigned and left political life, not pushed from office in the usual way but made irrelevant as other actors dismantled the state. The Soviet flag—the hammer and sickle symbolizing the nation that for fifty years had kept half of Europe in thrall—was lowered for the last time over the Kremlin.

The mighty fall left mighty problems in its wake. Food shortages worsened during the winter of 1992. The value of the ruble plummeted. The republics could not agree on common military policies or resolve difficult and dangerous questions concerning the control of nuclear warheads. Yeltsin's pleas for economic assistance from the West resulted in massive infusions of private and public capital, which nevertheless failed to prevent serious economic hardship and dislocation. Free enterprise brought with it unemployment and encouraged profi-

> Throughout the fall of 1991, as Gorbachev struggled to hold the union together, Yeltsin joined the presidents of the other large republics to capitalize on the discontent.

teering through crime. Yeltsin's determination to press ahead with his economic program met with stiff resistance from a parliament and citizenry alarmed by the ruthlessness and rapidity of the change they were experiencing. When the parliament balked at Yeltsin's proposals in September 1993, he dissolved it. This helped provoke an attempted coup two months later, staged by conservative politicians and army officers. Officials loyal to Yeltsin put the revolt down with far more force than the 1991 coup attempt—television viewers worldwide watched artillery shells slam into the rebel-occupied parliament building in Moscow during a bloody shootout. When the parliament was restored, elections in 1995 served as a benchmark of discontent: the resurgent communists claimed roughly one third of the seats, while xenophobic nationalists led by Vladimir Zhirinovsky also took a notable bloc of the vote, thanks to the steady blame he heaped on the West for Russia's troubles.

Meanwhile, ethnic and religious conflict plagued the republics. In the first years after the dissolution of the Soviet Union, warfare flared in Georgia, Armenia, and Azerbaijan. The most serious conflict arose in the predominantly Muslim area of Chechnya, bordering Georgia in the Caucasus, which had declared its independence from Russia in late 1991. The Chechen rebels were heirs to a tradition of banditry and separatism against Russian authority that stretched into the nineteenth century. In 1994 the Russian government, weary of this continuing challenge to its authority, launched a concerted effort to quash resistance. As Russian forces moved into the Chechen capital, Grozny, they were ambushed with firepower largely stolen from disused Russian armories. The result was a massacre of the invading Russians, followed by a long and bloody siege to take the city. This in turn fueled a long and particularly bloody guerrilla war between Russian and Chechen forces, marked by repeated atrocities on both sides. After brief pauses in 1995 and 1997, this Chechen war dragged on into the new century, echoing Russia's conflict in Afghanistan (see Chapter Twenty-Seven) on a scale that was both bloodier and closer to home.

The Iron Curtain had established one of the most rigid borders in European history. The collapse of the Soviet Union opened up both Russia and its former imperial dominions. That transformation brought the cold war to an end. It also created a host of unforeseen problems throughout Eastern Europe and the advanced industrial world: ethnic conflict, diplomatic uncertainty about the new Russian government, and single superpower domination, sometimes called American

unilateralism. Within the Russian and several of the former Soviet republics there emerged a new era that some called the Russian "Wild West." Capitalist market relations began to develop without clearly defined property relations or a stable legal framework. Former government officials profited from their positions of power to take over whole sectors of the economy. Corruption ran rampant. Organized crime controlled industries, stock exchanges, a thriving trade in illegal drugs, and even some local governments. Even the most energetic central governments in the large republics such as Russia, Ukraine, and Kazakhstan found themselves faced with enormous problems. Post-Soviet openness could lay the groundwork for a new democratic Russia; it could also set in motion the resurgence of older forms of tyranny.

POSTREVOLUTIONARY TROUBLES: EASTERN EUROPE AFTER 1989

The velvet revolutions of Central and Eastern Europe raised high hopes: local hopes that an end to authoritarian government would produce economic prosperity and cultural pluralism, and Western hopes that these countries would join them as capitalist partners in an enlarged European Community. The reality was slower and harder than the optimists of 1989 foresaw. The largest struggle, one with continuing implications for the European continent, has been the reunification of Germany. The euphoria of reunification masked uncertainty even among Germans themselves. The foundering East German economy has remained a problem. Piled onto other economic difficulties in the former West Germany during the 1990s, it has produced much resentment of the need to "rescue" the east. What the writer Günter Grass described as the "wall in the mind" still divided the countries. Though there has been great progress in integrating elections and the bureaucracies of the two German states, economic and cultural unity has been much harder to come by.

Adapting to change has been difficult throughout eastern Europe. Attempts to create free-market economies have brought inflation, unemployment, and—in their wake—anticapitalist demonstrations. Inefficient industries, a workforce resistant to change, energy shortages, lack of venture capital, and a severely polluted environment have combined to hinder progress and dash hopes. Uprisings in Bulgaria and Albania in early 1997 were fueled by the inability of those governments to resolve basic economic and social problems. In addition, racial and ethnic conflicts have continued to divide newly liberated democracies, recalling the divisions that led to World War I and that have plagued Eastern Europe throughout its history. Minorities waged campaigns for autonomous rights or outright secession that often descended into violence.

Czechoslovakia's velvet revolution collapsed into a velvet divorce, as Slovakia declared itself independent from the Czechs, forcing Havel's resignation and slowing down the promising cultural and economic reforms begun in 1989. Poland enjoyed an upswing in its economy during the 1990s, after many years of hardship, but most of the rest of Eastern Europe continues to find transformation rough going. These difficulties have been accompanied by revived ethnic tensions formerly suppressed by centralized communist governments. There has been violence against non-European immigrants throughout Eastern Europe, against gypsies (Romani) in the Czech Republic and Hungary, and against ethnic Hungarians in Romania.

The most extreme example of these conflicts came with the implosion of the state of Yugoslavia. After the death of Tito in 1980 the government that had held Yugoslavia's federalist ethnic patchwork together came undone. The 1960s and 1970s brought uneven economic growth, benefiting the capital, Belgrade, and the provinces of Croatia and Slovenia the most; but heavy industrial areas in Serbia, Bosnia-Hercegovina, and the tiny district of Kosovo began to lag far behind. A number of Serb politicians, most notably Slobodan Milosevic, began to redirect Serbs' frustration with economic hardship toward subjects of national pride and sovereignty.

Nationalism, particularly Serb and Croat nationalism, had long dogged Yugoslavia's firmly federal political system. Feelings ran especially deep among Serbs. Serbian national myths reach back to the Middle Ages, the country also has more recent traditions of political separatism on ethnic grounds. Milosevic and the Serb nationalists who gathered around him ignited those political flashpoints in ways that caught the fears and frustrations of his times. More important for Milosevic, it catapulted him into crucial positions of authority. In these posts, he alienated representatives from the non-Serb republics. Inspired by the peaceful transformations of 1989, representatives of the small

province of Slovenia declared they had been denied adequate representation and economic support inside the republic. In 1991, on a tide of nationalism and reform, the Slovenes seceded from Yugoslavia. After a brief attempt to hold the union together by force, the Yugoslav government relented and let Slovenia claim its independence. Ethnic nationalists in the other republics followed suit. A much deeper, bloodier process of disintegration had begun.

The large republic of Croatia, once part of the Habsburg Empire and briefly an independent state allied with the Nazis during World War II, cited injustices by Serb officials in the Yugoslav government and declared independence as a free, capitalist state. War broke out between federal Yugoslav forces and the well-armed militias of independent Croatia, a conflict that ended in arbitration by the United Nations. The religious nature of the conflict—between Catholic Croats and Orthodox Serbs—and the legacies of fighting in World War II produced violence on both sides. Towns and villages where Serbs and Croats had lived together since the 1940s were torn apart as each ethnic group rounded up and massacred members of the other.

The next conflict came in the same place that in 1914 had sparked a much larger war: the province of Bosnia-Hercegovina. Bosnia was the most ethnically diverse republic in Yugoslavia. Its capital, Sarajevo, was home to several major ethnic groups and had often been praised as an example of peaceful coexistence. When Bosnia seceded from Yugoslavia in 1992, ethnic coexistence came apart. Bosnia began the war with no formal army: armed bands equipped by the governments of Serbian Yugoslavia, Croatia, and Bosnia battled each other throughout the new country. The Serbs and Croats, both of whom disliked the Muslim Bosnians, were especially well equipped and organized. They rained shells and bullets on towns and villages, burned houses with families inside, imprisoned Muslim men in detention camps and starved them to death, and raped thousands of Bosnian women. All sides committed atrocities. The Serbs, however, orchestrated and carried out the worst crimes. These included what came to be called ethnic cleansing. This involved sending irregular troops on campaigns of murder and terror through Muslim or Croat territories to encourage much larger populations to flee the area. During the first eighteen months of the

Bosnia was the most ethnically diverse republic in Yugoslavia. Its capital, Sarajevo, was home to several major ethnic groups and had often been praised as an example of peaceful coexistence. When Bosnia seceded from Yugoslavia in 1992, ethnic coexistence came apart.

Legend:
- ✴ Sites of popular demonstrations
- ✪ Capital cities

EASTERN EUROPE IN 1989

What political changes in the Soviet Union allowed for the spread of demonstrations throughout Eastern Europe? Why did the first political upheavals of 1989 occur in Poland and East Germany?

fighting as many as 100,000 people were killed, including 80,000 civilians, mostly Bosnian Muslims. Although the campaigns appalled Western governments, those countries worried that intervention would result only in another Vietnam or Afghanistan with no clear resolution of the horrific ethnic slaughter itself. The outside forces, mostly European troops in United Nations blue helmets, concentrated on humanitarian relief, separating combatants, and creating safe areas for persecuted ethnic populations from all parties.

Mass Funeral in Kosovo, 1999. Ethnic Albanians bury victims of a Serbian massacre toward the end of Yugoslavia's ten years of fighting.

The crisis came to a head in the autumn of 1995. Sarajevo had been under siege for three years, but a series of mortar attacks on public marketplaces in Sarajevo produced fresh Western outrage and moved the United States to act. Already Croat forces and the Bosnian army had turned the war on the ground against the Serb militias, and now they were supported by a rolling wave of American air strikes. The American bombing, combined with a Croat-Bosnian offensive, forced the Bosnian Serbs to negotiate. Elite French troops supported by British artillery broke the siege of Sarajevo. Peace talks were held at Dayton, Ohio. The agreement divided Bosnia, with the majority of land in the hands of Muslims and Croats, and a small, autonomous "Serb Republic" in areas that included land ethnically cleansed in 1992. Stability was restored, but three years of war had killed over 200,000 people.

The legacy of Bosnia flared into conflict again over Kosovo, the medieval homeland of the Orthodox Christian Serbs, now occupied by a largely Albanian, Muslim population. Milosevic accused the Albanians of plotting secession and of challenging the Serb presence in Kosovo. In the name of a "greater Serbia," Serb soldiers fought Albanian separatists rallying under the banner of "greater Albania." Both sides used terrorist tactics. Western nations were anxious lest the conflict

might spread to the strategic, ethnically divided country of Macedonia and touch off a general Balkan conflict. Western political opinion was outraged, however, as Serbian forces used many of the same murderous tactics in Kosovo that they had employed earlier in Bosnia. Talks between Milosevic's government and the Albanian rebels were sponsored by the NATO powers but fell apart in early 1999. That failure was followed by a fresh wave of American-led bombing against Serbia itself, as well as against Serbian forces in Kosovo. A new round of ethnic cleansing drove hundreds of thousands of Albanians from their homes. Unwilling to fight a war on the ground in the mountainous, unforgiving terrain of the southern Balkans, the United States and its European allies concentrated on strategic attacks on bridges, power plants, factories, and Serbian military bases. The Russian government, bothered by this unilateral attack on fellow Slavs, nonetheless played an important part in brokering a cease-fire. Milosevic was forced to withdraw from Kosovo, leaving it in the hands of another force of armed NATO peacekeepers.

Finally, Serb-dominated Yugoslavia, worn by ten years of war and economic sanctions, turned against Milosevic's regime. Wars and corruption had destroyed Milosevic's credentials as a nationalist and populist. After he attempted to reject the results of a democratic election in 2000, his government fell to popular

Legend

- Soviet Union to 1991
- Soviet-dominated Eastern Europe to 1989
- German Democratic Republic (GDR) united with Federal Republic of Germany 1990
- Czechoslovakia to December 1992
- Yugoslavia to 1991
- Other communist states before 1991
- **1990** Date of first free election

Area of detail

EUROPE

AFRICA

NORWAY

SWEDEN

FINLAND

DENMARK

NORTH SEA

BALTIC SEA

RUSS. FED.

GERMANY

EAST GERMANY 1990

POLAND 1991

CZECH REPUBLIC 1992

SLOVAKIA 1992

SWITZ.

AUSTRIA

HUNGARY 1990

SLOVENIA 1992

CROATIA 1992

ITALY

BOSNIA AND HERZEGOVINA 1992

YUGOSLAVIA 1992

ADRIATIC SEA

ALBANIA 1991

MACEDONIA 1990

GREECE

BULGARIA 1990

ROMANIA 1990

MOLDAVIA 1994

ESTONIA 1992

LATVIA 1993

LITHUANIA 1990

BELORUSSIA 1995

UKRAINE

BLACK SEA

RUSSIAN FEDERATION 1993

TURKEY

GEORGIA 1991

ARMENIA 1995

AZERBAIJAN 1995

to AZERBAIJAN

IRAN

CASPIAN SEA

ARAL SEA

KAZAKHSTAN
1991: President Nazarbayev runs in election unopposed
1995: Nationwide referendum extends his term to 2000

UZBEKISTAN

TURKMENISTAN

KYRGYZSTAN

TAJIKISTAN

AFGHANISTAN

1992: Tensions between Russia and Ukraine over whether Black Sea Fleet is part of strategic forces controlled by CIS

1993: Joins the CIS to secure Russian military support against ousted President, Gamsakhurdia

500 Miles

500 Kilometers

250

250

0

THE POST–COLD WAR WEST

How did the collapse of the Soviet Union and the end of the cold war allow for the reemergence of certain forces in the political landscape of Europe? Examine closely the geography of southeastern and central Europe. How were political boundaries reorganized?

protests. He died in 2006, while being tried by a UN tribunal for war crimes.

As we gain perspective on the twentieth century, it is clear that the Yugoslavian wars of the 1990s were not an isolated instance of Balkan violence. The issues are thoroughly Western. The Balkans form one of the West's borderlands, where cultures influenced by Roman Catholicism, Eastern Orthodoxy, and Islam meet, overlap, and contend for political domination and influence. Since the nineteenth century, this region of enormous religious, cultural, and ethnic diversity has struggled with the implications of nationalism. We have seen how conflicts over the creation of new national states drawn mostly on ethnic lines were worked out in Central Europe, with many instances of tragic violence. The Yugoslav wars fit into some of the same patterns.

CONCLUSION

The Eastern European revolutions of 1989 and the subsequent collapse of the Soviet Union were a revolutionary turning point. Like the French Revolution of 1789, they brought down not only a regime, but an empire. Like the French Revolution, they gave way to violence. And again like the French Revolution, they had sweeping international consequences. These revolutions and the fall of the Soviet Union marked the end of the cold war, which had structured international politics and shaped the everyday lives of millions of people since the end of World War II. In the last chapter of this book, we consider how the cold war itself has given way to more complex global relations.

KEY TERMS

abstract expressionism	*The Feminine Mystique*	*perestroika*	Boris Yeltsin
Americanization	NAACP	velvet revolutions	Yugoslavia
French new wave	Prague spring	Slobodan Milosevic	

SELECTED READINGS

Bailey, Beth. *From Front Porch to Back Seat: Courtship in Twentieth-Century America.* Baltimore, Md., 1988. Good historical perspective on the sexual revolution.

Beschloss, Michael, and Strobe Talbott. *At the Highest Levels: The Inside Story of the End of the Cold War.* Boston, 1993. An analysis of the relationship between presidents Gorbachev and George H. W. Bush and their determination to ignore hard-liners.

Brown, Archie. *The Gorbachev Factor.* Oxford and New York, 1996. One of the first serious studies of Gorbachev, by an Oxford scholar of politics.

Caute, David. *The Year of the Barricades: A Journey through 1968.* New York, 1988. A well-written global history of 1968.

Charney, Leo, and Vanessa R. Schwartz, eds. *Cinema and the Invention of Modern Life.* Berkeley, Calif., 1995. Collection of essays.

Dallin, Alexander, and Gail Lapidus. *The Soviet System: From Crisis to Collapse.* Boulder, Colo., 1995.

Echols, Alice. *Daring to Be Bad: Radical Feminism in America, 1967–1975.* Minneapolis, Minn., 1989. Good narrative and analysis.

Eley, Geoff. *Forging Democracy: The History of the Left in Europe, 1850–2000.* Oxford and New York, 2002. Among its other qualities, one of the best historical perspectives on the 1960s.

Fink, Carole, Phillipp Gassert, and Detlef Junker, eds. *1968: The World Transformed.* Cambridge, 1998. A transatlantic history of 1968.

Fulbrook, Mary, ed. *Europe since 1945* (The Short Oxford History of Europe). Oxford, 2001. Particularly good articles on economics and political economy. Structural analysis.

Garton Ash, Timothy. *In Europe's Name: Germany and the Divided Continent.* New York, 1993. An analysis of the effect of German reunification on the future of Europe.

Glenny, Misha. *The Balkans, 1804–1999: Nationalism, War and the Great Powers.* London, 1999. Good account by a journalist who covered the fighting.

Horowitz, Daniel. *Betty Friedan and the Making of the Feminine Mystique: The American Left, the Cold War, and Modern Feminism.* Amherst, Mass., 1998. A reconsideration.

Hosking, Geoffrey. *The Awakening of the Soviet Union.* Cambridge, Mass., 1990. The factors that led to the end of the Soviet era.

Hughes, H. Stuart. *Sophisticated Rebels: The Political Culture of European Dissent, 1968–1987*. Cambridge, Mass., 1990. The nature of dissent on both sides of the disintegrating Iron Curtain in the years 1988–1989.

Hulsberg, Werner. *The German Greens: A Social and Political Profile.* New York, 1988. The origins, politics, and impact of environmental politics.

Jarausch, Konrad. *The Rush to German Unity.* New York, 1994. The problems of reunification analyzed.

Judah, Tim. *The Serbs: History, Myth, and the Destruction of Yugoslavia.* New Haven, Conn., 1997. Overview of Serbian history by journalist who covered the war.

Judt, Tony. *Postwar.* London, 2005. The most thorough and sophisticated account.

Kaplan, Robert D. *Balkan Ghosts: A Journey through History.* New York, 1993. More a political travelogue than a history, but very readable.

Kotkin, Stephen. *Armegeddon Averted: The Soviet Collapse, 1970–2000.* Oxford, 2001. Excellent short account.

Lewin, Moshe. *The Gorbachev Phenomenon.* Expanded ed. Berkeley, Calif., 1991. Written as a firsthand account, tracing the roots of Gorbachev's successes and failures.

Lieven, Anatol. *Chechnya, Tomb of Russia Power.* New Haven, Conn., and London, 1998. Longer view of the region, by a journalist.

Maier, Charles S. *Dissolution: The Crisis of Communism and the End of East Germany.* Princeton, N.J., 1997. Detailed and sophisticated.

Mann, Michael. *The Dark Side of Democracy: Explaining Ethnic Cleansing.* New York, 2005. Brilliant essay on different episodes from Armenia to Rwanda.

Marwick, Arthur. *The Sixties.* Oxford and New York, 1998. An international history.

Pells, Richard. *Not Like Us: How Europeans Have Loved, Hated, and Transformed American Culture since World War II.* New York, 1997. From the point of view of an American historian.

Poiger, Uta G. *Jazz, Rock, and Rebels: Cold War Politics and American Culture in a Divided Germany.* Berkeley, Calif., 2000. Pioneering cultural history.

Sheehan, Neil. *A Bright Shining Lie: John Paul Vann and America in Vietnam.* New York, 1988. A study of the war and its escalation through one of the U.S. Army's field advisers.

Strayer, Robert. *Why Did the Soviet Union Collapse? Understanding Historical Change.* Armonk, N.Y., and London, 1998. A good introduction, with bibliography.

Suri, Jeremi. *Power and Protest.* New ed. Cambridge, Mass., 2005. One of the best of the new global histories of the 1960s, looking at relations between social movements and international relations.

Wright, Patrick. *On Living in an Old Country: The National Past in Contemporary Britain.* New York, 1986. The culture of Britain in the 1980s.

CHAPTER TWENTY-NINE

A WORLD WITHOUT WALLS: GLOBALIZATION AND THE WEST

IN THE TWENTY-FIRST CENTURY, the world has reentered a period in which basic assumptions about the role of nation-states, the roots of prosperity, and the boundaries of cultures are changing fast. We say *reentered* because, as we have seen, a disconcerting sense of seismic and little-understood change has been central to Western culture during several different historical periods. The Industrial Revolution of the nineteenth century is an example, and just as *industrial revolution*, a term coined in the early nineteenth century, seemed to capture contemporaries' perceptions of changes in their own time, so *globalization* seems to capture ours. Globalization is not new, but our acute consciousness of it is.

We know, intuitively, what globalization means: the Internet, protests against the World Trade Organization (WTO), outsourcing of jobs and services, Wal-Mart in Mexico, the dismantling of the Berlin wall. All of these are powerful images of larger, enormously significant developments. The Internet represents the stunning transformation of global communication, the media, and forms of knowledge. The Berlin wall once stood for a divided cold war world; its fall marked a dramatic reconfiguration of international relations, an end to the ideological battle over communism, the creation of new alliances, markets, and communities. The attack on the World Trade Center in 2001 gave the term *globalization* a new and frightening meaning as well. It shattered many Americans' sense of relative isolation and security. Globalization, then, conjures up new possibilities but also new vulnerabilities.

What, precisely, does the term mean? What causes or drives globalization, and what are its effects? To begin simply, globalization means integration. It is the process of creating a rising number of networks—political, social, economic, and cultural—that span larger sections of the globe. New technologies, new economic imperatives, and changing laws have combined to make global exchange faster and, by the same token, to intensify economic, social, and cultural relationships. Information, ideas, goods, and people now move rapidly and easily across national boundaries. Yet *globalization* is not synonymous with *internationalization*, and the distinction is important. International relations are established between nation-states. Global exchange can be quite independent of national control: today trade, politics, and cultural exchange often happen "underneath the radar of the nation-state," in the words of one historian.

FOCUS QUESTIONS

- What is globalization?
- Why did postcolonial development unfold differently in different regions?

- What have been the major forces for political, religious, and social change in the Middle East?
- How has globalization changed the politics of terrorism?

Globalization has radically altered the distribution of industry and patterns of trade around the world, as Asian nations in particular emerge as industrial giants and Western powers become increasingly dependent on energy resources drawn from former colonies. Globalization has forced the reorganization of economic enterprises from banking and commerce to manufacturing. Supranational economic institutions such as the International Monetary Fund are examples of globalization and also work to quicken its pace. Likewise, the International Criminal Court represents an important trend in law: the globalization of judicial power. New, rapid, and surprisingly intimate forms of mass communication (blogs, Internet-based political campaigns, and so on) have spawned new forms of politics. International human-rights campaigns, for instance, owe an enormous debt to global communications and the communities they create. Perhaps most interesting, the sovereignty of nation-states and the clear boundaries of national communities seem to be eroded by many globalizing trends.

All these developments seem to be characteristic of our time. But are they new? For centuries, religion, empire, commerce, and industry have had globilizing impulses and effects. The East India Companies (Dutch and English), for instance, were to the seventeenth century what Microsoft is to the early twenty-first: the premier global enterprises of the time. Chartered and granted monopolies by the crown, they organized trade, investment of capital, manufacturing enterprises, and commercial agriculture. The Dutch East India Company's networks reached from Amsterdam to South Africa, through to India and Southeast Asia. The economic development of Europe in general was thoroughly enmeshed in global networks that supplied raw materials, markets, and labor. It has always been hard to strip the "West" of its global dimensions. The movement to abolish slavery was certainly transatlantic, if not global.

For another striking example, consider migration and immigration. We think of the contemporary world as fluid, characterized by vast movements of people. Mass, long-distance migration and immigration, however, peaked during the nineteenth century. Between 1846 (when the first reliable statistics were kept) and 1940, 55 to 58 million people left Europe for the Americas, especially for the United States, Canada, Argentina, and Brazil. During that same period, 48 to 52 million Indians and southern Chinese migrated to Southeast Asia, the Southern Pacific, and the areas surrounding the Indian Ocean (many of the Indian

migrants went to other parts of the British Empire). Roughly another 50 million people left northeastern Asia and Russia for Manchuria, Siberia, central Asia, and Japan. Faster long-distance transportation (railways and steamships) made these long journeys possible; the industrialization of the receiving regions provided the economic dynamics. As the scholar Adam McKeown writes, the nineteenth century was "a world on the move, flowing into factories, construction projects, mines, plantations, agricultural frontiers, and commercial networks across the globe." The demographic, social, economic, and cultural effects of these migrations were transformative. As McKeown also points out, after World War I, governments set out to close their gates; from the 1920s on, laborers (and refugees) found it much harder to move. If migration is a measure of globalization, our world is less "globalized" than it was a century ago.

What is more, to equate globalization with integration may be misleading. Globalizing trends do not necessarily produce peace, equality or homogeneity. Their effects are hard to predict. During the early 1900s many Europeans firmly believed that the world, at least the part of the world dominated by Western empires, would become harmonious, that Western culture would be exported, and that Western standards were universal. History defied those expectations. Some scholars argue that the term *globalization* should be jettisoned because it suggests a uniform, leveling process, one that operates similarly everywhere. Globalization has very different and disparate effects, effects shaped by vast asymmetries of power and wealth among nations or regions. In the last several decades, worldwide inequality has increased. Global processes encounter obstacles and resistance; they sow division as well as unity. At the level of everyday human contact, globalization has hastened new kinds of cultural blending and new forms of sociability, but it has also produced a backlash against that blending. The heady word *global* can distort our analyses or point us in the wrong direction. As one historian argues, although it is crucial to be able to think outside of "national or continental containers," it would be misleading to believe "that there is no container at all, except the planetary one."

In this chapter we explore three subjects crucial to our early efforts to understand globalization, especially as it relates to the post–cold war world of the twenty-first century. The first subject is the set of global changes that have accelerated the free flow of money, people, products, and ideas. The second subject is what we have come to call postcolonial politics—the varied trajectories that mark the contemporary experience of former colonies. Finally, we will consider in greater depth the complex and important role of Middle Eastern politics in contemporary global affairs. Throughout, we hope to suggest ways in which recent developments relate to familiar historical issues we have already examined in other contexts.

LIQUID MODERNITY? THE FLOW OF MONEY, IDEAS, AND PEOPLES

What is globalization?

A key feature of late-twentieth-century globalization has been the transformation of the world economy, highlighted by the rapid integration of markets since 1970. In a series of historic changes, the international agreements that had regulated the movement of people, goods, and money since World War II were overturned. To begin with, the postwar economic arrangements sealed at Bretton Woods (see Chapter Twenty-Seven) steadily eroded in the late 1960s, as Western industrial nations faced a double burden of inflation and economic stagnation. A crucial shift in monetary policy occurred in 1971, when the United States abandoned the postwar gold standard and allowed the dollar—the keystone of the system— to range freely. As a result, formal regulations on currencies, international banking, and lending among states faded away. They were replaced with an informal network of arrangements managed autonomously by large private lenders, their political friends in leading Western states, and independent financial agencies such as the International Monetary Fund and the World Bank. The economists and administrators who dominated these new networks steered away from the interventionist policies that shaped postwar planning and recovery. Instead they relied on a broad range of market-driven models dubbed "neoliberalism." In a

Industrial development in the globalized economy has created jarring juxtapositions of development and deterioration across entire continents and even within single cities—a phenomenon described as a "checkerboard of poverty and affluence."

variation on classic liberal economics, neoliberal economists stressed the value of free markets, profit incentives, and sharp restraints on both budget deficits and social welfare programs, whether run by governments or corporations. The new systems of lending they backed had mixed results, funding breakneck growth in some cases and bringing catastrophic debt in others. Industrial development in the globalized economy has created jarring juxtapositions of development and deterioration across entire continents and even within single cities—a phenomenon described as a "checkerboard of poverty and affluence."

At the same time, the world's local, national, and regional economies became far more connected and interdependent. Export trade flourished and, with the technological advances of the 1960s and 1980s, came to include an increasing proportion of high-technology goods. The boom in export commerce was tied to important changes in the division of labor worldwide. More industrial jobs emerged in the postcolonial world, not just among the Asian "tigers" but also in India, Latin America, and elsewhere. Although such steady, skilled manual employment started to disappear in Western nations—often replaced by lower-paying menial work— financial and service sector employment leaped ahead. The exchange and use of goods became much more complex. Goods were designed by companies in one country, manufactured in another, and tied into a broader interchange of cultures. Taken together, these global economic changes had deep political effects, forcing painful debates about the nature of citizenship and entitlement inside national borders, about the power and accountability of transnational corporations, and about the human and environmental costs of global capitalism.

Another crucial change involved not only the widespread flow of information but also the new commercial and cultural importance attached to information itself. Electronic systems and devices designed to create, store, and share information multiplied, becoming staggeringly more powerful and accessible—none with so great an impact on the everyday lives of men and women around the world as the personal computer. By the early 1990s increasingly sophisticated computers brought people into instant communication with each other across continents, not only by new means but also in new cultural and political settings. Electronic

"Checkerboard of Poverty and Affluence." Scenes of slums confronting towering skylines, such as this one from Argentina in 2000, are visible around the world as one of the side effects of development and deterioration.

communications over the Internet gave a compelling new meaning to the term *global village.* The Internet revolution shared features of earlier print revolutions. It was pioneered by entrepreneurs with utopian ambitions and lavished attention on with culturally illicit and politically scandalous materials that could be published easily and informally. It offered new possibilities to social and political groups, constituting new "publics." And it attracted large, established corporate interests, eager to cash in on new channels of culture and business.

However common their use seems, the Internet and similar technologies have had wide-ranging effects on political struggles around the globe. Embattled ethnic minorities have found worldwide audiences through online campaign sites. Satellite television arguably sped the sequence of popular revolts in eastern Europe in 1989. That same year, fax machines brought Chinese demonstrators at Tiananmen Square news of international support for their efforts. Meanwhile, leaps forward in electronic technologies provided new

Since 1945, the widespread migration of peoples, particularly between former colonies and imperial powers, has changed everyday life around the world.

worldwide platforms for commercial interests. Companies such as Sony, RCA, and others produced entertainment content, including music, motion pictures, and television shows as well as the electronic equipment to play that content. Bill Gates's Microsoft emerged as the world's major producer of computer software—with a corporate profit margin that surpassed Spain's gross domestic product. At the level of production, marketing, and management, information industries are global, spread widely across the United States, India, western Europe, and parts of the developing world. Their corporate headquarters, however, typically remain in the West and support neoliberal politics. The international media, news, and entertainment conglomerates run by the Australian Rupert Murdoch or by Time Warner, for example, are firmly allied to U.S. institutions and worldviews, edging aside state-run companies.

Like the movement of money, goods, and ideas, the flow of labor has become a central aspect of globalization. Since 1945, the widespread migration of peoples, particularly between former colonies and imperial powers, has changed everyday life around the world. Groups of immigrant workers have filled the lower rungs of expanding economies not only in Europe but also in oil-rich Arab states that attracted Asian and Filipino laborers and in the United States, where both permanent and seasonal migrations from Mexico and other Latin American nations have spread across the continent. This fusion of peoples and cultures has produced striking new blends of music, food, language, and other forms of popular culture and sociability. These seem novel until we think of Creole cultures formed in the New World from the sixteenth to the eighteenth centuries.

An Afghan Girl Weeds a Poppy Field, 2004. Though Afghanistan was historically a center for the silk trade, opium is its most important cash crop today.

It has also raised tensions over the definition of citizenship and the boundaries of political and cultural communities—familiar themes from modern history. As a result, cycles of violent xenophobic backlash, bigotry, and political extremism have appeared in host countries and regions, but so too have new conceptions of civil rights and cultural belonging.

As suggested earlier, sharp divides exist between the most successful global players and the poorer, disadvantaged, sometimes embattled states and cultures. In one particular area of manufacture, however, poorer postcolonial regions have been able to respond to a steady and immensely profitable market in the West. The production of illegal drugs such as opium, heroin, and cocaine is a thriving industry in countries such as Colombia, Myanmar (formerly Burma), and Malaysia. Though the trade in such substances is banned, the fragile economies of the countries where they are produced have encouraged public and private powers to turn a blind eye to their production—or even to intervene for their own profit. Other, similar forms of illegal commerce have also grown far beyond the old label of "organized crime" in their structure and political importance. Trafficking in illegal immigrants, the management of corrupt financial dealings, trade in illicit animal products, and "conflict" diamonds from several brutal postcolonial civil wars are all indicative of this trend. The organizations behind these criminal trades grew out of the political violence and economic breakdown of failing postcolonial states or from the human and commercial traffic between these parts of

the world and leading Western economic powers. They have exploited cracks, loopholes, and unsupervised opportunities in the less regulated system of global trade and carved out centers of power not directly subject to the laws of any single state.

DEMOGRAPHICS AND GLOBAL HEALTH

The developments of globalization are tied in complex ways to the evolving size and health of the world's population. Between 1800 and the middle of the twentieth century, the worldwide population roughly tripled, rising from 1 to 3 billion. Between 1960 and 2000, however, population doubled again, to 6 billion or more. Huge, if uneven, improvements in basic standards of health, particularly for young children and childbearing women, contributed to the increase—as did local efforts to improve the urban-industrial environment. Asia's population as a whole has increased nearly fourfold since 1900, to nearly two thirds of the world's present population. Such growth has strained underdeveloped social services, public-health facilities, and urban infrastructures, increasing the potential for epidemic disease as well as for cycles of ethnic and ideological violence nursed by poverty and dislocation.

A different type of demographic crisis confronts parts of the West, where steadily shrinking populations erode social welfare systems. Longer life spans, broadened welfare programs, and rising health-care costs have contributed to the challenge. Populations in

Government Efforts to Curtail the Spread of Severe Acute Respiratory Syndrome (SARS). In May 2003, migrant workers at a Beijing railway station line up to have their temperatures checked before boarding the trains.

demics of the Middle Ages. Such fears were confirmed by the worldwide spread of infection by HIV, whose final stage is AIDS, which first appeared at the end of the 1970s. As HIV-AIDS became a global health crisis—particularly in Africa, where the disease spread catastrophically—international organizations recognized the need for an early, swift, and comprehensive response to future outbreaks of disease, as evidenced by the successful global containment of severe acute respiratory syndrome (SARS) in 2003.

Meanwhile, the work of multinational medical research firms continued to extend the ability to prevent and treat disease. One of the most powerful tools in this endeavor was the development of genetic engineering, which stemmed from the monumental discovery of DNA in the 1950s. By the 1990s, several laboratories were engaged in the most ambitious medical research ever attempted: the mapping of the human genome—that is, the entire architecture of chromosomes and genes contained in basic human DNA. Through this process and alongside it, genetic engineers developed methods to alter the biology of living things. Infertile couples, for instance, could now conceive through out-of-body medical procedures. Genetic engineers developed—and patented—strains of mice and other laboratory animals that carried chemical markers, cells, even organs, of other species. By 1997 British researchers succeeded in producing a clone (an exact genetic copy) of a sheep. Genome research also broadened and deepened medical understanding of biological "defects" and diversions from the genetic norms of human development. As a new form of knowledge in an age of global interconnection, genetic engineering leaped across the legal and moral boundaries of human societies. The question of who would govern these advances—nations, international bodies, or local cultural and religious communities—was opened to passionate debate. So were fresh arguments about where to draw lines between lifesaving intervention and cultural preference, between individual agency and biological determinism. Like past scientific investigations directed at humankind, genetics has raised fundamental questions about ethics, citizenship, and the measure of humanity.

the United States and Great Britain have been stable or have been slowly expanded by immigration; in Italy, Scandinavia, and, recently, Russia, sharp drops in the birth rate have lead to population decline. Declining birth rates have been accompanied by growing populations of older adults, whose health and vitality resulted from decades of improved medical standards and state-run entitlement programs. Maintaining the long-term solvency of such programs poses difficult choices for European countries in particular, as they struggle to balance guarantees of social well-being with fiscal and political realities.

Globalization has also changed public health and medicine, creating dangerous new threats as well as promising new treatments. Better and more comprehensive health care has generally accompanied other kinds of prosperity and has thus been more accessible in the West. In Africa, Latin America, and elsewhere, political chaos, imbalances of trade, and the practices of some large pharmaceutical companies have often resulted in shortages of medicine and a rickety medical infrastructure, making it difficult to combat deadly new waves of disease. Indeed, the worldwide risk of exposure to epidemic diseases is a new reality of globalization—a product of increased cultural interaction, exposure of new ecosystems to human development, and the speed of intercontinental transportation. By the 1970s the acceleration of airplane travel led to fears that an epidemic would leapfrog the globe much faster than the pan-

AFTER EMPIRE: POSTCOLONIAL POLITICS IN THE GLOBAL ERA

Why did postcolonial development unfold differently in different regions?

Even after the superpower rivalry of the cold war collapsed, another legacy of the postwar era continued to shape international relations into the twenty-first century. The so-called postcolonial relationships between former colonies and Western powers emerged from the decolonization struggles detailed in Chapter Twenty-Seven. Former colonies, as well as other nations that had fallen under the political and economic sway of imperial powers, gained formal independence at the least, along with new kinds of cultural and political authority. In other respects, however, very little changed for people in the former colonies. The very term *postcolonial* underlines the fact that colonialism's legacies endured even after independence. Within these regions, political communities new and old handled the legacies of empire and the postcolonial future in a variety of ways. In some cases the former colonizers or their local allies retained so much power that formal independence actually meant very little. In others, bloody independence struggles poisoned the political culture. The emergence of new states and new kinds of politics was sometimes propelled by economic goals, sometimes by the revival of cultural identities that preceded colonization, and in other cases by ethnic conflict. The results ranged from breakneck industrial success to ethnic slaughter, from democratization to new local models of absolutism. During the cold war, these postcolonial regions were often the turf on which the superpower struggle was waged. They benefited from superpower patronage but also became the staging ground for proxy wars funded by the West in the fight against communism. Their various trajectories since 1989 point to the complex legacy of the imperial past in the post–cold war world of globalization.

> The emergence of new states and new kinds of politics was sometimes propelled by economic goals, sometimes by the revival of cultural identities that preceded colonization, and in other cases by ethnic conflict.

EMANCIPATION AND ETHNIC CONFLICT IN AFRICA

The legacies of colonialism weighed heavily on sub-Saharan Africa. Most of the continent's former colonies came into their independence after World War II with their basic infrastructures deteriorating after decades of imperial negligence. The cold war decades brought scant improvement, as governments across the continent were plagued by both homegrown and externally imposed corruption, poverty, and civil war. In sub-Saharan Africa, two very different trends began to emerge around 1989, each shaped by a combination of the end of the cold war and volatile local conditions.

The first trend can be seen in South Africa, where politics had revolved for decades around the brutal racial policies of apartheid, sponsored by the white minority government. The most prominent opponent of apartheid, Nelson Mandela, who led the African National Congress (ANC), had been imprisoned since 1962. Intense repression and violent conflict continued into the 1980s and reached a dangerous impasse by the end of the decade. Then the South African government chose a daring new tack: in early 1990 it released Mandela from prison. He resumed leadership of the ANC and turned the party toward a combination of renewed public demonstrations and plans for negotiation. Politics changed within the Afrikaner-dominated white regime as well when F. W. de Klerk succeeded the P. W. Botha as prime minister. A pragmatist who feared civil war and national collapse over apartheid, de Klerk was well matched to Mandela. In March 1992 the two men began direct talks to establish majority rule. Legal and constitutional reforms followed, and in May 1994, during elections in which all South Africans took part, Nelson Mandela was chosen the country's first black president. Although many of his government's efforts to reform housing, the economy, and public health foundered, Mandela defused the climate of organized racial violence. He also gained and kept tremendous personal popularity among black and white South Africans alike as a living symbol of a new political culture. Mandela's popularity extended abroad, within sub-Saharan Africa and worldwide. In a number of smaller postcolonial states such as Benin, Malawi, and Mozambique, the early 1990s brought political reforms that ended one-party or one-man

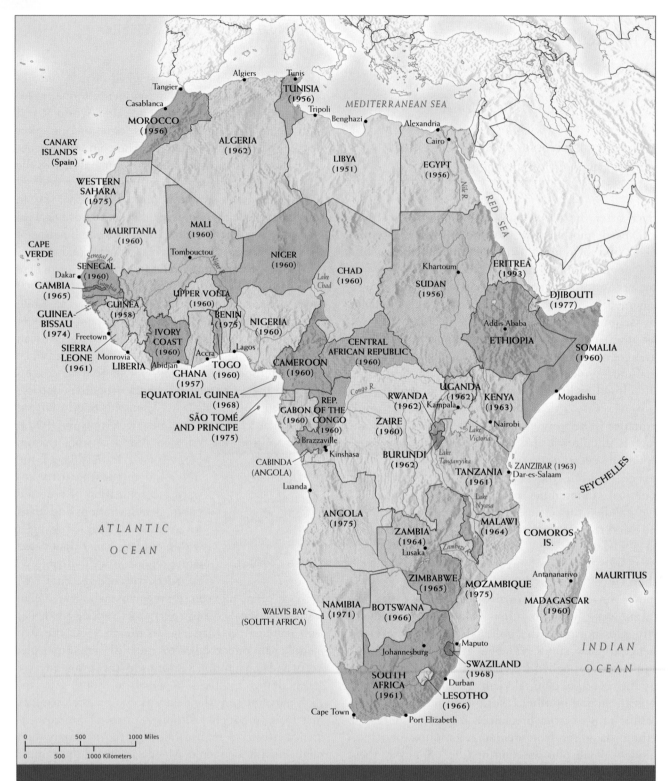

DECOLONIZATION IN AFRICA TO 1980

How do the modern borders of African nations still bear the stamp of European colonization? What effect do you suspect this has had on ethnic tensions within these nations?

Nelson Mandela Votes in South Africa's First Democratic Elections, 1994. He would be elected the country's president.

rule in favor of parliamentary democracy and economic reform.

The other major trend ran in a different, less encouraging direction. Some former autocracies gave way to calls for pluralism, but other states across the continent collapsed into ruthless ethnic conflict. In Rwanda, a former Belgian colony, conflicts between the Hutu and Tutsi populations erupted into a highly organized campaign of genocide against the Tutsi after the country's president was assassinated. Carried out by ordinary Hutus of all backgrounds, the ethnic slaughter left over 800,000 Tutsi dead in a matter of weeks. International pressure eventually turned local Rwandan politics against the perpetrators. Many of them fled to neighboring Zaire and became hired mercenaries in the many-sided civil war that followed the collapse of Mobutu Sese Seko, the country's long-time dictator, infamous for diverting billions of dollars in foreign aid into his personal bank accounts. A number of ambitious

neighboring countries intervened in Zaire, hoping not only to secure its valuable resources but also to settle conflicts with their own ethnic minorities that spilled over the border. Fighting continued through the late 1990s into the new century, dubbed "Africa's world war" by many observers. Public services, normal trade, even basic health and safety inside Zaire—renamed the Democratic Republic of Congo by an ineffective government in Kinshasa—collapsed. With a death toll that reached into the millions from combat, massacre, and disease, the fighting remained unresolved in the next decade.

ECONOMIC POWER ON THE PACIFIC RIM

By the end of the twentieth century, East Asia had become a center of industrial and manufacturing production. China, whose communist government began to establish commercial ties with the West in the 1970s, was the world's leading heavy industrial producer by the year 2000. Its state-owned companies acquired contracts from Western firms to produce products cheaply and in bulk, for sale back to home markets in the United States and Europe. In a deliberate reversal of Europe's nineteenth-century intrusions on the China trade, Beijing established semicapitalist commercial zones around major port cities like Shanghai, a policy whose centerpiece was the reclamation of Hong Kong from Britain in 1997. The commercial zones were intended to encourage massive foreign investment on terms that left China a favorable balance of trade for its huge volume of cheap exports. In practice, they enjoyed only mixed success. Downturns in farming and a looming energy crisis hampered prosperity and economic growth inland, but Hong Kong worked to maintain its economic and cultural middle ground with the rest of the world as it had since the days of the opium trade (see Chapter Twenty-Two).

Other Asian nations emerged as global commercial powers as well. Industry flourished in a string of countries, starting with Japan and extending along Asia's Pacific coastline into Southeast Asia and Oceania, during the decades after World War II. By the 1980s their robust industrial expansion and their apparent staying power earned them the collective nickname of "the tigers," taken from the ambitious, forward-looking tiger in Chinese mythology. These Pacific rim states collectively formed the most important industrial region in the world outside the United States and

Industrialization in China, 2002. The Three Gorges Dam on the Yan River in Yichang is the largest hydroelectric dam in the world. It has been called the largest construction project in China since the Great Wall.

Europe. Among them, Japan not only led the way but also became the most influential model of success, with a postwar revival that eventually surpassed West Germany's economic miracle (see Chapter Twenty-Eight). Japanese firms concentrated on the efficiency and technical reliability of their products: fuel-efficient cars, specialty steel, small electronic goods, and so on. Japanese diplomacy and large state subsidies supported the success of Japanese firms, while a well-funded program of technical education hastened research and development of new goods. Japanese firms also appeared to benefit from collective loyalty among civil servants and corporate managers, attitudes that were encouraged by Japan's long experience of trade guilds and feudal politics. Other East Asian nations, newer or less stable than Japan, tried to mimic its success. Some, such as South Korea and the Chinese Nationalist stronghold of Taiwan, treated the creation of prosperity as a fundamental patriotic duty. In postcolonial nations such as Malaysia and Indonesia, governments parlayed their natural resources and expansive local labor pools (which had made them attractive to imperial powers in earlier times) into investment for industrialization. As in China, the factories that emerged were either subsidiaries of Western companies or operated on their behalf in new multinational versions of the putting-out system of early industrialization.

The Pacific rim's boom, however, also contained the makings of a first "bust." During the 1990s a confluence of factors resulted in an enormous slowdown of growth

and the near collapse of several currencies. Japan experienced rising production costs, overvalued stocks, rampant speculation on its high-priced real estate market, and the customary kickbacks that rewarded staunch corporate loyalty. In Southeast Asia, states such as Indonesia found they had to pay the difference on overvalued industrial capital to Western lenders who set rigid debt repayment schedules. Responses to the economic downturn varied widely. In South Korea, an older generation that remembered economic catastrophe after the Korean War responded to national calls for sacrifice, frequently by investing their own savings to prop up ailing companies. Japan launched programs of monetary austerity to cope with its first serious spike in unemployment in two generations. In Indonesia, inflation and unemployment reignited sharp ethnic conflicts that prosperity and violent state repression had dampened in earlier times. This predominantly Muslim country, with a long tradition of tolerance and pluralism inside the faith, also saw outbursts of violent religious fundamentalism popularly associated with another region—the Middle East.

A NEW CENTER OF GRAVITY: ISRAEL, OIL, AND POLITICAL ISLAM IN THE MIDDLE EAST

What have been the major forces for political, religious, and social change in the Middle East?

Perhaps no other region has drawn more attention from the West in the age of globalization than the Middle East, where a volatile combination of Western military, political, and economic interests converged with deep-seated regional conflicts and transnational Islamic politics. The results of this ongoing confrontation promise to shape the twenty-first century. Here we consider

WHAT HAVE BEEN THE MAJOR FORCES FOR POLITICAL, RELIGIOUS, AND SOCIAL CHANGE IN THE MIDDLE EAST?

A NEW CENTER OF GRAVITY: ISRAEL, OIL, AND POLITICAL ISLAM IN THE MIDDLE EAST   1061

three of the most important aspects of recent history in the region. First is the unfolding of the Arab-Israeli conflict. Second is the region's vital development as the global center of oil production. The third emerges from inside the Arab world, largely as a reaction against the recent relations with the West. This is the development of a specific, modern brand of Islamic radicalism that challenges the legacies of imperialism and promises revolutionary and sometimes apocalyptic change in postcolonial nations and whose most violent elements generate a cycle of fear, anger, and ultimately direct conflict with Western governments.

THE ARAB-ISRAELI CONFLICT

As we saw in Chapter Twenty-Seven, Israel's existence was a battleground from the start. The national aspirations of Jewish immigrants from Europe fleeing the Holocaust and violent postwar anti-Semitism clashed with the motives of pan-Arabists—secular, anticolonial nationalists who urged Arab pride and self-reliance against European domination. By the late 1970s, in the aftermath of two Arab-Israeli wars, it appeared that a generation of fighting might come to an end. American mediators began sponsoring talks to prevent further, sudden outbursts of conflict, while Soviet leaders remained neutral but supportive of peace efforts. Most notably, the Egyptian president Anwar Sadat, who authorized and directed the 1973 war against Israel, decided that coexistence rather than the destruction of Israel was the long-term answer to regional conflict. Aided by the American president Jimmy Carter, Sadat brokered a peace between Egypt and Israel's staunchly conservative leader, Menachem Begin, in 1978. Leaders on both sides of the conflict believed the potential rewards were greater than the obvious risks.

Hopes for a lasting peace were soon dashed. Hostilities escalated between Israel and the Palestinian Arabs displaced by Arab-Israeli warfare, a confrontation that increasingly polarized a much larger group of people. On each side of the Israeli-Palestinian conflict, a potent blend of ethnic and religious nationalism began to control both debate and action. Conservatives in Israel played to a public sentiment that put security ahead of other priorities, particularly among the most recent Jewish immigrants, often from the former Soviet Union. On the other side, younger Palestinians, angered by their elders' failures to provoke revolution, turned against the secular radicalism of the Palestinian Liberation Organization (PLO) and toward radical Islam.

In this combustible political environment, the Palestinians living on the West Bank and in the desperately overcrowded Gaza Strip revolted in an outburst of street rioting in 1987. This rebellion—called the *intifada* (literally, a "throwing off" or uprising)—continued for years in daily battles between stone-throwing Palestinian youths and armed Israeli security forces. The street fights escalated into cycles of Palestinian terrorism, particularly suicide bombings of civilian targets, and reprisals from the Israeli military. International efforts to broker a peace produced some results, including the official autonomy of a Palestinian authority led by the PLO chief, Yasser Arafat. Yet the peace was always fragile at best—suffering perhaps fatal damage from the assassination of Israel's reformist prime minister Yitzhak Rabin in 1995 by a reactionary Israeli and from continued attacks by Islamist terrorists. By the turn of the twenty-first century the cycle of violence flared again, with a "second intifada" launched by Palestinians in late 2000. Thus continued the war of riots and bombings fought by next-door neighbors.

OIL, POWER, AND ECONOMICS

The struggles between the state of Israel and its neighbors have been important in their own right. Yet one of the most compelling reasons that this conflict mattered to outside powers was material: oil. The global demand for oil skyrocketed during the postwar era and has accelerated since. Starting with the consumer boom in the cold war West, ordinary citizens bought cars and other petroleum-powered consumer durables, while industrial plastics made from petroleum by-products were used to manufacture a wealth of basic household items. Those needs, and the desires for profit and power that went with them, drew Western corporations and governments steadily toward the oil-rich states of the Middle East, whose vast reserves were discovered in the 1930s and 1940s. Large corporations conducted joint diplomacy with Middle Eastern states and their own home governments to design concessions for drilling, refining, and shipping the oil. Pipelines were laid by contractors based around the world, from California to Rome to Russia.

The enormous long-term economic value of the Middle Eastern oil reserves made oil a fundamental tool in new struggles over political power. Many producer states sought to turn their resources into leverage with the West's former imperial powers. In 1960, the leading Middle Eastern, African, and Latin American producers banded together in a cartel to take advantage of this vital resource, forming the Organization of the Petroleum Exporting Countries (OPEC) to regulate the production and pricing of crude oil. During the

THE ARAB-ISRAELI WARS OF 1967 AND 1973

Note the changes in the political geography of the Middle East as a result of the Arab-Israeli conflicts of 1967 and 1973. What factors led to the Arab attacks on Israel in these two wars? Why did the Israelis wish to occupy the Sinai and West Bank regions at the end of the 1967 war? What problems did this create, and how might it have led to the conflict in 1973? Study the distribution of Israeli-occupied and Egyptian-occupied territory at the end of the 1973 war. Why was the resolution of the Sinai problem considered a top priority by many political figures in the West?

1970s, OPEC played a leading role in the global economy. Its policies reflected not only the desire to draw maximum profits out of bottlenecks in oil production but also the militant politics of some OPEC leaders who wanted to use oil as a weapon against the West in the Arab-Israeli conflict. After the 1973 Arab-Israeli war, an embargo inspired by the hard-liners sparked

spiraling inflation and economic troubles in Western nations, triggering a cycle of dangerous recession that lasted nearly a decade.

In response, Western governments treated the Middle Eastern oil regions as a vital strategic center of gravity, the subject of constant Great Power diplomacy. If conflict directly threatened the stability of oil production or

WHAT HAVE BEEN THE MAJOR FORCES FOR POLITICAL, RELIGIOUS, AND SOCIAL CHANGE IN THE MIDDLE EAST?

A NEW CENTER OF GRAVITY: ISRAEL, OIL, AND POLITICAL ISLAM IN THE MIDDLE EAST   1063

friendly governments, Western powers were prepared to intervene by force, as the 1991 Gulf War demonstrated. By the 1990s another new front of competition and potential conflict emerged as the energy demands of other nations also grew. In particular, the new industrial giants China and India eyed the Middle Eastern oil reserves with the same nervousness as the West. The oil boom also generated violent conflict inside Middle Eastern producer states. Oil revenue produced an uneven form of economic development. The huge gaps between or inside Middle Eastern societies that divided oil's haves and have-nots caused deep resentments, official corruption, and a new wave of radical politics. With the pan-Arab nationalists fading from the scene, the rising revolutionary force gathered instead around modern readings of Islamic fundamentalism, now tied to postcolonial politics.

> With the pan-Arab nationalists fading from the scene, the rising revolutionary force gathered instead around modern readings of Islamic fundamentalism, now tied to postcolonial politics.

THE RISE OF POLITICAL ISLAM

In North Africa and the Middle East, processes of modernization and globalization produced tremendous discontents. The new nations that emerged from decolonization often shared the characteristics of the "kleptocracies" south of the Sahara: corrupt state agencies, cronyism based on ethnic or family kinship, decaying public services, rapid increases in population, and constant state repression of dissent. Disappointment with these conditions ran deep, perhaps nowhere more so than in the seat of pan-Arabism, Nasser's Egypt. During the 1960s, Egyptian academics and cultural critics leveled charges against Nasser's regime that became the core of a powerful new political movement. Their critique offered modern interpretations of certain legal and political

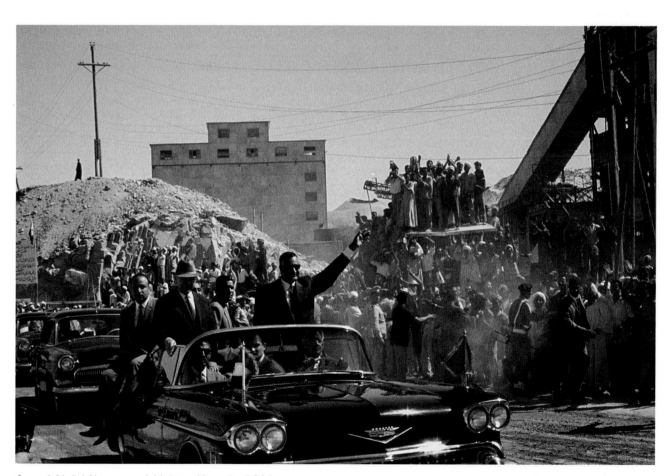

Gamal Abdel Nasser and Aleksey Kosygin, 1966. As the most prominent spokesman for secular pan-Arabism, Nasser became a target for Islamist critics, such as Sayyid Qutb and the Muslim Brotherhood, angered by the Western-influenced policies of his regime.

currents in Islamic thought, ideas linked loosely across centuries by their association with revolt against foreign interference and official corruption. They denounced Egypt's nationalist government as greedy, brutal, and corrupt.

There was a twist to their claims, however: that the roots of the Arab world's moral failure lay in centuries of colonial contact with the West. The most influential of these Islamist critics, Sayyid Qutb (*Kutb*; 1906–1966), presented these ideas in a series of essays for which he was arrested several times by Egyptian authorities and ultimately executed. His argument ran as follows. As a result of corrupting outside influences, the ruling elites of the new Arab states pursued policies that frayed local and family bonds, deepening economic divides while abandoning the government's responsibility for charity and stability. What was more, the nation's elites were morally bankrupt—their lives defied codes of morality, self-discipline, and communal responsibility rooted in Islamic faith. To maintain power, the elites lived in the pockets of Western imperial and corporate powers. From Qutb's point of view, this collaboration not only caused cultural impurity but also eroded authentic Muslim faith. This dire judgment of Arab societies—that they were poisoned from without and within—required an equally drastic solution. Arab societies should reject not only oppressive postcolonial governments but also all the political and cultural ideas that traveled with them, especially those that could be labeled "Western." After popular revolts, the Arab autocracies would be replaced by an idealized form of conservative Islamic government—a system in which a rigid form of Islam would link law, government, and culture.

In a formula familiar to historians of European politics throughout the nineteenth and twentieth centuries, this particular brand of Islamist politics combined popular anger, intellectual opposition to "foreign" influences, and a highly idealized vision of the past. By the 1970s it began to express itself openly in regional politics. Qutb's ideas were put into practice by Egypt's Muslim Brotherhood, a secretive but widespread society rooted in anticolonial politics, local charity, and violently fundamentalist Islam. The same ideas spread among similar organizations in other urbanized Arab countries and leading Islamic universities, which were historically centers of debate about political theory

> In a formula familiar to historians of European politics throughout the nineteenth and twentieth centuries, this particular brand of Islamist politics combined popular anger, intellectual opposition to "foreign" influences, and a highly idealized vision of the past.

and religious law. Radical Islam emerged as a driving force in criticism and defiance of autocratic Arab regimes. Secular critics and more liberal Islamists, who called for open elections and a free press, were more fragmented and thus easier to silence, whereas the new wave of fundamentalists gained concessions that allowed them to preach and publish in public so long as they did not launch actual revolts. Despite the movement's steady rise, the most dramatic turn still managed to surprise observers. Like Protestantism's emergence in the fractious German states, for example, or communism's successful revolution in Russia, radical Islam's defining moment as a political force came in an unexpected place: Iran.

IRAN'S ISLAMIC REVOLUTION

Iran offered one of the most dramatic examples of modernization gone sour in the Middle East. Despite tremendous economic growth in the 1960s and 1970s, Iranians labored with legacies of foreign intervention and corrupt rule at the hands of the shah, Reza Pahlavi, a Western-friendly leader installed during a 1953 military coup supported by Britain and the United States. In exchange for the shah's role as a friend to the West during the cold war and for providing a steady source of reasonably priced oil, the Iranian government received vast sums in oil contracts, weapons, and development aid. Thousands of Westerners, especially Americans, came to Iran, introducing foreign influences that not only challenged traditional values but also offered economic and political alternatives. The shah, however, kept these alternatives out of reach, consistently denying democratic representation to Westernizing middle-class Iranian workers and deeply religious university students alike. He governed through a small aristocracy divided by constant infighting. His army and secret police conducted regular and brutal campaigns of repression. Despite all this, and the public protests it spurred in the West, governments such as the conservative Nixon administration embraced the shah as a strategically vital ally: a key to anti-Soviet alliances and a safe source of oil.

Twenty-five years after the 1953 coup, the shah's autocratic route to an industrial state ended. After a lengthy economic downturn, public unrest, and personal illness, the shah realized he could not continue in power. He re-

What have been the major forces for political, religious, and social change in the Middle East?

A New Center of Gravity: Israel, Oil, and Political Islam in the Middle East   1065

Two Iranians symbolically substitute a picture of the shah with one of the ayatollah Khomeini after the Iranian Revolution, 1979.

The new Iranian government also defined itself against its enemies: against the Sunni religious establishment of neighboring states, against "atheistic" Soviet communism, but especially against Israel and the United States. Iranians feared the United States would try to overthrow Khomeini as it had other leaders. Violence in the streets of Tehran reached a peak when militant students stormed the American embassy in November 1979 and seized fifty-two hostages. The act quickly became an international crisis that heralded a new kind of confrontation between Western powers and postcolonial Islamic radicals. Democratic president Jimmy Carter's administration ultimately gained the hostages' release, but not before the catalog of earlier failures led to the election of the Republican Ronald Reagan.

tired from public life under popular pressure in February 1979. Eight months of uncertainty followed, most Westerners fled the country, and the provisional government appointed by the shah collapsed. The strongest political coalition among Iran's revolutionaries surged into the vacuum—a broad Islamic movement centered on the ayatollah Ruhollah Khomeini (1902–1989), Iran's senior cleric and theologian, returned from exile in France. Other senior clerics and the country's large population of unemployed, deeply religious university students provided the movement's energy. Disenfranchised secular protestors joined the radical Islamists in condemning decades of Western indifference and the shah's oppression. Under the new regime, some limited economic and political populism combined with strict constructions of Islamic law, restrictions on women's public life, and the prohibition of many ideas or activities linked to Western influence.

A massive crowd awaits the ayatollah Khomeini after the Iranian Revolution, 1979.

IRAN, IRAQ, AND UNINTENDED CONSEQUENCES OF THE COLD WAR

Iran's victory in the hostage crisis was fleeting. During the later part of 1980, Iran's Arab neighbor and traditional rival Iraq invaded, hoping to seize Iran's southern oil fields during the revolutionary confusion. Iran counterattacked. The result was a murderous eight-year conflict marked by the use of chemical weapons and human waves of young Iranian radicals fighting the Soviet-armed Iraqis. The war ended with Iran's defeat but not with the collapse of its theocratic regime. In the short term, their long defense of Iranian nationalism left the clerics more entrenched at home, while abroad they used oil revenues to back grass-roots radicals in Lebanon and elsewhere who engaged in anti-Western terrorism. The strongest threats to the Iranian regime ultimately came from within, from a new generation of young students and disenfranchised service workers who found their prospects for prosperity and active citizenship had not changed much since the days of the shah.

The Iran-Iraq conflict created another problem for Western interests and the governments of leading OPEC states: Iraq. Various governments—including an unlikely alliance of France, Saudi Arabia, the Soviet Union, and the United States—supported Iraq during the war in an effort to bring down Iran's clerics. Their patronage went to one of the most violent governments in the region, Saddam Hussein's dictatorship. Iraq exhausted itself in the war, politically and economically. To shore up his regime and restore Iraq's influence, Hussein looked elsewhere in the region. In 1990 Iraq invaded its small, oil-rich neighbor Kuwait.

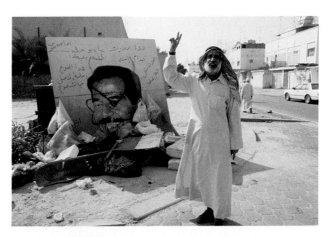

After American forces drove out his Iraqi occupiers, a Kuwaiti celebrates with the victory sign, 1991. Behind him, a defaced poster of Sadam Hussein sits in a garbage heap.

With the cold war on the wane, Iraq's Soviet supporters would not condone Iraqi aggression. A number of Western nations led by the United States reacted forcefully. Within months Iraq faced the full weight of the United States military—trained intensively since Vietnam to rout much more capable Soviet-armed forces than Iraq's—along with forces from several OPEC states, French troops, and armored divisions from Britain, Egypt, and Syria. This coalition pummeled Iraqi troops from the air for six weeks, then routed them and retook Kuwait in a brief, well-executed ground campaign. This changed the tenor of relations between the United States and Arab oil producers, encouraging not only closeness between governments but also anti-American radicals angry at a new Western presence. It was also the beginning rather than the end of a Western confrontation with Iraq, centered on Hussein's efforts to develop nuclear and biological weapons.

Elsewhere in the region, the proxy conflicts of the cold war snared both superpowers in the new and growing networks of Islamic radicalism. In 1979 the socialist government of Afghanistan turned against its Soviet patrons. Fearing a result like Iran, with a spread of fundamentalism into the Muslim regions of Soviet Central Asia, Moscow responded by overthrowing the Afghan president and installing a pro-Soviet faction. The new government, backed by more than 100,000 Soviet troops, found itself immediately at war with fighters who combined local conservatism with militant Islam and who attracted volunteers from radical Islamic movements in

Iranian guards keep watch over Iraqi prisoners during the Iran-Iraq war.

Egypt, Lebanon, Saudi Arabia, and elsewhere. These fighters, who called themselves *mujahidin*, viewed the conflict as a holy war. The mujahidin benefited from advanced weapons and training, given by Western powers led by the United States. Those who provided the aid saw the conflict in cold war terms, as a chance to sap Soviet resources in a fruitless imperial war. On those terms the aid worked; the war dragged on for nearly ten years, taking thousands of Russian lives and damaging the Soviet government's credibility at home. Soviet troops withdrew in 1989. After five years of clan warfare, hard-line Islamic factions tied to the foreign elements in the mujahidin took over the country. Their experiment in theocracy made Iran's seem mild by comparison.

Violence beyond Bounds: War and Terrorism in the Twenty-First Century

How has globalization changed the politics of terrorism?

The global networks of communication, finance, and mobility discussed at the beginning of this chapter gave radical political violence a disturbing new character at the end of the twentieth century. In the 1960s, organized, sectarian terrorist tactics had become an important part of political conflict in the Middle East, Europe, and Latin America. Most of these early terrorist organizations (including the Irish Republican Army, the Italian Red Brigades, and the different Palestinian revolutionary organizations) had specific goals, such as ethnic separatism or the establishment of revolutionary governments. By the 1980s and increasingly during the 1990s, such groups were complemented and then supplanted by a different brand of terrorist organization, one that ranged freely across territory and local legal systems. These newer, apocalyptic terrorist groups called for decisive conflict to eliminate their enemies and grant themselves martyrdom. Some such groups emerged from the social dislocations of the postwar boom, others were linked directly to brands of radical religion. They often divorced themselves from the local crises that first spurred their anger, roaming widely among countries in search of recruits to their cause.

CHRONOLOGY

Major Developments in the Middle East, 1948–Present

Israeli state formed	1948
First Arab-Israeli war	1948–1949
Egypt gains independence	1952
Israeli-Egyptian war	1956
Formation of OPEC	1960
Six-Day War; Israel occupies West Bank	1967
Second Arab-Israeli war	1973
Camp David peace accords	1978
Iran-Iraq war	1980–1988
Persian Gulf War	1991
Palestinians granted self-rule	1995
9/11 terrorist attacks; U.S. action against al Qaeda and the Taliban in Afghanistan	2001
U.S. invasion of Iraq; fall of Saddam Hussein	2003
Israeli-Palestinian conflict continues	present

A leading example of such groups, and soon the most famous, was the radical Islamist umbrella organization al Qaeda. It was created by leaders of the foreign mujahidin who had fought against the Soviet Union in Afghanistan. Its official leader and financial supporter was the Saudi-born multimillionaire Osama bin Laden. Among its operational chiefs was the famous Egyptian radical Ayman al-Zawahiri, whose political career linked him directly to Sayyid Qutb and other founding thinkers in modern revolutionary Islam. These leaders organized broad networks of largely self-contained terrorist cells around the world, from the Islamic regions of Southeast Asia to Europe, East Africa, and the United States, funded by myriad private accounts, front companies, illegal trades, and corporate kickbacks throughout the global economy. Their organization defied borders, and so did their goals. They did not seek to negotiate for territory, or to change the government of a specific state. Instead, they spoke of the destruction of the state of Israel and American, European, and other non-Islamic systems of government worldwide and called for a united, apocalyptic revolt by fundamentalist Muslims to create an Islamic community bounded only by faith. During the 1990s they involved themselves in a variety of local terrorist campaigns in Islamic countries and organized large-scale suicide attacks against American targets, notably the American embassies in Kenya and Tanzania in 1998.

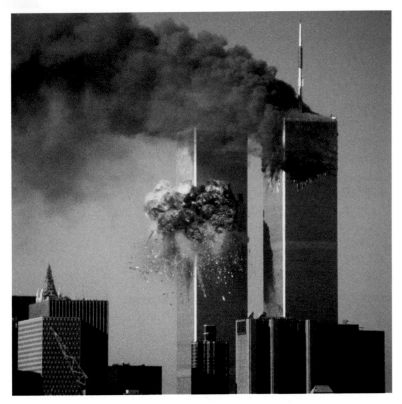

New York's World Trade Center towers, September 11, 2001.

At the beginning of the twenty-first century, al Qaeda's organizers struck again at their most obvious political enemy, the symbolic seat of globalization: the United States. Small teams of suicidal radicals, aided by al Qaeda's organization, planned to hijack airliners and use them as flying bombs to strike the most strategically important symbols of America's global power. On September 11, 2001, they carried out this mission in the deadliest series of terrorist attacks ever to occur on American soil. In the space of an hour, hijacked planes struck the Pentagon, the headquarters of the U.S. military, and the World Trade Center towers in New York City. A fourth plane, possibly aimed at the U.S. Capitol, crashed in open farmland in Pennsylvania, its attack thwarted when the passengers fought back against their captors. The World Trade Center towers, among the tallest buildings in the world, crumbled into ash and wreckage in front of hundreds of millions of viewers on satellite television and the Internet. In these several simultaneous attacks roughly 3,000 people died.

The attacks were at once a new brand of terror, deeply indebted to globalization in both its outlook and its method, and something older: the extreme, opportunistic violence of marginal groups against national cultures during a period of general dislocation and uncertainty. The immediate American response was action against al Qaeda's central haven in Afghanistan, a state in total collapse after the warfare of the previous thirty years. The United States' versatile professional soldiers and unmatched equipment, along with armed Afghan militias angry at the country's disarray quickly routed al Qaeda's Taliban sponsors and scattered the terrorists. That effort, however, failed to pinpoint and eliminate the hidden networks of leadership, finance, and information that propel apocalyptic terrorism. The rebuilding and rehabilitation of Afghanistan, a necessary consequence of American and European action, began from almost nothing in terms of administration and infrastructure. Pressing crises elsewhere and the changeable nature of Western popular concerns made a recovery difficult.

One reason for the persistent fears about such groups as al Qaeda has to do with the increasing power and availability of weapons they might use: chemical substances, biological agents that could kill millions, even portable nuclear weapons. With the end of the cold war, methods and technologies that the superpowers employed to maintain their nuclear balance of terror became more available on the margins to displaced groups with the financial or political leverage to seek them out. Other major arms races, centered, for example, around Israel or the conflicts between India and Pakistan, helped spread the availability of production sites and resources for weapons of horrific power, no longer governed absolutely by the legal conventions and deterrent strength of superpowers. Fear that the Iraqi government of Saddam Hussein was reaching for biological and nuclear capabilities helped propel the Gulf War of 1991 and active international efforts to disarm Iraq thereafter. Anxiety that states such as Iraq might transfer such weapons to apocalyptic terrorists, a fear given new life after the attacks on New York and Washington, provided the rationale for an American-led invasion of Iraq in the spring of 2003. The campaign, which used a remarkably small force both on the ground and in the air, quickly took Iraq over and deposed Hussein. No immediate evidence of recent, active weapons development programs was found, however; and in the process, the United States inherited the complex reconstruction of a broken state, fractured by guerilla violence and anti-Western terrorism.

A similar threat remained present in North Korea. After the loss of Soviet patronage in 1991, the isolated North Korean state careened from one economic disaster to another, with verified reports of local starvation in some regions of the country and a breakdown of government into military and political fiefdoms. The North Korean government pursued the development of a nuclear arsenal as a bargaining chip against the other major states of northeast Asia and the United States. Those neighbors each understood the grim chance that North Korea might break the last and perhaps most crucial nuclear threshold, providing nuclear weapons not to hard-pressed states but instead to stateless organizations. In short, by the early twenty-first century, warfare and the terrifying killing power of modern technology threatened to elude the control of national states and clearly defined political communities.

TRANSFORMATIONS: HUMAN RIGHTS

Some of the same globalizing processes have dramatically expanded our conception of citizenship, rights, and law. High school halls and college walkways are crammed with the tables of international organizations, such as Amnesty International, that promote universal human rights. How has this notion of human rights become so familiar? What older traditions has it built on or replaced?

The contemporary language of human rights is anchored in a tradition of political thought that reaches back to at least the seventeenth century. It took its present form in response to the atrocities of World War I and, especially, World War II. Atrocities and people's shocked responses to them, however, did not create either a new concern with human rights or the institutions dedicated to upholding them. Enforcing *universal* human rights challenges the sovereignty of nation-states and an individual nation-state's power over its citizens. International courts and human rights organizations thus require and hasten what political thinkers call the globalization of judicial power.

Human rights are part of the Western political tradition. So is opposition to them. The belief that rights were embedded in "nature," "natural order," or "natural law" formed a powerful strain of early modern political thought. John Locke understood natural law as the law of reason (see Chapter Fifteen); others understood it to be the law of God. However conceptualized, it represented a higher authority to which men owed their obedience. Opponents

Human rights are part of the Western political tradition. So is opposition to them.

of absolutism in seventeenth- and eighteenth-century Europe were driven by motives that were economic, religious, and social. Natural rights, however, became one of their rallying cries. The English Bill of Rights of 1689, accepted by William and Mary after the Glorious Revolution, insisted on "the true, ancient, and indubitable rights and liberties of the people of this kingdom." A century later, the American Declaration of Independence and the French Declaration of the Rights of Man more broadly proclaimed the "natural, inalienable and sacred rights of man," which in their eyes belonged to all men—not just the colonists of North America or the citizens of France. In point of fact, of course, those bold declarations of rights were not universal: women, slaves, people of color, and people of different religions were excluded, wholly or partially, and many nineteenth-century political theorists and scientists dedicated countless volumes to the proposition that these groups were *not* created equal. Which human beings might receive the "rights of man," then, was bitterly contested for the better part of the nineteenth and twentieth centuries, and only slowly did a more inclusive conception of human rights displace a narrower historical tradition of the rights of man.

Even the rights of man, relatively limited by present-day standards, met with opposition and skepticism. The distinguished conservative Edmund Burke (1730–1797) denounced the French Declaration of the Rights of Man as danger-ous metaphysical nonsense, which rested on "paltry blurred shreds of paper" rather than on well-grounded institutions and customs (see Chapter Eighteen). The equally distinguished radical Karl Marx (1818–1883) considered the French and American declarations illusory because the political rights they promised were eviscerated by social and economic inequality.

As far as the history of human rights is concerned, perhaps the most important development of the nineteenth century was the rise of nationalism and nation-states. Rights, and political movements claiming them, became increasingly inseparable from nationhood. "What is a country . . . but the place in which our demands for individual rights are most secure?" asked the Italian nationalist Giuseppe Mazzini. For nineteenth-century Italians, Germans, Serbs, and Poles and for twentieth-century Indians, Vietnamese, and Algerians —to name just a few—fighting for national independence was the way to secure the rights of citizens. National sovereignty, once achieved, was tightly woven into the fabric of politics and international relations and would not be easily relinquished.

The world wars marked a turning point. World War I, an unprecedented global conflict, almost inevitably fostered dreams of global peace under the auspices of international organizations. The Peace of Paris aimed for more than a territorial settlement: with the League of Nations it tried, tentatively, to establish an organization that would transcend the power of individual nations and uphold the (ill-defined) principles of "civilization." (Despite this commitment, the League bowed to British and American objections to a statement condemning racial discrimination.) The experiment failed: the fragile League was swept aside by the surge of extreme nationalism and aggression in the 1930s. The shock and revulsion at the atrocities of the war that followed, however, brought forth more decisive efforts. World War II's aftermath saw the establishment of the United Nations, an International Court of Justice at the Hague (Netherlands), and the UN's High Commission on Human Rights. Unlike anything attempted after World War I, the Commission on Human Rights set out to establish the rights of individuals—against the nation-state.

Mahtma Gandhi, asked to comment on Western civilization, replied that he thought it was a "good idea."

This Universal Declaration of Human Rights, published by the High Commission in 1948, became the touchstone of our modern notion of human rights. It was very much a product of its time. Its authors included Eleanor Roosevelt and the French jurist René Cassin, who had been wounded in World War I (and held his intestines together during a nearly 400-mile train ride to medical treatment), lost his family in the Holocaust, and had seen his nation collaborate with the Nazis. The High Commission argued that the war and the "barbarous acts which have outraged the conscience of mankind," showed that no state should have absolute power over its citizens. The Universal Declaration prohibited torture, cruel punishment, and slavery. A separate convention, also passed in 1948, dealt with the newly defined crime of genocide. The Universal Declaration of 1948 built on earlier declarations that universalized the rights to legal equality, freedom of religion and speech, and the right to participate in government. Finally, it reflected to postwar period's effort to put democracy on a more solid footing by establishing *social* rights—to education, work, a "just and favorable remuneration," a "standard of living," and social security, among others.

Few nations were willing to ratify the Universal Declaration of Human Rights. For decades after the war, its idealistic principles could not be reconciled with British and French colonialism, American racial segregation, or Soviet dictatorship. For a long as wars to end colonialism continued, declarations of universal principles rang hollow. (Mahtma Gandhi, asked to comment on Western civilization, replied that he thought it was a "good idea.") For as long as the cold war persisted, human rights seemed only a thinly veiled weapon in the sparring between the superpowers. Thus decolonization and, later, the end of the cold war began to enhance the legitimacy and luster of human rights. International institutions set up after World War II matured, gaining expertise and stature. Global communications and media dramatically expanded the membership and influence of organizations that, like Amnesty International (founded in 1961), operated outside the economic or political boundaries of the nation-state. Memories of World War II, distorted or buried by the cold war, continue to return, and the force of those memories helped drive the creation of International Criminal Tribunals for Yugoslavia and Rwanda in 1993. Finally, as one historian points out, at a time when many feel vulnerable to the forces of globalization, human rights offers a way of talking about rights, goods, and protections (environmental, for example) that the nation-state cannot—or can no longer—provide. The language of human rights, then, captures both the aspirations and some of the precariousness of globalization.

CONCLUSION

The loss of familiar moorings makes fundamental questions about human behavior and political community difficult to answer. History offers no quick solutions. Historians are reluctant to offer what historian Peter Novick calls "pithy lessons that fit on a bumper sticker." As Novick puts it:

> If there is, to use a pretentious word, any wisdom to be acquired from contemplating an historical event, I would think it would derive from confronting it in all its complexity and its contradictions; the ways in which it resembles other events to which it might be compared as well as the way it differs from them. . . . If there are lessons to be extracted from encountering the past, that encounter has to be with the past in all its messiness; they're not likely to come from an encounter with a past that's been shaped so that inspiring lessons will emerge.

The untidy and contradictory evidence that historians discover in the archives rarely yields unblemished heroes or unvarnished villains. Good history reveals the complex processes and dynamics of change over time. It helps us understand the many layers of the past that have formed and constrain us in our present world. At the same time, it shows again and again that these constraints do not preordain what happens next or how we can make the history of the future.

KEY TERMS

globalization	DNA	human rights	OPEC	al Qaeda
rights of man	Nelson Mandela	intifada	Sayyid Qutb	

SELECTED READINGS

Achebe, Chinua. *Things Fall Apart.* Expanded edition with notes. Portsmouth, N.H., 1996. An annotated edition of the now classic novel about postcolonial Africa.

Cmiel, Kenneth, "The Recent History of Human Rights." *American Historical Review.* (February 2004). One of the first scholars to treat human rights historically.

Coetzee, J. M. *Waiting for the Barbarians.* London, 1980. A searing critique of apartheid-era South Africa by a leading Afrikaner novelist.

Cooper, Frederick. *Colonialism in Question: Theory, Knowledge, History.* Los Angeles and Berkeley, Calif., 2005. Excellent collection of essays and valuable critical analysis of the term globalization.

Epstein, Helen. *The Invisible Cure: Africa, the West, and the Fight Against AIDS.* New York, 2007. One of the best recent studies.

Geyer, Michael, and Charles Bright. "World History in a Global Age." *American Historical Review* (October 1995). An excellent short discussion.

Glendon, Mary Ann. *A World Made New: Eleanor Roosevelt and the Universal Declaration of Human Rights.* New York, 2001. A fascinating study of the High Commission in its time by a legal scholar.

Held, David, et al. *Global Transformations: Politics, Economics, and Culture.* Stanford, Calif., 1999. Major survey of the globalization of culture, finance, criminality, and politics.

Hopkins, A. G., ed. *Globalization in World History.* New York, 2002. Excellent introduction, written by one of the first historians to engage the issue.

Hunt, Lynn. *Inventing Human Rights: A History.* New York, 2007. A short study of the continuities and paradoxes in the West's human rights tradition, by one of the foremost historians of the French revolution. On 1776, 1789, and 1948.

Keddie, Nikki. *Modern Iran: Roots and Results of Revolution.* New Haven, Conn., 2003. A revised edition of her major study of Iran's 1979 revolution, with added perspective on Iran's Islamic government.

Lacqueur, Walter. *The Age of Terrorism.* Boston, 1987. An important study of the first wave of post-1960s terrorism.

Landes, David. *The Wealth and Poverty of Nations: Why Some Are So Rich and Some So Poor.* New York, 1998. Leading economic historian's account of globalization's effects on the international economy.

Lewis, Bernard. *The Crisis of Islam: Holy War and Unholy Terror.* New York, 2003. Conservative scholar of the Arab world discussing the political crises that fueled terrorism.

McNeill, J. R. *Something New under the Sun: An Environmental History of the Twentieth-Century World.* New York and London, 2000. Fascinating new approach to environmental history.

Mckeown, Adam. "Global Migration, 1846–1940." *Journal of World History* 15.2 (2004). Includes references to more work on the subject.

Novick, Peter. *The Holocaust in American Life.* Boston, 1999.

Power, Samantha. *The Problem from Hell: America in the Age of Genocide.* A prize-winning survey of the entire twentieth century, its genocides, and the different human rights movements that responded to them.

Reynolds, David. *One World Divisible: A Global History since 1945.* New York and London, 2000. Excellent study of the different dimensions of globalization.

Shlaim, Avi. *The Iron Wall: Israel and the Arab World.* New York, 2000. Leading Israeli historian on the evolution of Israel's defensive foreign policy.

Stiglitz, Joseph E. *Globalization and Its Discontents.* New York, 2002. A recent and important consideration of contemporary globalization's character and the conflicts it creates, particularly over commerce and culture.

Shilts, Randy. *And the Band Played On: Politics, People, and the AIDS Epidemic.* New York, 1987. An impassioned attack on the individuals and governments that failed to come to grips with the early spread of the disease.

Turkle, Sherry. *Life on the Screen: Identity in the Age of the Internet.* New York, 1995. An important early study of Web culture and the fluid possibilities of electronic communication.

Winter, Jay. *Dreams of Peace and Freedom: Utopian Moments in the Twentieth Century.* New Haven, Conn., 2006. One of the leading historians of war and atrocity turns here to twentieth-century hopes for peace and human rights.

RULERS OF PRINCIPAL STATES

THE CAROLINGIAN DYNASTY

Pepin of Heristal, Mayor of the Palace, 687–714
Charles Martel, Mayor of the Palace, 715–741
Pepin III, Mayor of the Palace, 741–751; King, 751–768
Charlemagne, King, 768–814; Emperor, 800–814
Louis the Pious, Emperor, 814–840

MIDDLE KINGDOMS
Lothair, Emperor, 840–855
Louis (Italy), Emperor, 855–875
Charles (Provence), King, 855–863
Lothair II (Lorraine), King, 855–869

WEST FRANCIA
Charles the Bald, King, 840–877; Emperor, 875–877
Louis II, King, 877–879
Louis III, King, 879–882
Carloman, King, 879–884

EAST FRANCIA
Ludwig, King, 840–876
Carloman, King, 876–880
Ludwig, King, 876–882
Charles the Fat, Emperor, 876–887

HOLY ROMAN EMPERORS

SAXON DYNASTY
Otto I, 962–973
Otto II, 973–983
Otto III, 983–1002
Henry II, 1002–1024

FRANCONIAN DYNASTY
Conrad II, 1024–1039
Henry III, 1039–1056
Henry IV, 1056–1106
Henry V, 1106–1125
Lothair II (Saxony), 1125–1137

HOHENSTAUFEN DYNASTY
Conrad III, 1138–1152
Frederick I (Barbarossa), 1152–1190
Henry VI, 1190–1197
Philip of Swabia, 1198–1208 ⎫
Otto IV (Welf), 1198–1215 ⎭ Rivals
Frederick II, 1220–1250
Conrad IV, 1250–1254

INTERREGNUM, 1254–1273

EMPERORS FROM VARIOUS DYNASTIES
Rudolf I (Habsburg), 1273–1291
Adolf (Nassau), 1292–1298
Albert I (Habsburg), 1298–1308
Henry VII (Luxemburg), 1308–1313
Ludwig IV (Wittelsbach), 1314–1347
Charles IV (Luxemburg), 1347–1378
Wenceslas (Luxemburg), 1378–1400
Rupert (Wittelsbach), 1400–1410
Sigismund (Luxemburg), 1410–1437

HABSBURG DYNASTY
Albert II, 1438–1439
Frederick III, 1440–1493
Maximilian I, 1493–1519
Charles V, 1519–1556
Ferdinand I, 1556–1564
Maximilian II, 1564–1576
Rudolf II, 1576–1612

Matthias, 1612–1619
Ferdinand II, 1619–1637
Ferdinand III, 1637–1657
Leopold I, 1658–1705
Joseph I, 1705–1711
Charles VI, 1711–1740

Charles VII (not a Habsburg), 1742–1745
Francis I, 1745–1765
Joseph II, 1765–1790
Leopold II, 1790–1792
Francis II, 1792–1806

RULERS OF FRANCE FROM HUGH CAPET

CAPETIAN DYNASTY
Hugh Capet, 987–996
Robert II, 996–1031
Henry I, 1031–1060
Philip I, 1060–1108
Louis VI, 1108–1137
Louis VII, 1137–1180
Philip II (Augustus), 1180–1223
Louis VIII, 1223–1226
Louis IX (St. Louis), 1226–1270
Philip III, 1270–1285
Philip IV, 1285–1314
Louis X, 1314–1316
Philip V, 1316–1322
Charles IV, 1322–1328

VALOIS DYNASTY
Philip VI, 1328–1350
John, 1350–1364
Charles V, 1364–1380
Charles VI, 1380–1422
Charles VII, 1422–1461
Louis XI, 1461–1483
Charles VIII, 1483–1498
Louis XII, 1498–1515
Francis I, 1515–1547

Henry II, 1547–1559
Francis II, 1559–1560
Charles IX, 1560–1574
Henry III, 1574–1589

BOURBON DYNASTY
Henry IV, 1589–1610
Louis XIII, 1610–1643
Louis XIV, 1643–1715
Louis XV, 1715–1774
Louis XVI, 1774–1792

AFTER 1792
First Republic, 1792–1799
Napoleon Bonaparte, First Consul, 1799–1804
Napoleon I, Emperor, 1804–1814
Louis XVIII (Bourbon dynasty), 1814–1824
Charles X (Bourbon dynasty), 1824–1830
Louis Philippe, 1830–1848
Second Republic, 1848–1852
Napoleon III, Emperor, 1852–1870
Third Republic, 1870–1940
Péain regime, 1940–1944
Provisional government, 1944–1946
Fourth Republic, 1946–1958
Fifth Republic, 1958–

RULERS OF ENGLAND

ANGLO-SAXON DYNASTY
Alfred the Great, 871–899
Edward the Elder, 899–924
Ethelstan, 924–939
Edmund I, 939–946
Edred, 946–955
Edwy, 955–959
Edgar, 959–975
Edward the Martyr, 975–978
Ethelred the Unready, 978–1016

Canute, 1016–1035 (Danish Nationality)
Harold I, 1035–1040
Hardicanute, 1040–1042
Edward the Confessor, 1042–1066
Harold II, 1066

HOUSE OF NORMANDY
William I (the Conqueror), 1066–1087
William II, 1087–1100

Henry I, 1100–1135
Stephen, 1135–1154

HOUSE OF PLANTAGENET
Henry II, 1154–1189
Richard I, 1189–1199
John, 1199–1216
Henry III, 1216–1272
Edward I, 1272–1307
Edward II, 1307–1327
Edward III, 1327–1377
Richard II, 1377–1399

HOUSE OF LANCASTER
Henry IV, 1399–1413
HenryV, 1413–1422
Henry VI, 1422–1461

HOUSE OF YORK
Edward IV, 1461–1483
Edward V, 1483
Richard III, 1483–1485

HOUSE OF TUDOR
Henry VII, 1485–1509
Henry VIII, 1509–1547
Edward VI, 1547–1553
Mary, 1553–1558
Elizabeth I, 1558–1603

HOUSE OF STUART
James I, 1603–1625
Charles I, 1625–1649

COMMONWEALTH AND PROTECTORATE, 1649–1659

HOUSE OF STUART RESTORED
Charles II, 1660–1685
James II, 1685–1688
William III and Mary II, 1689–1694
William III alone, 1694–1702
Anne, 1702–1714

HOUSE OF HANOVER
George I, 1714–1727
George II, 1727–1760
George III, 1760–1820
George IV, 1820–1830
William IV, 1830–1837
Victoria, 1837–1901

HOUSE OF SAXE-COBURG-GOTHA
Edward VII, 1901–1910
George V, 1910–1917

HOUSE OF WINDSOR
George V, 1917–1936
Edward VIII, 1936
George VI, 1936–1952
Elizabeth II, 1952–

RULERS OF AUSTRIA AND AUSTRIA-HUNGARY

*Maximilian I (Archduke), 1493–1519
*Charles V, 1519–1556
*Ferdinand I, 1556–1564
*Maximilian II, 1564–1576
*Rudolf II, 1576–1612
*Matthias, 1612–1619
*Ferdinand II, 1619–1637
*Ferdinand III, 1637–1657
*Leopold I, 1658–1705
*Joseph I, 1705–1711
*Charles VI, 1711–1740
Maria Theresa, 1740–1780

*also bore title of Holy Roman Emperor

*Joseph II, 1780–1790
*Leopold II, 1790–1792
*Francis II, 1792–1835 (Emperor of Austria as Francis I after 1804)
Ferdinand I, 1835–1848
Francis Joseph, 1848–1916 (after 1867 Emperor of Austria and King of Hungary)
Charles I, 1916–1918 (Emperor of Austria and King of Hungary)
Republic of Austria, 1918–1938 (dictatorship after 1934)
Republic restored, under Allied occupation, 1945–1956
Free Republic, 1956–

RULERS OF PRUSSIA AND GERMANY

*Frederick I, 1701–1713
*Frederick William I, 1713–1740
*Frederick II (the Great), 1740–1786
*Frederick William II, 1786–1797
*Frederick William III,1797–1840
*Frederick William IV, 1840–1861
*William I, 1861–1888 (German Emperor after 1871)
Frederick III, 1888

*Kings of Prussia

*William II, 1888–1918
Weimar Republic, 1918–1933
Third Reich (Nazi Dictatorship), 1933–1945
Allied occupation, 1945–1952
Division into Federal Republic of Germany in west and
    German Democratic Republic in east, 1949–1991
Federal Republic of Germany (united), 1991–

RULERS OF RUSSIA

Ivan III, 1462–1505
Vasily III, 1505–1533
Ivan IV, 1533–1584
Theodore I, 1534–1598
Boris Godunov, 1598–1605
Theodore II,1605
Vasily IV, 1606–1610
Michael, 1613–1645
Alexius, 1645–1676
Theodore III, 1676–1682
Ivan V and Peter I, 1682–1689
Peter I (the Great), 1689–1725
Catherine I, 1725–1727
Peter II, 1727–1730

Anna, 1730–1740
Ivan VI, 1740–1741
Ellzabeth, 1741–1762
Peter III, 1762
Catherine II (the Great), 1762–1796
Paul, 1796–1801
Alexander I,1801–1825
Nicholas I, 1825–1855
Alexander II,1855–1881
Alexander III, 1881–1894
Nicholas II, 1894–1917
Soviet Republic, 1917–1991
Russian Federation, 1991–

RULERS OF SPAIN

Ferdinand ⎰ and Isabella, 1479–1504
⎱ and Philip I, 1504–1506
⎱ and Charles I, 1506–1516
Charles I (Holy Roman Emperor Charles V), 1516–1556
Philip II, 1556–1598
Philip III, 1598–1621
Philip IV, 1621–1665
Charles II, 1665–1700
Philip V, 1700–1746
Ferdinand VI, 1746–1759
Charles III, 1759–1788
Charles IV, 1788–1808

Ferdinand VII, 1808
Joseph Bonaparte, 1808–1813
Ferdinand VII (restored), 1814–1833
Isabella II, 1833–1868
Republic, 1868–1870
Amadeo, 1870–1873
Republic, 1873–1874
Alfonso XII, 1874–1885
Alfonso XIII, 1886–1931
Republic, 1931–1939
Fascist Dictatorship, 1939–1975
Juan Carlos I, 1975–

RULERS OF ITALY

Victor Emmanuel II, 1861–1878
Humbert I, 1878–1900
Victor Emmanuel III, 1900–1946

Fascist Dictatorship, 1922-1943 (maintained in northern Italy until 1945)
Humbert II, May 9–June 13, 1946
Republic, 1946–

PROMINENT POPES

Silvester I, 314–335
Leo I, 440–461
Gelasius I, 492–496
Gregory I, 590–604
Nicholas I, 858–867
Silvester II, 999–1003
Leo IX, 1049–1054
Nicholas II, 1058–1061
Gregory VII, 1073–1085
Urban II, 1088–1099
Paschal II, 1099–1118
Alexander III, 1159–1181
Innocent III, 1198–1216
Gregory IX, 1227–1241
Innocent IV, 1243–1254
Boniface VIII, 1294–1303
John XXII, 1316–1334
Nicholas V, 1447–1455
Pius II, 1458–1464

Alexander VI, 1492–1503
Julius II, 1503–1513
Leo X, 1513–1521
Paul III, 1534–1549
Paul IV, 1555–1559
Sixtus V, 1585–1590
Urban VIII, 1623–1644
Gregory XVI, 1831–1846
Pius IX, 1846–1878
Leo XIII, 1878–1903
Pius X, 1903–1914
Benedict XV, 1914–1922
Pius XI, 1922–1939
Pius XII, 1939–1958
John XXIII, 1958–1963
Paul VI, 1963–1978
John Paul I, 1978
John Paul II, 1978–2005
Benedict XVI 2005–

Glossary

Peter Abelard (1079–1142) Famed French theologian, logician, and university lecturer.

abolition of feudalism The end of the feudal system in France, which was brought about by the popular revolts of 1789. Louis XVI and other nobles established the National Assembly, which abolished all forms of privilege, such as the church tax on harvests, the labor requirement of peasants (known as the corvee), the nobility's hunting privileges, and a variety of tax exemptions and monopolies.

absolutism Form of government in which one body, usually the monarch, controls the right to make war, tax, judge, and coin money. The term was often used to refer to the state monarchies in seventeenth- and eighteenth-century Europe.

abstract expressionism The mid-twentieth-century school of art based in New York that included Jackson Pollock, Willem de Kooning, and Franz Kline. It emphasized form, color, gesture, and feeling instead of figurative subjects.

acid rain Precipitation laced with heavy doses of sulfur, mainly from coal-fired plants.

African National Congress (ANC) Multiracial organization founded in 1912 whose goal was to end racial discrimination in South Africa.

Afrikaners Descendants of the original Dutch settlers of South Africa; formerly referred to as Boers.

AIDS Acquired immune deficiency syndrome. AIDS first appeared in the 1970s and has developed into a global health catastrophe; it is spreading most quickly in developing nations in Africa and Asia.

Akhenaten The fourteenth-century B.C.E. pharaoh who developed a sun-oriented religion and ultimately damaged Egypt's position in the ancient world.

Alexander (356–323 B.C.E.) The Macedonian general who conquered northwest Asia Minor, and Persia, and built an empire that stretched as far east as the Indus River.

Algerian War The war in the 1950s and 1960s between France and Algerians seeking independence. Led by the National Liberation Front (FLN), guerrillas fought the French army in the mountains and desert of Algeria. The FLN also initiated a campaign of bombing and terrorism in Algerian cities that led French soldiers to torture Algerians and attract world attention and international scandal.

Allied Powers The World War I coalition of Great Britain, Ireland, Belgium, France, Italy, Russia, Portugal, Greece, Serbia, Montenegro, Albania, and Romania.

al Qaeda The radical Islamic organization founded in the late 1980s by former *mujahedin* who had fought against the Soviet Union in Afghanistan. Al Qaeda carried out the 9/11 terrorist attacks and is responsible as well for attacks in Africa, Southeast Asia, Europe, and the Middle East.

Americanization The fear of many Europeans from the 1920s and on that U.S. cultural products, such as film, television, and music exerted too much influence. Many of the criticisms centered on America's emphasis on mass production and organization. The fears about Americanization were not limited to culture. They extended to corporations, business techniques, global trade, and marketing.

Amnesty International Nongovernmental organization formed in 1961 to defend "prisoners of conscience"—those detained for their beliefs, color, sex, ethnic origin, language, or religion.

Anabaptists Swiss Protestant movement that began in 1521 and insisted that only adults could be baptized Christians. The movement's first generation, who had been baptized as infants according to Catholic practice, was "re-baptized," hence the name.

anarchism The social and political movement that began in the mid-nineteenth century and advocated the destruction of the state through violence and terrorism.

Apartheid The racial segregation policy of the Afrikaner-dominated South African government. Legislated in 1948 by the Afrikaner National Party, it existed in South Africa for many years.

appeasement The policy pursued by Western governments in the face of German, Italian, and Japanese aggression leading up to World War II. The policy, which attempted to accommodate and negotiate peace with the aggressive nations, was based on the belief that another global war like World War I was unimaginable, a belief that Germany and its allies had been mistreated by the terms of the Treaty of Versailles, and a fear that fascist Germany and its allies protected the West from the spread of Soviet Communism.

aqueducts   Engineering system that brought water from the mountains down to Roman cities.

Saint Thomas Aquinas (1225–1274)   Italian Dominican monk and theologian whose intellectual style encouraged the study of ancient philosophers and science as complementary to theology.

Arians   The fourth-century followers of a priest named Arius, who rejected the idea that Christ could be equal with God.

Aristotelian   The system of thought based on the ideas of the Greek philosopher Aristotle. Aristotelian ideas distinguished between the works of humans and those of nature and posited that as God's creation, nature belonged to a different, higher order.

Asiatic Society   A cultural organization founded in 1784 by British Orientalists who lauded native culture but believed in colonial rule.

Assyrians   A Semitic-speaking people that emerged around 2400 B.C.E. in northern Mesopotamia. Their highly militarized empire dominated Near-Eastern politics for close to two thousand years.

astrolabe   An ancient navigational instrument, thought to have been invented in 150 B.C.E., that was used to find latitude while at sea.

Atlantic system   A system of trade and expansion that linked Europe, Africa, and the Americas. It emerged in the sixteenth century in the wake of European voyages across the Atlantic Ocean.

Saint Augustine (c. 354–397)   One of the most influential Christian theologians of all time, Saint Augustine described his conversion in his autobiographical *Confessions* and formulated new aspects of Christian theology in *On the City of God*.

Augustus (63 B.C.E.–14 C.E.)   The grandnephew and adopted son of Julius Caesar and first emperor of the Roman empire.

Auschwitz-Birkenau   The Nazi concentration camp in Poland that was designed to systematically murder Jews and gypsies. Between 1942 and 1944 over one million people were killed in Auschwitz-Birkenau.

Austro-Hungarian empire   The dual monarchy established by the Habsburg family in 1867; it collapsed at the end of World War I.

authoritarianism   A centralized and dictatorial form of government, proclaimed by its adherents to be superior to parliamentary democracy and especially effective at mobilizing the masses. Authoritarianism was prominent in the 1930s.

Avignon   City on the southeastern border of France. Between 305 and 378 it was the seat of the papacy.

Aztecs   Native American people of central Mexico; their empire was conquered by the Spanish in the sixteenth century.

baby boom (1950s)   The post–World War II upswing in U.S. birth rates; it reversed a century of decline.

Francis Bacon (1561–1626)   British philosopher and scientist who pioneered the scientific method and inductive reasoning. In other words, he argued that thinkers should amass observations and then make general observations or theories.

Baghdad Pact (1955)   The Middle Eastern military alliance among countries friendly with America who were also willing to align themselves with the Western countries against the Soviet Union.

balance of power   Initated by the League of Augsburg in 1689, a new diplomatic goal emerged in western and central Europe to preserve a balance of power to prevent any single country from becoming so powerful as to threaten the position of the other major powers within the European state system.

Balfour Declaration   A letter dated November 2, 1917, by Lord Arthur J. Balfour, British Foreign Secretary, that promised a homeland for the Jews in Palestine.

Baroque   An ornate style of art and music associated with the Counter Reformation (from the French word for "irregularly shaped pearl").

Battle of the Marne   A major World War I battle in September 1914, which stifled German advancement in France and led to protracted trench warfare on the western front.

Bay of Pigs (1961)   The unsuccessful invasion of Cuba by Cuban exiles, supported by the U.S. government. The rebels intended to incite an insurrection in Cuba and overthrow the Communist regime of Fidel Castro.

Beer Hall Putsch (1923)   The Nazi invasion of a meeting of Bavarian leaders and supporters in a Munich beer hall; Adolf Hitler was imprisoned for a year after the incident.

Saint Benedict of Nursia (c. 480–c. 547)   Considered the father of western monasticism, Saint Benedict created the Benedictine rule that became the guide for nearly all western monks. Monks were required to follow the rules laid down by Saint Benedict: poverty, sexual chastity, obedience, labor, and religious devotion.

Berlin Airlift (1948)   The supply of vital necessities to West Berlin by air transport primarily under U.S. auspices. It was initiated in response to a blockade of the city that had been instituted by the Soviet Union to force the Allies to abandon West Berlin.

Berlin blockade   From June 1948 until May 1949, the Soviets cut all road, train, and river access from the Western zone of Germany to West Berlin. Unwilling to cede control of their portion of the capital, France, Britain, and the United States airlifted supplies over Soviet territory to the Western zone of Berlin.

Berlin Wall   The wall built in 1961 by East German Communists to prevent citizens of East Germany from fleeing to West Germany; it was torn down in 1989.

Bill of Rights   The first ten amendments to the U.S. Constitution; it was ratified in 1791.

Otto von Bismarck (1815–1890)   The prime minister of Prussia and later the first chancellor of Germany, Bismarck helped consolidate the German people's economic and military power.

Black Death   The epidemic of bubonic plague that ravaged Europe, East Asia, and North Africa in the fourteenth century, killing one-third of the European population.

Black Jacobins   A nickname for the rebels in Saint Domingue, including Toussaint L'Ouverture, a former slave who in 1791 led the slaves of this French colony in the largest and most successful slave insurrection.

Black Panthers   A radical African American group that came together in the 1960s; the Black Panthers advocated black separatism and pan-Africanism.

Blackshirts The troops of Mussolini's fascist regime; the squads received money from Italian landowners to attack socialist leaders.

Black Tuesday (October 24, 1929) The day on which the U.S. stock market crashed, plunging the U.S. and international trading systems into crisis and leading the world into the "Great Depression."

Blitzkreig The German "lightning war" strategy used during World War II; the Germans invaded Poland, France, Russia, and other countries with fast-moving well-coordinated attacks using aircraft, tanks and other armored vehicles, followed by infantry.

Bloody Sunday On Sunday, January 22, 1905, the Russian tsar's guards killed 130 demonstrators who were protesting the tsar's mistreatment of workers and the middle class.

Giovanni Boccaccio (1313–1375) Italian prose writer famed for his *Decameron*, one hundred short stories about the human condition, mostly from a comic or cynical point of view.

Boer War Conflict between British and ethnically European Afrikaners in South Africa, 1898–1902, with terrible casualties on both sides.

Simon de Bolivar (1783–1830) Venezuelan-born general called "The Liberator" for his assistance in helping Bolivia, Panama, Colombia, Ecuador, Peru, and Venezuela win independence from Spain.

Bolsheviks Former members of the Russian Social Democratic Party who advocated the destruction of capitalist political and economic institutions and started the Russian Revolution. In 1918 the Bolsheviks changed their name to the Russian Communist Party.

Napoleon Bonaparte (1769–1821) Corsican-born French general who seized power and ruled as dictator 1799–1814. After successful conquest of much of Europe, he was defeated by Russian and Prussian forces and died in exile.

bourgeoisie The French term for the middle class, which emerged in Europe during the Middle Ages. The Bourgeoisie sought to be recognized not by birth or title, but by capital and property.

Boxer Rebellion (1899–1900) Chinese peasant movement that opposed foreign influence, especially that of Christian missionaries; it was finally put down after the Boxers were defeated by a foreign army comprised mostly of Japanese, Russian, British, French, and American soldiers.

British Commonwealth of Nations Formed in 1926, the Commonwealth conferred "dominion status" on Britain's white settler colonies in Canada, Australia, and New Zealand.

Brownshirts Troops of young German men who dedicated themselves to the Nazi cause in the early 1930s by holding street marches, mass rallies, and confrontations. They engaged in beatings of Jews and anyone who opposed the Nazis.

bubonic plague An acute infectious disease caused by a bacterium that is transmitted to humans by fleas from infected rats. It ravaged Europe and parts of Asia in the fourteenth century. Sometimes referred to as the "black death."

Julius Caesar (100–44 B.C.E.) The Roman general who conquered the Gauls, invaded Britain, and expanded Rome's territory in Asia Minor. He became the dictator of Rome in 46 B.C.E. and was murdered by Brutus and Cassius, which led to the rise of Augustus and the end of the Roman republic.

caliphs Rulers of the Islamic community who claimed descent from Muhammad.

John Calvin (1509–1564) French-born Protestant theologian who stressed the predestination of all human beings according to God's will.

Canary Islands Islands off the western coast of Africa conquered by Portugal and Spain in the mid-1400s. Used to supply expeditions around the African coast and across the Atlantic.

Canterbury Tales Middle English verse stories by Geoffrey Chaucer (c.1340–1400) that reflect different classes and experiences in late medieval England.

caravans Companies of men who transported and traded goods along overland routes in North Africa and central Asia; large caravans consisted of 600 to 1,000 camels and as many as 400 men.

caravels Sailing vessels suited for nosing in and out of estuaries and navigating in waters with unpredictable currents and winds.

Carthage A great maritime empire that rivaled Rome; at its height, it stretched across the northern coast of Africa from modern-day Tunisia to the Strait of Gibraltar. Carthage fought against Rome in the Punic Wars that began in 264 B.C.E. The wars ended with the destruction of Carthage in 146 B.C.E.

Cassiodorus (490–583) Author of the *Institutes*, which instructed medieval readers on the essential works of literature a monk should know before moving on to more intensive study of theology and the Bible.

caste system A hierarchical system of organizing people and distributing labor, often based on heredity or regional origin.

Baldassare Castiglione (1478–1529) Author of *The Book of the Courtier*, a popular treatise on upper-class social graces.

Catherine the Great (1729–1796) German-born empress of Russia who maintained an absolutist feudal system but encouraged Enlightenment philosophy and the arts at court.

Catholicism Branch of Christianity headed by the pope.

Camillo Benso di Cavour (1810–1861) Anti-papist Italian leader who led the initial stages of revolution against the Habsburgs.

Central Powers The World War I alliance between Germany, Austro-Hungary, Bulgaria, and Turkey.

Charlemagne (742–814) Frankish ruler 767–813 who consolidated much of western Europe by adding Lombardy and Saxony to the Frankish kingdoms. With a strong sense of divine purpose, he forced the Christian conversion of pagan peoples and sponsored arts and learning at court. In 800 he became the first Roman emperor in the west since the 5th century.

Chartist movement (1834–1848) Mass democratic movement to pass the Peoples' Charter in Britain, granting male suffrage, secret ballot, equal electoral districts, and annual Parliaments, and absolving the requirement of property ownership for members of Parliament.

Chernobyl (1986) Site of the world's worst nuclear power accident; in Ukraine, formerly part of the Soviet Union.

chivalry From the word for "horsemanship"; an aristocratic ideology originating with the knights of eleventh-century Europe that encouraged military prowess and social graces.

Christine de Pisan (c. 1364–c. 1431) Born in Italy and spending her adult life in France, Pisan was the first lay woman to earn her living by her writing. While she wrote treatises on chivalry and warfare, she also wrote popular literature such as *The City of Ladies* and pamphlets debating the misogynistic claims made against women.

Winston Churchill (1874–1965) The British prime minister who led the country during World War II. He also coined the phrase "Iron Curtain" in a speech at Westminster College in 1946.

Church of England Founded by Henry VIII in the 1530s after his excommunication from the Catholic Church by Pope Clement VII, it is the established form of Christianity in England.

Cicero (106–43 B.C.E.) The most famous Stoic philosopher and orator of Rome.

Civil Constitution of the Clergy Issued by the French National Assembly in 1789, the Civil Constitution of the Clergy provided that all bishops and priests should be subject to the authority of the state. Their salaries were to be paid out of the public treasury, and they were required to swear allegiance to the new state, making it clear they served France rather than Rome. The Assembly's aim was to make the Catholic Church of France a truly national and civil institution.

Civil Rights Act (1964) U.S. legislation that banned segregation in public facilities, outlawed racial discrimination in employment, and marked an important step in correcting legal inequality.

Civil War (1861–1865) Conflict between the northern and southern states of America that cost over 600,000 lives; this struggle led to the abolition of slavery in the United States.

Cluny A Benedictine monastery, founded in 910, whose reform ideology tried to separate its network of religious houses from control by lay people.

Cold War (1945–1990) Ideological conflict in which the U.S.S.R. and Eastern Europe opposed the United States and Western Europe.

collectivization The process under Stalin in the 1920s and 1930s where peasants were forced to give up private farmland and join collective farms, which were supported by the state.

Colons French settler population in Algeria that ran the colonial government between 1830 and 1962.

Christopher Columbus (1451–1506) The Italian sailor who persuaded King Ferdinand and Queen Isabella of Spain to fund his expedition across the Atlantic to discover a new trade route to Asia. He miscalculated the size of the Earth and rather than landing in China or Japan, Columbus reached the Bahamas and the island of Hispaniola in 1492.

Committee of Public Safety Political body during the French Revolution that was controlled by the Jacobins, who enforced party rule by executing thousands during the Reign of Terror, September 1793–July 1794.

The Communist Manifesto **(1818–1883)** Radical pamphlet by Karl Marx that predicted the downfall of the capitalist system and its replacement by a system that operated in the interests of the working class (proletariat).

Compromise of 1867 Agreement between the Habsburgs and the peoples living in Hungarian parts of the empire that the Habsburg state would be officially known as the Austro-Hungarian Empire.

concession areas Territories, usually ports, established by the 1842 Treaty of Nanjing, where Chinese emperors allowed European merchants to trade and European people to settle.

Congo Independent State Large colonial state in Africa created by Leopold II, king of Belgium, during the 1880s, and ruled by him alone. After reports of mass slaughter and enslavement, the Belgian parliament took the land and formed a Belgian colony.

Congress of Vienna (1814–1815) and Restoration International conference to reorganize Europe after the downfall of Napoleon. European monarchies agreed to respect each other's borders and to cooperate in guarding against future revolutions and war.

conquistador Spanish term for "conqueror," applied to European leaders of campaigns against indigenous peoples in central and southern America.

conservativism Reactionary mode of thinking that held that tradition, including hereditary monarchy, would dispel the divisive ideas of the Enlightenment.

Constantinople Former capital of the Byzantine empire, eventually renamed Istanbul after its conquest by the Ottomans in 1453.

Constitutional Convention (1787) Meeting to formulate the Constitution of the United States of America.

Nicholas Copernicus (1473–1543) Polish astronomer who advanced the radical idea that the earth moved around the sun in *De Revolutionibus*.

Corn Laws Laws that imposed tariffs on grain imported to Great Britain, intended to protect British farming interests. The Corn Laws were abolished in 1846 as part of a British movement in favor of free trade.

Council of Trent Intermittent meeting of Catholic leaders (1545–1563) that reaffirmed Catholic doctrine against Protestant criticisms while also reforming the church.

Counter Reformation Movement To counter the spread of the Reformation, the Counter Reformation was initiated by the Catholic Church at the Council of Trent in 1545.

coup d'état Overthrow of established state by a group of conspirators, usually from the military.

courtly love Codes of refined romantic behavior between men and women of high station.

courtly romances Long narrative poems written in vernacular languages based on myths and legends but expressing ideals of medieval aristocratic conduct.

creoles Persons of European descent who were born in the West Indies or Spanish America.

Crimean War (1854–1856) War waged by Russia against Great Britain and France. Spurred by Russia's encroachment on Ottoman territories, the conflict revealed Russia's military weakness when Russian forces fell to British and French troops.

Oliver Cromwell (1599–1658) Puritan leader of the Parliamentary army that defeated the royalist forces in the English Civil War. After the 1649 execution of King Charles I and dispersion of Parliament, Cromwell ruled as self-styled Lord Protector from 1653 until his death.

Crusades (1096 to 1291) Series of wars undertaken to free Jerusalem and the Holy Lands from Muslim control.

Cuban Missile Crisis (1962) Diplomatic standoff between the United States and the Soviet Union that was provoked by the Soviet Union's attempt to base nuclear missiles in Cuba; it brought the world closer to nuclear war than ever before or since.

cult of domesticity Concept associated with Victorian England that idealized women as nurturing wives and mothers.

cult of the Virgin Mary A surge in veneration of the mother of Jesus beginning in the twelfth century that seemed to portend a change in how women were regarded as religious and moral beings.

cuneiform One of the earliest writing systems, beginning around 3500 B.C.E., it was the Mesopotamian form of writing on clay tablets using a stylus.

Cyrus (c.585–529 B.C.E.) The ruler of the Persians from circa 559 B.C.E. until 529 B.C.E.

Charles Darwin (1809–1882) British naturalist who wrote *Origin of the Species* and developed the theory of natural selection to explain the evolution of organisms.

David King of the Hebrews from around 1000 B.C.E. to 973 B.C.E. David united Israel and made Jerusalem his capital.

Leonardo da Vinci (1452–1519) Florentine painter, architect, musician, and inventor whose breadth of interests typifies Renaissance ideals.

D-Day (June 6, 1944) Date of the Allied invasion of Normandy under General Dwight Eisenhower to liberate Western Europe from German occupation.

Decembrists Russian army officers who were influenced by events in France and formed secret societies that espoused liberal governance. They were put down by Nicholas I in December 1825.

Declaration of Independence Historic U.S. document stating the principles of government on which America was founded.

Declaration of the Rights of Man and of the Citizen (1789) French charter of liberties formulated by the National Assembly that marked the end of dynastic and aristocratic rule. The seventeen articles later became the preamble to the new constitution, which the Assembly finished in 1791.

Olympe de Gouges (1745–1793) French political radical and feminist whose *Declaration of the Rights of Women* demanded an equal place for women in the new French republic.

Dhimmis "Peoples of the Book"; i.e., Jews and Christians, who were given a protected but subordinate place in Muslim society.

Charles Dickens (1812–1870) Hugely popular English novelist whose fiction exposed urban crime, poverty, and injustice but maintained Victorian domestic ideals.

Dien Bien Phu (1954) Defining battle in the war between French colonialists and the Viet Minh that secured North Vietnam for Ho Chi Minh and his army and left the south to form its own government to be supported by France and the United States.

Diet of Worms Examination of Luther by a church council in 1521. The council condemned him, and Luther was rescued by Frederick of Saxony.

Directory Temporary military committee that took over the affairs of the state of France in 1795 from the radicals and held control until the coup of Napoleon Bonaparte.

Discourse on Method Philosophical treatise by René Descartes (1596–1650) proposing that the path to knowledge was through logical speculation, beginning with one's own self: "I think, therefore I am."

Divine Comedy Italian verse narrative by Dante Alighieri (1265–1321); its complex themes exemplify the concerns of medieval learning.

DNA (deoxyribonucleic acid) Discovered by James Watson and Francis Crick in 1953, DNA contains an organism's genetic information and hereditary characteristics.

Dominican Order Founded by the Spaniard Saint Dominic (1170–1221) and approved by Innocent III in 1216, the order was dedicated to the fight against heresy and the conversion of Jews and Muslims. Many members of the order gained teaching positions in the infant European universities and contributed much to the development of philosophy and theology. The Dominicans always retained their reputation for learning, but they also came to believe that stubborn heretics were best controlled by legal procedures. Accordingly, they became the leading medieval administrators of inquisitorial trials.

Dominion in the British Commonwealth Canadian promise to keep up their fealty to the British crown, even after their independence in 1867. Later applied to Australia and New Zealand.

Don Quixote Comical adventure by Spanish writer Miguel de Cervantes (1547–1616) that mocks chivalric ideas.

Dreyfus Affair The 1894 French scandal surrounding accusations that a Jewish captain, Alfred Dreyfus, sold military secrets to the Germans. Convicted, Dreyfus was sentenced to life in prison. However, after public outcry, it was revealed that the trial documents were forgeries and Dreyfus was released.

Il Duce Term designating the fascist Italian leader Benito Mussolini.

Duma The Russian parliament.

Dunkirk The French port on the English Channel where the British and French forces retreated after sustaining heavy losses against the German military. Between May 27 and June 4, 1940, the Royal Navy evacuated over three hundred thousand troops using commercial and pleasure boats.

Earth Summit (1992) Meeting in Rio de Janeiro between many of the world's governments in an effort to address international environmental problems.

Eastern Front Battlefront between Berlin and Moscow during World War I and World War II.

East India Company (1600–1858) British charter company created to outperform Portuguese and Spanish traders in the Far East; in the eighteenth century the company became, in effect, the ruler of a large part of India. There was also a Dutch East India Company.

Edict of Nantes (1598) Edict issued by Henry IV to end the French Wars of Religion. The edict declared France a Catholic country, but tolerated some Protestant worship.

Eiffel Tower   Named after its creator, Gustave Eiffel, the tower was completed in 1889 for the Paris Exposition. This steel monument was twice the height of any other building at the time.

Albert Einstein (1879–1955)   German physicist who developed the theory of relativity, which states that space and motion are relative to each other instead of being absolute.

Elizabeth I (1533–1603)   Protestant daughter of Henry VIII, Queen of England 1558–1603. During her long reign, the doctrines and services of the Church of England were defined and the Spanish Armada was defeated.

Enabling Act (1933)   Emergency act passed by the *Reichstag* (German parliament) that helped transform Hitler from Germany's chancellor, or prime minister, into a dictator, following the suspicious burning of the *Reichstag* building and a suspension of civil liberties.

enclosure   Long process of privatizing what had been public agricultural land in the eighteenth century that changed the nature of economic activity in England.

The *Encyclopedia*   Joint venture of French *philosophe* writers, helmed by Denis Diderot (1713–1784), which proposed to summarize all modern knowledge.

Endeavor   Ship of Captain James Cook, whose widely celebrated voyages to the South Pacific at the end of the eighteenth century supplied Europe with information about the plants, birds, landscapes, and people of this uncharted territory.

Friedrich Engels (1820–1895)   German social and political philosopher who collaborated with Karl Marx on many publications.

English Navigation Act of 1651   Act stipulating that only English ships could carry goods between the mother country and its colonies.

Enlightenment   Intellectual movement stressing natural laws and classifications in nature, in eighteenth-century Europe.

Epicureanism   Greek philosophy that emphasized the individual, denied the existence of spiritual forces, and proposed that the highest good is pleasure.

Desiderius Erasmus (c. 1469–1536)   Dutch-born scholar and social commentator who proclaimed his humanist views in lively treatises like *In Praise of Folly* and the *Colloquies*.

Estates-General   French quasi-parliamentary body called in 1789 to deal with the financial problems that afflicted France at the time. It had not met since 1614.

Etruscans   Non-Indo-European-speaking settlers of the Italian peninsula who dominated the region from the late Bronze Age until the rise of the Romans in the sixth century B.C.E.

Euclid   Hellenistic mathematician whose book *Elements of Geometry* was the basis of modern geometry.

eugenics   Term, meaning "good birth," referring to the project of "breeding" a superior human race. It was popularly championed by scientists, politicians, and social critics in the late nineteenth and early twentieth centuries.

Eurasia   The combined area of Europe and Asia.

European Union (EU)   An international political body that was organized after World War II to reconcile Germany and the rest of Europe as well as to forge closer industrial cooperation. Over time, member states of the EU have relinquished some of their sovereignty, and cooperation has evolved into a community with a single currency, the euro, and a common European parliament.

Exclusion Act of 1882   U.S. congressional act prohibiting nearly all immigration from China to the United States; fueled by animosity toward Chinese workers in the American West.

existentialism   The philosophy that arose out of World War II and emphasized the human condition. Led by Jean Paul Sartre and Albert Camus, existentialists encouraged humans to take responsibility for their own decisions and dilemmas.

fall of the Bastille   On July 14, 1789, the sans culottes, led by the electors of Paris, stormed the Bastille, an ancient fortress, in search of weapons to protect themselves from Louis XVI's troops rumored to be heading toward the city. The fall of the Bastille was the first popular revolt in the French Revolution.

Fascism   The doctrine founded by Benito Mussolini. It emphasized three main ideas: statism ("nothing above the state, nothing outside the state, nothing against the state"), nationalism, and militarism.

Fascists   Radical right-wing group of the disaffected that formed around Mussolini in 1919 and a few years later came to power in Italy.

February Revolution (1917)   The first of two uprisings of the Russian Revolution, which led to the end of the Romanov dynasty.

Federal Deposit Insurance Corporation (FDIC)   Created in 1933 to guarantee all bank deposits up to $2,000 as part of the New Deal in the United States.

Federalists   Supporters of the ratification of the U.S. Constitution, which was written to replace the Articles of Confederation.

Federal Republic of Germany (1949–1990)   Country formed of the areas occupied by the Allies after World War II. Also known as West Germany, this country experienced rapid demilitarization, democratization, and integration into the world economy.

Federal Reserve Act (1913)   U.S. legislation that created a series of boards to monitor the supply and demand of the nation's money.

The Feminine Mystique   Groundbreaking book by feminist Betty Friedan (b. 1921), which tried to define "femininity" and explored how women internalized those definitions.

Fertile Crescent   An area of fertile land in what is now Syria, Israel, Turkey, eastern Iraq, and western Iran that was able to sustain settlements due to its wetter climate and abundant natural food resources. Some of the earliest known civilizations emerged there between 9000 and 4500 B.C.E.

feudalism   A loose term reflecting the political and economic situation in eleventh- and twelfth-century Europe. In this system, lords were owed agricultural labor and military service by their serfs, and in turn owed allegiance to more powerful lords and kings.

First Crusade (1095–1099)   Forces were sent by Pope Urban II to assist Byzantine emperor Alexius Comnenus in fighting Turkish forces in Anatolia. The struggle to recapture Jerusalem for western Christianity was eventually successful. This crusade prompted attacks against Jews throughout Europe and resulted in six subsequent military campaigns to the Holy Land.

First World War A total war from August 1914 to November 1918, involving the armies of Britain, France, and Russia (the Allies) against Germany, Austria-Hungary, and the Ottoman empire (the Central Powers). Italy joined the Allies in 1915, and the United States joined them in 1917, helping to tip the balance in favor of the Allies, who also drew upon the populations and material of their colonial possessions. Also known as the Great War.

Five-Year Plan Soviet effort launched under Stalin in 1928 to replace the market with a state-owned and state-managed economy in order to promote rapid economic development over a five-year period and thereby "catch and overtake" the leading capitalist countries. The First Five-Year Plan was followed by the Second Five-Year Plan (1933–1937), and so on, until the collapse of the Soviet Union in 1991.

Flagellants European social group that came into existence during the bubonic plague in the fourteenth century; they believed that the plague was caused by the wrath of God and chose to beat and mutilate themselves as a form of religious penance.

Franciscan order Order of monks established in 1209 by Saint Francis of Assisi (1182–1226); its members strove to imitate the life and example of Jesus.

Frankfurt Assembly An 1848 gathering of delegates from all German states that attempted to unify them into one nation. The liberal agenda and squabbling over whose plan for the nation was best led to the failure of the gathering.

Franz Ferdinand (1863–1914) Archduke of Austria and heir to the Austro-Hungarian empire; his assassination led to the beginning of World War I.

Frederick the Great (1740–1786) Prussian ruler who engaged the nobility in maintaining a strong military and bureaucracy, and led Prussian armies to notable military victories. He also encouraged Enlightenment rationalism and artistic endeavors.

French new wave A group of filmmakers in the 1950s and 1960s that emphasized naturalistic and unsentimental portrayals of ordinary life. Famous new wave directors included Francois Truffaut (1932–1984), Jean-Luc Godard (b. 1930), and Eric Rohmer (b. 1920).

French Revolution of 1830 The French popular revolt against King Charles's July Ordinances of 1830, which dissolved the French Chamber of Deputies and restricted suffrage to exclude almost everyone except the nobility. After several days of violence, Charles abdicated the throne and was replaced by a constitutional monarch, King Louis Philippe.

French Revolution of 1848 Brief uprising caused by economic grievances; it was violently quelled by the government.

Sigmund Freud (1865–1939) The Austrian physician who founded the discipline of psychoanalysis and suggested that human behavior was largely motivated by unconscious and irrational forces.

***Front de Libération Nationale* (FLN)/Algerian Revolutionary National Liberation Front** An anti-colonial, nationalist party that waged an eight-year war, beginning in 1954, against French troops for Algerian independence; the war forced nearly all of the 1 million French colonists to leave.

Galileo Galilei (1564–1642) Italian physicist and inventor. The implications of his ideas raised the ire of the Catholic Church, and he was forced to retract most of his findings.

Mohandas K. (Mahatma) Gandhi (1869–1948) The Indian leader who advocated nonviolent noncooperation and helped win home rule for India in 1947.

Giuseppe Garibaldi (1807–1882) Italian revolutionary leader who led the fight to free Sicily and Naples from the Habsburg empire; the lands were then peaceably annexed by Sardinia.

garrisons Military bases inside cities that were often used for political purposes, such as protecting the rulers and putting down domestic revolt or enforcing colonial rule.

Gaul The region of the Roman empire that is modern Belgium, Germany west of the Rhine, and France.

Gdansk shipyard Site of mass strikes in Poland that led to the formation in 1980 of the first independent trade union, Solidarity, in the Communist bloc.

Geneva Peace Conference (1954) International conference to restore peace in Korea and Indochina. The chief participants were the United States, the Soviet Union, Great Britain, France, the People's Republic of China, North Korea, South Korea, Vietnam, the Viet Minh party, Laos, and Cambodia. The conference resulted in the division of North and South Vietnam.

German Democratic Republic Nation founded from the Soviet zone of occupation of Germany after World War II; also known as East Germany.

German Social Democratic Party Founded in 1875, it was the most powerful Socialist party in Europe before 1917.

Gilgamesh The hero of the Sumerian epic, which was recorded in written form around 2000 B.C.E. Gilgamesh was a powerful ruler who, along with his friend Enkidu, battled monsters and gods and searched for immortality.

Girondins Liberal revolutionary group that supported the creation of a constitutional monarchy during the early stages of the French Revolution.

globalization The term used to describe political, social, and economic networks that span the globe. These global exchanges are not limited by nation states and often rely on new technologies, international laws, and economic imperatives.

Arthur de Gobineau (1816–1882) French writer whose pseudoscientific, racist ideology provided a rationale for European imperialism.

Gold Coast Name that European mariners and merchants gave to that part of West Equatorial Africa from which gold and slaves were exported. Originally controlled by the Portuguese, this area later became the British colony of the Gold Coast.

Gothic style Period of graceful architecture emerging after the Romanesque style in twelfth- and thirteenth-century France. The style is characterized by pointed arches, delicate decoration, and large windows.

Great Depression Period following the U.S. stock market crash on October 29, 1929, and ending in 1941 with America's entry into World War II.

great divide Refers to the division between economically developed nations and less developed nations.

Great East Asia Co-Prosperity Sphere   Term used by the Japanese during the 1930s and 1940s to refer to Hong Kong, Singapore, Malaya, Burma, and other states that they seized during their run for expansion.

Great Terror   The systematic murder of nearly a million people and the deportation of another million and a half to labor camps by Stalin's regime during 1937 in an attempt to consolidate power and remove perceived enemies.

The Great War (1914–1918)   World War I.

Greek Civil War (1821–1827)   Conflict between Greek Christians and Muslim Ottomans.

Pope Gregory I (540?–604)   Roman Catholic Pope 590–604. Used his political influence and theological teachings to separate the western Latin from the eastern Greek church. He also encouraged the Benedictine monastic movement and missionary expeditions.

Guerrillas   Portuguese and Spanish peasant bands who resisted the revolutionary and expansion efforts of Napoleon; after the French word for war, *guerre.*

Guernica   The Basque town bombed by German planes in April 1937 during the Spanish Civil War. It is also the subject of Pablo Picasso's famous painting from the same year.

guest workers   Migrants looking for temporary employment.

guilds   Professional organizations in commercial towns that regulated the business conditions and privileges of those practicing a particular craft.

gulag   The vast system of forced labor camps under the Soviet regime; it originated in 1919 in a small monastery near the Arctic Circle and spread throughout the Soviet Union and to other Soviet-style socialist countries. Penal labor was required of both ordinary criminals and those accused of political crimes (counterrevolution, anti-Soviet agitation).

Gulf War (1991)   Armed conflict between Iraq and a coalition of thirty-two nations, including the United States, Britain, Egypt, France, and Saudi Arabia. The seeds of the war were planted with Iraq's invasion of Kuwait on August 2, 1990.

gunpowder   An explosive mixture of nitrates, sulfur, and charcoal that can be used in firearms. The use of gunpowder transformed warfare in the late middle ages and played a major role in the creation of European empires in Africa and the Americas.

Habsburg empire   Ruling house of Austria, which once ruled the Netherlands, Spain, and Central Europe but came to settle in lands along the Danube River. It played a prominent role in European affairs for many centuries. In 1867, the Habsburg empire was reorganized into the Austro-Hungarian Dual Monarchy, and in 1918 it collapsed.

Hadith   Sayings attributed to the Prophet Muhammad and his early converts. Used to guide the behavior of Muslim peoples.

Hagia Sophia   The largest house of worship in all of Christendom, located in Constantinople and built by the emperor Justinian. When Constantinople fell to Ottoman forces in 1453, it was turned into a mosque.

Hajj   The pilgrimage to Mecca; an obligation for Muslims.

Hammurabi   The ruler of Babylon from 1792 to 1750 B.C.E. Hammurabi issued a collection of laws that were greatly influential in the Near East for centuries.

harem   Secluded women's quarters in Muslim households.

Harlem Renaissance   Cultural movement in the 1920s that was based in Harlem, a part of New York City where a large African American population resided. The movement gave voice to black novelists, poets, painters, and musicians, many of whom used their art to protest racial subordination; also referred to as the "New Negro Movement."

heliocentric   The sun-centered view of the planetary system, which displaced the Earth from the center of the universe.

Henry VIII (1491–1547)   Oft-married English monarch who broke with the Roman Catholic church when the pope refused to grant him an annulment. The resulting modified version of Christianity became the Church of England, or Anglicanism.

Henry of Navarre (1553–1610)   Crowned King Henry IV of France, he renounced his Protestantism but granted limited toleration to Huguenots (French Protestants) with the 1598 Edict of Nantes.

Prince Henry the Navigator (1394–1460)   Portuguese noble who encouraged conquest of western Africa and trade in gold and slaves.

hero cults   Important ancient Greek families would claim that an impressive Mycenean tomb was that of their own famous ancestor and would practice sacrifices and other observances to strengthen their claim. This devotion could extend to their followers, and eventually whole communities would identify with such local heroes.

Hiroshima   Japanese port devastated by an atomic bomb on August 6, 1945.

Adolf Hitler (1889–1945)   The author of *Mein Kampf* and leader of the Nazis. Hitler and his Nazi regime started World War II and orchestrated the systematic murder of over five million Jews.

Hittites   An Indo-European-speaking people that migrated into Anatolia (now Turkey) around the beginning of the second millennium B.C.E.

Ho Chi Minh (1890–1969)   The Vietnamese communist resistance leader who drove the French out of Vietnam and controlled North Vietnam after the Geneva Accords divided the region into four countries.

Holy Roman Empire   The collection of lands in central and western Europe ruled over by the kings of Germany (and later Austria) from the twelfth century until 1806.

Holy Russia   Name applied to Muscovy, and then to the Russian empire, by Slavic Eastern Orthodox clerics who were appalled by the Muslim conquest in 1453 of Constantinople (the capital of Byzantium and of Eastern Christianity), and who were hopeful that Russia would become the new protector of the faith.

home charges   Fees India was forced to pay to Britain as its colonial master; these fees included interest on railroad loans, salaries to colonial officers, and the maintenance of imperial troops outside India.

Homo sapiens   Term defined by Linnaeus in 1737 and commonly used to refer to fully modern human beings.

hoplite   A Greek foot soldier armed with a spear or short sword and protected by a large round shield (a hopla). In battle, hoplites stood shoulder to shoulder in a close formation called a phalanx.

Huguenots   French Protestants who endured severe persecution in the sixteenth and seventeenth centuries.

Human Comedy   Masterpiece of French novelist Honoré de Balzac (1799–1850) that criticized materialist values.

humanism   Medieval program of study built around the seven liberal arts: grammer, logic, rhetoric, arithmetic, music, geometry, and astronomy.

human rights   The belief that all people have the right to legal equality, freedom of religion and speech, and the right to participate in government. Human rights laws prohibit torture, cruel punishment, and slavery.

Hundred Years' War (1337–1453)   Long conflict, fought mostly on French soil, between England and France, centering on English claims to the throne of France.

Saddam Hussein (b. 1937)   The former dictator of Iraq who invaded Iran in 1980 and started the eight-year-long Iran-Iraq War; invaded Kuwait in 1990, which caused the Gulf War of 1991; and was overthrown when the United States invaded Iraq in 2003. Involved in Iraqi politics since the mid-1960s, Hussein became the official head of state in 1979.

Il-khanate   Mongol-founded dynasty in thirteenth-century Persia.

Imam   Muslim religious leader and also a politico-religious descendant of Ali; believed by some to have a special relationship with Allah.

Imhotep   The chief adviser to the Pharaoh Djoser, who ruled in the 27th century B.C.E. Often considered to be the first architect, Imhotep designed tombs and other structures to express the power of the Egyptian pharaohs.

Indian National Congress   Formed in 1885, this political party was deeply committed to constitutional methods, industrialization, and cultural nationalism.

Indian Rebellion of 1857   The uprising began near Delhi, when the military disciplined a regiment of Indian soldiers employed by the British for refusing to use rifle cartridges greased with pork fat—unacceptable to either Hindus or Muslims. Rebels attacked law courts and burned tax rolls, protesting debt and corruption. The mutiny spread through large areas of northwest India before being violently suppressed by British troops.

Indo-Europeans   A group of people that spoke variations of the same language and moved into the Near East and Mediterranean shortly after 2000 B.C.E.

indulgences   Remissions of the penances owed by Catholics as part of the process by which their sins are forgiven.

Inkas   The highly centralized South American empire that was toppled by the Spanish conquistador Francisco Pizarro in 1533.

Inquisition   Tribunal of the Roman Catholic Church that aimed to enforce religious orthodoxy and conformity.

International Monetary Fund (IMF)   Established in 1945 to promote the health of the world economy, the IMF is a specialized agency of the United Nations.

intifada   Uprising in the Palestinian occupied territories from 1987 to 1993, in protest against the Israeli occupation and politics. The Oslo Agreement (1993) helped to reduce the tension between the two sides and the Intifada all but ceased by the end of 1993. In early 2000, the Intifada resumed.

Investiture Conflict   A disagreement between Pope Gregory VII and Emperor Henry IV of Germany that tested the power of kings over church matters. After years of diplomatic and military hostility, it was settled by the Concordat of Worms in 1122.

invisible hand   Described in Adam Smith's *The Wealth of Nations*, the idea that the operations of a free market would produce economic efficiency and economic benefits for all.

Irish home rule   The late-nineteenth- and early-twentieth-century movement, led by Sinn Fein (established 1905), for Irish self-government.

Irish potato famine   Period of agricultural blight from 1845 to 1849 whose devastating results prompted a mass emigration to America.

Iron Curtain   Term coined by Winston Churchill in 1946 to refer to the division of Western Europe, under American influence, from Eastern Europe, under the domination of the Soviet Union.

Ivan the Great (1440–1505)   Emperor of Russia who annexed neighboring territories and began Russia's career as a European power.

Jacobins   Radical French political group that came into existence during the French Revolution, executed the French king, and sought to remake French culture.

Jacquerie   Violent 1358 peasant uprising in northern France, incited by disease, war, and taxes.

James I (1566–1625)   Monarch of Scotland and England from 1603 to 1625. He oversaw the English vernacular translation of the Bible known by his name.

Janissaries   Corps of enslaved soldiers recruited as children from the Christian provinces of the Ottoman empire and brought up with intense loyalty to the Ottoman state and its sultan. The sultan used these forces to curb local autonomy and to serve as his personal bodyguards.

Jesuits   Religious order founded in 1540 by Ignatius Loyola to counter the inroads of the Protestant Reformation; the Jesuits were active in politics, education, and missionary work.

Jihad   A struggle and, if need be, a holy war toward the advancement of the cause of Islam.

Joan of Arc (c. 1412–1431)   French teenager, supposedly divinely inspired, who led forces against the English during the Hundred Years' War. Burned at the stake for heresy by the English and later made a Catholic saint.

Justinian (527–565)   Emperor of eastern Rome. Justinian codified Roman law in the Corpus Juris Civilis and tried to reunify the eastern and western halves of the old Roman empire.

***Das Kapital* (Capital)**   The 1867 book by Karl Marx that outlined the theory behind historical materialism and attacked the socioeconomic inequities of capitalism. Mixing economic theory and revolutionary politics, the book became the preeminent socialist critique of capitalism.

Johannes Kepler (1571–1601)   Mathematician and astronomer who elaborated on and corrected Copernicus's theory and is chiefly remembered for his discovery of the three laws of planetary motion that bear his name.

Keynesian Revolution   Post-Depression economic ideas developed by the British economist John Maynard Keynes, wherein the state took a greater role in managing the economy, stimulating it by increasing the money supply and creating jobs.

KGB   Soviet political police and spy agency, first formed as the Cheka not long after the Bolshevik coup in October 1917. It grew to more than 750,000 operatives with military rank by the 1980s.

Chingiz Khan (c. 1167–1227)   Title taken by Mongol chief Temujin meaning "The Oceanic Ruler." Began dynasty that conquered much of southern Asia.

Khanate   Major political unit of the vast Mongol empire. There were four Khanates, including the Yuan empire in China, forged by Chingiz Khan's grandson Kubilai in the 13th century.

Nikita Khrushchev (1894–1971)   Leader of the Soviet Union during the Cuban Missile Crisis, Khrushchev had quickly reached power soon after Stalin's death in 1953. His reforms and criticisms of the excesses of the Stalin regime led to his fall from power in 1964.

Kremlin   Once synonymous with the Soviet government, it refers to Moscow's walled city center.

Kristallnacht   The Nazi destruction of seventy-five hundred Jewish stores and two hundred synagogues on November 9, 1938.

kulaks   Originally a pejorative term used to designate better-off peasants, it was used in the late 1920s and early 1930s to refer to any peasant, rich or poor, perceived as an opponent of the Soviet regime. Russian for "fist."

Labour Party   Founded in Britain in 1900, this party represented workers and was based on socialist principles.

League of Nations   International organization founded after World War I to solve international disputes through arbitration; it was dissolved in 1946 and transferred its assets to the United Nations.

Vladimir Lenin (1870–1924)   Leader of the Bolshevik Revolution in Russia (1917) and the first leader of the Soviet Union.

Leonardo da Vinci (1452–1519)   The ultimate Renaissance man, Leonardo was a painter, architect, musician, mathematician, engineer, and inventor. He set up an artist's shop in Florence by the time he was twenty-five and gained the patronage of the Medici ruler of the city, Lorenzo the Magnificent.

Leopold II (1835–1909)   Belgian king who sponsored colonizing expeditions into Africa.

Leviathan   A book by Thomas Hobbes (1588–1679) that recommended a ruler have unrestricted power.

liberalism   Political and social theory that advocates representative government, free trade, and freedom of speech and religion.

lithograph   Art form that involves putting writing or design on stone and producing printed impressions.

Long March (1934–1935)   Trek of over 10,000 kilometers by Mao Zedong and his Communist followers to establish a new base of operations.

lord   Privileged landowner who exercised authority over the people who lived on his land.

lost generation   Refers to the 17 million former members of the Red Guard and other Chinese youth who were denied education from the late 1960s to the mid-1970s as part of the Chinese government's attempt to forestall political disruptions.

Louis XIV (1638–1715)   The "Sun King," known for his opulent court and absolutist political style.

Louis XVI (1754–1793)   Well-meaning but ineffectual king of France, finally deposed and executed with his family by revolutionaries.

Luftwaffe   Literally "air weapon," this is the name of the German air force, which was founded during World War I, disbanded in 1945, and reestablished when West Germany joined NATO in 1950.

Lusitania   The passenger liner that was secretly carrying war supplies and was sunk by a German U-boat (submarine) on May 7, 1915.

Martin Luther (1483–1546)   A German monk who led the Reformation movement. At the center of his ideas is the doctrine, "justification by faith alone," which challenged many of the medieval practices of the Catholic Church and led to the religious wars between Protestants and Catholics.

Lutheranism   Branch of Protestantism that followed Martin Luther's (1483–1546) rejection of the Roman Catholic "doctrine of works."

lycées   System of high schools instituted by Napoleon as part of his domestic reform campaign.

madrassas   Muslim schools devoted to the study of the Quran and Islam.

Magna Carta   "Great Charter" of 1215 signed by King John of England, which limited the king's fiscal powers and is seen as a landmark in the political evolution of the West.

Moses Maimonides (1135–1204)   Spanish-born Jewish scholar, physician, and scriptural commentator.

mandate system   Administered by the League of Nations after the Treaty of Versailles, the mandate system legitimized Europe's dominance of territories in the Middle East, Africa, and the Pacific. Mandate territories were divided into groups based on location and their "level of development."

Nelson Mandela (b. 1918)   The South African opponent of *apartheid* who led the African National Congress and was imprisoned from 1962 until 1990. After his release from prison, he worked with Prime Minister Frederik Willem De Klerk to establish majority rule. Mandela became the first black president of South Africa in 1994.

Manhattan Project   The secret U.S. government research project in Los Alamos, New Mexico, to develop the first nuclear bomb. The first test of a nuclear bomb was near Los Alamos on July 16, 1945.

manorialism   System common to England, northern France, and Germany in the Middle Ages of communal peasant farming under the protection of a landholding lord.

Mao Zedong (1893–1976) The leader of the Chinese Revolution who defeated the Nationalists in 1949 and established the Communist regime in China.

Marshall Plan Economic aid package given to Europe after World War II in hopes of a rapid period of reconstruction and economic gain and to secure the countries from a Communist takeover.

Master Eckhart (c. 1260–1327) Dominican monk who preached an introspective and charismatic version of Christian piety.

Karl Marx (1818–1883) German philosopher and economist who believed that a revolution of the working classes would overthrow the capitalist order and create a classless society. Author of *Das Kapital* and *The Communist Manifesto*.

Maxim gun Invented in 1885 by an American, Hiram Maxim, the Maxim gun was the first portable machine gun. Quickly adopted by the majority of European armies and capable of firing 500 rounds per minute, it played a major role in the imperial conquests of the African continent.

Mayans Native American peoples whose culturally and politically sophisticated empire encompassed lands in present-day Mexico and Guatemala.

Giuseppe Mazzini (1805–1872) Founder of Young Italy and an ideological leader of the Italian Nationalist movement.

Mecca Major commercial city of the Arabian peninsula in the sixth century C.E., at which time the founder of Islam, Muhammad, was born and achieved prominence. From the earliest days of the spread of Islam, the city was the destination of the chief religious pilgrimage for Muslims, and it is now considered the holiest site in the Islamic world.

Medici Dynasty of Florentine bankers and politicians known for their patronage of the arts.

Meiji empire Empire created under the leadership of Mutsuhito, emperor of Japan from 1868 until 1912. During the Meiji period Japan became a world industrial and naval power.

Menander (342 B.C.E.?–292 B.C.E.) Ancient Greek dramatist who wrote over 100 plays, many of which were standards of Western literature for hundreds of years. Only one complete surviving play is known, *The Grouch*, which was rediscovered in 1957.

mercantilism A popular Western belief between 1600 and 1800 that a country's wealth and power was based on a favorable balance of trade (more exports and fewer imports) and the accumulation of precious metals.

Michelangelo (1475–1564) Virtuoso artist, best known for the Sistine Chapel ceiling in Rome and his sculptures *David* and *Pieta*.

John Stuart Mill (1806–1873) English radical philosopher whose writings advocated aspects of socialism and civil liberties.

Slobodan Milosevic (b. 1941) The Serbian nationalist politician who took control of the Serb government and orchestrated the genocide of thousands of Croatians, Bosnian Muslims, Albanians, and Kosovars. After ten years of war, he was ousted by a popular revolt in 2000.

Minoans A sea empire that flourished on Crete and in the Aegean Basin from 1900 B.C.E. until the middle of the second millennium B.C.E.

modernism The series of artistic movements, manifestos, innovations, and experiments that redefined art in the first half of the twentieth century. Modernism rejected history and tradition in favor of expressive and experimental freedom.

Michel de Montaigne (1533–1592) French philosopher known for his *Essays*.

mosque Place of worship for the people of Islam.

Wolfgang Amadeus Mozart (1756–1791) Austrian child prodigy and composer of instrumental music and operas.

Muhammad (570–632 C.E.) The founder of Islam, he claimed to be the prophet whom God (Allah) had chosen for his final revelation to mankind.

Mullahs Iranian religious leaders who led the opposition movement against the shah and denounced the depravity of late-twentieth-century American materialism and secularism.

multinational corporations Corporations based in many different countries that have global investment, trading, and distribution goals.

Muslim Brotherhood Egyptian organization founded in 1938 by Hassan al-Banna. It attacked liberal democracy as a façade for middle-class, business, and landowning interests and fought for a return to a purified form of Islam.

Muslim League National Muslim party of India.

Benito Mussolini (1883–1945) The Italian founder of the Fascist party who came to power in Italy in 1922 and allied himself with Hitler and the Nazis during World War II.

Mutiny of 1857 Uprising of Indian soldiers against the ruling British, sometimes called the Sepoy Rebellion.

Mycenaens The ancient Greek civilization that settled in Greece during the second millennium B.C.E. and organized around powerful citadels.

Nagasaki Second Japanese city on which the United States dropped an atomic bomb. The attack took place on August 9, 1945; the Japanese surrendered shortly thereafter, ending World War II.

Napoleonic Code Legal code drafted by Napoleon in 1804; it distilled different legal traditions to create one uniform law. The code confirmed the abolition of feudal privileges of all kinds and set the conditions for exercising property rights.

National Assembly of France Governing body of France that succeeded the Estates-General in 1789 during the French Revolution. It was composed of, and defined by, the delegates of the Third Estate.

National Association for the Advancement of Colored People (NAACP) Founded in 1910, this U.S. civil rights organization was dedicated to ending inequality and segregation for black Americans.

nationalism Movement to unify a country based on a people's common history and social traditions.

NATO The North Atlantic Treaty Organization, which was a 1949 agreement between the United States, Canada, Great Britain, and 8 European countries that declared that an armed attack against any one of the members would be regarded as an attack against all. Other European countries have since joined.

"navvies"   Slang for laborers who built railroads and canals.

Nazi Party   Founded in the early 1920s, the National Socialist German Workers' Party (NDSAP) gained control over Germany under the leadership of Adolf Hitler in 1933 and continued in power until Germany was defeated in 1945.

Nazism   The National Socialist Workers Party led by Adolf Hitler which advocated a violent anti-Semitic, anti-Marxist, pan-German ideology.

Nefertiti   The wife of Akhenaten, the fourteenth-century B.C.E. Egyptian pharaoh.

Neolithic   The "New" Stone Age, which began around 11,000 B.C.E., saw new technological and social developments, including managed food production, the beginnings of semipermanent and permanent settlements, and the rapid intensification of trade.

New Deal   President Franklin Delano Roosevelt's package of government reforms that were enacted during the 1930s to provide jobs for the unemployed, social welfare programs for the poor, and security to the financial markets.

new imperialism   Expansion of colonial power by Western European nations, especially in Asia, in the last three decades of the nineteenth century.

Isaac Newton (1642–1727)   One of the foremost scientists of all time, Newton was an English mathematician and physicist; he is noted for his development of calculus, work on the properties of light, and theory of gravitation.

New World silver   The most lucrative export from the Spanish colonies in Central and South America was silver. The massive infusion of New World Silver into the sixteenth-century European economy accelerated inflation and eventually caused the collapse of the Spanish economy and widespread misery for the rest of Europe's poorest inhabitants who could not afford the rising prices of goods.

Nicholas I (1796–1855)   Russian tsar who executed the leaders of the 1825 December Revolution and pursued an absolutist reign.

Tsar Nicholas II (1868–1918)   The last Russian tsar, who abdicated the throne in 1917. He and his family were executed by the Bolsheviks on July 17, 1918.

Nicomachean Ethics   The treatise on moral philosophy by Aristotle, which teaches that the highest good consists of the harmonious functioning of the individual human mind and body.

Friedrich Nietzsche (1844–1900)   The German philosopher who denied the possibility of knowing absolute "truth" or "reality," since all knowledge comes filtered through linguistic, scientific, or artistic systems of representation. He also criticized Judeo-Christian morality for instilling a repressive conformity that drained civilization of its vitality.

Non-governmental organizations (NGOs)   Private organizations like the Red Cross that play a large role in international affairs.

North American Free Trade Agreement (NAFTA)   Treaty negotiated in the early 1990s to promote free trade among Canada, the United States, and Mexico.

Novum Organum   Work by English statesman and scientist Francis Bacon (1561–1626) that advanced a philosophy of study through observation.

October Revolution   The October 1917 uprising in Russia led by Lenin and the Bolsheviks to overthrow the provisional Russian government, withdraw Russia from the First World War, and establish a one-party Bolshevik state.

OPEC (Organization of Petroleum Exporting Countries)   Organization created in 1960 by oil-producing countries in the Middle East, South America, and Africa to regulate the production and pricing of crude oil.

Operation Barbarossa   The codename for Hitler's invasion of the Soviet Union.

Opium Wars (1839–1842)   War fought between the British and Qing China to protect British trade in opium; resulted in the ceding of Hong Kong to the British.

oracle at Delphi   Dating to 1400 B.C.E., the oracle was the most important shrine in ancient Greece. A priestess of Apollo who attended the shrine was believed to be able to predict the future. The shrine ceased to function in the fourth century C.E.

Ottoman slavery   Social system of using slave labor for domestic, administrative, and military work that permitted social advancement and religious diversity within the Muslim empire.

Pan-African Conference   1900 assembly in London which sought to draw attention to the sovereignty of African people and their mistreatment by colonial powers.

pan-Slavism   Cultural movement that sought to unite native Slavic peoples within the Russian and Habsburg empires.

papal   Of, relating to, or issued by a pope.

Patria   Latin, meaning "fatherland."

patricians   The uppermost elite class of ancient Rome.

Paul   One of the twelve apostles of Jesus, Paul spread Christianity throughout the Near East and Greece.

Peace of Paris   The 1919 Paris Peace Conference established the terms to end World War I. Great Britain, France, Italy, and the United States signed five treaties with each of the defeated nations: Germany, Austria, Hungary, Turkey, and Bulgaria. The settlement is notable for the territory that Germany had to give up, including large parts of Prussia to the new state of Poland, and Alsace and Lorraine to France; the disarming of Germany; and the "war guilt" provision, which required Germany and its allies to pay massive reparations to the victors.

Pearl Harbor   The American Navy base in Hawaii that was bombed by the Japanese on December 7, 1941, which brought the United States into World War II.

Peloponnesian War   The ancient Greek war between Sparta and Athens that began in 431 B.C.E. and ended with the destruction of the Athenian fleet in 404 B.C.E.

People's Charter   An action of the Chartist Movement (1839–1848); between 1839 and 1842 over 3 million British signed this document calling for universal suffrage for adult males, the secret ballot, electoral districts, and annual parliamentary elections.

perestroika   Introduced by Soviet leader Mikhail Gorbachev in June 1987, *Perestroika* was the name given to economic and political reforms begun earlier in his tenure. It restructured the state bureaucracy, reduced the privileges of the political elite, and instituted a shift from the centrally planned economy to a mixed economy, combining planning with the operation of market forces.

Pericles The fifth-century B.C.E. Athenian leader who served as strategos for thirty years and pushed through reforms to make Athens more democratic by giving every citizen the right to propose and amend legislation and making it easier for citizens to participate in the assembly and the great appeals court of Athens by paying an average day's wage for attendance.

Peterloo Massacre (1819) The killing of 11 and wounding of 460 following a peaceful demonstration for political reform by workers in Manchester, England.

Peter the Great (1672–1725) Energetic tsar who transformed Russia into a leading European country by centralizing government, modernizing the army, creating a navy, and reforming education and the economy.

Francesco Petrarch (1304–1374) Italian scholar and writer who revived interest in classical writing styles and was famed for his love sonnets.

Pharisees A group of Jewish teachers and preachers that emerged in the third century B.C.E. and insisted that all of Yahweh's (God's) commandments were binding on all Jews.

Philip II (382–336 B.C.E.) The Macedonian king who consolidated the southern Balkans and the Greek city-states; he was the father of Alexander.

Phoenicians The semitic-speaking residents of present-day Lebanon from around 1200 to 800 B.C.E. The Phoenician cities were centers for trade throughout the Mediterranean.

Plato's *Republic* The first systematic treatment of political philosophy ever written, it argued for an elitist state in which most people would be governed by intellectually superior "philosopher-kings."

plebians The citizen population of ancient Rome that included farmers, merchants, and the urban poor; plebians comprised the majority of the population.

plebiscite A common tool of authoritarian leaders where they put a question directly to popular vote. This allows the head of state to bypass politicians or legislative bodies who might disagree with him—as well as permitting local officials to tamper with ballot boxes. For example, in 1802, Napoleon was proclaimed consul for life by a plebiscite.

Plotinus (204–270 C.E.) The neo-Platonist philosopher who taught that everything that exists proceeds from the divine and that the highest goal of life should be the mystic reunion of the soul with the divine, which can be achieved through contemplation and asceticism.

polis One of the major political innovations of the ancient Greeks was the Polis, or city-state. They were independent social and political structures, organized around an urban center, containing markets, meeting places, and a temple; they controlled a limited amount of the surrounding territory.

Marco Polo (1254–1324) Venetian merchant who traveled through Asia for twenty years and published his observations in a widely read memoir, *Travels*.

Populists Members of a political movement that supported U.S. farmers in late nineteenth-century America. The term is often used generically to refer to political groups who appeal to the mass of the population.

potato famine (1845–1850) Severe famine in Ireland that led to the migration of large numbers of Irish to the United States.

Prague Spring A period of political liberalization in Czechoslovakia between January and August 1968 that was initiated by Alexander Dubček, the Czech leader. This period of expanding freedom and openness in this Eastern bloc nation ended on August 20, when the USSR and Warsaw Pact countries invaded with 200,000 troops and 5,000 tanks.

The Praise of Folly 1511 satire by Erasmus that attacked the corruption of the papacy.

pre-Socratics A group of philosophers on the Greek island of Miletus, including Thales, Anaximander, and Anaximenes, who raised questions about the relationship between the natural world, the gods, and humans, and formulated rational theories to explain the physical universe they observed.

Primitivism Movement in Western art forms in the late nineteenth and early twentieth centuries that used the so-called primitive art forms of Africa, Oceania, and pre-Columbian America to inspire a break with the established art world.

The Prince Influential treatise by Niccolo Machiavelli (1469–1527) that attempts to lay out methods to secure and maintain political power.

Protestantism Division of Christianity that emerged in sixteenth-century western Europe at the time of the Reformation. It focused on individual spiritual needs and rejected the social authority of the papacy and the Catholic clergy.

Ptolemy (c. 85–165 C.E.) One of the most influential ancient Greeks; he was a leading astronomer, mathematician, and geographer who lived his entire life in Alexandria and helped to transform that city into a center of scientific study and scholarship.

puppet states Governments that have little power in the international arena and follow the dictates of their more powerful neighbors or patrons.

Puritans Seventeenth-century reform group of the Church of England; also known as dissenters or nonconformists.

Qur'an (often ***Koran***) Islam's holy book, comprised of Allah's revelations.

Sayyid Qutb (1906–1966) The Egyptian critic who became one of the most important intellectual leaders of the Muslim Brotherhood and whose writings are often cited as philosophical inspiration for Osama bin Laden and other Islamic radicals.

François Rabelais (c. 1494?–1553) French humanist satirist best known for his crudely comic *Gargantua and Pantagruel*, in which he espouses the "eat, drink, and be merry" lifestyle. Originally a novice in the Franciscan order, later a Benedictine monk who left the order to study medicine, Rabelais spent time in hiding for fear of being labeled a heretic, and some of his books were banned.

radicals Widely used term in nineteenth-century Europe that referred to those individuals and political organizations that favored the total reconfiguration of Europe's old state system.

Raj Term referring to the British crown's administration of India following the end of the East India Company's rule after the Indian Mutiny of 1857.

Ramadan Ninth month of the Muslim year, during which all Muslims must fast during daylight hours.

Raphael (1483–1520)   Italian painter noted for his warmly human treatment of religious subjects, particularly his Madonnas and large-figure compositions in the Vatican in Rome.

realism   Artistic and literary style which sought to portray common situations as they would appear in reality.

Realpolitik   Political strategy advancing power for its own sake.

reason   According to thinkers like Descartes, reason is a subjective faculty, or unaided ability, to form concepts.

Rebellion of 1857   Indian rebellion against the English East India Company to bring religious purification, an egalitarian society, and local and communal solidarity without the interference of British rule.

Reds   The Bolsheviks.

Reformation   Religious and political movement in sixteenth-century Europe that led to the breakaway of Protestant groups from the Catholic Church; notable figures include Martin Luther and John Calvin.

Reich   A term for the German state. The first Reich corresponded to the Holy Roman Empire (9th century to 1806), the second Reich was from 1871 to 1919, and the third Reich lasted from 1933 through May 1945.

Reign of Terror   Campaign at the height of the French Revolution (1793–1794) in which violence, including systematic executions of opponents of the Revolution, was used to purge France of its "enemies" and to extend the Revolution beyond its borders; radicals executed as many as 40,000 persons who were judged enemies of the state.

Religious Peace of Augsburg   1555 settlement between factions within the Holy Roman Empire that stated a territory would follow the religion of its ruler, whether Catholic or Protestant.

Renaissance   Term meaning "rebirth" that historians use to refer to the expanded cultural production of European nations between 1300 and 1600.

Restoration period (1815–1848)   European movement after the defeat of Napoleon to restore Europe to its pre-French revolutionary status and to prevent radical movements from arising.

Richard II (1367–1400)   King of England (r. 1377–1399), chiefly remembered for his successful resolution of the Peasants' Rebellion (1381) and as a vacillating, yet tyrannical monarch. He was deposed by his cousin Henry Bolingbroke (Henry IV) and assassinated.

Cardinal Richelieu (1585–1642)   First minister to French King Louis XIII, who centralized political power and deprived the Huguenots of many rights.

Rights of Man   A declaration by the French National Assembly in 1789 that declared property to be a natural right, along with liberty, security, and "resistance to oppression." It declared freedom of speech, religious toleration, and liberty of the press inviolable. All citizens were to be treated equally before the law. No one was to be imprisoned or punished without due process of law. Sovereignty resided in the people, who could depose officers of the government if they abused their powers.

Rembrandt Van Rijn (1606–1669)   A Dutch painter famous for his portraits, Biblical scenes, and imaginative experiments with light and shading.

Romanticism   Beginning in Germany and England in the late 18th century and continuing up to the end of the 19th century, a movement in art, music, and literature that countered the rationalism of the Enlightenment by stressing a highly emotional response to nature.

Jean-Jacques Rousseau (1718–1778)   Philosopher and radical political theorist whose *Social Contract* attacked privilege and inequality. One of the primary principles of Rousseau's political philosophy is that politics and morality should not be separated.

Russification   Programs designed to assimilate people of over 146 dialects into the Russian empire by the tsars in the late 19th century.

Rwanda   A former Belgian colony in central Africa that has been torn by ethnic violence between the Hutus and the Tutsis since before the country's independence in 1962.

Saint Bartholomew's Day Massacre   Massacre of French Protestants (Huguenots) by Catholic crowds that began in Paris on August 24, 1572, spreading to other parts of France and continuing into October of that year. More than 70,000 were killed.

St. Domingue   Former French Caribbean colony and site of a slave rebellion in 1791, which embroiled English and French forces until 1804, when St. Domingue was declared the independent nation of Haiti.

salons   Informal gatherings of intellectuals and aristocrats that allowed discourse about Enlightenment ideas.

Santa Sophia   The Byzantine church in Constantinople, constructed by emperor Justinian I in the sixth century, and famous for its dome, which rested on the keystones of four great arches.

Sappho (c. 620–c. 550 B.C.E.)   One of the most famous Greek lyric poets, she wrote beautiful poetry about romantic longing and sexual lust, sometimes about men, but more often about women.

Sargon (r. 2334–2279 B.C.E.)   The Akkadian leader who unified Mesopotamia.

Schlieffen Plan   Devised by Count Alfred von Schlieffen in 1905 and put into operation on August 2, 1914, the Schlieffen Plan required France to be attacked first through Belgium and a quick victory to be secured so that the German army could fight Russia on the Eastern Front.

scientific societies   Organizations that emerged in the seventeenth century to promote the improvement of scientific knowledge, experiments, and collaboration by scientists and philosophers.

Scramble for Africa   European rush to colonize parts of Africa at the end of the nineteenth century.

second industrial revolution   The technological developments in the last third of the nineteenth century, which included new techniques for refining and producing steel; increased availability of electricity for industrial, commercial, and domestic use; advances in chemical manufacturing; and the creation of the internal combustion engine.

Second World   Term invented during the cold war to refer to the Communist countries, as opposed to the West (or First World) and the former colonies (or Third World).

Second World War   Worldwide war that began in September 1939 in Europe, and even earlier in Asia (1930s), and that pitted Britain, the United States, and especially the Soviet Union (the Allies) against Nazi Germany, Italy, and Japan (the Axis).

Seleucus (d. 280 B.C.E.) The Macedonian general who ruled the Asian territory of Alexander the Great's empire and founded Greek colonies such as Antioch and Selsucia.

Semitic The Semitic language family has the longest recorded history of any linguistic group and is the root language for most of the languages of the Middle and Near East. Ancient Semitic languages include the language of the ancient Babylonians and Assyrians, Phoenician, the classical form of Hebrew, early dialects of Aramaic, and the classical Arabic of the *Quran.*

sepoys Hindu and Muslim recruits of the East India Company's military force.

serfdom Slavery-like system of customs and laws whereby peasants were kept poor and stationary by their manor lords; it had spread throughout the West by the 10th century and its peak was the Middle Ages.

Seven Years War (1756–1763) Worldwide war that ended when Prussia defeated Austria, establishing itself as a European power, and when Britain gained control of India and many of France's colonies through the Treaty of Paris. It is known as the French and Indian War in the United States.

Shah Traditional title of Persian rulers.

William Shakespeare (1564–1616) The greatest Elizabethan playwright, Shakespeare worked as actor before becoming a dramatist. The author of *Hamlet, King Lear,* and *Much Ado About Nothing* wrote nearly 40 plays and over 150 sonnets.

Shiism One of the two main branches of Islam. Shiites recognize Ali, the fourth caliph, and his descendants as rightful rulers of the Islamic world; practiced in the Safavid empire.

Shiites An often-persecuted minority religious party within Islam that insists only descendants of Ali can have any authority over the Muslim community. Today, Shiites rule Iran and are numerous in Iraq but make up only 10 percent of the worldwide population of Islam.

Silicon Valley Valley between California's San Francisco and San Jose, known for its innovative computer and high-technology industry.

Sinn Féin The Irish revolutionary organization that formed in 1900 to fight for Irish independence.

Sino-Japanese War (1894–1895) Conflict over the control of Korea in which China was forced to cede the province of Taiwan to Japan

Adam Smith (1723–1790) Scottish economist and philosopher who proposed that individual self-interest naturally promoted a healthy national economy. He became famous for his influential book, *The Wealth of Nations* (1776).

Social Darwinism Belief that Charles Darwin's theory of natural selection (evolution) was applicable to human societies and justified the right of the ruling classes or countries to dominate the weak.

social democracy The belief that democracy and social welfare go hand in hand, and that diminishing the sharp inequalities of class society is crucial to fortifying democratic culture.

socialism Political ideology that calls for a classless society with collective ownership of all property.

Social Security Act (1935) New Deal act that instituted old-age pensions and insurance for the unemployed in the United States.

the Social Question In the wake of the Industrial Revolution and rapid urbanization, topics such as criminality, water supply, sewers, prostitution, tuberculosis and cholera, alcoholism, wet nursing, wages, and unemployment were studied by political leaders, social scientists, and public health officials throughout Europe and collectively referred to as the "Social Question." Reformers and politicians believed that these issues needed to be addressed to avoid popular revolts in Europe's cities.

Society of Jesus Also called the Jesuit order, a group of priests influenced by military discipline. The society was founded by Saint Ignatius of Loyola (1491–1556) and is still very active in the field of education.

Socrates (469–399 B.C.E.) The ancient Greek philosopher who emphasized the reexamination of all inherited assumptions and tried to base his philosophical speculations on sound definitions of words. He also wished to advance to a new system of truth by examining ethics rather than by studying the physical world.

Solidarity The communist bloc's first independent trade union; it was established in Poland at the Gdansk shipyard in 1980.

Solon (d. 559 B.C.E.) Elected archon in 594 B.C.E., this ancient Greek aristocrat enacted a series of political and economic reforms that made Athenian democracy possible.

Aleksandr Solzhenitsyn (b. 1918) This Soviet novelist was a critic of the Soviet regime and wrote *The Gulag Archipelago,* which was published in 1974.

Sophists Ancient Greek professional teachers who taught that sense perception was the source of all knowledge and that only particular truths could be valid for the individual knower.

South African War (1899–1902) Often called the Boer War, this conflict between the British and Dutch colonists of South Africa resulted in bringing two Afrikaner republics under the control of the British.

Soviet bloc International alliance that included the East European countries of the Warsaw Pact as well as the Soviet Union, but also came to include Cuba.

Spanish-American War (1898) War between the United States and Spain in Cuba, Puerto Rico, and the Philippines. It ended with a treaty in which the United States took over the Philippines, Guam, and Puerto Rico; Cuba won partial independence.

Spanish Armada Supposedly invincible fleet of warships sent against England by Philip II of Spain in 1588, but routed by the English and bad weather in the English Channel.

Spartiate A full citizen of Sparta who was a professional soldier of the hoplite phalanx.

spinning jenny Invention of James Hargreaves (c. 1720–1774) that revolutionized the British textile industry.

S.S. (*Schutzstaffel*) Formed in 1925 to serve as Hitler's personal security force and to guard Nazi party (NDSAP) meetings, the SS were notorious for their participation in carrying out Nazi policies.

Joseph Stalin (1879–1953) The Bolshevik leader who succeeded Lenin as the leader of the Soviet Union in 1924 and ruled until his death.

Strategic Defense Initiative (Stars Wars)   Master plan initiated by President Ronald Reagan that envisioned the deployment of satellites and space missiles to insulate the United States from nuclear bombs missiles.

Stoicism   The ancient Greek and Roman philosophy that held that the cosmos is an ordered whole in which all contradictions are resolved for ultimate good. Everything that happens is rigidly determined in accordance with rational purpose, and no individual is master of his or her fate. Founded in the fourth century B.C.E. and still popular well into the fifth century C.E.

Suez Canal   Built in 1869 across the Isthmus of Suez to connect the Mediterranean Sea with the Red Sea and to lower the costs of international trade.

Sufism   Emotional and mystical form of Islam that appealed to the common people.

sultan   An Islamic political leader. In the Ottoman empire, the sultan combined a warrior ethos with an unwavering devotion to Islam.

Sumerians   The civilization and people that arose in southern Mesopotamia (modern Iraq and Kuwait) around 4000 B.C.E. and developed one of the first written languages.

Sunnis   Orthodox Islam, as opposed to Shiite Islam.

supranational organizations   International organizations such as NGOs, the World Bank, and the IMF.

survival of the fittest   A main concept of Charles Darwin's theory of natural selection (evolution), which holds that as animal populations grow and resources become scarce, a struggle for existence arises, the outcome of which is that only the "fittest" survive.

sweatshops   Textile factories with poor pay and work conditions.

Syndicalism   Late-nineteenth-century organization of workplace associations that included unskilled labor.

tabula rasa   Term used by John Locke (1632–1704) to describe man's mind before he acquired ideas as a result of experience; Latin for "clean slate."

Testament of Youth   The memoir by Vera Brittain about the home front and the changing social norms during World War I.

tetrarchy   Diocletian's political reform, which divided the Roman empire into two halves ruled by two rulers and two lieutenants.

Third Estate   Delegates from the common class to the Estates General, the French legislature, whose refusal to capitulate to the nobility and clergy in 1789 led to the Revolution.

Third Reich   The German state from 1933 to 1945 under Adolf Hitler and the Nazi party.

Third World   Nations—mostly in Asia, Latin America, and Africa—that are not highly industrialized and developed.

Thirty Years' War (1618–1648)   Beginning as a conflict between Protestants and Catholics in Germany, it escalated into a general European war fought in Germany by Sweden, France, and the Holy Roman Empire.

The Three Estates   Eighteenth-century French society was divided into three estates. An individual's status determined his or her legal rights, taxes, and so on. The First Estate was the clergy; the Second was the nobility; and the Third Estate included everyone from wealthy merchants to poor peasants.

Tiananmen Square   Largest public square in the world, located in Beijing, the site of the Chinese pro-democracy movement in 1989 that resulted in the killing of as many as 1,000 protesters by the Chinese army.

Timur the Lame (1336–1405)   Mongol ruler who was the last leader of the Khans' south Asian empire. Also known as Tamerlane.

total war   All-out war involving civilian populations as well as military forces, often used in reference to World War II.

Treaty of Brest-Litovsk (1918)   Separate peace between imperial Germany and the new Bolshevik regime in Russia. The treaty acknowledged the German victory on the Eastern Front and withdrew Russia from the war.

Treaty of Nanjing (1842)   Treaty between China and Britain following the Opium War; it called for indemnities, the opening of new ports, and the cession of Hong Kong to the British.

Treaty of Utrecht (1713)   Resolution to the War of Spanish Succession that redistributed territory among the warring nations of Europe and encouraged England's colonial conquests.

Treaty of Versailles   Signed on June 28, 1919, this peace settlement ended World War I and required Germany to surrender a large part of its most valuable territories and to pay huge reparations to the Allies.

trench warfare   The twenty-five thousand miles of holes and ditches that stretched across the Western Front during World War I and where most of the fighting took place.

Triangular trade   The eighteenth-century commercial Atlantic shipping pattern that took rum from New England to Africa, traded it for slaves taken to the West Indies, and brought sugar back to New England to be processed into rum.

Tripartite Pact (1940)   A pact that stated that the countries of Germany, Italy, and Japan would act together in all future military ventures.

Triple Entente   Alliance developed before World War I that eventually included Britain, France, and Russia.

Truman Doctrine (1947)   Declaration promising U.S. economic and military intervention, whenever and wherever needed, for the sake of preventing further communist expansion.

Truth and Reconciliation Commission   Quasi-judicial body established after the overthrow of the apartheid system in South Africa and the election of Nelson Mandela as the country's first black president in 1994. The commission was to take evidence about the crimes committed during the apartheid years. Those who showed remorse could appeal for clemency. The South African leaders believed that an airing of the grievances from this period would promote racial harmony and reconciliation.

tsar   Russian translation, similar to the German *kaiser*, of the Roman title "caesar" (emperor), a title claimed by the rulers of medieval Muscovy and then the Russian empire.

Mary Tudor (1516–1558)   Catholic daughter of Henry VIII who reinstituted Catholicism in England when she acceded to the throne; she was called "Bloody Mary" for her violent suppression of Protestants during her five-year reign.

Two Treatises on Government   Published in 1690, this work by John Locke (1632–1704) defended humans' right to freedom against absolutist ideas and served as one of the underpinnings of the U.S. Constitution.

Ubaid   This culture flourished in Mesopotamia between 5500 and 4000 B.C.E., characterized by large village settlements and the first temples built in that area. A precursor to the Sumerians and the development of "urban" civilizations.

UFA   The German film company that produced films by expressionist directors like F. W. Murnau and Fritz Lang during the 1920s. Under Hitler, it was controlled by the state and began turning out Nazi propaganda.

Universal Declaration of Human Rights (1948)   United Nations declaration that laid out the rights to which all human beings were entitled.

Utopia   Humanist social critique by English statesman Thomas More (1478–1535).

utopian socialism   The most visionary of all Restoration-era movements, Utopian socialists, like Charles Fourier, dreamt of transforming states, workplaces, and human relations, and proposed actual plans to do so.

velvet revolutions   The peaceful political revolutions throughout Eastern Europe in 1989.

Versailles   Splendid palace outside Paris where Louis XIV and his nobles resided.

Versailles Conference (1919)   Peace conference between the victors of World War I; resulted in the Treaty of Versailles, which forced Germany to pay reparations and to give up its colonies to the victors.

Queen Victoria (1819–1901)   Influential monarch who reigned from 1837 to her death; she presided over the expansion of the British empire as well as the evolution of English politics and social and economic reforms.

Viet Cong   Vietnamese communist group formed in 1954; committed to overthrowing the government of South Vietnam and reunifying North and South Vietnam.

A Vindication of the Rights of Woman   Noted work of Mary Wollstonecraft (1759–1797), English republican who applied Enlightenment political ideas to issues of gender.

Virgil (70–19 B.C.E.)   One of the most influential Roman authors, his surviving works include the Eclogues and the Roman epic poem, the *Aeneid*.

Visigoths   The German "barbarians" who sacked Rome in 410.

Voltaire   Pseudonym of French philosopher and satirist Francois Marie Arouet (1694–1797), who championed the cause of human dignity against state and church oppression. Noted Deist and author of *Candide*.

Voting Rights Act (1965)   Law that granted universal suffrage in the United States.

Wars of the Roses   Fifteenth-century conflict between the English dynastic houses of Lancaster and York (each symbolized in heraldry by the rose), ultimately won by Lancastrian Henry VII.

Warsaw Pact (1955–1991)   Military alliance between the U.S.S.R. and other Communist states that was established as a response to the creation of the NATO alliance.

James Watt (1736–1819)   Scottish inventor and scientist who developed the steam engine.

The Wealth of Nations   1776 treatise by Adam Smith, whose *laissez-faire* ideas predicted the economic boom of the Industrial Revolution.

Weimar Republic   The government of Germany between 1919 and the rise of Hitler and the Nazi party.

Western Front   Military front that stretched from the English Channel through Belgium and France to the Alps during World War I.

Whites   Refers to the "counterrevolutionaries" of the Bolshevik Revolution (1918–1921) who fought the Bolsheviks (the "Reds"); included former supporters of the tsar, Social Democrats, and large independent peasant armies.

William and Mary (1650–1702 and 1662–1694)   Dutch noble couple who supplanted the deposed Catholic King James II in 1688 as monarchs of England.

William of Ockham (d. 1349)   An English Franciscan monk, Ockham denied that human reason could prove fundamental theological truths such as the existence of God. He argued that there was no necessary connection between the observable laws of nature and the unknowable essence of divinity, and no hope of reason from the laws of nature to the nature of God. Ockham's ideas encouraged intellectuals to investigate the natural world without reference to the supernatural and encouraged empiricism.

William the Conqueror (1027–1087)   Duke of French Normandy who crossed the English Channel and defeated Harold for the English throne in 1066. Imposed a centralized feudal system on England and introduced French as the official language.

woman suffrage   The movement to win legal and political rights, including the right to vote for all women.

Works Progress Administration (WPA)   New Deal program instituted in 1935 that put nearly 3 million people to work building roads, bridges, airports, and post offices.

World Bank   International agency established in 1944 to provide economic assistance to war-torn and poor countries. Its formal title is the International Bank for Reconstruction and Development.

Yalta Accords   Meeting between President Franklin D. Roosevelt, Prime Minister Winston Churchill, and Premier Josef Stalin that occurred in the Crimea in 1945 to to prepare for the postwar order.

yellow press   Newspapers that sought increased circulation by featuring sensationalist reporting that appealed to the masses.

Boris Yeltsin (1931–2007)   The President of Russia who led the country after the disintegration of the Soviet Union in 1991.

Young Turks   The 1908 Turkish nationalist movement to depose Sultan Abdul Hamid II.

Yugoslavia   The Eastern European country that broke apart after the fall of the Soviet Union. Driven by nationalism and ethnic rivalries, the former Yugoslavia divided into six countries: Bosnia-Herzegovina, Croatia, Macedonia, Montenegro, Serbia, and Slovenia.

Zionism   Formally founded in 1897, a political movement holding that the Jewish people constitute a nation and are entitled to a national homeland, originally advocating the reestablishment of a Jewish homeland in Palestine.

Zoroastrians   Founded by Zoroaster around 600 B.C.E., this Persian religion urged people to be truthful, to help each other, and to practice hospitality. Those who did would be rewarded in an afterlife after a "judgment day."

Zulus   African tribe that, under Shaka, created a ruthless warrior state in southern Africa in the early 1800s.

Ulrich Zwingli (1484–1531)   A former Catholic priest from Zurich, Zwingli joined Luther and Calvin in attacking the authority of the Catholic Church. Zwingli's reforms resembled those of Luther's except that Zwingli believed that the Eucharist conferred no grace at all. At his peak, Zwingli converted much of northern Switzerland. After Zwingli's death in a battle with Catholic forces, most of his supporters began following John Calvin.

TEXT CREDITS

Leon B. Alberti: "On the Importance of Literature" from *University of Chicago Readings in Western Civilizations*, eds. Cochrane & Krishner. Copyright © 1986, University of Chicago Press. Reprinted by permission. "On the Family" from *The Family in Renaissance Florence*, trans./ed. by Renee Watkins. Copyright © 1969, University of South Carolina Press. Reprinted by permission.

Armand Bellée (ed.): *Cahiers de plaintes & doleances des paroisses de la province du Maine pour les Etats-generaux de 1789*, 4 vols. (Le Mans: Monnoyer, 1881–92), 2: 578–82. Translated by the American Social History Project, "Liberty, Equality, Fraternity: Exploring the French Revolution" by Jack R. Censer and Lynn Hunt.

Henry Bettenson (ed.): "Obedience as a Jesuit Hallmark" from *Documents of the Christian Church*, 2nd Edition. Copyright © 1967, Oxford University Press. Reprinted by permission of Oxford University Press.

Jacques Bossuet: "Bossuet on the Nature of Monarchical Authority" from *Politics Drawn from the Very Words of Holy Scripture*, trans. Patrick Riley. Copyright © 1990, Cambridge University Press.

Boyer, Baker & Kirshner (eds): "Declaration of the Rights of Man and of the Citizen," "Napoleon's Letter to Prince Eugene," and "Circular Letter to Sovereigns" from *University of Chicago Readings in Western Civilizations, Volume 7: The Old Regime and the French Revolution*, pp. 238–239; 419–420; 426–427, Copyright © 1987 University of Chicago Press. Reprinted by permission.

Louis Chevalier: From *Laboring Classes and Dangerous Classes in Paris During the First Half of the Nineteenth Century*. Copyright © 1973 by Howard Fertig, Inc. Reprinted by permission.

James Cracraft: "Alexander II's Decree Emancipating the Serfs, 1861," *Major Problems in the History of Imperial Russia*. Copyright © 1994 by D.C. Heath and Company. Reprinted with permission of Houghton Mifflin Company.

David Brion Davis: From *Encyclopédie*, Vol. 16, Neuchâtel, 1765, p. 532 as cited in David Brion Davis, *The Problem of Slavery in Western Culture* (Ithaca, N.Y.: Cornell University Press, 1966), p. 416. Copyright © 1966 by David Brion Davis. Reprinted by permission.

Simone de Beauvoir: From *The Second Sex* by Simone de Beauvoir, translated by H. M. Parshley, Copyright © 1953 and renewed 1980. Published by Jonathan Cape & by Alfred A. Knopf, a division of Random House, Inc. Reprinted by permission of The Random House Group Ltd & by permission of Alfred A. Knopf, a division of Random House, Inc. A new English translation is due to be published in 2008 by Jonathan Cape (London) and Knopf (New York).

Michel de Montaigne: From *Montaigne: Selections from the Essays*, translated and edited by Donald M. Frame (Harlan Davidson, Inc., 1973). Reprinted by permission of Harlan Davidson, Inc.

Alexis de Tocqueville: *Recollections: The French Revolution of 1848*; trans. George Lawrence, ed. J. P. Mayer, pp. 436–437. Copyright © 1987 by Transaction Publishers. Reprinted by permission of the publisher.

Auguste Debay: "Hygiène et physiologie de marriage" from *Victorian Women*, Hellerstein, Hune and Offen, pp. 175–177, Document 37i. Copyright © 1981 by the Board of Trustees of the Leland Stanford Junior University. Reprinted by permission.

Frantz Fanon: From *The Wretched of the Earth*, translated by Constance Farrington. Copyright © 1963, by *Présence Africaine*. Used by permission of Grove/Atlantic, Inc.

Gregory L. Freeze (ed.): From *From Supplication to Revolution: A Documentary Social History of Imperial Russia*. Copyright © 1988, Oxford University Press, Inc. Reprinted by permission of Oxford University Press.

Betty Friedan: From *The Feminine Mystique* by Betty Friedan. Copyright © 1983, 1974, 1973, 1963 by Betty Friedan. Used by permission of W. W. Norton & Company, Inc and Victor Gollancz, Ltd., a division of the Orion Publishing Group.

Galileo Galilei: From *Discoveries and Opinions of Galileo* by Galileo Galilei, translated by Stillman Drake, copyright © 1957 by Stillman Drake. Used by permission of Doubleday, a division of Random House.

Mohandas K. Gandhi: From *Hind Swaraj* or Indian Home Rule by M.K. Gandhi, pp. 24–27, 43–46, 56–63, 71–76 (Ahmedabad: Navajivan Trust, 1946).

Henry Bertram Hill: "Cardinal Richelieu on the Common People of France" from *The Political Testament of Cardinal Richelieu*. Copyright © 1961. Reprinted by permission of The University of Wisconsin Press.

Anton Kaes, Martin Jay, and Edward Dimendberg: *The Weimar Republic Sourcebook* (Los Angeles: University of California Press, 1994), pp. 137–138, 142. Copyright © 1994 by The Regents of the University of California. Reprinted by permission of the University of California Press.

Nikita Khrushchev: "Report to the Communist Party Congress (1961)" from *Current Soviet Policies IV*, eds. Charlotte Saikowski and Leo Gruliow, from the translations of the Current Digest of the Soviet Press. Joint Committee on Slavic Studies, 1962, pp. 42–45. Reprinted by permission of the Current Digest of the Soviet Press.

PHOTO CREDITS

Chapter 11: 416: *Army of Suleiman the Magnificent conquering Europe* (The Art Archive/Topkapi Museum, Istanbul/Dagli Orti); **420:** John Massey Stewart Picture Library; **421, 425, 432, 437:** *Persian panel of mosaic tilework, 14th–15th century* (Victoria & Albert Museum, London. Photo: Victoria & Albert Museum/Art Resource, NY); **423:** Werner Forman Archive/Topkapi Palace Library, Istanbul/Art Resource, NY; **424:** Mansell/TimePix/Getty Images; **431:** Royal Armouries Museum; **433:** José Pessoa, Arquivo Nacional de Fotografia, Instituto Português de Museus; **435:** The Art Archive/Biblioteca Nacional de Madrid/Dagli Orti.

Chapter 12: 440: *The School of Athens,* by Raphael (Scala/Art Resource, NY); **444, 447, 450:** detail from *Ceiling of Sala di Giove* (Palazzo Farnese, Caprarola, Italy. Photo: Scala/Art Resource, NY); **446:** Art Resource, NY; **448:** Réunion des Musées Nationaux /Art Resource, NY; **451:** Erich Lessing/Art Resource, NY; **452:** Erich Lessing/Art Resource, NY; **453 (top):** Réunion des Musées Nationaux /Art Resource, NY; **453 (bottom):** Scala/Art Resource, NY; **454:** Thyssen-Bornemisza Collection, Madrid, Spain/Art Resource, NY; **455:** Scala/Art Resource, NY; **456:** Scala/Art Resource, NY; **457:** Nimatallah/Art Resource, NY; **458 (left):** Scala/Art Resource, NY; **458 (right):** Erich Lessing/Art Resource, NY; **459:** Sandro Vannini/Corbis; **463:** © Frick Collection, New York; **464:** Réunion des Musées Nationaux /Art Resource, NY; **466:** Vanni/Art Resource, NY; **467:** Bildarchiv Preussischer Kulturbesitz/Art Resource, NY;

Chapter 13: 472: *Martin Luther preaching to faithful and communion and baptism from altarfront from Torslunde, 1561, Denmark* (The Art Archive / Nationalmuseet Copenhagen Denmark / Dagli Orti (A)); **474:** Scala/Art Resource, NY; **476:** Gemaldegalerie, Staatliche Museen zu Berlin, Berlin. Photo: Erich Lessing/Art Resource, NY; **477:** Alinari/Art Resource, NY; **478:** Staatsbibliothek, Bern; **480:** Bayerische Staatsgemäldesammlungen/Alte Pinakothek, Munich; **481: (left)** Staatliche Museen zu Berlin—Preußischer Kulturbesitz Kupferstichkabinett; **481: (right)** By permission of the British Library; **483:** The Warder Collection, NY; **484:** Erich Lessing/Art Resource, NY; **485:** The Warder Collection, NY; **489, 492, 498:** *Reformation monument on front of Vor Frue Kirke, Copenhagen, Denmark.* Photo: Bridgeman Art Library; **491:** National Trust/Art Resource, NY; **494: (left)** Erich Lessing/Art Resource, NY; **494: (right)** Scala/Art Resource, NY; **496:** Scala/Art Resource, NY; **497:** Kunsthistorisches Museum, Vienna; **499:** Archivo Iconografico, S.A./Corbis

Chapter 14: 502, 511, 516, 520, 524: *View of Toledo* by El Greco (The Metropolitan Museum of Art, H.O. Havemeyer Collection,

Bequest of Mrs. H.O. Havemeyer, 1919 (29.100.6) Photograph © 1992 The Metropolitan Museum of Art); **505:** Bettmann/Corbis; **506:** Gianni Dagli Orti/Corbis; **507:** Archivo Iconografico, S.A./Corbis; **509:** The New York Public Library. Astor, Lenox and Tilden Foundations; **514:** Archivo Iconografico, S.A./Corbis; **518:** Courtesy of the National Portrait Gallery, London; **519:** Photo Bulloz Collection, Privèe; **523:** Bibliotheque des Arts Decoratifs, Paris. Photo: Bridgeman Art Library; **528:** Scala/Art Resource, NY; **529:** Museo del Prado, Madrid; **530: (top)** Erich Lessing/Art Resource, NY; **530: (bottom)** Nimatallah/Art Resource, NY; **531: (left)** © English Heritage Photo Library; **531: (right)** Gift of Mr. and Mrs. Robert Woods Bliss, © 1997 Board of Trustees, National Gallery of Art, Washington, D.C.

Part V: 534: *Last Naval Battle in the Dutch-English War. August 11, 1637,* by Backhuyzen Ludolf, 1631–1708 (Erich Lessing/Art Resource, NY)

Chapter 15: 538: *Marriage a la Mode* by William Hogarth (National Gallery Collection; By kind permission of the Trustees of the National Gallery, London/Corbis); **541, 549, 574 :** *A fountain at Versailles* (Giraudon/Art Resource, NY); **543:** Courtesy of the National Portrait Gallery, London; **544:** Scottish National Portrait Gallery, Edinburgh, Scotland/Bridgeman Art Library; **545:** Bridgeman Art Library; **546:** Erich Lessing/Art Resource, NY; **547:** Giraudon/Art Resource, NY; **553:** The Art Archive/Musee du Chateau de Versailles/Dagli Orti; **554:** Erich Lessing/Art Resource, NY; **555:** by Friedrich Wilhelm Kurfürst von Brandenburg/Ullstein; **557:** The Art Archive/Russian Historical Museum Moscow/Dagli Orti (A); **560:** Giraudon/Art Resource, NY; **561:** Giraudon/Art Resource, NY; **564:** Ali Meyer/Corbis; **567:** John R. Freeman & Co.; **569:** Corbis; **570:** Gianni Dagli Orti/Corbis; **571:** The Warder Collection, NY

Chapter 16: 578: *The Comet of December 1680* by Lieve Verschuier (Courtesy of Historisch Museum, Rotterdam); **582:** Erich Lessing/Art Resource, NY; **583:** Bettmann/Corbis; **584: (top)** Stapleton Collection/Corbis; **584: (bottom)** Bettmann/Corbis; **587, 590, 596:** *Celestial map of planets by George Christoph Eimmert II. 17th century.* (O'Shea Gallery, London/Bridgeman Art Library); **588:** Erich Lessing/Art Resource, NY; **591:** Réunion des Musées Nationaux/Art Resource, NY; **592:** Bodleian Library; **594:** Bettmann/Corbis; **597:** Bodleian Library; **598:** Chateau de Versailles et de Trianon, Versailles, France. Photo: Erich Lessing/Art Resource, NY; **599: (left)** Bettmann/Corbis; **599: (right)** The Print Collector/Alamy

vate Collection/Ken Walsh/The Bridgeman Art Library; 890: Bettmann/Corbis; 891: Bettmann/Corbis; 893: Hulton-Deutsch Collection/Corbis; 894: Bettmann/Corbis; 895: Bettmann/Corbis; 897: The National Archives

Chapter 25: 902: *The Funeral Procession*, by George Grosz (Erich Lessing/Art Resource, NY. Art © Estate of George Grosz/VAGA, New York, NY); 904: Staaliche Museen zu Berlin/Preßischer Kulturbesitz; 905: The Museum of Modern Art, New York. Gift of the Judith Rothschild Foundation. Photo: Digital Image © The Museum of Modern Art, NY/Licensed by Scala/Art Resource, NY. © Estate of Gustav Klutsis/Artists Rights Society (ARS), New York; 908: Courtesy Schickler-Lafaille Collection; 909: Hoover Institution Archives, Stanford University; 910, 923, 934: *Detroit Industry* by Diego Rivera (Gift of Edel B. Ford. © 1998 Instituto Nacional de Bellas Artes, Mexico City. Photograph © The Detroit Institute of Arts. © 2007 Banco de México Diego Rivera & Frida Kahlo Museums Trust. Av. Cinco de Mayo No. 2, Col. Centro, Del Cuauhtémoc 06059, Mexico, D.F.); 912: Hoover Institution Archives, Stanford University; 916: Brown Brothers; 918: Hulton-Deutsch Collection/Corbis; 921: Stefan Lorant/The Warder Collection, NY; 925: Hulton-Deutsch Collection/Corbis; 928: Arthur Rothstein/Corbis; 930 (top): CNAC/MNAM/Dist. Réunion des Musées Nationaux/Art Resource, NY. ©Artists Rights Society (ARS), New York/ADAGP, Paris/Succession Marcel Duchamp; 930 (bottom): The Museum of Modern Art, New York. Photograph courtesy the Museum of Modern Art, New York; 932: Musee National d'Art Moderne, Centre Georges Pompidou, Paris, France. Photo: CNAC/MNAM/Dist. RMN/Art Resource, NY. Art © Estate of George Grosz/VAGA, New York, NY; 933: Kunstbibliothek, Staatliche Museen zu Berlin. Photo: Dietmar Katz/BPK/Art Resource, NY; 935: The Granger Collection, New York

Chapter 26: 938: *The War*, by Marc Chagall (Musee National d'Art Moderne, Centres Georges Pompidou, Paris. Photo: CNAC/MNAM/Dist. RMN/Art Resource, NY © Artists Rights Society (ARS), New York/ADAGP, Paris); 943 (top), 958, 962, 972: *Guernica* by Pablo Picasso (Giraudon/Art Resource, NY. ©Estate of Pablo Picasso/Artists Rights Society (ARS), New York); 943 (bottom): The Southworth Collection, The Mandeville Special Collections Library, University of California San Diego; 944: Stiftung Archiv der Kunste, Berlin. ©Artists Rights Society (ARS), New York/ VG Bild-Kunst, Bonn; 945; The National Archives/Corbis; 948: Corbis; 950: Hulton-Deutsch Collection/Corbis; 951: Corbis; 954: Hoover Institution Archives, Stanford University; 957: The Warder Collection, NY; 961 (top): AP Images; 961 (bottom): Jewgeni Chaldej/Voller-Ernst; 966: Public Record Office Image Library; 968: National Archives/Corbis; 969: Bettmann/Corbis; 970: The Imperial War Museum, London; 971: Bettmann/Corbis; 974: Bettmann/Corbis

Part VIII: 976–77: *A scene from the fall of the Berlin Wall* (David and Peter Tumley/Corbis)

Chapter 27: 980: *The Berlin airlift* (Bettmann/Corbis); 984: Corbis; 985: Bettmann/Corbis; 986: Yerevan, Armgosizdat/AP Images; 988: AP Images; 989, 999, 1005, 1009, 1012: *A scene from the Soviet occupation of Czechoslovakia* (Hulton-Deutsch Collection/Corbis); 991: German Information Center/The Warder Collection, NY; 994: Bettmann/Corbis; 997: © Xinhua/Sovfoto; 1006: Corbis; 1007 (top): Marc Garanger/Corbis; 1007 (bottom): Marc Garanger/Corbis; 1010: Hulton-Deutsch Collection/Corbis; 1013: Blue Lantern Studio/Corbis; 1014: Corbis

Chapter 28: 1016: *Striking Communist students demonstrate* (Bettmann/Corbis); 1019: Bettmann/Corbis; 1020 (top): Keystone/Corbis; 1020 (bottom): Paul Almasy/Corbis; 1021 (top): Bettmann/Corbis; 1021 (bottom): Bettmann/Corbis; 1022: Jerry Schatzberg/Corbis; 1023: Martha Holmes/Time & Life Pictures/Getty Images; 1024: Studio Patellani/Corbis; 1025: Bettmann/Corbis; 1027, 1033, 1035: (Tim Graham/Getty Images); 1029: AP Images; 1032: Patrick Chauvel/Sygma/Corbis; 1034: Abbas/Magnum Photos; 1036: Bettmann/Corbis; 1038: Bettmann/Corbis; 1040: Peter Turnley/Corbis; 1041: Wally McNamee/Corbis; 1042: Peter Turnley/Corbis; 1046: Patrick Robert/Sygma/Corbis

Chapter 29: 1050: Peter Parks/AFP/Getty Images; 1054: Michale Brennan/Corbis; 1055: Shaul Schwarz/Corbis; 1056: Reuters/Corbis; 1059: Reuters/Corbis; 1060: Reuters/Corbis; 1063: Bettmann/Corbis; 1065 (left): Alain DeJean/Sygma/Corbis; 1065 (right): Alain DeJean/Sygma/Corbis; 1066 (top): Peter Turnley/Corbis; 1066 (bottom): Jean Guichard/Sygma/Corbis; 1068: Sean Adair/Reuters/Corbis

INDEX